PRINCIPLES OF EUROPEAN CONSTITUTIONAL LAW

While politics wrestles with the Constitutional Treaty, this volume presents a European constitutional law—not as a mere project but as binding law. There are good reasons to treat the European Union's current primary law as constitutional law: it establishes public power, legitimates legal acts, provides a citizenship, protects fundamental rights, and regulates the relationships among legal orders as well as between law and politics. Reconstructing primary law as constitutional law yields useful insights, as this volume seeks to demonstrate.

This volume presents European constitutional law as it stands and, on that foundation, the Treaty establishing a Constitution for Europe. The contributions present its theoretical and doctrinal fundamentals from the perspective of German-speaking scholarship, reflect the state of research, clarify methodological approaches, illuminate legal doctrines and assumptions, and identify research desiderata. The perspectives on offer are not uniform, but encompass varying methodologies and differing political approaches to integration.

Volume 8 in the Series Modern Studies in European Law

Modern Studies in European Law

1 Soft Law in European Community Law *Linda Senden*

2 The Impact of European Rights on National Legal Cultures *Miriam Aziz*

3 Partnership Rights, Free Movement and EU Law *Helen Toner*

4 National Remedies Before the Court of Justice *Michael Dougan*

5 The National Courts Mandate in the European Constitution *Monica Claes*

6 EU Environmental Law *Maria Lee*

7 European Union Law and Defence Integration *Martin Trybus*

8 Principles of European Constitutional Law *Armin von Bogdandy and Jürgen Bast*

Principles of European Constitutional Law

Edited by

Armin von Bogdandy
and
Jürgen Bast
Max Planck Institute for Comparative Public Law and International Law

•HART•
PUBLISHING

OXFORD AND PORTLAND, OREGON
2006

Published in North America (US and Canada)
by Hart Publishing
c/o International Specialized Book Services
920 NE 58th Avenue, Suite 300
Portland, OR 97213-3786
USA
Tel: +1 503 287 3093 or toll-free: (1) 800 944 6190
Fax: +1 503 280 8832
E-mail: orders@isbs.com
Web Site: www.isbs.com

Hart Publishing, Salter's Boatyard, Folly Bridge, Abingdon Rd,
Oxford, OX1 4LB
email: mail@hartpub.co.uk
Telephone: +44 (0)1865 245533 Fax: +44 (0) 1865 794882

WEBSITE: http//:www.hartpub.co.uk

British Library Cataloguing in Publication Data
Data Available

ISBN-13: 978-1-84113-464-2 (hardback)
ISBN-10: 1-84113-464-3 (hardback)

Typeset by Compuscript, Shannon
Printed and bound in Great Britain by
TJ International, Padstow, Cornwall

Preface

WHILE POLITICS WRESTLES with the Constitutional Treaty as the founding legal document *de lege ferenda*, this volume presents a European constitutional law—not as a mere project but as binding, valid law, as *lex lata*. Of course, no document in force carries this designation. Scholarly terminology, however, does not require the blessing of politics. There are good reasons to treat the European Union's current primary law as constitutional law. After all, it establishes public power, legitimates legal acts, provides a citizenship, protects fundamental rights, and regulates the relationships among legal orders as well as between law and politics. Constitutional law is conceivable without a state, a nation, or an instrument that fulfils all the traditional requirements of a constitution. Reconstructing primary law as constitutional law yields useful insights, as this volume seeks to demonstrate. Such an endeavour does not imply a justification of primary law in force—rather, both achievements and deficits become apparent.

This volume presents European constitutional law as it stands and, on that foundation, the Draft Treaty establishing a Constitution for Europe as agreed upon by the European Convention (CONV 850/03 of 18 July 2003, hereinafter CT-Conv) as well as the Treaty establishing a Constitution for Europe finally adopted by the ensuing Intergovernmental Conference (CIG 87/04 of 6 August 2004, hereinafter CT-IGC). The work on the chapters was finalised in October 2004, the book reflects the European state of affairs of that time. The contributions present the theoretical and dogmatic fundamentals of European constitutional law from the perspective of German-speaking scholarship, reflect the state of research, clarify methodological approaches, illuminate legal doctrines and assumptions, and identify research *desiderata*. This volume brings together authors of varying methodologies and differing political approaches to integration; they are united by the desire to protect—and even to develop further—the existing constitutional culture within the Union.

This project is deeply indebted to the Fritz Thyssen Stiftung, which generously financed the extensive collaboration of the authors. Stephan Bitter, Andreas Magnusson, Julia Schwartz, Michael Rötting, Robert Stelzer, Markus Wagner, and Joseph Windsor provided valuable assistance in the completion of the volume.

Summary of Contents

Contents

Table of Cases

Court of First Instance

European Court of Justice (Judgments and Decisions)

European Court of Justice (Opinions)

European Commission of Human Rights/ European Court of Human Rights

Permanent Court of International Justice/International Court of Justice

National Courts and Tribunals

Table of European Founding Treaties

Table of National Constitutions

Table of Legislation

Decisions and Decisions sui generis

Directives

Regulations

Other European Acts

National Legislation

Table of International Treaties and Conventions

Part I
Defining the Field of Constitutional Law

1

Constitutional Principles

ARMIN VON BOGDANDY*

I. A THEORY OF A DOCTRINE OF PRINCIPLES

1. Principles and Constitutional Scholarship

A DOCTRINE OF PRINCIPLES, that is, a systematic exposition of the most essential legal norms of the European legal order, offers a fine method to develop European constitutional scholarship. In fact, this discipline still has to define its subject and to establish itself as a part of legal science.[1] Just as European law[2] and then European Community law[3] have become sub-disciplines, a further step in this differentiation is unfolding, irrespective of the fortunes of the Constitutional Treaty: the development of European constitutional law scholarship.[4] The potential contribution of a doctrine of principles can best be explained in the context of other approaches.

At first glance, a strict orientation to the sources of law offers a reliable approach to the determination of what is part of European constitutional law.[5] When using such an approach, the decisive criterion for identification

* Transl by Eric Pickett, revised by Markus Wagner and Joseph Windsor. The author would like to thank Stephan Bitter for valuable assistance.

[1] On legal science's function of constituting the object of study, G Jellinek, *Allgemeine Staatslehre* (3rd edn 1913, reprinted 1976) 50; N MacCormick, *Questioning Sovereignty. Law, State, and Nation in the European Commonwealth* (1999) 113.

[2] H Mosler, 'Der Vertrag über die Europäische Gemeinschaft für Kohle und Stahl. Entstehung und Qualifizierung', (1951–52) 14 *Zeitschrift für ausländisches öffentliches Recht und Völkerrecht* 1 at 23 *et seq*; H Mosler, 'Die Europäische Integration aus der Sicht der Gründungsphase', in: O Due, M Lutter and J Schwarze (eds), *Festschrift für U Everling* (1995), vol II, 911 *et seq*.

[3] HP Ipsen, *Europäisches Gemeinschaftsrecht* (1972) 4 *et seq*.

[4] On the step-by-step development of European administrative law, see E Schmidt-Aßmann, 'Strukturen des Europäischen Verwaltungsrechts: Einleitende Problemskizze', in: E Schmidt-Aßmann and W Hoffmann-Riem (eds), *Strukturen des Europäischen Verwaltungsrechts* (1999) 9 at 10 *et seq*.

[5] This contribution does not discuss whether the current primary law can be considered as the constitutional law of the European Union. It departs from the premise that this is the case. On the general issue, see the foreword and C Möllers's contribution in this volume.

is whether a provision or legal concept belongs to a body of law that can only be changed under qualified requirements—above all the procedures according to Article 48 EU, or, once the Constitutional Treaty has entered into force, Article IV-7 CT-Conv (Article 447 CT-IGC).[6] This is how Lenaerts and van Nuffel determine European constitutional law.[7] This learned but traditional portrayal of primary Union law neglects, however, important issues which, at least according to the German tradition, are crucial to the science of constitutional law: focusing on structuring elements and a corresponding core of legal doctrines that determine the discipline's identity. European constitutional scholarship should consist of more than a change of labels (i.e. presenting traditional works of European primary law as works of constitutional doctrine).[8] Rather, the treatment of primary law as constitutional law should bring about a new quality of understanding and exposition.

Not all the provisions of the Treaties and Protocols should be accorded the same importance. Rather, a selection must take place; the Constitutional Treaty changes nothing in this respect given its 448 Articles on 341 pages and a vast number of Protocols.[9] European constitutional scholarship should develop its field from those normative bases that HP Ipsen cautiously described as *Inbegriff des Primärrechts*, or the "core" of primary law.[10] Scholarship has responded to that call,[11] but nobody doubts that much remains to be done.

[6] On the amendment procedures as the decisive formal criterion, Jellinek, above n 1, 51; Kelsen's approach reaches similar results, H Kelsen, *Allgemeine Staatslehre* (1925, reprinted 1966) 249.

[7] K Lenaerts and P van Nuffel, *Constitutional Law of the European Union* (1999).

[8] F Snyder, The unfinished constitution of the European Union: principles, processes and culture, in: JHH Weiler and M Wind (eds), *European Constitutionalism Beyond the State* (2003) 55 at 58.

[9] The count is based on the document of 6 August 2004, CIG 87/04. The protocols to the Constitutional Treaty are not included in this document. No less than 36 protocols and two annexes are attached to the Constitutional Treaty, see CIG 87/04 ADD 1; moreover, the Euratom Treaty is not integrated into the Constitutional Treaty.

[10] Ipsen, above n 3, 64.

[11] Pathbreaking: J Frowein, 'Die Herausbildung europäischer Verfassungsprinzipien', in: A Kaufmann, E-J Mestmäcker and HF Zacher (eds), *Rechtsstaat und Menschenwürde: Festschrift für W Maihofer* (1988) 149; J Frowein, 'Wesentliche Elemente einer Verfassung', in: R Bieber and P Widmer (eds), *Der europäische Verfassungsraum* (1995) 71; R Bieber, B Kahl-Wolff and L Muller, 'Cours général de droit communautaire', in: Academy of European Law (ed), *Collected Courses of the Academy of European Law 1992* (1994), vol III-1, 49; J Gerkrath, *L'émergence d'un droit constitutionnel pour l'Europe* (1997) 183 *et seq*; F Toriello, *I principi generali del diritto comunitario* (2000); JHH Weiler, 'European Neo-constitutionalism: in Search of Foundations for the European Constitutional Order', (1996) *Political Studies* 517. The scholarship appears to be quite meager in particular with regard to the treatment of founding principles. A Arnull, *The General Principles of EEC Law and the Individual* (1990), contains a traditional presentation of primary law. J Usher, *General Principles of EC Law* (1999), as well as T Tridimas, *The General Principles of EC Law* (1999), restrict themselves largely to the principles protecting citizens. Research on the general principles of Community law has a long tradition (see P Pescatore, *Le droit de l'intégration* (1972) 70 *et seq*; H Lecheler, *Der Europäische Gerichtshof und die allgemeinen Rechtsgrundsätze* (1971)) but has largely

The relevance of a doctrine of principles to constitutional scholarship is confirmed by the better treatises on national constitutional law. Such expositions, which generally have much less of a problem identifying and structuring their subject, are often built upon a doctrine of principles.[12] By means of structuring and informing principles it is possible to understand the constitution as an "organic whole" and the constitutional text as the expression of a "grand", though only partially fixed, plan,[13] an idea perhaps alien to most Anglo-Saxon lawyers, but dear to continental scholarship.[14] Drafting such a "grand plan" for European constitutional law appears all the more urgent in view of the Treaties' generally recognised insufficient structure. The Constitutional Treaty, given its sometimes puzzling architecture, will not put many scholars out of business, but—on the contrary, because of its genesis—lends itself even more than the current Treaties to research on its underlying "plan".

2. Functions of a Doctrine of Principles

As a practical science, legal scholarship participates in law's function of settling conflicts. The development of a European doctrine of principles may channel and perhaps rationalise political and social conflicts, treating them as conflicts of principles which can be resolved according to the rules of legal rationality.[15]

Another important practical function of legal scholarship is the maintenance of an essential social "infrastructure" by creating and securing the

restricted itself to principles protecting the citizen. It has not led to a doctrine with the power to shape the law, like founding principles have, since it essentially concerns the limitation of governmental power. See eg, G Tesauro, 'Il ruolo della Corte di Giustizia nell'elaborazione dei principi generali', in: Associazione italiana dei costituzionalisti, *Annuario* (1999) 297 *et seq*.

[12] See K Hesse, *Grundzüge des Verfassungsrechts der Bundesrepublik Deutschland* (1999) Grundzüge, 2nd part; L Tribe, *American Constitutional Law* (2000) 2.

[13] GF Schuppert and C Bumke, *Die Konstitutionalisierung der Rechtsordnung* (2000) 28 at 39; see also Gerkrath, above n 11, 303.

[14] Most helpful, J Maxeiner, U.S. "methods awareness" (Methodenbewußtsein) for German jurists, in: B Großfeld *et al.* (eds), *Festschrift W Fikentscher* (1998) 114 at 117 *et seq*.

[15] This function is impressively confirmed by those who do not believe in "formalism", M Koskenniemi, *The Gentle Civilizer of Nations* (2002) 497 *et seq*; L Siedentop, *Democracy in Europe* (2000) 100. Certainly, a doctrine of principles will not advance the logical unity or pre-established harmony of primary European law. Rather, the diffuseness in the Union's constitutional law can to a large extent be explained by the partly hazy content of important constitutional principles and the ambiguous relationships between them. Case-law will not be able to resolve these problems alone. Yet there is something to be gained if the sizeable number of recognised principles and important elements of their legal concretisations are stipulated and controversial questions precisely defined. Last, but not least, a doctrine of principles as the offspring of jurisprudential (re-)construction cannot be identical to the actual legal practice. This is not a deficiency, but rather the proof of the critical content of jurisprudential constructions. A construction based on current law can develop elements for critique of current legal practices owing to abstraction and generalisation.

transparency and coherence of the law. In order to fulfil this task, a doctrine of principles provides a "framework for orientation".[16] Such a framework should be particularly helpful in the Union's fragmented legal order which lacks grand codifications such as the French Code Civil.[17]

The "infrastructure maintenance" function of legal scholarship is not static but demands participation in the development of the law to keep it in line with changing social relationships, interests and beliefs. This development happens to a great extent without the participation of the political realm—and often with recourse to constitutional principles. These principles can fulfil the function of "gateways" through which the legal order is attached to the broader public discourse. A doctrine of principles has the task of preparing and accompanying this process.

Furthermore, the constitutionalisation of European law, the process which lies at the heart of the legal development over the last forty years,[18] can probably only be completed by a doctrine of principles. A complete constitutionalisation of a legal order requires that the constitution "permeate"[19] all legal relationships, which is most easily accomplished through constitutional principles. By this means a doctrine of principles should participate in the completion of the development from a "law of integration" into a multifunctional framework.[20]

Yet a doctrine of principles as such does not necessarily suggest judicial activism on the basis of principles.[21] In particular, such activism, uncoupled from the concrete provisions of the Treaties, would misunderstand essential elements of the Union's Constitution: it is for many important questions a law of detail. Here again, the Constitutional Treaty does not change anything; the drafting of its Part I is most careful in this respect (e.g. Articles I-11(6), I-32(1) CT-Conv; Articles 12(6), 33(1) CT-IGC). The plethora of details is no coincidence, but rather expresses the Member States' (and thus the Union's founding authority's[22]) mistrust and desire for control. This

[16] Schuppert and Bumke, above n 13, 40.

[17] The term "constitutional chaos" is its best-known description, D Curtin, 'The constitutional structure of the Union', (1993) 30 *CML Rev* 17 at 67.

[18] JHH Weiler, 'The Reformation of European Constitutionalism', (1997) 35 *JCMS* 97.

[19] GFW Hegel, *Rechtsphilosophie* (1821, edn Moldenhauer and Michel 1970) § 274.

[20] Similarly, F Snyder, 'General Course on Constitutional Law of the European Union', in: Academy of European Law (ed), *Collected Courses of the Academy of European Law 1995* (1998), vol VI-1, 41 at 47 *et seq*.

[21] This is, by contrast, a *main* function of the Basic Law's principles according to the common German constitutional understanding, H Dreier, in: *id* (ed), *Grundgesetz-Kommentar* (1998), vol II (Articles 20–82), Art 20 (Einführung), para 10; GF Schuppert, 'Rigidität und Flexibilität von Verfassungsrecht', (1995) 120 *Archiv des öffentlichen Rechts* 32 at 51 *et seq*; for criticism, see eg M Bullinger, 'Fragen der Auslegung einer Verfassung', (2004) *Juristenzeitung* 209 at 211 *et seq*.

[22] See the utilisation of the term "founding authority of the Community" in Cases T-377/00, T-379/00, T-380/00, T-260/01 and T-272/01, *Philip Morris et al v Commission* [2003] ECR II-1, para 124.

must be taken into consideration when deducing legal consequences from constitutional principles.

A doctrine of principles plays a role in the creation of an emerging European identity. A European identity requires a common understanding of the polity by the citizens, something for which constitutional principles could be an important vehicle.[23] Here, some even see the path towards a European *demos*.[24] Certainly, a doctrine of principles developed by legal science cannot directly trigger the creation of an identity for broad parts of the population.[25] Yet it can be understood as a part of a public discourse through which the European citizenry ascertains the foundations of its polity.

The recent constitutional development tries to present the (legal) principles of the EU as the reflection of such convictions in the European citizenry. Efforts to represent the Union as an expression of the ethical convictions of Union citizens explain the rise of the term "value" as a key constitutional concept (see Article I-1(2) CT-Conv; Article 1(2) CT-IGC).

3. Integration as a Formation of Principles

If, notwithstanding these potentials, presentations of EC or EU law based on principles are rare, this is to be explained by the history of integration. The path to integration has not been constitutional, but rather functional.

This orientation decisively influenced the jurisprudential construction. The federal conception[26] failed to gain a larger following in legal science; economic law approaches and administrative law approaches were—at least in Germany—much more successful. Thus the first specific principles, as developed by Ipsen, namely integration and supranationality, were based squarely on the realisation of the tasks in Article 2 EEC Treaty and had little relation to the traditions of constitutional thinking. This dominance of the tasks continues up to the present. Thus Lenaerts' and van Nuffel's presentation of European constitutional law, for example, places Article 2 EC at the centre—in a study that explicitly attempts a systematic and principle-oriented exposition.[27] Principles qualifying as *structuring* constitutional principles developed only slowly.

[23] K Eichenberger, 'Vom Umgang mit Strukturprinzipien des Verfassungsstaates', in: J Burmeister (ed), *Verfassungsstaatlichkeit: Festschrift K Stern* (1997) 456 at 465 *et seq*; Siedentop, above n 15, 81, 94, 96 *et seq*, 101.

[24] D Fuchs, 'Demos und Nation in der Europäischen Union', in: H-D Klingemann and F Neidhardt (eds), *Zur Zukunft der Demokratie* (2000) 215 at 230 *et seq.*

[25] F Snyder, 'Editorial: Dimensions and precipitates of EU Constitutional Law', (2002) 8 *ELJ* 315 at 315.

[26] CF Ophüls, 'Quellen und Aufbau des Europäischen Gemeinschaftsrechts', (1963) *Neue Juristische Wochenschrift* 1697 at 1698.

[27] Lenaerts and van Nuffel, above n 7, 71 *et seq*.

The constitutionalisation of the Treaties can be perceived as the largely judicial and scholarly development of constitutional principles which were then codified in 1997 through the Amsterdam Treaty in Article 6 EU. This provision and its introduction can be understood as a call upon legal science to reconsider and reconstruct primary law according to enunciated constitutional principles.[28]

Principles figure even more prominently in the Constitutional Treaty, albeit not in a fully satisfactory way. The use in Article I-2 CT-Conv (Article 2 CT-IGC) of the term "value" instead of "principle", the sheer number of values enunciated as well as the unclear status of the "society of pluralism, tolerance, justice, solidarity and non-discrimination" show that the identification of European constitutional principles remains in an early stage of development.

II. GENERAL ISSUES OF A EUROPEAN DOCTRINE OF PRINCIPLES

1. The Subject Matter

For the purposes of this study it is not necessary to precisely define the concept "principle"[29] since the study will work with a broadly accepted minimal understanding: principles are legal norms laying down essential elements of a legal order.[30] The purpose of this study is above all to identify and clarify these principles, in particular on the basis of further legal concepts, more specific norms, settled case-law as well as established constitutional theories and doctrines.[31]

The doctrine of principles presented here will not discuss all principles of primary law. Rather, this study is concerned with *founding* principles

[28] Previously, such principles were to be found only in the 3rd recital to the Preamble of the EU Treaty (Maastricht version); on the importance of such principles in the legislative process, see Council Dir 2000/43/EC of 29 June 2000 implementing the principle of equal treatment between persons irrespective of racial or ethnic origin, OJ L 180, 19.7.2000, 22–6, 2nd recital; Council Dir 2000/78/EC of 27 November 2000 establishing a general framework for equal treatment in employment and occupation, OJ L 303, 2.12.2000, 16–22, 1st recital.

[29] For a good overview of the diverse understandings, R Alexy, *Theorie der Grundrechte* (1996) 71 *et seq*; ML Fernandez Esteban, *The Rule of Law in the European Constitution* (1999) 39 *et seq*; M Koskenniemi, 'General Principles: Reflexions on Constructivist Thinking in International Law', in: *id* (ed), *Sources of International Law* (2000) 359; R Dworkin, *Taking Rights Seriously* (1977) 24 *et seq*.

[30] See, in more detail, O Wiklund and J Bengoetxea, 'General Constitutional Principles of Community Law', in: U Bernitz and J Nergelius (eds), *General Principles of European Community Law* (2000) 119; on the status of principles within the hierarchy of Union law, see J Nergelius, 'General Principles of Community Law in the Future', in: *ibid*, 223 at 229 *et seq*.

[31] E Riedel, 'Der gemeineuropäische Bestand von Verfassungsprinzipien zur Begründung von Hoheitsgewalt', in: P-C Müller-Graff and E Riedel (eds), *Gemeinsames Verfassungsrecht in der Europäischen Union* (1998) 77 at 80 *et seq*, demonstrates that this is a "typical German" approach.

analogous to Article 20(1)[32] German Basic Law[33] or Article 1 Spanish Constitution.[34] Article 6 EU and Articles I-2, III-193(1) CT-Conv (Articles 2, 292 CT-IGC) are of great significance with regard to their identification.[35] They express an overarching normative frame of reference for all primary law, indeed for the whole of the Union's legal order. Although Article I-2 CT-Conv (Article 2 CT-IGC) uses the term "value", the tenets it lays down can be considered as principles. Usually, principles are to be distinguished from values, the latter being fundamental ethical convictions whereas the former are legal norms. Since the "values" of Article I-2 have legal consequences (Articles I-1(2), I-3(1), I-18 CT-Conv; Articles 1(2), 3(1), 19 CT-IGC) they are legal norms and can be considered as principles.[36]

This study examines only the European Union's constitutional principles. Although European constitutional law is closely intertwined with the national constitutions, forming the "European constitutional space", principles of the national constitutions will not be discussed. To focus almost exclusively on the European level is justified by the concept of autonomy of European primary law, analytical necessities and questions of space.

2. National and Supranational Principles: On the Question of Transferability

Many of the principles laid down in Article 6 EU are well-known from the national constitutions and have been the object of thorough research. A key question for a European doctrine of principles (and indeed for the whole of European constitutional law) is to what extent and with what provisos the relevant national jurisprudence can be used in order to develop the supranational principles.[37] More than a few scholars deny the possibility of such

[32] The decisions concerning Art 20 German Basic Law are considered to be "fundamental statements with respect to the constitutional identity", "the normative core of the constitutional order", provisions determining the "character of the Federal Republic of Germany" and "blueprints"; for more details, Dreier, above n 21, Art 20 (Einführung), paras 5 *et seq.*

[33] For an English version, see <http://www.bundesregierung.de/static/pdf/GG_engl_Stand_26_07_02.pdf> (8 April 2004).

[34] For an English version, see <http://www.oefre.unibe.ch/law/icl/sp00000_.html> (8 April 2004).

[35] M Scudiero, 'Introduzione', in: *id* (ed), *Il diritto costituzionale comune Europeo. Principi e diritti fondamentali* (2002) ix. Neither Art 6 EU nor Art 2 CT-Conv (Art 2 CT-IGC) contain an exhaustive list of the founding principles. Of further significance—under current law—are in particular Art 2 EU and Articles 2, 5 and 10 EC.

[36] For the reasons why the term "value" might have been chosen, see A von Bogdandy, 'Europäische Verfassung und europäische Identität', (2004) *Juristenzeitung* 53 at 58 *et seq.*

[37] In detail, R Dehousse, 'Comparing National and EC Law', (1994) 42 *AJCL* 761 at 762, 771 *et seq.*

recourse by claiming that the new form of governance requires "unprecedented thinking".[38]

Yet this demand clashes with the very nature of legal thinking, which, at its heart, is comparative and dependent on the repertoire of established doctrines of viable institutions.[39] Nor is it necessary to renounce any such comparison since there is sufficient similarity between the supranational and the national legal orders. The Union's and Member States' constitutions confront the same central problem: the phenomenon of public power as the heart of every constitutional order.[40] Most if not all constitutional principles are eventually concerned with this problem.[41] In view of this issue identity there is a sufficient degree of similarity to justify transferring the insights from the one order to the other.

Nevertheless, a simple transfer of concepts and insights from the national context in many instances will not be adequate for the issues that arise in the EU context. The transfer of constitutional concepts of one single Member State is already prohibited by the principle expressed in Article 6(3) EU, namely the equality of the 25 national constitutions.

Nor is it possible to simply project a common European denominator of national concepts onto the Union.[42] Every analogy and transfer must reflect the fact that the Union is not—according to the prevailing and convincing view—a state, but rather a new form of political and legal order.[43] The structuring principles must reflect this. A doctrine of European principles must therefore purify the content of the principles known from the national constitutions from those elements which apply only to a state.

Quite significantly in this respect, national constitutional law exhibits a far greater degree of political unity—that is, those phenomena which are traditionally subsumed under the term "political unity"—than does Union constitutional law, both conceptually and practically.[44] The exercise of power by the Union appears not as the will of a single sovereign, but rather

[38] GF Schuppert, 'Anforderungen an eine europäische Verfassung', in: Klingemann and Neidhardt, above n 24, 237 at 249. Schuppert himself demonstrates the utility of comparative thought in: GF Schuppert, 'Überlegungen zur demokratischen Legitimation des europäischen Regierungssystems', in: J Ipsen and E Schmidt-Jortzig (eds), *Recht—Staat—Gemeinwohl: Festschrift für D Rauschning* (2001), 201 at 207 *et seq*. On the theoretical aspect, see P Zumbansen, 'Spiegelungen von "Staat und Recht"', in: M Anderheiden *et al* (eds), *Globalisierung als Problem von Gerechtigkeit und Steuerungsfähigkeit des Rechts* (2001) 13.

[39] On the "memory function", E Schmidt-Aßmann, *Das allgemeine Verwaltungsrecht als Ordnungsidee* (2004) 4.

[40] MacCormick, above n 1, 138 *et seq*.

[41] Moreover, the Union enjoys the power to impose duties on Member States, which is the core feature of federal constitutional law.

[42] Yet a comparative approach is most useful in this respect; for a fine example, see Scudiero, above n 35.

[43] JHH Weiler, 'Introduction: The Reformation of European constitutionalism', in: *id*, *The Constitution of Europe* (1999) 221 at 221.

[44] On the development of this concept, T Vesting, *Politische Einheitsbildung und technische Realisation* (1990) 23 *et seq*; C Möllers, *Staat als Argument* (2000) 230 *et seq*.

as the common exercise of public power by various actors.[45] This idea underlies the very first normative enunciation of the Constitutional Treaty (Article I-1(1) CT-Conv; Article 1(1) CT-IGC): it founds a Union, "on which the Member States confer competences to attain objectives they have in common". Not only consensual and contractual elements and networks between various public authorities, but especially the prominence of the Member States and their peoples must decisively shape the understanding and concretisation of the structuring principles.

3. Constitutional Principles in View of Varying Sectoral Provisions

The principles set forth in Article 6(1) EU are valid for the whole of Union law. Yet numerous concretising figures are valid only in certain sectors, for instance the dual structure for democratic legitimation through the Council and Parliament. The Union's legal order reveals a significant fragmentation; the Constitutional Treaty mends this fragmentation to some extent (e.g. Article I-6 CT-Conv; Article 7 CT-IGC), but by no means in all areas.[46] This gives rise to doubts about the usefulness of an overarching doctrine of principles. It might even nurture the suspicion that a doctrine of principles is not the fruit of scholarly insight, but rather a policy instrument for more integration. Yet these doubts and suspicions are unfounded.

As the principles set forth in Article 6 EU apply to all areas of Union law, an overarching doctrine of principles built on Article 6 EU encompassing the entire primary law is a logical consequence. Unless *mis*interpreted as merely declaratory, the enactment of Article 6 EU in 1997 unavoidably requires its own expansion into a general doctrine of principles against which all areas of Union law and in particular the older layers of Community law must be assessed. Article 6 EU declares that the Union is "founded" on these principles. This contains an ambitious normative programme, the details of which probably only legal science and the courts are able to develop although the already mentioned limitations of a doctrine of principles as applied to a concrete legal situation must be respected.

In view of the fragmentation within primary law it might appear problematic to determine which provisions may be understood as concretising abstract principles. Theoretically, both the co-decision procedure under Article 251 EC as well as the Council's autonomous decision-making

[45] This may explain the renaissance of contractual thinking in constitutional theory. See G Frankenberg, 'The Return of the Contract', (2001) 12 *King's College Law Journal* 39; I Pernice, FC Mayer and S Wernicke, 'Renewing the European Social Contract', (2001) 12 *King's College Law Journal* 61.

[46] At a less abstract level, there are significant differences between individual sectors in all legal orders. See A Hanebeck, 'Die Einheit der Rechtsordnung als Anforderung an den Gesetzgeber', (2002) 41 *Der Staat* 429.

competence under the requirement of unanimity (e.g. Article 308 EC) can be understood as realisations of the principle of democracy. Yet the co-decision procedure, conceived as the "standard" by the model of supranational federalism,[47] applies to ever more situations.[48] The Constitutional Treaty backs this thesis in Articles I-19(1), I-33(1) CT-Conv (Articles 20, 34(1) CT-IGC).

An overarching doctrine of principles targeted in this "standard" manner must not, however, downplay sectoral rules which follow different rationales. To do otherwise would infringe upon an important constitutional principle: Article 6(3) EU in conjunction with Article 48 EU clearly shows that the essential constitutional dynamics are to remain under the control of the respective national parliaments.[49]

III. FOUNDING PRINCIPLES OF SUPRANATIONAL AUTHORITY

1. Equal Liberty

Article 6(1) EU names liberty as the first of the principles upon which the Union is founded.[50] This principle must transcend the various specific freedoms if it is to have an independent normative meaning, since the latter can be fully inferred from the words "respect for human rights and fundamental freedoms, and the rule of law", which appear later in this provision.[51] The fact that liberty is named separately should be understood as meaning that "liberty" is a principle which goes beyond the others. It cannot be reduced to the mere rejection of a social order based on privilege or of repressive forms of government, such as national socialism, fascism, communism or other forms of authoritarianism. That would be a minimal reading.

Rather, it can be understood as a declaration that the liberty of the individual is the starting and reference point for all European law: everyone within the EU's jurisdiction is a free legal subject and all persons meet each other as legal equals in this legal order.[52] Conceptually it leads to an

[47] On the model of supranational federalism in detail, A von Bogdandy, 'The European Union as a Supranational Federation', (2000) 6 *Columbia Journal of European Law* 27.

[48] See also K Lenaerts, in: Sénat et Chambre des représentants de Belgique (eds), *Les finalités de l'Union européenne* (2001) 14 at 15.

[49] Opinion 2/94, *ECHR* [1996] ECR I-1763, paras 10 *et seq*; Case C-376/98, *Germany v Parliament and Council* [2000] ECR I-8419.

[50] Art I-2 CT-Conv (Art 2 CT-IGC) places human dignity before liberty. According to a Kantian understanding, the latter is the immediate characteristic of the former and is sometimes even used as a synonym thereof. See W Kersting, *Wohlgeordnete Freiheit* (1993) 203 *et seq*.

[51] An independent meaning is not rarely disputed. See S Griller *et al.*, *The Treaty of Amsterdam* (2000) 186.

[52] Hegel, above n 19, § 4; Siedentop, above n 15, 200 *et seq*.

individualistic understanding of law and society.[53] This understanding of a person is by no means imposed by nature, but is rather the most important artefact of European history, fundamental for the self-understanding of most individuals in the Western world.

One may object that this liberty is the universal principle *par excellence*. This may well be. Yet one cannot deny that this principle has by no means found a footing in all legal orders. And the law of the European Union is the only transnational legal order that effectively realises this principle in concrete legal relations on a broad scale.

In light of this principle, fundamental yet often technically (mis)understood concepts of European law become closely connected to the European constitutional tradition. The first is the concept of direct effect, according to which the individual is not only the object but also the subject of Union law. It is no coincidence that this idea initiated the transformation of the EC Treaties into a constitutional law for Europe.[54]

The principle of individual liberty has been a core element of integration theory from its earliest stages. W Hallstein understood European integration, with its tendency to a continental scope, as a significant expansion of the individual's space of autonomous action. The constitutional dimension of this expansion is based on the attribution of a constitutional function to private law, above all contract law: many consider private law as the systematic order of individual liberties.[55] Even though the early Community enacted practically no rules pertaining to private law, since its inception it has had an important private law dimension as it helped the individual to conclude contracts on a much wider scale. From this perspective, one can understand the fundamental importance of the market freedoms and competition law as well as Article 4(1) EC. After all, the goal of a free, autonomous, continental area cannot be realised within the respective Member States—such an area thus embodies a particular value of integration.[56]

This private autonomy has a particular significance in a heterogeneous political community of nearly continental scope such as the Union. The

[53] I Kant, 'Über den Gemeinspruch: Das mag in der Theorie richtig sein, taugt aber nicht für die Praxis', in: I Kant, *Kleinere Schriften zur Geschichtsphilosophie, Ethik und Politik* (1964, ed by K Vorländer) 67 at 87; E Gellner, *Nationalismus und Moderne* (1983, reprinted 1991) 89; see also J Drexl in this volume.

[54] Case 26/62, *van Gend & Loos* [1963] ECR 1 at 12; P Pescatore, 'The Doctrine of "Direct Effect",' (1983) 8 *EL Rev* 155 at 158.

[55] W Hallstein, 'Die Wiederherstellung des Privatrechts', (1946) 1 *Schriften der Süddeutschen Juristen-Zeitung* 530; E-J Mestmäcker, 'Die Wiederkehr der bürgerlichen Gesellschaft und ihres Rechts', 10 *Rechtshistorisches Journal* (1991) 177.

[56] *Entscheidungen des Bundesverfassungsgerichts* 89, 155 at 174 (*Maastricht*); this explains the special importance of the economic constitution.

larger and more diverse a political community is, the harder it is to understand politics and law as instruments of free self-governance. Areas of private autonomy, thus, become all the more imperative.

Yet the concept of liberty would be misunderstood if one were to understand it only formally as private autonomy: such liberty is always in danger of being transformed into privilege.[57] True liberty can only be conceived as the same liberty for all legal subjects. It is this conception of *equal liberty* that explains a most important line of the ECJ's case-law: equalising the legal status of the European legal order's subjects in view of a concrete freedom.[58] It finds expression in the case-law on discrimination, particularly with respect to freedom of movement of workers, the general prohibition of discrimination, rights deriving from Union citizenship[59] and the right of association.[60] This case-law shows the great potential for emancipation which this principle still contains after decades of integration.[61] It is from this perspective of equal liberty that the objective of establishing an area of freedom, security, and justice (Article 2 EU) is to be understood, rather than by narrowly focusing on its use for the single market.[62]

The criteria for accession to the EU according to Articles 49 and 7(1) EU (or Articles I-1(2), I-2, I-57 CT-Conv; Articles 1(2), 2, 58 CT-IGC) can be substantiated: a state's legal order and social culture must be founded on this conception of the individual and there must be no internal segregation, such as irreconcilable religious, ethnic or social divisions, that leads to legal inequality among individuals.[63]

[57] G-P Calliess, 'Die Zukunft der Privatautonomie', (2001) *Jahrbuch junger Zivilrechtswissenschaftler 2000* 85 at 90 *et seq.*

[58] Accordingly, Art I-2 CT-Conv (Art 2 CT-IGC) counts equality as a value of its own. It remains open to discussion if this supplementation of liberty with dignity and equality leads to a modification of the concept of liberty. Following Kant, liberty is derived from dignity, and both terms may be used almost synonymously; above n 50. The combination of dignity with equality through the French concept of *égale dignité* highlights the intertwining of the three concepts; see AG Stix-Hackl, Opinion of 18 March 2004 in Case C-36/02, *Omega* [2004] ECR I-0000, para 80. For criticism with regard to the possible attenuation of the content of dignity by the concept of *égale dignité*, see M Borowsky, in: J Meyer (ed), *Kommentar zur Charta der Grundrechte der Europäischen Union* (2003) Art 1, paras 8, 18.

[59] above n 171 and accompanying text.

[60] Path breaking, Case C-268/99, *Jany* [2001] ECR I-8615; Case C-162/00, *Pokrzeptowicz-Meyer* [2002] ECR I-1049; Cases 317/01 and 369/01, *Abatay* [2003] ECR I-12301; in detail, M Hofmann, 'The Right to Establishment for Nationals of the European Union Associated Countries in the Recent Jurisprudence of the ECJ', (2001) 44 *German Yearbook of International Law* 469.

[61] A Somek, 'A Constitution for Antidiscrimination: Exploring the Vanguard Moment of Community Law', (1999) 5 *ELJ* 243.

[62] In this sense, Cases C-187/01 and C-385/01, *Gözütok* [2003] ECR I-1345, paras 36 *et seq.*

[63] Explicitly so in Articles 1(2), 2 CT-Conv (Art 1(2), 2 CT-IGC).

2. The Rule of Law

The basic elements of the rule of law were the first aspects of European constitutional thought in the 1960s that coalesced into principles of primary law. JH Kaiser declared programmatically in 1964 that the creation of a European state based on the rule of law is the task of our time.[64] Most legal systems subsume the pertinent elements under a term equal or similar to *Rechtsstaatlichkeit* or *l'État de droit*; almost all language versions of the Treaty similarly use terminology linked to the state. This terminology is imprecise, due to the inclusion of the element of statehood.[65] It seems more accurate to use the term "rule of law" (*prééminence du droit* or *Herrschaft des Rechts*) in the loaded sense of the word "law" as the ECJ has derived from Article 220 EC.[66] Establishing a culture of law has been of crucial importance to European development and integration.

a) A Community of Law

Perhaps the theoretical concept which has had the most far-reaching consequences for legal integration is that of the *Rechtsgemeinschaft*, "community of law",[67] the various elements of which establish *both* continuity *and* innovation with respect to national constitutional thought. As a principle it has had the greatest independent influence on the extensive legal development of the Treaties' content. Apparently, the responsible legal actors feel that, whereas issues of democracy must be left to the politicians, many aspects of the rule of law need not be.

A legal norm regulates social relationships. Its correlative (actual) effectiveness and nonpartisan application are constitutive for the rule of law. They are—in normative terms—the first expression of the legal equality of individuals.[68] The effectiveness of legal norms, at least in a functioning state, is usually beyond question. Due to the common origin of a state's authority to legislate and to enforce, this aspect of the rule of law is mostly a marginal topic or simply presumed to be self-evident. It is only with

[64] JH Kaiser, 'Bewahrung und Veränderung demokratischer und rechtsstaatlicher Verfassungsstruktur in den internationalen Gemeinschaften', (1966) 23 *Veröffentlichungen der Vereinigung der Deutschen Staatsrechtslehrer* 1 at 33. There is thus a striking parallel with the constitutional developments of the 19th century; see E-W Böckenförde, *Recht, Staat, Freiheit* (1992) 143 *et seq*.

[65] M Zuleeg, in: H von der Groeben and J Schwarze (eds), *Kommentar zum EU-/EG-Vertrag* (2003), Art 1 EC, para 4.

[66] Gerkrath, above n 11, 347.

[67] W Hallstein, *Die Europäische Gemeinschaft* (5th edn 1979) 51 *et seq*; on the reception, see M Zuleeg, 'Die Europäische Gemeinschaft als Rechtsgemeinschaft', (1994), *Neue Juristische Wochenschrift* 545; Esteban, above n 29, 154 *et seq*.

[68] M Nettesheim, 'Der Grundsatz der einheitlichen Wirksamkeit des Gemeinschaftsrechts', in: A Randelzhofer *et al* (eds), *Gedächtnisschrift für E Grabitz* (1995) 447 at 448 *et seq*.

respect to the equal application of the law that this question enjoys any constitutional attention in the domestic legal orders.[69]

As Community law was public international law in origin, its first problem has been and still is precisely its effectiveness and equal application to social relationships. This is the first aspect of Hallstein's term "community of law": the EU is *only* a community of law and not also a community of coercion by means of its own.[70] The situation is therefore different than that of a state's legal system. In a transnational community of law the community's systemic interest in the effectiveness of its law and the individual's corresponding interest in the enforcement of a norm that benefits him or her are consonant: the legislator (EU) and the beneficiary (citizen) both need the nation-state's domestic courts. The relevant legal concepts, above all direct applicability,[71] primacy[72] as well as the principles of effective and uniform application ("equivalence"),[73] indissolubly serve both interests. The widespread assertion that European law "instrumentalises the individual" for the advancement of European integration[74] (with the implicit reproach of an infringement of human dignity) expresses a misunderstanding of this basis of Community law.

Perhaps the Union is even more dependant on the rule of law than an established nation-state. When W Hallstein said that the Community is a *creation* of law,[75] this must be understood against the dominant understanding of the nation-state, which attributes to the nation-state a "pre-legal substratum" (e.g. a people, an established organisation). One can contest the pre-existence of the state before the constitution[76] as well as the explication of integration solely by the binding force of law.[77] Yet the outstanding importance of a common law as a bond which embraces all Union citizens is, in view of

[69] Art 3(1) German Basic Law; on the phenomenon of selective application as a legal problem, *Entscheidungen des Bundesverfassungsgerichts* 66, 331 at 335 *et seq*; 71, 354 at 362.

[70] Hallstein, above n 67, 53 *et seq*.

[71] Case 26/62, above n 54; Case C-8/81, *Becker* [1982] ECR 53, paras 29 *et seq*; Pescatore, above n 54.

[72] Case 6/64, *Costa* [1964] ECR 585 at 593 *et seq*; Case 92/78, *Simmenthal v Commission* [1979] ECR 777, para 39; Case C-213/89, *Factortame* [1990] ECR I-2433, para 19; Case C-285/98, *Kreil* [2000] ECR I-69 (presuming primacy as unproblematic).

[73] Cases 205/82–215/82, *Deutsche Milchkontor* [1983] ECR 2633, para 22; Case C-261/95, *Palmisani* [1997] ECR I-4025, para 27; Case C-404/97, *Commission v Portugal* [2000] ECR I-4897, para 55; S Kadelbach, *Allgemeines Verwaltungsrecht unter europäischem Einfluß* (1999) 117 *et seq* and 267 *et seq*.

[74] T von Danwitz, *Verwaltungsrechtliches System und Europäische Integration* (1996) 175; J Masing, *Die Mobilisierung des Bürgers für die Durchsetzung des Rechts* (1997).

[75] Hallstein, above n 67, 53; U Everling, 'Bindung und Rahmen: Recht und Integration', in: W Weidenfeld (ed), *Die Identität Europas* (1985) 152.

[76] Informative, H Schulze-Fielitz, 'Grundsatzkontroversen in der deutschen Staatsrechtslehre nach 50 Jahren Grundgesetz', (1999) 32 *Die Verwaltung* 241.

[77] R Dehousse and JHH Weiler, 'The legal dimension', in: W Wallace (ed), *The Dynamics of European Integration* (1990) 242.

the dearth of other integrating factors such as language or history, hardly contestable. Moreover, as already pointed out by de Tocqueville, the bigger and freer a polity is the more it must rely on the law.[78] This is also recognised in political science.[79]

Some aspects of European law seem rigidly at odds with the European value of diversity. This is partially due to the difficulty of securing the effectiveness of transnational law that conflicts with national provisions or practice. In view of the degree of effectiveness already achieved and the development of principles that attribute constitutional weight to colliding interests, it is now possible to find more balanced solutions according to general doctrines on the collision of principles.[80]

Law requires that conflicts be settled by an unbiased third party.[81] The principle of a community of law implies correspondingly that "neither its Member States nor its institutions can avoid a review of the question whether the measures adopted by them are in conformity with the basic constitutional charter, the Treaty. In particular, ... the Treaty established a complete system of legal remedies."[82] This is now reinforced by Article II-47(1) CT-Conv (Article 107 CT-IGC). The principle of comprehensive legal protection at the Community as well as at the Member State level has led to legal developments of the highest importance.[83] Against this background and in view of obvious loopholes in legal protection, the ECJ's restrictive interpretation of Article 230(4) EC seems unjustifiable.[84]

[78] A de Tocqueville, *Über die Demokratie in Amerika* [*Democracy in America*] (1835, reprinted 1985) 78 *et seq*, 99 *et seq*; G Bermann, 'The Role of Law in the Functioning of Federal Systems', in: K Nicolaidis and R Howse (eds), *The Federal Vision* (2001) 191.

[79] Siedentop, above n 15, 94.

[80] Kadelbach, above n 73, 270 *et seq*; M Zuleeg, 'Deutsches und Europäisches Verwaltungsrecht—Wechselseitige Einwirkungen', (1994) 53 *Veröffentlichungen der Vereinigung der deutschen Staatsrechtslehrer* 154 at 165 *et seq*; M Zuleeg, *Der rechtliche Zusammenhalt in der Europäischen Union* (2004) 104 *et seq*. For a rigid, pro-integration view, see C Kakouris, 'Do the Member States Possess Judicial "Procedural" Autonomy?', (1997) 34 *CML Rev* 1389.

[81] A Kojève, *Esquisse d'une phénoménologie du droit* (1982) § 13.

[82] Case 294/83, *Les Verts v Parliament* [1986] ECR 1339, para 23; Case T-17/00 R, *Rothley et al v Parliament* [2000] ECR II-2085, para 54.

[83] Kadelbach, above n 73, 368 *et seq*; D Classen, *Die Europäisierung der Verwaltungsgerichtsbarkeit* (1996) 182 *et seq*; see eg, Case 222/84, *Johnston* [1986] ECR 1651, paras 13 *et seq*; Cases C-6/90 and 9/90, *Francovich* [1991] ECR I-5357, para 31; Case C-70/88, *Parliament v Council* [1990] ECR I-2041, paras 15 *et seq*; Case 2/88 Imm, *Zwartveld* [1990] ECR I-3365, para 16.

[84] The approach taken in Case T-177/01, *Jégo-Quéré v Commission* [2002] ECR II-2365 *et seq*, paras 41 *et seq*, is to be welcomed; see also AG Jacobs, Opinion of 21 March 2002 in Case C-50/00 P, *Unión de Pequeños Agricultores v Council* [2002] ECR I-6677, paras 59 *et seq*. The ECJ, unfortunately, refused to follow the interpretation given by the CFI and the AG considering this step as requiring a Treaty amendment, Case C-50/00 P, *ibid*, paras 40 *et seq*, in particular para 45; see also the appeal judgement by the ECJ in Case C-263/02 P, *Commission v Jégo-Quéré* [2004] ECR I-3425, para 36; in detail, S Bitter, 'Procedural Rights and the Enforcement of EC Law through Sanctions", in: A Bodnar *et al* (eds), *The Emerging Constitutional Law of the European Union* (2003) 15 at 29 *et seq*.

The rule of law is not uncontested.[85] Titles V and VI EU hardly live up to this principle. The European Council's role is particularly problematic. Although, legally speaking, it is an institution of the Union, its self-understanding is that of an institution operating outside the ambit of the Union,[86] as demonstrated by its failure to proclaim the Charter of Fundamental Rights of the European Union. Similar to the king in the constitutional regimes of the 19th century, it is not answerable to any other institution and can do no wrong.[87] This institution, which often decisively shapes legislative projects, places itself outside the constitutional order and beyond legal and political responsibility.[88] The Constitutional Treaty remains most ambiguous in this respect. On the one hand, it squarely declares the European Council as an institution of the Union (Article I-18(2) CT-Conv; Article 19(1) CT-IGC). Yet it allows the European Council to elude many mechanisms of legal and political scrutiny (Articles I-20(1)(2), III-282(1) CT-Conv; Articles 21(1)(2), 376(1) CT-IGC)[89] and fortifies it, e.g., through a more efficient presidency (Article I-21 CT-Conv; Article 22 CT-IGC).[90]

b) Principles of Protection for the Individual and of Rational Procedure

The principle of the rule of law contains numerous (sub-)principles that aim at the rational exercise of public power and protect qualified interests of its subjects.[91]

At an early stage of integration, much effort was dedicated for that reason to the principle of the separation of powers. This is hardly surprising: its importance emerges from Article 16 of the French Declaration of the Rights of Man and of the Citizen of 1789. In the 1950s the ECJ used the principle of the separation of powers to protect the citizen and to rationalise the exercise of public power by the Community institutions.[92] Yet separation of

[85] For a pessimistic view on whether the "Community of law" is still a working premise to develop EU law, see C Joerges, 'The Law in the Process of Constitutionalizing Europe', (2002).4 *EUI Working Paper LAW*.

[86] JP Jacqué, in: von der Groeben and Schwarze, above n 65, Art 4 EU, para 5.

[87] C von Rotteck, *Lehrbuch des Vernunftrechts und der Staatswissenschaften* (2nd edn 1840, reprinted 1964), vol 2, *Lehrbuch der allgemeinen Staatslehren*, 249–51.

[88] Case T-584/93, *Roujansky v Council* [1994] ECR II-585, para 12; Case C-253/94, *Roujansky v Council* [1995] ECR I-7, para 11; R Lauwaars, *Constitutionele Erosie* (1994), cited by Gerkrath, above n 11, 150.

[89] Art 365 CT-IGC allows for a review of acts of the European Council which are intended to produce legal effects vis-à-vis third parties. Originally, the Convention had not foreseen the possibility of reviewing acts of the European Council in Art III-270(1) CT-Conv. Interestingly, this fundamental change has been presented as merely technical in character, see Editorial and Legal Comments on the Draft Treaty Establishing a Constitution for Europe of 6 October 2003 <http://ue.eu.int/igcpdf/en/03/cg00/cg00004.en03.pdf> (8 April 2004).

[90] For a constitutional classification of the European Council, see F Boschi Orlandini, 'Principi costituzionali di struttura e Consiglio europeo', in: Scudiero, above n 35, 165.

[91] Hallstein, above n 67, 55 *et seq*.

[92] Case 9/56, *Meroni v High Authority* [1957/58] ECR 133 at 152.

powers has lost much of its meaning, probably because it could not adequately respond to certain issues.[93] More specific requirements replaced it when the ECJ—and subsequently the CFI—developed, beginning in the late 1960s, principles for the protection of fundamental rights and rational procedure as well as principles of sound administration[94]; they are far more precise and effective.

The development of the numerous (sub-)principles which aim at a rationalisation of the exercise of public power and the protection of the individual is the part of the constitutional development which has received the most scholarly dedication.[95] These principles display a high degree of differentiation[96] and development, as demonstrated not least by the Charter of Fundamental Rights of the European Union.[97] The relevant discussions show how a European doctrine of principles takes recourse to the developed repertoire of national fundamental rights yet at the same time must take account of the Union's specific constitutional framework as a supranational authority.[98]

Although the improvement of the rule of law was not a core task of the European Convention, the Constitutional Treaty contains numerous elements that might provide for a better realisation of that principle.[99] It might even lead to a fundamental shift in the Union's legal order. In particular, Part II of the Constitutional Treaty, which incorporates the slightly changed Charter of Fundamental Rights, will raise the issue whether fundamental rights should be shifted from being simple constraints on the Union's public action to informing all public power, whether national or supranational.[100]

[93] But see H-J Seeler, 'Die rechtsstaatliche Fundierung der EG-Entscheidungsstrukturen', (1990) *Europarecht* 99; K Lenaerts, 'Some Reflections on the Separation of Powers in the European Community', (1991) 28 *CML Rev* 11.

[94] On the latter, Case T-54/99, *max.mobil v Commission* [2002] ECR II-313, para 48.

[95] A Arnull, *The General Principles of EEC Law and the Individual* (1990); I Pernice, *Grundrechtsgehalte im Europäischen Gemeinschaftsrecht* (1979); T Schilling, 'Bestand und allgemeine Lehren der bürgerschützenden allgemeinen Rechtsgrundsätze des Gemeinschaftsrechts', (2000) *Europäische Grundrechte-Zeitschrift* 3; J Schwarze, *European Administrative Law* (1992); T Tridimas, *The General Principles of EC Law* (1999); J Usher, *General Principles of EC Law* (1999); see also J Kühling in this volume.

[96] On the level of protection, see J Limbach, 'Die Kooperation der Gerichte in der zukünftigen europäischen Grundrechtsarchitektur', (2000) *Europäische Grundrechte-Zeitschrift* 217 at 219 *et seq*.

[97] Charter of Fundamental Rights of the European Union, OJ C 364, 18.12.2000, 8; for its detailed interpretation, see I Pernice and F Mayer, in: E Grabitz and M Hilf (eds), *Das Recht der Europäischen Union* (looseleaf, last update 2003), after Art 6 EU; see also Meyer, above n 58.

[98] Weiler, above n 43 (1999) 102 *et seq*.

[99] Eg, the extension of judicial review to former "third pillar policies" (*argumentum e contrario* Art III-283 CT-Conv, Art 377 CT-IGC), the entrenchment of requirements for a rational exercise of public authority (eg, good administration, Art II-41 CT-Conv; Art 101 CT-IGC); transparency and publicness (Art I-49(1) and (2) CT-Conv; Art 50(1) and (2) CT-IGC); access to documents (Articles I-49(3), (4) and (5), II-42 CT-Conv; Art 50(3) and (4), 102 CT-IGC), the new order of legal instruments (Art I-32 CT-Conv; Art 33 CT-IGC).

[100] In detail, A von Bogdandy, 'The EU as a Human Rights Organization?', (2000) 37 *CML Rev* 1307.

The ECJ has already taken important steps in this direction. Whenever there is the faintest link to the Union, the ECJ requires the national legal orders to respect the European Convention on Human Rights and its Protocols as interpreted by the Strasbourg Court.[101]

A doctrine of principles has to regulate conflicts between the rule of law and other principles that such a development will produce. In particular, the various principles protecting diversity demand restraints on a principle- or value-based homogenisation through the judiciary.[102] Moreover, the specific features of the Union's organisational constitution, for instance the lack of a constitutional founding authority organised at the Union level, must be taken into account when determining the principles' normative reach and depth. Considered in light of the full range of constitutional principles, expanding the reach and the depth of supranational fundamental rights in the current Union is by no means an unequivocally positive development, but rather a deeply ambiguous one.[103] Perhaps the ECJ is trying to respond to this danger by not developing its own fundamental rights case-law, but rather incorporating the ECHR's standards. Yet it is doubtful whether the ECHR is more responsive to issues of constitutional diversity and more acceptable for the national constitutional systems.

3. Democracy

a) Development and Basic Features

For over 30 years legal science focused not on the principle of democracy, but rather on the rule of law. The thesis that the Community *should* have its own democratic legitimacy started to develop only as a *political* request of some and not as a legal principle. Until the 1990s the view was held that the supranational authority did not legally require democratic legitimacy beyond the general requirements for an international organisation.[104] Then, a rapid development took place which followed two different, albeit connected paths: one, based on civil rights thinking, focusing on Union citizenship,[105] and another,

[101] Case C-60/00, *Carpenter* [2002] ECR I-6279, paras 41 *et seq*; Cases C-465/00, C-138/01 and C-139/01, *Österreichischer Rundfunk* [2003] ECR I-4989, paras 71 *et seq*; Case C-109/01, *Akrich* [2003] ECR I-9607, paras 58 *et seq*; Case C-101/01, *Lindqvist* [2003] ECR I-12971, para 90; Case C-117/01, *K.B.* [2004] ECR I-541, paras 33 *et seq*; on this case-law in detail, G Britz, 'Bedeutung der EMRK für nationale Verwaltungsgerichte und Behörden', (2004) *Neue Zeitschrift für Verwaltungsrecht* 173. In order to grasp its magnitude, this development has to be seen in relation to the equally activist case-law on Union citizenship; on the latter, below n 171 and accompanying text.

[102] Von Bogdandy, above n 100.

[103] For details, see S Kadelbach and J Kühling in this volume.

[104] A Randelzhofer, 'Zum behaupteten Demokratiedefizit der Europäischen Gemeinschaft', in: P Hommelhoff and P Kirchhof (eds), *Der Staatenverbund der Europäischen Union* (1994) 39 at 40 *et seq*.

[105] This path will not be presented here; see in detail S Kadelbach in this volume.

based on institutional thinking, oriented at the legitimacy of the Union's organisational set-up.

The development, from political demand for an independent democratic legitimacy; to *legal* principle, has been arduous. Tellingly, even the 1976 Act concerning the election of the representatives of the Parliament by direct universal suffrage does not contain the term "democracy".[106] Beginning in the 1980s, the ECJ very cautiously started to use the concept of democracy as a legal principle.[107] The Treaty of Maastricht then employed this term, although it mentions its role on the supranational level only in the 5th recital of the Preamble. With Article F EU Treaty in the Maastricht version democracy found its way into a Treaty text—yet not as a basis for the Union, but rather with a view to the Member States' political systems. The leap was not made until the Treaty of Amsterdam whose Article 6 EU then laid down that the principle of democracy also applies to the Union. This internal constitutional development is buttressed by external provisions. Of particular importance is Article 3 Protocol No 1 to the ECHR in its recent interpretation by the Strasbourg Court,[108] as well as—albeit less clearly—national provisions such as Article 23(1) German Basic Law.[109]

The Convention's draft of the Constitutional Treaty tried to make another leap, which, however, almost certainly would have failed. In selecting democracy as the theme of the introductory quotation,[110] the Convention's draft distinguished it as the highest value of the Union. This primacy, though, arose not solely from the prominent placement. The quotation comes from Pericles's funeral oration for the soldiers who died in the Peloponnesian War—in which speech democracy is elevated as the value that even justifies sacrifice of human lives.[111] To suggest democracy as the

[106] Act concerning the election of the representatives of the Parliament by direct universal suffrage, OJ L 278, 8.10.1976, 1.

[107] The principle has been used very carefully and above all to strengthen existing provisions; see especially Case 138/79, *Roquette Frères v Council* [1980] ECR 3333, para 33; Case C-300/89, *Commission v Council* [1991] ECR I-2867, para 20; Case C-65/93, *Parliament v Council* [1995] ECR I-643, para 21; Case C-21/94, *Parliament v Council* [1995] ECR I-1827, para 17; Case C-392/95, *Parliament v Council* [1997] ECR I-3213, para 14. But see the CFI judgement Case T-135/96, *UEAPME v Council* [1998] ECR II-2335, para 89, that interprets the principle of democracy with greater liberty. See G Britz and M Schmidt, 'Die institutionalisierte Mitwirkung der Sozialpartner an der Rechtsetzung der Europäischen Gemeinschaft', (1999) *Europarecht* 467 at 481 *et seq*; K Langenbucher, 'Zur Zulässigkeit parlamentsersetzender Normgebungsverfahren im Europarecht', (2002) *Zeitschrift für europäisches Privatrecht* 265.

[108] ECHR, *Matthews v United Kingdom* Rep 1999-I 251; see G Ress, 'Das Europäische Parlament als Gesetzgeber', (1999) *Zeitschrift für Europarechtliche Studien* 219 at 226.

[109] On similar provisions in other constitutions see C Grabenwarter's contribution in this volume and I Pernice, in: Dreier, above n 21, Art 23, paras 9 *et seq*; on the requirements of Art 23 German Basic Law, see *ibid*, paras 49–57.

[110] The text read as follows: "Our Constitution ... is called a democracy because power is in the hands not of a minority but of the greatest number."

[111] Thucydides, *History of the Peleponnesian War*, II, 42 and II, 44. The idea that the readiness to make sacrifices is a key element of a collective identity is often found in US-American constitutional theory; for the viewpoint of a leading proponent of the "cultural study of law", see P Kahn, 'American Hegemony and International Law', (2000) 1 *Chicago JIL* 1 at 8; see also U Haltern in this volume.

Union's primary value is risky. Certainly, most Union citizens value democracy highly, yet the introductory use seemingly intimated that the Union—at least as the Convention's draft would have it—exists for the purpose of realising democratic ideals. Many citizens, however, may—rightly—believe that democracy's status in the Union is not fully satisfactory; moreover, considering the institutional alterations, the Constitutional Treaty is unlikely significantly to improve this democratic deficit. Thus, discord was likely between the most prominent declaration of the Convention's draft and the everyday experience of Union citizens. This would not have helped to foster identity; on the contrary, some might have seen the inconsistency as a deceptive manoeuvre, which fostered not identification but alienation and cynicism. Fortunately, the IGC deleted the reference to Thucydides' narrative thereby attenuating the apparent inconsistency. With the more classical approach of extending the co-decision procedure to more fields of EU action and the adoption of the more innovative—yet still not fully convincing—articles on the democratic life of the Union (Articles I-44 *et seq* CT-Conv; Articles 45 *et seq* CT-IGC), the IGC thus takes steps which might prove more successful than the overambitious Convention's draft.

The word "democracy" in Article 6 EU carries no definition. It has yet to be determined what the principle of democracy means precisely on the European level. Nothing better depicts the uncertainties of how to understand the union principle of democracy than Part I Title VI and Part II Title V Constitutional Treaty. Under the headings "The Democratic Life of the Union" and "Citizens' Rights" respectively, a number of seemingly unconnected provisions are amassed; it will require a singular intellectual effort to reconstruct them as a meaningful whole.[112]

However, such innovative scholarship is needed anyway. More than for any other constitutional principle, it is beyond question that the principle of democracy requires a *specific* concretisation for the European Union and that any analogy to nation-state institutions must be carefully argued. A remarkably complex interdisciplinary discussion on European democracy has developed on the basis of this insight.[113]

From the perspective of a European doctrine of principles the preliminary question of the possibility of democracy at the Union level can be neglected.[114] First, a doctrine of principles can hardly say anything about this

[112] For the first comprehensive effort, see A Peters, 'European Democracy after the 2003 Convention', (2004) 41 *CML Rev* 37.

[113] For the identification of 64 positions on the European democracy problem, see F Schimmelpfennig, 'Legitimate Rule in the European Union. The Academic Debate', (1996), 27 *Tübinger Arbeitspapiere zur Internationalen Politik und Friedensforschung*, <http://www.uni-tuebingen.de/uni/spi/taps/tap27.htm> (8 April 2004).

[114] See P Graf Kielmansegg, 'Integration und Demokratie', in: M Jachtenfuchs and B Kohler-Koch (eds), *Europäische Integration* (1996) 47; C Offe, 'Demokratie und Wohlfahrtsstaat', in: W Streek (ed), *Internationale Wirtschaft, nationale Demokratie* (1998) 99; F Scharpf, 'Demokratieprobleme in der europäischen Mehrebenenpolitik', in: W Merkel and A Busch

question which rather belongs to the realm of political sociology. More importantly, the Union's constitutional law has normatively, and thus for a doctrine of principles decisively, decided the question in Article 6(1) EU: democracy *is* a constitutional principle of the Union.

A European doctrine of principles has to define the unional principle of democracy. The easier part of that exercise is to discard inappropriate understandings which are prominent in numerous national legal discourses on the concretisation of the principle of democracy. This is particularly true for the theory which understands democracy as being the rule of "the people" in the sense of a "*Volk*" insofar as the term is to be understood in a substantive sense. Such an understanding implies empirical bases that scarcely emerge at the European level; it would also be difficult to square with manifold provisions of the current Treaties (e.g. Articles 1(2) EU, 189 EC) although the substitution of the word "peoples" with "citizens" in the Constitutional Treaty might point to a shift in this conception in its Articles I-1(1), I-19(2) and I-45(2) CT-Conv (Articles 1(1), 20(2), 46(2) CT-IGC). Of course it is possible to proceed formally and conceive "*das Volk*" as being the sum of all Union citizens,[115] yet even such a strategy to concretise the principle of democracy would create severe strains on other central Union principles, in particular Articles 1(2) and 6(3) EU and Art 189 EC. These norms suggest that the principle of democracy within the context of the Union must be concretised independently from the (pre-legal and problematic) concept of "people".[116]

As an alternative, the individual's opportunities to participate come into the foreground. PM Huber conceives the European principle of democracy as giving the individual through unional as well as national procedures a sufficiently effective opportunity to influence the basic decisions of European policy. The European principle of democracy thus contains an optimisation requirement insofar as it aims at the full utilisation of possibilities to participate at both levels.[117] This understanding of democracy does not necessarily require breaking with understandings developed under the national constitutions, but rather correlates with the civil rights

(eds), *Demokratie in Ost und West* (1999) 672; D Grimm, 'Does Europe Need a Constitution?', (1995) 1 *ELJ* 282; Fuchs, above n 24, 222 *et seq*; but see M Zuleeg, 'Demokratie ohne Volk oder Demokratie der Völker?', in: J Drexl *et al* (eds), *Europäische Demokratie* (1999) 11; J Habermas, 'Warum braucht Europa eine Verfassung?', (2001) 27 *Die Zeit*, <http://www.zeit.de/2001/27/Politik/200127_verfassung_lang.htmllst (8 April 2004).

115 A Augustin, *Das Volk der Europäischen Union* (2000) 62 at 110 *et seq*.

116 For a detailed analysis, see S Dellavalle, 'Für einen normativen Begriff von Europa: Nationalstaat und europäische Einigung im Lichte der politischen Theorie', in: A von Bogdandy (ed), *Die Europäische Option* (1993) 217.

117 PM Huber, 'Demokratie ohne Volk oder Demokratie der Völker? Zur Demokratiefähigkeit der Europäischen Union', in: Drexl *et al*, above n 114, 27 at 55 (author's translation).

understanding of democracy. This strategy of concretising the principle of democracy finds confirmation in the legal concept of Union citizenship (Article 17 EC).

Yet it would be a misunderstanding of the unional principle of democracy to place *only* the individual Union citizen in the centre. The Union does not negate the democratic organisation of the citizens in and by the Member States (Article 17(1) EC). Thus, alongside the Union citizens, the Member States' democratically organised peoples (Articles 1(2) and 6(3) EU, Article 189 EC) are to be active in the Union's decision-making process as organised associations. A concretisation strategy should build on these two textual elements: the current Treaties speak on the one hand of the peoples of the Member States and on the other hand of the Union's citizens insofar as the principle of democracy is at issue.[118]

The central elements which determine the Union's principle of democracy at this first level are thus named. The Union is based on a dual structure of legitimacy[119]: the totality of the Union's citizens *and* the peoples of the European Union as organised by their respective Member State constitutions.

At the conceptual level, the understanding of the unional principle of democracy suggests abandoning the conception of democracy as the self-determination of a people. Yet the Constitutional Treaty depicts the Union as such an instrument of self-determination.[120] This conception becomes implausible since the peoples of the Member States, as members of the Union, no longer exercise such self-determination (if they ever did). In addition, conceptions that consider democracy as an instrument of individual self-determination[121] do not have much of a chance for success within the Union context. On all levels the civil rights and control oriented conceptions of democracy appear more appropriate.[122]

[118] The Constitutional Treaty alters this picture: although "peoples" remains a constitutional concept, the Constitutional Treaty always uses the term "citizens" in the context of democracy. This should not, however, alter the concept of dual legitimacy, as already expressed in Art I-1(1) CT-Conv (Art 1(1) CT-IGC).

[119] On the model of dual legitimacy, see A Peters, *Elemente einer Theorie der Verfassung Europas* (2001) 556 *et seq*; see also S Oeter and P Dann, both in this volume.

[120] This is underlined by the 3rd recital of the Preamble (4th recital of the Convention's draft) which states that the peoples of Europe are determined, "united ever more closely, to forge a common destiny".

[121] G Frankenberg, *Die Verfassung der Republik* (1997) 148 *et seq* and *passim* tends in this direction; J Habermas, *Faktizität und Geltung* (1992) 532 *et seq* and *passim*; I Pernice, 'Europäisches und nationales Verfassungsrecht', (2000) 60 *Veröffentlichungen der Vereinigung der Deutschen Staatsrechtslehrer* 148 at 160.

[122] Augustin, above n 115, 246 *et seq*, 319 *et seq*, 388 *et seq*; A Wallrabenstein, *Das Verfassungsrecht der Staatsangehörigkeit* (1999) 138 *et seq*. The dichotomies used herein are developed in A von Bogdandy, 'Globalization and Europe: How to Square Democracy, Globalization, and International Law', (2004) 15 *EJIL* 885.

b) The Principle of Democracy and the Institutional Structure

Under almost all understandings of democracy, the most important element lies in the choice of the political personnel through free elections by the citizens. There is no reason why there should be a different starting point for the Union. Elections provide two lines of democratic legitimacy for the Union's organisational structure.

These lines are institutionally represented respectively by the European Parliament (EP), which is based on elections by the totality of the Union's citizens, and by the Council and the European Council, whose legitimacy is based on the Member States' democratically organised peoples. In the current constitutional situation there is a clear dominance of the line of legitimacy from the national parliaments, as shown in particular by Article 48 EU as well as the preponderance of the Council and the European Council in the Union's procedures. The Constitutional Treaty increases the relative weight of the EP, without, however, equalising the two lines of democratic legitimacy.

One may even doubt whether a principle of dual legitimacy as a concretisation of the principle of democracy can be formulated at all since the co-decision of the EP has by no means been incorporated into all areas of competence, nor do all important personnel decisions require its approval, nor are the other institutions answerable to it for all acts. Nevertheless, there is broad consensus that the EP's current scope of competences already permits the assumption of a principle of dual legitimacy.[123] The decision on appointments to the Commission and thus the "political motor of integration" is based on dual legitimacy pursuant to Article 214 EC (Article I-26 CT-Conv; Article 27 CT-IGC) as are not only the greater part of the legislative process pursuant to Article 251 EC (Article III-302 CT-Conv; Article 396 CT-IGC), but also the budget according to Article 272 EC (Articles I-55, III-310 CT-Conv; Articles 56, 404 CT-IGC) and the decision on accepting a new Member under Article 49 EU (Article I-57(2) CT-Conv; Article 58 CT-IGC).

Yet, in view of the current legal situation, the principle can only be understood as meaning that the democratic legitimacy of Union acts *can* be derived by way of the Council and the EP. The European legal system does *not*, however, specify *which* institution in any concrete case *must* take a concrete decision.[124] The legitimacy of any specific act is a question of procedure, based on the relevant competence: for such sectoral regulation, the principle of democracy can promote stability but cannot modify procedure itself.[125] The

[123] *Entscheidungen des Bundesverfassungsgerichts* 89, 155 at 184 (*Maastricht*); see A von Bogdandy, 'Das Leitbild der dualistischen Legitimation für die europäische Verfassungsentwicklung', (2000) *Kritische Vierteljahresschrift für Gesetzgebung und Rechtswissenschaft* 284; see also above II 4.

[124] This notwithstanding the political demand that, at least in those areas in which the Council decides by majority decision, the Parliament should be involved by way of the co-decision procedure.

[125] The principle of democracy is thus not a criterion for the horizontal distribution of competences; see Case C-300/89, above n 107, paras 20 *et seq*; but see AG Tesauro, *ibid*, I-2892 *et seq*.

demand to expand parliamentary powers remains in the political sphere; it can scarcely be based on the Union's principle of democracy.[126]

If the legal impact of the principle of democracy is limited, its implications are enormous. A transnational parliament can confer democratic legitimacy although it does not represent a people. Moreover, a *governmental* institution (e.g. the Council) is also able to do so. This contrasts sharply with national constitutional law, where such decisions are usually considered democratically problematic.[127] Even in federal constitutions the representative institutions of the sub-national governments are rarely acknowledged to have a role in conferring democratic legitimacy.[128] The idea of a *unitary* people is too strong.[129] The modification of traditional strategies to realise democracy is especially evident at this juncture.

In Member States' constitutional law the principle of democracy is further concretised by the parliament's specific position in the overall constitutional structure. At this point, European democracy remains hazy. One encounters an open situation, displaying this principle's lesser degree of development.

Some aspects should be briefly highlighted. One concern is whether and to what extent the system of European government is a parliamentary one.[130] Applied to the Union this concerns the relationship between the EP and the Commission. Legally the EP's control over the Commission's composition is, in certain respects, greater than that of the French National Assembly over the government.[131] Yet, whereas a semi-parliamentarian system of government has been realised on the weak French basis, nothing of

[126] However, the approach taken by the CFI in its judgment in Case T-353/00, *Le Pen v Parliament* [2003] ECR II-1729, paras 90 *et seq*, and by the President of the ECJ in his Order in Case C-208/03 P-R, *Le Pen v Parliament* [2003] I-7939, paras 95 *et seq*, is too cautious in that it rejected an autonomous, extensive right of Parliament to verify the vacancy of the seat of one of its members as not having separate legal effects. The reasoning is based on the state of Community law after the 1976 Act. The principle of democracy enshrined in Art 6(1) EU could and should have been of more significance in this regard. See M Nettesheim, *Juristenzeitung* (2003) 952 at 954.

[127] On the discussion, see A von Bogdandy, *Gubernative Rechtsetzung* (2000) 108 *et seq*; HP Ipsen, 'Zur Exekutiv-Rechtsetzung in der Europäischen Gemeinschaft', in P Badura and R Scholz (eds), *Wege und Verfahren des Verfassungslebens: Festschrift für P Lerche* (1993) 425; on the controversial democratic legitimacy of the German Federal Council, see J Jekewitz, in E Denninger *et al* (eds), *Alternativ-Kommentar zum Grundgesetz für die Bundesrepublik Deutschland* (2001), before Art 50 GG, para 11; M Bothe, in *ibid*, Art 20 paras 1–3, II (Bundesstaat), para 27; but see H Bauer, in Dreier, above n 21, Art 50 GG, para 18.

[128] ECHR, above n 108, para 52.

[129] Similarly, E-W Böckenförde, 'Sozialer Bundesstaat und parlamentarische Demokratie', in J Jekewitz (ed), *Festschrift für F Schäfer* (1980) 182 at 190.

[130] See P Dann in this volume.

[131] According to Art 8(1) French Constitution, the president nominates the prime minister; the prime minister's dependence on Parliament results from Art 49 in conjunction with the obligation to resign according to Art 50. The parliamentary competences contained in Art 214 EC are to some extent greater, yet the 2/3 quorum required for a motion of censure according to Art 201 EC is too high to establish a parliamentary system of government.

the sort has occurred on the European level. It is quite conceivable that the Union's constitutive plurality prevents such a system from developing. Thus, the congressional model is also being discussed as an option for the EP.[132] It appears to be an empirically, constitutionally and politically open question, what form the European parliamentary system will finally take.[133]

The Parliament's lack of a right to legislative initiative might also become characteristic. It gives support to a conception grounded in the realistic parliamentary theories of the 20th century.[134] The lack of a right to legislative initiative can be construed in such a way that a society gives up the understanding of legislation as *self*-legislation, dear to important strands of democratic thinking.[135] The EP's whole organisation can be understood as a safeguard against the gubernative bureaucracy's becoming overly autonomous.[136] This conception points to a sober understanding of the principle of democracy but may have good prospects for that very reason. This fluidity shows that the ECJ has been wise not to use the principle of democracy for far-reaching developments of the law in the inter-institutional area, since, in contrast to the principle of the rule of law, sufficiently concretised strategies are needed.

c) Transparency, Participation, Deliberation and Flexibility

The principle of democracy, whether understood as an opportunity to participate, as a check on governmental abuse or as self-determination of the citizens, faces greater challenges under the Union's organisational set-up than it does within the nation-state context. Greater *private* freedom in the Union is bought at the cost of less democratic self-determination. Contrasted with the nation-state, the Union's sheer size and constitutive diversity, the physical distance of the central institutions from most of the Union's citizens and the complexity of its Constitution, which can only be modestly reduced, are only some of the factors that place greater restrictions on the realisation of the principle of democracy by way of electing representative institutions. In light of this insight, further strategies for the realisation of the principle of democracy have received far greater attention than within the national context, where even the potential of such strategies is not always perceived. This is especially true of transparency, participation of those affected, deliberation and flexibility.

[132] J Coultrap, 'From Parliamentarism to Pluralism', (1999) 11 *Journal of Theoretical Politics* 107; S Hix, 'Elections, Parties and Institutional Design: A Comparative Perspective on European Union Democracy', (1998) 21 *West European Politics* 19.

[133] On the issue of consociational democracy as a possible understanding, see Peters, above n 112, 83 *et seq*; see also S Oeter and P Dann in this volume.

[134] Peters, above n 119, 639; MG Schmidt, *Demokratietheorien* (1995) 115 *et seq*.

[135] See Frankenberg, above n 121, *passim*, in particular 80 *et seq*; A Verhoeven, *The European Union in search of a democratic and constitutional theory* (2002) *passim*, in particular 34 *et seq*.

[136] In more detail P Dann in this volume.

Sometimes the discussion about these concretising strategies appears to be carried by the hope that they might "compensate" for the Union's "democratic deficit". However, such considerations can only be useful in the "political realm", but not in the constitutional context. There are no criteria as to how a deficit in electoral legitimacy could be legally offset.[137] Yet the following concepts permit remarkable strategies for the realisation of the principle of democracy.[138]

The transparency of governmental action, that is its comprehensibility and the possibility of attributing accountability, is only peripherally associated with the principle of democracy in the domestic context.[139] European constitutional law places itself at the forefront of constitutional development when it requires that decisions be "taken as openly as possible", i.e., transparently. The Amsterdam Treaty first declared this, placing it prominently, namely in Article 1(2) EU. The specifically democratic meaning of transparency in European law was already to be found in the 17th Declaration to the Maastricht Treaty on the right to obtain information, which states that the decision-making procedure's transparency strengthens the institutions' democratic character. Article I-49 CT-Conv (Article 50 CT-IGC) confirms this understanding.

Transparency requires knowledge of the motives. From the beginning, Community law has recognised a duty to provide reasons even for legislative acts (Article 190 EEC Treaty, now Article 253 EC; Article I-37(2) CT-Conv; Article 38(2) CT-IGC), something which is hardly known in national legal orders.[140] Of course this duty was first conceived primarily from the perspective of the rule of law,[141] yet its relevance for the principle of democracy has meanwhile come to enjoy general acknowledgement.[142] The access to documents, which now also enjoys the dignity of being laid down in primary law in Article 255 EC, is also of great importance to the realisation of transparency. It has further become the subject of a considerable body of case-law,[143]

[137] E Klein, 'Die Kompetenz- und Rechtskompensation', (1981) *Deutsches Verwaltungsblatt* 661; G Britz and M Schmidt, 'Die institutionalisierte Mitwirkung der Sozialpartner an der Rechtsetzung der Europäischen Gemeinschaft', (1999) *Europarecht* 467 at 490 *et seq.*

[138] On the duty to provide reasons, T Müller-Ibold, *Die Begründungspflicht im europäischen Gemeinschaftsrecht und deutschen Recht* (1990) 53 *et seq*; on transparency, G Lübbe-Wolff, 'Europäisches und nationales Verfassungsrecht', (2000) 60 *Veröffentlichungen der Vereinigung der Deutschen Staatsrechtslehrer* 246 at 278; on participation, D Curtin, *Postnational Democracy* (1997) 53 *et seq.*

[139] Expressly so in Lübbe-Wolff, above n 138, 276 *et seq.*

[140] For a comparison, von Bogdandy, above n 127, 440 *et seq.*

[141] H Scheffler, *Die Pflicht zur Begründung von Maßnahmen nach den europäischen Gemeinschaftsverträgen* (1974) 44 *et seq* and 66 *et seq.*

[142] Peters, above n 112, 63 *et seq*; *eadem*, above n 119, 694 *et seq*; Verhoeven, above n 135, 268.

[143] Case C-349/99 P, *Commission v Arbeitsgemeinschaft Deutscher Tierzüchter* [1999] ECR I-6467; Cases C-174/98 P and C-189/98 P, *Netherlands et al v Commission* [2000] ECR I-1; Case C-41/00 P, *Interporc v Commission* [2003] ECR I-2125, para 39; Case T-309/97, *The Bavarian Lager Company v Commission* [1999] ECR II-3217; Case T-92/98, *Interporc Im- und Export v Commission* [1999] ECR II-3521; S Kadelbach, Annotation, 38 *CML Rev* (2001) 179 at 186 *et seq.*

which is slowly eroding the still powerful "tradition of secretiveness".[144] A further aspect is the openness of the Council's voting record on legislative measures.[145] The Constitutional Treaty develops these elements further with its provisions on the transparency of the institutions' proceedings and the access of the individual to the institutions' documents in Articles I-49, II-42, III-305 CT-Conv (Articles 50, 102, 399 CT-IGC).[146]

The second complex concerns forms of political participation beyond elections. Popular consultations appear as an obvious instrument, and referenda have occasionally been used to legitimatise national decisions on European issues (such as accession to the Union or the ratification of amending treaties). To extend such instruments to the European level has been proposed for some time,[147] and the citizens' initiative figures among the innovations of the Constitutional Treaty (Article I-46(4) CT-Conv; Article 47(4) CT-IGC). It is, however, carefully circumscribed, and it is difficult to evaluate at this moment its possible importance as a way to give life to the democratic principle.

Whereas the Union has no experience with popular consultations, it has much experience in allowing special interests to intervene in the political process. Comparative research between the Union and the independent regulatory agencies under the US Constitution has indicated that such participation of interested and affected parties might be a further avenue to realise the democratic principle.[148] Article I-46(1)–(3) CT-Conv (Article 47(1)–(3) CT-IGC) is based on this understanding, while such inclusion is still waiting to be generally recognised as a strategy for the realisation of the principle of democracy at the nation-state level.[149] There is, however, no principle in primary law that gives a right to affected parties to participate in the legislative process[150] but there are secondary legal provisions which are understood in this light.[151] This concretisation of the principle of democracy requires much further elaboration.

[144] Committee of Independent Experts, *Second Report on Reform of the Commission*, 10 September 1999, para 7.6.3, <http://www.europarl.eu.int/experts/default_en.htm> (8 April 2004).

[145] Art 207(3)(2) EC; in detail, C Sobotta, *Transparenz in den Rechtsetzungsverfahren der Europäischen Union* (2001) 144 *et seq* and 198 *et seq*; Commission, *White Paper European Governance* COM(2001) 428 final, 25 July 2001, 15 *et seq*.

[146] In detail Peters, above n 112, 64 *et seq*.

[147] H Abromeit, 'Ein Vorschlag zur Demokratisierung des europäischen Entscheidungssystems', (1998) *Politische Vierteljahresschrift* 80; M Zürn, 'Über den Staat und die Demokratie im Europäischen Mehrebenensystem', (1996) *Politische Vierteljahresschrift* 27 at 49.

[148] Pathbreaking, G Majone, 'Regulatory Legitimacy', in G Majone (ed), *Regulating Europe* (1996) 284 in particular at 291. The Commission has displayed considerable interest; see Commission, above n 145, 13 *et seq*.

[149] For a comparison, von Bogdandy, above n 127, 67 *et seq* and 391 *et seq*.

[150] Case T-521/93, *Atlanta et al v Council and Commission* [1996] ECR II-1707, paras 70 *et seq*; Case C-104/97 P, *Atlanta v Council and Commission* [1999] ECR I-6983; S Peers, 'WTO Dispute Settlement and Community Law', (2001) 26 *EL Rev* 605.

[151] Commission, above n 145, 19; see also FW Scharpf, 'European Governance: Common Concerns vs The Challenge of Diversity', (2001) 6 *Jean Monnet Working Paper*.

An interesting development in this regard is the use of the so-called "convention method" for the creation of fundamental European law, as was the case with the Charter of Fundamental Rights and the Constitutional Treaty. The instrument of the Convention allows for the inclusion of interested parties and experts in the law-making process.[152] Article IV-7(2) CT-Conv (Article 443(2) CT-IGC) now even introduces a compulsory Convention for the revision of the Constitutional Treaty.

The issue of how to guarantee political equality is still unanswered, as is the question of how to avoid political gridlock or the so-called agency capture by strong, organised groups. A related approach sees the principle of democracy to be realised in the deliberative quality of supranational administrative co-operation.[153]

The most important task in this regard is making the Union more flexible, something which was introduced as a general strategy by the Treaty of Amsterdam and considerably expanded by the Treaty of Nice (Articles 40 *et seq*, 43 *et seq* EU, Articles 11 *et seq* EC) as well as the Constitutional Treaty (Articles I-43, III-322 CT-Conv; Articles 44, 416 CT-IGC). It allows a democratic national majority to be respected without, however, permitting this national majority, which is a European minority, to frustrate the will of the European majority. However, there are difficult questions of competitive equality in the internal market as well as of guaranteeing democratic responsibility in ever more complex decision-making processes, an area legal science has scarcely shed light on so far.[154] Also, the possibility to leave the Union, as foreseen in Article I-59 CT-Conv (Article 60 CT-IGC), upholds at least the prospect of national self-determination as an important aspect of democracy.[155]

d) Supranational Democracy: An Evaluation

The preceding considerations demonstrate that the principle of democracy is only slowly taking form at the European level, building on some established conceptions while at the same time introducing a number of innovative accentuations and far-reaching modifications in order to make them fit for the European level.

[152] In detail, J Shaw, 'Process, Responsibility and Inclusion in EU Constitutionalism', (2003) 9 *ELJ* 45.

[153] C Joerges and J Neyer, 'Vom intergouvernementalen Bargaining zu deliberativen politischen Prozessen', in B Kohler-Koch (ed), *Regieren in entgrenzten Räumen* (1998) 207; see also C Joerges and J Falke (eds), *Das Ausschußwesen der Europäischen Union* (2000).

[154] J Wouters, 'Constitutional Limits of Differentiation', in B de Witte, D Hanf and E Vos (eds), *The Many Faces of Differentiation in EU Law* (2001) 301.

[155] On this provision, I Nicotra, 'Il diritto di recesso e il Trattato che istituisce la Costituzione europea', in A Lucarelli and G Buccino Grimaldi (eds), *Studi sulla Costituzione europea* (2003) 447.

The most important conceptual modification of established, national constitutional doctrine regards political unity, which most scholars consider foundational for the democratic constitutional state (even for the federal variant). The Union lacks such political unity; rather, it comprises discrete, nationally organised peoples and, thus, structurally related minorities without any majority.[156] This understanding finds its constitutional expression in the guarantee of respect for the Member States' peoples, the lack of will to found a state, the want of a comprehensive community of solidarity and defence (see, however, Articles I-40, I-42 CT-Conv; Articles 41, 43 CT-IGC) as well as the central role of the Council and the European Council in the decision-making process, to name a few.

Whereas in national constitutional law the principle of democracy—in the sense of the political equality of all citizens—greatly influences the organisational constitution,[157] the Union's constitutional organisation must place diversity at the same level.[158] It is this characteristic which explains and probably justifies, for example, some limitations placed on the principle of political equality[159] or the relative weakness of the EP. Perhaps these elements can even be seen as defining elements of a supranational understanding of democracy. However, the redefinition and emasculation of democratic equality in Article I-44 CT-Conv (Article 45 CT-IGC) can hardly be considered satisfactory.

Another legal question is whether the principle of democracy invites judicial activism. Within the organisational set-up and the inter-institutional relationships, in particular between the Council and the Parliament, judicial activism is only possible within the narrowest limits. Indeed, the Council is also dually legitimated to realise the principle of democracy, and nothing in unional constitutional law seems to prefer the EP's democratic legitimacy.[160] Judicial developments in the areas of transparency, participation by affected interests[161] and intra-institutional law[162] could be more significant.

[156] RM Lepsius, 'Die Europäische Union als Herrschaftsverband eigener Prägung', in C Joerges, Y Mény and JHH Weiler (eds), *What Kind of Constitution for What Kind of Polity?* (2000) 203 at 210.

[157] Hesse, above n 12, paras 125, 130.

[158] On this relationship, G Frankenberg, in Denninger, above n 127, Art 20, paras 1–3, I (Republik), para 37; C Schmitt, *Verfassungslehre* (1928, 8th edn 1993) 388 *et seq*; Craig, above n 132, 36 *et seq*.

[159] The question is what the fundamental concept of democracy entails: equality, self-governance, qualified participation by the norm's addressee or elite competition?

[160] Such approaches in the ECHR's case-law (in particular ECHR, *Matthews v United Kingdom* Rep. 1999-I, 251 *et seq*) are not convincing under Union law.

[161] See the CFI's first attempts regarding the participation of special partners, Case T-135/96, above n 107, paras 88 *et seq*, critical Britz and Schmidt, above n 107, 491.

[162] See the CFI's approach, Cases T-222/99, T-327/99 and T-329/99, *Martinez et al v Parliament* [2001] ECR II-2823, para 195.

4. Solidarity

The last of modern Europe's classical, structural principles is solidarity. Its constitutional basis is not Article 6 EU, but rather Article 1(3) EU and Article 2 EC, which formulate it not as a (mere) principle, but as one of the Union's fundamental tasks. This was a noteworthy textual development. In the original formulation, Article 2 EEC Treaty called only for the closer relationship between the Member States, weakly reminiscent of the first Preamble, according to which the Treaty aimed at "an ever closer union among the peoples of Europe". Later developments approached the preamble's lofty goal. The Treaty of Maastricht introduced the current text. The substitution of the term "relations" with the term "solidarity" can be understood as a conceptual transition from a Union based on international relations to the Union as a federal polity. The centrality of solidarity is underscored by the Charter of Fundamental Rights of the European Union, which devotes an entire Title (Title IV) to this principle. The Constitutional Treaty goes, at least rhetorically, further down this road. According to the 2nd recital of its preamble (3rd recital of the Convention's draft), the reunited Europe acts "for the good of all its inhabitants, including the weakest and most deprived". As stated by Article I-2 CT-Conv (Article 2 CT-IGC), justice, solidarity and non-discrimination are defining features of the European society.[163] Based hereon, Article I-3(3)(2) CT-Conv (Article 3(3)(2) CT-IGC) commits the Union to pursuing the objective of social justice.[164]

However, the unional principle of solidarity contains elements beyond the conventional understanding. The Constitutional Treaty introduces in Article I-42 CT-Conv (Article 43 CT-IGC) a "solidarity clause" in cases of terrorist attacks or disasters: the community of defence is considered an issue of solidarity. Moreover, Part II Title IV on "Solidarity" lists "environmental protection" (Article II-37 CT-Conv; Article 97 CT-IGC) or "access to services of general economic interest" (Article II-36 CT-Conv; Article 96 CT-IGC). At the same time, the Constitutional Treaty attenuates the relevant wording of the Charter of Fundamental Rights in Article II-52(5) CT-Conv (Article 112(5) CT-IGC).

The principle of solidarity has for a long time not been the basis for much judicial activism.[165] However, it has served to reinforce important legal concepts: the community of law,[166] the principle of loyal

[163] The singular in Art I-2 ("society") can only be understood as the assumption that there is only one European society.

[164] These provisions are part of an attempt to depict a European social model in the Constitutional Treaty.

[165] See Case C-149/96, *Portugal v Council* [1999] ECR I-8395, paras 83 *et seq*; Case 126/86, *Giménez Zaera* [1987] ECR 3697, para 11.

[166] Case 39/72, *Commission v Italy* [1973] ECR 101, paras 24 *et seq*. Here, solidarity serves as the basis for founding the duty to obey the law. Apparently, the ECJ felt that the formal legal duty needed a material basis.

co-operation,[167] the diverse mechanisms of redistribution,[168] European social law and certain aspects of the fundamental freedoms.[169] Recently, the principle of solidarity has acquired a much higher profile, being a key element of a most important line of the ECJ's case-law. The ECJ, perhaps in order to confute critical voices,[170] considers Union citizenship the "fundamental status" of Union citizens which requires equal treatment with national citizens under national systems.[171] The ECJ bases this seminal decision explicitly on the assumption that there is "a certain degree of financial solidarity between nationals of a host Member State and nationals of other Member States".[172] It thereby takes the understanding of the principle much further than Article 2 EC which only refers to solidarity among Member States. Obviously, this principle as understood within the Union leaves the often meaningless international conception of solidarity far behind. Perhaps these different aspects of solidarity are meant by the as yet enigmatic "duties" of Article 17 EC.

Yet the limits of the European community of solidarity in comparison to that of a nation-state can be discerned in the lack of a full defence community, the liability exclusions—slightly weakened by the Treaty of Nice—contained in Articles 100, 103 EC, the structure of net contributing and net receiving Member States as well as the relatively small volume of redistribution organised by and through the Union.[173]

A construction of Union law based on the principle of solidarity is particularly promising since the financial constitution is the Achilles' heel of a

[167] Case C-72/95, *Kraaijeveld* [1996] ECR I-5403, para 58; Case C-165/91, *Van Munster* [1994] ECR I-4661, para 32; Case C-378/98, *Commission v Belgium* [2001] ECR I-5107, para 31.

[168] This idea was introduced by Title V of the Single European Act, Articles 130a EEC Treaty *et seq*, now Articles 158 EC *et seq*. In modification of the original conception as expressed by Art 2 EEC Treaty this reveals that the single market does not automatically bring the same advantages to everyone. This idea speaks against a legal principle of *juste retour* regarding budgetary distributions; see M Lienemeyer, *Die Finanzverfassung der Europäischen Union* (2002) 263 *et seq*.

[169] In detail, T Kingreen in this volume.

[170] Outspoken, JHH Weiler, 'The Selling of Europe', (1996) 3 *Jean Monnet Working Paper* 11: "little more than a cynical exercise in public relations."

[171] Case C-184/99, *Grzelczyk* [2001] ECR I-6193 para 31; Case C-413/99, *Baumbast* [2002] ECR I-7091, para 82; see also the Opinion of AG Jacobs in Case C-85/96, *Martínez Sala* [1998] ECR I-2691, para 18; in detail, Verhoeven, above n 135, 180 *et seq*; T Kingreen, *Das Sozialstaatsprinzip im europäischen Verfassungsverbund* (2003), 414 *et seq*; S Kadelbach in this volume; for possible further developments in social democratic thinking, see D Scheuing, 'Freizügigkeit als Unionsbürgerrecht', (2003) *Europarecht* 744 at 770 *et seq*; AG Ruiz-Jarabo Colomer, Opinion of 11 December 2003 in Case C-386/02, *Baldinger* [2003] ECR I-0000, paras 45 *et seq*. On the ramifications of this case-law for the application of the Charter of Fundamental Rights, see P Eeckhout, 'The EU Charter of Fundamental Rights and the Federal Question', (2002) 39 *CML Rev* 945 at 969 *et seq*.

[172] Case C-184/99, above n 171, para 44.

[173] Council Dec 2000/597/EC, Euratom on the System of the Communities' Own Resources, OJ L 253, 7.10.2000, 42.

federal system. With the exception of Union citizenship, however, there are few studies on this subject.[174] Further legal scholarship could yield beneficial insight into the tensions between competitive and solidaristic federalism or between the welfare oriented aims of Article 2 EC and the liberal market orientation of Article 4(1) EC.

IV. THE FEDERAL BALANCE BETWEEN UNITY AND DIVERSITY

There is a red thread that runs through the preceding presentation: the Union's constitutional law establishes principles known from the national constitutions yet substantially modifies them in order to respond to the Union's constitutive diversity. Predictably, thus, the Union is particularly shaped by the principles which balance the relationships between unity and diversity, centre and periphery, the whole and its parts, higher and lower levels, the national and supranational elements of the European constitutional area.[175] This concerns the most critical aspect of the Union's Constitution, which hitherto has not been able to produce a long term-federal balance convincing to everyone. Consequently, even more unanswered questions will arise in this section than in the preceding section.

1. Diversity in a System of Complementary Constitutions

Unity is constitutive for diversity.[176] Consequently, principles advancing unity were the first to be developed in the history of integration. Those principles which secure diversity could achieve substance only as a second step. Yet their exposition can only succeed on the basis of an understanding of the relationship between the national constitutions and that of the Union.

Europe's community of law developed as an autonomous legal order.[177] Its nature as such was not merely one principle among others, but rather a normative axiom, defended by the ECJ with utmost resolve.[178] In fact, this

[174] C Tomuschat, 'Solidarität in Europa', in F Capotorti *et al* (eds), *Du droit international au droit de l'integration: Liber Amicorum P Pescatore* (1987) 729 *et seq*; C Calliess, in C Calliess and M Ruffert (eds), *Kommentar zu EU- und EG-Vertrag* (2002), Art 1 EU, paras 44 *et seq*; R Bieber, 'Solidarität als Verfassungsprinzip', in A von Bogdandy and S Kadelbach (eds), *Solidarität und Europäische Integration* (2002) 38 *et seq*; Zuleeg, above n 80, 153 *et seq*. However, recently an important monograph has been published; see Kingreen, above n 171, in particular 422 *et seq*, 438 *et seq*.

[175] It will remain to be be seen which metaphors and terminologies are the most appropriate.

[176] GWF Hegel, *Wissenschaft der Logik* (1812, edn 1923 by Lasson), vol I, 59.

[177] Case 26/62, above n 54; Case 6/64, above n 72; C-287/98, *Linster* [2000] ECR I-6719, para 43.

[178] Opinion 1/91, *EEA I* [1991] ECR I-6084, paras 30 *et seq*; Opinion 1/00, *ECAA* [2002] ECR I-3493, paras 12 *et seq*.

concept of separate legal orders was fundamental to the supranational legal order's establishment. This autonomy of the legal order corresponds to Monnet's conception for the Community's political-administrative system.

The actual development both in the political-administrative and in the legal realm led, however, not to separation, but rather to a close-knit interlocking or networking of the Union and the Member States.[179] In the wake of this development, scholars have put forth considerations of how to understand this networking. Some argue in favour of conceptions of the unity of the supranational and Member State realms.[180] Yet even those who do not follow these conceptions can hardly deny that an adequate understanding of both the Union and of the Member States must take into account the *whole* of the Union and the Member States.

There are three fundamental ways to conceive the relationship between the national and the supranational constitutions: tension, distance or complementarity. Of these, the latter attracts most support, not least because the dependence of the Union's constitution on the Member States' constitutions is greater, in law and in fact, than that of a federal state on its constituent states.[181] In terms of positive law this results from, for instance, Article 6(2) and (3) EU, and conceptually from the principle of dual legitimacy, which implies that the Union's legitimacy depends on the legitimacy transmitted through the national constitutions. The Constitutional Treaty, for its part, stresses complementarity through such crucial provisions as Articles I-1(1), I-5(1), I-7(3), and I-8(1) CT-Conv (Articles 1(1), 5(1), 9(3), and 10(1) CT-IGC).

This development has not yet led to an independent principle. Moreover, significant aspects of the concept of complementary constitutions are in dire need of further clarification. Nevertheless, it is certain that, in a system of complementary constitutions, principles protecting diversity carry much greater weight than under a conception of an "autonomous legal order" which is basically "blind" to the national constitutions. This perspective of

[179] GC Rodriguez Iglesias, 'Gedanken zum Entstehen einer Europäischen Rechtsordnung', (1999) *Neue Juristische Wochenschrift* 1; on the political relations and intransparency, F Scharpf, *Regieren in Europa* (1999) 70 *et seq*.

[180] For a political-science perspective, see W Wessels, *Die Öffnung des Staates* (2000) 122 *et seq* and 413 *et seq*; M Zürn, *Regieren jenseits des Nationalstaats* (1998) 235; for a legal science perspective, see especially I Pernice, 'Europäisches und nationales Verfassungsrecht', (2000) 60 *Veröffentlichungen der Vereinigung der Deutschen Staatsrechtslehrer* 148 at 163; GF Schuppert, 'Zur Staatswerdung Europas', (1994) 5 *Staatswissenschaften und Staatspraxis* 35; L Torchia, 'Una costituzione senza stato', (2001) *Diritto pubblico* 405; S Cassese, *La crisi dello stato* (2002) 67 *et seq*.

[181] J Frowein, 'Die rechtliche Bedeutung des Verfassungsprinzips der parlamentarischen Demokratie für den europäischen Integrationsprozeß', (1983) *Europarecht* 301 at 315 *et seq*; *id*, 'Die Verfassung der Europäischen Union aus der Sicht der Mitgliedstaaten', (1995) *Europarecht* 315 at 318 with the concept of partial constitutions; P Häberle, *Europäische Verfassungslehre* (2001/2002) 220 *et seq*; A Pace, 'La dichiarazione di Laeken e il processo costituente europeo', (2002) *Rivista Trimestrale di diritto pubblico* 613 *et seq*.

a common constitutional space of complementary constitutions offers a good approach to develop principles of unity and diversity.

2. Principles Promoting Unity

a) Realisation of Goals or Integration Tout Court?

The Community Treaties and the European Union Treaty were concluded to overcome the national limitations placed on many areas of life and to Europeanise the national societies. Although the Constitutional Treaty asserts the existence of a European society (Article I-2 CT-Conv; Article 2 CT-IGC), this process is by no means finished. European primary law has been, more than most national constitutions, an explicit instrument for far-reaching political and social projects[182]: the single market, a common currency, a common area of freedom, security and justice, a common external and defence policy, supplemented by numerous, further common policies. In European history, the promotion and realisation of such goals have always represented important elements in the creation of unity in a nation-state. Within the framework of the Union their realisation is more neutrally characterised by the term "European integration".

This project's legal importance flows from Articles 2 and 3 EC and Article 2 EU. A state constitution could not confer the same prominence on task-distribution norms that the EU and EC Treaties do in their respective Articles 2.[183] The listed goals can be conceptualised as principles, as basic concerns of the European legal order. Yet the ECJ has not derived duties of the institutions solely on the basis of Articles 2 and 3 EC.[184]

Nevertheless, these principles do have an influence on the European legal order that is hard to overestimate. They permit progressive interpretation of Treaty provisions based on the object and purpose,[185] particularly in view of such a relatively clearly described goal as the single market, thus providing for the dynamic character of the European legal order.[186] They provide

[182] This led to the conception of a "planning constitution"; see CF Ophüls, 'Die Europäischen Gemeinschaftsverträge als Planverfassungen', in JH Kaiser (ed), *Planung* (1965), vol I, 229 at 233; Ipsen, above n 3, 128 *et seq*.

[183] The lack of scholarly interest that these provisions have earned is surprising. Only C Stumpf's monograph *Aufgabe und Befugnis: Das wirtschaftsverfassungsrechtliche System der europäischen Gemeinschaftsziele* (1999), explores the right to an exemption from prohibited undertakings pursuant to Art 81(3) EC in light of Art 2 EC.

[184] See the action for wrongful failure to act Case 13/83, *Parliament v Council* [1985] ECR 1513, paras 49 *et seq* and 72 *et seq*.

[185] Opinion 1/78, *International Agreement on Natural Rubber* [1979] ECR 2871, para 44; Case C-35/90, *Commission v Spain* [1991] ECR I-5073, para 9; R Streinz, 'Der "effet utile" in der Rechtsprechung des Gerichtshofs der Europäischen Gemeinschaften', in *Festschrift U Everling*, above n 2, 1491 at 1509.

[186] C Alder, *Koordination und Integration als Rechtsprinzipien* (1969) 311 *et seq*; Ipsen, above n 3, 66 *et seq*; H Kutscher, 'Thesen zu den Methoden der Auslegung des

one basis for the *effet utile* interpretation. Framing the Union's goals as principles ultimately prohibits substantial re-nationalisation, which would materially endanger those goals.[187] These goals underline the importance of legitimacy through achievements (out-put legitimacy), something on which, according to widespread opinion, the Union depends more heavily than the Member States.[188] If the Union is *de facto* more dependent on out-put legitimacy than a state is, it appears reasonable constitutionally to require that certain achievements be secured.

On this basis one might assume a principle of integration in European law: integration understood as a fusion of heretofore nationally organised areas of life into one of European dimensions. Some authors even assert an abstract legal principle of "more Europe" as "more unity".[189] The first recital of the preamble to the EC Treaty, which speaks of "an ever closer union among the peoples of Europe", does indeed at first glance appear to recommend unity as a goal in itself.[190] However, such a principle would be highly problematic. First, it lacks a sufficient basis in the provisions of the Treaties. Moreover, a central function of European constitutional law, namely the stabilisation of the vertical relationship between the Union and Member States, would not be well served by such a principle. For this reason alone one should reject an independent legal principle of

Gemeinschaftsrechts aus der Sicht eines Richters', in ECJ (ed), *Begegnung von Justiz und Hochschule 27–28 September 1976* (1976) I-41; Pescatore, above n 11, 20 at 97; M Zuleeg, 'Die Gemeinschaft als Integrationsverband', in B Börner *et al* (eds), *Einigkeit und Recht und Freiheit: Festschrift für K Carstens* (1984) 289 at 301.

[187] E Grabitz, *Stillhalte-Verpflichtungen vor dem Binnenmarkt* (1988), 45 *et seq*. The concept of integration in Art 43 lit a EU as introduced by the Treaty of Nice should be understood in this sense. This does not exclude the abolishment of core elements of the Common Agricultural Policy, especially as they have recently endangered the single market; see Case C-289/97, *Eridania* [2000] ECR I-5409, para 78.

[188] Scharpf, above n 179, 20 *et seq*; Stumpf, above n 183, 119 *et seq*.

[189] A Bleckmann and S Pieper, 'Rechtsetzung und Vollzug des EG-Rechts: Rechtsquellen', in MA Dauses (ed), *Handbuch des EU-Wirtschaftsrechts* (looseleaf, last update 2003), B I, paras 162 *et seq*, in particular para 164; A Bleckmann, 'Die Rechtsquellen des Europäischen Gemeinschaftsrechts', (1993) *Neue Zeitschrift für Verwaltungsrecht* 824 at 827; Opinion of AG Reischl in Case 32/79, *Commission v United Kingdom* [1980] ECR 2403 at 2460 *et seq*. Those views are generalised in *Entscheidungen des Bundesverfassungsgerichts* 89, 155 at 210 (*Maastricht*); T von Danwitz, 'Die gemeinschaftsrechtliche Staatshaftung der Mitgliedstaaten', (1997) *Deutsches Verwaltungsblatt* 1 at 2, 4; similarly, J Isensee, 'Integrationsziel Europastaat?' in *Festschrift U Everling*, above n 2, 567 at 568.

[190] The Constitutional Treaty abolishes the finality of the "ever closer union among the peoples of Europe" which is enshrined in the 1st recital of the EC Treaty. However, defenders of national competences have no reason to feel triumphant: the 3rd recital of the Preamble contemplates the determination of the peoples of Europe (and not merely of the Heads of State, as in the EC Treaty) "united ever more closely, to forge a common destiny". Moreover, the 1st recital of the Preamble to the Charter of Fundamental Rights, which forms Part II of the Constitutional Treaty, reuses the language of "an ever closer union"; in detail, H-J Blanke, 'Essentialia des Entwurfs des Europäischen Verfassungsvertrages', (2003) *Rivista europea di cultura e scienza giuridica* 95 at 147.

integration.[191] Recent presentations only rarely feature the principle of integration prominently.[192]

In sum, the tasks laid down in Articles 2 and 3 EC and Article 2 EU can be understood as principles promoting unity, principles whose great importance in the Treaties contributes to the uniqueness of unional constitutional law.[193] As the objectives represent permanent tasks that are to be realised under constantly changing economic, political and social conditions, it furthermore follows that the Union is a dynamic process, not a static situation. An abstract legal principle of "more Europe", on the other hand, cannot be deduced from the Treaties. To avoid misunderstandings, one should speak of a principle of fulfilment of Treaty objectives and not of an abstract principle of integration *tout court*.

b) Structural Compatibility or Outright Homogeneity?

Early in the integration process, a certain structural compatibility among the Member States with respect to the market economy, democracy and rule of law was recognised as essential for the operation of the Community. These conditions were correspondingly formulated as normative requirements, though they only had a minimal character.[194] In the wake of the realisation of a common constitutional space, the question arises whether these requirements demand a legal principle of constitutional homogeneity to promote unity.[195]

Article 7(1) EU demands structural compatibility between the interrelated constitutional orders. It could function as a normative anchor for the development of a principle of constitutional homogeneity, replete with substantive requirements and unifying guidelines for the national

[191] See R Bieber and G Ress (eds), *Die Dynamik des Gemeinschaftsrechts* (1987); M Nettesheim and P Schiera (eds), *Der integrierte Staat* (1999); see also the authors in n 186, who understand "integration" solely as the realisation of the single market. C-D Ehlermann, 'How Flexible is Community Law?', (1984) 82 *Michigan L Rev* 1274 at 1279 *et seq*; U Everling, 'Rechtsvereinheitlichung durch Richterrecht in der Europäischen Gemeinschaft', (1986) 50 *Rabels Zeitschrift für ausländisches und internationales Privatrecht* 193 at 195; B Langeheine, 'Rechtliche und institutionelle Probleme einer abgestuften Integration in der Europäischen Gemeinschaft', in E Grabitz (ed), *Abgestufte Integration* (1984) 47 at 68 *et seq*.

[192] See, eg, P Manin, *Les Communautés européenne l'Union europénne* (1999) 309 *et seq*; going further, J González Campos, 'La posición del Tribunal Constitucional en la articulación entre Tribunales comunitarios y Tribunales nacionales', in E García de Enterría and R Alonso García (eds), *La Encrucijada Constitucional de la Unión Europea* (2002) 493 at 494.

[193] This is also underscored by the current constitutional discussion which concentrates on the organisation, competences and fundamental rights.

[194] HP Ipsen, 'Über Verfassungs-Homogenität in der Europäischen Gemeinschaft', in: *Festschrift G Dürig* (1990) 159; P Richter, *Die Erweiterung der Europäischen Union* (1997) 37 *et seq*, 57.

[195] On the concept, Schmitt, above n 158, 65; applied to the Union, *Entscheidungen des Bundesverfassungsgerichts* 89, 155 at 186 (*Maastricht*).

constitutional systems.[196] Yet such a principle would face significant objections.

To begin with, such a constitutional principle is not currently practicable, at least not in the constitutional landscape. Such a principle could hardly be reconciled with the current diversity among the national constitutions: republics and monarchies, parliamentary and semi-presidential systems, strong and weak parliaments, competitive and consensual democracies, strong and weak partisan structures, strong and weak social institutions, unitary and federal systems, strong, weak or absent constitutional courts as well as significant divergences in the content and level of protection of fundamental rights. The Union's eastward and southward expansion will increase this heterogeneity.

Neither does the postulation of such a principle withstand close scrutiny.[197] Even the norm's wording implies a structural consonance only at a rather abstract level, not, however, constitutional homogeneity. Systematically, such a principle of homogeneity could scarcely be justified in light of Article 6(3) EU, as national identity finds expression precisely in the peculiar, individual constitutional arrangements,[198] as explicitly stated in Article I-5(1) CT-Conv (Article 5(1) CT-IGC). This understanding is confirmed not least by the controversy over sanctions against Austria by the other 14 Member States and the debate about the concretisation of Article 51 of the Charter of Fundamental Rights of the European Union (Article II-51 CT-Conv; Article 111 CT-IGC).[199]

Legal science, then, must concretise Article 6 EU on a three-level regulatory system: the first level, with the highest regulatory density, concerns the Union's own design; the second level, which has significantly less regulatory density, concerns the general requirements placed on the Member States; and the minimally regulated third level informs the Union's foreign policy.[200] Only the second level imposes a duty of structural compatibility—it

[196] In detail, Bieber, Kahl-Wolff and Muller, above n 11, 57 *et seq*; T Schmitz, *Integration in der Supranationalen Union* (2001) 301 *et seq*; F Schorkopf, in Grabitz and Hilf, above n 97, Art 7 EU, para 32; A Verhoeven, 'How Democratic Need European Union Members Be?', (1998) 23 *EL Rev* 217 *et seq*; see the Communication from the Commission to the Council and the European Parliament on Article 7 of the Treaty on European Union "Respect for and promotion of the values on which the Union is based", COM(2003) 606 final.

[197] LM Díez-Picazo, *Constitucionalismo de la Unión Europea* (2002) 140 *et seq*; with the same result, even though the term "constitutional homogeneity" is kept, Frowein, above n 11, 157 *et seq*; M Heintzen, 'Gemeineuropäisches Verfassungsrecht in der Europäischen Union', (1997) *Europarecht* 1 at 8.

[198] M Hilf, 'Europäische Union und nationale Identität der Mitgliedstaaten', in *Gedächtnisschrift Grabitz*, above n 68, 157 at 166 *et seq.*

[199] On the former, see W Hummer and W Obwexer, 'Die Wahrung der "Verfassungsgrundsätze" der EU', (2000) *Europäische Zeitschrift für Wirtschaftsrecht* 485 at 492; on the latter, see Eeckhout, above n 171, 979 *et seq*; R Alonso García, 'Las cláusulas horizontales de la carta de los derechos fundamentales', in García de Enterría and Alonso García, above n 192, 151 at 158 *et seq.*

[200] On this model, von Bogdandy, above n 100, 162 *et seq.*

does not, however, require a principle of homogeneity. These considerations apply also to the Charter of Fundamental Rights of the European Union, which should not be misused to smuggle constitutional homogeneity into the EU.[201]

The Constitutional Treaty is deeply ambivalent in this respect. On the one hand, the protection of the national constitutions is a red thread running through many of its core provisions (e.g. Articles I-1(1), I-5(1), IV-7, IV-8 CT-Conv; Articles 1(1), 5(1), 443–445, 447 CT-IGC). On the other hand, the very denomination of the document as a "Constitution for Europe" provides for a unifying strand. "Europe" is more than the EU; the concept necessarily embraces the Member States. Combined with the term "Constitution", it will be easy to apply its principles to any public authority exercised within its territorial jurisdiction. In that event, the vision of complementary constitutions[202] will also be left behind.[203]

c) Supranationality?

Supranationality was Jean Monnet's slogan for effectuating integration, and in its original form it was a code word for the goal of statehood.[204] A corresponding principle could therefore substantially further unity. In the meantime, the concept of supranationality has mutated, now depicting integration as primary and supreme but simultaneously dissociating it from state influence—particularly in its polycentrism and its lack of means of enforcement.[205] In this form, the concept quite suitably distinguishes the Union's character from that of international organisations.[206]

Nonetheless, supranationality has not evolved into an independent legal principle.[207] The objections are the same as those against a legal principle of integration: the lack of roots in the normative tradition of European modernity and the abstract one-sidedness in the Union's stressed federalism speak against a normative elevation of this concept.

[201] Problematic, Case C-60/00, above n 101, paras 42, 46; see Britz, above n 101, 176 *et seq*.

[202] See above IV 1.

[203] On the effects of the Constitutional Treaty on homogeneity and national identity, see V Atripaldi and R Miccù, 'La Costituzione Europea "Multilivello" tra Garanzie di Omogeneità e Identità Plurali', in R Miccù and I Pernice (eds), *The European Constitution in the Making* (2004) 53.

[204] F Rosenstiel, 'Reflections on the Notion of Supranationality', (1963) 2 *JCMS* 127 *et seq*.

[205] Grimm, above n 114, 288 *et seq*.

[206] See Ipsen, above n 3, 67 *et seq*; M Zuleeg, 'Wandlungen im Begriff der Supranationalität', (1988) *integration* 103 *et seq*.

[207] Ipsen, above n 3, 67 *et seq*; the normative quality is unclear in Weiler, above n 98, 94 *et seq*, 250 *et seq*. The newest monograph on the subject, W Hertel, *Supranationalität als Verfassungsprinzip* (1999), does not, despite the title, elevate the concept of "supranationality" to a principle, but rather examines the constitutional quality of primary law.

d) The Single and Primary Legal Order

By regulating innumerable social relations through one common and supreme set of rules, the Union's legal order itself is by far the most important factor promoting unity.[208] In particular, the principle of equal freedom is the legal order's real centripetal force. Correctly, it is a general custom in legal science to mark the "real beginning" of Community law with the *van Gend & Loos* and *Costa* decisions, because the direct effect and primacy doctrines are the most important concretising legal doctrines of the principle of equal liberty. Primacy is of particular importance, because this principle, far more than the principle of direct effect, raises the question of hierarchy, the most important instrument for advancing unity.[209] First merely conceived as an expression of an autonomous legal order,[210] its constitutional[211] and federal[212] meanings were rapidly realised.

The development of the concept of primacy traces the Union's own progression into a supranational federation. Significant to the Union's development was the decision that Community law is not *supreme* (that is, it does not render conflicting national law void; supremacy, *Geltungsvorrang*) but is instead *primary* (that is, it is applied before national law, leaving inconsistent national law valid but unapplied; primacy, *Anwendungsvorrang*).[213] This shows far greater respect for the integrity of the Member States' legal orders. Nevertheless, primacy has been applied at times to extreme degrees, leading to vehement criticism from the national perspective. This extreme application may be partly explained by the problems of a supranational legal order in establishing itself against obstinate national legal orders. Together with the principle of equal liberty and the tasks in Article 2 EC, this approach may be justifiable. Yet in a developed and established community of law, with a view to the federal balance, it is important to conceive primacy as a principle (and not in all situations as a strict rule) so that

[208] In detail above, III 2 a; emphatically, Hallstein, above n 67, 51 *et seq*; sceptically, Dehousse and Weiler, above n 77, 242. The question of the extent to which law alone can effect "integration" is set aside here; see M Cappelletti and D Golay, 'The Judicial Branch in the Federal and Transnational Union: Its Impact on Integration', in M Cappelletti, M Seccombe and JHH Weiler (eds), *Integration Through Law* (1986), vol I, book 2, 261 at 300, 344, 348 *et seq*.

[209] Case 6/64, above n 72.

[210] The reference to the constitutional function can be found as early as AG Lagrange's Opinion in Case 6/64, above n 72, 585 at 606.

[211] E Grabitz, *Gemeinschaftsrecht bricht nationales Recht* (1966) 100.

[212] E Stein, 'Lawyers, Judges and the Making of a Transnational Constitution', (1981) 75 *AJIL* 1 at 12; Kadelbach, above n 73, 54.

[213] On supremacy in the strict sense (*Geltungsvorrang*), see Grabitz, above n 211, 113; in contrast, M Zuleeg's conception is essentially the primacy of application (*Anwendungsvorrang*), M Zuleeg, *Das Recht der Europäischen Gemeinschaften im innerstaatlichen Bereich* (1969) 140 *et seq*; the denomination *Anwendungsvorrang* itself apparently stems from G Hoffmann, 'Das Verhältnis des Rechts der Europäischen Gemeinschaften zum Recht der Mitgliedstaaten', (1967) *Die öffentliche Verwaltung* 433 at 439.

conflicts can be handled by weighing opposed principles.[214] In this perspective, the principles of effectiveness (*effet utile*) and equivalence also have to be understood as principles open to such a balancing test.[215]

Primacy of Union law cannot be fully understood from the perspective of Union law alone. As is well known, the ECJ and meanwhile also the Treaties assume an unconditional primacy even with regard to Member State constitutional law,[216] whereas most Member State high courts do not fully accept such primacy of Union law.[217] The principle of primacy does not succeed in creating complete unity by establishing a strict hierarchy; rather, the centre of the constitutional interplay is an "unregulated" relationship due to the competing jurisdictional claims. The situation is likely to remain the same under the Constitutional Treaty. Although it lays down unconditional primacy in Article I-10(1) CT-Conv (Article 6 CT-IGC), provisions such as Articles I-1(1), I-5(1), I-9(1), II-51, II-52(6), IV-8 CT-Conv (Articles 1(1), 5(1), 11(1), 111, 112(6), 447 CT-IGC) as well as the relevant national constitutional law will allow the national courts to uphold their current understanding.

From here, one can especially clearly perceive the polycentric structure as a decisive feature of the federation composed of the Union and the Member States. A number of authors understand it not as flawed but as reasonable for both the Union and the Member States.[218] If this relationship remains "unregulated", principles of the participating legal orders should help to avoid actual conflicts, in particular the obligations of mutual co-operation.

Despite the current problematic basis of the primacy of Union law, the Union's legal order has, due to its enormous expansion in almost all areas of law, achieved such a considerable centripetal force that the development of principles to safeguard diversity has become one of the central tasks of the nascent field of European constitutional law.

3. Principles Protecting Diversity

Principles protecting diversity became necessary when principles furthering unity began to shape reality. With the emerging success of the single market

[214] In more detail, Kadelbach, above n 73, 54 *et seq*; Case C-201/02, 7 January 2004, *Wells* [2004] ECR I-723, para 67; J Delicostopoulos, 'Towards European Procedural Primacy in National Legal Systems', (2003) 9 *ELJ* 599.

[215] Kadelbach, above n 73, 115 *et seq*.

[216] Recently, Case C-285/98, above n 72, without even discussing the problems of primacy; the Treaty makes mention of this issue in point 2 of the protocol on subsidiarity and proportionality (Amsterdam Treaty); see also Cases C-465/00, C-138/01 and C-139/01, above n 101, paras 90 *et seq*.

[217] For a detailed analysis, see FC Mayer in this volume; see also J Schwarze (ed), *Die Entstehung einer europäischen Verfassungsordnung* (2000).

[218] B de Witte, 'The Nature of the Legal Order', in Craig and de Burca, above n 11, 177 at 201; Peters, above n 119, 263 *et seq*.

programme, a lively scholarly and political discussion began concerning European tasks, the effectiveness of European law, its democratic legitimacy as well as the respect for national autonomy and identity. The discussion resulted in the insight that respect for diversity is an essential condition for justice and therefore a condition for the legitimacy of supranational authority. This insight then led to considerable innovations in primary law: Articles 1(2), 6(3) EU, Article 5 EC and the subsidiarity Protocol as well as the newly formulated competence provisions to reinforce autonomy (e.g., Articles 129, 149(4), 151(5), 152(4) lit c EC). A principle of cultural diversity can be deduced from Articles 3(1)(q), 149(1), (4) and 151(1) EC. The sensitive question of language, which was first placed within the discretion of the Community's legislator according to Article 290 EC,[219] has become at least partly constitutionalised in favour of diversity according to Article 21(3) EC.[220] Some of the single market principles are also quite open to an interpretation respectful of diversity, for instance, the principle of the equality of different national rules (principle of mutual recognition), especially as an indirect, harmonising effect has not materialised.[221] Nevertheless, the first indent of the Treaty of Nice's Declaration on the Future of the Union shows that these innovations do not completely satisfy the need to respect diversity.

a) Doctrine of Competences

The first of the principles protecting diversity is that the competence of constitutional amendment is reserved to the Member States acting jointly. This principle finds expression in Articles 48 and 49 EU as well as in the principle of attributed (conferred) powers. It comes forward with particular clarity in Article 5 EU and Article 5(1) EC and has developed into an independent principle of interpretation[222]; the "passerelle"-provision in Article I-24(4) CT-Conv (Article 444 CT-IGC) does not alter this situation in substance. In the past, substantiated doubts were raised as to whether

[219] Council Reg No 1 determining the languages to be used by the European Economic Community, OJ 1952–58 (I), 59; see T Oppermann, 'Das Sprachenregime der Europäischen Union – reformbedürftig?', (2001) *Zeitschrift für Europarechtliche Studien* 1 at 8.

[220] However, this provision does not embrace agencies. The ECJ decided in Case C-361/01 P, *Kik v OHIM* [2003] ECR I-8283, paras 81 *et seq*, the first major language case in a "shallow and narrow" and therefore extremely careful manner; in detail, FC Mayer, 'The Language of the European Constitution – beyond Babel?', in Bodnar *et al* (eds), above n 84, 359.

[221] On the principle of origin, Case 120/78, *Rewe* [1979] ECR 679, para 14; most recently, Case C-238/98, *Hocsman* [2000] ECR I-6623, paras 23 *et seq*; for a summary, see M Hoffmann, *Die Grundfreiheiten des EG-Vertrags als koordinationsrechtliche und gleichheitsrechtliche Abwehrrechte* (2000) 61 *et seq* and 151 *et seq* (on Art 28 EC), 172 *et seq* (on Articles 39, 43 and 49 EC).

[222] Cases 281/85, 283/85–285/85 and 287/85, *Germany et al v Commission* [1987] ECR 3203, paras 30 *et seq*; Opinion 1/94, *WTO* [1994] ECR I-5267, para 9; Opinion 2/94, above n 49, para 30; Case C-376/98, above n 49, para 83; Case C-50/00 P, above n 84, paras 40 *et seq*, in particular para 45; Case C-263/02 P, above n 84, para 36.

the Union's institutions had always respected the principle of limited competences.[223] More recent legal developments should meet these doubts,[224] even if important points still await confirmation. A substantial doctrine of the vertical competences has been developed only in the last several years.[225] The Constitutional Treaty contains some innovative elements in this respect.[226]

Since the Union's competences are broad, national autonomy can be considerably limited even when the limitations on the Union's competences are observed. The most important safeguard for the respect of Member State autonomy is organisational in nature: the Council's central role in the Union's decision-making process is protecting the Member States' interests. However, there are numerous examples of Council acts that demonstrate that it does not always convincingly fulfil this role.

Many proposals have been made to improve this principle's observance.[227] The principles of subsidiarity and proportionality in Article 5(2) and (3) EC as introduced by the Treaty of Maastricht are of central importance. The Article guarantees an application of the Union's competences which is respectful of the Member States' autonomy.[228] In particular with regard to subsidiarity, one can scarcely gain an overview of the literature published.[229] Although this provision has thus far not achieved an important role in the ECJ's case-law,[230] it has nonetheless successfully shaped the legislative culture: nobody has been able to demonstrate recently that the Union has passed legislation that substantially collides with the principle of subsidiarity.[231] Obviously, this is a rather successful innovation protecting the Member States' autonomy.

[223] Problematic, Opinion 1/91, above n 178, para 21; on the development, A Tizzano, 'Lo sviluppo delle competenze materiali delle Communità europee', (1981) *Rivista di Diritto Europeo* 139 *et seq*; R Dehousse, *La Cour de justice des Communautés européennes* (1994) 53 *et seq*.

[224] See the annotations in n 222.

[225] D Triantafyllou, *Vom Vertrags- zum Gesetzesvorbehalt* (1996); J Martín y Pérez de Nanclares, *El sistema de competencias de la Comunidad Europea* (1997).

[226] In detail, see A von Bogdandy and J Bast in this volume.

[227] I Boeck, *Die Abgrenzung der Rechtsetzungskompetenzen von Gemeinschaft und Mitgliedstaaten in der Europäischen Union* (2000); A von Bogdandy and J Bast, 'The European Union's Vertical Order of Competences', (2002) 39 *CML Rev* 227 at 251 *et seq*; MP Chiti, 'Delimitación o reparto de competencias entre Unión Europea y estados miembros?', in García de Enterría and Alonso García, above n 192, 69 *et seq*.

[228] Since the Treaty of Amsterdam it has been concretised by the protocol on subsidiarity and proportionality, which is adventurous with regard to its formulation; see Griller *et al*, above n 51, 96 *et seq*.

[229] C Calliess, *Subsidiaritäts- und Solidaritätsprinzip in der Europäischen Union* (1999).

[230] For the beginnings, see Case C-84/94, *United Kingdom v Council* [1996] ECR I-5755; Case C-233/94, *Germany v Parliament and Council* [1997] ECR I-2405; Cases C-36/97 and 37/97, *Kellinghusen* [1998] ECR I-6337; for possible further implications on all levels of government in the EU, see G de Búrca, 'Proportionality and Subsidiarity as General Principles of Law', in Bernitz and Nergelius (eds), above n 30, 95 at 108 *et seq*.

[231] See the subsidiarity report of the German federal government of 18 August 2000, BT-Drs. 14/4017.

b) A General Principle of Diversity?

Yet some think that this focus is too narrow. Thus, one line of European constitutional scholarship is trying to develop a general principle of diversity that, at the level of Union law, tries to establish diversity as an independent value to be legally protected against unifying Union measures. It would be a principle with the same level of abstraction as the principles of integration and homogeneity. A normative starting point could be found in Article 6(3) EU. The Constitutional Treaty adds Article IV-1(3) CT-Conv (Article 8(3) CT-IGC), the motto of the Union: "United in diversity".

It is constitutive for the Union not to be a vehicle of hegemonic aspirations of a people or a state; the entire constitution is infused with this idea.[232] The current debate does not engage this rather horizontal problem, but addresses itself to supranational homogenisation. JHH Weiler tries to capture the constitutional order's pluralistic, non-hierarchical, discursive, post-national character with a principle of constitutional tolerance.[233] Some authors propose a paradigmatic change from a diversity endangering paradigm of "uniformity, homogeneity and one-directional integration" to a diversity protecting paradigm of "flexibility, mixity and differentiation".[234] J Shaw attempts to conceptualise phenomena such as "disintegration", "flexibility" and "fragmentation"—which have thus far been perceived as a threat to the integration process—as principles that shape European constitutional law as much as integration and uniformity; this would sever the connection between supranational law and integration, thereby bringing a more balanced constitutional framework to the law of the Union, one corresponding to the diversity of the Union's members.[235] A properly understood principle of federalism could also function as a protection of diversity.[236]

The assumption of abstract legal principles such as diversity, difference, flexibility[237] or tolerance appears to be as problematic as an abstract legal

[232] Hallstein, above n 67, 45; on the hegemonic aspirations of the French policy and the Anglo-American culture, Siedentop, above n 15, 111, 113, 133.

[233] JHH Weiler, 'Federalism without Contitutionalism: Europe's *Sonderweg*', in Nicolaidis and Howse, above note 78, 54 at 65 *et seq*. The principle of "tolerance" in Art I-2 CT-Conv (Art 2 CT-IGC) does not appear to refer to Weiler's concept of "constitutional tolerance" but is rather of a more general nature.

[234] G de Búrca and J Scott, 'Introduction', in *id* (eds), *Constitutional Change in the EU* (2000) 1 at 2.

[235] J Shaw, 'European Union Legal Studies in Crisis?', (1996) 16 *OJLS* 231 at 240 *et seq*; J Shaw, 'Citizenship of the Union', in Academy of European Law (ed), *Collected Courses of the Academy of European Law 1995* (1998), vol VI-1, 237; J Shaw, 'Postnational constitutionalism in the European Union', (1999) *JEPP* 579.

[236] Siedentop, above n 15, 26.

[237] The current Union Constitution is eloquently silent on this point. It permits closer co-operation and thus flexibility (Articles 43 *et seq*, 40 EU, 11 EC) but does not attribute any value to it. Nor has European constitutional law established any serious hindrances to forms of flexible, closer co-operation outside the Treaties; B de Witte, 'Old Flexibility', in de Búrca

principle of unity or integration *tout court*. The contributions thus far have failed to show what such abstract principles could practically achieve beyond the doctrine of competences, the protection of national interests by means of the Union's organisational set-up and the legal principles regarding rational procedure and the protection of the citizen. Significant problems already arise with the concretisation of Article 6(3) EU. Such legal principles would only have a positive role to play as counterweight to contrary abstract principles such as unity, integration or homogeneity. Yet the European legal order does not support the assumption of such principles advancing unity. Consequently, there is no need for contrary principles to balance these principles. While the primary law clearly demands respect for diversity, it does not go so far as to support a legal principle, above and beyond the various legal norms.[238] Diversity is thus a political and ethical postulate but not a legal principle that has an operative function in the legal order.

c) Protection of Diversity Through Organisation and Procedure

The most important safeguard of European diversity is the Union citizens' will to assert their diversity and a responsive political structure of the European Union. The most important concretisation strategy for the protection of diversity is thus the organisation and procedures of the Union's political system. The postulate of diversity determines not only the vertical relationship between the Union and the Member States but also the Union's internal structure, be it the institutions' internal laws or the horizontal interinstitutional relationships.

The polycentric nature of the Council's internal organisation, along with the European Council the Union's most powerful institution, may serve as an example. The Council has a pluralistic composition, meets in over twenty different constellations and does not have at its disposal the central mechanism for building unity: a hierarchy.[239] In many respects it appears to be more a multifaceted and fragmented consensus-building process of 26 different political-administrative systems (25 national and the Commission's) than a single, harmonised institution. The political process

and Scott, above n 234, 31 at 39 *et seq*. This notwithstanding numerous possible conflicts and problems; see A Kliemann, 'Auf dem Wege zur Sozialunion?' in T von Danwitz *et al* (eds), *Auf dem Wege zu einer Europäischen Staatlichkeit* (1993) 171, 181 *et seq*. An examination of the diverse forms of flexibilisation with a view to structuring principles appears to be urgently required. Here, legal science has thus far not fulfilled its duty; but see the contributions by J Wouters, D Curtin and J-V Louis in B de Witte, D Hanf and E Vos (eds), *The Many Faces of Differentiation in EU Law* (2001).

[238] Equally for the German Federal Constitutional Court, E Denninger, *Menschenrechte und Grundgesetz* (1994), 13 *et seq*, 44 *et seq*, 61.

[239] F Grevisse, 'A propos de quelques institutions', (1998) *Revue du Marché commun et de l'Union européenne* 569 at 572 *et seq*.

is characterised not by hierarchical decree, but rather by contract-like co-operation between different political-administrative systems that are largely independent of each other.[240] The innovations of Article 207(2) EC and the strengthening of the Council Secretariat's administrative competences by the Treaty of Amsterdam[241] do not change this. The Constitutional Treaty introduces some elements which might provide for more "leadership", in particular the general strengthening of the European Council (Articles I-20 *et seq* CT-Conv; Articles 21 *et seq* CT-IGC), possibly of the presidency of the Council (Article I-23(4) CT-Conv, Article 24(7) CT-IGC) and of the General Affairs Council (Article I-23(1) CT-Conv; Article 24(2) CT-IGC). Yet it appears unlikely that the system's general operational mode will change from contractual to hierarchical.[242]

The diversity protecting nature of this arrangement, in its present and envisaged form, is evident when compared to analogous state institutions, that is, either the national parliament or the government.[243] The national government and the national parliament, the latter due to its partisan political structure, represent more highly hierarchical institutions. The governing majority, which is embodied in a more or less clear personal hierarchy, is of particular importance. A party structure as well as a personification of political power are largely missing at the European level. The Constitutional Treaty tries to mend this last point through three posts with high visibility: the President of the European Council (Article I-21 CT-Conv; Article 22 CT-IGC), the President of the Commission (Article I-26 CT-Conv; Article 27 CT-IGC) and the Union Minister for Foreign Affairs (Article I-27 CT-Conv; Article 28 CT-IGC). Yet the Constitutional Treaty does not provide these posts with such competences or other resources of power that the incumbents will emerge in the public similarly to leading national politicians.

One may object that even in national systems a strict hierarchy is no longer the rule and that federal states in particular generate further centres of power—for example the German Federal Council—representing regional governments.[244] Nevertheless, a qualitative difference remains: the

[240] F Scharpf, 'Introduction: The Problem Solving Capacity of Multi-Level Governance', (1997) 4 *JEPP* 520 *et seq*.

[241] On the proposals, A Dashwood, 'Effectiveness and Simplification of Decision-Making by the Council', in JA Winter *et al* (eds), *Reforming the Treaty on European Union* (1996) 147 at 156 *et seq*.

[242] P de Schoutheete, 'Forces et faiblesses du Conseil européen', in *Mélanges en hommage à J-V Louis* (2004), vol I, 109 at 115 *et seq*.

[243] A development on the part of the Commission towards a government in the sense of a centralisation of authority is not discernable and would hardly be consistent with the Union's structure; see P VerLoren van Themaat, 'The internal powers of the Community and the Union', in Winter *et al*, above n 241, 249 at 251 *et seq* and 258 *et seq*.

[244] R Steinberg, *Der ökologische Verfassungsstaat* (1998) 396 *et seq*; Vesting, above n 44, in particular 211 *et seq*.

national systems certainly show a tendency to focus political power at the top of the government, not least because of the *domestic* consequences of European integration.[245]

The lack of overarching hierarchical structures, or, to put it another way, the political system's polycentric and horizontal character, can be formulated as an independent constitutional principle protecting diversity. The relevant scholarship is still in its early stages.[246] Nevertheless, this insight indicates that the distribution of powers in the Union, which generally does not aim at separation but at co-operation, is not a problematic deformation, but rather an appropriate expression of the Union's peculiar system of authority.[247] This situation is normatively underpinned by the principle of institutional balance: it serves to stabilise the lines of responsibility established by the Treaties[248] as well as compliance with procedural rules[249] without, however, pushing the inter-institutional relationships toward any specific normative principle.[250] At any rate, it is unlikely that the organisational constitution's individual rules will prove to be the organic unfolding of a *single* principle: the provisions concerning the competences and co-operation of the European Council, the Commission, the Council and Parliament are too convoluted, uneven and scattered.[251] The individual rules are largely explained as the haphazard results of negotiating strategies and power politics. Thus far the success of legal science in grasping the Treaties' procedural law has been meagre[252] and can only be described as unsatisfactory.[253] The Constitutional Treaty mends this situation only at a first glance. In Part I emerges a more transparent

[245] What is initially seen as a loss of sovereignty is, on closer inspection, the loss of power of individual actors. The governments exchange the loss of national autonomy for opportunities to exercise influence at the supranational level and thereby achieve an extra profit, namely, the increase of autonomy with respect to other domestic institutions, such as the national parliament. See A Moravcsik, 'Warum die Europäische Union die Exekutive stärkt', in D Wolf (ed), *Projekt Europa im Übergang?* (1997) 211.

[246] See especially the authors cited above at nn 233 and 235.

[247] D Simon, *Le système juridique communautaire* (1997) 97, 107.

[248] Case 9/56, above n 92, 152; Case 25/70, *Köster* [1970] ECR 1161, para 9; on the correlative agency problems, E Vos, 'Reforming the European Commission: What Role to Play for EU Agencies?', (2000) 37 *CML Rev* 1113 at 1120; E Chiti, 'The Emergence of a Community Administration', (2000) 37 *CML Rev* 309.

[249] Case C-139/79, *Roquette Frères v Council* [1980] ECR 3333, para 33; Case C-70/88, *Parliament v Council* [1990] ECR I-2041, paras 22 *et seq*.

[250] Further considerations centre on apportioning competences according to the specific profile of the institution with a view to its legitimacy structure and out-put potential; in detail, Gerkrath, above n 11, 388 *et seq*; M Kaufmann, *Europäische Integration und Demokratieprinzip* (1997) 224 *et seq*; Lenaerts and van Nuffel, above n 7, 418.

[251] The term "organised irresponsibility" is apt; S Oeter, 'Vertrag oder Verfassung?', in T Bruha, K Hesse and A Nowak (eds), *Welche Verfassung für Europa?* (2001) 243 at 262, correctly states that the reform of the institutions and their co-operation is the fateful question.

[252] See especially R Bieber, *Das Verfahrensrecht von Verfassungsorganen* (1992) 240 *et seq*.

[253] A good example of the woeful state is offered by M Axmann, *Genese Europäischer Rechtsetzungsverfahren* (2001).

organisational set-up. However, the relevant rules in Part III are hardly less convoluted than their current equivalents.[254]

Additional procedural safeguards for national diversity include an early warning mechanism with respect to the principle of subsidiarity, according to Article I-9(3) CT-Conv (Article 11(3) CT-IGC) and the Protocol on the Application of the Principles of Subsidiarity and Proportionality, as well as the duty to inform the national parliaments of all legislative proposals according to the Protocol on the Role of National Parliaments in the European Union.[255]

4. The Principle of Loyalty and the Federal Balance

Whereas national law brings with it the threat of a sanctioning power,[256] one searches in vain for a European counterpart. Much of European law—namely all legal norms that represent, at their core, a communication between different public authorities—is not even symbolically sanctioned by possible coercion.[257] This aspect shows that loyalty plays a central, indeed even founding role in European law.

Moreover, loyalty as a legal principle has a seminal role in shaping the various relationships between public authorities. Especially in view of the lack of hierarchies[258] and because the legal provisions are often only fragmentary, these relationships must be embedded in supplementary duties that secure the law's effectiveness yet at the same time ease tensions. The principle of loyalty, usually described by the Court as the principle of co-operation, generates such duties.[259] The relevant judgements are based mainly on Article 10 EC, but the principle can now be extended to all the

[254] In detail, A Maurer, 'Orientierungen im Verfahrensdickicht?', (2003) *integration* 440.

[255] U Mager, 'Die Prozeduralisierung des Subsidiaritätsprinzips im Verfassungsentwurf des Europäischen Konvents', (2003) *Zeitschrift für Europarechtliche Studien* 471 at 480 *et seq*; Peters, above n 112, 61 *et seq*.

[256] Kelsen speaks of the "law as coercive norm"; see H Kelsen, *Introduction to the Problems of Legal Theory* (1999) 26.

[257] Of course, the compulsion foreseen in Art 37 German Basic Law has also never been exercised. Symbolic value, nevertheless, can be enormous as the US-American example shows. See US Supreme Court, *Brown v Board of Education*, 347 US 483 (1954); on the positions of the relevant jurisprudential discussions, A von Bogdandy, 'A Bird's Eye View on the Science of European Law', (2000) 6 *ELJ* 208 at 221 *et seq*.

[258] On the co-ordinating structure of European administrative law, W Hoffmann-Riem, 'Strukturen des Europäischen Verwaltungsrechts – Perspektiven der Systembildung', in Schmidt-Aßmann and Hoffmann-Riem, above n 4, 319 at 321 *et seq*.

[259] Case 230/81, *Luxembourg v Parliament* [1983] ECR 255, para 37; Case 54/81, *Fromme* [1982] ECR 1449, para 5; Cases 358/85 and 51/86, *France v Parliament* [1988] ECR 4821, para 34; Case 14/88, *Italy v Commission* [1989] ECR 3677, para 20; Case 2/88 Imm, above n 83, para 17; similarly, 3rd Declaration to Art 10 of the Treaty of Nice; O Due, 'Article 5 du traité CEE: Une disposition de caractère fédéral?', in Academy of European Law (ed), *Collected Courses of the Academy of European Law 1991* (1992), vol II-1, 15 at 35; J Mischo, *Der Beitrag des Gerichtshofes zur Wahrung der föderalen Balance in der Europäischen Union* (1999).

Union's activities,[260] which is now explicitly stated in Article I-5(2) CT-Conv (Article 5(2) CT-IGC). This principle shapes the manifold interactions between the Union institutions and the national authorities within the yet unnamed aggregate of Union and the Member States. Accordingly, it can both facilitate unity and protect diversity.[261]

The principle of loyalty is the basis of many important, sometimes highly differentiated legal concepts often with strongly unifying effects, for instance the requirements regarding judicial co-operation or the domestic implementation of Union law.[262] In light of the protection of diversity, however, the principle remarkably protects generally *only* the integrity of the results of European legislation against *subsequent* disobedience by individual Member States. In contrast, duties to formulate "Union friendly policies" are not derived from this principle.[263] This is by no means necessarily so; after all, German public officers are directly bound by the Union's goals (Article 2 EU, Articles 2 and 3 EC) when they participate in the Union's institutions, otherwise indirectly by Art 10 EC. These norms require them to further the interests of *all* Union citizens. Moreover, the principle of primacy might apply in case of conflict between "national" and "supranational" interests. Nevertheless, it has never come to a legal rejection of "national positions". This can be explained by the understanding of the Union's political system presented above: the European commonwealth is achieved through synthesis of the various standpoints which are usually brought into the European process by the national governments. The principle therefore only requires participation in the Union's political process.[264]

The principle of loyalty also imposes duties on the Union's institutions with regard to the Member States, as explicitly stated in Article I-5(2) CT-Conv (Article 5(2) CT-IGC).[265] These duties extend to the protection of

[260] U Everling, 'From European Communities to European Union', in A von Bogdandy *et al* (eds), *European Integration and International Co-ordination: Studies in Transnational Economic Law in Honour of C-D Ehlermann* (2002) 139 at 157; A Hatje, *Loyalität als Rechtsprinzip in der Europäischen Union* (2001) 39 *et seq*; Verhoeven, above n 135, 306.

[261] See generally Verhoeven, above n 135, 304 *et seq*, 358 *et seq*.

[262] Cases 205/82–215/82, above n 73, para 19.

[263] Case 57/72, *Westzucker* [1973] ECR 321, para 17.

[264] An "empty chair" policy, as conducted by France from July 1965 to January 1966, is thus a violation of Art 10 EC; Hatje, above n 260, 67, 77; in detail, JH Kaiser, 'Das Europarecht in der Krise der Gemeinschaften', (1966) *Europarecht* 4 *et seq*. Also, internal participatory procedures that largely deprive the representatives in the Council of their ability to conduct or conclude compromises and thus disproportionately compromise the European legislative process are inconsistent with this principle; U Everling, 'Überlegungen zur Struktur der Europäischen Union und zum neuen Europa-Artikel des Grundgesetzes', (1993) *Deutsches Verwaltungsblatt* 936 at 946; FC Mayer, 'Nationale Regierungsstrukturen und europäische Integration', (2002) *Europäische Grundrechte-Zeitschrift* 111 at 119.

[265] From the extensive case-law, see Case 230/81, above n 259, paras 37 *et seq*; Case 52/84, *Commission v Belgium* [1986] ECR 89, para 16; Cases 358/85 and 51/86, *France v Parliament* [1988] ECR 4821, paras 34 *et seq*; Case 94/87, *Commission v Germany* [1989] ECR 175, para 9; Case C-75/97, *Belgium v Commission* [1999] ECR I-3671, para 88; Case C-404/97, *Commission v Portugal* [2000] ECR I-4897, para 40; Case C-261/99, *Commission v France* [2001] ECR I-2537, para 24; Case C-378/98, *Commission v Belgium* [2001] ECR I-5107, para 31; Case C-263/98, *Belgium v Commission* [2001] ECR I-6063, paras 94 *et seq*.

diversity, though they still await further clarification. It is certain that Article 6(3) EU, as an expression of the principle of loyalty, requires the Union to take the Member States' constitutional principles and fundamental interests into account (Article I-5(1) CT-Conv; Article 5(1) CT-IGC).[266] However, there cannot be a prohibition on Union action for every infringement of a domestic constitutional position. Otherwise, in view of the fact that, for example, Germany deals with innumerable questions constitutionally, independent Union politics would be impossible. Rather, the principle is to be applied in case of concrete and serious interference with the fundamental requirements of the national constitutional order. Such determination will have to be made by the ECJ, probably in a procedure involving the national constitutional or high court.[267] The fact that this difficult and contentious road has never been taken demonstrates the effectiveness of the Union's institutions and its constitutional law. Loyalty thus appears to be key to understanding the Union. Just as the European legal order ultimately rests on the voluntary obedience of its Member States, and therefore on their loyalty, the principle of loyalty is also capable of generating solutions to open questions and thus containing the conflicts that arise in a polycentric and diverse polity.

V. CONCLUDING REMARKS

This exposition has revealed to what extent a doctrine of the unional founding principles can build on established constitutional scholarship and also where innovation is still necessary. In some important issues, continuity is possible only based on still controversial understandings of national constitutional law. Continuity increases as the national position is loosened from the postulate of unity. That is, continuity increases, if concepts such as people, state and sovereignty are not central but rather peripheral, if representation is not the mere visualisation of some unseen entity but rather an instrument for the aggregation of interests, if legal provisions are not the higher truth of the *volonté générale* but rather negotiated results, if law itself is not the expression of but rather a functional equivalent of common values. The more national constitutional law is seen as a constitutional law of social and political pluralism, the sooner a theoretical and normative connection can be established.

A European doctrine of principles remains a project that will occupy many legal scholars before a sufficient consensus emerges. Established

[266] *Entscheidungen des Bundesverfassungsgerichts* 89, 155 at 174 (*Maastricht*); A Epiney, 'Gemeinschaftsrecht und Föderalismus', (1994) *Europarecht* 301 at 318; C Schmid, *Multi-Level constitutionalism and constitutional conflicts* (2001) 222 *et seq*.

[267] P Kirchhof, 'Gegenwartsfragen an das Grundgesetz', (1989) *Juristenzeitung* 453 *et seq*; Schmid, above n 266, 228.

doctrines concretise unional principles in only few areas. Many principles remain largely abstract, or their nature as principles is even contested. Legal science's design for the European legal order on the basis of principles remains a programme for the future.

The principle of democracy and the relationship between principles furthering unity and those protecting diversity have proven to be philosophically problematic and antinomic.[268] Legal science alone will not be able to pacify the underlying tension. However, conceiving such tension as conflicts of principles introduces legal reasoning into the process. Moreover, the principle of loyalty can check unresolved, political tensions. Definite solutions, though, should not be expected. C Schmitt was likely right on one point: *substantial* stability is largely impossible in a real—that is, heterogeneous—federation.[269] Yet it is even likelier that, in a rapidly changing, interdependent world, substantial stability is an out-dated, illusory pipe-dream. Fortunately, what really matters is not substantial stability, but the realisation of the principles discussed in this contribution. Their realisation appears demanding, but eventually promising.

[268] I Kant, *Kritik der reinen Vernunft* (1787, 2nd edn 1956), B 392, 444; Frowein, above n 181, 317.
[269] Schmitt, above n 158, 370.

2

Federalism and Democracy

STEFAN OETER

I. INTRODUCTION: "UNDERSTANDING THE EUROPEAN UNION AS A FEDERAL POLITY"

REFERENCES TO CONCEPTS of federalism currently enjoy a certain popularity in the political and constitutional debate on the future architecture of the European Union (EU). The slogan "From a Commonwealth of Nations to a Federation" has become a means of gaining positive profile as visionaries[1] for some politicians (particularly from Germany). Similarly, but in a diametrically opposed fashion, such visions serve to antagonise politicians with a different orientation, in particular from France and the United Kingdom. Consequently, it is rather easy for them to mobilise masses of voters concerned with the preservation of traditional statehood in terms of the nation-state. Federalist concepts thus consolidate ever more the already existing rift dividing the various factions in the constitutional-political debate on the future shape of a united Europe. "Understanding the European Union as a Federal Polity", to borrow the title of a recently published article of an American political scientist,[2] proves to be a position far from a potential consensus. This is striking if one takes into consideration that for the founding father generation of European federalists, enthused by the project of founding the "United States of Europe", concepts of federalism from the beginning had served as guideline for their visions of a "European Constitution".[3] This was a group which had been very influential in the early years of the European project but which became marginalised in later years. The opponents of such vision have always dismissed the use of federal concepts in European politics (and in scientific

[1] See the speech by the German Minister for External Affairs Fischer at Humboldt University, Berlin, 12 May 2000, printed as: J Fischer, 'Vom Staatenbund zur Föderation', (2000) *integration* 149 at 154.

[2] R Koslowski, 'Understanding the European Union as a Federal Polity', in T Christiansen, KE Jørgensen and A Wiener (eds), *The Social Construction of Europe* (2001) 32.

[3] See the fundamental work of M Burgess, *Federalism and European Union* (2000) 55.

analysis of European integration) as a "hopelessly impractical or even utopian" misconception, if not as a horror scenario.[4]

For a long time, using the "dirty F-word" in the upper echelons of European politics has been the equivalent of breaking a taboo. What are the reasons for this? "Why has federalism provoked such an obviously irrational response"—a question recently formulated by the British political scientist Michael Burgess, a leading authority in the debate—"and why does it continue today to upset even well-informed observers of the evolving European Union (EU)?"[5] Burgess identifies primarily—and I find this convincing—a distorted perception of federalist experiences. Federalism constitutes, according to a widespread understanding of the basic experiences of federal systems like the USA, Germany or Switzerland, a decisive part of the complex historical process of state formation and of national integration of heterogeneous polities. Federalism thus seems to be inseparably linked to the dialectical process of forming an own nation and an own state. Accordingly, the formation of a federally structured European Union would inevitably end up—this is implicitly assumed—in the formation of a European state, thus dissolving the traditional nation-states and national cultures into the melting pot of a newly formed "European Nation".[6]

In contrast to such an "oversimplified and chimerical" misconception, one must make clear that the construction of a united Europe in federal categories does not constitute an enterprise of destroying the inherited nation-state, but is an enterprise intended to save these traditional polities.[7] If this is possible at all, the inherited nation-states will only be able to survive in a world increasingly characterised by international entanglement of economies, societies and political entities if they manage to integrate into a bigger, overarching polity. Such a polity would enable public authorities to find suitable answers to the challenges of "globalisation", whilst at the same time preserving in its federal division of functions the existence of traditional states and their (limited) capacity to act.

If one has managed to overcome the first barrage of completely tabooing federalist concepts as a tool for the discussion of European integration, a new problem arises. In analysing the federalist discourse more in detail, one becomes aware that there is not a definitive discourse on "federalism and the European Union", but a multitude of discourses which are only loosely related to one another. The discourse on the future shape

[4] *Ibid*, xi.

[5] *Ibid.*

[6] *Ibid*; see also T Fischer and N Schley, *Europa föderal organisieren* (1999) 38.

[7] See especially P Hoffmann, 'Reflections on the Nation-State in Western Europe Today', (1982) 21 *JCMS* 21; also AP Milward, *The European Rescue of the Nation-State* (1992) in particular 2–9, 438–42.

of "federal Europe"—envisioned as a constitutional project—is inspired by a completely different set of guiding ideas, concepts and arguments than the more analytical, politically scientific discourse on the possibilities of theoretically modelling the existing institutional framework of the EU upon the categories of a federal or federative composite system. While one school of thought attempts to overcome the "half measures" of the existing "union of states" by integrating states through a federal constitution (in its genuine sense), leading to a "genuinely united" European federal state, another school of thought already perceives the existing multi-level system of the European Union as a structure of federal (composite) statehood. Furthermore, economists pursuing totally different cognitive interests and using different theoretical concepts on the European Union, describe the EU as a paradigmatic case of "fiscal federalism", i.e. a system of organised competition between public entities and states.

Accordingly, as a first step I will attempt to give a brief summary of the various theoretical approaches and models using federalist concepts as a tool of conceptualising the European Union. Naturally, as a lawyer with a particular interest in political science, I will show a marked preference for the institutionalist discourse, inspired by concepts of political science and European Community law. This is a logical consequence of implicit cognitive interests. Also, due to my background, I have a personal preference for the description, analytical screening and theoretical reconstruction of the existing multi-level system of "composite" European statehood and consequently a marked scepticism towards any "visionary" call for a "constitutional revolution", i.e. an overcoming of the institutional status quo by the "grand design" of a completely new institutional arrangement.

The core of the synthetical reconstruction of European federalism debates on which this study focuses deals with the basic questions and guiding concepts of the political science and Community law discourses on "federalism and European Union", eg the controversy over whether and to what degree it is possible to model the (existing) European Union as a federal system of "composite" statehood. This controversy is full of conceptual flaws since the debate is a complex myriad of divergent theoretical concepts and notions. Such concepts and notions will have to be evaluated and partly reconstructed in the course of a basic revision and synthesis of the discourse. This is particularly evident with the (delicate) debates on sovereignty and on democracy in the European Union. Any serious attempt to reconstruct the inherited notions (and the underlying theoretical concepts), inevitably exemplifies how much our theoretical and constitutional thinking on state and constitution is still dominated by the legacy of 19th century ideas and one begins to question whether these inherited notions and concepts are still relevant to the challenges of transforming statehood in the 21st century.

II. THE DIFFERENT FEDERALISM DISCOURSES—AN OUTLINE

For the founding fathers of the European Community (EC) the problem of modelling European integration just described did not exist to the same degree as it exists now. They constructed a new form of "supranational" integration which they developed out of the traditional forms of international organisation—a new arrangement which on completion was perceived to fit easily into the established categories of traditional political theory. Without unduly simplifying, one can state that the founding generation envisaged a step by step process of "thickening" integration, a largely consent-based process which had a clear final vision: a "United States of Europe", in the classical form of federal statehood.[8] "The unfinished federal state"[9]—a noteworthy book, by Walter Hallstein, the first president of the Commission—programatically called for the project to be brought to its logical end, with regards to the common objective underlying the enterprise. The founding fathers of the Community therefore were practically all "federalists". The EEC was borne out of the disappointment over the failure of the (much more ambitious) project of a European Defence Community, a project which carried, even more visibly than the follow-up project EEC, the mission of serving as a fundamental and "first pillar" of the aspired European federal state.[10] The most important actors of European integration policy of these years—from Robert Schuman and Jean Monnet to Walter Hallstein, Konrad Adenauer and Alcide De Gasperi—were undoubtedly inspired by the same vision when they started the surrogate project of a European Economic Community in 1955.[11] Their position was not without controversy. The famous German Federal Minister of the Economy at the time, Ludwig Erhard, often complained about the "Europe-romanticists" in the Foreign Office, a group which incidentally had strong backing from Adenauer.[12] The "federalist" camp proved to have stronger support and was in the end victorious. The result was a treaty which contained an institutional structure that was conceived to serve as a blueprint for a "federal" system. Even more, in the first composition of the Commission, the central organ of the EEC became a bulwark of declared "federalists"[13], with Walter Hallstein at its head[14] and open advocates of a European federal state, like Hans von der Groeben and Jean Rey, as influential members.

[8] See Burgess, above n 3, 64–70.

[9] W Hallstein, *Der unvollendete Bundesstaat* (1969).

[10] See only F Duchene, *Jean Monnet: First Statesman of Interdependence* (1994) 340–6.

[11] Burgess, above n 3, 72–7.

[12] HJ Küsters, 'Walter Hallstein und die Verhandlungen über die Römischen Verträge 1955–1957', in Loth *et al* (eds), *Walter Hallstein: Der vergessene Europäer*? (1995) 81 at 93.

[13] Burgess, above n 3, 73, 76–9.

[14] See concerning the "federalist" ideas of Hallstein his influential work *Der unvollendete Bundesstaat* (1969) as well as W Hallstein, *Europe in the Making* (1972).

However, this vision soon suffered setbacks, beginning with De Gaulle's initiatives of a purely intergovernmental "Political Union"[15]. The result was a confrontation between the French government on the one hand, the Commission and the majority of the Council on the other. The outcome was the (French) "empty chair policy"[16] consequently stagnating any further phases of integration in the late sixties, seventies and early eighties[17]. The federalist teleology which had been shared by most activists of European integration seemed to have been proven illusory. Thus the competing paradigm to the initial federal vision, based upon the construction of the European Community as a (limited) project of "functional integration" with a primarily economic objective, got the upper hand. The federal paradigm never completely vanished, but became the profession of faith for a sectarian group of convinced idealists. Documents, such as the 1975 report of the Commission on the reform of the Community inspired by Altiero Spinelli,[18] which served as the basis for the Tindemans Report, as well as the introduction of direct elections for the European Parliament in 1979,[19] showed "federalist" ambitions going well beyond the dominant approach of pure functionalism. The clearly visible resistance of national politics against such far-reaching objectives as well as the deliberate change to an approach of cautious incrementalism led to a nearly complete disappearance of federalist programmes in politics, however. Only the discussion on the necessity of a European Constitution in the 1990s has revived the federalist argument to the point that now even the most important politicians tend to perceive it as opportune to gain profile as "progressives" by using federalist concepts.

The big disappointment of the late 1960s had transformed the federal paradigm from a powerful political eschatology to a much more modest, more status quo-oriented "cognitive pattern". "The unfinished federal state", by Walter Hallstein, is again perhaps a good point of reference. Based upon his disillusioning experience as President of the Commission, Hallstein advocated an understanding of the existing Community arrangement as the nucleus of a federal type of institutional arrangement, oriented towards the vision of a federal system, towards the "United States of Europe". The ambiguity of such federal concept has been voiced with utmost clarity already by Hallstein:

[15] Burgess, above n 3, 78–82 and very detailed PJ Bodenheimer, *Political Union* (1967).

[16] See again Burgess, above n 3, 83–7, but also W Loth, 'Hallstein und De Gaulle: Die verhängnisvolle Konfrontation', in Loth *et al* (eds), above n 12, 171–88, and HH Götz, 'Die Krise 1965/66', in *ibid*, 189.

[17] Burgess, above n 3, 85–8, 101–4.

[18] *Ibid*, 108–12.

[19] *Ibid*, 116–18.

> The federal concept is ... not only an objective. It is at the same time the most simple—and in this sense the most adequate—description of a (partial) reality, namely the European Community.[20]

Observers have characterised this perspective as a "Kantian constitutionalist strategy, directed towards a federative supra-state"[21], a strategy which intends to portray the integration to the reader as something effective as well as reasonable, with the aim of taking effect as some kind of "self-fulfilling prophecy".

The dominant "functionalist" paradigm of the decades after 1970,[22] however, has resulted in all concepts of the EC as a "federal" arrangement receding into the background. One should seriously question, however, whether Hallstein's construction of the "real-existing" Community does not include more than one grain of truth. Recent writings, in particular with a German background, increasingly raise this question.[23] Inspired by historical analogies to the construction of the German Empire of 1867/1871[24], the federal features of the Community's construction are increasingly elaborated upon within the relevant literature. This approach can also be increasingly found in the anglo-saxon literature, albeit with a more comparative orientation. It is fuelled by the growing research on comparative federalism.[25] This line of debate (re)introduces an important new dimension in European constitutional discourse, and corrects not only traditional intergovernmentalist perceptions, but also the narrow sides of "supranational-functionalist" thought. It also reassesses and deconstructs, in a critical

[20] W Hallstein, *Die Europäische Gemeinschaft* (5th edn 1979) 439.

[21] See W Wessels, 'Walter Hallsteins integrationstheoretischer Beitrag—überholt oder verkannt?', in Loth *et al* (eds), above n 12, 281.

[22] See as a fundamental work EB Haas, *The Uniting of Europe* (2nd edn 1968); see in addition PC Schmitter, 'Three Neofunctional Hypotheses about International Integration', (1969) 23 *International Organization* 161.

[23] See U Everling, 'Zur föderalen Struktur der Europäischen Gemeinschaft', in K Hailbronner (ed), *Staat und Völkerrechtsordnung: Festschrift für K Doehring* (1989) 179; P Badura, 'Die "Kunst der föderalen Form"', in P Badura (ed), *Wege und Verfahren des Verfassungslebens: Festschrift für P Lerche* (1993) 369; P Lerche, 'Europäische Staatlichkeit und die Identität des Grundgesetzes', in B Bender (ed), *Rechtsstaat zwischen Sozialgestaltung und Rechtsschutz: Festschrift für K Redeker* (1993) 131 at 143–4; R Kopp, *Föderalismus—Modell für Europa* (1993); S Mazan, *Das föderative Prinzip in der Europäischen Union* (1996); H Laufer and T Fischer, *Föderalismus als Strukturprinzip für die Europäische Union* (1996) 41 *et seq*; K Heckel, *Der Föderalismus als Prinzip überstaatlicher Gemeinschaftsbildung* (1998); P Häberle, 'Föderalismus und Regionalismus in Europa', (1998) 10 *Revue europénne de droit public* 299; A von Bogdandy, *Supranationaler Föderalismus als Wirklichkeit und Idee einer neuen Herrschaftsform* (1999); D Thürer, 'Föderalistische Verfassungsstrukturen für Europa', (2000) *integration* 73; M Nettesheim, *EU-Recht und nationales Verfassungsrecht* (2002) 28.

[24] See A Böhmer, *Die Europäische Union im Lichte der Reichsverfassung von 1871* (1999) 35 *et seq*, 125 *et seq*, 144 *et seq*; S Oeter, 'Souveränität und Demokratie als Probleme in der "Verfassungsentwicklung" der Europäischen Union', (1995) 55 *Zeitschrift für ausländisches öffentliches Recht und Völkerrecht* 659.

[25] See the recently published collective work edited by K Nicolaidis and R Howse, *The Federal Vision* (2001) 1.

sense, the assumptions and conceptual pre-judgments dominating the debate. The following sections will attempt to undertake such a reconstruction of the most recent "revisionist" approaches.

III. THE EUROPEAN UNION AS A MIXED SYSTEM OF A FEDERATIVE CHARACTER

The real-existing "Constitution" of the European Community (and of the Union) contains features of a hybrid system.[26] As a treaty community founded by a treaty of public international law, the Community displays strong traits of a confederal, "unional" arrangement and of a "functional community" with limited purposes. The constructive fundament of the Community (and the Union) remains a series of classical inter-state treaties under public international law.[27] From this perspective, the Community can easily be recognised as a type of international organisation, albeit one with particularly strong competences. The international organisation model clearly inspired the founders in the 1950s when they designed the details of the institutional arrangements of the Community, in particular the basic features of the organs. The Council of Ministers as the main decision-making institution of the Community and the Parliament—as a marginalised consultative organ—were clearly based upon the typical institutional structure of international organisations. The other classical organ of an international organisation, the secretariat, has admittedly found a very peculiar form within the European Commission. The Commission might still be perceived, however, as a special variant of a traditional bureau or secretariat facilitating inter-state co-operation. Therefore the "secretariat" has only been adapted to the particular needs of a supranational community.[28] Even the European Court of Justice has some parallels in the founding treaties of more recent international organisations as it can settle disputes regarding the intepretation of the founding Treaties.

[26] See with particular clarity the assessment by Burgess, which argues "that the EU represents something distinctly new in the world of both inter-state and intra-state relationship. It is not yet a union of individuals in a body politic but it is more than merely a union of states in a body politic. It is not a federation but it is also more than a confederation understood in the classical sense. It exists, then, in a kind of conceptual limbo, a twilight zone where the firm boundaries that once defined it have been gradually eroded, reducing many of its distinct features to a blurred and indistinct union which has no name."—Burgess, above n 3, 41–2.

[27] See, regarding the differences between such a "treaty constitution" and a constitution in a narrow sense, S Oeter, 'Vertrag oder Verfassung', in T Bruha, JJ Hesse and C Nowak (eds), *Welche Verfassung für Europa?* (2001) 243 at 245 *et seq*; but also M Dickstein, *Der Verfassungsbegriff der Europäischen Union* (1998) 10 *et seq*, 142 *et seq*; as well as D Grimm, 'Vertrag oder Verfassung', (1995) 6 *Staatswissenschaften und Staatspraxis* 509 at 510 *et seq*.

[28] See A Böhmer, *Die Europäische Union im Lichte der Reichsverfassung von 1871* (1999) 53, 125 *et seq*.

A larger group of political scientists accordingly tends to analyse and construct the institutional arrangement of the Community as a mere variant of an "international regime[29]"—a construction which has become characteristic for the developing system of global governance during the last fifty years.[30] Consequently, the European Community (and now the Union) could perhaps be described as the most elaborate and refined treaty regime of regional integration.[31] The supranational character of the Community, however, does not really fit into this picture. The Commission, for example, clearly contains features of a supranational organ. Likewise, the Parliament has not remained a classical parliamentary assembly, but has become, first through the shift to direct elections and secondly through the gradual increase of parliamentary participation in law-making, a body with genuine powers of (co-)decision.[32]

With the elements of supranationality becoming stronger during the evolution of the Community system, the Community develops increasingly more federal features. This is a remarkable contrast from the originally dominant confederal features of the system of European integration. Although it seems logical to understand—according to the classical theoretical categorisations of "confederations of states" and "federal states"—"confederal" and "federal" as mutually exclusive theoretical notions, the Community system undoubtedly demonstrates features of both categories in a mixture which is changing over time.[33] The dichotomy of "confederation" and "federal state", in addition, has always been a theoretical artefact. The German Union of the

[29] Concerning the application of institutionalist approaches from the sphere of international relations to the analysis of European integration see R Keohane and P Hoffman, 'Institutional Change in Europe in the 1980s', in R Keohane and P Hoffman (eds), *The New European Community* (1991) 25.

[30] See as fundamental works of reference concerning the regime theory E Haas, 'Why Collaborate? Issue-Linkage and International Regimes', (1979-80) 32 *World Politics* 357; PD Krasner (ed), *International Regimes* (1983); OR Young, *International Cooperation* (1989) 13 *et seq*; V Rittberger, *Regime Theory and International Relations* (1993); A Hasenclever, P Mayer and V Rittberger, *Theories of International Regimes* (1997).

[31] As most important advocate of such an approach see A Moravcsik, 'Negotiating the Single European Act', (1991) 45 *International Organization* 19; also *id*, 'Preferences and Power in the European Community', (1993) 31 *JCMS* 473.

[32] See CD Classen, 'Europäische Integration und demokratische Legitimation', (1994) 119 *Archiv des öffentlichen Rechts* 238; W Kluth, *Die demokratische Legitimation der Europäischen Union* (1995) 87 *et seq*; R Bieber, 'Demokratische Legitimation in Europa', (1999) *Zeitschrift für europarechtliche Studien* 141; J Pinder, 'Steps towards a Parliamentary Democracy for Europe', in F Breuss, G Fink and P Griller (eds), *Vom Schuman Plan zum Vertrag von Amsterdam* (2000) 194.

[33] See on that point recently also Burgess, above n 3, 41 *et seq*, in particular 42, who points to the fact "that the established concept of federation may no longer be helpful and the federation-confederation antithesis may prove to be completely misleading. ... The future may not lie in an outmoded state sovereignty but in a new theory of association ... The established concept of federation has also been challenged because it is simply too constricting and is unable to encapsulate the complex realities which now exist. The theoretical implication is obvious: we have to expand our conceptual categories or we will simply fail to grasp and accommodate global empirical change."

early 19th century ("*Deutscher Bund*"), for example, at its origin could be described as a basic model of a confederation (*Staatenbund*), but when examined in more detail it constituted much more than a mere confederation. Indeed it not only possessed supranational, but one could also say federal characteristics, as opposed to the North German Union ("*Norddeutscher Bund*") of 1867 and its successor, the German Empire in 1871, which still possessed strong confederal features. However, there were other motives behind the reduction of both models into new theoretical categories. The leading authors of German constitutional law after 1871 did not want to take into consideration the hybrid character of both constitutional arrangements, as their agenda was to denounce the German Union in an attempt to reinterpret the Constitution and ultimately purify the "federal state" of 1867/1871 from all its confederal rudiments.

The use of the theoretical concepts such as confederation and federal state aims to establish a dominant normative *Leitmotiv* in order to adequately conceptualise the European Union's construction and hence exclude some political-strategic ideas. It is thus not possible to lead a meaningful debate over the "federal" features of the European Community if one does not direct attention to the political implications and implicit discursive strategies linked to the use of the concepts just described. The discussion on parallels, analogies and also direct potentials of explication that has sprung up in the last years is very much driven by such political implications and deliberate discursive strategies. While the debate in the German-speaking area concentrates in particular upon similiarities, analogies, and also contrasting models with a view to the German Empire of 1871, the anglo-saxon literature refers to many more examples. These include the federal Constitution of the United States of America, the federal "dominion" Constitutions of Canada and Australia, in addition to the postcolonial federal Constitutions of India, Nigeria, Burma and Malaysia. Furthermore, recent political science literature, particularly in the field of nationalism, questions how a decidedly multinational community might be integrated at all levels of a state—coming to a clear conclusion that this is possible only in a federal form, if at all! Here Switzerland, Belgium and Canada serve as good points of reference.

While the first idea which is strongly represented in German speaking literature aims primarily at a deconstruction of guiding ideas and basic concepts of the debate on the "European Constitution", the more comparative literature on European federalism, primarily of anglo-saxon background, tries to draw constructive consequences from the rich experience which might be found in an empirical analysis of the functioning of federal systems all over the world.[34] The constructive orientation is even more openly

[34] See the exemplary contributions by DJ Elazar, JHH Weiler, JD Donahue, MA Pollack, GA Bermann, G Majone und K Nicolaidis, in K Nicolaidis and R Howse (eds), *The Federal Vision* (2001) 31, 54, 73, 191, 252 and 439.

displayed with the debate inspired by nationalism studies, a debate which covers the chances of federal integration of a multitude of national entities and/or peoples in a multinational arrangement of a federal nature. The debate struggles with the question of whether under conditions of national heterogeneity it is possible to avoid giving the federal structure strong "consociational" characteristics. In the end, this leads to the question of what might be the potential collective subject of such a conglomerate of nations—culminating in a work such as "A Theory of the Necessity of a Federal "Staatsvolk", and of Consociational Rescue"[35].

IV. THE BENEFIT OF FEDERAL ANALOGIES—OR THE CENTRAL STATE AS A "LEITMOTIV" OF POLITICAL THEORY

Let us begin with the deconstructivist potential which is inherent to any comparative look at federal parallels. One of the most interesting aspects of the debate on form and content of a European Constitution is the choice of theoretical assumptions. It should not come as a surprise that such a choice in states like France, characterised for centuries by experiences and traditions of a rigid centralisation, demonstrate an instinctive fixation on centralist models and categories. In contrast, the orientation towards centralist models that characterises the German debate should be of greater surprise. The strong fixation of the German debate on the traditionalist concept of sovereignty is conspicuous in this regard, coupling this concept with classical ideas of people's sovereignty and of parliamentary democracy.[36] On the basis of such construction, a lot of authors conclude that it is not possible to successfully "parliamentarise" an arrangement like the European Union, or that—seen from a perspective of German constitutional law—such "parliamentarisation" would mean an infringement of the constitutional guarantee of democracy. The peculiarity of the arrangement created during decades of gradual integration does not allow—so it is argued—for a complete parliamentary codetermination in political decision-making without destroying the balance of the overall system.

If viewed through the lenses of German constitutional history, such debate raises strange analogies to the constitutional discourse of the late 19th century over the nature and character of the federal state, a debate which suggests that there exist common problems and structures in such arrangements of a federal type.[37] The search for the ultimate place of sovereignty

[35] B O'Leary, 'An Iron Law of Nationalism and Federation?', (2001) 7 *Nations and Nationalism* 273.

[36] See I Pernice, 'Maastricht, Staat und Demokratie', (1993) *Die Verwaltung* 449 at 451 *et seq*.

[37] On the question what might be the common structure of such confederal systems see A Weber, 'Zur künftigen Verfassung der Europäischen Gemeinschaft', (1993) *Juristenzeitung* 325; as well as Everling, above n 23, 179.

became almost an obsession in the late 19th and early 20th centuries, particularly whether sovereignty had gone over to the *Reich* with its foundation or whether it had remained in the hands of the individual monarchs jointly forming this entity. A second question closely linked to this point was the debate over whether a parliamentary system would be compatible with the federal character of the *Reichsverfassung* (imperial constitution). The majority of German constitutional scholars took a rather negative stance in the second debate, dismissing any such compatibility.[38]

The return of this archaic debate about the place of sovereignty is irritating, if one takes into consideration its background. In pursuing the debate to its conclusion, in particular current ideas about the "special nature" of a confederal system (perceived as incompatible with a consequent parliamentarisation), one cannnot avoid the strange impression of experiencing a revival of the theories of the late 19th century. The German debate of that time nevertheless offers insights into the fallacies of a theoretical debate based upon traditional patterns of "positivist" deduction. The recourse to seemingly outdated "historical" debates over basic concepts may be used to prove that notions and categories perceived as secure and beyond argument contain more problems than the users of such concepts are ready to admit.

1. The Question of Sovereignty

The specific construction of the federal Constitution of 1867, which had been deliberately worked out in this form by Bismarck,[39] had left open the question that seemed so central for constitutional lawyers of that time—the question of where real sovereignty was placed. The Constitution had created a fragile balance not only between monarchical sovereignty—of the individual princes, embodied in the organ of the Federal Council (*Bundesrat*)—and the people's sovereignty—of the entire German people, embodied in the Imperial Diet (*Reichstag*)—but had also left open the question whether the Empire had become a fully sovereign state on its own by marginalising the member states to dependent entities or whether the individual States that had formed the Empire continued to exist as sovereign states. This "deliberate confusion" was easy to understand because at the time when the states unified to form the Empire, the dominant thought of the old liberal constitutionalism worked with the assumption of a shared or

[38] See E Kaufmann, *Bismarcks Erbe in der Reichsverfassung* (1917) 6–9, 64–7, 96–101; see also O Mayer, 'Republikanischer und monarchischer Bundesstaat', (1903) 18 *Archiv des öffentlichen Rechts* 337 at 366–8.

[39] See only T Nipperdey, *Deutsche Geschichte 1866–1918* (1992), vol II, 109; GA Craig, *Deutsche Geschichte 1866–1945* (1981) 45 *et seq.*

joint sovereignty, distributed upon federation and member states.[40] The sovereignty of the (compound) state was perceived as being simply divided between the different levels of state authority.

Under the influence of a new theoretical school which had gained prominence soon after 1871 and which was working on the basis of the "juridical-formal" method later called legal positivism, the question of sovereignty was immediately readdressed. Constitutional positivism forced an outcome on the issue of sovereignty. State sovereignty—thus was the widely shared belief in constitutional law doctrine—is indivisible according to its nature and legal concept and can accordingly only be attributed to either the federal state or the member states[41] According to methodological perspective (and political preference) one could either construe the federal (imperial) Constitution as a more confederal, "unional" arrangement, or perceive the federal (imperial) Constitution as the founding act of a new state (the Empire) marginalising the member states which had entered into such a union. Following the latter understanding, the Federation (*Reich*) had thus been transformed into a state which had become the exclusive bearer of sovereignty.[42]

The old liberal line of constitutional thinking which had been dominant up to 1871[43] soon disappeared. The liberal thinkers had argued that the nature of a federation lies in shared sovereignty.[44] Robert von Mohl, eg, had explained even in 1873:

[40] See G Waitz, *Grundzüge der Politik* (1862) 42–5, 162–6; see also R von Mohl, *Encyclopädie der Staatswissenschaften* (2nd edn 1872) 367; G Meyer, *Staatsrechtliche Erörterungen über die Deutsche Reichsverfassung* (1872)12 at 74 et seq; JC Bluntschli, *Allgemeine Staatslehre* (6th edn 1886) 560; F von Martitz, 'Das Staatsrecht des deutschen Reichs von P Laband', (1876) 32 *Zeitschrift für die gesamte Staatswissenschaft* 555. As a survey of the state of opinion in late 19th century see the description by A Haenel, *Deutsches Staatsrecht I* (1892) 201–5; H Preuß, *Gemeinde, Staat, Reich als Gebietskörperschaften* (1889) 33–40; see finally M Stolleis, *Geschichte des öffentlichen Rechts in Deutschland* (1992), vol II, 365–8.

[41] See in this sense P Laband, *Das Staatsrecht des Deutschen Reiches* (1876), vol I, 73–9; A Haenel, *Studien zum Deutschen Staatsrechte, Erste Studie: Die vertragsmäßigen Elemente der Deutschen Reichsverfassung* (1873) 239–49; P Zorn, *Staatsrecht des deutschen Reiches* (2nd edn 1895) 61–9; M von Seydel, 'Der Bundesstaatsbegriff', 28 *Zeitschrift für die gesamte Staatswissenschaft* (1872) 185; id, *Kommentar zur Reichsverfassung* (2nd edn 1897) 13–6; see also ER Huber, *Deutsche Verfassungsgeschichte* (1963), vol III, 786–7, 791, 794–6; Stolleis, above n 40, 366 *et seq*.

[42] See as a summary of this controversy von Martitz, above n 40, 560 *et seq*.

[43] In 1876 Laband still wrote of the "terminology of Waitz which has until recently claimed the nearly absolute and undisputed supremacy"—above n 41, 73.

[44] As founder of this doctrine German literature refers to G Waitz, who was strongly influenced by A de Tocqueville's *De la démocratie en Amérique*—see particularly G Waitz, *Grundzüge der Politik* (1862) 162–78; see also HA Zachariä, *Deutsches Staats- und Bundesrecht, Erster Theil*, (2nd edn 1853) 93–6; as another important advocate of this approach see von Mohl, above n 40, 367; *id, Das deutsche Reichsstaatsrecht* (1873) 29–32, 50–1; see also CF von Gerber, *Grundzüge eines Systems des Deutschen Staatsrechts* (2nd edn 1869) 238–49; JC Bluntschli, *Allgemeine Staatslehre* (6th edn 1886) 560–68; concerning the doctrinal evolution of this theory see, with a lot of detail, the historical study of S Brie, *Der Bundesstaat. Eine historisch-dogmatische Untersuchung* (1874) 92–104; as well the professorial dissertation of H Preuß, above n 40, 20–35.

> Nevertheless, the member states do not cease to exist as separate entities, having their own constitution and administration, pursuing a certain part of the objectives of a state independently and with their own means and according to their own rules; only a specific part of sovereignty, determined by the competence of the federal authority, is lost by them and is shifted to the federal organs.[45]

The positivist thinking which quickly gained ground after 1871, a school of thought which was obsessed with systematic stringency, logical consequence and rigid use of terminology, accused the liberal school with deforming the important concept of sovereignty completely, thus creating a chimera.[46] According to this view, sovereignty must be construed as "the highest, supreme, only itself directing power"—a concept that includes "logically the characteristic of unrestrictedness and accordingly also the characteristic of indivisibility".[47] Or—reformulated in terms of the famous question of the *Kompetenz-Kompetenz* (competence-competence):

> In the authority of the state over its competence lies the highest condition of its self-sufficiency, the core point of its sovereignty.[48]

However, such a sovereignty, according to the perception of the majority of constitutional lawyers, could belong only to one collective subject or state, that of the Empire (*Reich*). The German science of constitutional law thus had become entangled "in the web of the concept of sovereignty ... like a fly in the web of a spider".[49]

2. "Divided Sovereignty" and the Principle of People's Sovereignty

The old liberal constitutionalism could imagine only the principle of people's sovereignty as a suitable basis and guiding principle of a modern state.[50] When constitutional theory based itself upon the assumption of people's sovereignty, a construction of "shared sovereignty" made a lot of sense. The people, as the ultimate owner of sovereignty, are not capable of acting independently. People's sovereignty must always be organised by a constitution and must be channelled in an institutional arrangement in

[45] Von Mohl, *Reichsstaatsrecht*, above n 44, 29 *et seq*.
[46] See specifically blunt Laband, above n 41, 73–8.
[47] Thus the critique of Laband, above n 41, 73; see in the same direction also von Seydel, *Kommentar zur Reichsverfassung*, above n 41, 3.
[48] Haenel, above n 41, 149.
[49] Preuß, above n 40, VI.
[50] So—as an accusation—Mayer, above n 38, 337.

order to work.[51] However, in a constitutional system based upon the separation of powers such an organisation always rests upon a division of labour in the exercise of public authority. The state—organised on the basis of a formal constitution—by definition does not know a state organ which could be, as the bearer of an organ-specific sovereignty, supreme to the other organs, i.e. endowed with absolute authority.[52] On the contrary: in such a constitutional system, the organisational bearer of sovereign rights can only be a multitude of organs which exercise the state's public authority jointly—if one does not think in categories of the centralisation of powers inherent to classical doctrines of "sovereignty of parliament".[53] Absolute sovereignty of parliament, however, is the constitutional doctrine of a unitarian state, and not of federal states. The division of labour in the exercise of sovereign rights in federal constructions is the corresponding construction to the principle of separation of powers safeguarding the distribution of state authority to several state organs.

A completely different image emerges if one takes as a starting point a divergent theoretical construction, like German constitutional theory of the late 19th century did. The indisputed axiom of the system of constitutional monarchy had always been the unlimitedness—and indivisibility—of sovereignty.[54] Monarchical sovereignty—understood in the absolutist intellectual tradition of Bodin's doctrine as *suprema potestas* of a monarch representing the state—logically tended to a construction of unitary and absolute power. State authority was always derived power—derived from the "supreme, absolute power", the sovereignty of the monarch. Such uniform and centralised power, however, could only belong to one source of authority, even in a federal state. This had not been changed by the compromise formula found in the era of constitutionalism, the formula replacing the monarch as genuine bearer of sovereignty by the state[55]—a compromise solution which has had a lasting influence on German

[51] See on this—essentially undisputed—assumption of any modern theory of the state K Stern, *Das Staatsrecht der Bundesrepublik Deutschland* (2nd edn 1984), vol I, 604–7; E-W Böckenförde, 'Demokratische Willensbildung und Repräsentation', in J Isensee and P Kirchhof (eds), *Handbuch des Staatsrechts der Bundesrepublik Deutschland* (1987), vol II, 33, in particular paras 9 to 11—both with further references to the relevant literature.

[52] See more in detail K Stern, *Das Staatsrecht der Bundesrepublik Deutschland* (1980), vol II, 527–41, in particular at 532–6.

[53] As a classical emanation of the doctrine of "sovereignty of the parliament" see JC Bluntschli, *Allgemeines Staatsrecht* (6th edn 1885) 134–8; from a comparative perspective see also S Oeter, 'Die Beschränkung der Normenkontrolle in der schweizerischen Verfassungsgerichtsbarkeit', (1990) 50 *Zeitschrift für ausländisches öffentliches Recht und Völkerrecht* 545 at 556–8; with a critical distance to the classical British perspective I Harden, 'The Constitution of the European Union', (1994) *Public Law* 609 at 614–18.

[54] See only Laband, above n 41, 73; von Seydel, *Kommentar zur Reichsverfassung*, above n 41, 3.

[55] Concerning the victory of this construction see the historical study of W Pauly, *Der Methodenwandel im deutschen Spätkonstitutionalismus* (1993) in particular 23–9, 46, 66–7, 77–9.

constitutional doctrine right up to this day. The state as a collective subject in those days had been raised to the position of a genuine owner of sovereignty.[56]

The German debate on the impending loss of national sovereignty following the Maastricht Treaty only becomes understandable if one takes these intellectual legacies into consideration. Various conceptual peculiarities derive from this legacy, like the formula of the "proper and ultimately responsible statehood of the Federal Republic" ("eigenen und letztverantwortlichen Staatlichkeit der Bundesrepublik")[57] or the "constitutional necessity of an indivisible responsibility" ("Verfassungsnotwendigkeit einer unteilbaren Verantwortlichkeit") as well as the "guiding idea of an ultimate responsibility" of the German State ("Leitbild einer Letztverantwortlichkeit").[58] The drama which has unfolded in the eyes of a powerful faction of German constitutional scholars by the transfer of certain additional competences to the European Union is understandable only if one starts from the inherited, unitarian concept of a uniform and indivisible sovereignty. If one were to take the old construction of "shared sovereignty" as a starting point, the arrangement of the European Union founded with the Maastricht Treaty and further developed with the Amsterdam and Nice Treaties and now the Constitutional Treaty would be reduced to a rather banal operation of rounding off the competences of the Community system.

3. People's Sovereignty and the "Constitution" of the European Union

The supranational arrangement of the European Communities raises questions on the construction of the federal state. These questions concern in particular the division and grading of "sovereigns" and the change of the concept of sovereignty. It is disputed whether the European Union already possesses "state-like" or "parastatal" characteristics. But in many aspects the existing "Constitution" of the European Union—in the form of the Treaties of Maastricht, Amsterdam and Nice—demonstrates striking similiarities to the constitutional arrangement of the German Empire of 1867/1871, which also rested on a series of compromises in the distribution of powers. In hindsight and with good reason, the German *Reich* has also been described as a "community of states" or a "union of states" (*Staatenverbund*),[59] due to its confederal characteristics. This is true in particular for the form in which the member states participated in the central decision-making of the *Reich*. The arrangement designed by Bismarck in

[56] See A Peters, *Elemente einer Theorie der Verfassung Europas* (2001) 126–9.

[57] R Breuer, 'Die Sackgasse des neuen Europaartikels (Art. 23 GG)', (1994) *Neue Zeitschrift für Verwaltungsrecht* 417 at 425.

[58] V Götz, 'Das Maastricht-Urteil des Bundesverfassungsgerichts', (1993) *Juristenzeitung* 1081 at 1082.

[59] See KE Heinz, 'Das Bismarck-Reich als Staatengemeinschaft', (1994) 5 *Staatswissenschaften und Staatspraxis* 77; as well as Böhmer, above n 28, 35 *et seq.*

1867 was far from being typical for federal states at that time.[60] The most telling part of the construction is the Federal Council. The Council was designed as a surrogate of the (missing) executive of the *Reich*. It was intended (according to Bismarck's original concept) to serve as a kind of joint governmental organ of the "allied monarchical governments" of the princely member states.[61] With that construction, Bismarck deliberately tried to preserve the independence of the individual States' executives.[62] The "allied governments", as bearer of the monarchical sovereignty, constituted the real sources of legitimacy in the bureaucratic model of an authoritarian state dominant at that time in Germany. By preserving the political predominance of the monarchical executives, Bismarck at the same time hoped to block—and this was a deliberate part of the construction—any victory of parliamentarism. One could say something similiar concerning the construction of the European Community which in its approach is also a very technocratic construction. By attributing to the national governments (through the predominance of the "intergovernmental" Council) the decisive saying in the decision-making of the Community, the whole construction secures the hegemony of the executive. If seen in this perspective, it is amazing how the pragmatic arrangement of the Council is given a sacred meaning as an emanation of democracy. The Council is often elevated to being the centre of the European democratic process, which means that the project of European integration is in danger of becoming an instrument for safeguarding the autonomy of executives in political decision-making. This has an ironic consequence. The European project, still to some degree an idealistic concept, becomes hijacked by the "intergovernmental" predominance in its institutional arrangement, which in turn means that the Community construction can easily bypass democratic participation.

The role of the parliament accordingly poses particularly difficult questions. From the beginning, the role of the federal parliament (*Reichstag*) was in stark contrast to the more bureaucratic authoritarian constitutional arrangement characterising the *Reich* in general—a contrast that was deliberately built into the federal Constitution of 1867.[63] The *Reichstag*

[60] The differences between the federal constructions of the German Empire on the one hand and the classical federations like the USA and Switzerland have been recognized already by several contemporaries, so eg with particular clarity JC Bluntschli in his state theory—Bluntschli, above n 44, 561–2; see also G Anschütz, *Bismarck und die Reichsverfassung* (1899) 13–7; H Triepel, *Die Reichsaufsicht* (1917) 71–5.

[61] On the Bismarckian thesis of a "League of Princes" ("Fürstenbund") see eg the declaration of Bismarck before the Federal Council on 5 April 1884, printed in: *Hirth's Annalen* (1886) 350–4; on the political function of the thesis see Craig, above n 39, 50; Nipperdey, above n 39, 87–8; Huber, above n 41, 788–9.

[62] See only Nipperdey, above n 39, 92.

[63] The Constitution of the Empire was—as Thomas Nipperdey has formulated it—"truce and compromise". The Constitution has "balanced federalist and parliamentary principles. It has indeed limited, if not blocked the potential power of the parliament and the position of the government by the decidedly federalist organ of the Federal Council, but it has also created and consolidated a dynamic parliament on the basis of general elections."—Nipperdey, above n 39, 79.

represented the principle of people's sovereignty of the German people, a principle which stood in a marked contrast to the conserved institution of monarchical (i.e. bureucratic) sovereignty of the "allied governments". Bismarck had used the appeal to the people's sovereignty of the German people as a kind of "joker" in the struggle over hegemony. It was also a useful catalyst of further integration in the aspiration for legal unity.

Something similiar could be said concerning the position of the European Parliament. The institutional arrangement of the European Community is to a comparable degree characterised by a compromise between persisting Member States' "sovereignty" (as classical state sovereignty) and direct representation at the European level (as an expression of the principle of people's sovereignty). It is thus based on two pillars of democratic legitimation: a national one by way of national parliaments and governments and a Community-related one grounded in the directly-elected European Parliament. Although in its original version as a "Parliamentary Assembly", the European Parliament did nothing more than incorporate the national parliaments in the decision-making procedures of the Communities, it still "represented" the national peoples as the undisputed subjects of a (Member State-related) people's sovereignty through the inclusion of national MPs in the decision-making process. The introduction of a scheme of direct elections, however, shifted in a very peculiar way, the institutional role of the European Parliament.[64] It is not possible any more to understand the members of the European Parliament as simple "representatives" of individual nations or peoples constituting the Union, as an expression of a—separate—people's sovereignty of each nation united with the other nations in the Union.[65] They are not trustees of (a German or another national) state authority any more, legitimated through the national parliamentary systems, as much as the members of the German federal Parliament are not representatives of a specific "people" of a *Land* any more, although they are elected in this *Land*. The Members of the EP are "representatives" of the people of the European Union ("people" understood as the totality of all the citizens of the Union) with a view to a public authority extending to the whole Union.

The identification of people and nation is a possible, but not necessarily the only cogent interpretation of the concept of people's sovereignty. In a generic perspective the concept of people's sovereignty has not been

[64] See only Burgess, above n 3, 116–18.

[65] Parts of the doctrine are still of the opinion that by definition only the traditional statenations, which are capable of delivering a genuine democratic legitimation through their national parlaments, can be bearer of people's sovereignty—see eg PM Huber, 'Die Rolle des Demokratieprinzips im europäischen Integrationsprozeß', (1992) 3 *Staatswissenschaften und Staatspraxis* 349 at 354; F Ossenbühl, 'Maastricht und das Grundgesetz—eine verfassungsrechtliche Wende?', (1993) *Deutsches Verwaltungsblatt* 629 at 634; HP Ipsen, 'Europäische Verfassung—nationale Verfassung', (1987) *Europarecht* 195 at 209 *et seq*.

intrinsically based upon the concept of nation, but rested (at least at the beginning) upon the idea of free self-determination of a citizenry. The consensus of citizens was needed to legitimate state authority; but these were the citizens of a given political entity, not the members of a pre-existing national community. Therefore, the individual citizens must not have constituted a people or nation prior to the act founding a political community, but may have altogether found themselves as a collective entity (and a *pouvoir constituant*) by the act of constitution-making.[66]

Accordingly there is probably only one plausible option left, if one does not want the European Parliament to fade into a *quantité négligeable*, like the advocates of national sovereignty prefer to argue.[67] This option tells us that the European Parliament is an elected representative organ, a symbolic embodiment of a principle of representation (in the sense of people's sovereignty) oriented towards the entirety of the European Union,[68] even if such people's sovereignty does not belong to a uniform "European people" (*Staatsvolk*), but a "people" in the pre-national, authentic sense of the term, as *demos*, as the totality of the citizenry living in a given polity.[69] If it is possible at all to construct the concept in traditional categories, we could speak of the European peoples united in the Union as a compound polity of multinational character.

This element of representation which until now is inherent to each directly elected parliament has only a relatively weak embodiment in the institutional structure of the Union and is largely overshadowed by the statal sovereignty of Member States embodied in the Council of Ministers. In principle, the Member States formally continue to be the "Masters of the

[66] H Steinberger in particular has pointed out this, 'Der Verfassungsstaat als Glied einer europäischen Gemeinschaft', (1991) 50 *Veröffentlichungen der Vereinigung der Deutschen Staatsrechtslehrer* 9 at 23.

[67] As an example for this tendency see only Ossenbühl, above n 65, 634–5 who claims that the European Parliament is "not a parliament in the traditional sense of popular representation". Despite the identity of names (as parliament) one should not "identify it with the constitutional position of national parliaments". According to him, it remains unclear from which source the European Union should ever obtain its democratic legitimiation; see also PM Huber, above n 65, 356 who—in modifying the famous words of Montesquieu—calls the role of the European Parliament as "en quelque façon nulle" and writes of a "democratic decorum"; see in addition the literature listed in G Lübbe-Wolff, 'Europäisches und nationales Verfassungsrecht', (2001) 60 *Veröffentlichungen der Vereinigung der Deutschen Staatsrechtslehrer* 246 at 263 n 44.

[68] See Classen, above n 32, 246–7; and also Pernice, above n 36, 477–9; the sociologist MR Lepsius has spoken in this context of a "double basis of legitimation" of the Community, which on the one hand is rooted in the Treaties, but on the other hand derives from a "direct representation of the "people of the European Community" modelled through the European Parliament"—MR Lepsius, 'Nationalstaat oder Nationalitätenstaat als Modell für die Weiterentwicklung der Europäischen Gemeinschaft', in R Wildenmann (ed), *Staatswerdung Europas?* (1991) 19 at 22.

[69] See Pernice, above n 36, 477–8 and also in a recent scholarly study in detail A Augustin, *Das Volk der Europäischen Union* (2000), in particular 63 *et seq*, 393 *et seq*; also Peters, above n 56, 657–66, 700–8.

Treaties" ("Herren der Verträge"), since changing the treaties (as the "Constitution" of the Union) formally does not require consent of the European Parliament.[70] But the stronger European Parliament and the more important its participation in decision-making becomes, the stronger the element of an all-European people's sovereignty embodied in the parliament comes to the fore.[71]

In view of the current state of integration, in particular the European Parliament's degree of participation in political decision-making, one might ask whether the European Union does not constitute a state with "shared" or "dual" sovereignty.[72] The reference to the (missing) *Kompetenz-Kompetenz* of the Union which usually serves as a counter-argument, does not really help here. Such competence to decide upon the distribution of competences remains, according to the common construction, with the Member States as "Masters of the Treaties".[73] But the assumption that there exists such a *Kompetenz-Kompetenz* in theory presupposes the existence of an ultimate decisional prerogative which is far from being self-evident in a federal or confederal system. The institute of an unlimited *Kompetenz-Kompetenz* transfers the model of the hierarchically organised unitarian state to any sort of federal structure, since it claims that public authority and sovereignty are always attributed to one central organ, originally to the monarch, then to the central parliament. However, this transfer of unitarian theoretical categories to a federal structure is, by definition, problematic.

The deliberately unitarian orientation of the theoretical concept of *Kompetenz-Kompetenz* should urge us to be cautious. Any precipitate transfer of the concept to federal constructions like the European Union will inevitably be misleading, since any form of deepened integration sub-

[70] See only Ipsen, above n 65, 202 and HJ Blanke, 'Der Unionsvertrag von Maastricht', (1993) *Die Öffentliche Verwaltung* 412 at 418 *et seq*; but also U Everling, 'Zur Stellung der Mitgliedstaaten der Europäischen Union als "Herren der Verträge"', in U Beyerlin (ed), *Recht zwischen Umbruch und Bewahrung: Festschrift für R Bernhardt* (1995) 1161.

[71] Such strengthening of the "central" people's sovereignty embodied in the parliament will not necessarily lead to a transformation of the entire arrangement into a genuine federal state. The federal state is based upon certain external formalities, like constitution-making (resting upon the *pouvoir constituant* of the people). A "central" people's sovereignty accordingly can coexist with a traditional "union of states" or confederation as long as the form of a treaty community is kept. See for this point only Oeter, above n 27, 258–9.

[72] On the undecided situation resulting from such an approach see H Steinberger, 'Aspekte der Rechtsprechung des Bundesverfassungsgerichts zum Verhältnis zwischen Europäischem Gemeinschaftsrecht und deutschem Recht', in Hailbronner (ed), above n 23, 951 at 968; see also Peters, above n 56, 144–7 with further references to the relevant literature in fn 241.

[73] See only U Everling, 'Sind die Mitgliedstaaten der Europäischen Gemeinschaft noch Herren der Verträge?', in R Bernhardt (ed), *Völkerrecht als Rechtsordnung, internationale Gerichtsbarkeit, Menschenrechte: Festschrift für H Mosler* (1983) 173 at 189 and *id*, above n 70, 1161; also M Heintzen, 'Die "Herrschaft" über die Europäischen Gemeinschaftsverträge', (1994) 119 *Archiv des öffentlichen Rechts* 564 at 567 *et seq*; as well as Peters, above n 56, 140–4.

sequently can only be understood in categories of unitarian statehood or at its best in categories of the German "unitarian federalism". This is not really plausible, taking into consideration that a united Europe may not be constructed according to the model of the modern unitarian nation-state with a centralised bureaucracy and a parliament understood as omnipotent.

If the project of building a European polity is only conceivable in form of the confederal "union of peoples", the sovereignty of the Member States continues to exist, at least at its core. This is due to the states continuing to possess an autonomous, (non-derived) original ("originäre") public authority (which we could call also sovereignty). Such sovereign power, however, is not unlimited any more, as the traditional doctrine of sovereignty demanded. Rather it is only a partial authority over its citizens, since other parts of its sovereign powers are irrevocably bound in the system of supranational integration.[74] The corresponding level of supranational authority also possesses only a limited power—a fact which would not change even after a potential "constitutionalisation" of the system, through the formal introduction of a European Constitution.

V. THE ROLE OF THE PRINCIPLE OF DEMOCRACY IN A FEDERAL COMMONWEALTH

The question of sovereignty and the principle of democracy thus prove to be a conundrum of inseparably linked questions, like Siamese twins.[75] In an arrangement of modern constitutionalism the question of sovereignty is always linked to the construction of people's sovereignty. The construction of people's sovereignty, however, is at its core a question of moulding the principle of democracy.[76] How one solves the question of who should be the ultimate bearer of sovereignty in a system of federal integration will depend upon the chosen model of procuring democratic legitimacy. If one is thinking in unitarian categories, one will tend to construct a sovereignty of the federation, in contrast to a system of "shared" sovereignty. However, if one accepts as subjects of people's sovereignty only the individual peoples of the member states forming a confederation, sovereignty will be attributed exclusively to the member states.

The response to the question of democratic legitimation does not only depend upon the theoretical understanding on which the implicit model of

[74] Such finding is described by K Doehring with the formula "amputated sovereignty"—K Doehring, 'Staat und Verfassung in einem zusammenwachsenden Europa', (1993) *Zeitschrift für Rechtspolitik* 98 at 99; see, however, in the sense of a positive reassessment Peters, above n 56, 144 *et seq*.

[75] See only E-W Böckenförde, 'Demokratie als Verfassungsprinzip', in J Isensee and P Kirchhof (eds), *Handbuch des Staatsrechts der Bundesrepublik Deutschland* (1987), vol I, 887–9, 892.

[76] See Böckenförde, above n 75, 893–6.

construction of the European integration rests, but also upon the assumed theory of democracy. If one perceives the Community under a traditionalist perspective, i.e. constructing the arrangement exclusively as a commonwealth of sovereign nation-states, the source of democratic legitimacy can only be the parliamentary system at the national level. But what then is the role of the European Parliament? It undoubtedly is no longer a simple form of a consultative "parliamentary assembly", but a directly elected parliamentary representation of the European citizens and accordingly a genuine organ of parliamentary representation which possesses direct democratic legitimacy. In taking into account such a changed role for the European Parliament, it is not possible any more to deny that the European Parliament has acquired aspects of a common European people's sovereignty. Similarly to the federal parliament of the German *Reich*, the *Reichstag*, the foundations of a people's sovereignty throughout the whole European polity remains constricted by the fact that the overall arrangement of the European Constitution does not establish a genuinely parliamentary system, but attempts to consolidate the predominance of the "allied governments". It will depend mainly upon the concrete modelling of the position of the European Parliament as to how strong the core of an evolving "European people's sovereignty" will further develop. Rey Koslowski has recently spoken in that regard of a process of "unintentional constitutionalisation of power-sharing", in contrast to the classical founding act of federal systems, i.e. the "intentional federalism by treaty".[77]

A change in the functional distribution of roles between the organs of the Community and a transmission of the system of political parties will therefore go hand in hand. A growing importance of the Parliament will force the parties at the European level to a deeper internal integration, a process which is necessary in order to enable the European Parliament to do justice to its new function. Such an increased role for the Parliament will also raise the interest of the media in "European internal politics", i.e. the decisions in rule-making, budgetary and administrative control attributed to the Parliament. Intensified reporting (heightened interest by the public), however, would lead to more public knowledge of parallel debates in the medial publics of other Member States, which would result in a growing interdependency and interlocking of hitherto rather separated "national" publics. The more the Parliament and the Commission deal with questions of European politics of public interest, in the sense of a "European common good", the more the current national political perspectives will develop into an all-encompassing "European" discourse. In such European discourses, the same questions, if perceived with a view to the arguments of the others and with an orientation of common goals, would have a chance to become

[77] Koslowski, above n 2, 39–40.

fused to a "European common good", overarching the individual nations with its constructs of "national interest". None of this will happen quickly, but will be a tortuous and protracted process. The "constitutionalisation" of the European Union to a federal polity should accordingly be construed in this perspective as a slow and in its essence dialectical process. If the project of European integration is to be a success, it will not suffice to develop the institutional arrangements of a "European democracy", but—parallel to the shift in balance of the institutional roles—the social and organisational preconditions of a functioning democracy at the European level will have to develop. It is exactly in this dual nature, where the real challenge of a creeping process of gradual "federalization" lies, of an—to use the words of Koslowski—"institutionalization of a federal legal framework through the routinization of practices".[78]

As a consequence, it becomes questionable whether it is justified to claim that the founding of genuine people's sovereignty at European level should happen as a "revolutionary act" in the shape of formulating a formal Constitution. Moulding a Constitution in this case is perceived as requiring an act directly legitimised by the people, usually instituted through the election of a constitutent assembly or at least the confirmation of a Constitution by referendum.[79] In reality, however, the process of European constitution-making will have a gradual character. Accordingly, the establishment of a European democracy resting on a common European people's sovereignty will happen beyond public attention. The idea of a "revolutionary" act of a singular nature, meant as the setting of a new "foundational rule" (*Grundnorm*), thus proves to be highly problematic.[80] In conclusion, one should imagine "constitution-making" in the European Union in a totally different manner, more as a process of creeping accumulation of important fundamental decisions according to the style of British constitutional evolution, and not as formal exercise of a revolutionary *pouvoir constituant* by a constituent assembly.[81]

Nevertheless, the concept of a revolutionary shift of sovereignty serves as the main point of attack for the critics of further integration. An ongoing "parliamentarisation" of the Union would inevitably erode national sovereignty and marginalise national parliaments. The European Community and Union accordingly qualify in the perspective of this line of thinking as a mere system of international law-based regional integration, as a "commonwealth" of confederal nature, not suited to democratisation. Democracy requires in this view the existence of a recognised people as

[78] Koslowski, above n 2, 41.

[79] So eg Huber, above n 65, 360 *et seq*; J Wolf, 'Die Revision des Grundgesetzes durch Maastricht', (1993) *Juristenzeitung* 594 at 598–600.

[80] See Peters, above n 56, 360–78, in particular at 372–77, 487–95.

[81] See to that point also R Bieber, 'Verfassungsentwicklung und Verfassungsgebung in der Europäischen Gemeinschaft', in Wildenmann (ed), above n 68, 393 at 408–9.

bearer of people's sovereignty.[82] A "European people", some argue, does not exist or cannot exist since the diversity and heterogeneity of its peoples is constituent for Europe. A "people" as a subject of popular sovereignty does not necessarily require a common language, culture and history, but needs at least a collective which is convinced of it belonging together, prepared to form a legal union and ready to accept common decisions taken by organs responsible for the whole entity. Only on the basis of such commonalities might a political public agree to support an overarching people's sovereignty and enjoy the ultimate control within a democracy. The preservation of particularities of the peoples and states united in the Union is thus seen as requiring renunciation of any further democratisation of the Union, is seen in fact as the very reverse, as requiring stronger inclusion and participation of national parliaments.[83]

At first glance this argument seems plausible. A "European people", in the sense of a nation with pre-existing collective identity oriented towards creating its own, homogeneous nation state, indeed does not exist. But is this statement really the end of the debate? Does this starting-point really justify the conclusions derived from it? The response should not be given too hastily. The assumptions of the described line of argument should not be presumed as self-evident without further questioning.[84] The current argument of a missing "European people" as an insurmountable obstacle in democratising the European Community shows a problematic understanding of the construction of modern statehood. It demonstrates that it is erroneous to identify without any further reflection people's sovereignty and the traditional nation-state with one another.[85] Most of European nations are results of a common statehood in history, from which they derived, and did not constitute pre-existing conditions of a national state founded upon the basis of such a prior nation.[86] During the French revolution, France was declared to be a nation-state, although most of the inhabitants of France

[82] See only the references to the relevant literature given by Lübbe-Wolff, above n 67, 263 in n 44. On the difficulties of the notion "people", in particular regarding the "treaty constitution" of the European Union, see in detail Augustin, above n 69, 29–35, 196–204, 393–8; and Peters, above n 56, 105–7, 651 *et seq.*

[83] See only Fischer and Schley, above n 6, 34; on the practical problems of such an understanding see in particular U Everling, 'Überlegungen zur Struktur der Europäischen Union', (1993) *Deutsches Verwaltungsblatt* 936 at 945–7; Pernice, above n 36, 466–70.

[84] See in this sense also Peters, above n 56, 651–5; R Lepsius, '"Ethnos" und "Demos"', (1986) 38 *Kölner Zeitschrift für Soziologie und Sozialpsychologie* 751 at 756; J Habermas, 'Remarks on Dieter Grimm's "Does Europe Need a Constitution?"', (1995) 1 *ELJ* 303 at 305; JHH Weiler, 'The Reformation of European Constitutionalism', (1997) 35 *JCMS* 97 at 118–21.

[85] With particular openness this is done by U Di Fabio, 'Der neue Art. 23 des Grundgesetzes', (1993) 32 *Der Staat* 191 at 202, who refers for the construction of "democratic sovereignty" to the "idea of the modern European nation state".

[86] See in particular EJ Hobsbawm, *Nationen und Nationalismus* (German edn 1991) 25–31; also E Gellner, *Nationalismus und Moderne* (1991); as well as EJ Hobsbawm and T Ranger (eds), *The Invention of Tradition* (1983).

were far from feeling members of a uniform nation; it was only the centralised state enthused by the national idea that has formed France into a uniform nation[87] in just over a century. The same could be said for most of the other nation-states of Western Europe.[88] The popular identification of people's sovereignty and nation-state thus contains at its core an element of ethnic fundamentalism and demonstrates traits of mythological thinking.[89] Historically, people's sovereignty works without any problem where the unifying relationship of common "ethnos" does not exist[90]—one only need think of Switzerland or classical immigrant countries like the USA and Canada.[91]

The current argument against democratising a confederal system like the European Union contains ahistorical irony, as the German constitutional scholars in the late 19th and early 20th century, particularly during World War I, had also objected to such an idea. These objections were raised in order to "defend" Germany against any further parliamentarisation. The Allied Powers favoured a parliamentary system which German scholars argued was completely alien to the German constitutional tradition. The "genuine" German model of statehood embodied in the "constitutional monarchy" was perceived as being incompatible with a dependency of government from parliament. Moreover, the diversity of German statal and cultural traditions—preserved in the federal model—was seen as incompatible with parliamentarisation, because parliamentary sovereignty in the *Reich* would inevitably mean the final marginalisation of the individual States' monarchies.[92]

Some authors argue in a rather similiar fashion today. They claim that the construction of people's sovereignty and hence democracy is inherent to the traditional unitarian nation-state of Western European origin and is therefore not compatible with the concept of a further democratisation of the Union. This is not objectionable insofar as people's sovereignty and

[87] See only Hobsbawm, above n 86, 75; G Ziebura, 'Nationalstaat, Nationalismus, supranationale Integration. Der Fall Frankreich', in HA Winkler and H Kaelble (eds), *Nationalismus—Nationalitäten—Supranationalität* (1993) 34 at 42–5.

[88] Hobsbawm, above n 86, 97–105.

[89] So with good arguments BO Bryde, 'Die bundesrepublikanische Volksdemokratie als Irrweg der Demokratietheorie', (1992) 5 *Staatswissenschaften und Staatspraxis* 305 at 309; JHH Weiler, 'Der Staat "über alles"', (1996) 44 *Jahrbuch des öffentlichen Rechts der Gegenwart Neue Folge* 91.

[90] On the friction which exists between the concept of the modern "statenation" relying upon the principle of non-identification and the nation-state principle see in particular J Delbrück, 'Global Migration—Immigration—Multiethnicity', (1994) 2 *Global Legal Studies Journal* 45; as an interesting attempt to apply certain findings of recent political theory to the problems of the social and cultural fundaments of European integration see also S Howe, 'A Community of Europeans', (1995) 33 *JCMS* 27; also S Choudhry, 'Citizenship and Federations', in Nicolaidis and Howse (eds), above n 34, 377.

[91] See on that point Bryde, above n 89, 312.

[92] See eg Kaufmann, above n 38, 98–9.

democracy are understood as being exclusively oriented towards the concept of the nation-state. "Democratisation" of the Community in the sense of a classical parliamentary majority rule would result in the creation of a European "suprastate" and would be doomed to destroying the balance of the Community system that is based upon continuing self-determination in the framework of the "national" state and upon the preservation of heterogeneity and diversity of the European national cultures. The underlying tenet, however, is questionable—namely the assumption that a gradual progress of European integration is only possible in the organisational structures of the classical nation-state. The argument completely disregards the wealth of—empirically gained—experiences with the construction of non-nation-state-based compound systems which have been found by the research on comparative federalism. The compound of different levels of statehood with a division of labour between these various levels, a structure typical for federal systems, does not abolish the polities united in its institutional framework, but preserves the (albeit functionally limited) decisional autonomy and self-determination of the relevant nation-state in the multi-level system of a federal nature. It thus consolidates and secures the political autonomy of its subjects. Only the tasks which must be pursued by a central authority are transferred to the newly created, overarching level of the federative commonwealth; the decentralised powers of the member states preserved in the federal compound remain at the same time intact, which also preserves "regulatory competition" of member states as a disciplining element of federative unions of states.

In contrast to such a cautious approach characteristic of federalism, the inherited model of unitarian statehood of the nation-state is often misunderstood as an *a priori* value in the model of the "eurosceptics", instead of dealing with federalism as a question of the functional adequacy of a certain institutional order.[93] Such perseverance with the ideal of the given ideal, however, tends to avoid the decisive question: does the renunciation of any further consolidation of the role of the European Parliament and the compensatory strengthening of the national parliaments really solve the problems hidden behind the slogan of the "democratic deficit"?

VI. THE CONSTRUCTION OF DEMOCRATIC RESPONSIBILITY—EXPERIENCES OF FEDERAL SYSTEMS

The persistence on historical peculiarities and on a presumed "being different" tends to hide the decisive questions. The bureaucracies of the individual States, Max Weber argued in 1918, perceived the *Reich* primarily as an "insurance institution for safeguarding their own position".[94]

[93] See Peters, above n 56, 93–9.

[94] M Weber, *Parlament und Regierung im neugeordneten Deutschland* (1918) 146.

What always stood and still stands, he argued behind the slogan of "protection of federalism" in Germany continues to be a kind of dynastic-bureaucratic insurance of privileges, which practically finds its expression in a guarantee of far-reaching freedom of control enjoyed by the bureaucracy. Freedom of control in particular in the interior of the administration of individual States.[95]

By shifting politically delicate questions to the federal level, the bureaucracy at State level had largely got rid of any control by State parliaments. The lack of a functioning parliamentary control of the executive at the federal level resulted in a system of completely uncontrolled bureaucratic decision-making.

Uncontrolled power of the bureaucracy is necessarily a corrolary of unclear attribution of political responsibility.[96] Clear political responsibility will be avoided or obscured, with the result that political decisions need not be justified publicly by its authors as part of a coordinated strategy but develop more or less accidentally, partly in coexistence, partly in confrontation between bureaucratic suborganisations.[97] Against the misery of such a bureaucratic decision-making there is, according to Max Weber, only one remedy. Only genuine parliamentary control of government can secure a clear attribution of political responsibility and force the executive to put its decisions to the scrutiny of the public.[98]

I admit, the general public today is disillusioned to a large degree with the virtues of parliamentarism. However, an efficient alternative to the inevitable growth of bureaucratic organisations, not to mention an alternative mechanism of public scrutiny and clear attribution of political responsibility, remain absent. Such an observation definitely applies to a confederal arrangement like the European Union, the construction of which was originally based upon a primarily intergovernmental "commonwealth of nations". The problems of confederal systems on a bureaucratic basis which were stated so eloquently by Max Weber in 1918 are also visible to a frightening extent with the project of European integration. The bureaucracies of the Member States in the system of the European Union manage rather successfully to bypass the control of their national parliaments, by shifting problems of decision-making to the European level.[99] At the European level the bureaucracies are not subject to a form of political accountability comparable to the system of parliamentary control at the

[95] *Ibid.*

[96] See *ibid*, 13–18

[97] See *ibid*, 33–6.

[98] See *ibid*, 39–43, 99–105.

[99] There is a widespread agreement on this fact, even among "euro-sceptics"—see only Ossenbühl, above n 65, 635–6, 640; Steinberger, above n 66, 39; U Fastenrath, 'Die Struktur der erweiterten Europäischen Union', (1994) *Europarecht, Beiheft 1* 101 at 119; PM Huber, *Recht der Europäischen Integration* (1996) 81.

national level.[100] Political responsibility accordingly becomes diffused, until it vanishes in its entirety.[101] What develops then is a system of "organised irresponsibility", as Max Weber has demonstrated in the example of the external policy apparatus of the German *Reich*. There is no lack of concrete examples in the Community system of such apparent dangers to any specialist of organisational sociology, as a superficial glance at the European policy arenas demonstrates, e.g. the Common Agricultural Policy or the EC's trade policy. And there is no indication that inter-governmental co-operation according to the model of the second and third pillar of the EU, which some suggest as a means of preserving sovereignty, is devoid of such problems. Attention to the beginnings of a Common Foreign and Security Policy may suffice here. This project attempts to insulate a decisive field of politics against the mechanisms of (national) parliamentary control whilst not creating an adequate (surrogate) mechanism of public responsibility that could replace the national mechanisms. Politics accordingly is left to the grey-zone of bureaucratic policy-making, with the corresponding losses of transparency as well as efficiency.

This should not be misunderstood in meaning that the European Union must necessarily, in order to create clear channels of public responsibility, convert to a system of pure parliamentary majority rule, as was advocated for the German *Reich* by Max Weber. The heterogeneity of the nations and societies united in the European Union is unarguably so large that it is not possible to rely exclusively on the mechanisms of majority rule. Majority decisions alone would not lead to decisions generally accepted as legitimate in a multinational confederation like the EU.[102] Federal systems like the European Union, which must attempt to integrate an enormous amount of societal diversity, cannot avoid incorporating strong elements of a consociational system in its arrangement of political decision-making.[103] More far-

[100] With some justification, however, Steinberger, above n 66, 40–1, points to the fact that the governments in current parliamentary systems are not comparable with the monarchical executives of the 19th century, because they constitute in practice a kind of governing committee of parliamentary majority; nevertheless it remains doubtful whether parliamentary groups, even when a partner in government, have enough expertise as well as working capacity to really enable them to control the executive apparatus in its activities in the field of European law-making.

[101] This is admitted as problem even by the authors who are sceptical towards a further strengthening of the European Parliament—see eg Huber, above n 65, 356–7.

[102] See only FW Scharpf, *Regieren in Europa* (1999) 16–9; *id*, 'Democratic Legitimacy under conditions of Regulatory Competition', in Nicolaidis and Howse (eds), above n 34, 355.

[103] This point was made rather early—within a normative perspective—by Steinberger, above n 66, 47; JA Frowein, 'Verfassungsperspektiven der Europäischen Gemeinschaft', (1992) *Europarecht, Beiheft 1* 63 at 72; P Badura, 'Bewahrung und Veränderung demokratischer und föderativer Verfassungsprinzipien der in Europa verbundenen Staaten', (1990) 109 *Zeitschrift für Schweizerisches Recht Neue Folge* 115 at 133; for political scientists, the concept of consociationalism serves more as an analytical model in the description of the institutional structure of the Community—see P Taylor, 'Consociationalism and Federalism as Approaches to International Integration', in AJR Groom and P Taylor (eds), *Frameworks for International Cooperation* (1990) 172 at 173–7; DN Chryssochoou, 'Democracy and

reaching conclusions, however, like the claim that the integrated Europe will, by definition, not be capable of developing a democratic system at the European level, are based upon a problematic distortion of perspective.[104] One should bear in mind that decision-making on the basis of national arrangements of democracy is not a genuine alternative to "democratising" the European Union, since significant policy fields have long ago been placed under the jurisdiction of the Community, with the result that joint decisions are taken in any case by the institutions of the Community. The whole project is path-dependent and the path taken with the transfer of important policies to the arena of the Community is no longer reversible. There are many problems which the Member States could no longer deal with in the "splendid isolation" of the classical nation-state.[105] The solution therefore is not a return to traditional policy-making at the national level, but ought to be the creation of an international treaty regime enabling an institutionalised co-operation of states. But the accountability of politicians in such regimes is often even worse than in the European Community. The political choice is thus rather limited. One can choose between the established form of purely bureaucratic decison-making in the framework of intergovernmental negotiation procedures, either institutionalised in the Community system or insulated in a separate treaty regime, or between a political decision-making systematically made subject to public scrutiny and to political responsibility on the basis of prior public debate and parliamentary decision.[106] The question is no longer "whether" one wants to have a structure of integrated decision-making at an international level, because the list of state functions which cannot be exercised without international co-operation has grown so long that the matter has largely got out of hand. States would be overburdened if they attempted seriously to "re-nationalise" all these policies and keep them under strict national control. This leaves us with the question of *how* we want to organise the institutional arrangements of common decision-making, to counteract the indisputable lack of homogeneity that blocks the simple solution of classical majority rule?[107]

Symbiosis in the European Union', (1994) 17 *West European Politics* 1 at 4–7; JHH Weiler, UR Haltern and FC Mayer, 'European Democracy and its Critique', (1995) 18 *West European Politics* 4 at 31–4; A Lijphart, *Patterns of Democracy* (1999) 34–47; PC Schmitter, *How to Democratize the European Union ... And Why Bother?* (2000) 78–89.

[104] See Bryde, above n 89, 307–10.

[105] See only KH Ladeur, 'Towards a Legal Theory of Supranationality', (1997) 3 *ELJ* 33 at 47–8, and JHH Weiler, *The Constitution of Europe* (1999) X.

[106] See also FL Graf Stauffenberg and C Langenfeld, 'Maastricht—ein Fortschritt für Europa?', (1992) *Zeitschrift für Rechtspolitik* 253 at 258.

[107] Classical forms of international negotiations between national bureaucracies are not a priori better equipped to cope with these problems than parliamentary procedures formed according to the models of "internal politics", which shift the question of aggregation of interests from the classical "statal" (bureaucratic) actors to the political parties, the elections and the parliamentary process. See in this direction, however, the sceptical reflections by FW Scharpf, 'Europäisches Demokratiedefizit und deutscher Föderalismus', (1992) *Staatswissenschaften und Staatspraxis* 293 at 297–301.

Two findings seem to be beyond dispute at this point. The first is that the Council is indispensible as a decisive organ and must keep its function in the political process of the Community;[108] moreover, it is also an instrument to secure participation of the Member States in law-making and executive governance of the European Union. The second is that political decisions must be taken in such a way that all relevant social groups have a chance to be heard in decision-making. There are good reasons, for instance as in Switzerland as an elaborate multinational state, for developing a model of consensual democracy with a collegial structure of government. A collegial directorate ensures representation of all important social groups in governmental decision-making. It is beyond doubt in my opinion that the European Union will have to strive for something similiar, even when instituting a framework of co-decision by the European Parliament. The Union already possesses, through the Commission, a collegial organ that according to its institutional position and composition strikingly resembles the Swiss Federal Council.[109] It would be a folly to transform such a collegial executive, the composition of which ensures that the different peoples, traditions and political preferences of the member nations are represented in the executive centre of the institutional system, into a parliamentary government based on the Westminster system. Unfortunately, there are tendencies towards doing just this, which seem to reflect the lack of comprehension and fantasy in European politics. If federal experiences with the institutional problem of how to incorporate linguistic and cultural diversity into a decision-making structure teach us anything, it is that a parliamentary government according to the Westminster-model, entrusting the decision-making to a simple parliamentary majority, or even worse a presidential executive like the American model, would not be capable of producing convincing results under the conditions of the European Union.[110] Efficiency within the procedure of decision-making is only one parameter when measuring the success of an institutional system, whilst the other is the perceived legitimacy of the decisions taken. Only legitimacy ensures that decisions taken and rules enacted by the institutions are respected in society. The legitimacy of a simple arrangement of majority rule in the European framework, however, would be worse than fragile. The classical models of

[108] See on that point the convincing reasons given by P Raworth, 'A Timid Step Forward', (1994) 19 *EL Rev* 16 at 23–5; in addition also the reflections of Fastenrath, above n 99, 114–6.

[109] Concerning the institutional construction of the Federal Council as a collegial organ see JF Aubert, *Bundesstaatsrecht der Schweiz* (1995), vol II, paras 1587 to 1609; Y Hangartner, *Grundzüge des schweizerischen Staatsrechts* (1980), vol I, 122–9; B Ehrenzeller, 'Kollegialität und politische Verantwortlichkeit im schweizerischen Konkordanzsystem', (1999) 100 *Schweizerisches Zentralblatt für Staats- und Verwaltungsrecht* 145; see also the recently published contribution by L Mader, '§ 67: Bundesrat und Bundesverwaltung', in D Thürer, JF Aubert and JP Müller (eds), *Verfassungsrecht der Schweiz / Droit constitutionnel suisse* (2001).

[110] See in this sense also Fischer and Schley, above n 6, 32.

parliamentary majority rule and of presidentialism presume a social condition which is lacking in European Union: the consent (usually presumed as self-evident) of the outvoted minority to recognise as legitimate the decisions taken against their will. If this basic condition does not exist, majority decisions mean for the losing minorities nothing else but brutal domination by external rulers—a finding which becomes even more evident if the division between majority and minority follows clear-cut national, ethnic or cultural cleavages. A political minority under these conditions is in danger of becoming entrapped in a structural minority position, denying it any chance of ever winning a majority. Federal arrangements of a multinational character accordingly need strong elements of consensus. Consensual (or "consociational") patterns admittedly must avoid an unconditional veto of various ethnic groups or "nations", while at the same time seeking a consensus as broad as possible including the views of all involved. Otherwise the union is in danger of breaking apart exactly along the cleavages upon which it was constructed.[111]

The comparison with Switzerland, however, must take several problems into consideration. As long as the centre of gravity of political decision-making lies with the Council, the Commission continues to be dependent upon boxing up national interests in package deals often with rather unconvincing content in detail.[112] The Commission still does not have the privilege of making use of the balancing act which is available to the executive in classical federal systems, due to the inherent tension between a Parliament oriented towards integration and Member State bureaucracies taking shelter behind the principle of "subsidiarity". Policies that are defined and formed exclusively in the informal negotiation procedures of "intergovernmental co-operation" will always contain an element of opaqueness and will bear the traits of package deals.[113] Such policies always tend to show more features of an aggregation of bureaucratic particular interests than the aspired overall transformation of particular interests in the formulation of an independent "common good" of the entire Community. Political decisions of a certain consistency probably will be achieved only by political accountability of the political leadership towards a central parliament as representative of the "compound people"[114]—that is Max Weber's genuine insight that led to his polemic being used against the Constitution of the late German Empire.

[111] See Fischer and Schley, above n 6, 33, 40.

[112] See concerning the dialectic of the relations between Commission and national bureaucracies HC Röhl, 'Die Beteiligung der Bundesrepublik Deutschland an der Rechtsetzung im Ministerrat der Europäischen Union', (1994) *Europarecht* 409 at 415–8.

[113] This is true in particular as long as the deliberations (like in the Council) take place under exclusion of the public. Accordingly the public accessibility of Council sessions is one of the most important demands for reform—see only Lübbe-Wolff, above n 67, 256.

[114] See Lübbe-Wolff, above n 67, 259–63.

VII. THE UNITED EUROPE AS A FEDERAL SYSTEM—WHERE DOES THE FEDERAL "STAATSVOLK" COME FROM?

At last the question remains: does the association of consolidated nation-states (each with a marked national identity) meet the basic social preconditions to bring about an effectively integrated political structure centred around a federal arrangement of institutions? The various facets of this changing debate may be found in the numerous writings on European constitutionalism. The common feature of all these variants is the implicit question: where do the people of a common European polity, the European "*Staatsvolk*", come from? One might be tempted to reject such a question as overly naïve, and being too much oriented towards the traditional model of the nation-state. But research into the theory of federalism tells us that behind this underlying "prejudice" a good deal of truth can be found. The recent discussion on the social preconditions of functioning statehood—a discussion that is to a certain degree inspired by the findings of current studies into nationalism—begins with the assumption that a process of "nation-building" must precede the constructive act of constitution-making if a federation is to develop the necessary social cohesion to function (and the solidarity nourished by such a feeling of "belonging together"). Social cohesion and a spirit of solidarity are indeed needed if the constructed polity is to be of a lasting nature—and particularly if the polity is organised in federal forms. Mere power alone, institutionalised in statal forms, in a "state authority", is not enough to sustain a state through times of crisis and problems. Only such state constructions are capable of gaining the required stability and basic legitimacy which are perceived as an organisation of power not only "from the people" and "by the people", but also "for the people".[115] But under what circumstance would the peoples of Europe give up the solidarity and cohesion of the world of nation-states which has stood the test of time and instead run the risks of the experiment of a European federation?

The question is not formulated fairly, I admit. The cohesion, the traditional feeling of solidarity and safety enjoyed in the inherited structures of national statehood, must not be given up for the European experiment. They should only be supplemented by the advantages of the overarching federal polity of the "European Union". It is undoubtedly a strength of the model of federal association of peoples (and States) that the advantages and the stability of the traditional state institutions will not be abandoned but continue their existence, with the "added value" of an additional level of state authority. The federal organisation above the state takes over functions which hitherto had been exercised formally by the interaction of individual states in the context of international co-operation or where states, due to its territorial limitations, could not efficiently reach a solution.

[115] See Fischer and Schley, above n 6, 27 *et seq*.

What remains unclear is whether such a form of confederal institutionalised co-operation is really in need of common social traditions and feelings of solidarity? Does such an arrangement need the often-mentioned "community of communication, experience and memory"? Or does this common understanding imply that the federal arrangement is advantageous? The debate on these questions remains unclear even in the international arena. There are federal systems which are held together by the nationalistic "sense of belonging together" of a dominant "*Staatsvolk*" of the classical model of the nation-state. But there exist also federal polities which lack any kind of a dominant "*Staatsvolk*"´, which are created from a multitude of rather different "peoples" in an ethnic-cultural sense. Such federal polities are only stable, however, if a kind of balance of power between the relevant ethnic groups evolves. A balance of power that is then encapsulated and consolidated institutionally by a specific arrangement that lies at the basis of all the formal constitutional mechanisms that govern the state. Historical experiences of a dependency upon consensus as a precondition of successful collective action must belong to the core of the federal construction in such situations.[116] As a leading exponent of nationalism studies stated recently, in reference to Ernest Gellner:

> A majoritarian democratic federation requires a Staatsvolk, a demographically, electorally and culturally dominant nation. This lends weigh to Ernest Gellner's theory about the power of nationalism. But the theory has a corollary: the absence or near absence of a Staatsvolk does not preclude democratic federation, but a democratic federation without a clear or secure Staatsvolk must adopt (some) consociational practices if it is to survive.[117]

In light of this finding, it is anything but a miracle that multinational federations accordingly tend to develop strong consensual elements, if they do not opt for a wholesale system of consociational democracy.[118] This will not sound very reassuring to proponents of federalism, since consociational systems go along with a high degree of interlocking of political institutions, with the ensuing phenomenon that political responsibility becomes blurred in the course of tiresome processes of building a broad consensus. In the result, this leads to political processes of an inevitably ponderous and slow character. The efficiency of decision-making with the federal construction suffers considerably. The big advantage of the creation of a separate level of federal statehood with its own competences and its own, institutionally independent, decison-making procedures as well as its own chain of democratic legitimation thus tends to become obsolete. The desired transparency suffers significantly, and the ideals of a "pure" democratic legitimation

[116] *Ibid*, 31.
[117] O'Leary, above n 35, 291.
[118] See in this sense Fischer and Schley, above n 6, 47–48.

through representation and decision-making under the scrutiny of voters is countered by the dictates of consociational arrangements. But we should be realistic. The "real existing" alternatives to such a consensual system are far from being preferable. It is not the clear arrangement of orderly democratic responsibility of a parliamentary democracy with majority rule that is the real alternative, but the problems associated with the sheer impenetrable quagmire of institutions and the labyrinthine decision-making of the usual international co-operation in treaty regimes which constitutes the competing option. I admit that the advantage of the federal construction vis-à-vis the procedures of intergovernmental co-operation tends to vanish in the consensual mode of consociationalism. Webs of informal agreements and consensus routines tend to dominate formal institutions, but only such mechanisms ensure—as important writings have made plausible—the cohesion and undisturbed functioning of multinational federations.[119] At the same time, the system maintains its high degree of flexibility in decision-making which is much higher than in traditional forms of purely intergovernmental co-operation. The absolute veto power of any member, which in traditional forms of international regime formation tends to make the majority hostage to those stubbornly pursuing particular interests significantly lessens in the federal system. The federal system is still burdened with strong consensual elements. If in a first phase of negotiations the search for a consensus remains the decisive orientation, the possibility of majority decision, however, increases the readiness of potential veto candidates to make concessions and to reach a compromise; if they remain too stubborn and stick too uncompromisingly to their blocking position, they run the risk of having no influence at all on the contents of the final decision, and being outvoted.[120] The decision-making system is not necessarily forced to show consideration for the voice of every single member in every case, if that voice is stubbornly particularistic and shows no respect for common purposes. What the system must avoid, however, is the danger that the elementary interests of important states, political entities or peoples are disregarded altogether, because such a systematic neglect would endanger the cohesion of the federal polity in general.

VIII. CONCLUSIONS: THE FEDERAL "UNION" AS A PROMISING CONSTRUCTION

In reviewing the arguments, one comes across a series of marked ambiguities. Without parliamentary responsibility it is impossible, even in the European Union, to ensure political transparency and a form of decision-making responsible towards the common good of the entire

[119] *Ibid.*
[120] *Ibid*, 40.

community.[121] At the same time it is obvious that a future Constitution of the European Union will not be able to follow any "pure" doctrine of a parliamentary system, but must search—with a view to its own functional requirements—for its own solutions, solutions that inevitably will contain strong elements of a consensual system. This does not necessarily imply a pleading for the "grand design" of a "European draft constitution"; on the contrary, the revolutionary founding act of a constructivist constitution-making will remain a mere illusion—a utopia with its inherent danger. If such a utopia came near realisation, it would bring with it an enormous temptation of a constructivist exuberance, with the ensuing risk of overstraining the given will to enter into statal unity. The existing "compound arrangement" of integration, which might be placed somewhere between the classic poles of "federal statehood" and "league of states" or "confederation", might be described as the decisive virtue of the existing European Constitution, a Constitution which is in constant change. From this perspective, the peculiar Constitution of the EU is much more than a deficient construction. The "compound constitution", preserving in its core strong elements of a confederation, represents a decisive safeguard of decentralised prerogatives in political decision-making. It ensures the peaceful coexistence of the divergent peoples of Europe, without depriving them of the advantages of a deepened co-operation in federal forms. In contrast, constitutions according to the model of modern constructions of federal statehood always contain a strong dose of deliberately advanced "creation of unity", since they constitute at least as strong a central authority oriented towards unitarisation as they safeguard a (rudimentary) allocation of competences in favour of the subdivisions of the federal state.[122] The citizens of the European Union do not want a process of unitarisation, however, in the sense of a forced "nation-building". A radical restructuring in pursuit of such an objective would potentially destroy the complex arrangement of the European "compound of states" (or confederation), without replacing it by something really better than the existing union.

Accordingly, the gentle evolution of the arrangement along the lines mentioned above seems to be without real alternatives in political practice.[123] Even careful reform of the existing Union needs its guiding stars at

[121] On the interdependency of transparency and accountability see also *ibid*, 11.

[122] In this sense see the pleading of DJ Elazar for continuing a confederal construction of the European Union, which he perceives—in a certain way nearly ironically—as recollection to the federalist-consociational heritage of "Ancient Europe", and as a *volte-face* against statist patterns of continental European nation statehood—see DJ Elazar, 'The United States and the European Union', in Nicolaidis and Howse (eds), above n 34, 31–53.

[123] See also the pleading of J Pinder for an "incrementalist", gradual process of "federalization" of the Community—J Pinder, 'The New European Federalism', in M Burgess and AG Gagnon (eds), *Comparative Federalism and Federation* (1993) 46.

which point the basic problem remains the same with all the special solutions tailored to the specific situation of the Community. Therefore the European Union will either accept the challenge of finding an adequate solution to the problem of attribution of clear political responsibility and find a system of transparent political decision-making at European level, or the project of European integration will be frustrated by the immense challenges that lie ahead. Terminological debates on sovereignty, democracy, federalism, the incompatibility of a federally construed commonwealth with parliamentarism are not going to help in coping with these challenges, any more than discussions among constitutional scholars over the compatibility of parliamentary structures in the European Union with the principle of democracy under the German Basic Law. The theoretical fundamentals are so problematic in this field that workable constitutional legal conclusions should not be derived by means of logical deductions according to the traditional patterns of legal positivism. Even the structural safeguard clause of Art 23 Basic Law does not oblige the German state organs to preserve a "sovereignty" or "ultimately responsible statehood", but provides for certain structural objectives of a European "constitutional evolution" and obliges the German state organs to strive for an optimisation of the future "Constitution" of the Union in the sense of the structural principles such as federalism and democracy, characteristic of the Basic Law.[124]

What the best realisation of these objectives might look like is a question that has to be decided primarily from a political perspective.[125] The European democracies will have to consider what they want: preservation of "national autonomy" as far as possible, which in a system of intergovernmental co-operation will necessarily be to the detriment of the efficiency of common action, but also to the mechanisms of democratic control, or strengthening of the mechanisms of the formation of a common will and of the coupled democratic mechanisms of scrutinising the exercise of public authority. The second alternative, however, would come at the expense of the autonomy of national systems and bureaucracies.[126] But can the lack of clear political responsibility characteristic of bureaucratic confederal systems really be a valuable alternative? If dependency upon consensus is unavoidable, then we should prefer the openly political search for consensus of the federal system which is also accountable to the public and not the

[124] Concerning the structural safeguard clause of Art 23 Basic Law and the resulting problems see only Breuer, above n 57, 421–4.

[125] On the political dilemma of any further development of the European Union see FW Scharpf, 'Kann es in Europa eine stabile föderale Balance geben?', in Wildenmann (ed), above n 68, 415 at 418–20.

[126] This should not be misunderstood as a plea for a further expansion of the EU to a European federal state or for a further extension of the competences of the EU. The question of the adequate structures of political decision-making is independent from an aspired legal quality as state or a quality as federal "compound polity"—see Graf Stauffenberg and Langenfeld, above n 106, 259; Oeter, above n 27, 248 *et seq*.

classical intergovernmental system based upon the veto which has no option but relying upon the "lowest common denominator". The patterns of decision-making in the Community suffer less with a "democratic deficit" in a proper sense, but with a "transparency deficit".[127] Without elements of transparency, however, there may never exist a proper mechanism of democratic control, which by definition needs a certain degree of accountability in public affairs. Ultimately one needs a public scrutiny that forces political actors to routinely justify their actions. Such a scheme of clear attribution of political responsibility will be possible only to a limited extent if one takes into consideration the necessity to incorporate elements of consensual democracy into the system. But the collective of citizens will become—merely by the fact of being integrated in a common polity that takes decisions determining over their weal and woe—a "community of fate" ("Schicksalsgemeinschaft")[128], to use a popular term of German constitutional theory. Such a community needs to be able to influence the decisions of the political leadership to ensure that power does not become structurally independent (and thereby lacking responsibility towards the "people").[129]

This is a result which is not easy for constitutional lawyers and those adhering to the theory that is exclusively centered upon the state in its traditional form to accept. Based on the paradigm of the "sovereign state" we have difficulties, even nowadays, imagining another polity outside that of the nation-state. Municipalities, counties, regions, member states can be understood, if perceived from the perspective of the *Kompetenz-Kompetenz*, only as dependent subdivisions of the state; international and supranational organisations can be conceived only as dependent "functional communities" centered upon the state.

As long as legal doctrine perpetuates its distorted assumptions, it will remain practically impossible to comprehend in theoretical terms institutional arrangements like the European Community.[130] If taken seriously, this should be understood as a challenge to reassessing the assumptions of constitutional theory and to adapting them to real developments.[131] "Understanding the European Union as a Federal Polity" expresses the challenge for modelling the institutional structure of the EU—a formula which should not be misunderstood in the sense that the European Union

[127] See Fischer and Schley, above n 6, 31; see as well as Peters, above n 56, 626–9, 694–8.

[128] "People" here understood in the sense of the notion modelled by E-W Böckenförde as "democratic notion of people: people as political community of fate"—*id*, above n 75, 903–5.

[129] From the perspective of "Union citizenship" S Choudhry, 'Citizenship and Federations', in Nicolaidis and Howse (eds), above n 34, 377–402; but also D Lacorne, European Citizenship, *ibid*, 427–38.

[130] See also GF Schuppert, 'Zur Staatswerdung Europas', (1994) 5 *Staatswissenschaften und Staatspraxis*, 35 at 53–7.

[131] See to this point also I Pernice, 'Carl Schmitt, Rudolf Smend und die europäische Integration', (1995) 120 *Archiv des öffentlichen Rechts* 100.

should be forced into the Procrustean bed of classical federalist constructions. "Federal Polity" does not necessarily mean "federal state", but may comprise of other constructions of a "confederal nature". The call for escape from the inherited ideals of constitutional theory accordingly does not mean to proclaim the "end of the state". The nation-states that founded the Union would persist also in an openly federal construction as states, would continue as bearers of genuine statehood and symbols of national identity, equipped with important competences and a wide spectrum of statal institutions and instruments; they would, however, lose their "exclusivity" as the only imaginable bearers of sovereignty. The Union, as the federal roof, with the exception of a Common Foreign and Security Policy and coordinating institutions of a common protection of internal security will—even in the future—not be able to exercise more functions than the Community does now. The European Union, however, would not just be a mere variable, a simple construction of national "internal" politics any more. It needs to develop something like an all-European "common good" and to persuade the peoples of the Union to actively embrace it.[132]

This enterprise should not be an elitist project, no constructivist experiment of well-meaning technocrats, no matter how sincere their intentions may be. The enterprise must respect the conditions, opinions and elementary interests of the peoples of the Union and must constantly include the citizens in order to gain their approval. At the same time, it must not be a populist image of national clientelisms, lest its purpose be forgotten. Such a struggle for a common European interest cannot be organised in purely intergovernmental forms. Accordingly, it is no accident that the project of European integration has demonstrated from the beginning features of a federal construction.[133] The task of a federalist theory of European integration must be to strengthen and expand these features gradually, without overstraining the still fragile will of the citizens of Europe to live in a European federation. It must not be the foundation of a "European Federal State" modelled on a copy of American, German or other federal state constructions. The united Europe of the European Union for quite a time will not be a federal state in the classical sense, but will remain a treaty-based hybrid; a mixed system that will gradually develop more

[132] See Peters, above n 56, 174.

[133] See the lucid formulation by W Wallace—the European Community is "a constitutional system which has some state attributes, but which most—or all—of its constituent governments do not wish to develop into a state, even while expecting it to deliver outcomes which are hard to envisage outside the framework of an entity which we would recognize as a (federal) state."—W Wallace, 'Theory and Practice in European Integration', in P Bulmer and A Scott (eds), *Economic and Political Integration in Europe* (1994) 272; see also *id*, 'Less than a Federation, More than a Regime', in H Wallace and W Wallace (eds), *Policy-Making in the European Community* (2nd edn 1983) 403–8.

federal characteristics, but at the same time will keep some traits of an arrangement of international co-operation.[134]

The dictates to preserve "confederal" elements derived from regimes of international co-operation will be particularly visible in the attribution of competences to Member States, the Community and the Union. In contrast to classical federations, the European Community was deliberately limited within its powers to achieve certain fixed objectives, without detail to the means by which it may exercise its tasks.[135] Such an approach often requires, as is routine in the ambit of international organisations, a recourse to the instrument of "implied powers" to deduce its concrete competences. It might be seen as problematic with regard to legal certainty and positivity of the ordering of competences. Nevertheless, for an international legal regime, which requires a laborious procedure to change its "basic Constitution", a flexible working of the treaty is essential. An adherence to the attributed competences without the possibility of amendments to the Constitution through a qualified majority would deprive the system of any potential to adapt in the future. No doubt, federal constitutions seek to protect minorities against arbitrary decisions of the majority by incorporating specific obstacles that make it burdensome to achieve constitutional amendments. For good reasons they deny, however, its individual Member States comprehensive veto positions. In addition, one should not have too many illusions concerning the precision of traditional federal catalogues of competence. Replacing the existing system of specific empowerments in the treaty with a detailed catalogue of Community competences would not bring about substantial improvements in legal certainty,[136] if such a catalogue were to be characterised (like the German Basic Law) by competential titles with few contours. The best example for this is the competence for regulating the "economic law" ("Recht der Wirtschaft") in Art 74(1) No 11 of the Basic Law.

The system of administrative implementation of Community law also refers to the hybrid character of the Community and Union. Such a system is characterised by the model of the Member States' administrations implementing Community law with its own resources and with its own responsibilities. The system indeed demonstrates considerable similiarities to the German constitutional arrangement with its "state-based" (*landeseigener*)

[134] See generally concerning the problems of theoretical categorisation Burgess, above n 3, 46–9; AM Sbragia, 'Thinking about the European Future', in AM Sbragia (ed), *Euro-Politics* (1992) 262–3; also PC Schmitter, 'Some Alternative Features for the European Polity and their Implications for European Public Policy', in Y Meny, P Muller and JL Quermonne (eds), *Adjusting to Europe* (1996) 25.

[135] See U Leonardy, 'The Political Dimension, German Practice, and the European Perspective', in JJ Hesse and V Wright (eds), *Federalizing Europe?* (1996) 73 at 85; W Hertel, 'Formen des Föderalismus', in W Graf Vitzthum (ed), *Europäischer Föderalismus* (2000) 13 at 238.

[136] Hertel, above n 135, 25.

implementation. Under the German Constitution, however, the implementation by federal agencies is an alternative to the implementation by State authorities. This is different within the Community. An extension of "direct implementation" of Community law beyond the field of competition policy is only imaginable, at least in the short term, in very specific cases.[137] There are credible arguments of subsidiarity that militate against an expansion of "direct implementation", not to speak of the regularisation of this form of administrative activity of the Community as a regular form of implementation of Community law.

The character of the European "compound of constitutions" (*Verfassungsverbund*)[138] as a hybrid should be understood more as a virtue than a weakness of the European Union. For aesthetic purists such a hybrid system will always be problematic; for political practice, however, the ambivalent character of the federal construction has indisputable advantages, since such a construction allows for gradual progress towards further integration without compromising the place of genuine "statehood". In conclusion, more confidence in the dynamics of the existing Union, without aspiring to overturn the achievements of our predecessors, could guide us in reforming its obvious shortcomings. If one accepts that the European Union is already a "federal" construction, a lot of arguments speak in favour of the position that it is best to build upon this construction in the hope that we will optimise the inherited institutional structures, instead of overturning the Union structure in a completely "revolutionary" act which would transform it into a state artificially created by technocratic elites. It may be that the political elites are not capable of imagining a reformed Union without approximating it to the common model of the nation-state. This is no argument, however, for propagating a reformed Union according to the institutional model of traditional "statehood". Just the reverse: a "social construction" of the Community and Union as a federally construed polity of a compound character will give us the calm which is needed in order to ensure that the "united Europe" will not be undone by a controversial constitutional utopia. In order to prevent such fierce constitutionalist actions, we should strive for a careful and gradual way of consolidating and reforming the existing institutional structures, towards a federally constituted "Union" of the European peoples with a government accountable to the people, and a parliamentary arrangement securing Europe its own schemes of democratic responsibility and control. The experience with federal constructions tells us that, should the Community not manage to develop into an efficiently organised federal polity, driven towards achieving an

[137] See much more in detail Hertel, above n 135, 31–2.

[138] See concerning the concept of a *Verfassungsverbund* I Pernice, 'Die Dritte Gewalt im europäischen Verfassungsverbund', (1996) *Europarecht* 27 at 29–33; and *id*, 'Der europäische Verfassungsverbund auf dem Wege der Konsolidierung', (2000) 48 *Jahrbuch des öffentlichen Rechts der Gegenwart Neue Folge* 205 at 214–17; also Peters, above n 56, 207–15.

overarching "common good", the entire project of European integration will fail in the long run.[139] The European Union will either conserve its federal characteristics and will strengthen these features in its institutional reforms, or it will as a kind of *monstro simile* suffer a comparable fate to the Holy Roman Empire of the German Nation which was swept away by the Napoleonic project of a hegemonial reconstruction of a "Roman Empire" covering all of Europe. Those who believe in the vision of a free association of the European peoples in a functioning "compound" of States, should rally for a strengthening of the federal traits of the European Community. But there is another battlefield, beyond the trenches of political decision-making. In the "social construction of reality" regarding the existing Union, the advocate of a federal Europe will have to strive—if he thinks in constructivist terms—for an intellectual "reconstruction" of the existing arrangement of integration into federal categories. The European Union must not only in the future be conceived as a federal polity, but should already—in its current state—be perceived as a federal structure. For such a "reconstruction", this contribution has attempted to demonstrate, there are many more arguments than the "mainstream" of European studies was, until recently, ready to accept.

The current constitutional debate over the necessary reforms of the European institutions takes a very peculiar shape in view of the thoughts and findings outlined here. Perhaps the vision of the "United States of Europe" is not as utopian as is usually assumed. There is however one certainty—a "United States" as a federal polity will (and should) be different to the United States of America. The rather strange "compound constitution" of the Union, the "distinct constitutional arrangement", as Joseph Weiler has called it, must be understood as a potential treasure, in its future development. The deviation from traditional forms of statehood organised in federal forms is anything but accidental.[140] Even the long-term objective of the Union expressed in the Preamble of the Treaty departs from a continued existence of the different peoples of Europe distinguished by language, culture and historical experience. As Joseph Weiler has recently stressed, to unite these peoples in an overall arrangement without depriving them of their diversity (and accordingly their "distinctness"), is a civilising project of the highest order. We should become aware of this particularity of the project of European integration and looking from a federalist perspective helps us to do this. The call to enter with "completely different" people into an "ever closer union" requires an extremely high degree of tolerance, individually as well as socially. "Living the Kantian categorical imperative is most meaningful when it is extended to those who

[139] See in this sense also Fischer and Schley, above n 6, 8.

[140] JHH Weiler, 'Federalism Without Constitutionalism', in Nicolaidis and Howse (eds), above n 34, 54–70.

are unlike me".[141] Therefore a characteristic feature of the Union is "constitutional tolerance". Such inherent tolerance of differences, however, is inextricably linked to the construction of the "European Constitution". Not that this Constitution could (and should) not be reformed in detail as is demonstrated sufficiently throughout this contribution. But the "federalist paradigm" should create some sensibility for a lesson which all too easily gets lost in times of loud calls for a "new", "final" Constitution for Europe: Europe already has a Constitution that corresponds rather well to its current state. Or—as Joseph Weiler concludes in one of his recent publications: "Europe has charted its own brand of constitutional federalism. It works. Why fix it?"[142]

[141] *Ibid*, 67.
[142] *Ibid*, 70.

3

National Constitutional Law Relating to the European Union

CHRISTOPH GRABENWARTER

I. INTRODUCTION

THE DEVELOPMENT OF national constitutional law which deals with the European Union is related in a specific way to the relationship between national constitutional law and Union law. This contribution considers changes in national constitutional law resulting from accession to the Communities or Union, the continuing confrontation with Union law and developments in Union law. This involves the contents of written and unwritten legal rules and their changes over the course of time as well as the way in which such changes take place. This contribution will investigate the extent to which individual Member States pursue specific strategies in order to cope with increasing European integration.

Constitutions and their development reflect the strategies of constitutional organs and therefore form the main subjects of investigation. This contribution will not use the term "constitution" too narrowly, bearing in mind the aim of the investigation. Often, changes do not reveal themselves in textual mutations of constitutional documents but rather in secondary constitutional law, implementing laws or realisation of constitutional law (constitution in the material sense).

The interesting changes represent certain "adaptation processes". Initially, adaptation appears to be a unilateral process implying that the national constitution is altered in compliance with Union law. However, this interpretation formulates "adaptation" too narrowly. At least in this context, adaptation contains two components, i.e. a "conformity aspect" and a "creative aspect". The former aspect describes the capitulation to the pressure of adaptation emanating from Union law. The creative aspect refers to the creative management of adaptation conditioned by law and politics. Adaptation relationships within the network of the current 25 Member States are more complex, however: adaptations can also occur in the sense of a unification relating to Member States' constitutions and which are not caused but simply induced by Union law. The effect of "adaptation" in this sense may by no means be reduced to that of "unification". Such unification can be both the aim and, where successful, the result of an adaptation process. However, *e contrario* it can also be diversity and therefore any (legal) condition which facilitates the juxtaposition and co-operation of two legal levels on a regular basis. This effect of adaptation is conveyed by the English term of (institutional) "adaptation", which is often used in political science,[1] and which does not refer to a unilateral process—as does not the German term "*Anpassung*".[2]

This investigation consists of three stages. The first stage clarifies the starting point between national constitutional law and the most important part of Union law, i.e. the question whether Community law takes primacy over national constitutional law. The second stage describes the typical contents of those parts of constitutional law which are particularly related to Union law. Finally, the third stage identifies similarities and differences in strategies and consequences for Union law.

II. THE RELATIONSHIP BETWEEN UNION LAW AND NATIONAL CONSTITUTIONAL LAW

Consideration of what is depicted here as "Union constitutional law of the Member States" starts with the relationship between Union law, in particular Community law, and national constitutional law. It determines the form which adaptations of Union constitutional law take. The adaptation strategies of national constitutional law are influenced and sometimes even determined by the dogmatic management of the relationship. The relationship between national constitutional law and Community law assumes significance both for contractual amendments and the continuing development of domestic law in relation to Community law.

Today, it is generally accepted that European Community Law takes primacy over the national law of Member States.[3] As early as 1964 the ECJ made it clear that Community law takes primacy over national law at every

[1] Cf eg the terminology in T Börzel, States and Regions in the European Union: Institutional Adaptation in Germany and Spain (2001) 27 *et seq*.

[2] In French literature, one can also find the (more neutral) term "mutation", "adaptation", as well as "adéquation". Cf the subtitle of the book by J Rideau, *Les États Membres de l'Union Européenne*: "*Adaptations—Mutations—Résistances*" (1997), or S Muñoz Machado, *La Unión Europea y las mutaciones del Estado* (1993).

[3] T Oppermann, *Europarecht* (1999), paras 615 *et seq*.

level, i.e. including the constitutional law of Member States.[4] Although in principle this starting point is nowadays accepted with regard to ordinary statutory law, views on the relationship between national constitutional law and Union law are controversial and inconsistent. In this respect, Member States differ considerably. States can be divided into three groups: States in which Community law enjoys full primacy, States in which Community law has limited primacy and those in which national constitutional law takes primacy over Community law.

1. Full Primacy of Community Law

The first group comprises states in which the primacy of Community law is largely undisputed and recognised by the courts even in relation to constitutional law. *The Netherlands* is the main example in this respect. Leading opinion assumes unqualified primacy because, according to the view of the adjudicating division of the Raad van State (Afdeling Bestuursrechtspraak), the primacy of Community law is derived not from the Dutch Constitution but directly from European law.[5]

In *Austria* too, the opening up of the Austrian legal system for EU membership was made in awareness and recognition of the primacy of Community law (cf Article 2 of the Act of Accession), independently of the status of conflicting national law. The Austrian Constitutional Court appears to take the primacy of Community law for granted even in relation to constitutional law.[6] However, in line with those states which place limits on primacy, "basic principles" of constitutional law are not "subordinate" to Community law.[7]

[4] Case 6/64, *Costa* [1964] ECR 585 at 594: Community law cannot be overridden "by domestic legal provisions, however framed". See also Case 106/77, *Simmenthal II* [1978] ECR 629, where the ECJ states that in case of conflict domestic legal provisions do not get reversed by Community law but must not be applied. Referring expressly to fundamental rights: Case 11/70, *Internationale Handelsgesellschaft* [1970] ECR 1125; critical of the ECJ's argumentation: A Schmitt Glaeser, *Grundgesetz und Europarecht als Elemente Europäischen Verfassungsrechts* (1996) 156 *et seq.*

[5] Decision Metten v Minister van Financiën of 7 July 1995, *NJB-katern* (1995) 426; on this see FC Mayer, *Kompetenzüberschreitung und Letztentscheidung* (2000) 191; LFM Besselink, 'An Open Constitution and European Integration', in (1996) *F.I.D.E. 17 Congress*, vol 1, 361 at 390 *et seq.*

[6] Austrian Constitutional Court, Verfassungssammlung 15427/1999, on the replacement of the organisational provision of Art 133 No 4 of the Federal Constitution by a Directive; for a discussion on this topic S Griller, 'Introduction to the Problems in the Austrian, the Finnish and the Swedish Constitutional Order', in AE Kellerman, JW de Zwaan and J Czuczai (eds), *EU Enlargement* (2001) 147 at 169 *et seq*; P Jann and B Schima, 'Bemerkungen zum Gebot der richtlinienkonformen Auslegung des nationalen Rechts', in N Colneric *et al* (eds), *Une communauté de droit* (2003) 283 at 289 *et seq.*

[7] Rejection of the "subordination" of fundamental principles of constitutional law in P Pernthaler, *Der Verfassungskern* (1998) 14 *et seq*; T Öhlinger, 'Die Transformation der Verfassung', (2002) *Juristische Blätter* 2 *et seq.*

2. Limited Primacy of Community Law over Constitutional Law

In the second group of states, it is assumed for different reasons that Community law has a partial primacy, which is limited by constitutional law. In terms of numbers, this is by far the largest group.

First of all, the constitutional courts of *Italy*, *Germany*, *Denmark* and *Belgium* have highlighted limits to the primacy of Community law in relation to national law—constitutional law, in particular.

In 1984, the Italian *Corte Costituzionale* acknowledged the primacy of Community law in principle.[8] However, the court expressly reserved to itself the right to check the observance of fundamental rights and personal freedoms.[9] A decision of December 1995 is interpreted to the effect that the *Corte Costituzionale* will only consider exercising this power of review if the ECJ previously rejects the protection given by fundamental rights within the framework of a reference for preliminary ruling.[10]

The German Federal Constitutional Court *(Bundesverfassungsgericht)* recognised the primacy of Community law over national law relatively early on.[11] However, over time it formulated different restrictions on full primacy in relation to constitutional law. The effect of primacy was initially subject to the protection of structural principles. Thereby the right to review Community legislative acts was recognised[12] at least by implication. However, the Federal Constitutional Court later qualified this to the effect that it did not wish to review Community measures *vis a vis* their compatibility with the German Constitution, the *Grundgesetz* (Basic Law), provided

[8] Sen Decision 170/1984 of 8 July 1984, Granital, *Il Foro Italiano* 1984 I, 2062, Engl transl in (1984) 21 *CML Rev* 756 *et seq*, with commentary by G Gaja, 764 *et seq*; further details on this in A La Pergola, 'Costituzione ed integrazione Europea', in A Pace (ed), *Studi in onore di L Elia* (1999), vol I, 815 at 826 *et seq*; see also Muñoz Machado, above n 2, 50; A Adinolfi, 'The Judicial Application of Community Law in Italy', (1998) 35 *CML Rev* 1313 at 1314 *et seq*; AM Aronovitz and B Cottier, 'Italie', in B Cottier (ed), *Staatsrechtliche Auswirkungen der Mitgliedschaft in den Europäischen Gemeinschaften* (1991) 287 *et seq*.

[9] Sen Decisions 117 of 31 March 1994, *Il Foro Italiano* 1995 I, 1077; Sen Decision 170/1984 of 8 July 1984, Granital, *Il Foro Italiano* 1984 I, 2062, (1984) 21 *CML Rev* 756. Admittedly, this principle was already proclaimed in Sen Decision 183/73 of 27 December 1973, Frontini, (1974) 11 *CML Rev* 2 at 372 (389, 405). On this decision see C Maestripieri, 'The application of Community law in Italy in 1973', (1975) 12 *CML Rev* 431 *et seq*; PF Lotito, 'Die italienische Corte Costituzionale und die Anwendung der Gemeinschaftsnormen in der innerstaatlichen Rechtsordnung', in C Tomuschat, H Kötz and B von Maydell (eds), *Europäische Integration und nationale Rechtskulturen* (1995) 259 *et seq*; Adinolfi, above n 8, 1313, 1317 *et seq*, 1322.

[10] Sen 509 December 1995, (1996) *Rivista italiana di diritto pubblico comunitario* at 764; on this see Adinolfi, above n 8, 1324 *et seq*.

[11] Concerning this cf *Entscheidungen des Bundesverfassungsgerichts* 22, 293 at 296 (*EEC regulations*); 31, 145 at 174. On the question whether Community law takes primacy of validity or application over national law, the Federal Constitutional Court appears to prefer the latter in its more recent decisions, cf R Streinz, *Europarecht* (2001) para 207.

[12] *Entscheidungen des Bundesverfassungsgerichts* 37, 217 at 279 (*Solange I*); 58, 1 at 40 (*Eurocontrol*); see also J Schwarze, 'Deutscher Landesbericht', in *id* (ed), *The Birth of a European Constitutional Order* (2001) 109 at 170 *et seq*.

that the standard of fundamental rights achieved at Community level was generally guaranteed.[13] In the Maastricht judgment passed in 1993, the court deliberately left open the question whether it had the power to review Community measures to ensure that they remained within the framework of Community law jurisdiction.[14] In its "Banana-market Decision" of 2000, the Federal Constitutional Court distanced itself from or at least did not enforce the claim for review.[15] In the meantime, the constitutional legislator laid down limits to the power of integration contained in Article 23(1) Basic Law.[16]

In its judgment on *Denmark's* Act Ratifying the Maastricht Treaty of April 1998, the *Højesteret*, the Supreme Court in Copenhagen, stated that Danish courts could still exercise their right to review whether an EC legal act observed limits on the transfer of sovereignty laid down by the Act of Accession.[17]

Belgium also belongs to this group. The earlier case law of the *Cour de Cassation*[18] gave the impression that Community law took primacy over all measures of national law. However, the *Cour d'Arbitrage* (arbitration tribunal), established in 1983, clearly rejected this approach. In its judgment of 16 October 1991, the court held that the power to review international treaties also extended to the inherent constitutionality of treaty provisions (material constitutionality).[19]

Spain can be included in the same group of states, even if the starting point suggests something different. The Spanish Constitutional Court

[13] *Entscheidungen des Bundesverfassungsgerichts* 73, 339 at 387 (*Solange II*).

[14] *Entscheidungen des Bundesverfassungsgerichts* 89, 155 at 188 (*Maastricht*). Critical eg M Kumm, 'Who is the final arbiter of constitutionality in Europe?', (1999) 36 *CML Rev* 351 *et seq*, and C Tomuschat, 'Die Europäische Union unter der Aufsicht des Bundesverfassungsgerichts', (1993) *Europäische Grundrechte-Zeitschrift* 489.

[15] *Entscheidungen des Bundesverfassungsgerichts* 102, 147 at 164 (*Bananenmarktordnung*); cf R Hofmann, 'Zurück zu Solange II! Zum Bananenmarktordnungs-Beschluß des Bundesverfassungsgerichts', in HJ Cremer *et al* (ed), *Tradition und Weltoffenheit des Rechts: Festschrift für H Steinberger* (2002) 1207.

[16] See III 2.

[17] Højesteret of 6 April 1998, pursuant to I 361/1997 (1999) *Europäische Grundrechte-Zeitschrift* 49; on this see the examination by R Hofmann, 'Der Oberste Gerichtshof Dänemarks und die europäische Integration', (1999) *Europäische Grundrechte-Zeitschrift* 1; F Thomas, 'Das Maastricht-Judgment des dänischen Obersten Gerichtshofs vom 6. April 1998', (1998) 58 *Zeitschrift für ausländisches öffentliches Recht und Völkerrecht* 879 *et seq*; H Koch, 'The Danish Constitutional Order', in Kellermann, de Zwaan and Czuczai (eds), above n 6, 109 at 114 *et seq*; Mayer, above n 5, 213 *et seq*; P Lachmann, 'The Treaty of Maastricht vs the Danish Constitution', (1998) 67 *Nordic Journal of International Law* 365 *et seq*; G Ring and L Olsen-Ring, 'Souveränitätsübertragung nach dänischem Verfassungsrecht', (1998) *Europäische Zeitschrift für Wirtschaftsrecht* 589 *et seq*.

[18] Cf Cour de Cassation, Judgment of 27 May 1971, Le Ski, *Journal des Tribunaux* (1971) 460 (1972) 9 *CML Rev* 330; cf also Oppermann, above n 3, para 625. However, this case concerned an ordinary legal rule and not a constitutional provision. The force of the judgment is accordingly qualified.

[19] Decision of 16 October 1991, (1992) *Journal des Tribunaux* 6670, cf Mayer, above n 5, 179 *et seq*.

(*Tribunal Constitucional*) expressly reserved to itself the power to review the constitutionality of Community law.[20] For this purpose the Court referred to Article 95.1 of the Constitution in its fundamental Maastricht Decision of 1 July 1992. This provision states that the conclusion of an international treaty which contains unconstitutional provisions requires the prior amendment of the constitution. The Court took the view that the application of Article 93 which grants the power to transfer sovereign rights could not undermine the protective function of Article 95 and thereby could not result in implied changes to the Constitution.[21] However, since this judgment the Constitutional Court has tended to adopt a Community-friendly interpretation and has increasingly referred to Community law as an aid to interpretation.[22] However, this Community-friendly interpretation does not extend to those parts of the Constitution classified as "particularly sovereign". Besides the fundamental rights of the Constitution, this includes the fundamental principles of the state: democracy; separation of powers; distribution of jurisdiction between the nation-state and autonomous communities as well as the parliamentary monarchy as the form of government; unity of the state; and Spanish as the official language.[23]

In *Sweden* it is generally suggested that Community law has primacy over any national law including constitutional law.[24] However, the constitutional rule of Chapter 10 § 5, which was enacted for the purpose of accession, clearly reflects the "Solange" case law of the Federal Constitutional Court. Accordingly, the Swedish parliament can transfer decision-making rights to the European Community "provided this has a protection of

[20] E García de Enterría and R Alonso García, 'Spanischer Landesbericht', in J Schwarze (ed), *Die Entstehung einer europäischen Verfassungsordnung* (2000) 287 at 298; Muñoz Machado, above n 2, 37 *et seq*; G Garzón 'Clariana, The Spanish Constitutional Order', in Kellermann, de Zwaan and Czuczai (eds), above n 6, 117 at 121 *et seq*.

[21] Declaration of the *Tribunal Constitucional* of 1 July 1992 (1993) *Europäische Grundrechte-Zeitschrift* 285; on this see A López Castillo and J Polakiewicz, 'Verfassung und Gemeinschaftsrecht in Spanien', (1993) *Europäische Grundrechte-Zeitschrift* 277 at 281; A Estella de Noriega, 'A Dissident Voice: The Spanish Constitutional Court case law on European Integration', (1999) 5 *European Public Law* 269 at 279; A Jiménez-Blanco Carillo de Albornoz, 'Die verfassungsrechtlichen Auswirkungen des Vertrages über die Europäische Union in Spanien und Frankreich', (1995) *Die Verwaltung* 225 at 230; Muñoz Machado, above n 2, 39 *et seq*; A Ruiz Robledo, 'Las implicaciones constitucionales de la participación de España en el proceso de integración Europeo', (2000) 183 *Noticias de la Unión Europea* 9 at 10.

[22] García de Enterría and Alonso García, above n 20, 298 *et seq*.

[23] Cf Arts 1 to 3 of the Spanish Constitution; admittedly, this has not yet been expressly decided by the *Tribunal Constitucional*, but the leading opinion in literature presumes this, cf García de Enterría and Alonso García, above n 20, 299; Estella de Noriega, above n 21, 298.

[24] U Bernitz, Swedish Report, in Schwarze (ed), above n 20, 389 at 422 *et seq*, in accordance with Ch 4 § 3 of the Constitution, the legislative committee, which investigated the necessity of constitutional changes before Sweden's accession, did not regard it necessary to entrench the primacy in the constitution. See the Committee's Report in the official governmental series *Statens offentliga utredningar* (SOU) 1993: 14, EG och våra grundlagar, at 88, 169.

liberty and law which corresponds to the protection of human rights and fundamental freedoms given in this constitution and in the European Convention on Human Rights".[25] Accordingly, the "Solange" case law of the Federal Constitutional Court is established in the constitution as positive law and forms the basis of Swedish membership.[26]

In *Ireland,* it is also assumed that Community law takes primacy over the constitution, at least in principle.[27] The Irish Constitution contains provisions both in Article 29(4) No 3 (Accession to the EC) and Article 29(4) No 4 (Maastricht Treaty) according to which no existing or future part of Community law may be deemed to contravene the Irish Basic Law.[28] As a result, Irish statutes which serve to implement indirectly applicable EC law cannot be declared invalid on the basis of Irish constitutional law. Any measure of Community law is also protected against a judicial review of its compatibility with the Irish Constitution. There is however a significant exception to this: it is generally accepted that Community law relating to Ireland can be set aside where human rights protected by the constitutional statute may be infringed.[29]

Finally, *Great Britain* can also be classified within this group even if it represents a special case. In contrast to Ireland, Great Britain initially accepted the primacy of EC law without making any amendment to the constitution. In any case, British constitutional law is largely uncodified and hardly receptive to a formal amending act.[30] Accordingly, commentators were content to point out that British constitutional law hardly contained any provisions which could infringe EC law anyway.[31]

[25] Griller, above n 6, 154 *et seq.*

[26] Cf U Bernitz, 'Sweden and the European Union: On Sweden's Implementation and Application of European Law', (2001) 38 *CML Rev* 903 at 910 *et seq.*

[27] G Hogan, 'Ireland and the European Union: Constitutional Law and Practice', in Kellerman, de Zwaan and Czuczai (eds), above n 6, 89 at 101; also Mayer, above n 5, 201 *et seq.*

[28] "No provision of this Constitution invalidates laws enacted, acts done or measures adopted by the State which are necessitated by the obligations of membership of the European Union or of the Communities, or prevent laws enacted, acts done or measures adopted by the European Union or by the Communities or by the institutions thereof, or by bodies competent under the Treaties establishing the Communities, from having the force of law in the State." Cf Hogan, above n 27, 90 *et seq*; M Sychold, 'Irischer Landesbericht', in B Cottier (ed), *Staatsrechtliche Auswirkungen der Mitgliedschaft in den Europäischen Gemeinschaften* (1991) 257 at 264.

[29] This is taken from the decision of the Supreme Court in the case *Society for the Protection of Unborn Children* (Ire) *Ltd v Grogan* (1989) IR 753. This case concerned the question whether distributing information in Ireland on the possibilities of abortion in Great Britain was covered by the freedom in Community law to provide services, cf Case C-159/90, *Society for the Protection of Unborn Children* [1991] ECR I-4685. Owing to the exceptional sensitivity of this subject in Ireland, the case is not classified as establishing a general rule; cf Hogan, above n 27, 101; Sychold, above n 28, 264 *et seq.*

[30] N Foster, 'Grossbritannien und die Europäische Union: Verfassungsrechtliche Aspekte des Beitritts und der Mitgliedschaft', (1998) *Aktuelle Juristische Praxis* 409 at 412; see also P Birkinshaw, 'British Report', in Schwarze (ed), above n 12, 205 at 221 *et seq.*

[31] See eg Sychold, above n 28, 264.

Admittedly, the unwritten constitutional principle of sovereignty of parliament contains considerable potential to conflict with Community law.[32] The question of primacy and whether it complied with this principle was repeatedly discussed during the first twenty years of British membership in the EC, but was never resolved. The resolution of the dispute was left to the Courts which had always found pragmatic solutions in compliance with Community law by avoiding dogmatic questions.[33] Accordingly, since the decision *Macarthy's Ltd v Wendy Smith* of the English Court of Appeal, Section 2 (4) of the European Communities Act (ECA) was generally regarded as having established the principle that national law was to be interpreted broadly in order to avoid a direct collision between a measure of Community law and a national measure adopted subsequently.[34] The decision of the House of Lords in the 1991 *Factortame Ltd* cases proved to be an acid test where the resolution of a collision proved unavoidable:[35] For the first time the House of Lords decided not to apply a subsequent national rule owing to its incompatibility with Community law. This break with case law heralded the Courts' recognition that Community law took primacy over national law.[36] The question as to whether it would be lawful for Parliament to expressly declare its intention to infringe Community law and whether such a decision would also bind the Courts owing to the sovereignty of Parliament remains undecided. It is debatable whether such a "reservation of sovereignty"—i.e. the power to expressly adopt legislation in contravention of Community law—exists and, if so, to what extent.[37]

[32] Cf on this set of questions: PP Craig, 'Sovereignty of the United Kingdom Parliament after Factortame', (1991) 11 *Yearbook of European Law* 221 *et seq*; S Davis, *Theorie und Praxis der Bewältigung des Verhältnisses zwischen EG-Recht und englischer Rechtsordnung (unter Einbezug der EMRK)* (1991) 9; Mayer, above n 5, 194 *et seq.*

[33] S Rajani, *Die Geltung und Anwendung des Gemeinschaftsrechts im Vereinigten Königreich von Großbritannien und Nordirland* (2000) 27.

[34] *Macarthy's Ltd v Wendy Smith*, (1979) 16 *CML Rev* 3 at 44; (1979) 3 All ER, 325. Concerning this basis of conform interpretation see the speech of Lord Oliver in the case *Litster v Forth Dry Dock and Engineering Co Ltd*, 21 *CML Rev* (1989) 194: "If the legislation can reasonably be construed so as to conform with those obligations—obligations which are to be ascertained not only from the wording of the relevant directive but from the interpretation placed upon it by the European Court [...]—such a purposive construction will be applied even though, perhaps, it may involve some departure from the strict and literal application of the words which the legislature has elected to use". For more details on the significance of the ECA see PJ Birkinshaw, 'British Report', in Schwarze (ed), above n 20, 205 at 235 *et seq*; Schwarze, in *ibid*, 463 at 507 *et seq*; A Dashwood, 'The British Way', in Kellerman, de Zwaan and Czuczai (eds), above n 6, 81 at 84.

[35] House of Lords, *Factortame Ltd v Secretary of State* (1991) 1 AC, 603.

[36] Cf Lord Bridge: "If the supremacy within the European Community of Community Law over the national law of member states was not always inherent in the E.E.C. Treaty it was certainly well established in the jurisprudence of the European Court of Justice long before the United Kingdom joined the Community. Thus, whatever limitation of its sovereignty Parliament accepted when it enacted the European Communities Act 1972 was entirely voluntary" (*ibid* 658 *et seq*). However, the other Law Lords did not expressly support his view.

[37] Lord Denning supported this in his opinion in the *Macarthy* case (1979) 3 All ER, 325; cf also Craig, above n 32, 221; Dashwood, above n 34, 87; C Filzwieser, *Ausgewählte rechtliche Aspekte der Mitgliedschaft des Vereinigten Königreichs bei den Europäischen Gemeinschaften* (1999) 100 *et seq*; Rajani, above n 33, 195 *et seq.*

3. Primacy of the Constitution

The third group concerns those states which assume that their constitutional law takes primacy over Community law either predominantly or in principle. These states are *France* and *Greece*.

French constitutional law is characterised by a complex interaction between constitutional requirements, the practice of executive and legislative organs and the jurisdiction of the *Conseil constitutionnel*.[38] Nowadays it is accepted that Community law has the same status as international agreements, that is to say between constitution and law on the basis of Articles 54 and 55 of the Constitution.[39] In accordance with Article 54, the *Conseil constitutionnel* has the power of preventative control over the constitutionality of primary Community law.[40] The limits to constitutional change created thereby suggest that the Constitution takes primacy over national law.[41] Article 55 grants Community law primacy over national legislation but subjects this primacy to certain conditions thereby making it clear that only a moderate form or qualified monism exists in France. Therefore, according to Articles 54 and 55, Community law ranks below the Constitution but above national law.[42]

[38] For a description of the development of the discussion of primacy in France see K Alter, *Establishing the Supremacy of European Law* (2001) 124 *et seq* and JF Flauss, 'Auf dem Weg zu einer europäischen Verfassung', in J Schwarze and PC Müller-Graff (eds), *Europäische Verfassungsentwicklung,* (2000) *Europarecht,* supp I 31 *et seq*; Schwarze, above n 34, 502; T de Berranger, *Constitutions nationales et construction communautaire* (1995) 333 *et seq*; J Gundel, *Die Einordnung des Gemeinschaftsrechts in die französische Rechtsordnung* (1997) 70 *et seq*.

[39] Gundel, above n 38, 480. By contrast, no conclusion on the primacy relationship is drawn from paras 14 and 15 of the Preamble. These paragraphs are merely referred to as a measure for the constitutionality of the integration treaties, *id*, 49, 55. For a slightly different understanding de Berranger, above n 38, 215 *et seq*, 247, who advocates activating para 15 of the Preamble as an "integration lever" in favour of Community law.

[40] See the procedure of the *Conseil constitutionnel* prior to ratification of the Maastricht Treaty, Decision no 92-308 DC of 9 April 1992 (1993) *Europäische Grundrechte-Zeitschrift* 187 and then the Decision no 92-312 DC of 2 September 1992 (1993) *Europäische Grundrechte-Zeitschrift* 193. This possibility of preventative control was introduced by the Constitution of the 5th Republic, Gundel, above n 38, 57.

[41] Gundel, above n 38, 72.

[42] Gundel, above n 38, 70. The basic structure of the classification of international treaties in the French legal system resembles the solution which applies in relation to the classification of international obligations of the Community in its "internal legal area". In Community law too, international treaties are considered an autonomous source of law. However, they do not take primacy over primary law as a "constitution" of the Community. They are subordinate to primary law but superior to secondary legislation. In addition, there is a procedural parallel: preventative control of a treaty which still has to be concluded, cf Art 54 French Constitution and the opinion procedure according to Art 300(6) EC; however, a subsequent review of conformity with primary law is also possible in accordance with Art 230 EC, see Gundel, *ibid*, at 67, 68, 70 *et seq*. Concerning the extent to which the constitution has primacy cf the decisions of the *Conseil constitutionnel* on the constitutionality of European Community law see J Dutheil de la Rochère, 'The French *Conseil constitutionnel* and the constitutional development of the European Union', in M Kloepfer and I Pernice (eds), *Entwicklungsperspektiven der europäischen Verfassung im Lichte des Vertrages von Amsterdam* (1999) 43 at 46 *et seq*; Flauss, above n 38, 31, and C Walter, 'Die drei Entscheidungen des französischen Verfassungsrates zum Vertrag von Maastricht über die Europäische Union', (1993) *Europäische Grundrechte-Zeitschrift* 183 *et seq*.

Community law does not take precedence over *Greek* constitutional law either, according to the leading opinion. This was justified by the wording and genesis of Article 28(1) of the Constitution, which only grants Community law primacy over ordinary law. This suggests *e contrario* that Community law does not enjoy any primacy over the constitution, otherwise the legislature of 1975, who was aware of Community law's claim to primacy, would have formulated the provision differently.[43] In July 1997, the State Council confirmed this approach in the "DI.KATSA"-decisions. Contrary to Article 149 EC and the Diploma Directive, the Court held that the prohibition of private universities anchored in the Constitution excluded the recognition of diplomas awarded by foreign universities.[44]

4. The Situation in the Legal Systems of New Member States

For the sake of completeness, the situation in the ten new Member States has to be considered although the legal situation does not lead to a different conclusion for the analysis in general. First of all, European Union law was already engendering "pre-effects" of the later realised membership in the legal systems of the former "accession candidates". On the eve of their accession, the Constitutional Courts of the Czech Republic, Hungary and Poland already declared their position in principle vis-à-vis the relationship between Community law and national law.[45] The Hungarian Constitutional Court was more reserved[46] in declaring that the requirements of the bilateral European agreement did not belong to the "generally recognised rules of international law" according to Article 7 of the Constitution. The requirements of Community law had a dynamic character as developed according to the application practice of Community organs. The Community formed a system of public power independent of and separate from the Hungarian Republic; Hungary did not exercise any influence over its legislation. Accordingly, the Hungarian Constitution would have to be amended before Community law took direct effect.[47]

[43] C Bernasconi and C Spirou, 'Griechischer Landesbericht', in B Cottier (ed), *Staatsrechtliche Auswirkungen der Mitgliedschaft in den Europäischen Gemeinschaften* (1991) 155 at 169. Cf contra D Evrigenis, 'Legal and constitutional implications of Greek accession to the European communities', (1980) 17 *CML Rev*, 157 at 167, who, taking account of Greece's receptiveness towards Europe, expects Greek courts to affirm Community law's primacy over constitutional law on the basis of Art 28(1) and (2).

[44] Cf Mayer, above n 5, 220 *et seq*.

[45] Cf M Hofmann, 'Gemeinschaftsrecht in der Rechtsprechung des ungarischen und des tschechischen Verfassungsgerichts', in Hanns Seidel Stiftung and Ùstavny súd Slovensky republiky (ed), *Euròpske právo v judikatúre ústavnych súdov* (2001) 34 at 36 *et seq*.

[46] Cf J Zemánek, 'Mittel- und Osteuropa vor dem EU-Beitritt', in Kloepfer and Pernice (eds), above n 42, 132 at 137.

[47] Decision 30/1998 (IV 25) AB of 25 June 1998, *Magyar Közlöny* 1998/4565; repr in German trans in *Gewerblicher Rechtsschutz und Urheberrecht Internationaler Teil* (1999) 1.

The *Czech Constitutional Court* was unable to declare that law determined by the European Community was unconstitutional despite there being a substantive conflict between the competition rules in the EC Treaty and national constitutional law. The court justified this by arguing that the Treaty of Association like the Treaty establishing the European Union rested on the same values and principles as the constitutional order of the Czech Republic.[48] As a result, the Constitutional Court emphasised that it could not be unconstitutional to interpret national law in compliance with European competition law. This result does not differ any more from Community law taking primacy over constitutional law in accordance with the case in question. Nevertheless, there are no express regulations governing the primacy of European Union law over constitutional law in this respect either. Accordingly, the constitutional courts of most new Member States will have to determine the primacy of Community law more or less on a case-to-case basis.[49]

5. Similarities and Differences in Justifications

From a comparative perspective one can define a number of similarities and differences that contribute to the explanation of the relationship between national constitutional law and the law of the Union.

As with the primacy of Community law over national law in general, the relationship between Community law and constitutional law depends on the relevant reference system to which primacy applies. From the viewpoint of Community law, the ECJ derives primacy from the autonomy of Community law,[50] whereas from the viewpoint of national law primacy is justified by a specific power of constitutional law.[51] In terms of legal theory, one can explain this distinction using two different basic rules[52] without actually resolving the conflict for a judicial body (court or administrative authority) that has to deal with the conflict in practice. In this respect,

[48] Decision No 66 of 29 May 1997, III. ÚS 31/97, *Sbírka nálezu a usnesení* 6 (1996-II Pt) 149; repr in German trans in G Brunner, M Hofmann and P Holländer, *Die Verfassungsgerichtsbarkeit in der Tschechischen Republik* (2001) 444 *et seq*.

[49] Cf Mayer, above n 5, 358.

[50] Of fundamental importance in this respect: Case 6/64, *Costa* [1964] ECR 585; Case 26/62, *Van Gend & Loos* [1963] ECR 1; Case 11/70, *Internationale Handelsgesellschaft* [1970] ECR 1125; Case 106/77, *Simmenthal II* [1978] ECR 629; T Giegerich, *Europäische Verfassung und deutsche Verfassung im transnationalen Konstitutionalisierungsprozeß* (2003) 678 *et seq*.

[51] On this see Streinz, above n 11, paras 180 *et seq* with further references.

[52] Cf W-D Grussmann, 'Grundnorm und Supranationalität', in T von Danwitz *et al* (eds), *Auf dem Wege zu einer Europäischen Staatlichkeit* (1993) 47 at 56; J Isensee, 'Vorrang des Europarechts und deutsche Verfassungsvorbehalte—offener Dissens', in J Burmeister (ed), *Verfassungsstaatlichkeit: Festschrift für K Stern* (1997) 1239 at 1262.

authorities will have to search for strategies of avoiding conflicts and strategies for co-operation given the fact that there are different rules of primacy in European and national law.[53]

Finally, the principle of Community law refers to the constitutions of Member States in order to determine its limits.[54] National constitutional legislatures do not have unqualified discretion, having subjected themselves to restrictions during their accession and/or even sometimes subsequently. Balancing the interest in the uniform effect of Community law and the interest in having intact, functioning and accepted constitutions of Member States sometimes leads to different results in Member States. In most of the countries investigated, the case law of the (constitutional) courts determines the relationship or exact demarcation between constitutional law and European Community law. Comparing and distinguishing three groups of constitutional orders shows four phenomena:

1. Different solutions determine the relationship in most Member States.
2. Although aspects which serve to highlight limitations to primacy are characterised by national peculiarities, they essentially amount to the same constitutional principles. The vast majority of Member States have an inviolable core of basic constitutional principles or emphasise the autonomy of fundamental rights.
3. Those states which formally grant unlimited primacy to one legal level also recognise limits to primacy.
4. The acceptance of Community law's primacy over constitutional law is more difficult in those states that joined the Community early on,[55] where constitutional organs (especially constitutional courts)[56] have protected national identity more strongly and—to a certain extent—the more important a country is to Europe, particularly in terms of its size.

6. The Legal Situation According to the Constitutional Treaty

The Constitutional Treaty would not lead to a change in the relation between European law and national (constitutional) law. It would rather confirm the existing relation in a twofold manner. On the one hand, Article I-10(1)

[53] Cf M Jestaedt, 'Der Europäische Verfassungsverbund—Verfassungstheoretischer Charme und rechtstheoretische Insuffizienz einer Unschärferelation', in R Krause, W Veelken and K Vieweg (eds), *Recht der Wirtschaft und der Arbeit in Europa: Gedächnisschrift für W Blomeyer* (2004) 637 at 666 *et seq*.

[54] M Nettesheim, 'Der Grundsatz der einheitlichen Wirksamkeit des Gemeinschaftsrechts', in A Randelzhofer (ed), *Gedächtnisschrift für E Grabitz* (1995) 447 at 457.

[55] Cf the analysis conditional on the time of accession by FG Jacobs, 'The Constitutional Impact of the Forthcoming Enlargement of the EU' in Kellermann, de Zwaan and Czuczai (eds), above n 6, 183 *et seq*.

[56] Schwarze, above n 34, 502 *et seq*.

CT-Conv (Article 6 CT-IGC) codifies the existing principle of primacy of EU law: the Constitution, and law adopted by the Union's Institutions in exercising competencies conferred on them, shall have primacy over the law of the Member States. On the other hand, according to Article I-5(1) CT-Conv (Article 5(1) CT-IGC) the Union shall respect the national identities of its Member States inherent in their fundamental structures, political and constitutional, inclusive of regional and local self-government. In particular, it shall respect their essential State functions. Moreover, Article I-5(2) CT-Conv (Article 5(2) CT-IGC) stipulates that following the principle of loyal co-operation, the Union and the Member States shall, "in full mutual respect", assist each other in carrying out tasks which flow from the Constitution.

It would no longer be the autonomy of Community law which forms the basis for primacy of EU law, but an explicit norm of Union law. From the viewpoint of Union law and constitutional law, it appears now clear that an "all or nothing" approach is both unwarranted and inappropriate considering the aims of Union law. The assumption of a full primacy of Community law over constitutional law would neglect the dependence of Community law on "intact, functioning and accepted constitutional orders of Member States".[57] On the contrary, the Constitutional Treaty refers to the constitutions of Member States in order to determine its limits.[58]

In conclusion, it would be confirmed by the Constitutional Treaty that the national constitutional legislators do not have any unqualified discretion, having subjected themselves to restrictions through their accession and even sometimes subsequently. The Constitutional Treaty would explicitly give the criteria that are relevant when a balance between the interest in the uniform effect of Union law and the interest in having intact, functioning and accepted constitutions of Member States has to be struck.

III. CONTENTS OF NATIONAL CONSTITUTIONAL LAW RELATING TO THE EUROPEAN UNION

The adaptation of Member States' constitutional law and the strategies pursued thereby depend first of all on the subject of the constitutional regulation to be adapted. The following analysis focuses on central contents and principles of the constitutions, namely the question of sovereignty (1.), structural safeguard clauses (2.), the federal state (3.) and questions concerning democracy (4.) and fundamental rights (5.). This section does not aim to reappraise and record all adaptation procedures individually, rather to portray the way in which changes have taken place and to what extent.

[57] Concerning this and the following see Nettesheim, above n 54, 457; Gundel, above n 38, 30 *et seq.*

[58] Nettesheim, above n 54, 457.

Furthermore, this section aims to highlight differences in the intensity of adaptation depending on constitutional content (state organisation law on the one hand and fundamental rights on the other) together with differences revealed when comparing countries—besides those genuinely caused by national law (e.g. the system of legal sources etc).

1. Sovereignty and Transfer of Sovereign Rights

In the vast majority of Member States it is assumed that accession to the EC or EU and "integration impetus" engendered by amendments to the Treaty affect their national sovereignty and prevailing notions of sovereignty.[59] The intensity of the related debates depends on the importance that the country concerned attaches to sovereignty. In France and the United Kingdom (the latter case also involving the question of parliamentary sovereignty) the loss of sovereignty was regarded as a central problem of the necessary adaptation. For different reasons it proved less of an issue in other countries—including Germany.[60]

The initial years of European integration provoked only sporadic reactions by Member States. At any rate, express provision for the transfer of sovereign rights to international organisations had existed in the German Basic Law (Article 24) since 1949, in the Danish Constitution since 1953 (Article 20)[61] and in the Dutch Constitution since 1956 (Article 67(1), now Article 92). Other European constitutions subsequently adopted comparable clauses.[62]

However, many states found that the usual provisions allowing them to enter into "normal" international obligations exceeding those of international agreements no longer offered an adequate constitutional basis for transferring sovereign rights within the framework of increasing European integration. The inadequacy of such provisions became clear when states acceded to the Communities or Union, or even subsequently—for instance when making an amendment to a treaty. Besides general powers, the constitutions of many Member States now contain specific provisions regulating the transfer of jurisdiction to the European Union.

In *France*, the first Maastricht decision of the *Conseil constitutionnel* dating from 9 April 1992 led to the adoption of Title XV (Articles 88-1 to 88-4) by the Constitution.[63] It lays down constitutional limits to integration

[59] See also J Kokott, 'Die Staatsrechtslehre und die Veränderung ihres Gegenstandes', (2004) 63 *Veröffentlichungen der Vereinigung der Deutschen Staatsrechtslehrer* 11 at 17 *et seq.*

[60] For the reasons see Schwarze, above n 34, 514.

[61] See the Judgment of the Supreme Court in Copenhagen of 6 April 1998, (1999) *Europäische Grundrechte-Zeitschrift* 49.

[62] For instance, Sweden 1965, see Bernitz, above n 26, 910. Detailled references in de Berranger, above n 38, 47 *et seq*; R Bieber, 'Die Europäisierung des Verfassungsrechts', in K Kreuzer, D Scheuing and U Sieber (eds), *Die Europäisierung der mitgliedstaatlichen Rechtsordnungen in der Europäischen Union* (1997) 71 at 77.

[63] *Conseil constitutionnel*, Decision no 92-308 DC of 9 April 1992, above n 40, 187.

where "essential conditions of the exercise of national sovereignty"[64] are affected by integration. As such, it is crucial for the understanding and substance of amendments to constitutional law. The *Conseil constitutionnel* held that it was necessary to amend constitutional law owing to negative effects on sovereignty in three respects even though it regarded participation in the European Community as fundamentally compatible with the protection of national sovereignty, i.e. the right to vote in municipal elections,[65] currency union[66] and visa policy (Articles 61 *et seq* EC).[67] The Court's decision led to new regulations being adopted in all three cases.[68] Article 88-1 expressly points out in relation to Union membership that the European Communities and European Union are "constituted by States that have freely chosen, by virtue of the treaties that established them, to exercise some of their powers in common", although the continued existence of the states must be safeguarded, depending on the issue in question.[69] Article 88-2 (Currency Union, Visa policy) contains a proviso of reciprocity as does Article 88-3. This latter article also "intensifies the national state" in the parliamentary procedure in two respects. First, the national assembly transformed the constitutional right of EC-foreigners to vote in municipal elections into a mere legislative power. According to the version at the senatorial reading this power could only be exercised by the national assembly and senate acting in tandem. Second, besides parliamentary participation in the legislative process of the European Union (discussed below) in Article 2-2 a new constitutional provision was adopted declaring French as the language of the French Republic. All amendments—the language provision in particular[70]—suggest an attempt to protect national identity and sovereignty.[71]

[64] See 14th Consideration: "au cas où des engagements internationaux souscrits à cette fin contiennent une clause contraire à la Constitution ou portent atteinte aux conditions essentielles d'exercice de la souveraineté nationale, l'autorisation de les ratifier appelle une révision constitutionelle".

[65] Cf Considerations 21 *et seq*. The Municipal Elections Act (Art 8 EC) contravened Art 3 of the Constitution whereby the matter is discussed as a sovereignty problem: The election of the municipal parliament also decides the constitution of the senate, which also takes part in the exercise of national sovereignty. For more details on this problem see below 5 a) and J Hecker, *Europäische Integration als Verfassungsproblem in Frankreich* (1998); Walter, above n 42, 183; Gundel, above n 38, 132.

[66] Cf Consideration 36 at 43, see Gundel, above n 38, 133.

[67] Cf Consideration 46 at 49, see Gundel, above n 38, 133.

[68] See again *Conseil constitutionnel*, Decision no 92-312 DC of 2 September 1992 (1993) *Europäische Grundrechte-Zeitschrift* 193.

[69] Flauss, above n 38, 38; Hecker, above n 65, 248; Muñoz Machado, above n 2, 29; V Constantinesco, 'Der Beitrag nationaler Verfassungen zur Entwicklung eines zweistufigen europäischen Verfassungssystems', in U Battis *et al* (eds), *Das Grundgesetz im Prozeß europäischer und globaler Verfassungsentwicklung* (2000) 61 at 70.

[70] For extensive information on this see J Rideau, 'France', in J-C Masclet and D Maus (eds), *Les constitutions nationales à l'épreuve de l'Europe* (1993) 67 at 110; a similiar provision is mentioned within Art 11(3) of the Constitution of Portugal ("the official language is Portuguese") inserted by the "Lei Constitucional 1/2001 de 12 de Dezembro".

[71] Hecker, above n 65, 248; Alter, above n 38, 171.

In *Greece*, the constitutional basis for EU membership is Article 28(2) of the Constitution. This provision displays the principle of open statehood. In addition, the provision constitutes an interpretative guide as a "fundamental decision", i.e. a fundamental aim of state policy.[72] Article 28(3) expresses the inherent limits to Article 28(2). It contains substantive requirements for limiting the exercise of sovereignty which results from accession to the EC.[73] Article 28(2) and (3) was adopted in 1975 as part of a substantial amendment of the Constitution, and in view of the following (a few days) application of Greece to join the European Communities. The provision was proposed following the pretext of similar provisions in the constitutions of existing or potential Member States which had already passed constitutional reviews before national courts.[74] The loss of sovereignty, which membership of the European Community entailed, was considered a fair price for the immediate and future advantages promised by Greek participation in the process of European unification.[75]

The *Italian* Constitution only contains a very short regulation: according to Article 11 of the Italian Constitution, it is constitutional for Member States to restrict their sovereignty by transferring their sovereign rights to the Community established by the founding treaties.[76]

Austria ensured the constitutionality of accession to the European Union by a separate Federal Constitutional Act of Accession which empowered the responsible organs to conclude the necessary international treaty. This constitutional Act therefore forms the basis for the transfer of sovereign rights to the European Union. Although it had also been subject to a referendum owing to constitutional reasons, the question of sovereignty played only a subordinate role at most.[77] Entrenching participation in the common foreign and security policy by means of an accompanying constitutional amendment was due not so much to sovereignty as to the constitutional

[72] T Antoniou, *Europäische Integration und griechische Verfassung* (1985) 205; Evrigenis, above n 43, 159.

[73] Antoniou, above n 72, 208.

[74] Evrigenis, above n 43, 160. T Antoniou does not regard membership of the EC creating the problem of an irredeemable loss of sovereignty since the States have agreed not to exercise specific state powers but have not forfeited the substance of their state power. Rather, in accordance with Art 1(3) Greek Constitution, the substance of state power lies directly and inalienably with the people, whilst their exercise is distributed between different holders as stipulated by the constitution (Art 26 or in relation to international organisations Art 28(2) Greek Constitution), Antoniou, above n 72, 209.

[75] G Papadimitriou, 'Europäische Integration und nationales Verfassungsrecht in Griechenland', in U Battis, D Tsatsos and D Stefanou (eds), *Europäische Integration und nationales Verfassungsrecht* (1995) 149 at 160.

[76] Lotito, above n 9, 261.

[77] Further details in H Schäffer, 'Österreichischer Landesbericht', in Schwarze (ed), above n 20, 339 at 372 *et seq.*

principle of permanent neutrality, which resembles an international restriction on foreign policy and possibility of military action.[78]

Finally, as an example of the last generation of acceding countries, it is worth taking account of the discussion in *Poland* that was held on the eve of its accession to the European Community. Sovereignty undoubtedly assumed great importance in the debate concerning Article 90 of the Polish Constitution of 1997 which grants the power to transfer sovereign rights to the European Union.[79] It also raised further issues, in particular linking the accession procedure to a referendum and Polish notions of sovereignty. In particular the national ratification procedure of the Treaty on the accession of Poland to the European Union was accompanied by controversies of a constitutional nature: pursuant to Article 90 of the Constitution of Poland the consent for ratification of an international agreement, on the basis of which the Republic of Poland delegates to an international organisation or international institution the competence of organs of State authority in certain matters ("European clause"), may be granted by parliament in form of a statute—passed by a qualified majority vote of two-thirds in both houses of parliament[80]—or by a nation-wide referendum.[81] The choice of one of these procedures has to be taken by the Sejm (the lower house of the Polish parliament) by an absolute majority vote taken with at least half of the statutory number of Deputies (Article 90(4)). On 17 April 2003, one day after the signing of the Treaty on accession of ten states, the Polish Sejm chose to call a referendum—the most important form of direct democracy and therefore a special form of expression of the state sovereignty[82]—to grant consent for the ratification of this Treaty by the President of the Republic of Poland pursuant to Article 90 of the Polish Constitution.[83] The

[78] T Öhlinger, 'BVG Neutralität', in K Korinek and M Holoubek (ed), *Österreichisches Bundesverfassungsrecht, loose-leaf* (2001) para 13; Art 23f Austrian Federal Constitutional Law, which in this respect was originally created to justify in constitutional terms the participation in embargo decisions of the EU council, has been amended on ratification of the Treaty of Amsterdam in order to do justice to the "Petersberg tasks": see W Hummer, 'Österreichs dauernde Neutralität und die "Gemeinsame Außen- und Sicherheitspolitik" (GASP) bzw "Gemeinsame Europäische Sicherheits- und Verteidigungspolitik" (GESVP) in der Europäischen Union', (2001) *Schweizerische Zeitschrift für internationales und europäisches Recht*, 443 at 465 *et seq*.

[79] Cf M Wyrzykowski, 'European Clause: Is it a Threat to Sovereignty?', in *id* (ed), *Constitutional Cultures* (2000) 267 at 268, 279 *et seq*.

[80] I.e. the so called "legislative procedure", pursuant to Art 90(2) of the Polish Constitution; cf Wyrzykowski, above n 79, 271 *et seq*.

[81] I.e. the so called "ratification procedure", cf Art 90(3) Polish Constitution; cf Wyrzykowski, above n 79, 274 *et seq*. According to Art 125(1) of the Polish Constitution, such a referendum should only be held "in respect of matters of particular importance of the state".

[82] Cf Wyrzykowski, above n 79, 278.

[83] The referendum was held on 7 and 8 June 2003. 58,85% of the citizens having the right to vote took part in the referendum whereby 77,45% of the valid votes were cast in favour of ratification of the Treaty. In accordance with the result of the referendum, the President ratified the Accession Treaty.

Nation-wide Referendum Act 2003,[84] that regulates the principles and procedures of holding a nation-wide referendum, provides in Article 75 that if the result of the ratification of the referendum was not binding (less than half of the citizens having the right to vote participated therein), the Sejm could again adopt a resolution to hold another referendum or to initiate the parliamentary procedure to grant consent for ratification. *Inter alia*, the constitutionality of this provision as well as the interpretation of Article 90 of the Constitution led to political and legal controversies (the main fear of the opponents of the European clause of Article 90 was the loss of State sovereignty)[85] and was proofed by the Constitutional Tribunal of Poland on 27 May 2003. On the basis that the interpretation of binding statutes should take into account the constitutional principle of favourable predisposition towards the process of European integration,[86] the Constitutional Tribunal decided that the Nation-wide Referendum Act 2003 was neither incompatible with Article 4 (the principle of sovereignty of the Nation) nor with Article 90 of the Constitution.[87]

2. Structural Safeguard Clauses

In the constitutions of many Member States, provisions on *inter alia* the power of accession and the transfer of other sovereign powers are accompanied by "structural safeguard clauses". Such clauses are often connected to a power to enter into or confirm membership or to the accession of a state to the European Union. They also serve to demarcate the limits to integration or the development of Union law by withdrawing even a core area of constitutional law from the scope of European measures aimed at integration ("constitutional reserve clause", "Verfassungsbestandsklauseln").

[84] Although the Act does not only refer to referenda in respect of the ratification of international agreements described in Art 90 of the Constitution the legal and political debate that accompanied the adoption of the Act, was dominated by problems concerning the accession referendum. The reason for this lies in the fact that the Act was adopted in the final stage of the debate on Poland's accession to the EU with the intention of enacting rules regarding the accession referendum and the referendum campaign proceeding it.

[85] Cf Wyrzykowski, above n 79, 268 *et seq*.

[86] Cf the Preamble and Art 9 of the Constitution ("The Republic of Poland shall respect international law binding upon it"); Judgment of the Polish Constitutional Tribunal of 27 May 2003, K 11/03 (*referendum on Poland's accession to the European Union*).

[87] According to the Constitutional Tribunal the "representative democracy as a basic form of democracy in Poland" is expressed by Art 90 of the Constitution and the referendum is only a facultative procedure to grant consent for ratification. The Nation has to express its will, either directly or through its representatives (Art 4(2) of the Constitution) and if the Nation does not express its will by more than the half of the entitled citizens, the referendum is only of advisory significance. Such a result should be treated at the same time as the lack of acceptance by the Nation-sovereign of the proposition to hold a referendum itself. Accordingly, the Sejm could make the choice again, whether to hold a new referendum or to initiate the parliamentary procedure. See Judgment of the Polish Constitutional Court of 27 May 2003, K 11/03 (*referendum on Poland's accession to the European Union*).

In this respect, the primacy of Community law also encounters *constitutional* limits.

Article 23(1) of the German Basic Law clearly expresses the connection between the reception clause and the purpose of the structural guarantee.[88] At the same time, it requires the Union to obey certain principles by participating in the development of the European Union. They constitute substantive limits to the power of integration. Article 23(1) lays down these principles thereby subjecting the European Union to structural requirements which display parallels to the structural principles of the Basic Law. However, this does not require structural congruence; rather, the postulates must be structurally modified in order to comply with the peculiarities of the EU structure concerned.[89] These structural safeguard clauses display clear parallels to the case law of the Federal Constitutional Court, at least with regard to the protection of fundamental rights.[90] They provide normative reference points for future decisions of the Federal Constitutional Court in reinforcing the limits and establishing the consequences of their infringement.[91]

The extent to which the Federal Republic of Germany may participate in the integration process without abandoning its constitutional *essentialia* is determined by the constitutional reserve clause of Article 23(1) Basic Law by reference to Article 79(3) Basic Law. The administrative principles covered by this "permanent guarantee" largely include the same principles which should bind the Union as a whole according to the Basic Law—albeit in modified form—i.e. constitutional principles under Article 20, in particular.[92]

Sweden and *Austria* adopted aspects of German constitutional law when they acceded to the Union in 1995. Admittedly, the constitutional legislator did not display the same confidence towards Europe so that the result was rather different. The Austrian constitutional legislator sometimes refers literally to the limits on integration which the Federal Constitutional Court

[88] See eg R Breuer, 'Die Sackgasse des neuen Europaartikels (Art 23 GG)', (1991) Neue Zeitschrift für Verwaltungsrecht 417 at 422; F Ossenbühl, 'Maastricht und das Grundgesetz—eine verfassungsrechtliche Wende?', (1993) *Deutsches Verwaltungsblatt* 629 at 633; K Schmalenbach, *Der neue Europaartikel 23 des Grundgesetzes im Lichte der Arbeit der Gemeinsamen Verfassungskommission* (1996); D König, *Die Übertragung von Hoheitsrechten im Rahmen des europäischen Integrationsprozesses* (2000) 279 *et seq*; C Dorau, *Die Verfassungsfrage der Europäischen Union* (2001) 168 *et seq*.

[89] See U Everling, 'Überlegungen zur Struktur der Europäischen Union und zum neuen Europa-Artikel des Grundgesetzes', (1993) *Deutsches Verwaltungsblatt* 936 at 944; König, above n 88, 282, 413.

[90] In particular *Entscheidungen des Bundesverfassungsgerichts* 74, 339 at 378 *et seq* (*Solange II*).

[91] *Entscheidungen des Bundesverfassungsgerichts* 89, 155 at 179, 182 *et seq* (*Maastricht*).

[92] Isensee, above n 52, 1257 *et seq*; GB Oschatz, 'Verfassungsrechtliche Grenzen der Weiterentwicklung Europas', in D Merten (ed), *Die Stellung der Landesparlamente aus deutscher, österreichischer und spanischer Sicht* (1997) 33 at 36; Schwarze, above n 12, 134 *et seq*.

had laid down in its Maastricht judgment. However, it does not do so in the text of the Federal Constitutional Act of Accession, but merely in the explanatory memorandum to the law. It is therefore generally suggested that limits comparable to those in Germany do not exist in Austria.[93] Similarly, Ch 10 § 5 of the Swedish Constitution refers to an equivalent standard of protection of fundamental rights as a constitutional condition for the Law of the Union.

Article 28(3) of the *Greek* Constitution also contains a type of structural safeguard clause. Like Article 79(3) of the German Basic Law, it also contains substantive requirements and thereby limits the transfer of sovereignty by protecting the fundamental core of the principles contained in Article 110(1) of the Greek Constitution. Article 28(3) subjects limitations on sovereignty to the substantive requirements of *inter alia* the protection of human rights and foundations of the democratic system. In this respect, the structure of the EC should not adopt the specific form of the nation-state as an expression of democracy but instead the guarantee of the foundations and principles of democracy in general. Nor should it seek to protect fundamental rights as laid down by the Greek Constitution, but instead human rights *per se*.[94]

Article 11 of the *Italian* Constitution only allows limitations of sovereignty insofar as these serve to establish a system ensuring peace and justice between states.[95] In 1973, the Italian Constitutional Court confirmed the compatibility of the EC Treaties with this objective.[96]

A similar provision exists within Article 7(6) of the Portuguese Constitution which provides that Portugal contributes to European integration in respect of both the principle of reciprocity and subsidiarity and with regard to the realisation of economic and social cohesion. But according to this provision, Community law can be reviewed on the basis of national constitutional law. As a result, this provision represents constitutional limits to integration.

Article 88(1) of the *French* Constitution contains a structural safeguard clause insofar this provision, established in the wake of the Maastricht I Decision, presupposes a Community structure which is based on independent Member States. However, substantive limits on the transfer of sovereign rights to the Union are still determined by the case law of the *Conseil constitutionnel* and embrace the "conditions essentielles d'exercice de la souveraineté nationale" and the protection of fundamental rights.[97] The idea of

[93] T Öhlinger, 'EU-Beitritts BVG', in K Korinek and M Holoubek (eds), *Österreichisches Bundesverfassungsrecht, loose-leaf* (2001), paras 19 *et seq*.

[94] Antoniou, above n 72, 207 *et seq*.

[95] Bieber, above n 62, 78.

[96] Sen Decision 183/73 of 27 December 1973, Frontini (1974) 11 *CML Rev* 372 at 389 or 405.

[97] Mayer, above n 5, 146 *et seq*; Rideau, above n 2, 118.

a permanent core within the French legal order, unalterable even by constitutional amendment, is still largely rejected.[98]

The new Member States had already adapted their constitutional systems for membership of the European Union before the accession process itself took place.[99] The *Polish* Constitution played a leading role in this respect: Article 90 of the new Polish Constitution of 1997 grants the power to transfer sovereign rights and is described in Polish literature as the "European clause".[100] Para 1 provides that the Republic of Poland may, by virtue of international agreements, delegate to an international organisation or international institution the competence of organs of State authority "in relation to certain matters". In light of the discussion concerning the provision,[101] it is clear that it is conceived for accession to the European Union, notwithstanding its limitation to "certain matters". It also appears accepted that the provision resembles a structural safeguard clause.[102]

Constitutional development in *Slovakia* has not only followed this example but goes one step further.[103] Extensive constitutional amendments were already adopted in February 2001, of which the most important related to EC accession. According to Article 7 of the Constitution, the Republic of Slovakia may "by an international treaty or on the basis of such treaty, transfer part of its powers to an international organisation of which it is a member." This provision therefore resembles Article 90 of the Polish Constitution because it establishes that Community law will take direct effect upon accession. In general terms, legal acts of this international organisation are directly applicable and take primacy over statute.

3. Federal and Decentralised Entities

National legislators display different approaches depending on whether they belong to federal or decentralised entities of Member States. The crucial factors in this respect appear to be the weight of national sub-divisions together with the federalist culture of a Member State. Processes of constitutional adaptation are determined by disputes concerning the protection of national jurisdiction which is subject to change owing to growing integration. In

[98] Gundel, above n 38, 172 *et seq*.

[99] Cf M Hofmann, 'Die Europa- und Völkerrechtsdimension der geänderten slowakischen Verfassung', in M Hofmann and H Küpper (eds), *Kontinuität und Neubeginn* (2001) 398 *et seq*, with further references on Hungary and Bulgaria; concerning Slovenia cf M Skrk, 'The European Union Law and the Constitutional Order of Slovenia', in Hanns Seidel Stiftung and Ùstavny súd Slovensky republiky (eds), above n 45, 70 at 75; concerning other states of central and eastern Europe cf the contributions in Kellerman, de Zwaan and Czuczai (eds) above n 6, 267 *et seq*.

[100] Cf Wyrzykowski, above n 79, 268 *et seq*.

[101] See 3 1.

[102] Wyrzykowski, above n 79, 280.

[103] Cf Hofmann, above n 99, 398, 405 *et seq*.

retrospect, it becomes clear that the Maastricht Treaty once more marked a turning point in this respect which encouraged crucial constitutional developments at Member State level.

It is primarily federal entities, with the exception of communities and regions of Belgium, which seek compensation for the transfer of their jurisdiction "to Brussels". German states in particular are seen as the losers in an increasing unification of Europe. This particularly affects state parliaments because also the legislative powers of the German states are transferred to the European Union along with national sovereign powers. The loss of power within the jurisdiction of the Federation as a whole is partly compensated by participation in the European organs. In the case of the states, however, compensation in European law is initially limited to a right to participate within the Member States.[104] In Germany, national compensation is awarded to state governments and not state parliaments,[105] whereby European integration indirectly reinforces the development of Federal statehood into executive federalism.[106]

Regarding the participation rights of federal or decentralised entities in the European legislative process, three categories of constitutional adaptations can again be distinguished.[107]

Belgium belongs to the first category. The federal entities were empowered to represent Belgium in the Council of the European Union within the framework of their jurisdiction following the great constitutional reform of 1993. This gave rise to a highly complicated system of co-operation between the state and its federal entities. Article 1 of the Constitution declares that Belgium is a federal state made up of communities and regions. This results in a complicated network of altogether six constituent states each of which has its own executive and legislative organs.[108] These

[104] The European Union is therefore often told to be "blind" with regard to the states. Cf only Streinz, above n 11, 61, para 152.

[105] In Austria, this question is left to the state constitutions. The integration agreement of the states provides that the organ consists of the state heads and the presidents of the state councils. However, the right to vote is only to be exercised by the heads of state executive organs; cf H Schambeck, 'Föderalismus und Parlamentarismus in Österreich', in Merten (ed), above n 92, 15 at 26 *et seq*.

[106] J Isensee, 'Der Bundesstaat—Bestand und Entwicklung', in P Badura and H Dreier (eds), *Festschrift 50 Jahre Bundesverfassungsgericht* (2001), vol 2, 719 at 751 *et seq*; R Halfmann, *Entwicklungen des deutschen Staatsorganisationsrechts im Kraftfeld der europäischen Integration* (2000) 323; E Iltgen, 'Bundesstaatliche Ordnung und Europäische Union aus der Sicht der (neuen) deutschen Landtage', in Merten (ed), above n 92, 45 at 47; R Müller-Terpitz, *Die Beteiligung des Bundesrates am Willensbildungsprozess der Europäischen Union* (1999) 357; K Pabel, *Grundfragen der Kompetenzverteilung im Bereich der Kunst* (2002) 201 *et seq*.

[107] The regions (decentralised expanded administrative entities) in Greece which were established at the end of the 1980s are not comparable to the German States: Papadimitriou, above n 75, 178.

[108] See G Roller, 'Die Mitwirkung der deutschen Länder und der belgischen Regionen an EG-Entscheidungen', (1998) 123 *Archiv des öffentlichen Rechts* 21 at 47; see also A Alen, 'Belgien: Ein zweigliedriger und zentrifugaler Föderalismus', (1990) 50 *Zeitschrift für ausländisches öffentliches Recht und Völkerrecht* 501.

constituent states are granted wide rights to participate in the creation of both primary and secondary law. Two co-operative agreements between the federal state, communities and the regions establish procedures regarding the expression of will of the Belgian state.[109] According to this, prior co-ordination of Belgian opinion takes place at a council meeting within the framework of the "Administrative Direction of European affairs" established in the Foreign Office. Executive representatives from all levels are invited to such co-ordination meetings, i.e. representatives of the Prime Minister, the respective Deputy Prime Minister, Minister for European Affairs, chairpersons of community and regional governments, members of the same, the permanent representation at the European Communities together with the attachés of the communities and regions. In addition, the agreement establishes a special measure on representation at the Council of Ministers. Annex I to the Treaty lists the areas of jurisdiction and sets out the individual powers of representation, although the latter can always be amended. Altogether, four categories of representation are provided: exclusive federal representation (Cat I), federal representation with assessors of the federated areas (Cat II), representation by the federated areas with federal assessors (Cat III) and, finally, exclusive representation by federated areas (Cat IV).[110] According to the Annex, justice, energy research and culture are therefore subject to categories I, II, III and IV respectively. Cases where the communities and regions have the power to represent Belgium are, in turn, characterised by a bi-annual rotation principle (Annex II of the Treaty).

A second category of constitutions is governed by the notion of co-operative federalism. Federal entities are indeed granted rights of representation but with the proviso that they remain subject to the interests of the nation-state. This category includes *Germany* and *Austria* with their respective *Länder* and, again as a special case, the *United Kingdom* following *devolution*.

As far as Germany is concerned, Article 23(2), (4), (5) and (6) of the Basic Law provide for the "participation" of the Federal Council. Action by the Federation, in particular the Federal Government, is always provided for, in which case the Federal Council is involved. Even in the extreme case that the exclusive legislative powers of the states are affected in terms of subject, the power to enforce the rights of the Federal Republic as an EU Member State can be transferred to a representative of the German states. However, here too the rights are exercised "with the participation

[109] Co-operative agreement of the Federal State, the Communities and the Regions on the representation of the Kingdom of Belgium at the Council of Ministers of the European Union of 8 March 1994, *Belgisches Staatsblatt of 17 November 1994*, 28217; as well as co-operative agreements of 8 March 1994, under the influence of the "Joint Community Commission" of the Brussels region, *Belgisches Staatsblatt of 17 November 1994*, 28224.

[110] Cf Roller, above n 108, 53.

and concurrence" of the Federal Government and subject to "the responsibility of the Federation for the nation as a whole".[111]

Federal state participation in Austrian constitutional law is quite similar, the regulation of which has clearly been influenced by the German example.[112] Article 23d Austrian Federal Constitutional Law establishes a duty of information incumbent on the Austrian Federal Republic (para 1). The federal states have the right to express their views with differing binding effect (para 2) and, concerning matters within the federal states' legislative jurisdiction, the participation at Council meetings can be delegated to a federal state representative (para 3). The most important departure from the German system is that the organ acting for the states is not the Federal Council,[113] but an "Integration Conference of the Federal States" ("Integrationskonferenz der Länder", "IKL"), assembled from the heads of federal state governments and councils.[114] At the same time, the Austrian states are also obliged to ensure that standards of Community law are implemented within their jurisdiction.[115] Austria had already established the relevant mechanisms and procedures before accession as part of its membership of the EEA in compliance with the requirements of European Union membership. The Federation undoubtedly paid a price for the required agreement of the Federal Council to the Accession Treaty by Article 23d Federal Constitutional Law. Nevertheless, this accounted for half the price at most. The other half, namely a full reform of the Federal State with jurisdictional shifts to the benefit of the states has not yet been paid.[116] What is noticeable about the Austrian regulation is that the municipalities also gained access to participation: Like the states, towns and municipalities also

[111] The *Länder* Participation Act governs the details, see Müller-Terpitz, above n 106, 267 at 294 *et seq*; König, above n 88, 332 *et seq;* Giegerich, above n 50, 1366 *et seq*.

[112] W Dax, 'Die Bedeutung der Landesparlamente in Österreich', in Merten (ed), above n 92, 71 at 76 *et seq*. Concerning the amendments of 1992 and 1994, cf H Schäffer, *Information und Entscheidungsabstimmung zwischen Landesparlament und Landesregierung*, in: *ibid*, 105 at 117 *et seq*.

[113] The position of the Austrian Federal Council is considerably weaker than that of its German counterpart in political and legal terms. In political terms because it is constituted from politicians of the "second set", who are not government members but elected by state parliaments; in legal terms because the Austrian Federal Council has considerably less power in legislative procedure at the federal level.

[114] The crucial legal foundations are Art 23d Austrian Federal Constitutional Law, the Agreement between the Federal Republic and States according to Art 15a Federal Constitutional Law (BGBl 1992/775) and the Intermediate State Agreement, LGBl Wien 1992/29. For details see C Grabenwarter, 'Änderungen der österreichischen Bundesverfassung aus Anlaß des Beitritts zur Europäischen Union', (1995) 55 *Zeitschrift für ausländisches öffentliches Recht und Völkerrecht* 166 at 171; Schäffer, 'Österreichischer Länderbericht', in Schwarze (ed), above n 12, 375 *et seq*.

[115] Art 23d(5) Austrian Federal Constitutional Law.

[116] The states considered withholding their consent but in the event did not do so. The pressure upon them not to delay the entry into force of the Accession Treaty was too great.

have the right to be informed and to express their views (Article 23d(1) Federal Constitutional Law).[117]

The devolution of Scotland and Wales in 1998 also raised the question concerning the participation rights of these decentralised entities within the United Kingdom.[118] Admittedly, the peculiarity here is that the *transfer of jurisdiction* to the devolved parts of the country took place at a time when European integration had already been completed. Therefore, the issue did not concern the defence of existing jurisdiction with regard to constituent states; rather, it concerned the allocation or "decentralisation" of centralised state jurisdiction. A legally non-binding agreement was made between the government of the United Kingdom on the one hand and the regional governments of Scotland (*Scottish Ministers*) and Wales (*Cabinet of the National Assembly for Wales*) on the other. This agreement comprises a *memorandum of understanding* and individual *supplementary agreements*.[119] Accordingly, a *Joint Ministerial Committee* (JMC) was established as a central co-ordination board consisting of representatives from the executives of the bodies involved. Nevertheless, co-ordination largely takes the form of co-operation between the relevant ministries for the case in question. As additional regulations, separate *Concordats on Co-operation of European Union Policy Issues* together with further *Concordats* between the individual ministries for individual matters were concluded for Scotland and Wales. These *Concordats on Co-operation of European Union Policy Issues* are expressly non-binding ("intended to be binding in honour only"). They enact *inter alia* information duties, participation rights in the expression of the British opinion on different policies together with the right to attend meetings of the Council of Ministers and other meetings. According to such *Concordats*, the Scottish and Welsh executives are completely and continuously involved within the framework of the development, negotiation and implementation of political opinions which affect the jurisdiction of the constituent bodies. In this respect, an effective and uniform negotiation strategy should be guaranteed particularly in light of negotiations held

[117] The extra-political participation of the Swiss cantons is also mentioned in this respect. According to Art 55 of the Federal Constitution of 1999 (BV) the cantons are granted a right to participate in extra-political decisions "which concern their responsibilities or their significant interests". The Federation is obliged to notify the cantons punctually and comprehensively and to hear their views. Finally, Art 55(3) BV establishes that: "The position of the Cantons shall have particular weight when their powers are concerned. In these cases, the Cantons shall participate in international negotiations as appropriate." Cf T Cottier and C Germann, 'Die Partizipation bei der Aushandlung neuer völkerrechtlicher Bindungen', in D Thürer, J-C Aubert and JP Müller (eds), *Verfassungsrecht in der Schweiz* (2001) § 5, particularly para 27.

[118] Cf R Grote, 'Regionalautonomie für Schottland und Wales', (1998) 58 *Zeitschrift für ausländisches öffentliches Recht und Völkerrecht* 109 *et seq.*

[119] Memorandum of Understanding and supplementary agreements between the United Kingdom Government, Scottish Ministers and the Cabinet of the National Assembly for Wales, October 1999, Cm 4444. This also governs the participation rights of the Northern Ireland Executive Committee.

under time pressure. Even if the leadership of negotiations remains the right of central government, Scottish or Welsh representatives can represent the previously agreed British position in the Council under certain circumstances.

The Spanish Constitution adopts a third method by means of the autonomous communities (*Comunidades Autónomas*, "CCAA"). This method basically protects the character of the nation state and grants decentralised entities only limited participation rights.

Since the accession of Spain, there have been differences in opinion between the government and the CCAA concerning the latter's participation in the European legislative process. All attempts at co-operation failed during the first years of membership. Initially, the autonomous Communities attempted to make contact with European institutions by informal means mainly in order to avoid further centralisation at the national level.[120] Once the communities had recognised that such means met with little success, a parliamentary initiative at the beginning of 1989 during the Spanish EC presidency persuaded the government to adopt agreements according to the area or theme concerned. The most obvious example of this phase was a conference on European affairs which took place towards the end of 1988. Only in 1994 was a model for co-operation created which was subsequently enacted.[121] This also bears strong similarities to the German model. Nevertheless, there are substantial differences. The organs involved in enforcing interests of the autonomous communities are the *Conferencia para Asuntos Relacionados con las Comunidades Europeas* together with the subject-related *Conferencias sectoriales*, which most closely resemble the German Ministers Conference. Like the Austrian Integration Conference, they do not have any influence on legislation at the nation level. Moreover, the representative of central government is also a member and commands the right of veto. Accordingly, the Spanish state structure clearly resembles a politically decentralised nation-state. It does not constitute a federal state consisting of Member States but a "complex nation-state".[122]

A comparison of Belgium, Germany, Austria, Great Britain and Spain shows very clearly that any differences in the extent of constitutional amendments and the degree of participation are mainly determined by the weight of the federal entities. In a state where the federal bodies exercise a strong centrifugal force as in Belgium, the corresponding entities could assume complete representation in some cases. In addition, it succeeds

[120] On this and the following Börzel, above n 1, 113 *et seq*.

[121] Ley 2/1997, de 13 de marzo, por la que se regula la Conferencia para Asuntos Relacionados con las Comunidades Europeas: see B Fernández Pérez, 'La Ley 2/1997, de 13 de marzo, por la que se regula la Conferencia para Asuntos Relacionados con las Comunidades Europeas', (1997) XLIX *Revista Espanola de Derecho Internacional* 314.

[122] F Segado quoted in IC Ibán, *Einführung in das spanische Recht* (1995) 84.

where such entities as in Germany and Austria are better able to prevent themselves from being bought off by compensatory concessions, accomplished by ratifying an agreement which takes the further development of Union law into account.[123] However, the relationship between these two states differs greatly which is explained by the comparatively weaker position of the Austrian states, in particular, of the Federal Council.

If one looks for similarities in the adaptation procedure and its result, then two interrelated modifications become apparent. The first one concerns a defining characteristic of federal statehood, i.e. that the federal bodies exercise their legislative powers within a certain system of jurisdiction. These powers are exercised insofar as European legislation now takes place in this area by the "extended" procedure and, in particular, by involvement in the participation of the Federal Republic in the EU. Participation federalism is replacing jurisdictional federalism:[124] the Federal Council's rights to exclusive decision-making by consent or objection or in general by federal states exercising their legislative powers are being exchanged for participation rights.

This introduces the second modification which concerns the separation of powers between the legislative and executive. Participation rights are created by the Federal Council itself or by leading representatives of the executive of federal entities directly. This is achieved either via representatives nominated by the Federal Council or via members of "State Conferences" and, in particular, by co-operating with the Federal Republic. In Belgium this depends on which "category" representatives of federalised constituent areas fall under. The "losers" are the state parliaments and the relevant legislative organs. In the end, what they are left with is that the state governments and their relevant organs are also responsible for European policy and that they are allowed to implement Directives into law.[125] The participation procedure therefore serves to reinforce executive federalism.[126]

[123] Concerning Germany see Börzel, above n 1, 68 *et seq.*

[124] Cf Müller-Terpitz, above n 106, 357; D Reich, 'Zum Einfluss des Europäischen Gemeinschaftsrechts auf die Kompetenzen der deutschen Bundesländer', (2001) *Europäische Grundrechte-Zeitschrift* 1 at 11 *et seq*; T Stein, 'Europäische Union: Gefahr oder Chance für den Föderalismus in Deutschland, Österreich und der Schweiz', (1994) 53 *Veröffentlichungen der Vereinigung der Deutschen Staatsrechtslehrer* 26 at 36 *et seq*; M Schweitzer, *ibid*, 48 at 62 *et seq.*

[125] Sometimes, the state constitutions provide for the involvement of state parliaments in resolutions for the Federal Council. Eg Art 34a of the State Constitution of Baden-Württemberg: the State Council has to be informed of and involved in all plans relating to the European Union which are of paramount political importance and substantially affect significant state interests or the legislative jurisdiction of the states directly. On this and further examples: K Zwicker, *Als Bundesstaat in die Europäische Union* (2000) 225 *et seq.*

[126] This tendency is also noticeable in Switzerland where the cantons established the so-called "Conference of Canton Governments" [*Konferenz der Kantonsregierungen* (KDK)] in October 1993 in order to represent the cantons' interests in the formation of foreign policy in a co-ordinated way in relation to the federation: cf T Fleiner and N Töpperwien, 'Chancen und Probleme für den schweizerischen Föderalismus nach einem Beitritt zur Europäischen Union', in T Cottier and A Kopše (eds), *Der Beitritt der Schweiz zur Europäischen Union* (1998) 323 at 334 *et seq*; K Nuspliger, 'Vernetzung führt zum Erfolg', in T Cottier and A Caplazi (eds), *Die Kantone im Integrationsprozess* (2000) 29.

Altogether, the participation rights of federal entities appear to provide some compensation for the loss of legislative autonomy. However, such compensation is by no means adequate.[127] All the same, however, following erosive tendencies, particularly in the 1970s, the federal entities were reinforced by adaptation to national constitutions in the 1990s. This reinforcement is, in turn, supported by the European Union owing to constitutional development in the wake of the Maastricht Treaty.

4. The Position of National Parliaments

According to the principles of democratic constitutions, adaptation can be noticed in three areas, *viz* the adoption of plebiscite elements, the participation of national parliaments in Community legislation and changes relating to the right to vote in municipal elections induced by European legal development. At this point, only the second area will be subject to a comparative investigation, the right to vote in municipal elections will be discussed in connection with fundamental rights,[128] plebiscite elements are referred to in the concluding chapter.[129]

To a large extent, constitutional adaptations aim to protect the democratic legitimisation of the legislative process in the European Union. This aim is clearly expressed by the structural guarantee clauses of the Member States' constitutions. Such an example is Article 23(1) of German Basic Law, which not only obliges the Union to protect democratic principles (*structural guarantee directed towards the Union*), but also imposes qualified obligation on the Basic Law to protect these principles in conjunction with Union law *via* the reference to Article 79(3) Basic Law. The Federal Constitutional Court expresses the reciprocal effect between Union law and national constitutional law by its demand that national parliaments assume "tasks and powers of substantial importance".[130] In this respect, the rights of national parliaments to participate in the legislative process can largely perform the function of compensation provided that democratic legitimisation is still deficient at the European level in comparison with that at the national level.[131]

How do constitutional legislators in Member States react to the national parliaments' loss of powers? Regulations have been adopted in this respect at the constitutional level in Germany, France, Denmark as well as in the most recent accession states of Sweden, Austria and Finland. Besides this, there are extra-constitutional participation rights, one example being those of the parliament in Great Britain. The motive for corresponding

[127] So too König, above n 88, 415.
[128] See 5 a).
[129] See IV 1.
[130] *Entscheidungen des Bundesverfassungsgerichts* 89, 155 at 186 (*Maastricht*).
[131] *Ibid*; HD Jarass and B Pieroth, *Grundgesetz* (2002), Art 23, para 28; R Scholz, *Europäische Union und nationales Verfassungsrecht* (1994) 12 at 16 *et seq*.

constitutional amendments resembles that in relation to federalism. This also aims to compensate the loss of influence by granting parliaments the right to participate in the European legislative process.

The regulations of Member States certainly differ in detail. However, they are similar in principle. The instrument employed by the constitutions in order to protect the influence of parliaments essentially consists of two components, *viz* information rights and participation rights in the form of rights to express their opinion.[132] Under certain circumstances, the Member State's representative can be obliged to express Parliament's opinion to the Council in a given case.

The constitutions of almost all Member States grant the Parliament *information rights*. Only Luxembourg does not provide for such a legal obligation[133] and in Great Britain and Ireland it exists on the basis of *convention*.[134]

The second component, i.e. the *participation of the parliament* in the decision-making process is common to all constitutions. However, the instruments of participation are to varying degrees developed. They encompass the mere reports of the *Select Committee on European Legislation* in Great Britain,[135] the consideration of opinions in Germany,[136] the (essentially unqualified) binding effect of opinions in Austria[137] and the reservations of consent or mandates for the benefit of the Parliament in Denmark.[138] Ultimately, there are two constitutions which also recognise duties of the government to report to Parliament in order to facilitate an ex-post control in conjunction with the updating of ministerial responsibility.[139] Finally, one noticeable peculiarity is the participation of the Austrian parliament in personnel decisions within the framework of the European Union.[140]

[132] Eg Art 23(3) German Basic Law; Art 161 Portuguese Constitution; Art 23e Austrian Federal Constitutional Law.

[133] D Bossaert, 'The Luxembourg Chamber of Deputies: From a Toothless Tiger to a Critical Watchdog?', in A Maurer and W Wessels (eds), *National Parliaments on their Ways to Europe* (2001) 301 at 306; HG Kamann, *Die Mitwirkung der Parlamente der Mitgliedstaaten an der europäischen Gesetzgebung* (1997) 148.

[134] Cf Kamann, above n 133, 124 *et seq*, 136. In the United Kingdom "conventions of the Constitution" are regarded as extra-legal rules of constitutional conduct which are binding but not directly enforceable by the courts or the presiding officers in Parliament.

[135] Cf P Weber-Panariello, *Nationale Parlamente in der Europäischen Union* (1995) 47 *et seq*.

[136] Cf Art 23(3) German Basic Law.

[137] Cf Art 23e(2) Austrian Federal Constitutional Law; H Schäffer, 'Österreichs Beteiligung an der Willensbildung in der Europäischen Union, insbesondere an der europäischen Rechtssetzung', (1996) 50 *Zeitschrift für öffentliches Recht* 3 at 54 *et seq*; *id*, 'Österreichischer Länderbericht', in Schwarze (ed), above n 12, 377 *et seq*.

[138] On the resultant legal situation in Denmark, see Kamann, above n 133, 60 *et seq*; F Laursen, 'The Danish Folketing and its European Affairs Committee,' in Maurer and Wessels (eds), above n 133, 99 at 104 *et seq*.

[139] Cf concerning Denmark: Kamann, above n 133, 61; on Austria: Arts 23e(4) and 142(2)(c) Federal Constitutional Law, in detail: Grabenwarter, above n 114, 180 *et seq*.

[140] Art 23c(2) of the Austrian Federal Constitutional Law.

Differences in details notwithstanding, the procedure is characterised by a great degree of uniformity. The essential documents must be delivered regularly as required by constitutional law; the governmental representative only gives his opinion once the national participation procedure has been concluded. Once the Parliament has formed an opinion this is usually not binding.[141]

When comparing countries, the *Danish* and *Austrian* parliaments (*Folketing* and *Nationalrat* respectively), which have the right to issue a binding opinion according to national law, display the strongest participation rights. The legal situation in Denmark results from the parliament's traditionally strong position in relation to foreign affairs.[142] However, the adoption of the Austrian regulation which otherwise followed the Danish model was the result of a temporary shift of power in the national council.[143]

At the opposite end of the spectrum are the French and Greek parliaments. In France, the parliament's right to participate in its present form was only achieved in proceedings before the *Conseil constitutionnel*. The court held that constitutional amendment was necessary in order to grant the Parliament an (indirect) channel of influence over the French government's attitude in the Council.[144] According to Article 88-4 of the Constitution, which did no more than implement the standards of the *Maastricht I*-Decision, the government submitted to the national assembly and the senate those bills or proposals for legal acts of the EC and the European Union containing legal measures. The two chambers could (only) pass resolutions on such drafts and proposals as well as other documents.[145]

The participation of the *Greek* parliament is also weakly developed. Initially, Article 3 of the Act Ratifying Accession only required the government to submit a report on the development of European affairs to the parliament before the end of its annual term.[146] In 1990, a Commission for

[141] Concerning the Federal Council practice: KD Schnapauff, 'Der neue Europaartikel in der staatlichen Praxis', (1997) 12 *Zeitschrift für Gesetzgebung* 188 at 190 *et seq*; F Pflüger, *Die Beteiligung der Parlamente in der europäischen Verfassungsentwicklung*, presentation held at the Walter Hallstein Institute for European Constitutional Law of the Humboldt-Universität in Berlin on 24 April 2001, available under <http://www.whi-berlin.de/pflueger.htm> (15 May 2004).

[142] Cf Kamann, above n 133, 55; J Albaek Jensen, 'Prior Parliamentary Consent to Danish EU Policies', in E Smith (ed), *National Parliaments as Cornerstones of European Integration* (1996) 40.

[143] Immediately following the referendum on EC accession and prior to accession, the coalition government lost its Parliamentary majority of two thirds which is the proportion necessary for constitutional amendments. The opposition was then able to demand a price for its consent both to the other constitutional changes necessary and the Treaty of Accession. It demanded stronger rights for the Parliament and was also able to enforce them.

[144] Eg Gundel, above n 38, 479.

[145] In more detail Kamann, above n 133, 102 *et seq*; Weber-Panariello, above n 135, 162 *et seq*.

[146] Evrigenis, above n 43, 168; Bernasconi and Spirou, above n 43, 186.

European Affairs was established consisting of 25 members. The Commission has consultative powers only. It follows current affairs in the Community and general European policy and issues a report in which it can also make recommendations.[147] However, the government does not provide prior information on a regular basis. Similarly, the government is not bound to follow the recommendations and its practical influence is extremely low.[148]

At the constitutional level, there are two aspects relating to adaptations of the traditional legislative procedure in Parliament. Plans within the framework of the participation procedure are dealt with by individual committees. As a rule, their members are specialists in European affairs in order to ensure effective participation by their compact size, specialisation and expertise which is increased thereby. The second aspect of adaptation is related to this: In order to comply with the legislative process at European level, plans in Parliament must be dealt with within short periods. Constitutions or the laws to be implemented sometimes stipulate precise periods or are content with approximate stipulations such as "at the earliest opportunity",[149] "immediately" or "reasonable".[150]

On paper, Parliaments sometimes appear to have extensive powers; nevertheless, participation in the legislative procedure of the European Union does not adequately compensate the loss of legislative powers. In Germany, for example, provisions such as Article 23(1) Basic Law show that only the government really has the institutional and functional legitimisation to participate in supranational legislation. This represents a shift in the functional order contained in the German *Grundgesetz*. Parliament's control over government replaces autonomous legislation.[151] Additionally, the practice in states which recognise greater powers of the Parliament does not differ from that of other states as greatly as constitutional texts may suggest. Accordingly, there has never been any serious resistance or restriction of governmental discretion, not to mention genuine conflict during the six years of Austria's membership.[152] In Denmark, the mandates of the Market Committee of the *Folketing* are broadly interpreted following a case of conflict. Consequently, the governmental representative is left with a certain freedom of negotiation which serves to avoid conflict.[153] The realisation that infringements of the bond in national constitutional law do not affect

[147] Bernasconi and Spirou, above n 43, 186 *et seq*; Papadimitriou, above n 75, 168; P Zervakis and N Yannis, 'The Parliament of Greece', in Maurer and Wessels (eds), above n 133, 147 at 160.

[148] Kamann, above n 133, 118.

[149] § 3 Implementing Act (AusfG) to Art 23(2) German Basic Law, also § 5.

[150] Art 23d(1) of the Austrian Federal Constitutional Law.

[151] M Kaufmann, *Europäische Integration und Demokratieprinzip* (1997) 485 *et seq*.

[152] See also the first interim balance by Schäffer, above n 137, 60 *et seq*.

[153] Weber-Panariello, above n 135, 308.

the validity of a legal act at Union level may also contribute to the fact that Parliaments have little practical influence.

The Constitutional Treaty would incorporate a number of elements of national constitutional law defined above in a general way that matches the provisions of national constitutional law. In two protocols national Parliaments appear in a very prominent way that is partly based on existing national constitutional law or will call for respective provisions in the future.

First of all the *Protocol on the Application of the Principles of Subsidiarity and Proportionality* provides in its No 3 that the Commission shall send all its legislative proposals and its amended proposals to the national Parliaments of the Member States at the same time as to the Union legislator. Upon adoption, legislative resolutions of the European Parliament and positions of the Council of Ministers shall be sent to the national Parliaments as well. Within six weeks the national Parliament may submit a reasoned opinion stating why it considers that the proposal in question does not comply with the principle of subsidiarity (No 5). With regard to regional parliaments with legislative powers, the Protocol provides for the possibility to consult them without any legal obligation ("it will be for each national parliament ... to consult, where appropriate...").[154] This must be understood in such way that European law is open for a legal obligation under national (constitutional) law.

The procedure to be followed in case of a reasoned opinion includes the obligation to take account of the reason (No 6 para 1 of the Protocol), the number of votes allocated to the various parliaments and chambers (para 2), and the Commission's obligation to review the proposal in the case of a "qualified opinion", i.e. when it represents one third of all the votes of parliaments which is roughly eight national parliaments where there is no bicameral system. Whatever the Commission decides it has to give reasons for its decisions. Finally, in order to ensure some effectiveness of the principle of subsidiarity, the Protocol provides for a right to bring actions on grounds of an alleged infringement of this principle. However, actions may only be brought by the Member States or "notified by them in accordance with their legal order on behalf of their national Parliament or a chamber of it (No 7 of the Protocol).

The Protocol on the Role of National Parliaments in the European Union refers in its preamble to the control of national parliaments over their respective governments and their activities in the European Union and expresses the will to increase the involvement of national Parliaments in the activities of the Union. For this purpose the Protocol contains a number of obligations on the side of European institutions to inform national

[154] Cf P Straub, 'Der Verfassungsentwurf des EU-Konvents aus Sicht der Länder und ihrer Parlamente', in J Schwarze (ed), *Der Verfassungsentwurf des Europäischen Konvents* (2004), 37 at 38 *et seq.*

Parliaments (Part I). Moreover, Part II provides for interparliamentary co-operation between the European Parliament and national parliaments.

These two examples are significant for a stronger mutual interrelation between national institutions and European institutions and as a consequence between national constitutional law and European law in the field of organisational law.

5. Fundamental Rights

That fundamental rights were and are directly affected by Community law is shown most clearly by the case law of the Federal Constitutional Court on individual powers of revision relating to the protection of fundamental rights. The accession of France to the Human Rights Convention, the joint declaration of the Council, Commission and Parliament of 1977, the case law accumulating on the fundamental rights of the ECJ with increasing references to the Human Rights Convention, amendments of primary Community law relating to fundamental rights and finally the proclamations of the Charter of Fundamental Rights represent the most important milestones. This development also affects national constitutions. In contrast to the areas hitherto described, changes in this area—with the exception of the right to vote in municipal elections—are expressed less by the wording of the constitutional texts than changes to the case law of the constitutional and supreme courts.

Concerning the legal mechanisms of effect emanating from Union law, five different types of changes can be distinguished:

a) Expanding the scope of national guarantees of fundamental rights directly demanded by Community law,
b) changes and expansions effected by Community law to the protection of fundamental rights within its scope,
c) reinforcing and changing the effect of the Human Rights Convention within the national area,
d) indirect effects of Community law on the scope of national guarantees of fundamental rights and finally,
e) matching national fundamental rights with increased standards at European level.

a) Expanding the Scope of National Guarantees of Fundamental Rights Demanded by Community Law: The Example of the Right to Vote in Municipal Elections

Classifying the right to vote in elections at municipal level as a fundamental right might not be immediately obvious. However, this classification is justified by the fact that this right is governed by the same principles which apply in Germany to the right to vote at federal and State levels and the corresponding classification in the constitutions of other Member States.[155] The Charter of Fundamental Rights also classifies the right to vote in municipal elections contained in Article 38 under Citizens' Rights in its 5th Chapter.

The guarantee of voting rights for EU foreigners at municipal level and its detailed form in Directive 80/94 first anchored in Article 8b(1) EC Treaty and subsequently in Article 19(1) EC required a series of amendments in a number of states because foreigners were, for democratic reasons, not permitted to participate in elections. During the run-up to amendments at Union level, the constitutional courts dealt with this question in order to clarify the amendments required and not least with regard to the issue of sovereignty and the state. By way of example, developments in Germany, France and Spain show the different amendment strategies.

In *Germany*, the Federal Constitutional Court clarified the requirements of constitutional adaptations on different grounds but at a time when the Directive on the right to vote in municipal elections was already looming. In 1990 two judgments of the Federal Constitutional Court declared that the right to vote granted to foreigners by statute in Schleswig-Holstein and Hamburg at municipal levels was unconstitutional.[156] The Court interpreted Article 20(2) Basic Law to the effect that the "people" legitimising state authority is the people of the Federal Republic of Germany. The state could not be conceived without the entirety of the people who were the holders and subjects of state power.[157] Membership of the German state people is bestowed by nationality.[158] According to the Federal Constitutional Court's interpretation, the Constitution merely granted the right to vote on federal and State levels to German nationals and that a right to vote for foreigners was accordingly unconstitutional.[159] At municipal level, the Court decided that municipal self-government was also the (indirect) exercise of state authority and that therefore the required democratic legitimisation, provided by Article 28(1) Basic Law, could similarly only be conveyed by German nationals.[160] At the same time, the Court stated in an *obiter dictum* that the introduction of a right to vote in municipal elections for EU foreigners discussed at the time could be the subject of a valid amendment to the constitution according to Article 79(3) Basic Law.[161] Owing to the clear statement of the Constitutional Court's judgment on the right to vote in municipal

[155] Cf, eg, Art 14 Finnish Constitution; Art 15(4) Portuguese Constitution.

[156] *Entscheidungen des Bundesverfassungsgerichts* 83, 37 at 60 *et seq* (*foreigners electoral law*); cf, eg, K Sieveking, 'Die Umsetzung der Richtlinie des Rates zum Kommunalwahlrecht der Unionsbürger in den deutschen Ländern', *Die öffentliche Verwaltung* (1993) 449.

[157] *Entscheidungen des Bundesverfassungsgerichts* 83, 37 at 50 (*foreigners electoral law*).

[158] *Ibid*, 51.

[159] *Ibid*, 51 *et seq* and head note 3.

[160] *Ibid*, 53 *et seq*.

[161] *Ibid*, 59; cf also Schwarze, above n 12, 149.

elections for foreigners, Article 28(1) was amended to implement the Maastricht Treaty.[162] According to sentence 3 of the newly formulated article, nationals of a Member State of the European Union are also entitled to vote and stand for election in district and municipal elections in compliance with Community law. Thereby, the Basic Law grants access to a provision of Community law and a more detailed form of the right to vote in municipal elections for EU citizens (Article 28(1) sentence 3 Basic Law as an "opening clause"[163]).

In *France*, the constitutional situation before the introduction of the right to vote in municipal elections for EU citizens was similar. The Constitutional Council held in the *Maastricht I* decision that Article 3(4) of the French Constitution only granted French citizens the right to vote and stand for election.[164] With reference to Articles 3(1) and (2), 24 and 72 of the Constitution the *Conseil constitutionnel* held that it was unconstitutional for EU citizens to participate in municipal elections because the election of senators by the municipal councils would indirectly result in non-French Union citizens participating in elections of the state senate.[165] This suggests that the *Conseil constitutionnel* judges regional and state elections differently.[166] The introduction of the right to vote in municipal elections for EU citizens, following the conclusion of the Maastricht Treaty, meant that the constitution had to be changed in France as well.[167] This amendment is notable largely because Article 88-3 of the Constitution only authorises the legislator, subject to reciprocity, to grant EU foreigners resident in France the right to vote in municipal elections.[168] The *Conseil constitutionnel* quickly showed that this discretion of the legislator had apparently relaxed the restrictions in the *Maastricht II* decision by warning the legislator to adhere to the Directive's standards when adopting the transposing Act.[169]

In *Spain*, implementation took place with fewer conflicts and ultimately went considerably further in terms of constitutional law as well. At the time of the implementation of European standards, the adaptation procedure had already been half carried out anyway, because the active right to vote for foreigners subject to the requirement of reciprocity already existed.

[162] Amending Act of 27 October 1994, BGBl I, 3146.
[163] R Scholz, in T Maunz and G Dürig (eds), *Grundgesetz: Kommentar* (loose-leaf 2001), Art 28, para 41 b.
[164] *Conseil constitutionnel*, Decision no 92-308 DC of 9 April 1992, above n 40, 187 at 190.
[165] *Ibid*.
[166] Walter, above n 42, 186.
[167] *Conseil constitutionnel*, Decision no 92-308 DC of 9 April 1992, above n 40, 187 at 192; cf also Constantinesco, above n 69, 68.
[168] Regardless of this, at constitutional level foreigners are already excluded from the office of mayor and councillor, from nomination by electors to the senate and from the senate elections themselves.
[169] *Conseil constitutionnel*, Decision 92-308 DC of 9 April 1992, above n 164, 187.

Besides, the Constitutional Court held that according to constitutional law, the right of EU citizens to vote in municipal elections did not contravene Article 23.1 of the Spanish Constitution which guaranteed citizens the right to political participation. This guarantee is, in principle, limited to Spanish nationals but can also be extended to foreigners on the basis of the general clause of Article 13.1 of the Constitution. However, this required Article 13.2 of the Constitution to be changed which only granted foreigners the right *to vote in elections*. The new article now grants foreigners the right to stand for elections and—like the existing regulation—without restriction to Union citizens. As to whether foreigners' participation in municipal elections infringes Article 1.2, according to which the Spanish people are the sole holders of sovereignty, the Constitutional Court held that the municipalities do not exercise powers which are connected to the exercise of Spanish sovereignty.[170]

b) Increased Protection of Fundamental Rights within the Scope of Community Law: The Example of Equal Treatment of Men and Women

Community law recognises different special principles of equal treatment which are found in both primary and secondary law. The equal treatment of men and women in relation to education, appointments, working conditions and payment is guaranteed by Article 141 EC and the Equal Treatment Directive.[171] Article 12 EC prohibits discrimination on grounds of nationality in relation to cross-border cases, the details of which are more precisely structured in the fundamental freedoms of the internal market. Further prohibitions on discrimination can be found in connection with the fundamental freedoms of the internal market.[172] Prohibitions on discrimination and principles of equal treatment located at different levels have influenced national constitutional law in different ways and complement each other.

Community law exercises considerable influence over national (constitutional) law particularly in relation to the equal treatment of men and women.[173] Without the facts of any case needing to possess a cross-border dimension, women and men must be equally treated in relation to education, appointments, working conditions and payment in accordance with Article 141 EC and the equal treatment Directive—anywhere from training as a tax-advisor to recruitment by the army.[174] This is often connected to a

[170] Cf A López Castillo and J Polakiewicz, 'Verfassung und Gemeinschaftsrecht in Spanien', (1993) *Grundrechte-Zeitschrift* 277 at 282; Muñoz Machado, above n 2, 32 *et seq*.
[171] Dir 76/207/EEC, OJ L 39, 14.2.1976, 40.
[172] M Holoubek, in: J Schwarze (ed), *EU-Kommentar* (2000) Art 12 EC, paras 7 *et seq*.
[173] Cf J Kokott, 'Zur Gleichstellung von Mann und Frau', (1995) *Neue Juristische Wochenschrift* 1049.
[174] See Case C-1/95, *Gerster* [1997] ECR I-5253; Case C-273/97, *Sirdar* [1999] ECR I-7403; Case C-285/98, *Kreil* [2000] ECR I-69.

change in or at least a supplement to the national reserve of fundamental rights. This influence is particularly apparent in Germany and Ireland.

Using Germany as an example, the effects on the scope of protection according to Article 3(2) Basic Law can be clearly shown by two examples. First, Article 141 EC and the equal treatment Directive extend to the whole of working life and thereby do not only bind the state—in contrast to Article 3(2) Basic Law. Only in its decision to prohibit night work did the Federal Constitutional Court transfer this protective policy to the interpretation of Article 3(2) by the notion of protective duty.[175] Second, the ECJ's consideration of factual discrimination influenced the case law of the Federal Constitutional Court on Article 3(2) Basic Law. If at first only rules relating to gender[176] were believed to infringe Article 3(2) Basic Law, the Federal Constitutional Court now interprets the article to the effect that it demands the creation of *de facto* equality of the sexes.[177] In a further decision following the amendment of Article 3 in 1994, the Federal Constitutional Court also regarded positive discrimination as constitutional[178] in order to create *de facto* equality, whilst the ECJ continues to interpret the principle of equal treatment in the sense of strict equality.[179]

In relation to German constitutional law, the equal treatment regime of Community law has entailed further consequences. Until 2000, women were barred from military service in the Bundeswehr according to Article 12a(4) Basic Law. According to the prevailing opinion in legal scholarship[180] and the case law of the Federal Administrative Court (Bundesverwaltungsgericht)[181] they were only allowed to be employed in the Bundeswehr as medics or military musicians. The ECJ held that this practice was incompatible with the equal treatment Directive 76/207/EEC in a decision which caused great excitement in Germany. According to the Luxembourg Court, the Directive also applied to the areas of internal and external security, gender did not constitute any essential requirement for the employment relationship and the complete exclusion from armed service

[175] *Entscheidungen des Bundesverfassungsgerichts* 85, 191 at 207 (*prohibitition of night work*); cf CD Classen, 'Wechselwirkungen zwischen deutschem und europäischem Grundrechtsschutz', in G Manssen (ed), *Grundrechte im Umbruch* (1997) 61 at 70 *et seq.*

[176] *Entscheidungen des Bundesverfassungsgerichts* 85, 191 at 207 (*prohibition of night-work*); 52, 369 at 375 *et seq* (*day off for housewives*); 92, 91 at 109 (*fire-service contribution*).

[177] *Entscheidungen des Bundesverfassungsgerichts* 85, 191 at 207 (*prohibition of night-work*); *Entscheidungen des Bundesverfassungsgerichts* 89, 276 at 285 (*see 611a German civil code*); cf Classen, above n 175, 72; *id*, 'Wie viele Wege führen zur Gleichberechtigung von Männern und Frauen?', (1996) *Juristenzeitung*, 921 at 922.

[178] *Entscheidungen des Bundesverfassungsgerichts* 92, 91 at 109 (*fire-service contribution*).

[179] Case C-450/93, *Kalanke* [1995] ECR I-3051, paras 21 *et seq*; Case C-409/95, *Marschall* [1997] ECR I-6363, paras 25 *et seq*; cf Classen, above n 175, 73.

[180] In preference to many, R Scholz, in: Maunz and Dürig (eds), above n 163, Art 12a, paras 196 *et seq*; F Kirchhof, 'Bundeswehr', in J Isensee and P Kirchhof (eds), *Handbuch des Staatsrechts der Bundesrepublik Deutschland* (2000), vol III, § 78, para 42.

[181] Eg *Entscheidungen des Bundesverwaltungsgerichts* 103, at 301.

was neither reasonable nor necessary in order to achieve the aim of guaranteeing public security.[182] In German legal scholarship it was debated whether Article 12a(4) Basic Law prevented women from performing military service on a voluntary basis. Accordingly, the constitutional legislator made a minor amendment to the wording of the relevant sentence in Article 12a(4) to make clear that women also have voluntary access to the Bundeswehr even though such service is military in nature.[183]

c) Reinforcing and Changing the Effect of the European Convention on Human Rights in the National Area

Union law also influences the constitutions of Member States in relation to fundamental rights, insofar as this area gives rise to an increase of the influence of the Human Rights Convention or changes in the content of fundamental rights' guarantees of the Human Rights Convention.

The reinforcement of the protection of fundamental rights at national level induced by Union law can be illustrated by many examples: for instance the enactment of the Human Rights Act in Great Britain, which transformed the Human Rights Convention into national law, while in Sweden the incorporation of the Human Rights Convention into national law was directly connected with EU accession which took place at the same time.[184] The ratification of the Protocol No 6 to the Human Rights Convention by Belgium, Great Britain and Greece is the direct consequence of the first Declaration of the governmental conference on the ratification of the Amsterdam Treaty on the abolition of the death penalty.[185]

Where the Human Rights Convention takes precedence over national law or influences the interpretation of fundamental rights,[186] Union law increasingly serves to modify the substance of fundamental rights. Examples are the "reception terms", such as "aliens" in Article 16 Human Rights Convention and "legislative institution" in the guarantees of the right to vote contained in Article 3, Protocol No 1 to the Human Rights

[182] Case C-285/98, *Kreil* [2000] ECR I-69, paras 15 *et seq*. Concerning the judgment see R Streinz, 'Frauen an die Front', (2000) *Deutsches Verwaltungsblatt* 285 *et seq*; R Scholz, 'Frauen an die Waffe kraft Europarechts?', (2000) *Die öffentliche Verwaltung* 417 *et seq*; C Koch, 'Commentary', (2000) *Deutsches Verwaltungsblatt*, 476 *et seq*; Schwarze, above n 12, 152 *et seq*.

[183] According to the new legal situation, women may not "under any circumstances be obliged to perform armed service."

[184] U Bernitz, The Incorporation of the European Human Rights Convention into Swedish law, 38 *German Yearbook of International Law* (1995) 178 at 181.

[185] When the Treaty of Amsterdam was signed, the governmental conference accepted Declaration no 1 on the abolition of the death penalty in which it was pointed out, with reference to Art 6(2) EU, that the 6th Protocol had been signed and ratified by a large majority of Member States.

[186] Cf C Grabenwarter, 'Europäisches und nationales Verfassungsrecht', (2001) 60 *Veröffentlichungen der Vereinigung der Deutschen Staatsrechtslehrer,* 292 at 299 *et seq*.

Convention. Article 16 of the Convention allows the political activity of aliens to be restricted in relation to Articles 10, 11 and 14 Human Rights Convention. However, the legal development in Union law leads to the term "aliens" in Article 16 of the Convention being restricted to nationals of third party states. Consequently, EU foreigners are placed on an equal footing to citizens when exercising rights according to Articles 10, 11 and 14 of the Convention at least for canvassing purposes before elections to the European Parliament. The term "legislature" in Article 3 Protocol No 1 to the Human Rights Convention, which was originally only intended to constitute a guarantee for national parliaments, refers to national constitutional law. Its interpretation must take the constitutional structures of the state concerned into account.[187] On this basis, the ECHR has confirmed the applicability of Article 3 Protocol No 1 to elections for the European Parliament.[188] The ECHR held that the European Parliament did not fall outside the scope of Article 3 Protocol No 1 only because it was a supranational and not a purely national organ. By referring to the relevant provisions prior to and following the entry into force of the Maastricht Treaty, the ECHR concluded that the European Parliament was sufficiently bound into the general democratic supervision of activities of the European Communities to represent part of the legislative body for the Member States of the Community.

d) Indirect Effects of Community Law on the Scope of National Guarantees of Fundamental Rights

Effects on the scope of national guarantees of fundamental rights stem finally from the interplay between the fundamental freedoms of the EC treaty on the one hand and national fundamental rights on the other. The latter concern those rights which apply to nationals and EU foreigners equally as well as those limited to state citizens.

In the first case, the improved position of foreigners ("reverse discrimination") required by EC law could conflict with the general principle of equality. The legal position of EU foreigners as a comparable group has been withdrawn from the regulatory power of national legislators and is governed by supranational law.[189] National constitutional law sees itself confronted with the problem that Community law is not part of national law but part of the legal system applicable in the Member State.

187 Cf *Mathieu-Mohin et Clerfayt v Belgien* ECHR [1987] Series A No 113, para 53; *X v Österreich* ECHR [1976] DR 6, 120; *Timke v Germany* ECHR [1995] DR 82-A, 158.

188 ECHR, *Matthews v United Kingdom* Rep 1999-I 251, paras 39 and 54.

189 H Weis, 'Inländerdiskriminierung zwischen Gemeinschaftsrecht und nationalem Verfassungsrecht', (1983) *Neue Juristische Wochenschrift* 2721 at 2725.

Assuming that Article 3(1) Basic Law applies to cases of reverse discrimination,[190] then it also extends to Community law as a full principle of equality within the legal system of the Federal Republic. Even if the unequal treatment of nationals and EC foreigners is ultimately based on Community law, then the national legislator can satisfy its international obligation in different ways. Both national and Community law also leave open the possibility of releasing nationals from an oppressive regulation. Therefore, national legislators remain responsible for the distinction between nationals and foreigners[191] and this constitutes a disadvantage in the rights according to Article 3(1) Basic Law. However, discrimination can be justified if there is sufficient objective justification and the disadvantage of nationals is kept within limits.[192]

The Austrian Constitutional Court did not have any doubt that the national principle of equality applied to cases of reverse discrimination from the outset. It assumes that Austrian laws are bound both to Community law on the one hand and national constitutional law *viz* the national principle of equality on the other.[193] National law must therefore be in conformity with the principle of equality; the fact that Community law has been implemented does not constitute sufficient justification.[194]

Only a few days before Poland's accession to the European Union, the Constitutional Tribunal held that the scope of the freedom the legislator enjoys in enacting regulations concerning restrictions on economic freedom, its delimitation and the interpretation of the notion of "important public interest", as contained in Article 22 of the Constitution, must be assessed in keeping with the fact of Poland's participation in the European Common Market. This has particular consequences in relation to the constitutional assessment of reverse discrimination—enacting restrictions on economic freedom applying only to national subjects, as their application to foreign entities from the EU is prohibited by community law. Even though discrimination acting against national entities is irrelevant in the light of community law, protection against such discrimination is the constitutional duty of national authorities.[195]

190 W Heun, in H Dreier (ed), *Grundgesetz: Kommentar* (1996), Art 3, para 10; L Osterloh, in Sachs (ed), *Grundgesetz* (1999), Art 3, para 1; contra D König, 'Das Problem der Inländerdiskriminierung', (1993) 118 *Archiv des öffentlichen Rechts* 591 at 599 *et seq*. The Federal Constitutional Court deliberately left undecided the question whether Art 3 Basic Law applied to cases of domestic discrimination, Federal Constitutional Court, Devisional Court Decision of 8th November 1989, *Neue Juristische Wochenschrift* (1990) 1033.

191 Herdegen, *Europarecht* (2001), para 100; Streinz, above n 11, para 685.

192 A Epiney, in C Calliess and M Ruffert (eds), *EUV/EGV* (2002), Art 12 EC, paras 33 *et seq*; Herdegen, above n 191, para 100; C Starck, in H von Mangoldt, F Klein and C Starck (eds), *Das Bonner Grundgesetz* (1999), Art 3(1), para 213.

193 Eg Verfassungssammlung 15106/1998.

194 Verfassungssammlung 15683/1999.

195 Judgment of the Polish Constitutional Tribunal of 21 April 2004, K 33/03 (*biocomponents in gasoline and diesel*).

The second group of indirect adaptations concerns the protection of EU foreigners' fundamental rights which are found in the scope of a fundamental freedom, but which do not come within the protection of a corresponding fundamental right of national law. In this respect, Community law may require EU foreigners to be placed in a position which is no worse than that of EU nationals. Cases of application are, for example, the fundamental rights limited to state nationals of occupational freedom in accordance with Article 12 German Basic Law or freedom of association pursuant to Article 8 Basic Law as well as the principle of equality under Austrian constitutional law.

Here, the question arises as to the way in which a guarantee of fundamental rights applicable to nationals can be granted to the EU foreigner. This may be necessary in order to take account of a principle of Community law, for instance a freedom of the internal market, or to avoid discrimination, particularly in legal protection.[196] The most convincing[197] way of solving this problem is to extend the protection of state citizens' fundamental rights to EU foreigners.[198]

In Greek constitutional law, one example of the indirect influence of Article 191 EC (ex-Article 138 EEC Treaty) on Article 29 of the Greek Constitution is the provision which grants Greek citizens the right to found and become members of political parties. Whilst the constitutional legislator originally only intended to include national parties, it is now argued—on the basis of the integration clause of Article 28(2) and (3) of the Constitution—that Union as well as Greek citizens can be active in political parties.[199]

On the level of the limits of interference with fundamental rights the fact that nationals are disadvantaged in relation to co-competitors from EC Member States might also have to be taken into account when judging the proportionality of a measure which restricts occupation (contained in the regulation disadvantaging the national). The criteria of suitability and necessity might also have to be re-evaluated in light of domestic discrimination.[200]

[196] In relation to the fundamental rights guaranteed by the German Basic Law, see A Siehr, *Die Deutschengrundrechte des Grundgesetzes* (2001) 329 *et seq*.

[197] Cf preferably the objections of H Dreier, in *id* (ed), above n 190, Preamble to Art 1, para 17; E Klein, 'Gedanken zur Europäisierung des deutschen Verfassungsrechts', in Burmeister (ed), above n 52, 1301 at 1309 *et seq*; Jarass and Pieroth, above n 131, Art 19, para 10.

[198] In relation to Art 12 German Basic Law see R Breuer, in J Isensee and P Kirchhof (eds), *Handbuch des Staatsrechts der Bundesrepublik Deutschland* (1989), vol VI, § 147, para 21; further references in PM Huber, 'Europäisches und nationales Verfassungsrecht', (2001) 60 *Veröffentlichungen der Vereinigung der Deutschen Staatsrechtslehrer* 194 at 201.

[199] Papadimitriou, above n 75, 173.

[200] Example in König, above n 190, 603 *et seq*.

e) Matching National Fundamental Rights with Increased Standards at European Level

Using the fundamental right to asylum as an example, it becomes clear how increasing co-operation at European level influences definitions of fundamental rights. It is no coincidence that the reference to safe third-party states in Article 16a(2) German Basic Law and the provision of international agreements in Article 16a(5) Basic Law emphasise EC Member States. Rather, it includes the Convention Implementing the Schengen Agreement[201] and, with regard to para (5), the Dublin Convention determining the State responsible for examining applications for asylum lodged in one of the Member States.[202]

The constitutional amendment contained in Article 53-1 of the French Constitution on the participation of France in the Schengen system is to be similarly evaluated even if it does not directly concern a provision relating to fundamental rights. The legislator amending the constitution thereby responded to the decision of the *Conseil constitutionnel* on 13 August 1993, i.e. that only a "lagging" participation granting admission, i.e. renewed review of applications for asylum already rejected in other Member States complied with the constitutional guarantee of asylum.[203]

That co-operation in the field of asylum rights still suffers from harmonisation deficiencies, is shown by the House of Lords' decision in the case *Secretary of State for the Home Department v Adan und Aitseguer.*[204] In this case, Algerian and Somalian nationals were protected from deportation to Germany or France on the grounds that these states did not qualify as safe third-party states. This is because they interpreted Article 1A of the Geneva Refugee Convention in a way which did not take into account persecution by non-state groups. As far as Germany is concerned, an approximation of judicial practice appears to be taking place following the decision of the Federal Constitution Court of 10 August 2000[205] or the judgment of the Federal Administrative Court of (Bundesverwaltungsgerichts) of 20 February 2001[206].

[201] So, too, *Entscheidungen des Bundesverfassungsgerichts* 94, 49 at 86 (*safe third-party states*).

[202] Cf B Huber, 'Das Dubliner Übereinkommen', (1998) *Neue Zeitschrift für Verwaltungsrecht* 150 *et seq*; G Lübbe-Wolf, in Dreier (ed), above n 190, Art 16a, para 102; U Davy, in E Denninger *et al* (eds), *Kommentar zum Grundgesetz für die Bundesrepublik Deutschland* (loose-leaf 2001) Art 16a, para 58.

[203] Cf Gundel, above n 38, 63 *et seq.*

[204] Judgment of 19 December 2000—R 9441 (2/2002) *Neue Zeitschrift für Verwaltungsrecht*, supp I, 17 *et seq.*

[205] (2000) *Europäische Grundrechte-Zeitschrift* 388.

[206] *Entscheidungen des Bundesverwaltungsgerichts* 114, 27.

IV. CONCLUSIONS: THE RELATIONSHIP BETWEEN NATIONAL CONSTITUTIONAL LAW AND UNION LAW

1. Bodies Acting under the Constitutional Order

The extent to which the *constitutional legislators* are active depends on the constitutional tradition in question. Whilst a series of states such as Germany, France or Ireland, as well as the more recent Member States, have predominantly made their own—partly detailed—regulations on the transfer of sovereign powers,[207] other constitutional orders are more reserved[208] without containing a general "European Article". Instead, they apply general regulations for transfers of sovereign rights. However, this does not provide any indication as to how "pro-European" the constitution is. Rather, shifts in sovereignty can be limited by a regulation specifically dealing with Europe.

If, against this background, one considers the relationship between the constitutional legislator and *constitutional courts*, then it becomes obvious that the balance of power depends on the subject. In many states, the constitutional legislators still hold the reigns of constitutional legislation as far as the law governing state organisation is concerned. In several states, constitutional changes have taken place which have adopted some detailed regulations in the constitutional text concerning the participation of parliaments and, in the case of federally organised states, the federal states or comparable entities as well. With regard to the separation of powers, a comparable situation would exist if the constitution only contained one basic rule and the ordinary legislator issued implementing regulations.

Certainly constitutional courts also help to establish the rules' starting points and basic conditions, to differing degrees. Accordingly, the Federal Constitutional Court has expressly linked parliamentary participation to the requirements of Article 23 of the German Basic Law concerning the democratic structure of the Union's legislative process.[209] The French *Conseil constitutionnel* even transformed a regulation corresponding to the later Article 88-4 of the French Constitution into a constitutional requirement for ratification of the Maastricht Treaty.[210] By comparison, regulations in other states have sometimes become constitutional law owing to the constitutional legislator's interest in protecting its own powers, and sometimes influenced by the example of other countries.

This suggests that there are two different views concerning the role of constitutional jurisdiction and legislation which are connected to the system of constitutional jurisdiction. In the French system, constitutional jurisdiction

[207] See Ch 10 § 5 Swedish Constitution; Art 93 Finnish Constitution; Arts 23a to 23f Austrian Federal Constitutional Law, as well as the Federal Constitutional Accession Act.

[208] Mainly the Benelux-States but also Spain.

[209] *Entscheidungen des Bundesverfassungsgerichts* 89, 155 at 184 *et seq* (*Maastricht*).

[210] *Conseil constitutionnel*, Decision no 92-308 DC of 9 April 1992, above n 40, 190.

usually establishes the requirements of constitutionality prior to ratification and other acts of transfer. However, in the system of *ex-post* control, as practised by the Federal Constitutional Court in compliance with the concept of the German *Grundgesetz*, the constitutional legislator plays the major role. Nevertheless in this area too, borders become blurred especially between French and German constitutional control. Whereas the Federal Constitutional Court reviewed the compatibility of the Maastricht Treaty with the standards of the *Grundgesetz* prior to its ratification by the Federal Republic of Germany, the French *Conseil constitutionnel* increasingly assumes the role of an *ex post facto* review court by subjecting past legislation or Acts of ratification to review when amending statutes or treaties.[211]

In general constitutional courts play a greater role in developing the content of fundamental rights than in the law governing state organisation. The reasons for this are less European than domestic. In most constitutions, the constitutional courts have repeatedly interpreted the texts of fundamental rights, which have remained unaltered for many years. Such texts are formulated in a relatively general way as befits the nature of a fundamental right. Throughout Europe, recourse to the constitutional courts is replacing the legislator's discretion. European courts have also contributed to this trend.

In interpreting the law, constitutional courts are coming into conflict with the ECJ. As far as the courts of Member States are concerned, such conflicts are resolved by the preliminary reference procedure found in Article 234 EC. What has today become the rule for "ordinary courts"—regardless of national differences in the willingness to make a reference[212]—still encounters considerable reservations in constitutional courts. Indeed most constitutional courts feel themselves obliged to adopt an interpretation in compliance with European law but either they do not regard themselves as a court at all pursuant to Article 234 EC[213] or avoid making a reference by concluding that—e.g. because the legal question is sufficiently clear—they are neither justified nor obliged to make a reference or to hold that non-reference by a lower court amounts to an infringement of constitutional law. In this respect, the Austrian Constitutional Court is different because in 1999 it was the first constitutional court to make a reference according to the procedure under Article 234 EC[214]; this practice has since continued in other cases.[215]

211 Cf references in Hecker, above n 65, 110 *et seq*.

212 Cf CO Lenz, 'Die Rolle des EuGH im Prozeß der Europäisierung der mitgliedstaatlichen Rechtsordnungen', in K Kreuzer, D Scheuing and U Sieber, *Die Europäisierung der mitgliedstaatlichen Rechtsordnungen in der Europäischen Union* (1997) 161 at 162 *et seq*, 174.

213 *Entscheidungen des Bundesverfassungsgerichts* 92, 203 at esp 236 *et seq* (*EEC television directive*); U Everling, 'Vorlagerecht und Vorlagepflicht nationaler Gerichte nach Art 177 EWG', in G Reichelt (ed), *Vorabentscheidungsverfahren vor dem EuGH*, 11 at 14.

214 Constitutional Court Decision, 12 December 2000, KR 1-6, 8/00, (2001) *Europäische Grundrechte-Zeitschrift* 83.

215 The House of Lords has also shown itself to be willing to make a reference, cf C Filzwieser, *Ausgewählte rechtliche Aspekte der Mitgliedschaft des Vereinigten Königreichs bei den Europäischen Gemeinschaften* (1999) 127 *et seq*.

If one considers the practice of constitutional organs in amending or interpreting constitutional law, one often gains the impression that arguments relating to the protection of democratic standards to ensure the rule of law or state sovereignty are motivated, at least in part, by the need to protect their respective powers. This can be seen most clearly in the participation of the parliaments or federal entities, primarily the German and Austrian *Länder* and the Federal Council.

Concerning amendments to treaties, the "constitutional organ" of the people still plays a role where referendums decide the development of Union law just as much as the development of the national constitution.[216] Referendums are not only held for constitutional reasons.[217] They are held partly for the political symbolism of legitimising fundamental decisions (acts of accession and amendments to treaties).[218] As a way of effecting important amendments to treaties referenda represent democratic legitimisation but their effect on other Member States can also make the ratification procedure unpredictable. Ultimately, they have consequences not only for the substance of amendments but also for the ratification procedure.[219] Structural imbalances are thereby caused in the Member States which are by no means unusual in federal systems: A few votes in a referendum can decide on whether a treaty is entered into, or in less spectacular cases, whether a treaty takes effect with or without adjustments.[220]

2. Interdependencies Between the Constitutional Orders of Member States

Many adjustments to the constitutions of Member States only appear to be directly influenced by Union law. In fact, adjustment here makes a detour being guided either by constitutional law of other Member States or influences emanating from international treaties, which bind all Member States but which do not form part of Union law.[221]

[216] See also the general overview by R Grote, 'Direkte Demokratie in den Staaten der Europäischen Union', (1996) *Staatswissenschaften und Staatspraxis* 317 *et seq.*

[217] Eg Ireland and Denmark as well as Poland from the Group of the new Member States.

[218] Eg France and Sweden; cf Bernitz, above n 24, 435 *et seq.*

[219] An example is Denmark's ratification of the Maastricht Treaty. Since in Parliament the bill did not get the required majority of 5/6, but the government stuck to the bill, according to § 20(2) sentence 2 of the Constitution, a referendum became necessary. Only in a second referendum on an amended bill a majority voted in favour of ratification. For details see H Zahle, 'Europäische Integration und nationales Verfassungsrecht in Dänemark', in U Battis, D Tsatsos and D Stefanou (eds), *Europäische Integration und nationales Verfassungsrecht* (1995) 47 at 49 *et seq.*

[220] Cf the Irish referendum of 7 June 2001, according to which 53.87% of the electorate rejected the ratification of the Treaty of Nice, see A Kellermann, 'Postscriptum–The Irish referendum on the Treaty of Nice and Article 10 EC', in *id*, de Zwaan and Czuczai (eds), above n 6, 499.

[221] On these see R Uerpmann-Wittzack, in this volume. For a typology of adaptations in the relationship between several constitutions in the wider sense Bieber, above n 62, 76 *et seq*; *id*, 'Der Verfassungsstaat im Gefüge europäischer und insbesondere supranationaler Ordnungsstrukturen', in D Thürer, JF Aubert and JP Müller (eds), *Verfassungsrecht der Schweiz* (2001) 97 at 102.

The first area concerns the reciprocal effects between the constitutional orders of Member States. Since accession took place at different times, the constitutional order had to satisfy completely different adjustment requirements in each case. In the founding Member States, certain questions arose when Community law had not yet reached its current state of development. This is shown most clearly in respect of the primacy of Community law and competition in protecting fundamental rights. A decision such as *Solange I* will no longer be possible in the next group of accession countries provided that the written law of the European Union contains a catalogue of fundamental rights at the time of their accession.

On the other hand, the constitutional legislator, courts and legal science developed in one state responds to tensions between the national and European legal systems, which could be and, promoted by legal comparison, actually are received in other states. In light of comparable political systems and constitutional cultures, new accession states are often attracted to ideas in one state which have already proved their worth over decades of membership at least as a basis for their own solutions. This can be observed from the accessions of 1995 and also in developments that took place in the new Member States of 2004.[222]

Besides this, later accessions also proved to be "psychologically soothing" in relation to national organs. Constitutional courts and other constitutional organs which, for example, developed limits to the primacy of Community law over decades of dialogue with organs of the European Union, have as a rule greater difficulties in recognising a more extensive *acquis* than a constitutional court of a new Member State, which, in this respect, is confronted by completed facts in the creation of which it has not contributed. This may explain the difference between the Federal Constitutional Court of Germany on the one hand and the Austrian and Polish Constitutional Courts on the other hand.

However, shifts necessitated by differing durations of exposure to Community law can occur in the relationship between the constitutional legislator and constitutional jurisdiction as well. Accordingly, the courts in one Member State may develop, slowly and gradually without a written basis in constitutional law, principles that other states later implement by written constitutional law.[223]

Where interdependencies in Article 6(2) EU are not already stipulated as mandatory, then they are nevertheless considerably encouraged. General legal principles are (at least as far as the fundamental claim is concerned)

[222] For Poland cf Wyrzykowski, above n 79, 267. For Hungary see eg A Harmathy, 'Constitutional Questions of the Preparation of Hungary to Accession to the European Union', in Kellermann, de Zwaan and Czuczai (eds), above n 6, 315 at 316 *et seq*.

[223] Cf the demise of Art 10 § 5 of the Swedish Constitution which was influenced by the Maastricht-Judgment of the Federal Constitutional Court.

ascertained by taking the constitutions of *all* Member States into account rather than those of individual countries, which is not the case with the reciprocal relationships already described.

The situation does not significantly differ in relation to international treaties that bind all Member States but that do not form part of Union law. As the most important example the Human Rights Convention mainly influences the constitutional orders of Member States and not only in terms of membership of the European Human Rights Convention but also conveyed, modified and even reinforced by the law of the European Union.[224]

3. Typology According to Substantive Orientation: Adaptations Which are Receptive and Defensive Towards Integration

In substantive terms, adaptations of national constitutional law can be classified into two groups, i.e. those "receptive to integration" and those which are "defensive". The classification is not always straightforward and the wording alone occasionally leads to incorrect results. Often, the only source of information is the genesis of a rule of European constitutional law.

Article 7(5) of the Portuguese Constitution clearly recognises European integration and commits Portugal, "to the reinforcement of the European identity and to the strengthening of the European States' action towards peace, economic progress, and justice in the relations amongst peoples." A similar impression is conveyed by the duty in Article 23(1) Basic Law, *viz* to participate in the development of the European Union "in order to realise a united Europe".[225]

Nonetheless, these tasks of integration are only one side of the coin. If one can unhesitatingly classify these as pro-integration adaptations, then the structural guarantee clauses accompanying them must belong to the defensive adaptations. This is shown more clearly in the case of Germany but also features in the Portuguese Constitution, albeit that here, as in other constitutions, the principle of subsidiarity is referred to just as much as the principle of reciprocity.[226]

The defensive strategy of the French legislator is especially clear in relation to amendments prior to the ratification of the Maastricht Treaty. Certainly, Article 88-1 of the French Constitution contains a formulation comparable to the introductory passage of Article 23(1) German Basic Law concerning participation in the EC and the EU but there is no reference to a united Europe. Instead of this, the EC and the EU are described as interstate

[224] For details see (Sec III 5 c).

[225] Further references in I Pernice, in H Dreier (ed), *Grundgesetz: Kommentar* (1998), Art 23, para 8.

[226] Art 7(6) Portuguese Constitution; Art 23(1) sentence 1 German Basic Law; Art 28(3) Greek Constitution; Art 11 Italian Constitution; Art 20 Danish Constitution.

organisations, "*constituted by states* that have *freely chosen, by virtue of the treaties* that established them, to exercise *some* of their powers in common."[227] The Member States as "rulers of the Treaties" obtain this powerful confirmation by the approval of national legislators.

Austria's way of adapting constitutional law to the Foreign and Defence Policy is offensive only at first sight. According to Article 23f(1) Federal Constitutional Law, Austria participates in the common foreign and security policy of the European Union. In reality, this provision hides all those complex—hardly rational—sensitivities which exist in relation to the "permanent neutrality" of Austria which many still consider as the condition for the existence of the independent state. This is because it also serves as a constitutional signal to remove any doubts in the Union and other Member States as to the ability of Austria to participate in the European Community. Within Austria, however, the provision has the effect of reducing the constitutional obligation of neutrality.[228] The defensive character of adaptation becomes clear mainly in the qualified procedural provisions of Article 23f(1) last sentence and in the requirement of Article 23f(3) Federal Constitutional Law, *viz* that the Federal Chancellor and the Foreign Minister reach agreement.

4. Development Towards a Reciprocal Linking of Constitutions

The involvement of Member States in the European integration process has become a significant component of constitutional development for all national constitutions.[229] European law, which was once developed from the principles and traditions of Member States, now forces national constitutions to adapt in the course of European integration. Owing to the increasing influence of European law, national constitutions have started to approximate each other in central areas[230] even if the strategies employed are different insofar as they are strongly characterised by national peculiarities. Amendments to the EU Treaty and advances in integration also give rise to substantive constitutional amendments at national level which are not always expressed in text.[231]

[227] Emphasis added.

[228] C Grabenwarter, 'Permanent Neutrality and Economic Integration', in *Encyclopaedia of Public International Law* (1997), vol 3; *id*, above n 114, 166; T Öhlinger, 'BVG Neutralität', in: K Korinek and M Holoubek (eds), *Österreichisches Bundesverfassungsrecht* (2001) para 13; S Griller, 'Die GASP und das Ende der immerwährenden Neutralität', in W Hummer (ed), *Rechtsfragen in der Anwendung des Amsterdamer Vertrages* (2001) 261 at 265; *id*, above n 6, 158 *et seq*.

[229] A Peters, *Elemente einer Theorie der Verfassung* (2001) 210 *et seq*.

[230] Cf also Schwarze, above n 34, 463.

[231] JA Frowein, 'Wesentliche Elemente einer Verfassung', in R Bieber and P Widmer (eds), *Der europäische Verfassungsraum* (1995) 71 at 83.

However, such standards are not the artificial products of European law but substantively sustained by Member States' constitutions. Therefore, its interpretative development again takes place under the influence of national constitutions and particularly in relation to their structural guarantee clauses. These make constitutions receptive to the process of supranational constitutional legislation and determine the procedure and organs by which the process of supranational constitutional legislation is formulated in accordance with democratic principles.[232]

First of all, this involves the mutual reference to and consideration of the requirements of procedure and decision-making concerning the participation of national legislators and federal entities in the legislative process of the European Union. These are expressed both in national constitutions, e.g. in Article 23(2) Basic Law, and in Union law, eg in Article 203 EC and Section I of the Protocol annexed by the Treaty of Amsterdam on the role of national parliaments in the European Union.[233] The two Protocols to the Constitutional Treaty, the Protocol on the Role of National Parliaments and the Protocol on the Application of the Principles of Subsidiarity and Proportionality, are the most substantial legal instruments in this respect so far.

However, the principles which establish a dialectic relationship between the national and European constitutional development are more important.[234] Union law and Member States' constitutions are linked with each other on the basis of the law of the Union.[235] Consequently, the constitutional autonomy of Member States is limited. The homogeneity clause of Article 6(1) EU and the respective provisions in Part I of the Constitutional Treaty (in particular Article I-2 CT-Conv; Article 2 CT-IGC) contain the most essential criteria for a common standard of democracy, fundamental rights and the constitutional state which Member States' constitutions must satisfy under the threat of sanctions contained in Article 7 EU. This forms a "structural link"[236] with the constitutions of Member States which, according to national constitutional law, cannot be dissolved unilaterally.[237]

This mutual relation may be described as a system of reciprocal constitutional stabilisation,[238] which has in German legal scholarship been

[232] I Pernice, *Kompetenzabgrenzung im europäischen Verfassungsverbund*, Presentation held at the Humboldt University Berlin on 6 Juli 2000, available under <http://www.whi-berlin.de> (15 May 2004).

[233] Cf eg Müller-Terpitz, above n 106, 47 with further references.

[234] Frowein, above n 231, 83; cf also Schwarze, above n 34, 464 *et seq*.

[235] Huber, above n 198, 209.

[236] U Di Fabio, *Das Recht offener Staaten* (1998) 99.

[237] For Germany: Art 23(1) Basic Law; for Austria: the Federal Constitutional Act on Accession which involved a complete amendment to the Federal Constitution and which could only be repealed in the (more difficult) procedure of complete amendment in connection with a departure from the Union.

[238] A von Bogdandy and M Nettesheim, 'Die Europäische Union: Ein einheitlicher Verband mit eigener Rechtsordnung', (1996) *Europarecht* 1.

described as the "existential condition of the European constitutional association".[239] The concept of a "constitutional association" has been developed to emphasise the legal unity of supranational and national levels. It is meant to emphasise the particular make-up of this system in which there are multiple institutional, personal, functional, procedural and substantive law references of both levels, and the citizens in their different capacities as national, state and Union citizens are both the subject of legitimisation and addressees of the respective rules issued at the different levels.[240] However, this concept has been subject to substantial criticism which leaves a question mark over the accuracy and value of concepts like the "constitutional association" or "multilevel constitutionalism".[241] The concept of "constitutional association" is in part not a normative category but an expression that describes the legal *and factual* interrelation between constitutions as a consequence of provisions in different legal orders that refer to the other one without creating a system of dependence like in federal states.

For the moment this mutual connection, still *sui generis* in nature and difficult to describe in an adequate definition, forms the basis both for further developments of national constitutional law relating to the European Union and for Union law referring to national constitutional law. The Constitutional Treaty would enhance those links.

[239] I Pernice, 'Bestandssicherung der Verfassungen', in Bieber and Widmer (eds), above n 231, 225 at 261 *et seq*; *id*, 'Europäisches und Nationales Verfassungsrecht', (2001) 60 *Veröffentlichungen der Vereinigung der Deutschen Staatsrechtslehrer* 148 at 186.

[240] Cf I Pernice, in Dreier (ed), above n 225, Art 23, paras 20 *et seq*; *id*, above n 239, 163 *et seq*.

[241] Jestaedt, above n 53, 666 *et seq*.

4

The Constitutional Role of Multilateral Treaty Systems

ROBERT UERPMANN-WITTZACK

I. A CONSTITUTIONAL QUESTION: THE EXPOSURE OF A LEGAL ORDER TO INTERNATIONAL LAW*

THIS CHAPTER DEALS with the constitutional effects of multilateral treaty systems within the EC legal order. Treaty systems with such effects may be called international supplementary constitutions. An international supplementary constitution is a multilateral treaty system that acts alongside the constitutional order of a community. Christian Tomuschat coined the phrase with regard to German constitutional law in 1977 when he presented a paper to the Association of German Constitutional Law Professors.[1] In this paper he described international instruments for the protection of human rights as the principal examples of supplementary constitutions for the Federal Republic of Germany. In a later article he applied the concept even exclusively to codifications of human rights.[2] Ernst-Ulrich Petersmann took up the concept in 1989 in order to describe the function of GATT.[3] Both Tomuschat and Petersmann employed the German term *völkerrechtliche Nebenverfassungen*. This is best translated as "international supplementary constitutions".

Such treaty systems can fulfil various functions. Sometimes national constitutional law contains gaps, which are filled by referring to international law. This is especially the case in the area of human rights. Thus the

* A previous version of this contribution entitled "International Law as an Element of European Constitutional Law", which is available as *Jean Monnet Working Paper* No 9/03 at <http://www.jeanmonnetprogram.org/papers/03/030901-02.html> (2 September 2005), was translated by Kathryn Bly. I thank Alexander Hohl for his linguistic support in finalising the present version.

[1] C Tomuschat, 'Der Verfassungsstaat im Geflecht der internationalen Beziehungen', (1978) 36 *Veröffentlichungen der Vereinigung der deutschen Staatsrechtslehrer* 7 at 51 *et seq.*

[2] C Tomuschat, 'Die staatsrechtliche Entscheidung für die internationale Offenheit', in J Isensee and P Kirchhof (eds), *Handbuch des Staatsrechts* (1992), vol VII, § 172, para 73.

[3] E-U Petersmann, 'Wie kann Handelspolitik konstitutionalisiert werden?', (1989) *Europa-Archiv* 55 at 62.

European Convention on the Protection of Human Rights (ECHR) has taken on a gap-filling role in several European countries. For example, the Convention compensates in different ways for deficiencies in the national protection of basic rights in Austria,[4] in the United Kingdom[5] and also in France.[6] In contrast to these countries Germany possesses an almost complete and legally defensible catalogue of fundamental rights, which are enshrined in the German Constitution. Consequently, the ECHR's gap-filling function scarcely shows itself in Germany. Here the ECHR instead provides inspiration in the development of internal law.[7]

International supplementary constitutions are also an expression of "openness of the state" (*offene Staatlichkeit*).[8] The community does not retreat from international influences; rather it fits itself, as a section, into an international community and accepts international constitutional law[9] as part of its own constitution. The internal constitution no longer consists of a single domestic document[10]; instead it opens itself up to international specifications. International treaty systems on human rights and the Charter of the United Nations form the hard core of international constitutional law. According to some authors, the law of the World Trade Organisation (WTO) also has a constitutional quality,[11] although others reject this.[12]

[4] See H Tretter, 'Austria', in R Blackburn and J Polakiewicz (eds), *Fundamental Rights in Europe* (2001) 103 *et seq*.

[5] See R Blackburn, 'United Kingdom', in Blackburn and Polakiewicz, above n 4, 935 *et seq*.

[6] See J Gundel, 'Der Status des Völkerrechts in der französischen Rechtsordnung nach der neueren Rechtsprechung des Conseil d'Etat: Von der Öffnung zum Rückzug?', (1999) 37 *Archiv des Völkerrechts* 438 at 439 *et seq*; see also JF Flauss, 'Auf dem Wege zu einer europäischen Verfassung–Wechselwirkungen zwischen europäischem und nationalem Verfassungsrecht aus französischer Sicht', (2000) *Europarecht Beiheft 1* 31 at 35 *et seq*; C Grewe, 'Das Verständnis des Rechtsstaates in Frankreich und in Deutschland', in H Jurt, G Krumeich and T Würtenberger (eds), *Wandel von Recht und Rechtsbewusstsein in Frankreich und Deutschland* (1999) 157 at 165 *et seq*.

[7] R Uerpmann, 'Völker- und Europarecht im innerstaatlichen Recht', in C Grewe and C Gusy (eds), *Französisches Staatsdenken* (2002) 196 at 202 *et seq*.

[8] This phrase originates from K Vogel, *Die Verfassungsentscheidung des Grundgesetzes für eine internationale Zusammenarbeit* (1964) 33 *et seq*.

[9] See R Uerpmann, 'Internationales Verfassungsrecht', (2001) *Juristenzeitung* 565.

[10] For a narrow understanding of the concept of a constitution see C Möllers in this volume.

[11] T Cottier, 'A Theory of Direct Effect in Global Law', in A von Bogdandy, PC Mavroidis and Y Mény (eds), *European Integration and International Co-ordination* (2002) 99 at 113; E-U Petersmann, 'Rights and Duties of States and Rights and Duties of Their Citizens', in U Beyerlin, M Bothe, R Hofmann and E-U Petersmann (eds), *Recht zwischen Umbruch und Bewahrung: Festschrift für R Bernhardt* (1995) 1087 *et seq*; also T Cottier, 'Dispute Settlement in the World Trade Organization', (1998) 35 *CML Rev* 325 at 326; with regard to GATT 1947 see Petersmann, above n 3, 58 *et seq*; on the constitutional contents of the Law of the WTO see Uerpmann, above n 9, 569, 571.

[12] See, eg: M Nettesheim, 'Von der Verhandlungsdiplomatie zur internationalen Verfassungsordnung', in CD Classen, A Dittmann *et al* (eds), *"In einem vereinten Europa dem Frieden der Welt zu dienen ...": Liber amicorum T Oppermann* (2001) 381 at 392 *et seq*; see also the critical analysis of Petermann's theory of constitutional functions by M Krajewski, *Verfassungsperspektiven und Legitimation des Rechts der Welthandelsorganisation (WTO)* (2001) 161 *et seq*; similarly A von Bogdandy, 'Law and Politics in the WTO', in JA Frowein and R Wolfrum (eds), (2001) 5 *Max Planck Yearbook of United Nations Law* 609 at 655 *et seq*.

Whether or not a community incorporates multilateral treaty systems as international supplementary constitutions into its domestic constitutional system implies a certain vision of its position in the world. Tomuschat's theme in 1977 was: "The Constitutional State within the Network of International Relations".[13] He was able to base his argument on Klaus Vogel, who in 1964 described the question of the integration of an individual state into the international community as a question of constitutional law.[14] The present contribution details how the EC behaves within the network of international relations. A state that wants to emphasise its independence and autonomy will have a reserved attitude towards international law. It will not be inclined to integrate international supplementary constitutions into its own constitution. The situation is different for a community that sees itself as a part of the international community. In this case it is to be expected that the community's constitution will be characterised quite strongly by components of international law.

The ECHR comes primarily into consideration when deliberating about international supplementary constitutions of the European Community. Its guarantees represent a common European standard of basic rights.[15] Meinhard Hilf describes it as the "agreed heart of a common European constitutional order".[16] Even though the EC has not acceded to the ECHR, the Convention is unquestionably of significance to Community law as a point of reference for human rights questions. Originally, Community law completely lacked a human rights catalogue. The ECHR was an important aid in rectifying this deficiency.[17] In this way the Convention has fulfilled the gap-filling function of an international supplementary constitution. The treaty system of the WTO shall be examined as a second example of an international supplementary constitution. Its constitutional quality is far less certain,[18] but this is not of importance for the present analysis. This chapter does not intend an abstract determination of which multilateral treaty systems have a constitutional quality. It is European constitutional law that this project is concerned with. Consequently this chapter is about the multilateral treaty systems which the EU and EC have integrated into

[13] Above n 1.

[14] Vogel, above n 8, 30.

[15] HC Krüger and J Polakiewicz, 'Proposals for a Coherent Human Rights Protection System in Europe', (2001) 22 *HRLJ* 1 at 3 and 8 *et seq*; German version: 'Vorschläge für ein kohärentes System des Menschenrechtsschutzes in Europa', (2001) 28 *Europäische Grundrechte-Zeitschrift* 92.

[16] M Hilf, 'Europäische Union und Europäische Menschenrechtskonvention', in U Beyerlin, M Bothe, R Hofmann and E-U Petersmann (eds), *Recht zwischen Umbruch und Bewahrung: Festschrift für R Bernhardt* (1995) 1193 at 1194: "*konsentierten Kern einer gesamteuropäischen Verfassungsordnung*".

[17] See J Kühling in this volume; D Shelton, 'The Boundaries of Human Rights Jurisdiction in Europe', (2003) 13 *Duke Journal of Comparative International Law* 95 at 111 *et seq*, as well as Section V.

[18] Above n 11 *et seq*.

their own legal regime so that they become parts of European constitutional law.

Both the ECHR and the WTO can be distinguished considerably from other sources of international law. Both instruments provide external standards of review for EC law, and international courts or quasi-judicial bodies observe their domestic implementation. As a result, their impact on the domestic legal order is higher than that of customary international law or ordinary treaties. Indeed, they might actually threaten the autonomy of EC law and EC institutions.

From this point of view the law of the WTO is particularly interesting because it has struggled to establish its position in Community law in recent years. However, the Charter of the United Nations can be disregarded. While the Charter is part of international constitutional law, it affects Community law only indirectly and only in connection with certain points via the two-tiered mechanism for the adaptation of UN sanctions according to Article 301 EC (Article III-224 CT-Conv; Article 322 CT-IGC) and Articles 11 *et seq* EU (Articles III-193, III-195 *et seq* CT-Conv; Articles 292, 294 *et seq* CT-IGC).[19] Association agreements pursuant to Article 310 EC also remain to one side. Their aim is to bring non-Member States closer to the EU.[20] The extension of Community law regulatory content to non-Member States is thus to the fore. This is also the case for the agreement on the European Economic Area, which associates the EFTA-countries.[21] By contrast, this chapter has as its theme the import of external, foreign regulatory content into the law of the Community.

The aim of the following is to determine whether or not the law of the Community has absorbed the ECHR and the law of the WTO into its constitutional order as international supplementary constitutions. For this purpose it is necessary to investigate which mechanisms Community law provides for the incorporation of international law. The classical mechanism of compliance with an international treaty is accession. This will be dealt with first (see II). Nevertheless, this mechanism was used neither with the ECHR nor with GATT 1947. As a result of this the question of further incorporative mechanisms is raised. The contracting states, the European Court of Justice (ECJ) and academics have developed various mechanisms for this purpose. The different mechanisms can be grouped around three

[19] See T Stein, 'Außenpolitisch motivierte (Wirtschafts-) Sanktionen der Europäischen Union – nach wie vor eine rechtliche Grauzone?', in U Beyerlin, M Bothe, R Hofmann and E-U Petersmann (eds), *Recht zwischen Umbruch und Bewahrung: Festschrift für R Bernhardt* (1995) 1129 at 1136 *et seq*; W Wormuth, *Die Bedeutung des Europarechts für die Entwicklung des Völkerrechts* (2004) 200–8.

[20] According to the ECJ, the non-Member State "must, at least to a certain extent, take part in the Community system" (Case 12/86, *Demirel* [1987] ECR 3719, para 9); see also A Weber, in H von der Groeben and J Schwarze (eds), *Kommentar zum Vertrag über die Europäische Union und zur Gründung der Europäischen Gemeinschaft* (2004), Art 310 EC, para 1.

[21] See T Oppermann, *Europarecht* (1999) paras 137 at 139.

basic concepts, which will be considered consecutively. Following accession, the concept of legal succession will be dealt with next (see III), then incorporation by means of express reference, as found in Article 6(2) EU for the ECHR (see IV), and finally, the concept of general principles of law (see V). The original question will be returned to in a concluding evaluating section on how the constitution of the EC and EU relates to international supplementary constitutions (see VI). This section will also address the ongoing constitutional process.

To begin with two issues relating to terminology should be clarified:

1 The relationship between the EC and the EU cannot and need not be determined in this chapter. The EC acts within the framework of the WTO. Likewise, it is the EC that is of prime importance in relation to the ECHR. EC and Community law will therefore be the primary focus of the discussion below. However, the reference to human rights in Article 6(2) EU shows that the EU must also be considered. Therefore, the way terms are used will not be quite uniform. Euratom and the former ECSC need not be considered in this chapter.

2 The internal effect of international law has generally been discussed in relation to nation states. If the EC now integrates international law into its internal system of laws, the law of the Community, it takes on a role that was previously reserved for states. The effects of international law within national law and within Community law should accordingly be seen as parallel phenomena. Given that the term "internal effect" can be applied in relation to both, it will generally be preferred to other terms. However, it is sometimes difficult to use vocabulary developed in relation to the impact on the legal systems of nation states to describe the influence on EC law. As a result, terminology used in this paper relating to the Member States and national law should be understood as applying equally to the EC where appropriate.

II. ACCESSION

1. WTO

The normal way to make an international treaty binding is via accession. The EC complies with the WTO in this way. The EC is one of the founding members for which the agreements establishing the World Trade Organisation came into force on 1 January 1995.[22] Subsequently the parties to the agreements are obliged under international law to keep to the contractual rules. International law leaves the choice of means by which this is

[22] See the notification of the WTO General Secretary pursuant to Art XIV(3) WTO Agreement, WTO-Doc WT/Let/1/Rev 2; available at <http://www.wto.org/>.

achieved to the contracting parties. In particular, there are no rules of general international law to determine whether and how the parties have to incorporate a treaty into their internal law.[23] The parties to a treaty can determine together whether they require a direct effect within internal law or whether they want to exclude it.[24] This corresponds to freedom of contract, which governs international relations. In the case of the WTO, though, this did not occur.[25] The decision remained with the individual parties to the treaty.[26] Article 1(1)(3) TRIPS clarifies this.[27] For the EC, Article 300(7) EC stipulates that the WTO agreements are binding on the institutions of the Community and on the Member States. It is, however, debatable what this means.

a) Article 300(7) EC as a Starting Point

Taking the literal meaning of the wording of Article 300(7) EC as a starting point, it is initially unclear what the legal nature of the binding effect is. The international legal obligation of the EC as such follows directly from the contractual conclusion pursuant to Article 300(2) EC. Community law has no influence on this binding effect. Article 300(7) EC can, therefore, only place an obligation on the individual Community institutions, which goes beyond the international obligations of the Community.

The obligation of the institutions under Article 300(7) EC is not restricted. The institutions are consequently also bound when they are active as the Community's legislator.[28] The internal effect of international treaties within the Community follows from this. As a result of the fact that international treaties derive their binding effect from primary law, they rank below primary law within the Community legal order. On the other hand the fact that Article 300(7) EC binds the Community's legislator shows that it allocates to international treaties a place above secondary law.[29] The treaties,

[23] Case 104/81, *Kupferberg* [1982] ECR 3641, para 18; G Betlem and A Nollkaemper, 'Giving Effect to Public International Law and European Community Law before Domestic Courts', (2003) 14 *EJIL* 569 at 573.

[24] Cottier, above n 11, 121; PE Holzer, *Die Ermittlung der innerstaatlichen Anwendbarkeit völkerrechtlicher Vertragsbestimmungen* (1998) 35 *et seq.*

[25] GM Berrisch and H-G Kamann, 'WTO-Recht im Gemeinschaftsrecht', (2000) 89 *Europäisches Wirtschafts- und Steuerrecht* 92 *et seq*; W Meng, 'Gedanken zur Frage unmittelbarer Anwendung von WTO-Recht in der EG', in U Beyerlin, M Bothe, R Hofmann and E-U Petersmann (eds), *Recht zwischen Umbruch und Bewahrung: Festschrift für R Bernhardt* (1995) 1063 at 1085; this is also confirmed by ECJ, Case C-149/96, *Portugal v Council* [1999] ECR I-8395, paras 34 *et seq*, 41.

[26] A von Bogdandy and T Makatsch, 'Collision, Coexistence, or Cooperation?', in G de Búrca and J Scott (eds), *The EU and the WTO* (2001) 131 at 143; German version: 'Kollision, Koexistenz oder Kooperation?' (2000) *Europäische Zeitschrift für Wirtschaftsrecht* 261.

[27] See also Case C-89/99, *Schieving-Nijstad* [2001] ECR I-5851, paras 33 *et seq.*

[28] C Timmermans, 'The EU and Public International Law', (1999) 4 *European Foreign Affairs Review* 181 at 189.

[29] A Epiney, Zur Stellung des Völkerrechts in der EU, *Europäische Zeitschrift für Wirtschaftsrecht* (1999) 5 at 7.

therefore, fit in between primary law and secondary law within the Community legal order.

The internal primacy of international treaties over secondary law is not a self-evident truth. In Germany, for example, Article 59(2)(1) of the Basic Law allocates international treaties merely the rank of an ordinary federal law.[30] If a constitution places international law above ordinary law it takes the freedom to pass laws that do not comply with international law away from the internal legislator.[31] This is becoming the norm more and more in Europe. Article 55 of the French Constitution, Article 94 of the Dutch Constitution and Article 91(2) of the Polish Constitution are examples of this. Article 300(7) EC also opts for this solution, which is particularly friendly to international law.

This is, in principle, broadly acknowledged. Academics are not the only ones to derive the primacy of international treaties over secondary Community law from Article 300(7) EC.[32] The ECJ also recognises this primacy by means of its willingness to review secondary Community legislation by reference to the standards laid down in international treaties.[33] Yet, the ECJ hesitates to do so in the sphere of WTO law. The legitimacy of this reserved attitude towards WTO law is still to be tested.

In short, international treaties are binding within the Community legal order and rank between primary and secondary law. However, it has not yet been clarified under which circumstances international treaty norms can regulate the legal relationships of individuals within the Community. This is determined by the theory of direct effect.

b) The Theory of Direct Effect

Although international law does not regulate its own internal effect, a general concept about its direct internal effect has been developed. This concept is common to many countries.[34] Following the leading decisions of the ECJ in *Haegemann*[35] and *Kupferberg*,[36] the academics of European Law

[30] O Rojahn, in I von Münch and P Kunig (eds), *Grundgesetz-Kommentar* (2001), Art 59, para 37.

[31] C Tomuschat, in von der Groeben and Schwarze, above n 20, Art 300 EC, para 74.

[32] See H Krück, in J Schwarze (ed), *EU-Kommentar* (2000), Art 281 EC, para 30; Tomuschat, above n 31, para 74.

[33] Case C-377/98, *Netherlands v Parliament and Council* [2001] ECR I-7079, paras 53 *et seq*; see also Case C-61/94, *Commission v Germany* [1994] ECR I-3989, para 52, in which the ECJ expressly acknowledged the primacy of international agreements.

[34] For France D Alland, 'Jurisprudence en matière de droit international public', (1998) 102 *Revue générale de droit international public* 203 at 219 *et seq*; for the USA CM Vázquez, 'The Four Doctrines of Self-Executing Treaties', (1995) 89 *AJIL* 695 *et seq*; for Switzerland Holzer, above n 24, 103 *et seq* as well as D Würger, 'Die direkte Anwendbarkeit staatsvertraglicher Normen', in T Cottier, A Achermann, D Würger and V Zellweger, *Der Staatsvertrag im schweizerischen Verfassungsrecht* (2001) 93 at 97 *et seq*; for a German comparative perspective G Buchs, *Die unmittelbare Anwendbarkeit völkerrechtlicher Vertragsbestimmungen* (1993) 31 *et seq*.

[35] Case 181/73, *Haegemann* [1974] ECR 449, para 2/6.

[36] Case 104/81, *Kupferberg* [1982] ECR 3641, paras 9–27.

quite predominantly assume that these rules are equally valid within the framework of Article 300(7) EC.[37] The concept of direct effect is also described as the theory of self-executing treaties.[38] One particular manifestation of this theory is found in the theory of direct effect of Community law within its Member States. However, the law of the Community constitutes a special development distinct from general international law.[39] It is closer in many respects to internal law rather than international law.[40] If the internal effect of international law is to be examined here, it is of paramount importance to look at the general theory of self-executing treaties.

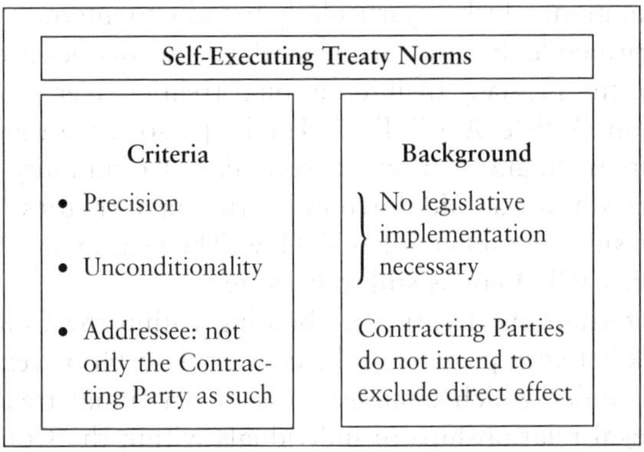

The diagram shows an overview of the requirements of direct effect. Accordingly, a self-executing norm is a norm that is sufficiently certain and absolute to be used internally in national courts. In this context the ECJ examines whether the purpose of the agreement "contains a clear, precise and unconditional obligation which is not subject, in its implementation or effects, to the adoption of any subsequent measure".[41] The German Federal Administrative Court emphasises the comparability with an internal legal act.[42] If the international norm requires implementation through state

[37] P Hilpold, *Die EU im GATT/WTO-System* (2000) 171; Meng, above n 25, 1067 at 1070 and 1072; as well as Cottier, above n 11, 104; for the same result see A Peters, 'The Position of International Law Within the European Community Legal Order', (1997) 40 *German Yearbook of International Law* 9 at 42–5, who, however, would prefer to avoid the concept of "self-executing" and emphasises in particular the intentions of the contracting parties; a conflicting point of view is apparently taken by J Sack, 'Noch einmal: GATT/WTO und europäisches Rechtsschutzsystem', (1997) *Europäische Zeitschrift für Wirtschaftsrecht* 688.

[38] On the identity of the concepts Buchs, above n 34, 26 *et seq.*

[39] Hilpold, above n 37, 168–70; Peters, above n 37, 55 *et seq.*

[40] P Eeckhout, 'The Domestic Legal Status of the WTO Agreement', (1997) 34 *CML Rev* 11 and 56.

[41] Cases C-300/98 and 392/98, *Dior et al* [2000] ECR I-11307, para 42, with reference to Case 12/86, *Demirel* [1987] ECR 3719, para 14; Case 162/96, *Racke* [1998] ECR I-3655, para 31.

[42] *Entscheidungen des Bundesverwaltungsgerichts* 80, 233 at 235; 87, 11 at 13.

legislation before it can be applied, it is not a self-executing norm.[43] In this situation the international norm leaves a normative gap, which the national courts cannot fill. The separation of competences between the political organs of the first and second powers on the one hand and the judiciary on the other hand stands as a background to the theory of direct effect.[44] Norms are on the whole only self-executing if the courts can interpret and apply them without taking on political functions. An international treaty can, through its formulation, also express that it requires normative implementation. This is to be assumed if an international norm expressly addresses the states as such and requires them to act in a certain way. The answer as to whether a norm has direct effect can, therefore, turn out quite differently for different provisions belonging to one and the same treaty.

Yet, direct effect does not depend on whether a norm confers an individual right.[45] It is true that the right of action will frequently depend on the assertion of an individual right. It is not necessary, however, that this right arises from the international treaty. For example if an administrative act, which is contrary to international law, conflicts with a constitutional human rights norm, the constitutional norm confers the required right of action.

If these principles are applied in relation to the law of the WTO, directly effective provisions are easy to find.[46] There is hardly any doubt, for example, that Article 50 TRIPS, which contains rules on provisional legal protection through the courts, has direct effect.[47] The norm is directly addressed to the courts, and it does not require further normative implementation. Each court can remedy possible doubts about the content of WTO law by means of legal interpretation. Other rules, such as the ban on non-tariff trade barriers according to Article XI GATT and the exceptions

[43] See *Entscheidungen des Bundesverwaltungsgerichts* 87, 11 at 13, where a need for "further normative completion" was deemed to exclude direct effect, as well as Art 91(1) of the Constitution of the Republic of Poland enacted on 2 April 1997, according to which an international treaty "shall be applied directly, unless its application depends on the enactment of a statute" (*The Constitution of the Republic of Poland/The Constitutional Tribunal Act*, ed by the Cabinet of the President of the Constitutional Tribunal, Warsaw 2001).

[44] These aspects are emphasised by Cottier, above n 11, 115 *et seq*.

[45] Buchs, above n 34, 40 at 88 *et seq*; Vázquez, above n 34, 719 *et seq*; Würger, above n 34, 109 *et seq*.

[46] See also S Mauderer, *Der Wandel vom GATT zur WTO und die Auswirkungen auf die Europäische Gemeinschaft* (2001) 117; A Ott, *GATT und WTO im Gemeinschaftsrecht* (1997) 223 *et seq*; E-U Petersmann, 'Darf die EG das Völkerrecht ignorieren?', (1997) *Europäische Zeitschrift für Wirtschaftsrecht* 325 at 327; *id*, 'GATT/WTO-Recht: Duplik', (1997) *Europäische Zeitschrift für Wirtschaftsrecht* 651 at 652 *et seq*.

[47] The German Federal Government in its memorandum concerning the ratification of the WTO agreements also assumes that at least some sections of TRIPS have direct effect (Printed matter of the Federal Parliament [Bundestags-Drucksache] 12/7655 [new], 345); with specific regard to the direct effect of the TRIPS agreement see R Duggal, 'Die unmittelbare Anwendbarkeit der Konventionen des internationalen Urheberrechts am Beispiel des TRIPs-Übereinkommens', (2002) *Praxis des internationalen Privat- und Verfahrensrechts* 101 at 104–7.

that are laid down in Article XX GATT, are much less precise. Armin von Bogdandy draws attention to the legal uncertainty which could arise for market participants in the application of such complex rules.[48] However, these rules also allow the individual states no scope for implementation. According to the WTO Dispute Settlement Understanding, any state can initiate a procedure with the assertion that another state has violated its GATT obligations. In this case a panel, and, if need be, the appellate body, decides whether GATT has actually been violated. The panel and appellate body are not political institutions, and instead decide using a court-like procedure. If the panel and appellate body are in a position to make a decision of a judicial nature, the same must be true for the state courts. Piet Eeckhout suggests that it could be asking too much of the national courts if they had to apply WTO law directly.[49] However, the courts are frequently required to apply complex law. In Europe the ECJ is the court most concerned with the application of WTO law. Even more than other courts, the ECJ should be in a position to adapt to working with the legal system of the WTO in an adequate way.

c) Interconnecting Different Jurisdictions

Of course it is often difficult to determine how judicial bodies will finally interpret and apply a norm of WTO law. Divergences between decisions of the different national courts[50] or between national decisions and later decisions within the WTO Dispute Settlement Procedure[51] might often arise if the national courts were to apply WTO law directly. However, this problem is not limited merely to WTO law.[52] National constitutional law is often uncertain to a degree in that constitutional court decisions are frequently unpredictable. It is no oddity for decisions of the constitutional courts to deviate from earlier decisions of the lower courts. Other international treaties also allow considerable scope for interpretation. This is aimed principally at the ECHR. The danger that judgments of the European Court of

[48] A von Bogdandy, 'Legal Equality, Legal Certainty, and Subsidiarity in Transnational Economic Law', in A von Bogdandy, PC Mavroides and Y Mény (eds), *European Integration and International Co-ordination* (2002) 13 at 29 *et seq*; German version: 'Rechtsgleichheit, Rechtssicherheit und Subsidiarität im transnationalen Wirtschaftsrecht', (2001) *Europäische Zeitschrift für Wirtschaftsrecht* 357.

[49] Eeckhout, above n 40, 50.

[50] This is emphasised by C Schmid, 'Immer wieder Bananen: Der Status des GATT/WTO-Systems im Gemeinschaftsrecht', (1998) *Neue Juristische Wochenschrift* 190 at 195; see also HG Krenzler, in E Grabitz and M Hilf (eds), *Das Recht der Europäischen Union* (looseleaf, last update 1999), vol III, E 1, para 85; H-D Kuschel, 'Die EG-Bananenmarktordnung vor deutschen Gerichten', (1995) *Europäische Zeitschrift für Wirtschaftsrecht* 689 at 690.

[51] This is emphasised by Krajewski, above n 12, 65; P Royla, 'WTO-Recht—EG-Recht: Kollision, Justiziabilität, Implementation', (2001) *Europarecht* 495 at 500 even concludes that the establishment of international sanction mechanisms is not consistent with the concept of direct effect.

[52] Meng, above n 25, 1086.

Human Rights might differ from earlier national decisions on the ECHR has been well known for a long time. Nevertheless more and more countries are deciding to integrate the ECHR into their internal law as a yardstick for judicial review.[53]

Markus Krajewski considers it to be an essential difference between the ECHR and the WTO that the law of the WTO contains no mechanisms to regulate conflicts between, on the one hand, decisions within the framework of WTO dispute settlement and, on the other, decisions of national courts. As a result of this deficiency, he claims that it ought to be concluded that the contracting states wanted to exclude the direct effect of WTO law. By contrast, the ECHR regulates the relationship between different jurisdictions with the so-called local remedies rule as laid down in Article 35(1) ECHR.[54] This argument is not completely convincing. Article 35(1) ECHR does not avoid diverging decisions. Rather the rule guarantees that the European Court of Human Rights can essentially only judge cases in which national courts have definitely excluded an infringement of the law. Whenever the Court of Human Rights then detects an infringement, this results in conflict with national decisions. Under these circumstances, it cannot be concluded from the silence of WTO law that the Member States of the WTO wanted to exclude the direct effect of WTO law in the interest of avoiding conflicts. Rather this silence supports the conclusion that the law of the WTO has not decided the question of its internal effect.[55]

The ECJ cites the fact that the law of the WTO allows the Member States a broad scope for negotiations as a decisive argument against direct effect.[56] In particular Article 22(2) of the Dispute Settlement Understanding (DSU) provides that if a member cannot remedy a violation that has been determined by the Dispute Settlement Body (DSB) within a reasonable period of time, it ought to negotiate and subsequently agree on compensation with the state concerned.[57] The ECJ gives no theoretical foundation for its argument. The theory of direct effect would bring the criterion of a lack of unconditionality into consideration. A norm may only have direct internal effect if its requirements are unconditional.[58] If the EC were free to decide whether it should follow rules of the WTO or instead pay compensation, this would result in the rules of the WTO actually lacking unconditional application.[59] Such an understanding of WTO law is, however,

[53] See Krüger and Polakiewicz, above n 15, 2.

[54] Krajewski, above n 12, 63 *et seq*, 270.

[55] Above n 25.

[56] Case C-149/96, above n 25, para 36; Cases C-27/00 and C-122/00, *Omega Air et al* [2003] ECR I-2569, paras 89–90; cautious agreement from M Hilf and F Schorkopf, 'WTO und EG: Rechtskonflikte vor den EuGH?', (2000) *Europarecht* 74 at 85 *et seq*, 90; similarly Schmid, above n 50, 195.

[57] Case C-149/96, above n 25, para 39; Hilpold, above n 37, 272–7 also argues this.

[58] Above nn 41 *et seq*.

[59] To this effect see J Sack, 'Von der Geschlossenheit und den Spannungsfeldern in einer Weltordnung des Rechts', (1997) *Europäische Zeitschrift für Wirtschaftsrecht* 650.

hardly tenable.[60] Article XVI(4) of the WTO Agreement underlines the obligation of adhering to the law of the WTO. Article 22(1)(2) DSU confirms that a member is always ultimately obliged to harmonise its law with its obligations that arise from the WTO agreements.[61]

In the recent *Biret v Council* judgments of 2003,[62] the ECJ added a new element to this reasoning. After having confirmed its settled case-law according to which WTO law has no direct effect,[63] the Court indicated that DSB decisions on WTO law might have direct effect, but it did not decide on that point.[64] Instead, it referred to Article 21(3) DSU. Under this provision a member shall have a reasonable period of time in which to comply with a DSB decision if it is impracticable to do so immediately. For this purpose, the DSB may approve a period of time proposed by the member concerned in conformity with Article 21(3)(3)(a) DSU. According to the ECJ in *Biret*, no direct effect is possible before the end of such a period of time, as otherwise the Court would render "the grant" of a reasonable period for implementation superfluous.[65] This leads back to Krajewski's question whether there is a mechanism to regulate conflicts between DSB decisions and decisions of domestic courts.[66] According to the logic of *Biret*, Article 21(3) DSU might imply the rule that national authorities are only obliged to comply with WTO law after a corresponding DSB ruling and after a reasonable period of time has elapsed. However, Article XVI(4) of the WTO Agreement makes WTO law binding right from the beginning. Article 22(3) DSU does not "grant" a right to infringe upon WTO law, but rather accepts that bringing national rules into conformity with WTO law may take some time. Article 22(3) DSU therefore does not hinder domestic courts from giving full effect to WTO law.

d) The Principle of Reciprocity

In *Portugal v Council*, the ECJ introduced another argument for the rejection of direct effect.[67] It has relied since then on a lack of reciprocity. Indeed,

[60] J Pauwelyn, 'Enforcement and Countermeasures in the WTO', (2000) 94 *AJIL* 335 at 341 *et seq*.

[61] Berrisch and Kamann, above n 25, 92; Eeckhout, above n 40, 54 *et seq*; Mauderer, above n 46, 133 at 160–2; Petersmann, above n 46, 653; W Schroeder and P Schonard, 'Die Effektivität des WTO-Streitbeilegungssystems', (2001) 43 *Recht der internationalen Wirtschaft* 658 at 659–62.

[62] Case C-93/02 P, *Biret International v Council* [2003] ECR I-10497 and, nearly identical, Case C-94/02 P, *Établissements Biret v Council* [2003] ECR I-10565.

[63] Case C-93/02 P, above n 62, para 52.

[64] Case C-93/02 P, above n 62, paras 56–9.

[65] Case C-93/02 P, above n 62, para 62.

[66] Above n 54.

[67] Case C-149/96, above n 25, paras 42–7; confirmed by Cases C-300/98 and 392/98, above n 41, para 44; Case C-307/99, *OGT Fruchthandelsgesellschaft* [2001] ECR I-3159, paras 24 *et seq*; in agreement Hilf and Schorkopf, above n 56, 84 *et seq*, 90; as well as Hilpold, above n 37, 262–71.

the important trade partners of the EC likewise grant WTO law no internal effect.[68]

This argument is not convincing within the context of international law. If another country violates WTO law, the EC can initiate dispute settlement proceedings and, should the situation arise, suspend its own obligations in a precisely regulated procedure according to Article 22 DSU. Such a suspension of international law can also be carried out internally. The doctrine of direct effect is no obstacle to this. If a rule is suspended in international law the parallel internal effect does not apply either.[69] However, outside of the special procedures of the DSU, the EC cannot make its own legal compliance with international law dependent on the faithfulness of other states to international law.[70]

Admittedly, the internal effect of WTO law is not established by international law anyway.[71] Internal law is crucial. Here reciprocity can be raised perfectly as a requirement for direct effect, as verified by Article 55 of the French Constitution.[72] Nevertheless the French example shows that the precondition of reciprocity is problematic. French courts have increasingly restricted the application sphere of this precondition.[73] If the international treaty itself provides for a dispute settlement and implementation mechanism, the reservation of reciprocity as a form of pressure can be refrained from.[74] If this were to be followed the WTO dispute settlement mechanism would exclude the reservation of reciprocity even under French law. Above all though, Community law lacks a rule that would correspond to Article 55 of the French Constitution. Article 300(7) EC does not recognise a proviso of reciprocity.[75] Certainly Article 300(7) EC does not offer any indication that reciprocity is required only from a specific type of agreement. This is, however, what the ECJ did.[76] The argument's inconsistency is further illustrated by the fact that the ECJ does not apply the reciprocity argument to association agreements,[77] although Article 310 EC expressly demands reciprocal rights and obligations for this type of agreement.

It seems that the ECJ recognised the weakness of the reciprocity argument in *Omega Air*, where it essentially relied on the argument that WTO

[68] This is confirmed and relativised by T von Danwitz, 'Der EuGH und das Wirtschaftsvölkerrecht', (2001) *Juristenzeitung* 721 at 726–8.

[69] Meng, above n 25, 1076 *et seq*.

[70] Mauderer, above n 46, 180 *et seq*; Schroeder and Schonard, above n 61, 660 *et seq*.

[71] Above n 25.

[72] See also von Danwitz, above n 68, 726; further see Buchs, above n 34, 101–4 where she draws a parallel to American case-law.

[73] D Alland, 'Le droit international "sous" la Constitution de la Ve République', (1988) 114 *Revue du droit public* 1649 at 1664–6; J Gundel, 'Der Status des Völkerrechts in der französischen Rechtsordnung', (1999) 37 *Archiv des Völkerrechts* 438 at 460 *et seq*.

[74] Alland, above n 73, 1665.

[75] Von Danwitz, above n 68, 726.

[76] Berrisch and Kamann, above n 25, 93.

[77] Case 87/75, *Bresciani* [1976] ECR 129, para 22/23; Case C-469/93, *Chiquita Italia* [1995] ECR I-4533, paras 31–5.

members should keep the possibility of finding negotiated solutions open[78]. This comes close to the reasoning of some academics who object that direct effect would deprive the Community of a means of political pressure in negotiations with other states.[79] According to Helen Keller's analysis, such reasoning is based on a political-diplomatic understanding of international law. Although the legal character of international norms is not completely denied, compliance with international law ultimately becomes a question of political choice.[80] Following this school of thought the ECJ does not feel entitled to divest the legislative and executive Community institutions of the scope, which the corresponding institutions of trading partners of the Community have at their disposal.[81] The loss of this form of political pressure is, nevertheless, inherent in the theory of direct effect. If a constitution arranges direct effect within the state it decides in favour of a comprehensive observance of international law. It does this without making its own faithfulness to international law dependent on the behaviour of other states. This decision is particularly friendly towards international law. Many national constitutional orders and also Article 300(7) EC have made this decision. The case-law of the ECJ indicates that this friendliness towards international law is not sought after politically.[82] Typically, Article 300(7) EC is not once referred to by the ECJ.[83]

From the silence regarding Article 300(7) EC it may be possible to infer that the ECJ does not construct its arguments around substantial law. The ECJ might prefer instead to use procedural arguments. The wording of the ECJ in stating that the WTO agreements "are not in principle among the rules in the light of which the Court is to review the legality of measures adopted by the Community institutions", may also speak in favour of this.[84] If this statement is understood procedurally the ECJ does not doubt that the Community institutions are substantially bound by WTO law. Rather the scope of review of the ECJ is limited so that the substantial obligation cannot be updated procedurally. However, this procedural approach is not satisfactory either. It merely shifts the problem from the substantial law level to the procedural level. The scope of review of the ECJ is in principle just as broad as the substantial obligations laid down in Community

[78] Above n 56.

[79] S Peers, 'Fundamental Right or Political Whim?', in De Búrca and Scott, above n 26, 111 at 122 *et seq*; Sack, above n 59, 651.

[80] H Keller, *Rezeption des Völkerrechts* (2003) 700.

[81] Case C-149/96 above n 25, para 46.

[82] For analysis of the political dimension see Mauderer, above n 46, 170 *et seq*; the economical and political context is examined by Hilpold, above n 37, 212–52.

[83] This is also emphasised by Berrisch and Kamann, above n 25, 91 as well as C Schmid, 'Ein enttäuschender Rückzug, Anmerkungen zum "Bananenbeschluss" des BVerfG', (2001) *Neue Zeitschrift für Verwaltungsrecht* 249 at 256.

[84] Case C-149/96, above n 25, para 47; Cases C-27/00 and C-122/00, above n 56, para 93; Case C-93/02 P, above n 62, para 52.

law. Dealing with public international law in *International Fruit Company*[85] and in *Racke*[86], the ECJ confirmed that its jurisdiction cannot be limited by the grounds on which the legality of a Community act is contested. Furthermore, neither Article 230(2) EC nor Article 234(1)(b) EC permits any distinction in the scope of judicial review depending on the type of international treaty at issue.

e) Unilateral Council Action

Some authors discuss whether the Council has excluded the internal effect of the WTO agreements by using its decision of approval.[87] According to the 11th and last recital in the preamble of the decision, "by its nature, the Agreement establishing the World Trade Organisation, including the Annexes thereto, is not susceptible to being directly invoked in Community or Member State Courts".

It is recognised that the contracting parties have the authority to limit or exclude the internal effect of an agreement by means of a provision that is enacted at the international level.[88] This qualifies the principle that the internal effect of a treaty is a question for internal law and complies with the concept of freedom of contract under international law. The decision of the Council of the European Union is, however, a purely internal act, which produces no effect in the sphere of international law.[89] At the international law level the EC accepted the WTO agreements on 30 December 1994. According to the notification issued by the Director-General of the WTO[90], it did so without reservation or other additional declarations.[91]

Because of this the question arises as to whether the Council of the European Union can take the internal effect away from a treaty through an act that belongs to Community law alone.[92] This is a question of primary EC law. Article 300(2) EC grants the Council of the European Union the authority to decide on the international obligations of the Community. The Council can adopt a treaty, reject it or limit its scope by a reservation under public international law. Insofar as the Council accepts the international

[85] Cases 21 to 24/72, *International Fruit Company* [1972] ECR 1219, paras 5 *et seq.*

[86] Case 162/96, *Racke* [1998] ECR I-3655, paras 26 *et seq.*

[87] Council Dec 94/800/EC concerning the conclusion of the agreements reached in the Uruguay Round multilateral negotiations, OJ L 336, 23.12.1994, 1.

[88] Von Danwitz, above n 68, 725; Tomuschat, above n 31, para 79.

[89] According to its Art 1(3), Council Dec 94/800/EC, above n 87, only contains the Community law authorisation to grant the subsequent declaration of accession under international law; see also von Danwitz, above n 68, 725.

[90] Above n 22.

[91] Moreover, a unilateral declaration ought not to be sufficient anyway. According to draft guideline No 1.4.5 of the International Law Commission on Reservations to Treaties of 2003 (UN-Doc A/58/10, 165 at 171 *et seq*) such a declaration would not be a reservation, rather merely an informative statement.

[92] Confirmatory of this Tomuschat, above n 31, para 81.

obligation, Article 300(7) EC, however, arranges its internal effect.[93] At this level the Council has no freedom. In fact international law leaves the determination of the internal effect up to the respective contracting party,[94] i.e. the EC in this situation. In Community law, however, the question is regulated at the primary law level in Article 300(7) EC and is subsequently binding for the Council of the European Union.[95] Werner Meng refers to the contrast with German law.[96] In Germany the order of internal application of a ratified treaty (*Rechtsanwendungsbefehl*) is not contained in the constitution itself, but rather in the assenting law, which the German federal legislator enacts according to Article 59(2)(1) of the Basic Law. In this way, the German legislator is theoretically capable of excluding the internal effect. In Community law, by contrast, primary law enacts the order of internal application. The EC Treaty is in this respect friendlier towards international law than the German Basic Law.[97] Under these circumstances, the above-mentioned consideration in the preamble of the Council decision qualifies only as a mere expression of opinion.[98] Thus, when the ECJ cites the recital of the preamble in *Portugal v Council*[99] as confirmation of its argumentation, it provides a political justification of its decision according to Thomas von Danwitz.[100]

f) Internal Effect Short of Direct Effect

In view of the persistence with which the ECJ denies WTO law direct effect, it is of special importance to consider those internal effects, which can befit the international treaties to which the EC accedes without direct effect. Some German authors deal with these effects under the concept of internal validity (*interne Geltung*). According to these authors, a treaty becomes automatically internally valid as soon as it has been incorporated into the domestic legal order. This internal validity does not depend on a treaty's self-executing nature. Therefore, a treaty may be valid within Community

[93] R Arnold, in: MA Dauses (ed), *Handbuch des EU-Wirtschaftsrechts* (looseleaf), K I, para 61; von Danwitz, above n 68, 726; W Schroeder and M Selmayr, 'Die EG, das GATT und die Vollzugslehre', (1998) *Juristenzeitung* 344 at 348. A von Bogdandy, 'Rechtsgleichheit, Rechtssicherheit und Subsidiarität im transnationalen Wirtschaftsrecht', (2001) *Europäische Zeitschrift für Wirtschaftsrecht* 357 at 361, stresses that the Council of the European Union toned down the wording in the preamble of its later decision of approval 1999/61/EC concerning the conclusion of the results of the World Trade Organisation negotiations on financial services, OJ L 20, 27.1.1999, 38.

[94] Tomuschat, above n 31, para 81; above also n 25.

[95] Krajewski, above n 12, 69 *et seq*; Meng, above n 25, 1070, 1072; Mauderer, above n 46, 193; against Tomuschat, above n 31, para 81.

[96] Meng, above n 25, 1070, 1072; as well Mauderer, above n 46, 192.

[97] On the specific friendliness of Art 300(7) EC towards international law also Hilpold, above n 37, 187 *et seq*.

[98] For this result also von Bogdandy, above n 48, 24.

[99] Case C-149/96, *Portugal v Council* [1999] ECR I-8395, para 48.

[100] Von Danwitz, above n 68, 724; similarly Mauderer, above n 46, 136 *et seq*.

law even if it produces no direct effect.[101] Even though this is true, the concept of internal validity seems to be too narrow to cover all cases of internal effect. For instance consistent interpretation of domestic law with international law is possible even if the international norm is only binding at an international level but does not come into force internally. The mere interest in avoiding responsibility under international law can be a sufficient motive for an interpretation of internal law that concurs with international law.[102] French academics list the various forms of internal effect under the generic term of *invocabilité*.[103] Von Danwitz translates this concept as "cause to sue" (*Einklagbarkeit*).[104] However, this could too greatly restrict its understanding to the perspective of procedural law. That is why internal effect should be spoken of here in a way that is as neutral as possible.

As a means of avoiding getting bogged down in the precedents of the ECJ, some authors refer to the previously mentioned theory of interpretation that complies with international law.[105] According to this theory, internal law should be construed as far as possible in conformity with international law (*völkerrechtsfreundliche Auslegung*).[106] The ECJ initially cautiously approached this method of consistent interpretation in *Werner*[107] and *Leifer*[108] and confirmed it in *Hermès*.[109] This method has the potential to become a highly effective means of avoiding conflicts between international and European law and of integrating international standards into the European legal order. Yet, its success depends on whether the norms of Community law open up a corresponding scope for interpretation. In this, the Community's legislator remains master of the internal effect of WTO law.[110]

In addition, such rules that do not have direct effect could also function as yardsticks for internal law.[111] This is recognisable from the relationship between Community law and national law. An EC directive, which is not directly effective as a result of its contents, is, nevertheless, able to render

[101] See for example Schroeder and Selmayr, n 93, 345 *et seq*.
[102] Uerpmann, above n 7, 200.
[103] Alland, above n 34, 234 *et seq*; P Manin, 'L'influence du droit international sur la jurisprudence communautaire', in Société Française pour le Droit International (ed), *Droit International et Droit Communautaire* (2000) 153 at 163 *et seq*.
[104] Von Danwitz, above n 68, 722.
[105] Berrisch and Kamann, above n 25, 95; von Bogdandy and Makatsch, above n 26, 147; Cottier, above n 11, 109–11; Hilf and Schorkopf, above n 56, 88; GA Zonnekeyn, 'The Status for WTO law in the EC Legal Order', (2000) 34/3 *JWT* 111 at 124 *et seq*.
[106] See also Betlem and Nollkaemper, above n 23, 574–5.
[107] Case C-70/94, *Werner Industrie-Ausrüstungen* [1995] ECR I-3189, para 23.
[108] Case C-83/94, *Leifer et al* [1995] ECR I-3231, para 24.
[109] Case C-53/96, *Hermès International* [1998] ECR I-3603, para 28; further confirmed in Cases C-300/98 and 392/98, above n 41, para 47; Case C-76/00 P, *Petrotub and Republica v Council* [2003] ECR I-79, para 57.
[110] Cottier, above n 11, 122, states that the "prerogative of democratic legislation" is preserved.
[111] Epiney, above n 29, 11.

contradictory internal law inapplicable.[112] WTO law also ought to be able to annul a contradictory EC regulation by means of its internal validity according to Schroeder and Selmayr even if it is not directly effective.[113] The concept is coherent. As Jan Klabbers observes, legality and direct effect are logically unrelated.[114] The ECJ recognised it with regard to the Convention on Biological Diversity of 5 June 1992.[115] Yet, in WTO law the Court has not proceeded in this way. According to *Fediol* and *Nakajima*, the Court recognises WTO law only in exceptional cases as a yardstick for Community law. This occurs when Community law either implements a particular obligation that was entered into within the framework of the WTO[116], or refers expressly to specific provisions of WTO law.[117, 118] Von Bogdandy points out that the internal effect here depends on a retractable act of the EU institutions so that the institutions do not bind themselves.[119] WTO law, which is internationally binding on the EC, would, therefore, only have an internal effect insofar as and so long as the Community institutions wanted this.

g) Monism and Dualism Revisited

The relationship between international law and internal law has been traditionally described in terms of monism and dualism. Article 300(7) EC has been said to express a monist view.[120] This is only partially true. A strictly monist conception would imply that international law automatically takes precedence over all norms of internal law including constitutional law. By contrast, the legal scope of international law within Community law is determined by a norm of European law, and there is hardly any doubt about the internal primacy of primary EU law.[121] Coming from the point of view of French constitutional law, which is said to stand in a

[112] Alland, above n 34, 234–7.
[113] Schroeder and Selmayr, above n 93, 345.
[114] J Klabbers, 'International Law in Community Law: The Law and Politics of Direct Effect', (2002) 21 *Yearbook of European Law* 263 at 291.
[115] Case C-377/98, above n 33, paras 53 *et seq*.
[116] Case C-69/89, *Nakajima v Council* [1991] ECR I-2069, paras 27–31.
[117] Case 70/87, *Fediol v Commission* [1989] ECR 1781, paras 19 *et seq*; along these lines above also Case C-377/98, above n 33, para 55.
[118] This is confirmed in Case C-149/96, above n 25, para 49; Case C-93/02 P, above n 62, para 52; Case C-76/00 P, above n 109, para 54.
[119] Von Bogdandy, above n 48, 26.
[120] V Constantinesco and D Simon, 'Quelques problèmes des relations extérieures des Communautés européennes', (1975) 11 *Revue trimestrielle de droit européen* 432 at 440–3; P Pescatore, 'Die Rechtsprechung des Europäischen Gerichtshofs zur innergemeinschaftlichen Wirkung völkerrechtlicher Abkommen', in R Bernhardt, WK Geck, G Jaenicke and H Steinberger (eds), *Völkerrecht als Rechtsordnung, Internationale Gerichtsbarkeit, Menschenrechte: Festschrift für H Mosler* (1983) 661 at 680–7.
[121] Above Section II 1 a.

monist tradition,[122] Denis Alland remarks that all constitutional concepts of the integration of international law are in essence dualist ones. What varies from one constitutional order to the other is the degree of monist influence.[123] These observations are also true for EU law.

The well-established reading of Article 300(7) EC is inclined to a monist interpretation as it automatically integrates international treaties into the European legal order and gives them a rank above secondary law. When dealing with WTO law, the ECJ does not follow this line. Instead, the *Fediol* and *Nakajima* case-law turns out to be strongly inspired by dualism. It denies WTO law automatic effect within the European legal order. The internal effect of WTO law depends on a specific Community act, which may be freely retracted by the relevant Community institutions.[124] This is not compatible with the traditional understanding of Article 300(7) EC.

This disturbing lack of doctrinal coherence may be solved in different ways. The ECJ could give up *Portugal v Council* and bring its WTO case-law into line with the general doctrine of direct effect. As the Court does not seem inclined to go in this direction, another option would be to revise the established interpretation of Article 300(7) EC. Its wording is sufficiently open to permit a different reading.[125] Such a revision cannot be limited to WTO law but must take into account public international law as a whole. This does not exclude the possibility of making distinctions between different types of international treaties. A new doctrine of direct effect could be limited to certain types of treaties. Von Bogdandy has proposed a series of criteria that may help to build up such a new doctrine.[126] The relationship of law and politics and the question of democratic legitimacy are of particular importance in this context.[127] This is not a question that can be addressed here.

What must be retained from this chapter is the shift from monism to dualism. Whereas the Community legal order was thought to stand in a monist tradition, the ECJ chooses a strongly dualist approach with regard to WTO law. In this school of thought, the autonomy of the EU legal order takes precedence over its integration into an overarching international legal order.

122 Nguyen Quoc D, P Daillier and A Pellet, *Droit international public* (1999) para 148.
123 Alland, above n 34, 220.
124 Above n 119.
125 See Klabbers, above n 114, 270 *et seq*.
126 Von Bogdandy, above n 48, *passim*; for a discussion of these criteria, see R Uerpmann, 'International Law as an Element of European Constitutional Law', *Jean Monnet Working Paper* No 9/03, 15–8, available at <http://www.jeanmonnetprogram.org/papers/03/030901-02.html> (2 September 2005).
127 See von Bogdandy, above n 48, 33; also von Bogdandy, above n 12, 614 *et seq*; Cottier, above n 11, 115; JH Jackson, 'Status of Treaties in Domestic Legal Systems', (1992) 86 *AJIL* 310 at 330 *et seq*; Krajewski, above n 12, 223–5.

2. ECHR

The EC has not, as yet, acceded to the ECHR. Therefore, it might seem unnecessary to examine the mechanism of accession with regard to the ECHR. Nevertheless, the ECHR is indisputably a central reference text for the protection of fundamental rights in Europe and also in the European Union. At the same time the European Court of Human Rights as protector of the ECHR increasingly occupies the position of the highest and ultimate guarantor of human rights in the states of the Council of Europe. The European Union is the only important European public authority that stands outside this system. This could make an accession pressing.[128] Hence, an analysis of the reasons against the accession promises further information about the attitude of the EC towards international law.

The first obstacle arises from international law. The ECHR is only open to accession by members of the Council of Europe[129], and only states can join the Council of Europe.[130] In order to make the accession of the EC possible, an additional protocol to the ECHR or an amendment of the Charter of the Council of Europe is, therefore, required. Although this would be costly,[131] it would be practicable. It is striking that the EC and its Member States have as yet made few efforts in this direction.

From the point of view of Community law, it is doubtful whether the EC Treaty confers the competence to accede. It is well known that the ECJ has denied this.[132] According to the opinion of the ECJ, Article 308 EC is not sufficient to found such a competence because an accession would have "equally fundamental institutional implications for the Community and for the Member States" and, therefore, "would be of constitutional significance".[133] This has been interpreted as implying that the ECJ fears above all subjection to the European Court of Human Rights.[134] Krüger and Polakiewicz object that Community law does not exclude the establishment of an external judicial power, as the first opinion of the ECJ on the European Economic Area and the ECJ opinion

[128] See Krüger and Polakiewicz, above n 15, 3 *et seq*, for an emphatic view on this.
[129] Art 59(1) ECHR; see also Winkler, *Der Beitritt der Europäischen Gemeinschaften zur Europäischen Menschenrechtskonvention* (2000) 46–50, but see now Art 17 Additional Protocol No 14 amending Art 59 ECHR (not yet in force).
[130] Art 4 of the Charter of the Council of Europe.
[131] Krüger and Polakiewicz, above n 15, 13.
[132] Opinion 2/94, *ECHR* [1996] ECR I-1759, para 36.
[133] Opinion 2/94, above n 132, para 35.
[134] See Mathieu, 'L'adhésion de la Communauté à la CEDH', (1998) *Revue du marché commun* 31 at 34; to this effect see also G Ress, 'Menschenrechte, Europäisches Gemeinschaftsrecht und nationales Verfassungsrecht', in H Haller, C Kopetzki *et al* (eds), *Staat und Recht: Festschrift für G Winkler* (1997) 897 at 919; JHH Weiler and SC Fries, 'A Human Rights Policy for the European Community and Union: The Question of Competences', in P Alston (ed), *The EU and Human Rights* (1999) 147 at 160 talk about the "hallowed position" of the ECJ in this context; Winkler, above n 129, 129, questions this motive.

concerning accession to the WTO showed.[135] Although the assessments are very different, they do agree on the starting point that the relationship of both European jurisdictions to each other constitutes the main problem.[136] In essence, the independence of the ECJ as the highest protector of Community law is at stake.

The Member States could have reacted to this without any problem by embedding the necessary competence expressly in the Treaty at a revision conference[137], as Finland suggested in September 2000.[138] The attitude of the majority,[139] which declined to make such an amendment to the Treaty which prevailed until recently,[140] may have had two reasons. The ECHR was created as a system to regulate state power. A community that accedes to this system would become increasingly similar to a state.[141] The position as guarantor for civil rights and freedoms, from which a state derives part of its legitimacy, would then equally befit the EC. The significance of the Member States would decrease. According to Sebastian Winkler, it is especially because of this effect of integration that some of the Member States disapproved of accession to the ECHR.[142] The alternative reason points in the opposite direction. A participant who can be called to account before an international court loses part of its self-righteousness. In the case of the Human Rights Court, the intervention is especially serious because this court does not merely judge relations between states. The Court of Human Rights is also of prime importance in internal occurrences. For states, which as the original subjects of international law are sovereign, it has been long settled that their subjection to international jurisdiction is compatible with their sovereignty. Extensive ideas of absolute sovereignty have been overhauled. The EC, as a non-state subject of international law, has never been granted sovereignty anyway. Nevertheless, it does not appear to be out of the question that opposition to an ECHR accession is based on the fear that subjection to the jurisdiction of the Court of Human Rights could impair the independence of the Community. This idea will be further considered below.

[135] Krüger and Polakiewicz, above n 15, 10; on the permissibility of an external jurisdiction see also Winkler, above n 129, 77–84.

[136] As stated by M Ruffert in a note to Opinion 2/94, above n 132, (1996) *Juristenzeitung* 624 at 626.

[137] See S Alber and U Widmaier, 'Die EU-Charta der Grundrechte und ihre Auswirkungen auf die Rechtsprechung', (2000) *Europäische Grundrechte-Zeitschrift* 497 at 505 *et seq*.

[138] The Finnish suggestion of 22 September 2000 is printed in: (2000) 21 *HRLJ* 487.

[139] For the different agendas of the Member States see Winkler, above n 129, 115 *et seq*.

[140] For latest developments see Section VI 2 and L Wildhaber, 'A constitutional future for the European Court of Human Rights', (2000) 23 *HRLJ* 161 at 165.

[141] Winkler, above n 129, 118 *et seq*.

[142] Winkler, above n 129, 116.

III. LEGAL SUCCESSION BY VIRTUE OF FUNCTIONAL SUCCESSION

1. Legal Succession in International Law

a) GATT 1947

A further mechanism that could make international law binding on the EC is the concept of legal succession. By taking over certain functions from its Member States, the EC could participate in their obligations under international law. This possibility has been discussed above all in connection with GATT 1947. Schroeder and Selmayr talk of a "functional succession" (*Funktionsnachfolge*) that has established obligations of the EC in international law.[143] Tomuschat describes what has happened as "functional legal succession" (*funktionelle Rechtsnachfolge*).[144]

Public international law contains rules on the succession of states. Such a succession has not taken place, however, with regard to the EC.[145] The rules of state succession find application if the territorial sovereignty over an area is passed from one state to another.[146] In the case of the EC, it has not come to this. The EC is not a state. It has not ousted its Member States as territorial sovereignties, rather merely taken over certain of their functions. This substitution of Member States by the EC may be described as a functional succession. It could be considered whether such a functional succession also allows for the obligations of international law to be transferred. Yet, currently such functional succession has been recognised neither by international treaties nor by customary international law as a reason for a legal succession. Also the role that the EC has played in GATT 1947 hardly results in this being rated as a precedent. The EC was actually integrated into GATT 1947 as a Member State under international law. However, consent to this existed amongst all of the participants.[147] Consequently the position of the EC within GATT 1947 could be explained by the concept of implied accession.[148]

Since the foundation of the WTO, which the EC formally joined in 1994, questions of the legal succession in GATT 1947 have played no real role

[143] Schroeder and Selmayr, above n 93, 344.

[144] C Tomuschat, in von der Groeben and Schwarze, above n 20, Art 281 EC, paras 53 *et seq*.

[145] GM Berrisch, *Der völkerrechtliche Status der Europäischen Wirtschaftsgemeinschaft im GATT* (1992) 93 *et seq*; K Osteneck, *Die Umsetzung von UN-Wirtschaftssanktionen durch die Europäische Gemeinschaft* (2004) 216 *et seq*.

[146] See Art 2(1)(b) Vienna Convention on succession of states in respect of treaties of 23 August 1978, 1946 *UNTS* (1996) 3 at 5.

[147] Cases 21 to 24/72, n 85, paras 16 *et seq*.

[148] R Bernhardt, 'Die Europäische Gemeinschaft als neuer Rechtsträger im Geflecht der traditionellen zwischenstaatlichen Beziehungen', (1983) *Europarecht* 199 and 205; Ott, above n 46, 117–9; for details on the possible contractual and contract-like interpretations Berrisch, above n 145, 212 *et seq*.

anyway. The mechanism of legal succession by virtue of functional succession, however, remains interesting as a legal option for other cases. A succession of the EC in the duties that arise from the Geneva Convention on Refugees of 1951 and the accompanying Protocol of 1967 may be considered with regard to the planned harmonisation of the law on asylum. Under international law, the Geneva Convention binds only the EU Member States as yet but not the EC. Nevertheless, the question of succession also has only a limited meaning here because Article 63(1)(1) EC makes the Geneva Convention on Refugees substantially binding under Community law.[149] Even more interesting is a possible legal succession of the EC in the obligations that arise out of the ECHR.

b) ECHR

Mechanisms which can be assigned more or less to the concept of functional succession have also been discussed with regard to the ECHR. They are based on the basic idea that it would not be acceptable for the Member States to deprive individuals of the human rights guarantees enshrined in the ECHR by transferring important state functions to the EC.

aa) The Member States' Responsibility to Guarantee the Observance of Human Rights by the European Community In *M & Co v Germany*[150], the European Commission of Human Rights proposed a means to achieve a general protection of human rights. According to the Commission's decision, the ECHR accepts that the Member States, in striving for co-operation and integration, create supranational organisations. At the same time, the ECHR States will only do justice to their own responsibility for human rights if they guarantee that the supranational organisation observes a human rights standard that corresponds to the ECHR. This extension is similar to the so-called *Solange* case-law of the German Federal Constitutional Court concerning the relationship between EC law and German constitutional law.[151] According to this decision, it is incumbent on the German Federal Constitutional Court not only to guarantee the protection of fundamental rights as against the German State, but also to guarantee the comprehensive protection of fundamental rights in Germany.[152] Thus EC law would also be measured against the German Basic Law. This requirement of effectiveness and control is, however, not required as long as the EC guarantees a protection of fundamental rights which is structurally comparable to that of the Basic

[149] See Section IV.

[150] EComHR, *M & Co*, Decisions and Reports 64, 138 at 145; confirmed by EComHR, *KE Heinz*, Decisions and Reports 76-A, 125 at 127 *et seq* and recently ECHR, *Bosphorus Hava Yollari Turizm v Ireland* (45036/98), judgement of 30 June 2005, paras 149 *et seq*, not yet reported.

[151] This parallel is also depicted by Hilf, above n 16, 1198.

[152] *Entscheidungen des Bundesverfassungsgerichts* 89, 155 at 174 *et seq* (*Maastricht*).

Law.[153] The European Commission of Human Rights argues in a similar way with regard to the applicability of the ECHR.

Strictly speaking, however, this is not concerned with legal succession by virtue of functional succession. The states alone remain obligated. They are required to ensure that the EC guarantees the protection of fundamental rights. The legal sources and texts on which this protection is based remain open.

bb) Legal Succession in a Narrower Sense Legal succession in a narrower sense applies to the ECHR in the same way that it applies to the GATT 1947.[154] According to Hilf, it is quite clear that the Member States can only transfer national jurisdiction by simultaneously passing on the related legal obligations.[155] Advocates of this concept thus maintain that the national jurisdiction which the Member States transferred to the EC carries with it the obligation to adhere to human rights (*Hypothek*).[156] It is difficult to explain this in legal theory. First of all, the idea referred to contradicts the general view that the EC exercises original jurisdiction and not a bundle of Member State jurisdictions.[157] The creation of a new jurisdiction, however, does not necessarily stand in the way of legal succession. In cases of dismemberment, fusion or secession, the rules on state succession also apply to a new, original jurisdiction, which is thus bound by the obligations of the predecessor state. More importantly, the temporal sequence of the ECHR is not as clear as that of GATT 1947. Although the ECHR is older than the EC, the ECHR only came into force in France in 1974, a long time after the EC Treaty. This means that in this respect no legal succession could have occurred at any rate until 1974. The French accession to the ECHR cannot have triggered legal succession either because the transfer of sovereign rights to the EC had already taken place. In 1974 there was no functional transition. Just as difficult to establish would have been why the EC should have been bound by additional protocols to the ECHR, which came chronologically after the conclusion of the EC founding Treaties. The well-established concepts of the international succession of states would require considerable further development in order to provide a solution for this.

153 *Entscheidungen des Bundesverfassungsgerichts* 102, 147 at 162 *et seq* (*Bananenmarktordnung*) in connection with *Entscheidungen des Bundesverfassungsgerichts* 73, 339 at 374 *et seq* (*Solange II*).

154 The text in which this idea first appeared was P Pescatore, 'La Cour de justice des Communautés européennes et la Convention européenne des Droits de l'Homme', in F Matscher and H Petzold (eds), *Protecting human rights: the European dimension: Studies in honour of GJ Wiarda* (1988) 441 at 450 *et seq*; as an overview see Winkler, above n 129, 29–32.

155 Hilf, above n 16, 1197.

156 A Bleckmann, *Die Bindung der Europäischen Gemeinschaft an die Europäische Menschenrechtskonvention* (1986) 113–6; similarly Pescatore, above n 154, 450.

157 *Entscheidungen des Bundesverfassungsgerichts* 37, 271 at 280 (*Solange I*); C Tomuschat, in *Bonner Kommentar* (1981), Art 24, para 15.

Moreover, Rodriguez Iglesias objects to a legal succession by stating that the EC could not be treated as an equal with contracting parties without their agreement.[158] Indeed, international law in principle exempts treaties that establish membership in an international organisation from the succession of states.[159] It is in accordance with this that the advocates of the concept of a legal succession limit this mostly to the substantial guarantees of the ECHR.[160] Subjection to the control mechanism that includes the possibility of individual applications to the Court of Human Rights is reserved for the accession of the EC to the ECHR.

cc) Direct Responsibility of EC Member States The direct responsibility of EC Member States is another idea that has been increasingly discussed recently. This theory states that it should not be possible for the contracting states of the ECHR to evade their responsibility for the protection of human rights through the establishment of an international organisation as a form of interstate co-operation.[161] The Member States of the EC therefore take full responsibility under the ECHR for the conduct of the EC institutions. This mechanism does not imply a legal succession in the strict sense. The Member States do not pass any of their duties to the EC. Rather the conduct of the Community institutions is attributed to the Member States. This approach relies on the general rules on state responsibility, as they are now laid down in the draft articles adopted by the International Law Commission in 2001.[162] According to Draft Article 5, the conduct of entities which are not organs of the state but which are empowered by the law of that state to exercise elements of the governmental authority shall be considered acts of the state under international law if the entities are acting in that capacity. Following this logic then, the conduct of the EC institutions which are not organs of the EU Member States but which are empowered by the laws of these states to exercise public authority can be considered as conduct of the Member States. Article I-9(2) CT-Conv (Article 11(2) CT-IGC) even strengthens this argument by stressing that powers have been conferred upon the EU by its Member States.

Although this mechanism may appear radical, the underlying theoretical concept is simple. The EC is no longer seen as an independent subject of

[158] GC Rodriguez Iglesias, 'Zur Stellung der Europäischen Menschenrechtskonvention im europäischen Gemeinschaftsrecht', in U Beyerlin, M Bothe, R Hofmann and E-U Petersmann (eds), *Recht zwischen Umbruch und Bewahrung: Festschrift für R Bernhardt* (1995) 1269 and 1274.

[159] V Epping, in K Ipsen (ed), *Völkerrecht* (2004), § 31, para 22.

[160] Bleckmann, above n 156, 81; also Hilf, above n 16, 1197 *et seq*, speaks merely of the material binding effect; for a different view see Pescatore, above n 154, 453.

[161] C Grabenwarter, 'Europäisches und nationales Verfassungsrecht', (2001) 60 *Veröffentlichungen der Vereinigung der deutschen Staatsrechtslehrer* 290 at 329–31; the considerations of Ress, above n 134, 920 *et seq* and 932, follow the same trend.

[162] UN-Doc A/RES/56/83 at 2 *et seq*.

international law from the perspective of the ECHR.[163] As soon as the EC is not considered a responsible entity in international law anymore, the conduct of the Community institutions is attributed to the Member States, which founded the EC and which support it. The EC's "veil of legal personality" is lifted.[164] Academics have drawn a parallel to indirect state administration.[165] If a state transfers national jurisdiction to sub-state entities, international law ascribes the conduct of the entities to the state as its own.[166] A similar mechanism is used with regard to the EC. So long as the EC itself has not acceded to the ECHR, the conduct of the Community institutions can be ascribed to the Member States from the point of view of the ECHR.

The European Court of Human Rights has not, as yet, ventured to take these steps. In the *Matthews* judgment of 1999, it explained that the transfer of competences to an international organisation, such as the EC, does not liberate the Member States from their responsibility under the ECHR.[167] At the same time, however, the Court emphasised that legally relevant acts of the Community institutions could not form the subject matter of an action before the Court of Human Rights.[168] In the end, the decision did not depend on this question because the responsibility of the United Kingdom arose from its approval of a decision of the Member States meeting within the Council and of the Treaty of Maastricht.[169]

It may be objected that it would be impractical to hold individual, or indeed all[170], EU Member States responsible for the conduct of the EC, which they can scarcely control. Such considerations of practicability can, however, hardly determine the legal extent of human rights protection. Besides the problems can be solved. For instance, it might be possible for the EC Member States to allow themselves to be represented by a delegate of the EC in cases where acts of the EC are challenged. The mere suggestion that the Human Rights Court actually follows the route of attributing EC acts to the Member States might also exert considerable pressure to clear up the legal position by means of a formal accession of the EC to the ECHR.[171]

[163] Winkler, above n 129, 170.

[164] A similar concept was applied by the ICJ in the context of diplomatic protection; ICJ, *Barcelona Traction* [1970] Rep 3, para 56.

[165] Winkler, above n 129, 170; see further Bleckmann, above n 156, 93.

[166] See also Draft Arts 4 and 5 on Responsibility of States, above n 162.

[167] ECHR, *Matthews v United Kingdom*, Rep 1999-I, 251, para 32.

[168] Above n 167.

[169] Above n 167, para 33; in Application No 56672/00, *Senator Lines v 15 EU Member States*, the question of Member State responsibility for EC acts was directly raised; see the applicant's memorial to the Court, (2000) 21 *HRLJ* 112 at 116–8; however, the Court's decision on inadmissability of 10 March 2004 left the question open.

[170] On the question of whether all Member States may be jointly claimed against see Winkler, above n 129, 180 *et seq*.

[171] See also R Harmsen, 'National Responsibility for European Community Acts Under the European Convention on Human Rights: Recasting the Accession Debate', (2001) 7 *European Pubic Law* 625 at 645–8.

2. Legal Succession under Community Law

International law may not, as yet, be developed enough to accept the idea of functional succession and to derive from it a legal succession of the international ECHR obligations of the Member States to the EC. However, a legal succession under Community law may still be considered. This mechanism would likewise lead to the EC institutions being bound by the ECHR. Yet, the obligation would no longer be one of international law. Rather, the EC institutions would only be bound under Community law. Rudolf Bernhardt reasons along these lines when he speaks of the phenomenon that the EC is substantially bound by treaty rules without being a contracting party itself. He explains this by the principle that Community law must be interpreted and applied in accordance with the international commitments of the Member States.[172]

The starting point of such considerations is Article 307 EC. Article 307(1) EC expresses the self-evident truth that accession to the EC did not affect the obligations under the ECHR that most Member States had previously undertaken. As seen above[173], these obligations can be understood in such a way that the Member States are also responsible for ensuring that the conduct of the EC conforms with the ECHR.[174] Potential incompatibilities between the ECHR and the EC Treaty should be remedied in accordance with Article 307(2) EC. The normal normative consequence of Article 307(2) EC is to obligate Member States to modify conflicting pre-Community treaties or, if this is not possible, to denounce them.[175] An amendment or even termination of the ECHR in favour of the EC Treaty is not at issue. It is true that Toth suggested in 1997 that all EU Member States should withdraw from the ECHR.[176] According to his proposal, the ECJ could take over the task of protecting human rights within the EU. However, this concept runs counter to the very idea of the ECHR system, which was to subject any exercise of public authority within Europe to an external control. There is a consensus that national constitutional courts cannot replace the external control exercised by the Court of Human Rights. Nor can any judicial body of the EU. One author even described the idea of terminating ECHR membership as "absurd".[177] The only solution is, therefore, to oblige the EC institutions to follow the ECHR in

[172] Bernhardt, above n 148, 214.
[173] Above n 150 *et seq* and nn 161 *et seq.*
[174] To the same effect see Bleckmann, above n 156, 87.
[175] P Manzini, 'The Priority of Pre-Existing Treaties of EC Member States within the Framework of International Law', (2001) 12 *EJIL* 781 at 788 *et seq.*
[176] AG Toth, 'The European Union and Human Rights: The Way Forward', (1997) 34 *CML Rev* 491 at 512 and 518–27.
[177] Winkler, above n 129, 146 *et seq*; along these lines see also AVMW Busch, *Die Bedeutung der Europäischen Menschenrechtskonvention für den Grundrechtsschutz in der Europäischen Union* (2003) 174 *et seq*; C Grabenwarter, 'Entwicklungen zu einer Europäischen Verfassung', in G Hohloch (ed), *Wege zum Europäischen Recht* (2002) 87 at 97 *et seq.*

Community law so that it does not come to Member State responsibility under international law.[178]

The concept of legal succession under Community law permits the obligations of the Member States to bind the institutions of the EC in Community law. It does this without needing to further develop the international rules on legal succession and without having to rely on the involvement of non-member states, as would be the case with the accession of the EC to the ECHR. At the same time, the autonomy of the Community remains unaffected because the EC is not obligated under international law. However, this mechanism may turn out to be superfluous. It is not needed if the observance of the ECHR by the EC institutions can be guaranteed by an alternative means. Here Article 6(2) EU comes into consideration.

IV. EXPRESS INCORPORATION IN PRIMARY LAW—IN PARTICULAR ARTICLE 6(2) EU

A third way of incorporating international law into Community law is through the use of primary law references to international law. The most important example of this is Article 6(2) EU with regard to the ECHR. On examination of Article 6(2) EU, it should first of all be noted that the mechanism is a purely European one. European Union law invests a text of international law with the role of yardstick without establishing an international obligation. Article 6(2) EU, therefore, facilitates the reception of international law standards without creating external obligations or subjecting the Community or the Union to the jurisdiction of an organ that stands outside the Union. Article 6(2) EU consequently preserves the independence of the EC and its institutions.

Beyond this the scope of Article 6(2) EU is unclear. Some would like to see Article 6(2) EU as making the ECHR binding at least within the Community. Hilf talks of "a substantial obligation" in this context.[179] He emphasises that Article 6(2) EU does not refer generally to international human rights norms, rather specifically to the ECHR. He also stresses that the article mentions first the ECHR as an independent guarantee and only afterwards the constitutional traditions of the Member States.[180] Others, however, emphasise once more the independence of Community law. Thus

[178] To the same effect Grabenwarter, above n 161, 331, who wants to interpret Art 6(2) EU in this sense. Winkler, above n 129, 147 *et seq*, goes even further: according to him, Art 307(2) EC requires the accession of the EC to the ECHR because this would be the only way to establish a right of complaint against the EC under Arts 33 and 34 ECHR. However, this does not follow because the ECHR does not require a subjection of the EC to the jurisdiction of the ECHR. As explained in III 1 b, it is already doubtful whether the ECHR applies to EC acts. Even if this is approved of, the competence of the ECHR is safeguarded by putting the responsibility for EC acts on the Member States.

[179] Hilf, above n 16, 1206 *et seq*: "materielle Bindung"; this concept is taken up by Busch, above n 177, 24.

[180] Hilf, above n 16, 1205 *et seq*.

the Court of First Instance (CFI) has stated that the ECHR is "not itself part of Community law"; the ECJ and CFI merely allow themselves "to draw inspiration from the guidelines" that the ECHR provides.[181] This has led authors to the conclusion that the ECHR is not a source of law for the EC, rather merely a subsidiary source for the determination of EC law.[182]

Eckhard Pache assesses the ruling of the CFI by stating that it avoids the danger of an external domination of EC human rights protection by the European Court of Human Rights.[183] As an observation this may be true.[184] However, this raises the question of why control by that Court should be considered to be a dangerous domination. It is not astonishing that Alber and Widmaier reason in the opposite direction and consider a future provision in primary law, which would make the ECJ's observance of the case-law of the Human Rights Court compulsory.[185] If all EU Member States have voluntarily subjected themselves to control by the Court of Human Rights, the same should not be too alarming for the EC anyhow.

The Charter of Fundamental Rights of the European Union shows once more the ambivalent attitude of the Community and the Union towards the ECHR as an international supplementary constitution. The basic decision to formulate a specific EU text on fundamental rights instead of incorporating international human rights texts formally into Community law corresponds with other efforts to safeguard and emphasise the independence of Community law. As regards content, the references in the Charter of Fundamental Rights to the ECHR go further than Article 6(2) EU. Article 52(3)(1) of the Charter synchronises the Charter guarantees with parallel guarantees of the ECHR.[186] Moreover, Article 53 of the Charter declares the ECHR to be the European minimum standard, in connection with other guarantees of fundamental and human rights.[187] However, this incorporation

[181] Case T-347/94, *Mayr-Melnhof v Commission* [1998] ECR II-1751, para 311 *et seq*; Case T-112/98, *Mannesmannröhrenwerke v Commission* [2001] ECR II-729, paras 59 *et seq.*

[182] T Kingreen, in C Callies and M Ruffert (eds), *Kommentar zu EU-Vertrag und EG-Vertrag* (2002), Art 6 EU, paras 35 and 40; R Streinz, *Europarecht* (2003) para 361: "Rechtserkenntnisquelle"; see also J Kühling in this volume, at II 1 b.

[183] E Pache, in a note to the Case T-112/98, above n 181, (2001) *Europäische Zeitschrift für Wirtschaftsrecht* 351.

[184] See also Cases T-305/94 *et al, Limburgse Vinyl Maatschappij et al v Commission* [1999] ECR II-931, para 420, where the CFI emphasises the independence from the case-law of the European Court of Human Rights.

[185] Alber and Widmaier, above n 137, 507 *et seq.*

[186] With regard to the consequences of this article, see Section VI 2 as well as C Grabenwarter, 'Die Charta der Grundrechte für die Europäische Union', (2001) *Deutsches Verwaltungsblatt* 1 at 2; O Le Bot, 'Charte de l'Union Européenne et Convention de sauvegarde des droits de l'homme', (2003) 55 *Revue trimestrielle des droits de l'homme* 781 at 800–1; P Lemmens, 'The Relation between the Charter of Fundamental Rights of the European Union and the European Convention on Human Rights', (2001) 8 *Maastricht Journal of European and Comparative Law* 49 at 50 *et seq*; R Uerpmann, 'Doppelter Grundrechtsschutz für die zukünftige Europäische Union', (2005) *Die Öffentliche Verwaltung* 152 at 155 *et seq.*

[187] Grabenwarter, above n 186, 11.

of the ECHR into Community law remains merely an agenda so long as the Charter of Fundamental Rights lacks a legally binding nature.

An essentially stronger incorporation at primary law level can be found in Article 63(1)(1) EC. The Treaty of Amsterdam added this rather concealed provision. It gives the European legislator the task of harmonising the law on asylum. At the same time, it binds the legislator to the Geneva Convention on Refugees of 1951, to its Protocol of 1967 and also to other relevant treaties. Here a multilateral treaty system is integrated at the primary law level into Community law. Whilst Article 6(2) EU merely requires a more or less narrow orientation towards the ECHR, Article 63(1)(1) EC demands behaviour "in accordance with" international law. The Geneva Convention thus becomes a direct standard against which decisions are to be measured. It is not just a subsidiary source. Rather it becomes a source of law by virtue of a reference to it in primary Community law. This achieves practical meaning, however, only in the context of harmonisation of asylum law by Community legislation, which has to comply with the Convention.

V. GENERAL PRINCIPLES OF LAW

A final approach to incorporating international law into Community law is the use of general principles of law. The ECJ had already started to use the ECHR as an expression of general principles of law well before Article 6(2) EU was adopted. According to some authors, Article 6(2) EU simply confirmed this jurisprudence.[188] The gaps in the written legal order of the Community are the starting point for this concept. As European integration reached a certain level, an irrefutable need arose to guarantee fundamental rights protection against acts of the Community institutions. Fundamental rights had to be derived from other sources because there was a lack of these rights in written Community law. The use of general principles of law seemed practical. The ECHR, which guarantees a common European standard of fundamental rights,[189] was employed as a reference text.

The ECJ nonetheless avoided making the ECHR directly binding.[190] The Convention is not the point of reference; rather, the unwritten legal principles it expresses are. These are inferred from common constitutional tradition. German academics have described this method as one of comparing and evaluating systems of law (*wertende Rechtsvergleichung*).[191] According

[188] D Kugelmann, *Grundrechte in Europa* (1997) 25; Streinz, above n 182, para 358; also Rodriguez Iglesias, above n 158, 1281.

[189] Above nn 15 *et seq*.

[190] Kingreen, above n 182, Art 6 EU, para 35; J Kühling, *Die Kommunikationsfreiheit als europäisches Gemeinschaftsgrundrecht* (1999) 55.

[191] Kingreen, above n 182, Art 6 EU, para 39; H-W Rengeling, *Grundrechtsschutz in der Europäischen Gemeinschaft* (1993) 224 *et seq*; J Schwarze, in: Schwarze (ed), above n 32, Art 220 EC, para 16.

to earlier leading decisions of the ECJ, international agreements on human rights could provide "guidelines" for the unwritten principles of constitutional law.[192] Later, the ECJ emphasised the "particular significance" of the ECHR.[193] As a result, the independence of the evolution of Community law remains guaranteed despite the dominant function of the ECHR. Jürgen Schwarze talks of a "*Reservoir*" from which the ECJ draws.[194]

The incorporation mechanism of general principles of law thus identifies itself not only by its great flexibility but also by the fact that it leaves the independence of the Community untouched. Obligations in international law are not established. The extent to which the standards of international law are gradually taken over within the Community depends on the Community institutions alone. The case-law of the ECJ is of prime importance. The analysis, which this chapter suggests agrees with that which Jürgen Kühling emphasises in his contribution to this volume[195] from the viewpoint of EU fundamental rights protection.

VI. ASSESSMENT AND PERSPECTIVES

1. The Status Quo

At the beginning of this chapter, the question was raised how the constitution of the EC and the EU relates to international supplementary constitutions. The results of the above analysis allow two interpretations that are not mutually exclusive. One explanation addresses the rule of law within the Community, the other concerns the position of the Community in the world.

Because of the restrictive attitude which the ECJ takes towards WTO law, it is frequently stated that the Court does not wish to restrict the scope of action of the Council of Ministers and the European Commission.[196] Underlying this is an understanding of the separation of powers which exempts the exercise of foreign-political powers from judicial control.[197] Josef Drexl describes this as a tension between judicial control on the one hand and adherence to the freedom to disregard a treaty on the other

[192] Case 4/73, *Nold v Commission* [1974] ECR 491, para 13; Case 44/79, *Hauer* [1979] ECR 3727, para 15.

[193] Cases C-97/87, C-98/87 and C-99/87, *Dow Chemical Ibérica et al v Commission* [1989] ECR 3165, para 10; see also Case C-299/95, *Kremzow* [1997] ECR I-2629, para 14: "special significance".

[194] Above n 191.

[195] At II 1 c.

[196] Berrisch and Kamann, above n 25, 94; von Danwitz, above n 68, 728 *et seq* and also Petersmann, above n 46, 327 are critical of this; along these lines, although less critical, Hilf and Schorkopf, above n 56, 89.

[197] To this effect see also the analysis of Peters, above n 37, 59 *et seq*.

hand.[198] He comes out in favour of judicial control for policy-orientated reasons.[199] Legal contemplation of European constitutional law leads to the same result. In national law the idea that foreign policy is exempt from judicial control has been increasingly abandoned.[200] In France the significance of international law in the judicial application of law in recent years has considerably increased.[201] German courts have repeatedly emphasised that it is one of the tasks of national courts to avoid situations that could lead to international responsibility of the state.[202] Legal control of foreign-policy powers is also laid down in the EC Treaty in Article 300(7) and in the rules on judicial control in Articles 220 *et seq*. The Community institutions do not, as yet, appear to have reached this stage of legal development.

The restrictive attitude taken towards international law also concerns the EC's position in the world. Naturally, the EC is a member of the international community, and it is one of the important actors in the context of the WTO. The ECHR guarantees a common European standard of fundamental rights. It is obvious that the EC and the EU cannot, in principle, evade this standard. Nevertheless, the EC consistently pursues a policy of maintaining as much independence as possible from the international community and international law obligations. The EC has at its disposal mechanisms to efficiently incorporate the human rights standards of the ECHR into Community law as required. At first there was the concept of the general principles of law, which is now supplemented by the autonomous reference in Article 6(2) EU. The EC has, however, always avoided international obligations, which could have restricted its freedom of action. An accession to the ECHR has not, as yet, taken place, and the idea of a legal succession under international law has only been proposed by a few authors. The situation is similar with regard to the WTO. Although the EC has formally acceded to this system in international law, the almost inevitable consequence of granting WTO law an extensive internal effect via Article 300(7) EC has not been set up by the crucial institutions. As formulated by Berrisch and Kamann, the ECJ decided in favour of the protection of the Community's sovereignty within the WTO.[203] A committee report of the

[198] J Drexl, 'Unmittelbare Anwendbarkeit des WTO-Rechts in der globalen Privatrechtsordnung', in B Großfeld, R Sack *et al* (eds), *Festschrift für W Fikentscher* (1998) 822 at 836.

[199] Drexl, above n 198, 839 *et seq*, 845 *et seq*.

[200] See also von Danwitz, above n 68, 728; F Mayer, 'Angriffskrieg und europäisches Verfassungsrecht', (2003) 41 *Archiv des Völkerrechts* 394 at 406.

[201] Grewe, above n 6, 165 *et seq*.

[202] *Entscheidungen des Bundesverfassungsgerichts* 58, 1 at 34 and 59, 63 at 89 (*EUROCONTROL*); *Entscheidungen des Bundesgerichtshofs in Strafsachen* 45, 321 at 339.

[203] Berrisch and Kamann, above n 25, 92 "Bewahrung der gemeinschaftlichen Souveränität innerhalb der WTO"; von Danwitz, above n 68, 729, comments on the adherence to the WTO agreements by stating that the legally unbridled sovereign power of the Community institutions still prevails behind the façade of the concluded agreements ("Hinter der Fassade der geschlossenen Abkommen herrscht ... immer noch die rechtlich ungezügelte Hoheitsmacht der Gemeinschaftsinstitutionen.").

European Parliament from 1997 toes exactly this line. It calls for the Community to provide for a "sovereignty shield" in the course of Treaty amendments.[204]

Thus one is faced with the image of a European Community which seeks to preserve a conception of sovereignty which modern European states have long since outgrown. Many states are prepared to confer on international law an internal effect that noticeably restricts the freedom of action of the state institutions. The constitutional courts of European states lost their roles as sole supreme protectors of fundamental rights long ago. The Court of Human Rights stands next to and above them.[205] It seems odd that the European Community, which has never been regarded as a sovereign state, should have greater difficulty in subjecting itself to international obligations. Perhaps, however, an explanatory approach lies exactly here. Nation states such as Germany or France do not seriously jeopardise their identity if they subject themselves to international obligations and revoke their claim to autonomous legislation and application of the law. The situation is different with the EC. The EC is a relatively young construction that is, in essence, conceived to be a Community of law.[206] If Community law loses its autonomy, this could endanger the Community's identity.

The Community's aspiration for autonomy, therefore, appears to be an attempt to achieve and strengthen an identity of its own. The identity deficit of the EU and the EC is well known.[207] The EU Treaty considers this in the context of the Common Foreign and Security Policy (CFSP). In the 10th recital of its Preamble, the EU Treaty describes the CFSP as a means of reinforcing the European identity and its independence. It is remarkable that identity and independence are expressly associated with each other here. Article 2(1) EU takes up the theme of the Preamble in its second sub-paragraph. It declares the assertion of identity on an international level to be an objective of the European Union. Article 2(1) EU conceives the Union as a political actor on the international stage. This effort of European integration is intended to strengthen the European identity. A second strategy is based on emphasising independence: marking differences and autonomy can also establish identity. The ECJ proceeded in this second way as long ago as 1964 in *Costa v ENEL*. In that case, the Court extracted Community law as an autonomous legal order from the legal orders of the Member States.[208] The

[204] European Parliament, Committee on Legal Affairs and Citizen's Rights, *Report on the Relationships between International Law, Community law and the Constitutional Law of the Member States* adopted on 24 September 1997 (rapporteur: S Alber), A4-0278/97, PE 220.225/fin, 14.

[205] With regard to this parallel also Alber and Widmaier, above n 137, 506; Krüger and Polakiewicz, above n 15, 8 *et seq*.

[206] See A von Bogdandy in this volume, at III 2 a.

[207] See W Graf Vitzthum, 'Die Identität Europas', (2002) *Europarecht* 1 at 5 *et seq*; FC Mayer and J Palmowski, 'European Identities and the EU—The Ties that Bind the Peoples of Europe', (2004) 42 *JCMS* 573 *et seq*. as well as UR Haltern in this volume.

[208] Case 6/64, *Costa* [1964] ECR 585.

ambivalent attitude of the Community towards international supplementary constitutions reflects the same strategy. The Community institutions endeavour to make the legal order of the Community independent from international law. This aspiration for autonomy seems to a certain extent outdated, since the nation states are increasingly prepared to withdraw prevailing ideas of sovereignty and to open their national constitutional orders to international influences. The policy of the Community, which runs contrary to this, is explicable in that the Community has not yet found its permanent place in the international community.

According to this analysis, the constitutional order that is examined in this volume appears to be an order *in statu nascendi*. It cannot do without international supplementary constitutions. However, as long as the European constitutional order has not established itself, the Community will endeavour to play down the significance of international supplementary constitutions and to place its own claims to autonomy in the foreground.

2. Constitutional Perspectives

a) The Constitutional Treaty

The Constitutional Treaty brings with it a radical change of attitude as regards the European system for the protection of human rights. Article I-7 CT-Conv (Article 9 CT-IGC) introduces two additional sources of human rights law. Article I-7(1) CT-Conv (Article 9(1) CT-IGC) refers to the Charter of Fundamental Rights which now forms Part II of the Constitutional Treaty. Thus, future EU constitutional law will contain its own written catalogue of human rights, which is legally binding. At the same time, Article I-7(2) CT-Conv (Article 9(2) CT-IGC) is a reaction to ECJ Opinion 2/94[209], as it provides an express competence for joining the ECHR. Article I-7(2) CT-Conv (Article 9(2) CT-IGC) not only opens the door for accession, but it urges the EU institutions to undertake the necessary steps.

Under the future Constitution, the ECHR will be relevant in two different ways. Accession under Article I-7(2) CT-Conv (Article 9(2) CT-IGC) will make the ECHR internationally binding on the EU, and it will subject the EU institutions to external legal control. Article III-225(2) CT-Conv (Article 323(2) CT-IGC), which follows Article 300(7) EC, incorporates the international treaty into the Union's legal order and assigns it a rank above Union laws but below the Constitution.[210] However, the relevance of the ECHR does not stop there, as Article II-52(3) CT-Conv (Article 112(3)

[209] Above n 132.
[210] Section II 1 a with regard to Art 300(7) EC.

CT-IGC) provides a second means of incorporation. According to this norm, rights contained in Part II which correspond to rights guaranteed by the ECHR shall have the same meaning and scope as those of the ECHR. The explanations, which were prepared by the Praesidium of the Charter Convention and later updated by the Praesidium of the European Convention on the Future of Europe, contain a list of corresponding rights.[211] According to the 5th recital of the revised Preamble of the Charter, these explanations are to serve as a means of interpretation.[212] They show that the guarantees of the ECHR and its Protocols are almost entirely mirrored in Part II of the Constitutional Treaty. Article II-52(3) CT-Conv (Article 112(3) CT-IGC) is of particular importance when Charter guarantees are impinged upon. According to this provision, any limitation of Charter rights must meet not only the general criteria laid down in Article II-52(1) CT-Conv (Article 112(1) CT-IGC), but also the specific criteria laid down in the ECHR.[213] When it comes, for instance, to an interference with the right to a private life, Article II-7 CT-Conv (Article 67 CT-IGC) has to be seen in the light of Article 8 ECHR. The interference is only justified if it complies both with Article II-52(1) CT-Conv (Article 112(1) CT-IGC) and with Article 8(2) ECHR, the latter having been incorporated into EU constitutional law by means of Article II-52(3) CT-Conv (Article 112(3) CT-IGC). So, though at first glance it would seem otherwise, Part II of the Constitutional Treaty does not contain an autonomous Charter of Fundamental Rights. In order to determine the true scope of Charter guarantees both the Charter and the ECHR have to be read together. Insofar as Article II-52(3) CT-Conv (Article 112(3) CT-IGC) incorporates the ECHR, the international treaty acquires the rank of EU constitutional law. Under Articles I-7 and II-52(3) CT-Conv (Articles 9 and 112(3) CT-IGC), the ECHR will become a supplementary constitution of the EU in the full meaning of the term.

However, the Constitutional Treaty's positive stance towards external influences is restricted to European human rights law. There is no significant change with regard to WTO law. Article 300(7) EC, which should be the starting point of any debate on direct effect,[214] is simply reproduced in Article II-225(2) CT-Conv (Article 323(2) CT-IGC). The opportunity to resolve open questions has not been taken.[215] While external action and foreign policy are given considerable attention, the Constitutional Treaty focuses most particularly on the external influence of the EU. According to

[211] CONV 828/1/03 REV 1 of 18 July 2003 at 50 *et seq*.

[212] See also Art 112(7) CT-IGC.

[213] M Mahlmann, 'Die Grundrechtscharta der EU', (2000) *Zeitschrift für Europarechtliche Studien* 419 at 442.

[214] See Section II 1 a.

[215] C Herrmann, 'Die Außenhandelsdimension des Binnenmarktes im Verfassungsentwurf', in A Hatje and J Terhechte (eds), *Das Binnenmarktziel in der Europäischen Verfassung*, (2004) *Europarecht Beiheft* 2 175.

Article I-3(4), 1st sentence CT-Conv (Article 3(4), 1st sentence CT-IGC), the Union shall uphold and promote its values and interests in the world. The norm expresses the will to export the Community's standards, whereas the possibility of importing international standards into its own order is not given any consideration. Article I-3(4), 2nd sentence CT-Conv (Article 3(4), 2nd sentence CT-IGC), mentions the EU contribution to free and fair trade, but it must be presumed that the standards of what is free and fair are, once again, to be defined by the EU. The same sentence deals with the EU contribution to the strict observance and development of international law. The wording suggests that international law is not unequivocally accepted with its present content. Instead, it is to be developed according to EU standards. Article III-193(1) CT-Conv (Article 292(1) CT-IGC) confirms the intention to promote EU standards outside Europe in the context of the Union's foreign policy. European integration is described as a model for the wider world.[216] In these provisions the Constitutional Treaty paints an image of a Union which is self-sufficient and which does not expect to be significantly influenced from the outside, be these influences from the WTO or from other institutions. Aside from the ECHR, it does not seem inclined to accept any supplements to its constitution originating from the international sphere.

b) Anticipating the Constitution

The Constitutional Treaty's change of attitude towards the European system for the protection of human rights has been anticipated by the ECJ. Although the ECJ still upholds the concept of general principles derived from common constitutional traditions,[217] it seems to be ready to give full effect to ECHR guarantees within the EC legal order. Moreover, the ECJ has begun to rely on the case-law of the Human Rights Court in the same way as it relies on its own case-law.[218] This is even more striking given that the ECJ virtually never refers to any authority other than itself and, more recently, the Human Rights Court. Statistics confirm that the ECJ has become more and more willing to accept the ECHR and European Court of Human Rights case-law in recent years. The diagram below shows a clear evolution in this regard.

216 Herrmann, above n 215, under III 2.

217 Eg Case C-112/00, *Schmidberger* [2003] ECR I-5659, para 71.

218 Eg Case C-112/00, above n 217, para 79; Case C-245/01, *RTL Television*, [2003] ECR, I-12489, para 73.

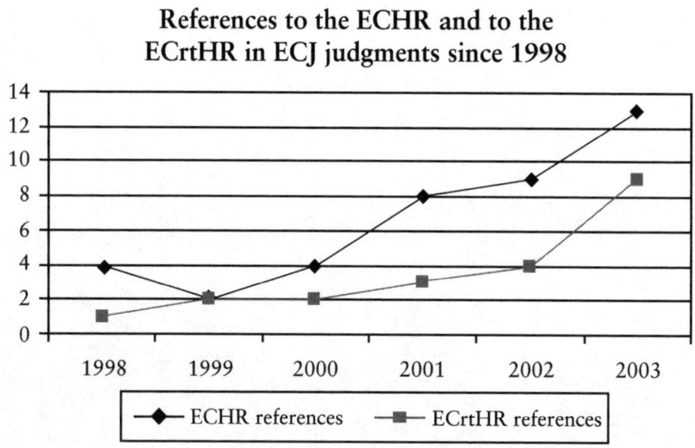

There are unambiguous signs that the conservative attitude of the Luxembourg judges towards the Strasbourg Court belongs in the past.[219] Obviously, the time is ripe for accession to the ECHR.

The absence of a similar evolution with regard to WTO law reflects the silence of the Constitutional Treaty in this field. However, even here a more open attitude is potentially visible. The recent *Biret* judgments, where the ECJ alluded to a possible direct effect of DSB decisions,[220] could be a sign that the last word on the intra-Union effects of WTO law has not yet been heard. If the ECJ were to accept that DSB decisions have direct effect,[221] the WTO would be considerably strengthened. At the same time, the argument of reciprocity, which is the Court's main argument against giving WTO norms direct effect,[222] would be seriously challenged.

[219] J Callewaert, 'Die EMRK und die EU-Grundrechtecharta', (2003) *Europäische Grundrechte-Zeitschrift* 198 at 203; also F Sudre, 'L'apport du droit international et européen à la protection communautaire des droits fondamentaux', in Société Française pour le Droit International, above n 103, 169 at 185–6 and 192–3.

[220] Above n 62.

[221] Against Cases T-64/01 and T-65/01, *Afrikanische Frucht-Compagnie v Council and Commission* [2004] ECR I-0000, paras 139–41.

[222] Above n 67.

5

Pouvoir Constituant—Constitution—Constitutionalisation

CHRISTOPH MÖLLERS

I. CONSTITUTIONAL RHETORIC: LEVELS OF MEANING

THE AMBIGUITY OF the term "constitution" is well-known and infamous.[1] "Constitution" can describe a norm but also a political condition, an object, the document itself or even a function. Mostly a few, but seldom all, of these meanings are addressed simultaneously when the term is used. This difficulty creates vagueness. This vagueness increases when different constitutional traditions meet and there is neither consensus whether there is already a constitution nor agreement if there should be one at all. This is the case in Europe. It causes a blend of legal and political questions that currently lends political significance to every theoretical statement.

These complications cannot be avoided by simply limiting the concept to one possible meaning. Such a terminological reduction threatens to improperly level a discussion that is now simultaneously revolving around the European ability to have a constitution and the content of this notion. For this reason, it may also turn out to be unproductive to conceptually close the connection between the concept and the state of European integration, i.e. just to determine that the European Union[2] had or needed a constitution or did not have or need one. Rather, the term "constitution" offers opportunities for analysis on different levels.

[1] D Grimm, 'Verfassung', in *id, Staatslexikon* (1989), vol 5, para 634; K Loewenstein, *Verfassungslehre* (1969) 140 *et seq*; C Schmitt, *Verfassungslehre* (1928) 3 *et seq*.

[2] This article will only make use of the term European Union for all of the three pillars of the Treaty of Maastricht. For reasons: A von Bogdandy and M Nettesheim, 'Die Europäische Union: Ein einheitlicher Verband mit eigener Rechtsordnung', (1996) *Europarecht* 3 at 12 *et seq*; W Schroeder, 'Verfassungsrechtliche Beziehungen zwischen Europäischer Union und Europäischen Gemeinschaften', in A von Bogdandy (ed), *Europäisches Verfassungsrecht* (2003) 373; English version: W Schroeder, 'European Union and European Communities', *Jean Monnet Working Paper* 9/03, available at <http://www.jeanmonnetprogram.org/papers/03/030901-08.html> (19 July 2004).

Besides its political connotations, three levels of meaning are connected with the term constitution: a theoretical level that reflects the term with regard to history and legitimacy; a normative level that applies the term as an element of the legal system; and a descriptive level that uses constitution as a term to analyse institutions. Only a reflection of the conceptual level applied can lend consistency to the discussion about the constitution of European integration. At the same time, it is important to see that the distinction between these levels does not imply their separation: theoretical terms may become legal concepts. Legal implications can be applied to the European Treaties if they are labelled as a "constitution" as it is done in the Constitutional Treaty.

The following considerations will attempt to expose different traditional meanings of the concept of "constitution" and examine their applicability to the European integration. In this, they take their starting point from two premises: First, a meaningful contemporary use of the constitutional concept cannot ensue without a historical-systematic referral to its meanings.[3] This is particularly important in a juridical context which is always asymmetrically oriented towards the past.[4] Second, the function of constitutions will be understood as the reciprocal connection of politics and law, i.e. the connection of law-making to a political process, on the one hand, and of the legalisation of political processes on the other hand.[5]

A juridical confrontation with the term constitution must, on the one hand, study the usage of the term and, on the other hand, check for conclusiveness. For this, the historic-systematic development of the concept must first be pursued (II.). A critical investigation of the discussion about constitutionalisation of Europe can follow this (III.), which can finally lead to the construction on the three levels of meaning—theory, legal doctrine, descriptive analysis (IV.). All this may help to finally give an assessment of the Constitutional Treaty (V.).

II. THEORETICAL PREREQUISITES: TWO TYPES OF CONSTITUTIONS

If the term "constitution" is used to describe all kinds of normative structures from the *Magna Carta* to the UN Charter, then this broad use remains too unspecific to lend any analytical value to the discussion about the European constitution. In order to develop a more precise usage of the category, without restraining oneself to a certain definition too early, two

[3] The necessity for historical account of constitutional arguments is impressively underlined in J Derrida, *L'université sans condition* (2001) 66 *et seq*.

[4] S Kirste, *Die Zeitlichkeit des positiven Rechts und die Geschichtlichkeit des Rechtsbewußteins* (1998) 352 *et seq*; F Ost, *Le Temps du Droit* (1999) 43 *et seq*.

[5] See UK Preuß, 'Der Begriff der Verfassung und ihre Beziehung zur Politik', in *id* (ed), *Zum Begriff der Verfassung* (1994) 7 at 9.

constitutional traditions have to be distinguished in the following. The chosen distinction is not new.[6] It owes its conceptual background to the seminal but in the legal literature too little used work of *Hannah Arendt* about history and theory of the revolution,[7] but it is—and this is different from Arendt—orientated towards the correlation between law and politics: the first French-American tradition created a specific democratic stock of traditions that are still crucial for Europe—as was shown in 1989. Its theme is the democratic politicisation of law-making through the founding of an entirely new system of government (1.) An older form of constitutionalism that, conversely, places the juridification of an already existing governmental system in its centre (2.) This tradition can be found—with many differences between the individual cases—for instance in the German and the British constitutional traditions. As will be shown, both constitutional traditions are necessary for a European constitutional theory (3.).

1. Founding of a New Order: Constitution as Politicisation of Law

What are the common characteristics of the constitutional idea that arose at the end of the 18th century from the American and French Revolutions? Two basic features can be systematically extracted:[8]

a) Foundation of a New Political Order

The new constitutions founded an entirely new order. They did not just limit already existing powers.[9] This point—often, and probably not accidentally, overlooked in the German discussion[10]—is crucial for the theory of the liberal constitutional state: in the organisation of revolutionary constitutions every form of the exercise of public power requires an immanent

[6] For these two traditions: H Brunkhorst, *Solidarität* (2002) 84 *et seq*; Preuß, above n 5, 11 *et seq*; I Pernice, 'Europäisches und nationales Verfassungsrecht', (2001) 60 *Veröffentlichungen der Vereinigung der Deutschen Staatsrechtslehrer* 148 at 159; H Vorländer, *Die Verfassung. Idee und Geschichte* (1999) 15; Ost, above n 4, 211–2.

[7] H Arendt, *On Revolution* (1963).

[8] For differing accounts H Hofmann, 'Zur Idee des Staatsgrundgesetzes', in *id*, *Recht—Politik—Verfassung* (1986) 261 at 266 *et seq*; G Stourzh, 'Staatsformenlehre und Fundamentalgesetze in England und Nordamerika im 17. und 18. Jahrhundert', in R Vierhaus (ed), *Herrschaftsverträge, Wahlkapitulationen, Fundamentalgesetze* (1977) 294 at 294–5; for a short history of the notion: T Ball and RL Hanson (eds), *Political Innovation and Conceptual Change* (1989) 50.

[9] This founding character has been extensively described by Arendt, above n 7, 139 *et seq*. Furthermore: E-W Böckenförde, 'Geschichtliche Entwicklung und Bedeutungswandel der Verfassung', in *id*, *Staat, Verfassung, Demokratie* (1991) 29 at 42–3; H Brunkhorst, *Einführung in die politische Ideengeschichte* (2000) 253 *et seq*; UK Preuß, *Revolution, Fortschritt und Verfassung* (1994) 19–20; GS Wood, *The Creation of the American Republic* (1969).

[10] See III 2 a.

form of justification defined by the constitution. The constitution determines the form and the content of the sovereign power and, in doing so, terminates the previous political order: it founds a discontinuity, a rupture, that finds its institutional correspondence in France in the Revolution and in the United States in the Revolutionary War of Independence. With this, constitution becomes an exclusive concept: certain forms of order are now no longer labelled as faulty or wrong constitutions; rather, their claim to be constitutions at all is denied.[11]

The concept of the democratic *pouvoir constituant* can be affiliated with the foundation of a new order, though it hardly plays a role in the American tradition.[12] The idea of a *pouvoir constituant* designates the subject of the founding act, the people, and it guarantees, that the process of constitution-making can be transformed into a perpetual process[13]—in France, through the institution of the parliamentary democratic law that is responsible for the scope of subjective rights.[14] This perpetuation is guaranteed by procedures, not by specific purposes of sovereign power. Because the basis of sovereignty is self-determination, sovereignty becomes an end in itself.[15]

The tradition's egalitarian concern for the individual (democratic equality) also follows from its founding character.[16] Only this concern, enables, at least in theory, a radical break from the authoritarian status quo. Because the constitution must ignore and abolish already existing political power structures, it must make individual freedom its systematic reference point. The addressees of the constitution are those who are individually subjected to the new authority without any interference of other intermediate corporations.[17] This does not necessarily result in less governmental power towards society than before: both the French Revolution and the founding of the United States may have more likely led to an increase in public power, and the time before and after the Revolution in France may be portrayed as

[11] The notorious example is of course Art 16 of the *Déclaration des Droits de l'homme* (1789): "Toute societé dans laquelle la garantie des droits n'est pas assurée, ni la séparation des pouvoirs déterminée, n'a point de constitution". For the American tradition, see the contemporary quote in Wood, above n 9, 267: "All countries have some form of government, but few, or perhaps none, have truly a constitution"; below also n 27.

[12] EJ Sieyès, *Qu'est-ce que le tiers état?* (1789); an American reception: B Ackerman, *We the People* (1991, 1998).

[13] E-W Böckenförde, 'Die Verfassunggebende Gewalt des Volkes', in *id*, *Staat, Verfassung, Demokratie* (1991) 90 at 100.

[14] Raymond Carré de Malberg, *La loi, expression de la volonté générale* (1931); Vorländer, above n 6, 55–6. The revolutionary idea of separated powers is analysed in M Gauchet, *La Révolution des Pouvoirs* (1995) 55 *et seq*.

[15] The democratic clou of the idea of public power as an aim in itself has been widely misunderstood. But see: H Kelsen, *Allgemeine Staatslehre* (1925) 39–40.

[16] L Henkin, 'Revolutionen und Verfassungen', in Preuß above n 5, 213 at 214 *et seq*; for democratic equality elaborating Kant: I Maus, *Zur Aufklärung der Demokratietheorie* (1994) 176 *et seq*.

[17] Its most severe expression was the prohibition of any form of association or corporation between state and individual in the revolutionary *Loi Le Chapelier*.

an administrative continuum.[18] However, the constitution organises, establishes and justifies these interventions through the invention of citizenship, through the right to vote and through civil rights. The constitution founds a new form of sovereignty that is limited from the start by the rights of the individual. It does not organise an already existing sovereignty.

b) Normativity, Supremacy and Written Form of the Constitution

The normative claim of this constitutional tradition is implied in its founding character.[19] The constitutional revolution eliminates the recognition of the status quo as a legitimate consideration. As a result, tradition loses its justifying value.[20] It is replaced by "new traditions" that are specific to the constitution. This disengagement from the past is, at the same time, a disengagement from the previously existing political practice and, therefore, an intensification of the difference between political practice and the normative demands of the constitution: the pre-constitutional inventory of privileges must be forgotten.[21] In doing so, the constitution opens up a horizon for the future that, along with the perpetuation of the democratic *pouvoir constituant*, also works towards the perpetuation of changes.[22]

Beginning in the United States this emphatic normativity developed into the legal concept of the constitution as the supreme law. The establishment of supremacy is successful under certain institutional premises: besides having interpretable constitutional contents, it also requires institutions of review that are specific to the constitution—constitutional courts.[23] The example of France shows, on the other hand, that a revolutionary constitutional tradition can also develop over a long period of time without this sort of pronounced constitutional supremacy.

Not only the political-utopian content but also the legal supremacy of the constitution are favoured through its written form.[24] The written documentation of the constitutional content has a formalising effect. The objectification of the constitution in one text makes the constitution an autonomous piece of sense and the reference to its content again and again open for new interpretation. This creates its specific political normativity.

[18] This has famously been elaborated for the case of France by A de Tocqueville, *L'ancien régime et la révolution* (1851). See the analysis of F Furet, *Penser la Révolution française* (1978) 209 *et seq*.

[19] Preuß, above n 9, 20–1.

[20] The classical critique is of course E Burke, *Reflections on the Revolution in France* (1789) (ed JCD Clark 2001) 181 *et seq*.

[21] WH Sewell Jr, *A Rhetoric of Bourgeois Revolution* (1994) 109, writes with a view on *Sieyès* of a "Rhetoric of Amnesia".

[22] Preuß above n 9, 24 *et seq*; Ost, above n 4, 175 *et seq*.

[23] Looking to the United States the seminal contribution of N Luhmann, 'Verfassung als evolutionäre Errungenschaft', (1990) 9 *Rechtshistorisches Journal* 176.

[24] SE Finer, *The History of Government* (1997), vol III, 1503 *et seq*; Preuß, above n 9, 21–2; Stourzh, above n 8, 318 *et seq*.

Similar to a piece of art, its objective character enables it to portray potential oppositions to "social reality".[25] The objectification of the constitution in a text calls forth its symbolisation.[26] The function of the written form is not necessarily the fixing of a certain content, because the textual understanding obviously changes quite considerably over time and this change is by no means undesirable.[27] However, the documentation of the constitution enables its political-utopian demand to become independent of political practice. Yet, the written form also has meaning for the supremacy of the constitution: if constitutional changes are tied to changes in the constitutional text, then this increases the constitutional distance from specific present political problems and emphasises its demand for supremacy.

c) Result

The revolutionary constitutional tradition demands a comprehensive democratic politicisation of law-making. The discontinuity that is at least feigned through the revolutionary foundation of constitutional law justifies the necessity to focus the law production on a single democratic reference-point, in which all citizens must be able to participate as free and equal individuals. The central meaning of the democratic law (*loi*, *Gesetz*) for the democratic state results from this. The availability of democratic proceedings, alone, justifies the legal system and can even—as strived for in the figure of the *pouvoir constituant* of the people—legitimise its abolition in favour of another political system.

2. Shaping of the Powers: Constitution as Juridification of Politics

The profile of the revolutionary concept becomes clearer when contrasted with another constitutional tradition that does not strive towards founding a new political order, but towards the legalisation or juridification of the already existing one. In the European constitutional tradition England and Germany can be named as examples of this tradition—of course with substantial differences in detail.[28]

[25] N Luhmann, *Die Kunst der Gesellschaft* (1995) 229–30.

[26] ES Corwin, 'The Constitution as Instrument and as Symbol', (1936) 30 *American Political Science Review* 1071 at 1072–3.

[27] In *McCulloch v Maryland,* 4 Wheaton 316 (1819) this is exactly the problem John Marshall refers to in writing the famous phrase: "In considering this question, then, we must never forget that it is a constitution we are expounding."

[28] Worth mentioning are the different parliamentary and, respectively, anti-parliamentary traditions. For the notorious German misunderstanding of parliamentarianism see E Fraenkel, 'Historische Vorbelastungen des deutschen Parlamentarismus', in *Deutschland und die westlichen Demokratien* (1991) 23. Also worth mentioning is the different concept of statehood.

a) Limiting Powers by Legalisation of Government

Since its beginnings, German constitutionalism has not aimed at the erection of a new democratic order, but rather at the limitation of the already existing governmental system which was conceptually identified with the person of the king and later with the legal personality of the state.[29] The constitutions "do not constitute a new polity; rather, they represent a system of limitations to the sovereign power".[30] A structurally similar constitutional understanding arose in England in a completely different historical context.[31] The gradual juridification of the legitimate power apparatus also functioned as the "constitution".

The original constitutional situation in the United States was the existence of a representative body, a parliament, without an administration.[32] It was just the opposite in Germany and England: a representative body with gradually increasing importance was allocated to the already existing monarchy.[33] The king's "original" power was to be put in its place through the constitution.[34] This starting point has always been the common denominator in two important traditions: the German "Rechtsstaat" and the British rule of law.[35] Therefore, it is not a coincidence that both constitutional traditions, different from those in France[36] and the United States,[37] have not developed a democratic theory within their constitutional system: in Germany the constitution as a power-limiting institution lacked a principle of justification, a legitimising process. Until 1918 the legitimacy of government remained merely a background topic for German public jurisprudence, which did not accidentally call itself "Staatsrecht" instead of constitutional law. In England, on the other hand, the established legitimacy[38] of the traditional theory of sovereignty was successfully united with a modernisation of the institutions. British parliamentarianism was the result.[39]

[29] For the German case H Boldt, *Deutsche Staatslehre im Vormärz* (1975) 25 *et seq*, 133 *et seq*; Böckenförde, above n 9, 33 *et seq*; Dreier, above n 9, 30 *et seq*.

[30] H Brandt, *Landständische Repräsentation im Vormärz* (1968) 46.

[31] The origins are analysed in JGA Pocock, *The Ancient Constitution and the Feudal Law* (1957) 46 *et seq*.

[32] On the construction of a federal administration by early Congress see SM Elkins and EL McKitrick, *The Age of Federalism* (1993) 50 *et seq*.

[33] C Schönberger, *Das Parlament im Anstaltsstaat* (1997) 56 *et seq*, 148 *et seq*; GA Ritter, *Parlament und Demokratie in Großbritannien* (1972) 69 *et seq*.

[34] On the British idea of the rule of law see AV Dicey, *Introduction to the Study of the Law of the Constitution* (10th edn 1959) 183 *et seq*; K Loewenstein, *Staatsrecht und Staatspraxis von Großbritannien* (1967) 74 *et seq*; Preuß, above n 5, 13–4; on the American rule of law in comparison to German *Rechtsstaatlichkeit* see O Lepsius, *Verwaltungsrecht unter dem Common Law* (1997) 207 *et seq*.

[35] In Germany influentially used by R von Gneist, *Der Rechtsstaat und die Verwaltungsgerichtsbarkeit* (2nd ed 1879).

[36] J-J Rousseau, *Du contrat social* (1762) para I, 7 and II; Sieyès, above n 12.

[37] J Madison and A Hamilton and J Jay, *The Federalist Papers* (1788) No 51.

[38] On English constitutionalism see M Weber, *Wirtschaft und Gesellschaft* (1974) 189.

[39] Since the very beginning of European integration the British Government has had doubts about the compatibility of the European institutions with Parliamentary Rule: K Adenauer, *Erinnerungen 1945–1953* (1965) 499.

The question of legitimacy was practically solved as a matter of parliamentary election and deliberation.[40]

The historic fear of unrestrained tyranny is closely connected to this idea of limitation of power. However, for a modern variation of power-limiting constitutional theory it is important to see that limitation of power does not weaken public institutions, but just legalises them. This shaping of political power through juridification must in no way lead to a decrease, rather more likely to an increase, in its influence,[41] just as the modern constitutional state may have infinitely more precise control over its citizens than an absolutist ruler.[42] The juridification of the power apparatus may improve organisational rationality,[43] increasing executive powers. For this reason, the constitutional tradition developed here will be called a power-shaping—not a power-limiting—tradition in what follows.

b) Restricted Normativity of the Constitution

Lacking a revolutionary rupture, the normative demand of the power-shaping constitutional tradition remained limited. Starting even before the Weimar discussion the attempt has been regularly made in Germany to integrate social reality into the concept of constitution. Influential concepts like "Verfassungswirklichkeit"[44], "Verfassungwandel"[45], "Materielle Verfassung"[46] or constitution as "politische Grundentscheidung"[47] have been the witnesses to this tradition up to the present time.[48] Reflected in this are the lack of experience with a revolutionary change in government as well as the doubts concerning the ability of legal forms to grasp social reality as a "whole". The constitution is not the text, the constitution "is" the total condition of society. At the same time, the fact that the concept of constitution reaches out to the entire society makes it more and more similar to another notorious concept, that of the "state". State and constitution developed into integral, but interchangeable categories.[49] At this juncture the allegedly compelling correlation between state and constitution that has become of such

[40] The classical source is E Burke, 'Speech to the Electors of Bristol (3 November 1774)', in D Bromwich (ed), *On Empire Liberty and Reform* (2000) 39 at 45–6. For the distinction between deliberation and democracy see the analysis in JM Bessette, *The Mild Voice of Reason* (1994) 40 *et seq*.

[41] Legal forms and separated branches do not necessarily decrease the power of the state: M Foucault, *Il faut défendre la société* (1997) 21 *et seq*.

[42] For a historical comparison: BS Silberman, *The Cages of Reason* (1993).

[43] Weber, above n 38, 468 *et seq*; S Breuer, *Der Staat* (1998) 161 *et seq*; W Reinhard, *Geschichte der Staatsgewalt* (1999) 291 *et seq*.

[44] F Lasalle, *Über Verfassungswesen* (1862).

[45] D-L Hsü, *Die Verfassungswandlung* (1932); B-O Bryde, *Verfassungsentwicklung* (1982).

[46] R Smend, *Verfassung und Verfassungsrecht* (1928).

[47] Schmitt, above n 1, 23 *et seq*.

[48] For an important critique using the Anglo-Saxon tradition as a counterpart W Hennis, *Verfassung und Verfassungswirklichkeit* (1968) 24 *et seq*.

[49] C Möllers, *Staat als Argument* (2000) 141 *et seq*.

central importance in the discussion of the European constitution arises in German constitutional theory.[50]

In England the idea of constitutionalism also remained limited but in quite another way.[51] The development appears less in the dogma of the parliamentary sovereignty[52] and in the modest juridification of constitutional supremacy. We can also find these phenomena in France.[53] More significant is the absence of a constitutional document[54] and the corresponding identification of the constitution with a certain inventory of tradition[55] that has to be continuously developed. Constitution "is" an evolutionary process of political practice. Therefore, in both traditions, the constitution does not raise a normative demand for absoluteness with respect to the existing political system. As a result, the concept experiences an evolutionary rather than a revolutionary design over time. It is the idea of continuous constitutionalisation, not of a supreme constitution.

c) Result

Accordingly, the power-shaping constitutional tradition does not require a concept of democracy—again here it is different to the order-founding tradition. Rather, its central theme is limiting a pre-democratic sovereignty through legal form. In connection with this, a special function is assigned to the courts not only in the German but also in the English tradition. As legal protection in Germany compensated for the lack of democratisation,[56] so did (and still does) jurisdiction in England guarantee that the sovereign is obligated to certain standards of justice that especially originate from the tradition of Common Law[57] and represent a specific form of constitutionalisation without constitutional text. With this, constitution describes, in both traditions, the result of a process of juridification, not a process of politicisation.

[50] See III 1.
[51] Vorländer, above n 6, 34–5.
[52] Canonised by Dicey, above n 34, 37 *et seq*; and ECS Wade, 'Introduction', in *ibid*, XXXIV *et seq*; for the present state: E Barendt, *An Introduction to Constitutional Law* (1998) 86 *et seq*.
[53] Above n 14.
[54] Dicey, above n 34, 4 *et seq*; Loewenstein, above n 34, 43 *et seq*; AW Bradley and KD Ewing, *Constitutional and Administrative Law* (1997) 7 *et seq*.
[55] J Hatschek, *Das Staatsrecht des Vereinigten Königreichs Großbritannien-Irland* (1914) 7 *et seq*; FW Maitland, *The Constitutional History of England* (1908, 1961) 526 *et seq*.
[56] D Jesch, *Gesetz und Verwaltung* (1961) 24 *et seq*.
[57] Legal analysis in TRS Allan, 'Constitutional Rights and Common Law' in *id*, *Law, Liberty and Justice* (1993) 135 at 136 *et seq*; for the history of ideas: RG Asch, 'Das Common Law als Sprache und Norm der politischen Kommunikation in England', in H Duchhardt and G Melville (eds), *Im Spannungsfeld von Recht und Ritual* (1997) 103.

d) In Particular: Constitutional Treaties

Constitutional treaties[58] also belong to the power-shaping constitutional tradition.[59] Constitutional treaties are not social contracts.[60] Different from the latter, the former do not represent a theoretical construction for justifying public power.[61] Constitutional treaties deal, rather, with a certain form of constitutional norms that have emerged from a treaty, not from a representative constitutional assembly. Constitutional treaties belong to the power-shaping tradition because the parties who make the treaty are sovereigns who do not completely dispose of their sovereign power at the time the treaty is concluded, but rather legally bind their power, or transfer it to a higher level, like the states during the founding of the *Norddeutscher Bund* as the first modern German state.[62]

Occasionally, the establishment of the first German nation-state is used as a model in the European constitutional discussion. The reason for this is that the European Treaties were also established by sovereigns whose existence was not rescinded, but was and is specifically recognised by these Treaties (Article 5(2) EC, Article 6(1), 2nd sentence EU).[63]

The central problem of a constitutional treaty is represented in the question to what extent the subject that emerges through the treaty can become legally independent of the parties to the treaty. To put it another way: is the constitutional treaty really a constitution or only a treaty? Therefore, it is not a coincidence that in Germany the autonomy of European law was, at first, established with a theoretical design that originates from the theory of the German *Kaiserreich*: Ipsen's "Gesamtaktstheorie".[64] The problem of this doctrine can also be represented as one of the problems of the power-shaping constitutional theory in general: according to its own premise this tradition cannot claim a complete discontinuity, a real new establishment that can be traced back to a democratic act. But the autonomy of a new legal system is less plausible if the old legal systems continue to exist and are specifically recognised by the new system. Ipsen's "Gesamtaktstheorie" proves to be—just like more recent theories that postulate the existence of a European "Grundnorm"[65]—a doctrine of *pouvoir constituant* without the people.

[58] G Frankenberg, 'The Return of the Contract', (2000) 6 *ELJ* 257; A Peters, *Elemente einer Theorie der Verfassung Europas* (2001) 234 *et seq.*

[59] Böckenförde, above n 9, 36 *et seq.*

[60] Rousseau, above n 36, II/36.

[61] JW Gough, *The Social Contract* (1957); W Kersting, *Die politische Philosophie des Gesellschaftsvertrags* (1994) 19 *et seq.*

[62] E-R Huber, *Deutsche Verfassungsgeschichte* (3rd edn 1988), vol 3, 743 *et seq.*

[63] Structural parallels between the foundation of the German Reich and the European integration are a much rehearsed theme in the German discussion, see A Böhmer, *Die Europäische Union im Lichte der Reichsverfassung von 1871* (1999) 39 *et seq*; S Oeter in this volume; P Dann in this volume.

[64] HP Ipsen, *Europäisches Gemeinschaftsrecht* (1972) 61; convincing critique of this German doctrine HF Köck, *Der Gesamtakt in der deutschen Integrationslehre* (1978) 50 *et seq.*

[65] N MacCormick, 'The Maastricht-Urteil: Sovereignty now', (1995) 1 *ELJ* 259 at 262 *et seq.*

3. The Traditions Correlated: Constitution as Coupling of Politics and Law

The ideal-typical confrontation of the two constitutional traditions allows a more exact description of their mutual relationship and of their applicability to the European integration. Order-founding and power-shaping constitutional traditions do not principally contradict one another; moreover, both traditions can be seen in the Member State constitutional systems of the present. However, the aspect of democratic creation and the legal formality of the political process can unfold in antagonistic directions.[66] Such contradictions have been known to constitutional theory for a long time, and they have occupied—for instance in the question of democratic legitimacy of constitutional courts[67] or the question of the statutory interpretation of civil rights—much academic discussion, which continues to the present day. Within the academic literature the attempt is frequently made to resolve this antagonism in favour of one of the two traditions and in this way display constitutional law's "political character".[68] Conversely, the current academic debate on constitutionalisation seems to privilege juridification over politicisation.[69]

The supposition behind such approaches—that democratisation and juridification necessarily clash at one another's expense—underlies the thesis of a zero-sum game between politics and legal form. In contrast, one may point out that western legal systems have long been familiar with the antagonism of two forms of law: one driven by politics and one that arose autonomously. This dualism, which gives courts the scope to create law and legislatures the general power to correct the courts, is also necessary for the adequate functioning of the legal and political systems.[70]

On a theoretical level this necessary correlation between the two constitutional traditions can be described by quite a diversity of theories and terminology—for instance as the structural coupling of politics and law,[71] as the deliberative circle of law and democracy[72] or simply as the juridification of democratic-parliamentary law-making[73]—so that both points of view

[66] C Möllers, 'Steps to a Tripartite Model of Multilevel Government', *Jean Monnet Working Paper* 5/03, sub 1.2. <http://www.jeanmonnetprogram.org/papers/03/030501.html> (30 June 2004).

[67] For the question of counter-majoritarian difficulty JB Thayer, 'The Origin and Scope of the American Doctrine of Constitutional Law', 7 (1893) *Harv L Rev* 129, 137; A Bickel, *The Least Dangerous Branch* (1962); comparative approach: UR Haltern, *Verfassungsgerichtsbarkeit, Demokratie und Mißtrauen* (1998) 169 *et seq.*

[68] See C Schmitt's attempt to construe a contradiction between rule of law and democracy, and between law and politics: above n 1, 125 *et seq.*

[69] See IV 3 and V.

[70] H Hofmann, *Das Recht des Rechts, das Recht der Herrschaft und die Einheit der Verfassung* (1998) 40 *et seq.*

[71] Luhmann, above n 23, 193 *et seq*, 204 *et seq.*

[72] J Habermas, *Faktizität und Geltung* (1992) 167 *et seq*; O Gerstenberg, *Bürgerrechte und Demokratie* (1997) 27 *et seq.*

[73] Kelsen, above n 15, 234.

can be understood as having equal rights. Finally, this also allows for the hypothesis that legal form and democratic law-making can reciprocally strengthen each other.[74] In contrast, abatements in the juridification of the political process lead to deficits that can be portrayed as both malfunctions and as deficits in legitimacy. For example, political "considerations" in court reasoning question the legitimacy of the political system that exerts influence on the court and the legitimacy of the legal system that submits itself to such an influence. A too extensive constitutional adjudication can, on the other hand, lead to an over-juridification of political processes that overuse constitutional texts. This diminishes the normative power of the constitution and, at the same time, calls into question the ability of the political system to function properly.

In order to apply both constitutional traditions to European integration, the question is not, therefore, which of the two is the "better" tradition. More accurately, on the European level one observes both; new forms of political law-making processes with specific claims to a legitimacy of their own, and intensive forms of legalisation of the original intergovernmental political process. The European Parliament is an example of the first phenomenon, and procedural standards, developed by the European Court of Justice (ECJ), are an example of the second trend.

If the coupling of politics and law through constitutions is not a zero-sum game, as shown, then there are many reasons to believe that the European institutions lack both: not only structures of democratic law-making but also suitable forms of juridification. In this way, the Council's arcane legislative techniques are neither legalised nor democratic.[75] If we are dealing insofar with a double deficit in the democratic foundation of the order and in its legal form, then the distinction between an order-founding and a power-shaping constitutional concept can present a form of analysis of the European constitutional state of mind that cuts across the question whether Europe "has" or "should have" a constitution. This also allows for a more exact reconstruction of the normative cost-benefit balance of the notion of a European constitution. In this certain phenomena can be traced back to the one, and some to the other, constitutional tradition. At the same time, these traditions should also submit a critical scale against which European integration can be evaluated.

III. BASIC POSITIONS IN THE CONSTITUTIONAL DISCUSSION—A CRITICAL INVENTORY

The basic positions in the current academic discussion about the European constitution are not totally compatible with the conceptual and historical

[74] This insight can be described on different theoretical bases, see Möllers, above n 66, sub 1 3.

[75] See IV 2 a.

requirements previously mentioned: they revolve around assigning the constitutional concept to the nation-state (1), around reducing the constitutional concept to constitutional elements or constitutional functions (2) and around the question of the autonomy of European law (3). But it remains dubious how helpful these questions are (4).

1. Assignment of the Constitution to the Nation-State

Large portions of the discussion about the European constitution focus on the relationship between constitution and state. This strand of the debate discusses whether the idea of constitution must be limited to the state[76] or whether it may also be applied to Europe.[77]

If one first looks at the historical classification, then very little speaks for placing the concepts of state and constitution in a necessary correlation. This is true, for example, for the German tradition: German constitutional history is familiar with constitutionalism without a nation-state and without *pouvoir constituant* and is, therefore, pre-nationally familiar with the supposedly new model of the post-national constitution.[78] Despite this historical experience, the discussion about the relationship between state and constitution proceeds in a remarkably non-historical fashion on both sides of the front, especially since the nation-state is not a typical model in German history. In the words of a prophetic observer from the early 1930s, German history demands a form of government in the sense of the pre-national imperial idea or of the post-national United States of Europe.[79] British constitutional history also hardly possesses a strong concept of the state, at least if what is meant by this is the institutional concept of the state oriented towards administration.[80] England is a "stateless society" that remains distant from administration-centered legal thinking.[81] In European

[76] O Beaud, *La Puissance de L'État* (1994) 209; E-W Böckenförde, 'Begriff und Probleme des Verfassungsstaates', in *id*, *Staat, Nation, Europa* (1999) 127 at 135 *et seq*; D Grimm, 'Does Europe need a Constitution?', (1995) 3 *ELJ* 292.

[77] U Di Fabio, 'Eine europäische Charta', (2000) *Juristenzeitung* 737 at 738 *et seq*; J Gerkrath, *L'émergence d'un droit constitutionel pour l'Europe* (1997) 87 *et seq* (but *ibid*, at 127 *et seq*); Pernice, above n 6, 155 *et seq*; P Pescatore, 'Die Gemeinschaftsverträge als Verfassungsrecht', in WG Grewe (ed), *Europäische Gerichtsbarkeit und nationale Verfassungsgerichtsbarkeit* (1981) 319 at 322; L Torchia, 'Una costituzione senza Stato', (2001) *Diritto Publico* 405; distinguishing the French and English traditions: I Harden, 'The Constitution of the European Union', (1994) *Public Law* 609 at 613–14.

[78] Pernice, above n 6, 155 *et seq*; D Curtin, 'Civil Society and the European Union', in *Collected courses of the Academy of European Law* 7 (1996) 185; J Habermas, 'Die postnationale Konstellation', in *id*, *Die postnationale Konstellation* (1998) 91.

[79] H Plessner, *Die verspätete Nation* (1933) 27; *R Koselleck*, 'Deutschland—eine verspätete Nation? ', in *id*, *Zeitschichten* (2000) 359 at 373 *et seq*.

[80] Weber, above n 38, 29–30.

[81] KW Dyson, *The Western State Tradition* (1980).

constitutional history any identification of nation-state and constitution is unconvincing.[82]

Consequently systematic arguments for state-oriented constitutionalism often refer to the French nation-state, namely the "universal" category of *pouvoir constituant*. The term constitution is only used where a democratic *pouvoir constituant* brought about the formation of a new order in a revolutionary[83] act of democratic self-determination.[84] This view quickly leads, however, to the question of the sociological requirements of European state formation, which cannot be solved with jurisprudential tools. The reference to the necessity of a homogenous state citizenry does not lead any further here.[85] The argument involves sociological questions of the state of European integration and the public sphere.[86]

The proof of a necessary correlation between state and constitution does not even succeed on a theoretical level. The argument insinuates a notion of democratic homogeneity that is not part of the democratic tradition of the French Revolution.[87] The concept of nation as a self-determining subject is confounded with statehood.[88] The invocation of statehood remains without democratic elaboration. Consequently, the argument would have eventually to deny many other constitutions—possibly even that of the second German Empire—their constitutional character. The necessary correlation of state and constitution does not follow from the fact that a certain tradition of the constitutional concept was manifested in the French nation-state.

Despite these objections, the question remains at what level law and politics can be re-united beyond the nation-state, and which constitutional concepts will be adequate for the approaching politicisation of the European level.[89]

2. Constitutional Elements—Constitutional Functions

However, no positive claim can be deduced from the rejection of a statist idea of constitutionalism: even if constitutions do not necessarily limit

[82] Pernice, above n 6, 156 *et seq*.
[83] Beaud, above n 76, 359 *et seq*.
[84] Grimm, above n 76, 870 *et seq*; M Kaufmann, *Europäische Integration und Demokratieprinzip* (1997) 38, 48 *et seq*; P Kirchhof in this volume.
[85] Schmitt, above n 1, 228 *et seq*.
[86] MR Lepsius, 'Nationalstaat oder Nationalitätenstaat als Modell für die Weiterentwicklung der Europäischen Gemeinschaft', in *id, Demokratie in Deutschland* (1993) 265; P Häberle, *Europäische Verfassungslehre* (2002) 162 *et seq*, 213 *et seq*.
[87] Brunkhorst, above n 6, 91 *et seq*; Preuß, above n 5, 24.
[88] Möllers, above n 49, 422–3; for the distinction between state and nation: F Mancini, 'Europe: the Case for Statehood', (1998) 4 *ELJ* 29.
[89] For a critique of the actual state of European integration: J Habermas, 'Braucht Europa eine Verfassung?', in *id, Die Einbeziehung des Anderen* (1996) 185.

themselves to the nation-state, the proposition that it makes sense to apply the category to European integration has still to be proved. In order to answer this question in a positive sense, the academic literature has emphasised constitutional functions and elements of EU law. However, both can only justify a very modest concept of constitution.

The reference to certain constitutional functions fulfilled by EU law, especially by the Treaties, often serves as a complementary element of reasoning in favour of the Union's constitutional character.[90] In this context, functions like legitimacy, power-fragmentation or organisation are cited. However, the deduction of such functions is planned with relatively little systematic or historical effort. Usually, no attempt is made to systematise the various functions into a concept. The meaning of "function" is simply assumed.

Conceptually, at least, it does not seem necessary to conclude from the fact that an institution fulfils the function of another, that both should be described by the same term. On the contrary, the functional concept refers specifically to structurally similar services of different institutions; otherwise, "function" could be replaced by "identity". In other words, not every legal structure that fulfils constitutional functions is therefore a constitution. One must ask whether assigning a multiplicity of functions without a compelling internal system actually provides a particular descriptive value.[91] This is best clarified using the example of the correlation between two constitutional functions mentioned in the discussion: constitutive legitimising functions.

An influential voice in the debate tries to tie the "constitutive" and "legitimising" functions of the European Treaties together. The Treaties constitute the European Union and they grant individual rights. The exercise of these rights determines the state of legitimacy of the Union.[92] However, under these conditions it becomes necessary to explain why the European Treaties presuppose the existence of its Member States[93] and do not directly address its citizens in a constitution-creating situation. The observation that the democratic Member States are also, in the end, committed to the individual freedoms of the citizens[94] cannot refute this objection: this statement defines democracy without government[95] and therefore

[90] A von Bogdandy, 'Skizzen zu einer Theorie der Gemeinschaftsverfassung', in T von Danwitz *et al* (eds), *Auf dem Wege zu einer europäischen Staatlichkeit* (1993) 9 at 24–5; MLF Esteban, *The Rule of Law in the European Constitution* (1999) 7 *et seq*; Pernice, above n 6, 158 *et seq*; J Schwarze, 'Verfassungsentwicklung in der Europäischen Gemeinschaft', in J Schwarze and R Bieber (eds), *Eine Verfassung für Europa* (1984) 15 at 25 *et seq*; Peters, above n 58, 76 *et seq*.

[91] The ambivalence of the notion has been recognised for a long time: RK Merton, 'Manifest and Latent Functions', in *id*, *Social Structure and Social Theory* (1968) 73 at 79 *et seq*.

[92] Pernice, above n 6, 159, 167–8.

[93] See II 2 d.

[94] Pernice, above n 6, 164.

[95] For the connection between democracy and public power O Lepsius, 'Die erkenntnistheoretische Notwendigkeit des Parlamentarismus', in M Bertschi *et al* (eds), *Demokratie und Freiheit* (1999) 123.

denies the difference between individual freedom and public authority. Democracy's paradoxical achievement[96] lies, however, in the fact that it does not make government disappear, but organises it in a particular form. The European citizens' democratic self-determination cannot simply be identified with decisions of the Member States. Here functional concepts conceal terminological contradictions and the plural legitimacy of the EU. To express this in terms of the concept outlined above: democratic foundation and legalisation, and their basically antagonistic institutional tendencies, are not differentiated in this line of argument, but are improperly identified with one another. The complex triangular relationship between European authorities, government by the Member States and citizens' rights in Europe disappears in functional terminology.

At first glance it seems more helpful to allocate the limitation and organisation of pre-existing governmental power to Union law as a "classic" constitutional function.[97] Because the European Union is consciously tied to the power of the Member States, this function seems more appropriate for European law. However, such a determination secretly reduces the idea of a constitution to a power-shaping understanding and withholds, for one, the democratic constitutional tradition[98] and, for another, the fact that "power shaping", in this sense, can lead to an increase in the exercise of power.[99] The European exercise of political power is marginalised via this functions-process. Even less helpful is the organisational function: the Treaties do indeed define the organisation of the European Union,[100] but quite evidently organisational rules are not enough to elevate a norm to the level of a constitution.

The line of argument examined here shows basic flaws. It cannot, for instance, identify the losses that the concept of constitutionalism has suffered in regard to the revolutionary constitutional tradition. Constitution "is", according to the functional understanding, the power correlation between Union and Member States,[101] "is" a constitutional system or "is" a multi-level system[102] that one can recognise by looking at the political reality. With this, the normative—and indeed the utopian—content of constitutionalism gets completely lost.[103] Via the functional concept, constitutionalism becomes a synonym for the status quo of integration. The European constitution is the collective state of the European institutions, nothing

[96] N Luhmann, *Die Politik der Gesellschaft* (2000) 357–8.
[97] Pernice above n 6, 158 talks of limitation as the "classical" concept.
[98] See II 1.
[99] See II 3.
[100] M Hilf, *Die Organisationsstruktur der Europäischen Gemeinschaften* (1982).
[101] Pernice, above n 6, 165 *et seq*.
[102] I Pernice, 'Multilevel Constitutionalism and the Treaty of Amsterdam', (1999) 36 *CML Rev* 703 at 708 *et seq*.
[103] It is remarkable that the pre-democratic theorist Jellinek regularly serves in this context as a source for defining the term constitution: G Jellinek, *Allgemeine Staatslehre* (3rd edn 1912) 505.

more. At the same time, it remains unclear exactly what is to be described under a functional constitutional concept: the political system of the Community, with or without Member States, or just the norms of the Treaties.

Equally serious are the descriptive losses. A functional interpretation of the constitutional concept only then offers an individual explanatory value if the function in question is exactly specified.[104] This is lacking when different, partly exchangeable, partly dispensable functions are taken from the national legal system and transposed to the European level. The attempt to consistently specify constitutional functions within the context of the relationship between politics and law[105] retreats in favour of a more associative connection of functions.

The same can be said of the reference to constitutional *elements* of European law. The notion of constitutional elements can refer to Article 16 of the revolutionary Declaration,[106] which declared civil rights and separation of powers as conditions necessary for a constitution. But these elements, as defined by the French revolutionaries, are understood cumulatively. A constitution that contains only organisational rules is, according to this understanding, not a constitution—a constitution that contains the specified elements can be one, but does not have to be. In any case, civil rights must be legally effective and kept up to date by a democratic legislator.[107]

Article 16 had a radical-democratic momentum.[108] This is diminished by the fact that the reference to organisational rules or basic freedoms in the European Treaties ought to justify their constitutional character.[109] Such an argument does not do justice to the tradition it refers to. It also ignores the difference between basic freedoms and human rights.[110]

Reducing constitutionalism deprives the constitutional concept not only of its legitimising contents but also of its theoretical descriptive value and covers up a deficient end result.[111] Although the applicability of the term 'constitution' within European law has, in the meantime, received extensive recognition, the reference to constitutional functions or elements may not be sufficient to justify it.

3. Heteronomy or Autonomy of EU Law

The discussion about the European constitution continues on another different conceptual level, calling for the autonomy of European law. Does it

104 Above n 91.
105 See II 3.
106 Above n 11.
107 Above n 14.
108 Grimm, above n 76, 868.
109 See III 2 a.
110 J Kühling and T Kingreen, both in this volume.
111 M Höreth, *Die Europäische Union im Legitimationstrilemma* (1999) 171 *et seq.*

enjoy autonomy,[112] or is it only valid through the intervention of national law?[113] At least in Germany this question is more controversial in respect of the use of the term constitution than it is in the EU. But the question of autonomy cannot be answered "correctly" here; instead its pertinence must be questioned. Two aspects provoke doubts: the Treaties are the undisputed basis of European law, but the legal consequences of this observation are debatable (1), and is it at all productive to include the complex relationship between national law and Union law in a binary scheme of autonomy or dependence (2)?

1. The construction of an individual autonomous fundament for European law, perhaps as a "Grundnorm", is often used in order to justify the ultimate authority of the ECJ.[114] One must, however, question whether such a construction will be successful. The Kelsenian "Grundnorm" is not a norm, but an extra-judicial fact[115] like the act of constitution-making. It is hardly convincing to assume a "Grundnorm" simply by pointing to the adjudication of the ECJ. And even if one did this, it would not be possible to construct a logical correlation between a certain ECJ standard of review for an "ultimate" decision and the autonomy or constitutional character of European law. Even a strictly international concept of European law does not exactly speak for a sovereign reservation of national law or national courts.[116]

2. The correlation between Union law and national legal systems—or more generally between different legal systems[117]—can, in the second place, hardly be squeezed into any dichotomy between autonomy and heteronomy.[118] In other words, the autonomy of a legal system is always relative.[119] In substance,

[112] Ipsen, above n 64, 62 *et seq*, 100; L-J Constantinesco, *Das Recht der Europäischen Gemeinschaften* vol I (1977), 180 *et seq*; CF Ophüls, 'Staatshoheit und Gemeinschaftshoheit', in CH Ule (ed), *Recht im Wandel: Festschrift C Heymanns Verlag* (1965) 519 at 558 *et seq*.

[113] *Entscheidungen des Bundesverfassungsgerichts* 73, 339 at 375 (*Solange II*); 89, 155 at 183–4, 190 (*Maastricht*); but see also 45, 142 at 169 (*Rückwirkende Verordnungen*); C-D Ehlermann, 'Die Europäische Gemeinschaft und das Recht', in B Börner (ed), *Eingkeit und Recht und Freiheit: Festschrift für K Carstens* (1984) 81 at 83; Kaufmann, above n 84, 428 in fn 69.

[114] For other legal orders of the old Member States FC Mayer, *Kompetenzüberschreitung und Letztentscheidung* (2000) 87 *et seq*.

[115] H Dreier, *Rechtslehre, Staatssoziologie und Demokratietheorie bei Hans Kelsen* (1990); Möllers, above n 49, 398.

[116] Convincing JHH Weiler and UR Haltern, 'The Autonomy of the Community Legal Order Through the Looking Glass', (1996) 37 *Harv IntLJ* 411; against T Schilling, 'The Autonomy of the Community Legal Order', (1996) 37 *Harv IntLJ* 389.

[117] Be it within federal states in public international law or in private law making procedures.

[118] The same question arises if one wonders what the community administration might be—whether the Member States are implementing EU law or the Commission and its sub-division, or whether both are rather co-operating: E Schmidt-Aßmann, 'Verwaltungskooperation und Verwaltungskooperationsrecht in der Europäischen Gemeinschaft', (1996) *Europarecht* 270 at 275 *et seq*.

[119] M van de Kerchove and F Ost, *Le système juridique entre ordre et désordre* (1988) 154 *et seq*.

the body of European law has undoubtedly become a methodically and systematically autonomous structure—much more autonomous than, say, the legal systems of the German Länder or the Spanish *comunidades autónomas* are from their national laws.[120] However, this autonomy cannot be equated with a detachment from the contractual basis.

Formally the decisive criterion for the degree of autonomy—also covered by the term competence-competence[121]—lies in the relationship between treaty-making and treaty amendment. The picture here appears unclear: on the one hand the Member States remain, according to Article 48 EU, the only deciding factors for the amendment of the Treaties—in other words the treaty amendment procedure has not become independent. On the other hand, the first independent tendencies have emerged regarding the obligation to hear the European Parliament,[122] above all, in the accession procedure according to Article 49 EU. This is different from federal national constitutions in that a single Member State can prevent a treaty amendment. It is possible to recognise the survival of Member State sovereignty in this, insofar as one does not actually understand sovereignty[123] as the nation-states' unrestrained ability to act,[124] but normatively as the ability to obligate themselves.[125] This remaining element of state sovereignty does not have to remain in existence, but it has, until further notice, to be mentioned.

The newly created right to leave the Union in Article I-59 CT-Conv (Article 60 CT-IGC) has an ambivalent meaning. At first glance, this provision expresses the greatest possible respect for the sovereignty of the Members States, but looking deeper, the fact that European constitutional law grants this option changes this impression. Two effects of the provision can be mentioned that do rather diminish the influence of single Members States. The provision may give the opportunity to draw a distinction between legal and illegal forms of secession.[126] Secondly, the alternative to leave the Union may weaken an individual Member State position in a

[120] Perhaps the highest degree of autonomy within a federal system can be found in the US Supreme Court's actual understanding of dual federalism. An interesting comparative account including the US, the EU and Germany: D Halberstam, 'Comparative Federalism and the Issue of Commandeering', in K Nicolaidis and R Howse (eds), *The Federal Vision* (2001) 213.

[121] To the history of this German concept P Lerche, '"Kompetenz-Kompetemz" und das Maastricht-Urteil des Bundesverfassungsgericht', in *Festschrift C Heymanns Verlag*, above n 112, 409 at 409 *et seq*.

[122] Pernice, above n 6, 171–2.

[123] This concept can only be applied within a plurality of states, S Langer, *Grundlagen einer internationalen Wirtschaftsverfassung* (1995) 23.

[124] An idea of power that historically never has been realised, SD Krasner, *Sovereignty* (1999) 3 *et seq*.

[125] See U Di Fabio, *Der Verfassungsstaat in der Weltgesellschaft* (2001) 92; Möllers, above n 49, 400.

[126] I have to thank J Bast for this point.

negotiation process.[127] The provisions about treaty ratification in Article IV-7(4) CT-Conv (Article 443(4) CT-IGC) seem to underline the suspicion that the Constitutional Treaty may be the first step in a development towards treaty amendment by qualified majority.

4. Limited Relevance of the Discussion Fronts

The discussion that has been presented so far stays, for the most part, within a binary conceptual framework: the question whether or not Europe has a constitution always also deals with whether it should have a constitution and, in the end, how the status of integration is politically assessed. These discussions may, moreover, owe their limited productivity to their conceptual polarisation strategy that cannot exhaust the concept of constitution. The discussion often falls back upon a misstated version of the constitutional traditions developed above: limiting constitutionalism to the nation-state proved to be an etatist reduction of the revolutionary constitutional tradition. Reducing constitutionalism to functions or elements has proven to completely disregard the different constitutional traditions.

However, even if one cannot ask European integration to duplicate legendary democratic revolutions as in France, much still speaks for not excluding the idea of constitutionalism from the European integration and not identifying it with the integration process. Rather the traditions have to be carefully adapted to the peculiarities of the integration process in a way that retains a normative value.

IV. THREE CONCEPTS OF THE CONSTITUTION IN EUROPE

If the central theme of constitutional theory is the institutionalised relationship between politics and law, or more exactly the legalisation of politics and the democratisation of law-making,[128] then this correlation must be developed on three conceptual levels. (1) On a theoretical level the notion of the *pouvoir constituant* for Europe will be reconsidered. This is the component of the tradition that most uncompromisingly stands for the democratic politicisation of law-making. (2) At the level of positive law, the use of a formal concept of constitution, i.e. of a written supreme norm, will be applied and examined regarding the European Treaties. (3) Finally, on a descriptive level, the concept of the constitutionalisation of European law has to be distinguished from the idea of a constitution itself and made fruitful for some phenomena of the integration. Referring to the categorisation

[127] To have another option can be a disadvantage. This point was discovered by TC Schelling, *The Strategy of Conflict* (1960).

[128] See II 3.

developed in the first part, the first level can be understood as an update of the revolutionary tradition, and the third point as making use of a power-shaping concept. Formal constitutionalism, the second point, stands between these two traditions.

1. *Pouvouir Constituant*—the Criterion for Equal Freedom

If it were possible to apply the revolutionary constitutional tradition to the European Union, the question about the existence of a European *pouvoir constituant* would have to be raised. However, is this admissible without distortions? In the academic discussion the category of *pouvoir constituant* is often formalistically equated with the question regarding the autonomy of European law:[129] if European law is heteronomous, then the Member States constitute the *pouvoir constituant*;[130] if it is autonomous, the citizens do.[131] However, this approach misjudges the radical-democratic content of the doctrine of the *pouvoir constituant*.

The concept of *pouvoir constituant* refers to the democratic form of the emergence of a democratic system; it therefore contains two closely linked democratic elements. However, the paradoxical structure of the doctrine of *pouvoir constituant*[132] makes it susceptible to misuse. On the one hand, its effect is only recognisable *ex post*, when a constitution has come into being. On the other hand, it cannot be regulated through law.[133] The *pouvoir constituant* is quintessentially not controllable through law,[134] it is the theoretical utopia of democratic self-determination.[135] After all, the actual practice of constitution-making almost never satisfies the democratic principles contained in the constitution through which the practice is decided.[136] We will have to come back to this point when we look at the Convention and its "method".[137]

Sieyès labels as *pouvoir constituant* the act of a nation of free and equal citizens, uncommitted and willing to bind themselves through the creation of a constitution.[138] In whatever way this is constituted, at least certain minimum

[129] See III 3.

[130] Huber, *Maastricht—ein Staatsstreich?* (1992) 214 *et seq*; Kaufmann, above n 84, 534–5.

[131] C Dorau, *Die Verfassungsfrage der Europäischen Union* (2001) 66 *et seq*; Pernice, above n 6, 171.

[132] J Derrida, 'Declarations of Independence', (1986) 15 *New Political Science* 7; F Müller, *Fragment (über) Verfassunggebende Gewalt des Volkes* (1995); Hofmann, above n 8, 292–3.

[133] Beaud, above n 76, 321 *et seq*; Böckenförde, above n 13, 91.

[134] A Augustin, *Das Volk der Europäischen Union* (2000) 318.

[135] A Negri, *Il potere costituente* (1992); critical analysis of this approach in G Agamben, *Homo Sacer* (2002) 50 *et seq.*

[136] See accounts of the often dubious historical practices in K von Beyme, *Die verfassunggebende Gewalt des Volkes* (1968) 7 *et seq*; J Elster, 'Deliberation and Constitution Making', in J Elster (ed), *Deliberative Democracy* (1998) 97 at 100 *et seq.*

[137] See V.

[138] Sieyès, above n 12; Sewell Jr, above n 21, 45 *et seq*; Brunkhorst, above n 6, 102 *et seq*; A Zweig, *Die Lehre vom Pouvoir Constituant* (1909) 116 *et seq.*

requirements may also be derived from this concept for the European level: the existence of a political mechanism for participation, in which the European citizens as a whole (not as parts of national or regional constituencies)[139] have an equal and free right to participate. In this, the central requirement for democratic equality results from the Republican idea of justification that is oriented towards the individual and in which political self-determination must always be a medium for the individual perception of freedom. Democratic processes for securing individual freedom must, according to this, grant all individuals whose freedom may be addressed a strictly equal chance to participate.[140]

If these requirements are accepted, it seems somewhat problematic to allocate the European *pouvoir constituant*, in its current phase, to European citizens. Only this kind of allocation would permit one to speak of a *pouvoir* of the people in the demanding democratic sense that goes beyond the technicalities of treaty-making or amendment. Therefore, in a democratically demanding sense the European Union does not have any *pouvoir constituant*.[141] A European-wide plebiscite about the constitution would radically change this. However, such a plebiscite would require European national societies that are ready to succumb to a majority of "foreigners" in a national sense and to accept them as co-Europeans. This does not seem to be the state of integration. But among the diverse political processes that take place on the European level, there is not one that corresponds to these strict criteria.

First, the Member States' representation, according to the principle of sovereign equality, must be distinguished from the citizens' representation, according to the principle of strict individual equality.[142] Not only does the original act forming the Roman Treaties—the actual act of a *pouvoir constituant sans peuple*—conform to the first principle of representation, but also does the treaty amendment in Union law found in Article 48 EU. The states' representation disrupts democratic equality.[143] In the debate about international relations this problem has been long recognised under the heading of foreign policy's lack of democratic coherence.[144]

But the argument does not end here. The legitimacy of constitutional law does not end with laying down the constitution,[145] but is perpetuated in the law-making procedures set up by the constitution.[146] Assuming this, one

[139] Augustin, above n 134, 401–2.
[140] EJ Sieyès, *Essai sur les privilèges* (1788); E-W Böckenförde, 'Demokratie als Verfassungsprinzip', in *id*, above n 9, 289 at 327 *et seq*; Maus, above n 16.
[141] See HP Ipsen, *Fusionsverfassung Europäische Gemeinschaften* (1969) 35, 51; Gerkrath, above n 77, 127; less rigid Häberle, above n 86, 232 *et seq*.
[142] Kaufmann, above n 84, 344–5.
[143] Above nn 16 and 140.
[144] M Zürn, *Regieren jenseits des Nationalstaates* (1998) 237–8.
[145] Augustin, above n 134, 319 *et seq*; Böckenförde, above n 13, 105–6; Peters, above n 58, 379 *et seq* (with differing normative implications).
[146] See II 1 a.

can conversely examine European law-making mechanisms, without confusing the fact that the Union's is more or less accepted with a positive "plébiscite des tous les jours".[147] Lack of revolt does not justify an existing political order.

The idea of a *pouvoir constituant* refers to the legal institutionalisation of a political process according to the principles of democratic equality. Political process means procedures that generate possible alternative decisions and that are at least regularly controversial (i.e. allow themselves to be broken down into a dichotomous scheme—e.g. right-wing/left-wing or government/opposition). Furthermore, as Hannah Arendt has stressed, politics is dependent on the possibility of action, i.e. political processes must be able to create something new, to cause a disruption, to detach themselves from context and history.[148] But the possibility of fresh action[149] needs an institutional frame, mechanisms in which actors can be changed—such as elections. Therefore, the distinction between government and opposition is crucial for any legitimate political process. With this, the legitimate idea of a *pouvoir constituant* is radically input-oriented[150] and cannot be satisfied by introducing deliberative structures that do not lead to the ability to act.[151]

Understood this way, the doctrine of a *pouvoir constituant* takes quite a clear position between intergovernmental, supranational and federal theory in the discussion about the legitimacy and finality of Europe: it is not in favour of the nation-state and thus in favour of a primarily intergovernmental Union structure;[152] rather the opposite, it is in favour of an extensive federalisation of integration.[153]

If one scrutinises the institutional system against this background, the results remain negative. The supranational contribution of the ECJ cannot be integrated into such a model; indeed it should not be, since it, after all, stands for juridification. Also, the deliberative environment of the committee system cannot be allowed to belong to this due to the democratic inequality of those involved in it.[154] Finally, political discretion which the

[147] Pernice, above n 6, 161 referring to E Renan, *Qu'est-ce qu'une nation?* (1882); criticism: Augustin, above n 134, 349 *et seq.*

[148] H Arendt, *Responsibility and Judgment* (2003).

[149] HC White, *Identitiy and Control* (1992).

[150] This distinction was developed by FW Scharpf, *Demokratietheorie zwischen Utopie und Anpassung* (1970) 21 *et seq*; applied on Europe FW Scharpf, *Governing Europe* (1999) 20 *et seq* and by Peters, above n 58, 580 *et seq*; a short critique of the idea of output-democracy: H Brunkhorst, 'Globale Solidarität', in L Wingert (ed), *Die Öffentlichkeit der Vernunft und die Vernunft der Öffentlichkeit: Festschrift für J Habermas* (2001) 605 at 621 in fn 48.

[151] B Manin, 'On Democracy and Political Deliberation', (1987) 15 *Political Theory* 338 at 351 *et seq*; J Habermas, 'Preface to the 2nd edn', in *The Structural Transformation of the Public Sphere* (1991); J Bohman, *Public Deliberation* (2000) 23 *et seq.*

[152] Above n 151.

[153] A critique of any federal legitimacy of the EU is in Kaufmann, above n 84, 260 *et seq.*

[154] A critique JHH Weiler, 'Epilogue: "Comitology" as Revolution', in C Joerges and E Vos (eds), *EU Committees* (1999) 339 at 347 *et seq*; also below n 256.

Commission possesses in relation to initiative and implementation competences also does not fit into this reconstruction.[155] A different paradigm could only be valid for the Commission insofar as it is accountable to the European Parliament. This is discussed under the heading "parliamentarianisation".[156] However, the shattered electoral law of the European Parliament hardly satisfies the standards of democratic equality.[157]

The doctrine of *pouvoir constituant* does not assume the existence of a somehow pre-legally characterised people. The democratic subject is a normative concept in the revolutionary tradition. It emerges in a normative sense as soon as the legal system addresses it.[158] Conversely, the genuinely normative construction of *pouvoir constituant* permits understanding the establishment of a parliament, elected according to the criteria of democratic equality, as the prerequisite for a democratic citizenry. Further substantial requirements are foreign to the radical-democratic concept of demos.[159] Thus, institutions that satisfy the minimal requirements for the doctrine of *pouvoir constituant* could only arise in the establishment of a parliament, instituted according to standards of equality, or in the introduction of a Union-wide plebiscite.[160]

If the doctrine of *pouvoir constituant* of the people stands for the democratic politicisation of legislation,[161] then its institutional realisation in Europe faces two problems—first, the lack of democratic institutionalisation as described above; and second, the open question as to what extent a political process that makes integration its main object can be institutionalised on the European level.[162] If one generally understands a political process as an open-ended form of decision-making that leads to binding law, and is in turn organised through binding law, then independent political processes are, indeed, located at the Union level. They are, however, hardly such that satisfy the democratic demands developed above.

[155] For the technocratic legitimacy of the Commission, G-D Majone, 'The European Commission as Regulator', in *id* (ed), *Regulating Europe* (1996) 61.

[156] P Magnette, 'Appointing and Censuring the European Commission', (2001) 7 *ELJ* 292; P Dann in this volume.

[157] Precise analysis in Kaufmann, above n 84, 251 *et seq*; C Gusy, 'Demokratiedefizite postnationaler Gemeinschaften', (1998) 45 *Zeitschrift für Politik* 267 at 269.

[158] Here use can be made of Hans Kelsen´s work: H Kelsen, *Vom Wesen und Wert der Demokratie* (2nd edn 1929) 14 *et seq*; Kelsen, above n 15, 310 *et seq*; and O Lepsius, 'Staatstheorie und Demokratiebegriff in der Weimarer Republik', in C Gusy (ed), *Demokratisches Denken in der Weimarer Republik* (2000) 366 at 403 *et seq*.

[159] Brunkhorst, above n 9, 256 *et seq*; in particular about Europe: Brunkhorst, above n 6, 227 *et seq*. This may imply a complete abandonment of the notion of the people: Augustin above n 134, 377 *et seq*.

[160] Beaud, above n 76, 477 *et seq*.

[161] See II 1 a.

[162] Optimism and good reasons for it can be found in P Steinberg, 'Agencies, Co-Regulation and Comitology—and what about politics?', in C Joerges, Y Mény and JHH Weiler (eds), *Mountain or Molehill? A Critical Appraisal of the Commission White Paper on Governance* (2002) 139 at 141 *et seq*.

Yet, essential aspects of the integration process were deliberately withdrawn from any political realm and given over to the responsibility of the ECJ as the most effective supranational actor.[163] Despite the often extended parallel between European integration and legal integration in the USA,[164] there is a decisive difference in terms of the establishment of democratic procedures. In the United States the constitutional conflict between the national and State level had already changed, early on, into a political conflict at the national level.[165] The crucial distinction between government and opposition[166] was coupled with the differentiation of the two levels. The process for creating constitutional law represented the conflict between the national and State level through the tendency of one party, in the two-party system, to side with the Federal Government and the other to side with the State Governments. The European level lacks this interconnection of democratic conflict and integration, at least for the moment. This can be seen in the Parliament's institutional behaviour, which does not know political conflict on the question of how much more integration is necessary, but shows political consensus concerning its own institutional position.[167] But only a political confrontation over integration itself within the European Parliament can create democratic legitimacy for integration, in a demanding sense. It has to be kept in mind that democratic institutions must combine an institutional and procedural consensus with material dissent.[168] Such a dissent on the European level might push the development and the factual relevance of (almost) egalitarian political institutions like the EP. Maybe the conflict over the EU's relationship with the United States during the war on Iraq will be seen as a first indication of such a conflict—as was the relationship with England in the early history of the United States.

Accordingly, what does this perspective on the doctrine of *pouvoir constituant* mean for European constitutional discussion? It reminds us, first of all, that the demanding radical-democratic heritage of the late eighteenth century must not be limited to the institution of the nation-state. Also, it provides substantial criteria for a further development of the Union that wants to keep abreast of its own democratic rhetoric. With this, the figure of *pouvoir constituant* serves as a theoretical thorn for the development of European integration with concrete institutional implications. But only under the condition of European-wide political dissent can this institution work.

[163] An institutional comparison in J Tallberg, 'The Anatomy of Autonomy', (2000) 38 *JCMS* 843.

[164] Analyses in M Cappelletti, J Secombe and JHH Weiler (eds), *Integration through Law* (1985–88), 3 vols; T Sandalow and E Stein (eds), *Courts and Free Markets* (1982), 2 vols.

[165] Elkins and McKitrick, above n 32, 258 *et seq.*

[166] About the early United States: R Hofstadter, *The Idea of a Party System* (1970).

[167] A Héritier, 'The White Paper on European Governance', in Joerges, Mény and Weiler, above n 162, 73.

[168] M Neves, *Zwischen Themis und Leviathan* (2001).

2. Constitution: The European Treaties as a Formal Constitution for the Union

It seems plausible to understand the European Treaties as a formal constitution[169] of Europe. The Treaties constitute autonomous forms of law-making at the European level, and they are supreme above all other layers of Union law. The Treaties are "law-making norms",[170] and with this they couple the relation of politics and law at the level of the Union.

There are two reasons for taking a closer theoretical look at this formal constitutional structure: for one, this structure brings up the element of the written form of the constitution that is often underestimated especially in the discussion about European law. Second, dealing with formal aspects is also *e contrario* advisable because the search for a substantial constitution for Europe hardly leads to a systematic concept. Indeed, there are apparently necessary connections between the idea of the constitution and all imaginable legal principles.[171] If one emphasises the individual mobilisation of the court, then a connection with the concept of rule of law[172] lies close at hand. If one focuses on the organisational structures, then one can turn to the federal organisation,[173] the subsidiarity principle[174] or forms of differentiated integration.[175] Functional considerations, finally, suggest declaring the open domestic market[176] or the basic freedoms as the constitutional core of integration.[177] However, important as all these principles are for the consistent and complete description of the European legal system, it is far from clear that there is an urgent or necessary connection of any one principle to the idea of constitution or a connection to all of them. This also corresponds to the widely spread use in European legal literature of talk about a European constitution, without any theoretical elaboration of the term.[178]

Limiting the analysis to its formal aspects leads to a more modest and selective result. Moreover, this seems to correspond to the ECJ, which

[169] For the concept of a formal constitution: Kelsen, above n 15, 251–2

[170] Kelsen, above n 15, 98, 234.

[171] On the basis of Art 6 EU: A von Bogdandy in this volume; Gerkrath, n 77, 325 *et seq.*

[172] See II 2 a.

[173] P Hay, *Federalism and Supranational Organization* (1966); K Lenaerts, 'Constitutionalism and the Many Faces of Federalism', (1990) *AJCL* 205; JHH Weiler, 'Constitutionalism and Federalism', in R Howse and K Nicolaidis (eds), *The Federal Vision* (2001) 54; S Oeter in this volume.

[174] C Calliess, *Subsidiaritäts- und Solidaritätsprinzip in der Europäischen Union* (1999) 65 *et seq.*

[175] C-D Ehlermann, 'Engere Zusammenarbeit nach dem Amsterdamer Vertrag', (1997) *Europarecht* 362.

[176] PC Müller-Graff, 'Die wettbewerbsverfaßte Marktwirtschaft als gemeineuropäisches Verfassungsprinzip?', (1997) *Europarecht* 433 at 439 *et seq.*

[177] M P Maduro, *We the Court* (1998) 7; A Hatje in this volume.

[178] Eg J Boulois, *Droit institutionel de L'Union Européenne* (1995); K Lenaerts and P van Nuffel, *Constitutional Law of the European Union* (1999); TC Hartley, *The Foundations of European Community Law* (1999).

referred to the Treaties as to a "constitutional charter".[179] The investigation of the formal constitutional characteristics also represents an opportunity to completely restructure the programmatically overloaded European constitutional debate.

However, before a systematic investigation of the formal constitutional characteristics of the Treaties can begin, we need to set clear terminological limits to the formulation of the ECJ. The words that appear in the French translations of the judgments are "charte constitutionelle de base qu'est le traité". This not only reveals ambiguities in the translation[180] but also gives a historical indication of the legally compromising character of the European Treaties. For in the French constitutional history this term refers to the "Charte Constitutionelle" of 4 June 1814, which is emphatically not a "constitution" that the people gave themselves, but a basic law given by the king. The term indicates a democratic deficit and introduces the idea of royal constitutionalism into European history, holding back the democratic achievements of the Revolution for the time being.[181]

Formal constitutionalism—different from the doctrine of *pouvoir constituant* already dealt with, and different from the concept of constitutionalisation yet to be dealt with—cannot clearly be assigned to one of the two constitutional traditions developed above. Written form and constitutional supremacy indeed first took on their central meaning when the revolutionary constitutional concept appeared.[182] However, they can also be integrated into an evolutionary constitutional understanding, though it is no necessary part of it.[183]

a) The Treaties in Written Form

The written aspect of a constitution has two functions.[184] On a political level the constitutional text is a program against which the reader can repeatedly measure and criticise social reality. The constitution—and this is a heritage of the revolutionary constitutional tradition that can still be clearly observed in the United States—develops an important symbolic

[179] GA Lagrange to Case 6/64, *Costa* [1964] ECR 600, 605: "the constitution of the Community"; Case 294/83, *Les Verts v Parliament* [1986] ECR 1339, para 23: "the basic constitutional charter"; Opinion 1/91, *EEA 1* [1991] ECR 1991 I-6079, para 1: "albeit concluded in the form of an international agreement, none the less constitutes the constitutional charter of a Community based on the rule of law." Similar *Entscheidungen des Bundesverfasungsgerichts* 22, 293 at 296 (*EWG-Verordnungen*). But see also Opinion 1/76, *Laying Up-Fund* [1977] ECR 741, para 5, where the court talks about the "internal constitution ... of the Community". A careful analysis can be found in Gerkrath, n 77, 124–5.

[180] "Charte" can be translated as constitutional document or as constitution of the Treaties. The adjective "constitutionelle" seems rather to weaken than to underline its constitutional character.

[181] F Furet, *La Révolution, tome II 1814–1880* (1988) 24 *et seq.*

[182] See II 1 b.

[183] This shows the English constitutional tradition.

[184] See II 1 b.

function for a society, a normativity for the polity that it regulates.[185] The text of the constitution is read again and again and reinterpreted, demanding and requiring new efforts of a society to improve itself. The general dissemination of a readable constitutional text promotes this claim. Furthermore, the requirement for documentation strengthens the de-coupling of constitutional guarantees from specific political matters. Ad hoc amendments to the constitution are avoided, and it provides a guarantee that the entire constitutional status quo is preserved and that no unwritten sub-constitutions can emerge.[186] These important functions of a constitutional text must at least be put into perspective in regard to the European Treaties. The written form of the Treaties is precarious for a variety of reasons that can be traced back to the continuously functioning intergovernmental origins of European law.

First, the division of the founding charters into different treaties at the community's founding moment has restricted their formal constitutional character. This problem has been deepened through the division of European Treaties since the Maastricht Treaty. The system of protocols and declarations intensifies this problem. According to Article 311 EC the Protocols become part of the Treaty. Even though they are part of the juridification of the treaty amendment process,[187] they are suspect, especially in cases in which their content violates core rules of Union law, like the ban on discrimination or the retention of the *acquis communautaire*[188] in the Barber Protocol.[189] The protocol system is the European equivalent of the practice found in some Member States of allowing constitutional amendments that do not change the constitutional text.[190] Less serious, but nevertheless belonging in this context are the Member States' final declarations in the appendices to the Treaties. They are, however, restricted in their legal effect to being interpretation aids.[191] Also belonging in this context are the powers of Article 308 EC as well as the existence of special rules for the

[185] See II 1 b.

[186] U Hufeld, *Die Verfassungsdurchbrechung* (1997) 208 *et seq*.

[187] For the applicability of 48 EU on protocols, see W Meng, in von der Groeben and Schwarze (eds), *Kommentar zum EU-/EG-Vertrag* (2003), Art 48 EU, para 38.

[188] D Curtin, 'The Constitutional Structure of the Union: a Europe of Bits and Pieces', (1993) 30 *CML Rev* at 22 *et seq*.

[189] D Curtin, 'Scalping the Community Legislation: Occupational Pensions and "Barber"', (1990) 27 *CML Rev* 475.

[190] For Austria in Art 44 Federal Constitutional Law. A special case is of course the United Kingdom.

[191] U Everling, 'Zur rechtlichen Wirkung von Beschlüssen, Entschließungen, Erklärungen und Vereinbarungen des Rates oder der Mitgliedstaaten der Europäischen Gemeinschaft', in G Lücke (ed), *Rechtsvergleichung, Europarecht und Staatenintegration: Gedächtnisschrift für L-J Constantinesco* (1983) 133 at 153; arguing against any application by the ECJ: AG Toth, 'The Legal Status of the Declarations Annexed to the Single European Act', (1986) 23 *CML Rev* 803 at 810–11.

simplified treaty amendments in Articles 22(2), 190(4) and 269(2) EC, and Article 42 EU.[192]

The complexity of the entire treaty system corresponds to the much disliked complexity of the single treaties, principally the Community Treaty. This is also the result of intergovernmental negotiation processes and diminishes the positive effects of a written constitution. In their current form, because of problems of style, the treaties cannot be used as the political catechism of a democratic polity.

Finally, the written form experiences its most extensive modification through specific forms of differentiated intergovernmental integration (e.g. through the "enhanced cooperation" according to Article 43 EU and Article 11 EC,[193] and through the "open method of co-ordination").[194] The latter procedure is particularly questionable because it leaves absolutely no formalised written traces in Union law: it is neither planned for in the Treaties nor does it lead to an edict of Union legal acts. The integration proceeds separate from the Treaties' texts and remains invisible to their readers.

From a theoretical viewpoint these mechanisms are similar in that they constitute a political valve on the Union's intergovernmental side with a quasi-constituent effect. This valve crystallises institutionally in the European Council, Article 4 EU.[195] Such a valve function, however, disturbs the balanced coupling of political process and legal form that is expected from constitutions. It is deficient even from an inter-nationalist point of view because the national parliaments remain partially excluded.[196] As a result, a look at the official side of the Treaties yields problematic answers regarding their material ability to function as a constitution. Beyond this, the structuring of the Treaties reduces the political-symbolic function of the constitutional charter until it is unrecognisable.[197]

A legal solution to these structural problems could lie in the generalisation of the rule in Article 48 EU, which—like the ECJ argumentation using the constitutional concept[198]—could be ascribed a unifying effect for the entire Union law system. But the inclusion of all forms of intergovernmental subconstitutional law in the amendment procedure of Article 48 EU[199] cannot

[192] Lenaerts and van Nuffel, above n 178, 262–63.

[193] T Bender, 'Die Verstärkte Zusammenarbeit nach Nizza', (2001) 61 *Zeitschrift für ausländisches öffentliches Recht und Völkerrecht* 729 at 738 *et seq*; for the Constitutional Treaty: A López-Pina, 'Enhanced Cooperation as European Form of Government', in I Pernice and M Maduro (eds), *A Constitution for the European Union* (2004) 119.

[194] Lisbon European Council, *Presidency Conclusions*, sub I 7, <http://www.europarl.eu.int/summits/lis1_de.htm> (30 June 2004).

[195] P Dann in this volume.

[196] C Koenig and M Pechstein, 'Die EU-Vertragsänderung', (1998) *Europarecht* 130 at 139–40.

[197] See II 1 b.

[198] See b) aa.

[199] A restrictive interpretation is proposed by Koenig and Pechstein, above n 196, 133 *et seq*, referring to the General Principles of public international law.

be legally justified. At least, an amendment to the Treaties is not possible outside of the amendment procedure.[200] Again one may recognise the analytical deficiencies of an approach that wants to completely detach European law from its intergovernmental roots.[201] As seen above, the Constitutional Treaty may change this.[202]

b) Supremacy of the Treaties

Supremacy is part of a formal constitution.[203] Regarding the Treaties, two levels of hierarchy are recognisable:[204] a possible hierarchy within the law of the Treaty, and second, the supremacy of Treaty law with respect to other Member State laws and Union law. At this point, the "metaphor"[205] of the European Treaties as a constitution takes a concrete legal meaning.

aa) Constitution as a Legal Argument—the ECJ and Hierarchies within the Treaties The possible internal hierarchy (or the immanent amendment limits of the Treaties) lead to one of the classic problems of European law, to the issue of the consensual revocability of the Treaties. But the conflict between treaty-rules of public international law and a supranational ban on leaving the Union[206] proves to be merely illusory.[207] The discussion mirrors the ambiguities of the concept of sovereignty,[208] oscillating between a normative right and a factual capability. The following observation may be sufficient. If a State is able to leave the EU, if the costs of withdrawal are worthwhile, then an opposing obligation will not play a practical role. If this ability does not exist, the question of law does not become relevant.[209]

The problem of internal hierarchy of certain treaty contents may be of major significance in the future. The court used the notion of the constitution at this point in its first Opinion on the EEA[210] to interpret the current

[200] Case 22/70, *Commission v Council* [1971] ECR 263, para 17 about an agreement with third states; Case 43/75, *Defrenne* [1976] ECR 455, para 58; Case 59/75, *Manghera* [1976] 91, paras 19/21 about a Council resolution; Case 68/86, *UK v Council* [1988] ECR 855, para 38: "the Treaty rules to change the Treaties are not *jus dispositivum*"; Opinion 2/94, *ECHR* [1996] ECR I-1759, para 30 about an amendment according to Art 308 EC.

[201] See III 3.

[202] See n 124.

[203] Kelsen, above n 15, 252–3.

[204] This is stressed as a constitutional element of the Treaties by GC Rodríguez Iglesias, 'Zur "Verfassung" der Europäischen Gemeinschaft', (1996) *Europäische Grundrechte-Zeitschrift* 125 at 125–26; F Schorkopf, *Homogenität in der Europäischen Union* (2000) 219–20.

[205] A von Bogdandy, 'Beobachtungen zur Wissenschaft vom Europarecht', (2001) 40 *Der Staat* 1 at 12.

[206] Contra the right to secession: U Everling, 'Sind die Mitgliedstaaten der Europäischen Gemeinschaft noch Herren der Verträge?', in R Bernhardt (ed), *Völkerrecht als Rechtsordnung, internationale Gerichtsbarkeit, Menschenrechte: Festschrift für H Mosler* (1983) 173 at 183 *et seq*; pro: W Meng, *Das Recht der internationalen Organisation* (1979) 119 *et seq*, 162 *et seq*.

[207] JHH Weiler, *The Constitution of Europe* (1999) 18.

[208] M Koskenniemi, *From Apology to Utopia* (1989) 192 *et seq*.

[209] Critique: Möllers above n 49, 399–400.

[210] Opinion 1/91, above n 179.

Article 310 EC.[211] In this controversial decision the court seals the EC legal system off from another legal order by using the term constitution. According to the court, the prerequisite for homogenising the Union legal system follows from the constitutional qualities of the Treaties. The notion of constitution serves in this context as a tool to close and unify the European legal order.

Although the decision *Les Verts*[212] is rarely discussed under the heading of internal hierarchy,[213] it is similar in its invocation of "constitutional" qualities of the EC. The Court deduces a comprehensive demand for legal protection from the constitutional qualities of the Treaty. In an astonishing parallel argument to Justice Marshall's in *McCulloch v Maryland*,[214] the invocation of constitutional qualities serves to widen the content of the norm text and the jurisdiction of the court. Constitution here means to close EC law towards the outside and to complete it inwardly. This occurs at the expense of the systematic coherence of the reasoning.[215] However, such circular arguments may often mark the beginning of a constitutional adjudication,[216] and its practical power to establish a legal system should at least not depend on its argumentative conclusiveness. Despite this, the use of the term offers a solution to a problem unforeseen by the text that is convincing in the result, an interpretation that is more *praeter* than *contra legem*.

bb) Supremacy of the Treaty Law The supremacy of the Treaties over all levels of Member State law, including constitutional law, is often understood as an important constitutional element of the European legal order.[217] But in public international law international courts generally apply and enforce international law obligations without regard to state law.[218] The enforcement of European law in respect to the Member States is, in this sense, not unusual. However, this enforcement becomes particularly visible because of the quantity of European law, on the one hand, and because of its direct applicability on the other.[219]

In federal structures the constitutional supremacy of the higher level constantly proves to be a precarious phenomenon because decisions concerning

[211] A critical analysis in M Heintzen, 'Hierarchisierungsprozesse des Primärrechts in der europäischen Gemeinschaft', (1994) *Europarecht* 35; Hertel, above n 77, 238.
[212] Case 294/83, above n 179.
[213] But see PP Craig, 'Constitutions, Constitutionalism, and the European Union', 7 (2001) *ELJ* 125 at 133–34.
[214] Above n 27.
[215] Similar circular reasoning in the founding period of Community law are analysed in B de Witte, 'Direct Effect, Supremacy and the Nature of the Legal Order', in P Craig and G de Búrca (eds), *The Evolution of EU Law* (1999) 177 at 208.
[216] PW Kahn, *The Reign of Law* (1997) 134 *et seq.*
[217] Hartley, above n 178, 233 *et seq*; Ipsen, above n 64, 266–67, 277 *et seq.*
[218] Art 46(1) WCT; Weiler and Haltern, above n 116.
[219] Similar Weiler, above n 207, 20–21.

the relationship between the levels are also regularly assigned to a court of the higher level. It is, therefore, not easy to compare the effects of constitutional supremacy within one level and between different levels. Despite these difficulties it is necessary to undertake this comparison within an investigation of the supremacy of European Treaty law.

If the Treaties serve to juridify European law-making structures in a similar way to national constitutions, then they must prevail over secondary law. In this way the ECJ review of European law seems to be less intensive than that of Member State acts. It is also oriented, at least in the result, towards political majorities in the Council.[220] A similar observation can be made for the delegation of legislative competences from the Council to the Commission, on the one hand, and to the Member States on the other.[221] There is undoubtedly a reason for these distinctions. If the core of the basic freedoms is anti-discrimination, then Member State acts are more likely to infringe upon them than European acts. A similar situation can be observed in the function of delegated rules as securing a homogenous system of implementation,[222] especially since written limits of delegation are unknown to the EC. Seen this way, a large part of the Treaty law focuses specifically on the Member States and legitimately differentiates between national and Union law. However, this justification of different supremacy structures has its limits. If one also understands basic freedoms as a ban on limitations[223] and if Community law's implementation structure is increasingly designed homogeneously, then different standards of review may lose plausibility. But despite the growing level of integration, the judicial enforcement of European primary law with regard to the European level remains the exception. This can be clearly seen in the fact that a lack of competence at the European level has hardly ever been accepted by the ECJ.[224]

Modifications of Treaty supremacy can also be observed in other ways: Union law lacks a canon of legal forms that can formally portray the difference between various norm hierarchies.[225] This affects not only the sub-treaty law, which does not have separate forms for basic and implementing rules,[226] but also the Treaties, whose contents are materially overloaded and which contain a multiplicity of secondary rules in this matter.

[220] Maduro, above n 177, 78 *et seq*; for the collaboration between ECJ and Commission: E Stein, 'Lawyers, Judges, and the Making of a Transnational Constitution', (1981) 75 *AJCL* 1.

[221] An analysis in C Möllers, 'Durchführung des Gemeinschaftsrechts', (2002) *Europarecht* 483.

[222] K Lenaerts, 'Regulating the regulatory process: "delegation of powers" in the European Community', (1993) 18 *EL Rev* 23 at 29 *et seq*; Möllers, above n 221, 503 *et seq*.

[223] Similar: T Kingreen in this volume.

[224] Beyond the decisions concerning the external powers of the EU see Case C-376/98, *Germany v Parliament and Council* [2000] ECR I-8419; B Simma, MC Zöckler and JHH Weiler, *Kompetenzen und Grundrechte* (1999).

[225] J Bast in this volume.

[226] R Bieber and I Salomé, 'Hierarchy of Norms in European Law' (1996) 33 *CML Rev* 907 at 920–21, 926–27.

Both are harmful to the supremacy of Treaty law. The functioning of Treaty supremacy is not based on the isolated demand for supremacy of a complex of norms above all others. It must, rather, be appropriately designed for application. Specifically, the question whether primary or secondary law is the actual standard of review, i.e. whether the supremacy of the Treaties is applied or not, is hardly discernible in the jurisprudence of the ECJ.

This may change gradually via the Constitutional Treaty, because in a move which is at least symbolically important,[227] the Constitutional Treaty starts to draw the legal distinction between laws and rules in Article I-32(2) CT-Conv (Article 33(2) CT-IGC).[228] The effects of the change are uncertain, but real changes are indeed most likely on the level of the standard of review by the European Courts, that may lead to a more fine-tuned constitutional supremacy of the Treaties.

c) The Treaties as a Formal Constitution: Supranational Over-juridification and Intergovernmental Politicisation

Even if there are good reasons for understanding the European Treaties as the formal constitution of the European Union, this categorisation allows, at the same time, the development of a critical account defining deficits: the Treaties' quality as a constitutional document is limited by their division, by their overloaded contents, by the annex system and by continuously working intergovernmental super-legislative processes. Also, under closer scrutiny, the Treaties' supremacy proves to be limited, in that the ECJ does not apply the same standards of review towards the Member State and the European levels. In both cases the Treaties only partially fulfil the task of coupling political process and legal form: in terms of written form, they prove to be intergovernmentally politicised; in terms of Treaty supremacy they prove to be supranationally over-juridified. To put it another way, the Treaties insufficiently bundle the rules according to which the supreme law should originate. They bind the simple legislative processes through an excess of substantial law that has been decided upon inter-governmentally. The Treaties are underformalised and over-materialised. The connection of both constitutional traditions, the democratisation of law-making and the juridification of the political process, has yet to prove itself in the formal constitutional qualities. It is only partially successful in terms of the European Treaty system.

3. Constitutionalisation

The concept of constitutionalisation, which is ubiquitously used in the literature on European law, cannot be completely separated from the term

[227] See VI 3.
[228] J Bast in this volume.

constitution. But it should be clearly distinguished from it.[229] To understand this distinction, one may return to the constitutional traditions categorised above. The concept of constitutionalisation can be assigned to the second, power-shaping tradition: it receives its emphasis less from the democratisation of law-making than from the incremental juridification of the political exercise of power. Regarding the British constitutional tradition that is shaped by the Common Law, constitutionalisation results in executive control through the courts, which develop general standards of procedural justice. This enables spontaneous forms of juridification without a legislative process. It is important to note that the distinction between public law and private law plays a minimal role in this constitutional tradition,[230] if it plays a role at all.

Similarly, in the context of supranational and international law the concept of constitutionalisation describes the developing autonomy of international regimes from intergovernmental action.[231] Constitutionalisation can, therefore, be understood as a phenomenon of the gradual formation of a new legal level. It may be described as the unorganised intensification of a legal regime, whose increasing quantity of norms finally enables the emergence of normative structures—of legal principles—that can be generalised and that are also, at least factually, difficult to amend due to their generality.[232] In this way, a spontaneous internal hierarchy of norms arises that increases and accelerates through the multiplication of adjudicative authorities.[233]

Such a broad understanding of constitutionalisation also enables the inclusion of private law phenomena. In particular the development of the Common Law demonstrates a constitutionalisation phenomenon in its amalgamation of private law and "constitutionally legal protections".[234] The central role of subjective rights is a decisive factor for the advanced constitutionalisation of the European Union. This also results from the direct applicability of Community law[235] that provides for an intensive

[229] Similar Craig, above n 213, 126–27.

[230] JWF Allison, *A Continental Distinction in the Common Law* (1997).

[231] This is significant for the discussion in International Economic Law: EU Petersmann, *Constitutional Functions and Constitutional Problems of International Economic Law* (1991). More careful C Walter, 'Constitutionalizing (Inter)national Governance', (2001) 44 *German Yearbook of International Law* 170 at 192 *et seq*; M Nettesheim, 'Von der Verhandlungsdiplomatie zur internationalen Verfassungsordnung', (2000) 19 *Jahrbuch für Neue Politische Ökonomie* 48 at 58 *et seq*. For the United Nations AL Paulus, *Die internationale Gemeinschaft im Völkerrecht* (2001) 293 *et seq*. The phenomenon of an autonomous supra- or international judicial process without a legislative complement is well described for the WTO by A v Bogdandy, 'Law and Politics in the WTO', (2001) 5 *Max Planck Yearbook of UN Law* 609 at 615 *et seq*.

[232] This important observation can be found in Heintzen, above n 211, 36.

[233] Weiler, above n 207, 9.

[234] G Teubner, 'Societal Constitutionalism: Alternatives to State-centred Constitutional Theory?', in C Joerges, I-J Sand and G Teubner (eds), *Constitutionalism and Transnational Governance* (2004).

[235] Hartley, above n 178, 187 *et seq*; Weiler, above n 207, 19–20.

juridification of European law.[236] With this, the concept of constitutionalisation can be interpreted as a complementary concept to the figure of *pouvoir constituant*—the two constitutional traditions introduced above can be found again here: while the one tradition assumes a political basis for the establishment of the entire legal system in a revolutionary discontinuity, in political action in an Arendt sense, emphasising the legislature. The concept of constitutionalisation, with the complementary tradition, describes a gradual and self-referential[237] process of juridification. This process is particularly pushed by the courts but also by an administrative practice that is structuring itself and that is also structured by academic legal doctrine. Such processes of evolving constitutionalisation are of major importance for European law.

a) Common European Constitutional Law—Establishing Principles

The discussion about the formation of a Common European Constitutional Law[238] can serve as an example of a constitutionalisation process in Europe. Against the background of homogenisation requirements that run in both directions from the European level to the Members States and vice versa (Article 6(1) EU[239], Article 23(1) German Basic Law[240]), common structures of constitutional law could be developed horizontally among the Member States or vertically among them and the Union. Certainly, one will have to declare doubt as to the use of the notion of a common law,[241] especially for organisational rules.[242] While comparable structures arise in the relationships between governmental bodies and citizens in the Member States and the Union, this applies less to the organisational norms. In concrete terms, while the legal protection of legitimate expectations[243] or the proportionality principle[244] could lead to common solutions,[245] this does not apply in the same way to either the issue of democratic legitimacy or to separation of powers, or rather the "institutional balance". Indeed, comparisons can also be made here, but potential solutions are so strongly influenced by the

[236] For a private law understanding of the fundamental freedoms: J Drexl in this volume.
[237] In the sense of a law of the law, not a law of politics: Hofmann, above n 70, 40–41.
[238] A concept developed by P Häberle, 'Gemeineuropäisches Verfassungsrecht', (1991) *Europäische Grundrechte-Zeitschrift* 261 at 268 *et seq.*
[239] Schorkopf, above n 204, 69 *et seq.*
[240] For other Member States Schorkopf, above n 204, 45 *et seq*; C Grabenwarter in this volume.
[241] Häberle above n 238, 268.
[242] The attempt to define a common concept of separation of powers regarding the EU, the United States and Germany is made in C Möllers, *Gewaltengliederung* (2005), forthcoming.
[243] W Bernhardt, *Verfassungsprinzipien—Verfassungsgerichtsfunktionen—Verfassungsprozeßrecht im EWG-Vertrag* (1987) 70 *et seq*; T Tridimas, *The General Principles of EC Law* (1999) 89 *et seq.*
[244] E Ellis (ed), *The Principle of Proportionality in the Laws of Europe* (1999).
[245] A Schmitt Glaeser, *Grundgesetz und Europarecht als Elemente europäischen Verfassungsrechts* (1996) 191 *et seq.*

prevailing regulatory context that a common European legal doctrine may hardly result. Additionally, the organisational structures of the Member States are only selectively affected by the Union law. The development of a common canon of argumentation will most likely be limited to civil rights.

Yet, something different could most likely apply to the unwritten rules of loyalty to the Union and between the Member States that is anchored in Article 10 EC as well as in national constitutions. Rules that can be generalised for the conduct of courts[246] and other public authorities may also arise from this concept.[247]

b) Charter of Fundamental Rights

The introduction of the Charter of Fundamental Rights[248] and its integration into the Constitutional Treaty also belongs within the context of constitutionalisation and with that, for their part, to the power-shaping constitutional tradition. The charter that is proclaimed without any democratic act places European actions under further legal control without complementary democratic processes being available. With that, it institutionally transfers the further extension of the legal system to the courts and is clearly part of the continuity of European development since its beginnings. This raises the question as to whether a further level of civil rights could lead to restricting the political discretion too much—creating a problem that is specifically known in German constitutional law.[249]

On the other hand, introducing the charter also fulfils a symbolic function that is tied to the revolutionary constitutional tradition in that it documents the European civil rights protection. However, as long as the charter is not made obligatory, its symbolic content is limited to being the most noticeable symbol of the love of the European Union for constitutional folklore.[250]

c) Administrative Constitutionalisation

If constitutionalisation is understood as a spontaneous form of juridification that leads to a legal order without legislative intervention, then the administration also comes into view as an actor. Even though it is difficult to identify an independent "European Administration" between European and Member State organs,[251] systematic structures are nevertheless recognisable.

[246] FC Mayer in this volume.

[247] M Blanquet, *L'article 5 du traité C.E.E.* (1994).

[248] EO Eriksen, JE Fossum and AJ Menéndez (eds), *The Chartering of Europe—The Charter of Fundamental Rights in Context* (2003).

[249] GF Schuppert and C Bumke, *Die Konstitutionalisierung der Rechtsordnung* (2000).

[250] UR Haltern in this volume.

[251] E Schmidt-Aßmann, 'Europäische Verwaltung zwischen Kooperation und Hierarchie', in H-J Cremer (ed), *Tradition und Weltoffenheit des Rechts: Festschrift für H Steinberger* (2002) 1375 at 1380 *et seq*.

The development of a European administrative law can then be understood as a phenomenon of constitutionalisation.[252] At the first level, such structures result from principles of administration in an inductive comparison of Member State administrative legal systems.[253] But systematic structures emerge also from the actions of Union organs.[254]

There have been diverse discussions about the codification of a European administrative procedure,[255] about the legitimacy of comitology,[256] about inter-national administrative action,[257] and about a European General Administrative Law.[258] The Commission's White Paper on Governance, that quite specifically argues on the basis of the existing Treaties, keeping the political process of legislation out, is closely connected to this.[259] These discussions care less about legislative programs than about the reconstruction of administrative practices in order to satisfy certain standards of procedural justice.

The concept of constitutionalisation that is applied here, the construction of administrative legitimacy, is largely independent from a free and equal democratic process. Indeed, not all concepts correspond to a merely "expertocratic" model of legitimacy.[260] However, the political environment of the named administrative structures is definitely not coupled with a general equal chance of participation for all citizens. It is not accidental that this facet of the constitutionalisation discussion, although it maintains its claims to novelty, remains quite clearly within an English conceptual and theoretical tradition, and its critique[261] of a French concept of law-bound hierarchical administration.[262] Like the evolution of Common Law, constitutionalisation is understood as spontaneous social process[263] that is not limited to private actors but is also applied to public authorities.[264]

[252] J Schwarze, *Administrative Law under European Influence* (1992).

[253] E Schmidt-Aßmann, *Das allgemeine Verwaltungsrecht als Ordnungsidee* (1998) 323 *et seq.*

[254] M Everson, 'The Constitutionalisation of European Administrative Law', in C Joerges and E Vos (eds), *European Committees* (1999) 281 at 289 *et seq*; S Kadelbach, 'European Administrative Law and the Law of a Europeanized Administration', in C Joerges and R Dehousse (eds), *Good Governance in Europe's Integrated Markets* (2002) 167 181 *et seq.*

[255] C Harlow, 'Codification of the EC Administrative Procedures?' (1996) 2 *ELJ* 3.

[256] C Joerges and J Neyer, 'From Intergovernmental Bargaining to Deliberative Political Process' (1997) 3 *ELJ* (1997) 273 at 293 *et seq.*

[257] Weiler, above n 207, 96 *et seq*, 283 *et seq.*

[258] HP Nehl, *Principles of Administrative Procedure in EC Law* (1999) 13 *et seq.*

[259] European Governance, 25.7.2001, COM(2001) 428 final; see the critiques in Joerges, Mény and Weiler, above n 162.

[260] Majone, above n 155.

[261] Explicit criticism is in C Harlow, 'European Administrative Law', in Craig and Búrca (eds), above n 215, 261 at 264 *et seq.*

[262] T Groß, *Das Kollegialprinzip in der Verwaltungsorganisation* (1999) 111 *et seq.*

[263] Eg N Walker, 'European Constitutionalism and European Integration', (1996) *Public Law* 266; J Shaw, 'Postnational Constitutionalism in the European Union', (1999) 6 *JEPP* 579 at 582 *et seq*, both on the basis of J Tully, *Strange Multiplicity: Constitutionalism in the Age of Diversity* (1995).

[264] For the criticism of the hidden common law context of certain theories of European constitutionalism: C Möllers, 'Transnational Governance without a Public Law?' in: C Joerges, IJ Sand and G Teubner (eds), *Constitutionalism and Transnational Governance* (2004).

The two constitutional traditions that were reconstructed above can, therefore, be portrayed as two possible concepts of a European administration. On the one hand, there is a pluralistic concept, on the other hand, the idea of a hierarchical unitarian administration. The academic discussion moves more along the lines of the first model, the adjudication of the ECJ may speak more for the second model.[265] The dilemma in this is that the guardian of a European administrative unity is not a politically accountable government, but a Commission that is still operating with a technocratic self-image.[266]

d) The Legitimacy of Evolutionary Constitutionalisation

Juridification without democratic politics: the forms of constitutionalisation introduced here are, without a doubt, well-suited to increasing the legitimacy of European law. They have in common that they foster rationality, systemic approaches and transparency of law through the development of principles as well as through the institutionalisation of deliberative procedures. Such developments are necessary in a legal system that is, institutionally and in terms of legitimacy, split like that of the EU. The plurality of the European legal system hampers a hierarchical understanding as it is indicated by the constitutional ideal of a democratic *pouvoir constituant*.[267]

The concept of constitutionalisation originates from a tradition that shows its great sensitivity through the evolutionary development of legal principles on the basis of case-by-case problem solving. However, for precisely this reason it is doubtful in what way this concept is suited to lay claim to legitimacy among legal developments at large. It is quite possible that the chosen path of constitutionalisation is only considered legitimate because it was indeed chosen. Spontaneous constitutionalisation processes without attributable political decisions construct the integration as an almost naturally grown "evolution",[268] i.e. a development that can neither be fundamentally changed nor democratically answered for. Herein lies the danger of a concept of constitution that is limited to constitutionalisation.

V. EUROPEAN CONSTITUTIONAL LAW—A LEGAL FIELD AND ITS ACADEMIA

The difficulties in defining what European Constitutional Law could be are, at second glance, less Europe-specific than one may presume. In this way,

[265] Case 9/56, *Meroni* [1958] ECR 133; Case T-369/94 and T-85/95, *DIR* [1998] ECR II-357, para 52.

[266] This is made very clear by the Commission's White Book on Governance: FW Scharpf, 'European Governance', in Joerges, Mény and Weiler, above n 162.

[267] See II 1 a and IV 1.

[268] So the title of Craig and de Búrca (eds), *The Evolution of EU Law*, above n 215.

for example, German public law jurisprudence has never succeeded in giving a consistent meaning to the expressly maintained difference between constitutional law and "Staatsrecht".[269] Moreover, it is not always possible in federal structures to clearly assign a certain body of law to a certain level of law production.[270] This is also true for the European Union.[271]

What is really addressed when European constitutional law is being discussed? Even if this question cannot be unambiguously answered for national structures, determining this branch of law on the European level raises additional problems. This is practically a result of the intense association of primary and secondary law in the ECJ standards of review, and in the blend of Union law and national law that is particularly typical for directives.[272] The degree to which European constitutional law can be determined is, consequently, completely dependent upon very concrete institutional correlations.[273] The fact that selective demarcations regarding national law as well as secondary law are not always possible should, however, not prevent a discussion around "European Constitutional Law". Thus far it makes sense to talk about constitutional law at a time when a supranational regulatory context exists that is able to establish law-making structures that go beyond selective dispute resolution. If this is the case, legal hierarchies emerge. A specific field of juridical questions is then connected to the term European Constitutional Law. These questions can be reasoned from the three-part concept that has been developed here:

To begin with, what belongs to this is—true to the revolutionary constitutional tradition and the doctrine of *pouvoir constituant* affiliated with it—the reconstruction of Union law's democratic legitimacy. This question can neither be left to political philosophers nor to empirical social scientists: it represents a genuine juridical problem to the extent that the concept of legitimacy joins democratic theory with the codification and interpretation of positive law. The question as to where political processes are located on the European level, and whose rights of participation are in play, is a focus of a European constitutional law. This means that European constitutional law cannot limit itself to positive law but also must use theoretical tools.

Furthermore, any collision between the primary Treaty-law and other Union and national legal rules continue to belong to a European constitutional law—true to a formal constitutional concept. The questions regarding the dogmatic and the institutional resolution of conflicts between Union

[269] Möllers, above n 49, 173.

[270] For the German federal system: P Lerche, 'Bundesverfassungsnormen mit landesverfassungsrechtlicher Qualität?' in F Ruland (ed), *Verfassung, Theorie und Praxis des Sozialstaats: Festschrift für HF Zacher* (1998) 529 at 530.

[271] Weiler, above n 207, 12.

[272] PP Craig, 'Directives: Direct Effect, Indirect Effect and the Construction of National Legislation', (1997) 3 *EL Rev* 519.

[273] Häberle, above n 85, 123 *et seq.*

and Member State law,[274] and regarding the standard-setting function of primary law with respect to secondary law, are the focus here. A wealth of specific problems can be tacked on to this: for example, the delegation structure within the Community law or the implications of various understandings of Union basic freedoms and civil rights have for the competences of the European level.

Finally, the development of legal principles for Community law that result from judicial and administrative practice belongs to a European constitutional law—true to the power-shaping constitutional tradition, and the understanding of constitution as an evolutionary constitutionalisation process that belongs to this. The chaotic complexity of secondary law demands—not only for practical-systematic, but also legitimacy reasons—structures that stand out from mere single regulations and can be recognised as principles.

Considering the definition of a European constitutional law, three different aspects must be considered regarding the duties of the academic jurisprudence in the European constitutional discussion: first of all, the types of constitutions reconstructed here, revolutionary and power-shaping constitutional understandings, assign various tasks to academic jurisprudence: while evolutionary constitutionalisation processes allow jurisprudence to become an important legal source through establishment of principles and systems, the influence of the discipline is repressed not only through revolutionary incidents but also through the activity of the democratic legislator—jurisprudence's restrained "positivist" self-image is the methodical correlate here. This correlation explains the importance of juridical law-making and of arguments inspired in a philosophical manner, that is growing again specifically in international and supranational regulatory contexts.[275] This affinity is, certainly, just another formulation for a democratic deficit because legal expertise—like every other expertise—lacks a mandate for legitimate law-making. Against this background jurisprudence must be careful not to privilege certain constitutional concepts, only because they could strengthen its own institutional role. Concretely, this means that the recommendation for the problem of coupling politics and law on the level of the European Union cannot simply be "law". Many aspects speak much more for the fact that the Union has hit the "limits of informal constitutional development"[276] which presents itself, above all, as a phenomenon of juridification without corresponding political processes.

[274] CU Schmid, 'From Point d'Avignon to Ponte Vecchio: The Resolution of Constitutional Conflicts between the European Union and the Member States through Principles of Public International Law', (1998) 18 *Yearbook of European Law* 415 at 449 *et seq*.

[275] To this and the following C Möllers, 'Globalisierte Jurisprudenz: Einflüsse relativierter Nationalstaatlichkeit auf das Konzept des Rechts und die Funktion seiner Theorie', (2001) *Archiv für Rechts- und Sozialphilosophie* suppl 79, 41 at 43 *et seq*, 49 *et seq*.

[276] Peters, above n 58, 478.

Besides the danger of privileging certain forms of constitutionalisation, jurisprudence also faces the danger of a lack of temporal distance to the European constitutional project. This results from interventions in primary law that are comparatively frequent and intense, and from the multiplicity of official proposals for a European constitution.[277] It is particularly important for the legal sciences, which necessarily work with a retrospective view,[278] to uncover the basic and longer-term trends among current developments.

Finally, the theoretical discussion is suffering quite evidently from a lack of distance: the constitutional concept still serves as a kind of shibboleth[279] that is supposed to express a fundamental position on the European constitution.[280] Yet, the amalgamation of constitutional politics and constitutional theory is nothing new. A glance at the history of legal science shows that even objective contributions took sides in a political sense. However, this taking of sides, if it is to have a theoretically intrinsic value, cannot on the one hand be reduced to making the constitutional concept a taboo, and on the other hand it also may not stretch the concept to complete status-quo submissiveness. Inevitably, every use of the concept on the European level feeds on the pathos transferred to it by the history of nation-states.[281] Thus, the question in what way this pathos is deserved requires theoretical critique.

VI. EPILOGUE: THE CONSTITUTIONAL TREATY

The Constitutional Treaty has found consensus in the Intergovernmental Conference in Brussels. Though its ratification will be a cumbersome process, it is possible to offer a first assessment of the constitutional process so far. Three points emerge as being relevant for a constitutional theory of European integration: the deliberative process in the European Convention and the Intergovernmental Conference (1), the search for "constitutional moments" in the European process of constitutionalisation (2) and, finally, the value of the label "constitution" for the result of this process (3).

1. Constitutional Deliberation: Convention and Intergovernmentalism

The development of the European Convention[282] was a reaction to the practical failure of the Intergovernmental Conference in Nice. Nice seemed to

[277] See the constitutional drafts, OJ C 77, 14.2.1984, 33 (Spinelli); OJ C 61, 10.2.1994, 155 (Herman).
[278] Above n 4.
[279] Book of Judges 12, 6.
[280] Von Bogdandy, above n 205, 14.
[281] UR Haltern in this volume.
[282] <http://european-convention.eu.int> (30 June 2004).

prove the deficiencies of intergovernmental decision-making procedures, as long since analysed by political scientists. A "real" constitution, therefore, should not be the result of an intergovernmental pork barrel compromise but of a genuine deliberative procedure: Habermasian virtues instead of intergovernmental vices. The European Convention should remind us of Paris and Philadelphia, not of Amsterdam and Nice. One important consequence of this insight was the integration of a great number of European and national MPs in the Convention. And indeed, it seems to be the case that the discussion in the Convention was, at least in some of the working groups, more constructive and problem-oriented than in the IGC.[283] And as we know from historical research, none of the legendary constitutional conventions lived up to the democratic qualities they were defining for the constitution to be written.[284] There is no reason to be too critical of the discussion culture within the Convention.

Yet, the process remains peculiar: an intergovernmental body empowers a deliberative body to write a legal text that can be modified and has to be decided upon by the intergovernmental body. This irritating structure underlines the unsolved political dilemmas of European integration. On the one hand, there is no legitimate power that can make constitutional decisions beyond the Member States. All academic speculation about deliberation as a substitute (and not only a supplement) to national political processes remains mere talk. But on the other hand, there is a deep and well-founded mistrust in the way in which these national processes co-operate on the European level. The Convention shows that Europe has no trust in the only decision-making procedures that Europe can accept as legitimate.

The Convention method, therefore, reveals a certain irony: the deliberations within the Convention do not add any democratic legitimacy to the constitutional process. The Convention remained distant from the political consciousness of the overwhelming majority of European citizens. But the Convention produced a result that—though it deserves critique—was in any case much better than any purely intergovernmental result would have been. The "deliberative" Convention did not work as a legitimate but as a functional problem-solving body.

2. Constitutional Moments: The Political Remaining Outside

The incremental character of the process of European integration is notorious. Hannah Arendt's credo that politics needs disruption and acts of creation[285] seems to be rather far from the European polity and its political organs: obvi-

[283] A Maurer, 'Die Methode des Konvents: Ein Modell deliberative Demokratie?', (2003) *integration* 1309.

[284] Above n 136.

[285] The term has religious overtones but may be unavoidable for an analysis of the social practices of politics and art: G Steiner, *Grammars of Creation* (2001).

ously far from the Council, that knows no form of disruption whatsoever but works in steady political continuity, but also from Parliament and Commission whose work seems to be only mildly irritated by change to its membership or elections. Yet, European politics still dreams of such an Arendtian disruption, of its own constitutional moments. And the Constitutional Treaty seems to be the result of this dream, giving the primary law a new name, but without changing the contents of European law more radically than, for example, the Treaty of Maastricht. The Constitutional Treaty brings a nominal innovation, but it most certainly does not create a constitutional moment.[286]

But this is not the whole story: It is one of the mysteries of European integration that the lack of constitutional moments is accompanied by the fact that the character of the European polity has dramatically changed in the space of 20 years. One just has to compare its status before the Single European Act with its status after enlargement and the European Convention. Major changes without a major change? A rapid institutional evolution without constitutional moments? Or are there still constitutional moments that can be attached to this development? Does the evolution have its revolutionary elements?

One of the first constitutional moments of the new European Union is obviously the year 1989. And the way this event worked for Europe may be typical for the future. In Eastern Europe the end of the Cold War was perceived as a national act, as the rebirth of democratic nation states. But of course this event had its own political meaning for European integration. And this connection between national events and their European meaning seems to be the way in which "the political" in Europe will work in the future, as has been the case in many political disruptions at the national level, such as the elections in Austria and in Spain. It was the attack in Madrid that influenced the outcome of the Spanish Parliamentary elections. And it was the change of the Spanish Government that isolated resistance against the Constitutional Treaty. Would there be a Constitutional Treaty without the attack in Madrid? This speculation shows how disconcerting constitutional moments can be.

Similar observations can be made at the global level. The war in Iraq created a genuine political conflict within the European Council, a conflict that did not adhere to the right/left distinction. As analysed above,[287] it is such a conflict, and not any form of consensus, that may enable the making of a genuine European democratic process. But this illustrates again how dangerous the making of a real supranational democratic process can be. The making of the United States resulted in a democratic conflict between two parties that finally led to a civil war.

At the moment, procedures within the European institutional framework are not ready to produce such a political momentum of their own. One has just to compare the relevance of the above events with the political relevance

[286] But see I Pernice, 'The Draft Constitution of the European Union', in *id* and Maduro (eds), above n 193, 13; N Walker, 'After the Constitutional Moment', in *ibid*, 23.

[287] See IV 1.

of the elections to the European Parliament in June 2004. The political process within the institutions only gains genuine political relevance by means of national or international political conflicts.

3. Constitutional Honesty: The Constitutional Treaty as a Semantic Constitution

Is the Constitutional Treaty a constitution? After the Second World War, the German immigrant Karl Loewenstein developed the notion of a "semantic constitution",[288] so as to give a name to political systems in which the text of the constitution is only a masque, behind which a completely different political system is hidden. The European Union is by no means a totalitarian system,[289] but the fact that it wants to give itself a constitution also means that it submits its political order to a very demanding tradition. At least as regards the democratic-revolutionary tradition[290] that served as the ideological blueprint of the political events in 1989, one will have to accept that the Constitutional Treaty is not a constitution.

However, as shown, the constitutional traditions are manifold and the term constitution is open to change. Regarding the Constitutional Treaty the problem of a semantic constitution or that of constitutional honesty lies deeper. The whole structure of the Constitutional Treaty seems to promise more than it can deliver. Parts I and II look like a constitution in the sense that they provide general law-making procedures and fundamental rights. But the relationship between these Parts and Part III illustrates the whole problem of a constitution that is not semantic towards political realities but towards its own contents. The political process opened up in the legislative procedure between Parliament and the Council is closed for important exceptions, such as the definitions of prices in agriculture, Article III-127(3) CT-Conv (Article 231(3) CT-IGC), competition law, Articles III-52(1) and III-58 CT-Conv (Articles 163 and 169 CT-IGC), and in parts of the "area of freedom, security and justice", Article III-164 CT-Conv (Article 263 CT-IGC). If these exceptions express the political state of integration, then that state does not correspond to the truly constitutional, i.e. general, law-making procedure that is pretended in Part I.

But constitutional semantics may develop a life of its own, and may function as a self-fulfilling prophecy[291] in the hands of the ECJ. The political dishonesty of Part I may some day become a constitutional truth.

[288] K Loewenstein, *Political Power and the Governmental Process* (1957) 203 *et seq*.

[289] But see the interesting comparison between the EU and authoritarian Austria of the 1930s in A Somek, 'Authoritarian Constitutionalism', in C Joerges and NS Ghaleigh (eds), *Darker Legacies of Law in Europe* (2003) 361 at 381 *et seq*.

[290] See II 1.

[291] RK Merton, *Social Theory and Social Structure* (1968) 475 *et seq*.

Part II
Institutional Issues

6

The Political Institutions

BY PHILIPP DANN

I. INTRODUCTION AND PURPOSE

ANALYSING THE INSTITUTIONS of the European Union is doing research on a moving object. Central parts of what is now the core of the Union's institutional system were not there at the beginning of the process of European integration. The European Council or the European Parliament, for example, are today central actors in the institutional setting, but the former was not even mentioned in the Treaty of Rome and the latter dramatically changed its role. Looking at this profound change, one might assume that the institutional system is still in flux, not yet matured—and thus difficult to interpret in a coherent way.

Yet, another view is possible. The institutional development of the Union can also be seen as variations on a fixed tune, a development inspired by the same melody, although in different keys and tempi. This will be the approach of this article. It will try to analyse the institutions as being shaped by a generally unchanged tune or, as might be the more appropriate term in this context: structure. This structure, so the underlying thesis here, works its way into the shape of the institutions, their inter-institutional dynamic, and at the same time poses inherent and thus recurrent problems. This structure is that of executive federalism.

The aims and purpose of this article are threefold. First, it will reflect upon past research that has been carried out in Germany on the topic of the European institutions. It will thereby try to describe how our current understanding of European institutions has been shaped (II).

On this basis, the second aim will be pursued. The present article tries to analyse the institutional setting within a coherent conceptual frame. To that end, this frame will be presented first; it is the system of executive federalism (III). The basic feature of this concept is a system of interwoven competences, by which Union and Member States are knit together in the tasks of law-making and driven into an institutional dynamic of co-operation. The Council of Ministers is considered the institutional counterpart to this system of competences. The next part of the article, describing the institutional setting (IV), will thus begin with the Council (IV.1) and then analyse the other institutions, as they perform their tasks "under the spell" of the institutional dynamic arising from the system of executive federalism: the European Parliament (IV.2), the European Commission (IV.3) and finally the European Council (IV.4). The article will then turn away from single institutions and focus on the major principled question concerning the institutions: the question of legitimacy (V). It will present different aspects of this issue and propose a new label for the distinctly European situation: the label of a "semi-parliamentary democracy".

Finally, a third aim of this article is to reflect on the possible future development of the institutional system, as it can be anticipated from the Constitutional Treaty. Although its central aspects concerning the institutions will also be considered throughout, its general implications will be assessed in a final chapter (VI).

But before we embark on time-travel to past research, some clarifications are necessary. First to the notion of institution. This article will use a more traditional and legal approach than Antje Wiener does in this volume. Whereas Wiener employs the notion of "soft institutions", covering social and cultural norms, rules or routine practices,[1] here "institutions" mean the organs of the Union as they are mentioned in the Treaties, Art 7 EC and Art 4 EU. These institutions are described as part of constitutional and sub-constitutional law.[2]

This article will not cover all institutions, though. It will focus on those organs that are part of the regular political process of policy- and law-making. The Court of Auditors will therefore not be a topic here, and neither will be the European Court of Justice (ECJ). Certainly, one can argue that the ECJ is a political organ. It serves as a constitutional court and its case law has set fundamental factors for the political process. Nevertheless, the ECJ is not an organ which is part of the regular process of policy- and law-making. The rules for appointing its members, its principle task and, last but not least, its self-understanding are sufficiently different from institutions, which evolve from party competition, elections, and which act proactively to shape policy.[3]

One final remark may be permitted. This article will try to develop a systematic and coherent perspective on the institutional system in the structure of executive federalism. To this end, it will stress those aspects, which make the system work, and focus less on its evident failures. To some, this

[1] See A Wiener, Institutionen, in: A von Bogdandy (ed), *Europäisches Verfassungsrecht* (2003) 121; also *eadem* in this volume.

[2] The terms "organ" and "institution" are used synchronically in this text.

[3] As to the ECJ, see generally F Mayer in this volume with references to further literature.

perspective will come across as apologetic; some might suspect Dr. Panglos at work.[4] Perhaps that is true. It could also be the German mindset of the author, as such always struggling to build systems and to detect reason in accidental realities. Alternatively, it could be that there actually is some sense behind this setting. Let's see.

II. PAST RESEARCH AND RECURRENT QUESTIONS

This volume aims to describe not only the current constitutional law of the European Union, but to reflect upon the ways in which the understanding of this law has been formed. Theoretical approaches or scientific self-understandings, so the assumption, influence today's analysis and perception of the law as well as major previous studies.

However, examining past German legal science on institutions requires a careful look. A first search for books on Community institutions seems to produce disappointing results. A German monograph, analysing only the Commission as arguably the most original piece in the new institutional setting, was published for the first time in 1980.[5] The Council, the most powerful of the new institutions, has stimulated monographic treatment only in the early 1960s.[6]

But this first look is deceptive. Typically for German, perhaps for any legal approach to institutions, is that it does not tackle them directly but has instead often been fuelled by debates on legal principles. Especially the separation of powers doctrine and the democratic principle have been starting points for legal examinations of the supranational institutional system. Also, German legal science has focused on procedures and the law that involves the institutions. Here, material in the form of norms governing such procedures enables legal analysis and provides perspectives on dynamic aspects of the institutional setting. This first became relevant with respect to Council and Commission.

1. To Council and Commission Through Principles and Procedures

By the 1950s, the debate on European institutions was characterised by the view of institutions seen through the lens of legal principles. In those days, heated debate arose with respect to the European Defence Community.

[4] Voltaire, *Candide* (1998).

[5] H Schmitt von Sydow, *Die Organe der erweiterten Gemeinschaft—die Kommission* (1980).

[6] KH Friauf, *Die Staatenvertretung in supranationalen Gemeinschaften* (1960); S Buerstedde, *Der Ministerrat im konstitutionellen System der Europäischen Gemeinschaften* (1964); for later literature on the Council, see below n 31.

The point in question was whether the new organisation had to observe the separation of powers principle. The debate was sparked by the argument that the German Constitution, which generally allowed the transferral of sovereign rights to international organisations, requires that the newly erected organisation must observe a "structural congruence" with German constitutional law.[7] As the Defence Community project collapsed, this debate spread to the EEC.

Probably, this debate was, at its core, more concerned with German constitutional law (and lawyers[8]) than on the EEC. Nevertheless, it initiated the first intense discussion of the institutional setting of the EEC, thus bringing the new organisation to the centre of attention in the German legal science.[9] In 1964, the preservation of the rule of law in international organisations even became topic of the annual meeting of public law scholars,[10] always a certain indicator that a topic had made it to the main stage. However, by then the heat had cooled off. The opinion prevailed that the new Communities presented a new form of governmental and legal structure, in which the idea of separation of powers was applicable but had found a new form.[11]

Early research on the institutions beyond this debate provided groundwork, without inspiring legal scholars to more conceptual aspirations. The analysis of the Council by Sigismund Buerstedde, to take the best example, gives a knowledgeable account of the foundation, organisation and mechanisms of this institution.[12] It also shows that the struggle with the Council's complex organisation and cumbersome procedure is as old as the institution itself.

After receiving heightened attention in the first decade, research on Council and Commission slipped from general attention—to which it would not return until the 1990s. The field became one of experts and practitioners.

[7] H Kraus, 'Das Erfordernis struktureller Kongruenz zwischen der Verfassung der Europäischen Verteidigungsgemeinschaft und dem Grundgesetz', in: Veröffentlichungen des Instituts für Staatslehre und Politik (ed), *Der Kampf um den Wehrbeitrag* (1953), vol 2, 545; as to this debate KH Friauf, above n 6, 77.

[8] Hans Peter Ipsen later scathingly remarked that the whole debate was yet another sign of the introverted nature of German legal science, HP Ipsen, 'Diskussionsbeitrag', (1964) 23 *Veröffentlichungen der Vereinigung der Deutschen Staatsrechtslehrer* 130.

[9] See, eg J Seeler, *Die europäische Einigung und das Problem der Gewaltenteilung* (1957); H Petzold, *Die Gewaltenteilung in den Europäischen Gemeinschaften* (1966), with further references.

[10] *Tagung der Vereinigung der Deutschen Staatsrechtslehrer.*

[11] JH Kaiser and P Badura, 'Bewahrung und Veränderung demokratischer und rechtsstaatlicher Verfassungsstrukturen in den internationalen Gemeinschaften', (1964) 23 *Veröffentlichungen der Vereinigung der Deutschen Staatsrechtslehrer* 1, 34.

[12] Buerstedde, above n 6.

Another transformation took place. By the early 1970s there was general agreement that the EC institutional system was dysfunctional and needed reform. The question of how to change the institutions became a dominant topic. The work of Christoph Sasse is representative for this time.[13] He saw two main problems: a lack of leadership and a lack of legitimacy. The Commission was regarded as the victim of a miscalculation according to which technocratic expertise alone would convince national publics, and suffice as basis for leadership. The Council, on the other side, was marked as the villain. The dominance of national self-interest in its deliberations and disrespect for the role of the Commission were seen as causes of the bleak situation.

In a different class was Hans Peter Ipsen's handbook on European law.[14] Presenting a whole theory of European integration and its law, it also came close to offering a conceptual framework for the institutions. However, from today's perspective, the Ipsen book seems more like a dinosaur than a Minervian owl. Voluminous in its form, it was unable to grasp the changes that had occurred in the institutional system since the mid-60s. Although Ipsen acknowledges the central role of the Council as an organ that presents at the same time "potency and risk", he has no answer to the problems of the Commission.

Perhaps wary of conceptual approaches in times of perceived stagnation, legal literature in the late 1970s and 1980s turned to topics that were located more at the core of legal analysis.[15] The proliferation of organisations under the EC Treaty raised questions about how this growing organisational structure could be understood and legally ordered.[16] Meinhard Hilf's major study of the organisational structure of the EC provides a formidable overview of the immense differentiation of the institutional system below the level of Treaty organs.[17]

At the same time, the creation of new inter-institutional procedures was discussed intensely, mainly the concerted action between Council,

[13] See C Sasse, 'Die institutionellen Fortentwicklung der Gemeinschaften', in: Wissenschaftliche Gesellschaft für Europarecht (ed), *Die institutionellen Entwicklung der europäischen Gemeinschaften in den siebziger Jahren* (1973) 61; also C Sasse, *Regierungen, Parlamente, Ministerrat* (1975).

[14] HP Ipsen, *Europäisches Gemeinschaftsrecht* (1972).

[15] For another general approach see L-J Constantinesco, *Recht der Europäischen Gemeinschaften* (1977).

[16] See already U Everling, 'Zur Errichtung nachgeordneter Behörden der Kommission der EWG', in: W Hallstein and HJ Schochauer (eds), *Zur Integration Europas: Festschrift für CF Ophüls* (1965) 33.

[17] M Hilf, *Die Organisationsstruktur der Europäischen Gemeinschaften* (1982); as to other questions of this development see R Priebe, *Entscheidungsbefugnisse vertragsfremder Einrichtungen im Europäischen Gemeinschaftsrecht* (1979).

Commission and EP, which was agreed upon in 1975.[18] This is the beginning of an intense examination of law-making procedures in German legal science.[19] However, it is also part of the attention, which the pet object of German institutional scholarship the European Parliament has received.

2. European Parliament: the Pet Object

Research on the EP has always played a special role in German institutional research. Self-sustained interest produced a constant flow of literature. Nevertheless early research was also driven by a principled question. The above-mentioned debate on a requirement of congruence between German and European constitutional law also raised the question of the democratic principle. However, this question was fenced off quicker than with respect to the separation of powers doctrine. The limited scope of autonomous Community powers, the role of national parliaments and different forms of popular involvement, especially through the Economic and Social Committee, were regarded as safeguards of democracy.[20] Hence, the EP was not (yet) considered the proper place to expect democratic reassurance.

Nevertheless, interest in the EP itself began to spread and to produce a number of detailed studies.[21] This research faced a dilemma, though. The current legal position of the EP obviously deviated from the picture of "normal", i.e. national parliaments and caught observers between the description of the current and the prescription of an envisioned state of the law. But although the literature is carried by sympathy for the experiment

[18] See, eg B Beutler, 'Rechtsfragen des Konzertierungsverfahrens', in: R Bieber (ed), *Das Europa der zweiten Generation: Gedächtnisschrift für C Sasse* (1981) 311; R Bieber, 'Kooperation und Konflikt', in: *ibid*, 327; Bothe, 'Soft law in den Europäischen Gemeinschaften', in: I Münch (ed), *Staatsrecht, Völkerrecht, Europarecht: Festschrift für HJ Schochauer* (1981) 65; M Gauweiler, *Die rechtliche Qualifikation interorganschaftlicher Absprachen im Europarecht* (1988); T Läufer, *Die Organe der EG* (1990).

[19] See, eg J Wuermeling, *Legislativer Trilog im institutionellen Dreieck der Europäischen Gemeinschaften* (1990); R Bieber, *Das Verfahrensrecht der Verfassungsorgane* (1992); HP Folz, *Demokratie und Integration* (1999).

[20] See again the reports given on the 1964 meeting of the public law section, Kaiser, above n 11, 31, paras 3, 6, 9; Badura, above n 11, paras 20–2; also U Oetting, *Bundestag und Bundesrat im Willensbildungsprozeß der Europäischen Gemeinschaften* (1973).

[21] Only for the time before the direct election see A Reifferscheidt, *Die Ausschüsse des Europäischen Parlaments* (1966); T Harms, *Die Rechtsstellung des Abgeordneten in der beratenden Versammlung des Europarates und im Europäischen Parlament* (1968); C Sachsee, *Die Kompetenzen des Europäischen Parlaments und die Gewaltenteilung* (1971); A Schaub, *Die Anhörung des Europäischen Parlaments im Rechtsetzungsverfahren* (1971); R Bieber, *Organe der erweiterten Gemeinschaft—das Parlament* (1974); E Reister, 'Parlamentarische Budgetrecht und Rechnungshof', (1976) *Europarecht* 69.

of a supranational parliament, most authors do not simply echo the high-flying political rhetoric, which pictured the EP as future parliament of a European Federation—and thus as a copy of national parliaments.[22] Instead, sober warnings against a schematic transferral of national systems onto the European level and against unrealistic expectations were manifold. Manfred Zuleeg warned against the mechanic reproduction of a system of parliamentarism, which already at the national level was confronted with severe problems.[23] As early as 1971 Roman Herzog pointed to the discrepancies between formal and social legitimacy, a trap in which the EP could be caught, if its formal powers were enhanced without it enjoying the support of European civil society.[24]

Research changed with the announcement of direct elections to the EP. Not only did this step initiate the development of an election law. It also provoked new studies into the general nature of the Parliament. It is mainly the research of Eberhard Grabitz, which set new standards here.[25] Together with other researchers, he started to re-think the EP beyond traditional paths. Trying to locate it in the dynamic system of governance, as it emerged in the Communities, they developed an analytical framework that would reflect this unique environment.[26]

3. Changing Tides: Institutional Research in the 1990s

The late 1980s and 1990s saw breathtaking political and institutional change in the EU. This dynamic changed the field of institutional research. Only a few general remarks need be made.

First, the new dynamic meant a shift in stage. For the first time since the early 1960s, questions about European institutions again became a regular topic for general German public law scholars. Thus, the circle of authors changed. EC law specialist and practitioners, who used to dominate the

[22] Interesting on the self-understanding of the EP, which itself claimed this role, see KH Neunreither, 'Bemerkungen zum gegenwärtigen Leitbild des Europäischen Parlaments', (1971) 2 *Zeitschrift für Parlamentsfragen* 321.

[23] M Zuleeg, 'Die Anwendbarkeit des parlamentarischen Systems auf die Europäischen Gemeinschaften', (1972) *Europarecht* 1.

[24] R Herzog, 'Zur Legitimation der Willensbildung in den Gemeinschaften', in: Wissenschaftliche Gesellschaft für Europarecht (ed), above n 13, 35; also JA Frowein, 'Zur Legitimation der Willensbildung in den Gemeinschaften', in: *ibid*, 83.

[25] See E Grabitz and T Läufer, *Das Europäische Parlament* (1980); E Grabitz, W Schmuck, S Steppat and W Wessels, *Direktwahl und Demokratisierung* (1988).

[26] See also O Schmuck and W Wessels (eds), *Das Europäische Parlament im dynamischen Integrationsprozeß* (1989); W Wessels, 'Wird das Europäische Parlament zum Parlament?', in: A Randelzhofer *et al* (eds), *Gedächtnisschrift für E Grabitz* (1995) 879.

field were now complemented by regular public law scholars. This also contributed to an immense increase in the number of studies undertaken.[27]

Second, again the motor of the new debate was a question of principle. Not this time the rule of law as in the 1960s, but instead the democratic principle aroused German scholars in the 1990s.[28] The debate also kicked off a new wave of studies on the institutions themselves. Within this literature, once again the EP has attracted most attention. Although one might say that modern research lacks a convincing theoretical concept of the Parliament as a whole,[29] the detailed studies together constitute a European parliamentary law.[30] In addition, other organs and institutions have found new attention.[31]

And finally, another change set in. Surprisingly, German legal science on European institutions for years neglected a comparative perspective. There has been especially no reflection on European institutions in contrast to institutions of evolving federations. This seems particularly astonishing in the German context, since German constitutional and institutional history itself provides a major example of such an evolving entity. However, the 1990s have brought about a growing awareness of the value of comparative approaches, if only for a deeper understanding of German federal history.[32]

In sum, the past fifty years have produced a number of imminent studies on European institutions and their law—with particular attention to the law of the EP and inter-institutional procedures. Against this background, we may now turn to the analysis of the current institutional system.

[27] As for an overview A von Bogdandy, 'Beobachtungen zur Wissenschaft vom Europarecht', (2001) 40 *Der Staat* 3.

[28] As best overview see M Kaufmann, *Europäische Integration und Demokratieprinzip* (1997); see also A von Bogdandy in this volume.

[29] See V Saalfrank, *Funktionen und Befugnisse des Europäischen Parlaments* (1995); B Suski, *Europäisches Parlament* (1996); D Reich, *Rechte des Europäischen Parlaments* (1999).

[30] Only books see R Fleuter, *Mandat und Status des Abgeordneten im Europäischen Parlament* (1991); C Schultz-Bleis, *Die parlamentarische Immunität der Mitglieder des Europäischen Parlaments* (1995); I Beckedorf, *Das Untersuchungsrecht des Europäischen Parlaments* (1995); V Neßler, *Europäische Willensbildung - Fraktionen im EP* (1997).

[31] A Egger, *Das Generalsekretariat des Rates der EU* (1994); M Mentler, *Der Ausschuß der Ständigen Vertreter bei den Europäischen Gemeinschaften* (1994); D Fischer-Appelt, *Agenturen der Europäischen Gemeinschaft* (1999); F Rutschmann, *Der europäische Vermittlungsausschuß* (2002); J Wuermeling, 'Streicht die Räte und rettet den Rat', (1996) *Europarecht* 167; HC Röhl, 'Die Beteiligung der Bundesrepublik an der Rechtsetzung im Ministerrat der EU', (1994) *Europarecht* 409.

[32] S Oeter, 'Souveränität und Demokratie als Probleme in der Verfassungsentwicklung der Europäischen Union', (1995) 55 *Zeitschrift für ausländisches öffentliches Recht und Völkerrecht* 659 at 688; A Boehmer, *Die EU im Lichte der Reichsverfassung von 1871* (1999) 73; also P Dann, *Parlamente im Exekutivföderalismus* (2004) 8, 43 *et seq.*

III. CONCEPTUAL FRAMEWORK: THE SYSTEM OF EXECUTIVE FEDERALISM

The institutions of a political system do not stand separately and for themselves. Their interplay is as much a defining mark of them as their powers and interior organisation. In addition, another wider frame has to be taken into account, as institutions are also embedded in the general constitutional order.

Looking at the institutions of the EU from this perspective, the multilayered or federal nature of the Union is the first landmark to be seen.[33] And indeed, the federal structure plays a pivotal role in explaining the institutional setting of the EU. Particularly important is the distinct form of this federal order. The EU is shaped by a system, which we shall call an executive federalism.[34] What characterises this federal scheme to make it of such importance for the institutions? Abstractly speaking, it is the dynamic interplay between a vertical structure of interwoven competences and the horizontal set up of separated but co-operating institutions. And concretely speaking?

The concept of executive federalism can be described as having three basic characteristics. First, it is rooted in a vertical structure of *interwoven* competences. That means that making laws in the EU occurs at the federal (supranational) level but implementing that same law occurs at the level of the Member States. Simply: union laws are executed by Member States. Legally based on Art 10 EC, this structure places on Member States the duty to "take all appropriate measures ... to ensure fulfilment of the obligations arising out of this [EC] Treaty", entailing a principle of loyal co-operation.[35] In effect, it means that the EU has almost no original competences to implement EU law, but the Member States do.[36] The Union, instead, has the duty to supervise the implementation of its law.[37] It should be noted, though, that the EC Treaty does not necessarily proscribe this system of competences.

[33] Using the phrase "federal" does not imply a state-like construct. Instead, federalism is regarded here as a general principle of organising multi-layered structures of governance, be they in a national, supranational or international sphere, see D Elazar, *Exploring Federalism* (1987) 34; A von Bogdandy, 'The European Union as a Supranational Federation', (2000) 6 *Columbia Journal of European Law* 27 at 51–2; see also S Oeter in this volume.

[34] As to the notion of executive federalism, see below at the end of this chapter III.

[35] Case C-476/93, *Nutral v Commission* [1995] ECR I-4125, para 14; K Lenaerts and P van Nuffel, *Constitutional Law of the European Union* (1999) para 8-010, also para 11-042.

[36] Exceptions are, understandably, in the field of internal organisation (Art 274 EC) and most prominently in the field of competition law (Arts 81, 82, 86(3) EC), see J Suerbaum, *Kompetenzverteilung im Verwaltungsvollzug* (1998) 110.

[37] Arts 211, 1st indent, 226 EC; K Lenaerts, 'Some Reflections on the Separation of Powers in the European Community', (1991) 28 *CML Rev* 15.

Another system of sharing competences could be equally lawful under the EC Treaty. However, the political and legal development has confirmed the system of interwoven competences, so that today it is in practical terms a virtually unchangeable part of the constitutional order. It is as telling as it is consequential that the Constitutional Convention did not discuss, and the Constitutional Treaty will not alter, this system of competences.[38]

Initially, this first characteristic of executive federalism might seem like a subtle and after all rather dry aspect of the constitutional set up. Nevertheless, it entails far-reaching consequences for the institutional system. Most of all, the system of interwoven competences requires extensive co-operation: co-operation in the process of negotiating and adopting law, co-operation in the procedures of implementing law, even co-operation in the process of reviewing the law.[39] Moreover, equally important, the system predetermines *who* has to co-operate. It requires not only vertical co-operation between actors from both levels, but also requires the involvement of *executive actors*, especially at the Member State level. Since EU law is implemented by national administrations, it makes perfect sense to give these administrations a voice in the process of making these laws.[40]

This leads to two further characteristics of executive federalism. The second characteristic is the existence of an institution that organises and harbours the necessary co-operation as just described, the Council of Ministers, regarded as the institutional counterpart of the system of competences. And finally, as a third characteristic a decision-making mode of consensus facilitates co-operation in the Council and beyond.

Before we turn to the more detailed analysis of the institutions, beginning with the Council, a few remarks are necessary to set the notion and concept of executive federalism in context.[41] The structure of executive federalism can most clearly be contrasted with the American model of "dual federalism", where every level autonomously organises the making and implementation of its laws at the federal and state level.[42]

At the same time, "executive federalism" itself can be understood in two ways. The regular understanding would be in the sense of the German "Vollzugsföderalismus". It means that the federal system is characterised

[38] A von Bogdandy, J Bast and D Westphal, 'Die vertikale Kompetenzordnung im Entwurf des Verfassungsvertrages', (2003) *integration* 414 at 423; A von Bogdandy and J Bast in this volume.

[39] I Pernice, 'Multilevel Constitutionalism and the Treaty of Amsterdam', (1999) 36 *CML Rev* 703 at 724.

[40] See H Wallace, 'Institutions of the EU', in: W Wallace and H Wallace (eds), *Policy Making in the EU* (1996) 58; further explanation of this system, see below section IV. 1. a/b.

[41] In detail Dann, above n 32, 117 *et seq*.

[42] K Lenaerts, 'Constitutionalism and the many Faces of Federalism', (1990) 38 *American Journal of Comparative Law* 205 at 231; MJC Vile, *Structure of American Federalism* (1961) 64; to the limits of this autonomy D Elazar, *The American Partnership* (1962).

only by the interwoven structure of competences, as described above. The main examples of this system are found in Switzerland, Austria and Germany.[43]

However, the notion of "executive federalism" is used here with a more specific meaning. The difference occurs with a look at and inclusion of an institutional aspect, that is the design of the federal chamber. Executive federalism here means that the system of interwoven competences is complemented by the institution of a Council, which is composed of the executives of the Member States (therefore *executive* federalism). Through this organ the Member States are directly involved in the making of the law, which they have to execute. Such systems of executive federalism can be found not only in the EU, but also and traditionally in Germany since the Constitution of 1866/1871.[44]

On this basis, we can now turn to the analysis of separate institutions.[45]

IV. THE INSTITUTIONAL SETTING

1. Council of Ministers

a) Form Follows Function: Members, Organisation and Competences

In the system of executive federalism, the Council of the European Union[46] is the institutional counterpart to the specific division of competences. Its composition, organisation and powers offer what the interwoven competences require, that is a meeting point for actors from the national and supranational level, a meeting point for politicians and bureaucrats, a place

[43] JA Frowein, 'Integration and the federal experience in Germany and Switzerland', in: M Cappelletti *et al* (eds), *Integration through Law* (1986) 573 at 586; Lenaerts, above n 42, 230–3.

[44] As to its historical roots see S Oeter, *Integration und Subsidiarität im deutschen Bundesstaatsrecht* (1998); G Lehmbruch, *Parteienwettbewerb im Bundesstaat* (1998); comparing federal structures in EU and Germany FW Scharpf, 'Community and Autonomy', (1994) 1 *JEPP* 219; S Oeter, 'Föderalismus', in: von Bogdandy, above n 1, 59 *et seq*; Dann, above n 32, 43 *et seq*. As to a Swiss functional equivalent in the *Vernehmlassungsverfahren*, see W Linder, 'Das politische System der Schweiz', in: W Ismayr (ed), *Die politischen Systeme Westeuropas* (1999) 468 at 470.

[45] Two disclaimers have to be posted: first, the concept proposed here is based on the analysis of the 'Community system'. Thus it does not directly apply to the two intergovernmental pillars of the Union. Second, the following analysis describes primarily the institutions, and only to a certain extent the decision-making procedures that are played out between these institutions. To focus on the latter would require another article, or book. See, eg P Craig and C Harlow (eds), *Lawmaking in the European Union* (1998); see Folz, above n 19.

[46] The former "Council of the European Communities" decided after the ratification of the Maastricht Treaty to call itself the "Council of the European Union", a term applicable to all its activities (Dec 93/591/EU, Euratom, ECSC, EC of 8 November 1993). In order to simplify the text, this term will be used here synchronically with the term 'Council'.

to negotiate and to legislate. As such, it is the central institution of this federal system.[47]

The Council's special role derives, first, from its composition. The Council "consists of a representative of each Member State at ministerial level".[48] Thus, its members are not directly elected but sent in their function as ministers of national governments. As such, they are mostly appointed or nominated by their Prime Minister. This forms a sharp contrast to most other federal chambers, the members of which are directly elected, e.g. in the US Senate.[49]

Specific to the nature of the Council is the mandate and self-understanding of its members. US Senators are elected politicians, free to take any position they want. Council members, in contrast, are representatives of their home government; they are "authorised to commit the government of the Member State".[50] Thus, they have to follow the guidelines agreed upon in their cabinet and have to negotiate within these margins.[51]

Yet, the Council is much more than the round of national ministers. They are only the top of a complex system, best described as a pyramid (or rather 'funnel') of groups, in which national actors convene. This funnel has three principal tiers: the Council as meeting place of the ministers, the Committee of Permanent Representatives (COREPER[52]) and the Working groups. Their composition and functioning is best explained by tracing the negotiations on a new bill, as this demonstrates the procedural logic evolving from the interwoven competences, the logic of executive co-operation:

It is the sole right of the Commission to introduce bills. Yet its first[53] and most important reality test comes when a bill is discussed in a Council Working group, composed of national civil servants from each Member State, who are responsible for the specific matter.[54] They check how the

[47] The best overviews of the Council are: F Hayes-Renshaw, 'The Council of Ministers', in: J Peterson and M Shackleton (eds), *The Institutions of the European Union* (2002) 47; F Hayes-Renshaw and H Wallace, *The Council of Ministers* (1997); M Westlake, *The Council of the European Union* (1999).

[48] Art 203 EC.

[49] G Löwenberg and SC Patterson, *Comparing Legislatures* (1979) 121; G Sartori, *Comparative Constitutional Engineering* (1999) 185.

[50] Art 203 EC.

[51] A von Bogdandy, 'Information und Kommunikation in der Europäischen Union', in: W Hoffmann-Riem and E Schmidt-Aßmann (eds), *Verwaltungsrecht in der Informationsgesellschaft* (2000) 168; D Spence, 'Negotiations, coalitions and the resolution of inter-state conflicts', in: Westlake, above n 47, 369, 372.

[52] This French acronym is the one most commonly used in respect of this committee. It stands for Comité des representants permanentes.

[53] Not even counting that these proposals are often already prepared in close co-operation with national experts and bureaucrats, see W Wessels, 'Dynamics of Administrative Interaction', in: W Wallace (ed), *The dynamics of European Integration* (1990) 229.

[54] There are roughly 250 groups, see Westlake, above n 47, 303 *et seq*.

proposal fits into the administrative and legal systems of their respective state. This can often take a long time, but it also clears most of the often very technical complications arising with a bill which has to be implemented in 25 different legal systems. A proposal then goes to the COREPER, which consists of the national ambassadors to the EU (thus career diplomats who stay for long terms in Brussels). Whereas Working Groups are put together flexibly and for a short term to discuss one specific proposal, the COREPER is a permanent body.

The COREPER, sometimes regarded as the most powerful part of the EU, serves as a clearing point: it checks every proposal, and negotiates those issues which remain unresolved in the working groups.[55] Since it is not split into specialised groups for every proposal,[56] it gathers a supreme overview and accumulates immense expertise. Finally yet importantly, it is this aspect which allows its members to strike more deals and settle more political issues than the Working Groups.[57] Only what is highly political and not negotiable stays undecided and finally has to be negotiated by the national ministers.[58]

One more important characteristic of the Council structure has to be added: the Council has no plenary. The ministers convene in accordance with their field of responsibility, as Ministers of Finance, as Ministers of the Environment, etc.[59] As a consequence there is no place for general discussion but only for sectoral negotiation. It is an extremely complex system with barely any hierarchy or hegemony to streamline processes.[60] Previous attempts to change the situation did not succeed in the envisioned way.[61]

[55] On the COREPER: J Lewis, 'National Interests: Coreper', in: J Peterson and M Shackleton (eds), above n 47, 277; Mentler, above n 31.

[56] This is a simplification: The COREPER convenes in two formations, Coreper II being composed of the permanent representatives themselves and being responsible for foreign, financial and horizontal matters, Coreper I being composed of deputies from the permanent representations dealing with most of the more technical legislation (Lewis, above n 55, 282–6). There are also other Committees, like the Political and Security Committee or the Economic and Finance Committee, which act beside the Coreper (Lewis, above n 55, 286; Westlake, above n 47, 299).

[57] For the best account of the negotiating methods within the Council see Spence, above n 51, 364 *et seq*.

[58] Neither COREPER nor working groups have the competence to formally decide a matter. Yet, about 80 % of the matters are already materially decided before the ministers convene. These so-called A points are decided without any further negotiation in the Council, Hayes-Renshaw, above n 47, 54; but Lewis, above n 55, 287.

[59] See Hayes-Renshaw, above n 47, Table 3.1 at 50; also Council Communication on Council formations, OJ C 174, 23.6.2000, 1.

[60] Von Bogdandy, above n 33, 41–4; generally D Curtin, 'The Constitution of the Union', (1993) 30 *CML Rev* 17 at 26; as to the growing informality of Council negotiations see U Puetter, 'Informal circles of Ministers', (2003) 9 *ELJ* 109 at 114.

[61] See W Wessels, *Öffnung des Staates* (2000) 227; instead, two other institutions serve as buckle to fasten the Council system so far: the rotating presidency and the Secretariat, Westlake, above n 47, 165, 317.

This overall structure remains generally untouched by the Constitutional Treaty.[62] Changes that had been envisioned by the Convention's Draft, e.g. the introduction of a "Legislative and General Affairs Council" or a modified system of Council Presidencies, were not confirmed by the final IGC.[63] A hierarchy of Council formations to streamline procedures is not envisioned.

Although composition and internal organisation are of salient importance, it is the powers which render the Council the central institution in the institutional setting of the EU. And it is this aspect which also renders it a highly characteristic feature of executive federalism in the EU: the Council's powers are spread from legislative to executive areas, thus defying any sort of traditional separation of power scheme, but serving the structure of interwoven competences.

With regard to law-making, the Council of Ministers plays a dominant role, although it is not (as often falsely portrait) the sole centre of it. However, despite the important influence of both Commission[64] and European Parliament,[65] the Council is the only institution that has decision-taking powers in all procedures.[66] Nevertheless, the Council also plays a major role with regard to the executive function, as it is involved in the taking of implementing decision.[67]

It is crucial to realise that composition and powers are closely connected to the structure of interwoven competences. The Council has to participate in law-making (and facilitates executive tasks), because it is the national authorities, which finally implement and administer these policies. The early as well as influential involvement of national actors is a necessary ingredient to make these mechanisms work—and thus entrenched in the interwoven structure of competences, hence the system of executive federalism. Yet, it is a third element that renders this system workable: the specific decision-making method.

[62] See A Maurer and S Matl, 'Steuerbarkeit und Handlungsfähigkeit', (2003) *integration* 483 at 488–90.

[63] Cp Art I-23(1) CT-Conv to Art 24(1) CT-IGC, and Art I-23(4) CT-Conv to Art 24(7) CT-IGC; see W Wessels, 'Die institutionelle Architektur der EU der nach der europäischen Verfassung', (2004) *integration* 161 at 165.

[64] The Commission is a major law-maker; it is roughly half of all laws, which are enacted directly by the Commission, hence more than by the Council, see A von Bogdandy, J Bast and F Arndt, 'Handlungsformen im Unionsrechts', (2002) 62 *Zeitschrift für ausländisches öffentliches Recht und Völkerrecht* 78 at 139.

[65] As to the role of the EP, see below, IV. 2.

[66] Arts 250 *et seq* EC.

[67] Art 202, 3rd indent EC, and the Comitology Dec 99/468/EC, see K Lenaerts and A Verhoeven, 'Towards a Legal Framework for Executive Rule-Making in the EU?', (2000) 37 *CML Rev* 645.

b) Mode of Decision-Taking: Consensus and its Reasons

It has often been highlighted as specific to the supranational nature of the EU that the Council as one of its major decision-making bodies does not act by unanimity, but by majority rule, distinguishing the EU from any form of international organisation.[68] Yet, it is evenly well-known, that this is not the whole truth. Despite an often-applicable majority rule,[69] the Council mostly acts according to a decision-making method, which has been described as consensus or simply the Community method.[70] Here, solutions are sought through ongoing negotiations, openness to compromise and the incorporation of as many parties as possible. This method is based on mutual trust and the expectation of gaining more by giving in to a certain extent, and being re-paid in another round. Moreover, it is in no minor part based on the secrecy and confidentiality of these negotiations.[71] In a sense, the Council thus adheres to two rules: behind the formal majority rule there is an informal consensus method.[72]

Looking at the EU's institutional system through the lens of executive federalism, the Council seems to be almost necessarily a non-majoritarian system.[73] Put differently, as long as the EU has interwoven competences and a Council structure as just described, the Council has to work on a consensual basis. There are mainly three reasons for this connection:

1 There is, first, the federal heterogeneity of the EU, which seems to simply require an inclusive, consensus-based decision-making method. The theory of consensus democracy shows that culturally, religiously, linguistically or otherwise divided societies developed an original mode

[68] Ipsen, above n 14, para 2/44.

[69] As to the different forms of majority votes in the Council, see Westlake, above n 47, 88. As to the rules of majority vote in the Treaty of Nice X Yataganas, 'The Treaty of Nice', *Jean Monnet Working Paper* No 1/01, ch B 1 <http://www.jeanmonnetprogram.org/papers/01/010101.html> (3 July 2004); in broader perspective W Wessels, 'Nice Results', (2001) 39 *JCMS* 197.

[70] Thus referring to the name of the EC as first and most integrated or supranational pillar of the Union, Wallace and Hayes-Renshaw, above n 47, 253; on the methods employed see Spence, above n 51, 364; on voting patterns see M Mattila and JE Lane, 'Why unanimity?', (2001) 2 *European Union Politics* 31.

[71] Cf Arts 5 and 6 Rules of Procedure of the Council, which proscribe that meetings are closed to the public and that participants have to stay silent about the content of the negotiations, cf Westlake, above n 47, 146; C Sobotta, *Transparenz in den Rechtsetzungsverfahren der EU* (2001) 63.

[72] Both are intertwined, as decision-making in consensus is facilitated by the possibly of a dispute-settling majority decision. This has been called decision-making "under the shadow of the vote", JHH Weiler, 'The transformation of Europe', in: *id*, *The Constitution of Europe* (1999) 72; see also TC Hartley, *The Foundations of European Community Law* (1998) 19; M Mattila, 'Contested decisions: Empirical Analysis of Voting in the European Union', (2004) 43 *European Journal of Political Research* 29.

of decision-making, which enables them to find a peaceful way of dealing with conflicts.[74] This method is based on inclusion, i.e. on compromise in decision-making and on proportionate accommodation of all parties in responsible offices of government. Thus, it forms a contrast to competition and exclusion, which shape systems organised by majority rule.[75]

2 If consensus method in the Council is required by the diversity of interests, it is facilitated by the similarity of the Council's members. As described above, negotiations in the Council are mostly a deliberation of national and supranational civil servants. Despite linguistic, political or other differences, these civil servants very often share a common education (law, political science), a common professional background (national administrations) and grow closer over their ongoing contact. This common habit creates a certain Club spirit, as it is called (or *Esprit du Corps* or *Fachbruderschaft*) that facilitates compromise and consensus.[76]

3 Finally, the issue of implementation explains why the consensus method is entrenched in the structure of executive federalism. It is an obvious observation, that a solution is more acceptable, if the different parties agree on it. In the EU, the implementation of norms rests with the Member States, their legislatures as well as their bureaucracies. Thus, Union regulations and directives will have a greater chance of being properly implemented by the national bureaucracies, if they were decided upon in consensus.[77]

With regard to these observations, the consensus method can be regarded as a complementary element of executive federalism.

[73] R Dehousse, 'Constitutional Reform in the European Community', (1995) 18 *Western European Politics* 125.

[74] See G Lehmbruch, *Proporzdemokratie* (1967); A Lijphart, *The Politics of Accommodation* (1968); as to these two researchers H Daalder (ed), *Comparative European Politics* (1997) 197–9, 248–50; M Schmidt, *Demokratietheorie* (2000) 327 *et seq*.

[75] It might be added, that this method may prevail even after these cleavages are gone. Best example is the case of Germany, see H Abromeit, *Der verkappte Einheitsstaat* (1992); D Elazar, above n 33, 66.

[76] The master of studies of bureaucracies, Max Weber, has called this phenomenon "*Kompromisskollegialitaet*", M Weber, *Wirtschaft und Gesellschaft* (5th edn 1972) 164; Wessels, above n 61, 224; D Chrysoochou, *The Consociational Dimension of European Integration* (1994) 26.

[77] J Schwarze *et al*, *Die Implementation von Gemeinschaftsrecht* (1993) 13; S Krislov, C-D Ehlermann and JHH Weiler, 'The Political Organs and the Decision-Making Process in the United States and the European Community', in: M Cappelleti, M Seccombe, JHH Weiler (eds), *Integration through Law* (1986), vol 1, book 2, 3 at 63; N Nugent, *The Government and Politics of the European Community* (1994) 145.

This puts in perspective the debate about qualified majority voting, which has dominated the Nice IGC as well as the Convention and its following IGC. The Nice Treaty proscribes a complex system of triple majorities.[78] In bright contrast to this, the Convention envisioned a radical reform: abolishing the weighted votes and introducing a system of double-majorities, first of Member States, and, secondly, representing three fifths of the population.[79] But even though these are "majority votes", they are in fact highly sophisticated super-majorities, which could also be classified as a form of consensus.[80] From that perspective, even majority votes require a level of agreement which is very high—and underlines the consensual character of Council decision-making.

This point can be taken even further. Not only is the consensus method prominent in all layers of Council decision-making. The EU in general can be characterised as a consensus democracy.[81] The method in the Council has a spillover effect on decision-making procedures in other organs as well as between the organs. Perhaps the most striking example of this spillover effect can be observed in the European Parliament.

2. European Parliament

In an almost revolutionary development, the EP has developed from a mere consultant assembly into an equal counterpart to Council and Commission.[82] At the same time, the EP has been something like a pet object at least of German institutional scholarship.[83] Yet despite ample material and analytical attention, a coherent interpretation of role and structure of the EP has not emerged.

[78] Triple majority stands for a majority of weighted votes, of Member States and in some cases of population, Art 3 of the Protocol on the Enlargement (2001), see Yatanagas, above n 69, ch B 2.

[79] See Art I-24(1) CT-Conv; see also n 80; A Peters, 'European Democracy after the 2003 Convention', (2004) 41 *CML Rev* 37 at 55–8; W Wessels, 'Der Verfassungsvertrag im Integrationstrend', (2003) *integration* (2003) 293.

[80] And the IGC has even raised the threshold for a majority. Now 55% of the members of the Council, comprising at least 15 of them and 65% of the population of the Union have to agree, Art 25(1) CT-IGC; Wessels, above n 63, 166–9.

[81] A Lijphart, *Patterns of democracy* (1999) 42–7; D Chryssochoou, *The Consociational dimension of European Integration* (1994); A Peters, *Elemente einer Verfassungstheorie* (2001) 728, 758; B Kohler-Koch, *The Evolution and Transformation of European Governance* (1998) 12; S Oeter in this volume; and see below, V. 2.

[82] Describing this truly astonishing development D Judge and D Earnshaw, *The European Parliament* (2003) 26–64; A Kreppel, *The European Parliament and Supranational Party System* (2002) 52–90; also B Rittberger, 'The Creation and Empowerment of the European Parliament', (2003) 4 *JCMS* 203.

[83] See above, II. 2.

2 A second argument derives from the way in which the EP conducts the approval procedure of a new Commission.[96] It would be the "natural" behaviour in a debating parliament for the majority party (or coalition) to elect the government without further discussion. In the EP, instead, there is no majority which perceives itself as a loyal parliamentarian base of the Commission. Especially in the hearings of the candidates, which the EP conducts before it approves of a new Commission, the EP presents itself rather as a critical counter-weight than as a loyal supporter of the Commission.[97]

3 A final argument against a parliamentarisation concerns the fusion between EP and Commission, which would be a necessity in a parliamentary system and a debating parliament. Empirically, there is no fusion between both institutions.[98] Also legally, a fusion would not be possible. An incompatibility rule between a mandate in the EP and a seat in the Commission formally prohibits the appointment of MEPs to the Commission.[99] De lege ferenda this could be changed. In addition, its historical roots in the technocratic origins of the Commission are weak today. However, the incompatibility rule fits perfectly well into the structure of executive federalism. Here, the divide runs not between the political parliament and the technocratic Commission, but between the legislature and the executive branch.

In sum, a development into a parliamentary system seems unlikely. This thesis has been underlined by the Constitutional Treaty. Despite several proposals and strong support from the more federalist side, the role of the EP in appointing the Commission according to the Constitutional Treaty will not change significantly.[100] Although the Constitutional Treaty now states that the Commission President "shall be elected by the European Parliament", Art 27(1) CT-IGC, this does not abridge the right of the European Council to choose the candidate to be voted on. In effect, the Constitutional Treaty only exchanges words, but does not alter the procedure.

[96] S Hix and C Lord, 'The making of a president', (1996) 31 *Government and Opposition* 62; A Maurer, *Parlamentarische Demokratie in der Europäischen Union* (2002) 172 *et seq*.

[97] But see Magnette, above n 91, 298–9.

[98] Corbett *et al*, above n 84, 250; Magnette, above n 91, 298.

[99] Art 6(1), 2nd indent, of the Act concerning the election of the representatives of the Assembly by direct universal suffrage (OJ L 278, 8.10.1976, 5). This provision is based on Art 213(2) EC, which does not explicitly mention an incompatibility but prohibits that "members of the Commission engage in other paid activities" and is interpreted as incompatibility rule (Dann, above n 94, 27).

[100] Arts 20(1), 27(1) and (2) CT-IGC; see also J Kokott and A Rüth, 'The European Convention and its Draft Treaty Establishing a Constitution for Europe', (2003) 40 *CML Rev* 1315 at 1332–3.

Nevertheless, the elective powers of the EP today or tomorrow are neither unimportant nor meaningless. Quite to the contrary, they tell a lot about the specific role of the parliament in the EU. Although it cannot autonomously elect any Commission, it can always prevent one. Thus, it functions as a controlling force, holding a negative elective competence. This power makes perfect sense in the specific institutional and political setting of the EU. First of all, possessing this negative competence might ensure at least a basic standard of democratic accountability. More importantly from the perspective of the overall system, an increased influence on the election of the Commission would also require a stable coalition in the EP to carry this Commission. This is not only very difficult to achieve (or maintain!) but would endanger the federal diversity of the party system in the EP. And, thirdly, the fact that the EP or its majority is not bound to the Commission by party loyalty has positive effects on its independence when it comes to questions of control and law-making. Thus, the current position of the EP might not only describe it adequately, but also seems to fit normatively into the broader political system of the EU.

However, this interpretation of the EP's elective powers should not obscure a deep flaw in the elective system of executive federalism. This is the question of accountability. It is a central principle of democratic government that the people shall have a say in who is governing. Democratic government is self-government. But looking at the EU, this principle is grossly violated. Here, the executive, located in the Commission and to some extent in the Council, is not elected by the EP but appointed by EP and Council together. The Council itself is composed of national governments, thus elected separately by the respective national parliaments and their elections. Hence, every vote is several times counterbalanced and dispersed by other elections—and it is barely possible to get rid of the governing, since there is a factually permanent all-party-government.[101]

But if parliamentarisation is prevented by the structure of executive federalism, would then the direct election, namely of the President of the Commission, remedy the problem? This could be argued, since it would enhance the transparency of the system and strengthen a clear line of responsibility.[102]

Yet, the problem of accountability in the EU runs deeper. It is rooted in the federal structure, which necessarily demands co-operation between the federal levels and different governments. The problem of accountability and

[101] JHH Weiler, 'To be a European citizen', in: Weiler, above n 72, 350; KH Neunreither, 'Governance without Opposition', (1998) 33 *Government and Opposition* 419.

[102] Lord, above n 84, 131.

the federal structure of the EU are deeply intertwined.[103] Even a directly elected President of the Commission would have to bargain and make compromises with the national governments in the Council. It lies in the nature of executive federalism to entail this somewhat murky and non-transparent situation. What seems like an obvious violation of democratic principles on one side turns out to be the life insurance of the federal system on the other side.[104]

b) Oversight Function: Control via Organisation

The structure of executive federalism has also important consequences for the oversight function. Coming back to both types of parliaments, they differ remarkably in their approaches: a *debating parliament* scrutinises the government foremost in public debate in the plenary. A *working parliament* does it more in detailed control of government proposals, exercised by specialised committees.[105]

How does the EP fare with respects to these types? Looking from a formal standpoint, the EP could easily qualify as a debating parliament. It has several formal powers to interrogate and scrutinise the Commission in plenary.[106] The actual use of these powers, however, alters the picture. Although interrogation powers are undoubtedly popular,[107] their usage has relatively shrunk, especially since the EP has gained legislative powers.[108] Hence, these powers do not add up to be the living part of EP procedures.[109]

[103] See also Oeter, above n 44, 101 *et seq.*

[104] See for precisely this problem in another executive federalism, the German: E-W Böckenförde, 'Sozialer Bundesstaat und parlamentarische Demokratie', in: J Jekewitz (ed), *Politik als gelebte Verfassung: Festschrift für F Schaefer* (1980) 188; C Moellers, 'Der parlamentarische Bundesstaat', in: J Aulehner (ed), *Föderalismus: Auflösung oder Zukunft der Staatlichkeit?* (1997) 81; as to the relation between Bundestag and Bundesrat see also K von Beyme, *The Legislator* (1998) 95–102.

[105] K Bradshaw and D Pring, *Parliament and Congress* (1972) 355; G Löwenberg and S Patterson, *Comparing Legislatures* (1979) 148.

[106] See Art 197(3) EC, Arts 42, 44; 43, 50 Rules of Procedure of EP (RoP-EP); Corbett *et al*, above n 84, 248; Beckedorf, above n 30, 126. The EP also has extended powers to scrutinise the Council, which finds an explanation only in the special role that the Council plays in executive federalism, see Dann, above n 32, 360 *et seq*; also Beckedorf, *ibid*, 157; J Lodge, 'The European Parliament', in: SS Andersen and KA Eliassen (eds), *The EU: how democratic is it?* (1996) 198.

[107] In the fourth legislature (1994–99), the Commission had to answer not less than 21.096 parliamentary questions (Corbett *et al*, above n 84, 250). For regular updates on these numbers see the annual reports of the Commission; for an insightful early analysis, see L Cohen, 'The Development of the Question time in the EP', 16 (1979) *CML Rev* 46.

[108] A Maurer, *What next for the European Parliament?* (1999) 54.

[109] Two details underline this result: First, in the time schedule of the EP there is only one out of four weeks reserved for plenary discussions (Corbett *et al*, above n 84, 32). And secondly, it is interesting to note that the EP Committees don't convene at the seat of the plenary in Strassbourg, but in Bruxelles where the other institutions have their seats.

Instead, the working parliament approach grasps the EP much better. This approach is primarily based on organisational pre-conditions, namely an effective committee structure,[110] exemplified in the US Congress.[111] And indeed, the EP's committees are of paramount importance.[112] Two aspects shall highlight their central position:

First, their role in acquiring and analysing information and in formulating political positions is central to the policy-formulation in the EP. Committees have the right to interrogate the Commission[113] and to hold hearings with special experts.[114] Through these instruments, committees have acquired specific expertise in their fields.[115] On this basis, they file reports for the plenary, thereby pre-determining most of the outcomes.[116]

Second, their internal structure plays a pivotal role. They are small, specialised and targeted in their scope at the division of subject matters in the Commission. Of salient importance is also their leadership structure. This consists of a chairperson and a *rapporteur.*[117] The latter is responsible for presenting a matter to the committee, drafting the report for the committee and arguing it in plenary and with other institutions. Therefore a highly influential figure, he is chosen in a complicated and hotly contested procedure.[118] Besides, this position creates clear responsibilities, giving the committee a distinct voice to communicate to the inside (between different committees and party groups) as well as to the outside (to other institutions). It renders committees especially suited to negotiate with other institutions.[119]

[110] From a comparative perspective K Strom, 'Parliamentary Committees in European Democracies', in L Longley and R Davidson (eds), *The new role of parliamentary committees* (1998) 21.

[111] See C Deering and S Smith, *Committees in Congress* (1997); M Shapiro, 'The politics of information', in: Craig and Harlow (eds), above n 45, 187.

[112] See Corbett *et al*, above n 84, 105–29; V Mamadou and T Raunio, 'The Committee System', (2003) 41 *JCMS* 333; C Neuhold, 'The 'legislative backbone' keeping the Institution upright?', (2001) 5 *European Integration online Papers* No 10; S Bowler and D Farrel, 'The Organizing of the European Parliament', (1995) 25 *British Journal of Political Science* 226.

[113] Art 164 RoP-EP.

[114] Art 166(2) RoP-EP.

[115] See K Collins, C Burn and A Warleigh, 'Policy Entrepreneurs', (1998) 19 *Statute Law Review* 1 at 9–10; Bowler and Farrel, above n 112, 226–35.

[116] Another important facet of the EP's scrutiny system are the Committees of Inquiry (Art 193 EC) that can be set up for special purposes and for a limited time, see Beckedorf, above n 31, *passim*; M Shackleton, 'The European Parliament's New Committees of Inquiry', (1998) 36 *JCMS* 115.

[117] Art 157 RoP-EP; see Mamadouh and Raunio, above n 112, 341–8; Bowler and Farrel, above n 112, 242–3; Neuhold, above n 112, 6.

[118] Cf Art 159 RoP-EP; Neuhold, above n 112, 7; Corbett *et al*, above n 84, 117–8.

[119] Another important aspect explaining their role is that EP committees convene and negotiate in public, and function as "windows of the parliament", Art 171(3) RoP-EP (above neuhold, above n 112, 8–9; Corbett *et al*, above n 84, 272–3).

The EP can finally be characterised as a working parliament with respect to its staff. It is one sign of a working parliament that it acquires its expertise and level of scrupulous scrutiny only because of the support from an extensive staff. Compared to the US Congress, of course, the EP's staff looks petty. But compared to all national parliaments in Europe, it is very well equipped.[120]

c) Co-Legislator: Law-making by Co-operation and Consensus-building

Finally, the EP has to be qualified as a working parliament with respect to the law-making function.[121] As such, it has a more powerful position as legislature than most national parliaments, acting in a parliamentary system.[122] Three aspects shall characterise its specific role: first the need for inter-institutional co-operation, second the need for intra-institutional consensus building within the EP and finally its role of a policy-*shaping*, not policy-making actor:[123]

1 Law-making in the EU is, above all, characterised by an overriding need for co-operation between the involved organs.[124] This follows (partly) from the strictly bicameral approach of Art 251 EC and its co-decision procedure, which can be regarded the standard law-making procedure—and will it be according to the Constitutional Treaty.[125] Through two readings in EP and Council, and possibly a conciliation committee, a bill has to be agreed upon by both organs, EP and Council.[126] In this often long bargaining process the Commission acts

[120] See Shapiro, above n 111, 199–207; Corbett *et al*, above n 84, 166–76; in a comparative perspective Löwenberg and Patterson, above n 105, 159–64. Altogether there are 4100 staff workers, although 1200 of them are actually translators. Nevertheless, there are even more sources: the EP has adopted a network concept to use external research institutions for European matters (the so-called STOA, Scientific and Technical Options Assessment, see Corbett *et al*, above n 84, 252). Moreover, there is the legal service of the EP which provides valuable support not only in judicial proceedings.

[121] As to the differing approaches of both types of parliament to law-making, see Dann, above n 84, 566; Bradshaw and Pring, above n 105, 293.

[122] As to the specific development of the EP's legislative competences see A Maurer, 'The Legislative Powers and Impact of the EP', (2003) 41 *JCMS* 227 at 231–6.

[123] There is not enough space here to spell out details of the lawmaking procedures; for a brief overview see Lenaerts and van Nuffel, above n 35, 442–54; A Dashwood, 'The constitution of the European Union after Nice', (2001) 26 *EL Rev* (2001) 215; for an empirical assessment, see Maurer, above n 96, 131 *et seq*.

[124] 'Co-operative mechanisms are common to all law-making procedures', Läufer, above n 18.

[125] Art III-302 CT-Conv (Art 396 CT-IGC); Peters, above n 79, 45 and 49.

[126] As to the conciliation committees, see extensively F Rutschmann, *Der europäische Vermittlungsausschuß* (2002); also Corbett *et al*, above n 84, 196–200.

as a broker. The triangular game is facilitated by a range of informal meetings between the institutions, in which package deals and other tactics find ample use.[127]

The need for ongoing co-operation has a second reason: Although the Commission has the sole power to initiate legislation,[128] it has no steady parliamentary base to carry its bills through the deciding organs.[129] This reflects the Commission's role as a politically (and nationally) balanced institution. However, even if there were one in the EP, structurally it cannot be in the Council, which is not prearranged along party lines. Hence, the Council forms a roadblock of executive federalism against a smooth government-lead legislative process, rendering it a highly consensual, co-operation-based process.[130]

2 But co-operation between organs is only one side. The other side is the fact that the EP in itself is a consensual system.[131] Its committees serve as small, specialised *fora* for negotiations between the different party groups as well as with the other institutions.[132] Besides, the general leadership structure of the EP provides it with a competent system to act in a consensual setting.[133]

The EP is also a dominantly consensual actor because its party structure is especially diverse.[134] To reach an agreement here already requires the art of compromise. Moreover, majority rules in the EP set particularly high standards for reaching agreement.[135] Both aspects force the

[127] M Shackleton and T Raunio, 'Codecision since Amsterdam', (2003) 10 *JEPP*, 171 at 176–81; J Garman and L Hilditch, 'Behind the scenes: an examination of the importance of the informal processes at work in conciliation', (1998) 5 *JEPP* 271; H Farrell and A Héritier, 'Formal and Informal Institutions under Codecision', 6 (2002) *European Integration online Papers* No 3, at 7.

[128] Cf Arts 250(1), 251(2), 252a EC; see C von Buttlar, *Das Initiativrecht der Kommission* (2003); G Edwards and D Spence, 'The Commission in Perspective', in: G Edwards and D Spence (eds), *The European Commission* (1997) 9; M Westlake, *The Commission and the Parliament* (1994) 19–21.

[129] Dehousse, above n 73, 126; S Hix and C Lord, *Political Parties in the European Union* (1997) 178.

[130] S Boyron, 'The Co-decision procedure', in: Craig and Harlow (eds) above n 45, 147.

[131] See also Farrel and Heritier, above n 127, 7; Kreppel, above n 82, 174–5, 215.

[132] The Commission is a regular participant of EP committee sessions, presenting and defending its proposals. Also the Council (represented by the minister of the incumbent presidency) is more and more often to be seen in these meetings to pave the way for later agreements, a situation legalised in Arts 137 RoP-EP; Neuhold, above n 112, 10; Collins *et al*, above n 112, 6.

[133] Judge and Earnshaw, above n 82, 173–6.

[134] Hix and Lord, above n 129, 77, 156 (table 6.7); Kreppel, above n 82, 215 *et seq.*

[135] Arts 198, 251(2)(b) and (c) EC.

EP to develop negotiating and compromise techniques for its interior arrangements, allowing it to also thrive in the broader inter-institutional process.[136]

This diverse and thus consensual character of the EP itself might explain why a parliamentary and majoritarian logic never really took root and thus does not conflict with the federal and consensual structure of the institutional process in the EU.[137] From this perspective, the political deficit of the EP, as Renaud Dehousse has called it,[138] turns out to be the "efficient secret" of the decision-making in the institutional setting of the EU.

3 A third point has to be made to characterise the EP's comparatively powerful role in law-making. Since the EP has no power to initiate legislation, its influence is principally of an amending or blocking nature.[139] The EP's general role is therefore less that of a policy-making legislature, but can rightfully be called a policy-*shaping* legislature. This does not, however, qualify it as a weak or incomplete parliament. In "normal" parliamentary systems today, it is nearly exclusively the government that introduces bills. Compared to that, the EP has developed not only an active agenda-setting behaviour. Due to its political independence from the Commission and a ruling majority party and due to its organisational features (namely the committees), the EP is better able to rigorously scrutinise and amend bills and thus shape legislation than parliaments in parliamentary systems, which have to loyally follow their government.[140]

In sum, the EP as parliament in a system of executive federalism can best be understood as a working parliament—acting out of strong committees, neither politically nor personally connected with the Commission, since it is only negatively involved in its election, and influential in law-making procedures through its political independence and veto power. However, its relation to the Commission is flawed by a lack of elective accountability, surely with consequences for the question of gubernative leadership.

[136] Corbett *et al*, above n 84, 152.

[137] As to different experiences in the German executive federalism see Lehmbruch, above n 44.

[138] Dehousse, above n 73, 124.

[139] As to its right to request that the Commission submits a proposal, Art 192 EC, and its rare use, see von Buttlar, above n 128, 190 *et seq*, 254; Corbett *et al*, above n 84, 209–10; M Westlake, 'The Commission and the Parliament', in G Edwards and D Spence (eds), above n 128, 244–5.

[140] Von Bogdandy, Prinzipien, in: *id* (ed), above n 1, 149 at 177; cf K von Beyme, *Die parlamentarische Demokratie* (1999) 282 *et seq*.

3. European Commission

a) The Problem of Leadership

Perceived through the lens of executive federalism, the gubernative function poses an inherent problem. The principal equality of Member States and the absence of ideological coherence in the Council withstand hierarchical leadership. Even though certain tandems or triangles of countries may serve as motor, there is no steady base for formal or informal hierarchy. In addition, the need for consensus veils responsibility. As most decisions are taken in agreement with all parties involved and negotiated confidentially, it is often hard to discern what party is responsible for what—a central mark of leadership. And finally, the demand for co-operation prevents quick action. Not only in the Union of 25, the agreement on policy initiatives and bills takes an enormous amount of time, thus slowing down any energetic attempt.[141] However, the institutional system of the EU offers two organs that have potentially gubernative functions, the European Commission and the European Council. How does the Commission, to start with the truly supranational organ, perform its gubernative function and how does it cope with the restraints of executive federalism?

Again, two approaches shall be applied. First, role and functions of the Commission are examined in the frame of executive federalism. Secondly, we will once again use a comparative approach to get a clearer view on what type of institution the Commission is.[142] To that end, two types of governments shall be outlined:[143]

The *majoritarian government* is composed along lines of political affiliation. Based on the majority in parliament, which elects and supports the government, the ministers are selected from one party or a coalition of parties; ideological coherence is the essential characteristic of a majoritarian government. The internal organisation of the cabinet government is structured by a clear hierarchy in which a prime minister forms the top. He takes

[141] This view shall not foreclose other explanations for the problem of leadership, namely of institutional rivalry between Commission and Council; N Nugent, *The European Commission* (2001) 202–4.

[142] This article will only examine the political top of the Commission, ie the College and its President, but not the bureaucratic base, ie the services; for further information on them above Nugent, above n 141, 134 *et seq*.

[143] Various concepts have been employed to grasp the Commission's nature, see D Rometsch, *Die Rolle und Funktionsweise der Kommission in der Ära Delors* (1999) 55; Nugent, above n 141, 8–9; L Cram, 'The European Commission as Multi-Organisation', (1994) 1 *JEPP* 195; JH Matlary, 'The role of the Commission', in N Nugent (ed), *At the Heart of the Union* (2000) 270.

ultimate responsibility in face of the parliament. Examples of this type can be found in the British government or the German Bundesregierung.[144]

The hallmark of the *consensual government*, as a second type may be called, is its proportionate composition, representing all relevant regional, cultural and political groups. It is not built on a parliamentary majority but based on the principle of fair representation of all parties and regions. Members of the government are equals and take collective responsibility. The federal government is elected by an assembly, composed of both houses of parliament, thus ensuring the federal balance of the election. This form of government is to be found in the Swiss *Bundesrat* (Federal Council).[145]

b) Organisational Structure: the Outlook of a Consensual Government

The composition of the Commission shows strong similarities to a consensual government. In the college of 25 members, every Member State is represented by one commissioner.[146] Also in terms of political composition, a form of proportionate representation (and not ideological coherence) is prevailing.[147] The holy status of these rules of proportionate composition can be estimated by following the discussions within the Convention on the Constitutional Treaty—and by taxing the result.[148] The principle of "one country—one commissioner" was not to be touched.[149]

With respect to its internal hierarchy, we can observe a development from a consensual to a more majoritarian type. The Commission has a collegiate nature with the Commission President traditionally being only marginally elevated.[150] Until today, the college takes decisions collectively.[151]

[144] For a description of this form see M Schröder, 'Bildung, Bestand und parlamentarische Verantwortlichkeit der Bundesregierung', in J Iseensee and P Kirchhof (eds), *Handbuch des Staatsrechts* vol II (1998), § 51; von Beyme, above n 140, 415 *et seq*.

[145] L Mader, 'Bundesrat und Bundesverwaltung', in D Thürer (ed), *Verfassungsrecht der Schweiz*, § 67.

[146] Art 213(1) EC, Art 4 Protocol on the Enlargement (2001).

[147] It is a telling detail that the bigger states, which used to send two commissioners, chose two from different political camps, eg Neil Kinnock and Chris Patten, cf Nugent, above n 141, 89; more explicit is the legal situation in the role model Switzerland, see Art 175(4) *Bundesverfassung* (Swiss Constitution).

[148] According to Art 26(5) CT-IGC, the Commission shall for the first term under the new Constitution consist of one national of each State. Art 26(6) CT-IGC then proscribes a reduction of the number of Commissioners corresponding to two thirds of the number of Member States—but leaves a backdoor open to the European Council to avert the reduction by a unanimous decision; see W Wessels, above n 63, 171.

[149] See also Convention's proposal in Art I-25(3) CT-Conv; also J Schild, 'Die Reform der Kommission', (2003) *integration* 498; Kokott and Rühl, above n 100, 1338–9.

[150] Nugent, above n 141, 68–71.

[151] Case 5/85, *AKZO Chemie v Commission* [1986] ECR I-2585, para 30; also Lenaerts and van Nuffel, above n 35, para 7-056.

However, past Treaty revisions have led to a stronger role of the President. The Commission works now "under the political guidance of its President", who can decide on its internal organisation and allocate responsibilities.[152] More important perhaps, the President can influence the choice of 'his' Commissioners[153] and can (at least with approval of the college) dismiss a member of the Commission.[154]

As to the mode of appointment, a close resemblance to the consensual type of government can be observed again. The Commission is appointed in an intricate procedure that intertwines the role of the Council with the EP. Whereas the former has the power to nominate first the President and then a list of Commissioners, the latter has to confirm first the choice of the President and then the college as a whole.[155] Thus, it is not the parliament that can autonomously elect the government, as in the majoritarian model, but a tandem of a unitary and a federal actor.[156]

The stability of the term of office is another indicator of a consensual government, as it is only curbed by impeachment. The Commission comes close to this. The Council, as one part of the bicameral elector, has no power to dismiss the Commission. The EP, on the other side, has the power to retire the Commission by a motion of censure,[157] a typical instrument of parliamentary regimes. Its use is seriously hampered, though, by the requirement of a two-third majority of cast votes.[158] Especially in a parliament which is characterised by a very heterogeneous mix of parties, such a majority is almost impossible to organise.

c) Functions: Agenda-setter, Mediator and Guardian

Although the consensual and federal aspects in the structure of the Commission have been demonstrated, the fingerprints of *executive* federalism have been less obvious so far. This changes, once we look at the functions of the Commission.

Every political system needs an institution that provides for orientation and leadership. Particularly the institutional dynamic of co-operation and

[152] Art 217(1)(2) EC, G Falkner and M Nentwich, 'The Amsterdam Treaty', in KH Neunreither and A Wiener (eds), *European Integration after Amsterdam* (2000) 15 at 23 *et seq*.

[153] Art 214(2) EC.

[154] Art 217(4) EC. The condition of obtaining the approval of the College will be dropped and the President's role again strengthened according to the Constitutional Treaty, see Art 27(3) CT-IGC.

[155] Art 214(2) EC; see Maurer, above n 96, 171 *et seq*; S Hix, 'Executive selection in the EU', in Neunreither and Wiener, above n 152, 98.

[156] Cf the Swiss *Bundesversammlung* (Federal Assembly), Art 157(1), 175(2) *Bundesverfassung* (Swiss Constitution); see Mader, above n 145, 1051.

[157] Art 201 EC.

[158] See Corbett *et al*, above n 84, 243 *et seq*.

consensual agreement within the EU creates such a need. But this furthered need is confronted with a specific relation between the Commission and the law-making organs, which is characterised by two aspects: first of all, the Commission has no political basis in the EP. In contrast to governments in parliamentary systems, it can therefore not rely on a steady partner to carry through its political concepts. Secondly, even if it would have such a parliamentary basis, this would not reach into the second house of the federal bicameral legislator, i.e. the Council. Hence, any institution of leadership in executive federalism must be able to reach out to both, EP and Council. With that in mind, powers and means of the Commission prove perhaps more convincing, because they fit more effectively into the institutional system of executive federalism.

Three functions of the Commission shall be highlighted:[159]

aa) Agenda Setting First of all, the Commission serves as agenda-setter.[160] To that end, it can command several means of communication.[161] Evenly important is its exclusive right of initiative in the law-making procedures.[162] The Commission can decide, whether, when and on which legal basis the Union should act. Even though Council and EP can request the Commission to submit proposals, the Commission cannot be obliged to do so.[163] The right of initiative also reaches into the legislative procedures and adds further powers to the Commission's ability of promoting and influencing legislation.[164]

bb) Mediating Interests Secondly, the Commission serves as a broker and mediator between parties and institutions. As a commanding leadership is hampered in executive federalism by a lack of hierarchy and a necessity for consensus, the need for a neutral third rises.[165] The Commission is well-equipped to serve this purpose.[166]

[159] As to other functions see Lenaerts and van Nuffel, above n 35, paras 7-045–7-049; JA Usher, 'The Commission and the Law', in Edwards and Spence (eds), above n 128, 155 at 162–5; Nugent, above n 143, 297 *et seq*.

[160] Above Nugent, above n 143, 217 *et seq*.

[161] Art 211, 2nd indent EC; Lenaerts and van Nuffel, above n 35, para 7-047.

[162] Lenaerts and van Nuffel, above n 35, para 11-011; von Buttlar, above n 128.

[163] Arts 208, 192 EC.

[164] See Lenaerts and van Nuffel, above n 35, para 11-014; von Buttlar, above n 128, 68 *et seq*; these powers will be untouched and even be strengthened by the Constitutional Treaty, Arts I-25(2), III-302(2) CT-Conv (Arts 26(2), 296(2) CT-IGC); Schild, above n 149, 494.

[165] Cf FW Scharpf, B Reissert and F Schnabel, *Politikverflechtung* (1976) 42 *et seq*.

[166] It should be underlined that the neutrality of the Commission is interpreted here not as technocratic legacy, nor is it defined as a-political task, but as a federal function.

Already its mandate and mantra is that of a neutral actor,[167] a first and decisive pre-condition for any broker. By law, Commission and Commissioners have to be completely independent and have to perform their duties only "in the general interest of the Community".[168] The Commission has mostly achieved to be seen in practice as just that, an independent broker for sound solutions in the common interest.[169]

Its capability of serving as a neutral third is also promoted by the Commission's procedural rights, as it takes part in all legislative procedures and has access to all institutions.[170] Following from its right of initiative, it also has the power to amend a draft at any time and without any further formalities, or to simply withdraw it. Thus, the Commission has utmost flexibility and superior information as to how an agreement between the actors involved could be achieved.

In this function as broker, the interplay between functional demand of the executive federalism and the Commission's structure as a consensual government appears most striking. The specific structure of the Commission seems exactly shaped to fit into and promote the institutional dynamic of this federal system.

cc) Federal Voice and Guardian A third function of the Commission pivotal in executive federalism is to serve as a voice of the federal interest. The structure of executive federalism does not provide for a voice that speaks not just as neutral third, but as advocate of the common interest.

The Commission, however, has several competences to serve as such a voice. Its role in the decision-making procedures has been mentioned already. Evenly important, the Commission has the power to ensure that the Treaties are applied by the other organs. Art 211, 1st indent EC obliges it to check that the other institutions comply with Union law and to bring an action for annulment or for failure to act in the Court of Justice.[171] These powers fit well into the system of executive federalism, in which the Member States implement Union law. It seems evident that a federal organ has to supervise the implementation. It is not only a question of efficiency, but also of fairness between the Member States that a neutral institution ensures that all Member States comply. In that perspective, the function as a federal voice and guardian is central to the functioning of the EU as executive federalism.

[167] Art 213(2) EC.
[168] As to the incompatibility rule between Commission and EP, see above, IV. 2. a.
[169] Nugent, above n 143, 210–1.
[170] Hayes-Renshaw and Wallace, above n 47, 180–1.
[171] Arts 230, 232 EC; Usher, above n 159, 165–8; Lenaerts and van Nuffel, above n 35, para 7-046; still informative Schmitt von Sydow, above n 5, 28 *et seq.*

d) Conclusion and an Unresolved Problem of Leadership

In sum, structure and powers of the Commission find a coherent explanation within the conceptual framework of executive federalism. As Walter Hallstein put it, the Commission is "at once a motor, a watchdog and a kind of honest broker".[172] It is interesting to observe how the organisational structure of the Commission and its tasks interplay and complement each other. Namely, the proportionate composition of the Commission seems irreplaceable in order to serve as the mediating and prosecuting third, which is an essential task in the consensual system of executive federalism.[173]

However, one question, which has not been directly answered yet, is the one question about of leadership. Considering the specific problems of leadership, arising from the structure of executive federalism as spelled out in the beginning, it seems that there are two answers—a more benevolent one, and a more sceptical one. In a more benevolent light one could argue, that a consensual system like the European Union needs a specific form of leadership. Leadership within this federal system cannot follow traditional (or majoritarian) ideas of command and top-down procedures. Instead, leadership here has to take on a more dialogical style, based more on the powers to initiate and to shape procedures. This type of leadership is not simply a softie version of power or yet another European disease. The powers of the President of the United States are mostly seen along these lines too.[174]

The more sceptical observer would point out, though, that leadership by the Commission is weak, caused by a tension between the task of political leadership and the task of mediation. The Commission is torn between politicisation and federal accommodation, and in effect unable to lead in a strong sense. It seems, so the sceptic could argue, that an institution can either serve as a political leader with political goals, or as a neutral third, but both together lead to an unsatisfying medium. The history of Commission can demonstrate this. Whenever it took a strong lead in whatever policy field, it had to disguise its (political) intentions behind a facade of expertise and wrap it in rhetoric of the common interest. According to this view, the Commission is structurally a hampered leader.

Whatever view one might prefer, one sure consequence of the Commission's role as neutral broker often is a political deficit. Where political goals are pursued by technical deliberations, the open competition of

[172] Nugent, above n 143, 28.

[173] As to a comparison between Swiss *Bundesrat* and Commission see also Oeter, above n 44, 105.

[174] Against popular believe on this side of the Atlantic, the US president has rather limited resources of power, among which the power of persuasion is central, as famously described by R Neustadt, *Presidential Power* (1960).

opinion is over. This consequence follows from the structure of executive federalism and is yet another demonstration of a fundamental dilemma inherent to it. A system as heterogeneous and as much based on consensual procedures as the EU gets less effective the more political and open a discussion is. Or as it has been put before: a certain political deficit ensures the working of the institutions of executive federalism.[175]

In that situation, an alternative could lie in a tandem-leadership with another institution, the European Council.

4. European Council

The European Council was not part of the original institutional set up of the European Communities. Instead, it grew out of a row of summits of the heads of governments in the 1960s, and was officially established as a regular meeting in 1974.[176] This development is of special importance to the understanding of what is today seen as the central stage for major policy decisions in the EU and has a lot to do with functional deficiencies of the federal institutional structure. At the same time, and that is interesting from our federal perspective, the creation of the European Council can be regarded as the ultimate confirmation of the structure and institutional logic of executive federalism in the EU.

a) Composition and Form: The Ideal of the "Fireside Chat"

A threefold impulse led to the creation of the European Council.[177] Domestic pressure on the organisation of the welfare state, combined with rising international economic instability and a leadership gap within the European Communities signalised an enhanced need for direct contact and co-operation between the heads of governments. However, the chance to create a truly helpful place for co-operation was crucially dependent on the institutional setting of the envisioned meetings.[178] At the heart of the European Council therefore lies its form. The European Council was meant to be something like a "fireside chat", a forum as informal and private as

[175] See above, IV. 2. c. (2).

[176] Communiqué of the Heads of States or of Governments meeting in Paris, 9/10 December 1974 (1974) 12 EC Bull Point 1104(3); it convened officially for the first time as "European Council" in Dublin in March 1975, see for the development Westlake, above n 47, 19; W Wessels, *Der Europäische Rat* (1980); J Werts, *The European Council* (1992).

[177] S Bulmer and W Wessels, *The European Council* (1987) 16.

[178] As to the models discussed, Bulmer and Wessels, *ibid*, 36; Werts, above n 176, 70 *et seq*.

possible, and at the same time cast as high-ranking as possible.[179] Today, the European Council has grown out of this original format, but its central organisational features still mirror this idea.

The European Council convenes only the most important actors, i.e. the heads of governments or of states as well as the President of the Commission, assisted by their foreign ministers and another member of the Commission.[180] Second and as important, the European Council adheres to special working methods, especially informality.[181] It is strictly observed that there are no written records of the meetings. Until today, only a very limited number of actors are allowed into the meeting room.[182] Central to the working methods of the European Council is also its strict use of a consensual form of decision-taking.[183]

However, the informal and almost private character of the meetings has found its limits as importance and agenda of European Councils have grown immensely. Considerable organisational problems are the consequence.[184] One central structural change is therefore planned by the Constitutional Treaty: in order to ensure the continuity and coherence of the European Council, the Constitutional Treaty introduces the post of a European Council President.[185] He or she shall be elected for a (renewable) two and a half years term.[186]

The original "fireside-chat" idea led to another consequence—with special meaning for the legal observer. The European Council is mainly kept beyond the law. Only 12 years after its creation, the European Council was first mentioned in primary law.[187] Today, it is vaguely described in Art 4 EU,

[179] This idea was based on the experiences that Giscard d'Estaing and Helmut Schmidt had made in the so-called "library group", Westlake, above n 47, 21; also Bulmer and Wessels, above n 177, 80.

[180] Art 4(2) EU.

[181] See the Decision of the European Council meeting in London (1977) 6 EC Bull point 2.3.1., which lays down the organisation and form of meetings; also P de Schoutheete, 'The European Council', in Peterson and Shackleton (eds), above n 47, 21 at 30.

[182] P Ludlow, *A View from Brussels*, (No 8) July 2000 (Brussels: CEPS), 15; see also the vivid description by de Schoutheete, above n 181, 25.

[183] Bulmer and Wessels, above n 177, 55; Art I-20(4) CT-Conv (Art 21(4) CT-IGC) even states consensus as the regular form of decision-taking of the European Council.

[184] De Schoutheete, above n 181, 41–4.

[185] Art I-21 CT-Conv (Art 22 CT-IGC); see P de Schoutheete, 'Die Debatte des Konvents über den Europäischen Rat', (2003) *integration* 468 at 478–80.

[186] But see Kokott and Rühl, above n 100, 1337–8; another organisational change is planned according to the Constitutional Treaty: the exclusion of the foreign ministers from the meetings, Art I-20(2) CT-Conv (Art 21(2)CT-IGC); as to the reasons de Schoutheete, above n 185, 473.

[187] Art 2 SEA.

but not mentioned in Art 7 EC, which establishes the institutional framework of the Communities. Thus, the European Council is not an institution of the Community and Community institution are not legally bound by its decisions.[188]

Here, the Constitutional Treaty proposes significant changes, as it will incorporate the European Council into the regular institutional and legal framework of the Union.[189]

As we look at the organisational structure, it is revealing to put on the glasses of executive federalism for a moment. It is not difficult to recognise those aspects that fit into the federal system. The need for extended co-operation, which led to the creation of the European Council, can be located in the lack of political leadership that has been named as characteristic of the federal system. Also, the consensual form of decision making between executives plays well into the general character of the system of executive federalism as consensual democracy. In a sense, the European Council can be seen as the re-birth of an original, that means confederate Council idea, serving as a meeting point of executives, where negotiations take place in strict confidentiality, and the consensual mode of decision-taking is adhered to. Hence, much less than the other institutions, the European Council is shaped by the Council; instead, it actually replicates it.[190]

b) Functions

Functions and powers of the European Council have originally not been fixed. Even today, they are legally of rather elusive form. Art 4(2) EU confers on the European Council the task of providing "the Union with the necessary impetus for its development" and with the task of defining "the general political guidelines".[191] Comprehension of its institutional role will therefore only follow from a closer look at its concrete functions. Three seem of special importance:[192]

[188] Lenaerts and van Nuffel, above n 35, para 2-011; to the legal force of its acts, see below, IV. 4. b. bb.

[189] Arts I-18(2), 20 CT-Conv (Arts 19(1), 21 CT-IGC); especially with regard to the question of whether its actions can be brought before the ECJ for infringement of the Treaty, see Art 365(1) CT-IGC.

[190] As to the relation between Council of Ministers and European Council, which are legally and institutionally to be distinguished, see Hayes-Renshaw and Wallace, above n 47, 159 *et seq*; Werts, above n 176, 105 *et seq*; Bulmer and Wessels, above n 177, 104; but see P Sherington, *The Council of Ministers* (2000) 40.

[191] See also its concrete powers as laid down in Arts 99(2), 128, 113(3), 128(5) EC, and in Arts 13(1) and (2), 17(1) EU.

[192] For an overview de Schoutheete, above n 181, 33–40.

aa) Steering Committee The central reason for creating the European Council has been a need for closer co-operation and concerted leadership. Hence, leadership by providing direction and enabling major decisions is the main function of the European Council. It has developed into the central stage for launching and directing major steps in the development of the integration project.[193] The European Council is thereby not confined to any special policy fields, but has taken action in every area, actually greatly enlarging the scope of Union activities.[194]

bb) Final Arbiter and Co-ordinator Yet, the European Council has not been confined to giving impulses. To an ever growing extent the European Council has taken on itself decision-making powers and has become a final arbiter of European affairs. Against its original intention,[195] the European Council has become involved in deciding major policy deals or leftovers from sectoral Councils.[196] Moreover, the European Council has asserted increasingly the position of a final arbiter for problems, for which the sectoral Councils were unable to find solutions.[197] This role as final arbiter falls naturally to it since the decisive method of making broad package deals is to that extent only available to the heads of governments sitting in the European Council.[198]

Besides, the European Council has become more and more involved in co-ordinating the policies of the Council. This also rather unintended function is mainly based on a failure on the side of the General Affairs Council (of Foreign Ministers), which is supposed to play to central co-ordinating role.[199]

The legal implications of these developments are tricky. As has been mentioned, the European Council itself is not an organ of the Community.

[193] Eg the impulses for the begin of the European Monetary System (1978–79), the start into the enlargement process with Eastern European countries (1993) or the Lisbon process (2000); an account of the actions taken by the European Council provide Bulmer and Wessels, above n 177, 85; Werts, above n 176, 177 *et seq*.

[194] The Solemn Declaration on European Union of 19 June 1983 even states this as task of the EC, see Point 2.1.2. of the declaration, *Bulletin of EC* 1983, No 6; see also Bulmer and Wessels, above n 177, 92.

[195] *Ibid*, Point A, at the end; this intention was also underlined again in Art I-20(1), 2nd sentence CT-Conv (Art 21(1), 2nd sentence CT-IGC).

[196] A precise account of these developments gives MT Johnston, *European Council* (1994) 75.

[197] This practice of shifting too difficult problems up to the EC (and thereby ensuring unanimity) has been even institutionalised in the area of the CFSP and JHA, see Arts 23(2), 40a(2) EU; Lenaerts and van Nuffel, above n 35, para 2-011.

[198] S Bulmer, 'The European Council and The Council of the European Union', (1996) 26 *Publius* 32.

[199] However, there is no clear division of tasks and of policy fields where which formation is leading, see Bulmer and Wessels, above n 177, 103; also Hayes-Renshaw and Wallace, above n 47, 163–5.

Thus, in the area of Community competences the European Council lacks the formal power to take binding decisions.[200] Instead, it could take Community decisions only, if it would act as a regular Council (thus excluding the Commission President). But in this case, it would also have to proceed in accordance with the requirements of the TEC, i.e. a vote based on a Commission proposal and in co-decision with the EP. The European Council has so far not made use of this track. Instead, the Council of Ministers formally enacts what follows from the conclusions of the European Council summits.[201]

However, the development towards the European Council as arbiter finds an explanation from the perspective of executive federalism. It is no surprise, that the growing complexity of the system through an expanded range of covered policy areas leads to an enhanced demand of co-ordination and requires a certain degree of consistency between the sectoral policies. Whether the European Council fills this gap convincingly might be another question.[202]

Surely more successfully, the European Council has answered to the need for a final decision taker. This need is imminent in the consensual nature of executive federalism, which is prone to be caught in blockades. But the "European Council has been able—not consistently but as the culmination of a cycle of package-dealing meetings—to provide an escape from the Council's earlier institutional 'gridlock'"[203].

cc) Treaty Negotiator and Constitutional Motor The European Council also has developed an increasing impact on the constitutional development of the Union, being today the "key forum for determining treaty reforms"[204].

This comes as a certain surprise. When the European Council was created, it had been feared, that the new institution would lead to a strengthening of intergovernmental politics in the Communities and thus block the supranational development.[205] But quite to the contrary, the European Council has turned out to be a major motor for the integrational development of the EU. Since the SEA, we can observe an ever-increasing speed of Treaty reforms. The role of foreign ministers, which has been crucial to the organisation and success of earlier Treaty negotiations, is now shrinking.[206]

[200] Lenaerts and van Nuffel, above n 35, para 2-012.
[201] *Ibid.*
[202] Bulmer and Wessels, above n 177, 94.
[203] Bulmer, above n 198, 31.
[204] H Wallace, 'The Institutional Setting', in W Wallace and H Wallace (eds), *Policy Making in the EU* (2000) 20.
[205] Bulmer, above n 198, 31.
[206] De Schoutheete, above n 181, 40.

Instead, the European Council has become the final and decisive point of negotiations.[207] To some extent, this development is confirmed in the Constitutional Treaty by the incorporation of special powers of constitutional amendment (so-called "passerelle"), granted to the European Council.[208]

In a comparative perspective, the European Council finds no equivalent as organ of constitutional change. However, there is an ironic twist to this situation, since the EEC, which was meant to be a system "in the making", from the outset lacked an institution or mechanism to actually "make it". In the European Council, at its inception feared as blockade against deepened integration, it seems to have invented a congenial institution that provides what an overloaded Council and restricted Commission cannot deliver.[209]

c) Conclusions

According to none other than Jean Monnet, "the creation of the European Council is the most important decision for Europe since the Treaty of Rome".[210] Here, at the end of this chapter we may briefly ask: why? To what extent did the creation of the European Council shift the institutional balance? How does the new institution fit into the structure and institutional system of executive federalism? And finally, which answer does it give to the question of leadership?

aa) An Institution Out of the Cookbook of Executive Federalism It has been suggested, that the creation of the European Council was not designed along the lines of the "founding fathers".[211] This was meant in the sense, that otherwise a reform would have been one in the existing institutional framework and probably more along the lines of technocratic reform. This may be true.

However, one can argue, that the creation of the European Council surely was along the lines of the founding fathers, at least, if their vision was one of executive federalism. Indeed, the creation of the European Council seems composed according to the cookbook of executive federalism. Instead of strengthening the Commission, empowering the parliament, or creating a European President, the solution has been a strengthening of the executive

[207] Bulmer, above n 198, 32.

[208] Arts I-24(4) and I-39(8) CT-Conv (Arts 444 and 40(7) CT-IGC).

[209] A practitioners insight in the need for the EC: C Tugendhat, *Making Sense of Europe* (1986) 166.

[210] Tugendhat, above n 209, 167.

[211] Bulmer, above n 198, 30.

branch. And not just that: the solution has been one of consensual executive co-operation. The European Council plays along the already well-known tune of co-operation and consensus, and thus decisively substantiates the logic and structure of executive federalism in the EU.

However, the European Council is not only a proof of this basic structure. It is also a response to its deficits: adding a powerful organ that can provide leadership, serving as a motor of development and (at least partly) remedying the danger of gridlock in the Council. Most interestingly, the creation of the European Council cannot be understood as being anti-federal, or anti-supranational. The European Council has played a decisive role in advancing this supranational system. If it needed a proof: the draft Constitution of the EP of 1984, often criticised as being one of dreaming federalism, acknowledges the role of the European Council, Art 32.

But how does the European Council relate to other institutions? The relation to the Council has been described above.[212] With respect to the EP, the answer is ambivalent. At its inception, the consent to the creation of the European Council was "bought" from the smaller states with the promise of the bigger states to direct elections of the EP.[213] Thus, the European Council stands at the cradle of the EP as the most directly legitimised institution of the EU. Moreover, the European Council as actor in constitutional politics has been immensely helpful in pushing towards stronger powers for the EP. The direct relations between EP and European Council are, however, not worth mentioning. Although Art 4(3) EU prominently mentions the duty of the European Council to report to the EP, the practical effect of that duty is almost zero.[214]

bb) European Council and European Commission as Twofold Gubernative

Original fears, the European Council would decisively diminish the role of the Commission,[215] have not come true.[216] Instead, today European Council and Commission can be regarded as two sides of a twofold gubernative, complementing each other in providing different yet crucial forms of leadership.

[212] See section IV. 4. a.

[213] Westlake, above n 47, 21; Werts, above n 176, 153; Bulmer and Wessels, above n 177, 44.

[214] To the practice of reporting even before Werts, above n 176, 158; also Bulmer and Wessels, above n 177, 114.

[215] Eg J Lodge, 'The role of EEC summits', (1974) 6 *JCMS* 337 at 339; Bulmer and Wessels, above n 177, 109–10.

[216] This seems to be the general perception, see already CD Ehlermann, 'Das schwierige Geschäft der Kommission', (1981) *Europarecht* 335 at 355; W Wessels and D Rometsch, 'The Commission and the Council of the Union', in Edwards and Spence (eds), above n 128, 233; P Craig, 'Some Thoughts on the role of the European Council', in JMB Pérez and I Pernice (eds), *The Government of Europe* (2003) 55.

The European Council ensures guiding political leadership and major decision-making, a role originally envisioned for the Commission. But only the European Council combines the power of its participants to command their domestic governments with their legitimacy to stand for the direction taken.

However, this dominant centre not only casts a shadow. It also offers the Commission a stage for launching ideas, since the Commission has learned to handle the European Council and to use it to its own ends.[217] First, the Commission greatly profits from the direct channel of information that it gets by being part of the European Council. Also, the Commission has attained an important role in providing the European Council with reports, memoranda and basic information, therefore described as "technical authority" in the European Council.[218] But in some aspects, the role of the Commission goes beyond that. More than once, the Commission was able to launch broad policy initiatives by using the European Council.[219] For this capacity, the Commission's role within the European Council has convincingly been called "promotional brokerage".[220]

d) A Threefold Gubernative? The Constitutional Treaty and the New Foreign Minister

The Constitutional Treaty will complement as well as complicate this twofold structure by introducing a third gubernative actor: a Minister of Foreign Affairs.[221] In response to the growing engagement of the Union in external matters and a confusing multitude of voices speaking for it, this new Minister "shall conduct the Union's common foreign and security policy". Its institutional locus, though, will be divided: elected by the European Council, the Minister will be a Vice-President of the Commission, will chair the Council of Minister when convening as Foreign Affairs council, and will take part in the meetings of the European Council. The Foreign Minister is thus planned to provide gubernative leadership in all foreign affairs.

However, the new office entails considerable risks. Its doubled institutional position will go well beyond the understanding of most observers. This poses a serious threat to the transparency of the institutional system. Together with the newly created President of the European Council and the Commission's President, there will be three "faces" (with at least three voices) to represent the Union. Moreover, the division of competences

[217] Wessels and Rometsch, above n 216, 233; Bulmer, above n 198, 34.

[218] Werts, above n 176, 143.

[219] This especially depends on the personal standing of the Commission president, though Werts, above n 176, 144.

[220] Rometsch and Wessels, above n 216, 233.

[221] Art I-27 CT-Conv (Art 28 CT-IGC).

between these three actors and their full system of instruments is not yet clear. Institutional rivalries between these gubernative actors are therefore likely.[222]

V. LEGITIMACY OF THE INSTITUTIONAL SYSTEM

A description and even more a concept of the institutional system of the EU would be incomplete, if it would not address the question of legitimacy. This holds especially true for the supranational experiment called EU. At the same time, approaches and opinions with regard to this topic are myriad. It would therefore ultimately overburden this article, if one would attempt to give a complete overview.[223]

Instead, this part will present two different aspects for an understanding of the question of legitimacy in the institutional system of the EU: first of all, parliaments matter. Thus, concept and perspectives of parliamentary democracy will be analysed first. In addition, the institutional system of the EU as an executive federalism is prone to function along the lines of consensual decision-making. This also has consequences for a concept of legitimacy in the EU, which will be noted in a second step. Finally, a conclusion will propose to label the European form of institutional setting and its form of legitimacy as a "semi-parliamentary democracy".[224]

1. Parliamentary Democracy

In a European context, it seems self-evident that public authority has to be legitimised by some form of representative democracy. Nevertheless, one has to acknowledge, that the principle of democracy, as mentioned in Art

[222] See Kokott and Rühl, above n 100, 1337–8.

[223] See for overviews: Lord, above n 84; Kaufmann, above n 28; FW Scharpf, *Governing Europe* (1999); P Schmitter, *How to Democratize the European Union?* (2000); Peters, above n 81; see also L Siedentopf, *Democracy in Europe* (2000).

[224] A third aspect that contributes to legitimacy cannot be spelled out here: the concept of separation of powers. Nevertheless, two things should be noted very briefly: First of all, the separation of powers concept has found a specific expression in the EU system. This is closely linked to the system of executive federalism, where the executive branch of the Member States is involved in the law-making at the central level, thereby purposely defying a classical separation of powers scheme. And secondly, within the EU institutional system the idea of separation of powers seems to be replaced by a concept of institutional balance, which is aimed at balancing interests through the balanced participation of institutions as agents of interests (see generally Montesquieu, *L'Esprit Des Lois* (1998), Book XI ch VI; R Bellamy, 'The Political Form of the Constitution', in R Bellamy and D Castiglione (eds), *Constitutionalism in Transformation* (1996) 25; as to this principle in the EU see A von Bogdandy in this volume; also C Möllers, 'Steps to a Tripartite Theory of Multi-level Governance', *Jean Monnet Working Paper* No 5/03, <http://www.jeanmonnetprogram.org/papers/030501.html> (3 July 2004); as to the concept within the EU see A Verhoeven, *The European Union in search of a Democratic and Constitutional Theory* (2002) 208–10; Lenaerts and van Nuffel, above n 35, paras 10-001 *et seq*).

6(1) EU, is rather vague and without any concrete implications for its institutional materialisation.[225]

Taking into account this open situation, we will turn the perspective around: we will not attempt to deduce any institutional consequences from the principle in Art 6(1) EU, but instead use the above analysis of the institutional setting and its inherent dynamic to ask, whether this institutional structure has any implications for the options that are available to organise parliamentary democracy in the EU.[226] The look turns hence to the dual path of parliamentary involvement in the EU, first to the national parliaments and secondly to the European Parliament.

a) The Dilemma of the National Parliaments

National parliaments are supposed to infuse democratic legitimacy to European governance by controlling the national governments as they are acting in the Council of Ministers.[227] They are also considered the sovereign actors in constitutional matters ratifying Treaty reforms or the accession of new members—in theory.[228] But in practice their supposed influence is dramatically undercut. Although this is well known, it is much less well explained. The structure and institutional logic of executive federalism can offer a coherent explanation and discloses an underlying dilemma. Three major problems arise:[229]

1 Most fundamentally, the federal structure renders Member State parliaments mediated actors in European affairs. It is not national parliaments but national *governments* that are involved in the regular procedures of supranational law-making. Seen through the lens of executive federalism, this makes perfect sense, as has been explained above.[230]

[225] Von Bogdandy, above n 140, 170; even the ECJ has not used the legal principle to shape the institutional structure in one direction or the other; on the ECJ case law, see S Ninatti, 'How do our judges conceive of democracy?', *Jean Monnet Working Paper* No 10/03, <http://www.jeanmonnetprogram.org/papers/03/031001.html> (3 July 2004).

[226] This instigates a short remark on a terminological problem: In contrast to the notion of a "parliamentary system" which is used *strictu sensu* here (above n 90), the term "parliamentary democracy" shall be understood broader, covering any form of legitimacy through the involvement of parliaments.

[227] The literature on the national parliaments is abundant, see eg A Maurer and W Wessels (eds), *National Parliaments on their ways to Europe* (2001); P Weber-Panariello, *Nationale Parlamente in der Europäischen Union* (1998); Dann, above n 32, 177–210.

[228] Kaufmann, above n 28, 337–403.

[229] See the detailed argument in Dann, above n 32, 210. These arguments target the current state of law. As to the envisioned changes for the national parliaments in the Constitutional Treaty, see below, V. 1. b.

[230] See section III., IV. 1; as to the notion of implementation in the EU, covering the adjudication but also and especially the implementing legislation of the Member States, see Dann, see 94, 10 note 45.

In consequence, national parliaments have to watch the complex European law-making procedures from the sidelines. The arising from that are lack of insight information, a timetable not geared towards the working rhythm of national parliaments, and finally often disadvantage in in-depth expertise all of which makes control cumbersome to ineffective.[231]

2 The inter-institutional decision-making process in the EU is often based on confidential negotiations. This poses another major problem for control through the national parliaments.[232] But, this confidentiality is a necessary ingredient of the institutional setting in executive federalism. Especially Lehmbruch's works on consensus democracy have demonstrated how compromise and consensus are based not only on mutual trust but also on the freedom of the actors to strike deals.[233] Thus, the urge of parliaments to publicly discuss and control collides with the confidentiality of EU negotiations.

3 And finally, executive federalism works largely by consensus, adding another two problems. First, the consensus method is based on fairly unbound actors. In order to reach agreements, every party has to be free to make a compromise and cannot be bound to a rigid mandate from their constituency. Parliaments, on the other side, will aim at giving mandates or setting stringent margins in order to actually influence the behaviour in negotiations.[234] Thus, parliamentary mandates collide with governmental freedom to negotiate.

Second and more fundamental, consensus is based on compromise. Yet, compromises are grey. They do not offer clear-cut options, but a complex combination. The logic of parliamentary politics, on the other side, is based on a majoritarian and mainly binary mode.[235] Parliaments display the contrast of government and opposition, of contrasting policy options and of winner and loser in concrete votes. National parliaments, which want to control what their governments do in Brussels, have to deal with a lot of consensual grey.[236]

[231] E Töller, *Europapolitik im Bundestag* (1995) 100; as to the exceptional Danish case, see F Laursen, 'The Danish Folketing and its European Affairs Committee', in Maurer and Wessels (eds), above n 227, 99; Maurer, above n 96, 259; A Moravcsik, 'Why the European Community strengthens the state', *Harvard Working Paper Series* No 52 (1994).

[232] P Birkinshaw and D Ashiagbor, 'National Participation in Community Affairs', (1996) 33 *CML Rev* 499 at 521; Oeter, above n 32, 695, 703.

[233] Lehmbruch, above n 44, 19.

[234] See A Benz, 'Compounded Representation in EU Multi-Level Governance', in B Kohler-Koch (ed), *Linking EU and National Governance* (2003) 82 at 91–2.

[235] See Dehousse, above n 73, 125; Lehmbruch, above n 44, 19.

[236] Weber-Panariello, above n 227, 310; Benz, above n 234, 105.

In sum, national parliaments face a dilemma between their own right to control and the efficiency of Union procedures. The more they try to get hold of their governments with strict means of supervision, the more they run the risk to block procedures.

A separate remark shall be added to comment on the changes that the Constitutional Treaty envisions for the national parliaments. These changes provide an innovative and convincing solution to the situation of national parliaments. However, they will not lift this fundamental dilemma. The Constitutional Treaty introduces an "early warning" mechanism.[237] National parliaments can thereby *ex ante* raise their concerns with respect to any legislative proposal from the Commission, if they see an infringement on the Union's behalf to the principle of subsidiarity. If at least a third of the Member State parliaments signal concerns about the proposal, the Commission is obliged to review (not to change) its proposal. The Member States parliaments can then, although this is not new, involve the ECJ on the grounds of an infringement of the principle of subsidiarity.

This new system is convincing, because it gives national parliaments a voice, which is already of considerable symbolic value. It also gives them a fair chance to halt European processes. However, the envisioned mechanism will only be used successfully if national parliaments invest the massive resources necessary to check early and competently, which legislative proposal might violate the principle of subsidiarity and endanger their competences. Here lies the dilemma. National parliaments will still be mediated actors in the ongoing legislative procedure. Hence, they have to invest resources on matters, which are not "theirs". For a normal national member of parliament, European matters will be "alien territory" and difficult to oversee. Therefore, I expect that the new system will mainly be of symbolic importance.

b) The EP and its Representational Limits

As national parliaments have legally and practically only a very limited influence on the decision-making in the EU, the focus turns to the EP. And as we have seen above, the EP has developed the organisational means and the competences to be taken seriously.[238] It surely offers the option for parliamentary legitimacy in the EU, even though or, as I would argue, because it is not likely to develop into a parliamentary system.

[237] See Protocol on the application of the principles of subsidiarity and proportionality; see also the Protocol on the role of national parliaments in the European Union; as to other changes see Peters, above n 79, 60–2.

[238] See above, IV. 2. b–d.

However, parliamentary legitimacy from the EP still has a weak spot. That is its representational function.[239] A first central aspect of this function is that parliaments are meant to serve as a public forum for society.[240] Parliaments are sounding boards for society. This aspect has traditionally been regarded as a specific problem of the EP, because it lacks a common language and a common civil society.[241] However, different types of parliaments show that the public forum function can be performed very differently. Whereas for countries with a *debating parliament*, to take up the two ideal types of parliaments that have been used above, the plenary debates are effectively the central stage of political discussion,[242] in countries with a *working parliament* the approach is very different:[243] Since the battle between government and opposition in parliament is at the outset prevented by the incompatibility rule which forbids ministers from sitting in parliament, it is thus not the plenary, but the parliamentary committees which serve as public sounding-boards.

Picturing the EP as a working parliament helps to better understand its representational function. It entails that the EP "naturally" does not have such a vivid plenary culture as debating parliaments. This might be a deficiency, but it is less a European one than a deficiency common to working parliaments. Looking at the committee culture in the EP easily underscores this point. It is the committees which attract most of the public recognition, by working openly, pooling expertise and involving the interested public via hearings.[244]

However, these arguments do not obscure the flaws of the EP. Conceptualising it as working parliament might explain some aspects, but it does not render it a stainless organ of representation. Rather the contrary is true: the situation of the EP appears worse because certain makeshift structures, which in national political systems help to remedy the weaknesses of such parliaments, are missing here. These problems are rooted in the representational role of parties and/or single parliamentarians.

[239] There are formal and more communicative aspects to this function, see for the first F Arndt, Distribution of Seats at the European Parliament, in: A Bodnar *et al* (eds), *The Emerging Constitutional law of the EU* (2003) 93; Lord, above n 84, 44; as to the latter Weiler, above n 72, 80–6; JHH Weiler, U Haltern and F Mayer, 'Five uneasy pieces: European Democracy and its critique', (1995) 18 *Western European Politics* 6.

[240] Bagehot, above n 85, 73–4; Löwenberg and Patterson, above n 105, 44–51, 182; E-W Böckenförde, 'Demokratie und Repräsentation', in Böckenförde, *Staat, Verfassung, Demokratie* (1992) 379.

[241] D Grimm, 'Does Europe need a Constitution?', (1995) 3 *ELJ* 292; P Kirchhof, 'Der deutsche Staat im Prozeß der europäischen Integration', in P Kirchhof and J Isensee (eds), *Handbuch des Staatsrechts* vol VII (1992), § 183; Weiler *et al*, above n 239, 12.

[242] A Adonis, *Parliament today* (1993) 130.

[243] Steffani, above n 84, 333; Bradshaw and Pring, above n 105, 360–2.

[244] Neuhold, above n 112, 9; Corbett *et al*, above n 84, 7, 272.

If the plenary as a sounding board is mute and committees reach out only to a specialised public, then there are normally specific agents of representation. There are mainly two models: Either political parties serve as "representative agencies", offering a clear and coherent program that is infused into the parliamentarian discussion and evaluated by the voters,[245] or there are individual parliamentarians, who are taken by their constituency as responsible delegate.[246] Especially where parties are rather loose and decentralised organisations, providing little orientation for the voter, single parliamentarians are considered delegates of a specific constituency.[247]

The problem with these two models in Europe is that both fail.[248] There are, first, only very loose European parties, which lack coherent European programs.[249] European election campaigns have therefore been dominated by national topics.[250] Moreover, empirical data shows that MEPs are only barely representative of their electorate since they are by far more "pro-European" than their constituencies.[251]

The model of single parliamentarians also fails, not only but mostly for one simple reason: the size of the constituency. Most of the Member States have electoral systems which provide for only one national constituency in EP elections. That rules out any local basis of the parliamentarians.[252] In addition, even if there are regional constituencies for European elections, then these are still huge. In effect, MEPs are hardly known in their constituencies. Thus, the model of parliamentarians being deeply entrenched in one region and thereby triggering feedback and accountability, is structurally hampered in the EU.[253]

[245] W Müller, 'Political parties in parliamentary democracies', (2000) 37 *European Journal of Political Research* 309; P Mair, 'Political parties, popular legitimacy and public privilege', (1995) 18 *Western European Politics* 40.

[246] M Marsh and P Norris, 'Political Representation in the European Parliament', (1997) 32 *European Journal of Political Research* 153; Löwenberg and Patterson, above n 105, 167.

[247] This model has been especially used to explain representation in the US Congress; for a path-breaking American study see W Miller and D Stokes, 'Constituency influence in the US Congress', (1963) 57 *American Political Science Review* 45; a classic also: R Fenno, *Home Style* (1978).

[248] See extensively Dann, above n 32, 41 *et seq*.

[249] For past and current political composition of the EP, see Hix and Lord, above n 129, 54; also Corbett *et al*, above n 84, 59.

[250] K Reif and H Schmitt, 'Nine second-order elections', (1980) 8 *European Journal of Political Research* 3; F van der Eijk and MN Franklin, *Choosing Europe?* (1996) 367.

[251] See J Thomassen and H Schmitt, 'Policy Representation', (1997) 32 *European Journal of Political Research* 165 at 181; see also Lord, above n 84, 67.

[252] Corbett *et al*, above n 84, 12–3; C Haag and R Bieber, in H von der Groeben and J Schwarze (eds), *Vertrag über die Europäische Union und Vertrag zur Gründung der Europäischen Gemeinschaft* (2004), after Art 190 EC, para 23.

[253] M Marsh and B Wessels, 'Territorial representation', (1997) 32 *European Journal of Political Research* 227.

In sum, none of the models to provide representation works properly in the European context. In fact, we face a puzzling situation. Institutionally, the EP has to be regarded as a strong parliament. However, sociologically, it is barely existent in the European political mindset. Only (yet surely) time will change this.

2. Consensual Democracy

Next to the avenue of parliamentary democracy, there is another path that can lead to the legitimacy of the institutional setting: the EU is generally qualified as a consensus democracy. This qualification is based on a number of features, which are typical for consensus democracies and to be observed in the functioning of all European institutions.[254]

However, despite the agreement on the character of the EU as consensus democracy, it has seldom been asked, how the consensual and the parliamentary path relate to each other.[255] This is surprising, since in the national context of executive federalism a friction between the modes of deciding by party-competition-based majority rule and consensus rule, between parliamentary and federal logic has been diagnosed long ago.[256] However, in contrast to national arenas, the traditional parliamentary logic of majority decisions and ideological battle is much less dominant in the EU and in the EP, where rather a "federal" logic of consensual agreements and co-operation takes over.[257] The reason for this may lie in the fact that the EP offers a heterogeneous party system and that it is itself not too strongly involved in the logic of a parliamentary system and its binary party competition.

The concept of consensual democracy, though, is less approachable for legal analysis than that of parliamentary democracy. Therefore, consensus democracy has not (yet) found its way into constitutional law concepts of democracy in a way that parliamentary democracy has. Nevertheless, a European concept of legitimacy will have to integrate both, if it wants to grasp the specific character of European democracy.

[254] Eg proportional accommodation of parties in organs, decision-making rules and veto powers, balancing of competences between institutions; for literature above n 81, also E Eriksen and JE Fossum (eds), *Democracy in the EU* (2000).

[255] As to the relation of several strands of legitimacy in the EU above now C Lord and P Magnette, 'E Pluribus Unum? Creative Disagreement about Legitimacy in the EU', (2004) 42 *JCMS* 183.

[256] Lehmbruch, above n 44; for a transfer of this analysis to the EU level Benz, above n 234, 84 *et seq*.

[257] Benz, above n 234, 103 *et seq*; see section IV. 2. c.

3. Conclusion and Proposal: a Semi-parliamentary Democracy

Looking back, it becomes obvious, why legitimacy poses such a sincere problem to the institutional system of the EU. Especially the questions of effective representation through parliamentary actors and of transparent lines of accountability are unresolved. At the same time, it is evident, that the institutional system of European executive federalism has clear implications for the concept of legitimacy. Alternatively, to put it less neutrally, the system of executive federalism and its institutional implications are part of the problem. As we just saw, the mediated role of national parliaments and thus their exclusion from effective control is part of this federal set up. Also, non-transparent responsibilities because of consensual agreements are typical for the federal system and render accountability a problem. But at the same time, this system is also part of the solution. The tendency towards consensus ensures a great deal of legitimacy. Also, the role of the EP is strong, because of the specific institutional division between itself and the executive branch.

Hence, in whatever way one sees it, the institutional system and its composed form of legitimacy represents a very distinct model. To highlight this form, I propose to give it a special label, and call it a semi-parliamentary democracy, for the following reasons:

The relation between the executive and the legislative branch, based on the existence or non-existence of appointment power, is normally used to label political systems.[258] Applying this yardstick to the EU, we see neither a directly elected presidential nor a parliamentary elected executive. Thus, the EU seems to be an undefined tertium. Looking closer, though, we find its characteristic: the negative appointment power of the EP. It is not enough to call it a parliamentary system. But the negative power, a sort of veto power in the appointment process and an emergency break in the running term, gives the parliament a decisive say—and the system a characteristic feature.

Even more with respect to the Council as part of the executive branch, the EU is "only" semi-parliamentary, because the Council as such and as a whole cannot be dismissed by the Parliament.[259]

The EU is semi-parliamentary also with respect to the influence of executive actors, in form of the Council, on the law-making function. Traditionally, a parliamentary system would be one, in which parliament is the supreme authority in making the laws. This is hardly the case here, where the EP in the best case is the semi-legislator.

[258] Sartori, above n 49, 84, 101, 131; Lijphart, above n 81, 116.
[259] It is this aspect on which Paul Magnette rests his qualification of the EU as semi-parliamentary democracy, Magnette, above n 91, 302.

All the above arguments speak for the semi, or even for less. However, there is a "parliamentary" aspect to it, and that is position and powers of the EP. The whole institutional and governmental system of the EU would not be precisely described, if one would ignore the EP's influence on the creation of the executive branch, its control of the executive branch, and most of all its participation in the process of law making. Quite to the contrary, the whole system gets a very specific twist through the participation of the EP. The label of a semi-parliamentary democracy might help to describe it.

VI. SUMMARY AND PROSPECTS: THE CONSTITUTIONAL TREATY AND ITS IMPLICATIONS

The institutional system of the EU is shaped by the structure of executive federalism. A system of interwoven competences and the Council of Ministers as its institutional counterpart create an institutional dynamic, that works its way into the shape of the institutions, their inter-institutional dynamic, and at the same time poses recurrent because inherent problems.

From this point, overlooking the current state of this institutional system, we can now take a general look at the Constitutional Treaty, as it may indicate into which direction this system might develop.[260] Is the Constitutional Treaty to be seen as a "point zero" for the institutional development? Or will it rather proscribe a continuation along the existing path? In which direction will the system develop?

Considering the underlying thesis of this article, it may not surprise to hear that the Constitutional Treaty proposes mainly a continuation along the existing institutional patterns. It is not a radical break, but leaves the basic structure and institutional dynamic of executive federalism untouched. However, the verdict on the Constitutional Treaty is more complex than this. Even a mere continuation along the existing patterns has a truly puzzling effect. It could well be that the Constitutional Treaty means polishing the advantages and prolonging the suffering at the same time. How come? The key to this puzzle lies in the dilemmatic nature of executive federalism. Its structure entails an *aporia*, which we have encountered time and again in the past pages. This *aporia* is rooted in the interwoven structure of competences, creating an institutional dynamic of co-operation

[260] See for overview articles on the Constitutional Treaty, eg Kokott and Rühl, above n 100; Peters, above n 79; Wessels, above n 63; also K Lenaerts and D Gerard, 'The structure of the Union according to the Constitution for Europe', (2004) 29 *EL Rev* 289; S Sieberson, 'The Proposed European Union Constitution', (2004) 10 *Columbia Journal of European Law* 173; PM Huber, 'Das institutionelle Gleichgewicht zwischen Rat und Europäischem Parlament in der künftigen Verfassung für Europa' (2003) *Europarecht* 574.

and consensus. This dynamic has a double-effect: it infuses legitimacy by inclusion and at the same time drains legitimacy by blurring responsibilities. These effects can be traced also in the institutional structure according to the Constitutional Treaty:

First, the system of interwoven competences between Union and Member States remains untouched. Hence, the starting point for the institutional dynamic of executive federalism and its logic of co-operation will not be disrupted.

In addition, the Council of Ministers in its organisation and competences rests mainly unchanged. The envisioned reforms might rationalise and streamline its working, but already in the question of qualified voting rules the changes seem much less decisive from the perspective of executive federalism than in the political arena. Even qualified majority votes require a high level of agreement and coalition-building. The consensual mode of decision-taking is therefore unlikely to fade.

The EP has been strengthened in its role as legislature, but not in its role in appointing the Commission. These changes fit well into the EP's character as a working parliament: it holds and extends considerable powers as legislature and centre of democratic control, becoming more powerful than most of its national counterparts. However, this does not result in a development towards parliamentarisation. Instead, the EP remains clearly separated from the executive branch, in its personal composition as well as in its political affiliation.

The changes with regard to the Commission, especially strengthening its procedural rights and administrative competences, underline its specific and sensitive role within the structure of executive federalism: its organisation as a consensual government is of central importance for its role as agenda setter and mediator in the context of federal heterogeneity and separated, politically non-coherent institutions. However, just as important are the roads not taken: the proposal to autonomously elect the Commission President by the EP has not found sufficient support, preventing a development away from the consensual and towards a majoritarian government.

The perhaps most striking changes occur with respect to the European Council, especially in the creation of a permanent President. They demonstrate and clarify the central position of this institution. Together with the creation of the new post of a Foreign Minister, they also imply a structural change in the institutional setting. Here lie the most fundamental uncertainties as to the functioning of this setting as a whole. The standing of the European Council President is mainly open. On one side, its visibility will be particularly high, hence creating an influential stage. However, on the other side its administrative and political positions seem rather weak. Whom can he actually mobilise? Which resources can he really rely on? Besides, its democratic accountability is more than doubtful. And finally, the relation between European Council President, Foreign Minister and

Commission President is unclear. A lot will depend here on personalities—and on the first years. But in any case it is likely that the gain in transparency by visibility of the European Council President will be eaten up by the rivalry between the three executive heads of the Union and the national heads of state and governments.

The indisputable achievement of the Constitutional Treaty, that is the creation of a new level of unity and transparency in the legal structure of this European Union, therefore does not spill over into its institutional system. Instead, strength and characteristic of this system will continue to lie in its co-operative and inclusive aspects. In any event, the structure of executive federalism, the root of these aspects, will most likely continue to accompany and shape the Union's institutional system.

7

The European Constitution and the Courts

FRANZ C MAYER*

INTRODUCTION

'IN EUROPE, THE judge has never been merely *la bouche qui prononce les paroles de la loi*',[1] exclaimed the German Constitutional Tribunal (the *Bundesverfassungsgericht* (*BVerfG*)) in 1987. This statement applies to European constitutional law as well, regardless of the distinct legal traditions of its Member States. The interplay of the respective courts is not only the subject of the study of European constitutional law doctrine, but the courts themselves are also active participants in the shaping of this same European constitutional law.

This analysis of the relationship between the two levels of courts therefore has to begin with an assessment of their jurisprudence (I.), followed by a theoretical breakdown of the case law (II.). I will conclude with observations on the prospects for the future of the relationship between European and national courts (III.).

* Dr jur, LLM (Yale). Walter Hallstein-Institut, Humboldt-Universität zu Berlin. Contact: fmayer@aya.yale.edu. I wish to thank Randi Goring (New York), Mark Beamish (London) and Wolfgang Mayer for their invaluable help in improving the English language version of this paper. For an earlier version of this text in German see: FC Mayer, 'Europäische Verfassungsgerichtsbarkeit', in A von Bogdandy (ed), *Europäisches Verfassungsrecht* (2003) 229.

[1] *Entscheidungen des Bundesverfassungsgerichts* 75, 223 at 243 (*Kloppenburg*), referring to the famous sentence by *Montesquieu* (English translation in 3 *CMLR* (1988) 1; and A Oppenheimer (ed), *The Relationship between European Community Law and National Law: The Cases* (1994) 496). See also I Pernice, 'Die Dritte Gewalt im europäischen Verfassungsverbund', (1996) *Europarecht* 27 at 35.

I. TAKING STOCK: THE ECJ AND THE HIGHEST NATIONAL COURTS—CONFLICT OR CO-OPERATION?

The highest court at the European level is the ECJ in Luxembourg.[2] The situation is less clear at the national level. Therefore, the first step is to identify the national adjudicating bodies that function as the ECJ's interlocutors.

The relevant adjudicating entities in the present context are constitutional courts and supreme courts.[3] Special constitutional courts exist, alongside specialised high courts in Austria (*Verfassungsgerichtshof*), Germany (*BVerfG*), Italy (*Corte Costituzionale*), Portugal (*Tribunal Constitucional*), Spain (*Tribunal Constitucional*), and, since 1996, also in Luxembourg (*Cour Constitutionnelle*). Ireland (Supreme Court) and Denmark (*Højesteret*) have supreme courts that are also constitutional courts. In Great Britain, it is the second chamber of Parliament, the House of Lords, that exercises the functions of a constitutional and a supreme court.

In the Netherlands, we can find a number of specialised courts of equal rank, *inter alia* the *Raad van State* and the *Hoge Raad*. The situation is similar in Sweden, where the highest (specialised) courts are the Supreme Court (*Högsta domstolen*) and the Supreme Administrative Court (*Regeringsrätten*), as well as in Finland (*Korkein oikeus*, Supreme Court, and *Korkein hallinto-oikeus*, Supreme Administrative Court). Swedish judges of the two supreme courts also form a Council (*Lagrådet*) to exercise a non-binding review of draft legislation, whereas Finland has a Constitutional Committee of Parliament (*Perustuslakivaliokunta*), to control its draft legislation.

In France, there is no formal constitutional court aside from the highest courts for administrative law (*Conseil d'Etat*[4]) and for civil and criminal

[2] The Court of First Instance is mentioned together with the ECJ in Art 220 EC as of the Treaty of Nice, but the ECJ's position as the highest court of the European Union is confirmed by Art 225 EC in the Treaty of Nice version. Art 29 CT-IGC (Art I-28(1) CT-Conv) states: "The Court of Justice of the European Union shall include the Court of Justice, the General Court [CT-Conv: "High Court"] and specialised courts. It shall ensure that in the interpretation and application of the Constitution the law is observed [CT-Conv: "shall ensure respect for the law in the interpretation and application of the Constitution"]".

[3] See for the supreme and constitutional courts in the respective Member States C Starck and A Weber (eds), *Verfassungsgerichtsbarkeit in Westeuropa I* (1986); European Parliament (ed), *Constitutional Courts in the Member States of the European Union* (1995); AM Slaughter, A Stone Sweet and JHH Weiler (eds), *The European Courts and National Courts* (1998); FC Mayer, *Kompetenzüberschreitung und Letztentscheidung* (2000) 71 *et seq*; C Tomuschat, 'Das Bundesverfassungsgericht im Kreise anderer nationaler Verfassungsgerichte', in P Badura and H Dreier (eds), *Festschrift 50 Jahre Bundesverfassungsgericht* (2001) 245.

[4] Institutions modelled on the structure of the French Council of State (*Conseil d'Etat*) in Belgium, Netherlands, Greece, and until 1996 also in Luxembourg typically have specialised adjudication-sections which exercise the functions of a supreme administrative court, while other sections have advisory functions. The specific names of the adjudication-section, eg, in France *Section du Contentieux*, in the Netherlands (since 1994) *Afdeling Bestuursrechtspraak*, are omitted here.

law (*Cour de cassation*). The *Conseil constitutionnel*, originally limited to the review of draft legislation, increasingly exercises the role of a constitutional court.

Finally, Belgium has specialised supreme courts (*Conseil d'Etat* and *Cour de cassation*), and since 1983 a constitutional court that specialises in, but is also limited to, controlling the exercise of competences, the *Cour d'arbitrage*.[5] In Greece, there are several supreme specialised courts, the *Symvoulio Epikrateias*[6] (Council of State), the *Elegktiko Synedrio*[7] (Court of auditors) and the *Areios Pagos*[8] (Supreme Court). Beyond that, there is a Special Supreme Court, the *Anotato Eidiko Dikastirio*,[9] which is composed of judges from the highest specialised courts.

To solve conflicts and contradictions between these courts, similar institutions can typically be found in other systems with specialised high courts of equal rank. In France, there is a *Tribunal des Conflits* between *Cour de cassation* and *Conseil d'Etat*, and in Germany, there is a *Gemeinsamer Senat der obersten Bundesgerichte* (Joint Chamber of the Highest Federal Courts).

Most of the states who entered the EU in 2004 have a constitutional Court: Hungary (*Alkotmánybíróság*), Latvia (*Satversmes tiesa*), Lithuania (*Konstitucinio Teismo*), Czech Republic (*Ústavní soud*), Slovakia (*Ústavny súd*), Slovenia (*Ustavno sodisce*) and Malta (*Qorti Kostituzzjonali*); or a constitutional Tribunal (Poland *Trybunal Konstytucyjny*). Supreme Courts exist in Estonia (*Riigikohus*) and Cyprus (*Anotato Dikastirio tis Dimokratias*[10]).

This summary of the highest courts of the Member States leaves us with a rather heterogeneous picture.[11] One way to improve the understanding of the relationship between the ECJ and the respective supreme national courts is to examine the procedural link between the court-levels as foreseen by the treaties: the preliminary reference procedure under Article 234 EC

[5] The jurisdiction of the Cour d'arbitrage has been modified in 2003, see Loi spéciale du 9 mars 2003 modifiant la loi spéciale du 6 janvier 1989 sur la Cour d'arbitrage, *Moniteur belge* 11 April 2003.

[6] Συμβούλιο της Επικρατείας.

[7] Ελεγκτικό Συνέδριο.

[8] Άρειος Πάγος.

[9] Ανωτάτο Ειδικό Δικαστήριο.

[10] Ανωτάτο Δικαστήριο της Δημοκρατίας.

[11] Of course, this heterogeneity extends to the role of the judge in the different legal cultures, see in that context P Pernthaler, 'Die Herrschaft der Richter im Recht ohne Staat', (2000) *Juristische Blätter* 691. Contrasts seem to prevail: traditional and venerable institutions (such as the House of Lords in Great Britain or the *Conseil d'Etat* in France) may be found alongside newly created institutions (the *Cour d'arbitrage* in Belgium or the *Cour Constitutionelle* in Luxembourg). Courts with comprehensive powers (the *BVerfG* in Germany, the *VfGH* in Austria) operate side by side with less powerful tribunals. Sometimes, there are no specific constitutional courts at all (Denmark, Ireland); sometimes, it is the mere idea of constitutional adjudication or judicial review that is not compatible with the constitutional traditions of a Member State (eg in France, Finland, and the Netherlands).

and Article 35 EU (1.). Apart from this, there are areas of substantive constitutional law that have shaped the relationship between the courts. These include the issue of fundamental rights protection as well as the question of who controls the limits of the EU's[12] competences (2.).

1. Adopting a Procedural Perspective: The Duty to Make Preliminary References under Article 234(3) EC

European law imposes a duty on national courts to make preliminary references, that is to request certification, to the ECJ in two situations. Any court or tribunal of a Member State that has doubts about the validity of European law has to make a reference, as the ECJ claims a monopoly as regards deciding upon the validity of European law.[13] Then, there is the duty to make references to the ECJ under Article 234(3) EC, which requires that "a court or tribunal of a Member State against whose decisions there is no judicial remedy under national law" shall also bring questions of mere interpretation of European law before the ECJ.[14] Thus, there are concrete obligations for supreme national courts flowing from primary law as interpreted by the ECJ (a). The national courts' obedience to these duties, however, will be scrutinised on an empirical basis (b).

a) Supreme National Courts and the Duty to Make References from the Perspective of European Law

Following attempts of national courts, in particular[15] the attempt of the French *Conseil d'Etat*,[16] to establish a category of clear and obvious interpretation' (*acte clair*[17]) in interpreting EC law, the ECJ decided the matter by means of its own EC law doctrine of *acte clair* which establishes an

[12] I will use European Union and EC/EU as umbrella terms for European integration. With the Treaty on a Constitution for Europe, the dichotomy between Union and Community will disappear (with the exception of the EAC).

[13] Case 314/85, *Foto-Frost* [1987] ECR 4199.

[14] See in that context Case C-99/00, *Lyckeskog* [2002] ECR I-4839, paras 10 *et seq*. See also Art 35 EU and Art III-274 CT-Conv (Art 369 CT-IGC).

[15] See also the German *Bundesfinanzhof* in BFH, *Europarecht* (1985) 191 (*Kloppenburg*). The ECHR took sides with the ECJ in these cases, see *Dangeville v France* (36677/97) ECHR 2002-III.

[16] CE 9 January 1970, *Sieur Cohn-Bendit*, Rec 15; CE Ass 22 December 1978, *Ministre de l'Intérieur c Sieur Cohn-Bendit*, Rec 524, Concl Genevois, *Revue Trimestrielle de Droit Européen* (1979) 157; *Europarecht* (1979) 292 (German translation); 3 *CMLR* (1980), 543 (English translation); see also Oppenheimer, above n 1, 317.

[17] For the notion see E Laferrière, *Traité de la juridiction administrative et des recours contentieux, vol 1* (1887) 449 *et seq*; B Pacteau, Note, *Recueil Dalloz-Sirey* (1979) 164. For more recent cases related to this concept see, in France, Cour de Cassation, chambre sociale, 16 January 2003, *Madame X v CMSA*, or in Spain, Tribunal Supremo, 7 March 2002, Sentencia del Tribunal Supremo, Sala de lo Contencioso-Administrativo, sección 2.ª, recurso de casación nº 9156/1996; Tribunal Supremo, 15 July 2002, Sala de lo Contencioso-Administrativo, sección 2.ª, recurso de casación nº 4517/1997.

extremely strict standard.[18] From the perspective of European law, a national court decision that violates this standard is a breach of the treaty in the sense of Articles 226 and 227 EC.[19] A court or tribunal of last instance that disregards its duties to make a preliminary reference violates Article 234(3) EC. The principle of the independence of the judiciary[20] notwithstanding, acts of courts or tribunals are attributed to the respective Member State.[21]

To date, there have been no Treaty infringement proceedings against Member States resulting from decisions of the national courts.[22] To the extent that the Commission has entered into the preliminary procedure foreseen in Article 226 EC,[23] it has confined itself to ensuring that its

[18] According to the *CILFIT* decision, the only cases in which it is safe to assume that there is no duty to refer a question to the ECJ is either when the question is not relevant for the national court's decision or when the interpretation of EC law is obvious. This is the case only when the correct application of Community law is so obvious as to leave no room for any reasonable doubt. Under the *CILFIT* criteria, the national court or tribunal has to be convinced that the matter is equally obvious to the courts of the other Member States and to the ECJ. The existence of such a possibility must be "assessed in the light of the specific characteristics of Community law, the particular difficulties to which its interpretation gives rise and the risk of divergences in judicial decisions within the Community.", Case 283/81, *CILFIT* [1982] ECR 3415, para 21. The ECJ will normally not make a statement on the relevance of the reference for the judgment of the national court, Case C-369/89, *Piageme* [1991] ECR I-2971. It does not have jurisdiction, though, to reply to questions which are submitted to it within the framework of procedural devices arranged by the parties in order to induce the Court to give its views on certain problems of community law which do not correspond to an objective requirement inherent in the resolution of a dispute: Case 244/80, *Foglia* [1981] ECR 3045, para 18. For recent objections to the strict *CILFIT* standard from a Member State perspective (Denmark) see Case C-99/00, *Lyckeskog* [2002] ECR I-4839 (see also Opinion of AG Tizzano, *ibid*, paras 51 *et seq*).

[19] See, eg, C Hillgruber, 'Grenzen der Rechtsfortbildung durch den EuGH', in T von Danwitz *et al* (eds), *Auf dem Wege zu einer europäischen Staatlichkeit* (1993) 45 at n 40.

[20] See for example Art 97(1) of the German Constitution; Art 6(1) ECHR; Art 47(2) Charter of Fundamental Rights.

[21] In that respect, European law adopts a public international law approach towards the Member States. See PICJ, *Polish Nationals in Danzig*, 1932, Series A/B, No 44, 24.

[22] Notorious Member State court decisions, such as the *Cohn-Bendit* decision of the French *Conseil d'Etat* (see n 16) or the *Maastricht* decision of the German *BVerfG* (*Entscheidungen des Bundesverfassungsgerichts* 89, 155) have not led the Commission to commence formal infringement proceedings. To the extent that the constitutional law reserve of power assumed by the *BVerfG* is an obiter dictum and thus lacking immediate legal effect (§ 31(1) *Bundesverfassungsgerichtsgesetz*), there may be no infringement of the treaties. A different view is adopted by H-P Folz, *Demokratie und Integration* (1999) 16 (the *Maastricht* decision itself is already an infringement of EC law). For English translations of the decision see Oppenheimer, above n 1, 526; 22 *ILM* (1994) 388; I Winkelmann, *Das Maastricht-Urteil des Bundesverfassungsgerichts vom 12 Oktober 1993* (1994) 751, this book also includes French and Spanish translations. The *BVerfG*'s case law is online at <http://www.bverfg.de> (16 July 2004) or in the DFR database at <http://www.uni-wuerzburg.de/glaw/> (16 July 2004).

[23] See G Meier, 'Zur Einwirkung des Gemeinschaftsrechts auf nationales Verfahrensrecht im Falle höchstrichterlicher Vertragsverletzungen', (1991) *Europäische Zeitschrift für Wirtschaftsrecht* 11; J Sack, 'Verstoßverfahren und höchstrichterliche Vertragsverletzungen', (1991) *Europäische Zeitschrift für Wirtschaftsrecht* 246; Editorial, 'Use of the preliminary procedure', (1991) 28 *CML Rev* 241 at 243.

view be made clear to the non-complying courts, thus acknowledging the principle of judicial independence, and only admonishing the respective national government to take legislative action in cases of continued or repeated violations.[24]

Answering a written question from a member of the European Parliament, the Commission stated in 1983 that infringement proceedings do not constitute an appropriate basis for co-operation between the ECJ and the national courts. According to the Commission, the procedure was not designed as a blanket means to review national court decisions, but rather for use only in cases of systematic and intentional disregard of Article 177 EEC Treaty (now Article 234 EC).[25]

With the decision in the *Köbler*-case,[26] the ECJ seems to have turned to the strategy of indirect enforcement which worked so well in the context of implementing directives.[27] In *Köbler*, the Court extended the principle of Member State liability for damage caused to individuals as a result of breaches of Community law for which the state was responsible to the national court's disobedience of European law. But the ECJ also acknowledged that the specific nature of the judicial function had to be taken into account, thus the breach could not be considered sufficiently serious if the infringement was not manifest.[28] Other recent decisions also indicate that the ECJ and the Commission remain very careful not to confront national courts head on.[29]

[24] Case *Hendrix* ("*Pingo-Hähnchen*"), Preliminary procedure under Art 169 EC Treaty [now Art 226 EC], A/90/0406, Reasoned opinion of the Commission SG (90)/D/25672 of 3 August 1990, Part V (dealing with a non-reference by the *Bundesgerichtshof (BGH)*, the German Supreme Court), see Meier, above n 23, 11.

[25] OJ C 268, 6.10.1983, 25. Note that the Commission establishes special criteria for infringements of EC law by the courts that are not foreseen in the treaties.

[26] Case C-224/01, *Köbler* [2003] ECR I-10239. The *Köbler*-case was referred to by the highest Spanish Civil court when holding the justices of the Constitutional tribunal responsible for a decision, Tribunal Supremo, Sala de lo Civil, 23 January 2004, N° 51/2004; the Constitutional tribunal overruled that decision, Tribunal Constitucional, Acuerdo, 3 February 2004. Critical of *Köbler*: PJ Wattel, '*Köbler*, *CILFIT* and *Welthgrove*: We can't go on meeting like this', (2004) 41 *CML Rev* 177.

[27] Cases C-6/90 and C-9/90, *Francovich* [1991] ECR I-5357.

[28] The situation for the domestic legal system in such a case is that the ECJ declares that there has been an infringement of European law, thus an illegal act, albeit not sufficiently manifest for state liability. Depending on the internal legal order, this may be sufficient to re-open the domestic proceedings.

[29] In Case C-129/00, *Commission v Italy* [2003] ECR I-14637, the responsibility of the Italian courts was camouflaged to some respect, as the primary target was Italian legislation—as applied by the courts. See also Case C-453/00, *Kühne and Heitz* [2004] ECR I-837 in that context. The Commission did start a preliminary procedure against Sweden though (No. 2003/2161), because of the highest courts' non-reference record.

b) The Preliminary Reference Practice of Supreme National Courts

The German *BVerfG* has to date[30] not made any reference to the ECJ.[31] It has stated in the *Solange I* decision of 1974 and in the *Vielleicht* decision of 1979 that it is in principal bound to Article 234 EC.[32] However, the *BVerfG* has not reviewed the issue of its own obligations under Article 234 EC following the ECJ's *CILFIT* decision [33] of 1982. It has limited itself to specifying the conditions under which the highest specialised German courts are obliged to make references.[34]

The German court is not alone, however. Other supreme courts have also avoided making references to the ECJ. The Italian *Corte Costituzionale* in its *Giampaoli* decision of 1991[35] admitted the possibility, albeit not the obligation, of making references under Article 234 EC, only to reverse itself at a later date: pointing to the fact that it is not a court in the sense of Article 234 EC and thus unable to enter into direct contact with the ECJ by

[30] The *BVerfG*'s reluctance to use Art 234 EC or even to clarify its own position on Art 234 EC was particularly noteworthy in the *Maastricht* decision of 1993, in which the *BVerfG* reserved for itself the right to review the exercise of competences of European institutions in light of the German Constitution. During the proceedings, the *BVerfG* utilised a rather original solution in solving questions of EC law interpretation, by hearing the Director General of the Commission Legal Service as a witness, instead of making a reference to the ECJ; see M Zuleeg, 'The European Constitution under Constitutional Constraints: The German Scenario', (1997) 22 *EL Rev* 19. Furthermore, in the *NPD*-proceedings of 2001, the *BVerfG* had the unique opportunity to make a principal statement on its obligations under Art 234 EC in a case where it was unquestionably the court of first and last instance (the proceedings to declare a political party unconstitutional under Art 21 of the German Constitution). The *BVerfG* also did not use this chance, Decision of 22 November 2001, *Europarecht* (2002) 236 (*NPD*); on that decision Mayer, below n 34. See also BVerfG, 1 BvR 1778/01, 16 March 2004, (*Fighting Dogs*), para 55.

[31] The highest German courts started to make references relatively early: the *Bundessozialgericht* in 1967 (Case 14/67, *Welchner* [1967] ECR 331); the *Bundesfinanzhof* also in 1967 (Case 17/67, *Neumann* [1967] ECR 441); the *Bundesarbeitsgericht* in 1969 (Case 15/69, *Südmilch* [1969] ECR 363 (German edn, no English trans); the *Bundesverwaltungsgericht* in 1970 (Case 36/70, *Getreide-Import* [1970] ECR 1107); the *Bundesgerichtshof* in 1974 (Case 32/74, *Haaga* [1974] ECR 1201). These courts have continued to use the preliminary reference procedure on a regular basis. For an example of *Länder* (State/Regional) constitutional courts see the reference from *Hessischer Staatsgerichtshof*, *Europäische Grundrechte-Zeitschrift* (1997) 213.

[32] *Entscheidungen des Bundesverfassungsgerichts* 37, 271 at 282 (*Solange I*) (English trans in Federal Constitutional Court (ed), *Decisions of the Bundesverfassungsgericht. Volume 1/Part II* (1992); and in Oppenheimer, above n 1, 440; 2 *CMLR* (1974) 540); *Entscheidungen des Bundesverfassungsgerichts* 52, 187 at 202 (*Vielleicht*).

[33] Above n 18.

[34] See for example BVerfG, 9 January 2001, *Europäische Zeitschrift für Wirtschaftsrecht* (2001) 255 (*Non-reference by the BVerwG*) (Case C-25/02, *Rinke* [2003] ECR I-8349), see also *Entscheidungen des Bundesverwaltungsgerichts* 108, 289. The *BVerfG* asks whether non-reference by a specialised court violates a fundamental right "to have access to the lawful judge" (Art 101(1) of the German Constitution). In addition to the *CILFIT*-criteria, the German constitutional law question hangs on whether the court acted arbitrarily ("willkürlich") in not making a reference. For more detail see FC Mayer, 'Das Bundesverfassungsgericht und die Verpflichtung zur Vorlage an den Europäischen Gerichtshof', (2002) *Europarecht* 239; for how one may construe an individual right to have a court make a reference see C Grabenwarter, 'Die Europäische Union und die Gerichtsbarkeit öffentlichen Rechts', in (2000) *14, I/2 Österreichischer Juristentag Wien* 15 (65).

[35] Decision No 168/91 (*Giampaoli*), *Foro italiano* I (1992) 660 paras *5 et seq*.

means of a preliminary reference, the *Corte Costituzionale* declared in the *Messagero Servizi*[36] decision of 1995 that it did not consider itself bound by Article 234 EC. Instead, the *Corte Costituzionale* ordered the court of the previous instance to make a reference to the ECJ.

The Spanish *Tribunal Constitucional* (TC) has also not made any references yet, and is even reluctant to involve itself in the cases of non-reference of the other Spanish courts.[37] According to the TC, the application of European law is not an issue of constitutional law, and thus not part of the TC's jurisdiction. Legal protection against Spanish acts that violate European law, the TC holds, is afforded by the regular Spanish courts and the ECJ.[38] The Portuguese *Tribunal Constitucional* considers itself bound under Article 234(3) EC,[39] but has yet to make a reference.

The French *Conseil d'Etat* has made references to the ECJ both before and after the *Cohn-Bendit*-case, dating back to 1970.[40] Still, the *Conseil d'Etat* issued decisions not compatible with ECJ jurisprudence and in disregard of Article 234(3) EC, even after the ECJ's *CILFIT*-decision.[41] The *Cour de cassation* made its first reference in 1967,[42] while the *Conseil constitutionnel* has not yet done so.[43]

The highest Belgian courts, the *Conseil d'Etat*[44] and the *Cour de cassation*[45] began to make references early, in 1967 and in 1968. The *Cour d'arbitrage*, created in 1983, first made a reference in 1997.[46] The highest Dutch courts started making references in the early seventies (the *Raad van State* in 1973,[47] the *Hoge Raad* in 1974[48]) and have continued doing so on a regular basis. The

[36] Decision No 536/95 (*Messagero Servizi*), *Gazzetta Ufficiale n 1 I*, 3 January 1996; see also Decision No 319/96 (*Spa Zerfin*), *Gazzetta Ufficiale n 34 I*, 21 August 1996.

[37] TC Decision 111/1993, 25 March 1993, *Boletín Oficial del Estado* 27 April 1993; TC Decision 180/1993, 31 May 1993, *Boletín Oficial del Estado* 5 July 1993—*FOGASA*; TC Decision 372/1993, 13 December 1993, *Boletín Oficial del Estado* 19 January 1994 (*Lao*).

[38] TC Decision 28/1991, 14 February 1991, *Boletín Oficial del Estado* 15 March 1991 (*EP-elections*) (English trans in Oppenheimer, above n 1, 702); TC Decision 64/1991, 22 March 1991, *Boletín Oficial del Estado* 24 April 1991 (*ASEPESCO*) (English trans in Oppenheimer, above n 1, 705).

[39] TC Decision 163/90, 23 May 1990, *Moreira da Costa e Mulher*, *Diàrio da República*, 2 No 240, 18 October 1990.

[40] The first reference 1970: Case 34/70, *Syndicat national du commerce extérieur des céréales* [1970] ECR 1233.

[41] For the (still) diverging approach of the *Conseil d'Etat* on Art 249(3) EC and the timely limitations of the effect of ECJ decisions, see *Commissaire du gouvernement* Savoie in his Conclusions in the *Tête*-case (CE Ass 6 February 1998, *Tête*, Rec 30, Concl 32) and P Cassia, 'Le juge administratif français et la validité des actes communautaires', (1999) *Revue Trimestrielle de Droit Européen* 409.

[42] Case 22/67, *Goffart* [1967] ECR 321.

[43] In CC 10 June 2004, *Loi pour la confiance dans l'économie numérique*, para 7, the *Conseil constitutionnel* emphasised the importance of the preliminary reference by the national courts, though.

[44] Since 1967, Case 6/67, *Guerra* [1967] ECR 219.

[45] Since 1968, Case 5/68, *Sayag* [1968] ECR 395.

[46] Case C-93/97, *Fédération belge des chambres syndicales de médecins* [1998] ECR I-4837.

[47] Case 36/73, *Nederlandse Spoorwegen* [1973] ECR 1299.

[48] Case 15/74, *Centrafarm* [1974] ECR 1147.

Luxembourg *Cour de Cassation* made its first reference in 1967,[49] and the Luxembourg *Conseil d'Etat* joined in only in 1981.[50] The *Cour Constitutionnelle* has not made any references yet.

The British *House of Lords* made a first reference in 1979. Further references have followed on a regular basis.[51] The Danish *Højesteret* may be one of the more sceptical courts as far as European integration is concerned, but it has made numerous references to the ECJ, the first one in 1978.[52] The Irish *Supreme Court* began to make references in 1983[53] and has continued such practice regularly since then. The highest Greek courts are also on record with references. The *Symvoulio Epikrateias* (Council of State) has made references on a regular basis, starting early in 1983.[54] Occasional references have been made by the *Elegktiko Synedrio* (Court of Auditors) since 1993,[55] and since 1996, there are also references every now and then from the *Areios Pagos* (Supreme Court).[56] The Supreme Special Court (*Anotato Eidiko Dikastirio*) has not made any references yet.

The Swedish *Högsta domstolen* made a first reference almost immediately after Swedish accession in 1995.[57] The Swedish *Regeringsrätten* followed just two years later in 1997.[58] The *Lagrådet*, which takes non-binding control of draft legislation, has not made any references to date. The supreme Finish administrative court *Korkein hallinto-oikeus* has been making references on a regular basis since 1996.[59] The supreme court *Korkein oikeus* is on record with its first question stemming from 1999.[60] The Constitutional Committee of Parliament (*Perustuslakivaliokunta*) has not made any references so far, while the Austrian Constitutional Court, the *VfGH*, early on acknowledged the option to submit references under Article 234 EC,[61] and it has first made a reference to the ECJ in 1999.[62] There is no reference from the States who joined the EU in 2004 yet.[63]

[49] Case 2/67, *De Moor* [1967] ECR 197.

[50] Case 76/81, *Transporoute* [1982] ECR 417.

[51] Case 34/79, *Henn and Darby* [1979] ECR 3795. The House of Lords is on the record with around 30 references.

[52] Case 151/78, *Sukkerfabriken Nykøbing* [1979] ECR 1.

[53] Case 182/83, *Fearon* [1984] ECR 3677.

[54] Case 142/83, *Nevas* [1983] ECR 2969.

[55] Case C-443/93, *Vougioukas* [1995] ECR I-4033.

[56] Case C-348/96, *Calfa* [1999] ECR I-11. In the following case of 1998, Case C-235/98, *Pafitis*, the procedings were not continued (OJ C 63, 4.3.2000, 21).

[57] Case C-43/95, *Data Delecta* [1996] ECR I-4661.

[58] Case C-241/97, *Försäkringsaktiebolaget Skandia* [1999] ECR I-1879.

[59] Case C-412/96, *Kainuun Liikenne* [1998] ECR I-5141.

[60] Case C-172/99, *Liikenne* [2001] ECR I-745.

[61] ÖVfGH, 11 December 1995, *Österreichische Zeitschrift für Wirtschaftsrecht* (1996) 24 (*Bundesvergabeamt*). See also K Heller and F Sinnl-Piazza, 'Verfassungsrechtliche Aspekte der Anwendung des Gemeinschaftsrechts in den Mitgliedstaaten der EU', (1995) *Juristische Blätter* 636 and 700 at 711.

[62] Case C-143/99, *Adria-Wien Pipeline* [2001] ECR I-8365.

[63] See the Swedish example, above n 57, for a fast post-accession reference.

c) The National Supreme Courts' Reference Practices—A Mixed Bag?

This brief assessment of the national courts' reference practices reveals several contradictory points. On the one hand, the strict standard imposed by the ECJ's *CILFIT*-formula is cushioned by a Commission practice that does not sanction non-certification as an infringement under the treaty infringement proceedings. On the other hand, there are important courts and tribunals at the Member State level that do not make references to the ECJ. A similar approach to the *BVerfG*'s non-reference practice[64] exists in Italy and in Spain. Thus, nations that established particularly strong constitutional courts in the aftermath of dictatorial regimes follow a different path in their dealings with the European court. These three courts remain a minority, however, when contrasted with other courts in the EU.[65] A closer look at the courts that have not yet made references reveals several motivations, ranging from the way these courts see themselves, to constraints imposed by their respective national constitutions, to a simple lack of opportunities to make references. There is also the question whether the ECJ's alleged self-constraint to dealing with matters of European law—as opposed to directly commenting on national law—is not a fiction,[66] which would also explain national courts' scepticism.[67] From these motivations, the hypothesis of the courts' self-image, i.e. seeing themselves as guardians of their (respective) constitutions,[68] seems to have the greatest weight.

In any case, an analysis of the national courts' procedural points of contact with the ECJ suggests that there are open questions. The sole binary empirical question of reference or non-reference is too simple to explain

[64] Which is arguably not compatible with the German Constitution's fundamental right of "access to the lawful judge" (*Recht auf den gesetzlichen Richter*, Art 101(1) of the German Constitution) and with Art 23 of the German Constitution.

[65] References are made by both the ancient British House of Lords and the rather Euro-sceptical Danish *Højesteret*, as well as from the Austrian *VfGH*, a genuinely specialised constitutional court in a similar position as the Spanish, Italian and German constitutional courts.

[66] See more on this in K Alter, *Establishing the Supremacy of European Law* (2001) 10, referring to ECJ judge Mancini.

[67] See in that context the *Arsenal*-case in Great Britain, where the High Court even decided to ignore a preliminary ruling of the ECJ (Case C-206/01 *Arsenal Football Club* [2002] ECR I-10273), stating that the ECJ had no jurisdiction to make findings of fact or reverse the national court on its findings of fact, [2002] EWHC 2695 (Ch); 1 All ER (2003) 137. This decision was overruled by the Court of Appeal, Court of Appeal (Civil Division), 21 May 2003, *Arsenal Football Club v Matthew Reed* (2003) EWCA Civ 96. The German *BVerfG* considers non-references as violating the German Constitution (above n 34) only when it is clear that there is a question of interpretation, as opposed to applying European law to a concrete case, see BVerfG, Decision of 30 January 2002, 1 BvR 1542/00, *Neue Juristische Wochenschrift* (2002) 1486 (*biobronch*); see also *Entscheidungen des Bundesverfassungsgerichts* 82, 159 (*Absatzfonds*); BVerfG, Decision of 10 December 2003, 1 BvR 2480/03.

[68] See the divergent opinions of H Kelsen, 'Wer soll Hüter der Verfassung sein?', (1931) *Die Justiz* 5, in favour of a constitutional court as the guardian of the constitution, and C Schmitt, *Der Hüter der Verfassung* (1931) 12 *et seq*, in favour of the head of the executive (the *Reichspräsident*) as the guardian of the constitution. Schmitt's position is severely weakened by the pathetic role President Hindenburg played in the final days of the Weimar Republic in Germany.

what exactly the constitutional law patterns are that drive the relationship between the national courts and the ECJ. To answer this question, one has to turn to a more substantive analysis.

2. Adopting a Substantive Perspective on the Courts' Relationship

a) The Perspective of the ECJ

The ECJ claims the monopoly on invalidating (secondary[69]) European law.[70] In 1987, the ECJ held in the *Foto-Frost*-case [71] that national courts are entitled to consider the validity of community acts and to conclude that a community act is completely valid, as "by taking that action they are not calling into question the existence of the Community measure".[72] But the ECJ also made it very clear that national courts do not have the power to declare acts of community institutions invalid,[73] arguing for the unity of the Community legal order and for the need for legal certainty.[74]

The proceedings outlined derive their conclusiveness from Article 292 EC, according to which the Member States commit themselves to not solving disputes over the interpretation or implementation of the Treaty in any other way than is provided for in the Treaty.[75] Moreover, the obligation of national courts to respect the interpretation of European law as established

[69] On the issue of primary law as incompatible with the treaties, see J da Cruz Vilaca and N Picarra, 'Y a-t-il des limites matérielles à la révision des Traités instituants les Communautés européennes?' (1993) *Cahiers de Droit Européen* 3; U Everling, 'Zur Stellung der Mitgliedstaaten der Europäischen Union als "Herren der Verträge"', in U Beyerlin *et al* (eds), *Recht zwischen Umbruch und Bewahrung: Festschrift für R Bernhardt* (1995) 1169.

[70] The ECJ reviews European acts under Art 230 EC, as either incidental questions under Art 241 EC or in the context of a reference under Art 234 EC. See also Art 35 EU. Member State administrations can only make references to the ECJ if they fall under the ECJ's European law definition of a court (for Public Procurement Awards Supervisory Boards, see Case C-54/96, *Dorsch Consult* [1997] ECR I-4961); see also Case C-431/92, *Commission v Germany* [1995] ECR I-2189, on the duties of administrations to respect European law.

[71] Case 314/85, *Foto-Frost* [1987] ECR 4199, paras 11 *et seq*.

[72] *Ibid*, para 14.

[73] *Ibid*, para 15.

[74] The Court points to the "necessary coherence of the system of judicial protection established by the Treaty" that gives the ECJ "the exclusive jurisdiction to declare void an act of a Community institution". The ECJ emphasises that it is in the best position to decide on the validity of Community acts, as all Community institutions whose acts are challenged are entitled to participate in the ECJ proceedings and can therefore supply the information that the ECJ considers necessary for the purposes of the case before it. As far as interim measures are concerned, the ECJ has given national courts some leeway to make statements on the validity of European law, all the while insisting on its exclusive powers to determine the validity of these acts as well, Cases C-143/88 and C-92/89, *Süderdithmarschen* [1991] ECR I-415, paras 14 *et seq*; Case C-465/93, *Atlanta* [1995] ECR I-3761. Apparently, the ECJ is not even willing to give national courts the right to decide upon legally non-existent acts, see for this concept Cases 1/57 and 14/57, *Société des usines à tubes de la Sarre v High Authority* [1957/58] ECR 105.

[75] See Opinion 1/91, *EEA* [1991] ECR I-6079, paras 2 *et seq*.

by the ECJ under Articles 220 *et seq* EC could also be justified as an obligation arising under Article 10 EC (the Member States' obligations arising out of the Treaty).

In addition to arguments provided by the ECJ in its relevant decisions, another possible explanation for the ECJ's restrictive approach lies in the Court's image of itself as the "driving force" behind European integration. If this was really the court's own perception, conflicts of interest with national courts would be unavoidable. The cautious attitude of the ECJ may also be explained by a certain distrust the ECJ harbours against national courts, which—given a wide latitude in their decision-making—could well try to resist increasing integration through jurisprudence.

The real argument behind the ECJ's reluctance to give the national courts more control, however, probably lies in the principle of the primacy or supremacy[76] of European law in the case of a conflict of laws as it was developed[77] by the ECJ. The ECJ's core justifications for the primacy of European law are independence, uniformity and efficacy of Community law.[78] In this perspective, Community law is "an integral part of [...] the legal order applicable in the territory of each of the Member States", provisions of Community law "by their entry into force render automatically inapplicable any conflicting provision of current national law".[79] This concept of primacy in application, *Anwendungsvorrang* (as opposed to primacy in validity, *Geltungsvorrang*), also applies to the Member States' constitutional law provisions: "The validity of a Community measure or its effect within a Member State cannot be affected by allegations that it runs counter to either fundamental rights as formulated by the constitution of that state or the principles of a national constitutional structure."[80]

[76] The fact that European law prevails over national law in case of conflict may be conceptualised as "supremacy" or as "primacy". Unlike European law textbooks and doctrinal writings, the ECJ has used the term "supremacy" only once in a judgment so far (Case 14/68, *Walt Wilhelm* [1969] ECR 1, para 5). The term appears as a keyword in a 1972 decision (Case 93/71, *Leonesio* [1972] ECR 287) and occasionally in Advocate General Opinions (in Case C-112/00, *Schmidberger* [2003] ECR 5659, para 5, AG Jacobs played it safe: "by virtue of the primacy or supremacy of Community law, they prevail over any conflicting national law"). "Primacy" can be found much more frequently in ECJ decisions, albeit often enough the Court just refers to what was said by parties or the national court. For an example of the ECJ clearly using "precedence" see Case C-256/01, *Allonby* [2004] ECR I-873, para 77. The Constitutional Treaty uses "primacy" (Art I-10 CT-Conv; Art 6 CT-IGC). It is hard to say for a non-native speaker to what extent there is a difference between primacy and supremacy, whether this difference is related to British versus American English or whether the term supremacy implies more of a hierarchy or of the German concept of *Geltungsvorrang*.

[77] Case 6/64, *Costa* [1964] ECR 585. For the definition and the typology of the conflict of laws see S Kadelbach, *Allgemeines Verwaltungsrecht unter europäischem Einfluß* (1999) 23 *et seq*.

[78] Case 11/70, *Internationale Handelsgesellschaft* [1970] ECR 1125, para 3.

[79] Case 106/77, *Simmenthal* [1978] ECR 629, paras 3 and 21 *et seq*. See also Case C-213/89, *Factortame* [1990] ECR I-2433, paras 20 *et seq*.

[80] Case 11/70, above n 78, para 3; Case C-473/93, *Commission v Luxembourg* [1996] ECR I-3207, para 38. See also Case C-285/98, *Kreil* [2000] ECR I-69.

The critics of the Court's primacy concept are numerous.[81] Among other things, they have pointed out a structural parallel between supreme European law and the law of (military) occupation[82] (!) and have criticised the "rigorous simplicity" of the concept of primacy.[83] The absoluteness of the ECJ's vision of European law primacy over each and every norm of municipal law—including any provision of the municipal constitutions—has raised the question of whether the ECJ might have overstepped its competences by establishing such an absolute concept of primacy.[84] According to this view, the ECJ's role is to interpret European law; but the question of how the Member States' legal orders handle conflicts between the Member States' legal orders and European law, so the critics say, goes beyond a mere question of interpretation.[85]

Admittedly, the ECJ has remained oddly unclear in its statements on the exact source of primacy and of European law itself, even relative to the limited language the ECJ normally utilises in its decisions,[86] merely alluding to what kind of organisation the EC/EU is. The formula used by the Court, however, has evolved over the years, from a new "legal order of international law" (1963),[87] followed by the formula "own legal system" (1964),[88] and the concept of the Treaty as "the basic constitutional charter" (1986)[89] or "the constitutional charter of a Community based on the rule of law" (1991).[90] This constitutional dimension of the European legal order does emphasise the autonomy of European law, but it does not clearly state a separation between EU law and the legal order of the Member States.

[81] See, for example, H-H Rupp, 'Die Grundrechte und das Europäische Gemeinschaftsrecht', (1970) *Neue Juristische Wochenschrift* 953. See Alter, above n 66, 88 *et seq*, for an account of how this article may have triggered subsequent developments such as the ECJ decision in Case 11/70, above n 78, which openly claimed primacy of European law over national constitutions, and the *BVerfG's* fierce reaction to that in 1974, *Entscheidungen des Bundesverfassungsgerichts* 37, 271 (*Solange I*). Rupp actually remains unconvinced, see H-H Rupp, 'Anmerkungen zu einer Europäischen Verfassung', (2003) *Juristenzeitung* 18. See also the references in HP Ipsen, *Europäisches Gemeinschaftsrecht* (1972) 267 *et seq*; another example of critique may be found in T Schilling, 'Zu den Grenzen des Vorrangs des Gemeinschaftsrechts', (1994) *Der Staat* 555. Alter, above n 66, 19, explains why the Italian Constitutional Court could not refute the initial primacy claim in the *Costa*-case.

[82] See the references in Pernthaler, above n 11, 700.

[83] R Abraham, *L'application des normes internationales en droit interne* (1986) 155. See also A Schmitt Glaeser, *Grundgesetz und Europarecht als Elemente Europäischen Verfassungsrechts* (1996) 156 *et seq*, with further references.

[84] Abraham, above n 83, 154 *et seq*.

[85] *Ibid*.

[86] For a critique and an explanation of the ECJ's style see for example Pernthaler, above n 11, 694.

[87] Case 26/62, *Van Gend en Loos* [1963] ECR 1.

[88] Case 6/64, *Costa* [1964] ECR 585.

[89] Case 294/83, *Les Verts v Parliament* [1986] ECR 1339, para 23. The French language version is "Charte constitutionnelle de base", in German "Verfassungsurkunde der Gemeinschaft".

[90] Opinion 1/91, *EEA* [1991] ECR I-6079, para 1.

Rather, this interpretation holds out European law as the overarching legal order within a community of law, which at the same time is taken up and complemented by the Member States' respective legal orders.

The primacy-principle is explicitly laid down in the Constitutional Treaty.[91] A declaration annexed to the final act of the IGC states that this provision reflects existing Court of Justice case law.[92]

b) The Perspective of the Highest National Courts

aa) The German BVerfG In its decision of 5 July 1967,[93] its first to discuss Community law in detail, the *BVerfG* emphasised a central role for the "act of assent" to the founding treaties.[94] Later commentators likened this central role to that of a bridge[95] between EC law and national law, in that—in the German view—the act of assent functions as the decisive "order to give legal effect"[96] to European law. That very same year, the *BVerfG* expressed its view of the Community as distinct public authority in a distinct legal order.[97] This view is still held today. The *BVerfG* qualified the EEC Treaty as a "constitution, as it were, of this Community"[98] and Community law as a "distinct legal order, whose norms neither belong to public international law nor belong to the national law of the Member States".[99] The *BVerfG* hinted, though, at

[91] Art 6 CT-IGC: "The Constitution and law adopted by the institutions of the Union in exercising competences conferred on it shall have primacy over the law of the Member States."

[92] CIG 60/03 add. 1; CIG 81/04.

[93] *Entscheidungen des Bundesverfassungsgerichts* 22, 134 at 142.

[94] The *Zustimmungsgesetz*, a federally enacted law under Art 24, today Art 23 of the German Constitution. The Art 23 provision dealing specifically with European integration was introduced in December 1992, replacing the old Art 23 which had served as the legal basis for German reunification. Both Art 23 and Art 24 foresee an act of assent for the transfer of public powers. Art 23 establishes two sets of limits; on the one hand, it institutes limits concerning the European construct, which for example has to guarantee a standard of fundamental rights protection essentially equal to that guaranteed by the German Constitution. On the other hand, Art 23(1) points to the limits of how European integration can affect Germany, as the principles mentioned in Art 79(3) are inalienable.

[95] This *Brückentheorie* is based on the metaphor suggested by Paul Kirchhof, for example in 'Die Gewaltenbalance zwischen staatlichen und europäischen Organen', (1998) *Juristenzeitung* 965 at 966. See for Great Britain the European Communities Act as the bridge, N Bamforth, 'Courts in a Multi-Layered Constitution', in N Bamforth and P Leyland (eds), *Public Law in a Multi-Layered Constitution* (2003) 277 at 288.

[96] "Rechtsanwendungsbefehl".

[97] "Gemeinschaft als eigenständige Hoheitsgewalt in einer eigenständigen Rechtsordnung".

[98] "gewissermaßen die Verfassung dieser Gemeinschaft".

[99] "eigene Rechtsordnung, deren Normen weder Völkerrecht noch nationales Recht der Mitgliedstaaten sind", *Entscheidungen des Bundesverfassungsgerichts* 22, 293 at 296 (*EWG-Vererdnungen*) (English trans in Oppenheimer, above n 1, 410). The reference to the EEC Treaty's "distinct legal order" can already be found in *Entscheidungen des Bundesverfassungsgerichts* 29, 198 at 210, although it is accompanied by a reference to the "numerous intertwinements of Community and national law". On autonomy, see also *Entscheidungen des Bundesverfassungsgerichts* 31, 145 at 174 (*Lütticke*) (English trans in Oppenheimer, above n 1, 415). Indeed, the formula is reminiscent of Alfred Verdross' formula of an internal law of a community of States, based on public international law, 30 *Recueil des Cours* (1929-V) 311, as Pernthaler, above n 11, 692, indicates.

constitutional limitations on the transfer of public authority rights[100] to the EC in the context of the German Constitution's guarantee of fundamental rights. An answer to this question, however, was not forthcoming at this stage.[101] Not yet.

(1) Fundamental Rights: The Solange I and Solange II Decisions (1974/1986)

In the *Solange I* decision of 29 May 1974, the *BVerfG* stipulated constitutional limits on the primacy of European law and reserved a right of judicial review in order to safeguard the fundamental rights guaranteed by the German Constitution. The *BVerfG* asserted that in a case of conflict between EC law and the fundamental rights of the German Constitution, the German Constitution's fundamental rights would prevail. A five to three majority of the second senate of the Court [102] supported the main elements of the decision.[103] In regard to the principal limits of EC law primacy, inalienable essentials of the German Constitution and the "division of labour" between the *BVerfG* and the ECJ, the decision still stands today.[104]

After indicating a change of its *Solange I* jurisprudence in July 1979,[105] twice in 1981[106] and then again in February 1983,[107] the *Solange II* decision of 22 October 1986[108] brought the long-expected supplement to the *Solange I* decision, which—without renouncing the principle of a constitutional law

100 "Übertragung von Hoheitsrechten".

101 *Entscheidungen des Bundesverfassungsgerichts* 22, 293 at 298 *et seq* (*EWG-Verordnungen*).

102 There are two senates at the *BVerfG*, each with eight judges.

103 *Entscheidungen des Bundesverfassungsgerichts* 37, 271 (*Solange I*). The dissenting opinion starts at p 291.

104 The position adopted by the dissenting minority deserves closer attention as it went much further than even the *BVerfG's Solange II* decision 12 years later. According to the minority, the German Constitution's fundamental rights standard cannot be applied to EC secondary law. The EEC Treaty has established an original legal order, whose law is safeguarded by the ECJ. The Community legal order, the dissenting judges continue, is autonomous and independent from national law. The ECJ's *Nold* decision is already mentioned, which the *BVerfG* would 12 years later in *Solange II* refer to as "an essential step" towards a sufficient fundamental rights protection standard at the European level. The minority also emphasises that the duty to acknowledge the acts of supranational institutions, recognised by the *BVerfG* itself (*Entscheidungen des Bundesverfassungsgerichts* 31, 145 at 174 (*Lütticke*)), excludes from the outset any kind of national control over these acts, as the Federal Republic relinquished this right by joining the EEC. The minority, however, confirms that EC law has primacy over domestic law only to the extent that the German Constitution allows a transfer of public authority to the Community institutions and that there are limits to that transfer. But the *BVerfG* does not have the right to apply the German Constitution's standards in general and the fundamental rights standard in particular to provisions of EC law in order to make statements on the validity of EC law. That the majority claims this power is in the opinion of the minority a clear infringement of the powers reserved to the ECJ and incompatible with Art 24(1) of the German Constitution. In conclusion, the minority considers the *BVerfG*'s reservation of a constitutional check on EC law—a reservation that the *Solange II* decision maintains—to be illegal.

105 *Entscheidungen des Bundesverfassungsgerichts* 52, 187 at 202 *et seq* (*Vielleicht*).

106 *Entscheidungen des Bundesverfassungsgerichts* 58, 1 (*Eurocontrol I*); 59, 63 (*Eurocontrol II*).

107 BVerfG, *Neue Juristische Wochenschrift* (1983) 1258—(*Mittlerweile*).

108 *Entscheidungen des Bundesverfassungsgerichts* 73, 339 (*Solange II*) (English trans in Federal Constitutional Court (ed), *Decisions of the Bundesverfassungsgericht. Vol 1/Part II* (1992) 613, and in Oppenheimer, above n 1, 461; 3 *CMLR* (1987) 225).

check—defused the fundamental rights issue "in a pragmatic sense".[109] The *BVerfG* did insist that the transfer of public authority to supranational institutions be subject to constitutional limits: there is no authorisation, it held, to give up the identity of the German constitutional order by means of transferring competences to supranational institutions with the result of an "intrusion into the fundamental architecture, the constituting structures" of the Constitution.[110] Nevertheless, the *BVerfG* holds after an extensive assessment of the development of EC law: "as long as" (*solange*) an effective protection of fundamental rights is guaranteed at the European level, with a level of protection which is substantially equivalent[111] to the inalienable minimum level of protection of fundamental rights under the German Constitution, including a general guarantee of the essential substance (*Wesensgehalt*) of the fundamental rights, the *BVerfG* "will no longer exercise its jurisdiction to decide on the applicability of derived Community law, that may constitute the legal basis for acts of German courts or authorities in the Federal Republic."[112]

The fundamental rights section of the 1993 *Maastricht* decision[113] and the 2000 *Banana* decision[114] have basically confirmed the *BVerfG's* statement of principle in *Solange II*.[115] In a decision of 2001, the *BVerfG* has re-confirmed its understanding that the standard of fundamental rights protection required by the German Constitution is safeguarded under the current system.[116]

(2) Powers and Competences: The German *Maastricht* Decision (1993)

With the *Maastricht* decision of 12 October 1993,[117] the *BVerfG* established a constitutional law reserve of power over the exercise of competences by

[109] G Hirsch, 'Kompetenzverteilung zwischen EuGH und nationaler Gerichtsbarkeit', (1998) *Neue Zeitschrift für Verwaltungsrecht* 907 at 909.

[110] "durch Einbruch in ihr Grundgefüge, in die sie konstituierenden Strukturen", *Entscheidungen des Bundesverfassungsgerichts* 73, 339 at 375 *et seq* (*Solange II*). Here, the Court refers to the jurisprudence of the Italian Constitutional Court.

[111] "im wesentlichen gleichzuachten".

[112] *Ibid*, 387. Since 1992, the two sets of constitutional limits have been explicitly mentioned in Art 23 of the German Constitution, including the *Solange II*-formula. Interestingly, this formula was also introduced into the 1975 Swedish Constitution (in 1994, Chapter 10(5)), see O Ruin, 'Suède', in J Rideau (ed), *Les Etats membres de l'Union européenne* (1997) 440 *et seq*.

[113] *Entscheidungen des Bundesverfassungsgerichts* 89, 155 at 175, Leitsatz 5 paras 3, 6 and 7 (*Maastricht*).

[114] *Entscheidungen des Bundesverfassungsgerichts* 102, 147 (*Banana case*).

[115] This is also the view of R Hofmann, 'Zurück zu Solange II!', in H-J Cremer *et al* (eds), *Tradition und Weltoffenheit des Rechts: Festschrift für H Steinberger* (2002) 1207 *et seq*. Any doubts the *Maastricht* decision may have raised are resolved by the *Banana* decision: the Court emphasised that an individual's constitutional complaint under Art 93(1) or a national court's reference under Art 100 of the German Constitution simply will be held inadmissible, unless the individual/ the referring court proves a complete erosion of fundamental rights in accordance with *Solange II*.

[116] Although the *BVerfG* does not contribute to this safeguarding of European fundamental rights by making references to the ECJ, it does contribute by supervising the duty to make references of the regular German courts, using as a basis the German Constitution's fundamental right of "access to the lawful judge", above n 34.

[117] *Entscheidungen des Bundesverfassungsgerichts* 89, 155 (*Maastricht*). The decision and the proceedings are well documented in I Winkelmann, above n 22; further references in Mayer, above n 3, 98 *et seq*.

the EC/EU. Accordingly, the *BVerfG* may examine whether acts at the European level conform to the boundaries set for the transfer of public powers to the EU.[118] The Court justifies its right of control over ultra vires acts (in the decision, the Court says *ausbrechende Rechtsakte*,[119] "acts breaking out") by pointing to the constraints of German constitutional law. What the Court actually does within that concept amounts to an independent interpretation of European law: according to the *BVerfG*, the plan of integration[120] outlined in the act of assent (*Zustimmungsgesetz*) and in the EU Treaty cannot be substantially altered later on by means of European ultra vires acts s.o. without losing the cover provided by the act of assent. Taking a closer look at this argument, one realises that this amounts to a doubling of the relevant standards. European acts have to be compatible with the guarantees of the German Constitution and, of course, with European law. This is the case because the *BVerfG* would actually review the act of assent to the extent that it covers a given European act. This European act would then thus be reviewed by the standard of a "German version" of European law (the "Constitutional-law-version" of EU law). The alleged limitation on scrutinising the act of assent under a German constitutional law standard thus only seems to be a trick: in actuality, the compatibility of a European act with German constitutional law depends on its compatibility with European law—that is, the way the *BVerfG* interprets European law.

As far as ECJ "acts" are concerned, the *Maastricht* decision remains unclear about how, in practice, to draw the line between the (permitted) development of the law by European judges and the (prohibited) development of judge-made European law, or between substantial alterations of the European competence provisions and still acceptable alterations.[121]

The legal consequences of deeming a European act ultra vires would be that this act would not be binding in Germany. This amounts to a German constitutional law-based reserve of power over European acts that restricts the primacy of European law. In such a situation, the *BVerfG* takes on the role of the guardian.

All things considered, one may well say that the *Maastricht* decision is within a certain continuity of the *BVerfG*'s prior jurisprudence on fundamental rights, as far as the concept of a constitutional law reserve of control

[118] *Entscheidungen des Bundesverfassungsgerichts* 89, 155 at 188 (*Maastricht*).

[119] For the terminology, literally "acts that break out" ("ausbrechender Rechtsakt"), see already the earlier decision *Entscheidungen des Bundesverfassungsgerichts* 75, 223 at 242 (*Kloppenburg*). For the distinction between ultra vires-acts in a narrow sense (ie, overstepping competences defined according to area) and in a broad sense (ie, the general illegality of an act) see Mayer, above n 3, 24 *et seq.*

[120] Strangely enough, the *BVerfG* also used the idea of an underlying "integration programme" in the context of the NATO Treaty, *Entscheidungen des Bundesverfassungsgerichts* 104, 151. See M Rau, 'NATO's New Strategic Concept', (2001) *GYIL* 545 at 570.

[121] See M Zuleeg, 'Die Rolle der rechtsprechenden Gewalt in der europäischen Integration', (1994) *Juristenzeitung* 1 at 3; C Tomuschat, 'Die Europäische Union unter der Aufsicht des Bundesverfassungsgerichts', (1993) *Europäische Grundrechte-Zeitschrift* 489 at 494.

that restricts the European law claim for primacy is concerned. What is striking though is the aggressive tone of the decision when compared to previous decisions.[122] One should also note a crucial difference between the fundamental rights issue (*Solange II*) and the competence issue (*Maastricht*): as for the competence issue, the reproach with which the European level is confronted in case of an ultra vires act goes beyond the bipolar relationship between the German constitutional order and the European legal order. The categories of an ultra vires act on the one hand and an act infringing upon the fundamental rights laid down in the German Constitution on the other hand are utterly different: the absence of a certain aspect of fundamental rights protection in the jurisprudence of the ECJ can already occur either for procedural reasons or because the range of a given fundamental right is defined differently at the European and national levels. In that case, the *BVerfG*'s formula for a co-operative relationship (*Kooperationsverhältnis*) between (*zwischen*[123]) the *BVerfG* and ECJ in the sense of a spare or reserve guarantee in line with the *Solange II* jurisprudence appears totally plausible. To uphold, in principle, the standard of fundamental rights protection guaranteed by the German Constitution does not necessarily imply a reproach against the European level; it does not go beyond the bipolar relationship between German and European legal orders.

This is different in the case of a reproach of an ultra vires act: there is no leeway for a relationship of co-operation between the *BVerfG* and ECJ where the question of the limits of European competences is concerned.[124] Declaring an act to be ultra vires always implies a defect in the act. It would also imply a reproach towards the European level and especially to the ECJ. Moreover, the reproach of an ultra vires act would also concern the validity and/or application of European law in all other Member States, as an act cannot be ultra vires only in the bipolar relationship between one Member State and the EU. This is hence a frontal attack on judge-made European law.[125]

Imposing the strict standard implicitly suggested by the *BVerfG* on the principles of interpretation of European law as developed by the ECJ would

[122] This view is also adopted by U Everling, 'BVerfG und Gerichtshof der Europäischen Gemeinschaften', in A Randelzhofer *et al* (eds), *Gedächtnisschrift für Eberhard Grabitz* (1995) 72.

[123] The actual wording in the decision is "Kooperationsverhältnis *zum* EuGH" (to), *Entscheidungen des Bundesverfassungsgerichts* 89, 155 at 175 and Leitsatz 7 (*Maastricht*).

[124] A different view is adopted by R Scholz, 'Zum Verhältnis von europäischem Gemeinschaftsrecht und nationalem Verwaltungsverfahrensrecht', (1998) *Die Öffentliche Verwaltung* 261 at 267. In fact Scholz establishes a relationship of competition, not co-operation between the ECJ and *BVerfG*.

[125] The concept of judge-made law, its limits and the controversies surrounding it are too broad to be explored here. See instead the references in Pernthaler, above n 11, 691; see also the contributions in *Richterliche Rechtsfortbildung: Festschrift der Juristischen Fakultät zur 600-Jahr-Feier der Rupert-Karls-Universität Heidelberg* (1986); U Everling, *Richterrecht in der Europäischen Gemeinschaft* (1988); and J Ukrow, *Richterliche Rechtsfortbildung durch den EuGH* (1995).

significantly reduce the ECJ's latitude. This kind of constraint reaches beyond the EU Treaty, the actual subject of the *Maastricht* decision,[126] and extends to European law in general. By implying a duty of the ECJ to police the principle of subsidiarity and proportionality at the European level in a specific way, the *BVerfG* claims the power to scrutinise[127] difficult balancing decisions undertaken by the ECJ as well as the development of European law influenced by the ECJ.[128]

The immediate effects of the *Maastricht* decision have been limited. Still, at least one court, a Financial Court of the first instance (the *Finanzgericht Rheinland-Pfalz*[129]) has declared an EC act to be ultra vires. Other courts (the *Bundesgerichtshof*, the *Oberverwaltungsgericht Münster*, the *Bundesfinanzhof* and also the *Verwaltungsgericht Frankfurt*[130]) have been extremely liberal in making use of the concept of EC ultra vires acts, without actually declaring any act to be ultra vires. These decisions have revealed quite different understandings of what an ultra vires act may be, extending to an understanding that would make any illicit European act an ultra vires act, no matter what nature the legal defect of the act in question actually is.

In doctrinal writings, the *BVerfG*'s concept of ultra vires acts has been severely criticised by some,[131] but welcomed by others, to the extent that it has been used as an argument against all kinds of alleged ultra vires acts stemming from the EC, in particular from the ECJ (the ECJ decisions in the *Süderdithmarschen*, *Alcan* and *Kreil* cases).[132] What is striking is the sharpness of the debate, at least among some German scholars in the past.[133] In any case, the Federal administrative court—the *BVerwG*—and

[126] Zuleeg, above n 121, 7.

[127] Winkelmann, above n 22, 52.

[128] See U Everling, 'Richterliche Rechtsfortbildung in der Europäischen Gemeinschaft', (2000) *Juristenzeitung* 217 at 227.

[129] Finanzgericht Rheinland-Pfalz, *Entscheidungen der Finanzgerichte* (1995) 378; see also *Entscheidungen des Bundesfinanzhofs* 180, 231 at 236.

[130] Further references in Mayer, above n 3, 120 *et seq.*

[131] JA Frowein, 'Kritische Bemerkungen zur Lage des deutschen Staatsrechts aus rechtsvergleichender Sicht', (1998) *Die Öffentliche Verwaltung* 806 at 807 *et seq.*

[132] The term *ausbrechender Rechtsakt* is used, for example, in *Sondergutachten 28* of the *Monopolkommission* [Opinion on a Commission White paper] in 1999, para 72 (against changing the system of European competition law), see in that context W Möschel, 'Systemwechsel im Europäischen Wettbewerbsrecht', (2000) *Juristenzeitung* 61 at 62, with further references; Scholz, above n 124 (against the *Alcan* decision as an *ausbrechender Rechtsakt*), 267; R Scholz, in T Maunz and G Dürig (eds), *Grundgesetz: Kommentar* (looseleaf), Art 12a, paras 189 *et seq* (against the ECJ's *Kreil* decision as an *ausbrechender Rechtsakt*); F Schoch, in F Schoch, E Schmidt-Aßmann and R Pietzner, *Verwaltungsgerichtsordnung* (looseleaf), § 80, paras 270 *et seq* (against the ECJ's *Süderdithmarschen* decision as an *ausbrechender Rechtsakt*).

[133] See first the newsmagazine-article "Sprengkraft der Banane", *Focus* 7/1999, 13 February 1999, 11; then by former ECJ judge U Everling, 'Richterliche Unbefangenheit?', (1999) *Europäische Zeitschrift für Wirtschaftsrecht* 225; followed by the answer in the German *Maastricht* case, P Kirchhof, 'Der Weg Europas ist der Dialog', (1999) *Europäische Zeitschrift für Wirtschaftsrecht* 353.

even the *BVerfG* itself have clearly rejected any attempt to depict the ECJ's *Alcan* decision as an invalid and thus irrelevant ultra vires act.[134]

One may ask, though, what the concept of competences is behind the ultra vires accusations concerning the ECJ's decisions in the *Süderdithmarschen* and *Alcan* cases. The argument that the ECJ does not have the "competences to regulate" in the sense of legislative powers suggests erroneously that the ECJ decisions in question contain some kind of quasi-legislative regulation of a competence area, such as court procedure or administrative procedure. Even if there may be some truth in depicting numerous decisions of the ECJ as blunt, to use a friendly word, especially those in which it insists and pretends that it is merely interpreting positive law,[135]—what the ECJ does in the *Alcan* case is simply enforcing the European control of state aids (subsidies).

Moreover, it is also doubtful whether the *Maastricht* decision's initial concept of ultra vires acts actually covers this kind of reasoning in the first place, as there is no doubt that eg the control of state aids (subsidies) is in the realm of European competences. The wording of the *Maastricht* decision seems to indicate that the *BVerfG* was aiming at ultra vires acts in a narrow sense, as acts beyond the scope of European competences, in other words, as acts that transcend the realm of European jurisdiction. It did not seem to aim at the separation of powers question of which institution at that level has what powers. And surely the *BVerfG* did not want to introduce some kind of general legality check on European law, to consider any kind of formal or substantial legal defect of European acts.

(3) The Consistency of the *BVerfG's* Case-law: Controlling the Bridge

In summary, one can say that, in spite of the *BVerfG*'s recognition of the autonomy of the Community legal order, the *BVerfG* has always seen the acts of assent to the respective treaties, based on the German Constitution, as the link between European law and national law, with the Member States remaining the "Masters of the Treaties".[136] Moreover, this is a linear, continuous link, and not a one-time link that becomes irrelevant once the German legal order has been "opened up" to European law. Policing this link, or, to come back to *Paul Kirchhof*'s metaphor, controlling this bridge, enables the *BVerfG* to effectuate far-reaching indirect control over the application of European law by applying to it the standard of German

[134] BVerwG, *Deutsche Zeitschrift für Wirtschaftsrecht* (1998) 503 (*Alcan*); BVerfG, Decision of 17 February 2000, *Europäische Zeitschrift für Wirtschaftsrecht* (2000) 445 (*Alcan*). The *BVerfG* has also refused to declare the Banana-regulation (*Entscheidungen des Bundesverfassungsgerichts* 102, 147) or the Broadcasting-directive (*Entscheidungen des Bundesverfassungsgerichts* 92, 203) ultra vires.

[135] On this aspect see Pernthaler, above n 11, 695.

[136] *Entscheidungen des Bundesverfassungsgerichts* 75, 223 (*Kloppenburg*).

constitutional law under the guise of interpreting and controlling the act of assent.

The alleged "auto-limitation" policy of the *BVerfG*, according to which the *BVerfG* and ECJ adjudicate in spheres independent of each other, merely acts to blur the fact that policing the constitutional limits imposed on transfers of public authority under Articles 23/24 of the German Constitution amounts to an indirect control of European law. And the *BVerfG* indeed consistently imposes constitutional law limits on the primacy of European law. These limits justify the *BVerfG*'s claim of entitlement to control European law as the guardian of the German Constitution.

It should be noted that the *BVerfG* has never relinquished its claim to a right to decide the point at which it would leverage its constitutional control; it merely modified this threshold. This is especially visible in the *Solange I/Solange II* shift, where the Court reversed what it considered to be the principle and what the exception. Only the dissenting opinion in the *Solange I* case[137] indicated a willingness to completely abandon a right of judicial review over the constitutionality of the European law, albeit insisting on constitutional law limits. Finally, the difference between the fundamental rights issue and the ultra vires issue should be borne in mind, as "ultra vires acts" and "acts violating fundamental rights as accorded by the German Constitution" are different categories.

bb) Other High Courts[138] Claims of some form of last instance reserve of power over the legality of European law can be found in Italy (in the *Corte Costituzionale's* decisions in the *Frontini*[139] and *Fragd* cases[140]); Ireland (in the Supreme Court cases on abortion[141]); Denmark (in the *Højesteret's* Rasmussen decision of 1998, the Danish *Maastricht* case[142]); Greece (in the Council of State's *DI.K.A.T.S.A.* decision 1998[143]); Spain (in the *Tribunal Constitucional's* Maastricht opinion of 1992 [144]) and, as

[137] Above n 104.

[138] For a more detailed account of the the jurisprudence of the different courts see Mayer, above n 3, 143–271.

[139] Decision No 183/73 (*Frontini*), *Foro italiano* I (1974) 314 (English trans in Oppenheimer, above n 1, 629; 2 *CMLR* (1974), 372).

[140] Decision No 232/89 (*Fragd*), *Foro italiano* I (1990) 1855 (English trans in Oppenheimer, above n 1, 653).

[141] SC *SPUC (Ireland) Ltd v Grogan* [1989] IR 753.

[142] Højesteret, Decision of 6 April 1998, *Carlsen et al v Rasmussen*, I 361/1997, *Ugeskrift for Retsvæsen* (1998) 800 (German trans *Europäische Grundrechte-Zeitschrift* (1999) 49).

[143] Council of State No 3457/98, *Katsarou v DIKATSA*; see in that context also the Opinion Council of State No 194/2000.

[144] TC Declaration 108/1992 1 July 1992 (*Maastricht*-Opinion), *Revista de Instituciones Europeas* (1992) 633 (English trans in Oppenheimer, above n 1, 712).

a special case,[145] France (in the *Conseil d'Etat's* Cohn-Bendit decision of 1978[146]).

Jurisprudential developments that may turn into similar claims of the right to judicial review over European law can be detected in Belgium (in the *Cour d'arbitrage*'s jurisprudence on treaty law[147]). Similar indications, which point at least to the remote possibility of courts claiming a reserve of power over European law, can be found in extrajudicial avenues in Sweden (in a statement from the highest court on the constitutional amendments in the context of accession to the EU[148]) and in Austria (in the Official Government Statement on accession[149]).

Other Member States have not fully developed a standard of national constitutional law control over European law, but such a possibility remains open. Portugal's constitutional law includes limits on European integration.[150] In addition, because of the primacy of parliamentary decisions in Great Britain, the British constitutional reserve of power over European law—which exists in principle with the claim to have retained parliamentary sovereignty—is unlikely to be activated by the courts alone.[151]

[145] Because of the constraints of the French legal order, which does not provide for a constitutional judicial review, the *Conseil d'Etat* cannot openly refer to constitutional law arguments. Nevertheless, in a legal order without a constitutional court, even the decision of a body not empowered with comprehensive judicial review may function as a leading decision of quasi-constitutional character. It thus has more weight than the non-references of specialised courts of last instance that occasionally happen in most Member States. These non-references are recorded in the annual Reports on monitoring the application of Community law, see for example the 17th report 1999, OJ C 30, 30.6.2001, 1; the 18th report 2000, COM(2001) 309 final, 16 July 2001; the 19th report 2001, COM(2002) 324 final, 28 June 2002; the 20th report 2002, COM(2003) 669 final, 21 November 2003; see in that context the references at <http://europa.eu.int/comm/secretariat_general/sgb/droit_com/index_en.htm> (16 July 2004).

[146] Above n 16. See also CE 30 October 1998, *Sarran, Revue française de droit administratif* (1998) 1081; Cass 2 June 2000, *Fraisse*; CE 3 December 2001, *SNIP*; CE 30 July 2003 *Association Avenir de la langue française (Loi Toubon)*. The issue of primacy concerning infra-constitutional law was settled with the *Nicolo* decision, CE 20 October 1989, Rec 190. The *Conseil constitutionnel* confirmed this in CC 10 June 2004, *Loi pour la confiance dans l'économie numérique*, para 7, still pointing to the possibility of a provision explicity incompatible with the French Constitution, thus not accepting unconditional primacy of European law.

[147] Decision 26/91, 16 October 1991 (*Commune de Lanaken*); (Dutch-Belgian double taxation treaty), *Journal des Tribunaux* (1992) 6670; see also Decision 12/94, 3 February 1994, *Ecole européenne* (school fees at European schools), *Moniteur Belge* 11 March 1994, 6142; Decision 33/94, 26 April 1994 (*ECHR*), *Moniteur Belge* 22 June 1994.

[148] 'EG och grundlagarna—sammanställning av remissyttranden över betänkandet' SOU 1993:14 och departementspromemorian Ds 1993:36, *Departementsserien* 1993:71.

[149] 'Erläuterungen zur Regierungsvorlage über das Bundesverfassungsgesetz über den Beitritt Österreichs zur Europäischen Union', 1546 *Beilagen zu den Stenographischen Protokollen des Nationalrates der Republik Österreich 18. GP.*

[150] Art 7(6) of the Portuguese Constitution. According to this provision, Portugal may—under the condition of reciprocity—enter into agreements for the joint exercise of the powers necessary to establish the European Union, in ways that have due regard for the principle of subsidiarity and the objective of economic and social cohesion.

[151] House of Lords, *Factortame v Secretary of State* [1991] 1 AC 603. See also House of Lords, *Macarthys v Smith (No 1)* [1979] 1 All ER 325 (329) and the "metric martyrs" case, High Court QBD, *Thoburn v Sunderland City Council et al* [2002] 4 All ER 156. See in that context N Bamforth, 'Courts in a Multi-Layered Constitution', in N Bamforth and P Leyland (eds), *Public Law in a Multi-Layered Constitution* (2003) 277.

Both the structural circumstances of the constitutional law and the general trend of the jurisprudence in regard to the European law/national law relationship make it highly improbable for a reserve of power to be claimed in Luxembourg (no possibility for national courts to control European law plus Community-friendly courts) and the Netherlands (no constitutional court, no judicial review of international agreements and unconditional precedence of international obligations, even over the constitution). For Finland, court claims of reserve of power over European law are equally unlikely because of the constitutional order (no possibility for courts to review European law compatibility with the constitution).

In most Member States where a power to control European law is either being claimed or merely discussed, this power is justified on constitutional law grounds. In other words, in these Member States, the primacy of European law over national law does not automatically extend to constitutional law. The Netherlands are a special case: not only do the Dutch courts lack the authority to judicially review European law, but there are no constitutional constraints on European law at all, as the Dutch constitutional order recognises without reservation the primacy of Community law.

In contrast, German and Italian jurisprudence establishes a link between a national court's finding a European act ultra vires and the violation of core constitutional law. In Germany, the argument centres on the German Constitution's principle of democracy,[152] while in Italy on the fundamental principals of the Italian Constitution known as counterlimits or *controlimiti*.[153] The jurisprudence of the *Højesteret* in Denmark points to a privileged position for constitutional provisions on liberties and on national independence.

What appears to be particularly threatening for legal unity and the uniform interpretation of European law in the case-law of the highest courts and tribunals is the phenomenon of interpreting European law from the perspective of the national constitutional order, generating a parallel version of European law (a constitutional law version of European law). Such power to engage in an autonomous parallel interpretation of European law on its compatibility with the respective constitutions (thus doubling the standard of scrutiny) is claimed by the *BVerfG* in Germany,[154] the *Corte Costituzionale* in Italy (in the *Frontini* case[155]), the Supreme Court in Ireland (*inter alia* in the *Campus Oil* decision[156]) and the *Højesteret* in Denmark (in the *Maastricht* decision *Carlsen/Rasmussen*[157]).

[152] *Entscheidungen des Bundesverfassungsgerichts* 89, 155 (*Maastricht*).

[153] M Cartabia, *Principi inviolabili e integrazione europea* (1995) 8 und 95 *et seq*.

[154] Above I 2 b.

[155] Above n 139.

[156] SC, *Campus Oil v Minister for Industry and Energy* [1983] IR 82, an example for the SC being "plus communautaire que les Communautés" (DR Phelan and A Whelan, Ireland, in FIDE (ed), *17th Congress 1996* (1996) 292 (302)), though.

[157] Above n 142.

Overall, considering the constitutional law framework and the case law of these courts, it seems fair to say that for some national supreme courts, developing a jurisprudence that would resemble the German *Maastricht* decision remains a possibility. The most important indications in that context are constitutional constraints imposed on the European law principle of primacy by a given Member States' constitutional order.

Thus, one can say that there are certain tendencies in the jurisprudence of a number of Member States that are not entirely insignificant. These tendencies are marked by an emphasis on elements of the national constitutional order that are unalterable, thus "primacy-proof". There is also evidence of an autonomous interpretation of European law by Member State courts that could lead to results that diverge from the ECJ's findings This autonomous interpretation of European law from a Member State perspective could be coined "parallel interpretation" of European law, establishing Member State constitutional law versions of European law.[158] In this respect, former German ECJ judge *Ulrich Everling*'s assessment of a "potential for conflict"[159] existing at the level of the Member States appears to be confirmed.

cc) The Highest Courts in the New and Prospective Member States With the accession of at least 10 states from Central, Eastern and Southern Europe as of 2004, the role of their highest courts in relation to the ECJ comes into question.[160] In Poland it is the Constitutional Tribunal that decides inter alia on the compatibility of international treaties with the Constitution, with the Constitution taking precedence over international law obligations (Article 90). In Hungary, the Constitutional Court has already made explicit reference to the German *BVerfG*'s *Maastricht* decision. As far as the Constitutional Court of the Czech Republic is concerned, there are no indications yet of the position that court will take on the relationship between constitutional law and European law. The Supreme Court of Estonia's case law on the association agreement with the EU indicates a willingness to bring the interpretation of the Constitution and the duties flowing from European law into line. Latvia has had a Constitutional Court since 1996. The statute on Latvia's international agreements of 1994 stipulates that

[158] See in that context O Dubos, *Les juridictions nationales, juge communautaire* (2001) 857 *et seq*, who openly suggest giving Member State courts EC law jurisdiction.

[159] Everling, above n 122, 68. See also R Streinz, 'Verfassungsvorbehalte gegenüber Gemeinschaftsrecht—eine deutsche Besonderheit?', in *Festschrift Steinberger*, above n 115.

[160] For the following overview, see the contributions in AE Kellermann *et al* (eds), *EU Enlargement: The Constitutional Impact at EU and National Level* (2001), by J Justynski (Poland), 279 at 283 *et seq*; A Harmathy (Hungary), 315 at 325; V Balas (Czech Republic), 243 at 246 *et seq*; T Kerikmäe (Estonia), 337 at 344; A Usacka (Latvia), 337; V Vadapalas (Lithuania), 347 at 349 *et seq*; P Vehar (Slovenia) 367 at 371 *et seq*; PG Xuereb (Malta), 229 at 239 *et seq*; N Emiliou (Cyprus), 243 at 246 *et seq*; V Kunová (Slovakia), 327 at 335; E Tanchev (Bulgaria), 301 at 306; A Ciobanu-Dordea (Romania), 311 at 312; M Soysal (Turkey), 267 at 272 *et seq*.

international obligations take precedence over statutes, but not over the Constitution. A similar statute (of 1999) and a Constitutional Court also exist in Lithuania. In Slovenia, the Constitution also claims precedence over the international obligations. The Slovenian Constitutional Court has confirmed this in several decisions. As for Malta, the Maltese Constitutional Court seems to have concerns about the relationship with the European Convention on Human Rights. According to the jurisprudence of the Supreme Court in Cyprus, international agreements take precedence over statutes, but not over the Constitution. In Slovakia, the constitutional amendment of February 2001 has introduced a specific, detailed provision dealing with European integration (Article 7), which provides for the supremacy or primacy of European law over domestic statutes. It is unclear, though, whether the Slovak Constitutional Court would also extend this provision to constitutional law.

In Bulgaria, the 1991 Constitution attributes international agreements a rank superior to statutes, but inferior to the Constitution, which would bind the Constitutional Court on this question. The situation appears to be similar in Romania and the Romanian Constitutional Court. In Croatia, another country with a Constitutional Court, international agreements become part of the internal legal order. Finally, in Turkey, it is expected that in the case of accession, the Turkish Constitutional Court would explicitly follow the way lead by the *Solange I* and *Solange II* jurisprudence of the *BVerfG* and the *Frontini* and *Fragd* decisions of the Italian *Corte Costituzionale*.

This summary overview indicates that almost all new Member States/accession candidates have a constitutional court and that in a number of cases, unconditional primacy of European law over the constitution is not compatible with the current constitution in these countries. It must be noted though that the constitutional order is not yet consolidated in some of these states, as constitutional reforms and amendments are intended or pending. Nevertheless, it seems fair to say that at least some of the highest courts and tribunals of these states may be reluctant to unconditionally accept the ECJ's claim to be the final arbiter on European law. The rather stunning Polish Constitutional Tribunal's decision on Polish EU membership from May 2005, Case K 18/04, seems to confirm this.

3. Interim Summary

One must not get carried away with the results of the analysis of the case law: after all, at this point, there is no open conflict in the relationship between the ECJ and the highest national courts. Still, the lack of willingness to engage in a conversation with the ECJ by means of references under Article 234 EC points to the potential for disobedience. It indicates to what extent national courts could be willing to insist on an original position vis-à-vis the ECJ.

And without crossing the threshold to open conflict, there are still some worrying tendencies in the case law of the highest courts and tribunals of the Member States. These tendencies may be coined "frictional phenomena". They include the insistence on primacy-proof elements of the national constitutional order (e.g. fundamental rights) and the autonomous interpretation of European law by Member State courts (in the context of competences and ultra vires acts), which may lead to an interpretation distinct from the ECJ's interpretation (a parallel interpretation, generating national constitutional law versions of EU law).[161]

Another tendency is the seeming connection between specialised constitutional tribunals and the issue of a constitutional law reserve of power over European law (Germany, Italy, and Spain). On the other hand, the absence of a central constitutional court in the Member State acting as the guardian of its constitution or, at least, the core of its constitution, against European law appears advantageous for European law.[162] Still, as the Danish example illustrates, this case does not exclude national claims to a final say over European law.

II. ADOPTING AN ANALYTICAL AND A THEORETICAL PERSPECTIVE

Although the frictional phenomena between the ECJ and the highest courts of the Member States detected in Part I have not so far crossed the threshold to open conflict, one may still reflect upon how to resolve the friction (1) and how to put these frictional phenomena into a theoretical perspective (2).

1. Dealing with the Question of Ultimate Jurisdiction

One way to approach the potential for conflict inherent in the question of ultimate jurisdiction is to identify a set of legal tools or instruments which may help shape the legal context or the legal basis of the respective courts, with a view to clarifying the respective positions, in order to rationalise and, along that line, resolve the conflict.[163]

[161] The relevant statements of the national courts are often made outside an actual legal question, as obiter dicta or in the context of a mere legal opinion. A plausible explanation for this is that the courts are emitting signals here that are also meant to be received by the ECJ, having an anticipatory effect on the ECJ. See Alter, above n 66, 118, who applies this category coined by E Blankenburg on European policy-making.

[162] A similar view is adopted by M Claes and B de Witte, 'Report on the Netherlands', in Slaughter *et al* (eds), above n 3, 190.

[163] See in more detail FC Mayer, 'The European Constitution and the Courts', *Jean Monnet Working Paper* 9/03 (2003), <http://www.jeanmonnetprogram.org/papers/03/030901.html> (16 July 2004).

Differences of opinion between the European and the national legal orders on the location of the ultimate control competence on European law could be defused by modifying the attribution of competences (in the broadest sense) or standards applied by a court. The "Irish solution" bears testimony to this: a primary law protocol annexed to the *Maastricht* treaty stipulates that nothing in the European treaties shall affect the application in Ireland of Article 40.3.3 of the Constitution of Ireland (prohibition of abortion). The most obvious solution to national courts' claims of jurisdiction is to take away jurisdiction from these courts, e.g. by an explicit statement inscribed into national law that even incidental questions of European law must be resolved under Article 234 EC and not answered by national courts.[164] One could also consider shifting the responsibility for the type of ultimate decisions that are problematic in the present context to distinct institutions. Institutional solutions are particularly noteworthy in relation to competence conflicts in the strict sense—the overstepping of competence boundaries which delimit specific areas (ultra vires acts). They may be conceptualised as judicial or as political mode of control. Judicial control (courts of competence) would mean the establishment of special courts for resolving competence conflicts.[165] Proposals in this context include suggestions to establish a European Supreme Court (*Europäischer Oberster Gerichtshof*) or a European Constitutional Tribunal (*Europäisches Verfassungsgericht*),[166] a Union Court of Review,[167] a Constitutional Council,[168] or a European Conflicts Tribunal.[169] A political

[164] This would amount to a reinforcement of obligations already existing under European law.

[165] This is something that was suggested early on in the history of the US federal system, but without success. The most recent suggestion to establish a Court of the Union dates from 1962, for the details Mayer, above n 3, 308. Comparable proposals have repeatedly been made for the EU, see the references in A Schwartze, 'Kompetenzverteilung und Entscheidungsverfahren in einer Europäischen Verfassung', in ME Streit and S Voigt (eds), *Europa reformieren* (1996) 136 *et seq*; M Hilf, 'Ungeschriebene EG-Kompetenzen im Außenwirtschaftsrecht', (1997) *Zeitschrift für Verwaltung* 295; in recent times even by acting judges of the German *BVerfG*. For the proposal of a special Treaty Arbitration Court composed out of 15 representatives of national courts and one ECJ representative, see judge S Bross, 'Bundesverfassungsgericht—Europäischer Gerichtshof—Europäischer Gerichtshof für Kompetenzkonflikte', (2001) *Verwaltungsarchiv* 425; see also more recently *id*, 'Überlegungen zum gegenwärtigen Stand des Europäischen Einigungsprozesses', (2002) *Europäische Grundrechte-Zeitschrift* 574; for a "Common Constitutional Court" bringing together members of "the Member State constitutional courts" see Judge U Di Fabio, 'Ist die Staatswerdung Europas unausweichlich?, *Frankfurter Allgemeine Zeitung*', 2 February 2001, 8.

[166] K Friedrich, 'Bundesfinanzhof contra Europäischen Gerichtshof', (1985) *Recht der Internationalen Wirtschaft* 794; S Magiera, in D Merten (ed), *Föderalismus und Europäische Gemeinschaften* (1990) 127.

[167] European Constitutional Group, *A Proposal for a European Constitution* (1993) 13.

[168] JHH Weiler, 'The European Union Belongs to its Citizens', (1997) 22 *EL Rev*, 150 at 155. See also JHH Weiler, UR Haltern and FC Mayer, 'European Democracy and Its Critique', (1995) 18 *West European Politics* 4 at 38; JHH Weiler *et al*, *Certain Rectangular Problems of European Integration* (1996) 14; JHH Weiler, 'In der Unterwelt der Ausschüsse', *Die Zeit*, 22 October 1998, 9.

[169] P Lindseth, 'Democratic legitimacy and the administrative character of supranationalism', (1999) 99 *Columbia L Rev* 628 at 731 *et seq*.

control of competences could be assigned to existing institutions such as the Council of Ministers and the European Parliament, or to institutions that would have to be newly created, such as a special parliamentary committee.[170]

Without entering into a detailed appraisal of the proposals, it seems fair to say that new institutions would have only a limited problem-solving capacity. First, it cannot be emphasised enough that there is a court of competence already—the ECJ. ECJ Judge Colneric has presented a detailed account of the jurisprudence of the court in the field of competences.[171] Introducing an additional court with comprehensive powers would amount to a complete reshuffle of the institutional setting at the European level. As to the suggested *ex ante* control of competences, they would fail to catch ECJ decisions. Moreover, an institution composed of European members and national members on an equal basis would probably be unable to solve or prevent conflicts. In sum: new institutions would not prove effective in resolving all possible conflict scenarios.

It seems to me that the crux of the competence issue in non-unitary systems is to ensure that all actors exercise a consistently high level of sensitivity in matters of competences. This can be achieved neither by the wording of competence provisions, however detailed they may be, nor by institutional arrangements alone.[172] This points to the importance of "soft" mechanisms (procedures, reports etc.) which aim at a structurally different and cautious approach towards competences, emphasising the importance of conflict avoidance by means of procedures and deliberation.[173] Nonetheless, a conceivable institution would be an additional forum for judicial dialogue[174] between courts of the different levels, but without the authority to take binding decisions.[175]

[170] I Pernice, 'Kompetenzabgrenzung im europäischen Verfassungsverbund', (2000) *Juristenzeitung* 866 at 874 and 876, suggests the establishment of a Subsidiarity Committee (*Subsidiaritätsausschuss*). Similar to this the proposal by J Schwarze, 'Kompetenzverteilung in der Europäischen Union und föderales Gleichgewicht', (1995) *Deutsches Verwaltungsblatt* 1265 at 1267 (a *Subsidiaritätsausschuss* as a body that would take binding decisions, though). See in that context also the debates in Working Group I of the Convention and the final report CONV 286/02.

[171] N Colneric, 'Der Gerichtshof der Europäischen Gemeinschaften als Kompetenzgericht', (2002) *Europäische Zeitschrift für Wirtschaftsrecht* 709.

[172] A different view is taken on the last point at least by A von Bogdandy and J Bast, 'Die vertikale Kompetenzordnung der Europäischen Union', (2001) *Europäische Grundrechte-Zeitschrift* 441 at 458, who emphasise the relevance of the European institutional structure.

[173] For the details see FC Mayer, 'Die drei Dimensionen der Europäischen Kompetenzdebatte', (2001) 61 *Zeitschrift für ausländisches öffentliches Recht und Völkerrecht*, 577 at 606 *et seq* (WHI-Paper 2/02 <http://www.whi-berlin.de/kompetenzdebatte.htm> (16 July 2004)).

[174] On this notion Pernice, above n 1, 29.

[175] It could be composed of ECJ judges and the highest-ranking national judges and could perhaps (also) deal with competence issues, without being an additional court taking binding decisions. In the past, judicial dialogue, the continuous conversation between the courts of the different levels by means of the Art 234 EC procedure, has proven to be a fundamental element of the constitutionalisation of the Community legal order driven forward by the ECJ. See also JHH Weiler, AM Slaughter and A Stone Sweet, 'Prologue', in Weiler, Slaughter and Stone Sweet (eds), above n 3, v und xii *et seq*; JHH Weiler, *The Constitution of Europe* (1999) 287 *et seq*, 322: "constitutional discourse".

Dialogue, discourse and conversation between the courts seem to bear a substantive problem-solving potential. In this sense, establishing a "Joint Senate of the highest courts and tribunals of the European Union" may be a good idea.

Beyond new institutions, another overall approach would be to strengthen structural safeguards of Member States' interests and specific safeguards of Member State courts that may play an indirect role in setting a threshold for national courts' claims of ultimate jurisdiction in questions of European law. There are two approaches that have been developed in the US in order to elucidate the relationship between federal level and state level, which may aid a better understanding of the EU. The theory of *Political Safeguards of Federalism*[176] emphasises the safeguards of state interests by means of structural characteristics of the overarching (federal) level, which in turn allows courts to exercise self-restraint. It has been noted by Koen Lenaerts that this approach actually suits the EC/EU constellation even better than the US situation.[177] The problem in the present context is, that in order to justify judicial self-restraint of Member State courts, it is the Member State courts themselves that have to be convinced that structural safeguards of Member State interests are adequate at the European level. Decisions such as the German *BVerfG's Maastricht* judgment however, demonstrate that such conviction is by no means forthcoming.

The basic concept behind *judicial federalism* in the US is the guarantee of autonomous and comprehensive powers for the state courts in a multilevel system. Some of the doctrines and mechanisms developed in the US in that context[178] may be of some interest for the EU. A procedure similar to the Certification procedure (whereby Federal courts submit references to State courts on questions of State law) could, for example, be helpful in all cases where provisions at the European level (e.g. Article 6(3) EU, see below) can be interpreted as referring to national law. Such a procedure would also emphasise the autonomy of Member State courts and counteract the impression of there being a hierarchy between the courts of the different levels.

Finally, re-conceptualising primacy may help. Unconditionally accepting primacy of European law over any national law has been equated to the creation of Federal statehood at the EU level.[179] The term that is used in the Swedish debate for the unconditional acceptance of primacy, *prostration*,[180] is even more graphic, as it symbolises the utmost kind of humble subordination. The surrender of possibilities of using constitutional law to fend off

[176] H Wechsler, 'The Political Safeguards of Federalism', (1943) 54 *Columbia L Rev* 543; D Shapiro, *Federalism* (1995) 116 *et seq*; see also US Supreme Court, *Garcia v San Antonio Metropolitan Transit Authority*, 469 US 528 (1985).

[177] K Lenaerts, 'Constitutionalism and the Many Faces of Federalism', (1990) 38 *AJCL* 205 at 222.

[178] For a detailled account Mayer, above n 3, 310 *et seq*.

[179] M Herdegen, 'Maastricht and the German Constitutional Court', (1991) 31 *CML Rev*, 235 at 240.

[180] O Ruin, 'Suède', in J Rideau (ed), *Les Etats membres de l'Union européenne* (1997) 440.

the primacy claim of European law is viewed as subordination under a "foreign" power. Note, though, that such subordination is not a merely theoretical idea, but, in the case of the Netherlands for example, part of the constitutional law of the land. The Irish solution of a protocol at the level of European primary law to preserve the sacrosanctity of national constitutional provisions on abortion could be regarded as simply being peculiar to the specific anti-abortion provision of the Irish Constitution. But it may be read more broadly as a revocation of European law's claim to primacy in respect of specific Member State interests, which are of particular importance in a given case. Consideration for Member State matters is not such an unusual concept. Indeed it may be found in the original treaties. Examples include the public service (Article 39(4) EC) and official authority exceptions (Article 45 EC) and the exceptions from the fundamental freedoms in Articles 30, 46 and 55 EC,[181] all of which are uniform concepts of Community law. It is also conceivable then that a common set of fundamentals of national constitutional law could be established, which could be declared exempt from the primacy of European law.[182]

Article 6(3) EU goes beyond mere Union-wide exceptions to European law. According to this provision, the European Union shall respect the national identities of the Member States. Here, a uniform European concept of national identities would be meaningless. This provision clearly refers back to the Member States. As national identity arguably includes constitutional identity,[183] Article 6(3) EU could be seen as a starting point on the European level to revoke the claim of primacy of European law over the Member States' constitutional identity. One may ask how the concept of national identity can be given meaning on the European level. One answer could be to include the Member States into the process of clarification of the concept: it is hardly surprising that it is an Irish academic contribution that develops the idea inherent to Article 6(3) EU of protecting fundamental (constitutional) national choices further into attributing to national courts of last instance the role of determining the content of such choices, as recognised and protected by European law.[184] This is where a European

[181] For an overview, see DR Phelan, *Revolt or Revolution* (1997) 422 *et seq*.

[182] See B de Witte, 'Droit communautaire et valeurs constitutionnelles nationales', (1991) *Droits* 87, who, attempting to define such a set of common fundamentals, acknowledges that the crucial problem of the respective Member States' specific constitutional provisions which shape national constitutional identity remains ("identité constitutionnelle nationale", *ibid*, 95).

[183] See Art I-5 CT-Conv (Art 5 CT-IGC).

[184] Phelan, above n 181, 416. In order to avoid a revolt or a (legal) revolution and to maintain the legitimacy of the national legal orders, *Phelan* suggests an amendment to the treaties which would give primacy (over European law) to basic principles of the Member States' constitutions relating to life, liberty, religion, and the family, which are predicated on visions of personhood and morality (not of the market or the proper distribution of goods) peculiar to each Member State. The rights through which these principles find expression would be regarded as superior to European law within their sphere of application. The exact range of this reservation would be established by the respective national courts or other institutions of

version of the American Certification procedure mentioned earlier could be helpful. The core idea of considerations for constitutional principles of the Member States on the European level can also be detached from Article 6(3) EU: one proposal suggests a duty for the Community, in conjunction with Article 10 EC, to consider and respect national constitutional structures when exercising European competences.[185]

To sum up: there is indeed a set of tools and instruments which could be used to minimise the friction between the highest national courts and the ECJ. Firstly, a modification of the law is a possibility, with a view to clarifying the scope of the primacy principle, particularly in relation to the national constitutions. Other, complementary legal options include adopting a type of judicial federalism and relying on the courts' self-restraint on the condition of political-structural safeguards of Member State interests. One may also consider institutional solutions with a view to the creation of juridical or political institutions that bring together the European and the Member State levels, or solving selected conflicts by modifying the allocation of competences.

2. Adopting a Theoretical Perspective

a) Existing Approaches

One way to approach differences between national courts and the ECJ is to reject either one or the other position by legal arguments.[186] The efficacy of this kind of approach is rather limited, as the indications are that neither national courts, such as the *BVerfG*, nor the ECJ are willing to surrender ground to the respective counter position.

last resort, *ibid*, 416, 417 *et seq*. Critical of *Phelan* MP Maduro, 'The Heteronyms of European Law', (1999) 5 *ELJ* 160 and N MacCormick, 'Risking Constitutional Collision in Europe?', (1998) 18 *Oxford Journal of Legal Studies* 517. See in that context also DR Phelan, 'The Right to Life of the Unborn v the Promotion of Trade in Services', (1992) 55 *MLR* 670.

[185] On that proposal Folz, above n 22, 387. In the German debate, the principle in Art 10 EC is typically referred to as Union loyalty (*Unionstreue*), a concept reminiscent of federal comity or loyalty (*Bundestreue*).

[186] This approach was adopted, for example, by commentators on the *Maastricht* decision, in that they repeatedly attempted to prove either the *BVerfG* or the ECJ "wrong" with arguments based either in constitutional law (for the position of the *BVerfG* Kirchhof, above n 95, 965; G Hirsch, 'Europäischer Gerichtshof und Bundesverfassungsgericht—Kooperation oder Konfrontation?', (1996) *Neue Juristische Wochenschrift* 2457, attempts to disprove the position of the *BVerfG* with arguments taken from the German Constitution) or in European law (see eg Tomuschat, above n 121, 494 *et seq*; for further references Mayer, above n 3, 117), and occasionally even in public international law, T Schilling, 'The Autonomy of the Community Legal Order', (1996) 37 *Harv Int LJ* 389; critical Weiler, above n 175, 286 *et seq*. See also A Paulus, 'Kompetenzüberschreitende Akte von Organen der Europäischen Union—Die Sicht des Völkerrechts', in B Simma and C Schulte (eds), *Akten des 23. Österreichischen Völkerrechtstages* (1999) 49. For a conciliatory interpretation of the divergent positions see eg I Pernice, Einheit und Kooperation, in *Gedächtnisschrift Grabitz*, above n 122, 523 (534 *et seq*).

A position seemingly inspired by this view touches upon the limits of legal reasoning. It considers this type of conflict unresolvable on a legal level. In terms of legal theory, this can be conceptualised as a conflict of *Grundnorms* in the Kelsenian sense, for which no further legal solution is available.[187] From this point of view, the ECJ and the highest national courts and tribunals could be considered *Grenzorgane*, or borderline institutions, in the Verdrossian sense: that is, institutions bound by law, but not subject to any legal control, so that the resolution of a conflict is a merely political or sociological matter,[188] and at the end of the day a "question of power".[189] This is also the core of the argument of those who propose leaving the "ultimate umpire" question open and unresolved.[190] The attraction of these latter approaches is without any doubt their level-headed pragmatism. It is likely that these approaches are inspired by some kind of calm confidence that the friction between the courts will not escalate into open conflict. And it cannot be denied that the frictions between the courts are easier to overlook than open conflicts.

What remains a problem, though, is that these approaches—in particular when referring to a conflict of *Grundnorms*—are probably too hastily giving up on what law, and constitutional law in particular, is all about: legal certainty and the legal constraint of power. After all, there is also some evidence that the national courts' positions have caused some harm in terms of legal certainty already. In Germany, some lower court judges can give a detailed account of how the *BVerfG's* concept of ultra vires acts did induce law-suits against European acts in national courts.

In search for concepts, one may also consider the "relationship of co-operation" (*Kooperationsverhältnis*) invented by the German *BVerfG* in its case law to describe the relationship between the ECJ and the highest national courts of Member States. One should note though that the *BVerfG* refers to the relationship of co-operation in the *Maastricht* decision only in the context of the protection of fundamental rights.[191] This leads back to the difference between the two categories "ultra vires acts" and "acts violating fundamental rights as accorded by the German

[187] See M Heintzen, 'Die "Herrschaft" über die Europäischen Gemeinschaftsverträge—Bundesverfassungsgericht und Europäischer Gerichtshof auf Konfliktkurs?', (1994) 119 *Archiv des öffentlichen Rechts* 564; N MacCormick, 'The Maastricht-Urteil: Sovereignty Now', (1995) 1 *ELJ* 259; W-D Grussmann, 'Grundnorm und Supranationalität', in von Danwitz *et al* (eds), above n 19, 47 *et seq*.

[188] See A Verdross, *Völkerrecht* (1950) 24 *et seq*, referring to *Hans Kelsen*.

[189] J Isensee, 'Vorrang des Europarechts und deutsche Verfassungsvorbehalte—offener Dissens', in J Burmeister (ed), *Verfassungsstaatlichkeit: Festschrift für K Stern zum 65. Geburtstag* (1997) 1265.

[190] See JA Frowein, 'Das Maastricht-Urteil und die Grenzen der Verfassungsgerichtsbarkeit', (1994) 54 *Zeitschrift für ausländisches öffentliches Recht und Völkerrecht*, 1 at 7.

[191] *Entscheidungen des Bundesverfassungsgerichts* 89, 155 at 175 and Leitsatz 7.

Constitution".[192] Although the *BVerfG* has used this concept of a relationship of co-operation since the *Maastricht* decision,[193] the nature and scope of this concept remain ill-defined and require further clarification.[194]

b) Embedding the Problem into a Modern Concept of Constitutionalism

As was explained earlier, possibilities for dealing with the differences between the courts by shaping the legal environment do exist. Article 35 EU and Article 68 EC, for example, suggest the possibility for the Member States to "clip the ECJ's wings".[195] The fact that the possibilities are not followed through may indicate that the problem simply is not serious enough or not taken seriously enough to change the law. Another explanation is that national governments simply do not understand the problem.[196] Or could it be that the conflict between the courts itself has a role to play in the relationship between EU and Member States—that of indirectly safeguarding Member State interests? On that reading, the claims of Member State courts of ultimate jurisdiction would allow Member States to circumvent European law obligations that are not in line with their interests. Leaving the question of ultimate jurisdiction open thus appears to be in the interest of Member States, as reserving the right of Member State courts to claim ultimate jurisdiction could be considered a kind of compensation for the ever-decreasing influence of Member States on decision-making at the European level. Thus, national court claims of ultimate jurisdiction may even bear some stabilising potential, as they may well lead to minority

[192] A different view seems to be adopted by R Scholz, 'Zum Verhältnis von europäischem Gemeinschaftsrecht und nationalem Verwaltungsverfahrensrecht', (1998) *Die Öffentliche Verwaltung* 261 at 267. He transfers the concept of a "relationship of co-operation" (*Kooperationsverhältnis*) from the realm of fundamental rights to the field of competences, assuming that a "similar relationship of co-operation" exists there as well. In fact, Scholz establishes a relationship of court-competition in the area of competences between ECJ and *BVerfG*. Academic writings before the *Maastricht* decision also suggested co-operation between *BVerfG* and ECJ in the context of fundamental rights only, and not for ultra vires acts, see R Streinz, *Bundesverfassungsgerichtlicher Grundrechtsschutz und Europäisches Gemeinschaftsrecht* (1989) 304 *et seq.*

[193] Above nn 114 and 34.

[194] See in that context M Zuleeg, in *Alternativkommentar zum Grundgesetz* (2001), Art 23, paras 32 *et seq* ("Verhältnis der Zusammenarbeit", a relationship of working together) and the recurring wording of the ECJ since the Order concerning the admissibility of third party interventions, Case 6/64, Order of 3 June 1964, *Costa v ENEL* [1964] ECR 614, on the "cooperation between the Court of Justice and the national courts" (in the German version "Zusammenarbeit des Gerichtshofes mit den staatlichen Gerichten", p 1307 (1309) of the German language edn of the ECR), see also "spirit of cooperation" in Case 244/80, *Foglia* [1981] ECR 3045, para 20, or the obligation of also the courts to promote "the principle of sincere cooperation" ("Grundsatz der loyalen Zusammenarbeit") laid down in Art 10 EC, Case C-50/00 P, *UPA v Council* [2002] ECR I-6677, para 42.

[195] See Alter, above n 66, 197. The first reference under Art 35 EU was Cases C-187/01 and 385/01, *Gözütok* [2003] ECR I-1345.

[196] See Alter, above n 66, 182 *et seq,* who points to the different time horizons and focuses of politicians and judges.

opinions among Member States, e.g. in a vote, to be taken into consideration at the European level,[197] contributing to maintaining the balance between the two levels.

The challenge for European constitutional legal science is to capture phenomena of European constitutional reality within a modern concept of constitutionalism. Friction between courts and the function of this friction are a part of this European constitutional reality.

aa) Clarification: What Constitution? Constitutions, Verfassungsverbund and Multilevel Constitutionalism

(1) Constitutions and the Concept of *Verfassungsverbund*

Whether it is accurate or desirable to speak of the existence of a European Constitution is subject to debate, to say the least. The introduction of a Constitutional Treaty would not settle this debate.[198] The critics do not only query the de-coupling of the concept of constitution from the concept of "State".[199] They also point to the risk of weakening the national constitution, inherent in the idea of a European Constitution, since the structural security built into national constitutions is called into question. And, the argument continues, a constitution is the enactment of an existing legal culture, which must be developed to some degree, and this level of development has not yet been achieved as regards the EU.[200] Such an emphatic approach to the concept of constitution may have numerous advantages, not least the familiarity of the interpreters of the constitution with this concept.

In consideration of the developments at the suprastate level throughout the second half of the 20th century, a different strand of constitutional thought has called for a "rethinking of the concept of constitution".[201] It seems to me that under the changed circumstances of a "post-national constellation" (*Jürgen Habermas*),[202] a more pragmatic concept of constitutionalism, emphasising that there is no state or public power beyond that

[197] For the exploitation of national constitutional courts' positions see M Hilf, 'Solange II: Wie lange noch Solange?', (1987) *Europäische Grundrechte-Zeitschrift,* 1 at 2: "In den politischen Beratungen vor allem des Rates wurde gelegentlich die Karte der Karlsruher Richter als letztes Mittel ausgespielt." [In the political deliberations in particular in the Council, occasionally pointing to the judges in Karlsruhe was used as a last resort].

[198] Technically, the Constitutional Treaty is still a treaty of public international law.

[199] See eg J Isensee, 'Staat und Verfassung', in J Isensee and P Kirchhof (eds), *Handbuch des Staatsrechts* (1987), vol I, § 13, paras 1, 3 *et seq*, and the references in C Grabenwarter, (2000) 60 *Veröffentlichungen der Vereinigung der Deutschen Staatsrechtslehrer* 290 at 292.

[200] P Kirchhof, 'Große Entwürfe und kleine Schritte', (2001) *Handelsblatt,* 8 August.

[201] P Badura, 'Bewahrung und Veränderung demokratischer und rechtsstaatlicher Verfassungsstruktur in den internationalen Gemeinschaften', (1966) 23 *Veröffentlichungen der Vereinigung der Deutschen Staatsrechtslehrer*, 34 at 95.

[202] J Habermas, *Die postnationale Konstellation* (1998) 91 *et seq*; see also M Zürn, 'The State in the Post-National Constellation', *ARENA Working Papers* WP 99/35, <http://www.arena.uio.no> (16 July 2004); see also D Curtin, *Postnational Democracy* (1997) 5, 48 *et seq*, 51 *et seq*; J Shaw, 'Postnational constitutionalism in the European Union', (1999) 18 *Journal of European Public Policy* 579 at 586 *et seq*.

established by the constitution,[203] is probably more helpful in explaining the phenomena relating to European integration.

As far as the European Union is concerned, there are two observations that seem to be relevant in the present context: First, there already exists European public authority or public power in the EU, which affects the individual directly in his or her legal status.[204] Second, at least the German Constitution points beyond itself by referring to the objective of a unified Europe[205] in the Preamble and in Article 23(1). With this in mind, one may answer the question of whether there is a constitutional dimension to European integration in the affirmative. One possible conceptualisation of this constitutional dimension is to depict "the" European Constitution as a complementary structure of national and European constitutions.[206] This concept is known as *Verfassungsverbund* (multilevel constitutionalism).[207] The closest literal

[203] A Arndt, 'Umwelt und Recht', (1963) *Neue Juristische Wochenschrift* 24 at 25: "In einer Demokratie gibt es an Staat nicht mehr, als seine Verfassung zum Entstehen bringt" [In a democracy, there is no more to a "State" than established by the constitution]; see also P Häberle, *Verfassungslehre als Kulturwissenschaft* (1998) 620.

[204] The description of *Gemeinschaftsgewalt* as *Herrschaftsgewalt* is already suggested by Badura, above n 201, 59.

[205] "zur Verwirklichung eines vereinten Europas".

[206] A different concept is, for example, the concept of a "dual-constitution" (T Öhlinger, 'Die Verfassung im Schmelztiegel der europäischen Integration: Österreichs neue Doppelverfassung', in *id*, *Verfassungsfragen einer Mitgliedschaft zur Europäischen Union* (1999) 165 *et seq*; P Pernthaler, 'Die neue Doppelverfassung Österreichs', in H Haller *et al* (eds), *Staat und Recht: Festschrift für G Winkler* (1997) 773); see in that context the Austrian VfGH, Decision of 9 December 1999, *Europäische Zeitschrift für Wirtschaftsrecht* (2001) 219 (222)—*Reverse discrimination.* For more references on the debate see A Peters, *Elemente einer Theorie der Verfassung Europas* (2001); P Craig, 'Constitutions, Constitutionalism, and the European Union', (2001) 7 *ELJ*, 125; D Blanchard, *La constitutionalisation de l'Union européenne* (2001).

[207] The term was coined by I Pernice, 'Bestandssicherung der Verfassungen', in R Bieber and P Widmer (eds), *L'espace constitutionnel européen* (1995) 225 at 261 *et seq*, see also *id*, 'Europäisches und nationales Verfassungsrecht', (2001) 60 *Veröffentlichungen der Vereinigung der Deutschen Staatsrechtslehrer* 163 *et seq*, with further references. Conceived in 1995 as an alternative concept to the *Staatenverbund* (above n 224), the notion is increasingly used detached from its original context, eg in PM Huber, (2001) 60 *Veröffentlichungen der Vereinigung der Deutschen Staatsrechtslehrer*, 194 *et seq*. On *Verbund* as a concept of order E Schmidt-Aßmann, 'Europäische Verwaltung zwischen Kooperation und Hierarchie', in *Festschrift Steinberger*, above n 115, 1375 at 1381 *et seq*. The term multilevel constitutionalism was introduced in I Pernice, 'Constitutional Law Implications for a State Participating in a Process of Regional Integration. German Constitution and "Multilevel Constitutionalism"', in E Riedel (ed), *German Reports. XV. International Congress on Comparative Law* (1998) 40 *et seq*; see also I Pernice, 'Multilevel constitutionalism and the Treaty of Amsterdam', (1998) 36 *CML Rev* 703 (WHI-Paper 4/99 <http://www.whi-berlin.de/pernice-cmlrev.htm> (16 July 2004)); I Pernice, FC Mayer and S Wernicke, 'Renewing the European Social Contract. The Challenge of Institutional Reform and Enlargement in the Light of Multilevel Constitutionalism', (2001) 12 *King's College Law Journal* 61 (WHI-Paper 11/01 <http://www.whi-berlin.de/socialcontract.htm> (16 July 2004)); I Pernice, 'Multilevel Constitutionalism in the European Union', (2002) 5 *EL Rev* 511; J Shaw, *Law of the European Union* (2000) 179 *et seq*. For a French version of the concept as *constitution composée* I Pernice and FC Mayer, 'De la constitution composée de l'Europe', (2000) *Revue Trimestrielle de Droit Européen* 623 (WHI-Paper 1/01 <http://www.whi-berlin.de/pernice-mayer.htm> (16 July 2004)), for an Italian version see 'La Costituzione integrata dell'Europa' in G Zagrebelsky (ed), *Diritti e Costituzione nell'Unione Europea* (2003) 43 (WHI-Paper 7/03 (2003) <http://www.whi-berlin.de/costituzione.htm> (16 July 2004)).

translation of this term is compound of constitutions.[208] According to this concept, a European constitution already exists, and arises out of both national and European constitutional levels. European and national constitutional law form two levels of a unitary system in terms of substance, function and institutions.[209] On this reading, the principle of primacy in application (*Anwendungsvorrang*) does not imply a hierarchy of norms in the sense of the general hierarchical superiority or inferiority of either European or national (constitutional) law:[210] "The hallmark of the *Verfassungsverbund* is its non-hierarchic structure".[211] One may identify as the deeper basis of validity for this European compound constitution the individual, to whom the public powers allocated to both the national and European component constitutions may be traced back.[212] This is different from classical international law constructs, and this is also where a justification of the concept of primacy may be found.[213]

(2) Multilevel Systems

Josef Isensee's comment that the EC/EU is slipping away from established, traditional typologies of public international and constitutional law[214] illustrates why one may have to try and go beyond the traditional typologies in an even more principled way, and establish new concepts such as "multilevel systems".

[208] See in that context the concept suggested by N Bamforth and P Leyland (eds), *Public Law in a Multi-Layered Constitution* (2003) 3 *et seq*, with power diffused "vertically upwards and downwards".

[209] Pernice, above n 207, 173

[210] This may be the difference between supremacy and primacy. On hierarchies see R Bieber and I Salomé, 'Hierarchy of Norms in European Law', (1996) 33 *CML Rev* 907 at 912. See on this Spanish Tribunal Constitutional, Case 6603/2004, Declaration 1/2004.

[211] Pernice, above n 207, 185, emphasising the difference between *Verbund* (compound) and *Verband* (association). Critical Nettesheim, *German report for the XX. FIDE conference 2002*, *Europarecht* suppl 2 (2004) 7 <http://www.fide2002.org> (16 July 2004).

[212] In that sense I Pernice, 'Die Europäische Verfassung', in *Festschrift Steinberger*, above n 115, 1319 at 1324; see also I Pernice, FC Mayer and S Wernicke, above n 207, 64 *et seq*, 68 *et seq*. The problematic nature of this approach's emphasis on the individual is highlighted inter alia by UK Preuss, 'Contribution to the discussion', (2000) 60 *Veröffentlichungen der Vereinigung der Deutschen Staatsrechtslehrer*, 384 *et seq*.

[213] All this cannot be explored here in more detail. On the concepts of European constitutionalism see also the contribution by C Möllers in this volume.

[214] J Isensee, ''Integrationsziel Europastaat?', in O Due, M Lutter and J Schwarze (eds), *Festschrift für U Everling zum 70. Geburtstag* (1995) 567. See also GF Schuppert's comment that the Community may only be understood with a way of thinking and a terminology which pays tribute to the specifics and the process-oriented nature of the EC: 'Zur Staatswerdung Europas', (1994) *Staatswissenschaften und Staatspraxis* 35 at 60.

(a) Objections to the Traditional Repertoire of Terms and Concepts

The objections raised against the "traditional repertoire of terms and concepts"[215] typically used to describe non-unitary systems within which there are competing public powers are numerous.[216]

Even concepts such as *Verfassungsverbund* (multilevel constitutionalism), which seek to avoid the trappings of traditional terms and concepts, encounter objections that point to the danger of blurring responsibilities, of

[215] Schuppert, above n 214, 53. See also E-W Böckenförde, *Staat, Nation, Europa* (1999) 8, according to whom we are in a state of transition, where traditional dogmatic categories and structures capture the changing realities only in part or not at all ["...wir in einer Situation des Übergangs stehen, in der überkommene dogmatische Kategorien und Strukturen die sich verändernde Wirklichkeit nur noch zum Teil oder gar nicht mehr normativ übergreifen"].

[216] *Staat* and *Staatlichkeit* (statehood) have been coined the "central complex of German constitutional psychology" from an outside observer's perspective, P Allott, 'The Crisis of European Constitutionalism', (1997) 34 *CML Rev* 439 at 444; see also JHH Weiler, 'The State "über alles"', in *Festschrift Everling, above* n 214, 1651; see on that C Möllers, *Staat als Argument* (2000) 407. Hugo Preuss considered the elimination of the term "sovereignty" from constitutional theory to be a precondition of any kind of development of a modern constitutional theory at the end of the 19th century—already more than 100 years ago, H Preuss, *Gemeinde, Staat, Reich als Gebietskörperschaften* (1889) 92, 135; see S Oeter, 'Souveränität und Demokratie als Probleme in der "Verfassungsentwicklung" der Europäischen Union', (1995) 55 *Zeitschrift für ausländisches öffentliches Recht und Völkerrecht* 659 at 704; on sovereignty in public international law also S Oeter, 'Souveränität—ein überholtes Konzept?', in *Festschrift Steinberger*, above n 115, 259 at 283 *et seq*. For the French debate F Chaltiel, *La souveraineté de l'Etat et l'Union européenne, l'exemple français* (2000). Concepts such as "autonomous legal order" or "independent legal system" will always lead back to equally unclear concepts such as "independent source of effectiveness" of a legal order. "Federalism" encounters the difficulty of finding some common understanding of this term and concept from the outset. The difficulties in discussing the concept of federalism are illustrated by the discussion on P Lerche, 'Föderalismus als nationales Ordnungsprinzip', (1964) 21 *Veröffentlichungen der Vereinigung der Deutschen Staatsrechtslehrer*, 66 at 105 *et seq*, in particular 109, 120 *et seq*, 124, 125, 136. See also T Koopmans, 'Federalism: The wrong debate', (1992) 29 *CML Rev*, 1047 at 1051; O Beaud, 'Föderalismus und Souveränität', (1996) *Der Staat* 45; or Armin von Bogdandy's attempt to develop the concept of a "supranational Union"—at least on a terminological level—into the concept of a "supranational Federation": A von Bogdandy, 'Die Europäische Union als supranationale Föderation', (1999) *integration* 95; A von Bogdandy, *Supranationaler Föderalismus als Wirklichkeit und Idee einer neuen Herrschaftsform* (1999) 63, n 280. See also the contributions to K Nicolaidis and R Howse (eds), *The Federal Vision* (2001). As for "constitution", any attempt to establish a substantive understanding of this term for non-statal entities meets with resistance and brings about a debate not only on the link between statehood and constitution, but also on the basis of a legal order, the exact location of sovereignty, the core of federalism etc. See already Carl Schmitt's critique of Alfred Verdross' attempt (*Die Verfassung der Völkerrechtsgemeinschaft*) to establish a constitution of the international community based on a *Grundnorm "pacta sunt servanda"*, C Schmitt, *Verfassungslehre* (1928) 69 and 363 *et seq*. For the concept of a constitution of the international community see also A Verdross and B Simma, *Universelles Völkerrecht* (1984) § 75 *et seq*, with further references. On the UN-Charter as a constitution of the international community also B Simma, 'From Bilateralism to Community Interest in International Law', 250 *Recueil des Cours* (1994-VI) 217 at 258 *et seq*. For tendencies of constitutionalisation at the WTO level see M Nettesheim, 'Von der Verhandlungsdiplomatie zur internationalen Verfassungsordnung', in CD Claasen *et al* (eds), *In einem vereinten Europa dem Frieden der Welt zu dienen...: Liber amicorum T Oppermann* (2001) 381 *et seq*; R Howse and K Nicolaidis, 'Legitimacy and Global Governance: Why Constitutionalizing the WTO is a Step too Far', in P Sauve *et al* (eds), *Equity, Efficiency and Legitimacy* (2001).

falling into joint decision traps,[217] of the "federal-state-kind-of-thought dependency of compound constructions", and of potential "blueprint traps".[218]

The comparative law context which is inherent in European integration also speaks in favour of referring to an analytical concept such as that of a "multilevel system", which is as neutral as can be. The variety of legal and constitutional concepts in Europe arising out of differences in language and legal culture (as may easily be illustrated by the different understandings of state, federalism, sovereignty and constitution), necessitates an enormous amount of conceptual and terminological clarification before one uses these terms and notions in the EU context.[219]

What is interesting is that the quest for neutral analytical concepts to elucidate new and recent phenomena is also taking place in the realm of social science,[220] with—in part—the same motivation as in law, namely to overcome the fixation with the state as the dominant form of political organisation.[221]

Moreover, what speaks in favour of trying to develop a more neutral concept such as that of a "multilevel system" is the very nature of the subject of scrutiny already: the particular conceptual form and shape of the EU, which is open and must remain so.[222] There are indications that the "traditional repertoire of terms and concepts" will be incapable of adequately explaining

[217] See the references to *Fritz Scharpf*'s work n 239 and 240.

[218] "föderalstaatliche Pfadabhängigkeit der Verbundkonstruktion", "Blaupausenfalle", GF Schuppert, 'Anforderungen an eine Europäische Verfassung', in H-D Klingenmann and F Neidhardt (eds), *Zur Zukunft der Demokratie* (2000), 207 at 216, 226; see also GF Schuppert, 'Contribution to the discussion', (2000) 60 *Veröffentlichungen der Vereinigung der Deutschen Staatsrechtslehrer*, 352.

[219] The mere translation of new terms and concepts such as *Staatenverbund* or *Verfassungsverbund*, for example into English, proves highly problematic: whereas *multilevel constitutionalism* (above n 207) carries at least the idea behind the concept, the English translation of *Staatenverbund* ("compound of states" is the term used in the ILM-translation of the *Maastricht* decision, 22 *ILM* (1994) 388) remains clumsy. Nuances between *Verbund* (compound) and *Verband* (association) pale into obscurity. Note in that context L Siedentop, *Democracy in Europe* (2000) 27, though, pointing to *Madison* in the Federalist papers, speaking of the "compound republic".

[220] See M Jachtenfuchs and B Kohler-Koch (eds), *Europäische Integration* (1996) 11 *et seq*; M Jachtenfuchs, 'Theoretical Perspectives on European Governance', (1995) 1 *ELJ* 115 at 119 *et seq*, pointing to the parallel legal debate; M Jachtenfuchs and B Kohler-Koch, 'Regieren im dynamischen Mehrebenensystem', *ibid*, 30. See also T König, E Rieger and H Schmitt (eds), *Das europäische Mehrebenensystem* (1996) 15. Donald Puchalla warned as early as 1971 in his influential article 'Of Blind Men, Elephants and International Integration', against destroying essentially new phenomena in international relations with blunt and inappropriate analytical instruments, (1971/72) 10 *JCMS* 267 at 269. Similar Ipsen, above n 81, 183 *et seq*, in 1972 on the dangers of thinking in categories of federal theory or public international law theory.

[221] Under the label of "New Institutionalism", there have been attempts to overcome the state-orientation of social science in general and of International Relations theory in particular, starting out from a broad concept of institutions, which includes formal and informal institutions as well as procedures. See S Bulmer, 'The Governance of the EU: A New Institutionalist Approach', (1994) 13 *Journal of Public Policy* 351; P Craig, 'The Nature of the Community', in P Craig and G de Búrca (eds), *The Evolution of EU law* (1999) 19 *et seq*.

[222] Ipsen, above n 81, 1050 *et seq*.

the specifics of this original "organisational reality" of the EU,[223] if, as is arguably the case for the EC/EU, this reality is a dynamic, ongoing process. This is because traditional and less traditional (*Staatenverbund*[224]) terms and concepts tend to be geared to static phenomena,[225] already presupposing a political unit and unity.[226] The EU as a "fluid system" may "hardly be described and circumscribed with rigid terms and notions".[227] This also applies to another concept, developed out of a perceived inadequacy of existing concepts[228] in the early days of European integration. It was first used by social scientists,[229] and was later taken on and developed further by lawyers:[230] the concept of supranationalism[231] or of a supranational Union.[232] Even if this term does manage to grasp the nature of the EC/EU,[233] it still tends to be oriented towards a concept of a static, already established entity.

The fact that there is "still no convincing concept" for the Community as a "*novum*" and, arguably, an "interim form",[234] may be another argument

[223] Schuppert, above n 214, 53.

[224] Thus the characterisation by the *BVerfG* in the *Maastricht* decision, *Entscheidungen des Bundesverfassungsgerichts* 89, 155 at 181, 190, and *Leitsatz* 8. The term *Staatenverbund* was initially coined by P Kirchhof, 'Contribution to the discussion', (1991) *Europarecht* suppl 1, 47; *id*, 'Der deutsche Staat im Prozeß der europäischen Integration', in Isensee and Kirchhof, above note 199, vol VII, § 183, para 69. B Kahl, 'Europäische Union: Bundesstaat—Staatenbund—Staatenverbund?', (1994) *Der Staat* 241, tells us that in terms of content, of system and of *telos*, the *Staatenverbund* corresponds to the *Staatenbund* (confederation), *ibid*, 245. U Di Fabio, *Das Recht offener Staaten* (1998) 140 *et seq*, describes the *Staatenverbund* as a transitory model in times of change. *Kirchhof* himself initially also used the term "*Staatenverband*", 'Deutsches Verfassungsrecht und Europäisches Gemeinschaftsrecht', (1991) *Europarecht* suppl 1, 11 at 16. The latter concedes at least an orginal form of its own to the European construct; the *Verbund* leaves this autonomy in the dark and deliberately emphasises that the States are the principal entities in European integration. Critical H Schneider, 'Die Europäische Union als Staatenverbund oder als multinationale "Civitas Europea"?', in *Gedächtnisschrift für E Grabitz*, above n 122, 677; uncritical M Kaufmann, *Europäische Integration und Demokratieprinzip* (1997) 214 *et seq*.

[225] Schuppert, above n 214, 53. For the process-driven nature of European integration see also R Pitschas, 'Europäische Integration als Netzwerkkoordination komplexer Staatsaufgaben', (1994) *Staatswissenschaften und Staatspraxis* 503 at 504.

[226] See I Pernice, 'Carl Schmitt, Rudolf Smend und die europäische Integration', (1995) 120 *Archiv des öffentlichen Rechts* 100 at 118.

[227] Isensee, above n 214, 567; for the problem of using "constitution" in that context Pernthaler, above n 11, 696.

[228] JHH Weiler, 'The Community System: the Dual Character of Supranationalism', (1981) 1 *YEL* 267 at 268.

[229] See EB Haas, *The Uniting of Europe* (1958) 59.

[230] In Germany, eg, by Badura, above n 201, 57 *et seq*; see also Ipsen, above n 81, 67 *et seq*.

[231] According to Ipsen, above n 81, 67 with further references, the term itself goes back to Nietzsche (*Der Wille zur Macht* (1885)). See in general also JHH Weiler, *Il sistema comunitario europeo* (1985).

[232] von Bogdandy, above n 216.

[233] K Stern, *Staatsrecht* (1984), vol I, 540 *et seq*; Isensee, above n 189, 1239 *et seq*.

[234] D Grimm, 'Europäischer Gerichtshof und nationale Arbeitsgerichte aus verfassungsrechtlicher Sicht', (1996) *Recht der Arbeit* 66 (English version 'The European Court of Justice and National Courts', (1997) 3 *Columbia J Eur L* 229). Grimm categorises the Community somewhere between State and International Organisation, not being a State because of the lacking self-determination on form and content of its political existence; not being an International Organisation because of a surplus of public authority.

related to European integration in favour of a concept more neutral than the traditional, established terms and concepts of traditional constitutional thought.[235]

(b) The Level Metaphor

Irrespective of the question of what exactly defines a multilevel system, one may already have doubts about whether the particular metaphor of distinct levels depicts the reality of non-unitary systems better than others. The metaphor of "levels" can typically[236] be found in theories of federalism and in social science descriptions of European integration.[237] There may be a problem with the image of different levels, used to describe non-unitary systems, though, as the term "level" suggests a super-/subordination and an impermeable separation of the levels.[238] The latter at least does not really correspond to the decision-making structure of the EC/EU, where, for example, the Council of Ministers is made up of members of the "other level" and where joint-decision trap phenomena[239] have reached a European dimension.[240]

Other common attempts to describe non-unitary systems include the centre-periphery model,[241] the pyramid model and the matrix model,[242] or the attempt to overcome the whole/components distinction by terming the Union and the Member States "centres" in the sense of a "polycentric system".[243] In the context of federal theory, the orthodox "layer model" has

[235] In the context of European integration, Pernice, above n 226, 120, considers an adaptation of the fundamental terms and concepts of constitutional theory to be possible though.

[236] In the field of law in Germany, Gunnar Folke Schuppert, Rainer Wahl and Udo Di Fabio have adopted the multilevel metaphor. See GF Schuppert, above n 218; R Wahl, 'Der Einzelne in der Welt jenseits des Staates', *Der Staat* (2001) 45 at 46 *et seq*; U Di Fabio, 'Mehrebenendemokratie in Europa. Auf dem Weg in die komplementäre Ordnung', Lecture given in the context of the FCE-series at Humboldt-University on 15. November 2001, <http://www.whi-berlin.de/difabio.htm> (16 July 2004). See also R Nickel, 'Zur Zukunft des Bundesverfassungsgerichts im Zeitalter der Europäisierung', (2001) *Juristenzeitung* 625 at 631. Critical P Badura, 'Contribution to the discussion', (2000) 60 *Veröffentlichungen der Vereinigung der Deutschen Staatsrechtslehrer* 353.

[237] Above n 220, in particular T König, E Rieger and H Schmitt, 16; see also R Mayntz, 'Föderalismus und die Gesellschaft der Gegenwart', (1990) 115 *Archiv des öffentlichen Rechts* 232; FW Scharpf, *Optionen des Föderalismus in Germany und Europa* (1994) 13; G Marks, L Hooghe and K Blank, *European Integration and the State (Manuscript)* (1994) 7, with further references. See also F Scharpf, 'Community and Autonomy. Multilevel Policy-Making in the European Union', *EUI Working Paper RSC* No 94/1.

[238] Schuppert reminds us that we are not the masters of the connotations of terms and concepts that we create, above n 218, 222.

[239] For more details on this concept FW Scharpf *et al*, *Politikverflechtung* (1976) 13 *et seq*; *id*, 'The joint-decision trap', (1988) 66 *Public Administration* 239; *id*, 'La trapolla della decisione congiunta', (1986) 17 *Stato e Mercato* 175.

[240] FW Scharpf, 'Die Politikverflechtungsfalle', (1985) 26 *Politische Vierteljahresschrift* 323.

[241] See eg JHH Weiler, 'The Transformation of Europe', (1991) 100 *Yale LJ* 2403 at 2408 *et seq*; see also D Elazar, *Exploring Federalism* (1987) 27 *et seq*

[242] Elazar, above n 241, 27 *et seq*.

[243] Von Bogdandy, above n 216, 217.

been complemented by a "marble cake model", where ingredients—meaning component entities—are less easy to distinguish.[244]

Compared to all these other models, the advantage of the "level" metaphor seems to be that it captures the horizontal juxtaposition of constituent entities better than, eg, the polycentric structure. Horizontal coupling is typical of complex social systems: *Renate Mayntz* refers to the work of American organisational theory scholar and Nobel prize winner *Herbert A. Simon* in that field,[245] who showed that this kind of structure corresponds to a structure principle typical of organic life forms that has been successful in evolution because of its effectiveness.

The objection which points to the joint-decision trap phenomenon can be rebutted in that even joint-decision traps and respective theories presuppose distinct and determinable units that develop into situations of joint-decision traps later on. It is in the sense of describing distinct and determinable units that "levels" are to be understood in the present context.

Furthermore, the image of distinct levels is not necessarily linked to "superordination", supervision and subordination. Levels may also be understood as platforms that may be at equal height in one case, at different heights in another, or even circling freely around each other.

(c) Multilevel Systems—Attempting a Definition

There are two empirical observations independent of concepts of constitution, state or federalism that appear to be beyond contestment: existing political entities are typically subdivided into component units for reasons of practicability.[246] Or existing political units unite to form a new political entity, without giving up their own quality as—now constituent—distinct, individual units. A sharing out of tasks between constituted or original overarching entities and their component sub-entities is agreed upon, which finds its legal expression in an allocation of powers or competences between the overarching unit and the sub-units.

Typically, there will be an overarching entity with a certain range of competences on one level and a multitude of entities each with an equally large range of competences—not, however, necessarily the same competences—on another level.[247] A (decision-making) level is characterised by one or

[244] M Grodzins, 'The Federal System', in A Wildavsky (ed), *American Federalism in Perspective* (1967) 257.

[245] 'The Achitecture of Complexity', in *Kommunikation* III/2, 1967, 55, quoted by Mayntz, above n 237, 241.

[246] On the aspect of size as a relevant factor for public authorities R Dahl, 'Federalism and the Democratic Process', in R Pennock and JW Chapman (eds), *Liberal Democracy* (1983) 95 *et seq*; R Dahl and E Tufte, *Size and Democracy* (1973) 137 *et seq*. From the perspective of organisational theories see in that context Mayntz, above n 237, 232 at 241 *et seq*, with further references.

[247] The term "overarching" is simply used to denote the relation of levels and entities towards each other. It is by no means used to suggest hierarchical superiority.

more (decision-making) entities with equal or similar competences. An entity may well be an overarching one, that covers several entities in the way just described, and itself be a component entity of another overarching entity.[248] Thus, in principle, multilevel systems may cover a multitude of levels. The entities in that context are political units with an original or attributed decision-making power and a certain degree of legal-organisational distinctiveness that makes them distinguishable in the first place.

Public power is thus not defined by the monopoly of power, the traditional concept used inter alia to define elements of sovereignty,[249] but rather by the mere decision-making power (leaving aside the question of enforcement capacity), typically expressed in the concrete form of norm- or law-making capacity. The decision-making power represents a subset of the elements that characterise the traditional concept of state and public power: the monopoly of force plus exclusive law-making powers.[250] The legal powers defined as competences take on a concrete form through a decision;[251] levels in the context of a legal multilevel system are decision-making levels.[252]

Decision in this context is a cipher for decision-making operating under the rule of law, i.e. determined by and organised according to law.[253] The emphasis on the element of decision instead of that of enforcement when defining public power may also be found elsewhere: The element of decision is the object and central paradigm of regime theory in social sciences, sometimes under the distinct label of "governance".[254]

A series of levels representing a multilevel system is distinguishable from the many other existing levels and entities by virtue of the factual and legal

[248] A German *Land* (state/region) is an overarching entity for municipalities and districts. The *Land*, in turn, is part of the Federal Republic, which is a Member State of the EU. For the emergence of new decision-making levels due to internationalisation Mayntz, above n 237, 243.

[249] The monopoly on the (legitimate) use of force as the basis for state and public authority structures is emphasised inter alia by M Weber, *Wirtschaft und Gesellschaft* (5th edn 1985) 835 *et seq*. See also von Bogdandy, above n 216, 211 *et seq*.

[250] Von Bogdandy, above n 216, 215.

[251] A similar approach is taken by R Stettner, *Grundfragen einer Kompetenzlehre* (1983) 73 *et seq*.

[252] For a similar concept Scharpf, above n 237, 25, 29 and Mayntz, above n 237, 232. See also Schuppert's description of the EC as a political entity with several decision-making levels, above n 214, 39, or as *Mehrebenenentscheidungssystem* (system of multilevel decision-making) by M Zürn, 'Über den Staat und die Demokratie in der Europäischen Union', *ZERP-Diskussionspapier* 3/95, 19 *et seq*. Whether one categorises entities with a relatively small norm- or law-making capacity, such as municipalities in Germany or French regions, as levels depends on how narrow one wishes the criteria of decision-making powers to be.

[253] See in this context the concept of the State suggested by H Heller, *Staatslehre* (1934) 228 *et seq*, according to whom the State is an organised entity of effective decision-making (*organisierte Entscheidungs- und Wirkungseinheit*); see also von Bogdandy, above n 216, 217.

[254] See S Krasner (ed), *International Regimes* (1983); F Kratochvil and JG Ruggie, 'International organization: a state of the art on an art of the state', (1986) 40 *International Organization* 753. A differentiated approach to the concept of decision is suggested by M Reisman and M McDougal, *International Law Essays* (1981) 4.

relationship between them. First, there is a specific factual relationship between the different levels of a multilevel system: Typically, a multilevel system will have one overarching unit on one side and a multitude of smaller entities on another level, the latter entities being a subset of the overarching unit in terms of territory and individuals. In addition to this factual relationship, there will typically be a specific legal bond among the entities and levels, which rests upon the factual link: the law of the distinct levels claims to be effective within the same territory—in principle, the individual may be granted rights and receive obligations from each of the levels. Legal acts of the different levels can thus cover identical or similar situations.

bb) The Role of Courts in a Multilevel System

(1) From Constitutional Court to Complementary Constitutional Adjudication?

If the European Constitution can be conceptualised as a complementary structure in the sense of multilevel constitutionalism (*Verfassungsverbund*), European constitutional adjudication may have to be conceptualised in a similar way.[255] On a positive reading, "the" European Constitutional Court would consist of both the highest national courts and tribunals and the ECJ. Since, from the theoretical perspective of multilevel constitutionalism, the national courts' and the ECJ's authority both stem from the individual, there is no presupposed hierarchy between the courts, but rather a duty of co-operation. The task of this composite European Constitutional Court would be that of a guardian and interpreter of the (composite) European Constitution. This concept of "the European constitutional court" clearly differs from the ideal that *Walter Hallstein* and others seemed to have in mind when they modelled the ECJ on the US Supreme Court.[256]

(2) Courts in a Multilevel System

Having chosen a neutral analytical concept, the multilevel system, and having merely observed that there is friction between the highest national courts and the ECJ, the fundamental consideration must be how to minimise the potential for conflict in the event of diverging claims of ultimate jurisdiction in multilevel systems. Empirical analysis indicates that ultimately, the subject of conflict in the relationship between the levels are the issue

[255] The German *BVerfG* stated already in *Entscheidungen des Bundesverfassungsgerichts* 73, 339 at 367 *et seq* (*Solange II*), that there is a "functional intertwinement of the European and Member State judiciaries", including a "partial functional incorporation of the ECJ into the domestic court system" ("funktionelle Verschränkung der Gerichtsbarkeit der Europäischen Gemeinschaften mit der Gerichtsbarkeit der Mitgliedstaaten" mit einer "teilweisen funktionalen Eingliederung des Europäischen Gerichtshofs in die mitgliedstaatliche Gerichtsbarkeit").

[256] W Hallstein, *Die Europäische Gemeinschaft* (5th edn 1979) 110. Pernthaler, above n 11, 693, also quotes J Monnet, *Les Etats Unis d'Europe Ont Commencé* (1955) 53.

of primacy and the question of the source of European law, its basis of validity. The latter question is controversial in the context of the concept of compound or multilevel constitutionalism (*Verfassungsverbund*), since the mere concept of constitutionalism implies a statement on the source of European law.[257] This question can be left open in the multilevel context.

As far as the primacy issue is concerned, the multilevel description exposes the minimum requirements for a conditional principle of primacy between distinct levels of public powers to function: the primacy question, at the end of the day, can be answered unambiguously only according to the content accorded to it at the overarching level. In the EU, this content is the principle of precedence in application (*Anwendungsvorrang*)[258] of the law of the overarching level. In order to avoid conflicts, though, any claims for elements of national law, in particular constitutions, to be exempt from the primacy of European law have to be recognised by both levels in principle, and determined consensually from both levels, in concrete cases.

This leads to the core question of where to locate ultimate jurisdictional claims of the highest *national* courts and tribunals at the *European* level. The answer points to Article 234 EC in a procedural perspective and to Article 6(3) EU in a substantive perspective. The interpretation of the latter norm has to be accomplished by both the highest national courts *and* the ECJ. The fundamental rights saga from *Solange I* up to the *Banana* decisions in front of the ECJ and the *BVerfG* seems to indicate that the respective courts of ultimate decision, guardians of the interests of the respective levels, are already working towards establishing a core of (constitutional) law exempt from the primacy of European law, and accepted as such from both levels.[259]

c) Objections to Complementary European Constitutional Adjudication[260]

Whether one starts out from multilevel constitutionalism or merely from a multilevel description of legal systems, the idea of a complementary structure of European constitutional adjudication raises numerous objections.

aa) Asymmetry The heterogeneity of the highest national courts and tribunals described earlier is not limited to the role of the judge, the language of the decisions and the acceptance of judge-made law in 25 and more Member States. There are also differences in the range of powers and jurisdiction of the highest national courts. Hence the concept of a complementary European

[257] See in that context H Hofmann, 'Von der Staatssoziologie zu einer Soziologie der Verfassung?', (1995) *Juristenzeitung* 1065.

[258] Though not in validity (*Geltungsvorrang*). above n 76 on the difference between primacy and supremacy in that context.

[259] See also Art 5 CT-IGC: "The Union shall respect the equality of Member States before the Constitution as well as their national identities, inherent in their fundamental structures, political and constitutional, inclusive of regional and local self-government."

constitutional judiciary leads to a very different shape of European constitutional law adjudication from Member State to Member State.

In Germany, for example, the strong constitutional court may claim exemption from European primacy for certain national constitutional law principles, whereas in the Netherlands, for lack of a constitutional court, this possibility does not exist.

One the one hand, this kind of asymmetry is intrinsic to the heterogeneity of the EU Member States, which is one of the crucial constitutional hallmarks of the Union.[261] On the other hand, proposals in some of the Member States for court reforms, going as far as the introduction of genuine constitutional courts may be part of a trend towards convergence,[262] promoted to some extent by the ultimate jurisdiction issue. This is indicated by the Swedish example, at least.[263] This may lead to an overall strengthening of influence of the courts in the EU.

Generally speaking, this is the point where the merits of the multilevel approach become apparent: the relevant borderline between public powers in the EU is the line between the European and the Member State levels. The way the fundamental rights issue developed is a good illustration that it may well be enough to have one single court of one level—in that case the German *BVerfG*—determining the constitutional interests of that level. This is not to say that the *BVerfG* may be some kind of role model for other courts in other Member States. It is simply to say that the reservations expressed by the *BVerfG* in the field of fundamental rights have contributed to making the case law of the ECJ clearer in this area. All Member States have benefited from this, whether or not they have a constitutional court which voiced similar national concerns as the *BVerfG*. In that sense, the *BVerfG* could be seen as not only the guardian of the German Constitution, but also a guardian of the interests of the Member State level generally. The same applies, of course, for the other highest national courts and tribunals in their respective positioning towards the ECJ.

[260] More general objections against the concept of (constitutional) judicial review as such and theories dealing with judicial review will not be addressed here, see for this debate U Haltern, *Verfassungsgerichtsbarkeit, Demokratie und Mißtrauen* (1998) in particular 169 *et seq*, with further references; for the American debate on judicial review A Bickel, *The Least Dangerous Branch* (1962); M Tushnet, *Taking the Constitution Away from the Courts* (1999).

[261] See in that context J Tully, *Strange multiplicity* (1995) 183 *et seq* (constitutions as "chains of continual intercultural negotiation"). According to Art IV-1 CT-Conv (Art 8 CT-IGC), the motto of the Union shall be: "United in diversity".

[262] Considering the number of States where judicial review of parliamentary decisions is still considered an anomaly, one cannot yet speak of a general convergence in Europe towards judicial review exercised by constitutional courts, but see Tomuschat, above n 3, 245 *et seq*. In any case, the new Member States and the candidates for accession to the EU have almost all established a constitutional court (see above, I).

[263] In the context of the constitutional reform required by accession to the EU, the Swedish government wanted to make sure that Swedish courts would have the same powers as far as European law is concerned as the German *BVerfG*, Justitiedepartmentet, 'Våra Grundlagar och EG—förlag till alternativ', *Departementsserien 1993:36*.

The objection that the ECJ and the highest national courts are not really comparable—in spite of occasional descriptions of the ECJ as a constitutional court[264]—carries particular weight. It possibly points to an asymmetry between the courts in question, which excludes any concept of complementary jurisdiction in respect of European constitutional law.[265] On that reading, the ECJ and the highest national courts and tribunals are just too different.

One fundamental difference, addressed earlier, is the absence of a "real" constitution. If constitutional adjudication can indeed be said to be characterised by a particularly large margin of interpretation, constitutional adjudication without a constitution could admittedly prove to be rather problematic.[266] I will not undertake a more detailed analysis of this problem at this juncture.

Other differences between national courts and the ECJ may be related to the fact that traditional concepts of separation of powers cannot simply be transferred to the European construct: such a view accords an entirely different role to the European judiciary in comparison to that of a supreme/constitutional national court.

Something that also distinguishes the ECJ from the highest national courts is the fact that it is an exception that individuals appear before the ECJ. In European procedural law, the Member States, the Commission and national courts (by way of references) are privileged parties. These are the ECJ's preferred interlocutors.[267] The ECJ has confirmed this in its recent case law, in opposition to the Court of First Instance and against the advice of the Advocate General.[268] This seems to indicate a conception of the ECJ's function as relating specifically to maintaining and strengthening European integration, rather than a concern for focusing on the protection of individual rights.[269] The Convention discussed introducing a fundamental rights

[264] J Schwarze (ed), *Der Europäische Gerichtshof als Verfassungsgericht und Rechtsschutzinstanz* (1983); O Due, 'A Constitutional Court for the European Communities', in D Curtin and D O'Keefe (eds), *Constitutional Adjudication in European Community and National Law* (1992) 3; K Alter, *Establishing the Supremacy of European Law* (2001) 225.

[265] A similar objection is made by P Badura, 'Contribution to the discussion', (2000) 60 *Veröffentlichungen der Vereinigung der Deutschen Staatsrechtslehrer* 353, against the multilevel concept, when pointing to the lack of comparability of the levels.

[266] Pernthaler, above n 11, 695, who opposes using the concept of constitution in the European context.

[267] See on this H Schepel and E Blankenburg, 'Mobilizing the European Court of Justice', in G de Búrca and JHH Weiler (eds), *The European Court of Justice* (2001) 9 (18 *et seq*). See also in that context the rather strict approach of the ECJ concerning the admissibility of third party interventions, Case 6/64, Order of 3 June 1964, *Costa* [1964] ECR 614.

[268] Case C-50/00 P, *UPA v Council* [2002] ECR I-6677; against AG Jacobs, Opinion of 21 March 2002, paras 59 *et seq*, and the Court of First Instance, Case T-177/01, *Jégo-Quéré v Commission* [2002] ECR II-2365, paras 41 *et seq*, 50; overruled by Case C-263/02 P, *Jégo-Quéré v Commission* [2004] ECR I-3425.

[269] H Rasmussen, *The European Court of Justice* (1998) 198 *et seq*. See also L Hooghe and G Marks, *Multi-Level Governance and European Integration* (2001) 26 *et seq*.

complaint,[270] modelled more or less on the German *Verfassungsbeschwerde*, as well as a substantial modification of Article 230(4) EC.[271] In the end, there was no agreement on opening up direct access to the European courts.[272]

The most serious objection in the present context is probably the one pointing to the differences in democratic legitimacy between the ECJ on the one hand and the highest national courts and tribunals on the other. Unlike the courts of some Member States, who take their decisions "in the name of the people",[273] the ECJ does not even reveal in whose name or on whose behalf it is speaking. This raises the question of who or what legitimises the ECJ. According to Article 223 EC, the European judges are appointed by the governments of the Member States without any parliamentary participation—neither of the European, nor of national parliaments.[274] In contrast, the judges of the German *BVerfG*, for example, are elected by the German *Bundestag* (Parliament) (Article 94 of the German Constitution). It is nevertheless true that the selection of ECJ judges can be democratically justified by chains of legitimacy, some of which are longer than others. However, it should be noted that European law does not prevent parliamentary participation at the Member State level, with the Austrian case providing an example.[275] The Constitutional Treaty slightly enhances transparency by introducing a panel which is to give an opinion on candidates' suitability to perform the duties of Judge and Advocate-General.[276]

[270] Suggested by N Reich, 'Zur Notwendigkeit einer Europäischen Grundrechtsbeschwerde', (2000) *Zeitschrift für Rechtspolitik* 375; see also Convention document CONV 72/02, point I3; CONV 354/02. For a possible consequence of a new focus on fundamental rights, a shift of paradigms, away from the market-driven economic community towards a fundamental rights community, see A von Bogdandy, 'Grundrechtsgemeinschaft als Integrationsziel', (2001) *Juristenzeitung* 157.

[271] See the final report of WG II, CONV 354/02 point C, and the debate within the Discussion circle on the Court of Justice (Circle I), CIRCLE I WD 08, para 17 *et seq;* CONV 543/03. See also the hearing of President of the ECJ *Rodríguez Iglesias* in Circle I on 17 February 2003, CONV 636/03 (against opening up Art 230(4) EC); the hearing of the President of the CFI *Vesterdorf* on 24 February 2003, CONV 588/03 (in favour of broadening Art 230(4) EC, similarly AG *Jacobs*, WG II WD 20, see also judge *Skouris*, WG II WD 19)). See also U Everling, 'Rechtsschutz im europäischen Wirtschaftsrecht auf der Grundlage der Konventsregeln', in J Schwarze (ed), *Der Verfassungsentwurf des Europäischen Konvents* (2004) 263; FC Mayer, 'Individualrechtsschutz im Europäischen Verfassungsrecht', (2004) *Deutsches Verwaltungsblatt* 606.

[272] See, however, Art I-28(1) CT-Conv (Art 29(1) CT-IGC) which guarantees access to justice.

[273] This aspect is highlighted in the comprehensive study by Dubos, above n 158, 855.

[274] The history of the recent appointments of the German judges Everling, Zuleeg and Hirsch is not exactly a success story, as all of them were one-term judges. This seems to indicate some deficiencies in the current procedure. Alter, above n 66, 200, reports that U Everling was initially seen as having a greater appreciation of the borders of EC authority, and that M Zuleeg, rather than being reappointed, was replaced by G Hirsch from Bavaria in part because of the perception that he was too willing to interpret European law expansively. The problem may simply be a lack of interest of the governments in the issue, though.

[275] Art 23c of the Austrian Constitution, the B-VG (*Bundes-Verfassungsgesetz*).

[276] Art 375 CT-IGC. There is still the problematic issue of former European Commission officials becoming judges or working for judges, which raises the question of informal channels between the Commission and the Court. This and the role of the judges' collaborators, the *référendaires*, who do not even appear on the Court's homepage, is something that has not attracted much scholarly attention so far.

Generally speaking, one will find numerous unanswered fundamental questions on the legitimacy of judges at the Member State level as well,[277] and the German procedure of selecting the highest judges by by way of parliamentary participation could itself be criticised for not being as transparent as, say, the US solution of public hearings of the prospective judges.

In the end, the utterly different understandings of and approaches to the nature and the range of democratic legitimacy of courts is probably simply the corollary of the heterogeneity of the Member States.

bb) The Evaporation of Responsibilities—Who is to Define the Common Good? There are more fundamental objections than asymmetry to a concept of complementary jurisdiction in European constitutional law. They concern the issue of accountability and the question of how to establish a concept of "common good" in such a complex system.

Just as a certain fuzziness or lack of clarity has developed over time in the realm of the executive between Council, national governments and administrative structures,[278] a composite structure of jurisdiction might be vulnerable to an unclear and ill-defined division of responsibilities and jurisdiction. This could lead to a vacuum of responsibility for fundamental rights protection *in concreto*, as the *Banana* cases[279] indicated. There, the principles were upheld, but the Banana importers went bankrupt. It would be a serious problem indeed if a forum for the definition of the common good,[280] the place where a concept of solidarity could also be developed, became less and less discernible. In this instance, solidarity-free individualisation would then have also reached the realm of constitutional law.

cc) Is there any Added Value in Theories of Composite Structures of Adjudication? The value of conceptualising what the courts in the EU do or should do by means of a non-hierarchic, composite multilevel structure may be summarised as follows: starting from a concept that covers the national and the European levels, and thus establishing responsibilities of adjudication on European constitutional law for both of them, the non-hierarchic relationship of the courts takes on a clearer form, constitutional clarity is enhanced and a reciprocal strengthening of constitutional bonds and limits is achieved.

[277] For a German perspective A Voßkuhle and G Sydow, 'Die demokratische Legitimation des Richters', (2002) *Juristenzeitung* 673. Pernice, above n 1, 36, emphasises the functional legitimacy of the European judiciary.

[278] See FC Mayer, 'Nationale Regierungsstrukturen und europäische Integration', (2002) *Europäische Grundrechte-Zeitschrift* 111 *et seq*.

[279] Above n 114.

[280] On the question of a "multilevel common good" ("Mehrebenen-Gemeinwohl") GF Schuppert, 'Die Zukunft der Daseinsvorsorge in Europa', in H-P Schwintowski (ed), *Die Zukunft der kommunalen EVU im liberalisierten Energiemarkt* (2002) 11 at 20 *et seq*; see also P Häberle, 'Gibt es ein europäisches Gemeinwohl?', in *Festschrift Steinberger*, above n 115, 1153 at 1166 *et seq*; R Uerpmann, *Das öffentliche Interesse* (1999) 266 *et seq*.

The multilevel approach can serve as a starting point to develop criteria for determining the limits of responsibilities and as a conceptual basis for the constitutional dialogue between the courts, which are allotted functions according to a specific concept of constitutionalism. That means rejecting the conflict paradigm and more readily accepting the co-operation paradigm. To some extent, the non-subordination of national courts could be explained and legitimised in terms of European constitutional law. It would no longer automatically be seen as an infringement of European law. In any case, there would be clear limits on how national courts may act, which would remove the foundations of misleading legal reasoning (particularly in respect of ultra vires acts[281]).

3. Interim Summary

The "frictional phenomena" that exist between the highest national courts and tribunals of the Member States and the ECJ can be legally analysed and their specific manifestations can be shaped by law. They have a function in the relationship between EU and Member States. There are theoretical tools which can help to constructively explain and conceptualise this function and the empirical findings of differences between the courts. By means of concepts such as the *Verfassungsverbund* or the multilevel system, the co-operation paradigm can be emphasised.

III. THE FUTURE OF THE RELATIONSHIP BETWEEN EUROPEAN AND NATIONAL COURTS

The courts have not been at the heart of the reform process between 2000 and 2004.[282] Neither the "Draft Treaty establishing a Constitution for Europe" of the 2002/2003 Convention[283] nor the modifications of that draft introduced along the ensuing Intergovernmental Conference in 2003/2004 and agreed upon in June 2004[284] contain substantive changes as far as the ECJ or the national courts are concerned. Numerous open questions remain.

[281] Above n 132 for examples of alleged "ausbrechende Rechtsakte".

[282] See in that context the Declaration (No 23) on the future of the Union annexed to the Treaty of Nice from 2000/2001 (Document CONFER 4820/00 and OJ C 80, 10.3.2001, 1); the Laeken declaration from 2001 (Conclusions of the Presidency, Laeken European Council, Annex I, 15 December 2001, Document SN 300/01, <http://ue.eu.int> (16 July 2004)).

[283] See document CONV 850/03. It is only at a very late stage that a forum for debating ECJ-related questions was introduced, albeit with a rather limited mandate. For the mandate of this "Discussion circle on the Court of Justice" (Circle I), see CONV 543/03. For the final report, see CIRCLE I WD 08.

[284] See CIG 50/03 as amended by CIG 81/04 and CIG 85/04.

1. The Courts and Core Topics of the Constitutional Debate Until 2004

In the context of the debate on the delimitation of European powers and competences[285] a new, additional Court of competence was suggested,[286] but not agreed upon. Still, the recurring—unsubstantiated[287]—accusation that the ECJ is not fulfilling its functions may have damaged the position of the ECJ, with destabilising side effects for the entire system of European constitutional law adjudication.

This is just one example of how debating constitutional topics that are not directly related to the courts may still generate side effects that affect the courts. This kind of side effect may also be detected in the institutional debate. The fact that in the future a more politicised Commission or, worse, a Commission more or less deprived of power, may no longer act as guardian of the treaties, could have an indirect effect on the Court, increasing its burden of responsibility to defend the supranational originality and independence of the entire integration project. The dichotomy of legislature and executive might be taken to imply that the separation of powers concept of the nation state can simply be applied to the EU. This is not necessarily the case. The judiciary may be the last remaining institution to be implementing the driving idea behind European integration of the last 50 years which was to mediate political conflict by means of law, and its (assumed) rationality.[288]

The extension of (qualified) majority voting (QMV) in the Council of Ministers is also an issue which is not prima facie dealing with courts, but which still affect the role of the courts. This is well illustrated by the Banana-regulation:[289] Germany actually voted against the regulation in the Council but was nonetheless bound by it, and then had to solve the massive fundamental rights problems that arose at home as a result. More generally speaking: extending QMV also means that governments may no longer be able to act as guardians of certain interests in the Council. To the extent

285 According to the "Declaration on the future of the Union" annexed to the Treaty of Nice, one point for discussion was "inter alia" the question of "how to establish and monitor a more precise delimitation of powers between the European Union and the Member States, reflecting the principle of subsidiarity".

286 Above n 165 for proposals made by two judges of the German *Bundesverfassungsgericht*. See also U Everling, 'Quis custodiet custodes ipsos?', (2002) *Europäische Zeitschrift für Wirtschaftsrecht* 357, rejecting this kind of proposal; for the debate in the Convention see document CONV 286/02.

287 Just see Case C-376/98, *Germany v Commission* [2000] ECR I-8419. See also Mayer, above n 173, 594 *et seq*, and German ECJ Judge Colneric, above n 171.

288 The *Carpenter* decision of July 2002, where the ECJ clearly disregards any limits that Art 51 of the Fundamental Rights Charter might impose on the *ERT*-case law, seems to indicate that it might not be easy to circumnavigate the ECJ. See Case C-60/90 *Carpenter* [2002] ECR I-6279; I Pernice and FC Mayer, in E Grabitz and M Hilf (eds), *Das Recht der Europäischen Union: Kommentar* (looseleaf), 'Grundrechtsschutz und rechtsstaatliche Grundsätze (after Art 6 EU)', paras 32 *et seq*.

289 See on this decision FC Mayer, 'Grundrechtsschutz gegen europäische Rechtsakte', (2000) *Europäische Zeitschrift für Wirtschaftsrecht* 685.

that these interests are well enough established to be covered by constitutional law (such as e.g. fundamental rights), the national courts may be forced into a more activist role as defenders of these interests against the EU, in particular when these interests can be designated integration-proof elements of national constitutional law. Moreover, the binding character of the Fundamental Rights Charter introduced by the new Constitution[290] would make more apparent the divergence in control, scrutiny and standards of protection between the European level and at least some of the Member States.[291]

2. Open Questions

There are numerous questions about the future of the courts which were not raised in the Convention or the IGC, but which still need answering.[292] There is not only the question already touched upon of how to establish a concept of the common good in the EU. There are also foreseeable logistical and infrastructural obstacles to a functioning ECJ in an EU of 25 or more Member States, with possible side effects for European constitutional law adjudication in the entire EU. These obstacles include the language problem[293] and the question of how to ensure a balanced composition of the Court and its component parts based on equal representation of Member States.

More generally, one may question whether the agenda of the Convention and the IGC did not ignore fundamental questions of European law, such as the range and limits of the (common) market. This issue does not only concern social and cultural specifics of the Member States, but also fundamental choices of a society on the market-state relationship, taking into consideration social and other preferences. The ECJ's *Preussen-Elektra* judgment illustrates in the area of the relationship between free movement

[290] In December 2000, the Charter was only announced as a solemn political proclamation, see OJ C 364, 18.12.2000, 1.

[291] On this point M Nettesheim, 'Grundrechtliche Prüfdichte durch den EuGH', (1995) *Europäische Zeitschrift für Wirtschaftsrecht* 106; P Selmer, *Die Gewährleistung der unabdingbaren Grundrechtsstandards durch den EuGH* (1998) 133 *et seq.*

[292] For the debate on the reform of the European court system, which strangely has been decoupled from the general constitutional debate, see *inter alia* JHH Weiler, 'Epilogue: The Judicial Après Nice', in G de Búrca and *id* (eds), *The European Court of Justice* (2001) 215 *et seq*; U Everling, 'Zur Fortbildung der Gerichtsbarkeit der Europäischen Gemeinschaften durch den Vertrag von Nizza', in *Festschrift Steinberger*, above n 115, 1103 *et seq*, with further references.

[293] The increasing number of languages may not be just a logistical problem, it may also adversely affect the clarity of Court decisions and contribute to the fuzziness of European law, see on that aspect I Pernice and FC Mayer, in E Grabitz and M Hilf (eds), above n 288, Art 220 EC, paras 86 *et seq*. See FC Mayer, 'The language of the European Constitution—beyond Babel?' in A Bodnar *et al* (eds): *The Emerging Constitutional Law of the European Union* (2003) 359; see also FC Mayer, 'Europäisches Sprachenverfassungsrecht', (2005) *Der Staat* 367.

of goods and environmental protection that, in spite of the pronouncement in *Keck*, the ECJ is finding it increasingly difficult to remain consistent in its case law on the limits of the market.[294]

The question of how to conceptualise public power in an era of globalisation and internationalisation reaches beyond European integration. Similar frictional phenomena as detected between the Member States and the EU may occur there, with similar lines of conflict. The ECJ may find itself in a position vis-à-vis courts or other adjudicating bodies outside the EU, which resembles the position national courts have adopted towards the ECJ.[295] Moreover, there are numerous new fundamental questions, ranging from the question of how to tame new, previously unknown threats to individual freedom relating to economic power to the question of how to legitimise new forms of governance.[296] The answers to these questions will also affect the role and the function of national and supranational courts.

SUMMARY AND CONCLUSION

The analysis of the conflicts between the highest courts and tribunals at the European and Member State levels goes far beyond the mere relationship between these courts. Looking at this relationship offers more general insights about how Member States deal with the tension between their national legal orders and the European legal order and where the crucial points for potential conflict are located within the European construct. Beyond the law, national courts also reflect changes in mood or opinion,

[294] Case C-379/98, *Preussen Elektra* [2001] ECR I-2099. See also the contribution by T Kingreen in this volume.

[295] See ECHR, *Bosphorus v Ireland* (45036/98), 30 June 2005. See also ECHR, *Matthews v United Kingdom* Rep 1999-I 251; ECHR, *Ermesa Sugar v The Netherlands*, (62023/00), following Case C-17/98, *Emesa Sugar* [2000] ECR I-665 (on the right to respond to the AG's opinion, see in that context ECHR, *Kress v France* (39594/98) ECHR 2001-VI); see also the case ECHR, *Senator Lines GmbH v 15 EU Member States* (56672/00), *Europäische Grundrechte-Zeitschrift* (2000) 334; following Case T-191/98 R, *Senator Lines v Commission* [1999] ECR II-2531 and Case C-364/99 P(R), *Senator Lines v Commission* [1999] ECR I-8733. The ECHR-proceedings were not continued following the CFI decision in Joined Cases T-191/98, T-212/98 to T-214/98, *Atlantic Container Line et al v Commission* [2003] ECR II-0000. Looking at the references to each other's cases that can be found in both ECJ and ECHR decisions and at cases such as *Dangeville v France* (36677/97) ECHR 2002-III, where the ECHR took sides with the ECJ, the relationship between the ECJ and the ECHR seems to be characterised by co-operation and mutual respect at this point. Note that the ECHR referred to the EU's Fundamental Rights Charter before the ECJ did, *I v United Kingdom* (25680/94) ECHR 2002-VI para 80; *Goodwin v United Kingdom* (28957/95) ECHR 2002-VI, para 10, pointing to Art 9 of the Charter. See for the WTO-'courts' Case C-377/02, *Van Parys* [2005] ECR I-0000.

[296] See on this point J Tully, 'The Unfreedom of the Moderns in Comparison to Their Ideals of Constitutional Democracy', (2002) 65 *MLR* 204 at 209, with further references; N Walker, 'The Idea of Constitutional Pluralism', (2002) 65 *MLR* 317.

regarding European integration, within the respective Member States.[297] The differences and conflicts between the courts can be considered representative of more general trends and differences of opinion.

In all, it is still premature to regard the relationship between the ECJ and the highest national courts and tribunals to be a consolidated relationship, but it is on the right path, heading towards a complementary structure of European constitutional law adjudication. This path is characterised by embracing co-operation instead of collision and by elements of a constitutional conversation between the courts, sometimes quite indirect, and variant in its characteristics, depending on the Member State in question. However, it remains to be seen, whether enlargement as of 2004 and the success or failure of the new Constitution will serve or hinder this positive development.[298]

Thus, in these times of change in Europe, what is true for European integration in general applies likewise to the relationship between the courts: when facing crucial decisions, all-important is to preserve and secure what has already been achieved. Offering concepts and ideas to this end is not the only, but a particularly befitting task for the science of European constitutional law.

[297] JHH Weiler, 'The Reformation of European Constitutionalism', (1997) 35 *JCMS* 97 at 107.

[298] The Constitution has already been and will be the subject of the constitutional law proceedings in a couple of Member States. See, e.g. for Great Britain in July 2003 already the court-decision not to decide on a referendum, Court of Appeal of England and Wales, *R v Seceratary of State for Foreign and Commonwealth Affairs, ex parte Southall and Anor, 3 CMLR* (2003) 18. The French *Conseil constitutionnel* (Decision 2004/505 DC, *Journal officiel* 273 24 November 2004, 19885), and the Spanish *Tribunal Constitucional* (Case 6603/2004, Declaration 1/2004, 13 December 2004, 1 CMLR (2005) 981) have declared that the European Constitution is compatiable with the respective domestic constitutions. Cases are pending in front of the German *Bundesverfassungericht* (Cases 2 BvR 839/05 and 2 BvE 2/05, filed on 27 May 2005 by MP Peter Gauweiler), the Slovak Constitutional Court (Decision of 14 July 2005 to halt the ratification), and the Czech Constitutional Court (filed on 2 February 2005 by President Vaclav Klaus). These decisions and the debate about them generate another round of discourse on European constitutional law, and they will contribute to further develop European Contitutional law, no matter whether in the end, the Constitutional Treaty will actually go into force or not.

8

The Vertical Order of Competences

ARMIN VON BOGDANDY AND JÜRGEN BAST*

I. INTRODUCTION

THE VERY HEART of the European Union is that it exercises public power. This power stems from its vertical competences (*Verbandskompetenzen* in German, literally "an association's competences"). These competences are the subject of a lively debate. According to the Declaration on the Future of the Union, the so-called post-Nice process should address the question of "how to establish and monitor a more precise delimitation of powers between the European Union and the Member States, reflecting the principle of subsidiarity".[1] Accordingly, the European Convention placed at the head of its draft the general rules for *Verbandskompetenzen*—rules which to some extent go beyond the mere codification of already established legal doctrines.

The attention for this subject reflects a strategy for dealing with the Union's crisis of legitimacy, which is attributed in part to the Union's citizens' perception of it being too amorphous and too large. It also addresses a core concern of the implementing national authorities and in particular of the German *Länder*: protection against unnecessary and dysfunctional infringements on their powers.[2] Moreover, there is a view that the Union's

* The text was translated by Eric Pickett and Joseph Windsor.

[1] [2001] OJ C 80/85. On the linguistic differences see G de Búrca and B de Witte, 'The Delimitation of Powers Between the EU and its Member States' in A Arnull and D Wincott (eds), *Accountability and Legitimacy in the European Union after Nice* (2002), 201 at 202 *et seq*.

[2] Cf in particular the resolution of the German Federal Council (Bundesrat), *Forderungen der Länder zur Regierungskonferenz 1996*, Bundesrat Drucksache 667/95, Anlage; W Clement, *Europa gestalten—nicht verwalten* (2001), <http://www.whi-berlin.de/clement.htm> (27 August 2004), para 4 with further references; E Stoiber, *Eckpunkte der europäischen Zukunftsdebatte* (2001), <http://www.whi-berlin.de/stoiber.htm> (27 August 2004), 8; furthermore Sénat et Chambre des représentants de Belgique (eds), *Les finalités de l'Union européenne* (2001); see also D Reich, 'Zum Einfluß des Europäischen Gemeinschaftsrechts auf die Kompetenzen der deutschen Bundesländer' [2001] *Europäische Grundrechte-Zeitschrift* 1.

competences steadily erode those of the Member States, thereby endangering their statehood.[3]

Until the end of the 1990s, there had been astonishingly little research on the vertical competences.[4] Legal literature on competence issues had almost exclusively focused on Art 235 EEC Treaty (now Art 308 EC).[5] Since then, however, a wealth of literature has been published, much already on the relevant parts of the Treaty establishing a Constitution for Europe.[6]

Two remarks should be made at this point. First, this contribution does not address the ECJ's competence to develop the law, even though this is unquestionably a significant aspect of the EU's *Verbandskompetenz*. This limitation is justified by the focus of the intense debate that led to Arts 11 *et seq* CT-IGC (Arts I-9 *et seq* CT-Conv); furthermore, a "restraint" on judge-made law requires other instruments than a modification of the order of competences.[7] Second, this contribution understands the Union as an

[3] *Entscheidungen des Bundesverfassungsgerichts* (Federal Constitutional Court) 89, 155 at 210 (*Maastricht*); on the debate see I Pernice, 'Kompetenzabgrenzung im Europäischen Verfassungsverbund' [2000] *Juristenzeitung* 866.

[4] But see H Jarass, 'Die Kompetenzverteilung zwischen der Europäischen Gemeinschaft und den Mitgliedstaaten' (1996) 121 *Archiv des öffentlichen Rechts* 173; D Triantafyllou, *Vom Vertrags- zum Gesetzesvorbehalt* (1996); cf also J Martín y Pérez de Nanclares, *El sistema de competencias de la Comunidad Europea* (1997); I Boeck, *Die Abgrenzung der Rechtsetzungskompetenzen von Gemeinschaft und Mitgliedstaaten in der Europäischen Union* (2000).

[5] U Everling, 'Die allgemeine Ermächtigung der Europäischen Gemeinschaft zur Zielverwirklichung nach Art. 235 EWGV' [1976] *Europarecht* special ed 2; C Tomuschat, 'Die Rechtsetzungsbefugnisse der EWG in Generalermächtigungen, insbesondere in Art 235 EWGV' [1976] *Europarecht* special ed 45; RH Lauwaars, 'Art 235 als Grundlage für die flankierenden Politiken im Rahmen der Wirtschafts- und Währungsunion' [1976] *Europarecht* 100; D-W Dorn, *Art 235 EWGV: Prinzipien der Auslegung* (1986); E Steindorff, *Grenzen der EG-Kompetenzen* (1990).

[6] P Craig, 'Competence: Clarity, Containment and Consideration' in I Pernice and M Poiares Maduro (eds), *A Constitution for the European Union* (2004), 75 and (2004) 29 *EL Rev* 323; C Trüe, 'Das System der EU-Kompetenzen vor und nach dem Entwurf eines europäischen Verfassungsvertrags' (2004) 64 *Zeitschrift für ausländisches öffentliches Recht und Völkerrecht* 391; V Michel, '2004: Le défi de la répartition des compétences' (2003) 39 *Cahiers de Droit Européen* 27; S Weatherill, 'Competence' in B de Witte (ed), *Ten Reflections on the Constitutional Treaty for Europe* (2003), 45; JM Beneyto, 'Die Kompetenzverteilung zwischen der Europäischen Union und den Mitgliedstaaten' in DH Scheuing (ed), *Europäische Verfassungsordnung* (2003), 87; R Bieber, 'Kompetenzen und Institutionen im Rahmen einer EU-Verfassung' in P Häberle, M Morlok and V Skouris (eds), *Festschrift für DTh Tsatsos* (2003), 31; U Di Fabio, 'Some Remarks on the Allocation of Competences between the European Union and its Member States' (2002) 39 *CML Rev* 1289; V Götz and J Martínez Soría (eds), *Kompetenzverteilung zwischen der Europäischen Union und den Mitgliedstaaten* (2002); U Leonardy, 'Kompetenzabgrenzung' in PA Zervakis and PJ Cullen (eds), *The Post-Nice Process* (2002), 129; S Magiera, 'Zur Kompetenzneuordnung zwischen der Europäischen Union und den Mitgliedstaaten' [2002] *Integration* 269; JM y Pérez de Nanclares, 'La delimitación de competencias entre la Unión Europea y los Estados Miembros' [2002] *Revista de Derecho Comunitario Europeo* 343; C Trüe, *Das System der Rechtsetzungskompetenzen der Europäischen Gemeinschaft und der Europäischen Union* (2002); FC Mayer, 'Die drei Dimensionen der europäischen Kompetenzdebatte' (2001) 61 *Zeitschrift für ausländisches öffentliches Recht und Völkerrecht* 577.

[7] U Everling, 'Rechtsfortbildung in der Europäischen Gemeinschaft' [1998] *Juristenzeitung* 217 at 225 *et seq*.

organisation that includes the Communities, so that Community law is a qualified part of Union law.[8] This allows applying insights, developed on the basis of the EC Treaties, to the EU Treaty.[9] The following exposition is based on the EC Treaty, so a certain degree of ambiguity with respect to the EU Treaty is inevitable. However, there is a presumption that those competence theories developed on the basis of the EC Treaty with a view to preserving the Member States' powers must apply all the more to the competences under the EU Treaty, given their impact on core national interests. The solution of the Constitutional Treaty with respect to the competences of Title V and Title VI EU Treaty builds on this premise.

This contribution will first outline the fundamental features of the current vertical order of competences (II). On that basis, it will present some aspects of the Constitutional Treaty's order of competences (III).

II. THE CURRENT ORDER OF COMPETENCES

1. Terminological and Theoretical Bases

Some terminological questions need to be mentioned first. There is a certain degree of linguistic uncertainty in the Treaties, in particular with respect to the terms "power" and "competence". For example, in Art 5(1) and Art 7(1)(2) EC the term "powers" is used; in the German version "*Befugnis*". Art 300(1), (2) EC uses the term "*Zuständigkeit*" in the German version, whereas in the English version the term "powers" is used. Yet in Art 230(2) EC the terms used are "*Kompetenz*" and "competence", respectively. In the provisional draft of the Treaty of Nice circulated on 12 December 2000, we find "how to establish and monitor a more precise delimitation of *competencies*"[10], the term being an alternative form to the plural of competence.[11] The usage in other languages varies in still different ways. Neither the terms "competence" and "power" in the Treaties[12] nor the terms

[8] In detail A von Bogdandy, 'The Legal Case for Unity' (1999) 36 *CML Rev* 887; the more precise relationship between the Union and the Communities is not relevant to this article; on the discussion see S Kadelbach, C Koenig, M Zuleeg, A von Bogdandy and U Everling in [1998] *Europarecht*, suppl 2.

[9] It is widely recognised that the latter's institutions are strictly bound by those competences under Titles V and VI EU Treaty: M Pechstein and C Koenig, *Die Europäische Union* (2000), para 193; in contrast see P Manin, *Les Communautés européennes, l'Union européenne* (1999), para 128.

[10] Doc SN 5333/00, emphasis added.

[11] B Garner (ed), *Black's Law Dictionary* (1999) contains five definitions for the term 'power'. Definitions one and three are of relevance here. The first definition is 'the ability to act or not to act', and the second 'the legal right or authorization to act or not to act; the ability conferred on a person by the law to alter, by an act of will, the rights, duties, liabilities, or other legal authorization'. Under the term 'competence' one finds as relevant definitions 'the basic minimal ability to do something' and 'the capacity of an official body to do something'.

[12] See also de Búrca and de Witte, above n 1, 202, who arrive at the same conclusion.

"empowering provision", "authorisation" and "legal basis" appear to have distinct legal meanings respectively. All these terms will therefore be used synonymously.

a) The Competence Requirement as an Evolutionary Achievement

The demand for a catalogue of European competences, a new order of competences or additional rules for the exercise of competences all build on a fundamental principle of European constitutional law: *the principle of constitutional legality*. This principle has two aspects: negative and positive legality. According to the *principle of negative legality*, every act that can be attributed to the Union must be consistent with higher ranking law.[13] Every act of secondary law must conform to the totality of the existing Treaty norms as well as to those general principles of law to be found at the same level.[14] This establishes a strict hierarchy of norms within Union law: all secondary law enacted by the Union's institutions is on one single level under primary law.[15] Art 5 EU formulates the Treaties' "yardstick character" as applying comprehensively to the Union's five main institutions and to all the Union's spheres of activity (i.e. including Titles V and VI EU Treaty); for secondary Community law this follows with particular clarity from Art 230(2) EC. The principle of negative legality is valid without exception: the Union's constitution takes absolute precedence.

The tremendous success of the constitutionalisation of the Treaties is revealed by the fact that the principle of negative legality appears trivial.[16] Yet, obvious as the validity of this legal concept may appear today, it was anything but evident for the early Community.[17] That the founding treaty of an international organisation can simultaneously function as the standard for the law produced by that organisation is a rather new phenomenon.[18]

[13] On the current state of common European constitutional law in this regard see A von Bogdandy, *Gubernative Rechtsetzung* (2000) 166.

[14] See Case 294/83 *Les Verts v Parliament* [1986] ECR 1339, para 23; Opinion 1/91, *EEA I* [1991] ECR I-6079, para 21.

[15] Only exceptionally does Union law permit the Union's institutions to enact primary law without the Member States' involvement (so-called autonomous Treaty amendment), eg, Art 213(1)(2) EC; the Constitutional Treaty avails itself of this amendment procedure more extensively, as in, for instance, Art 444 CT–IGC (Art I–24(4) CT–Conv).

[16] According to some authors, even today there is only a 'slight hierarchy' (*geringe Hierarchisierung*) between primary and secondary law; see, eg, C Schönberger, 'Normenkontrollen im EG-Föderalismus' [2003] *Europarecht* 600 at 601.

[17] Cf H-J Rabe, *Das Verordnungsrecht der Europäischen Wirtschaftsgemeinschaft* (1963), 50 *et seq*; H Wagner, *Grundbegriffe des Beschlußrechts der Europäischen Gemeinschaften* (1965), 236 and *passim*; K Carstens, 'Die kleine Revision des Vertrags über die Europäische Gemeinschaft für Kohle und Stahl' (1961) 21 *Zeitschrift für ausländisches öffentliches Recht und Völkerrecht* 1 at 14, 37; too optimistic for the early days of Community law is M Nettesheim, 'Kompetenzen' in A von Bogdandy (ed), *Europäisches Verfassungsrecht* (2003), 415 at 418.

[18] See J Brunnée, 'COPing with Consent: Lawmaking under Multilateral Environmental Agreements' (2002) 15 *Leiden Journal of International Law* 1.

A hierarchisation of the sources of law was essentially foreign to public international law (with the exception of *ius cogens,* in itself a new development).[19] Such hierarchisation in the EU is thanks to the ECJ's case law. Starting from the premise of an autonomous legal order, the ECJ consistently concluded that the procedures for amending the Treaties are exclusively those foreseen and provided for by the Treaties (now Art 48 EU). The Treaties' strict normativity does not permit the temporary suspension of the Treaties' provisions by informal agreements,[20] nor can a persistent practice by the institutions derogate primary law.[21] This jurisprudence prevents any extralegal influence on the part of the Member States. Even acts adopted unanimously by the Council are completely subject to primary law: in Community law, consensus is not a valid argument in favour of legality.[22] The ECJ's strict view equally applies when the Council based its act on a broadly defined authorisation like Art 235 EEC Treaty (Art 308 EC).[23] This provision can therefore hardly any longer be considered to be a competence to amend or "supplement" the Treaty.[24] When, however, it was not the Council but rather an intergovernmental conference that acted (the "Representatives of the Governments of the Member States, meeting within the Council"), then the principle of the primacy of Community law over *any* Member State law is applicable,[25] which, in the end, has the same effect with regard to the principle of negative legality.

This leads to a striking dichotomy, well-known in constitutional theory, pertaining to the Member States' status and their capacities to act. As constitution-amending actors they remain basically outside the scope of the Union's jurisdiction,[26] yet they can only exercise this capacity according to the procedure foreseen in Art 48 EU. In substance this means that the

[19] A Verdross and B Simma, *Universelles Völkerrecht* (1984), § 640; W Heintschel von Heinegg, 'Die weiteren Quellen des Völkerrechts' in K Ipsen, *Völkerrecht* (2004), § 20, para 1; S Kadelbach, *Zwingendes Völkerrecht* (1992), 26.

[20] See Cases 90/63 and 91/63, *Commission v Belgium and Luxembourg* [1964] ECR 625 at 631 *et seq*; Case 43/75, *Defrenne* [1976] ECR 455, paras 56–58; Case 59/75, *Manghera* [1976] ECR 91, para 21.

[21] See Case 68/86, *United Kingdom v Council* [1988] ECR 855, para 24; Case C–271/94, *Parliament v Council* [1996] ECR I–1689, paras 24, 34; Case C–27/04, *Commission v Council* [2004] ECR I–0000, para 81 (regarding the Stability and Growth Pact).

[22] C-D Ehlermann, 'How Flexible is Community Law?' (1984) 82 *Michigan Law Rev* 1274 at 1276.

[23] Case 38/69, *Commission v Italy* [1970] ECR 47, paras 12–13.

[24] Such was still the claim in HP Ipsen, *Europäisches Gemeinschaftsrecht* (1972), 22–15; see similarly, eg, JH Kaiser, 'Grenzen der EG-Zuständigkeiten' [1980] *Europarecht* 97 at 115; Steindorff, above n 5, 114; Herdegen, *Europarecht* (2003), para 193; today the dominant scholarly view holds that Art 308 EC is subject to the competence order's constraints: see, eg, R Streinz in R Streinz (ed), *EUV/EGV* (2003), Art 5 EC, paras 4 and 10; M Nettesheim in E Grabitz and M Hilf (eds), *Das Recht der Europäischen Union* (looseleaf), Art 249 EC, para 60.

[25] Case 44/84, *Hurd* [1986] ECR 29, paras 20 and 39; Case 235/87, *Matteucci* [1988] ECR 5589, para 14; Case C–55/00, *Gottardo* [2002] I–413, para 33.

[26] But cf Arts 6(1), 7(1) EU and the requirements of the ECHR: see ECHR, *Matthews v United Kingdom* Rep 1999-I 251.

Union's constitutional order is largely protected against any kind of ad hoc modification. At the same time, the Member States' representation through the Council means that they are at the focal point of the public power constituted by the Treaties. In this capacity, however, they are fully subject to the Union's primary law. This simultaneous exclusion and inclusion of the "masters of the Treaties" bears a remarkable resemblance to the foundation of constitutional legality in the Member States: the parliaments represent the sovereign, yet are strictly bound by their respective constitution.[27]

Only on the basis of this constitutional normativity does the *principle of positive legality* flourish. This principle implies that an empowering provision is a necessary proviso. Any act at the level of secondary Union law must rest on a legal basis which can be traced back to the Treaties. The legal basis can either be contained in the Treaties themselves or in an act of secondary law, which in turn is based on the Treaties.[28] Whereas negative legality is (only) concerned with delimiting an assumed public power, the requirement of an empowering provision is situated one step before and asks about the act's legal foundation. Thus—and this is an important point in the current debate—a modification of the order of competences can limit the EU's power virtually at its source. The legal consequences of an infringement on the negative or the positive aspect of constitutional legality are identical: the usual legal consequence of an act's illegality is that it is annulled when challenged, and in cases of especially serious and obvious defects the act may even be declared non-existent.[29]

b) On the Scope of the Principle of Attributed Powers

The principle of positive legality, viz that the Union may only exercise as much power as conferred on it by the Treaties, has been universally recognised and is known as the principle of attributed powers or principle of conferral.[30] More generally, one can speak of a competence requirement.

This requirement is occasionally questioned when the measure at issue does not infringe on the rights of the citizens or intervene in the Member States' legal orders.[31] Yet, the ECJ already declared at an early stage of the Community that an act benefiting any given party requires an empowering

[27] See N Luhmann, 'Verfassung als evolutionäre Errungenschaft' (1990) 9 *Rechtshistorisches Journal* 176.

[28] The question whether State actions must also always have a basis in national constitutions is very controversial: see C Möllers, *Staat als Argument* (2000), 256 *et seq*.

[29] Case C–137/92 P *Commission v BASF* [1994] ECR I–2555, paras 48 *et seq*; see for a different view, however, Nettesheim, above n 17, 430 (assuming that a lack of competence in any case leads to non-existence of a contested act).

[30] Sometimes the term 'enumerated powers' is used. The term is misleading, since it implies some form of a catalogue which is missing in the Treaties.

[31] See A Bleckmann, *Europarecht* (1997), para 382; also too narrow: H-P Kraußer, *Das Prinzip der begrenzten Einzelermächtigung im Gemeinschaftsrecht* (1991), 86 *et seq*; and B Biervert, *Der Mißbrauch von Handlungsformen im Gemeinschaftsrecht* (1999), 89 *et seq*.

provision.[32] In particular the expenditure of funds as an important resource of influence is by no means legally neutral,[33] so the Union does not possess a general competence to grant aids. Against the Commission's problematic practice, the ECJ correctly emphasised that the expenditure of EU money is subject to the cumulative requirements of a budgetary authorisation and an empowering legislative act.[34]

It has not yet been completely clarified whether those acts of institutions that by their very form produce no legal effects are subject to the competence requirement.[35] Institutional practice has developed non-binding instruments other than those foreseen in the Treaties,[36] such as Council resolutions and Commission communications. The need for legitimacy of any act by a public authority suggests that the competence requirement applies also to such acts. The ECJ correctly annulled Commission communications which appeared to impose obligations on the Member States, because the Commission did not have the competence (!) to make such communications.[37] The same rationale must apply to Council resolutions. The inclusion of non-regulative powers in Art 17 CT-IGC (Art I-16 CT-Conv; see below) supports the view that in Union law the competence requirement is to be understood broadly and is not limited to legal acts in a narrow sense. Hence, all types of Union actions, irrespective of their legal nature or form, need a legal basis, which explicitly or implicitly confers the relevant power to act. As an example of the latter, official announcements that, at an early stage in the law-making process, fix the (preliminary) results of consultations can be understood as supported by an unwritten competence, implied by the institutions' power of internal organisation.[38]

Deriving a competence from the institutions' power of internal organisation leads to the question how the principle of attributed powers relates to "creative" interpretation. Of particular importance are the doctrine of implied powers[39] and the deduction of powers from the tasks set out in the

[32] Case 111/63, *Lemmerz-Werke v High Authority* [1965] ECR 677 at 691.

[33] As pointed out by Nettesheim, above n 17, 429.

[34] Case C–106/96, *United Kingdom v Commission* [1998] ECR I–2729, paras 22 and 28. On this problem see A Dashwood, 'The Limits of European Community Powers' (1996) 21 *EL Rev* 113 at 126 *et seq*; on the previous practice cf J-L Dewost, 'Décisions des institutions en vue du développement des compétences et des instruments juridiques' in R Bieber and G Ress (eds), *Die Dynamik des Gemeinschaftsrechts* (1987), 321 at 328. See Art 53(4) CT–IGC (Art I–52(4) CT–Conv).

[35] See for sceptical views, eg, Oppermann, *Europarecht* (1999), para 517; B Biervert in J Schwarze (ed), *EU-Kommentar* (2003), Art 249 EC, para 12; Triantafyllou, above n 4, 73 *et seq*.

[36] These are the recommendation and the opinion: Art 249(5) EC.

[37] For instance in Case C–57/95, *France v Commission* [1997] ECR I–1627, para 25.

[38] On the Parliament's power to adopt resolutions see Case 230/81, *Luxembourg v Parliament* [1983] ECR 255, para 39; on the scope of the power of internal organisation see Case C–58/94, *Netherlands v Council* [1996] ECR I–2169, para 37.

[39] G Nicolaysen, 'Zur Theorie von den Implied Powers in den Europäischen Gemeinschaften' [1966] *Europarecht* 129; T Hartley, *The Foundations of European Community Law* (1998), 102–3.

Treaties, even in the absence of an explicit empowering provision. The very existence of Arts 5(1) and 308 EC commands to construe these two methods narrowly.[40] An implied powers doctrine within Union law can only have the status of a rule of interpretation for explicit authorising norms. The proviso is that a specific objective cannot be achieved without going beyond the explicit wording of a competence norm.[41] This is—beyond the power of internal organisation—especially relevant for the Union's external relations: parallel to its internal powers *and precisely on this legal basis* the Council is empowered to conclude international agreements.[42] The derivation of competences from general goals, on the other hand, does not respect the principle of conferral.[43] After some uncertainty in the 1980s,[44] this is now generally recognised. This has the unfortunate albeit unavoidable consequence that the Union is, e.g. obligated to facilitate civil protection (Art 3(1)(u) EC) but is not—due to a lack of an explicit empowering provision—permitted to do so in a targeted manner.[45]

c) Empowering Provisions and Standard-establishing Provisions

Both aspects of the principle of constitutional legality are constitutive for the Treaties' constitutional character. The division between empowering provisions and provisions that serve as standards delimiting the exercise of power runs along the same dividing line as between positive and negative legality.

Yet this theoretically clear distinction is not easily applicable to the Treaties: most empowering provisions not only specify an abstract title to act, as is the case in some national constitutions (e.g. Arts 73 *et seq* of the German Basic Law, or Arts 148 and 149 of the Spanish Constitution), but also contain substantive standards for the exercise of that power. The object of the latter is to inform, direct, channel and limit European power. Consequently, in some cases it is a question of convention and formulation technique whether a particular normative element is considered to be on the side of the *creation* of the competence or part of the standard for the power's *exercise*. This difficulty should not, however, be a reason generally to abandon the theoretical distinction between empowering and standard-establishing norms by conceiving the latter, e.g. fundamental rights, as "negative competence provisions".[46]

[40] See Dashwood, above n 34, 124 *et seq*.

[41] This was developed by the ECJ. See, in detail O Dörr, 'Die Entwicklung der ungeschriebenen Außenkompetenzen der EG' [1996] *Europäische Zeitschrift für Wirtschaftsrecht* 39 at 43.

[42] Case 22/70, *Commission v Council* [1971] ECR 263, paras 15–19; Opinion 1/94, *WTO* [1994] ECR I–5267, paras 76–77; for a thorough analysis see P Eeckhout, *External Relations of the European Union* (2004), 58 *et seq*.

[43] In particular M Zuleeg insisted on this early on: M. Zuleeg, 'Der Verfassungsgrundsatz der Demokratie und die Europäischen Gemeinschaften' (1978) 17 *Der Staat* 27.

[44] See Cases 281, 283–285 and 287/85, *Germany et al v Commission* [1987] ECR 3203, para 28.

[45] But see Arts 17(f) and 284 CT–IGC (Arts I–16(2) and III–184 CT-Conv).

[46] Yet this is FC Mayer's approach, see above n 6, 584.

The conceptual distinction between *if* there is a competence to act and *how* the competence may be legally exercised remains valuable, if for no other reason than because such a distinction is assumed in Art 230(2) EC. Thus the concept of a competence should not be bundled together with all the conditions on the legal exercise of the power, but rather should be limited to the abstract conferral of power. Competence norms, as they are defined here, are abstract titles conferring the power to act. Their exercise is directed and delimited by norms that specifically provide formal, procedural and material conditions for the proper exercise of the particular competence as well as by the general scheme relating to the proper exercise of power (such as fundamental rights). This conceptual proposal is consistent with the differentiation in Arts 111, 112 CT-IGC (Arts II-51, II-52 CT-Conv), which repeatedly confirm the distinction between the standards established in the Charter on Fundamental Rights and the competences conferred upon the Union in other Parts of the Constitution.[47]

d) Horizontal and Vertical Competences

Another important and clarifying distinction, yet often disregarded, is that between the competences of the Union as such (vertical competences, *Verbandskompetenzen*) and the distribution of competences among its institutions (horizontal competences, *Organkompetenzen*). The issue of vertical competences concerns the relationship between the Member States and the Union, whereas the issue of horizontal competences concerns the relationships between the Union's different institutions and therefore the internal division of powers.[48] The issue of vertical competences therefore describes different constitutional questions and conflict potentialities than the issues of horizontal competences.[49]

This distinction is, however, made difficult because the Union's vertical competences can (almost always) only be deduced from the competences attributed to its institutions. The Treaties' empowering provisions are usually so formulated that they do not authorise the Union or the Community as such, but rather name the institution(s) that are so empowered ("The Council shall adopt ...").[50] The rationale behind this drafting technique is

[47] For details, see J Kühling in this volume.

[48] The French theory uses the concept of *compétence* for the *Verbandskompetenz* and the concept of *pouvoir* for the institutions' competences: see in detail V Constantinesco, *Compétences et pouvoirs dans les Communautés européennes* (1974).

[49] There is a rich case law on the distribution of horizontal competences regarding the choice of the appropriate legal basis, summarised in Case C–281/01, *Commission v Council* [2002] ECR I–12049, paras 33 *et seq*; for an overview cf Trüe (2002), see above n 6, 511 *et seq*. It has usually not been disputed that the Union possesses the *Verbandskompetenz* for the challenged act in these cases.

[50] Art 6(4) EU, which has a different wording, is—tellingly—not considered to confer a competence: cf D Simon in V Constantinesco, R Kovar and D Simon (eds), *Traité sur l'Union européenne* (1995), Art F, paras 17–18.

that the Union has no single institution that is vested with the residual power to exercise a "non-specified" vertical competence (see Art 7(2) EC).[51] The categorical distinction between vertical and horizontal competences has, despite this difficulty, significant clarifying potential for the current constitutional debate. The debate on a "more precise delimitation of powers between the European Union and the Member States" regards, according to its clear formulation, only the *Verbandskompetenzen*; it is not about *which* institution of the Union should act under *which* procedural mechanism.[52] Broadly speaking, the issue of vertical competences regards the issue of mutually protecting the Member States and the Union against irregular interferences, whereas the issue of horizontal competences regards the effectiveness of the Union's decision-making system and its further democratisation. When an empowering Treaty provision providing for the Council to act unanimously has been amended, henceforth to allow the Council to act by qualified majority, this amendment does not change the vertical order of competences, although it significantly reduces a single Member State's capacity to block future European legislation. The distinction may become particularly relevant under Art 445(3) CT-IGC, which provides for a simplified Treaty amendment procedure subject to the requirement that the amending decision does not increase the vertical competences of the Union.

2. Fundaments of the Vertical Order of Competences

a) Union and Member State Competences

The Union's competences cannot be regarded separately from those of the Member States. This is due in the first place to the fact that the Union tends not towards the American model of the separation between the federal and state powers, but rather towards the German *Verflechtungsmodell*. The latter is based on interconnections, interdependence and co-operation between the various public authorities.[53] Generally speaking, the Member States and the Union closely co-operate, a fact which is usually affirmatively interpreted as a co-operative system of separation of powers.[54] This implies that

[51] The dominance of the institutions in the order of competences is also reflected in the 'final product'. The institution responsible for adopting an act leaves its fingerprints all over it: the act's title, preamble and signature all testify to the responsible institution. The legal authorship is attributed to the institution responsible for the act's final wording; with co-decision acts, this responsibility is shared between Parliament and the Council.

[52] It is to be stressed that redistributing the horizontal competences in favour of the Council does not offer any protection in the order of vertical competences. This can easily be concluded from acts passed under Art 235 EEC Treaty—the most critical and controversial provision within the order of vertical competences. It requires unanimity (!) in the Council.

[53] On the concept of executive federalism, see P Dann in this volume.

[54] See Pernice, above n 3, 871; P Kirchhof, 'Gewaltenbalance zwischen staatlichen und europäischen Organen' [1998] *Juristenzeitung* 965 at 969–70; see also his chapter in this volume.

there are narrow limits to disentangling the powers of the various (competence) levels in order to establish clearer lines of responsibility.

A proper understanding of the Union's *Verbandskompetenz* requires one to consider its impact on the Member States' competences. It should be recalled that the conferral of a competence upon the Union does not—according to what has in the meantime become the overwhelmingly majority opinion—lead to a loss of "ownership" of the competence by the Member State; this potentially "imperialistic" reading is no longer advocated.[55] Nevertheless, the Member States may be permanently prohibited from exercising their powers. At the Union's current stage of legal development, the Member States may no longer exercise many of their constitutional powers or may only exercise them within the confines of Union law.[56] Furthermore, the individual Member State has forfeited its right to determine its own competences (*Kompetenz-Kompetenz*) insofar as it is not permitted to extend its powers *unilaterally* to the detriment of the Union. The Member States acting jointly as the Contracting Parties may amend the Treaties and transfer powers back to the Member States, but they are bound by the procedures provided for in Art 48 EU. In return for these restraints, the principle of attributed powers safeguards the individual Member State's competences in all areas that have not been positively conferred upon the Union.

The observance of the order of competences, with the exception of measures under Title V and Art 7 EU, is fully subject to judicial review.[57] There is mistrust in the Member States as to whether the ECJ adequately fulfils this task. This mistrust is historically justified insofar as the Court did not oppose the Council's excessive recourse to Art 235 EEC Treaty in the 1970s and 1980s.[58] The Court has, however, become increasingly self-confident with regard to the Council.[59] In its *Tobacco Advertising* decision the ECJ confirmed that it is able to assert itself as the highest court in a constitutional order adjudicating on competences.[60]

What has not yet been clarified is to what extent the vertical distribution of competences is bipolar in nature, that is, whether, in addition to the

[55] E Grabitz, *Gemeinschaftsrecht bricht nationales Recht* (1966), 41 *et seq.* Also the opposite view that the Union is just a 'trustee' of the Member States'(!) competences has largely been abandoned. Rather, the Union enjoys autonomous competences that came into being with the Treaties, *Entscheidungen des Bundesverfassungsgerichts* 37, 271 at 280 (*Solange I*).

[56] The concept of a state as possessing 'omni-jurisdiction' (*Totalzuständigkeit*), that is, jurisdiction in all matters, will not be separately discussed here.

[57] Art 35(6) EU now confirms this for Title VI as well; the Treaty of Nice limits legal review of measures under Art 7 EU to procedural errors: Art 46(e) EU.

[58] On the details of the case law see A Tizzano, 'Lo sviluppo delle competenze materiali delle Communità europee' [1981] *Rivista di Diritto Europeo* 139; R Dehousse, *La Cour de justice des Communautés européennes* (1994), 53 *et seq.*

[59] The ECJ had already asserted its authority in opposition to the Commission, cf Cases 281, 283–285 and 287/85, above n 44.

[60] Case C–376/98, *Germany v Parliament and Council* [2000] ECR I–8419; see also Opinion 1/94, above n 42, para 9; Opinion 2/94, *ECHR* [1996] ECR I–1763, paras 10 *et seq.*

competences positively conferred upon the Union, there are also negative competence provisions deferring to the Member States. Art 5(1) EC can be interpreted as a general clause deferring to Member State competences, similar to Art 30 German Basic Law.[61] Other Treaty provisions are interpreted as conferring special negative competences.[62] Arts 149(1), 150(1) and 152(5) EC, which explicitly state that the Member States are responsible for the "content of teaching and the organisation of educational systems", "content and organisation of vocational training" and the "organisation and delivery of health services and medical care" respectively, are in particular considered to be true negative vertical competences. Granted, these provisions may be understood as safety clauses: the Treaty authors wanted to make sure that a particular distribution of powers would be maintained after the adoption of a new competence. The current distribution of powers in these fields is comparable to the situation under Arts 117, 118 EEC Treaty before the adoption of the Social Protocol. As recognised by the ECJ's case law, the Treaties at that time left the Member States with their original powers in the social area. This did not, however, prohibit Community acts with a social policy content based on other Treaty provisions.[63] This shows that negative competence provisions have only a limited reach: it is foreign to Community law to create areas that are hermetically sealed off from Community influence through measures based on recognised Community competences.[64]

A precise analysis of these types of provisions, which are conceived by some as negative competence norms, demonstrates that it is more convincing to understand them (only) as negative conditions belonging to a specific empowering provision. This interpretation has the advantage of avoiding unforeseeable legal consequences that a reconstruction of the Union's constitution as a bipolar order of competences might entail.[65] Consequently, they do not function as cross-sectoral norms limiting the Union's *Verbandskompetenz* as such; rather, they limit the scope of the concrete power given by a specific norm. For most of the relevant norms this understanding is the one which best corresponds to their wording.

This understanding is also appropriate for the harmonisation prohibitions contained, e.g. in Arts 149(4), 150(4) and 151(5) EC: they refer exclusively to measures based on those competences, not, however, to other legal bases. In other words, these Articles must be construed as being silent on

[61] See Mayer, above n 6, 584.

[62] Surveyed in, *ibid*, 588 *et seq*, and Pernice, above n 3, 874; see also the conception *de lege ferenda* in T Fischer and N Schley, *Organizing a Federal Structure for Europe* (2000), 17–18.

[63] See Cases 281, 283–285 and 287/85, above n 44, para 14.

[64] See Case 9/74, *Casagrande* [1974] ECR 773, para 6; Case C–285/98, *Kreil* [2000] ECR I–69, para 15.

[65] Hence the preference for the concept of complementary 'partial constitutions' rather than a comprehensive 'all-embracing constitution'.

the *Verbandskompetenz*.[66] Admittedly, the Treaty formulation is open to interpretation. The wording can, however, be explained by the evolutionary expansion of the Union's vertical competences through successive Treaty amendments. These amendments occurred under the strict observance of the *acquis communautaire*, as Art 32 SEA and Art 47 EU demonstrate. This means that the vertical competences have only been expanded, and never contracted. Of course, a reassessment of the Union's competences is not excluded, but it requires amending the Treaties and explicit wording. In the absence of such an amendment, it must be assumed that the *acquis* pertaining to the attribution of powers remains untouched, i.e. that the introduction of new competences does not affect the existing ones. There is, however, an important exception to this interpretation: because of its subsidiarity to every explicit or implicit competence norm,[67] the scope of application of Art 308 EC has been systematically reduced since the enactment of the Single European Act. Summing up, the thesis that the Treaties contain a bipolar division of powers beyond the general clause contained in Art 5(1) EC does not withstand close scrutiny.

b) Types of Vertical Competences

In what follows, an attempt is made to put order into the jungle of positive competences by categorising them according to various types. One differentiation often made is between competences based on aims (*zielbezogene Kompetenzen,* also termed *functional* competences) and those based on fields (*sachbezogene Kompetenzen*).[68] The differentiation is terminologically unfortunate since competences qualified as being based on fields (*sachbezogen*) usually also exhibit functional aspects, a phenomenon which also flows from the crucial role of Art 2 EU and Art 2 EC.[69] It is therefore more precise to distinguish between (1) *functional* competences with a *cross-sectoral character* (in particular Arts 88, 94, 95, 308 EC[70]), (2) *functional* competences *in a particular policy field* (which are most of the competences, e.g. Arts 37, 175 EC) and (3) other competences with respect to a particular field without functional elements, in particular in the institutional area (e.g. Arts 195(4), 255 EC). The cross-sectoral functional competences—which are considered to be the most critical type—have recently been given sharper contours by the ECJ.[71]

[66] For an explicit example see AG Fennelly in Case C–376/98 *Germany v Parliament and Council* [2000] ECR I–8419, para 71.

[67] Opinion 2/94, above n 60, para 29.

[68] M Zuleeg in H von d Groeben and J Schwarze (eds), *Kommentar zum EU-/EG-Vertrag* (2003), Art 5 EC, para 4.

[69] Cf Art 37 EC (agriculture), Art 175 EC (environmental protection) as two competences that are usually considered to be *sachbezogen*; P-C Müller-Graff, 'Kompetenzen in der Europäischen Union' in W Weidenfeld (ed), *Europahandbuch* (1999), 779 uses the same scheme as in this article.

[70] Cf AG Fennelly in his opinion, above n 60, paras 58, 62.

[71] See Opinion 2/94, above n 60, paras 23 *et seq*; Case C–376/98, above n 60, paras 83 *et seq.*

Another classification of the vertical competences can be made following elements of the separation of powers doctrine. The regular power of the Union is that of legislation, the adoption of abstract and general norms.[72] However, the Union's vertical competences do not include "constitutional legislation", as has been established in view of Art 308 EC[73] and Art 230(4) EC[74]. With respect to the executive function, it is clear that the Union's competences do not include coercive powers over the citizens.[75] Otherwise, however, the Union's power to apply the law (i.e. implementation of rules in individual cases) is not categorically excluded from the vertical competences; it depends entirely on the analysis of the respective empowering provisions.[76] The Union may set detailed rules on the national administrative application by means of secondary law; it is not limited to the enactment of general rules. Moreover, all Member State authorities must observe the general principles of Union law (e.g. the prohibition on discrimination), even if this impacts a sector for which the Union does not possess a competence.[77] However, the Union's institutions need a proper legal basis in order to implement Union law directly; the Commission in particular does not enjoy a general competence to apply the law.[78] Equally, the Union's institutions lack the authority to issue instructions to national authorities.[79] In certain cases this is compensated for by the Commission's authority to issue decisions addressed to the Member States. These decisions often largely determine the latter's administrative action directed at its citizen. Further instruments of

[72] Legislation and rule-making are treated as synonyms in this text. Whereas in the constitutional systems of the Member Sates the term 'legislation' is often reserved for parliamentary rule-making, at the transnational level it describes the enactment of all forms of abstract and general rules: see Case C–280/93 *Germany v Council* [1994] ECR I–4973, para 47. The Constitutional Treaty, however, opts for a narrower concept of 'legislative acts' (Art 34 CT–IGC; Art I–33 CT–Conv); see J Bast in this volume.

[73] See Opinion 2/94, above n 60, paras 26 *et seq*.

[74] See Case C–50/00 P, *Unión de Pequeños Agricultores v Council* [2002] ECR I–6677, para 45.

[75] See Manin, above n 9, para 140.

[76] See Jarass, above n 4, 182–3; it is significant this is always treated as a question of institutional balance within the context of the *horizontal* competences: cf K Lenaerts, 'Some Reflections on the Separation of Powers in the European Community' (1991) 28 *CML Rev* 11 at 19 *et seq*; K Lenaerts and P van Nuffel, *Constitutional Law of the European Union* (1999), 458 *et seq*; see also D Simon, *Le système juridique communautaire* (1997), 74.

[77] The ECJ has developed these conditions into detailed requirements: cf S Kadelbach, *Allgemeines Verwaltungsrecht unter europäischem Einfluß* (1999), 296 *et seq*; GC Rodríguez Iglesias, 'Zu den Grenzen der verfahrensrechtlichen Autonomie der Mitgliedstaaten bei der Anwendung des Gemeinschaftsrechts' [1997] *Europäische Grundrechte-Zeitschrift* 289. This case law has been in part strongly criticised; as discussed above (section I), this point is nevertheless beyond the current discussion.

[78] Few Treaty norms enable the Union to apply the law directly to the citizens; a proper legal basis may, however, be found in basic acts of the Council and the Parliament. The term 'implementation' in Art 202 EC encompasses individual measures as well as general rules: Case 16/88, *Commission v Council* [1989] ECR 3457, para 11; for details, see C Möllers, 'Durchführung des Gemeinschaftsrechts' [2002] *Europarecht* 483 at 493 *et seq*.

[79] See Kadelbach, above n 77, 337–8; A Hatje, *Die gemeinschaftsrechtliche Steuerung der Wirtschaftsverwaltung* (1998), 161 *et seq* and 438.

guidance of national authorities have been developed through obligations to consult the Commission and through budgetary mechanisms.[80]

The most important limitation in this respect comes from the principles of subsidiarity and proportionality. This solution is convincing: it is hardly possible to normatively distinguish the legislative and executive functions at the abstract *Verbandskompetenz* level with sufficient precision.[81]

aa) Exclusive Powers In this section the Union's competences will be classified according to the way that they affect the Member State's powers. According to Art 5(2) EC, European constitutional law distinguishes between exclusive and non-exclusive competences. Within the latter one can distinguish between concurrent and parallel (also termed cumulative-concurrent) powers. Within the parallel powers, one can conceive non-regulatory powers as a particular subgroup.

The concept of exclusive competences was introduced by the ECJ and has since been explicitly recognised in the Treaty of Maastricht in Art 3b(2) EC Treaty (now Art 5(2) EC). An exclusive competence of the Union means that *the mere existence of such a norm* prohibits the Member States from acting in that area.[82] From the point in time that such a competence is to be found in the Treaties, and as long as this particular provision remains in force, the Member States are basically prohibited from enacting any legislation in that field.

The Treaties themselves explicitly confer exclusive competences only in the monetary policy field (e.g. Art 106(1) EC). The qualification of other competences as exclusive is controversial, in particular after the introduction of Art 3b(2) EC Treaty.[83] The common commercial policy under Art 133 EC is, based on the ECJ's jurisprudence, recognised as being an exclusive competence, but the boundaries to other fields in which the Member States enjoy concurrent powers are often difficult to draw.[84] Given the important repercussions on national competences, classifying a competence as exclusive should only be done when: (1) the actions by the Member States would severely prejudice later Union action, (2) a common legal framework is necessary *in any case*[85], and (3) the decision-making system of

[80] There are detailed analyses in E Schmidt-Aßmann and W Hoffmann-Riem (eds), *Strukturen des Europäischen Verwaltungsrechts* (1999).

[81] From the Protocol on subsidiarity and proportionality one can deduce the principle that the application of the law of the Union should rest with the Member States. That implies that the Union has vertical competence to do otherwise.

[82] Cases 3/, 4/ and 6/76 *Kramer* [1976] ECR 1279, paras 30/33; Case 804/79 *Commission v United Kingdom* [1981] ECR 1045, paras 17 *et seq*; Case C–405/92, *Mondiet* [1993] ECR I–6133, para 12; Manin, above n 9, para 145.

[83] Cf the Commission's long list on this, published in *Agence Europe* No. 1804/05 on 30 October 1992.

[84] On the WTO Agreements, see Opinion 1/94, above n 42, paras 22 *et seq*.

[85] In more detail see A von Bogdandy in E Grabitz, A von Bogdandy and M Nettesheim (eds), *Europäisches Außenwirtschaftsrecht* (1994), 23–4; Zuleeg, above n 68, Art 5 EC, para 7.

the Union is able to cope with its sole responsibility. Accordingly, even in the common commercial policy field an exclusive competence would only exist in the core areas.

Alongside these exclusive powers the Union also enjoys exclusive competences regarding the internal organisation of its institutional system, sometimes because this is explicitly foreseen, sometimes based on an implicit competence. Here one can cite the right to promulgate staff regulations and conditions of employment under Art 283 EC, or the rules on judicial procedure in the European courts, which are exclusively governed by the CFI's and ECJ's Rules of Procedure.[86]

One consequence of granting the Union an exclusive competence is that the principle of subsidiarity is not applicable, as Art 5(2) EC expressly recognises. The principle of subsidiarity requires balancing the alternative of the Union's acting against the Member States acting alone. When the Union enjoys an exclusive competence, the latter alternative is lacking, i.e. the Member States acting alone is not an alternative.[87]

The Treaties' restraint in granting the Union exclusive competences is welcome. Exclusive competences are particularly problematic because the Union's cumbersome decision-making system cannot reliably satisfy the demands placed on the legislature.[88] The recognition of an implied "emergency legislative" power on the part of the Member States (as "defenders of the common interest"[89]) highlights this problem.

bb) Concurrent Powers When the ECJ qualifies competences, it generally does so by distinguishing only between "exclusive" and "parallel" competences, in which it includes *all* non-exclusive competences.[90] However, it is more convincing to distinguish first between exclusive and non-exclusive competences and, within the latter category, to further distinguish between *concurrent*, *parallel* and *non-regulatory* powers. Moreover, the ECJ does not clearly distinguish between an exclusive competence and a concurrent competence that has been exercised exhaustively ("secondary exclusivity").[91]

In contrast to exclusive competences, concurrent competences permit autonomous national legislation, provided the Union has not made use of its competence. If, however, the Union has taken action, a concurrent competence allows it to regulate the field exhaustively. In other words, the Member States retain their right to autonomously regulate a particular field

[86] There are, however, sections of institutional law that belong to the concurrent powers, eg, Art 190(4) EC.

[87] On further consequences, see Art 43(d) EU, Art 44(1) CT–IGC (Arts I–43(1) CT–Conv).

[88] The ECB Council, the ECB's main decision-making body, significantly and reasonably relies on the principle of a simple majority: Art 10.2 of the Statute of the ESCB.

[89] See M Pechstein, *Die Mitgliedstaaten als 'Sachwalter des gemeinsamen Interesses'* (1987), 75 *et seq*.

[90] Cf Zuleeg, above n 68, Art 5 EC, para 12.

[91] See, eg, Case 22/70 *Commission v Council* [1971] ECR 263, para 31.

as long as and to the extent the Union has not exercised its regulatory power. Only once the Union has exercised its regulatory power, are the Member States prevented from adopting additional rules.[92] That prohibition is usually unwritten and, from a systemic point of view, attributable to the primacy of Union law; this effect is also called pre-emption, after the American constitutional doctrine.[93] The extent to which the Member States may continue to enact legislation depends on the legal instrument the Union employed: the directive (Art 249(3) EC) requires the Member State to adopt national laws transposing it, whereas the same provision, if the Union chose the regulation (Art 249(2) EC), would largely prevent the adoption of national legislation. In both cases the Union can pre-empt the Member States from any autonomous action by occupying the field.[94] According to the implied powers doctrine, this prohibition extends to relations with third countries (ERTA case law).[95] Regarding the external relations, Member States may be pre-empted from any autonomous action much more easily than in the internal realm, since occupation of the field is not demanded.[96]

Concurrent competences can be found above all in the core sectors of the common market, in particular in the customs union, agriculture, transport and the various harmonisation powers for the establishment and development of the internal market. It is appropriate to exclude from the concept of concurrent competences those harmonisation powers that limit the Union to legislating minimum standards, e.g. Art 137 EC. It is the essence of minimum harmonisation that there is no pre-emption.[97] Applying these insights, the Union's important competence under Art 95 EC must be understood as a concurrent competence since legally exhaustive rules are possible.[98]

In sum, exclusive and concurrent competences fundamentally differ as long as the Union has not exercised its power. If, however, the Union has enacted exhaustive legislation, then the difference depends on a criterion that appears rather technical, namely, whether the norm that leads to the prohibition to enact autonomous national legislation is at the level of primary or secondary law. One may speak of primary and secondary exclusivity in order

[92] See Dashwood, above n 34, 126.

[93] For an overview see ED Cross, 'Pre-emption of Member State Law in the European Economic Community' (1992) 29 *CML Rev* 447.

[94] For an exhaustive regulation in the form of a directive see Case 278/85 *Commission v Denmark* [1987] ECR 4069, para 12. It can be very difficult to determine whether and to what extent a subject has been pre-empted or not.

[95] In summary form see Dörr, above n 41, 39 *et seq.*

[96] On external concurrent competences in detail see Nettesheim, above n 17, 453 *et seq.*

[97] M Dougan, 'Minimum Harmonization and the Internal Market' (2000) 37 *CML Rev* 853 at 854 *et seq*; S Weatherill, 'Beyond Preemption?' in D O'Keeffe and PM Twomey (eds), *Legal Issues of the Maastricht Treaty* (1994), 13 at 23 *et seq.*

[98] See Manin, above n 9, para 143; derogations by Member States are subject to an approval procedure under Art 95(6) EC, hence to the exercise of a Union competence; see in more detail W Kahl in C Calliess and M Ruffert, *Kommentar zum EU- und EG-Vertrag* (2002), Art 95 EC, para 7.

to demonstrate this affinity (and to contrast them with a mere parallel competence; see below). One must not, however, confuse the two types of competences, since the exhaustive use of a concurrent competence cannot transform it into an exclusive competence.[99]

Against this background a remarkable misunderstanding comes to the fore. In particular the assumption of German *Länder* that a return of power to national and sub-national entities requires a constitutional change is incorrect because their political demands regard only supranational legislation under the non-exclusive powers, i.e. withdrawal of existing secondary law. Their chances of attaining their objectives would be far greater if they pushed for the reform of secondary legislation rather than constitutional reform. One might also mention that this approach would be better targeted, thus increasing the chances of reaching their specific goals.

This is particularly true for the agricultural sector. Art 37 EC is constantly—and incorrectly—brought forward as the "outstanding example" of an exclusive competence.[100] It is true that practically all agricultural market organisation law has been exhaustively regulated based on Art 37 EC. The competence is not, however, exclusive, because there is no functional requirement that prevents the Member States from enacting legislation independently from Union acts. The limitations on national competences result instead solely from the density of the secondary regulations, which is by no means required by the agricultural Title's provisions in the EC Treaty.[101]

The description of the EU's competences as "dynamic" is another misunderstanding. It is, of course, true that concurrent competences make it difficult to draw a line between the competences of the Member States and the Union insofar as any additional Union legislation places further limits on the Member States' competence to regulate the subject matter autonomously.[102] The boundary is thus constantly moving as the Union enacts further legislation. This flexibility is not, however, an unusual effect of the vertical distribution of competences in multilevel (federal) systems.[103] This form of "dynamism" is nothing more than the logical consequence of the nature of concurrent competences, which allows Member States much greater autonomy than the "non-dynamic" exclusive competence. However, the charge that the Union has a dynamic order of competences in the sense that the

[99] See Trüe (2004), above n 6, 403 and 414; A Furrer, *Die Sperrwirkung des sekundären Gemeinschaftsrechts auf die nationalen Rechtsordnungen* (1994), 236 *et seq*; for a different view, however, see Weatherill, above n 97, 14 and 21.

[100] See the Commission's first paper on subsidiarity, cf above n 83; as here J-C Piris, 'Hat die Europäische Union eine Verfassung? Braucht sie eine?' [2000] *Europarecht* 311 at 332.

[101] R Bieber, 'Abwegige und zielführende Vorschläge: Zur Kompetenzabgrenzung der Europäischen Union' [2001] *Integration* 308 at 311.

[102] See Piris, above n 100, 332.

[103] Cf Art 74 German Basic Law; on this see R Stettner in H Dreier (ed), *Grundgesetz Kommentar* (1998), Art 74, para 12.

Union's institutions are able to change the *content* of a competence norm by their own legislative activity or even by binding interpretation is incorrect.[104]

Looking at the concurrent competences for harmonisation, one discovers that the ECJ has clarified the scope of Art 95 EC in its *Tobacco Advertising* decision, delimiting its problematic breadth. This harmonising competence is only applicable in those cases where, in order to foster the fundamental freedoms, a Union measure is necessary to eliminate distortions of competition with an appreciable effect or trade obstacles caused by differing Member State regulations.[105] This interpretation of Art 95 EC, in which the ECJ also incorporates services (Art 55 in conjunction with Art 47(2) EC), can be generalised as a comprehensive conception. The EU is empowered to harmonise only insofar as such action is necessary for the functioning of the internal market; the mere existence of disparities between national regulatory schemes does not justify a harmonisation.[106]

The basic logic is as follows. The fundamental freedoms, with their prohibitions on discrimination and market hindrance, extensively co-ordinate the national legal orders without, however, harmonising them. Yet, insofar as it emerges that the fundamental freedoms alone are not able to guarantee the functioning of the internal market, the individual Member States' regulations may be subject to European harmonising measures.[107] In particular, since the fundamental freedoms do not prevent Member States from unilaterally adopting measures in order to serve a common good (such as public health or consumer protection), they may not effectively prevent market fragmentation.[108] The ECJ thus uses the fundamental freedoms to define the scope of competences here. The Union's competence to enact approximations[109] with a view to realising the internal market extends as far as the fundamental freedoms' scope of application.[110] This conception

[104] On Art 128 EEC Treaty (Rome), see AG Tesauro in Cases C–51, C–90 and C–94/89, *United Kingdom et al v Council* [1991] ECR I–2757, para 2.

[105] See Case C–376/98, above n 60, paras 85; this is largely consistent with the demands of the German *Länder*, cf their reform proposal for Art 95 EC in Bundesrat Drucksache 667/95, 14.

[106] See HM Watt, 'Experiences from Europe: Legal Diversity and the Internal Market' (2004) 39 *Texas International Law Journal* 429 at 437.

[107] For cases after *Tobacco Advertising*, see Case C–377/98 *Netherlands v Parliament and Council* [2001] ECR I–7079, para 20; Case C–491/01 *British American Tobacco* [2002] ECR I–11453, para 60; Cases C–465/00, C–138/ and C–139/01, *Österreichischer Rundfunk* [2003] ECR I–4989, para 41.

[108] See, eg, Case C–262/02 *Commission v France* [2004] ECR I–0000, paras 23 *et seq*.

[109] The term 'approximation' (and its cognates) is used interchangeably with the term 'harmonisation' (and its cognates).

[110] Herein lies a hitherto undiscovered implication of the *Keck* case law, which removes rules concerning selling arrangements that are applied equally to domestic and foreign products from the reach of Art 28 EC. This also contains a (negative) statement on the scope of the Union's harmonisation competence; on this interrelation, see recently CD Classen, 'Die Grundfreiheiten im Spannungsfeld von europäischer Marktfreiheit und mitgliedstaatlichen Gestaltungskompetenzen' [2004] *Europarecht* 416 at 437; on *Keck*, see T Kingreen in this volume.

has the undeniable advantage that the issues of the vertical competences are linked to the far more detailed case law on the fundamental freedoms.[111]

Against this background one can further explain why the prohibition on approximation contained in Art 152(4)(c) EC is inapplicable under Art 95 EC. Harmonisation necessary for the internal market also includes the competence to harmonise national rules limiting the fundamental freedoms, including those national rules justified on the basis of a public good.[112] Once the legal and political case for harmonisation is made, the political decisions about the relative importance of the affected interests (here: the appropriate level of health protection) must be determined by the European legislative institutions, whereas the individual Member States—at least in cases of an exhaustive secondary regulation—are no longer able to rely on the primary law's protective clauses (e.g. Art 30 EC).[113] If the Union legislature were prevented from pursuing health policy itself, a problematic one-sidedness for Community law would result, since "negative integration" effected by the fundamental freedoms would not be counterbalanced by "positive integration" effected by European legislation.[114]

The conception proposed here, that internal market harmonisation under Art 95(1) EC is a concurrent competence,[115] is incompatible with the view that this provision founds an exclusive Union competence.[116] The qualification of Art 95(1) EC as an exclusive competence overlooks the fact that internal market harmonisation is consistent with the maintenance of autonomous Member State regulatory competence. The Union can even limit itself to enacting minimum standard legislation to foster mutual recognition. Moreover, the Member States' concurrent competence is even a logical precondition for a any action under Art 95 EC: it would make no sense to "approximate" a sector in which the Member States were no longer permitted to legislate.

As an overall assessment, one can say that concurrent competences as a category provide considerable advantages. The possibility of exhaustively

[111] Furthermore, this conception has the potential to simplify the issue insofar as the Union possesses vertical competence for the harmonisation of any measure that falls within the freedoms' scope of application. The more complicated question of the appropriate legal basis is only important for determining the horizontal competence. Due to differing procedural requirements, not all legal bases providing a power to harmonise can be cumulated, so that difficult problems of delimitation can arise.

[112] According to the so-called 'new approach', the logic of internal market harmonisation is driven precisely by the interplay of primary and secondary law: Commission, 'Completing the Internal Market': White Paper from the Commission to the European Council, COM(1985) 310 final, Nos 13 and 64; Council Resolution on a new approach to technical harmonization and standards [1985] OJ C 136/1.

[113] Case C–37/92 *Vanacker* [1993] ECR I–4947, para 9; Case C–324/99 *Daimler Chrysler* [2001] ECR I–9897, para 32; cf Weatherill, above n 97, 16 *et seq*.

[114] This is a common criticism, see F Scharpf, *Regieren in Europa* (1999), 70 *et seq*; but see Art 95(3) EC.

[115] See Case C–377/98, above n 107, paras 31 *et seq*.

[116] See AG Fennelly, above n 66, paras 135–42.

regulating a subject matter is advantageous from the point of view of legal security since it can avoid subtle questions of conflicting laws. The dynamics that reside in this type of competence have, however, led to the well-known problems with respect to the Member States' competences and the transparency problems connected to this. Yet, these disadvantages are counterbalanced by the fact that the Member States' competences are less affected than by exclusive competences and legal loopholes and uncertainty are avoided.

One can conclude that, insofar as concurrent competences are concerned, it is not necessary to amend the Treaties to return legislative competence to the Member States. The future debate should not, therefore, be conducted as one of *constitutional* reform. Political actors who desire an expansion of Member State powers should try to influence the European law-making process, but need not embark on the much more difficult process of amending the Treaties.

cc) Parallel Powers The third type of competence includes those empowering provisions under which the Union and Member State competences can be exercised alongside one another. In this case, the Union's exercise of a competence does *not* lead to the Member States' being prohibited from acting autonomously in the same field. These competences are variously termed parallel powers, cumulative-concurrent competences or shared competences.

Where the Treaties permit the Union and the Member State to enact parallel legislation, they assume that the measures enacted at each level are not in fundamental opposition, but rather strengthen each other. The relevant articles generally use the description of "complementing" the Member State activities (Art 164 EC) or "contributing" to the achievement of common objectives (Art 157 EC). Most of the new powers introduced in the EC Treaty since the Single European Act correspond to this type of competence. Some examples include industrial policy (Art 157 EC), economic and social cohesion (Arts 158 *et seq* EC), research and technological development (Arts 163 *et seq* EC) or development co-operation (Arts 177 *et seq* EC). The common foreign and security policy under the EU Treaty also corresponds to this type. The law on state aids (Art 87 *et seq* EC) plays a special role in the area of parallel powers. As a functional, cross-sectoral competence, it can, of course, only be exercised by the Union. However, the Member States retain a parallel competence, each according to its respective internal order of competences, to set the legal framework for aids granted by the Member State.

The parallel activity of the Union and Member States requires rules for the co-ordination of conflicting provisions. When both the Union and the Member State simultaneously enact requirements and prohibitions directed at the citizen, the latter must in principle satisfy both. When, however, the legal orders enact contradictory rules of conduct or require the Member

State authorities to act inconsistently, the primacy of Union law as a general co-ordinating rule is applicable.[117] The range of competences available to the national institutions can thus also be significantly reduced in areas where there is a parallel EU competence, as is readily evident from the example of the law of state aids. A general pre-emption of an entire regulatory field, however, is precluded.

A subgroup of parallel powers has already been mentioned: the Union's competence to establish minimum standards. The most important examples here are the minimum standards for asylum and immigration under Art 63 EC, the social policy provisions under Art 137(2)(b) EC, environmental standards under Art 175 EC and certain areas of criminal law under Arts 31, 34 EU. As a rule, minimum approximation permits the Member States to take stricter measures, departing from the "Community floor".[118] Limitations may arise from other provisions, however, in particular the fundamental freedoms. The difference between minimum and total harmonisation is fluid, as the case law on the details of the environmental field demonstrates.[119]

From the perspective of the Member States the advantages of parallel competences are evident. The national authorities are able to continue political activity even within the realm of European legislation and thereby remain visible to their citizens. As a rule, parallel competences are also unobjectionable from an integration perspective in areas where the measures only flank the internal market and are not of central importance to the disciplines of competition or market equality.[120] The concept of minimum standards may represent an acceptable compromise between necessary legal equality and regulatory competition, which tends to promote innovation. The goal of establishing clear lines of responsibility by decoupling the decision-making levels can hardly be achieved in this way, however. Furthermore, conflicts of law are pre-programmed.

dd) Non-regulatory Powers Those empowering provisions that permit the Union to act, yet restrict its institutions to actions with limited effects can be considered a subcategory of parallel powers. Under these competences the Union is prevented from regulating, therefore the term "non-regulatory powers"; they are also termed as "complementary" powers.[121] Here, the

[117] See Case 14/68, *Walt Wilhelm* [1969] ECR 1, para 6.

[118] F Tuytschaever, *Differentiation in European Union Law* (1999), 19 *et seq*.

[119] DH Scheuing, 'Regulierung und Marktfreiheit im Europäischen Umweltrecht' [2000] *Europarecht* 1; Dougan, above n 97, 866 *et seq*.

[120] S Krislov, C-D Ehlermann and JHH Weiler, 'The Political Organs and the Decision-Making Process in the United States and the European Community' in M Cappelletti, M Seccombe and JHH Weiler (eds), *Integration Through Law* (1986), i, bk 2, 95–6.; on the controversial conversion from parallelism to total harmonisation in competition law cf Council Reg (EC) No 1/2003 [2003] OJ L 1/1, on this C-D Ehlermann, 'The Modernization of EC Antitrust Policy' (2000) 37 *CML Rev* 537; see also J Drexl in this volume.

[121] See the Final Report of the Convention's Working Group V, 'Complementary Competencies', CONV 375/1/02 <http://register.consilium.eu.int/pdf/en/02/cv00/ 00375-r1en2.pdf>(1 September 2004).

Member States retain the primary legislative competence. Yet, it is worthwhile construing this type as a separate category since—under normal circumstances—a conflict of norms cannot arise. Therefore it does not require a co-ordination rule, which is different to the parallel competences in the narrow sense.[122] The non-regulative competences can be further subdivided into competences to provide incentives, to co-ordinate and to make recommendations. The Treaties often combine these different variants, which provides further justification for considering these instruments under a unique rubric.

Provisions that authorise the Union to undertake so-called "incentive measures", excluding any harmonisation, fall under the rubric of non-regulatory competences. They are a steering mechanism, providing the Member States and private parties with an incentive to take positive action, primarily through targeted subsidies, pilot projects and symbolic action. Examples can be found in employment, education, culture and health, Arts 129, 149(4), 151(5), 152(4)(c) EC respectively. The legal acts taken under these empowering provisions take the form of decisions *sui generis* (*Beschluss*) which are not addressed to particular persons. This legal instrument cannot create duties for either the Member States or citizens.[123] The Member States do, however, have an obligation arising from Art 10 EC to facilitate the achievement of the Union's undertaking.[124]

The co-ordinating competences also belong to this category.[125] The Treaties contain many mechanisms for co-ordinating the Member States' otherwise autonomous policies as well as mechanisms for facilitating co-operation between the Member States' authorities. The surveillance of economic policy (Art 99 EC) is one of the better known examples. Another example is the co-ordinated employment strategy under Arts 125 *et seq* EC. It is notable that the European Council is involved in the exercise of both of these co-ordinating competences. In most cases the horizontal competence to co-ordinate the Member States' authorities lies with the Commission.[126]

Lastly, the recommendation competences also belong to this category. It has already been noticed that non-binding instruments also require a Treaty

[122] However, the principle of sincere co-operation, Art 10 EC, plays a role in the exercise of the non-regulative competences. Moreover, the doctrine of consistent interpretation applies when the Member States decide to transpose a recommendation: Case C–322/88 *Grimaldi* [1989] ECR 4407, para 18.

[123] See J Bast in this volume; for details, see *id*, *Grundbegriffe der Handlungsformen der EU* (2006), part 2.

[124] See Case 242/87 *Commission v Council* [1989] ECR 1425, paras 11, 19.

[125] For the importance of the competence, see G Amato, 'L'Europa dal passato al futuro' [2004] *Il Mulino* 5.

[126] When the Treaties give the Commission a co-ordinating task, it is entitled to create a legally binding framework for its administration, which includes, for instance, the creation of reporting obligations by means of a decision addressed to the Member States: Cases 281, 283–285 and 287/85, above n 44, para 28.

authorisation. It is therefore worth remarking that the EC Treaty has conferred a broad competence upon the Commission to make recommendations and deliver opinions (Art 211 EC). In practice, the Commission has used this power cautiously; it might have done so with a view to preserving this special instruments.[127] The Council does not enjoy a general competence to make recommendations.[128] Aside from the recommendations for fiscal and economic co-ordination, it is worth mentioning Art 151(5) EC, which empowers the Council to unanimously (!) adopt recommendations.[129] In rare instances, Parliament and Council, acting jointly under the co-decision procedure, even adopt recommendations such as those on education policy based on Arts 149(4) and 150(4) EC. An explicit power to make recommendations under Art 33 Euratom Treaty may even give rise to an external power to conclude international agreements.[130]

Consequently the Union's institutions and the Member States take non-regulatory competences seriously: European constitutional scholarship should do so as well. Equipping the Union with limited non-regulatory competences allows the Union's institutions to undertake activities in sectors where the Member States are not prepared to accept further integration. The fact that non-regulatory competences are positively formulated in the Treaties has been a major factor in limiting the problematic practice of "complementary law", i.e. agreements and decision of the Member States adopted outside of the Union's constitutional framework. In particular, the competences to provide incentives, with all their respect for national autonomy, have an important impact through the various action programmes, e.g. the well-known ERASMUS-programme. It is thus all the more important to recognise that the Union's non-regulatory competences are based on specific attribution through the Treaties. Ad-hoc co-ordination of the Member States through the European Council, vaguely laid down in the conclusions of its Presidency, should be avoided. Rather, actions by the Union's legislative institutions, which demand a clear constitutional basis, should be favoured.

c) Rules Regarding the Exercise of Powers

Since the Treaty of Maastricht the task of Art 5 EC (ex Art 3b EC Treaty) has been to stabilise the exercise of vertical competences. This task was concretised by the Treaty of Amsterdam's Protocol on subsidiarity and proportionality.[131] The goal is to counter a supposed automaticity, which allegedly

[127] For empirical data, see A von Bogdandy, F Arndt and J Bast, 'Legal Instruments in European Union Law: A Systematic Approch on an Empirical Basis', (2004) 23 *YEL* 91.

[128] But see Art 35(3) CT–IGC (Art I–34(2) CT–Conv).

[129] On the duty to respect the relevant law-making procedure when amending an existing recommendation see Case C–27/04, above n 21, paras 91 *et seq* (regarding the Stability and Growth Pact).

[130] Case C–29/99, *Commission v Council* [2002] ECR I–11221, para 105.

[131] In more detail see S Griller *et al*, *The Treaty of Amsterdam* (2000), 96 *et seq*.

expands the Union's competences at the expense of the Member States'. An ocean of ink has been spilled on the subject of subsidiarity.[132] Even though this provision has so far not played a central role in case law,[133] it has marked the legislative culture. It has become difficult to demonstrate that Union legislation seriously endangers the subsidiarity principle.[134] It is obviously a successful innovation protecting the Member States' competences. As a rule for the *exercise* of competences it is based on an already existing *Verbandskompetenz*,[135] so it only indirectly touches on the question of drawing the boundaries separating the Union's competences from those of the Member States.

III. THE CONSTITUTIONAL TREATY'S ORDER OF COMPETENCES[136]

As stated above, three different sources of concern fuel the debate over competences. The first is the concern that there is an automatism that deprives the Member States of their powers and thereby undermines their political relevance, even their statehood; the following analysis of the Constitutional Treaty proceeds first from this perspective. A second concern—particularly, of the German *Länder*—deals with reclaiming some of the national or regional scope of action in the exercise of competences. Even if the limitations on the German *Länder* do not result from the vertical order of competences (as section II of this paper shows), this source nonetheless yields another angle of appraisal. The third source of concern involves the reality that Union legitimacy suffers from the fact that its citizens perceive it as a too diffuse conglomeration. This diffuseness results primarily from the horizontal order of competences (that is, the Union's institutional structure) and not from the vertical order. However, it is undisputed that the vertical order of competences, as well, could be arranged more transparently and comprehensibly.

1. The Protection of Member State Sovereignty

Whether and to what degree the term sovereignty continues to play a useful role in the relationship between the Union and Member States is

[132] For a fundamental work, see C Calliess, *Subsidiaritäts- und Solidaritätsprinzip in der Europäischen Union* (1999).

[133] See, eg, Case C–377/98, above n 107, paras 30 *et seq.*

[134] See R v Borries, 'Rechtsetzung in der Europäischen Gemeinschaft' [2001] *Zeitschrift für Gesetzgebung* 79.

[135] Art 5(1) EC concerns the 'can question', Art 5(2) EC the 'if question', Art 5(3) EC the 'how question': M Ruffert in Calliess and Ruffert, above n 98, Art 5 EC, para 6.

[136] An earlier version of this section was published in German with co-authorship of Dietrich Westphal: A von Bogdandy, J Bast and D Westphal, 'Die vertikale Kompetenzordnung im Entwurf des Verfassungsvertrags' [2003] *Integration* 414.

uncertain.[137] At any rate, the term still brings together basic issues of the vertical order of competences, since demands for its fundamental reform are most often formulated under the catchphrase "protection of national sovereignty". The following analysis does not, however, evaluate the new powers conferred upon the Union in Part III of the Constitutional Treaty; rather, it focuses only on the relevant provisions of Part I.

a) The Basis for Competence

The Constitutional Treaty's first operative clause, Art 1(1), displays its desire—at least symbolically—to address concerns about sovereignty. After much debate, the Convention decided against founding Union competence ultimately in the Constitutional Treaty itself. Instead, according to the final formula, the "Member States confer" them upon the Union.[138] Likewise, pursuant to Art 11(2) CT-IGC (Art I-9(2) CT-Conv), the Union shall act within the limits of the competences "conferred upon it by the Member States in the Constitution"; in an earlier version it was still the competences "conferred upon it by the Constitution".

Thus, the Convention adopted the terminology used in corresponding national constitutional law. European constitutional law comes into direct *terminological* (though not necessarily *conceptual*) consonance with national constitutional law. With echoes of Art 88-2 of the French Constitution ("transferts de compétences"), Art 93 of the Spanish Constitution ("se atribuya ... competencias derivadas de la Constitución"), and Art 23(1) German Basic Law ("Hoheitsrechte übertragen"), the Constitutional Treaty formulates its Art 1(1) (respectively, "confèrent des compétences", "confiren competencias", and "Zuständigkeiten ... übertragen") and Art 11(2) CT-IGC (respectively, "compétences ... attribuées", "competencias ... atribuyen", and "Zuständigkeiten ... zugewiesen"). This terminological correspondence between supranational and national levels—at such a fundamental point—can certainly be welcomed as intentionally "peacemaking".

This, then, would seem to foreclose an understanding of *Verbandskompetenz* under emphatic theories of constitution-making (*pouvoir constituant*).[139] Symbolic emphasis is placed on the political decision *not* to craft the Constitutional Treaty with a legitimacy separate from and independent of the Member States. One wonders, though, whether this method of establishing competence undermines Union law as it stands today—which has consisted of and been defined by the legal concepts of

[137] See S Oeter in this volume.

[138] Cp with the earlier proposal of the Praesidium the Draft of Art 1 to 16 of the Constitutional Treaty, CONV 528/03 <http://register.consilium.eu.int/pdf/en/03/cv00/cv00528en03.pdf> (8 September 2004).

[139] See C Möllers in this volume. On the weaknesses of emphatic theories, see T Herbst, *Legitimation durch Verfassunggebung* (2003), 28.

direct effect and primacy of Union law. The legal justification of primacy, in particular, has always been precarious. The ECJ and much of the legal scholarship have based it on the legal premise that Community law forms an autonomous legal order.[140] This autonomy conflicts with widespread notions of a "transfer of sovereign power", for example, in Arts 23(1) and 24(1) German Basic Law. The Constitutional Treaty, with its reiteration of the transfer formulation, seems itself to erode this autonomy.[141]

Such fears, however, fail to recognise that the doctrine of autonomy becomes superfluous insofar as the primacy of Union law is positively codified in Art 6 CT-IGC (Art I-10(1) CT-Conv), especially since the term "law of the Member States" comprehends the respective bodies of constitutional law, as well. To the degree that primacy of Union law is explicit, matters of autonomy become dispensable in legal practice. The legal concept of an autonomous legal order is problematic for numerous reasons (e.g. the intermingled complexity of national and Union legal orders); having lost much of its significance, the concept can be downgraded. Granted, to a certain degree it remains legally relevant, not least for the autonomy of interpretation of Union legal terms. Because this latter autonomy is unquestioned, the content of the Union term "transfer" or "conferral" can develop distinctly and separately from its various national counterparts. The continued application of the ECJ's established doctrines is certain, not least due to Art 438(4) CT-IGC (Art IV-3(2) CT-Conv). In the future, theoretical construction will have to shift the emphasis of these doctrines away from ideas of separating the legal orders and, thus, towards co-operative law-making within complementary constitutional orders.[142]

b) A Critically Narrow Concept of Competence?

If the protection of Member State sovereignty is thus symbolically underscored, counterbalancing aspects are also evident. For instance, the Constitutional Treaty does not seem to subsume all Union activities and measures under the order of competences. According to its Art 1(1), 2nd sentence, the Union shall not only "exercise on a Community basis the competences" conferred on it, but also shall act *beyond* this to "coordinate the policies by which the Member States aim to achieve" their common objectives. The notion of competence, therefore, seems to refer only to legal acts

140 On the debate, compare T Schilling, 'The Autonomy of the Community Legal Order: An Analysis of Possible Foundations' (1996) 37 *Harv Int'l LJ* 38 with JHH Weiler and U Haltern, 'The Autonomy of the Community Legal Order—Through the Looking Glass' (1996) 37 *Harv Int'l LJ* 411.

141 See E Brok and other members of the Convention in a suggested amendment of Art I–9(2) CT–Conv, see E Brok *et al*, 'Amendment Form', <http://european-convention.eu.int/Docs/Treaty/pdf/8/8_Art%20I%209%20Brok%20EN.pdf> (6 September 2004).

142 See AG Geelhoed in Case C–304/02 *Commission v France* [2004] ECR I–0000, para 29 (Opinion of 29 April 2004).

in a narrow sense, not to co-ordinating action. This, in turn, would leave important processes of policy co-ordination outside the order of competences and beyond its function of protecting Member States' jurisdictions against irregular interferences by Union institutions.

Nonetheless, Arts 15 and 17 CT-IGC (Arts I-14 and I-16(1) CT-Conv) provide a basis for a more reasonable understanding of competence, since its "coordinating action" also falls within the Title on Union competences. This broad understanding subordinates a wide scope of action to the competence regime. Thus, Art 1(1), 2nd sentence, should be read as presenting different types of Union competence, which range from competences for merely co-ordinating Member States' policies to supranational legislative competences to be exercised "on a Community basis". Such an understanding is to be preferred, since the Union's "soft" steering can massively influence the Member States' freedom to act.

In this context, it also is remarkable that Part I of the Constitutional Treaty neither regulates nor even mentions the so-called open method of co-ordination (OMC).[143] The proposal of the Convention's Working Group IX, that constitutional status should be assigned to the OMC,[144] was not implemented. Thus a significant realm of political activity—critical both to democracy and the rule of law—basically remains outside the order of competences, despite taking place within Union institutions.[145]

c) Preservation and Enlargement of a "Flexibility Clause"

For many critics of the Union's order of competences, Art 308 EC is an upsetting thorn in the side. Its abolition has long belonged to the central demands of, for example, representatives of the German *Länder*.[146] Indeed, the Article represents the weakest point in the limiting function of the current division of powers.

Nevertheless, the Convention's proposal maintains the substance of Art 308 EC in Art 18 CT-IGC (Art I-17 CT-Conv) and even extends its scope of application. Apparently, the members of the Convention could not calm the fears that unforeseen situations would repeatedly call for the Union to take action.[147] Even a Union that protects, as a matter of constitutional

[143] Although in Part III OMC is present, see the 'initiatives' the Commission may take: Arts 213(2), 250(2), 278(2), 279(2) CT–IGC (Arts III–107(2), III–148(2), III–179(2), III–180(2) CT–Conv).

[144] Final report of Working Group IX on Simplification, CONV 424/02, 7 <http://register.consilium.eu.int/pdf/en/02/cv00/00424en2.pdf> (1 September 2004).

[145] On formalising OMC see D Ashiagbor, 'Soft Harmonisation: The "Open Method of Coordination" in the European Employment Strategy' (2004) 10 *European Public Law* 305 at 330 *et seq*.

[146] Cf Clement, above n 2, para 34 (with further references).

[147] Eg, the establishment of a fund for German flood victims: see Council Reg (EC) 2012/2002 establishing the European Union Solidarity Fund [2002] OJ L 311/3. No minister-president of a German *Land* criticised this.

principle, national freedom to act needs a safety valve such as Art 308 EC. Moreover, the Convention succeeded in persuasively reformulating this empowering provision: the involvement of national parliaments as well as the required consent of the European Parliament better legitimate the exercise of this power.

In contrast to Art 308 EC, the new provision is not limited to the common market and applies henceforth to each of the political areas catalogued in Part III. This includes the common security and foreign policy as well as the previous third pillar, which was extremely controversial at the Convention.[148] The drafters' intention that the flexibility clause "could not be used to extend the competences of the Union by establishing a new policy"[149] is reflected in the text of Art 18(1) CT-IGC (Art I-17(1) CT-Conv). This provision, however, confers upon the legislator a considerable margin of discretion to determine which action proves "necessary within the framework of the policies defined in Part III". Safeguarding Member States' interests predominantly is a function of the relevant procedural requirements. The continued requirement of unanimity in the Council bestows their strong position, further strengthened by paragraph (2) and (3). The former entitles national parliaments to take part in the Union's legislative process and to monitor compliance with the principle of subsidiarity. Additionally, the latter paragraph establishes a prohibition on harmonisation in order to prevent the relevant prohibition under a specific competence being circumvented.[150] Finally, the flexibility clause is not subject to a simplified amendment procedure under Art 444 CT-IGC (Art I-24(4) CT-Conv) or Art 445 CT-IGC.

d) The ECJ as Guardian of the Order of Competences

An order of competences is only as good as its safeguarding instruments. As the institution representing the Member States' interests, the Council has certainly failed on occasion in this regard. Until the 1990s, even the ECJ hardly monitored the Council's exercise of *Verbandskompetenzen*. Since then, though, the ECJ has evolved into a court of competence.[151] Yet, the ECJ's recent sweeping jurisprudence on citizenship and fundamental

[148] Draft Text with Comment of the Praesidium, CONV 724/03, 84 <http://register.consilium.eu.int/pdf/en/03/cv00/cv00724en03.pdf> (1 September 2004).

[149] *Ibid*, 84.

[150] This prohibition has no relevance for the interpretation of Art 172 CT–IGC (Art III–65 CT–Conv, the successor to Art 95 EC), as demonstrated above: see II 2 a; this view is shared by M Dougan, 'The Convention's Draft Constitutional Treaty: Bringing Europe Closer to its Lawyers?' (2003) 28 *EL Rev* 763 at 769.

[151] The ECJ's case law corresponds almost verbatim with the statements of the German Federal Constitutional Court on the limiting function of the vertical order of competences; see Opinion 2/94, above n 60, para 30; Case C–376/98, above n 60, para 83; *Entscheidungen des Bundesverfassungsgerichts* 89, 155 at 210 (*Maastricht*).

rights[152] might create a need for later European legislation to harmonise these issues, which might, in turn, stretch the harmonisation competences and, thus, the principle of conferral.[153]

Even today, in the debate over adherence to competence limits, some claim that only a separate court could effectively prevent infringement of Member State sovereignty.[154] Most notably, Siegfried Broß, a judge at the German Federal Constitutional Court, has regularly come forward with such propositions.[155] This proposal did not find its way into the Constitutional Treaty. The Convention's concept on the "final say" regarding conflicts of competence actually leads in the opposite direction, namely, towards a normative (re)affirmation of the ECJ's jurisdiction over such matters. Previously only among the "general and final provisions" of the EC Treaty, Art 292 EC is henceforth positioned as Art 375 CT-IGC (Art III-284 CT-Conv) within the subsection on the ECJ. This is a strong indication that the ECJ is also empowered to make final determinations in conflicts of competence, as Art 438(4) CT-IGC (Art IV-3(2), 2nd sentence CT-Conv) confirms (keyword: *Foto-Frost* case law[156]).

Does the failure to establish a court of competence beside or above the ECJ represent a shortcoming in the Constitutional Treaty? The proposal to create a new court[157] received much scholarly attention and has been refuted by persuasive arguments, for example, in critiques by Ulrich Everling and Franz C Mayer.[158] Nonetheless, proponents persist without rebutting counterarguments or discussing the ECJ's case law on competence issues; thereby, they reveal the weakness of their own position. No current proposal sufficiently demonstrates the need for such a drastic reform as the introduction of another court. Critical extensions of the scope of Union law, likely to result from the case law on citizenship and fundamental rights, are

[152] Case C–184/99 *Grzelczyk* [2001] ECR I–6193, para 31; Case C–60/00 *Carpenter* [2002] ECR I–6279, paras 42, 46; Case C–413/99 *Baumbast* [2002] ECR I–7091, para 82; Case C–148/02 *Garcia Avello* [2003] ECR I–11613, para 27; Case C–117/01, *K.B.* [2004] ECR I–541, para 33.

[153] Also sceptical is CD Classen, 'Anmerkung (on Case 117/01)' [2004] *Juristenzeitung* 513 at 514.

[154] On the various proposals for the institutional and procedural shape of such competence tribunals, see FC Mayer, *Kompetenzüberschreitung und Letztentscheidung* (2000), 330 *et seq*.

[155] See, eg, S Broß, 'Grundrechte und Grundwerte in Europa' [2003] *Juristenzeitung* 429 at 431 *et seq*; *id*, 'Überlegungen zum gegenwärtigen Stand des Europäischen Einigungsprozesses' [2002] *Europäische Grundrechte-Zeitschrift* 574 at 578 *et seq*; *id*, 'Bundesverfassungsgericht—Europäischer Gerichtshof—Europäischer Gerichtshof für Kompetenzkonflikte' (2001) 29 *Verwaltungsarchiv* 425.

[156] Case 314/85 *Foto-Frost* [1987] ECR 4199, para 17.

[157] But see JHH Weiler, 'A Constitution for Europe?' in THH Weiler, I Begg and J Peterson (eds), *Integration in an Expanding European Union* (2003), 17 at 27 (concluding that the solution to conflicts of competence is 'the creation of a Constitutional Council for the Community, modelled in some ways on its French namesake').

[158] U Everling, 'Quis custodiet custodes ipsos?' [2002] *Europäische Zeitschrift für Wirtschaftsrecht* 357; Mayer, above n 154.

not covered by this proposal.[159] Considering all this, the Constitutional Treaty very judiciously declined to establish a new institution for the resolution of conflicts of competence.

2. Protection of Member States' Scope of Action

Apart from concerns about an abstract loss of sovereignty, another source of debate over competence deals with the desire to protect national, regional and local associations from the reins of the Union and especially of the Commission. The Constitutional Treaty devotes attention to this concern and incorporates methods to protect, or even increase, the Member States' scope of action.

a) A Revised Principle of Subsidiarity and a Reconstructed Protocol

Some progress was made with the definition of the principle of subsidiarity in Art 11(3) CT-IGC (Art I-9(3) CT-Conv). The principle, of course, corresponds to Art 5(2) EC, but the new formulation is to be preferred. Firstly, the Constitutional Treaty no longer speaks only of the Member States but now mentions "regional and local level". Secondly, the formulation "but can rather" replaces the nonsensical "and can therefore". Therewith, it is clear and unambiguous that a two-step test is required: the first step requires determination of an insufficiency at the national, regional or local level to solve the problem, and the second requires determination of the Union's problem-solving capacity.

Significant improvement can be found in the Protocol on the Application of the Principles of Subsidiarity and Proportionality, which omits the dubious soft standards in the form of "guidelines" (see No 5 of the existing Protocol). As a result, the proposed new Protocol contains primarily procedural rules and obligations to give reasons. The Convention thereby implements legal science's insight that adherence to the principle of subsidiarity is most effectively secured through procedure and organisation.[160]

b) Involvement of National Parliaments

National parliaments, widely seen as the "loser" of Europeanisation, gain access to primary law via Art 11(3) CT-IGC (Art I-9(3) CT-Conv) and the above mentioned Protocol; they act as an instance of political control,

[159] Rather, this demonstrates the interaction of substantive law and competence law that would make it ill-advised to establish a separate court to adjudicate competences: Classen, above n 110, 437.

[160] See, eg, U Mager, 'Die Prozeduralisierung des Subsidiaritätsprinzips im Verfassungsentwurf des Europäischen Konvents' [2003] *Zeitschrift für Europarechtliche Studien* 471.

monitoring compliance with the principle of subsidiarity. Thus, "for the first time in the history of European construction, it involves national parliaments in the European legislative process".[161] Of course, their role is notably "only" that of a subordinate safeguard-mechanism. Also remarkably, No 5 of the Protocol does not grant national parliaments a direct right of action to the ECJ.[162] The Commission, under No 4 of the Protocol, continues to have a special duty to state reasons only for legislative proposals, which could—given the narrow definition of "legislative acts" in Art 34 CT-IGC (Art I-33 CT-Conv)—significantly compromise the effective safeguarding of subsidiarity in other legal instruments, especially in the form of European regulations and decisions.[163]

Recapitulating the relevant debate,[164] one clearly sees that here, as well, the Convention had the foresight to avert certain doubtful suggestions. Above all, the idea was frequently suggested to create a subsidiarity committee with consultative powers out of national parliamentarians and to work it into the legislative process.[165] In our view, institutional isolation of subsidiarity outside the political institutions is unconvincing: the questions, whether the national level is "insufficient" and, moreover, whether the European level might "better" handle the problem, are not meaningfully separable from the political questions arising from the concrete issue. The evaluation of subsidiarity is, to a high degree, a matter of political discretion, for which the political institutions must be accountable to the European public. Additionally, such a committee would further complicate the Union's institutional structure would further hamper the localising of political responsibility.

Against this backdrop, the Convention's solution becomes clearly advantageous. It permits less potential for blockade. It avoids further complicating the institutional structure of the Union, in that it provides for formalised inclusion of the national parliaments in scrutinising legislative proposals instead of setting up an additional institution.[166] The national parliaments' participation in this "early warning system" can be seen as an institutional experiment, whose functioning cannot yet be foreclosed. One should also not underestimate its symbolic relevance for the Member States. Hopefully, with the Convention's proposal, which the IGC did not call into question, a lasting constitutional compromise on subsidiarity was finally reached.

[161] Conclusions of Working Group I on the Principle of Subsidiarity, CONV 286/02, 5 <http://register.consilium.eu.int/pdf/en/02/cv00/00286en2.pdf> (1 September 2004).

[162] R Barents, 'The Court of Justice in the Draft Constitution' (2004) 11 *Maastricht Journal of European and Comparative Law* 121 at 135: 'this phrase is of purely cosmetic significance'.

[163] See J Bast in this volume.

[164] Cf S Weatherill, 'Using National Parliaments to Improve Scrutiny of EC/EU action' (2003), <http://www.fd.unl.pt/je/edit_pap2003-02.htm> (6 September 2004).

[165] See Pernice, above n 3, 876; see also L Siedentop, *Democracy in Europe* (2000), 147; J Schwarze, 'Kompetenzverteilung in der Europäischen Union und föderales Gleichgewicht' [1995] *Deutsche Verwaltungsblätter* 1265 at 1268 *et seq.*

[166] Cf also the proposed new Protocol on the role of national parliaments.

c) Revocability of Union Legal Acts

In contrast, the Convention neglected a weighty problem. The category of concurrent competence brings with it a grave problem in terms of legal technique and the democratic principle. According to a general principle of law the withdrawal of a legal act requires the same law-making procedure as the original enactment. As a consequence, a Union act can remain valid and Member State action remain pre-empted despite the fact that support for the Union act may later become insufficient. This may appear trivial at first glance. In the Member State governmental systems, a simple majority usually decides, thus making it procedurally relatively easy to amend or repeal existing legislation that lost sufficient political support. In contrast, a Union legislative act can only be amended or repealed by a new qualified majority, or even unanimity, in the Council. Hence, a *minority* can block both the amendment of Union law and the release of Member States' legislatures from pre-emption. This problem has become particularly virulent in the agricultural sector.

The resulting rigidity represents a significant constraint on restructuring the current secondary law in light of the subsidiarity principle. There is an important lesson here: it would be a grave error to assume that qualified majorities, let alone unanimity, in the Council are principally autonomy-friendly, as the criticism of many acts under Art 308 EC sufficiently demonstrates.[167] Proposed solutions for managing this rigidity have not been accepted. One possible solution would be to relax the conditions under which a legislative act adopted under a concurrent competence can be repealed. For example, if the act's passage required unanimity, then its abolition may require only a qualified majority after the measure has been effective for some specified period of time. Although it was not agreed on, the comparable proposal of Working Group V of the Convention (if only for Art 308 EC) was commendable and should be maintained as a proposition for future reform.[168]

d) The Institutional Structure as Central Problem

The institutional structure is the key to a constitutional order that both protects the Member States' scope of action and is sufficiently transparent to the citizenry. Deficits in the protection of *Verbandskompetenz* are predominantly operational deficits in the European Council and the Council. The Convention's Draft contained a plethora of institutional changes, most of them upheld by the IGC, but an assessment is beyond the tasks of this

[167] The criticism by Kaiser (see above n 24) referred almost exclusively to measures that fall under this competence and thus were enacted unanimously by the Council.

[168] Final report of Working Group V, CONV 375/02, 16 <http://register.consilium.eu.int/pdf/en/02/cv00/00375en2.pdf> (1 September 2004).

article.[169] However, the innovations as regards the European Council and the Council have not apparently strengthened their protective role in the vertical order of competences. On the contrary, the possible narrow interpretation of competence, discussed above, largely disregards political co-ordination and intergovernmental co-operation and, thereby, forebodes a troubled future for competence law.

3. Transparency

The last issue is the transparency of the vertical order of competences. With the provisions of the Title on competence, the Constitutional Treaty succeeds in raising the current level of transparency, despite a series of unresolved, critical points.

a) The New Order of Vertical Competences

At the outset, it should be noted that the Title's heading "Union Competences" is misleading. Title III only contains one competence norm (Art 18 CT-IGC, Art I-17 CT-Conv); aside from this, the "scope of and arrangements for exercising the Union's competences" (that is, competence in its sense of legal authorisation to enact unilateral measures) "shall be determined by the provisions relating [CT-Conv: "specific"] to each area in Part III" (Art 12(6) CT-IGC, Art I-11(6) CT-Conv). The provisions, building on the relevant work of the German Federal Council,[170] deal mostly with general questions of categorisation and delimitation of Union and Member State competences. The nerve centre of categorisation is Art 12 CT-IGC (Art I-11 CT-Conv). In conjunction with Arts 13 to 17 CT-IGC (Arts I-12 to I-16 CT-Conv), it contains general rules for the application and construction of the empowering provisions in Part III. This new arrangement of the order of competences certainly is an improvement, since it helps to identify the applicable rules governing a particular policy field.[171] Further progress is made in that the competences from the EU Treaty are henceforth subject to the competence regime already known from the EC Treaty.

It follows from this approach that Title III of Part I does not include a catalogue of competences. In view of the current complexity of the competences,

[169] For an overview, see GA Bermann, 'The Institutions under the New Draft Constitution' in Pernice and Maduro (eds), above n 6, 45; see also P Dann in this volume.

[170] Entschließung des Bundesrates zur Vorbereitung der Regierungskonferenz, Bundesrat Drucksache 169/95 (1996); Entschließung des Bundesrates, 'Forderungen der Länder zur Regierungskonferenz 1996', Bundesrat Drucksache 667/95 (1996); see also A von Bogdandy and J Bast, 'The European Union's Vertical Order of Competences' (2002) 39 *CML Rev* 227 at 266.

[171] See D Hanf and T Baumé, 'Vers une clarification de la répartition des compétences entre l'Union et ses États Membres?' (2003) 39 *Cahiers de Droit Européen* 135 at 153.

any catalogue, no matter how well-formulated, would have been less precise than the detailed provisions that currently confer competences.[172] A simplification of the individual empowering provisions would have very likely come at a great political cost, since the complexity of a competence provision usually directly reflects the underlying complex political compromises.[173] The margin for technical consolidation was practically reduced to zero. It follows that Arts 73 to 75 German Basic Law or Arts 148 and 149 of the Spanish Constitution do not represent a useful example for a catalogue of Union competences: the competences attributed by these constitutional provisions are far more indefinite than the current competence provisions. If a catalogue of competences does not come into question, they could only be reproduced in simplified form. The Constitutional Treaty avoids *mere* repetition of the relevant provisions—which would possibly lead to legal problems—by determining the specific type of competence.

In principle, the systematisation in Art 12 CT-IGC (Art I-11 CT-Conv) is to be welcomed, but a number of critical questions remain. For instance, under Art 12 CT-IGC, the Union order of competences has three categories, namely, exclusive, shared and supplementary[174] competences. According to Art 14(1) CT-IGC (Art I-13(1) CT-Conv), Union competences are, as a rule, shared competences. Consequently, the list of "Areas of shared competence" in Art 14 CT-IGC is non-exhaustive, as opposed to the lists in Arts 13 and 17 CT-IGC (Arts I-12 and I-16 CT-Conv).[175] The non-comprehensive character of the categorisation is evident from the mere fact that Art 18 CT-IGC (Art I-17 CT-Conv) is not mentioned. Furthermore, the three categories do not cover the co-ordination of certain Member State policies (Art 15 CT-IGC; Art I-14 CT-Conv) and the common foreign and security policy (Art 16 CT-IGC; Art I-15 CT-Conv). Taken seriously, the wording of Art 14(1) CT-IGC would require assignment of Arts 15 and 16 CT-IGC to the category of shared competences—a poor fit for the systematics of the Title. In view of the manifold peculiarities of these policy sectors and the related political sensibilities, the categorisation of the relevant powers in Part III is left in the dark.[176]

Moreover, Arts 12(2) and 14 CT-IGC (Arts I-11(2) and I-13 CT-Conv) lay down a single category of "shared competence". Yet, on closer inspection, two types of competences can be found hiding under the category. First, "shared competence" refers to those competences classified above as

[172] See De Búrca and de Witte, above n 1, 207–8.

[173] In more detail see A von Bogdandy and C-D Ehlermann, 'Guest Editorial: Consolidation of the European Treaties' (1996) 33 *CML Rev* 1107 at 1109; C Schmid, 'Konsolidierung und Vereinfachung des europäischen Primärrechts' [1998] *Europarecht* suppl 2, 17.

[174] Art 17 CT–IGC (Art I–16 CT–Conv), under the heading 'Areas of supporting, coordinating or complementary action' pertains to areas such as industry and culture; any harmonisation is excluded: Art 12(5) CT–IGC (Art I–16(3) CT–Conv).

[175] The Convention Praesidium made this point explicitly: CONV 724/03, see n 148, 70, 73, 82.

[176] See Craig, above n 6, 87 *et seq*.

concurrent,[177] because they can be used in such an exhaustive way that, eventually, no room is left for autonomous law-making by the Member States, Art 12(2) CT-IGC (Art I-11(2) CT-Conv). Second, "shared" also describes some Union competences that do *not* prevent the Member States from exercising theirs, Art 14(3) CT-IGC (Art I-13(3) and (4) CT-Conv). Thus, the legal difference between the two categories developed in section II of this paper, i.e. concurrent and parallel competences, continues to exist.[178] In view of transparency, this drafting technique is questionable, since Art 14(3) CT-IGC provokes an *e contrario* argument that under any other "shared competence", in particular under those related to the areas listed in Art 14(2) CT-IGC, Union legislation *may* result in Member States being prevented from exercising their powers.[179] This is not always compatible with the provisions in Part III, e.g. regarding environmental policy (see Art 234(6) CT-IGC; Art III-131 CT-Conv).[180]

Finally, and most critically, some policy areas are for the first time classified as being areas of exclusive Union competence. In Art 12(1) CT-IGC (Art I-11(1) CT-Conv), the Constitutional Treaty defines the legal consequences of this classification in conformity with current Union law. Yet, in view of the findings in section II of this paper, a surprisingly long list of areas is included in Art 13(1) CT-IGC (Art I-12(1) CT-Conv). Classifying competition law as an exclusive legislative competence is certainly not a mere restatement of current law,[181] nor is this categorisation supported by the content of Arts 161 *et seq* CT-IGC (Arts III-50 *et seq* CT-Conv). The same holds true for the common commercial policy, since Art 315 CT-IGC (Art III-217 CT-Conv) significantly broadens its scope, compared with the law as it stands. Overall, the Constitutional Treaty adopts a wide concept of exclusive Union competence, which is, for reasons explained above, highly problematic.

b) The Persistent Entanglement of Union and Member States

As observed above, most of its citizens perceive the Union as a diffuse conglomeration, resulting in serious legitimacy problems. This diffuseness has vertical and horizontal dimensions. Horizontally, the diffuseness flows from the complex organisational constitution: how many actually have an even

[177] See above II. 2. b) bb).

[178] The 'trans-European proposal on amending the draft Constitutional Treaty for the European Union' <http://www.umich.edu/~iinet/euc/MiscHTML/EUnews.html> (6 September 2004), overlooks this distinction, although it proceeds consistently to propose deleting Art I–13(3) and (4) CT–Conv. See also F Chaltiel, 'Une Constitution pour l'Europe' (2003) 471 *Revue du Marché commun et de l'Union européenne* 493 at 501.

[179] See C Trüe, 'EU-Kompetenzen für Energierecht, Gesundheitsschutz und Umweltschutz nach dem Verfassungsentwurf' [2004] *Juristenzeitung* 779 at 786.

[180] See Trüe, above n 179, 786; cf Craig, above n 6, 84.

[181] See Case 14/68, above n 117, para 9; Dougan, above n 150, 770.

elementary idea of who does what and who is responsible for what in the Union? Whether the personalisation of Union politics, which the Constitutional Treaty strives for, or the envisaged reformed interaction among the political institutions will alleviate this, is beyond the scope of this paper. Likewise, the vertical dimension of Union diffuseness reveals a problem of transparency: citizens can hardly discern the fine line between Union and national activity—and, thus, responsibility.

Many demand clarification of the boundary between areas of Union and national responsibility.[182] This, though, is only possible by way of exclusive competences—a road wisely not travelled by the Convention. It necessarily would have led to a critical expansion of Union activities far beyond the already critical conception underlying Art 13(1) CT-IGC (Art I-12(1) CT-Conv).

As already mentioned, the Union and the Member States are interlinked in a way that can be coined a system of co-operative division of powers. The Union has tended to develop not after the American model of separation of powers, but after the German model of interweavement. This entails that in most policy fields both EU and national competences are exercised, both in law-making and in the application of the law.[183] This places a decoupling under narrow constraints. The goal of disentangling the competences could only be achieved at the price of restructuring the Union's system from the ground up, uprooting the current networks of authorities[184] and, moreover, providing the Union with its own administrative substructures. The political costs of such an undertaking would be prohibitively high and hardly consistent with the subsidiarity principle. Rightly, the Constitutional Treaty left this the road not taken.

4. The Outlook

The Constitutional Treaty submits several remarkable innovations with its vertical order of competences, thereby addressing the three concerns that have fuelled the debate over competence. It does not incorporate all the proposals which were made for a restructuring of the competence order; in particular, potentially damaging modifications were prudently avoided. The provisions in Title III of Part I and their relationship to the relevant provisions in Part III do raise new questions; but these questions should find their timely answers in future case law and legal scholarship.

[182] See, eg, J Fischer, 'Vom Staatenverbund zur Föderation' [2000] *Integration* 149; reacting to this speech, see C Joerges, Y Mény and JH Weiler (eds), *What Kind of Constitution for What Kind of Polity Competences?* (2001).

[183] See Pernice, above n 3; Kirchhof, above n 54.

[184] The Commission's proposals on better governance in Europe rely precisely on the expansion of such networks between the Union and Member State authorities, European Commission, 'European Governance: A White Paper', COM(2001) 428 final.

Hence, this contribution emphasises the continuity between the current order of competences and the one of the Constitutional Treaty. Yet, it is well possible that the enlarged and refounded Union evolves into quite a different polity and its political activity might undergo substantial mutations. That would transform the context in which the Union's competences are to be interpreted. It would be a grave error to consider the Union's vertical order of competences as finally settled; it remains in a flux, it remains scholarly exciting.

9

Legal Instruments

JÜRGEN BAST*

INTRODUCTION

WHEN BRITAIN'S FOREIGN secretary Jack Straw defended the failure to propose a "pocket-sized" Constitution for Europe, stating that only a European superstate could have a short, clear-cut constitutional document,[1] he probably underestimated the complexities of writing a federal state constitution.[2] In view of legal instruments, however, he had a point. The instruments of action currently at the disposal of the Union are different from those common in national constitutional law, and their complexity may be explained by a unique constitutional environment. Nobody could have seriously expected the Constitutional Treaty to bring major change in this respect. The following discourse presents some of the patterns of the Union's instruments, identifies the relevant legal concepts and reflects on how an adequate theory of instruments could perform. The main emphasis lies in reconstructing the current law; on that basis, aspects of the proposed reform in the Constitutional Treaty are evaluated.

As to terminology, this study employs "instrument" (or "type of act", in German "*Handlungsform*", literally "form of action") as a concept to classify legal acts, or groups of legal acts. An instrument is understood as an abstract category that is defined by a coherent set of legal attributes, e.g. the type of act "regulation" in the sense of Art 249(2) EC. A concrete act can be affiliated with a certain instrument, which implies that the act then shares its legal attributes. One can also say that the enacting institution has chosen that instrument, or that an act is "in the form of a regulation" (Art 230(4) EC), or simply that it "is" a regulation.

* For a more detailed version, not yet covering the Constitutional Treaty, see J Bast, 'On the Grammar of EU Law: Legal Instruments' in A von Bogdandy and JHH Weiler (eds), *New German Scholarship*, Jean Monnet Working Paper 9/03 <http://www.jeanmonnetprogram.org/papers/03/030901-05.html>. The translation is based on a draft by Eric Pickett, Frankfurt am Main, revised by Andreas Magnusson and Joseph Windsor, Heidelberg. Comments are welcome to <jbast@mpil.de>.

[1] J Straw, 'By invitation', *The Economist*, 10 July 2004, 49.

[2] For a striking example, see G Austin, *The Indian Constitution* (2nd ed 1999).

The terms may seem peculiar to some readers. In the constitutional context, one usually speaks of "sources", whereas some traditions reserve the term "type of act" to administrative law. In the context of the latter, it includes both legal and factual actions. Such a distinction is not intended here. Within the context of this chapter, all the relevant instruments are legal instruments and all the relevant acts are legal acts. Thereby a broad concept of law is employed, encompassing individual measures as well as non-binding statements. Consequently, the term "law-making" applies to all kinds of acts, be they individual or general in nature, and whether they have binding or non-binding effects. This terminological conception is based on the language of the Treaties, which use the term "acts" regardless of their nature or form.[3] This broad scope also clarifies why the term "sources" is inappropriate here: in most theoretical contexts the term is reserved for instruments that contain binding rules of general application.

Due to the complexities mentioned above, it may be helpful to restrict the study. Hence, only those instruments that are valid under the founding Treaties will be taken into account; primary law itself and so-called complementary law (i.e., agreements of international law concluded between the Member States)[4] are not included. Additionally, international instruments that form a part of the Union legal order (i.e., external agreements, or acts adopted by co-operation bodies set up by such an agreement) will not be addressed, even though this negatively impacts the ability to generalise certain results. Finally, this study will confront the problems at the centre of the legal order, so that almost only *Community* instruments will be considered; the special instruments of secondary law under the EU Treaty will be mentioned only peripherally.[5]

The chapter is divided into five sections. First, an overview of the current understanding of the theory of instruments is presented by outlining the discipline's development (I.). The second section turns to the provisions of primary law governing legal instruments and structuring secondary law. This section concludes with a look at the Court's handling of the instruments (II.). An analysis of the respective lawfulness requirements of the instruments is the subject of the following section (III.). Next, the instruments' different legal effects are examined and, on that basis, a proposal for systematising them is presented (IV.). Finally, the paper briefly focuses on recent moves for reforming the legal instruments, in particular in the context of the Constitutional Treaty (V.).

[3] See, eg, Arts 230(1), 232(3) and 234(1)(b) EC; in French, the term *actes* is used; in German, the interchangeable terms *Akte* and *Handlungen*.

[4] Eg, acts of the 'Representatives of the governments of the Member States meeting in Council'.

[5] The reader should therefore bear in mind that this article conceives Community law as a qualified part of Union law; on this conception see A von Bogdandy, 'The Legal Case for Unity' (1999) 36 *CML Rev* 887.

I. OUTLINE OF THE DISCIPLINE'S DEVELOPMENT

For the past fifty years, legal science has been trying to understand and clarify the instruments of Community law. As the community of scholars went through different phases, its interest in different instruments changed accordingly. The following brief history of the theory of instruments can *en passant* serve to bring together some of the insights into the legal profile of these instruments.

1. European Coal and Steel Community: Focus on the Decision

In the early European Coal and Steel Community (ECSC), decisions directly addressed to undertakings in the coal and steel sector dominated the discussion. With this instrument to regulate the mining markets, the ECSC Treaty provided the supranational High Authority (which later became the Commission of the European Communities) with a legal potential that had heretofore been reserved to states.[6] The scholarship on this new entity of public international law used doctrines of national administrative law as if to do so were self-evident.[7] Constitutional law could not serve as a reference point, because the ECSC's law-making institution, the High Authority, was not yet considered a legislator according to the separation of powers doctrine. Consequently, it could only enact *actes administratifs* in the sense of French law.

French administrative law had a large bearing upon the Treaty text and the development of Community law in general.[8] One could cite the four grounds of review (*moyens*) contained in Art 33(1) ECSC Treaty, the logic of which can hardly be understood without knowing the *Conseil d'Etat*'s case-law. The standing of private applicants against a general decision (Art 33(2) ECSC Treaty) should also be mentioned here. This is quite different from, for example, German administrative law, where the distinction between a rule of general application (*Rechtssatz*) and an individual measure (*Einzelakt*) is decisive. Under the ECSC Treaty, the executive nature of the law-making body was essential, so that an action for annulment was opened for all *actes administratifs*, whether they were *actes règlementaires* or *actes individuels*.[9]

6 See G Jaenicke, 'Die Europäische Gemeinschaft für Kohle und Stahl (Montanunion)' (1951/2) 14 *Zeitschrift für ausländisches öffentliches Recht und Völkerrecht* 727 at 744 *et seq*; H Mosler, 'Die europäische Integration aus der Sicht der Gründungsphase' in O Due *et al* (eds), *Festschrift für U Everling* (1995), 911 at 920.

7 See CH Ule, 'Der Gerichtshof der Montangemeinschaft als europäisches Verwaltungsgericht' [1952] *Deutsches Verwaltungsblatt* 66 at 67 *et seq*; B Börner, *Die Entscheidungen der Hohen Behörde* (1965), 1 *et seq*, 29 *et seq*, 107 *et seq*.

8 See, eg, P Becker, *Der Einfluß des französischen Verwaltungsrechts auf den Rechtsschutz in den europäischen Gemeinschaften* (1963); M Fromont, *Rechtsschutz gegenüber der Verwaltung in Deutschland, Frankreich und den Europäischen Gemeinschaften* (1967).

9 R Chapus, *Droit du contentieux administratif* (2001), paras 629 *et seq*.

The German tradition of administrative law with its key category of the administrative act (*Verwaltungsakt*) was introduced only with difficulty. One point of entry was the distinction between individual and general decisions, which was still necessary because the ground of review against the latter was—impractically—limited to misuse of powers.[10] On this issue, insights of German jurisprudence concerning general administrative acts (*Allgemeinverfügungen*) proved fruitful, particularly by applying the conceptual pairs general/individual and concrete/abstract to the *décision* under the ECSC Treaty.[11]

The subject of reviewable decisions also dominated the Court's case-law from the beginning. Which measures the private individual enjoys legal protection against has been a dogmatic controversy since these early days.[12] Some years later, the discussion about the differentiation between general and individual decisions[13] was superseded by the controversy about reviewable regulations under the EEC Treaty.[14] Furthermore, reviewable binding decisions had to be differentiated from non-binding acts. After the Court began to declare that informal letters and communications could constitute reviewable decisions,[15] the High Authority attempted to reserve to itself the power of definition: undertakings could rely on the fact that only statements that had a certain *form* were intended to create legal obligations. To this end the High Authority established binding criteria concerning the form of acts in its Dec No 22/60 of 7 September 1960.[16] Among other prerequisites, the terminology used in the heading was to indicate whether the act was a "decision". The ECJ decisively rejected these efforts, although Art 15(4) ECSC Treaty provided the basis for a convincing argument in favour of such a power of the High Authority.[17] The Court's steadfast position favouring legal protection was already evident in these early judgments. To preclude the danger of a political institution arbitrarily foreclosing legal protection, formal criteria for the qualification of a reviewable act were to play only a limited role. The ECJ was prepared to accept the consequences of decoupling the system of legal protection from the system of legal instruments.[18] The hope that Dec No 22/60 would be able to structure the various types of acts with a single stroke was thus scuttled; the Court's conception of an act's

[10] A Schüle, 'Grenzen der Klagebefugnis vor dem Gerichtshof der Montanunion' (1955/6) 16 *Zeitschrift für ausländisches öffentliches Recht und Völkerrecht* 227 at 230 *et seq*; BW Meister, *Ermessensmissbrauch oder détournement de pouvoir als Fehlertatbestand der Nichtigkeitsklage des Montanvertrags* (1971).

[11] E-W Fuß, 'Rechtssatz und Einzelakt im Europäischen Gemeinschaftsrecht (pt 2)' [1964] *Neue Juristische Wochenschrift* 945 at 946 *et seq*; Börner, above n 7, 117 *et seq*.

[12] See, eg, G Bebr, *Judicial Control of the European Communities* (1962), 68 *et seq*.

[13] On the criteria of delimitation, see Case 8/55 *Fédéchar v High Authority* [1955] ECR 245 at 256 *et seq*.

[14] See below, II. 3. b.

[15] Cases 7/56 and 3–7/57 *Algera et al v Common Assembly* [1957] ECR 39 at 54 *et seq*.

[16] [1960] OJ 61/1248.

[17] Cases 53 and 54/63 *Lemmerz-Werke et al v High Authority* [1963] ECR 239 at 247 *et seq*.

[18] See Cases 8–11/66, *Cimenteries Cementbedrijven et al v Commission* [1967] ECR 75 *et seq*.

"legal nature" held sway. Nevertheless, the appearance and the formal organisation of Union acts as they are known today and as they are set forth in Annex IV of the Council's Rules of Procedure[19] were developed on the basis of Dec No 22/60.

It should be briefly mentioned that the Court's early case-law continues to influence Community law and the theoretical understanding of its instruments in many respects. For instance, delegating legislative powers to bodies that are not fully politically and legally responsible is prohibited to this day.[20] Of continuous importance is also the comprehensive incidental control, which implied that the High Authority was strictly bound by its own general decisions.[21] This can be understood as a strategy to cope with the lack of a hierarchy between law-making institutions, something that is even more important under the EC Treaty. Finally, under the ECSC Treaty it was already apparent that the Court would have to create elements of a European administrative law through its case-law, as it did, for instance, when it developed the criteria for the retroactive withdrawal of decisions.[22] The theory of instruments thus still has the coal dust of the early days of Community law on its clothes, so to speak.

2. The EEC in the 1960s and 1970s: Focus on the Regulation

The agricultural sector most occupied the Court after the EEC was founded. In this second phase, academic interest in the Community's instruments was overwhelmingly devoted to the regulation, the general decision's more sophisticated successor. Until the end of the 1960s numerous publications on this legal instrument were presented,[23] among them notably the monographic study by J-V Louis.[24] The regulation, with its ability to affect the legal position of the market citizen in the same way a national statute does, fascinated scholars: it was considered to be an expression of the new public authority's supranationality and autonomy.[25] Its qualification as a Community statute was prevented only by the separation of powers doctrine, which requires that a statute be enacted according to parliamentary

[19] Council Decision of 22 July 2002 adopting the Council's Rules of Procedure (2002/682/EC, Euratom) [2002] OJ L 230/7.

[20] Case 9/56 *Meroni v High Authority* [1958] ECR 133 at 146 *et seq.*

[21] *Ibid*, 140 *et seq.*

[22] Cases 7/56 and 3–7/57, above n 15, 55 *et seq.*

[23] H-J Rabe, *Das Verordnungsrecht der Europäischen Wirtschaftsgemeinschaft* (1963); GL Tosato, *I regolamenti delle Comunità europee* (1965); JR Haase, *Die Kompetenzen der Kommission im Verordnungsrecht der Europäischen Wirtschaftsgemeinschaft* (1965); W Möller, *Die Verordnung der Europäischen Gemeinschaften* (1967); JA Perez Bevia, *El reglamento como fuente de derecho en las Comunidades Europeas* (1973).

[24] J-V Louis, *Les règlements de la Communauté économique européenne* (1969).

[25] C-F Ophüls, 'Staatshoheit und Gemeinschaftshoheit' in CH Ule (ed), *Recht im Wandel* (1965), 519 at 550.

procedures. Nonetheless, from then on national constitutional law was a point of reference for the understanding of Community instruments.

The relationship between Community law and national law took centre stage. The Commission's and the Council's law-making powers unmistakably began to compete with the national parliaments, a situation that required conceptual clarification. More specifically, the regulation and its claim to be directly applicable in all Member States brought up the problem of a collision with national law.[26] HP Ipsen cogently theorised that the regulation as set forth in the Treaty was an expression of the new quality of Community law separating it from public international law: the Community character of the regulation is found in the inviolable uniqueness of its uniform application throughout the Community.[27] M Zuleeg saw in Art 189(2), 2nd sentence EEC Treaty (Art 249(2), 2nd sentence EC) the positive law solution to the problem of collisions of national and supranational law.[28]

The power to make regulations also played a significant role for the ECJ when it proclaimed the autonomy of the Communities' legal order. The "establishment of institutions endowed with sovereign rights, the exercise of which affects the Member States and also their citizens"[29] is a central argument which the ECJ relied on for the direct effect of Community law. In *Costa* the ECJ reasoned that Community law was supreme, making explicit reference to the unqualified binding force of the regulation and its direct applicability.[30] On the other hand, the ECJ has always rejected the *e contrario* argument that, since the regulation by its very nature has direct effect, other categories of acts can never have similar effects.[31]

Art 189(2) EEC Treaty provided a key concept for the system of legal protection under Art 173 EEC Treaty (now Art 230 EC), namely that of general application (in German, *allgemeine Geltung*; in French, *portée générale*), which functioned as the counterpart to the individual applicability of a decision. At first, the ECJ only reluctantly accepted the rule laid down in Art 230(4) EC that, in principle, individuals have no standing against a regulation. However, it required that the act must "have the character of a regulation" according to its substance.[32] The ECJ also answered

[26] Quite a few contributions focused solely on the regulation when discussing the primacy of Community law; see K Carstens, 'Der Rang europäischer Verordnungen gegenüber deutschen Rechtsnormen' in B Aubin *et al* (eds), *Festschrift für O Riese* (1964), 65; RH Lauwaars, *Lawfulness and Legal Force of Community Decisions* (1973), 14 *et seq*.

[27] See HP Ipsen, *Europäisches Gemeinschaftsrecht* (1972), paras 10–41.

[28] See M Zuleeg, *Das Recht der Europäischen Gemeinschaften im innerstaatlichen Bereich* (1969), 154 *et seq*.

[29] See Case 26/62 *van Gend & Loos* [1963] ECR 1 at 12.

[30] See Case 6/64 *Costa* [1964] ECR 585 at 594.

[31] See Case 9/70 *Grad* [1970] ECR 825, para 5; Case 41/74, *van Duyn* [1974] ECR 1337, para 12.

[32] See Cases 16 and 17/62 *Producteurs de fruits v Council* [1962] ECR 471 at 479.

the question of whether an individual can challenge a decision addressed to a Member State by referring to the concept of general application.[33] It took some time before the ECJ freed itself from the chains of this conception and finally rejected the premise that an act cannot simultaneously be of general application and of individual concern to certain natural or legal persons.[34]

With respect to the legal effects of regulations, the ECJ held that national measures which "alter [the regulation's] scope or supplement its provisions" are not permissible.[35] The Member States are prohibited from taking any action that would conceal the Community nature and the uniform entry into force of a regulation.[36] On the other hand, the choice of a regulation does not oblige the Community legislator to create an exhaustive regime, so that a regulation may permit the Member States some legislative discretion or oblige them to take further implementing action to fill in the gaps.[37] The path has thus been cleared for the regulation's direct application and, at the same time, its suitability as an instrument of harmonisation, the presumptive domain of the directive. The ECJ has in general accepted the multifarious use of the regulation, e.g. for the conclusion of international agreements, the adoption of organisational rules and even for autonomous Treaty amendment.[38] The thesis based on Art 189(2) EEC Treaty that regulations are reserved for general rules[39] was unable to gain acceptance. General applicability is not a necessary precondition for the legality of a regulation. Typically, regulations are drafted in general and abstract terms, but this is not a legal requirement. The ECJ has displayed little inclination to review the institutions' discretion regarding the choice of instrument.[40]

The differentiation developed by the Court in the 1970s concerning the scope of the duty to provide reasons pursuant to Art 190 EEC Treaty (Art 253 EC) is remarkable as well. With regard to acts of general application, the enacting institution may limit itself to indicating the situation which led to the adoption of the measure and the general objectives it intended to achieve.[41] The Community legislator's discretion corresponds to a less demanding duty to provide reasons than the case is with individual acts. With this argumentation, the ECJ modified its jurisprudence on the ECSC,

[33] See Case 231/81 *Spijker Kwasten v Commission* [1983] ECR 2559, para 10; Case 206/87 *Lefebvre v Commission* [1989] ECR 275, para 13.

[34] See below, II. 3. b.

[35] See Case 40/69 *Bollmann* [1970] ECR 69, para 4.

[36] See Case 39/72 *Commission v Italy* [1973] ECR 101, para 17; Case 34/73 *Variola* [1974] ECR 981, paras 10–11.

[37] See Case 31/78 *Bussone* [1978] ECR 2429, paras 28–33; Case 230/78 *Eridania* [1979] ECR 2749, para 34; Case 237/82 *Jongeneel Kaas* [1984] ECR 483, para 13.

[38] For the latter, see Case 185/73 *König* [1974] ECR 607, paras 5 *et seq.*

[39] U Everling, 'Die ersten Rechtsetzungsakte der Organe der Europäischen Gemeinschaften' [1959] *Betriebs-Berater* 52 at 53.

[40] See Case 5/73 *Balkan-Import-Export* [1973] ECR 1091, para 18; Case C–70/88 *Parliament v Council* [1991] ECR I–4529.

[41] See Case 5/67 *Beus* [1968] ECR 83 *et seq*; Case 78/74 *Deuka* [1975] ECR 421, para 6; Case 166/78 *Italy v Council* [1979] ECR 2575, para 8.

which balanced limited review of discretionary decision-making with a general increase of the demand to provide reasons.[42] The background for this change was the mass of routinely adopted regulations: the regulation had become the instrument of choice for the administration's daily norm production, especially in the agricultural field.[43] Under these circumstances, the dominant task of the duty to provide reasons was to help the Court to review the legality of an act.[44] In contrast, the right of those concerned to information as an expression of accountability to the European public has only limited significance. The ECJ's often criticised lax scrutiny of the formulaic phrases used later when giving reasons relating to subsidiarity has its origins here.[45]

3. The Discussions in the 1980s and 1990s: Focus on the Directive

A third phase, which started in the 1980s and continued well into the 1990s, focused on the directive. It had taken a long time for the scholarly community to construe the directive as a "truly legislative" instrument.[46] Until then, the directive was considered to be "by its nature" a "decision addressed to the Member States"[47] and thus an individual measure, not a general norm. As late as 1973 RH Lauwaars stated that a directive "in fact do[es] not contain norms .... It only establishes legal relationships between the member State concerned and the Community".[48]

This picture changed dramatically when specialised academia and, for the first time, the broader legal community turned to the innovations developed by the Court regarding the effects benefiting the individual when directives were improperly transposed.[49] Particularly in the German literature, one could witness a steady increase in publications[50] in the wake of the conflict between the ECJ and German courts concerning the direct effect of the 6th VAT directive (*Becker* decision).[51] The *Grad* case,[52] which concerned

[42] Cases 36–38 and 40/59, *Geitling et al v High Authority* [1960] ECR 423 at 439.

[43] See, eg, Case 29/77 *Roquette Frères* [1977] ECR 1835, paras 13–18.

[44] The duty to state the legal basis serves this objective: see Case 45/86 *Commission v Council* [1987] ECR 1493, paras 8–9.

[45] See, eg, Case C–233/94 *Germany v Parliament and Council* [1997] ECR I–2405, paras 22 *et seq*.

[46] As for early endeavours, see E-W Fuß, 'Die "Richtlinie" des Europäischen Gemeinschaftsrechts' [1965] *Deutsches Verwaltungsblatt* 378; N Weber, *Die Richtlinie im EWG-Vertrag* (1974).

[47] Everling, above n 39, 52.

[48] Lauwaars, above n 26, 32.

[49] See Case 41/74, above n 31, para 12; Case 152/84 *Marshall* [1986] ECR 723, para 49.

[50] See, eg, U Everling, 'Zur direkten innerstaatlichen Wirkung der EG-Richtlinien' in B Börner (ed), *Einigkeit und Recht und Freiheit: Festschrift für K Carstens* (1984), i, 95; M Hilf, 'Der Justizkonflikt um EG-Richtlinien: gelöst' [1988] *Europarecht* 1.

[51] See *Entscheidungen des Bundesfinanzhofs* 133, 470; Case 8/81 *Becker* [1982] ECR 53, para 21; Case 70/83 *Kloppenburg* [1984] ECR 1075, para 14; *Entscheidungen des Bundesfinanzhofs* 143, 383; *Entscheidungen des Bundesverfassungsgerichts* 75, 223 at 245 (*Kloppenburg*).

[52] See Case 9/70, above n 31, para 5.

a decision addressed to the Member States, did not receive such attention, although E Grabitz already outlined the consequences for the vertical direct effect of directives in 1971.[53] The doctrine of indirect effect, which requires national law to be construed in light of Community directives,[54] and the doctrine of Member State liability for improper transposition[55] further fuelled the debate.[56]

During this phase, the legal community anxiously followed the innovations introduced into Community law by the ECJ, splitting the former into true believers and sharp-tongued critics.[57] The ECJ's apparently restless activism scarcely left time to systematically work through and critically analyse the consequences of the recent judgments for the system of legal instruments. Many observers felt that it was only a question of time before the ECJ recognised the horizontal direct effect of directives.[58] However, they underestimated the ECJ's readiness to preserve the unique profile of the directive.[59] The legal concepts developed in these days (namely, direct effect, consistent interpretation, and state liability) tie in with a Member State's breach of Community law and could thus be founded on Art 5 EEC (Art 10 EC), which protects Community legislation from being unilaterally challenged by extralegal means.[60] It was therefore hardly to be expected that the Court would respond to the call to recognise the direct effect of a recommendation. Such non-binding "directives" do not carry with them a duty to implement; thus the idea of sanctioning the failure to act does not apply.[61]

The reasons for the remaining dissatisfaction with the contours given to the directive by the Community legislator and the ECJ are not to be found in the doctrine of legal defects.[62] The underlying conflict dates back to the early days of Community law. Particularly German authors, arguing from

[53] E Grabitz, 'Entscheidungen und Richtlinien als unmittelbar wirksames Gemeinschaftsrecht' [1971] *Europarecht* 1.

[54] See Case 14/83 *Colson* [1984] ECR 1891, para 26; Case C–106/89 *Marleasing* [1990] ECR I–4135, para 8; D Curtin, 'The Province of Government' (1990) 15 *EL Rev* 195 at 220 *et seq*; W Brechmann, *Richtlinienkonforme Auslegung* (1994); P Craig, 'Direct Effect, Indirect Effect and the Construction of National Legislation' (1997) 22 *EL Rev* 519.

[55] See Cases C–6 and C–9/90 *Francovich* [1991] ECR I–5357, para 31; R Caranta, 'Governmental Liability after Francovich' (1993) 52 *Cambridge Law Journal* 272.

[56] For a detailed survey, see S Prechal, *Directives in European Community Law* (1995), 155 *et seq*.

[57] For the latter see, eg, H Rasmussen, *The European Court of Justice* (1998).

[58] Construed as an element of constitutionalisation by E Stein, 'Lawyers, Judges and the Making of a Transnational Constitution' (1981) 75 *AJIL* 1; a distinct call to the Court was made in the Opinion of AG Lenz in Case C–91/92 *Faccini Dori* [1994] ECR I–3325, paras 43 *et seq*; see AL Easson, 'Can Directives Impose Obligation on Individuals?' (1979) 4 *EL Rev* 67; T Tridimas, 'Horizontal Direct Effect of Directives' (1994) 19 *EL Rev* 621.

[59] See Case C–91/92, above n 58, para 24; Case C–192/94 *El Corte Ingles* [1996] ECR I–1281, para 17.

[60] A von Bogdandy, 'Rechtsfortbildung mit Art 5 EG-Vertrag' in A Randelzhofer *et al* (eds), *Gedächtnisschrift für E Grabitz* (1995), 17 at 26 *et seq*.

[61] See Case 322/88 *Grimaldi* [1989] ECR 4407, para 16.

[62] Cf M Hilf, 'Die Richtlinie der EG—ohne Richtung, ohne Linie?' [1993] *Europarecht* 1.

the wording of Art 189(3) EEC, claim that the Member States must retain a considerable amount of discretion when implementing directives.[63] Confronted with the presumption that the directive is an instrument exclusively reserved for framework legislation, the current usage of the directive does seem to indicate an abuse of discretion.[64] Law-making practice and case-law, however, have never accepted this premise.[65] Instead, the directive has always been used as *loi uniforme* as needed, which can impose detailed instructions on the Member States as to the legal state of affairs to be created.[66] Today the admissibility of the directive as a "truly legislative" instrument with a two-step implementation structure is widely recognised.[67] Without further clarification, the ECJ and CFI can assume that a directive normally is an act of general application.[68] The decisive difference from the regulation is the directive's inability to impose obligations of itself on an individual, a difference that must also be taken into account when considering the legal consequences of deficient transposition.[69]

Significantly, within the Constitutional Convention no serious proposals were raised to alter the definition of that instrument, or even abolish it. Moreover, after some discussion it became clear that a directive-type instrument would be needed both for legislative and implementing acts.[70] Solely the new designations of the directive-type instruments under the Constitutional Treaty are hardly convincing. According to its legal definition

[63] See, eg, M Kaltenborn, 'Rahmengesetzgebung im Bundesstaat und im Staatenverbund' (2003) 128 *Archiv des öffentlichen Rechts* 412 and 443; R Oldekop, *Die Richtlinien der EWG* (1968), 161 *et seq*; see also P Kirchhof in this volume.

[64] Cf B Biervert, *Der Mißbrauch von Handlungsformen im Gemeinschaftsrecht* (1999), 138 *et seq*.

[65] See, eg, Case 38/77 *ENKA* [1977] ECR 2203, paras 15–17; Case 102/79 *Commission v Belgium* [1980] ECR 1473, para 11.

[66] See Ipsen, above n 27, paras 21–29; M Zuleeg in H von der Groeben and J Schwarze (eds), *Kommentar zum EU-/EG-Vertrag* (2003), Art 5 EC, para 20; M Nettesheim in E Grabitz and M Hilf (eds), *Das Recht der Europäischen Union* (looseleaf, last update 2003), Art 249 EC, para 133.

[67] This is an important difference from the instruments under most national constitutional legal systems: in Union law an act's maximum regulatory density does not depend on the instrument used (eg, there is no instrument like the German framework statute under Art 75 Basic Law), nor does Union law set requirements for minimum regulatory density depending on the instrument at issue (eg, there is no rule comparable to that under German constitutional law that all 'essential' decisions must take the form of a parliamentary statute).

[68] See Case C–10/95 P *Asocarne v Council* [1995] ECR I–4149, para 28; Cases T–172 and T–175–T–177/98 *Salamander et al v Parliament and Council* [2000] ECR II–2487, para 29. This applies equally and without qualification to Commission directives: Cases 188–190/80 *France et al v Commission* [1982] ECR 2545, para 6.

[69] See Case C–97/96, *Verband deutscher Daihatsu-Händler* [1997] ECR I–6843, para 24; Case C–443/98, *Unilever* [2000] ECR I–7535, para 50; see S Weatherill, 'Breach of Directives and Breach of Contract' (2001) 26 *EL Rev* 177; M Lenz, DS Tynes and L Young, 'Horizontal What? Back to Basics' (2000) 25 *EL Rev* 509; K Lackhoff and H Nyssens, 'Direct Effect of Directives in Triangular Situations' (1998) 23 *EL Rev* 397.

[70] On the Convention Praesidium's failed plan to restrict the directive to so-called legislative acts, see Draft Text with Comment of the Praesidium, CONV 724/03, 84 <http://register.consilium.eu.int/pdf/en/03/cv00/cv00724en03.pdf> (29 October 2004).

the "European framework law" is as little restricted to low-density "framework" rules as its EC successor was.[71] Be that as it may, the directive proves to be a felicitous invention that has worked its way into the core of Union law-making.

4. The Perceived Lack of Coherence: Focus on Reform

The discussion since the 1990s has been characterised by remarkable incongruity. On the one hand, European legal scholarship—after the difficulties experienced in ratifying the Treaty of Maastricht—is being pressed, indeed shaken, by great disputes: the Union's democratic legitimacy, the limits of its competences, the role of the judiciary, the Union's future shape.[72] On the other hand, the theory of instruments has not been able to make an independent contribution to these discussions. Typically, even fundamental constitutional changes—the Economic and Monetary Union, the development of the co-decision procedure, the numerous new competences—have scarcely been analysed from the perspective of the theory of instruments. A similar decoupling from the general discipline can be seen with respect to secondary law. Legislation and case-law are the subject of intensive academic study, but it is dominated by the specialised sectoral disciplines that—for obvious reasons—are hardly interested in the abstract questions related to legal instruments. One looks mostly in vain for the intersectoral view of the structures of secondary law from the perspective of a theory of instruments. At any rate, it currently appears that scholarly attempts to systematise the legal instruments are dismissed with a mere shrug of the shoulders.[73]

This, in turn, stands in stark contrast to the claim of many that a reform of the instruments is needed to introduce order into a chaotic situation.[74] Since the mid-1990s, scholarly attention as regards legal instruments has focused more and more on a perceived need to alter their bases in primary law. One can identify two main approaches in the debate: a tendency towards hierarchy and a tendency towards simplification.

The call for hierarchisation came first from the political sphere. At its core, this debate was (and is) about the role of the European Parliament in the Union's constitutional scheme—introducing a hierarchy of instruments

[71] As to the non-legislative directive, which henceforth operates under the name of 'regulation', see below V.

[72] Cf A von Bogdandy, 'A Bird's Eye View on the Science of European Law' (2000) 6 *ELJ* 208.

[73] E Grabitz's contribution in the anthology *Thirty Years of Community Law* still by and large represents the cutting edge of the theory of instruments: see Commission of the European Communities (ed), *Thirty Years of Community Law* (1981), ch V.

[74] See, eg, M Ruffert in C Calliess and M Ruffert (eds), *Kommentar zu EU-Vertrag und EG-Vertrag* (2002), Art 249 EC, paras 14–15; R Lukes, 'Rechtsetzung und Rechtsangleichung' in M Dauses (ed), *Handbuch des EU-Wirtschaftsrechts* (looseleaf, last update 2001), sec B II, para 49.

aims at reshuffling the institutional balance. The 1991 draft Treaty of the Luxembourg Presidency expressly foresaw a "Community statute" prevailing over all other legal instruments.[75] Legal academia, then, took up this topic,[76] "leftover" by the Maastricht IGC.[77] The hierarchy motif played no role at the conferences of Amsterdam and Nice but made a surprise appearance in the Laeken Declaration on the future of Europe.[78] Eventually, at the Convention the instruments had become another stage on which the institutional actors played out their drama on the great constitutional questions.

The call for simplification of the instruments seems to have its source elsewhere. This approach is only loosely connected with the Union's self-confident claim that its instruments should reflect the separation of legislative and executive powers, thereby copying patterns of national constitutionalism. Instead, the call for simplification came from the deep-seated uncertainty that has shadowed European integration ever since the near failure of the Maastricht Treaty. The proliferation of instruments under the EU and EC Treaties, as well as the confusing correlation of institutions, competences, and instruments, are now suspected of contributing to the Union's crisis of legitimacy.[79] Hence, reforming the instruments seems necessary in order to present the Union, vis-à-vis its citizens, as a well-ordered polity.

Both approaches aim at redefining the Union's legislative output and therefore touch upon the basic structures of the legal order. Unfortunately, in its current state, the theory of instruments is poorly equipped to assist such fundamental reforms by providing empirical and dogmatic knowledge about the law as it stands. In particular regarding the lesser known phenomena beyond Art 249 EC, it has yielded only minimal academic output. Today, the theory of instruments can hardly fulfil its basic task of providing an overview of the arsenal of legal instruments, let alone actually systematise them.[80] It is probably owing to legal science's traditional disfavour

[75] Non-Paper of the Luxembourg presidency of 17 April 1991, published in: W Weidenfeld (ed), *Maastricht in der Analyse* (1994), 265 at 288.

[76] See A Tizzano, 'La hiérarchie des normes communautaires' [1995] *Revue du Marché Commun et de l'Union Européenne* 219; S Magiera, 'Zur Reform der Normenhierarchie im Recht der Europäischen Union' [1995] *Integration* 197 at 200; P-Y Monjal, 'La Conférence intergouvernementale de 1996 et la hiérarchie des normes communautaire' (1996) 32 *Revue Trimestrielle de Droit Européen* 681; R Bieber and I Salomé, 'Hierarchy of Norms in European Law' (1996) 33 *CML Rev* 907; R Kovar, 'La déclaration No 16 annexée au Traité sur L'Union européenne' (1997) 33 *Cahiers de Droit Européen* 3; H Hofmann, *Normenhierarchien im europäischen Gemeinschaftsrecht* (2000).

[77] See Declaration No 16 to the Maastricht Treaty on the hierarchy of Community acts.

[78] European Council, 'Laeken Declaration on the Future of the European Union' 14./15. December 2001, SN 300/1/01 REV 1.

[79] For an example of this new uncertainty, see T Koopmans, 'Regulations, Directives, Measure' in Due *et al* (eds), above n 6, 691; A Tizzano, 'The Instruments of Community Law and the Hierarchy of Norms' in JA Winter *et al* (eds), *Reforming the Treaty on European Union* (1996) 207 at 211: 'the ... technique utilized by the Treaty in order to define the instruments ... has gradually produced the greatest confusion'.

[80] On the tasks of a theory of instruments, see E Schmidt-Aßmann, 'Die Lehre von den Rechtsformen des Verwaltungshandelns' [1989] *Deutsches Verwaltungsblatt* 533 at 540.

for empiricism that numerous new developments in legal practice have been neglected.[81] Two illustrations sufficiently demonstrate the point.

One area still awaiting empirical research and theoretical systematisation is the non-binding acts in their various forms. The codified instruments—opinions and recommendations—enjoy a privileged attention that is hardly justifiable on substantive grounds. Comparatively little attention is given to the instrument most frequently used in practice: the resolution.[82] Perhaps the most intense debate in the realm of non-binding instruments concerns the Commission's communication and its use as an administrative guideline addressed to the Member States.[83] Another line of discussion draws parallels to the sources of international law, using particularly the concept of soft law as an analytical device.[84] As yet, the need persists for a systematic overview that distinguishes the non-binding instruments and describes their correlative functions as well as their interrelation with binding acts.

A second and even wider gap in research involves the addresseeless decision (in German *Beschluss*, in contrast to a decision in the sense of Art 249(4) EC that has an explicit addressee and is designated as *Entscheidung*).[85] A binding Community instrument was developed that in practice is far more frequently used even than the directive.[86] Decisions without a specified addressee are adopted in all policy fields and find a legal basis in nearly all of the empowering provisions.[87] In terms of its formal structure, the addresseeless decision is a single-stage instrument that has

[81] The lack of empirical research weakens even advanced proposals for reform: see G Winter, 'Reforming the Sources and Categories of European Law' in *id* (ed), *Sources and Categories of European Unions Law* (1996), 13.

[82] For statistics and case-law, see A von Bogdandy, J Bast and F Arndt, 'Handlungsformen im Unionsrecht' (2002) 62 *Zeitschrift für ausländisches öffentliches Recht und Völkerrecht* 77 at 120 *et seq* (updated English version (2004) 23 *YEL* 91); for a comprehensive study on non-binding instruments, see now L Sender, *Soft Law in EC Law* (2004).

[83] G della Cananea, 'Administration by Guidelines' in I Harden (ed), *State Aid* (1993), 61; F Snyder, 'Soft Law and Institutional Practice in the European Community' in S Martin (ed), *The Construction of Europe* (1994), 197 at 205 *et seq*; J Gundel, 'Rechtsschutz gegen Kommissions-Mitteilungen zur Auslegung des Gemeinschaftsrechts' [1998] *Europarecht* 90; H Adam, *Die Mitteilungen der Kommission* (1999); A-M Tournepiche, 'Les Communications: instruments privilégiés de l'action administrative de la Commission européenne' (2002) 454 *Revue du Marché Commun et de l'Union Européenne*, 55.

[84] M Bothe, '"Soft Law" in den Europäischen Gemeinschaften?' in I von Münch (ed), *Staatsrecht, Völkerrecht, Europarecht: Festschrift für H-J Schlochauer* (1981), 761; KC Wellens and GM Borchardt, 'Soft Law in European Community Law' (1989) 14 *EL Rev* 267; F Beveridge and S Nott, 'A Hard Look at Soft Law' in P Craig and C Harlow (eds), *Law Making in the European Union* (1998), 285.

[85] The author's doctoral thesis contributes to the doctrine of the addresseeless decision: J Bast, *Grundbegriffe der Handlungsformen der EU* (2006), part 2.

[86] According to the official 'Directory of Community legislation in force' about 10 per cent of all acts that actually form current Union law are designated as *Beschluss* in their German heading. One has to add roughly the same number of addresseeless decisions which were used to conclude external agreements. For further statistics, see von Bogdandy, Bast and Arndt, above n 82, 90.

[87] They are, for instance, of great importance for institutional self-organisation, for concluding external agreements and for the establishment of incentive programmes.

constitutive effect *erga omnes*. As to its legal effects, an addresseeless decision cannot impose, either directly or indirectly, duties or obligations on private parties or Member States, but it can create actionable individual rights vis-à-vis the Union's institutions.[88] However, as the ECJ found in its famous ERASMUS judgment, the Member States do have the duty to facilitate the practical results intended by an addresseeless decision.[89] It is telling that publications recognising the addresseeless decision as an independent legal instrument come from experts close to the institutions.[90] It is a harsh verdict on the current state of the theory of instruments that even though the institutions have had established knowledge of this instrument for quite some time it has, due to a lack of scholarly attention,[91] remained the "secret knowledge" of their legal services.[92] Constructing conceptions by abstraction, a primordial task of the theory of instruments, can no longer be left to the institutions as their "in-house" doctrine.

II. CONSTITUTIONAL FRAMEWORK

1. Art 249 EC as the Central Provision

In view of the uncertain and incomplete theoretical basis, it appears appropriate to take a step back and reconsider the constitutional basis for the Union's legal instruments. Art 249 EC is the undisputed central provision for the system of instruments and has itself only been amended once, namely, when the Maastricht Treaty introduced the co-decision procedure. Art 249 EC served as the model for Art 110 EC, which recognises the power of the ECB to adopt regulations, decisions, recommendations and opinions by its decision-making bodies.[93] The legal effects attributed to ECB instruments are precisely those of Art 249 EC, and therefore Art 110 EC contains identical instruments.[94]

[88] See Case C–58/94 *The Netherlands v Council* [1996] ECR I–2169, para 38; Case T–105/95, *WWF UK v Commission* [1997] ECR II–313, para 55.

[89] See Case 242/87 *Commission v Council* [1989] ECR 1425, paras 11 and 19.

[90] J-L Dewost, 'Décisions des Institutions en vue du développement des compétences et des instruments juridiques' in R Bieber and G Ress (eds), *Die Dynamik des Gemeinschaftsrechts* (1987), 321 at 327; IE Schwartz in von der Groeben and Schwarze (eds), above n 66, Art 308 EC, paras 204 *et seq*; for the traditional conception, see T Oppermann, *Europarecht* (1999), paras 536 and 577; B Biervert in J Schwarze (ed), *EU-Kommentar* (2000), Art 249 EC, para 5.

[91] For an exception, see W Schroeder in R Streinz (ed), *EUV/EGV* (2003), Art 249 EC, paras 29 ff.

[92] Until recently the Council's Rules of Procedure ignored addresseeless decisions in its annexed 'Provisions concerning the form of acts'. For the first time, Council Decision of 22 July 2002 (see above n 19) recognises the addresseeless decision as a regular Community instrument (cf the German, Dutch, and Danish versions of Annex IV, letter B).

[93] The Statute of the European System of Central Banks invented two further instruments, whose operating mode was unknown to the Treaties: guidelines and instructions of the ECB: Art 12.1 ESCB Statute. These instruments are binding upon the national central banks to which they are addressed: Art 14.3 ESCB Statute.

[94] C Zilioli and C Kroppenstedt in von der Groeben and Schwarze (eds), above n 66, Art 110 EC, para 2.

a) Normative Contents of Art 249 EC

In view of its remarkable stability and ramifications, there is surprising uncertainty as to the legal meaning of Art 249 EC. It has already been mentioned that Art 249 EC reflects aspects of the legal quality of EC law and how collisions with national law are to be resolved.[95] Quite a few authors saw in the formulation "in accordance with the provisions of this Treaty" an expression of the principle of attributed powers, now enacted into positive law in Art 5(1) EC.[96] Moreover, this formula expresses a strict hierarchy between (primary) Treaty law and (secondary) derived law, which is a precondition that makes the principle of attributed powers work.[97] Furthermore, by placing its instruments in the hands of the Commission, of the Council, or of the Council and Parliament acting jointly "in order to carry out their tasks", Art 249(1) EC qualifies these institutions as the Union's regular law-making institutions.[98] But what is the legal content of Art 249 EC with regard to the types of acts? Which legal requirements are connected to which legal consequences?

A minimalist interpretation reads the catalogue in Art 249 EC as parenthetical definitions, concretising other Treaty provisions that use its terminology.[99] Convincing results can be achieved by this approach for empowering provisions that specify the instrument to be used: thus Art 249(5) EC specifies that recommendations and opinions which Art 211 EC empowers the Commission to adopt "have no binding force". Yet, in this reading Art 249 EC has only a limited function since most Treaty provisions do not mention any particular legal instrument. According to more prevalent constructions, Art 249 EC denotes the "essential characteristics"[100] or the "structure and effects"[101] of its instruments. Art 249(2)–(5) EC thus designates what *legal effects* are caused (or potentially caused) by a concrete act, once its affiliation with the abstract instrument defined in the respective paragraph is established. However, the question then arises as to which elements indicate affiliation with a certain instrument. The common understanding, when confronted with this question, reverses its logic and deduces the instrumental identity of the act in question from the presence of certain elements contained, again, in Art 249 EC. In other words, it is claimed that a measure must be a directive because it has the legal effects of a directive, and that it must have these legal effects because it is a directive.

[95] G Schmidt in von der Groeben and Schwarze (eds), above n 66, Art 249 EC, para 1; Nettesheim, above n 66, Art 249 EC, para 1.

[96] See Ipsen, above n 27, paras 20–21; Biervert, above n 90, Art 249 EC, para 12.

[97] See Ruffert, above n 74, Art 249 EC, para 9; on the interrelation between the principles of positive and negative legality, see A von Bogdandy and J Bast in this volume.

[98] In exact terms this should read: two institutions and one combination of institutions. Acts adopted under the co-decision procedure are attributed both to Parliament and the Council.

[99] See AG Lagrange in Cases 16/ and 17/62, above n 32, 483.

[100] G Schmidt in von der Groeben and Schwarze (eds), above n 66, before Arts 249–256 EC, para 5.

Such circular logic can only be avoided if the instrumental identity of an act can be determined by a method other than that of simply attributing to it precisely that instrument's legal effects. In law-making practice, the institutions have, at least for all practical purposes, solved this problem from the beginning by expressly designating in its title what instrument the act is supposed to be, complementing this practice by using fixed introductory and concluding clauses. It is significant that in almost all cases in which the legal effects of an act were contested before the Court—e.g. the direct effect produced by the provisions of a directive—the instrumental identity of the act (the fact that it *is* a directive) was not in dispute. However, where the category that the act belongs to was contested—e.g. where one party claimed that the act was a directive and the other claimed it was a non-binding act—the ECJ tried to avoid the circular argument above, usually resorting to competence issues. Thus the Court answered the question whether an act designated as a recommendation was a "true recommendation" by reference to the fact that the legal basis given for the act does not provide for the adoption of a binding measure.[102] Not even the ECJ can derive an act's "legal nature" from its pure content.

b) Limitations Imposed by Art 249 EC

The cross-referencing of Community instruments with its defined legal effects was never so strict that the legal effects set forth in Art 249(2)–(5) EC could not be attributed to instruments other than those catalogued in Art 249 EC. Both in practice as well as in legal literature there is broad consensus that Art 249 EC does not establish a *numerus clausus* of instruments.[103] The usual argument for the incompleteness of the listing is that the Treaties contain empowering provisions that do not specify what type of act shall be used.[104] On closer inspection this turns out to be as circular as the argument that the instruments foreseen in Art 249 EC are not entirely adequate under some legal bases:[105] in both cases it is simply assumed that an alternative form of action is a lawful option. A more substantial intimation is the instrument-neutral formulation "act" found in Arts 230(1), 232(3)

[101] See Biervert, above n 90, Art 249 EC, para 1.

[102] See Case 322/88, above n 61, para 15.

[103] M Kaltenborn, 'Gibt es einen numerus clausus der Rechtsquellen?' [2003] *Rechtstheorie* [2003], 459 at 473 *et seq*; S Douglas-Scott, *Constitutional Law of the European Union* (2003), 113 *et seq*; K Lenaerts and P Van Nuffel, *Constitutional Law of the European Union* (1999), para 14–089; G Isaac and M Blanquet, *Droit communautaire général* (2001), 156; Schmidt, above n 95, Art 249 EC, para 15; Nettesheim, above n 66, Art 249 EC, para 74; for a different opinion, see R Streinz, *Europarecht* (2003), para 375.

[104] Nettesheim, above n 66, Art 249 EC, para 74; M Schweitzer and W Hummer, *Europarecht* (1996), para 412; Biervert, above n 64, 73.

[105] R Bieber, *Verfahrensrecht von Verfassungsorganen* (1992) 286; *Rabe*, above n 23, 48 *et seq*.

and 234(1) EC.[106] Yet once again it must first be demonstrated why the term "act" in these articles should not—beyond the scope of Art 249 EC—be limited to specialised instruments expressly foreseen in the Treaties, such as the budget or the institution's Rules of Procedure. Nonetheless, the open wording "act" ensures that the development of new instruments will not present the system of legal review with insurmountable challenges. Legal science's willingness to accept the institutions' dynamism in creating and using new instruments stands in awkward counter-position to the theory of instruments' alleged function of assisting the principle of attributed powers.[107] An implied power of the institutions to create new legal instruments is, of course, a plausible assumption; but the limits placed on the Union's competence have to be respected. A Community instrument developed in practice is only permissible insofar as its legal effects fall within the spectrum of legal effects already foreseen by Art 249(2)–(5) EC. It would therefore be *de constitutione lata* impermissible, for example, if the Council were to empower the Commission to adopt a new type of "decision" giving direct instructions to the Member States' administrative authorities instead of formally addressing the Member States as such.[108] The further development of the system of legal instruments should be limited to newly combining those legal effects acknowledged by the Treaties with each other. Additionally, the principle of legal certainty will serve as a criterion for material review,[109] since it requires clarity with regard to the legal effects of the instrument chosen.[110]

Perhaps the most important normative content of Art 249 EC concerns not the relationship between the types of acts and their specific legal effects, but rather that between the instruments and the enacting institution(s). Since Art 249 EC entrusts specific institutions with these instruments, it prevents their use by all other institutions and bodies, be they foreseen in the Treaties or auxiliary bodies created by the Treaty institutions.[111] The common mantra that Art 249 EC is not exhaustive is thus imprecise since, in relation to the institutions that may make use of the instruments listed in Art 249(2)–(5) EC, it *is* exhaustive. This exclusivity is also strictly observed in practice. Of course the Treaties empower other institutions to create binding rules in specific cases, e.g. the European Parliament in Art 190(5)

[106] See Schroeder, above n 91, Art 249 EC, para 10; Gaitanides in von der Groeben and Schwarze (eds), above n 66, Art 230 EC, para 12; H-W Daig, *Nichtigkeits- und Untätigkeitsklagen im Recht der Europäischen Gemeinschaften* (1985), para 22.

[107] See Ipsen, above n 27, paras 20–23 *et seq*; H-P Kraußer, *Das Prinzip begrenzter Ermächtigung im Gemeinschaftsrecht als Strukturprinzip des EWG-Vertrags* (1991), 86.

[108] On guidelines and instructions of the ECB, see above n 93.

[109] See Nettesheim, above n 66, Art 249 EC, para 76.

[110] See Opinion of AG Tessauro, Case C–325/91 *France v Commission* [1993] ECR I–3283, paras 21.

[111] See Schmidt, above n 95, Art 249 EC, para 15; for the opposite view, see Biervert, above n 90, Art 249 EC, para 2.

and 195(4) EC, or expressly permit them to adopt binding acts, e.g. the law-making bodies set up by international agreements, Art 300(2)(2) EC. For these types of acts, those instruments contained in Art 249 EC are not available. This limitation obviously applies to the Member State acting jointly through their representatives meeting in Council. Finally, Art 249(1) EC requires a legal basis in "*this* Treaty", so that the Council acting on a legal basis of the EU Treaty is unable to avail itself of this provision.[112]

2. The Unity of Secondary Law

In addition to these normative contents, Art 249 EC sheds light on the structure of secondary law. For the order of instruments foreseen in Art 249 EC, hierarchy plays a far lesser role than is the case under national constitutional law.

a) Equality of Law-making Institutions

To begin with, the Union has, as can be seen in Art 249(1) EC, not just one, but several law-making institutions. This is not as such unusual. All European states, in some form and to some degree, have non-parliamentary law-making, be it delegated legislation or other kinds of law-making by governmental institutions, and some constitutions even permit legislation by sub-national authorities, for example statutes adopted by the parliamentary assembly of a German or Austrian *Bundesland* or of a Spanish *communitad autonoma*. In national constitutional law, however, these concurrent law-making authorities are typically vested with their own instruments different from the parliamentary statute.[113] Art 249 EC provides no basis for such a distinction, and the Court has rejected all attempts to distinguish the legal effects of an instrument according to the acting institution.[114] Contrary to the national states, in which the plurality of the sources of law was developed on the basis of different modes of creation or instances of legislation,[115] Community law decouples the process of law-making from the legal regime of its instruments.

[112] As registered by the 'Directory of Community legislation in force', the instruments of Art 249 EC compose 71 per cent of current law. Another 9 per cent is taken up by Community agreements under Art 300 EC. The largest group falling outside the scope of Art 249 EC is acts designated as *Beschluss*, with a share of 10 per cent. Roughly two thirds of the latter are attributed to the regular law-making institutions cited in Art 249 EC: see von Bogdandy, Bast and Arndt, above n 82, 136.

[113] Cf FB Callejón, 'Das System der Rechtsquellen in der spanischen Verfassungsrechtsordnung' (2001) 49 *Jahrbuch des öffentlichen Rechts der Gegenwart NF* 413 at 427.

[114] See Case 41/69, *ACF Chemiefarma v Commission* [1970] ECR 661, paras 60–62; Cases 188–190/80, above n 68, para 6.

[115] See A Merkl, 'Prolegomena einer Theorie des rechtlichen Stufenbaus' in A Verdross (ed), *Gesellschaft, Staat und Recht: Festschrift für H Kelsen* (1931), 252 at 253.

This insight can be made even more radical. The institutions not only make use of the same instruments, there is also no hierarchy among the law-making institutions.[116] Community law does not employ the hierarchical concept of the separation of powers but rather the non-hierarchical concept of institutional balance, that is, the balance among the main Treaty institutions. Accordingly, each institution may only act within the limits of the powers attributed to it by the Treaties, and the horizontal order of competences, so established, may not be modified by action of any institution.[117] As the inter-institutional relationship is thus based on the autonomy and the equality of the institutions created by the Treaties,[118] there is no hierarchy of norms among the legal acts adopted by them.[119]

Consequentially, assuming a sufficient legal basis, nothing prevents an act adopted by one institution from being amended or even repealed by another institution: the rule of *lex posterior derogat legi priori* applies.[120] Acts of secondary law are able to derogate from earlier acts of secondary law, irrespective of the enacting institutions involved.[121] This unfamiliar consequence could only be avoided if the horizontal order of competences perfectly apportioned the institutions' powers so that any derogation from the act of another institution would be ultra vires. In fact Community law tries to realise this strict delimitation of powers in many areas,[122] but there are also counterexamples where the horizontal order of competences intentionally provides overlapping empowering provisions so that different institutions may legislate concurrently. The relationship between Art 137(2) and Art 139(2) EC is an obvious (and extreme) example of that, since the articles provide for alternative options of law-making within an *identical* scope of application. A similar technique of allocating powers is frequently used in basic acts of secondary law whenever the Council reserves to itself the right to override implementing acts adopted by the Commission.[123]

[116] R Bieber and I Salomé, 'Hierarchy of Norms in European Law' (1996) 33 *CML Rev* 907 at 915.

[117] Case 25/70 *Köster* [1970] ECR 1161, para 4; Case 138/79 *Roquette Frères v Council* [1980] ECR 3333, para 33; Case C–70/88 *Parliament v Council* [1990] ECR I–2041, para 21.

[118] Cases 7/56 and 3–7/57, above n 15, 57: 'the institutions are autonomous within the limits of their powers'; Case 204/86 *Greece v Council* [1988] ECR 5323, para 17.

[119] The critical case of delegated legislation will be discussed below, II. 2. d.

[120] The *lex posterior* rule prevails over substantive considerations: see Case C–46/98 P *Petrides v Commission* [1999] ECR I–5187, paras 40–41.

[121] See Möller, above n 23, 112 *et seq*; see otherwise, however, Schmidt, above n 95, Art 249 EC, para 24; Ruffert, above n 74, Art 249 EC, para 11; Biervert, above n 90, Art 249 EC, para 10.

[122] For instance, the ECJ held that the powers under Art 88(2) EC of the Commission and the Council respectively do not overlap at any given point in time: Case C–110/02 *Commission v Council* [2004] I–0000, paras 32 *et seq*.

[123] See Art 4(3) and (4) of Council Decision of 28 June 1999 laying down the procedures for the exercise of implementing powers conferred on the Commission (1999/468/EC) [1999] OJ L 184/23; the Court upheld this practice: Case 30/70 *Scheer* [1970] ECR 1197, para 21.

b) Equality of Law-making Procedures

Even more important is the ability to derogate from or amend an act adopted under a different procedure: Community law does not recognise a hierarchy of law-making procedures.[124] For instance, the *lex posterior* rule applies when the law-making procedure, which a particular empowering provision provides for, has later been changed by Treaty amendment. In any case, it is the procedure under the provision *in force* that is relevant, even if an earlier act was adopted under a stricter procedure. The same mechanism can be observed when two empowering provisions, contemporaneously in force, overlap *ratione materiae*. As the rich case-law on the choice of the appropriate legal basis shows, this is surprisingly often the case.[125] The ECJ does not assume that empowering provisions have no overlapping scope of application, but rather that there is, in order to protect the institutional balance of the Treaties, a need to define as clearly as possible which legal basis shall apply to the measure to be adopted. If a measure's content falls predominantly within an empowering provision's scope of application, even though other provisions are incidentally or indirectly affected, the measure must be founded on a single legal basis, namely that required by the main or predominant purpose or component.[126] The incidental aims or effects do not require a double legal basis, which would necessitate that the material and procedural requirements of both empowering provisions be observed.[127] This "centre of gravity" doctrine entails a tacit assumption that has significant ramifications for the structure of secondary law: an act legally adopted has the potential of derogating from previous acts that fall within the scope of other empowering provisions, without fulfilling the procedural requirements of the latter.[128] Obviously, the application of the *lex posterior* rule does not require that the law-making procedures be parallel.[129]

[124] See Bieber and Salomé, above n 116, 916: 'each procedure has the same formal status'; the opposite view is still dominant in legal literature: see Schmidt, above n 95, Art 249 EC, para 24; Biervert, above n 90, Art 249 EC, para 10; Magiera, above n 76, 200.

[125] For an overview, see N Emiliou, 'Opening Pandora's Box' (1994) 19 *EL Rev* 488; C Trüe, *Das System der Rechtsetzungskompetenzen der Europäischen Gemeinschaft und der Europäischen Union* (2002), 511 *et seq*.

[126] See Case C–42/97 *Parliament v Council* [1999] ECR I–869, para 40; Cases C–164 and C–165/97 *Parliament v Council* [1999] ECR I–1139, para 14; Case C–491/01 *BAT et al* [2002] ECR I–11453, para 94.

[127] When recourse to such a dual legal basis is not permissible because the law-making procedures are incompatible with one another, and at the same time the act simultaneously pursues a number of inseparable objectives, a main objective must even be achieved under a 'wrong' legal basis: Case C–300/89 *Commission v Council* [1991] ECR I–2867, paras 17–21; Opinion 2/00, *Cartagena Protocol* [2001] ECR I–9713, para 23.

[128] Cf Case 165/87 *Commission v Council* [1988] ECR 5545, para 17; *in nuce* already in Case 111/63 *Lemmerz-Werke v High Authority* [1965] ECR 677 *et seq*.

[129] Hence, the principle in French public law known as the *parallélisme des formes* is not applicable in Union law when concurrent empowering provisions need to be dealt with. Cf Opinion of AG Darmon in Case 16/88 *Commission v Council* [1989] ECR 3457, para 26. Indisputably this principle applies when only one empowering provision is relevant, Case C–292/95 *Spain v Commission* [1997] ECR I–1931, para 30; Opinion of AG Mischo in Cases C–248/ and C–365/89 *Cargill* [1991] ECR I–2987, para 38.

This unique constitutional situation has not been changed by the introduction of the co-decision procedure (Art 251 EC). Rather, co-decision has been seamlessly added to the various equal-ranking law-making procedures. This became particularly clear when the ECJ held that an act adopted by Parliament and Council acting jointly under the co-decision procedure may later be amended by the Council acting alone in a simplified procedure.[130] Hence, the Maastricht conference introduced co-decision as the future standard method for securing democratic legitimacy, but it refrained from introducing a hierarchical distinction within secondary Community law. Instead, it opened the spectrum of regular instruments to the co-decision legislator by amending Art 249(1) EC. Thus, the incremental process of expanding the scope of application of Art 251 EC to other areas was made possible without requiring that a new hierarchy of norms be worked out for every Treaty amendment. The Treaties' allocation of procedures and competences has never been and is not now an expression of a coherent "grand scheme", but rather reflects political compromises between different national interests and constitutional politics. A vertical ordering principle for secondary law cannot be derived from the horizontal order of competences.

c) Equality of Binding Instruments

If a hierarchy of secondary law can be derived neither from the acting institution nor from procedural aspects, could one perhaps be established based on the type of instruments? To some authors, the development of criteria for a hierarchical order of instruments is an absolute necessity.[131] However, *de lege lata* a convincing demonstration of this thesis has yet to be produced.[132] In contrast to national constitutional law,[133] Community law must largely forego the structuring order a dominant instrument would bring. Nor can the regulation do this. Apodictic assertions—for instance, that a directive can never derogate from a regulation[134]—probably arise from a desire to elevate the regulation to a place of pride similar to that of a parliamentary statute.[135] However, when reform of existing secondary law is

[130] See Case C–259/95 *Parliament v Council* [1997] ECR I–5303, para 27.

[131] Eg, E-W Fuß, 'Rechtssatz und Einzelakt im Europäischen Gemeinschaftsrecht (pt 1)' [1964] *Neue Juristische Wochenschrift* 327 at 330; J Schwarze, *Europäisches Verwaltungsrecht* (1988), 235.

[132] Bieber and Salomé, above n 116, 917; Schroeder, above n 91, Art 249 EC, para 18; such a superior/inferior relationship cannot be read out of Art 249 EC, although the arrangement of the instruments' listing sometimes is construed in this manner: Louis, above n 24, 144; R Geiger, *EUV/EGV* (2004), Art 249 EC, para 3.

[133] See A Ross, *Theorie der Rechtsquellen* (1929, reprint 1989) 34 *et seq*, Callejón, above n 113, 421 *et seq*.

[134] Nettesheim, above n 66, Art 249 EC, para 235; Schroeder, above n 91, Art 249 EC, para 21.

[135] See P Laband, *Das Staatsrecht des deutschen Reichs* (1911, reprint 1964), ii, 68.

on the agenda, there is no convincing argument against using a different instrument than previously.[136] In practice there are innumerable examples of regulations, directives, addresseeless decisions and decisions addressed to Member States that amend or repeal each other.[137] A certain conservatism as to the choice of instruments observed in practice is not an expression of a legal inability.

Yet, some limitations on the interchangeability of instruments result from the specific "operating mode" of the instruments involved, that is, the legal effects an act entails precisely due to its affiliation with a given type of act. Binding force is the legal effect most relevant in this context. Art 249 EC indicates that a clear division can be made between binding and non-binding instruments. With the inclusion of recommendations and opinions, Art 249 EC opted for an extensive concept of law. Thus, their non-binding character actually constitutes part of their *legal* effect. Nonetheless, a non-binding act cannot derogate from a binding act.[138] Therefore the totality of acts in the form of a non-binding instrument compose a group that ranks below all binding instruments.[139]

d) Do Implementing Measures Have a Separate Rank?

The foregoing analysis of the structure of secondary law depicted a horizontally organised body of law.[140] But so-called implementing acts seem to provide a strong counterargument to the concept of single-level secondary law. The term refers to legal acts that do not find their legal basis directly in the Treaty, but rather in an act of secondary law.[141] The exercise of implementing powers requires the delegation of power in a preceding act. The latter is usually called a "basic act" or, borrowing from Latin terminology, an "act of habilitation". Arts 202 and 211 EC indicate that this conferral of powers is the normal case in Community law.[142] Art 202 EC names both the

[136] The principle of proportionality requires this possibility to be considered: see Protocol on the application of the principles of subsidiarity and proportionality (1997), No 6; affirmed by Arts 10(4) and 38(1) CT–IGC (Arts I–9(4) and I–37(1) CT–Conv).

[137] In fact, there are only a few examples of directives amending a regulation, eg, Art 38(1) of Dir 2004/38/EC of the European Parliament and of the Council of 29 April 2004 on the right of citizens of the Union and their family members to move and reside freely within the territory of the Member States *amending* Reg (EEC) No 1612/68 ... [2004] OJ L 158/77 (emphasis added).

[138] See Case C–149/96, *Portugal v Council* [1999] ECR I–8395, para 56.

[139] R Baldwin, *Rules and Government* (1995), 226.

[140] One should recall that this contribution does not address instruments of international law; for the hierarchisation effected by Art 300(7) EC, see R Uerpmann–Wittzack in this volume.

[141] The implementing measures of the Union's institutions must not be confused with implementing measures of the Member States, the latter concept bundling together legislative transposition and administrative application; see C Möllers, 'Durchführung des Gemeinschaftsrechts' [2002] *Europarecht* 483.

[142] For a general discussion on habilitated decision-making, see M Andenas and A Türk (eds), *Delegated Legislation and the Role of Committees in the EC* (2000); C Joerges and E Voss (eds), *EU Committees* (1999); for the procedural aspects, see K Lenaerts and A Verhoeven, 'Towards a Legal Framework for Executive Rule-Making in the EU?' (2000) 37 *CML Rev* 645.

Commission and the Council as institutions exercising delegated (habilitated) powers.[143] In addition, there is habilitated law-making practised by the ECB.[144] The Court has declared the conferral of powers on Treaty institutions *prima facie* permissible,[145] thereby employing a broad concept of "implementation", encompassing legislation in the form of all instruments as well as partial amendment of the basic act.[146] A habilitated act must, however, be consistent with the procedural as well as the material requirements set forth in the basic act, even if the acting institution is the same that delegated the power.[147] In case of conflict, the basic act prevails.[148]

Does not this bifurcation of secondary law into basic acts and implementing acts indicate that there is a full-fledged hierarchy of norms within secondary law?[149] Many authors come to this conclusion without, however, expressly arguing their case.[150] According to this conception, a habilitated act must be consistent not only with the act it is based on, but also with all other acts of the same rank as that basic act. A habilitated act would be subject to each and every act based directly on the Treaties: such strict rigidity follows necessarily from conceptualising a separate rank for implementing measures. The unmistakable model for this conception is the relationship between statutes and regulations, common in the Member States' constitutional orders.[151] This analogy also fits well in the familiar terminology of separation of powers: implementing measures could be attributed to the executive branch, whereas legislation directly based on the Treaty could be understood as legislative.[152]

There are, however, considerable concerns *de lege lata*. On closer inspection, the relationship between statutes and regulations in national legal orders proves to be the wrong point of reference. The Spanish and Italian model of "delegated laws" solves the problem of habilitated acts in a far

[143] Council self-authorisation is a common practice: roughly 10 per cent of the Council's acts in force are founded on a legal basis in secondary law.

[144] See Art 110(1) EC.

[145] See Case 25/70, above n 117, para 6; Case 23/75 *Rey Soda* [1975] ECR 1279, paras 10–14.

[146] See Case 41/69, above n 114, paras 60–62; Case 16/88, above n 129, para 11; Case C–417/93 *Parliament v Council* [1995] ECR I–1185, paras 29–30.

[147] See Case 38/70 *Tradax* [1971] ECR 145, para 10; Case 46/86 *Romkes* [1987] ECR 2671, para 16.

[148] Cases 6/ and 7/88 *Spain v Commission* [1989] ECR 3639, para 15; Case C–156/93 *Parliament v Commission* [1995] ECR I–2019, para 13; Case C–103/96 *Eridania Beghin-Say* [1997] ECR 1453, para 20.

[149] See H Kelsen, *Reine Rechtslehre* (1960, reprint 1992), 228 *et seq*; Ross, above n 133, 308 *et seq*.

[150] See Isaac and Blanquet, above n 103, 148 *et seq*; H Schmitt von Sydow in von der Groeben and Schwarze (eds), above n 66, Art 211 EC, para 77; Schmidt, above n 95, Art 249 EC, para 24.

[151] A von Bogdandy, *Gubernative Rechtsetzung* (2000) 227 *et seq*; on the exceptional case of Arts 34 and 37 Constitution française, see *ibid*, 262 *et seq*.

[152] K Lenaerts, 'Some Reflections on the Separation of Powers in the European Community' (1991) 28 *CML Rev* 11 at 17 *et seq*, 30 *et seq*; Douglas-Scott, above n 103, 125.

more convincing manner.[153] In Spanish constitutional law, a *decreto legislativo*—a law-making power delegated to the government—has the legal force of a statute (not of a regulation) and can thus amend or repeal parliamentary statutes. The only exception is that it cannot derogate from the delegating statute itself.[154] This is exactly the legal relationship between a habilitated act of Community law and all other acts directly or indirectly derived from the Treaties. Following the model of the *decretos legislativos*, there are partial hierarchies within secondary law insofar as a habilitated act cannot derogate from its specific basic act unless the latter explicitly permits this.[155] Such legal primacy is only *relative* and does not imply a general hierarchy with respect to other acts of secondary law.[156] In case of conflict with other acts of derived law, the normal *lex posterior* rule applies, so none of the latter can serve as standards for the legality of the habilitated act. The extent to which a habilitated act is able to amend an older act of secondary law depends solely on the scope of the powers conferred by the basic act.

e) Is the Lack of Hierarchy an Anomaly of the System?

Apart from the marginalised group of non-binding acts, secondary law appears to be a surprisingly modern, democratic society, where there are no differences according to class or origin—one nation under Treaty law. Not all, however, are ready to pledge allegiance to this non-hierarchical order, and the absence of an "appropriate hierarchy between the different categories of act" is considered a systemic deficiency of Community law.[157]

Nonetheless, one should bear in mind that the hierarchical order of instruments in national constitutional law accompanies the distribution of governmental functions to various constitutional organs. The higher rank of a statute is both historically and systematically explained by the fact that this instrument usually is assigned to a parliamentary procedure.[158] In Union law,

[153] Arts 82 *et seq* Constitutión Española, Arts 76 *et seq* Costituzione italiana; see I de Otto, *Derecho constitutional: Sistema de fuentes* (1987), 182 *et seq*; E Virgala Foruria, *La delegación legislativa en la Constitución y los decretos legislativos como normas con rango incondicionado de ley* (1991), 33 *et seq*; G Zagrebelsky, *Manuale di diritto costituzionale* (1990), i, 208 *et seq*.

[154] See von Bogdandy, above n 151, 295.

[155] A habilitated act may amend provisions of its basic act if the amended provision is 'non-essential', J Kalbheim and G Winter, 'Delegation Requirements for Rule-Making by the Commission' in Winter (ed), above n 81, 585 at 598; cf Art 2(b) of Council Dec 1999/468/EC, above n 123. According to Art 36(1) CT–IGC, the 'essential elements of an area shall be reserved for the European law or framework law' (similar Art I–35(1) CT–Conv).

[156] The conception of partial hierarchy between acts of secondary law equally applies when primary law so orders; on the partial hierarchy effected by Art 202 EC see Case C–378/00 *Commission v Parliament and Council* [2003] ECR I–937, paras 39–40.

[157] Declaration No 16, above n 77.

[158] H Heller, 'Der Begriff des Gesetzes in der Reichsverfassung' (1928) 4 *Veröffentlichungen der Vereinigung der Deutschen Staatsrechtslehrer* 98 at 118.

the decoupling of legal instruments from respective procedures and enacting institutions finds its logical extension in the equality of rank among all binding instruments. A hierarchical order of instruments would require a complete reconstruction of the current Union legal order; the justification for such a fundamental change would have to been impressive, indeed.

The reasoning behind a hierarchy of norms seeks an adequate normative regime via multi-phased and multi-layered legislation, but the current legal system already provides this. The model of partial hierarchies guarantees that the more demanding procedure is reserved for the preceding act fixing the essentials of a regulatory regime. The following step, which fleshes out the regime, can use streamlined procedures, but it does not call into question the compromises reached in the basic act. A cross-sectoral hierarchy of norms is not absolutely necessary. An essential objective of the Treaties is to find solutions to sector-specific problems by adequately distributing competences, so as to do justice to the interests involved and the projected need for legislation. Clearly, with the current distribution of institutional tasks and the multiplicity of law-making procedures, the Treaties do not always convincingly attain this objective. This does not change the fact that a polity with attributed powers must largely build on a horizontal organisation of its law, reflecting an array of empowering provisions. Under these circumstances, the concept of competence plays the key role in preventing and solving conflicts within the law. However, for the horizontal order of competences to achieve a level of rationality similar to that found in the vertical order of instruments under national constitutional law, a basic hierarchy is necessary: Treaty law must have strict primacy over secondary law.[159] So long as this commandment is observed, the egalitarian social order of secondary law will not devolve into anarchy.

3. The Court's Conception

The various aspects of legal protection have so far only been peripherally discussed. This appears to be a negligent omission, given that structuring the system of legal protection is considered to be one of the main tasks of Community legal instruments. The examination of acts from the perspective of judicial review is probably the dominant paradigm for the discussion about instruments.[160] The relevance of legal instruments for the regime of

[159] For a sceptical view, see C Schönberger, 'Normenkontrollen im EG-Föderalismus' [2003] *Europarecht* 600.

[160] On the discussion on effective legal protection of private parties, see, eg, K Lenaerts, 'The Legal Protection of Private Parties under the EC Treaty' in *Scritti in onore di Guisepppe Federico Mancini* (1998), ii, 591; A Ward, *Judicial Review of the Rights of Private Parties in EC Law* (2000); C Nowak, 'Das Verhältnis zwischen zentralem und dezentralem Individualrechtsschutz im Europäischen Gemeinschaftsrecht' [2000] *Europarecht* 724.

legal protection seems undeniable since Art 230 EC unmistakably operates with the terminology of Art 249 EC. The Court itself has from time to time emphasised the strong connection between the two provisions[161] and has still chosen another way since the beginning of the 1970s. By now the system of legal protection has been almost completely severed from the system of legal instruments. In the following section, it will be argued that the ECJ gives the law-making institutions far greater power to define the type of act than is generally recognised.

a) The Concept of an Act According to Art 230(1) EC

From the very beginning, the Court saw itself confronted with conflicting objectives. On the one hand, the autonomy of the Community legal instruments had to be protected. The Court's policy on legal instruments cannot be understood without understanding the fear that reference to instruments and practices common in public international law could compromise the Community's unique legal order.[162] The primacy of Community law serves as a firewall against all forms of Member State action, including those acts undertaken in the form of international law instruments, even if the agreement or "decision" in question is intended to enhance European integration.[163] The ECJ has also admonished the institutions that only through the instruments foreseen in the Treaties can they produce legal effects typical of Community law, or, as the ECJ put it, "uniform application of Community law can only be guaranteed if it is the subject of formal measures taken within the context of the Treaty".[164] This goal could happily be tied to another principle: the protection of the ECJ's monopoly on the authentic interpretation of Community law. The Court consequently rejects the notion that the Commission has the power to make binding interpretations of agricultural regulations via informal statements;[165] the Court even more strictly rejects the alleged binding force of interpretative "decisions" by the Administrative Commission on Migrant Workers,[166] an anachronistic anomaly of the institutional system in the social security sector.[167]

[161] Eg, Case C–298/89 *Gibraltar v Council* [1993] ECR I–3605, para 15.

[162] See Case 44/84 *Hurd* [1986] ECR 29, paras 20 and 39; Case C–6/89 *Commission v Belgium* [1990] ECR I–1595.

[163] See Case 130/73 *Vandeweghe* [1973] ECR 1329, paras 2 *et seq*; Case 235/87 *Matteucci* [1988] ECR 5589, para 14; Case C–55/00 *Gottardo* [2002] ECR I–413, para 33; only once was this principle set aside by the Court: it qualified the Brussels Convention on Jurisdiction and Judgments as being a part of Community law: Case 25/79 *Sanicentral* [1979] ECR 3423, para 5; Case C–398/92 *Mund* [1994] ECR I–467, paras 11–12.

[164] See Cases 90 and 91/63 *Commission v Belgium and Luxembourg* [1964] ECR 625 at 631 *et seq*; Case 74/69 *Krohn* [1970] ECR 451, para 9.

[165] See Case 132/77 *Société pour l'exportation des sucres v Commission* [1978] ECR 1061, paras 11–21; Case C–50/90 *Sunzest v Commission* [1991] ECR I–2917, para 13.

[166] See Case 19/67 *van der Vecht* [1967] ECR 345 *et seq*; Case 98/80 *Romano* [1981] ECR 1241, para 20.

[167] On the proposal to replace it with an advisory committee, see von Bogdandy, Bast and Arndt, above n 82, 150–1 and 157–8.

On the other hand, the ECJ has never seriously tried to prevent the institutions from having recourse to atypical instruments. If the Court had limited the canon of legal instruments, the law-making institutions would have found themselves in heavy chains. Applying this ideal would probably have proven to be counterproductive: numerous acts by the institutions would have been deprived of the effects of Community law. The number of informal agreements among the Member States would hereby have increased rather than decreased, and in both cases it would have been impossible for the Court to monitor Member States' compliance. Against this background, the Court formulated a broad conception of what could constitute a Community act. The jurisdiction of the Court should extend to virtually *all* actions of the Treaty institutions. This requires a concept of a legal act that is largely divorced from formal appearance. Even the most innocuous writings from a Commission department could potentially constitute a Community act.[168]

The conflict of goals becomes acute when the informal act is at the Council level. On the one hand, ordinary international law operating between Member States is not recognised as Community law, yet on the other hand, the Council cannot escape the jurisdiction of the ECJ whenever it wishes to, simply by calling itself an intergovernmental conference. The ECJ found the surprising solution in the doctrine of competences: irrespective of its designation or formal appearance, an act within the meaning of Art 230(1) EC is present when the subject matter, which the Member States' representatives agreed on in the institutional context of the Council, falls within the *exclusive* competence of the Community—the ERTA test was born.[169] If, to the contrary, authorship of an institution is undisputed, the act's contestability under Art 230 EC does not even require that the act in question have its legal basis in the EC Treaty.[170]

Such a broad approach, of course, needed a pacifying corrective, one that the ECJ found in the flexible category of "legal effects".[171] In the terminology of Art 249 EC, the term can be translated as "binding force".[172]

[168] Eg, Case 182/80 *Gauff v Commission* [1982] ECR 799, para 18; Case C–39/93 P *SFEI et al v Commission* [1994] ECR I–2681, para 27. A reviewable act may even lie in undated decisions of the Commission implicitly referred to in later action, eg, in a press release, Case C–106/96 *United Kingdom v Commission* [1998] ECR I–2729. However, in view of Art 232 EC mere silence does not constitute a reviewable act, save as expressly foreseen in secondary law: Cases T–189/95, T–39 and T–123/96 *SGA v Commission* [1999] ECR II–3587, paras 26–27.

[169] See Case 22/70 *Commission v Council* [1971] ECR 263, paras 3–4; Cases C–181 and C–248/91 *Parliament v Council and Commission* [1993] ECR I–3685, para 12; on the different types of vertical competences, see von Bogdandy and Bast in this volume.

[170] See Case C–316/91 *Parliament v Council* [1994] ECR I–625, para 9; Case C–170/96 *Commission v Council* [1998] ECR I–2763, paras 16–17.

[171] See Case 22/70, above n 169, paras 38–42; Case 60/81 *IBM v Commission* [1981] ECR 2639, para 9.

[172] K Lenaerts and D Arts, *Procedural Law of the European Union* (1999), para 7–007; TC Hartley, *The Foundations of European Community Law* (1998), 331.

A normative basis for this conception can be found in Art 230(1) EC, which opens the way for an action for annulment against acts "other than recommendations and opinions".[173] The ECJ ignores the methodological problems of determining whether an act is binding without regard to formal criteria. Concluding an act's legal effects from its instrumental identity (visible by its designation and other formal criteria) would have thwarted the Court's intentions. Nevertheless, both the use of an atypical designation as well as the lack of a signature on behalf of the institution suggest that the act is non-binding and therefore non-reviewable.[174]

Once again, the doctrine of competences plays a significant role, in this case in determining whether an act is binding: if an institution lacks the power to adopt an act with binding force in a certain area, this is a strong indication that the act does not have "legal effects", in which case an action for annulment is inadmissible.[175] In reaction to the growing flood of Commission communications interpreting Community law in general terms, the ECJ also turned this approach on its head: when an institution lacks the power to adopt a binding act in a given area and the act purports to impose obligations, it produces "legal effects". Hence, an action brought by a Member State is admissible and, due to lack of competence, well founded.[176] When the ECJ finally even recognised "legal effects" of a non-binding communication on a subject matter that the Commission could otherwise have regulated in the form of a binding instrument (the action was then admissible, but the claim not necessarily founded), the contradictions caused by the stubborn refusal to look at formal criteria to identify whether an act is binding or not became obvious.[177]

In the end, the theory of instruments must resign itself to the fact that the ECJ determines whether an act has "legal effects" mainly on a case-by-case basis. In doing so, the central question is whether judicial review is an appropriate outcome in the particular case. The Court consistently refers to the ERTA formula, according to which an action for annulment must be available for "all measures adopted by the institutions, whatever their nature or form, which are intended to have legal effects".[178] This formula

[173] Under Art 234(1) EC this corrective is not needed: see Case 113/75 *Frescassetti* [1976] ECR 983, paras 8–9; Case 90/76 *van Ameyde* [1977] ECR 1091, para 15; Case C–188/91 *Deutsche Shell* [1993] ECR I-363, para 18.

[174] See Cases 42 and 49/59, *SNUPAT v High Authority* [1961] ECR 53 at 72; Cases 90 and 91/63, above n 164.

[175] See Case 151/88 *Italy v Commission* [1989] ECR 1255, para 22; Case 175/84 *Krohn v Commission* [1986] ECR 753, para 21.

[176] See Case C–366/88 *France v Commission* [1990] ECR I–3571, para 12; Case C–303/90 *France v Commission* [1991] ECR I–5315, paras 10–11; Case C–57/95 *France v Commission* [1997] ECR I–1627, para 10; the Court is employing a concept of French administrative law: Gundel, above n 83, 97; on Case C–366/88 see G della Cananea, *Revista italiana di diritto pubblico comunitario* (1992), 691.

[177] See Case C–325/91, above n 110; the Opinion of AG Tesauro, *ibid*, para 14, confronted this problem.

[178] See Case 22/70, above n 169, paras 38–42.

offers the ECJ a sufficiently flexible tool. The price is the practically complete severing of the criteria for determining when there is a reviewable act from the doctrine of instruments. There is a connection only insofar as, once the institutions choose one of the binding instruments contained in Art 249 EC, the act is most assuredly subject to judicial review. This already indicates a 'division of labour' between the Court and the law-making institutions, something which can be even more clearly demonstrated with the reviewable decision under Art 230(4) EC: the institutions have far-reaching powers in their choice of instruments, including those that are beyond the scope of Art 249 EC. They are not, however, able to exempt themselves from legal review simply by using a certain legal instrument.

b) The Concept of a Decision According to Art 230(4) EC

On closer analysis, the "decision" in the sense of Art 230(4) EC turns out to be a procedural law concept like the term "act" in the sense of Art 230(1) EC. The qualification of an act as a decision means that a natural or legal person can challenge the act before the Court. This does not imply, however, that this act is affiliated with a particular legal instrument. The following reconstruction of this separation uses insights won in a study by HC Röhl, who was able to show that the concept of the reviewable decision belongs to procedural law and that this conception has its roots in French administrative law.[179]

The ECJ's dichotomy between measures of "general application" and those of "individual concern" has already been mentioned. If an act was found to be generally applicable, it was definitely not actionable by individual applicants.[180] According to the ECJ's early case-law, the decisive negative criterion was whether the number and identity of those who could be affected by its provisions was fixed.[181] An analysis of the ECJ's methodology shows that the first cracks between legal protection and the doctrine of instruments had already developed in this phase. The Court openly claims that it does not consider the type of act as a decisive criterion for an act's reviewability. The credo was: "The choice of form cannot change the nature of the measure."[182] The motivation for disregarding the act's formal qualification is clear: it would be an open contradiction to the ECJ's understanding of itself as the guarantor of the citizen's individual rights if the law-making

[179] HC Röhl, 'Die anfechtbare Entscheidung nach Art 230 Abs. 4 EGV' (2000) 60 *Zeitschrift für ausländisches öffentliches Recht und Völkerrecht* 331.

[180] See Cases 16 and 17/62, above n 32; Case 6/68 *Watenstedt v Council* [1968] ECR 409 *et seq*; Case 45/81 *Moksel v Commission* [1982] ECR 1129, para 17.

[181] See Cases 41–44/70 *International Fruit Company et al v Commission* [1971] ECR 411, paras 16–22; Cases 87, 130/77, 22/83, 9 and 10/84 *Salerno et al v Commission and Council* [1985] ECR 2523, para 30.

[182] See Case 101/76 *Koniklijke Scholten Honig v Council* [1977] ECR 797, paras 5–7; Cases 789 and 790/79 *Calpak et al v Commission* [1980] ECR 1949, para 7; Case 307/81 *Alusuisse Italia v Commission and Council* [1982] ECR 3463, para 7.

institutions could deny legal protection solely by "the choice of form". In this regard, when the ECJ claims for itself the exclusive power to determine whether or not the contested act is, in fact, a decision, it has already departed from an understanding of the decision as a legal instrument as set forth in Art 249(4) EC, its protests notwithstanding.[183] To all appearances, after the Court has found an act to be a decision, it has never attached to this finding legal consequences other than those of procedural law, in particular the action's admissibility. Thus a reviewable decision in the form of a regulation remains a regulation: it is equally valid in all official languages, it first enters into force with its publication (Art 254 EC)[184] and the Court's declaration of nullity has authority *erga omnes.*[185] By qualifying an act as a reviewable decision, the Court subjects the contested act to a specific regime of legal protection without, however, re-qualifying it as a different instrument.[186]

As a second step on the way to neutrality with regard to the type of act, "general application" lost significance as an indicator of whether an individual action lies.[187] It was gradually replaced with the concept of "individual concern" as the decisive criterion for access to the Court.[188] The ECJ thus uses the *Plaumann*-formula, according to which persons are individually concerned in the sense of Art 230(4) EC if the contested act "affects them by reason of certain attributes which are peculiar to them or by reason of circumstances in which they are differentiated from all other persons, and by virtue of these factors distinguishes them individually just as in the case of the person addressed"[189]. At first, however, this formula still served as an *e contrario* test to falsify the act's "normative" character, i.e. its general applicability.

The straw that broke the camel's back was the anti-dumping regulations. For the first time, the ECJ recognised that measures may "in fact, as regards their nature and scope, [be] of a legislative character," and yet "the provisions may none the less be of direct and individual concern" to some of the affected persons.[190] If it appeared at first that this new approach could be

[183] This became very clear in Cases 8–11/66, above n 18.

[184] The opposite view had no success, E-W Fuß, 'Rechtsatz und Einzelakt im Europäischen Gemeinschaftsrecht (pt 3)' [1964] *Neue Juristische Wochenschrift* 1600 at 1603.

[185] See Case 138/79 *Roquette Frères v Council* [1980] ECR 3333, para 37; this is different with regard to a collective decision in the meaning of Art 249(4) EC: see Case C–310/97 P *Commission v AssiDomaen Kraft Products et al* [1999] ECR I-5363, paras 52 *et seq*: that decision becomes definitive as against those addressees who did not bring an action for annulment within the time-limit.

[186] See Hartley, above n 172, 100.

[187] On the definition, see Cases 789 and 790/79, above n 182, para 9; Case 307/81, above n 182, para 9; it is still valid, see Case C–41/99 P *Sadam Zuccherifici et al v Council* [2001] ECR I–4239, para 24; Case C–171/00 P *Libéros v Commission* [2002] ECR I–451, para 31.

[188] See Case 100/74 *CAM v Commission* [1975] ECR 1393, para 19; Case 26/86 *Deutz et al v Council* [1987] ECR 941, para 9.

[189] See Case 25/62 *Plaumann v Commission* [1963] ECR 95, 107.

[190] See Cases 239 and 275/82 *Allied et al v Commission* [1984] ECR 1005, para 11.

explained solely by the peculiarities of trade-related protection measures,[191] it did not long remain limited to this sector. In the *Codorniu* case this development reached a new highpoint.[192] The *Plaumann*-formula now serves to identify a reviewable decision independently of the contested measure's "legal nature".[193] The instrument formally chosen and the legal nature of an act became preliminary questions, the answer to which could already positively determine the action's admissibility; it could not, however, definitively determine its inadmissibility.[194] In what has meanwhile become settled case-law of the CFI and ECJ, admissibility is first decided after an examination of whether there are any legal or factual aspects sufficiently individualising the plaintiff's concern.[195]

Albeit with a certain delay, the concept of a reviewable decision shows a parallel development to the concept of an act in the meaning of Art 230(1) EC. The type of act is only relevant for the act's contestability by individuals insofar as the adopting institution can positively open legal recourse for the explicit addressee by choosing the formal decision in the sense of Art 249(4) EC. As a balance, the addressee of this decision must expect that, after the deadline set forth in Art 230(5) EC has expired, the act's validity will be held against him or her.[196] Otherwise an act may not be rendered non-actionable simply due to the choice of instrument.[197]

The ECJ's conception results in a specific division of labour between the judiciary and the law-making institutions. The latter are responsible for the choice of the legal instrument and thus—within the limits foreseen by the Treaty—for the determination of the legal effects the act produces. It is not, however, within their power to decide whether and to what extent legal review against their acts may be possible. This leads to an irritating

[191] See Case 191/82 *Fediol v Commission* [1983] ECR 2913, paras 27 *et seq*; Case 264/82 *Timex v Council* [1985] ECR 849, para 16.

[192] See Case C–309/89 *Codorniu v Council* [1994] ECR I–1853, para 19; already prepared in Case C–358/89, *Extramet v Council* [1991] ECR I–2501, para 16.

[193] See Lenaerts and Arts, above n 172, paras 7–041 *et seq*; HG Schermers and D Waelbroeck, *Judicial Protection in the European Union* (2001), para 866.

[194] Verifying an act's 'legal nature' may be relevant for the substance of the case: see Cases T–480 and T–483/93 *Antillean Rice Mills et al v Commission* [1995] ECR II–2305, para 184; overly broad is D Booß in Grabitz and Hilf, above n 66, Art 230 EC, para 56, stating that the demarcation between a normative act and a decision has no practical relevance.

[195] See Case C–451/98 *Antillean Rice Mills v Council* [2001] ECR I–8949, para 46; Case T–109/97 *Mölkerei Großbraunshain et al v Commission* [1998] ECR II–3533, para 57; Case C–142/00 P *Commission v Nederlandse Antillen* [2003] ECR I–3483, paras 64 *et seq*; see in detail, A Arnull, 'Private Applicants and the Action for Annulment since Codorniu' (2001) 38 *CML Rev* 7 at 23 *et seq*; on the latest developments, see JA Usher, 'Direct and Individual Concern—an Effective Remedy or a Conventional Solution?' (2003) 28 *EL Rev* 575; P Craig, 'Standing, Rights, and the Structures of Legal Argument' (2003) 9 *European Public Law* 493; HC Röhl, 'Rechtsschutz gegen EG-Verordnungen' [2003] *Jura* 830.

[196] See Booß, above n 194, Art 230 EC, para 88.

[197] For an action against a directive, see Case T–135/96 *UEAPME v Council* [1998] ECR II–2335, para 63; against an addresseeless decision, see Case 297/86 *CIDA et al v Council* [1988] ECR 3531, para 13; Case 187/85 *Fediol v Commission* [1988] ECR 4155, para 6.

consequence, which the theory of instruments has yet to recognise, namely the judicial system's "blindness" to the type of act. The theory of instruments will have to sever itself from the paradigm of legal protection if it wishes to maintain its relevance.

An alternative approach could depart from the law-making institutions' exclusive power to define *ex ante* which instrument is employed for any given act. Through that choice of instrument an act is vested with specific legal characteristics, which in their totality constitute the legal regime of that instrument. Two lines of inquiry result. First, what specific requirements does Union law place on a particular instrument so that an act takes effect and is valid? Second, what are the specific legal effects of this particular instrument, that is, what capacities of modifying the Union's and Member States' legal orders characterise this instrument's operating mode? The following sections investigate both complexes, first the one concerning the variable conditions for an act to be legal and have effect (III.), then the question concerning the legal effects attached to the individual instruments (IV.).

III. VARIABLE CONDITIONS FOR LEGALITY AND EFFECT

Among the traditional tasks of a theory of instruments is identifying with which instrument an act is affiliated, in order to subject it to a specific legal regime. The instruments serve as a "memory cache" for insights and rules that apply to the respective act, without having to "download" them for each and every case.[198] Yet, as far as legal requirements are concerned, Union law does not utilise this "memory cache" function nearly as much as the national legal orders. In many areas where national public law brings order through its different instruments, Community law uses other means to impose order.[199] Nevertheless, it does not completely renounce this rationale. For its incontestable lawfulness, an act must fulfil certain conditions that stem solely from its affiliation with the legal regime of a particular instrument. Here one must distinguish between the conditions pertaining to the act's legality and the conditions for the act to have effect. Although Community acts, once adopted, often still take no effect unless certain further conditions are fulfilled, this in itself does not cast doubt on the legality of the act.[200] The reverse is also true. Except in cases where the measure exhibits particularly serious and manifest defects, an illegal act continues to have effect: it enjoys a presumption of validity.[201]

[198] E Schmidt-Aßmann, *Das allgemeine Verwaltungsrecht als Ordnungsidee* (2004), Ch 6, para 34.

[199] The opposite view—a dominant role of the concept of instrument within the Union legal order—is rather common: see Biervert, above n 64, 106 *et seq* ('*Handlungsformengerichtetheit der europäischen Rechtsordnung*').

[200] See Case 185/73, above n 38, para 6.

[201] See Case 15/85 *Consorzio Cooperative d'Abruzzo v Commission* [1987] ECR 1005, para 10.

1. Conditions for Effect

The conditions for a Community act to have effect are clearly differentiated according to the instrument at issue. This concerns the preconditions and the date of entry into force. For all instruments, the enacting institution must formally decide on a proposed text in accordance with its Rules of Procedure. Some instruments already take effect when this is done, unless the act itself specifies that it enters into force at a later time. Particularly the addresseeless decision can take effect immediately. However, the entry into force of most instruments is under the suspending condition that the act either be published in the Official Journal or notified to the specified addressee(s).

The publication requirement has always been applicable to regulations because of their potential to directly impose duties on an indeterminate number of persons. Art 191 EEC Treaty was considered to be an expression of a fundamental principle of law: a Community measure cannot be applied to those concerned before they have had the opportunity to make themselves acquainted with it.[202] The Treaty of Maastricht's reformulation of Art 254 EC (then still Art 191 EC Treaty) at least partially reflected the fact that the regulation is not the only "legislative" instrument at the Union's command. Art 254 EC uses two further criteria to establish publication as a condition for an act to have effect: the procedure according to which an act may be adopted, and its explicit addressee. Directives and decisions adopted in accordance with the co-decision procedure as well as those directives that are addressed to all Member States must be published. Directives and decisions that do not fall under Art 254(1) or (2) EC shall be notified to the specified addressee and take effect upon such notification, Art 254(3) EC.[203]

With respect to the addresseeless decision, the system of the conditions for effect seems to have a serious loophole: although it is binding, its publication is only on a voluntary basis. Without an addressee, notification is by definition impossible. An analogous application of Art 254 EC is only convincing for an addresseeless decision adopted under the co-decision procedure.[204] This unique regime of immediate effect of a binding instrument may be justified as the addresseeless decision is unable to impose obligations on private parties.[205] Yet, *de lege ferenda* a

[202] See Case 98/78 *Racke* [1979] ECR 69, para 15; however, belated publication does not affect the legality of the act: Case C–149/96, above n 138, para 54.

[203] Individual notification is not, however, a condition for the act's legality: irregularities in notification may be healed if the addressee otherwise acquires knowledge of the measure, though such a circumstance may have consequences for the time limit to bring action pursuant to Art 230(5) EC: Case 48/69 *ICI v Commission* [1972] ECR 619, paras 39–43.

[204] In practice all addresseeless decisions adopted under the co-decision procedure are published in the 'L' series of the OJ in the section that is reserved for 'acts whose publication is obligatory'.

[205] According to Art 17(4)(d) of its Rules of Procedure (see above n 19) the Council is free to decide, on a case-by-case basis, whether 'other Council acts, such as sui generis decisions or resolutions' should be published.

duty of subsequent publication would be more in line with the instrument's importance.[206]

2. Conditions for Legality

Certain conditions varying with the chosen instrument can touch on an act's legality.[207] Failing these conditions, an act may be declared void when challenged or withdrawn by the enacting institution under streamlined conditions. Interestingly, these consequences are not themselves specific to any one instrument: the Court assumes that there is a single system of legal consequences for all unlawful Community acts.[208] This conception implies that an illegal regulation remains valid if not timely challenged.[209] It is also surprising that an institution may retroactively withdraw an illegal act that is "normative" in character.[210]

The duties to give reasons and to refer to preparatory acts take centre stage among the conditions for legality varying with the instrument chosen.[211] Art 253 EC must be understood in light of the difference made in Art 249 EC between binding and non-binding instruments. Following this logic, addresseeless decisions come, by analogy, within the scope of the triad of "regulations, directives and decisions".[212] The duty to provide reasons thus applies to all Community acts which are intended to have "legal effects", that is, all binding acts. Whether this applies to the special instruments under Arts 12 and 34 EU still requires clarification: there is no express instruction in primary Union law (see Arts 28 and 41 EU). As already mentioned, within the family of binding acts, the scope of the duty to provide reasons varies according to the act's "legal nature", which is only in part defined by the instrument chosen.

This mostly covers the instruments' variable conditions for legality. In addition, there are the rules determining the languages of the institutions

[206] There is a similar problem with regard to association councils and similar co-operation bodies adopting decisions having legal effects: see Case C–192/89 *Sevince* [1990] ECR I–3461, para 24; Art 17(5) of the Council's Rule of Procedure is not convincing.

[207] The relevant point in time at which to examine an act's legality is the date of its adoption: see Cases 15/76 and 16/76 *France v Commission* [1979] ECR 321, para 7; Case T–115/94 *Opel Austria v Council* [1997] ECR II–39, paras 87–88.

[208] X Arzoz, 'Rechtsfolgen der Rechtswidrigkeit von Verordnungen der Europäischen Gemeinschaften' (2001) 49 *Jahrbuch des öffentlichen Rechts der Gegenwart NF* 299 at 308.

[209] Under the preliminary procedure the plea of illegality against a regulation is still permissible unless it is obvious that an action under Art 230 EC would have been admissible: see Case C–188/92 *Textilwerke Deggendorf* [1994] ECR I–833, paras 17–18.

[210] See Case C–248/89 *Cargill v Commission* [1991] ECR I–2987, para 20; Case C–365/89 *Cargill* [1991] ECR I–3045, para 18.

[211] See, in general, M Shapiro, 'The Giving Reasons Requirement' [1992] *University of Chicago Legal Forum* 179 at 197 *et seq*.

[212] See Case T–382/94 *Confindustria et al v Council* [1996] ECR II–519, para 49; that this should be so is certainly not obvious, as is evidenced by the German, Dutch and Danish wordings of the Treaty.

fixed in Reg No 1 of 15 April 1958.[213] Regulations and "other documents of general application" are to be drafted in all official languages pursuant to Art 4 of Reg No 1. Since these acts enter simultaneously into force in multiple languages, all versions must be the subject of the regular decision-making procedure.[214] The disregard of this rule constitutes an infringement of an essential procedural requirement.[215]

IV. OPERATING MODE AS THE CENTRAL CATEGORY

In stark contrast to the laconism of the specific requirements for legality, the instruments' legal effects are highly differentiated. Broadly speaking, in Community law legal instruments are about distinguishing legal effects. It is on this field that the theory of instruments must provide orientation and determine whether the differences in the operating modes can be described as a convincing 'division of labour' between the instruments.

1. An Attempt to Systematise the Instruments

There are at least four elements of great importance in classifying the legal effects of Community instruments. The first is whether the legal effects are binding or non-binding. A number of legal attributes that Union acts may have are dependent on a binding operating mode, most notable among them the capacity to create individual, actionable rights. The creation of individual rights resulting from the direct effect of an act presupposes, as a rule, the existence of a correlative duty,[216] something that can only be imposed by an act which has binding force.[217] It has long been established that the directive in its entirety belongs to the binding legal instruments; its ability to create individual rights follows from the Member States' duty to transpose the normative program laid down in the directive. However, the creation of individual rights is inappropriate as an independent classificatory criterion because, first, it is located at the "subatomic" level of an act's provisions and, second, it is not a necessary attribute of any Community instrument.

A second criterion also follows from Art 249 EC: the instrument which an act is affiliated with determines whether or not its legal effects

[213] Reg No 1 determining the languages to be used by the European Economic Community [1952] I OJ Spec. Ed. 8, 59.

[214] Cf Art 18 Rules of Procedure of the Commission, above n 92; the Council claims a more flexible rule, Art 14(1) Council's Rules of Procedures, above n 19.

[215] See Case C–137/92 P *Commission v BASF et al* [1994] ECR I–2555, para 76.

[216] See Cases C–6 and C–9/90, above n 55, para 31.

[217] The exclusion of direct effect of EU framework decisions and EU decisions pursuant to Art 34(2) EU is a systematic anomaly: see von Bogdandy, Bast and Arndt, above n 82, 111 *et seq* and 155 *et seq*.

are specific to a formally defined addressee. The formulations "to which it is addressed" and "to whom it is addressed" define directives, decisions addressed to Member States and decisions addressed to private persons through their addressee-specific operating mode, whereas the legal effects of regulations and addresseeless decisions arise vis-à-vis everyone (*erga omnes*). The same differentiation can be made amongst the non-binding instruments: recommendations work as non-binding directives and thus have (non-binding) legal effects only for their addressees, whereas resolutions and opinions have no specified addressee. Using an instrument with an addressee-specific operating mode makes it possible to limit the personal and/or territorial scope of an act's legal effects, something which is not possible for the regulation or the addresseeless decision.

A third criterion to classify the instruments according to their legal effects is only vaguely formulated in Art 249 EC, though it has been clearly elaborated by the Court as well as in law-making practice: whether an instrument shows a one-step or a two-step implementation structure. The legal effects of regulations and all kinds of decisions, including those without an addressee, emerge when the act enters into force, whereas directives and recommendations—unless they foresee pure omissions—require or recommend implementing acts on the part of the Member States. Consequently, these instruments first acquire their full legal effects in conjunction with subsequent Member State action.[218] Regulations and decisions addressed to Member States can foresee a two-step implementing procedure, depending on their substantive content. However, this is not necessarily attached to the operating mode of these instruments. The directive's two-step implementation structure correlates with two time periods (before and after the expiry of the time-limit for transposition); the legal effects are significantly different for each period.[219]

A fourth criterion concerns the varying capacities to impose legal duties and obligations. The category of obligatory force is a key to understanding the differences between the binding instruments: whereas regulations or decisions addressed to private persons can directly impose duties and obligations on anyone within the Union's jurisdiction, the addresseeless decision cannot oblige private parties or Member States. The obligatory force of an addresseeless decision does, however, go beyond mere self-binding of the adopting institution, because addresseeless decisions can, like every

[218] See now Art 137(3) EC (Nice).

[219] For an overview of the two-step operating mode, see A Scherzberg, 'Mittelbare Rechtssetzung durch Gemeinschaftsrecht' [1992] *Jura* 572, and A Schramm, 'Zweistufige Rechtsakte, oder: Über Richtlinien und Grundsatzgesetze' (2001) 56 *Zeitschrift für öffentliches Recht* 65; on the legal effects of a directive until the date on which it must be transposed, see Case 148/78 *Ratti* [1979] ECR 1629, paras 41 *et seq*; Case C–316/93 *Vaneetveld* [1994] ECR I–763, para 16; Case C–129/96, *Inter-Environnement Wallonie* [1997] ECR I–7411, paras 42 *et seq*.

binding instrument, impose duties and obligations for the Union's institutions and bodies. In terms of its obligatory force, the directive characteristically chooses a middle position: it directly imposes duties and obligations on the Member States to which it is addressed and, furthermore, it can, through the Member State's implementing act, indirectly impose duties and obligations on private parties. The very rationale of the directive lies in its inability to directly oblige private parties, not even after expiry of the time-limit for transposition. Non-binding instruments do not have obligatory force, though they can indirectly possess such a force in conjunction with other legal norms, in particular the principle of the protection of legitimate expectations.[220]

In view of their obligatory force, it is unclear how decisions addressed to Member States should be classified. It is beyond doubt that, in addition to their ability to directly impose duties and obligations on the Member State(s) to which they are addressed, they can also indirectly impose duties and obligations on citizens. The question of whether decisions addressed to Member States can also create obligations for private parties is critical. Legal literature tends to answer this question negatively, arguing with an analogy to directives.[221] The consequence of this thesis is that, at the level of the operating mode, no positive distinguishing criterion can be found: every directive would simultaneously be a decision addressed to Member States. At the same time it is claimed that there is a sharp distinction between regulations and decisions addressed to Member States, though there is no evidence that the Court is applying this conception.[222] A great deal speaks for the view that both the regulation and the decision addressed to Member States (which in practice often seem interchangeable) may serve as a legal basis for administrative acts by the national authorities that burden private parties. Hence, regulations and decisions addressed to Member States—in contrast to directives[223]—are directly executable.[224] In any case, compliance with a decision addressed to a Member State prevents application of contrary national provisions, even when the national provisions are favourable to citizens.[225] At the operating-mode level, an independent profile of decisions addressed to

[220] See Nettesheim, above n 66, Art 249 EC, para 214; on the impact of Art 10 EC, see Case 141/78 *France v United Kingdom* [1979] ECR 2923, paras 8 *et seq*.

[221] R Greaves, 'The Nature and Binding Effect of Decisions under Art 189 EC' (1996) 21 *EL Rev* 3 at 12 and 16; Nettesheim, above n 66, Art 249 EC, para 203; support comes from E Klein, *Unmittelbare Geltung, Anwendbarkeit und Wirkung von Europäischem Gemeinschaftsrecht* (1988), 21.

[222] Case 30/75 *Unil-It* [1975] ECR 1419, para 18, gave no answer to that question. On horizontal direct effect of regulations and decisions, see Case C–192/94, above n 59, para 17.

[223] A Scherzberg, 'Die innerstaatlichen Wirkungen von EG-Richtlinien' [1993] *Jura* 225 at 227.

[224] A Scherzberg, 'Verordnung—Richtlinie—Entscheidung' in H Siedentopf (ed), *Europäische Integration und nationalstaatliche Verwaltung* (1991), 17 at 37.

[225] See Case 249/85 *Albako* [1987] ECR 2345, para 17; Case C–24/95 *Alcan* [1997] ECR I–1591, para 38.

Member States and directives thus emerges: only the latter strictly bind the Member States and at the same time ensure that obligations on private parties first arise with the Member State's implementing measures.[226] Against this background, the differentiation made in Art 254 EC between a decision addressed to a Member State, which usually waives the publication requirement, and directives addressed to all Member States, for which publication is obligatory, appears to be unsatisfactory. In this instance, Union constitutional law does not coherently connect the conditions for an instrument to have effect with the legal effects the instrument entails. The fact that the preclusion period for challenging a decision addressed to a Member State begins to run only after the decision has come to the knowledge of the plaintiff[227] does not fully compensate for this deficiency.

2. The Multifunctionality of the Instruments

It has been demonstrated that clear definitions for the operating mode of the most important instruments of Community law can already be formulated with the help of the four criteria of binding force, formal addressee, implementation structure and obligatory force. One would, no doubt, encounter difficulties in trying to identify additional differentiating legal effects that follow from the choice of instrument and which are not merely typically associated with the instrument. In particular, the difference between a general and an individual act can hardly be mirrored within the system of instruments. True, decisions addressed to private parties and non-binding instruments certainly do not have a "normative" character.[228] However, certain decisions do have general scope, and certain regulations do constitute individual measures.

Granted, classifying the legal instruments at the abstract level of their operating mode remains strangely sterile in comparison to a characterisation that focuses on their typical use in practice and on specific supranational regulatory methods: it appears to be far more fruitful to understand the directive, for example, as an instrument for the harmonisation of laws, and the regulation as an instrument to create unitary law.[229] However, the gain in plasticity is bought at the expense of precision. The directive, for example, does not have a monopoly on harmonisation of Member States' laws. Regulations and decisions addressed to Member States are similarly suited

[226] For further differences, see U Mager, 'Die staatengerichtete Entscheidung als supranationale Handlungsform' [2001] *Europarecht* 661 at 679.

[227] See Case C–180/88 *Wirtschaftsvereinigung Eisen- und Stahlindustrie v Commission* [1990] ECR I–4413, para 22.

[228] In the language of the Court even non-binding acts can be of 'general application': see Case 92/78 *Simmenthal v Commission* [1979] ECR 777, summary, para 2; Case C–313/90 *CIRFS et al v Commission* [1993] ECR I–1125, para 44.

[229] See, eg, Biervert, above n 90, Art 249 EC, para 18.

and, indeed, are often used thus in practice. Directives can serve not only to stimulate national legislation but also just as well to activate administrative planning; directives can fully regulate a certain sector as well as confine themselves to setting minimum standards or obliging the Member States to make reports. Regulation are surely predestined normatively to direct an area of life, broadly and lastingly; yet a regulation is equally suited to highly specialised intervention in the administration of the agrarian sector or to the creation of a framework in which "open co-ordination" can take place. Overall, functional descriptions of instruments run the danger of raising mere empirical excerpts to normative rules, and they tend to underestimate the complexity of empirical law-making. A sound normative and empirical analysis of Union law argues for recognising all instruments as multifunctional. The legal regime of each instrument has to be construed in such a manner that it spans its various functions. Function follows legal potential, not vice versa.

But is it worthwhile to retain directives and various kinds of decisions when the Treaties permit the adoption of regulations in nearly all cases that require law-making activity? After all, the regulation's statute-like operating mode includes and surpasses all the other instruments' legal abilities. Hence, do we still need all the other instruments? The author's response rests on a dialectical argument, already anticipated in the above discussion of legal effects. Of course, a statute can do virtually "everything", and yet it also unable to do anything less than "everything". Seen from this perspective, the specific capacity that a directive has but a regulation does not is its inability to directly impose duties on private parties. The strength of this instrument lies in its built-in weakness that allows the legislator a nuanced use of powers. By choosing a "weaker" instrument, law-making institutions are able to make use of a "memory cache" of limitations, thereby excluding unwanted legal effects.[230] The performance profile of addresseeless decisions comes even more sharply into focus from this perspective. Its strength lies in its consistent protection of individual rights and the preservation of Member State autonomy. Connections to the doctrine of competences become apparent: with its specific operating mode, the addresseeless decision is predestined to be used when the Treaties empower the institutions to adopt "incentive measures, excluding any harmonisation".[231] The limits of such a non-regulatory competence can already be secured by the choice of instrument.

V. AN EDUCATIONAL CONSTITUTION—THE CONCEPT OF "EUROPEAN LAWS"

In its Arts 33 *et seq* CT-IGC (Arts I-32 *et seq* CT-Conv), the Constitutional Treaty proposes a revised nomenclature for the Union's legal instruments.

[230] Too pessimistic on the ability of Community instruments to serve as a 'memory cache': Röhl, above n 179, 363 *et seq*.

[231] Eg, Arts 149(4), 151(4) and 152(4)(c) EC.

As to simplification, the Convention and the ensuing IGC wisely decided to sustain the bulk of the current differentiations, with the very welcome exception of abolishing the sectoral instruments under Art 34(2) EU. Within the scope of Art 249 EC, the Constitutional Treaty even increases the number of instruments from five to, seriously counted, eight (not six, as Art 33(1)(1) CT-IGC suggests). The central aspect of the instruments' legal regime is still their operating modes, which are defined in Art 33(1), subparagraphs 2 to 5 CT-IGC in familiar wording. Reading these definitions of legal effects thoroughly, it becomes clear that both the European regulation and the European decision each make up not one but two instruments, since both comprise two different operating modes under a single designation. This pseudo-simplification certainly does not contribute to the system's transparency.[232]

The increased number of instruments is—beyond acknowledging the addresseeless decision in the first sentence of Art 33(1)(5) CT-IGC—due to a new distinction between legislative and so-called non-legislative acts (Arts 34, 35 CT-IGC). European laws and European framework laws are, by definition, legislative acts (Art 33(1) CT-IGC); this list of legislative instruments is exhaustive (Art 33(2) CT-IGC). Most notably, the Constitutional Treaty employs a notion which the drafters of the Treaties had carefully avoided to date: the concept of "the law" (*das Gesetz, la loi*). From the perspective of continental legal scholarship, this symbolises a quantum leap equal to that of the term "constitution".[233] Does the Constitutional Treaty meet the expectations it raises by employing the term "European law", or is this lexical revolution part of a purely symbolic constitutionalism?

First, drawing from national experience, a "law" is expected to be an act of Parliament. In this respect, the Constitutional Treaty fares quite well as far as the so-called ordinary legislative procedure is concerned. It defines, as a rule, that Parliament and Council co-decide upon a legislative act (Art 34(1) CT-IGC). This follows the bicameral approach gradually developed since the Maastricht Treaty and reflects the two strains of democratic legitimacy of the Union.[234] Had the Convention stopped at that point, it would have proposed a convincing classification based on a procedural concept of "law". But the rule has various exceptions called "special legislative procedures" (Art 34(2) CT-IGC). Whenever the Constitutional Treaty, in Part III, so provides, the Council acts as a legislator that does not necessarily need to reach agreement with the Parliament. Concerning the voting procedure, there need not be a difference between a European law and a European regulation of the Council.

[232] Editorial comment, (2004) 41 *CML Rev* 899 at 901: 'only the vocabulary, not the reality, was simplified'.

[233] See Ross, above n 133, 34 *et seq*; R Carré de Malberg, *La loi, expression de la volonté générale* (1931); J Habermas, *Faktizität und Geltung* (1992).

[234] Affirmed by Art 46(2) CT–IGC (Art 45(2) CT–Conv).

Second, a "law" is supposed to meet the expectation of being the (almost) supreme law of the land, ranking only below the Constitution but prevailing over other instruments enacted under that Constitution. This aspect is very much connected to the law's procedural legitimacy, since the basic decisions of a body politic, acting through its elected representatives, should not be called into question by any later act of a less legitimate authority. According to a widespread view, such a hierarchy necessarily results from the concept of European laws.[235] Yet, on closer inspection, no indication is found that such a revolution will happen. There is no provision stipulating a general hierarchy of instruments, and the Convention's Praesidium rejected requests from the floor to include such an article.[236] Consequently, the division of powers within the Constitutional Treaty is still governed by the individual empowering provisions of Part III and by partial hierarchies between basic and habilitated acts (Arts 36, 37 CT-IGC).[237] In particular the persistence of European regulations and decisions directly based on constitutional provisions—either of the Council or of the Commission or of the ECB—militates against the alleged supremacy of European laws.[238] Within the scope of their respective competences, European regulations and decisions prevail over interfering European laws.

A third aspect of what a "law" is commonly expected to entail is the legal concept which the French call *domaine de la loi*, the Germans *Gesetzesvorbehalt*. The "domain of the law" is formed by those subject areas reserved for rule-making by way of laws (that is, as described above, mostly for parliamentary law-making). The definitions vary significantly between the respective state constitutional orders. Yet, it is a common characteristic of these domains that they include constitutionally protected individual liberties: interference with these fundamental rights is only permissible on the basis of, or by order of, a law. Reading the text of the EU Charter of Fundamental Rights, now Part II of the Constitutional Treaty, suggests the existence of such a domain of the European law formed by individual liberties. According to Art 112 CT-IGC (Art II-52 CT-Conv), "any limitation on the exercise of the rights and freedoms recognised by this

[235] See, eg, FJ Carrera Hernández, 'Simplifición de los instrumentos jurídicos en el Proyecto de Tratado constitucional' (2003) 16 *Revista de Derecho Communitario Europeo* 1041 at 1058 *et seq*; J Schwarze, 'Ein pragmatischer Verfassungsentwurf' [2003] *Europarecht* 535 at 554; K Lenaerts, J-M. Binon and P Van Nuffel, 'L'Union européenne en quête d'une Constitution' [2003] *Journal des tribunaux—Droit Européen* 289 at 293.

[236] See, eg, Suggestion for amendment by Dr Silvia-Yvonne Kaufmann <http://european-convention.eu.int/Docs/Treaty/pdf/24/24_Art%20I%2032%20Kaufmann%20DE.pdf> (29 October 2004).

[237] See above, II. 2. d.

[238] For example, when Part III empowers the Council to adopt European regulations on fixing prices, levies, aid and quantitative restrictions relating to the common agricultural policy (Art 231(3) CT–IGC; Art III–127(3) CT–Conv), the Constitutional Treaty voluntarily forecloses these issues from the reach of the European laws establishing the common organisations of the agricultural markets (Art 231(2) CT–IGC; Art III–127(2) CT–Conv).

Charter must be *provided for by the law*" (emphasis added). Granted, there is a presumption of consistency telling us that the term "law" in Part II has the same meaning as in Part I. Regarding the general clause on permissible restrictions on fundamental rights, however, there are good reasons supporting a different solution. Firstly, one may point out that the phrase "provided for by the law" was taken from similar formulae in the European Convention on Human Rights.[239] This militates *prima facie* for the same meaning as under this Convention.[240] The Strasbourg Court, in its settled case-law, rejects the idea that the phrase was drafted in order to guard the prerogatives of a certain branch of government. Hence, the term "law" is to be understood in its substantive sense, not its formal one.[241] Secondly, there is an argument *ad absurdum* demonstrating that "the law" also includes "non-legislative" instruments like the European regulation. If the institutions of the Union could only interfere with constitutionally protected fundamental rights by using a European law, any such interference would be excluded in areas where the European law is not at the disposal of the institutions. Take, for example, competition law. There are no provisions conferring a competence to adopt European laws in order to establish the competition rules for the internal market. Rather, the Commission is empowered to make European regulations and decisions, and the Council is, in the form of European regulations, empowered to set up a legal framework, regulating, in particular, the relevant administrative procedures.[242] There is no doubt that these regulations and decisions potentially interfere with the rights and interests of private subjects. If that kind of action were lawful only when it takes the form of a European law, Part III would then provide a competence which Part II intends to suppress. That construction would make no sense. Overall, one may designate the sum of the empowering provisions of Part III of the Constitutional Treaty which provide for European laws and framework laws as "the domain of the law" under the Constitutional Treaty. This notion, however, does not meet the expectation that the domain of the European law extend to an area of specifically protected fundamental rights. In European constitutional law the chapter on legal instruments is still not interlinked with that on fundamental rights protection.

Fourth, in most national constitutional systems, the law enjoys a high degree of shielding against the judiciary. If not excluded completely, the right to declare an act of parliament void (or inapplicable) is most often

[239] Eg, Art 8(2) ECHR: 'in accordance with the law'; Art 9(2) ECHR: 'prescribed by law'.
[240] See Art 112(3) CT–IGC (Art II–52(3) CT–Conv).
[241] ECtHR, Appl No 37971/97, *Societe Colas Est v France* (2004) 39 EHRR 17, para 43; for further references, see JA Frowein, in *id* and W Peukert, *EMRK-Kommentar* (1996), before Arts 8–11 ECHR, paras 2 *et seq*.
[242] On the Council's powers, see Arts 163 and 169 CT–IGC (Arts III–52 and III–58 CT–Conv).

reserved to a special procedure or a special court. In Union law this conception is unknown, as demonstrated above.[243] The Constitutional Treaty clearly supports the conception of the ECJ, in particular by replacing the term "decision" of Art 230(4) EC with the term "act" in the relevant provision of the Constitutional Treaty, thereby finally clarifying the neutrality of legal protection regarding the choice of instrument. But the Constitutional Treaty raises new questions about linking legal instruments with legal review: henceforth, an individual action for annulment may be admissible, even though the individual concern requirement is not met, if the contested measure is a "regulatory act" (Art 365(4) CT-IGC; Art III-270(4) CT-Conv). Since this notion is neither defined nor used elsewhere in the Constitutional Treaty, its content is fairly hard to determine. Some authors construe it with a view to the similar term "European regulation".[244] They conclude that the streamlined conditions for legal protection against a "regulatory act" should not apply to European laws and framework laws. The author prefers a different view. The Constitutional Treaty's provisions on legal protection should be construed in the light of the right to an effective remedy (Art 107(1) CT-IGC; Art II-47(1) CT-Conv). One has to recall that the very moderate extension of legal standing was meant to close a serious gap between decentralised legal protection by the national courts and centralised protection by the ECJ. This gap pertaining to so-called self-executing EC regulations would continue to exist if the liberalised standing provisions were limited to non-legislative acts. Consequently, any act of general application should be considered as possibly constituting a "regulatory act"—including European laws.[245]

But what are the legal characteristics distinguishing a European law (or framework law) from other legal instruments, which the Constitutional Treaty classifies as "non-legislative"? In fact, the Constitutional Treaty rather sparingly attaches legal consequences to its "legislative" acts exclusively—such consequences do, however, exist. Constitutional rules applicable solely to "legislative acts" concern the transparency of the rule-making process, that is, its openness to the public. Not only the Parliament but also the Council shall deliberate and vote in public session when exercising legislative functions, i.e. deciding upon a draft European law or framework law.[246] Likewise, under the Protocol on the role of the national parliaments,

[243] See II. 3. a.

[244] See FC Mayer, 'Individualrechtsschutz im Europäischen Verfassungsrecht' [2004] *Deutsches Verwaltungsblatt* 606 at 610 *et seq*; J Temple Lang, 'Declarations, Regional Authorities, Subsidiarity, Regional Policy Measures, and the Constitutional Treaty' (2004) 29 *EL Rev* 94 at 102 *et seq*; W Cremer, 'Der Rechtsschutz des Einzelnen gegen Sekundärrechtsakte der Union gem. Art III–270 Abs. 4 Konventsentwurf des Vertrags über eine Verfassung für Europa' [2004] *Europäische Grundrechte-Zeitschrift* 577 at 582.

[245] See R Barents, 'The Court of Justice in the Draft Constitution' (2004) 11 *Maastricht Journal of European and Comparative Law* 121 at 134.

[246] Arts 24(6) and 50(2) CT–IGC (Arts I–24(1)(3) and I–49(2) CT–Conv).

any draft legislative act shall be forwarded to the national parliaments. The Protocol on subsidiarity and proportionality establishes an early warning system involving the national parliaments in order to foster subsidiarity compliance, which, again, is only applicable when a draft legislative act is at issue. A law under the Constitutional Treaty is, one can conclude, an act which is subject to special public scrutiny, since certain rules ensuring transparency of the proceedings of the Union institutions are mandatory (only) for legislative acts. Organised actors, including political parties in national parliaments, as well as individual Union citizens are better enabled to monitor and perhaps involve themselves in the process of European law-making.[247] The introduction of "the law" in Union affairs aims at selecting those rule-making projects which are of major relevance to the citizenry and the polity as a whole and concentrating public attention on them. Here a surprising parallel with the national constitutional system appears. On the national plane as well, the concept of a domain of the law ensures that, by requiring a parliamentary procedure, public deliberation is enabled, and at the same time that public attention—a scarce resource in contemporary societies—is focussed on issues of major importance.[248]

Hence, the thin line the Constitutional Treaty draws between legislative and non-legislative acts really does matter, both in legal and in political terms, since this delimitation is about the appropriate level of public scrutiny. Consequently, it is not for the institutions to decide whether an act is legislative or non-legislative in character—the decision is already made by the Constitutional Treaty itself by way of classifying the respective legal basis. This being true, then, only a careful analysis of Part III of the Constitutional Treaty can determine whether the distinction between legislative and non-legislative acts is based on reasonable criteria. Astoundingly, there was hardly any debate within the Convention about which empowering provisions of Part III should form part of the domain of the European law, and which of them could, alternatively, be assigned to European regulations and decisions of the Council. The outcome is, to put it mildly, not in all cases convincing. Competition law has already been cited as an example: is the Council really adopting an act of "non-legislative" nature when laying down the general rules for state aid control (Art 169 CT-IGC; Art III-58 CT-Conv)? When the Council defines the legal framework for administrative co-operation in the area of freedom, security and justice, i.e. for cross-border police co-operation (Art 263 CT-IGC; Art III-164 CT-Conv)? When it establishes the limits and conditions for the power of the ECB to impose sanctions on undertakings (Art

[247] The national parliaments, here, serve as a link between the Union institutions and the citizens.

[248] See von Bogdandy, above n 151, 199 *et seq.*

190(3) CT-IGC; Art III-82(3) CT-Conv)? All this appears, as Dougan correctly notes, "rather arbitrary"[249]. Bypassing the higher level of public scrutiny and of parliamentary involvement (both European and national) is precisely what seems to have motivated the drafters of the Constitutional Treaty in excluding those competences from the domain of the European law.[250]

One arrives at a mixed conclusion. Those who expected the twofold European law simply to replicate the laws of the national constitutional orders become disappointed (or even have the dim feeling of being cheated, since the new instruments are basically the old ones renamed). As in most other sections of European constitutional law, the proposed reform of the legal instruments heralds no revolution but mainly rests on established constitutional structures. However, the Constitutional Treaty brings significant change insofar as it uses legal instruments to decide the applicability of certain transparency rules. European laws and framework laws are adopted under mechanisms of enhanced public scrutiny and aim at attracting a higher degree of attention. This approach is to be welcomed, because it rests on the democratic ideal that a law shall be reserved for issues of major importance, and intense public debate is, therefore, worthwhile. But the distinction between legislative and non-legislative acts established in Part I is only as reasonable as the provisions of Part III which ultimately give meaning to it. Here the Constitutional Treaty certainly has its weaknesses, since important empowering provisions are classified as "non-legislative" on a rather arbitrary basis, let alone the activities of the European Council and the Council in the common foreign and security policy, which are completely excluded from the domain of the European law.

Do these deficiencies justify talk of a mere "semantic constitution", that is, according to a classification by Karl Loewenstein, a constitution unwilling to effectively shape and limit public power?[251] One may doubt that. Of course, an isolated reading of Parts I and II of the Constitutional Treaty is misleading. Since the real "power map"[252] of the European Constitution is drawn in Part III, the Constitutional Treaty is, to a certain degree, "dishonest towards its own contents"[253]. On the other hand, introducing a demanding concept like the European law has a normative potential which transcends the current regime of Part III. Attaching certain public scrutiny

[249] M Dougan, 'The Convention's Draft Constitutional Treaty: Bringing Europe Closer to its Lawyers?' (2003) 28 *EL Rev* 763 at 784.

[250] K Lenaerts, 'A Unified Set of Instruments' (2005) 1 *European Constitutional Law Review* (2005) 57 at 61.

[251] K Loewenstein, *Political Power and Governmental Process* (1957), 147 *et seq*; see C Möllers in this volume.

[252] ID Duchacek, *Power Maps: Comparative Politics of Constitutions* (1973).

[253] C Möllers in this volume.

mechanisms to legislative instruments may, in retrospect, prove to have marked only the beginning of a lasting development. Perhaps the Constitutional Treaty is neither a fully "normative" nor a merely "semantic" constitution. Perhaps it resembles the "nominal" type, which Loewenstein related to hopeful post-colonial constitutions of his time: "The primary objective of the nominal constitution is educational, with the goal, in the near or distant future, of becoming fully normative and actually governing the dynamics of the power process instead of being governed by it."[254]

[254] Loewenstein, above n 251, 149.

10

Soft Institutions

ANTJE WIENER*

INTRODUCTION[1]

James Tully points out that the social dimension that expressed the "customary" in ancient institutions has been eliminated with arguable success from modern institutions.[2] "[T]he Greek term for constitutional law, nomos, means both what is agreed to by the people and what is customary." It comprises "the fundamental laws that are established or laid down by the mythical lawgiver and the fitting or appropriate arrangement in accord with the preceding customary ways of the people."[3] Constitutional law, then, entails two types of practices; the first entails the process of reaching an agreement about the definition of the core principles, norms and procedures which guide and regulate behaviour in the public realm of a polity. The second type of practice refers to day-to-day interaction in multiple spaces of a community. Both types of practices are interactive and by definition social; as such they are constitutive for the "fundamental laws, institutions and customs" recognised by a community.[4] I will call the former *'organisational'* and the latter *'cultural'* practices. It can therefore be argued that ancient constitutionalism encompasses the social constitution of the nomos. In turn, modern constitutions are designed to provide

* Antje Wiener holds the Chair in International Relations at the School of Politics, International Studies and Philosophy and is the Director of the Jean Monnet Centre of Excellence at the Queen's University of Belfast.

[1] Earlier versions of this paper have been published as 'Institutionen' in A von Bogdandy (ed), *Europäisches Verfassungsrecht* (2003), 121; and as *Jean Monnet Working Paper 9/03*, New York Law School (2003) <http://www.jeanmonnetprogram.org/papers/index.html> For comments on previous versions of this paper I would like to thank the participants in the workshop series conducted within the European Constitutional Law project directed by Armin von Bogdandy at Frankfurt am Main and Heidelberg. Particular thanks go to Armin von Bogdandy, Neil Walker, Uwe Puetter and Guido Schwellnus. The responsibility for this version is the author's.

[2] See J Tully, *Strange Multiplicity: Constitutionalism in an Age of Diversity* (1995), 59.

[3] See Tully, above n 2, 60.

[4] *Ibid.*

guidelines for the organisation of a polity.[5] Tully therefore proposes to reconstruct multicultural dialogues by "looking back to an already constituted order under one aspect and looking forward to an imposed order under the other."[6] To accommodate diversity based on cultural recognition, the customary dimension needs to be brought back in.

This chapter highlights the impact of the societal underpinning of evolving constitutional law beyond the State. In doing so, it builds on Tully's insights and, indeed, shares the now increasingly familiar view that "the problems of the European Constitution are simply reflections of the limits of national constitutionalism"[7]. It differs, however, from Tully's focus on accommodating cultural diversity within the constitutional framework of *one State* (Canada), by addressing recognition in a constitutional framework *beyond the State* (European Union). That is, in addition to the vertical time axis in Tully's reconstruction of constitutional dialogues, a horizontal space axis requires analytical attention. Once constitutional norms are dealt with outside their socio-cultural context of origin, a potentially conflictive situation emerges. The conflict is based on de-linking the two sets of social practices that form the agreed-upon political aspect, on the one hand, and the evolving customary aspect of a constitution, on the other. The potential for conflict caused by moving constitutional norms *outside the bounded territory of states* (i.e. outside the domestic polity and away from the inevitable link with methodological nationalism) lies in decoupling the customary from the organisational. It is through this transfer between contexts, that the meaning of norms becomes contested as differently socialised actors such as politicians, civil servants, parliamentarians or lawyers trained in different legal traditions seek to interpret them. In other words, while in supranational contexts actors might well agree on the importance of a particular norm, say e.g. human rights matter, the agreement about a type of norm does not allow for conclusions about the meaning of that norm. As in different domestic contexts that meaning is likely to differ according to experience with "norm-use,"[8] it is important to recover the crucial interrelation

[5] According to Francis Snyder, four meanings of a constitution are possible including: first, the way in which a polity is, in fact, organised; secondly, the totality of fundamental legal norms of a legal order; thirdly, the fundamental legal act that sets forth the principal legal norms; and, fourthly, the written document as outcome of deliberations instead. See F Snyder, 'The Unfinished Constitution of the European Union' in JHH Weiler and M Wind (eds), *European Constitutionalism Beyond the State* (2003), 56; see also A Stone Sweet, 'Institutional Logics of Integration' in *id*, W Sandholtz and N Fligstein (eds), *The Institutionalization of Europe* (2001), 227; see also C Moellers in this volume for further details on distinct modern constitutions.

[6] See Tully, above n 2, 60–1.

[7] M Poiares Maduro, 'Europe and the Constitution: What if This is as Good as it Gets?' in Weiler and Wind, above n 5, 75.

[8] F Kratochwil, *Rules, Norms, and Decisions* (1989), 18; see also R Dworkin, *Taking Rights Seriously* (1973).

between both types of social practices, the cultural practices that generate the customary and organisational practices facilitated by public performance that interprets the norm for political and legal use. Both contribute to the interpretation of meanings that are entailed in constitutional norms.

To agree on a transnational constitutional law for the EU therefore requires awareness of multiplicity in meaning and subsequently mechanisms which allow for ongoing exchange about the multiple meanings of norms. This awareness depends on the proper analytical tools to capture how the complex interplay between the customary and the organisational is linked. To that end, this chapter proposes a focus on the role of institutions and how they facilitate and/or constrain the interpretation of meaning. It intends to facilitate an understanding of the flexible and contested role of institutions in relation to context and social practices. Following Peter Hall, institutions are defined as "formal and informal procedures, routines, norms and conventions embedded in the organisational structure of the polity or political economy."[9] The chapter elaborates on the dual challenge of accommodating diversity within modern constitutional frameworks that are, in addition, moved outside the territorial boundaries of modern states. While the title of this chapter suggests the discussion of the most important organs of the Union, I do however raise more substantial questions, focusing on the phenomenon of European constitutional law as such from a political science perspective. The respective organs of the Union are treated as "hard" institutions elsewhere in this book. In turn, the emergence of "soft" institutions such as ideas, social and cultural norms, rules and routinised practices and their impact on the evolution and success of the institutions of constitutional law are at the centre of this chapter. The first section identifies basic assumptions in political science in order to highlight differences between role and understanding of institutions offered by political science and law. The second section discusses the analysis of institutions in the process of European integration with a particular emphasis on the development of institutions until today's European constitutional debate from the changing political science perspective. Three phases can

[9] For this 'historical institutionalist' definition of institutions, see P Hall and R Taylor, 'Political Science and the Three New Institutionalisms' (1996) XLIV *Political Studies* 938. See also Lieber's definition of institutions, cited by Nicholas Onuf: '[I]t always forms a prominent element in the idea of an institution, whether the term be taken in the strictest sense or not, that it is a group of laws, usages and operations standing in close relation to one another, and forming an independent whole with a united and distinguishing character of its own. Even today, it would be difficult to improve on this definition, which makes rules working together "through human agents" the central feature of any institution': N Onuf, 'Institutions, Intentions and International Relations' (2002) 28 *Review of International Studies* 218 with reference to F Lieber, *On Civil Liberty and Self-government* (1859), 305.

be distinguished: first, integration through supranational institution-building, second Europeanisation through domestic institutional adaptation, and third, late politicisation as the more complex process of socio-cultural and legal institutional adaptation in vertical and horizontal dimensions. The third section discusses the role of institutions and their potential for accommodating diversity in the constitutional process. The two cases of European Union citizenship and the constitutional debate are introduced as examples to illustrate that role.

I. POLITICAL BEHAVIOUR AND THE ROLE OF INSTITUTIONS

At first sight, institution building in the integration process appears to rely most decisively on the founding treaties and their periodical revision at intergovernmental conferences. Yet, while the acts of treaty-making and revision are always exclusively submitted to final decisions within the institutional framework of the Council which grants voice and vote to the signatories of the treaties, the actual substance of treaty revisions is usually discussed, conceptualised and prepared by other European political organs. In particular the Commission as the guardian of the treaties, the Committee of Permanent Representatives, and increasingly the European Parliament as well as inter-institutional groups such as the Reflection Group and lobby groups had exerted considerable influence on treaty revisions during the negotiations prior to the Maastricht summit. In addition to producing factual accounts of institutional change regarding the four central organs of the EU, i.e. the Council, the Commission, the Court of Justice and the Parliament, it is therefore interesting for political scientists to identify and explain which actors' interests were most decisive in the process, and what motivated the changes, to what end and with which consequences for power relations. That is, in addition to identifying and categorising types of institutional change, it is deemed important to analyse the role of other actors, processes and organisational structures with a view to identifying interest aggregation, identity-formation and the transfer of action potential.

Within the framework of a volume which includes exclusively German approaches to European constitutional law, this chapter stresses the flexibility of political science analysis compared with the often dogmatically restricted interpretations of German law in particular. At the same time, it will also be demonstrated that the flexibility of political science analysis lies less in the discipline's generally favourable attitude and readiness towards questioning theoretical assumptions of specific approaches and more in the constant contestation of approaches in national and international discussions and debates between different schools of thought. The ongoing contest between different political science approaches is demonstrated particularly well in the discussion about "hard" and "soft" institutions within the framework of neoinstitutional approaches[10] in particular and most recently, in relation with the debate on constructivism in theories of international relations.[11] Different from law, political science can not begin from a general systemic approach entailing clearly defined rules for interpretation. Instead, it observes regularities or, indeed, laws that allow for systematic comparative or critical analysis of political behaviour with reference to polity, policy and politics.[12] A range of differing—and often not only contravening but heatedly debated—assumptions about legitimate research questions (epistemological focus) and/or convincing approaches and research objects (ontological focus) set the framework for the debate.[13] In the field of institutional analysis, it is helpful to roughly distinguish among agency oriented rational actor models, structural approaches and interactive approaches. Usually, agency oriented approaches work with the assumption that rational interests inform strategic behaviour based on exogenous preference formation[14] that is independent from societal or cultural factors. Political scientists who share this view work with the basic assumption that individual interest in increasing, stabilising or at the least, maintaining power motivates behaviour, based on the law that *A* is motivated by her interest in power over *B*. The central research question posed by this approach is therefore directed towards identifying the condition *X* under which that interest can be most effectively pursued. By contrast, structural approaches see actors as influenced by additional—structural—context conditions created by social, institutional and/or cultural environments and/or mechanisms. Structures, they argue, exert additional constitutive

[10] A Stone Sweet, *Judicialization and the Construction of Governance* (1996); J March and J Olsen, 'The Institutional Dynamics of International Political Orders' (1998) 52 *International Organization* 943; W Powell and P DiMaggio, *The New Institutionalism in Organizational Analysis* (1991); K Thelen and S Steinmo, 'Historical Institutionalism in Comparative Politics' in S Steinmo, K Thelen and F Longstreth (eds), *Structuring Politics—Historical Institutionalism in Comparative Analysis* (1992), 1; P Hall and R Taylor, 'Political Science and the Three New Institutionalisms' (1996) 44 *Political Studies* 936; P Pierson, 'The Path to European Integration: A Historical Institutionalist Analysis' (1996) 29 *Comparative Political Studies* 123; MA Pollack, 'The New Institutionalism and EC Governance: The Promise and Limits of Institutional Analysis in Governance' (1996) 9 *International Journal of Policy and Administration* 429; G Schneider and M Aspinwall (eds), *The Rules of Integration: Institutionalist Approaches to the Study of Europe* (2001).

[11] F Kratochwil and JG Ruggie, 'International Organization: A State of the Art on an Art of the State' (1986) 40 *International Organization* 753; B Zangl and M Zürn, 'Argumentatives Handeln bei internationalen Verhandlungen: Moderate Anmerkungen zur post-realistischen Debatte' (1995) *Zeitschrift für Internationale Beziehungen* 341; P Katzenstein (ed), *The Culture of National Security* (1996); T Risse, 'Let's Argue! Communicative Action in World Politics' (2000) 54 *International Organization* 1.

[12] For a systematic assessment of how these three areas matter for the analysis of European integration, see T Diez and A Wiener, 'The Mosaic of Integration Theory' in A Wiener and T Diez (eds), *European Integration Theory* (2003), 18.

[13] For an overview of the various theoretical positions involved in this debate, see in particular PC Schmitter, 'Neo-Neofunctionalism' in Wiener and Diez, above n 12, 48.

[14] See Thelen and Steinmo, above n 10, 9.

and/or regulative impact on behaviour. Actors thus behave in a power oriented and rational way, however, the additional variable of structure needs to be considered as influential for interest and preference formation. This approach seeks to identify the structures that are relevant for action, recognising their stability on the one hand, and critical junctures that are likely to induce possibilities for changing them, on the other. A third approach works with the assumption that interrelation between structure and agency is the key element. This approach emphasises the role of social interaction and cautions against the valuation of structure over agency, or vice versa, focusing on the concept of intersubjectivity. One key issue here is the additional consideration of changing identities and their influence on preference formation; another is the analytical challenge to conceptualise the mutual constitution of institutions and actor identities based on interaction.

The important insight conveyed by these approaches is that institutions are assigned different roles according to different academic perceptions of political behaviour. Different approaches to institutions thus develop significantly divergent arguments. While institutions are conceptualised as enabling for actors in that they entail an extension of behavioural options, they are, in principle, also considered as hard to control and therefore constraining behaviour. According to the respective basic assumptions and analytical framework, research questions and research design demonstrate considerable variation, a conceptual starting point which might come as a surprise to dogmatic lawyers. In European integration research, institutional analysis has gained importance not only since the Europolity's design depends crucially on supranationally constructed and evolving institutions, but also as a theoretical spill-over from the elaboration of institutional analysis in international relations theory and sociology as disciplines which share an interest in the expanding processes of governance beyond that nation-State.[15] Nonetheless, European integration crucially challenged the realist assumption of an international society of states that involves independent sovereign states governed by the principle of anarchy.[16] It raises questions about states' interest in institution building and co-operation, and in the influence exerted by these new institutions on structural constraints and opportunities for State behaviour.[17] The following sections summarise four substantially different approaches to institutional analysis in political science.

[15] See, eg J Jupille, JA Caporaso and JT Checkel, 'Integrating Institutions: Theory, Method, and the Study of the European Union' (2003) 36 *Comparative Political Studies* 7.

[16] See Hobbes' 'state of nature' as 'an institution that cannot become something else', Onuf, above n 9, 216. According to Hobbes it follows that 'deliberate action is the only hope', cf Onuf, above n 9.

[17] Theoretical discussions in political science integration research present the basic controversy entailed in these respective questions. See for example L Cram, 'Integration Theory and the Study of the European Policy Process' in J Richardson (ed), *European Union—Power and Policymaking* (1996).

1. Actor Oriented Approaches: Institutions as Strategic Context

Actor oriented approaches[18] like rational choice theory work with the "individualism assumption" which "treats individuals as the basic (elemental) units of social analysis. Both individual and collective actions and outcomes are explicable in terms of unit-level (individual) properties."[19] Accordingly, it is assumed that political institutions like international organisations, conventions, co-operation agreements, treaties or committees are established in order to provide manageable information for political actors in decision making processes. In other words, institutions are understood as providing a monitoring role. This view is based on the assumption that institution building is initiated as a consequence of actors' interests. It is therefore considered as potentially reversible.[20] Examples for this approach in political science, and to some extent, economics, are game theory and negotiation theory.[21] This approach has been challenged by work which identified path-dependent institutional impact on behaviour. That is, the strategic pursuit of interest was found to be constrained through lock-in effects produced by institutions which had been created following the strategic interests of actors whose was informed by different material resources.[22] Thus, a key problem has emerged e.g. from the routinisation of institutions beyond the time period in which they were considered appropriate and desirable. That is, while institution building at a point in time *(t1)* might reflect the interest of particular actors, it is likely that at another point in time *(t2)* interests, resources and power constellations have changed.[23] Subsequently, institutions may turn out as having a constraining impact on behaviour. Importantly then, the reversibility of institution building cannot be assumed as a given factor in institutional

[18] For approaches on agency-oriented institutionalism, see in particular the work by R Mayntz and FW Scharpf, *Regieren in Europa: Effektiv und demokratisch?* (1999), 10.

[19] See Jupille *et al*, above n 15, 12.

[20] JE Alt and KA Shepsle, *Perspectives on Positive Political Economy* (1990); G Garrett, 'International Cooperation and Institutional Choice: The European Community's Internal Market' (1992) 46 *International Organization* 533 *et seq*; G Garrett and G Tsebelis, 'An Institutional Critique of Intergovernmentalism' (1996) 50 *International Organization* 269 *et seq*; G Garrett and BR Weingast, 'Ideas, Interests, and Institutions: Constructing the European Community's Internal Market' in J Goldstein and RO Keohane (eds), *Ideas & Foreign Policy: Beliefs, Institutions and Political Change* (1993), 173 *et seq*.

[21] RM Axelrod, *The Evolution of Cooperation* (1984); M Zürn, 'Jenseits der Staatlichkeit: Über die Folgen der ungleichzeitigen Denationalisierung' (1992) 20 *Leviathan* 490 *et seq*; F Scharpf, 'The Joint-Decision Trap: Lessons from German Federalism and European Integration' (1988) 66 *Public Administration* 239.

[22] See Pierson, above n 10.

[23] DC North, 'The Path of Institutional Change' in DC North (ed), *Institutions, Institutional Change and Economic Performance* (1990); Pierson, above n 10.

[24] As Onuf writes, '[T]he alternative to institutions by design are those that arise as the unintended consequences of self-interested human action': Onuf, above n 9, 212.

analysis.[24] Actor oriented approaches work with the logic of consequentialism.[25] European integration research has documented this particular aspect of institutions most convincingly during the second and third phase of European integration.

2. Structure Oriented Approaches: Institutions as Guidelines for Social Behaviour

As opposed to the primacy of agency, structural approaches analyse institutions as structures with guiding and/or prescriptive impact on behaviour. Accordingly, "institutions constrain and shape politics through the construction and elaboration of meaning."[26] These approaches are based on macro-sociological and organisation sociology[27] which consider institutions as aggregated "rules" or, as sociological constructivists put it, as "single standards of behaviour."[28] The chapter turns to this difference in more detail later on; at this point, it is important to note that structural socio-cultural factors matter for behaviour, even in the absence of legal or formal political organs. It is assumed that social norms defined as "collective expectations for the proper behavior of actors with a given identity" guide behaviour.[29] International relations theorists are particularly interested in those institutions which have a significant impact on shaping actors' interests. Empirical research seeks to identify the role and function of specific institutions in this process.[30] Two types of institutions and their respective impact can be differentiated. On the one hand, international institutions are assigned the role of creating interactive spaces for elites who take an active role in diffusing norms, ideas and values through their interactions back

[25] See, eg, JG March and JP Olsen, *Rediscovering Institutions: The Organizational Basis of Politics* (1989); TA Börzel and T Risse, 'When Europe Hits Home: Europeanization and Domestic Change' (2000) 4 *European Integration online Papers* No 15 <http://eiop.or.at/eiop/texte/2000-015a.htm> (5 July 2004); H Müller, 'Arguing, Bargaining, and All That: Reflections on the Relationship of Communicative Action and Rationalist Theory in Analysing International Negotiation' (2004) 10 *European Journal of International Relations* 395.

[26] See March and Olsen, above n 25, 39.

[27] See Powell and DiMaggio, above n 10; A Kieser, *Organisationstheorien* (1993).

[28] M Finnemore and K Sikkink, 'International Norm Dynamics and Political Change' (1998) 52 *International Organization* 89.

[29] See P Katzenstein, 'Introduction' in Katzenstein, above n 11, 5; Finnemore and Sikkink, above n 28; March and Olsen, above n 10.

[30] So far this work has mainly focused on the role and function of institutions without putting much emphasis on their emergences. Thus, Ruggie writes, for example, that 'the origins of identities and other normative factors need to be better theorized'; see JG Ruggie, *Constructing the World Polity* (1998), 16; see also the critical question 'If norms are important, a second question naturally emerges: Where do norms themselves come from? While the preceding essays devote considerable effort to answering the first question, they rarely address the second one' raised by P Kowert and J Legro, 'Norms, Identity, and Their Limits' in Katzenstein, above n 11, 468; RA Payne, 'Persuasion, Frames and Norm Construction' (2001) 7 *European Journal of International Relations* 37.

into their respective domestic contexts. On the other hand, norms such as human rights norms are assigned regulative and constitutive influence themselves. For instance, drawing on organisational theory March and Olsen argued convincingly that under specific conditions actors behave according to the "logic of appropriateness"[31]. Institutions are considered as emerging within a particular socio-cultural environment; they are labelled as "soft institutions" or "social facts" (ideas, principled beliefs, social facts).[32]

Examples for the impact of such institutions have been provided by sociological constructivist work in international relations and international law as well as, more recently, by research on European integration. This work pursues the basic question of why actors obey the rules set by such soft institutions in the absence of legally binding rules and without decisive material push factors.[33] They demonstrate the diffusion of types of norms and cultures such as, e.g. administrative culture and co-operation on the one hand and the acceptance of a leading role of norms such as human rights norms, environmental and labour standards on the other.[34] Thus, John Meyer and his colleagues were able to demonstrate that the types of public administration, constitutional practices, educational institutions, welfare-State policies and even the role of particular branches of defence ministries were diffused into the domestic context of a number of states despite an absence of a plausible necessity for the implementation of these norms and practices.[35] For scholars who study institutional change in the context of European integration questions about the role of supranational institutions in diffusing and stabilising the emergence of norms and routinised practices are of particular interest. For example, studies on the "Europeanisation" of

[31] See March and Olsen, above n 25.

[32] See Katzenstein, above n 11; Ruggie, above n 30; Kratochwil, above n 8; A Wendt, *Social Theory of International Politics* (1999). See the original application of the concept of '*fait social*' (sociological facts) and the discussion about diverting opinions on this central term in Durkheim's '*Les règles de la méthode sociologique*', see E Durkheim, *Die Regeln der soziologischen Methode* (1999), 38.

[33] A Chayes and AH Chayes, *The New Sovereignty: Compliance with International Regulatory Regimes* (1995); HH Koh, 'Why do Nations Obey International Law?' (1997) 106 *Yale Law Journal* 2599; JT Checkel, 'The Constructivist Turn in International Relations Theory' (1998) 50 *World Politics* 324.

[34] On the effect of norm diffusion through international organisations see in particular the world-polity approach of the Stanford School around John Meyer, for example the work of YN Soysal, *The Limits of Citizenship: Migrants and Postnational Membership in France* (1994); D Jacobson, *Rights Across Borders: Immigration and the Decline of Citizenship* (1996); M Finnemore, 'Norms, Culture and World Politics: Insights from Sociology's Institutionalism' (1996) 50 *International Organization* 325; M Finnemore, *National Interests in International Society* (1996); for an excellent overview in German see T Wobbe, *Weltgesellschaft* (2000).

[35] The establishment of 'constitutional forms, educational institutions, welfare policies, human rights conventions, defense ministries in states that face no threat (including navies for landlocked states)' as well as 'science ministries in countries that have no scientific capability' offers evidence of this type of norm diffusion as Ruggie points out, above n 30, 15.

norms such as citizenship, water directives and environmental standards have demonstrated first that norms which entail prescriptive rules emerge through processes of learning and diffusion in supranational institutions, and second how these norms are diffused often with the additional pressure of advocacy groups. In sum, norms are found to exert pressure leading to policy change in domestic contexts of EU Member States.[36]

3. Intersubjective Approaches: Institutions Constituted Through Practice

Intersubjective approaches to institution building have been further developed as part of the literature that evolved around the "constructivist turn"[37] in international relations theories. These constructivist approaches proceed from the assumption that political action, identities and institutions are mutually constitutive. Institutions are not only assigned a regulative role in relation to behaviour, they are also considered as constitutive for actors' identities. Different from the rational actor approach which perceives institutions as exogenous factors that are mobilised according to actor's interests in decision making processes, the intersubjective approach questions that analytical separation of institutions, interests and identities. Instead, all three are considered as interrelated through, if strategic, yet communicative action.[38] The conceptual framework is offered by an, albeit selective reference to Habermas's theory of communicative action, based exclusively on communication as strategic action—not as a societal theory.[39] Communication, these approaches argue, is particularly important for exploring the impact of soft

[36] For an overview see the introduction to MG Cowles, JA Caporaso and T Risse-Kappen, *Transforming Europe: Europeanization and Domestic Change* (2001). For the focus on behavioural prescriptions in the case of European citizenship see eg Checkel's work on the extension of citizenship rights in Germany towards the inclusion of dual citizenship: JT Checkel, 'The Europeanization of Citizenship?' in *ibid*, 180. On the role of advocacy groups see in particular the work of A Klotz, 'Norms Reconstituting Interests' (1995) 49 *International Organization* 451; K Sikkink, 'The Power of Principled Ideas' in Goldstein *et al*, above n 20, 161; ME Keck and K Sikkink, *Activities Beyond Borders* (1998); B Locher, *Trafficking in Women in the European Union* (Unpublished, 2002).

[37] AE Wendt, 'The Agent-structure Problem in International Relations Theory' (1987) 41 *International Organization* 335; AE Wendt, 'Anarchy Is What States Make of It' (1992) 46 *International Organization* 391; Katzenstein, above n 11; E Adler, 'Seizing the Middle Ground: Constructivism in World Politics' (1997) 3 *European Journal of International Relations* 319; Checkel, above n 33. For a recent overview see E Adler, 'Constructivism in International Relations' in W Carlsnaes, T Risse and BA Simmons (eds), *Handbook of International Relations* (2002); for a critical perspective see S Guzzini, 'A Reconstruction of Constructivism in International Relations' (2000) 5/6 *European Journal of International Relations* 147; as well as S Guzzini and A Leander, 'Alexander Wendt's Social Theory for International Relations' (2001) 4 *Journal of International Relations and Development*.

[38] F Schimmelfennig, 'Rhetorisches Handeln in der internationalen Politik' [1997] *Zeitschrift für internationale Beziehungen* 219; and F Schimmelfennig, 'The Community Trap: Liberal Norms, Rhetorical Action, and the Eastern Enlargement of the European Union' (2001) 55 *International Organization* 47; as well as Risse, above n 11.

[39] See J Habermas, *Theorie des kommunikativen Handelns* (1981).

institutions such as e.g. norms. On the one hand, they demonstrate the complex framework of implementation and compliance with supranational norms;[40] on the other, they try to demonstrate that shared references are constructed arguing and bargaining in negotiating situations. Following Habermas, it is assumed that the negotiators are ready to be persuaded by the better argument brought to the fore through controversial debate. The rationale for norm-following then is considered as the logic of arguing.[41] This approach offers a helpful research platform for analysing ongoing and potentially long-lasting discussions about a European Constitution. In principle, and at its best, this approach could be developed towards a reflexive approach to norms.[42] After all, the full "constructivist ethic and politics relies on argumentation according to the dialogue model: conflicting goals and norms are clarified through communicative action, guiding norms are agreed. The *Grundnorm* works along the lines of the Kantian moral reasoning. In reconstructing the Kantian principle of moral reason, the principle of trans-subjectivity makes it possible to avoid subjective and arbitrary norm-setting."[43] By and large, however, despite the inclusion of speech, language, and controversy in the form of a principled yet open-ended argument, this approach tends to leave the impact of socio-cultural origin and generation of norms which would ultimately allow accounting for the customary dimension of the *nomos*, to one side. The *meaning* of norms therefore remains analytically disconnected from the very practices that are claimed to influence their identification and change.[44] Thus, little attention is paid to the social embeddedness of arguing processes about norm validity and facticity and hence the normative philosophical dimension of communicative action stressed by Habermas. Yet, it is precisely the analytical appreciation of societal embeddedness which offers information about the "customary" dimension of constitutional law. Analytically, its reconstruction develops from a precise understanding of evolving soft institutions in the process of constitutionalisation.

[40] For a general perspective on rule following within the context of international law, see Chayes and Chayes, above n 33; and with reference to the growing legalisation of environmental policy, see M Zürn, 'The Rise of International Environmental Politics' (1998) 50 *World Politics* 617; C Joerges and M Zürn (eds), *Compliance in Modern Political Systems* (2004).

[41] See Risse, above n 11.

[42] For an elaboration of the reflexive link between the 'individual' and 'sociality', see in particular Kratochwil, above n 8; Guzzini, above n 37; A Wiener, 'Contested Compliance: Interventions on the Normative Structure in World Politics' (2004) 10 *European Journal of International Relations* 189.

[43] D Nohlen, R-O Schultze and SS Schüttemeyer, 'Keyword "Verfassungsgerichtsbarkeit"' in D Nohlen (ed), *Lexikon der Politik*, vol 7, Politische Begriffe (1998), 274 (author's translation).

[44] For an elaboration of this critical assessment of the logic of arguing see A Wiener, 'The Dual Quality of Norms: Stability and Flexibility', Paper presented at the Workshop *Habermas and IR Theory* (University of Birmingham, 17 May 2004); Payne, above n 30.

4. Reflexive Approaches: Contested Meanings of Institutions

A reflexive approach presupposes that meanings—while stable over long periods of time and within particular contexts—are always in principle contested.[45] The analytical assessment of conflictive potential leads beyond a mere assessment of procedures and norms as causes for behaviour that tends to leave actors the role of "cultural dupes" with little impact on social change.[46] Social practices in context are therefore conceptualised as key factors for the assessment of social change. Shared cultural contexts are expected to produce shared interpretations of meaning and, therefore, high social legitimacy of rules. The analytical focus on social practices draws on critical observations about the structural inflexibility of the logic of arguing (see section II. 3) which, it is held, facilitates more information about the role of different types of norms than about the impact of variation in the meaning of one single type of norm. Most importantly for that undertaking is an understanding of the role of "*social context* within which identities and interests of both actor and acting observer are formed."[47] In sum, the argument borrows from reflexive sociology.[48]

The reflexive approach builds on the central assumption about the dual quality of structures as constituted by and changed through social practices, which has been developed by Anthony Giddens, Pierre Bourdieu and Charles Taylor. For example, according to Giddens' concept of structuration, the duality of structures stems from a procedural perception of practices. Taylor takes this notion further, noting that "the practice not only fulfils the rule, but also gives it concrete shape in particular situations. Practice is ... a continual "interpretation" and reinterpretation of what the rule really means."[49] To assess the meaning of a rule therefore implies going back to the practices that contributed to its creation. Importantly, these practices involve contestation by way of discursive intervention. They imply an ongoing process of (re-)construction. Guzzini summarises the interrelation between rules and practices with reference to political systems beyond the State. Thus, the

> international system ... is still a system whose rules are made and reproduced by human practices. Only these intersubjective rules, and not some unchangeable

[45] A turn towards reflexive sociology has, for example, been suggested by studies of 'law in context': see eg F Snyder, *New Directions in European Community Law* (1990); and constructivist approaches to international relations to assess how 'cultural context shapes strategic actions' and is shaped by them, M Barnett, 'Culture, Strategy and Foreign Policy Change' (1999) 5 *European Journal of International Relations* 8; Guzzini, above n 37; Payne, above n 30.

[46] See Barnett, above n 45, 7.

[47] See Guzzini, above n 37, 149.

[48] As Guzzini observes correctly, '[R]eflexivity is then perhaps the central component of constructivism, a component too often overlooked': above n 37, 150.

[49] C Taylor, 'To Follow a Rule' in C Calhoun, E LiPuma and M Postone (eds), *Bourdieu: Critical Perspectives* (1993), 57.

truths deduced from human nature or from international anarchy, give meaning to international practices.[50]

International relations scholars have addressed this empirical problem by focusing on discourse as the "structure of meaning-in-use," conceptualising discourse as "the location of meaning."[51] Empirically, this focus implies studying social practices as discursive interventions, e.g. in official documents, policy documents, political debates, and media contributions. As Milliken observes "discourses do not exist 'out there' in the world; rather, they are structures that are actualised in their regular use by people of discursively ordered relationships."[52] Discursive interventions contribute to establish a particular structure of meaning-in-use which works as a cognitive roadmap that facilitates the interpretation of norms. This structure exerts pressure for institutional adaptation on *all* involved actors; at the same time, discursive interventions that refer to this structure have an input on its robustness. This assessment of norms leads beyond a neo-Durkheimian perception of norms as social facts that exert structural impact on behaviour. It means studying norms as embedded in socio-cultural contexts that entail information about how to interpret a norm's meaning in context. The reflexive approach assumes that norms entail a dual quality. They are both constructed and structuring. Hypothetically, the meaning of norms evolves through discursive interventions that establish a structure of meaning-in-use. Compliance therefore depends on the overlap of that structure in the reference by norm setters and norm followers. It follows that studying social practices in context opens analytical access to the interpretation of meaning which is constitutive for sustained compliance with norms. The process of contestation sheds light on different meanings of a norm. It thus enhances the probability of establishing mutally acceptable understanding or shared meanings of that norm.

II. THREE PHASES OF CONSTITUTIONALISATION

Before turning to selected examples and subsequently focussing more in detail on the current constitutional debate, a distinction between different phases of constitutionalisation offers a systematic framework for explaining the role of institutions in the process of European integration. It reflects

[50] See Guzzini, above n 37, 155.

[51] See J Milliken, 'The Study of Discourse in International Relations' (1999) 5 *European Journal of International Relations* 231; and R Huelsse, *Metaphern der EU-Erweiterung als Konstruktionen europäischer Identität* (2003), 39, respectively.

[52] See Milliken, above n 51, 231; for an effectively similar, if methodologically less explicit, view of the importance of recovering meaning from discourse for constitutional analysis in the EU, see eg Weiler's interest in 'the normative values of which the constitutional and political discourse is an expression' in Weiler and Wind, above n 5, 13.

the attempts by various political science approaches to systematically assess massive institutional change beyond the State in an area which is traditionally assumed to be governed by the principle of anarchy in the absence of global government.[53] The following distinct research goals emerged during different phases of integration thus reflecting significant changes of research questions, often shifting emphasis of integration research from one sub-discipline to another. For example, during the first "integration" phase institutional changes on the supranational level, i.e. the establishment of "hard" institutions such as the European political organs and treaties, mattered most to researchers. In turn, during the second "Europeanisation" phase institutional change in domestic contexts such as adaptation, harmonisation and regulation mattered most. Finally the current phase of "late politicisation" has triggered an enhanced constitutional debate in relation with the impending massive enlargement process. It brings the issues of finality, enlargement, fundamental rights and democracy to the fore, thus raising questions about the robustness of theoretical assumptions generated to study institutional change during the first two phases, especially regarding the post cold war changes and the massive eastern enlargement.

According to **table 1**, the integration process is assessed as entailing three phases in which different research questions dominate the field. The phases are distinguished with reference to significant changes in *type*, *place* and *dynamics* of integration that caused institutional change within the European multi-level governance system. Accordingly the first phase is characterised by bottom-up institutional building, the central research interest being about more or less integration; the core theories involved the debate over "grand theory" among neo-functionalist and intergovernmentalist approaches in international relations theories. The second phase is distinguished by a top-down research perspective on institutional adaptation. Here research interest focused on the question of more or less

Table 1: *Three Phases of European Constitutionalisation*

Phase	Type	Place	Dynamic	Institutions
I	Integration (more/less)	Supranational Level	bottom-up	hard
II	Europeanisation (more/less)	Domestic, regional level in member and candidate countries	top-down	hard/soft
III	Politicisation (more/less)	Euro-polity; transnational spaces	trickle-across, bottom-up, top-down	hard/soft

[53] See K Waltz, *Theory of International Politics* (1979); H Bull, *The Anarchical Society* (1977); J Rosenau and EO Czempiel (eds), *Governance without Government* (1992).

Europeanisation. Theoretical reference for this perspective is provided by the potpourri of the descriptive and increasingly all-encompassing multi-level governance approach, organisation theory, the various neo-institutionalisms, and regime theory as well as constructivist research; theoretically, this phase brought a shift from international relations towards comparative governance and public administration. The third phase is characterised by the increasingly complex challenge of reintegrating bottom-up institution building, i.e. the changing institutional basis of the European political organs, as well as the parallel and interrelated process of top-down Europeanisation of formal institutions in politics, the market, and the legal and administrative structures in the respective candidate countries. Furthermore, in the face of massive enlargement this third phase also involves the necessity to reconsider, evaluate and define the role and meaning of values and norms that lie at the core of European governance and—most importantly—the possibilities of their eventual expression within a distinctly defined constitutional framework. The characterisation of "late politicisation" stresses the often conflictive and controversial processes and the lack of shared instruments or values to guide conflict solution and set shared standards of behaviour. During this phase, interdisciplinary theoretical work bringing together law, political science and sociology and, though still much less established, cultural studies has begun to tackle the more substantial normative, functional, legal and political questions of European integration as a process that might have surpassed its dynamics of institution-building and expansive potential as a process of consolidation both in domestic and world political matters. According to historical institutionalist analysis, among the expected outcomes of this phase are feed-back loops which result from a lack of norm resonance between different socio-cultural contexts, and unintended consequences of institution-building. Such feed-back loops follow strategic norm setting expressed by the accession *acquis*. Thus, it has been demonstrated that e.g. the protection of minority rights which had been added exclusively to the accession *acquis* for security reasons, are expected to develop contested meanings that will loop back into the western normative structure of the EU. Such strategic norm setting is likely to produce a boomerang effect of delayed political conflict.[54] According to these three phases and taking into account the push and pull factors of institution building, it is possible to distinguish between patterns of motivation for the actors involved. While push factors are constituted by structures or path-dependency such as decisions about institutional change made in the past which evolve towards exerting influence on present and future decision-making processes, pull factors develop through interest constellations of dominant actors with influence on the direction and development of the

[54] A Wiener and G Schwellnus, 'Contested Norms of European Enlargement' in G Bermann and K Pistor (eds), *Law and Governance in an Enlarged Europe* (2004), 455.

integration process. Controversies among political science approaches, in particular among the North American variety, have focused on the role and impact of these different factors early on as the ongoing debate among neo-functionalists and intergovernmentalists about interest formation and decision-making in the process of integration demonstrates.[55] While the empirical focus of theoretical debates among political scientists has been adapted over time according to the phases of integration, the central controversy regarding the difference in analytical perception of the structure/agency relation continues to exist. While neo-functionalist, constructivist and historical approaches understand actors as socially embedded,[56] intergovernmentalists and rational choice institutionalists work with the assumption that actors are in principle socially isolated, and accordingly operate based on individual rationally perceived interests which may or may not involve the choice of reference to institutions as monitoring or, in any case, information providing elements in the decision-making process.[57] The following elaboration on the three phases of integration is intended to summarise research interests which cumulated at particular times. It is not meant to work as an exclusive pattern. Instead it seeks to offer a frame of reference for assessing the key questions raised about the integration process and which coined the respective phase. The distinction according to phases does not necessarily preclude overlapping research issues and *foci*. The overlap is particularly relevant with a view to the sequence of the second and third phases of Europeanisation and late politicisation, respectively.

[55] For most recent contributions to this ongoing debate, see EB Haas, 'Does Constructivism Subsume Neofunctionalism?' in T Christiansen, KE Jørgensen and A Wiener (eds), *The Social Construction of Europe* (2001), 22; PC Schmitter, 'Neo-Neo Functionalism' in Diez and Wiener, above n 12; F Schimmelfennig, 'Liberal Intergovernmentalism' in Diez and Wiener, above n 12. On the analysis of 'push' and 'pull' factors in the implementation of European legal norms in domestic contexts, see in particular A Sbragia, 'Environmental Policy: The "Push-Pull" of Policy-making' in H Wallace and W Wallace (eds), *Policy-Making in the European Union* (1996), 235, as well as A Lenschow, 'Variation in EC Environmental Policy Integration' (1997) 4 *JEPP* 109.

[56] EB Haas, 'The Study of Regional Integration' (1970) 24 *International Organization* 607; A Sbragia (ed), *Euro-politics: Institutions and Policymaking in the 'New' European Community* (1992); JA Caporaso, 'Changes in the Westphalian Order' in JA Caporaso (ed), *International Studies Review: Continuity and Change in the Westphalian Order* (2000), 1; Pierson, above n 11; J Peterson, 'Decision-Making in the European Union' (1995) 2 *JEPP* 69; SJ Bulmer, 'New Institutionalism, The Single Market and EU Governance' (1997) 25 *Working Paper ARENA*; S Bulmer and M Burch, 'The "Europeanisation" of Central Government: the UK and Germany in Historical Institutionalist Perspective in Aspinwall and Schneider, above n 10; T Christiansen, KE Jørgensen and A Wiener, 'The Social Construction of Europe' (1999) 6 *JEPP* 528; M Jachtenfuchs, 'Theoretical Perspectives on European Governance' (1995) 1 *European Law Journal* 115; B Koch and M Jachtenfuchs (eds), *Regieren in der Europäischen Union* (1996); C Joerges and J Neyer, 'From Intergovernmental Bargaining to Deliberative Political Processes' (1997) 3 *ELJ* 273.

[57] S Hoffmann, 'Reflections on the Nation-State in Western Europe Today' (1982–83) 21 *JCMS* 21; A Moravcsik, 'Negotiating the Single European Act' (1991) 45 *International Organization* 19; Garrett, above n 20; Garrett and Tsebelis, above n 20; Pollack, above n 10; Schimmelfennig, above n 55.

1. Integration (1960–1985)

During the first two decades, the integration process raised questions about the motivation for building supranational institutions in a Hobbesian world, i.e. about European integration as such. Motives and the rationale behind the process were identified on the level of national governments based on security and economic interests, i.e. on establishing institutions which would stabilise peace based on integrated coal and steel industries and the Euratom Treaty.[58] Yet, neo-functionalists such as Ernst Haas, Karl Deutsch, Leon Lindberg and Philippe Schmitter stressed transnational and supranational interest formation by elites and their impact on the integration process.[59] While, as Andrew Moravcsik pointed out later on, the State interests were informed by societal preference formation, e.g. by domestic interest groups, the key decisions were nonetheless always taken on the level of intergovernmental negotiations, i.e. at the State level.[60] The question about more or less integration is hence ultimately pinned down on State interests according to the traditional neorealist perception of States as the only influential political actors in world politics. These interests were informed by interstate relations and bargaining, yet, institutions were considered as enabling rather than constraining behaviour (actor oriented approach). Contrary to this rather clear cut perception of interest formation, role and input, neo-functionalists took the theoretical challenge of regional complexity on board, understanding the integration process as pushed and informed by elites, yet as a process which was not exclusively subject to change according to strategic interests. Instead, integration was pushed by the dynamic of spillovers between policy areas that complicated parsimonious theorising considerably. Integration is understood as pushed by the interests of societal and business elites which are able to strategically use the new supranational institutions and, in doing so, at times unintendedly cause further integration due to the spillover effect that linked different policy areas with one another.

2. Europeanisation (since 1985)

While during the integration phase the influence of international relations theory was particularly salient, especially in the context of US-American work, the re-launch of the integration process and the "internal market 1992" initiative during the commission presidencies of Jacques Delors (1985–95)[61]

[58] See eg the intergovernmentalists that followed and expanded on the seminal work by Hofmann, above n 57.

[59] See Haas, above n 55; L Lindberg and S Scheingold (eds), *Europe's Would-Be Polity: Patterns of Change in the European Community* (1970).

[60] See Moravcsik, above n 58; A Moravcsik, 'Preferences and Power in the European Community' (1993) 31 *JCMS* 473; A Moravcsik, *The Choice for Europe* (1998).

[61] W Sandholtz and J Zysman, 'Recasting the European Bargain' (1989) 41 *World Politics* 95; G Ross, *Jacques Delors and European Integration* (1995).

contributed to a shift of emphasis in academic research as well. With the increasing density of regulations and decision-making procedures that followed from the Single European Act in 1986, the sub-disciplines of comparative government, public policy and public administration gained influence in integration research.[62] This administrative turn led to a closer focus on "Europeanisation" understood as the capacity for institutional adaptation with European conditions of regulation within the various EU Member States. In the beginning this research was primarily interested in identifying the conditions and the question of whether or not domestic institutions were "fit" to implement European directives within the common market initiative.[63] Building on the growing volume and density of regulations of domestic politics through European policy initiatives, questions of political participation, co-determination, transparency, and political organisation gained importance in political science integration research.[64] Overall, this phase of integration research demonstrates a significant change of focus from international relations theories towards comparative politics. However, it is important to note that this phase has not necessarily produced a convincing or generally accepted systematisation in theoretical approach. After all, different from the integration phase which was clearly structured by opposing theoretical positions of two camps and strongly influenced by the US-American sub-discipline of international relations, the second phase of integration is more clearly characterised by an absence of analytical clarity. Due to the enormous empirical breadth and diversity in research issues, research programs stand to be further consolidated. In addition, the frequently used term of "good governance" and/or "multi-level governance"[65] which is all too often applied as a catch-all approach that inevitably raises more questions than offering convincing theoretical answers. An important change in analytical perspective is the growing interest in the EU as a political system and not, as in the previous phase, as an international organisation.

It was not until recently that this phase has generated more systematic approaches which offer a more succinct analytical focus on the question of Europeanisation as a consequence of integration politics. Thus, it has been

[62] RM Czada and A Windhoff-Heritier, *Political Choice: Institutions, Rules, and the Limits of Rationality* (1991); G Majone, 'The Rise of the Regulatory State in Europe' (1994) 17 *West European Politics* 77; Scharpf, above n 21; Wallace and Wallace, above n 55.

[63] See Sandholtz and Zysman, above n 61; Wallace and Wallace, above n 55; K Armstrong and S Bulmer, *The Governance of the Single European Market* (1998); W Wessels, *Die Öffnung des Staates: Modelle und Wirklichkeit grenzüberschreitender Verwaltungspraxis 1960–1995* (2000); Richardson, above n 17.

[64] E Grande, 'Demokratische Legitimation und europäische Integration' [1996] *Leviathan* 339; PC Schmitter, *How To Democratize the EU And Why Bother?* (2000); B Kohler-Koch (ed), *Regieren in entgrenzten Räumen* (1998).

[65] See Kohler-Koch, above n 64; L Hooghe and G Marks, 'The Making of a Polity: The Struggle over European Integration' (1997) 1 *European Integration online Papers* No 4 <http://eiop.or.at/eiop/texte/1997-004a.htm> (6 July 2004) respectively.

convincingly demonstrated that situations of institutional or structural "mis/fit" caused institutional adaptation, hence justifying the term Europeanisation understood as institutional adaptation due to pressure which has been generated by European rules and norms, i.e. directives and regulations of the expanding *acquis*.[66] Consequently, pressure for Europeanisation is likely to be higher in those Member States with policy sectors that entail institutions (norms, rules procedures) which are not readily compatible with European institutions. However, the Europeanisation effect was found to differ in the area of identity politics. For example, research on variation in the impact of national identity options in the process of Europeanisation demonstrated that the Europeanisation of national "identity-options" was higher in Member States with a higher (rather than a lower) compatibility of socio-cultural tradition with European integration. In the end, Europeanisation research has produced a plethora of Europeanisation approaches.[67] While each offers sufficiently systematic elaboration on the issue, the numerous and often descriptive and empirically rich policy studies in the 1980s and 1990s still remain considerably fragmented.

3. Late Politicisation (since 1993)

With the constitutional turn which had been triggered by the impending eastern enlargement process and which was manifested by the Amsterdam Treaty, a new phase which I call late politicisation has, if gradually, taken shape in the process of European integration.[68] Enhanced, and possibly triggered, by German Foreign Minister Joschka Fischer's Humboldt Speech in Berlin in 2000, a pluralist debate about political finality and its constitutional frame has been brought to the fore of academic and public discourse. The Convention on the Future of Europe was one institutional expression of this process. Questions raised by the constitutional debate are above all directed to the forthcoming decision about either simplifying the treaties without changing their status, or revising them with the goal of creating a constitutional text. The constitutional debate is more interested in the judicial and political form than in the substance, i.e. contents and meanings of the final text. As a member of the European Parliament notes, "despite

[66] T Börzel, 'Non-compliance in the European Union: Pathology or Statistical Artifact?' (2001) 8 *JEPP* 803; Börzel and Risse, above n 25.

[67] M Marcussen *et al*, 'Constructing Europe? The Evolution of French, British and German Nation-State Identities' (1999) 6 *JEPP* 614. On a general assessment of research on Europeanisation, see JP Olsen, 'The Many Faces of Europeanization' (2002) 20 *JCMS* 581.

[68] See eg the overview of the legal, regulative and political thrust of these phases of integration offered by Joerges: see C Joerges 'The Law in the Process of Constitutionalising Europe, Arena Annual Conference' *ARENA* Oslo (2002), <http://www.arena.uio.no/events/Conference2002/Papers.html> (6 July 2004).

being agreed as international treaties, the treaties are something akin to the Constitution of the European Union. Therefore they accomplish the role of a constitution. For me the question is not, whether Europe has a constitution, but whether Europe has the constitution it needs. That is precisely the question. That's what this is all about. And ... the answer is clear: the European Union does not have the constitution it needs."[69]

In light of the first and second phases which made little reference to political processes and the respective societal contexts in which they were generated,[70] the constitutional debate was characterised by the added time pressure to produce a successful outcome; i.e. drafting a constitutional document that was acceptable to the 2004 IGC, within a relatively short period of time, appears as a puzzle. The old and often repeated issues of the role of the public sphere and public opinion, legitimacy and democracy as well as the appropriate means for establishing and safe-guarding these principles politically are reposed in a hurry. The answers, which were, e.g. offered by the European commission's White Paper on Governance[71] as well as numerous proposals regarding the reorganisation of European political organs, demonstrate the scarcity of conceptually convincing and politically feasible approaches to constitutional change. To lawyers, projects which aim to achieve the "constitutionalisation of the treaties"[72] after years of integration through law and a prospering practice of law in Europe, come as a surprise. After all, constitutionalisation has been an ongoing process for decades. The following elaborates on the late politicisation phase, focusing on the role of institutions.

After the shift in the analytical area from *politics* of integration to *policies* of institutional adaptation, i.e. Europeanisation, including constitutionally important changes brought about by the Maastricht and Amsterdam Treaties and the pressure to enlarge the EU at the end of the cold war, students of European integration are eventually pushed to face the *polity*

[69] Interview with a member of the European Parliament, Brussels, 29 August 2001. This interview and the following are cited anonymously; they are on file with the author.

[70] With the exception of neo-functionalists' interest in social interaction; yet this work received little attention during the 1970s and 1980s; see PC Schmitter, 'Three Neo-functional Hypotheses about International Integration', (1969) 23 *International Organization* 162; Lindberg and Scheingold, above n 59; EB Haas, 'Turbulent Fields and the Theory of Regional Integration' (1976) 30 *International Organization* 173.

[71] For a detailed view, see European Commission, *European Governance: A White Paper*, COM(2001) 428 final, <http://europa.eu.int/eur-lex/en/com/cnc/2001/com2001_0428en01.pdf> (6 July 2004); for critical assessments see the contributions in C Joerges, Y Meny and JHH Weiler (eds), *Mountain or Molehill? A Critical Appraisal of the Commission White Paper on Governance* (2001); in particular the contributions by FW Scharpf, 'European Governance: Common Concerns vs. The Challenge of Diversity' 1, and J Shaw, 'European Union Governance and the Question of Gender', 129.

[72] See eg the report by the European Parliament's Committee of Institutional Affairs, 2000: European Parliament, *Report on the Constitutionalisation of the Treaties*, Final A5-0289/2000, PE 286.949.

dimension. Questions of identity, democracy and security among others have been brought to the fore with the introduction of Union citizenship and the communitarisation of the Schengen agreement to abolish internal border controls. Foreign policy changes such as the Kosovo crisis, the attack on the World Trade Centre and the political crisis in the Middle East have increased the challenges confronting the EU on the world stage. In addition, the process of enlargement with new accession criteria settled in Copenhagen in 1993 has increased the pressure for institutional adaptation in the candidate countries, the European political organs and the Member States as well. The current phase of late politicisation presents a context of complex institutional change characterised by multiple processes of institutional adaptation. In addition to the familiar bottom-up and top-down perspectives on institutional change (compare table 1) the future-oriented debate over fundamental issues of political responsibility and a revised constitutional framework has gained precedence over day-to-day policy issues.[73] As a consequence, the EU is now approached as a political system. According to Joschka Fischer in his Humboldt speech, "the whole is at stake", and hence the pressure to face finality both in constitutional and political terms is on the rise. The underlying security and financial interests that informed the choice and definition of the Copenhagen accession criteria (e.g. in the areas of minority policy, agricultural policy, visa policy, and fundamental freedoms) raised questions about the political constitution, the leading principles and the value system within the EU as a polity. In this phase, legal work on European integration gains importance for political science approaches and *vice versa*. The largely hidden link between "integration through law"[74] as an approach that offered explanatory guidance for lawyers during the first phase of integration, on the one hand, and "integration through policy' which had substantiated political science research during the second Europeanisation phase, on the other,[75] stands to be scrutinised with a new focus on "integration through politics" in academic research during the late politicisation phase.

III. INSTITUTIONS IN SELECTED POLICY AREAS: CITIZENSHIP AND THE CONSTITUTIONAL PROCESS

Following the overview about central questions and research areas of European integration raised by political science, this section turns to the third—"late politicisation"—phase of European integration and, more in detail, to the process of evolving constitutional law in selected policy areas.

[73] See also J Habermas, 'Warum braucht Europa eine Verfassung?', *Die Zeit* (29 June 2001); later published in J Habermas, *Zeit der Übergänge* (2001), 104.

[74] See M Capelletti, M Seccombe and JHH Weiler (eds), *Integration Through Law* (1985).

[75] See Wallace and Wallace, above n 55.

In concluding, it raises critical questions about the analytical capacity to grasp the political impact of the constitutional process, in particular, the speedy process of drafting a constitutional document and the outcome of the negotiations leading up to the 2004 Intergovernmental Conference. In the following I draw on both analytical dimensions addressed in the first two sections of this chapter, including first, the distinction between the "customary" and "organisational" dimensions of the *nomos*; secondly, I apply the distinction between the three different types of action i.e. the rational actor model, the structural approach and the intersubjective approach. The argument builds on Tully's reference to ongoing "dialogue" under conditions of equality. I thus return to the core argument developed in this chapter about bringing the customary back into modern constitutions and its relevance for transnational constitutional settings. I suggest conceptualising the principle of contestedness as a fourth normative perspective on—constitutionally established—institutions. The principle follows the assumption of the analytical and political impact generated by the *dual quality of norms* as both socially constructed through interaction as well as structuring actors' behaviour.[76] It proposes the extension of institutional analysis towards the assessment of the origin and transformation of soft institutions in order to reconstruct the interpretation of their meaning. The model is based on the assumption that these norms are not sufficiently legitimised by exclusive reference to their facticity, i.e. the recognition of the powerful prescriptive rules they entail. In addition, successful norms entail socio-culturally generated validity.[77] Absent this validity, the likelihood of sustained norm resonance decreases. The principle of contestedness draws on theoretical arguments developed by deliberative approaches in political theory as well as in integration research.[78] It stresses the lack of a more pronounced and systematic empirical focus on the impact of socio-cultural trajectories on norms.[79] In addition, multiple path-dependencies of soft institutions are considered as gaining in importance and impact on the meaning and role of norms. The following paragraphs introduce a more detailed application on the impact, possibilities and change of institution building based on two examples of evolving norms and their respective

[76] The approach draws on the concepts of 'structuration': A Giddens, *Central Problems in Social Theory* (1979); 'constitutional recognition', see Tully, above n 1; see also J Tully, 'The Unfreedom of the Moderns in Comparison to their Ideals of Constitutionalism and Democracy' (2002) 65 *MLR* 204, as well as the facticity-validity tension as a *Grundnorm* based on Habermas's work: J Habermas, *Zur Logik der Sozialwissenschaften* (1985); and *id*, *Faktizität und Geltung* (1992).

[77] See Habermas (1992), above n 76, 35.

[78] J Cohen, 'Deliberation and Democratic Legitimacy' in J Bohman and W Rehg (eds), *Deliberative Democracy* (1997), 67; S Benhabib, *Democracy and Difference Contesting the Boundaries of the Political* (1996); Joerges and Neyer, above n 56.

[79] See eg Habermas (1992), above 76, 629, '[e]ven if the wording of norms remains the same, their interpretations are fluid'.

contested meanings in Europe. The first example refers to European citizenship, the second to the constitutional debate.

The starting point of this analysis is the assumption of a link between the social construction of institutions and the successful implementation of law. It draws on a sociological concept of constitutionalisation which is based on the culturally embeddedness of constitutional dynamics.[80] I thus seek to recover the customary aspect of constitutional law based on a reflexive approach to soft institutions favouring a thick concept of the *nomos* rather more closely than the lean concept of modern constitutional law.[81] While the gradual and rather long-lasting process of constitutionalisation in its interchange with the advancing progress of European integration entails both types of constitutionalisation,[82] this chapter's sociological understanding of constitutionalisation comprehends the concept as involving two types of institutions. First, constitutions offer an institutional context for the political community as a hole; second, they consist of an aggregation of institutions themselves.[83] Proposing to extend modern constitutionalism towards the customary offers a shift of focus from analysing the expanding formal *acquis* towards understanding the *acquis* as "socially embedded".[84] It conceptualises institutions as created through social practices within particular contexts. Absent social interaction, rules and norms do not exist. In addition, legal and social institutions are interrelated insofar as the former require the latter in order to be meaningfully implemented, or for that matter, in order to resonate with their respective context of implementation. This approach allows for the analytical inclusion of multiple socio-cultural trajectories which produce and transform the meaning of "European" ways and structures in analyses of constitutional issues based on the Aristotelian understanding of a constitution as "institution of institutions".[85] Crucially,

[80] See Habermas (1992), above n 76, 629; for an elaboration of this approach, see also the contributions in A Wiener and J Shaw (eds), *The Evolving Norms of Constitutionalism*, (2003) 9 *ELJ* Special Issue; A Wiener, 'The Embedded *Acquis Communautaire*: Transmission Belt and Prism of New Governance' (1998) 4 *ELJ* 294. See also contributions to the 'new legal dynamics' strand of British European lawyers, ie N Walker, 'The Idea of Constitutional Pluralism' (2002) 65 *MLR* 317, as well as the contributions in G De Burca and J Scott (eds), *Constitutional Change in the EU: From Uniformity to Flexibility?* (2000); and P Beaumont, C Lyons and N Walker (eds), *Convergence & Divergence in European Public Law* (2002).

[81] See for a helpful overview P Craig, 'Constitutions, Constitutionalism, and the European Union' (2001) 7 *ELJ* 125.

[82] See eg E Stein, 'Lawyers, Judges and the Making of a Transnational Constitution' (1981) 75 *AJIL* 1; explicitly see Case 294/83 *Les Verts v Parliament* [1986] ECR 1339; Opinion 1/91, *EEA* [1991] ECR I–6079; AG Lagrange speaks already of a 'genuine constitution' of the European Communities in Case 6/64 *Costa* [1964] ECR 1255 at 1289.

[83] As Onuf writes, for example '[C]onstitutions institutionalize the whole even as they themselves consist of an aggregate of institutions': Onuf, above n 9, 218 *et seq*, with reference to Lieber, above n 9, 343.

[84] See Wiener (1998), above n 80; M Merlingen, C Mudde and U Sedelmeier, 'The Right and the Rightous: European Norms, Domestic Politics and the Sanctions Against Austria' (2002) 39 *JCMS* 59.

[85] See Onuf, above n 9, 222.

it allows to focus on constitutional norms as evolving through social practices even before a constitutional text is identified as a constitution and labelled accordingly.

The late politicisation phase with its focus on the finality debate follows a long period of constitutional politics carried out without any particularly defined political goal for the Europolity. As one of the many unintended consequences of institution-building in the process of European constitutionalisation, the finality debate encapsulates the breathless constitutional process which is likely to generate even further unintended consequences. In the process, normative concerns against a European Constitution that would lead beyond the simple re-organisation of the treaties are raised.[86] In this context the understanding of institution building and its often path-dependent impact is crucial. In other words, the meaning of institutions and hence their constitutive and regulative influence on behaviour changes once it is transferred across the socio-cultural boundaries which forge the meaning of core constitutional norms. That is, facticity and validity of norms produce conflicting interpretations across national boundaries within the territory to which a European Constitution would apply. Historical institutional analyses have pointed out the significance of identifying institutional impact over long time periods[87] with reference to changed resource constellations (i.e. power constellations, market resources, interests). This problem of so-called "snap-shot" as opposed to "moving picture" analyses extends towards the impact of socio-cultural resources which also produce unintended consequences under the conditions of time and contexts change. As I have argued elsewhere, "associative resources" (i.e. expectations, interpretations, meanings) are subject to change and contestation as well.[88] The example of Union citizenship substantiates this particular effect.

The argument elaborates on the evolving meaning of soft institutions based on the discussion about norms which offers new ways of assessing the establishment of democratic and legitimate process of governance beyond the State.[89] It begins from an institutionally established safe-guard mechanism for

[86] See eg JHH Weiler, *The Constitution of Europe* (1999). Weiler is in particular referring to constitutional principles such as eg the principle of tolerance which is already encapsulated in the preamble to the EC Treaty: see *id*, 'Europe's Constitutional *Sonderweg*' in *id* and Wind, above n 5, 19.

[87] See on path-dependency in general North, above n 24; and with particular reference to European integration Pierson, above n 10; as well as A Wiener, 'Zur Verfassungspolitik jenseits des Staates: Die Vermittlung von Bedeutung am Beispiel der Unionsbürgerschaft' (2001) 8 *Zeitschrift für internationale Beziehungen* 73.

[88] See Wiener, above n 80.

[89] See H Müller, 'Internationale Beziehungen als kommunikatives Handeln: Zur Kritik der utilitaristischen Handlungstheorien' [1994] *Zeitschrift für Internationale Beziehungen* 371; Risse, above n 11; Joerges and Neyer, above n 56; C Joerges, 'Deliberative Supranationalism Two Defenses' (2002) 8 *ELJ* 133. But see also the more encompassing approach to 'constitutional recognition' in multicultural contexts developed by Tully, above n 1.

ongoing deliberation about the meaning of norms and rules. It hence establishes an institutional framework which allows for a flexible and equal assessment of the facticity-validity tension based on public participation, thus offering a constitutionally entrenched link between "[I]nstitutionalized deliberation and public debate" which "must, indeed, interact."[90] It is here where the Europolity's best and worst outcome may well be decided. Hence, the key problem of academic approaches to constitutional debate lies in the practice of analytically bracketing controversial associative connotations about the meaning of constitutional substance, i.e. in excluding the intangible factors that inform interpretation, and ultimately, resonance with contested socio-cultural norms from the analysis. For example, the debate focuses on the discussion of different constitutional models and their substantive aspects (vertical debate: Which model is considered legitimate?) Yet, shared constitutional norms inevitably acquire varying interpretations through associative connotations that are developed within different socio-cultural contexts (horizontal contestation: which meanings of a norm and which expectations?). It is ultimately the associative connotations within these contexts which are constitutive for unintended consequences of institution-building as the following will explicate further.

1. European Citizenship

The formal institutionalisation of European citizenship with the Maastricht Treaty in 1991 presents a classic example of institution building with unintended consequences. This is due to the fact that Union citizenship entails all but a scarce amount of prescriptive force which would allow for the identification of guiding capabilities and a behavioural performance expected by the logic of appropriateness expected by constructivist compliance research.[91] Yet, what must appear puzzling to the latter is that Union citizenship has caused political reaction, all the same and despite the absence of standardised rule for behaviour. Thus, political actors such as lobbying groups, associations and interest groups made explicit reference to Union citizenship following its stipulation in the Maastricht Treaty, indeed, even going so far as demanding its revision.[92] This case of mobilisation in reaction to a newly established institution was less puzzling for authors that analysed European citizenship as a *practice*, i.e. the politics and policymaking which institutionalise the terms and forge the meanings of citizenship than observers who analysed Union citizenship as a new legal norm. The practice oriented work was able to demonstrate that the institution of

[90] See Joerges, above n 68, 146.
[91] See Checkel, above n 33, 200.
[92] See Art 8a–e EC Treaty (Maastricht), now Arts 17–22 EC.

Union citizenship—as stipulated by the TEU—represents just *one* aspect of the multiple and fragmented meanings of European citizenship. The larger and more encompassing understanding of the meanings of citizenship have evolved in relation with European citizenship practice, involving socio-cultural spaces, i.e. transnational, national or international interactions that remain theoretically (and therefore also empirically) hidden by structure-oriented behaviourist approaches. Thus, more than twenty-five years of European citizenship practice have had an impact on the transformation of national citizenship. While modern nationally defined citizenship stipulates identity and regulates rights and access based on membership within a centrally organised constitutional State,[93] the European Union has forged a fragmented type of citizenship which is neither centrally defined nor centrally practised.[94] Indeed, Union citizenship is not thinkable without reference to national citizenship as the revision of the Amsterdam Treaty explicates.[95] This fragmentation of citizenship rights within the Europolity has created a new meaning of citizenship that challenges the meaning of modern concepts of citizenship. Based on the particular meaning that is specific to Union citizenship and has evolved through citizenship practice, it thus challenges modern conceptions of citizenship that are deduced from the universal norm of citizenship.[96] This transformation of meaning is however not readily visible as a prescriptive force which guides behaviour based on an exclusive investigation of the citizenship articles (Arts 17–22) in the EC Treaty. Instead, the meaning must be empirically explicated and *mediated* in order to facilitate understanding.[97] Absent a successful mediation of meaning and the understanding about where to locate them, the political reactions to Union citizenship must remain a puzzle for actor-oriented and

[93] R Grawert, *Staat und Staatsangehörigkeit* (1973); R Bendix, *Nation Building and Citizenship* (1964); WR Brubaker, *Citizenship and Nationhood in France and Germany* (1992); UK Preuss, 'Citizenship and Identity: Aspects of a Political Theory of Citizenship' in: R Bellamy, V Bufacchi and D Castiglione (eds), *Democracy and Constitutional Culture in the Union of Europe* (1995), 107; B Turner, 'Outline of a Theory of Citizenship' (1990) 24 *Sociology* 189; R Beiner (ed), *Theorizing Citizenship* (1995).

[94] See the current constitutional stipulation of citizens' rights in Arts 17–22 EC, as well as in a number of EU Treaty Articles, eg Arts 13, 119 EU etc.

[95] See Art 17(1) EC.

[96] On the particularity of citizenship see especially TH Marshall, who emphasises the importance of the emergence of a citizenship ideal within particular societal contexts: TH Marshall, *Citizenship and Social Class* (1950); on the EU see E Meehan, *Citizenship and the European Community* (1993); A Wiener, 'Assessing the Constructive Potential of Union Citizenship' (1997) 1 *European Integration online Papers* No 17 <http://eiop.or.at/eiop/texte/1997-017a.htm> (6 July 2004); A Wiener, *'European' Citizenship Practice—Building Institutions of a Non-State* (1998); A Wiener, 'Citizenship' in M Cini (ed), *European Union Politics* (2003), 397. On the crucial importance of the difference between universal and particular aspects of citizenship and its contextual application, see also M Bös, 'Die Europäisierung nationaler Gesellschaften' [2000] *Kölner Zeitschrift für Soziologie und Sozialpsychologie*, Special Issue, 429.

[97] See Wiener, above n 80; on the mediation of meaning see more generally Kieser, above n 27, ch 9.

structure-oriented approaches of institution-building. After all, in the absence of prescriptive force, behavioural change is not expected. (From the perspective of law the more controversial and hence interesting question is not about the "why" of political reaction to Union citizenship, but about the substance and possible reactions to institutionalisation with a view to legal practice, on the one hand, and the consequences of institutionalisation for the final political shape of the Union, on the other.)[98] Based on the premise of the dual quality of norms as structuring and constructed, it is however possible to shed light on the puzzle. Once the principle of contestedness is taken as the starting point, norm implementation is always interrelated with deliberation about the meaning of norms. It is this perspective which eventually allows for an analytical approach to the fragmented meaning of diverse norms of citizenship.

2. The Constitutional Debate

If the customary dimension of constitutional law matters, the principle of contestedness has two implications for the constitutional process. The first refers to considering the evolving norms of constitutionalism generated by social practices in the process of enlargement. While the constitutional debate which has been largely carried out in the old—western—Member States provides a framework for open and constructive thought, the enlargement process has for more than a decade been dictated by rule-following behaviour which allowed for all but "socialising into" the community. The former has been future oriented in style and dynamics, and it is evaluated according to democratic criteria with respect to procedure and substance alike. The yardstick for legitimacy refers to the principle of equal access to participation in the debate for all those potentially influenced by the outcome of the process. Here the logic of arguing and the principle of contestedness are central for actors' behaviour. The latter, in turn, is guided by the rule following logic of compliance; the enlargement process thus entails the expectation of strict rule following and implementation of the compliance criteria. Accordingly the logic of action that influence behaviour most decisively in the enlargement process is that of consequentialism and the that of appropriateness.[99] The behaviour of the candidate countries is determined by the guiding impact of the accession criteria which had been identified in 1993 in Copenhagen. Their substance is not renegotiable.

[98] See S Kadelbach in this volume.

[99] For a focus on the logics of appropriateness and the logic of consequentialism in the enlargement process as separated from the process of EU polity formation and constitution making, see F Schimmelfennig and U Sedelmeier (eds), 'European Union Enlargement—Theoretical and Comparative Approaches' (2002) 9 *JEPP* Special Issue, in particular the contributions by Schimmelfennig, 598, and Schimmelfennig and Sedelmeier, 500.

Nonetheless, it is expected that the constitutional settlement agreed in 2004 be accepted by all signatories of the Constitutional Treaty—including both old and new Member States. Accommodating diversity based on day-to-day experience in *all* social contexts is therefore vital. Academic research on the European Constitution thus requires a critical understanding of the interrelation between both, the constitutional debate about political finality of the EU, on the one hand, and the political process of enlargement, on the other.[100] The link between both processes offers an understanding of both processes not only as potentially conflictive but as producing additional hurdles towards the acceptance of a revised common constitution in an enlarged EU.

The constitutional debate, preparing for massive enlargement in 2004 has demonstrated the dual challenge of accommodating diversity in a modern constitution beyond the State. Beyond analytically linking the two processes the challenge consists in establishing a constitutionally entrenched institutional body that offers the possibility for ongoing transnational deliberation as a basis for democratic decision-making, recognition and constitutional revision on the long run.[101] While doubtful, it is worthwhile assessing the potential future role of the *Convention model* and its democratic potential regarding fair and equal participatory conditions of current and future Member States. After all, the candidate countries are expected to act according to the compliance rationale and practice rule following with a view to the policy of conditionality that governs enlargement; yet at the same time, they are/were called to constructively participate in the Convention and in the wider public debate on the future of Europe.[102] The candidate countries are thus forced into a process of opposing identity formation which paves the way for a fragmentation among the future members of the constitutional community which raises four central questions. First, are restricted participation and opposing identity formation favourable factors for a successful outcome of the finality debate (i.e. agreement about the form and substance, and resonance of both within the respective Member State); second, what is the contribution of the Convention to solve the dilemma; third, how could the situation be improved; and fourth, what are the long-term consequences for establishment of democratic legitimation in the process of European integration?

[100] For a detailed argument on the two rationales, see A Wiener, 'Finality vs Enlargement: Constitutive Practices and Opposing Rationales in the Reconstruction of Europe' in Weiler and Wind, above n 5, 157.

[101] On the principle of constitutional recognition and the proposal to institutionalise access to ongoing deliberation about constitutional issues, see J Tully's excellent work, in particular Tully, above n 1, 59.

[102] Thus, eg, German Minister of Foreign Affairs Joschka Fischer 'encouraged Poland and the other east and central European countries which apply for membership in the European Union, to *participate in the debate over EU finality*': *Frankfurter Allgemeine Zeitung* (26 January 2002) 4 (emphasis added).

With reference to the different logics of action presented earlier in this chapter, it is possible to conclude that, in principle, the following conditions are necessary for democratic governance. First, according to Habermas's ideal speech situation all participants of a debate must be able to debate under equal conditions, including information, voice and vote in order to be able to generate, identify and accept shared norms (i.e. all participants must, in principle, be ready for persuasion by the better argument developed by the others, and to revise their previously held position accordingly). The starting point of the finality/compliance situation in the EU differs from this basic scenario. For example, the criteria set up for accession in Copenhagen have been neither sufficiently defined by the EU so as to allow for uncontested implementation (e.g. in the area of administration) nor have the EU Member States been subjected to scrutiny as to whether they have implemented the criteria themselves (e.g. in the area of minority rights).[103] In addition, the so-called transition rules, e.g. in the area of freedom of movement for workers, will create unequal conditions among the group of future Union citizens. While perfectly legitimate from a political and legal position, these are examples of areas in which the public perception of equality may not agree with the agreements on the governmental level and may therefore cause political mobilisation as an unintended consequence of institution building. Furthermore, the candidate countries work with a considerable information deficit in all areas of EU policy-making and politics, including the Convention, in which they have the right to voice, but not to veto. They thus enter the union with a structural disadvantage.[104] In conclusion, the establishment of spaces for transnational deliberation remains a core issue on the agenda for constitutional revision. Indeed, given past experiences of constitutional change, the *main issue* appears to be less one of agreeing on a new constitutional model than establishing transnational fora for deliberation in selected policy areas in which elected representatives from political levels of governance and public associations are entitled to participate in equal and ongoing debates as European citizens.[105]

[103] See Schwellnus and Wiener, above n 54, 455.

[104] See also C Landfried, 'Difference as a Potential for European Constitution Making' paper presented at the European Forum, Robert Schuman Centre, European University Institute, Florence (Ms, 18 March 2004).

[105] See proposals by Joerges and Neyer (supranational deliberation), above n 56; U Puetter, 'Informal Circles of Ministers—A Way Out of the EU's Institutional Dilemmas?' (2003) 9 *ELJ* 109; H Abromeit and T Schmidt, 'Grenzprobleme der Demokratie' [1998] *Politische Vierteljahresschrift,* Special issue 293; on Maduro (pluralistic citizenship), see MP Maduro, 'Where To Look For Legitimacy?, Arena Annual Conference', *ARENA* Oslo (2002) <http:://www.arena.uio.no/events/conference2002/papers.html> (6 July 2004); and from a more theoretical perspective see Tully, above n 1, 59. See also recent proposals to include the 'Open Method of Coordination' in the revised constitutional treaty by G de Búrca and J Zeitlin, 'Constitutionalising the Open Method of Coordination' Paper 6 (2003) <http://www.fd.unl.pt/je/edit_pap2003-06.htm> (6 July 2004).

IV. CONCLUSION

The process of enlargement with the respective challenges towards institutional adaptation requires precise understanding of the institutional framework of the EU. The calculation of necessary and expected institutional changes creates an increasing challenge for both academia and politics. While in earlier enlargement rounds that basic information was relatively easy to convey, the current enlargement process evolves within a context of increasing density of governance processes beyond State boundaries such as the influence of supranational institutions on domestic political processes (regime building, norm diffusion). Moral and ethical questions matter in world politics in addition to arithmetic and geopolitics that suggest the prevalence of allocation and distribution of resources. It is not only the focus on hard institutions such as e.g. the political organs of the EU (Commission, Council, Parliament, Court of Justice) and the formal core of the *acquis communautaire*, but also the role of soft institutions such as values, social norms, routinised practices and ideas which factor into analyses of European integration and enlargement. While neo-institutionalists have been able to explain the social push by way of spill-overs among particular policy areas, negative integration, the democratic deficit debate and now the constitutional debate have demonstrated that processes of institutionalisation have spread well beyond the market and its logic. In light of the dramatic increase in prescriptions for behaviour, lawyers have already suggested to clean up the *acquis*.[106] Furthermore, Brussels officials have expressed the wish to "use a hatchet to change the *acquis*, to cut it down, to revise it towards its necessity today."[107] The point of these observations is that the *acquis* has acquired an institutional breadth and density that creates all sorts of unintended consequences which are in turn difficult to predict.[108]

Academic studies on hard institutions have been the standard for a long time. Different from theoretical work in International Relations theories, assessing the impact of soft institutions still has some way to go towards systematic and generalisable approaches in European integration studies, and particularly, in European legal studies despite a number of more recent contributions to the field.[109] This chapter sought to highlight the different

[106] See in more detail A von Bogdandy and J Bast, 'The European Union's Vertical Order of Competences' (2002) 39 *CML Rev* 227. Bogdandy also stresses the importance of consequently implementing majority decisions into secondary law: see A von Bogdandy, 'Europäische Prinzipienlehre' in A von Bogdandy (ed), *Europäisches Verfassungsrecht* (2003), 149.

[107] Interview with a member of the European Parliament, Brussels, 28 August 2001; on file with author.

[108] See Wiener, above n 80.

[109] See Olsen's critical perspective on the 'Europeanisation' literature: Olsen, above n 67; but see recent work by Börzel and Risse, above n 25; Cowles *et al*, above n 36; see the contributions in Christiansen *et al*, above n 55; as well as, eg, H Farrell and A Héritier, 'Formal and Informal Institutions under Codecision' (2002) 6 *European Integration online Papers* No 3 <http://eiop.or.at/eiop/texte/2002-003a.htm> (6 July 2004).

avenues of analytical access to an increasingly complex body of institutions from a political science perspective in order to offer guidelines for orientation on the success and risks of strategic institution building (hard institutions) in the process of integration based on the elaboration of a more distinct perspective on societally generated processes of institutionalisation (soft institutions). The chapter suggests that the latter play an important role in particular for interdisciplinary perspectives that are increasingly attractive to legal studies of European integration and offer a perspective that avoids the analytical shortcomings in inspiration and flexibility presented by dogmatic approaches in European constitutional law, arguing that the latter is likely to overlook possibilities for theoretical innovation that are necessary to include a sharper analytical perspective on changing institutional contexts and their respective impact. Including different approaches in international relations and studies of European integration allows for a dual perspective, e.g. from the nation-State up towards the EU and from world politics down towards the EU. This combination of theoretical standpoints based on the respectively different strategic rationales could eventually contribute to avoid the trap of methodological nationalism.[110] Different from the considerably more narrowly conceptualised boundaries in law, for which a link or even overlap between international law and national law is almost unthinkable and which therefore raises the issue of creating a new discipline of European constitutional law, the interdisciplinary link between sub-disciplines in political science, law and sociology offers reasonable and so far little used possibilities—in particular from the perspective of German law—for a more comprehensive study of the process of European integration, and of constitutionalism beyond the State.[111]

[110] M Zürn, 'Democratic Governance Beyond the Nation-State' (2000) 6 *European Journal of International Relations* 183.

[111] Note, however, the pronounced emphasis on interdisciplinarity in British legal approaches to European integration such as eg 'New Legal Dynamics of Integration' literature offered by Shaw, Moore, Armstrong, Scott, de Búrca, Benkowski, Chalmers, Walker, Eversen, among others.

Part III
Individual Rights

11

Union Citizenship

STEFAN KADELBACH*

A nation? Says Bloom.
A nation is the same people living in the same place
James Joyce, Ulysses**

I. INTRODUCTION

EUROPEAN COMMUNITY LAW is the product of a process of transformation. It has emerged as an autonomous legal order from a series of international treaties. The role of the European Court of Justice was crucial in this respect. Long-term treaty objectives have been attributed direct applicability and supremacy over municipal law,[1] individual rights have arisen from Member State duties,[2] and the EEC Treaty, the central document of European integration, has been re-interpreted as a constitution.[3] According to the Court, the law of the European Community—today the Union—has become a legal system whose subjects are not only the Member States but also their citizens.[4] The Treaty of Maastricht, by inserting a new part on union citizenship into the EC Treaty (now Articles 17–22 EC), suggested that this path would be further followed. The individual appears to have been placed in the centre of Union law.[5]

Investigations into the legal substance of Union citizenship have resulted in very heterogeneous assessments which differ according to the chosen reference point.[6] Restricting analysis to the existing rules of the EC Treaty will

* The author thanks Mr Christopher Dallimore for his assistance in translating the German version.

** Quote taken from the Bodley Head edition (1960) 430.

[1] Case 6/64, *Costa* [1964] ECR 585 at 593.

[2] Case 26/62, *van Gend* [1963] ECR 1 at 12.

[3] Case 294/83, *Les Verts v Parliament* [1986] ECR 1339, para 23; *Entscheidungen des Bundesverfassungsgerichts* 22, 293 at 296 (*EWG-Verordnungen*).

[4] Opinion 1/91, *EEA* [1991] ECR I-6079, para 21.

[5] See, eg, N Reich, *Bürgerrechte in der Europäischen Union* (1999) 5, 450 *et seq.*

[6] J Shaw, 'The Interpretation of European Union Citizenship', (1998) 61 *MLR* 293.

ensure a conservative conclusion,[7] and particularly so if such assessments are based on a comparison with rights available to national citizens. Such comparison, which is suggested by the wording of the Union Treaties, almost inevitably leads to disappointment.[8]

Others assess Union citizenship in light of its future potential. Here too, the national citizen stands in the background and encourages diverse projections. Many of these assessments reflect the debate concerning the endurance and prospects of a European people and a European constitution.[9] One line of enquiry traces the foundations of citizenship to pre-legal identities. The appreciation of Union citizenship then depends on what is deemed indispensable for a constituency with respect to pre-existing factors of a social nature that create identity.[10] Other contributions express the view that Union citizenship can be structured by law; it may thus constitute the prerequisite of an active European citizenship, the continuing development of which will be influenced by a gradual enhancement in legal status.[11]

It is tempting to juxtapose perspectives of citizenship relating to positive law and political theory, for two reasons. The first reason is methodical in nature. Strictly speaking, both views concern two different and unrelated discourses. The question arises whether this must be necessarily the case or whether there are links which should provide more mutual interest. The second reason lies in the pioneering role which Union citizenship plays in the discussion concerning a European constitution. Both initiatives share the idea of creating integration and identification by law. The overriding question is: What value can concepts employed by theories which have a connotation with the state as a reference point have at the European level?

This article will first consider the object and purpose of the rules governing Union citizenship (II). Thereupon, the positive law governing Union

[7] HU Jessurun d'Oliveira, 'European citizenship: its meaning, its potential', in R Dehousse (ed), *Europe after Maastricht: An ever closer Union?* (1994) 126 at 135 *et seq*; S O'Leary, *European Union Citizenship* (1996) 44 *et seq*; J-D Mouton, *La citoyenneté de l'Union: passé, présent et avenir* (1996) 18 *et seq*; JHH Weiler, 'European Citizenship and Human Rights', in JA Winter *et al* (eds), *Reforming the Treaty on European Union* (1996) 57 at 65 *et seq*; other commentators make a distinction according to individual rights, eg, V Constantinesco, 'La citoyenneté de l'Union', in J Schwarze (ed) *Vom Binnenmarkt zur Europäischen Union* (1993) 25; J Verhoeven, 'Les citoyens de l'Europe', (1993) *Annales de droit de Louvain* 165 at 172 *et seq*.

[8] A Wiener, 'Zur Verfassungspolitik jenseits des Staates', (2001) 8 *Zeitschrift für Internationale Beziehungen* 73; critical of the reception of national symbolism NW Barber, 'Citizenship, nationalism and the European Union', (2002) 27 *EL Rev* 241 at 256 *et seq*.

[9] A Augustin, *Das Volk der Europäischen Union* (2000) 41 *et seq*.

[10] See, eg, D Grimm, 'Braucht Europa eine Verfassung?' (1995) *Juristenzeitung* 581 at 587 *et seq*.

[11] C Tomuschat and S Kadelbach, 'Staatsbürgerschaft—Unionsbürgerschaft—Weltbürgerschaft', in J Drexl *et al* (eds), *Europäische Demokratie* (1999), 73 at 84 *et seq* and 89 at 104 *et seq*, respectively.

citizenship will be investigated in order to find the reasons for its negative evaluation in legal writing to date (III). The final section will consider the horizon of constitutional-political expectations opened up by the introduction of Union citizenship using the social-science debate as a basis (IV). Comparing the state of both the legal and the social-science discourse can prove rewarding in relation to the future structure of Union citizen rights.

II. THE NOTION OF UNION CITIZENSHIP

1. History

The story of the metamorphosis of the individual in the Community legal order has often been told.[12] It begins with the artificial birth of the "market citizen",[13] a "reduced functionalist concept of an individual".[14] This concept describes the individual as a holder of economic freedoms, the judicial enforcement of which serves to realise the Common market. The establishment of Union citizen rights in the EC Treaty represents the final chapter of this tale; for the time being, it must remain unfinished, since Union citizenship was introduced as open to development (Article 22 EC). Accordingly, the citizen's status in the new body politic of the European Union has yet to be defined. Confronting the market with the Union citizen may have an heuristic value. However, it is doubtful whether such comparison charts the development with sufficient clarity.

On the one hand, individuals under the Community legal order were never mere market citizens. The original EEC Treaty already provided for elections to the European Parliament (Article 138 (3), now Article 190 EC). In 1962, even before the Court of Justice had acknowledged the direct effect of fundamental freedoms, the Commission took the view that individuals in the Community legal order did not simply exercise their fundamental rights as mere factors of production but as holders of civil rights.[15] The case law

[12] E Grabitz, *Europäisches Bürgerrecht zwischen Marktbürgerschaft und Staatsbürgerschaft* (1970) 65 *et seq*; T Oppermann, Vom Marktbürger zum EG-Bürger?, in: G Nicolaysen and H Quaritsch (eds), *Lüneburger Symposion für HP Ipsen* (1988), 87; E Marias, From Market Citizen to Union Citizen, in: E Marias (ed), *European Citizenship* (1994), 1; A Randelzhofer, 'Marktbürgerschaft—Unionsbürgerschaft—Staatsbürgerschaft', in A Randelzhofer (ed), *Gedächtnisschrift für E Grabitz* (1995) 580.

[13] HP Ipsen and G Nicolaysen, 'Haager Kongreß für Europarecht und Bericht über die aktuelle Entwicklung des Gemeinschaftsrechts', (1964) *Neue Juristische Wochenschrift* 339 at 340, n 2; HP Ipsen, *Europäisches Gemeinschaftsrecht* (1972) 187, 250 *et seq*, 742.

[14] J Habermas, *Die postnationale Konstellation* (1998) 142 (author's trans).

[15] Commission Recommendation to the Member States on the activities of the social services in respect of workers moving within the Community, Journal Officiel, 16.8.1962, 2118.

relating to fundamental Community rights began in 1969 with the *Stauder* case which dealt with the personality right of a welfare recipient who wished to purchase products subsidized from EC funds at a reduced price without having to reveal his identity.[16] Notwithstanding his capacity as a beneficiary of a programme to dismantle agricultural surpluses, it was impossible to regard him as an actual holder of economic freedoms of the EC Treaty. At the same time, legislation on co-ordinating European welfare law was introduced which also granted pensioners as well as relatives of employees and the self-employed outside their country of origin equal access to national systems of social welfare at their place of residence.[17] The first Council initiatives with the aim of a "Europe of citizens" go as far back as 1969,[18] at a time when the customs union had been prematurely realised, but direct effect of some fundamental rights had not yet been finally recognised by the Court.[19]

On the other hand, fundamental freedoms are not constitutive for Union citizenship and therefore do not necessarily entail the latter. A Union citizen is a person who has the nationality of a Union State (Article 17(1), 2nd sentence EC). By contrast, holders of fundamental freedoms are all those upon whom the Community legal order has conferred such rights. The free movement of goods does not depend on the nationality of the trading partners. The right to free movement can also be extended by treaty to nationals of non-EU states, despite the fact that it is reserved to Union citizens according to the wording of the EC Treaty. Such treaties have been concluded with EFTA member states and accession countries, including Turkey.[20]

Comparing the status between market and Union citizens makes clear that in Community legislation and political initiatives, personal rights have become increasingly independent of fundamental freedoms. The most

[16] Case 29/69, *Stauder* [1969] ECR 419.

[17] AC Evans, 'European Citizenship', (1982) 45 *MLR* 496; U Everling, 'Von der Freizügigkeit der Arbeitnehmer zum Europäischen Bürgerrecht?', (1990) *Europarecht* suppl 1, 81; S O'Leary, *The Evolving Concept of Community Citizenship* (1996) 65 *et seq*; B Laubach, *Bürgerrechte für Ausländer und Ausländerinnen in der Europäischen Union* (1998) 21 *et seq*; U Becker, 'Freizügigkeit in der EU—auf dem Weg vom Begleitrecht zur Bürgerfreiheit', (1999) *Europarecht* 522.

[18] Third General Report on the Activities of the European Union (1969) 527 *et seq*.

[19] See, eg, Case 41/74, *van Duyn* [1974] ECR 1337, para 5/7 (free movement of employees); Case 2/74, *Reyners* [1974] ECR 631, para 29/31 (freedom of establishment); Case 33/74, *van Binsbergen* [1974] ECR 1299, para 24/26 (freedom to provide services).

[20] See especially Arts 28, 31 and 36 of the Agreement on the European Economic Area, OJ L 1, 3.1.1994, 3; with respect to Turkey, eg, Case C-262/96, *Sürül* [1999] ECR I-2685, para 60; concerning the right of establishment of Polish, Bulgarian and Czech nationals see Case C-63/99, *Gloszczuk* [2001] ECR I-6369, para 30; Case C-235/99, *Kondova* [2001] ECR I-6427, para 30; Case C-257/99, *Barkoci and Malik* [2001] ECR I-6557, para 30.

important impulses emanated from European labour law and social legislation, the subjective guarantees of which initially served the freedom of employees but gradually became independent of the existence of an employment contract.[21] At the same time, the demand for a political status of migrants within the EC arose. In 1974, the Council of Paris asked the Commission to review the special rights which citizens of Member States could be granted as members of the Community.[22] The notion of the right to vote and stand as a candidate at municipal elections in the place of residence dates from this time.[23] The Tindemans Report, submitted in 1975, recommended more citizens' rights, inter alia equal access to public offices, dismantling of border controls, promotion of school and student exchange programmes, mutual recognition of diplomas and improved consumer protection.[24] For the time being, however, the universal suffrage for the European Parliament and a uniform passport were the only obvious signs of a "Europe for citizens".[25]

The Draft Treaty Establishing the European Union produced under Altiero Spinelli was passed by European Parliament in 1984 and employed the term "Union citizenship" for the first time.[26] The European Council of Fontainebleau convened the Adonnino Committee—named after its chairman—which had the task of adopting Community measures "to strengthen and promote its identity and its image both for its citizens and for the rest of the world".[27] The subsequent reports of the group already contained most of the rights which Union citizens now have under the EC Treaty.[28] In the same year, the ECJ granted tourists the right to rely on (passive) freedom of services and, by widening the scope of the fundamental freedoms in this way, made an important step towards defunctionalising the freedom of

[21] See references above n 17.

[22] Eighth General Report on the Activities of the European Union (1974) 337 *et seq*; the starting-point for the description which differentiates between four phases in Wiener, see above n 8, 79 *et seq*.

[23] Commission of the European Communities, *Towards a Europe for Citizens*, Bull EC 7-75, 5 at 23 *et seq*.

[24] Bull EC Suppl 1-76, 29.

[25] Dec 76/787/ECSC, EEC, Euratom relating to the Act concerning the election of the representatives of the Assembly by direct universal suffrage, OJ L 278, 8.10.1976, 1; resolutions concerning the adoption of a uniform passport pattern OJ C 241, 19.9.1981, 1 and OJ C 179, 1.7.1982, 1 as amended in OJ C 200, 4.8.1995, 1.

[26] Resolution on the Draft Treaty Establishing the European Union, OJ C 77, 19.3.1984, 53; Art 3 DTEU: "The citizens of the Member States shall *ipso facto* be citizens of the Union. Citizenship of the Union shall be dependent upon citizenship of a Member State; it may not be independently acquired or forfeited. Citizens of the Union shall take part in the political life of the Union in the forms laid down by the Treaty, enjoy the rights granted to them by the legal system of the Union and be subject to its laws."

[27] Bull EC 6-84, 11: "A People's Europe".

[28] Bull EC Suppl 7-85, 1 at 9 *et seq*, 19 *et seq*.

persons.[29] The 1987 'Erasmus' Decision of the Council concerning student exchange was the first legal act to refer to a "Europe for citizens".[30] In the following year, the Commission submitted its proposal for the right to vote at municipal elections.[31] A little later, in 1990, the Council issued three directives on the right of persons with no occupation to reside outside their home state.[32]

These initiatives show that the freedom of movement and granting of political rights were seen as the most important elements in creating Union citizenship. Something of more recent provenance is a third component which has arisen from the efforts of the Union institutions to increase the identification with Europe, to make the Union more citizen-oriented and to create a sense of accountability vis-à-vis the individual. This attitude is reflected in Article 1(2) EU, which declares its aim to be "an ever closer union among the peoples of Europe"; decisions should be taken "as closely as possible to the citizen". According to Article 2(3) EU, one aim of the Union is "to strengthen the protection of the rights and interests of the nationals of its Member States through the introduction of a citizenship of the Union".

All three elements mentioned so far are reunited in the form of individual rights in the EC Treaty: Freedom of movement (Article 18 EC), the right to vote (Article 19 EC) and freedom of information rights in relation to Union institutions (Articles 21 and 255 EC). In its section on citizens' rights, the Charter of Fundamental Rights of the European Union,[33] which has been inserted as Part II of the Constitutional Treaty, also grants the right to "good administration" which is closely connected to the third group (Article II-41 CT-Conv; Article 101 CT-IGC). The right to protection abroad by diplomatic and consular authorities of other Member States additionally appears as a fourth component (Article 20 EC).

[29] Cases 286/82 and 26/83, *Luisi and Carbone* [1985] ECR 377.

[30] Dec 87/327 EEC adopting the European Community Action Scheme for the Mobility of University Students (Erasmus), OJ L 166, 25.6.1987, 20; on the competence of the EC see Case 242/87, *Commission v Council* [1989] ECR 1425. Tourists and students thus qualify as the first true Union citizens.

[31] Proposal for a Dir on voting rights for Community nationals in local elections in their Member States of residence, OJ C 246, 20.9.1988, 3; the directive was deferred owing to preparatory work on the Union Treaty.

[32] Dir 90/364/EEC on the right of residence, OJ L 180, 13.7.1990, 26; Dir 90/365/EEC on the right of residence for employees and self-employed persons who have ceased their occupational activity, *ibid*, 28; Dir 90/366/EEC on the right of residence for students, *ibid*, 30, was annulled by the ECJ for incorrect basis of competence (Case C-295/90, *Parliament v Council* [1992] ECR I-4193) and newly enacted as Dir 93/96/EEC, OJ L 317, 18.12.1993, 59.

[33] Charter of fundamental rights of the European Union, OJ C 364, 18.12.2000, 1; on the creation of the Charter see G de Búrca, 'The drafting of the Union Charter of fundamental rights', (2001) 26 *EL Rev* 126.

[34] Conclusions of the Council of Rome, Bull EC Suppl 2-91.

Union citizenship is not limited to these rights. It extends to all rights and duties of Union law (Article 17(2) EC). It therefore includes fundamental freedoms resulting from constitutional traditions common to Member States (Article 6 EU) and social rights which have hitherto mainly existed on the basis of secondary legislation[34] to which the Charter of Fundamental Rights refers (Articles II-27-38 CT-Conv; Articles 87-98 CT-IGC). The rights guaranteed in Articles 18-21 EC nevertheless have a special symbolic value. As a rule, only nationals enjoy complete freedom of movement within the state borders.[35] Likewise, the right to vote and to stand for election is usually reserved to them alone. Diplomatic and consular protection, the expression of the state's sovereignty over persons, forms an important component of the reciprocal relationship of protection and obedience which exists between citizens and the state according to classical political theory.[36]

Since the creation of the rights of market citizens, European citizens have thus been granted many attributes which resemble political rights. Therefore, an investigation as to how far the parallels between state citizenship and Union citizenship extend and how each relates to nationality appears to be unavoidable.[37]

2. The Legal Concept of European Citizenship

a) Nationality

Nationality and citizenship are dependent on each other but are not congruent.[38] Depending on the view taken in constitutional theory, nationality

[35] Compare Art 11(1) of the German *Grundgesetz*; Art 5(4) Greek, Art 16 Italian, Art 44 Portuguese, and Art 19 Spanish Constitutions; proviso in relation to the acquisition of real estate in § 44(2) of the Danish Constitution, which is allowed in terms of primary law by a Protocol. Belgium, Ireland, Luxembourg, the Netherlands and Sweden do not anchor national freedom of movement in constitutional law. Only § 7 of the Finnish Constitution places nationals and foreigners legally resident in Finland on an equal footing, providing, however, for further legislation with respect to aliens.

[36] T Hobbes, *Leviathan* (1651), ed by M Oakeshott (1960) 467 *et seq*.

[37] The Commission does not appreciate such comparisons, see Third Commission Report on Citizenship of the Union, COM(2001) 506 final at 9: "When considering the scope of citizenship of the Union, attempts to draw parallels with national citizenship should be avoided. Because of its origins and the rights and duties associated with it, citizenship of the Union is *sui generis* and cannot be compared to national citizenship of a Member State."

[38] In German, the terms "*Staatsangehörigkeit*" and "*Staatsbürgerschaft*" have to be distinguished, see R Grawert, 'Staatsangehörigkeit und Staatsbürgerschaft', (1984) 23 *Der Staat* 179 at 182; see also T Wobbe, 'Soziologie der Staatsbürgerschaft', (1997) *Staatswissenschaften und Staatspraxis* 205 at 207 *et seq*; the English and French pairing of the terms "citizenship"/ "nationality" or "*citoyenneté*"/"*nationalité*" does not wholly correspond, see B Guiguet, 'Citizenship and Nationality: Tracing the French Roots of the Distinction', in M La Torre (ed), *European Citizenship* (1998), 95; D Gosewinkel, 'Untertanschaft, Staatsbürgerschaft, Nationalität', (1998) *Berliner Journal für Soziologie* 507.

describes either a status or legal relationship owing to which the individual is subject to a state's jurisdiction.[39] It has consequences in international and constitutional law.

In terms of international law, nationality forms a basis of a state's jurisdiction and a crucial requirement for the exercise of diplomatic protection in relation to other states.[40] Essentially, states are free to establish the requirements governing acquisition of nationality. However, a merely formal attribution of nationality is not sufficient to create a legal relationship which third states are bound to recognise. In its famous *Nottebohm* judgment concerning the exercise of diplomatic protection on behalf of a naturalised citizen, the International Court of Justice held that the legal bond of nationality had to correspond to social reality. Nationality had to be supported by a genuine, existential and emotionally rooted commitment to the state; otherwise, it would be ineffective and not give rise to any obligations vis-à-vis the claimant state.[41] This restriction is primarily significant for individuals who possess more than one nationality. It accords with the conflict of laws statutes of many states to choose the effective nationality as a reference point in such cases.[42] Under international law, nationality therefore serves to resolve collisions of jurisdiction.

According to most constitutions, nationality alone does not establish any rights or duties of an individual. However, it does represent a necessary condition for some of them such as the right to vote in elections, access to public offices or compulsory military service. To this extent, nationality is a framework legal relationship, to be filled out by law.[43]

b) Citizenship

Citizenship, on the other hand, describes the adherence to a body politic in a way which identifies a person as a full member thereof.[44] *Citoyens*, creatures of the enlightenment, are united by freedom, equality and brotherliness.[45]

[39] A Makarov, *Allgemeine Regeln des Staatsangehörigkeitsrechts* (1962) 21 *et seq*; K Hailbronner and K Renner, *Staatsangehörigkeitsrecht* (1998), Introduction, paras C 1 *et seq*.

[40] A Randelzhofer, 'Nationality', in R Bernhardt (ed), *Encyclopaedia of Public International Law*, vol III (1997) 501 at 502; C Gloria, in K Ipsen (ed), *Völkerrecht* (1999), § 24 paras 2 and 34.

[41] Developed by the International Court of Justice in the *Nottebohm* Case, *Liechtenstein v Guatemala* [1955] ICJ Rep 4 at 23.

[42] See also Art 5(1) of the introductory law to the German civil code (*Einführungsgesetz zum Bürgerlichen Gesetzbuch*).

[43] Grawert, above n 38, 183; with respect to the term "stand-by status" ("*Bereitschaftsstatus*") A Randelzhofer, in T Maunz, G Dürig *et al* (eds), *Grundgesetz*, Art 16, para 9 (rev edn 1985).

[44] Grawert, above n 38, 182 *et seq*.

[45] M Stolleis, 'Untertan—Bürger—Staatsbürger', in R Vierhaus (ed), *Bürger und Bürgerlichkeit im Zeitalter der Aufklärung* (1980), 65.

Expressed in terms of rights, they necessarily include protective citizens' rights of the *bourgeois* which aim to protect the individual against arbitrary interference by state authority. Historically, however, such rights were only limited to the states' own nationals for relatively short periods of time.[46] What is constitutive for a citizen's status are political rights, i.e. primarily the right to vote and stand for election. In historical comparison and in political theory they constitute the criterion of exclusion which distinguishes the fully effective status of a citizen from other forms of membership, especially from that of mere subjects.[47] Having regard to the consequences of industrialisation, English sociology first recognised that the status of a citizen also incorporates social rights.[48]

Citizenship may have its origin in political philosophy but this does not mean that it is not a legal concept. The German Basic Law employs it twice. Article 33(3) draws a distinction between civil (*bürgerlich*) and citizens' (*staatsbürgerlich*) rights and makes clear that both are independent of religious or other affiliation. Article 33(1) Basic Law guarantees all Germans equal political rights. According to the prevailing opinion, the people from whom all state authority derives according to Article 20(2) Basic Law, are German citizens eligible to vote.[49] This is equally so in other Union States.[50]

Empirically and legally, therefore, only nationals can be in full possession of all political rights. Those who stress that nationality serves as a criterion of exclusion, point to this connection between nationality and citizenship.[51] Whereas political philosophy sometimes refers to citizens being those who

[46] On the limitation of libertarian rights to nationals in the 19th century see G Oestreich, *Geschichte der Menschenrechte und Grundfreiheiten im Umriß* (1978) 81 *et seq.*

[47] Aristotle, *Politics*, 1275 a: "[A] ... citizen in the strictest sense ... shares in the administration of justice and in offices", quoted here according to S Everson (ed), *Aristotle, The Politics* (1989); on the individual epochs W Eder, 'Who Rules? Power and Participation in Athens and Rome', in A Molho *et al* (eds), *City-States in Classical Antiquity and Medieval Italy* (1991) 169; E Isenmann, *Die deutsche Stadt im Spätmittelalter 1250–1500* (1988) 93 *et seq*; R Brubaker, *Citizenship and Nationhood in France and Germany* (1992) 21 *et seq*; M Troper, 'The Concept of Citizenship in the Period of the French Revolution', in La Torre (ed), above n 38, 27 *et seq.*

[48] TH Marshall, *Citizenship and Social Class* (1949), here cited according to: TH Marshall and T Bottomore, *Citizenship and Social Class* (1992) 3 *et seq*; see also R Dahrendorf, 'The Changing Quality of Citizenship', in B van Steenbergen (ed), *The Condition of Citizenship* (1994) 10 at 13.

[49] *Entscheidungen des Bundesverfassungsgerichts* 83, 37 at 59 (*Ausländerwahlrecht* I).

[50] Concerning Art 88-3, 2nd sentence in connection with Arts 24 and 3 French Constitution see Conseil constitutionnel, CC no 92-308 DC, Rec 55 (*Maastricht* I); see also, eg, Art 48 Italian Constitution; Arts 23, 13 Spanish Constitution.

[51] See, eg, DM Smith and E Wistrich, 'Citizenship and Social Exclusion in the European Union', in M Roche and R van Berkel (eds), *Citizenship and Social Exclusion* (1997) 227.

wish to live in the same system,[52] full citizenship—in terms of constitutional law—requires naturalisation.[53]

c) Union Citizenship

aa) Nationality as a Condition for Union Citizenship Taking account of the guarantees contained in Articles 17-21 EC, it becomes clear that parallels to nationality are neither possible nor intended.[54] Article 17(1), 2nd sentence EC requires *nationality* by granting Union citizenship to those who are nationals of a Member State. The two are inseparable: Union citizenship cannot be acquired alone,[55] nor can it be forfeited without giving up nationality.[56]

As the Declaration to the Final Act of the Maastricht Treaty makes clear, the concept of nationality is determined by national law and not autonomously according to Community law.[57] Member States decide who is a Union citizen. A peculiarity in comparison with general international law lies in the fact that Member States must recognise such decisions on a mutual basis. In one case, an Italian-Argentine dual national wished to establish himself as a dentist in Spain following his studies in Argentina, his country of origin. The ECJ regarded the fact that Spanish law required effective nationality as incompatible with the prohibition of discrimination underlying the fundamental freedoms.[58] It might follow that nationals who possess another EU nationality may not be prejudiced in comparison with

[52] E Meehan, *Citizenship and the European Community* (1993) 123 *et seq*; J Habermas, 'Citizenship and National Identity', in van Steenbergen, above n 48, 20 at 23; C Closa, 'Citizenship of the Union and Nationality of Member States', (1995) 32 *CML Rev* 487 at 488 *et seq*, 507 *et seq*.

[53] *Entscheidungen des Bundesverfassungsgerichts* 83, 60 at 72 *et seq* (*Ausländerwahlrecht* II).

[54] Closa, above n 52, 488 *et seq*, 515 *et seq*; see also S Magiera, 'Die neuen Entwicklungen der Freizügigkeit für Personen: Auf dem Wege zu einem europäischen Bürgerstatut', (1992) *Europarecht* 433 at 446, with parallels to the *lex patriae* (*Indigenat*) introduced by German States in the 19th Century; similarly S Hobe, 'Die Unionsbürgerschaft nach dem Vertrag von Maastricht', (1993) 32 *Der Staat* 245 at 258 *et seq*; Hailbronner and Renner, above n 39, Introduction para 50; G-R de Groot, 'The Relationship between the Nationality Legislation of the Member States of the European Union and European Citizenship', in La Torre (ed), above n 38, 115 at 117; R Hofmann, 'German Citizenship Law and European Citizenship: Towards a Special Kind of Dual Nationality?', *ibid*, 149 at 163 *et seq*.

[55] Commission, above n 37, 8.

[56] Bavarian High Administrative Court, *Neue Zeitschrift für Verwaltungsrecht* (1999) 197; concerning possible limits in Community law to the deprivation of nationality see S Hall, 'Loss of Union Citizenship in Breach of Fundamental Rights', (1996) 21 *EL Rev* 129.

[57] Final Act to the Maastricht Treaty, Part III, 2nd Declaration (on nationality of a Member State); see also Conclusions of the European Council in Edinburgh, Bull EC 12-92, 26 *et seq*; with respect to British nationality law see Case C-192/99, *Kaur* [2001] ECR I-1237.

[58] Case C-369/90, *Micheletti* [1992] ECR I-4239.

beneficiaries of personal fundamental freedoms from other Member States either. Therefore, *discrimination à rebours*—which is otherwise not ruled out in the case law of the ECJ—is impermissible in such cases.[59] These consequences represent a departure from the principles drawn up by the International Court of Justice and referred to earlier. A further limit to the Member States' jurisdiction with respect to nationality law is set by the duty of loyalty to the Community (Article 10 EC), which prohibits Member States from obstructing a common immigration policy (Article 63 EC).[60]

bb) Union Citizenship as a Complement to State Citizenship Union citizenship is therefore based on a familiar foundation if it makes the creation of citizens' rights dependent on nationality. Article 17(1), 3rd sentence EC makes clear that the guaranteed rights are attached to those of citizens: "Citizenship of the Union shall complement and not replace national citizenship." This complementary element constitutes one of its crucial features.[61]

Union citizenship certainly aims to create political rights of participation with regard to the Union's sovereign powers which correspond to political rights in the state. This certainly applies to the basic right to participate in European elections (Article 190(4) EC) as well as the rights of petition, information and access to documents (Articles 21 and 255 EC). However, Union citizenship extends beyond this for the rights of Union citizens are not solely levelled against the Union and its institutions. Addressees of the freedom of movement (Article 18 EC) and the right to participate in European and municipal elections at the place of residence (Article 19(1) EC) are the Member States. To this extent, Union citizenship aims to ensure equal rights between nationals and members of other Union States throughout the Union. The provision on diplomatic-consular protection (Article 20 EC), also addressed to Member States, extends this status to the intergovernmental field of foreign affairs.

Thus, according to these Treaty provisions, the Union represents not only a supranational organisation but also a compound unit consisting of

[59] Case 235/87, *Matteucci* [1988] ECR 5589; for a case with French/German dual nationality see Case 292/86, *Gullung* [1988] ECR 11; generally U Wölker and G Grill, in H von der Groeben and J Schwarze (eds), *Vertrag über die Europäische Union und Vertrag zur Gründung der Europäischen Gemeinschaft* (2003), Art 39 EC, paras 9 *et seq.*

[60] This is a consequence of the reference of the ECJ in Case C-369/90, above n 58, para 10, that the Member States must make use of their powers "having due regard to Community law"; see A Hatje, in J Schwarze (ed), *Europäische Union* (2000), Art 17 EC, para 4.

[61] C Closa, 'The Concept of Citizenship in the Treaty on European Union', (1992) 29 *CML Rev* 1137; D O'Keefe, 'Union Citizenship', in D O'Keefe and PM Twomey (eds), *Legal Issues of the Maastricht Treaty* (1994) 87 at 102 *et seq.*

Member States, the European Communities and an overarching superstructure, i.e. a multi-level system.[62] Parallel considerations between national and Union citizenship only make sense against this background.

III. ELEMENTS OF UNION CITIZENSHIP IN POSITIVE LAW

1. Individual Rights Based on EC Law

According to Article 17(2) EC, citizens of the Union enjoy the rights conferred by the Treaty and are subject to the duties imposed thereby. Therefore, the rights of Union citizens are not limited to Articles 18-20 EC. References made in the EC Treaty to "this Treaty" also include the secondary law issued on its basis.[63]

a) Fundamental Freedoms

Since the free movement of goods does not only relate to persons but also to products, it is available to anyone whose economic activity falls within the scope of the EC Treaty. It does not depend on Union citizenship. The same applies in relation to the free movement of payment and capital, certain restrictions notwithstanding. By contrast, personal fundamental freedoms are based on the nationality of Member States (Articles 39(2), 43 and 49 EC). However, they may be extended to nationals of third states by international agreement.

It is important for understanding the relationship between fundamental freedoms and Union citizenship that the former require a cross-border reference, at least according to the case law of the ECJ. European citizens can only claim fundamental freedoms as against their own state if the latter intends to prevent them from exercising such rights.[64] Otherwise, domestic discrimination remains permissible.[65] The introduction of Union citizenship

[62] The German Federal Constitutional Court uses the term *Staatenverbund*, which may probably be translated as compound association of states, see *Entscheidungen des Bundesverfassungsgerichts* 89, 155 at 184, 190 (*Maastricht*), and which has a certain connotation to types of international organisations as founded under international law; the reciprocal relationships between intertwined levels of states and supranational structure are better expressed by the notion of multi-level constitutionalism as suggested by I Pernice, 'Europäisches und nationales Verfassungsrecht', (2001) 60 *Veröffentlichungen der Vereinigung Deutscher Staatsrechtslehrer* 148 at 163 *et seq*.

[63] As it is the case in Art 220 EC.

[64] Case 175/78, *Saunders* [1979] ECR 1129, para 11; Case C-112/91, *Werner* [1993] ECR I-429, para 17.

[65] Overview and further references in S Kadelbach, *Allgemeines Verwaltungsrecht unter europäischem Einfluß* (1999) 263 *et seq*.

has left the case law in this respect unaffected.[66] Hence it appears that freedoms are still understood as serving the creation of the common market. This does not comply with the concept of all citizens being equal before the law. The question as to whether provisions constituting Union citizenship also benefit State nationals and will eventually lead to the removal of domestic discrimination can only be answered by investigating the single guarantees individually. In any event, there is no reason to believe that fundamental freedoms represent a constitutive dimension of European citizens' rights. They amount to nothing more than their historical beginning, one of several components but have not lost their original functionalist purpose.[67]

b) Secondary Law: Union Citizens as Taxpayers, Welfare Recipients and Consumers

Broad concepts of European citizenship also include secondary law.[68] Like citizens within the national legal order, European citizens also possess rights for which nationality and thereby Union citizenship are not required. European citizens are therefore beneficiaries of rights guaranteed by Community law not only as national citizens of Member States, but because of further roles and identities. In their capacity as employees they enjoy protective rules under labour law and, as do self-employed individuals, possess the right of equal access to national welfare systems. They are affected by rules of other Europeanised legal areas in their capacity as taxpayers, consumers, students, victims of adverse environmental effects, addressees of legal measures concerning foreign nationals, members of minorities or simply as persons who have, need or spend money in the form of the new common currency. Why should the status of European citizenship not result from the sum of these rights?

Behind all of this, there is no settled idea concerning the rights a person has or should have by law. This is because there are different reasons for guaranteeing rights. On the European level, the harmonisation of indirect taxation as well as the establishment of employment and environmental standards were designed to create similar conditions of competition. In addition, provisions concerning consumer transactions improve transparency of cross-border competition between prices and terms. European co-ordinating social law facilitates the free movement of employees, the mobility of trainees and students being one of its pre-effects. Accordingly, some rights

[66] Case C-64/96, *Uecker* [1997] ECR I-3171, para 23.
[67] See above part II.1.
[68] Reich, above n 5, 76 *et seq.*

are granted to all those who reside, trade or buy products within the Community. Other rights concern the treatment of nationals and therefore can only be claimed by foreigners with EU nationality.

All this only affects the status of citizen insofar as that status must include the enjoyment of relevant rights on the basis of a general prohibition on discrimination (Article 12 EC). In this respect such rights are not different from personal rights granted by statute in national legal systems. The connection to the rights of Union citizens produced by Article 17(2) EC is therefore misleading. One can hardly claim that citizens have a system of rights to which this Treaty clause appears to refer.

2. Rights of Union Citizens

Therefore, the provisions of Articles 18-22 EC primarily determine the substance of Union citizenship.[69] It is difficult to assess their significance since the provisions have formed the subject of scientific discourse in very different areas. As the following will show, the question of their implementation involves—besides European law—aspects of constitutional law, local government law, administrative procedural law, international law and social law.

a) Freedom of Movement

Union citizenship attributes central significance to the right to move and reside freely within the territory of Member States (Article 18 EC), since this forms the pre-condition for exercising most fundamental freedoms and basic rights.[70] It aims at a general freedom of movement, independent from economic freedoms. A more detailed consideration proves that this aim has not yet been achieved.

The dispute which had arisen upon the introduction of this provision as to whether Article 18 EC was directly applicable has been decided. The ECJ, having deliberately avoided this question at first,[71] has now expressly recognised its direct effect.[72] Similarly, the prevailing opinion in academic

[69] For a comprehensive analysis see J-M Acker *et al*, 'Citoyenneté européenne', in Ecole nationale d'administration (ed), *Mise en œuvre du traité de Maastricht et construction européenne*, vol. 1 (1994), 323 *et seq*.

[70] Commission, above n 37, 15.

[71] Case C-85/96, *Martínez Sala* [1998] ECR I-2691, para 60; Case C-378/97, *Wijsenbeek* [1999] ECR I-6207, para 43; and Case C-274/96, *Bickel* [1998] ECR I-7637, para 15.

[72] Tendency towards direct effect in Case C-466/00, *Kaba I* [2000] ECR I-2623, para 30; Case C-357/98, *Yiadom* [2000] ECR I-9265, para 23; Case C-28/00, *Kauer* [2002] I-1343, para 45; clearly stated in Case C-413/99, *Baumbast* [2002] ECR I-7091, para 84.

writing has assumed that Article 18 EC takes direct effect.[73] The aim of expanding citizens' rights and a systematic comparison with the provisions in Articles 19 and 20 EC support this conclusion. On the one hand, the Council "may" adopt provisions further facilitating freedom of movement in accordance with Article 18(2) EC, whilst Article 19(1) and (2) EC clearly require it to adopt secondary legislation; granting discretion would invalidate the guarantee if it were not given direct effect. On the other hand, the Maastricht version of Articles 19 and 20 EC (formerly Articles 8b and 8c EC Treaty) laid down transposition periods for the Council and Member States. By contrast, Article 18 EC, formerly Article 8a EC Treaty, did not.

This finding alone does not lead far, however, since Article 18 EC does not go beyond the *acquis communautaire* in terms of content. The provision can only be invoked if none of the fundamental freedoms including all of their limitations is at issue.[74] Thus, it does not help to solve the problem of domestic discrimination.[75] Furthermore, existing "limitations and conditions" continue to apply. Conditions limiting the area of protection are, e.g., the evidence of adequate basic provisions and health insurance required by secondary law.[76] The continuing validity of public policy exceptions in Articles 39(3), 46 and 55 EC establish limitations which a fortiori apply to all those who cannot rely on one of the fundamental freedoms and which are filled out by the Member States.

Accordingly, it seems as if one hand takes away what the other has just granted. However, there are four differences found in comparison to the former legal situation. The first is that the freedom of movement is being placed on a constitutional basis. Now, even persons who do not exercise any fundamental freedoms such as those seeking employment, students and pensioners whose rights of residence have hitherto been based on secondary law can claim a guarantee anchored in the Treaty which thus can be described as a fundamental right.[77] Secondary law is to be interpreted in

[73] J Wouters, 'European Citizenship and the Case Law of the Court of Justice of the European Communities on the Free Movement of Persons', in Marias, above n 12, 25 at 48 *et seq*; M Haag, in von der Groeben and Schwarze, above n 59, Art 18 EC, para 7; W Kluth, in C Calliess and M Ruffert (eds), *Kommentar EUV/EGV* (2002), Art 18 EC, para 9; Hatje, above n 60, Art 18 EC, para 5; M Hilf, in E Grabitz and M Hilf (eds), *Das Recht der Europäischen Union* (looseleaf, last update 2001), Art 18 EC, para 1; against M Degen, 'Die Unionsbürgerschaft nach dem Vertrag über die europäische Union unter besonderer Berücksichtigung des Wahlrechts', (1993) *Die öffentliche Verwaltung* 749 at 752; M Pechstein and A Bunk, 'Das Aufenthaltsrecht als Auffangrecht', (1997) *Europäische Grundrechte-Zeitschrift* 547.

[74] See, eg, Case C-92/01, *Stylianakis* [2003] ECR I-1291, para 18.

[75] See above nn 65, 66.

[76] Art 1 Dir 90/364/EEC, Dir 90/365/EEC and Dir 93/96/EEC, respectively, above n 32; see also Case C-466/01, *Kaba II* [2003] ECR I-2219, para 46.

[77] Art II-45 CT-Conv (Art 105 CT-IGC).

light of this freedom. Second, Article 18(2) EC now provides a uniform legal basis for the adoption of secondary law on the freedom of movement thereby removing existing uncertainty concerning the proper bases of competences.[78] For this purpose, Article 18(2) EC allows measures facilitating the freedom of movement but no new restrictions.[79] Third, the Court takes Article 18 EC as a reason to construe exceptions to free movement rights even more narrowly than before.[80] Fourth, Article 18 EC offers the ECJ a reference point to extend social and cultural rights to all those legally residing in the territory of the Member State concerned by means of judge-made law and on the basis of the general prohibition of discrimination contained in Article 12 EC.[81]

Therefore, Article 18 EC certainly heralds an enhancement and extension of the freedom of movement but has not changed its *acquis communautaire* in terms of substance. As of today, there are still restrictions on the freedom of movement within the Union.

b) Political Rights

Article 19 EC grants Union citizens resident in Member States, of which they are not nationals, the right to vote and to stand as candidates at municipal (Article 19(1) EC) and European elections (Article 19(2) EC). The bearings on Union law are different in each case. Whilst Article 19(1) EC is closely connected to the right of free movement (Article 18 EC), Article 19(2) EC is also important in relation to the legitimacy of the Union's exercise of powers—even if this is not immediately obvious.

aa) The Right to Vote and to be Elected on the Local Level The right to vote at municipal elections is regarded as facilitating the freedom of movement. It aims to compensate for the loss of political involvement at local level caused by leaving the country of origin and to make integration easier by ensuring equal rights with nationals of the host state.[82] The opportunity to participate in decisions at local level, which has the most obvious consequences for citizens at all levels of state organisation, can make it easier to accommodate in another environment.

The right to vote at municipal elections has an important constitutional aspect. As in France, Spain and Portugal, implementing that right in

[78] On the repeal of Dir 90/366/EEC above n 32; until recently, there existed two Regulations and nine Directives on the right to entry and residence; they are now consolidated in Dir 2004/38/EC on the right of citizens of the Union and their family members to move and reside freely within the territories of the Member States, OJ L 158, 30.4.2004, 77.

[79] Haag, above n 73, Art 18 EC, para 17; Hatje, above n 60, Art 18 EC, para 13.

[80] Cases C-482/01 and C-493/01, *Orfanopoulos* [2004] ECR I-5257, para 65.

[81] Case C-85/96, above n 71, para 60; see also below part III 3 c).

[82] Degen, above n 73, 749.

Germany required a constitutional amendment.[83] According to the leading interpretation of the relevant provisions of the Basic Law, only German nationals may exercise the right to vote at elections.[84] The sovereignty of the people (Articles 20(2) and 28(1) Basic Law), which refers to the German people, is indeed entrenched according to the eternity clause of Article 79(3) Basic Law, defining the core elements of the Constitution as unchangeable, but the dependency between nationality and the right to vote at municipal elections does not belong to this reserve.[85] This is basically because the representative bodies of municipalities are believed to form part of the executive and not the legislature.[86] The right of Union citizens to vote at municipal elections was therefore facilitated by introducing a new Article 28(1), 3rd sentence Basic Law. The transposition of the Directive on municipal elections[87] comes within the jurisdiction of the States and has now been accomplished. For now, the German *Länder* have resolved the dispute in literature as to whether the right to vote at municipal elections may also extend to local referenda,[88] pursuant to a right of participation.[89]

The introduction of the right to vote at municipal elections had been planned for a long time.[90] From a legal point of view it influenced the

[83] For France see R Kovar and D Simon, 'La citoyenneté européenne', (1993) *Cahiers de Droit Européen* 285 at 304 *et seq*; for Spain see A Lopez Castillo and J Polakiewicz, 'Verfassung und Gemeinschaftsrecht in Spanien', (1993) *Europäische Grundrechte-Zeitschrift* 277; for Portugal see Lopes Marinho, in F Laursen and S Vanhoonacker (eds), *The Ratification of the Maastricht Treaty* (1994) 231; with respect to the transposition in the other Union States see K Hasselbach, 'Europäisches Kommunalwahlrecht', (1997) *Zeitschrift für Gesetzgebung* 49 at 64 *et seq*.

[84] *Entscheidungen des Bundesverfassungsgerichts* 83, 37 (right of non-nationals to vote in the *Land* of Schleswig-Holstein); *Entscheidungen des Bundesverfassungsgerichts* 83, 60 (right of non-nationals to vote in Hamburg).

[85] *Entscheidungen des Bundesverfassungsgerichts* 83, 37 at 59 (*Ausländerwahlrecht* I); Federal Constitutional Court (*Bundesverfassungsgericht*), *Neue Zeitschrift für Verwaltungsrecht* (1998) 52.

[86] See, eg, *Entscheidungen des Bundesverfassungsgerichts* 65, 283 at 289.

[87] Dir 94/80/EC laying down detailed arrangements for the exercise of the right to vote and to stand as a candidate in municipal elections by citizens of the Union residing in a Member State of which they are not nationals, OJ L 368, 31.12.1994, 38, as amended in OJ L 122, 22.5.1996, 14.

[88] The opposite view was taken by the Federal Minister of the Interior in a circular addressed to the *Länder* of 30th January 1995, unpubl, quoted in K Engelken, 'Einbeziehung der Unionsbürger in kommunale Abstimmungen (Bürgerentscheide, Bürgerbegehren)?', (1995) *Neue Zeitschrift für Verwaltungsrecht* 432 at 433, n 6; furthermore see, eg, M Kaufmann, 'Kommunales Unionsbürgerwahlrecht und kommunaler Staatsaufbau', (1998) *Zeitschrift für Gesetzgebung* 25 at 31 *et seq*; but see as in the present text H-U Erichsen, *Kommunalrecht Nordrhein-Westfalen* (1997) 84; K Barley, *Das Wahlrecht der Ausländer nach der Neuordnung des Art. 28 Abs. 1 S. 3 GG* (1999) 73 *et seq*.

[89] See, eg, the Constitution of Baden-Wuerttemberg Art 72; the Local Communities Acts (*Gemeindeordnungen*) of Hesse § 30; of Rhineland Palatine §§ 17a, 13; of Saxony §§ 24, 16; of North-Rhine Westphalia §§ 26, 21, here in connection with § 7 Municipal Elections Act.

[90] Above n 31; concerning the pre-history until 1972 Haag, above n 73, Art 19 EC, paras 3 *et seq*.

organisation of the state and represented a clear break with the constitutional traditions of some Member States. Regardless of the practical importance which the right to vote at municipal elections has for the approximately five million citizens resident outside their country of origin, it indicates that the Union has become a constitutive factor in the organisation of sovereign power in the European multi-level system.

bb) Right to Vote and to Stand for Elections to the European Parliament

The right to vote at European elections is only related to the right to vote at municipal elections insofar as it guarantees certain rights of political participation in the place of residence. Article 19(2) EC enables, for example, a Portuguese to participate in the election of the 99 delegates allotted to Germany (Article 190(2) EC). Thereby, the right to vote at European elections only differentiates with respect to nationals of third party states according to nationality, but within the Union exclusively according to the place of residence. The electorate is constituted by the citizens of the Union and not by the peoples of European states. This exclusive link to Union citizenship is a natural consequence of establishing direct elections to the European Parliament. However, reservations are expressed in this regard, i.e. that the success threshold—distributed unequally between Member States anyway—will be further reduced to the detriment of under-represented states.[91] The German Federal Constitutional Court has nevertheless not pursued such objections.[92] They are also untenable, even more so in light of the insignificant participation at elections.[93]

Like the right to vote at municipal elections, the right to vote at European elections, according to the wording of Article 19(2) EC, only extends to Union citizens who reside outside their state of origin. However, that provision cannot intend to place citizens residing abroad in a privileged position so that it must also confer a right to vote on nationals as well. The case law of the European Court of Human Rights concerning Article 3 of the 3rd Protocol to the ECHR also suggests such a conclusion. It deems the European Parliament to be entrusted with genuine legislative functions so that contracting states must ensure an election to that end.[94]

The procedures are set forth in the Directive on European elections.[95] It stresses the intention behind Article 19 EC to expand the rights of Union

[91] See, eg, R Streinz, *Europarecht* (2003) paras 54, 306; similarly M Dürig, 'Das neue Wahlrecht für Unionsbürger bei den Wahlen zum Europäischen Parlament', (1994) *Neue Zeitschrift für Verwaltungsrecht* 1180 at 1181 *et seq.*

[92] See *Bundesverfassungsgericht*, *Europäische Grundrechte-Zeitschrift* (1995) 566.

[93] Figures in Commission, above n 37, 18.

[94] ECHR, *Matthews v United Kingdom* Rep 1999-I 251, para 52.

[95] Dir 93/109/EC laying down detailed arrangements for the exercise of the right to vote and to stand as a candidate in elections to the European Parliament for citizens of the Union residing in a Member State of which they are not nationals, OJ L 329, 30.12.1993, 34.

citizens by allowing citizens to exercise the right to vote at elections in the country of origin instead of the place of residence. However, it did not aim to establish the planned uniform election procedure (Article 190(4) EC). The Directive is limited to questions concerning the personal right to vote at elections such as the application principle and to excluding multiple elections and candidates.

Article 19(2) EC is significant because it grants a personal component to the right to vote at European elections which to date has been conceived in purely institutional terms at European level (Article 190(1) and (3) EC: "representatives ... shall be elected").[96] Nationality is no longer a crucial factor in that respect. Thus, the EC Treaty is moving towards the notion of a European *demos*.[97] More than any other component of Union citizenship, this provision triggers considerations concerning the role Union citizens could play in organising the expression of will in Europe. This will be investigated in detail under IV below.

c) Petition, Information, Access to Documents

Union citizens—like all residents within Union territory—are granted a series of rights which can and should be attributed an auxiliary function in connection with active citizens' rights. This is true for the right of petition and the right to appeal to an ombudsman (Article 21(1) and (2) in conjunction with Articles 194 and 195 EC), the right to information (Article 21(3) EC), introduced by the Treaty of Amsterdam, and access to documents (Article 255 EC), adopted by the EC Treaty at the same time. These rights are listed together in the Charter of Fundamental Rights (Articles II-42-44 CT-Conv; Articles 102-104 CT-IGC).

The right to file a petition contains a guarantee which performs two functions in a national context. On the one hand, it is regarded as a link between the citizens and their Parliament which opens up a certain possibility of political influence.[98] On the other hand, it provides legal protection since it offers the opportunity to pursue individual matters outside formal legal remedies. At the European level, it expressly refers to all matters for which the Community is responsible but it is the practice of the Parliament to extend it to the whole Union.[99] Therefore, the substance of the guarantee

[96] Kovar and Simon, above n 83, 307.

[97] See also A Rosas, 'Union Citizenship and National Elections', in A Rosas and E Antola (eds), *A Citizen's Europe* (1995), 135; Weiler, above n 7, 74; R Rubio Marín, 'Equal Citizenship and the Difference Residence Makes', in La Torre (ed), above n 38, 201; M-J Garot, 'A New Basis for European Citizenship: Residence?', *ibid*, 229.

[98] H Bauer, in H Dreier (ed), *Grundgesetz Kommentar*, vol I (1996), Art 17 para 12.

[99] Rule 174 of the Rules of Procedure of the European Parliament.

is widely drawn. Nevertheless, more than half of the petitions do not pass the threshold of permissibility.[100] Most cases will lack the required personal impact.

The right to appeal to an ombudsman stresses the protective aspect of the right to complain. On this procedural path, wrongs committed by Union institutions in the course of their activities can be investigated. The responsibilities of the ombudsman extend beyond those of the Community to the so-called third pillar, i.e. co-operation with police and the courts in criminal cases. The concept of maladministration in Article 21(2) EC closely corresponds with the principles of "good administration" to which Article II-41 CT-Conv (Article 101 CT-IGC) refers.[101] These guarantees may help to increase discipline in the performance of official tasks and form a core set of rights designed to implement the idea of democratic governance.[102]

The right to information contained in Article 21(3) EC fits into this context. At first glance, it offers nothing more than the right to use one's mother tongue before the Community institutions or the ombudsman and to receive an answer in that language provided it is one of the Community languages (Article 314 EC).[103] Whether the right is limited to this formal aspect depends on the conditions which the answer requested must satisfy. The Union has expressly committed itself to more citizens' rights and greater transparency (12th recital of the Preamble, Article 1(2) EU, and Article 255 EC), which suggests an interpretation extending beyond the right to use one's own language. It represents a claim to information,[104] the content of which will depend not only on the matter in question but also on legitimate interests in confidentiality (Article 287 EC).

[100] Commission, above n 37, 20 *et seq*; the numerical significance is low (958 in the 1999/2000 session), with a continuing downward tendency.

[101] R Bauer, *Das Recht auf eine gute Verwaltung im Europäischen Gemeinschafsrecht* (2002); M Bullinger, 'Das Recht auf eine gute Verwaltung nach der Grundrechtecharta der EU', in E Eberle *et al* (eds), *Der Wandel des Staates vor den Herausforderungen der Gegenwart: Festschrift W Brohm* (2003), 25; A Guckelberger, 'Das Petitionsrecht zum Europäischen Parlament sowie das Recht zur Anrufung des Europäischen Bürgerbeauftragten im Europa der Bürger', (2003) *Die öffentliche Verwaltung* 829 at 834 *et seq*; K Kanska, 'Towards Administrative Human Rights in the EU', (2004) 10 *ELJ* 296.

[102] S Kadelbach, 'Verwaltungskontrollen im Mehrebenen-System der Europäischen Gemeinschaft', in E Schmidt-Aßmann and W Hoffmann-Riem (eds), *Verwaltungskontrolle* (2001) 205 at 220.

[103] However, the guarantee is confined to the institutions referred to in that article or mentioned in Art 7 EC and cannot be invoked against agencies, see Case T-120/99, *Kik v Office for the Harmonisation of the Internal Market (OHIM)* [2001] ECR II-2235, para 64, sustained on appeal in Case C-361/01 P, *Kik v OHIM* [2003] ECR, I-8283, para 83.

[104] W Kaufmann-Bühler, in CO Lenz and K-D Borchardt (ed), *EU- und EG-Vertrag* (2003), Art 21 EC, para 2; Hatje, above n 60, Art 21 EC, para 4; Hilf, above n 73, Art 21 EC, para 1.

The claim to information overlaps in part with the right of access to documents in the possession of the institutions enumerated in Article 255, i.e. Council, Commission and Parliament. The personal right of citizens referred to in Article 255 EC forms a relatively new instrument of monitoring administrative practice.[105] It stems from self-commitments of the institutions and has been further defined in a Transparency Regulation based on Article 255(2) EC.[106] The rule is that individuals must be granted access without having to prove a special interest. However, the Transparency Regulation sets out interests in confidentiality which can be raised against this law. Such exceptions include public security, defence, foreign relations and financial, currency and economic policy, as well as the protection of privacy, in particular data protection.[107] In addition, access can be refused in order to protect economic interests of a judicial or investigative procedure. Finally, there is no right to access documents of a preparatory character or such information which may only be distributed with the consent of a Member State. This Regulation has been criticised for being too restrictive.[108] But case law interprets exceptions narrowly. The ECJ refers to the Transparency Regulation as a law that contributes substantially to a status of active citizenship, enhances participation of the Union's citizens in the decision-making processes, provides for more legitimacy, efficiency and accountability of public administration in a democratic system and strengthens respect for fundamental rights.[109]

Such rights to control and information are indispensable for an administration which is close to the citizens. Some of them can also breathe new life into the administrative traditions of many Member States which only recognise a restricted access of the public to information. As with the participation of Union citizens in elections, however, such rights are relatively little used.[110] This particularly applies in relation to the right of access to

[105] See J Shaw, 'European Citizenship: The IGC and Beyond', (1996) 3 *EPL* 413 at 430 *et seq.*

[106] Reg 1049/2001 regarding public access to European Parliament, Council and Commission documents, OJ L 145, 30.5.2001, 43; Art 255 EC itself does not have direct effect, see Case T-191/99, *Petrie et al v Commission* [2001] ECR II-3677, para 34.

[107] *Ibid*, Art 4(1) in connection with Dir 95/46/EC on the protection of individuals with regard to the procession of personal data and on the free movement of such data, OJ L 281, 23.11.1995, 31, as amended in OJ L 284, 31.10.2003, 1; see also Art I-50 CT-Conv (Art 51 CT-IGC); generally A Hatje, 'Datenaustausch und Datenschutz in der EU', in S Magiera and KP Sommermann (eds), *Verwaltung in der Europäischen Union* (2001) 193 at 205 *et seq.*

[108] ME de Leeuw, 'The Regulation on public access to European Parliament, Council and Commission documents in the European Union: are citizens better off?', (2003) 28 *EL Rev* 324.

[109] Case C-41/00 P, *Interporc* [2003] I-2125, para 39; for cases under the old law see S Kadelbach, Case Note, (2001) 38 *CML Rev* 179.

[110] For figures Commission, above n 37, 20 and 22, where, however, they are evaluated more optimistically.

information. The Commission is conscious of this problem and attempts to confront it by making citizens aware of their rights to participation.[111] Ultimately, the rapprochement of the Union to its citizens encounters non-legal limits.

d) Protection by Diplomatic and Consular Authorities

Article 20 EC aims to open up a completely different dimension of personal rights. Union States' diplomatic and consular authorities must grant all Union citizens protection in states outside the Union in which their home state is not represented. Co-operation between diplomatic and consular representatives forms part of the common foreign and security policy (Article 20 EU). Article 20 EC therefore expresses the joint responsibility of Union States. In order to understand this provision, it is useful to remind oneself that, when the Maastricht Treaty entered into force, there were only five states in which all Union States were represented.[112] The concern to improve the position of tourists and business people abroad appears citizen-friendly. However, the extent and applicability of this guarantee are fraught with uncertainties which mitigate its effectiveness.

To begin with, it is not wholly clear what kind of protection is to be provided. The German text version refers to "diplomatic and consular protection" (*diplomatischer und konsularischer Schutz*). According to practice in international law, consular protection primarily embraces administrative activity such as issuing passports, supporting citizens in matters relating to family and inheritance law, providing representation before a court and legal aid etc.[113] These tasks can be directly performed by other states acting in a representative capacity.[114]

By contrast, diplomatic protection, as a technical term, refers to the situation where a state supports its own nationals in relation to breaches of international law by another state.[115] This activity focuses on taking up compensation claims of individuals arising from a shortfall in the minimum established by legal practice with regard to the protection of life, personal integrity and property. If the home state assumes its national's demand for reparation against the responsible state, then, at least according to the traditional understanding of international law, it effectively pursues its own

[111] Discussion paper on public access to Commission documents of 23 April 1999, SG.C.2/VJ/CD D (99) 83.

[112] Second Commission Report Citizenship of the Union, COM(1997) 230 final, 11.

[113] See Art 5 Vienna Convention on Consular Relations of 24 April 1963 (VCCR), United Nations Treaty Series 596, 261.

[114] Art 8 VCCR.

[115] Gloria, above n 40, § 24 paras 32 *et seq.*

claim.[116] If a third state wishes to pursue this claim, the consent of the claimant and the defendant states is required.[117]

It thereby becomes clear that Article 20 EC cannot guarantee a right to diplomatic protection *strictu sensu* to individuals. However, the substance of that guarantee does not extend to diplomatic protection in the classical sense either—contrary to its German wording which is apparently clear but actually misleading.[118] This is borne out by the versions in other authentic languages which refer to "protection by the diplomatic or consular authorities" ("protection par la part des autorités diplomatiques et consulaires" etc.). The context in which the term "diplomatic protection" is used in international law also opposes such an interpretation. Diplomatic protection does not require the victim's state of origin to maintain an embassy in the defendant state nor must the claim be brought on that state's territory. By contrast, protection by diplomatic authorities can also be consular protection,[119] to which existing transposition law has been limited.[120]

Article 20 EC is limited not only in substance but also in effect. Sentence 2 of the provision obliges Member States to agree upon the "necessary rules" and to start "international negotiations". A view which attributes Article 20 EC direct effect is hardly tenable in the light of this provision.[121] The first steps to implement the claim to protection were three decisions by the Member States which, for their part, require adoption by national law.[122] This has not yet happened. More than a decade after what is now

[116] *Greece v United Kingdom (Mavrommatis Palestine Concessions)*, PCIJ Series [1924] A No 2 at 12; *Liechtenstein v Guatemala* , above n 41, 24.

[117] *Belgium v Spain (Barcelona Traction Light and Power)* [1970] ICJ Rep 2 at 47.

[118] On the intention C Jiménez Piernas, 'La protección diplomática y consular del ciudadano de la Unión Europea', (1993) 20 *Revista de las Instituciónes Europeas* 9 at 17 *et seq*; J Weyland, 'La protection diplomatique et consulaire des citoyens de l'Union européenne', in Marias, above n 12, 63 at 64; M Ruffert, 'Diplomatischer und konsularischer Schutz zwischen Völker- und Europarecht', (1997) 35 *Archiv des Völkerrechts* 459 at 465, 472, and 476; for a view following the international law concept of diplomatic protection Haag, above n 73, Art 20 EC, paras 6 *et seq*; T Stein, 'Die Regelung des diplomatischen Schutzes im Vertrag über die Europäische Union', in G Ress and T Stein (eds), *Der diplomatische Schutz im Völker- und Europarecht*, (1996) 97; S Magiera, in R Streinz (ed), *EUV/EGV*, Art 20 EC, para 6.

[119] Art 3 2nd sentence VCCR, above n 113; Art 3(2) of the Vienna Convention on Diplomatic Relations of 18 April 1961, United Nations Treaty Series 500, 95.

[120] Art 5(1) Dec 95/553 regarding protection for citizens of the European Union by diplomatic and consular representations, OJ L 314, 28.12.1995, 73; Dec on practical arrangements to be made by consular officials, unpubl; Dec 96/409 on the establishment of an emergency travel document, OJ L 168, 6.7.1996, 4; see also the "Guidelines for the Protection of Unrepresented EC Nationals by EC Missions in Third Countries", publ as Doc 7142/94, PESC 161, COCON 2 of the General Secretary of the Council of 24 May 1994.

[121] Similarly Closa, above n 52, 502 *et seq*; Kaufmann-Bühler, above n 104, Art 20 EC, para 3; against U Everling, in R Hrbek (ed), *Bürger und Europa* (1994) 49 at 62; Ruffert, above n 118, 471 *et seq*; P Szczekalla, 'Die Pflicht der Gemeinschaft und der Mitgliedstaaten zum diplomatischen und konsularischen Schutz', (1999) *Europarecht* 325 at 327 *et seq*.

[122] Above n 120.

Article 20 EC entered into force, Member States have still not been able to grant it effective force.

Accordingly, Article 20 EC—like Article 18 EC—seems to promise more than it can deliver for the time being. Consular protection and auxiliary services of diplomatic protection can already be provided by third states according to applicable international law. Article 20 EC may have potential insofar as it could serve as an incentive for the Member States to cut on expenditures for diplomatic missions and personnel.[123] However, this would not have much to do with the motive of strengthening citizens' rights.

3. Rights of Union Citizens and Prohibition of Discrimination

a) The Link Between Union Citizenship and the General Prohibition of Discrimination

The Commission regards the prohibition of discrimination because of nationality (Article 12 EC) as belonging to the catalogue of Union citizen's rights. In its report on Union citizenship the Commission also refers to initiatives against discrimination on other grounds.[124]

For an analysis of the impact Article 12 EC has on Union citizenship, it is useful to recall its wording. Accordingly, "without prejudice to any special provisions contained [in this Treaty], any discrimination on grounds of nationality shall be prohibited". Most rights of Union citizens aim at national treatment, either expressly (Articles 19 and 20 EC) or implicitly (Article 18 EC). Therefore, they in effect prohibit Member States from discriminating on grounds of nationality just like Article 12 EC. Technically, requirements of equal treatment contained in Articles 18-21 EC thus take precedence as "special provisions" over the general principle of equality under Article 12 EC. On the other hand, they also belong to the "scope of application of this Treaty", and Article 17(2) EC refers to the "rights conferred by this Treaty", which, in turn, include Article 12 EC.

The ECJ has derived far-reaching consequences from such reciprocal linking. The guiding idea of its case law is that Union citizens who reside in the territory of a Union State on a regular basis can rely on Article 12 EC in all cases within the objective scope of the EC Treaty.[125] The consequences are hard to predict. For now, they mainly concern social and cultural rights.

[123] Hilf, above n 73, Art 20 EC, para 3.

[124] Commission, above n 37, 26 *et seq*.

[125] Case C-85/96, above n 71, para 62; critical C Tomuschat, Case Note, (2000) 37 *CML Rev* 449.

b) Derivative Social Rights

Although Community law does not grant any original claims under social welfare law, it does establish the inclusion of certain groups of persons into the national systems of welfare benefits, subject to requirements which vary according to legal basis. Up to now, access to national social security schemes was open to beneficiaries of free movement rights and their relatives. The same rules can apply in relation to those seeking employment, trainees or retired persons. However, it was always necessary to display a connection to one of the personal fundamental freedoms.

In its case law following the *Sala* decision, the ECJ has uncoupled such benefits from the requirement of a right of residence which is connected to the fundamental freedoms and attached them to the status of Union citizen. Regardless of whether Article 18 EC directly confers a right of residence or not, the Court supports a claim to share social welfare rights by this provision in conjunction with Article 12 EC in relation to all Union citizens who legally reside in the relevant Member State.[126]

Since residence—as in the *Sala* case—can also be based on national law Member States are free to take measures terminating it. The flipside of this case law could therefore be a more restrictive practice by immigration authorities in the Member States than before.[127] However, it must be observed that Community law similarly governs domestic law regulating foreign nationals. Here, account is taken of the "limitations and conditions", referred to in Article 18 EC. However, the need for social aid is not by itself sufficient to justify expulsion.[128] In the *Grzelczyk* case, a French student had become dependent on social welfare in the fourth year of study after having financed himself for three years. The ECJ held that this could not lead to automatic expulsion because the receipt of benefit was only temporary in nature.[129] In a recent judgment, the Court affirmed that Member States are not prohibited to maintain statutes according to which the granting of aid

[126] Case C-85/96, above n 71, para 63.

[127] S Fries and J Shaw, 'Citizenship of the Union: First Steps in the European Court of Justice', (1998) 4 *EPL* 533 at 553; S O'Leary, 'European Communities and EEA', (1999) 24 *EL Rev* 68 at 78; H Toner, 'Judicial Interpretation of European Union Citizenship', (2000) 7 *MJ* 158 at 179 *et seq*.

[128] According to K-D Borchardt, 'Der sozialrechtliche Gehalt der Unionsbürgerschaft', (2000) *Neue Juristische Wochenschrift* 2057 at 2059 *et seq*, only if the right of residence is used in order to receive higher welfare benefits; in a narrower sense A Randelzhofer and A Forsthoff, in Grabitz and Hilf, above n 73, Art 39 EC, para 193.

[129] For an example of inadequate application of the residence principle see Case C-184/99, *Grzelczyk* [2001] ECR I-6193, paras 34 *et seq*, abandoning Case 197/86, *Brown* [1988] ECR 3205, according to which the guarantee of subsistence for students did not fall within the scope of what is now Art 12 EC according to the state of Community law at the time; see commentary by C Jacqueson, 'Union citizenship and the Court of Justice', (2002) 27 *EL Rev* 260 at 268 *et seq*.

to those seeking employment is restricted to persons who have resided for a minimum period of time within their respective territories, provided such laws are based on clear criteria known in advance and effective remedies are at hand.[130]

For those who reside lawfully in one of the Member States, the *Sala* doctrine might have considerable consequences in the area of social law. The prohibition of discrimination contained in Article 12 together with Article 18 EC constitutes a comprehensive general clause which covers virtually all areas where application of national law concerns the lawful presence of individuals in a Member State. In the *D'Hoop* case, where the Court held that nobody should suffer disadvantages from crossing borders within the Union with respect to transitional unemployment benefits, it becomes manifest that nationality loses its significance as a criterion of social welfare law and gradually gives way to the residence principle.[131] The general concept is that discrimination on the basis of residence requires special justification.[132] Based on the case law just outlined, some derive a legal right of Union citizens to basic social security.[133] However, analysis in legal writing is only at its initial stages and case law is constantly developing.[134]

c) Derivative Cultural Rights

The right to use one's own language provides a further example of the almost boundless potential of this case law. The ECJ granted German and Austrian defendants—against whom criminal proceedings had been commenced in the Trentino-South Tyrol region—a claim to have proceedings

[130] Case C-138/02, *Collins* [2004] ECR I-2703, paras 61 *et seq*.

[131] Case C-224/98, *D'Hoop* [2002] ECR I-6191, paras 27 *et seq*; see also N Reich and S Harbacevica, 'Citizenship and family on trial: a fairly optimistic overview of recent court practice with regard to free movement of persons', (2003) 40 *CML Rev* 615 at 619 *et seq*; F David, 'La citoyenneté de l'Union, statut fondamental des ressortisants des Etats members', (2003) *Revue Trimestrielle de Droit Européen* 561; A Iliopoulou and H Toner, 'A new approach to discrimination against free movers?', (2003) 28 *EL Rev* 389 at 395.

[132] In the *Pusa* Case, a retired Finnish citizen decided to take residence in Spain. Execution orders by Finnish authorities seized a considerable part of his pension. Since taxes collected in Spain were not taken into account in computing the amount which was free of seizure, the result was that the remainder was lower than it had been if he had stayed in Finland. The Court decided that such an effect amounted to indirect discrimination and violated Art 18 EC, see Case C-224/02, *Pusa* [2004] ECR I-5763, paras 29 *et seq*.

[133] S Staeglich, 'Rechte und Pflichten aus der Unionsbürgerschaft', (2003) *Zeitschrift für Europa-Studien* 485 at 517; against S Bode, 'Von der Freizügigkeit zur sozialen Grundsicherung aller Unionsbürger?', (2003) *Europäische Zeitschrift für Wirtschaftsrecht* 552.

[134] Extensive consequences are drawn by Borchardt, above n 128, 2057 *et seq*; more reserved Randelzhofer and Forsthoff, above n 128, paras 189 *et seq*; critical R Kanitz and P Steinberg, 'Grenzenloses Gemeinschaftsrecht?', (2003) *Europarecht* 1013 at 1016 *et seq*.

held in their mother tongue.[135] The basis for the prohibition on discrimination according to Article 12 in conjunction with Article 18 EC was provided by Italian law which granted such a claim to members of the German-speaking community resident in the province of Bolzano. The case was distinguishable from the existing decisions on social security law because criminal law does not come within the scope of the EC Treaty. Apparently, this legal development is borne by the status of Union citizen alone.

In another case, union citizenship was linked with aspects of privacy. Garcia Avello, a Spanish citizen residing in Belgium and married to a Belgian, wanted his children—who held dual nationality—to be named in the Spanish tradition; i.e. that they be given two second names which was contrary to Belgian practice. The Court held that it involved serious disadvantages if dual nationals would have to bear names under two different legal systems; this discrimination was not justified.[136]

Speculation abounds as to the consequences which such an extension of rights might have. The Court has repeatedly held that "Union citizenship is destined to be the fundamental status of nationals of the Member States, enabling those who find themselves in the same situation to enjoy the same treatment in law irrespective of their nationalities".[137] The case law allows for ambivalent analysis. On the one hand, this statement should not lead to the assumption that there is complete equality before the law. So far, Union citizenship has not created any original rights to social welfare benefit. With respect to minority rights, there is no reason for assuming a general claim to the use of one's mother tongue before national courts of other Member States[138] or to enhanced rights of defendants in procedures before EU institutions such as, for example, in EC competition law.[139] Finally, the cases decided to date do not contribute anything new to the long-known problem of domestic discrimination. On the other hand, this observation notwithstanding, the judgments reported demonstrate that the Court is knotting an ever tighter net between Union citizenship and fundamental rights.

[135] Case C-274/96, above n 71, paras 16, 23 *et seq*; A Gattini, (1999) 82 *Rivista di Diritto Internazionale* 106.

[136] Case C-148/02, *Garcia Avello* [2003] ECR I-11613, paras 35 *et seq*.

[137] Case C-184/99, above n 129, para 31; Case C-224/98, above n 131, para 28; C-413/99, above n 72, para 82; Case C-148/02, above n 136, para 22; Case C-138/02, above n 130, para 61; Cases C-482/01 and C-493/01, above n 80, para 65; Case C-224/02, above n 131, para 16.

[138] But see P Hilpold, 'Unionsbürgerschaft und Sprachenrechte in der EU', (2000) *Juristische Blätter* 93 at 99; N Reich, 'Union Citizenship—Metaphor or Source of Rights?', (2001) 7 *ELJ* 4 at 13 *et seq*; critical F Palermo, 'The Use of Minority Languages: Recent Developments in EC Laws and Judgments of the ECJ', (2001) 8 *MJ* 299 at 312 *et seq*. The right to obtain the free assistance of a translator still forms the minimum standard according to Art 6(3) lit a and e of the European Convention of Human Rights.

[139] Case T-9/99, *HFB Holding für Fernmeldetechnik et al v Commission* [2002] ECR II-1487, para 331.

4. The Relationship Between Union Citizenship and Fundamental Rights

As has been pointed out, Articles 18-21 EC do not define Union citizenship exhaustively. The general reference in Article 17(2) EC to all rights and duties of Community law has already been examined in connection with secondary law. Furthermore, it has been stressed that written primary and secondary law does not by itself enhance citizen status. This effect was only achieved by the Court's rulings. The linking of Union citizenship with freedom from discrimination, one of the few fundamental rights set forth in the EC Treaty, represents an important step towards a legal cross-connection between Union citizenship and fundamental rights.[140] This provision raises the question as to how each relates to the other. In this respect, the aim cannot be to reserve all fundamental rights—libertarian rights in particular—to Union citizens.[141] However, fundamental rights provide information as to how a body politic is constituted. In particular, the question arises as to whether the recognition of individuals as citizens corresponds to libertarian rights which fill the concept and aim of Union citizenship with substance.[142]

Initially, there were no connections between the case law on fundamental rights and Union citizenship. Whereas Union citizenship is derived from the initiatives of the Council and the Commission, Community legal rights owe their creation to a correction of the EC law's claim to supremacy. That is to say that, on the one hand, uniformity, prevalence and effectiveness particularly of secondary law cannot be placed in question by national fundamental rights. On the other hand, however, the legitimacy of the Community legal order will suffer adverse effects if this loss is not compensated.[143] This may be why Union citizenship and fundamental rights do not refer to each other in the Treaties either. The Treaty on European Union, in Articles 6 and 7, recognises fundamental and human rights in a rather general way whereas Union citizenship is regulated in the EC Treaty—an almost paradoxical distribution considering the current significance of each subject.

Commentators have criticised the lack of a conception of citizens' rights which is becoming ever more obvious behind this hitherto rather loose connection. Despite a basic recognition of the merits of the ECJ and its decisions concerning fundamental rights, it is accused of enforcing personal

[140] K Lenaerts and E de Smijter, 'A "Bill of Rights" for the European Union', (2001) 38 *CML Rev* 273 at 275.

[141] See I Pernice, 'Eine Grundrechte-Charta für die Europäische Union', (2000) *Deutsches Verwaltungsblatt* 847 at 856.

[142] See the interpretation of "civis europeus" by Advocate-General Jacobs in Case C-168/91, *Konstantinidis* [1993] ECR I-1191, para 46.

[143] Compare *Entscheidungen des Bundesverfassungsgerichts* 37, 271 (*Solange* I) and Case 11/70, *Internationale Handelsgesellschaft* [1970] ECR 1125, para 3.

rights not for their own sake but only where expedient for Community law, while otherwise subordinating them to Community interests.[144] Such objections hide the desire to intensify the protection of legal rights and to make them not a limitation to, but an end of the Community's activity so that they, just like other rules which implement objectives of the Treaty, would participate in the *effet utile*.[145] The corresponding attempts by the Parliament have not yet met with success.[146] Their realisation would mean reorganising the Union from a special-purpose association of economic integration into a genuine community of fundamental rights and values, as it were, a supranational version of the European Council. However, this is not on the agenda owing to the distribution of roles between Member States and Union.

Essentially, the Charter of Fundamental Rights has not changed this in any way. It attempts to increase the value of human rights without affecting the functionality of the Union.[147] Indeed, it brings fundamental rights into contact with citizens. In accordance with its Preamble, the Union "places the individual at the heart of its activities" and "strengthen[s] the protection of fundamental rights [...] by making those rights more visible in a Charter." However, until recently, this was not achieved by amending the Treaties but by creating a reference document which is not legally binding in itself.[148] Critics of Union citizenship will note that it shares with the Charter a comparable desire to promote identification of citizens with the Union by the formulation of rights whilst at the same time keeping their practical effectiveness in check.

[144] S O'Leary, 'The relationship between Community citizenship and the protection of fundamental rights in Community law', (1995) 32 *CML Rev* 519 at 544 *et seq*.

[145] See P Alston and JHH Weiler, 'An "Ever Closer Union" in Need of a Human Rights Policy', in P Alston (ed), *The EU and Human Rights* (1999) 658 *et seq*; against A von Bogdandy, 'Grundrechtsgemeinschaft als Integrationsziel?', (2001) *Juristenzeitung* 157 at 158 *et seq*.

[146] Bull EC Suppl 2-91; Bindi-Report on European Citizenship for the European Parliament, PE Doc A3-0300/91, 4; see UK Preuß, 'Grundrechte in der Europäischen Union', (1998) *Kritische Justiz* 1 at 4; see also the statement of the former federal minister of justice, H Däubler-Gmelin, 'Vom Marktbürger zum Unionsbürger', *Frankfurter Allgemeine Zeitung* of 10th January 2000, 11.

[147] Compare, with respect to the draft stage, C Tomuschat, 'Manche Rechte bedürfen der Konkretisierung', *Frankfurter Allgemeine Zeitung* of 7th August 2000, 13, considering the Charter, by and large, as a good compromise, with KA Schachtschneider, 'Ein Oktroi, nicht die gemeinsame Erkenntnis freier Menschen von ihrem Recht', *ibid*, 5 September 2000, 9–10, who refers to it as a manifesto of global capitalism ("Kampfschrift für die Interessen des globalen Kapitals"); for a more comprehensive analysis see M Wathelet, 'La charte des droits fondamentaux: un bon pas dans une course qui reste longue', (2000) *Cahiers de Droit Européen* 585.

[148] See S Alber, 'Die Selbstbindung der europäischen Organe an die Europäische Charta der Grundrechte', (2001) *Europäische Grundrechte-Zeitschrift* 349; the European Court of First Instance referred to the Charter as a source of fundamental rights for the first time in Case T-54/99, *max.mobil v Commission* [2002] ECR II-313, paras 48, 57.

Chapter V of the Charter is dedicated to the further development of Union citizenship but fails to provide any new perspectives in this respect. It paraphrases the rights of citizens contained in the second part of the EC Treaty and complements them by the right to "good administration" (Article II-41 CT-Conv; Article 101 CT-IGC) already mentioned—firmly established in case law long before—and the right to access documents (Article II-42 CT-Conv; Article 102 CT-IGC), which has hitherto been regulated outside Union citizenship in the institutional part of the EC Treaty (Article 255 EC).[149] Some provisions also cite Union citizens as beneficiaries of rights but do not go beyond the sands of positive law in this respect. Personal fundamental freedoms have been summarised into a quasi-right to exercise fundamental rights (Article II-15(2) CT-Conv; Article 75(2) CT-IGC). In addition, one paragraph in the Article on the freedom of assembly and of association refers to expression of political will of Union citizens in European parties (Article II-12(2) CT-Conv; Article 72(2) CT-IGC, which correspond to Article 191 EC). The Charter therefore entrenches the status quo.

However, many connections between the status of citizen and fundamental rights could result over time. Court decisions already point into that direction, connecting Union citizenship with rights to family life and privacy.[150] The potential is greater than that. Insofar as Article 19 EC grants a right to vote and to be elected, all rights must be enforced which are required to participate in elections. These are the rights to free speech, information, assembly, equal rights to media access and the free exercise of office and mandate. Article 12 EC provides the key granting access to rights which state constitutions often reserve to their nationals and, indeed, irrespective of the Charter's status. Therefore, even if the courts did not continue their new trend of using the Charter as a source of law,[151] and any changes to its present status notwithstanding, Article 12 EC has generally granted all Union citizens access to citizens' rights in state constitutions.

The European Convention on Human Rights provides further leverage for enhancing the value of fundamental rights for Union citizens. In this context, the impulses radiating from the European Court for Human Rights are all too often overlooked. In one case, where the public were not

[149] The right to freedom of movement (Art 45) appears at first glance to be drawn wider than in Art 18 EC because there is no reservation of conditions and limitations; however, this is contained in the general limitation of Art 52(2).

[150] Case C-413/99, above n 72; Case C-148/02, above n 136.

[151] Above n 148.

[152] On the connection between the participation of the public in industrial plant supervision according to the "Seveso-Directive", the freedom to receive and impart information (Art 10 ECHR) and the right to privacy (Art 8 ECHR) see ECHR, *Guerra v Italy* Rep 1998-I, 210.

involved as required by a Directive on environmental law, the Court expressly stated that this stage in the administrative procedure was connected to the substantive guarantees of the Convention.[152] Particular importance is attached to the publicity of administrative decisions as a requirement of transparency. The Strasbourg Court decided that nationals of the EC, within the Union, are not to be considered as foreigners so that their political rights could not be limited according to Article 16 of the Convention.[153] In the more familiar *Matthews* decision, the Court regarded the European Parliament as a legislative body pursuant to the 3rd Additional Protocol of the Convention and granted inhabitants of Gibraltar the right, as against the UK government, to participate in EP elections.[154]

5. Duties of Union Citizens?

Article 17(2) EC implies that Union citizens have rights as well as duties. The significance attributed to constitutional obligations in the texts of national constitutions varies according to the constitutional tradition in question but, in most cases, they play a secondary role to fundamental rights. They usually serve as an implied basis for constitutions expressing republican constitutional duties expected of national citizens in the sense of a contribution. Examples include the duty to obey the Constitution and law (Articles 9(2), 18, 21(2) and (4) Basic Law), the duty to work (Article 58 Portuguese Constitution, Article 35 Spanish Constitution), the duty to pay taxes (Article 31 Spanish Constitution) and the duty to perform compulsory military service (Article 12a Basic Law, Article 30 Spanish Constitution).[155] If Article 17(2) EC is determined by this understanding, then it awakens associations with the image of the state. It is doubtful whether it can plausibly be given substance.

Notwithstanding the agreement underlying all legal systems to observe the legal rules from which it is constituted, EC law does not contain any duties comparable with political duties. The Community legal order does not demand either direct or indirect taxes or compulsory military service.

[153] With respect to Art 10 ECHR (freedom of expression) *Piermont v France* ECHR [1995] Series A No 314, para 64; commentary by *J-F Flauss*, *Revue Trimestrielle des Droits de l'Homme* (1996) 364. The judgment is however based not only on the fact that the plaintiff possessed the nationality of a Member State of the EC but also on the latter's status as a Member of the Parliament; it did not depend on the lawfulness of the residence (see paras 44, 49).

[154] Above n 94.

[155] J Shaw, 'Citizenship of the Union: Towards Post-National Membership?', in The European University Institute (ed), *Collected Courses of the Academy of European Law*, vol VI-1 (1998) 237 at 343.

Even the prohibition of the abuse of law only constitutes an inevitable limit of law and not an autonomous duty.[156]

As with the expectation of diplomatic protection abroad, political duties (as they are usually described) also arise in the conflict between protection and loyalty.[157] There is pressure within the Union for such a sphere of protection—visibly so in the proposal for an area of freedom, security and justice (Articles 2(4) and 29 EU) and the proclamation of a European Social Charter.[158] There is little to suggest that there are any duties relating to loyalty. Accordingly, Article 10 EC can merely be interpreted as meaning loyalty to the federation within a federal system. The structural policy and other programmes of financial assistance might amount to a form of financial compensation but certainly not a duty of solidarity among citizens.[159] Moreover, despite surrounding itself with attributes of statehood such as a flag, an anthem etc., the Union does not expect personal duties of loyalty. The Union courts its citizens not because it expects them to perform duties, but because it wishes to be accepted as a body politic, for which everyone feels a sort of ethical responsibility.

It is not necessary to establish duties of Union citizens in order to realise the aims by which Union citizenship is to be pursued, i.e. the strengthening of personal rights, the promotion of freedom of movement and, thereby, the integration of the peoples of Europe together with an increase in legitimacy of the Union. In the same vein, a constitutional style modelled on that of the state leads to misunderstandings as well, the avoidance of which should be in the interests of the parties involved.

6. Interim Evaluation

The investigation provides a split picture. It suggests that a uniform legal analysis of Union citizenship is not possible unless one is prepared, from the outset, to measure it against a pre-defined vision of the role of citizens in Europe. Each of the rather disparate guarantees must be assessed individually—despite their common orientation towards images of political rights.

The freedom of movement granted by Article 18 EC not only incorporates the *acquis communautaire* into positive law but also helps it to achieve

[156] Reich, above n 138, 21 *et seq*.

[157] On "residual republican duties" H Hofmann, 'Grundpflichten und Grundrechte', in J Isensee and P Kirchhof (eds), *Handbuch des Staatsrechts* (1992), vol V, § 114 para 20; critical G Frankenberg, *Die Verfassung der Republik* (1997) 117 *et seq*.

[158] See, eg, J Shaw, 'The Many Pasts and Futures of Citizenship in the European Union', (1997) 22 *EL Rev* 554 at 565 *et seq*.

[159] See L Osterloh, 'Harmonization and Public Finance in Germany and Europe', (1996) 2 *Columbia Journal of European Law* 519 at 529 *et seq*.

significance in terms of constitutional law, a uniform basis for enacting new secondary law and a view to further development (Article 18(2) EC).

The right to vote (Article 19 EC) offers a starting point for further considerations concerning the legitimacy of sovereign power at the local and the European level. Active citizenship is no longer determined by nationality but by place of residence. However, it currently lacks significance in the real world.

The rights to petition, information and access to documents (Articles 21 and 255 EC) essentially refer to other provisions of the EC Treaty and confirm the vested rights which exist in any event. In this respect, the right to access documents introduced innovative accents since it was previously—and still is—unrecognised by many legal systems. At the same time, such rights help to implement the active rights of citizens which are not exercised to a significant degree.

On closer examination, the right to diplomatic and consular protection (Article 20 EC) only has a symbolic significance, overall. The right adds practically nothing to that already possible under applicable international law and it appears that it will not be implemented in the foreseeable future.

Thus, the Treaty concept of citizenship appears comparatively weak. As always, it has received dynamic force by the Court. The link between the prohibition of discrimination (Article 12 EC) and the right of residence (Article 18 EC) has considerable potential which transfers the concept of national treatment inherent in Union citizenship to social and cultural rights as well as to fundamental rights in general. It shows most clearly the resolution to overcome the long-standing tendency to model individual rights on economic freedoms. It is not for the first time in the history of European integration that judicial development has served to counteract the relative inaction of the Union's political institutions.[160] To date, links between Union citizenship and basic rights have only resulted from the case law of the European Court of Human Rights. However, civil liberties could complement citizens' active rights if the ECJ were to further develop its approach and transfer the fundamental idea of the Sala decision based on Article 12 EC to the latter.

If one takes the contents of the individual guarantees into account, then all of them attempt to place Union citizens on an equal footing within their scope. This concept is indebted to the principle of equality before the law which constitutes a genuine attribute of any modern concept of citizenship.[161]

[160] On this distribution of roles and their reasons see the classical exposition in JHH Weiler, 'The Transformation of Europe', (1991) 100 *Yale LJ* 403 *et seq*.

[161] Thus, the next step to realise that ideal will have to be to abandon domestic discrimination, which is still beyond the reach of Union law.

IV. UNION CITIZENSHIP IN THE CONSTITUTIONAL TREATY

It was one of the motives which induced the invocation of the Constitutional Convention and the negotiations around the new Constitutional Treaty to strengthen the ties between the Union and its citizens. The Preamble of the Charter of Fundamental Rights, now Part II of the Constitutional Treaty, announced the objective to place "the individual at the heart" of the Union's activities and ties the establishing of European citizenship up with the creation of an area of freedom, security and justice. The operative text of the Constitution expresses the wish to implement this goal by enhancing the weight of individual rights in various ways. The values on which the Union is based comprise, according to Article I-2 CT-Conv (Article 2 CT-IGC), human dignity, liberty [CT-IGC: "freedom"], democracy, equality, the rule of law and the respect for human rights. By the adoption of the Charter as a whole, that confession is spelled out in terms of legal rights. It expresses the same intent that, in the section of the Constitutional Treaty on the four freedoms, the order was reversed, attributing to the free movement of workers at least symbolically a higher priority than in the present EC Treaty where free movement of goods is mentioned first (Articles III-18 to III-49 CT-Conv; Articles 133 to 160 CT-IGC). In other Treaty provisions which take up what is existing law, the language was changed so that provisions which were addressed to the Member States or the Union's institutions now name the citizens as subjects of the Union's policies, principles and obligations. In Article I-3 CT-Conv (Article 3 CT-IGC) the Union offers "its citizens" an area of freedom, security and justice without internal frontiers, and a single market. The European Parliament shall no longer consist of representatives "of the peoples of the States brought together in the Community" (Article 189 EC), but of the citizens alone (Article I-45(2) CT-Conv; Article 46(2) CT-IGC). With a view to their political rights, the principle of democratic equality applies, and all "shall receive equal attention" from the Union's institutions (Article I-44 CT-Conv; Article 45 CT-IGC). New principles of participatory democracy like openness and transparency and new procedures such as public hearings and referenda are supposed to improve the legitimacy of the Union (Articles I-46(2) and 49 CT-Conv; Articles 47(2) and 50 CT-IGC).

Thus, a strong effort is made in the Constitutional Treaty to find a new rights-based legal language. Looking at the substance of the new provisions, not much has changed with respect to the specific citizens rights examined above.[162] An important exception, however, is Article III-9(2) CT-Conv (Article 125(2) CT-IGC). This provision is meant to replace Article 18(2)

[162] See Arts I-8, II-39 to II-46, III-9 to III-13 CT-Conv (Arts 10, 99 to 106, 125 to 129 CT-IGC).

and (3) EC which provides for a basis of Union competences in the field of free movement. Article III-9(2) CT-Conv (Article 125(2) CT-IGC) now not only allows for measures with respect to passports and other documents of a similar nature, but also "measures concerning social security or social protection". The exact impact of that power is not yet entirely clear. It may well be read as empowering the Union to harmonise social security schemes and welfare law.[163] This would go beyond the Court's case law and depart from the present character of EU social law which has hitherto been of a co-ordinating character, safeguarding that migrant workers and self-employed persons do not suffer discrimination under domestic law in comparison to nationals of the state in which they reside. The question is not as sensitive as may appear since Article III-9(2) CT-Conv (Article 125(2) CT-IGC) requires the Council to decide unanimously. But it appears as if the social dimension of citizenship has found its way into primary law.

First reactions on the Constitutional Treaty's provisions about Union citizenship are just as controversial as evaluations of the existing law have been. Critics deplore that the Convention missed a chance to offer new opportunities to identify with the Union, whereas more optimistic analysts hold that the Constitutional Treaty brings about a change of paradigm by making a step forward from state-oriented obligations as they are usually found in Treaties towards genuine subjective rights of a constitutional character.[164] Hence it appears that union citizenship will continue to permit different projections which depend on the perspective from which it is assessed.

V. THE FUTURE OF UNION CITIZENSHIP

1. Union Citizens in the European Multi-level System

Union citizenship has turned out to be fragmentary and, in its present state, needs further elaboration (Article 22 EC). It is an open concept in every respect. For this reason, its true potential cannot be revealed by an analysis of positive law alone.

The diverse projections based upon various evaluations are derived from different assumptions concerning the future of Europe. It is striking that this discussion is held exclusively in normative terms and scarcely takes

[163] Kanitz and Steinberg, above n 134, 1035.

[164] Compare M Nettesheim, 'Die Unionsbürgerschaft im Verfassungsentwurf', (2003) *integration* 428 with I Pernice, 'Der verfassungsrechtliche Status der Unionsbürger im Vorfeld des Vertrags über eine Verfassung für Europa', in N Colneric *et al* (eds), *Une communauté de droit: Festschrift für Gil Carlos Rodriguez Iglesias* (2003), 177.

empirical contributions into account. The following sections attempt to make some connections.

a) Citizen Status and Identity

Whether Union citizenship is merely a legal construction or whether it also exists in social reality is a question to which different scientific disciplines offer divergent answers, depending on the methodology used. Regardless of discipline, it is possible to distinguish two positions. The frontlines between the different camps in the disputes concerning democracy in Europe, Union citizenship and a European constitution are largely running in parallel. Essentially, a rough distinction can be drawn between "multi-national" and "universal" views.[165]

aa) The Multi-national Tradition A multinational picture of Europe—which is basically a traditional public international law perspective on the Union—presents Union Member States as the significant parties. In terms of legitimacy, the Union is a creation of the peoples of nation states. This view is sceptical of the social requirements and possible development of an overarching European *pouvoir constituant* with its own constitution, a European democracy and an active citizenship. The Union's subject of legitimacy, according to that view, requires a shared bond which does not exist.[166] The criterion regarded as crucial varies.

The German Federal Constitutional Court, in its famous Maastricht decision, points in this direction. With regard to the principle of democracy, the Court takes account of social and political homogeneity as a requirement of "people", the legitimising community.[167] The body politic of the

[165] See the juxtaposition in E Balibar, 'Kann es ein europäisches Staatsbürgertum geben?', (1994) 36 *Das Argument. Zeitschrift für Philosophie und Sozialwissenschaften* 621 at 623, French original in B Théret (ed), *L'Etat, la finance et le social. Souveraineté nationale et construction européenne* (1995); M Kaufmann, *Europäische Integration und Demokratieprinzip* (1997) 110; PA Kraus, 'Von Westfalen nach Kosmopolis?', (2000) *Berliner Journal für Soziologie* 203 at 204 *et seq*. In the following, I will not go into the "functionalist paradigm" in the version of the German special-purpose association doctrine (*Zweckverbandslehre*) and liberal economic approaches as considered in my contribution to Drexl *et al*, above n 11, 105. According to this view, the stand taken by the citizens has no consequence for the continuance of integration (E Haas, *The Uniting of Europe* (1958) 17); this attitude has ultimately been one of the reasons for replacing the concept of market citizenship with the idea of Union citizenship; see P Genschel, 'Markt und Staat in Europa', (1998) 39 *Politische Vierteljahresschrift* 55.

[166] So-called "no demos thesis", see JHH Weiler, U Haltern and F Mayer, 'European Democracy and its Critique', (1995) 18 *West European Politics* 4; see also S Korioth, 'Europäische und nationale Identität: Integration durch Verfassungsrecht?', (2003) 62 *Veröffentlichungen der Vereinigung der Deutschen Staatsrechtslehrer* 117 at 151 *et seq*.

[167] *Entscheidungen des Bundesverfassungsgerichts* 89, 155 at 186 (*Maastricht*); see also P Kirchhof, 'Deutsches Verfassungsrecht und Europäisches Gemeinschaftsrecht', (1991) *Europa-Recht* suppl 1, 11; criticism in B-O Bryde, 'Die bundesrepublikanische Volksdemokratie als Irrweg der Demokratietheorie', (1994) *Staatswissenschaften und Staatspraxis* 305.

Basic Law must accordingly retain an adequate reserve of its own fields of responsibilities. In this respect, the Court does not rule out complementary strands of legitimacy concerning areas over which the Union exercises sovereign authority: on the contrary, it regards them as the necessary consequence of further steps towards integration. However, the time when this can or should occur is still some way off. Thus, the Union regarded as a "compound of states" (*Staatenverbund*) cannot currently possess a legitimising community of its own. The people of Europe legitimise the Union by their respective national parliaments: in this respect, the European Parliament plays a merely complementary role.

Academic literature also refers to the importance of socio-cultural requirements for a European citizenship.[168] According to *Dieter Grimm*, formerly on the bench of the German Constitutional Court, there is no European public with a pan-European, cross-border discourse on "European" themes; cultural pluralism and linguistic variety are regarded as substantial obstacles.[169] Others believe evidence of European solidarity to be crucial: this alone made it possible to tolerate outvoting by majority decisions across borders. However, such evidence is said to be hard to provide.[170]

The present form of democratic accountability in the Union then appears the only plausible concept. The connection between Union citizens only exists in law—in their subjective rights, to be more precise.[171] According to this viewpoint, the citizens of Europe form a loose association of individuals wholly unconnected with the Union itself. Democracy in Europe would then be an arrangement organised by the Member States in their co-operation within the Union, legitimised by their people and which can be dispensed with at any time.

The basic assumptions of this model are empirically formulated, but are normatively intended. They are based on what is regarded as obvious and for this reason do not take results of empirical social research into account.

[168] Grimm, above n 10, 587 *et seq*; P Kielmansegg, 'Läßt sich die Europäische Gemeinschaft demokratisch verfassen?', (1994) 22 *Europäische Rundschau* 23 at 26 *et seq*; W Streeck, *Internationale Wirtschaft, nationale Demokratie?* (1998) 11 *et seq*; FW Scharpf, *Regieren in Europa* (1999) 167 *et seq*; systematic consideration of different approaches in Augustin, above n 9.

[169] Grimm, above n 10; but see P Häberle, 'Gibt es eine europäische Öffentlichkeit?', (1998) *Thüringische Verwaltungsblätter* 121 at 124 *et seq*.

[170] On this debate see FW Scharpf, 'Europäisches Demokratiedefizit und deutscher Föderalismus', (1992) *Staatswissenschaften und Staatspraxis* 293 at 296 *et seq*; see also UK Preuß, 'Nationale, supranationale und internationale Solidarität', and W Kersting, 'Internationale Solidarität', both in K Bayertz (ed), *Solidarität* (1998) 399 and 411, repectively; R Bieber, 'Solidarität als Verfassungsprinzip der Europäischen Union', in A von Bogdandy and S Kadelbach (eds), *Solidarität und Europäische Integration* (2002) 38.

Their weakness lies in the fact that they can be countered by contrary theses with the same justification. One objection is that it is almost impossible nowadays to satisfy the demand for social and political homogeneity derived from a preformulated picture of society even within the nation states.[172] However, a certain immunisation against such criticism is achieved by keeping crucial criteria vague. One exception is the contention that a common political discourse is impossible owing to the lack of a European public.[173] The counter-argument is that the required discourse could be produced and influenced by the occupation of certain political fields[174] and by the formation of procedures and institutions.[175]

A further objection is levelled against the exclusiveness with which conditions of state democracy are referred to as a reference model. A comparative consideration of the state and the Union tends to neglect the peculiarities of the Union as a supranational organisation. National sovereignty is regarded as indivisible. The notion is not entertained that the Union could be composed of complementary and supplementary elements of a connected whole in which sovereignty is exercised at several levels of power[176] as is the case in federal systems.[177]

bb) Universalist Visions Advocates of the opposing line of thought believe the state has been defeated as a reference point of identification and direct their attention towards establishing a body politic by a special

[171] PM Huber, 'Demokratie ohne Volk oder Demokratie der Völker?', in Drexl *et al*, above n 11, 27 at 33 *et seq*; M Heintzen, 'Die Legitimation des Europäischen Parlaments', (2000) *Zeitschrift für Europa-Studien* 377 at 384 *et seq*.

[172] With respect to the example of Switzerland see B Schoch, 'Eine mehrsprachige Nation, kein Nationalitätenstaat', (2000) *Friedens-Warte* 349.

[173] Grimm, above n 10.

[174] W Kluth, *Die demokratische Legitimation der Europäischen Union* (1995) 49 *et seq*.

[175] J Habermas, *Faktizität und Geltung* (1992) 643 *et seq*; M Zuleeg, 'What Holds a Nation Together? Cohesion and Democracy in the United States of America and in the European Union', (1997) 45 *AJCL* 505 at 524 *et seq*; UK Preuß, 'The Relevance of the Concept of Citizenship for the Political and Constitutional Development of the EU', in UK Preuß and F Requejo (eds), *European Citizenship, Multiculturalism, and the State* (1998) 11 at 22 *et seq*; M La Torre, 'European Identity and Citizenship', *ibid*, 87 at 96; similar from the view of positive law E Pérez-Vera, 'Citoyenneté de l'Union Européenne, nationalité et condition des étrangers', (1996) 261 *Recueil des Cours* 243 at 391 *et seq*.

[176] But see N MacCormick, *Questioning Sovereignty* (1999).

[177] With respect to the USA see Supreme Court, *Garcia v San Antonio Metropolitan Transit Authority* 469 US 528, 549 (1985) per Blackmun, J: "The States unquestionably do retain a significant measure of sovereign authority. They do so, however, only to the extent that the Constitution has not divested them of their original powers and transferred those powers to the Federal Government." In *US Term Limits, Inc v Thornton* 115 S Ct. 1842 (1995), the Supreme Court did not agree on whether the holder of sovereignty was an American people or the people of the States of the USA; the opinions of Judges Thomas, Rehnquist, O'Connor and Scalia decided in favour of the latter; see commentary by KM Sullivan, (1995) 109 *Harvard Law Review* 78.

legitimising community of citizens beyond statehood.[178] According to this idea, the origin of a body politic lies in voluntary agreement on constitutive elements. In the "post-national constellation", Union citizenship can form the nucleus of a federal system with a European constitution. However, seen from the conceptual basis of this theory, there is no justification for replacing the personal isolation of the state by that of the Union. Rather, their arguments are based on the notion of the universality of subjective rights, the granting of which does not depend on traditional memberships. Upon this basis, justification is required if Union State nationals alone are granted political rights at the State level.[179] From that perspective, Union citizenship replaces one criterion of exclusion (i.e. membership of a state) by another (i.e. nationality of a Member State).

If the attribution of political rights is mainly a postulate of equality, the consequence is a "post-national citizenship" which allocates rights not according to the legally established nationality but the place of residence.[180] Consequently, also Union citizenship would have to be overcome. For the Union, Article 63(4) EC offers a starting point according to which the Council can establish rights which nationals of third party states with a right of residence in a Member State also enjoy in other Union States.[181]

This view derives arguments from some tendencies to uncouple individual rights and duties from nationality. Human rights can be invoked by all who reside within the jurisdiction of a state which recognises them, as is spelled out in Article 1 ECHR. Similarly, many conventions of the International Labour Organisation and other treaties of international law

[178] See J-M Ferry, 'Die Relevanz des Postnationalen', in N Dewandre and J Lenoble (eds), *Projekt Europa*, (1994) 30 *et seq*; J Linklater, 'Citizenship and sovereignty in the post-Westphalian State', (1996) 2 *European Journal of International Relations* 77; Habermas, above n 14, 91 *et seq*; concerning further levels U Beck, *Politik der Globalisierung* (1998) 7 *et seq*; D Held, 'Rethinking Democracy: Globalization and Democratic Theory', in Streeck, above n 168, 59.

[179] H Lardy, 'The Political Rights of Union Citizenship', (1996) 17 *EL Rev* 611 at 619 *et seq*.

[180] YN Soysal, *Limits of Citizenship. Migrants and Postnational Membership in Europe* (1994); M Martiniello, 'European Citizenship, European identity and migrants: towards the post-national state?', in R Miles and D Thränhardt (eds), *Migration and European Integration* (1995) 37 at 49 *et seq*; T Kostakopoulou, 'Towards a Theory of Constructive Citizenship in Europe', (1996) 4 *Journal of Political Philosophy* (1996) 337 at 343 *et seq*; *eadem*, 'European Union Citizenship as a model of citizenship beyond the nation state', in A Weale and M Nentwich (eds), *Political Theory and the European Union* (1998) 158; MJ Garot, *La citoyenneté de l'Union européenne* (1999) 304; H Staples, *The Legal Status of Third Country Nationals Resident in the European Union* (1999) 335 *et seq*; R Davis, 'Citizenship of the Union ... rights for all?', (2002) 27 *EL Rev* 121 at 135 *et seq*; on such models generally V Ferrari, 'Citizenship: Problems, Concepts and Policies', in La Torre (ed), above n 38, 51; JD Galloway, 'Citizenship: A Jurisprudential Paradox', *ibid*, 65.

[181] Reich, above n 138, 18 *et seq*.

introduce social rights which attach to the characteristic of employment alone. The obligation to pay tax, which is occasionally cited as an example of a civil duty, mainly depends on residence and not on nationality.

Even within a national context, rights or duties as the ones referred to were at most temporarily constitutive elements of the status of citizen, if at all.[182] But objections go deeper than that. At its core, the point radical universalism makes is that (Union) citizenship should not depend on nationality. Critics complain that a body politic cannot be established on the basis of civil rights and belief in abstract norms alone and that the effect of common integrative factors is underestimated.[183] They parade many arguments which have played a role in the debate on liberalism vs communitarianism.[184]

This contribution cannot investigate the contingencies of a cosmopolitan extension of the status of citizenship. Taking Union citizenship as it is conceived in Article 17 EC as its starting point, it will restrict itself to the consequences of the framework positive law offers in this regard.

b) Identities of Citizenship in Multi-level Systems

Objections that the republican basis of the state is over-emphasised or neglected might overlook promising attempts to classify Union citizenship within the framework of the vertical structure provided.[185] As with some of the approaches discussed, such criticisms also follow a federalist paradigm but avoid placing normative demands on Union citizenship in relation to its requirements. The point of departure is the hypothesis that citizen status is simultaneously possible at the Union and State levels. Evidence must then show that there are sufficient common elements for a united expression of will with regard to the current responsibilities of the Union.

A common culture of Member States has always been accorded a crucial role.[186] Here, the attempt to track down pre-existent social foundations of a body politic repeats itself. However, it would be incorrect to view the *leitmotiv* of culture in the light of advancing homogenisation.[187] The Union is

[182] See above, part II 2 (b).

[183] Kraus, above n 165, 206.

[184] See the contributions in A Honneth (ed), *Kommunitarismus* (1995).

[185] Meehan, above n 52, 150 *et seq*; D Heater, *What is Citizenship?* (1999) 87 *et seq*.

[186] See Art 151(1) EC ("common cultural heritage"). The familiar statement of Monnet also comes to mind: "If I had the chance to begin again, I would start with culture", see T Oppermann, *Europarecht* (1999), para 1967.

[187] Compare H Lübbe, 'Europas Identität und die europäische Einigung', in M Bahr (ed), *Das geistige Erbe Europas* (1994) 193; M Nettesheim, 'Das Kulturverfassungsrecht der Europäischen Union', (2002) *Juristenzeitung* 157.

based on the diversity of European culture and has accepted this as the most important justification for the principle of subsidiarity.[188] Linguistic variety also forms part of the *acquis culturel* of the Union. Cultural diversity might be in constant conflict with nationality but it is constitutive for Union citizenship. This condition is necessary for enquiring as to its genuine identity.[189]

An approach orientated towards the aim of citizen participation assumes that awareness of identity entails that members of a group share its common fate and exercise dispositive rights granted to them for their influence. The relevant models would be those which connect cultural diversity to the recognition of equal and political rights together with the form of democratic expression of will.[190] In relation to the Union, they would have to be transferred to its own system of rule. Several disciplines describe this by the concept of multi-level system which is receptive to very different models.[191]

The search for empirical requirements for such a ruling model uncovers research relating to sociology and social psychology which investigates the European identity of Union citizens. 'Identity' means the self-perception and portrayal of a human being which results from the awareness of belonging to certain groups or having distinct characteristics. Identity is, to a large degree, based on contingent factors and for many is therefore based on contexts which are "non-homogenous" and graded according to different levels of identity. In this respect, several identities are cumulatively possible without one of them having to claim precedence.[192] Identity can also

[188] R Lepsius, 'Bildet sich eine kulturelle Identität in der Europäischen Union?', (1997) *Blätter für deutsche und internationale Politik* 948; for the influence of regional elements on a common "lifestyle culture" within the Internal Market see R Münch, 'Between Nation-State, Regionalism and World Society', (1996) 34 *JCMS* 379 at 394 *et seq.*

[189] On identity as a concept in constitutional law see E-W Böckenförde, 'Die Nation—Identität in Differenz', in K Michalski (ed), *Identität im Wandel* (1995) 129 at 134, 145 *et seq.*

[190] See the contributions in M Walzer, *Civil Society and American Democracy* (1992).

[191] See Commission, *European governance—A White Paper*, OJ C 287, 12.10.2001, 1 at 29; in relation to the political system M Jachtenfuchs and B Kohler-Koch, 'Regieren im dynamischen Mehrebenensystem', in *id* (eds), *Europäische Integration* (1996) 27; M Zürn, 'Über den Staat und die Demokratie im europäischen Mehrebenensystem', (1996) 37 *Politische Vierteljahresschrift* 27; Scharpf, above n 152, 81 *et seq*; with respect to administrative law E Schmidt-Aßmann, *Allgemeines Verwaltungsrecht als Ordnungsidee* (1999) 324; regarding constitutional law I Pernice, 'Multilevel Constitutionalism and the Treaty of Amsterdam: European Constitution-Making Revisited?', (1999) 36 *CML Rev* 703.

[192] Such ideas are, of course, not new; see the references to Durkheim in W Gephart, 'Zwischen "Gemeinsamkeitsglaube" und "solidarité sociale". Partikulare Identitäten und die Grenzen der Gemeinschaftsbildung in Europa', (1993) 14 *Zeitschrift für Rechtssoziologie* 190 at 195 *et seq*; and to Burke, Laski and TH Marshall in J Monar, Die Unionsbürgerschaft als konstitutives Element des Unionssystems, in: R Hrbek (ed), *Die Reform der Europäischen Union* (1997) 203 at 209.

be distinguished in terms of culture and region (besides gender-, age-, religion-, biography-, profession-specific etc.): it can therefore display local, regional, national and European reference points. Transferring this assumption to the Union, it can be established by empirical methods that the existing system of several tiers is reflected in the consciousness of Europeans.[193] Regular rises in the "Eurobarometer" also show that most Union citizens see essential parts of their identity in both their states of origin and "Europe".[194]

Empirical findings cannot indicate normative postulates such as moral requirements of solidarity. However, to the present author's knowledge, it is not claimed that the constitutional role of citizenship in Europe can be developed from the reserve of multi-level identities alone. Three results deserve emphasis:

- The view of the necessarily exclusive nature of the position of the individual in terms of citizenship does not do justice to the empirical facts; normative conclusions based thereon are problematic.
- One cannot presume that Union citizenship is lacking any kind of social basis.
- Such studies have shown that identities are particularly influenced by political discourses expressed in the media.[195]

Identity and discourse therefore exercise mutual influence over each other.[196] European public opinion does not have to be a pre-condition for

[193] O Angelucci, Die europäische Identität der Europäer: Eine sozialpsychologische Bestandsaufnahme, in: A von Bogdandy (ed), *Die Europäische Option* (1993) 303; J Kerkhofs, Les valeurs des Européens, in: R Picht (ed), *L'identité européenne* (1994) 41; GM Breakwell and E Lyons (eds), *Changing European Identities* (1996); S Immerfall and A Sobisch, Europäische Integration und europäische Identität, *Aus Politik und Zeitgeschichte* (1997), no 10, 25 at 32; W Loth, Die Mehrschichtigkeit der Identitätsbildung in Europa, R Elm (ed), *Europäische Identität: Paradigmen und Methodenfragen* (2002) 93; JHH Weiler, To be a European Citizen, in: *id*, *The Constitution of Europe* (1999), 324 at 328 ("differentity"); for a recent elaboration of the consequences for constitutional law see A von Bogdandy, Europäische und nationale Identität: Integration durch Verfassungsrecht?, 62 *Veröffentlichungen der Vereinigung der Deutschen Staatsrechtslehrer* (2003) 156 at 168 *et seq*.

[194] Recently, 57 per cent of all those questioned in the Union stated that they feel (exclusive ly or in addition to being a national) European, 40 per cent defined their identity solely by reference to nationality; the data varies considerably according to region, from a relation of 72/25 per cent in Italy, 59/38 per cent in Germany to 36/62 per cent in Great Britain. Source: Standard Eurobarometer 60, at 27, collected October/November 2003, published February 2004, <http://europa.eu.int/comm/public_opinion/archives/ eb_arch_en.htm> (5 July 2004). 61 per cent declared themselves proud of Europe, by contrast 28 per cent did not perceive any emotional affinity, *ibid*, 28.

[195] O Angelucci, 'Europäische Identitätsbildung aus sozialpsychologischer Sicht', in Elm, above n 174, 111.

[196] Shaw, above n 131, 563; Shaw, above n 6, 312 *et seq*.

active Union citizenship but can emerge in parallel. Therefore, Union citizenship can clearly be created by legal means as well. The decisive point is not whether active citizenship has already existed with adequate characteristics of identification in the social sense but whether chances of identification are opened up and accepted.

The question now turns to whether there are any models of accountability beyond the nation state which adequately reflect social reality and their possibilities of development.

c) The Complementary Relationship Between Citizen Status and Political Participation

This analysis would correspond with a multi-level model with different legitimising communities (*demoi*).[197] Depending on the level concerned, the group of active citizens is constituted according to individual or several different criteria. Nationality is decisive when allocating political rights at the national level; otherwise among Union citizens the matter only concerns the centre of their lives which is represented by the place of residence. However, citizenship outlined in Union law and expanded at European level can only promote its social reality by creating genuine opportunities to participate in European politics.[198] Here lies the real problem with its legal construction.

2. Union Citizenship and Democracy in Europe

If reference to the legal debate concerning democracy in Europe is sought, two options can be ruled out: (1) the present discussion is not concerned with the Utopia of a European federal state, the democratic organisation of which would have to be proposed;[199] (2) the model of deliberative democracy sustained by universalist moral philosophy, the voters of which are constituted by those who have decided in favour of life in the Union and accept the rules of shared expression of will,[200] exceeds the concept of Union citizenship.

[197] See for example, R Koslowski, 'Intra-EU Migration, Citizenship and Political Union', (1994) 32 *JCMS* 369 at 389 *et seq*; DN Chryssochoou, 'Europe's Could-Be Demos: Recasting the Debate', (1996) 19 *West European Politics* 787 at 793 *et seq*.

[198] On this connection UK Preuß, 'Problems of a Concept of European Citizenship', (1995) 1 *ELJ* 267 at 276 *et seq*.

[199] F Mancini, 'Europe: the case for Statehood', (1998) 4 *ELJ* 29.

[200] J Habermas, *Die Einbeziehung des Anderen* (1996) 277 *et seq*; D Curtin, *Postnational Democracy: The European Union in Search of a Political Philosophy* (1997).

It has been presumed here that European citizenship can co-exist with national citizenship.[201] Citizens must participate in decision-making processes at both levels. Proposals for improving existing rules will pursue this objective and aim at strengthening elements of active citizenship by legal means in order to promote a common identity, responsibility and solidarity, such as European referenda,[202] but also a genuine procedural involvement in the constitutional process which would go beyond separate ratification by Member States.

To a certain degree, the notion of an active citizenship has become the strategy of the European Commission which has made transparency, control and good administration the leading concepts of its administrative policy by different initiatives.[203] Some traces of the notion of an enhanced role of civil society can be seen in newly adopted Treaty provisions.[204] A first step into that direction was the amendment of Article 257 EC—which deals with the Economic and Social Committee—by the Treaty of Nice. Accordingly, the Committee shall consist of representatives "of the various components of organised civil society". The discovery of civil society becomes more visible in the Constitutional Treaty according to which the Union is supposed to "maintain an open, transparent and regular dialogue with representative associations and civil society" (Article I-46(2) CT-Conv; Article 47(2) CT-IGC). Social partners and churches are honoured as particularly important associations (Articles I-47 and I-51 CT-Conv; Articles 48 and 52 CT-IGC). Good governance, meaning administrative participation, is expressly mentioned in Article I-49 CT-Conv (Article 50 CT-IGC) which recognises transparency, openness and, once again, the right of access to documents.

A further point, rightly regarded as decisive, is the promotion of legal equality amongst Union citizens which must complement the recognition of diversity.[205] The Constitution expressly connects equality and democracy.

[201] Weiler, above n 177, 324 *et seq*. Accordingly, the national level represents the sphere of the affinitive emotionally rooted identity, the European level the empire of the rational, determined by the perception that tasks of common interest can only be solved peaceably and in a legally ordered procedure; against Barber, above n 8, 250 *et seq*.

[202] JHH Weiler, 'The European Union Belongs to its Citizens: Three Immodest Proposals', (1997) 22 *EL Rev* 150 at 152 *et seq*, with elements of direct democracy; see also A Héritier, 'Elements of democratic legitimation in Europe: an alternative perspective', (1999) 6 *Journal of European Public Policy* 269.

[203] P Craig, 'The constitutionalisation of Community administration', (2003) 12 *EL Rev* 841.

[204] For the importance of upgrading the role of civil society as a compensation for the legitimacy deficit of the Union see O De Schutter, 'Europe in Search of its Civil Society', (2002) 8 *ELJ* 198.

[205] It forms a focus of the Third Report, above n 36, at 2, 4 and 26 *et seq*; also Shaw, above n 99, 424 *et seq*.

No less than 35 provisions of the Convention's Draft stress equality of all citizens, freedom from all kinds of discrimination and the principle of equal treatment.[206] Certainly, no one will accuse the Convention to have neglected that issue.

Important as such means of participatory democracy and the high esteem of *egalité* may be, the value of citizen status can only be further enhanced if the institutional framework is transformed: in particular, if the European Parliament assumed the function of a genuine parliament within the jurisdiction of the Union. This demand is already suggested by the present Treaty's choice of wording. For if political rights form the decisive criterion with regard to citizen status and, furthermore, if the identity of European citizen can only be constituted and further developed by the creation of European discourse, then it must be matched by substantial democratic procedures and institutions. In the Constitutional Treaty, this demand has been passed by once again. At this point, political limits to further development of the status of Union citizen become visible. The divergence between the symbols chosen in the language of the Treaty and the institutional architecture of the Union leads to an *aporia*. This will continue to be one reason why citizens remain at a distance to the Union, despite attempts by the Commission, the Parliament and the Convention to bridge the gap.

3. Union Citizenship and European Constitution-making

The experience from Union citizenship threatens to repeat itself in the debate concerning the European Constitution. The choice of the term "Constitution" triggers associations to which the content ultimately agreed upon might not correspond.[207] The convention procedure can be interpreted as an attempt to organise a step towards consolidating the Union, for a change, not in the intergovernmental procedure hitherto pursued and to lend it an improved basis of legitimacy. Looked at from a public international law perspective, however, the members of the convention are not more than plenipotentiaries with the power to negotiate yet another treaty. As to the text of the Treaty, the Heads of States and Governments had the

[206] Arts I-3(3), I-4(2), I-8(2), I-44, I-45(3), I-51(2), II-preamble para 3, II-15(3), II-20, II-21, II-22, II-23, II-25, II-26, II-34(2), II-39(1), II-39(2), II-40, II-41, II-45(2), II-47, III-2, III-3, III-7, III-8, III-18(2), III-22, III-27, III-28, III-29, III-43, III-45, III-60, III-108, III-124(2) CT-Conv. In addition, general references to human rights and fundamental freedoms implicitly cover equal protection such as, eg, Arts I-2 and I-7(3) CT-Conv.

[207] See the critique developed in A von Bogdandy, 'Europäische Verfassung und Europäische Identität', (2004) *Juristenzeitung* 53.

final say, and the entering into force will depend on the result of the ratification procedures provided for by the constitutions of the Member States.

In the political system it has been widely underestimated or even consciously neglected that the role citizens play here is a question which has bearing on their European identity. The citizens themselves hardly ever adopted constitutions in a factual sense. Social contracts are philosophical fictions according to which constitutional practice can be subsequently interpreted.[208] However, to believe that citizens will accept a constitution over the course of time by practical experience risks making the basis of the Union a fiction. To offer a Europe-wide referendum or to link the next elections to European Parliament with a constitutional debate would have meant to take citizens more seriously.

VI. CONCLUDING REMARKS

There are two discussions concerning Union citizenship which are independent from each other. One concerns the positive law of the EC Treaty and the case law, the other concerns the future role of active citizenship in the Union.

Analyses of the legal substance of Union citizenship as it was set forth in the founding Treaties usually show its limitations. They bring together the lines of development relating to freedom of persons and the political rights of participation and control. However, the provisions inserted into the Treaty alone have only resulted in an insignificant enhancement to the status of European individuals. The driving force is the ECJ true to its tradition of transforming weakly conceived legal institutions into strong concepts of rights. The connection of Union citizenship with social and cultural participation rights developed by the Court lends Union citizenship new substance, the appraisal of which is only just beginning.

The scholarly discussion concerning the future form of union citizenship can refer to the cross-border legitimising community of the Union, the creation of which Article 19(2) EC appears to anticipate. It has many conditions because it is influenced not only by views on the continuance of the integration process but also by the communitarian/liberal debate concerning the position of the individual and by the discourse concerning the

[208] Pernice, above n 61, 167 *et seq*; G Frankenberg, 'Die Rückkehr des Vertrages. Überlegungen zur Verfassung der Europäischen Union', in L Wingert and K Günther (eds), *Die Öffentlichkeit der Vernunft und die Vernunft der Öffentlichkeit: Festschrift für J Habermas* (2001) 507.

make-up of body politics without socio-cultural unity. It verifies which projections the concept of citizen allows and contrasts sharply with stock-taking of positive law.

If one accepts that the status of citizen is defined by the granting of political rights, then cross-connections to the normative question concerning social basis, democratic make-up and the multi-level architecture of the Union necessarily result. The empirical contributions, which play a subordinate role in the normative debate, certainly do not allow any compulsory conclusions for the views of European active citizenship but they do show that identities are changeable and can be moulded by institutions and, not the least, by law.

Sovereignty, people and the identity of individual citizens can refer both to the European and the national level. Concerning further initiatives in the tradition of establishing a "European identity", this means that the Union will only come closer to its citizens if it further follows its recent policy to offer identification by real opportunities of participation. Otherwise, Union citizenship will remain a weak construction behind its ambitious facade.

12

Fundamental Rights

JÜRGEN KÜHLING*

I. INTRODUCTION

WHILE THE COMPETENCES of the European Union have steadily expanded, this process has also increased the number of possible conflict areas in the field of fundamental rights. Perhaps the German debate,[1] which sometimes unnecessarily dramatises fundamental rights conflicts, will eventually receive empirical material to support its claim subsequently.[2] Added to this are the organisational changes in constitutional law that form part of the Community legislative process, a process which is characterised by a shift from unanimous voting to majority decision-making. These changes make it more difficult to uphold fundamental rights standards of Member States in the Community legislative process.[3] Nevertheless, the debate regarding an appropriate level of fundamental rights protection at the level of the European Union has been stormy at times, showing how important such protection is in order to ensure and solidify the successes of integration. Therefore, debating the protection of fundamental rights in the European Union is of the utmost importance.

* The author thanks Katrin Mayer for translating most parts of this paper.

[1] See, eg R Scholz, 'Grundrechtsprobleme im europäischen Kartellverfahren', (1990) *Wirtschaft und Wettbewerb* 99 at 107 *et seq*, on the claim that the inviolability of the home is not sufficiently protected after the judgment of the ECJ in Cases 46/87 and 227/88, *Hoechst v Commission* [1989] ECR 2859, and R Scholz, 'Wie lange bis "Solange III"?', (1990) *Neue Juristische Wochenschrift* 941 *et seq* on the claim that negative freedom of expression is not sufficiently protected as regards the content of the obligatory warnings on tobacco products.

[2] See for a recent example Case C-377/98, *Netherlands v Parliament et al* [2001] ECR I-7079, paras 71 *et seq*, which seeks to determine the appropriate level of protection of human dignity as regards the patentability of isolated parts of the human body.

[3] In this context see F Mayer, 'Grundrechtsschutz gegen europäische Rechtsakte durch das BVerfG', (2000) *Europäische Zeitschrift für Wirtschaftsrecht* 685 at 687.

The proclamation of the Charter of Fundamental Rights of the European Union has given the European debate on fundamental rights new impetus.[4] The Charter is being increasingly associated with the discussion regarding a future Constitution of the Eur opean Union. This occurs in several ways: primarily, the catalogue of fundamental rights is viewed as an integral part of a European Union Constitution.[5] The Treaty establishing a Constitution for Europe has met this demand. Another very important question to be resolved concerns the review of the activities of the institutions of the Community and of the Union taking as its benchmark the standard of Union and Community fundamental rights. In that respect, the ending of the era of the "planned constitution" requires a stricter and more intense approach to examination. In this context, the phrase "planned constitution" is used as a reference to the priority of achieving the goals of integration.[6] These goals have to be achieved irrespective of the extent to which "radical changes to the laws of the Member States"[7] are required and to which negative effects are caused in areas relevant to fundamental rights. As a reaction to this approach and against the backdrop of the German

[4] In addition to the following footnotes, see only L Besselink, 'The Member States, the National Constitutions and the Scope of the Charter', (2001) *MJ* 68 *et seq*; G de Búrca, 'The drafting of the European Union Charter of fundamental rights', (2001) 26 *EL Rev* 126 *et seq*; W Dix, 'Charte des droits fondamentaux et convention?', (2001) *Revue du marché commun et de l'Union européenne* 305 *et seq*; C Grabenwarter, 'Die Charta der Grundrechte und die Europäische Union', (2001) *Deutsches Verwaltungsblatt* 1 *et seq*; P Lemmens, 'The Relation between the Charter of Fundamental Rights of the European Union and the European Convention on Human Rights', (2001) *MJ* 49 *et seq*; NF Sola, 'À quelle nécessité juridique répond la négociation d'une charte des droits fondamentaux de l'union européenne?', (2000) *Revue du marché commun et de l'Union européenne* 595 *et seq*; A Vitorino, 'La Charte des droits fondamentaux de l'Union européenne', (2001) *Revue du droit de l'union européenne* 27 *et seq*; J Wouters, 'The EU Charter of Fundamental Rights', (2001) *MJ* 3 *et seq*; see also D Ehlers (ed), *Europäische Grundrechte und Grundfreiheiten* (2002) J Meyer (ed), *Kommentar zur Charta der Grundrechte der Europäischen Union* (2003), and C Nowak and S Heselhaus (eds), *Handbuch des Grundrechtsschutzes in der Europäischen Union* (2006, forthcoming).

[5] See, eg U Di Fabio, 'Die europäische Charta', (2000) *Juristenzeitung* 737 *et seq*; D Curtin and R van Ooik, 'The Sting is Always in the Tail', (2001) *MJ* 102 at 112 *et seq*; for the concept of constitution see also C Möllers in this volume.

[6] See especially J Weiler, 'Eurocracy and distrust', (1986) 61 *Wash L Rev* 1103 at 1108; see also K Bahlmann, 'Der Grundrechtsschutz der Europäischen Gemeinschaft', (1982) *Europarecht* 1 at 3, who speaks of an area of conflict between fundamental rights and integration; furthermore A Clapham, 'A Human Rights Policy for the European Community', (1990) *YEL* 309 at 359; C Turner, 'Human Rights Protection in the European Community', (1999) *EPL* 453 at 460, claims that "the ECHR regards human rights protection as the norm and derogation as the exception, whereas the ECJ views respect of the economic provisions of the EC Treaty as the norm providing for restriction, inter alia, in the interests of human rights protection".

[7] U Everling, 'Brauchen wir "Solange III"?', (1990) *Europarecht* 195 at 196.

debate surrounding the directives on tobacco products,[8] the demand was developed that the German Bundesverfassungsgericht (Federal Constitutional Court) should review Community law employing the standards of national fundamental rights and, in case of non-conformity, the Court should declare Community law inapplicable.[9] Yet, such a solution would attack the problem described at the wrong level, in that the conflict between the achievement of the goals of integration and the respect for fundamental rights must be solved at the level of the EU by expanding the fundamental rights of the Community.[10] Therefore, the present practice of giving priority to the achievement of the goals of integration must be restricted since such goals may only be pursued within the limits of fundamental rights protection at Community level. The process of integration would be subjected to this restriction at a stage at which it has already attained a high level. Thus, the end of the era of the "planned constitution" and the corresponding strengthening of fundamental rights protection do not pose any threats to the achievement of the goals of integration. In the medium or the long term, it would be reasonable to assume that this development would lead to a shift from expanding fundamental (market) freedoms to strengthening fundamental rights. Such a strengthening of the protection of fundamental rights is also very necessary as the quickly developing integration processes in areas sensitive to fundamental rights such as European police co-operation are prone to providing new situations endangering fundamental rights.[11] The necessity of fundamental rights protection is also referred to in the context of discussions regarding the development of a European criminal law.[12]

The following analysis deals with the important issue of fundamental rights protection in EU constitutional law in three steps: the first section

[8] Cf C-D Ehlermann, 'Zur Diskussion um einen "Solange III" Beschluss', (1991) *Europarecht* suppl 1 27 at 30; the fundamental rights relevance of this directive is denied by Everling, above n 7, 204 *et seq*; C Tomuschat, 'Aller guten Dinge sind III?', (1990) *Europarecht* 340 at 341; of a different opinion R Scholz, 'Europäisches Gemeinschaftsrecht und innerstaatlicher Verfassungsrechtsschutz', in KH Friauf and R Scholz (eds), *Europarecht und Grundgesetz* (1990) 53 *et seq*.

[9] Eg Scholz, above n 1, 943 *et seq*. This debate has been taken up by M Seidel, (2003) *Europäische Zeitschrift für Wirtschaftsrecht* 97 against the background of Art II-53 CT-Conv (Art 113 CT-IGC). But the argument is rather weak; against Seidel, See U Everling, (2003) *Europäische Zeitschrift für Wirtschaftsrecht* 225; rejecting such an interpretation also with reference to the wording and the genesis of the norm M Borowsky, in Meyer (ed), above n 4, Art 53 Charter, para 10, and JB Liisberg, 'Does the EU Charter of Fundamental Rights threaten the Supremacy of Community Law?', (2001) 38 *CML Rev* 1171 at 1192.

[10] Everling, above n 7, 199.

[11] Cf L van Outrive, 'Polizeiliche Zusammenarbeit und Bürgerrechte in Europa', (2000) *Datenschutz und Datensicherheit* 23 *et seq*.

[12] See P-A Albrecht *et al*, '11 Thesen zur Entwicklung rechtsstaatlicher Grundlagen europäischen Strafrechts', (2001) *Kritische Vierteljahresschrift für Gesetzgebung und Rechtswissenschaft* 279 *et seq*.

(section II. below) is dedicated to the phases of development of fundamental rights protection and the second more detailed section contains the development of the legal doctrine of fundamental rights (section III. below). One can examine fundamental rights from a multitude of viewpoints. This paper mainly looks at the developing legal doctrine and argues that its development would be very helpful for the effective protection of fundamental rights within the EU. The concluding section takes a brief look at the need for institutional amendments (section IV. below).

II. PHASES OF DEVELOPMENT OF FUNDAMENTAL RIGHTS PROTECTION

The impetus provided by the proclamation of the Charter of Fundamental Rights allows for a two-stage interpretation of the phases of development of fundamental rights protection. The proclamation of the Charter is seen as a turning-point, although only the integration of the Charter into primary law of the EU—as provided for in the Constitutional Treaty—will tell whether this assertion is completely true. A catalogue of fundamental rights provides visibility and publicity for the fundamental rights guaranteed therein and leads to a higher degree of legal certainty.[13] It also facilitates the fundamental rights debate at European level and strengthens the legitimating force of fundamental rights.[14]

1. The Development of Fundamental Rights Protection by the ECJ Prior to the Proclamation of the Charter of Fundamental Rights

a) From Refusal to Recognition

The development of fundamental rights protection by the ECJ is well known and may be divided into three phases. The early stage of the case-law of the ECJ was shaped by a more or less negative attitude of the Court with regard to the recognition of fundamental rights as part of the Community legal order.[15] It was not until 1969, 15 years after its first session, that the ECJ recognised in an obiter dictum of its much discussed ruling in *Stauder* that fundamental human rights form an integral part of the general principles of Community law.[16] It is a well documented fact that the

[13] C Starck, 'Ein Grundrechtskatalog für die Europäischen Gemeinschaften', (1981) *Europäische Grundrechte-Zeitschrift* 545 at 548.
[14] On this legitimating function M Hilf, 'Ein Grundrechtskatalog für die Europäische Gemeinschaft', (1991) *Europarecht* 19 at 26; furthermore I Pernice, 'Gemeinschaftsverfassung und Grundrechtsschutz', (1990) *Neue Juristische Wochenschrift* 2409 at 2418.
[15] Especially clear in Cases 36/59–38/59 and 40/59, *Geitling* [1960] ECR 887 at 920.
[16] Case 29/69, *Stauder* [1969] ECR 419, para 7, followed by the seminal judgment in Case 25/70, *Einfuhr- und Vorratsstelle für Getreide und Futtermittel* [1970] ECR 1161, para 22.

Court undertook this expansion of legal principles as well as its later extension not least because of the critical dialogue with national (constitutional) courts, supported by initiatives of the other Community institutions, especially those of the European Parliament.[17] The ECJ had realised that the legitimacy, the primacy and the uniform application of Community law were endangered by the lack of fundamental rights protection under Community law. Regarding this development and the now quite impressive catalogue and scope of fundamental rights as developed by the Court, it is sufficient to refer to the extensive accounts contained in numerous essays and more recent literature.[18] The third phase of fundamental rights protection is shaped by the extension of its scope as regards the Member States as addressees of fundamental rights.[19]

b) An Autonomous Specification by the Community on the Basis of Common Constitutional Traditions and the ECHR

The intricate problem from what kind of sources fundamental rights are derived (sources of law or subsidiary sources) can be unravelled whenever the Charter of Fundamental Rights is incorporated into the primary law of the Union[20] and will therefore not be discussed here.[21] Even in the era of the Charter the method of specification the ECJ has to employ when developing Union fundamental rights will be open to discussion. Presently, the binding effect of the common constitutional traditions and of the ECHR is still contested, not least because of the vague wording employed in Article 6(2) EU. In order to determine the contents of fundamental rights of the individual, the ECJ has developed its own cognitive method. The method may be characterised as an autonomous specification by the Community based on common constitutional traditions and the ECHR. In its case-law, the Court does not consider itself bound in any way by the fundamental rights guaranteed by the Member States nor by the ECHR. Rather, the Court aims at preserving the widest possible degree of flexibility when specifying fundamental rights. Nevertheless, any specification

[17] Eg, Resolution on the Constitution of the European Union, OJ C 61, 28.2.1994, 155; on the catalogues of fundamental rights cf E Chwolik-Lanfermann, *Grundrechtsschutz in der Europäischen Union* (1994) 299 *et seq*.

[18] See, eg in addition to the following footnotes Chwolik-Lanfermann, above n 17, especially on the development of the case-law of the ECJ, 47 *et seq*; on the three-phase development of the case-law in relation to fundamental rights (refusal—recognition—extension with regard to actions by the Member States) also H Schermers, *Protection of Human Rights in the European Community* (1994) 3 *et seq*; furthermore T Kingreen, in C Calliess and M Ruffert (eds), *Kommentar zum EU-/EG-Vertrag* (2002), Art 6 EU, paras 16 *et seq*.

[19] See below III.3.b.

[20] However, if Art I-7(3) CT-Conv (Art 9(3) CT-IGC) will be part of the final Constitution of the EU, the problem would persist, see below II.2.c.bb.(2).

[21] See for this J Kühling, 'Grundrechte', in A von Bogdandy (ed), *Europäisches Verfassungsrecht* (2003) 583 at 587 *et seq*.

occurs against the background of comparing different legal systems: the aim is to develop a standard which does justice both to national values as well as to the ECHR, and which corresponds to the structure of the Community and its goals. It would be impossible to propagate a solution that runs contrary to the core values of a Member State; this may also be derived from the proviso to respect the national identities of the Member States in Article 6(3) EU. The method seems to suggest a tendency to orientate oneself towards a wide-ranging standard, but not a maximum standard in the sense of guaranteeing all national maxims of protection. The reason is that Community law also contains a reasonable compromise between justified interests of the Community—such as a functioning administration—and a far-reaching protection of the individual by fundamental rights. Furthermore, in multi-tier constellations, the fundamental rights of an individual collide with those of another individual (freedom of expression of a civil servant versus the protection of the honour of another civil servant) so that any attempt at "maximum expansion" would in any case soon reach its limits.

Regarding the application of the ECHR, it is generally accepted that it is of special importance and has achieved at least equal importance to the sources of inspiration of national legal systems.[22] Recent case-law of the ECJ demonstrates a growing recourse to the rights guaranteed by the Convention and their interpretation by the bodies of the ECHR[23] that for the most part results in a factually binding effect. However, this does not mean that differing legal doctrines may not be developed in individual cases. To take one example, the ECHR does not contain a right to freedom of profession, which has led to a corresponding dogmatic extension of the right to property. For the purposes of EU fundamental rights, cases concerning the right to property (such as the loss of a concession[24]) could be grouped under the EU fundamental right of freedom of profession. This also applies to the differences regarding the principle of self-incrimination: while the ECtHR has extended this principle to apply to legal persons,[25] the ECJ has not done so.[26]

[22] F Mancini and Di Bucci, 'Le développement des droits fondamentaux en tant que partie du droit communautaire', (1990) *AEL* vol I Book 1, 1 at 38, even claim that the ECHR is of prime importance. Regarding the relationship between the ECHR and the Charter cf Lemmens, above n 4, 49 *et seq*; Curtin and van Ooik, above n 5, 102 *et seq*.

[23] Recently in Case C-274/99 P, *Connolly* [2001] ECR I-1611, paras 39 *et seq*.

[24] See, eg *van Marle et al*, ECHR [1986] Series A No 101, para 55, which concerned a refusal to be placed on a register of chartered accountants; see also ECHR, *Iatridis v Greece*, Judgment of 25 March 1999 Application No 31107/96, para 54 <www.echr.coe.int> (5 May 2004).

[25] *Funke v France* ECHR [1993] Series A No 256A, para 44.

[26] Case C-60/92, *Otto* [1993] ECR 5683, para 11; earlier, to the same effect Case 347/87, *Orkem* [1989] ECR 3283, para 20.

This could be offset by a corresponding extension of Community legal principles such as the rights of defence and the right to fair legal process.[27]

However, the development of common European fundamental rights standards by means of analysis of national legal systems and of orientation towards the ECHR as interpreted by the ECtHR constitutes only the basis of a specification of fundamental rights. The process of specification is also largely influenced by the second step of ascertaining whether such a right is ensured within the framework of the structure and objectives of the Community.[28] This "Community reservation" is on the one hand a general legal reservation, as it constitutes the legal starting-point for possibilities of interference with recognised fundamental rights. On the other hand, it also constitutes a maxim of interpretation for the entire process of specification of fundamental rights, i.e. the determination of restrictions and especially of their restrictions respectively. Furthermore, any fundamental right must be fitted into the distinctive features of a supranational legal order. Finally, scope is provided for teleological considerations against the backdrop of the functions and the goals of the EC and thus for value judgments of the Community. It can safely be assumed that this method will not change significantly in the era of the Charter and particularly its Articles 52 and 53 (Articles 112 and 113 CT-IGC).

2. The Fundamental Rights Debate in the Era of the Charter of Fundamental Rights of the European Union

a) Time for a Radical Re-orientation of the Development of Fundamental Rights?

The drawing-up and subsequent proclamation of the Charter of Fundamental Rights has led to a deluge of opinions on the status of fundamental rights protection in the European Union.[29] The proclamation of the Charter constitutes a turning point in the Community system of fundamental rights protection that provides an opportunity for a fundamental re-orientation of the development of fundamental rights. The furthest reaching comments are by Alston and Weiler, who demand progressive

[27] Case 347/87, above n 26, para 35; see later Case T-112/98, *Mannesmannröhren-Werke v Commission* [2001] ECR II-729, paras 63 *et seq*; concerning possible new areas of conflict see below n 180.

[28] This wording was first employed in Case 11/70, *Internationale Handelsgesellschaft* [1970] ECR 1125, para 4.

[29] Cf the references in n 4 above.

and energetic politics of fundamental rights for the EU, which they believe requires shifting fundamental rights protection from the courts to the legislature and the executive.[30] Despite some of their criticisms being justified,[31] this approach does not correspond with the traditions of the Member States both as regards its general tendency and in numerous individual aspects. Thus, the introduction of a separate Directorate General on fundamental rights[32] would be a questionable novelty, as there are no ministries of fundamental rights in the Member States.[33] Overall, an undue elevation of fundamental rights is not advisable. It also seems somewhat dubious to assume that the institutions of the Community or of the Union could provide the legitimating force for expansive fundamental rights policies.[34] It is impossible to overlook the counterproductive potential for disintegration inherent in such an idea. Furthermore, this would mean glossing over the now established complimentary performance of fundamental rights protection by national, international and supranational organs.[35] Therefore, it seems more advantageous to place the emphasis on strengthening and developing present concepts on the protection of fundamental rights. Fundamental rights protection by the courts will receive a further impetus if the Charter becomes legally binding as is intended.

Nevertheless, Alston's and Weiler's warning should be heeded when developing a legal doctrine of fundamental rights: it is not advisable to focus solely on the judiciary when seeking fundamental rights protection. Thus, it must be realised that any attempt to transfer the particularly German method of obtaining fundamental rights protection through the courts (i.e. a judicial expansion of fundamental rights) to the Community or Union level would, in the constitutional reality, result in a shift of power from the legislature and the executive to the judiciary.

[30] P Alston and J Weiler, *The EU and Human Rights* (1999), *passim*; against this see the convincing critique of A von Bogdandy, 'Grundrechtsgemeinschaft als Integrationsziel?', (2001) *Juristenzeitung* 157 at 159 *et seq*.

[31] See especially the criticism with regard to difficulties in applying to the ECJ in the case of an alleged violation of fundamental rights: P Alston and J Weiler, *The EU and Human Rights* (1999), paras 178 *et seq*.

[32] Alston and Weiler, above n 31, paras 55 and 132 *et seq*.

[33] To the same effect von Bogdandy, above n 30, 159.

[34] However, it must be pointed out that Alston and Weiler refer to both the external and internal fundamental rights dimension, while this paper is only concerned with the internal dimension. It is certainly true that the main actors in the external dimension will comprise the Commission, Council and Parliament rather than the judiciary. The opposite is true of a fundamental rights review of internal sovereign acts, which are characterised by the tension between the judiciary and other powers.

[35] This will be elaborated below in IV.

b) Catalyst Effect, but not Legally Binding

To date, the Charter of Fundamental Rights does not carry legal force although its incorporation into primary law was aimed at from the beginning.[36] Therefore, at present the ECJ may only draw inspiration from the Charter:[37] its effect on the development of fundamental rights in the EU should not be underestimated, however. Firstly, those institutions of the EC subjected to the jurisdiction of the ECJ may declare themselves bound, although this is not justiciable by the Court.[38] Furthermore, the Charter constitutes the essence of the status quo obtained through a comparison of different legal systems. This was mainly guaranteed by the composition of the Convention, as 45 of the 62 members sit in the parliaments of the Member States or were appointed by the Member State governments. Compared to the European Parliament's previous catalogues of fundamental rights, this actually confers an entirely new legitimating force on the Charter. Therefore, it is not surprising that Advocates General have already referred to the Charter in order to confirm the protection of fundamental rights under EU law.[39] The CFI—unlike the ECJ—followed suit when specifying fundamental rights.[40] In this context, it is also important to remember the "as-if-approach" which shaped the drawing-up of the Charter. According to this approach, the Convention prepared the Charter as if the latter were subsequently to be incorporated into the Treaties and thus obtain the binding nature of primary law.[41] Therefore, it may be assumed that any legally binding catalogue of fundamental rights expected in the future will

[36] This option was already mentioned in the Presidency Conclusions, Cologne European Council of 4 June 1999, (1999) *Europäische Grundrechte-Zeitschrift* 364 at 365: [After the proclamation] "it will then have to be considered whether and, if so, how the Charter should be integrated into the Treaties."

[37] T Schmitz, 'Die EU-Grundrechtecharta aus grundrechtsdogmatischer und grundrechtstheoretischer Sicht', (2001) *Juristenzeitung* 833 at 835 *et seq.*

[38] However, this cannot distract from the fact that the Charter is not based in Community primary law as otherwise the Parliament would be guilty of an abuse of form and of procedure. Neither is the Commission permitted to perform "autolegislative functions" by independently declaring certain rules to be binding. Yet rules could become binding insofar as an administrative practice is established. Regarding the question of whether Community institutions may declare themselves bound by the Charter and how this might be reviewed by the ECJ, see S Alber, 'Die Selbstbindung der europäischen Organe an die Europäische Charta der Grundrechte', (2001) *Europäische Grundrechte-Zeitschrift* 349 at 350 *et seq.*

[39] First AG Alber in Case C-340/99, *TNT Traco* [2001] ECR I-4112, para 94 and more recently AG Jacobs in Case C-50/00 P, *Unión de Pequeños Agricultures v Council* [2002] ECR I-6677, para 39.

[40] Case T-54/99, *max.mobil v Commission* [2002] ECR II-313, paras 48 and 57. The judges of the ECtHR also refer to the Charter in their rulings, see the dissenting opinion by Judge Costa in *Hatton et al v United Kingdom*, Judgment of 2 October 2001 Application No 36022/97, para 7 <www.echr.coe.int> (5 May 2004).

[41] Commission Communication on the Charter of Fundamental Rights of the European Union of 11 October 2000, COM(2000) 664, 4, para 7; see also de Witte, above n 20, 81 *et seq.*

not contain vastly differing contents (an assumption confirmed by the Constitutional Treaty). This suggests that it would make sense to orientate the future development of fundamental rights towards the Charter. In any case, this prospect should provoke a new Union-wide debate on fundamental rights on the basis of a common document.

Even if some aspects of the Charter lack a compelling nature from a perspective of legal doctrine, it can have a catalyst effect on the development of a theory of EU fundamental rights. An impetus could be provided by the system of uniform restrictions pursuant to Article II-52(1) CT-Conv (Article 112(1) CT-IGC) although exceptions are possible.[42] This concept could prove a great success for the Convention. A system of uniform restrictions is supposed to avoid the development of an intransparent and frequently inconsistent system of restrictions which has occurred both with regard to the ECHR[43] and with regard to the German *Grundgesetz*.[44] Criticism to the effect that a uniform system of restrictions lacks the additional directive force of a system where restrictions are adapted to individual fundamental rights[45] is refuted by experience to date.[46] However, the first sentence of Article II-52(3) CT-Conv (Article 112(3) CT-IGC) begs the question of whether it will be possible to consistently apply a system of uniform restrictions. From its wording, the stipulation to interpret rights contained in the Charter which are identical to rights guaranteed by the ECHR employing the standard of the ECHR also applies to the system of restrictions ("the meaning and the scope... shall be the same"; "leur sens et leur portée sont les mêmes"). This results from the fact that the "scope" ("portée") of fundamental rights is mainly defined by applying the restrictions. Neither does the provision in the second sentence of Article II-52(3) CT-Conv (Article

[42] See Art II-8(2) CT-Conv (Art 68(2) CT-IGC) which only permits interference in the right to protection of personal data if there is a "legitimate basis laid down by law"; of a more serious nature are the unresolved reservations contained, inter alia, in Art II-16 CT-Conv (Art 76 CT-IGC) relating to the freedom to conduct a business, which is merely recognised "in accordance with Union law and national laws and practices".

[43] Consider only the restrictions contained in the respective second paras of Arts 8–11 ECHR: while interference in the right to respect for private and family life in the interest of the economic well-being of a country is explicitly permitted in Art 8(2) ECHR, this justification is not contained in the provisions on freedom of religion, freedom of expression or freedom of assembly. This suggests that the formulations employed for the restrictions are marred by historical coincidences.

[44] See, eg the criticism by KA Bettermann, *Grenzen der Grundrechte* (1976) 3, who speaks of a "Schrankenwirrwarr" (ie a muddle of restrictions); U Scheuner, 'Die Funktion der Grundrechte im Sozialstaat', (1971) *Die Öffentliche Verwaltung* 505 at 511, who is of the opinion that the system of restrictions employed by the Grundgesetz is more or less incomplete and failed.

[45] Of a different opinion Schmitz, above n 37, 838.

[46] Cf Kingreen, above n 18, para 70 and fn 197, against criticism regarding a system of uniform restrictions by M Kenntner, 'Die Schrankenbestimmungen der EU-Grundrechtecharta?', (2000) *Zeitschrift für Rechtspolitik* 423 at 424 *et seq.*

112(3) CT-IGC) preclude a further differentiation of the system of restrictions; rather, it serves to promote it. Thus, a system of restrictions which differentiates between fundamental rights corresponding to the ECHR and other fundamental rights contained in the Charter is necessary. Independent of this serious problem, a future legally binding catalogue of fundamental rights should make clear to what extent the general restriction also applies to the first Chapter of the Charter. Thus, it would have to be emphasised that the prohibition of torture in Article II-4 CT-Conv (Article 64 CT-IGC) is not subjected to the general restriction, to take one example.

The thematic classification of fundamental rights into six chapters (Dignity, Freedoms, Equality, Solidarity, Citizens' Rights and Justice) has also proved interesting for dogmatic theory. This attempt at a coherent system is to be welcomed, although some critics have already pointed to questionable results in individual cases.[47] However, this did not solve the problem of classifying fundamental rights according to their functions. To this extent, a lot of effort is still required for the development of a theory of fundamental rights. Yet, in future it will be possible to discuss these questions as part of a common European debate on fundamental rights based on the Charter as a prominent document. Therefore, it is to be expected that at the time of the incorporation of the Charter into primary law, the outlines of a common European "language" of a legal doctrine of fundamental rights will already exist.

The recent case-law of the ECJ may already be a consequence of this catalyst effect. Although the Court does not refer to the Charter, it evidently is more willing to use fundamental rights to protect EU citizens[48] even in situations where the link to EU law is rather weak (cf. below III.3.b.bb).

c) The Incorporation of the Charter in the Constitutional Treaty

The most striking positive result of the Constitutional Treaty as far as fundamental rights are concerned is the binding character of the Charter (aa) whereas the adaptations of the Charter within the constitutional context (bb) are less convincing.[49]

aa) The Legally Binding Character The present position of the Charter as a separate part has to be considered to be a success for those justifiably aiming at an upgrading of the Charter regarding the various proposals dealing

[47] This applies in particular to the protection of families, which was spread over several chapters of the Charter (Arts II-7, II-24, II-33 CT-Conv; Art 67, 84, 93 CT-IGC), see the critical comment by Schmitz, above n 37, 834.

[48] See especially Case C-117/01, *K.B.* [2004] ECR I-541, paras 25 *et seq.*

[49] Concerning the welcome clause to the accession to the ECHR, see R Uerpmann-Wittzack in this volume, VI.2.a. Concerning the missed chance of a fundamental rights complaint see FC Mayer in this volume.

with the incorporation of the Charter into the Constitutional Treaty.[50] This planned form of implementation preserves the main goals in respect to the Charter: it bears a binding character and gives the Charter constitutional status. For citizens of the Union from member states where fundamental rights can be found in the beginning of their Constitution, as the case is particularly in the German and the Dutch Constitutions, the "pole position" may be considered only natural. This, however, is not the case in several Constitutions of older members of the EU e.g. Denmark or Ireland. Moreover, regarding Constitutions of new member states, e.g. the ones of Latvia or Hungary, fundamental rights can also be found in one of the later chapters. In most of the old and the new member states of the Union, fundamental rights are placed at the very beginning after a short chapter dealing with fundamental provisions of the political system (e.g. dealing with the federal character of Belgium). Although in comparison, the fundamental rights of the Constitutional Treaty have not reached such a prominent position, their full textual incorporation and positioning before certain political issues as well as the explicit reference in Articles I-2 and I-7 CT-Conv (Articles 2 and 9 CT-IGC) demonstrates their importance.[51] Unfortunately, the decision not to place the fundamental rights at the beginning of the Constitution bears the disadvantage of some unnecessary repetitions between the first and second part. The fundamental right of protection of personal data can be found with exactly the same wording in Articles I-50 and II-8(1) CT-Conv (Articles 51 and 68(1) CT-IGC).[52]

bb) Adaptations of the Charter within the Constitutional Context—the Fear of Judicial Activism Less convincing, however, are the drafting adjustments in the Charter text within the constitutional context as well as their framework provisions. The fear that the incorporation of the Charter may lead to judicial activism, especially in the vertical sense (that is to the disadvantage of the Member States) is prevalent throughout the drafting adjustments. Considering the necessity of adaptation in order to secure consensus, they may be acceptable. However, they contain unnecessary repetitions and reflect some suspicion towards the Charter text.

(1) Field of Application of the Charter

The old version of Article 51(2) of the Charter (Article 111(2) CT-IGC) already emphasised that it does not establish any new competences or tasks of the Community and Union, nor does it modify existing ones. This provision

[50] CONV 354/02, at 3.

[51] Also referring to the importance of the full textual incoperation J Pietsch, 'Die Grundrechtecharta im Verfassungskonvent', (2003) *Zeitschrift für Rechtspolitik* 1 at 3.

[52] J Meyer and S Hölscheidt, 'Die Europäische Verfassung des Europäischen Konvents', (2003) *Europäische Zeitschrift für Wirtschaftsrecht* 613 at 619.

was supplemented with the superfluous remark that the Charter also does not extend the field of application of Union law beyond the competences of the Union. Moreover, Article 51(1), 2nd sentence of the Charter (Article 111(1) CT-IGC) is likewise supplemented unnecessarily by a reference to the limits of the powers of the Union. However the old version of Article 51(1), 1st sentence already included an explicit reservation for competences, and Article 51(1), 2nd sentence of the Charter precluded any competences arising from the Charter. Resulting from these supplements, the clear structure of Article II-51 CT-Conv (Article 111 CT-IGC), which outlines the scope of application in Article II-51(1) and prohibits the exceeding of competences in Article II-51(1), 2nd sentence, now appears diluted,[53] whereas the decisive question of concretising the term "field of application"[54] is not even approached.

(2) Constitutional Traditions and General Principles of Law

Additionally preventing the Union to usurp competences is the new inserted Article II-52(6) CT-Conv (Article 112(6) CT-IGC) by stipulating the due consideration of national laws and practices. According to the final report of Working Group II, this paragraph recalls the due consideration of the principle of subsidiarity, as is already clear from the Charter's Preamble, its Article 51(1) and from those Charter articles making references to national laws and practices. With Article II-52(6) CT-Conv (Article 112(6) CT-IGC) another redundant provision has been inserted, which emphasises the maintenance of competences of the member states. Obviously, the need for safeguarding clauses was generally increased.

However, the newly inserted para 4 in Article II-52 CT-Conv (Article 112 CT-IGC) represents a different approach. According to this provision, the fundamental rights resulting from constitutional traditions common to the Member States shall be interpreted in conformity with those traditions. This also serves the purpose of restraining the ECJ, however, less in regard of using the Charter as a tool for exceeding competences but rather in respect to an extensive interpretation of fundamental rights. The formulation chosen serves the purpose to secure a connection to the community of shared values based on common constitutional traditions. Simultaneously, it is emphasised that in conformity with the case-law of the ECJ the provision, does not imply orientation at "a lowest common denominator".[55] The ECJ is given a wide margin of appreciation concerning the concretisation of the fundamental rights and the provision has an important function regarding Article I-7(3) CT-Conv (Article 9(3) CT-IGC). This paragraph develops

[53] See also Pietsch, above n 51, 3.
[54] Cf below III.3.b.bb.
[55] CONV 354/02, at 7.

the currently valid Article 6(2) EU. In accordance to this provision, fundamental rights, as they result from the ECHR and the constitutional traditions common to the Member States, belong to the general provisions of Union law. Article II-52(4) CT-Conv (Article 112(4) CT-IGC) constitutes the parallel provision to this in the Charter. The article guarantees a parallel interpretation of general principles of law existing outside the Charter and of the fundamental rights of the Charter interpreted in conformity with constitutional traditions common to the member states.[56] The main problem of Article I-7(3) CT-Conv (Article 9(3) CT-IGC) is that it maintains a parallel universe of fundamental rights next to the fundamental rights of the Charter. Considering the complete guarantees of fundamental rights as contained in the Charter, the question arises whether this parallelism is necessary. The formulation that the clause serves the possibility of recognising additional fundamental rights that might emerge in future developments[57] allows the question why the ECJ should not fulfil this task in the frame of interpreting the Charter. Carefully examined, this possibility, however, bears the risk that the ECJ may not limit itself to a dogmatically founded interpretation of the Charter provisions but may rely on the dogmatically less clear structure of general principles of law. Thereby a stronger dogmatic founding of case-law concerning fundamental rights, based on the text of the Charter itself, might be endangered.[58]

(3) Limitation of Interpretation of the Provisions

Finally, as a last bulwark against judicial activism Article II-52 CT-Conv (Article 112 CT-IGC) has been supplemented with para 5. It refers primarily to the provisions included in the Charter. These require implementation by organs on the Member States level and on the supranational level. Courts may only use these provisions when interpreting and controlling legality of this implementation. This abandons the idea of those planning to conclude a guaranteed minimum standard from the provisions. The more interesting question whether the provisions—for instance Article II-36 CT-Conv (Article 96 CT-IGC)—can provide subjective rights, however, needs further explanation. This remains an issue to be dealt with by the ECJ[59].

In summary, one can recognise that the adaptations of the Charter are motivated by the fear that the ECJ may use the fundamental rights provisions to exceed competences. Since they are—with the exception of Article II-52(5) CT-Conv (Article 112(5) CT-IGC)—redundant, they hardly aggravate

[56] See also Pietsch, above n 51, 3.
[57] CONV 528/03, at 13.
[58] Pietzsch, above n 51, 3; in favour of maintaining Art I-7(3) CT-Conv (Art 9(3) CT-IGC) U Steiner, 'Unionsbürgerschaft und Grundrechte', in: ZEI (ed), *Der Verfassungsentwurf des EU-Konvents* (2003) 27 at 35 *et seq*.
[59] Also Streinz, in: Streinz (ed), *EUV/EGV: Kommentar* (2003) Art 52 Charter, para 13.

the provision as such but they do aggravate the clarity of the Charter text. Seriously alarming, however, is the maintenance of a parallel existing fundamental rights universe arising out of general principles according to Article I-7(3) CT-Conv (Article 9(3) CT-IGC), since they could undermine the effective role of the Charter and its dogmatic foundation.

III. CORE ELEMENTS OF THE LEGAL DOCTRINE OF FUNDAMENTAL RIGHTS

1. Preliminary Remark: Functions and Necessary Development of the Legal Doctrine of Fundamental Rights

a) Functions of the Legal Doctrine of Fundamental Rights Against the Background of Diverging Fundamental Rights Cultures

To date, it has proved difficult to further define the Union fundamental rights because of the relatively vague and partly diverging wordings of fundamental rights in the constitutions of the Member States, the ECHR and the catalogues of fundamental rights compiled by the European Parliament. As far as the wide and open-ended formulations are concerned, the same applies to the Charter of Fundamental Rights. The many differentiating ways to specify fundamental rights obstruct the development of a general consensus on fundamental rights jurisprudence. As part of system-transcending criticism regarding the treatment of fundamental rights, it is possible to argue against this background that the interpretation of fundamental rights should only occur by the courts concerned on a case-by-case basis.[60] Insofar, legal doctrine would be superficial, if one understands it as a science penetrating and systematising legal problems by providing theorems, fundamental rules and principles as part of a rational discourse. However, there is one obvious advantage of working with legal doctrine: a transparent, well-founded and definite fundamental rights jurisprudence based on a coherent legal doctrine provides essential points of orientation for those formulating a rule and those applying it as well as creating legal certainty for the addressees of a rule. Faced with the variety and complexity of new problems, developed legal doctrine may provide patterns of solution and aid categorisation. Furthermore, the solutions provided by legal doctrine set a standard, which may only be derogated from once better solutions have been offered. Therefore, working with legal doctrine leads to an optimisation of the patterns and solutions offered to solve a problem. The quality once achieved cannot be reduced because new solutions will

[60] On this debate J Kühling and O Lieth, 'Dogmatik und Pragmatik als leitende Parameter der Rechtsgewinnung im Gemeinschaftsrecht', (2003) *Europarecht* 371 at 383 *et seq.*

always be tested against the old standard.[61] Obviously, this does not result in conserving the old standard at all costs, at the contrary: the old standard serves as an incentive to develop better solutions. Legal doctrine constitutes both a common language to determine the compatibility in constitutional law of decisions made by the executive and the legislature as well as of rulings by the judiciary in the form of check and counter-check of the instance of control. Legal doctrine is the medium by which common and diverging values may be communicated and it provides a background against which correspondences and divergences may be explicitly analysed. Thus, legal doctrine confers substantial gains in efficiency and, ultimately, legitimating force.

At Community level, the development of a coherent legal doctrine in the area of fundamental rights is still in the very early stages. Besides the lack of a legally binding catalogue of fundamental rights, this is the main reason for the factual or perceived deficits of fundamental rights protection under EU law. The problem is exacerbated by the Eastern enlargement of the EU as many of the new Member States yet have to develop a tradition of fundamental rights. It is up to the EU to provide an impetus and this will be facilitated by being able to offer the new Member States a developed legal doctrine of fundamental rights based on which may grow a common European understanding of fundamental rights. Therefore, to develop a legal doctrine of fundamental rights is a value of its own, regardless of the specific features of such a doctrine. The development of a common European legal doctrine of fundamental rights need not occur from scratch although the Member State traditions regarding the development of legal doctrine in general and of legal doctrine of fundamental rights in particular are very heterogeneous. A corresponding fundamental rights debate is not only taking place in Germany, but also in Italy and Spain. In other Member States—for example in Austria or in Belgium—such a debate is about to commence. This means that it is possible to take account of the experience of those Member States. There is a strong argument in favour of following the more developed legal doctrines of fundamental rights at the level of the EU. At least in the cases of Germany, Italy and Spain, the system of protecting fundamental rights played an important role in inspiring confidence in the political systems. As democratic legitimacy is rather weak at the European level, a strong fundamental rights discourse might compensate this to a certain extent. Apart from the legal doctrines of the Member States, inspiration may be drawn from the rich source of case-law on the ECHR which contains numerous highly developed dogmatic figures and very detailed structures of examination.

[61] Regarding the individual functions of legal dogmatics cf R Alexy, *Theorie der juristischen Argumentation* (1996) 326 *et seq*; B Rüthers, *Rechtstheorie* (1999) paras 321 *et seq*.

However, the importance of doctrinal work should not be overestimated, either. The idea prevalent at the end of the 19th century in Germany that legal doctrine was capable of providing a system of concepts under which any new problems would only have to be subsumed, has today rightly been discarded.[62] Additionally, the Member States' differing cultures of fundamental rights have to be taken into account when developing fundamental rights protection. In comparison to the German tradition of fundamental rights, these point to a higher degree of caution as regards fundamental rights review of the legislature, to take just one example.[63]

b) The Necessity of Further Development of the Present Legal Doctrine of Fundamental Rights of the ECJ and the Light at the End of the Tunnel

Therefore, it is absolutely necessary to further develop the present legal doctrine of fundamental rights of the ECJ. Primarily, various legal considerations suggest a strict orientation towards the standard of the ECHR as regards the sources of inspiration, despite the fact that neither the EC nor the EU are directly bound by the ECHR. However, such an orientation is necessary since the Member States of the EC are bound by the ECHR with the result that a participation in the creation and implementation of Community law contrary to the ECHR would force the Member States to violate international law.[64] However pursuant to Article 307(1) EC, Community law does not affect agreements in international law concluded before 1 January 1958 and Article 307(2) EC obliges the Member States concerned to take all appropriate steps to eliminate any possible incompatibilities.[65] Taking into account the obligation of co-operation in Article 10 EC which places an obligation on the institutions of the Community to

[62] R Alexy, *Theorie der Grundrechte* (1986) also concludes by claiming that it is impossible to develop a theory of fundamental rights providing a cogent solution in each case (cf 520); cf furthermore the overview in Rüthers, above n 61, paras 462 *et seq*.

[63] Cf especially the French tradition, J Kühling, *Die Kommunikationsfreiheit als europäisches Gemeinschaftsgrundrecht* (1999) 252 *et seq*.

[64] See particularly ECHR, *Matthews v United Kingdom* Rep 1999-I 251, in which the ECtHR found a responsibility of the Member States regarding directly effective Community legislation; the scope of the judgment is discussed by S Winkler, 'Der Europäische Gerichtshof für Menschenrechte, das Europäische Parlament und der Schutz der Konventionsgrundrechte im Europäischen Gemeinschaftsrecht', (2001) *Europäische Grundrechte-Zeitschrift* 18 at 23 *et seq*. Additionally, particular problems arise in countries such as Austria and the Netherlands where the ECHR has constitutional status or takes priority over constitutional law respectively. Regarding the status of the ECHR in these countries see C Grabenwarter, 'Europäisches und nationales Verfassungsrecht', (2001) 60 *Veröffentlichungen der Vereinigung der Deutschen Staatsrechtslehrer* 291 at 300, who also gives further references.

[65] Grabenwarter, above n 64, 332, speaks of "soft normative effects"('weichen' normativen Auswirkungen); however, this would require in each individual case a distinction between the Member States as regards the date of accession to the ECHR and its Additional Protocols as well as a debate to determine the precise extent to which that Member State may be bound by international law, see the corresponding references, 295 *et seq*.

show consideration for the Member States' constitutional structures and obligations under international law,[66] it is necessary to show as much consideration as possible for the standards of the ECHR when developing the fundamental rights of the Union. Although this is only an obligation to guarantee the ECHR standard as a minimum standard, it is advisable for pragmatic reasons to also adopt the legal doctrine of the ECHR insofar as no specific amendments need to be made due to the distinctive features of the EC: after all, the easily traceable and rich source of experience of the ECHR as well as the highly advanced legal doctrine of the ECHR would prove advantageous. Furthermore, an orientation towards the standards of the ECHR as a minimum standard guarantees a much higher level of predictability than the development of fundamental rights standards by means of comparing the Member States' constitutional traditions which is of limited comprehensibility. Moreover, the Constitutional Treaty demands accession by the EU to the ECHR. This growing orientation towards the standard provided by the ECHR also corresponds to current case-law of the ECJ.[67]

The differing functions of the ECHR on the one hand, seeking to achieve a minimum consensus and the EU on the other, seeking a higher level of integration must not be ignored, however. This requires an additional consideration of the Member States' fundamental rights traditions as well as a definition of the contents of fundamental rights, which must fulfil the systematic imperatives of the Constitution of the Union and implies a tendency to strengthen fundamental rights. The specification of fundamental rights must occur in a critical dialogue with the legal community[68] and legal science must contribute by compiling the values embodied in national fundamental rights and by including these when critically following the process of fundamental rights specification. Issues at the core of future dogmatic development especially include the determination of the "horizontal and vertical" scope of fundamental rights, i.e. their binding force as regards the institutions of the EU and of the EC on the one hand and action by Member States on the other.

Recent case-law of the ECJ has not only proved that the Court is willing to take fundamental rights seriously, but also to consider aspects of the legal dogmatics of fundamental rights. The discussion whether there was an interference with private life (as protected by Article 8 ECHR) in

[66] Kahl, in: Calliess and Ruffert, above n 18, Art 10 EC, para 52, giving further references; A Bleckmann, *Europarecht* (1997) para 715.

[67] Recently in *Connolly*, Case C-274/99 P, above n 23, paras 39 *et seq*; see also R Uerpmann-Wittzack in this volume, VI.2.b.

[68] An enumeration of the persons belonging to the legal community is provided by J Bengoetxea, *The Legal Reasoning of the European Court of Justice* (1993) 126.

Österreichischer Rundfunk is just one example. In this case, the ECJ also scrutinises the scope of Article 8 ECHR.[69]

2. Functions and Classification of Fundamental Rights

a) Possible Classifications

An important element of legal doctrine of fundamental rights is the question of what functions fundamental rights fulfil and how they can be classified. The Charter, in the wording of the Constitutional Treaty, emphasises in Article II-52(5) CT-Conv (Article 112(5) CT-IGC) the difference between rights and principles. The future legal doctrine of fundamental rights will therefore have to classify the different guarantees of the Charter according to this category and explain the differences with reference to Article II-52(5) CT-Conv (Article 112(5) CT-IGC). A further classification could have a focus on the different possible situations in which fundamental rights may be invoked. So far, one can derive from the case-law of the ECJ that fundamental rights are basically used to check legislative and executive acts. Therefore, fundamental rights are used as "control norms". The case of *Connolly* illustrates this situation.[70] However, they can also be referred to when interpreting other norms ("interpretation norm"). Article II-52(5) CT-Conv (Article 112(5) CT-IGC) reduces principles to this function. Thirdly, they can be applied in order to limit other norms such as the fundamental freedoms ("limitation norm"). The case of *Schmidberger* is a recent example of this function.[71] Other situations may be classified additionally.

b) Subjective (Negative) Rights and Positive Obligations

aa) The Difference Between Subjective (Negative) Rights and Positive Obligations A further classification could refer to the different "protective functions" of fundamental rights. In the current case-law of the ECJ, the prime function is that of a subjective (negative) right or individual right (in German "subjektives Abwehrrecht"). One may (attempt to) apply fundamental rights in order to hinder interference by State authorities, e.g. in the case of *Connolly* in order to protect your freedom of opinion against interferences of the Commission.[72] In that respect, it is a negative right as it

[69] Cases C-465/00, C-138/01 and C-139/01, *Österreichischer Rundfunk et al* [2003] ECR I-4989, paras 73 *et seq.*
[70] Case C-274/99 P, above n 23, paras 37 *et seq.*
[71] Case C-112/00, *Schmidberger* [2003] ECR I-5659, para 74.
[72] Case C-274/99 P, above n 23, paras 37 *et seq.*

prohibits a certain State action.[73] Nevertheless, other functions do exist. Although the following categories are partly based in German legal doctrine of fundamental rights, which only to a limited extent correspond to the fundamental rights doctrines of other Member States, the legal doctrine of the ECJ to date and especially that of the ECtHR show that a parallel development on the international level and thus also at supranational level is possible, although one hardly finds explicit references to the different protective dimensions (yet). Nevertheless it is argued, that such dimensions should be made explicit in legal doctrine of fundamental rights of the EU as it allows a more rational discussion of what functions fundamental rights should fulfil. Therefore, the proposal to adopt and develop the following doctrinal concepts does not pursue a specific outcome of certain aims fundamental rights should reach. It is rather a proposal for a common language allowing a rational discourse of certain aims fundamental rights might fulfil.

You can classify the other functions under the heading "positive obligations" as they all oblige State authorities to act in a certain manner.[74]

bb) Duty to Protect as Central Positive Obligation The most developed positive obligation is the duty to protect (also against private parties).[75] In this context, there are two different dogmatic constructions possible. Firstly, it is possible to widen the concept of interference by qualifying approval by the State of private intrusion on fundamental rights as interference by the State. Secondly, objective or positive duties to protect may be derived from fundamental rights, which in specific cases become concrete duties to act and then correspond to similar rights of the individual to activity by the sovereign power (rights providing protection or "Schutzgewährrechte" in German[76]). In its recent judgment on a positive duty of a State to protect in *Hatton*, the ECtHR (both the Chamber and the Grand Chamber) explicitly took as its theme these two possibilities of construction. It rightly pointed out that the respective standards of justification both for a sovereign interference with fundamental rights and for a possible violation of a duty on the State to protect (or more generally to act) may be compared.[77]

[73] Within a strict classification of duties one may classify it as a "duty to respect"; see for this approach the General Comment No 12 of the CESCR, UN-Doc. <http://www.unhchr.ch/tbs/doc.nsf/(Symbol)/ca12c3a4ea8d6c53c1256d500056e56f?Opendocument> (9 June 2004)

[74] See for such an approach with respect to the ECHR C Grabenwarter, *Europäische Menschenrechtskonvention* (2003), § 19.

[75] See comprehensively L Jaeckel, 'The duty to protect fundamental rights in the European Community', (2003) 28 *ELRev* 508.

[76] In particular, this term is employed in relation to the fundamental rights of the EU by Kingreen, above n 18, para 129.

[77] ECtHR (Chamber), above n 40, para 96; ECtHR (Grand Chamber), Judgment of 8 July 2003, paras 98, 119; cf the earlier judgment *López Ostra v Spain* ECHR [1994] Series A No 303C, para 51.

However, the Chamber still prefers a construction using a positive duty to protect, whereas the Grand Chamber did not decide on this question.[78] The approach of the Chamber should also be employed for the legal doctrine of Union fundamental rights in order to emphasise the special nature of this constellation as well as the specific limits of a fundamental rights review thereof. When developing a dimension of duties to protect, the ECJ may take recourse to its parallel case-law on the fundamental freedoms.[79] Additionally, some approaches contained in the fundamental rights jurisprudence to date may also be interpreted to this effect, such as the judgment in *Familiapress* for the purposes of maintaining press diversity.[80] Thus, duties to protect may be derived from fundamental rights and may, in individual cases, become enforceable rights providing protection (also against private persons). The question of the effect of fundamental rights between private parties ("horizontal effect" or in German "Drittwirkung") must also be viewed in this context. Thus, duties on the State to protect may be invoked against actions by private parties without having to take recourse to the doubtful construction of private parties being bound by fundamental rights.[81]

From the perspective of horizontal division of powers, it must, however, be taken into account that the formulation of such duties constitutes a sensitive interference with the scope for evaluation and the margin of discretion of both the legislator and the executive respectively. There is a danger that these bodies may be reduced to being the executing organ of imperative duties of protection in constitutional law.[82] Thus, it is generally only possible to assume an obligation to take effective measures, but not to perform certain actions if more than one action proves effective. Nevertheless, in this context the development of concrete duties of protection must take place with regard to individual fundamental rights and their respective significance for the individual as well as the activities concerned.

To this extent, a development of fundamental rights protection by means of procedural safeguards seems advisable as well. Regarding the right to respect for private and family life and home (Article 8 ECHR) a duty to

[78] ECtHR (Chamber), above n 40, para 95; ECtHR (Grand Chamber), above n 77, paras 98 and 119.

[79] See especially Case C-265/95, *Commission v France* [1997] ECR I-6959, paras 30 *et seq*, commented upon by P Sczczekalla, 'Grundfreiheitliche Schutzpflichten', (1998) *Deutsches Verwaltungsblatt* 219 at 221 *et seq*.

[80] Case C-368/95, *Familiapress* [1995] ECR I-3689, para 26; J Kühling, 'Grundrechtskontrolle durch den EuGH', (1997) *Europäische Grundrechte-Zeitschrift* 296 at 301.

[81] This is also the approach taken in *Hatton*, above n 40; cf also Kühling, above n 63, 379 *et seq*; taking an even stricter approach Kingreen, above n 18, para 63, with further references including the dissenting opinion.

[82] To this effect CD Classen, 'Die Ableitung von Schutzpflichten des Gesetzgebers aus Freiheitsrechten', (1987) 36 *Jahrbuch des öffentlichen Rechts der Gegenwart* 44, referring to the legislature.

examine may be assumed in the event of expected interferences in fundamental rights: this has been confirmed by the ECtHR in *Hatton*, a case concerning possible health endangerments trough environmental conditions.[83] However, the proviso on environmental protection and the improvement of the quality of the environment in Article II-37 CT-Conv (Article 97 CT-IGC) probably merely constitutes the formulation of a general objective of only limited validity as regards positive duties on the State to act and particularly to protect (a "principle" in the sense of Article II-52(5) CT-Conv; Article 112(5) CT-IGC).[84]

From the perspective of vertical division of powers, it must be pointed out that, unlike a State, the Union is not subjected to an encompassing duty to protect its citizens because the Union only possesses a limited competence in specified areas. Yet, this still makes it possible to consider duties to protect when applying Community law, even if the EU does not possess competence in this area. Thus, an obligation to maintain diversity may be taken into account in the sphere of the fundamental freedoms (see *Familiapress*[85]), merger control[86] or the Telecommunications Framework Directive[87]. However, while institutions of the EU or of the EC may only be obliged to perform certain acts within their competences, Member States may only be obliged to do so if the area concerned is within the field of application of Community law.

cc) Derived Participatory Rights Corresponding with the Positive Obligation to Give Access From the ECJ's legal doctrine of equal treatment, positive duties on the State to give access to enjoy certain collective benefits and a corresponding derived participatory right (in German "derivative Teilhaberechte") may also be derived, as a further function of fundamental rights. Thus, the ECJ has pointed out that the principle of equal

[83] ECtHR (Chamber), above n 40, paras 97 *et seq*; ECtHR (Grand Chamber), above n 77, para 99; one can also distinguish organisational and procedural safeguards as another category, see for such an approach with respect to the ECHR Grabenwarter, above n 74, § 19 III.

[84] The EU system of fundamental rights is also provided with the challenge of developing a different scope for the provisions on the protection of health, the environment and the consumer contained in Arts II-35, II-37 and II-38 CT-Conv (Arts 95, 97, 98 CT-IGC), the wording of which differs. Thus, the first sentence of Art II-35 CT-Conv (Art 95 CT-IGC) contains a stricter wording in that it contains a "right of access to preventive health care and the right to benefit from medical treatment". This must be contrasted to the second sentence which—in accordance with the other provisions—merely stipulates a high level of human health protection in the definition and implementation of all Union policies.

[85] Above n 80.

[86] See D Frey, 'Die europäische Fusionskontrolle und die Medienvielfalt', (1998) *Zeitschrift für Urheber- und Medienrecht* 985 *et seq*.

[87] On Art 8(2)(d) of Dir 2002/21/EC, OJ L 108, 24.4.2002, 33, see J-D Braun and R Capito, in: C Koenig, A Bartosch and J-D Braun (eds), *EC Competition and Telecommunications law* (2002) 310 at n 6.

treatment requires that the granting of a certain right to a group of persons is extended to a comparable group of persons.[88] These rights are referred to as derived participatory rights because the right of the individual may only be derived from the rights of a group. The Charter of Fundamental Rights provides an array of rules that may be interpreted as such derived participatory rights. This applies to the right of access to placement services pursuant to Article II-29 CT-Conv (Article 89 CT-IGC) and to the right of access to services of general economic interest in Article II-36 CT-Conv (Article 96 CT-IGC). Some of the procedural rights such as the right to an effective remedy and to a fair trial in Article II-47(1) and (2) CT-Conv (Article 107(1) and (2) CT-IGC) can be classified as derived participatory rights, as well.[89] Classic negative rights may also contain a participatory right component, however: in its judgment in *VDSÖ*, the ECtHR stated with reference to freedom of expression that a refusal by an authority to allow members of the Austrian Army to distribute a satirical magazine constitutes a violation of the victims' rights arising from Article 10 ECHR.[90] This implies at least a dimension of derived participation.[91] Thus, it may be concluded that it is possible to develop elements of derived participatory rights from the individual fundamental rights, for the purposes of the legal doctrine of EU fundamental rights.

dd) Original Rights to Performance Corresponding with Positive Obligations to Provide Original duties to provide benefits on part of the State (in German "originäre Leistungsrechte") take yet another step: these confer a claim to sovereign performance of a service even if this has previously not been provided for by law. The provisions in Articles II-29 and II-36 CT-Conv (Articles 89 and 96 CT-IGC), which have been discussed earlier to the effect that they may be read as participatory rights, may also be understood as original duties of the state to provide benefits. This also applies to the granting of legal aid referred to in Article II-47(3) CT-Conv (Article 107(3) CT-IGC) or the right to social and housing assistance contained in Article II-34(3) CT-Conv (Article 94(3) CT-IGC). Furthermore, similar protective components may be found in general fundamental rights such as the deduction of a claim

[88] Regarding the prohibition of discrimination in Art 12 EC see Case 186/87, *Cowan* [1989] ECR 195, paras 10 *et seq*; critical comment by M Rossi, 'Das Diskriminierungsverbot nach Art 12 EGV', (2000) *Europarecht* 197 at 215, who points out that alternatively the exclusion of both groups from the right would be possible as well as equal but different treatment. This scope for action by the Member States is unnecessarily restricted by the interpretation of the ECJ.

[89] See also with respect to the ECHR Grabenwarter, above n 74, § 19 II.

[90] *Vereinigung demokratischer Soldaten Österreichs et al v Austria* ECHR [1994] Series A No 302, paras 37 *et seq* and 49.

[91] To this effect also M Holoubek, *Grundrechtliche Gewährleistungspflichten* (1997) 62.

to legal aid from the right to a fair trial in Article 6 ECHR.[92] Thus, these provisions form the basis for corresponding claims even if such guarantees are not provided for in other provisions of Community law or in the law of the Member States.

In this case, there is a special challenge for the legal doctrine of fundamental rights to differentiate between the core of participatory right and the layer of original rights to performance and to develop different standards. It must be taken into account that original rights to performance have only a limited tradition in constitutional law.[93] They cause particularly sensitive interferences in the margin of interpretation and the margin of discretion of the executive and especially the legislature because they result in strains on the public budget and thus restrict parliamentary budget sovereignty. Therefore, special caution is necessary when developing these rights. As with regard to the remarks on duties of protection, the restrictions of competence apply in vertical perspective.

3. Who is Bound by Fundamental Rights?—the Reach of Fundamental Rights

Next to the institutions of the EU and the EC (a), Member State authorities may also be considered (b) as being bound by fundamental rights. However, it is more convincing from a dogmatic point of view to reconstruct the effect of fundamental rights between private parties ("horizontal effect" or "Drittwirkung") within the framework of sovereign duties to protect.[94]

a) The Binding Effect on the Institutions of the EC and the EU

The binding effect of the fundamental rights of the EU on the Community institutions has been established by the case-law of the ECJ without any resistance having been offered. The obligation applies both to abstract-general as well as concrete-individual Community action.[95] National courts, especially the German *Bundesverfassungsgericht* and the Italian *Corte*

[92] *Granger* ECHR [1990] Series A 174, paras 44 *et seq*; *Boner v United Kingdom* ECHR [1994] Series A No 300B, paras 30 *et seq*; ECHR, *Benham v United Kingdom* Rep 1996-III, paras 60 *et seq*.

[93] Kingreen, above n 18, para 187.

[94] Cf the references in n 81.

[95] For general acts by the Community see the seminal judgments in Case 11/70, *Internationale Handelsgesellschaft* [1970] ECR 1125, para 4, and Case 44/79, *Hauer* [1979] ECR 3727, paras 13 *et seq*, which were concerned with the review of regulations; regarding individual Community acts addressed to a specified individual see the seminal judgment in Case 4/73, *Nold v Commission* [1974] ECR 491, paras 12 *et seq*, which examined a decision of the Commission.

Costituzionale, not only welcomed this development, but demanded and inspired it.[96] The binding effect of EU fundamental rights on the institutions of the EU has now been laid down in Article 6(2) EU.[97]

b) The Binding Effect on the Member States as Determinant of the Vertical Scope of the Fundamental Rights of the Union

Dealing with the question of the binding effect of fundamental rights of the Union upon the Member States, one has to keep in mind that this question is also one important aspect of the question of how far fundamental rights should reach and how far integration through fundamental rights should go.

aa) The Position of the ECJ It was not until a later phase in the case-law of the ECJ that the more difficult question of whether Member States were bound by fundamental rights of the EU in their actions first arose. This question constitutes the central issue of the important debate on the future scope of Union fundamental rights from a vertical perspective. It is quite possible that the respective case-law of the ECJ has not yet been fully developed.[98] However, important trends are emerging: the ECJ is neither employing the approach of utilising fundamental rights to review all actions by Member States, nor is it absolutely refusing to conduct such an examination. Rather, the ECJ compromises by stating in its case-law that if a rule falls within the scope of Community law, any fundamental rights review must employ as its standard those fundamental rights whose observance the Court ensures.[99] Thus, the main question appears to be how to determine when a national rule touches upon those fundamental rights whose observance is ensured by the ECJ. In the face of the growing extent of regulation by Community law, the potential scope of finding Member States to be bound is extraordinarily broad and clear criteria for the determination of the extent to which Member States may be bound will have to be established by the case-law of the ECJ.

To date, two situations in which such a binding effect is to be affirmed have arisen from the case-law of the ECJ. One situation concerns the

[96] This applies in particular to the famous first "Solange" decision of the German *Bundesverfassungsgericht* of 29 May 1974, (1974) 2 *CML Rev* 540 at 549 *et seq*, which implies a demand to this effect, cf Kühling, above n 80, 299 in footnote 37.

[97] See above II.1.b.

[98] To this effect Mancini and Di Bucci, above n 32, 39; also M Ruffert, 'Die Mitgliedstaaten der Europäischen Gemeinschaft als Verpflichtete der Gemeinschaftsgrundrechte', (1995) *Europäische Grundrechte-Zeitschrift* 518 at 528 *et seq*; this is also criticised by T Jürgensen and I Schlünder, 'EG-Grundrechtsschutz gegenüber Maßnahmen der Mitgliedstaaten', (1996) 121 *Archiv des öffentlichen Rechts* 200 at 201.

[99] First in Case C-260/89, *ERT* [1991] ECR I-2925, para 42; confirmed inter alia in Case C-159/90, *Grogan* [1991] ECR I-4685, para 31 and Case C-2/92, *Bostock* [1994] ECR I-955, para 16.

implementation of secondary Community law as well as the administrative enforcement of Community law. It is graphically referred to by Weiler as an "agency situation":[100] Member State authorities execute or implement an act initiated by Community law. The ECJ first explicitly formulated this line of reasoning in the *Wachauf* judgment, which concerned the execution of a regulation in the dairy sector.[101] Ultimately, this approach already formed the basis of the ECJ's very first judgment of its fundamental rights jurisprudence in which the Court merely hinted at a fundamental rights review in an obiter dictum, obliging the Member State to apply a Commission decision in such a manner as not to violate the fundamental rights of the individual.[102] However, it is necessary that such a binding effect on the Member States also applies to the implementation of a directive.[103] As regards measures by Member States in the implementation of administrative procedures, the judgment in *Hoechst* is referred to. The ECJ pointed out that national authorities affording assistance to the Commission in the implementation of administrative procedures must respect general principles of Community law.[104] It remains to be seen whether this category may be extended to include contested measures by the State which do not have the purpose of implementing secondary Community law but which show a clear connection thereto.[105]

Since the judgment in *ERT*, a second category of Member State measures is subject to a fundamental rights review by the ECJ: in ERT, the Court determined that if a Member State invokes an exemption to one of the fundamental freedoms, the justification must be interpreted in the light of fundamental rights.[106] The ECJ has extended this line of reasoning to include

[100] J Weiler, 'Fundamental Rights and Fundamental Boundaries', in: NA Neuwahl *et al* (eds), *The European Union and Human Rights* (1995) 51 at 67 *et seq*.

[101] As confirmed in *Bostock*, above n 99.

[102] Case 29/69, *Stauder* [1969] ECR 419, paras 4 *et seq*.

[103] The earlier judgment in *Johnston* was interpreted to this effect, Case 222/84, *Johnston* [1986] ECR 1651, paras 17 *et seq*, which was concerned with the review of the right to an effective judicial remedy under national law regarding an implemented directive; this was commented upon by J Weiler and N Lockhart, '"Taking Rights Seriously" Seriously', (1995) 32 *CML Rev* 579 at 609.

[104] Cases 46/87 and 227/88, *Hoechst v Commission* [1989] ECR 2859, fifth heading and para 33.

[105] Above n 103; cf R Lawson, 'The European Court of Justice and Human Rights', (1992) 5 *LJIL* 99 at 105 *et seq*; J Temple Lang, 'The Sphere in which Member States are Obliged to Comply with the General Principles of Law and Community Fundamental Rights Principles', (1991) *LIEI* 23 at 27; cf also the ECJ's reasoning in Case C-299/95, *Kremzow* [1997] ECR I-2629, paras 15 *et seq*, where it was stated that the applicable provisions of national law "were not designed to secure compliance with rules of Community law"; this dictum is emphasised by M Holoubek, 'Anmerkungen zum Urteil des EuGH vom 29.5.1997', (1998) *Justizblatt* 237 who argues that a new general category could be based thereon.

[106] Case C-260/89, above n 99, paras 42 *et seq*; confirmed in Case C-62/90, *Commission v Germany* [1992] ECR I-2575, para 23.

the inherent restrictions on the fundamental freedoms, i.e. "mandatory requirements" in the case of Article 28 EC and "overriding reasons relating to the public interest" in the case of Article 49 EC.[107] *Carpenter* is the most recent judgment confirming this case-law.[108]

bb) The Future Consolidation of the ECJ's Point of View A review of fundamental rights in the case of an "agency situation" is widely accepted. More disputed is the examination of the implementation of a directive, however. Sometimes, Member State protection of fundamental rights is seen as sufficient when making use of the scope of implementation associated with a directive, while the fact that the Community institutions are bound is emphasised when it comes to those parts of the directive that are mandatory.[109] While the later is true, the former is to be doubted. Thus, the concept of a directive which, according to Article 249(3) EC, leaves to the Member States a choice of form and methods when implementing set targets binding under Community law, is in favour of taking into account national distinctive features, also with regard to fundamental rights. However, Member State measures necessitated by directives are still caused by Community law: without the initial act under Community law, many cases of jeopardising fundamental rights due to Member State action would not occur. This provides support for the theory that Member States must adhere to the standard of Community fundamental rights if an interference with fundamental rights occurs when making use of the scope for implementation of directives, irrespective of parallel protection (which is not always available) under fundamental rights of the Member States. This is the only way in which an EU-wide uniform (minimum) standard of fundamental rights may be guaranteed against interference with fundamental rights caused by Community law. In an "agency situation", the victim obtains protection not only against direct measures of Community institutions, but also against measures caused by Community institutions which required national institutions for their realisation. The citizen also obtains a guarantee that rights granted by Community law will be implemented into national law in such a way as to ensure conformity with Community fundamental rights.

Taking this approach as a basis, the case-law on the review of Community fundamental rights with respect to the so-called "restrictions on the restrictions" ("Schranken-Schranken") of the fundamental freedoms is to be followed (i.e. particularly Articles 30, 39(3), 46, 46 in conjunction

[107] Case C-23/93, *TV 10 SA* [1994] ECR I-4795, para 222 *et seq*; Case C-368/95, above n 80, para 24.

[108] Case C-60/00, *Carpenter* [2002] ECR I-6279, para 40.

[109] To this effect Kingreen, above n 18, para 59.

with 55, and 58 EC). It must be conceded, though, that the arguments usually employed (such as primacy of Community law, uniform application of the law as well as the right to an effective remedy[110]) do not necessarily lead to this result. However, upon closer inspection, the argument to the effect that restrictions constitute areas of exception and are therefore outside the reach of Community fundamental rights[111] turns out to be a circular argument as that which is to be proved is in fact presupposed. Ultimately, it must be taken into account that the fundamental freedoms grant rights which are part of Community law and which—just as the whole of Community law—must therefore be interpreted in conformity with Community fundamental rights, also as regards their possibilities of restriction.[112] By employing a proportionality test, it is possible to preserve the necessary scope for action by Member States both in this case and when reviewing the use of the scope for implementation of directives. To this extent, a more precise definition of the standard of review may occur by means of adopting a modified version of the ECHR concept of margin of appreciation.[113]

At the present stage of integration, however, it does not seem appropriate to increase the situations in which Member States are bound by fundamental rights. This also applies to the suggestion of Advocate General Jacobs in the *Konstantinidis* judgment to declare that Member State actions are bound by fundamental rights vis-à-vis nationals of other Member States present in that Member State.[114] Even less desirable is a result which would

[110] Cf Ruffert, above n 98, 523.

[111] However, to this effect T Kingreen, *Die Struktur der Grundfreiheiten des Europäischen Gemeinschaftsrechts* (1999) 168.

[112] Cf also T Schilling, 'Bestand und allgemeine Lehren der bürgerschützenden allgemeinen Rechtsgrundsätze des Gemeinschaftsrechts', (2003) *Europäische Grundrechte-Zeitschrift* 3 at 34 *et seq*, who speaks of the Member States being indirectly bound in the light of such an application of Community fundamental rights under Community law.

[113] This will be discussed below under 5.c,cc(4); the proposal by Ruffert, above n 98, 529, to restrict review to a *prima facie* control must be rejected. Rather it should be aimed to at least preserve the standard of the ECHR; U Schildknecht, *Grundrechtsschranken in der Europäischen Gemeinschaft* (2000) 225, even believes that a uniform (Community) standard should be applied.

[114] AG Jacobs had assumed that there was a sufficient connection to Community law if a Community national goes to another Member State as a worker or self-employed person. Such a "*civis europeus*" would be entitled to assume that, "wherever he goes to earn his living in the EC, he will be treated in accordance with a common code of fundamental values" without having to prove a further connection to Community law: Case C-168/91, *Konstantinidis* [1993] ECR I-1198, para 46; also F Jacobs, 'European Community Law and the European Convention on Human Rights' in: *Essays in Honour of Henry G Schermers* (1994), vol II, 561 at 564; the ECJ did not comment on this opinion and did not follow it as the Court required an economic disadvantage in order for Community law to become applicable, Case C-168/91, *Konstantinidis* [1993] ECR I-1191, paras 13 *et seq*; see the critical annotation by R Lawson, (1994) 31 *CML Rev* 395 at 406 *et seq*.

declare all actions by Member States to be bound by fundamental rights—as has been established in the US by *Gitlow v New York*[115]—because this would constitute a fundamental step towards a federal order for which no basis is provided in Community primary law. Rather, such a step would have to be supported by a political impetus in the shape of a far-reaching catalogue of fundamental rights. Otherwise, a severe threat of disintegration is to be expected and the now established complimentary performance of fundamental rights protection by national, international and supranational interpreters would be endangered unnecessarily.[116] However, Article II-51(1) CT-Conv (Article 111 CT-IGC) only obliges the Member States to respect the fundamental rights of the Union when implementing Union law. No expansive tendencies may be derived from this formulation. There is, rather, a discussion that this formulation reduces the reach of fundamental rights to the "agency situation".[117] But as the wording allows a broader interpretation and the explanations of the Praesidium show that the formulation should preserve the present case-law including *ERT*, to which the Praesidium explicitly refers, this interpretation is not compelling. The Praesidium paraphrases the wording with the formulation "when they act in the context of Community law". As the fundamental rights of the Charter are supposed to be interpreted with due regard to the explanations prepared at the instigation of the Praesidium according to the Preamble of Part II of the Constitutional Treaty (5th recital, last sentence), the formulation "when they act in the context of Community law" will be the future starting-point.[118] The most recent judgments on fundamental rights have shown a willingness of the ECJ to interpret the reach of Union fundamental rights rather generously. Particularly in *Avello*, the Court implicitly overruled *Konstantinidis* and stated that "[s]uch a link with Community law does, however, exist in regard to persons in a situation such as that of the children of Mr Garcia Avello, who are nationals of one Member State lawfully resident in the territory of another Member State"[119]. One may doubt whether the link proposed in *Avello* is sufficient. In the end, it opens a

[115] *Gitlow v People of the State of New York*, judgment of 8 June 1925, Supreme Court Reporter 45, 625; cf in detail M Shapiro, 'Freedom of Expression' in: M Cappelletti *et al* (eds), *Integration Through Law* (1986) vol 1, pt 3, 249 *et seq*, who traces the gradual shift of review in the last instance from the constitutional courts of the individual states to the Supreme Court using as an example freedom of speech which has had a path-breaking function.

[116] See below IV.

[117] Especially M Borowsky, in: Meyer (ed), above n 4, Art 51 Charter, para 29.

[118] P Eeckhout, 'The EU Charter of Fundamental Rights and the Federal Question', (2002) 39 *CML Rev* 945 at 993; F Turpin, 'La Charte des droits fondamentaux dans la Constitution européenne', (2003) *Revue trimestrielle de droit européen* 615 at 622; against W Cremer, 'Der programmierte Verfassungskonflikt', (2003) *Neue Zeitschrift für Verwaltungsrecht* 1452, who consequently demands a modification of Art II-51(1) CT-Conv (Art 111(1) CT-IGC).

[119] Case C-148/02, *Garcia Avello* [2003] ECR I-11613, para 27.

fundamental rights control of every treatment of EU foreigners without taking into account if the specific measure has any particular relevance for EU foreigners. In any case, such an expansion should only be undertaken with great caution.[120] The same has to be said whenever it comes to an expansion of the two categories, for example in the "agency situation", to include situations which do not concern the implementation of a directive, but are closely related.[121] However, in the end, one has to admit that there is no "super-formula" indicating when the Member states "act in the context of Community law" as the possible areas are numberless and heterogeneous. The case-law of the ECJ will have to develop the criteria step by step.

4. Who May Assert Fundamental Rights?

Unlike the question of who is bound by fundamental rights, the question of who may assert them is less contested. Apart from some particular rights for Union citizens such as right to vote (see Article II-39(1) CT-Conv; Article 99(1) CT-IGC) all natural persons are "born" obligees of the fundamental rights of the EU (including officials). Moreover, legal persons are generally obligees as well.[122]

5. The Structure of Examination of Fundamental Rights

a) An Overview over the System of Examination

One of the main points of criticism in German legal literature levied against the present case-law of the ECJ concerns the lack of a suitable and coherent structure of examination of fundamental rights. Thus, it is often difficult to comprehend whether a sufficient consideration of the interests involved has occurred. Sometimes, when analysing the area protected by a fundamental right, it even remains unclear which right is being examined.[123] Not only does this produce negative results for the general orientation function of the fundamental rights review but problematic results may also be produced in individual cases. Therefore, the necessary further development of the ECJ's fundamental rights legal doctrine must include an improvement

[120] Eeckhout, above n 118, 971.
[121] Above n 100 *et seq*.
[122] For more details Kühling, above n 21, 611 *et seq*.
[123] See for the first case Case C-280/93, *Germany v Council* [1994] ECR I-4973, paras 94 *et seq*; for the second case cf the ruling in *Hoechst*, Cases 46/87 and 227/88, above n 104, para 19; for an example of the critique in German academic literature see M Nettesheim, 'Grundrechtliche Prüfdichte durch den EuGH', (1995) *Europäische Zeitschrift für Wirtschaftsrecht* 106 *et seq*; more positively U Kischel, 'Die Kontrolle der Verhältnismäßigkeit durch den Europäischen Gerichtshof', (2000) *Europarecht* 380 *et seq*.

of the structure of examination employed. Recent judgments of the ECJ already suggest such an improvement[124] and in general,[125] it is recommended that further improvements should be orientated towards the system of examination employed by the ECtHR as far as possible. Inspirations may also be found in the legal doctrine of the Member States.

The structure of examination may vary according to the different rights concerned. Particularly, the subjective (negative) rights differ in that respect from the positive obligations. The following explanations focus on the structure of examination of the subjective (negative) rights as they are of prime importance. Particularities of the examination of the equality principle and positive obligations will be dealt with separately (section III.5.d below).

As a first step, this requires a description of the area protected by the fundamental right in question. The second step of examination aims at determining whether there has been an interference with the exercise of a fundamental right. The ECtHR usually combines these steps (section b below). In a third step, it must be examined whether the interference may be justified (section c below). The Charter of Fundamental Rights also implies such a interplay of the exercise of a fundamental right, its restriction and the justification for the restriction in Article II-52(1) CT-Conv (Article 112(1) CT-IGC).[126] According to this provision, any restriction must be provided for by law and respect the essence of the right in issue as well as being proportionate.

b) The Area Protected by Fundamental Rights and Interference Therein

The area of protection of a fundamental right (its protective scope, or *Schutzbereich*) describes the area of action which is guaranteed by the fundamental right in principle and the sovereign restriction of which requires a justification. In other words, it defines its scope. It is to be regretted that the ECJ has only commented briefly on questions relating to the area protected by a fundamental right. However, this should change when the Charter of Fundamental Rights is incorporated into primary law. The influence of a fixed text on the analysis of the area of protection is not to be underestimated. Even without the incorporation of the Charter, the ECJ

[124] Cf eg the judgment in *Connolly*, Case C-274/99 P, above n 23, paras 40 *et seq*.

[125] Nevertheless one may wonder if the sharp distinction between subjective negative rights and procedural rights with respect to the structure of examination is justified and should be transferred to the Union fundamental rights, see for this difference in the case-law of the ECtHR Grabenwarter, above n 74, § 18 I.

[126] Applying the terminology prevalent in German dogmatic theory of fundamental rights one could talk of restrictions ("Schranken") and "restrictions on the restrictions" ("Schranken-Schranken"). But this might be a little too German.

should develop more clearly the legal positions, which are objectively protected and should examine whether it is possible to limit these. Thus, when specifying the fundamental rights of the Union, the Court may refer to the Charter of Fundamental Rights as the essence of the traditions of the Member States. Additionally, an orientation towards the case-law of the ECtHR is recommended. First corresponding indications may be found in the case-law of the ECJ.[127] The Court is more willing to analyse the area protected by the fundamental right.[128]

To date, the development of legal doctrine as regards the interference with the exercise of a fundamental right has been completely neglected. This becomes even more problematic as there exist certain problems specific to the Community that require the development of independent legal doctrine. An interference may be defined as any impairment of the legal position protected in principle by the fundamental right in question. In individual cases, it may be difficult to determine to what extent a mere danger to the position of a fundamental right may already constitute an interference.

This problem is especially prevalent as regards the review of the legal provisions contained in directives. The question arises of whether a provision in a directive itself or only a national implementing act constitutes an interference. If the Member State is obliged to implement the provision concerned, then the wording of the directive already contains an obligation to interfere in the exercise of specified fundamental rights. Therefore, the duty of implementation causes a situation endangering fundamental rights equal to an interference which must then become real in the process of implementation by the Member State.[129]

c) Justification of an Interference with Fundamental Rights

To date, the structure employed by the ECJ to examine justifications for interferences in fundamental rights has varied widely. However, a uniform system of examination in the area of central freedoms has emerged from the experience of the ECHR: this is regulated by the respective provisions on restriction (see especially the second paragraphs of Articles 8 to 11 ECHR). Accordingly, the formal requirement of whether the interference is covered by an enabling legal basis must first be examined (aa). It must then be

[127] See, eg Cases C-174/98 P and C-189/98 P, *Netherlands et al v Commission* [2000] ECR I-1, paras 17 *et seq*; Case C-7/98, *Krombach* [2000] ECR I-1935, para 39; Case C-274/99 P, above n 23, paras 39 *et seq*.

[128] Cases C-465/00, C-138/01 and C-139/01, above n 69, paras 73 *et seq*.

[129] This is also assumed by AG Fennelly in Case C-376/98, *Germany v European Parliament and Council* [2000] ECR I- 8419, paras 146 *et seq*, especially para 165: "the Advertising Directive imposes restrictions on freedom of commercial expression"; see more detailed Kühling, above n 21, 615 *et seq*.

substantively determined whether the interference pursues a legitimate objective (bb). Next, the proportionality of the interference must be assessed in a third step (cc). These requirements are also provided in the general restriction clause in Article 52(1) of the Charter of Fundamental Rights. To this the guarantee of the very substance of rights in the first sentence of Article 52(1) must be added (dd).

aa) Interference Must be Founded on a Legal Basis The requirement of a legal basis ("provided for by law" in Article II-52(1) CT-Conv, Article 112(1) CT-IGC) has already been picked up by the ECJ. In the *Hoechst* judgment, the ECJ argued that "in all the legal systems of the Member States, any intervention by the public authorities in the sphere of private activities of any person, whether natural or legal, must have a *legal basis*" and that this need "must be recognised as a general principle of Community law".[130] In EU law, the legal basis for an interference may be found in primary law and in regulations, but especially in directives in connection with national implementing measures thereof. However, if Member State measures are being examined which do not implement Community law, the concept of law as developed by the bodies of the ECHR will apply. This extensive concept also includes unwritten law not enunciated in legislation to encompass common law.[131]

In the practice of the ECtHR, other formal requirements concerning the legal basis have been tightened in the context of the freedoms mentioned as regards two aspects which are also relevant for the legal doctrine of Union fundamental rights: the enabling provision must be formulated with sufficient preciseness and must be adequately accessible. The addressees of a norm must be able to orientate their conduct towards specified rules and to foresee potential sanctions; this is referred to as "accessibility". This means that the relevant norms must be sufficiently publicised to enable the addressee to have an indication thereof without considerable (or even financial) effort. Yet, the norm must also be as precise as possible in order to show clearly for what purposes and with which tendency it may be employed. General clauses must be sufficiently clarified through case-law. In the period immediately following their introduction, it must be obvious to foresee the tendency of their becoming applicable. The development of the case-law of the bodies of the ECHR has clearly shown that the importance of these principles is increasing.[132]

130 Cases 46/87 and 227/88, above n 104, para 19 (italics added).
131 See, eg *Sunday Times I* ECHR [1979] Series A No 30, para 47.
132 To take the example of Art 10(2) ECHR, cf Kühling, above n 63, 168 *et seq* with further references.

These strict requirements, which have developed in a similar way in Germany and in other countries,[133] may be transferred to EU law. Regarding the criterion of accessibility or availability, the ECJ has already stated that the principle of legal certainty requires that regulations only enter into force once the relevant issue of the Official Journal de facto is available in that Member State.[134] Additionally, Union citizens must also have access to implementing legislation of directives before these directives may possess a negative legal effect. Furthermore, the ECJ affirmed in the *Könecke* judgment that "a penalty, even of a non-criminal nature, cannot be imposed unless it rests on a clear and unambiguous legal basis".[135] This must apply to the preciseness of the enabling legal basis of any sovereign action.[136] The requirements concerning the enabling provision for action apply as regards the isolated examination of the basis itself (e.g. the examination of the provisions of a directive) as well as regards the examination of the implementing measures based thereon. In the case of directives, however, it must then be distinguished as follows: the requirements concerning preciseness only fully apply to the formulation of the objective of the directive. Concerning the form and the methods of national possibilities for implementation, it is the characteristic feature of a directive that it leaves to the Member States "the choice of form and methods" pursuant to Article 249(3) EC. This causes a certain openness in the formulation of the elements of a rule. However, the precise formulation of a rule must then be guaranteed in the national implementing acts.

bb) Legitimate Objective The ECJ is of the opinion that fundamental rights may only be limited if "those restrictions in fact correspond to objectives of general interest pursued by the Community".[137] The scope of possible Community interests legitimating an interference has been interpreted very widely in the ECJ's case-law to date and ranges from economic considerations[138] to interests of the Community institutions.[139] Some opinions by Advocates General, however, suggest a stricter approach as regards the examination of the genuine pertinence of the objectives advanced. Thus, in his opinion on the *Aids test* case, Advocate General van Gerven doubted

[133] Cf for the German situation B Pieroth and B Schlink, *Grundrechte Staatsrecht II* (2002) para 312.

[134] Case 98/78, *Racke* [1979] ECR 69, paras 19 *et seq.*

[135] Case 117/83, *Könecke* [1984] ECR 3291, para 11.

[136] Cf Case 169/80, *Gondrand Frères* [1981] ECR 1931, para 17.

[137] Case 5/88, *Wachauf* [1989] ECR 2609, para 18; see also the seminal judgment in Case 4/73, *Nold* [1974] ECR 491, para 14.

[138] Cases C-143/88 and 92/89, *Zuckerfabrik Süderdithmarschen* [1991] ECR I-415, para 76, referring to the aim to ensure "that losses incurred by an economic sector are not borne by the Community".

[139] Case C-404/92 P, *X v Commission* [1994] ECR I-4739, paras 19 *et seq.*

whether, in a concrete situation, the "economic well-being of the country" may be invoked as a justification for an interference with a person's private life.[140] As regards the fundamental rights of the EU, a careful examination of the reasons advanced for restriction is recommended. This also corresponds to the formulation of the proportionality principle in the second sentence of Article II-52(1) CT-Conv (Article 112(1) CT-IGC), which requires that restrictions "genuinely meet objectives of general interest recognised by the Union or the need to protect the rights and freedoms of others". This test of examining whether objectives are "genuinely" promoted introduces a strict examination of whether the legitimate objectives advanced are capable of justifying the interference. However, this already refers to the criterion of suitability of a measure as one aspect of proportionality. Altogether, the question arises of whether the examination of the legitimate objective should not be included in the proportionality test as is usual in German legal doctrine of fundamental rights, but not in the legal doctrine of the ECtHR. However, an independent examination of the legitimate objective makes it possible to better carve out the objectives pursued, as may be seen from the case-law of the ECtHR.

cc) The Principle of Proportionality As regards the principle of proportionality, many important questions of legal doctrine remain to be solved: the proportionality test plays a central part in the development of the legal doctrine of fundamental rights. It seems advisable to adapt the structure of examination to the general three-part proportionality test (suitability, necessity, proportionality in the narrow sense) usually employed in the examination of fundamental rights in Germany. This test is mainly used by the ECJ within the framework of examining possible violations of the fundamental freedoms and in an isolated examination of the proportionality principle. However, the ECJ sometimes even employs this test when examining fundamental rights.[141] On the other hand, the ECtHR mostly conducts a one-step examination orientated directly towards a balancing of the conflicting interests and rights, i.e. the proportionality test itself. Yet, there

[140] *Ibid*, Opinion of AG van Gerven, para 27; Schildknecht believes that this results in a *de facto* restriction of admissible justifications for interference as provided for by the ECHR: above n 113, 164 and 197 *et seq*.

[141] For a critical comment on the deficiencies of the proportionality test as applied to fundamental rights see S Storr, (1997) 36 *Der Staat* 547 at 564 *et seq* with further references; more positive Kischel, above n 123, 380 *et seq*; for an extensive general discussion on the principle of proportionality see G de Búrca, 'The Principle of Proportionality and its Application in EC Law', (1993) *YEL* 105 (at 113 *et seq* especially on the structure of examination); E Pache, 'Der Grundsatz der Verhältnismäßigkeit in der Rechtsprechung der Gerichte der Europäischen Gemeinschaften', (1999) *Neue Zeitschrift für Verwaltungsrecht* 1033 *et seq*; furthermore Schildknecht, above n 113, 51 *et seq*, 95 *et seq*, 165 *et seq*, 198 *et seq* and 217 *et seq*.

are also some cases containing elements of the first two steps of examination.[142] The three-part structure of the test provides a useful framework in that the genuine capability to attain the objective as well as the recourse to alternatives to the sovereign action in question, which may prove less of an interference, may already be debated at the level of examining the suitability and necessity of a measure. Thus, even at these levels, the three-part test contributes to a substantive review of sovereign interference with fundamental rights while simultaneously contributing to the subsequent application of the proportionality test if this should still prove necessary. Therefore, this test should also be employed as regards the review of interferences with EU fundamental rights.

However, the most importance must be attached to the carving-out of the parameters for balancing interests within the framework of assessing proportionality itself. To date, this constitutes the greatest omission of the review function of the ECJ which has all too often also examined in the same step whether there has been an interference with the very substance of the fundamental right guaranteed. This is then curtly denied, based on principle, without a sufficient analysis of interests or a precise examination of the workability of the sovereign measure in question having occurred.[143] Incidentally, the principle of proportionality should be completely integrated into the examination of fundamental rights as this is the only way to guarantee a review specific to the fundamental right in question in individual cases. In view of Article II-51 CT-Conv (Article 111 CT-IGC) and the increasing orientation towards the rights of the ECHR, a separate examination of the proportionality principle, which had been recognised in the ECJ's case-law at an early stage, is now outdated.

(1) Suitability

Therefore, it must first be examined whether the sovereign measure is suitable for, i.e. is capable of, attaining the objective pursued. This shows how important it is to subject the reasons for interference to a close examination (above bb). These reasons are now reviewed to see whether they may be realised with the means employed and whether they are in fact used for

[142] See for an examination of necessity in relation to freedom of expression the judgment of the ECtHR in *Informationsverein Lentia v Austria* ECHR [1993] Series A No 276, para 39; it is pointed out that there is a growing convergence with the proportionality test employed by the ECJ, see D Kugelmann, 'Zur Zulässigkeit eines öffentlichen Rundfunkmonopols nach Art. 10 EMRK', (1994) *Zeitschrift für Medien- und Kommunikationsrecht* 281 at 286; when examining freedom of possession, however, there is no determination of necessity, see K Gelinsky, *Der Schutz des Eigentums gemäß Art 1 des Ersten Zusatzprotokolls zur Europäischen Menschenrechtskonvention* (1996) 104 *et seq* with further references.

[143] Cf the reference in n 123.

these purposes.[144] However, at this stage of examination, a wide margin of appreciation must be granted to sovereign authorities when judging the suitability of a measure. This is especially the case if it is necessary to determine the efficiency by empirical research and this does not provide much security. In this context, it must be pointed out that, seen from the perspective of a procedural guarantee of fundamental rights, there may exist a sovereign duty to improve knowledge of the suitability of interferences, to examine the measures and to change or adjust these if necessary.[145]

(2) Necessity

In a second step, it must be examined whether the means employed are in fact necessary. This will be the case if, at the time the measure was adopted, there were no other means available which were equally efficient but less onerous. The examination is performed from an ex ante perspective. At this stage, the sovereign authorities are once again at an advantage when judging the efficiency of alternative options for action: they must be granted a wide margin of appreciation. This corresponds to the procedure employed by the ECtHR, in Germany and to the approach of Community law.[146] Here, one may use comparative law to show alternative possibilities for regulation that are equally efficient in attaining the objectives pursued, but which prove less onerous. The reasoning employed by the ECtHR in *Informationsverein Lentia* constitutes an example of the relevance of such an examination.[147] Similarly in *Österreichischer Rundfunk,* the ECJ has asked whether a certain measure is necessary or could be substituted by a measure which is equally efficient but less onerous.[148]

(3) Proportionality

There is no doubt that the core of the entire proportionality test is constituted by the determination of proportionality itself ("proportionality in the narrow sense"), i.e. the examination of whether the means employed are in proportion to the objectives pursued. First indications for this assessment are provided by the results gained at the first two stages. Thus, the review of suitability has shown the degree of efficiency of the measure in question. Subsequently, another assessment of the objective pursued must occur showing which public or private interests serve to legitimate this objective.

[144] This "in fact" test ("Tatsächlichkeitstest") corresponds both to the approach taken in Art 52(1) of the Charter ("*genuinely* meet objectives of general interest", italics added) as well as the case-law of the ECJ on the principle of proportionality in areas other than fundamental rights, Case C-157/99, *Smits* [2001] ECR I-5473, paras 75, 90 *et seq*; Case C-262/99, *Paraskevas Louloudakis* [2001] ECR I-5547, paras 69 *et seq*.

[145] On such duties to examine cf ECtHR (Chamber), *Hatton*, above n 40, paras 97 *et seq*.

[146] Cf Kühling, above n 63, 402 *et seq* with further references.

[147] See the reference above in n 142.

[148] Cases C-465/00, C-138/01 and C-139/01, above n 69, para 88.

Next, the severity of the interference must be judged. Orientation may be provided by the results of the examination of necessity. It must be examined whether the measure entails a substantial reduction of central protected positions. After an assessment of the interests concerned, it is possible to balance these. The balancing act, including the determination of appropriate margins of discretion for the legislature and the executive, may be considerably controlled by the legal concept of the margin of appreciation.[149]

(4) Density of Control and Margin of Appreciation

However, the application of the proportionality test also shows the limits of making the case-law on fundamental rights more dynamic as fundamental rights must not lose their "framework character" for the entire legal order. Both in principle and as regards various details, a substantive consideration of the legal doctrine of the ECHR and especially of the concept of margin of appreciation (or "marge d'appréciation") is recommended. According to this concept of density of control, the Member States of the ECHR are generally left a margin when determining an appropriate level of balance either between private interests *inter se* or between public and private interests.[150] In this context, the term "margin of appreciation" is not understood in a narrow sense as to merely refer to the existence of discretion when choosing an appropriate measure, but refers to the discretion in assessing potentials for danger or other factors. The intensity of interference permissible and the discretion inherent in attributing values to be protected depends hereupon. The bodies of the ECHR ensure that all sovereign measures remain within the margin allowed. This concept plays a central role in establishing common European standards. Thus, by employing a margin of appreciation, the ECtHR has carved out areas in which a considerable development of common European standards is guaranteed already. This results in the Member States of the ECHR being accorded a smaller scope for evaluation. However, if there is no such "common ground" or if controversial questions of morality are concerned, the Member States of the ECHR will be left a greater margin.[151]

The legal concept of a margin of appreciation may also be employed for the benefit of Community law. It is capable of controlling the entire proportionality test, but especially the balancing process in the third step of examination. As under the ECHR, the margin of appreciation makes it possible

[149] More on this presently (4).

[150] This is discussed in detail by E Brems, 'The Margin of Appreciation Doctrine in the Case-Law of the European Court of Human Rights', (1996) *Zeitschrift für ausländisches öffentliches Recht und Völkerrecht* 240 *et seq*; C Picheral and A-D Olinga, 'La théorie de la marge d'appréciation dans la jurisprudence récente de la Cour Européenne des droits de l'homme', (1995) *Revue trimestrielle des droits de l'homme* 564 *et seq*.

[151] Cf recently repeated in the judgment of the ECtHR, *Nikula v Finland*, Judgment of 21 March 2002 Application No 31611/96, para 46 <www.echr.coe.int> (5 May 2004).

to distinguish between the different subject areas concerned, and it makes it possible to employ a density of control varying in time, which gives sufficient consideration to newly developing common opinions. Furthermore, the concept of a margin of appreciation which is variable has another crucial advantage in Community law. It makes it possible to differentiate between stricter standards as regards action by institutions of the Community and of the Member States when executing Community law on the one hand and, on the other, more lenient standards as regards other action by Member States merely connected to Community law. It has already been emphasised that, in this regard, it is not possible to apply the same standards if conflicts with core national opinions on the reconciliation of public and private interests are to be avoided and an organic development of common European standards is to be secured.[152]

The concept of a margin of appreciation may not only play a role in vertical delimitation of competences between the Community and the Member States, but also at the level of horizontal division of powers. The description of the individual steps of applying the proportionality principle has already shown that, in certain questions, it is for the Community legislator to perform the prerogative of assessment with regard to the determination of suitability, necessity and appropriateness of measures.[153] This prerogative goes much further in relation to the legislature than in relation to the executive. In the future, it will be important to develop a concept to answer the question of which aspects may be better assessed by Community institutions. Therefore, the application of the concept of margin of appreciation to Community law is to be welcomed. Already, this is discernible in some opinions and in recent judgments of the ECJ.[154]

However, when adopting the international law concept of a margin of appreciation into supranational Community law, it must be taken into account that the circle of Member States of the Community is much more homogeneous than that of the High Contracting Parties of the ECHR. Additionally, the Community possesses a much greater level of integration and a higher degree of common standards is therefore to be expected. Furthermore, a distinction must be made with regard to the type of measures to be examined. To take an example, it is absolutely necessary to develop a uniform standard in relation to executive action by the institutions of the Community.

[152] See above, 3.b.bb.
[153] This is extensively discussed by Schildknecht, above n 113, 51 *et seq*.
[154] This was supported already by AG van Gerven, C-159/90, *Grogan* [1991] ECR I-4703, para 37; clearly to be seen recently in *Connolly*, Case C-274/99 P, above n 23, para 49; however, it is to be doubted whether this case really required such a margin of appreciation as it was concerned with restrictions placed upon the expression of opinion of a civil servant for which a general standard at Community level must be developed. There were no obvious reasons for granting such a margin; this will be further discussed below.

Based on this approach, orientation may be provided by the figure of "democratic society" referred to by the proportionality test of several rights guaranteed by the ECHR (see especially the second paragraphs respectively of Articles 8—11 ECHR)[155]. A distinction as regards the fundamental rights concerned is also conceivable. However, a sweeping distinction must be rejected which would lead to a prima facie review for economic fundamental rights and an increased density of control with regard to other fundamental rights.[156] Also to be rejected is any line of argumentation which assumes a higher degree of intensity of an interference with regard to economic fundamental rights in the face of the original character of the Community treaties as a "planned constitution".[157] In view of the depth of integration achieved to date, a higher degree of intensity of a measure of interference may not be justified by referring to objectives of integration. However, this does not make it impossible to adhere to distinguishing on the topic concerned provided that this is controlled by primary law. Thus, the permissible degree of interference with a fundamental right is greater in an economic branch shaped by planned economy (such as agriculture) than in other economic branches. Nevertheless, it is under these circumstances not possible to do without an appropriate level of fundamental rights protection. A strict review of measures of interference with a high degree of intensity is indispensable for an appropriate protection of fundamental rights.[158] Furthermore, it is suggested to distinguish between the individual fundamental rights, carving out a central area of protection specific to each fundamental right. As regards freedom of expression, this could be considered for those contents of the freedom of communication referring to the *res publica*.[159]

A distinction of interference by the legislature dependent on whether or not the measure concerned was taken by a majority vote must however be rejected.[160] The density of control of sovereign interference may not be dependent on the relevant voting procedure under Community law. Neither may it be assumed that a measure adopted by a unanimous vote will constitute less of a danger to fundamental rights. Despite all Member States

[155] See fundamentally C Engel, 'Die Schranken der Schranken in der Europäischen Menschenrechtskonvention', (1986) *Österreichische Zeitschrift für Öffentliches Recht und Völkerrecht* 261 at 268 *et seq*.

[156] After extensively discussing whether this tendency is derived from the case-law of the ECJ, Schildknecht, above n 113, 259, tentatively concludes that this is the case.

[157] Schildknecht is critical of corresponding approaches to be found in the case-law of the ECJ which award too wide a margin of appreciation to the legislature if areas of special political responsibility are concerned: *ibid* 261; see also n 6.

[158] Kischel, above n 123, at 386 *et seq* with further references.

[159] Kühling, above n 63, 406 *et seq*.

[160] To this effect, however, see Mayer, above n 3, 687.

having thus been involved in scrutinising a measure, there is still the possibility that a compromise endangering fundamental rights may have been achieved.

dd) The Guarantee of the Essence of Rights (Wesensgehaltsgarantie) As yet, the precise content of the guarantee of the essence (or the very substance) of rights remains unclear. Little orientation is provided by the law of the ECHR. It may be derived from the case-law of the ECtHR that interferences which detract from the substance of a right are to be rejected categorically.[161] In German constitutional law, the debate surrounding the interpretation of the guarantee of the essence of rights (which is contained in the *Grundgesetz*) is mainly concerned with whether its relative or absolute theory should be followed.[162] If it is decided to follow the first approach in its more popular subjective variant, the guarantee of the essence of rights only possesses declaratory importance as the very substance must be determined by means of a balancing process in each individual case and thus, as a result, coincides with the proportionality test. On the contrary, the subjective variant of the absolute theory is based on the belief that in each individual case there must remain a core of the right for the individual, while the objective variant seeks to prevent an undermining of the right altogether and demands a conservation of the substance of each right. There is no determination of the essence of rights in most other legal systems. However, references to the essence of rights may be found in the Greek, Italian, Portuguese and Spanish Constitutions and in those countries' constitutional literature which indicate the conservation of the substance of rights.[163]

In this context, the remarks by Otto y Pardo are of special interest: with regard to Spanish constitutional law, he points out that it is inadmissible to reduce the protection of fundamental rights to a mere protection of the essence of these rights.[164] This must be especially emphasised in view of the sometimes cursory style of examination employed by the ECJ which briefly denies that the very substance of the rights guaranteed by a fundamental right has been infringed before concluding that the interference with the exercise of a fundamental right was admissible.[165] However, from this

[161] See the judgment of the ECtHR in the *Belgian Languages Case* ECHR [1968] Series A No 6, para 5; see also R Weiß, *Das Gesetz im Sinne der Europäischen Menschenrechtskonvention* (1996) 137 *et seq.*

[162] For an overview Alexy, above n 62, 267 *et seq.*

[163] Cf Kühling, above n 63, 288, 306, 315, 331, 343.

[164] I de Otto y Pardo, 'Die Regelung der Ausübung der Grundrechte', in: A López Pina (ed), *Spanisches Verfassungsrecht* (1993) 326 *et seq.*

[165] See, eg Case 265/87, *Schräder v Commission* [1989] ECR 2237, para 18; O Müller-Michaels, *Grundrechtlicher Eigentumsschutz in der Europäischen Union* (1996) 53, who discusses the way in which the Court guarantees the very substance of rights when protecting the fundamental right of property, claims that there is no real but only a verbal restriction.

approach of the ECJ, it is not possible to draw any definite conclusions as regards the function and the effect of the guarantee of the very substance of rights in Community law. Although this approach takes recourse to the guarantee of the very substance of rights, there is no precise definition nor delimitation vis-à-vis considerations of proportionality. In view of the plea expressed here in favour of a more highly-developed proportionality test and the fact that it is explicitly referred to in Article II-52(1) CT-Conv (Article 112(1) CT-IGC), the guarantee of the essence of rights should be accorded the status of an additional element of protection. However, no further review effect may be developed on the basis of the relative approach.

It may be noted that the essence of rights is mainly referred to by States whose catalogues of fundamental rights were developed as a response to totalitarian rule. This indicates the motivation for introducing an additional dogmatic figure in order to review interferences in human rights: law must be preserved from a complete loss of substance and must not be degraded to become an empty shell. Since the Union has overcome totalitarism and socialism, a reference to the essence of a right as an explicit (and independent) safeguard seems reasonable. Thus, as a further admissibility criterion, Community law should examine whether a specific interference results in the entire fundamental right being undermined. Therefore, an absolute and objective review of the essence of rights must be performed[166] which, in everyday life, will possess a cautionary function vis-à-vis those institutions interfering in the exercise of fundamental rights.[167]

d) Particularities of the Examination of the Equality Principle and Positive Obligations

The coherent structure of examination is even less developed than in the case of freedoms as the core element of negative rights regarding all other types of fundamental rights and dimensions of protection. The sole exception is constituted by the equality principle which has featured extensively in the case-law of the ECJ as Article 141 EC contains various aspects of the principle of equal treatment concerning equal rights for men and women in the workplace; additionally, the EC Treaty exhibits several other cases in which equal treatment is stipulated, especially the general prohibition on discrimination on grounds of nationality in Article 12 EC.[168] These

[166] Arguing for such an approach of Community law to freedom of profession R Stadler, *Die Berufsfreiheit in der Europäischen Gemeinschaft* (1980) 364 *et seq*.

[167] J Günter, *Berufsfreiheit und Eigentum in der Europäischen Union* (1998) 246 *et seq*.

[168] For an overview of the other equality principles see T Kingreen and R Störmer, 'Die subjektiv-öffentlichen Rechte des primären Gemeinschaftsrechts', (1998) *Europarecht* 263 at 265 *et seq*; U Kischel, 'Zur Dogmatik des Gleichheitssatzes in der Europäischen Union', (1997) *Europäische Grundrechte-Zeitschrift* 1.

provisions stipulating equal treatment form part of the general equality principle affirmed by the ECJ. This prohibits "treating like cases differently, [...] without such differentiation being justified by the existence of substantive objective differences".[169] The principle of equality is violated if essentially similar situations are treated differently or if essentially different situations are treated similarly. It must be further examined whether there is a valid justification for differing treatment: some reasons for unequal treatment are per se inadmissible, such as differentiating on grounds of nationality pursuant to Article 12 EC. Finally, it must be shown that the unequal treatment is proportionate.[170] It is thus possible to adopt essential aspects of the legal doctrine of fundamental freedoms. This also applies to the equality provisions in the third Chapter of the Charter. However, the affirmative action contained in Article II-23(2) CT-Conv (Article 83(2) CT-IGC) which permits measures providing for specific advantages in favour of the under-represented sex will require specific further development as regards its legal doctrine. This must occur by reference to existing case-law of the ECJ.[171]

It is also necessary to develop a separate coherent structure to examine violations of duties to protect. It has already been pointed out[172] that the examination of a right providing protection is parallel to that of an original right to performance by the State so that the corresponding (need to develop) legal doctrine may be referred to. However, a concrete right providing protection will only be justified in the (exceptional) case of a reduction of the State's scope for action to perform a specific act. In parallel to the examination of negative rights, it is probably more suitable to examine the violation of duties to act developed from the various fundamental rights, e.g. duties to examine. Similarly, in parallel to the examination of negative rights, a violation of a duty to protect may be examined in the event of total inactivity or of wholly inappropriate measures being taken. This corresponds to the approach to be found in the case-law of the ECJ on duties to protect under the fundamental freedoms and to the approach taken by the *Bundesverfassungsgericht* with regard to duties of protection in fundamental rights.

As regards its structure of examination, a derived participatory right is usually similar to an equality right. As in that case, it must firstly be

[169] See the seminal judgment in Cases 17 and 20/61, *Klöckner* [1962] ECR 325 at 345; in the later jurisprudence for example Case C-306/93, *SMW Winzersekt* [1994] ECR I-5555, para 30; see also Kischel, above n 168, 1 *et seq.*

[170] On the structure of examination usually employed by the ECtHR see eg ECHR, *Larkos v Cyprus* Rep 1999-I 559, para 29, and ECHR, *Mazurek v France* Rep 2000-II 25, para 48.

[171] Case C-450/93, *Kalanke* [1995] ECR I-3051; Case C-409/95, *Marschall* [1997] ECR I-6363; Case C-158/97, *Badeck* [2000] ECR I-1875; Case C-407/98, *Abrahamsson* [2000] ECR I-5539.

[172] See above III.2.b.

examined whether a certain group of persons may assert a certain claim and whether the petitioner belongs to that group of persons or whether the petitioner may be compared to the other group of persons. It must then be examined whether possibly differing treatment may be justified.

However, the examination of an original duty of provision regularly consists of a single-step determination of whether a corresponding claim exists. This structure of examination also applies to some of the judicial fundamental rights[173] and to various citizens' rights containing a positive duty on part of the State. As far as the duties of provision and the corresponding original rights to performance are concerned, there remains a considerable need for a further development of legal doctrine of fundamental rights.

IV. OUTLOOK: AN INSTITUTIONAL AND SUBSTANTIVE WORKING PROGRAMME

Both the existing basis and the substantive programme for developing the legal doctrine of fundamental rights have been outlined. The future case-law of the ECJ will especially need to further clarify the horizontal and vertical scope of fundamental rights, focusing on the development of the respective standards for review. In this context, an extension of the concept of margin of appreciation will prove of great use. Furthermore, numerous individual questions of legal doctrine will need to be solved, such as determining the contents of participatory rights and of rights to performance by the State or the protection of public entities. Additionally, further aspects will have to be discussed which have not been touched upon in this paper. From the perspective of the theory of the fundamental freedoms, the question of whether these contain elements of fundamental rights will be raised. The answer to this question largely depends on whether the fundamental freedoms continue to be extended as "limitation norms" and, as part of this process, on the extent to which they become independent of their functional (referring to the internal market) and transnational (cross-border) roots: the greater the extent to which this occurs, the bigger the areas of overlapping fundamental rights will become. On the other hand, if the fundamental freedoms are to be mainly employed as prohibitions on discrimination, then their importance will diminish with the growing integrationary force of the internal market while fundamental rights will simultaneously gain prominence as standards for the review of harmonisation through secondary law.

[173] On the structure of examination usually employed by the ECtHR in relation to judicial fundamental rights containing a positive duty, see for example ECHR, *Palumbo v Italy*, Judgment of 30 November 2000 Application No 15919/89, paras 42 and 47 <www.echr.coe.int> (5 May 2004).

Besides the expected incorporation of the Charter into primary Community law, it must also be considered—with regard to institutional law—which measures are to be taken to facilitate the ECJ discharging its function of protecting fundamental rights. The answer to this question must be found both within the Community law system of legal protection as well as in coexistence relationships outside the Community. Thus, within the Community, the possibilities for individuals and, if necessary, for groups to bring an action before the ECJ must be improved. Carried through to its logical conclusion, the introduction of a right to bring a complaint of unconstitutionality or of a violation of a fundamental right (in German "Verfassungsbeschwerde") will have to be deemed sensible.[174] This would provide the ECJ with the possibility to strengthen its role as a constitutional court. Also pointing in this direction is the continuous shift of functions to the CFI, which at the same time is being turned into a substantial specialist court by the increasing use of chambers.[175] Nevertheless, as such a procedure has not been accepted by the European Convention it will probably not be realised in the near future. Concerning the relationship of coexistence of various interpreters of fundamental rights[176] at European level between the ECJ, the ECtHR and national constitutional courts, a further expansion of the complimentary, sometimes parallel, exercise of functions is necessary. After an initial phase of conjuring up conflicts which may prove quite fruitful, the current efforts to jointly develop and expand an appropriate system of fundamental rights protection at Community or Union level will have to be intensified. Therefore, the dimension of conflicts still conceivable at present should not be overestimated.

From a German perspective, the relationship between the ECJ and the *Bundesverfassungsgericht* has thus developed very favourably as far as fundamental rights are concerned with the courts exercising complimentary functions. Pursuant to Article 23(1) of the *Grundgesetz*, the *Bundesverfassungsgericht* limits itself to co-operating in the realisation of a unified Europe which "provides a protection of fundamental rights essentially

[174] See the comment by H-W Rengeling, 'Brauchen wir die Verfassungsbeschwerde auf Gemeinschaftsebene?', in: O Due *et al* (eds), *Festschrift für U Everling* (1995) 1187 *et seq*; N Reich, 'Zur Notwendigkeit einer europäischen Grundrechtsbeschwerde', (2000) *Zeitschrift für Rechtspolitik* 375 *et seq*.

[175] As to the changes made by the Treaty of Nice, see Arts 220—225(a), 229(a), 245 EC; see the comment by T Wiedmann, 'Anmerkungen zum Vertrag von Nizza', (2001) *Juristische Schulung* (2001) 846 at 849 *et seq*.

[176] On the relationship of the ECJ to the ECtHR see HC Krüger and J Polakiewicz, 'Vorschläge für ein kohärentes System des Menschenrechtsschutzes in Europa', (2001) *Europäische Grundrechte-Zeitschrift* 92 *et seq*; Lenaerts and de Smijter, above n 31, 90 *et seq*; E Pache, 'Der Grundsatz des fairen gerichtlichen Verfahrens auf europäischer Ebene', (2000) *Europäische Grundrechte-Zeitschrift* 601 at 606; Turner, above n 6, 453 *et seq*; cf commenting on the entire picture FC Mayer in this volume.

equivalent to that" of the *Grundgesetz*. This restricts the *Bundesverfassungsgericht* in that it may only examine whether there are indications—in an individual case or in general—pointing to the existence of structural deficits in the ECJ's system of fundamental rights protection.[177] Even in the event of the *Bundesverfassungsgericht* finding such deficits to exist, all possibilities for co-operation would have to be exhausted in accordance with the mandate to participate in the development of the EU in Article 23(1) of the *Grundgesetz* before the *Bundesverfassungsgericht* could exercise its competence to quash Community law. This has been referred to by the former leading judge of the *Bundesverfassungsgericht*, J Limbach, as a "very theoretical reserve competence" ("sehr theoretische Reservekompetenz").[178] Especially, either this means that the *Bundesverfassungsgericht* would have to express such reservations itself and refer the case to the ECJ under the preliminary ruling procedure provided for in Article 234 EC or it would have to oblige the courts of specialised jurisdiction to do so.[179]

Upon closer inspection, (putative) conflicts between the ECHR and the fundamental rights of the EU may also substantially be dissolved. In any case, the potential for conflict conceivable is largely reduced by a factual orientation of the ECJ towards the ECHR as interpreted by the ECtHR.[180] Articles 52(3) and 53 of the Charter (Articles 112(3) and 113 CT-IGC) lead to the same result in that the standard of the ECHR is observed in the event of conflict.[181] Only if contradictions still remain at this point, the "worst case scenario" arises: the implementation and execution of Community law which violates the ECHR according to the *Matthews* line of judgments of the ECtHR[182] constitutes a violation of international law by one or several Member States[183] which entails a corresponding obligation to eliminate the provision violating international law.[184]

However, the everyday work of the various interpreters of fundamental rights is predominantly shaped by co-operation and inspiration with the

[177] This became clear in a recent judgment: *Entscheidungen des Bundesverfassungsgerichts* 102, 147 at 164 (*Bananenmarktordnung*).

[178] J Limbach, 'Die Kooperation der Gerichte in der zukünftigen europäischen Grundrechtsarchitektur', (2000) *Europäische Grundrechte-Zeitschrift* 417 at 420.

[179] It seems highly unlikely that the ECJ would not heed such a warning sign. Therefore, there is no point in deliberating what legal consequences this would incur.

[180] To date, all putative discrepancies have proven to be harmless; cf Kühling, above n 63 57 *et seq*, giving the example of the much discussed judgments in *Hoechst*, *Orkem* und *Otto*. It is disputed whether the order of the Court in C-17/98, *Emesa Sugar* [2000] ECR I-665, paras 8 *et seq* has given rise to a new conflict with the case-law of the ECtHR in *Vermeulen* Rep 1996-I, paras 27 *et seq*. For a sceptical comment, see S Winkler, *Der Beitritt der Europäischen Gemeinschaften zur Europäischen Menschenrechtskonvention* (2000) 35 *et seq*; however, Grabenwarter, above n 63, 327, believes that such a conflict is likely.

[181] Grabenwarter, above n 63, 340 *et seq*.

[182] See the reference in n 64 above; Lenaerts and de Smijter, above n 31, 93 *et seq*.

[183] In this situation, too, it is highly unlikely that the ECJ would refuse to yield; cf also Krüger and Polakiewicz, above n 176, 96.

[184] On this tension see in more detail R Uerpmann-Wittzack in this volume, III.1.b.cc.

aim of guaranteeing an optimal level of fundamental rights protection for all citizens.[185] To this extent, the dialogue on pending judgments which is always isolated only must be reinforced by institutional possibilities for exchange of ideas. This is already happening in the mild, yet effective form of informal exchange of opinions.[186]

[185] Similarly A Weber, 'Einheit und Vielfalt der europäischen Grundrechtsordnung(en)', (2003) *Deutsches Verwaltungsblatt* 220 at 227.

[186] As regards possible further reaching forms of a co-operative relationship between the ECtHR and the ECJ, see S Alber and U Widmaier, 'Die EU-Charta der Grundrechte und ihre Auswirkungen auf die Rechtsprechung', (2000) *Europäische Grundrechte-Zeitschrift* 497 at 507 *et seq*, who also believe in the value of informal contact, *ibid*, 510; Pache, above n 176, 606, who fears that showing consideration informally will not suffice in the future; Turner, above n 6, 466 *et seq;* on the possibility of a preliminary reference procedure Pache, above n 176, 606, and Krüger and Polakiewicz, above n 176, 101, who coin the term "Gutachtenkompetenz" (competence to deliver an expert opinion); Turner, above n 6, 466 *et seq*, suggests the setting-up of a "Chamber of Human Rights" at the ECJ which would further informal exchanges and which would result in a uniform level of human rights protection. If requested to do so, this Chamber would also give opinions as part of the legislative process on the human rights dimension of intended legislation.

13

Fundamental Freedoms

BY THORSTEN KINGREEN*

I. THE FUNDAMENTAL FREEDOMS IN A LEGAL CONTEXT

EVEN IF THE DISCOVERIES of today often form the mistakes of tomorrow, knowledge thrives from discovery. New insights generate new terms, which from thereon represent the insight. Only seldom do such new terms achieve the acceptance and dissemination envisaged by their initial creators.

The German expression *Grundfreiheiten* (fundamental freedoms) as a generic term for the free movement of goods (Arts 28 and 29 EC; Art III-42 CT-Conv; Art 153 CT-IGC), the free movement of workers (Art 39 EC; Art III-18 CT-Conv; Art 133 CT-IGC), the freedom of establishment (Art 43 EC; Art III-22 CT-Conv; Art 137 CT-IGC), the freedom to provide services (Art 49 EC; Art III-29 CT-Conv; Art 144 CT-IGC) and the free movement of capital (Art 56 EC; Art III-45 CT-Conv; Art 156 CT-IGC) is one of these rare cases. Although it is not utilised by the EC Treaty[1] and although only passing reference is made to it within the case law of the ECJ,[2] the term has become part of the classic repertoire on European law in the German-speaking world. In contrast, it appears that other languages have not developed such a commonly used term.[3]

* For the dedicated and patient assistance with the translation I thank Andreas Magnusson, Cornelia Mielitz, Michael Rötting, and Jen Turner.

[1] The Treaties speak of 'fundamental freedoms', yet with reference to the European Convention of Human Rights: see, eg, Art 177(2) EC; Art III–193(1) CT–Conv (Art 292(1) CT–IGC); Art 6(2) EU; Arts I–7(2), II–52(3) and II–53 CT–Conv (Arts 9(2), 112(3) and 113 CT–IGC). But see now the heading of Art I–4 CT–Conv (Art CT–IGC).

[2] See Case 203/80 *Casati* [1981] ECR 2595, para 8; Case 205/84 *Commission v Germany* [1986] ECR 3755, para 54; cf W Pfeil, *Historische Vorbilder und Entwicklung des Rechtsbegriffs der 'Vier Grundfreiheiten' im Europäischen Gemeinschaftsrecht* (1998), 3.

[3] In English, the term 'the four freedoms' is apparently only seldom used. The term does not appear in the indexes or in the actual texts of academic writings (eg P Craig and G de Burca, *The Evolution of EC Law* (Oxford, 1999) 349; A Arnull *et al*, *European Union Law* (2000), 317) and it is used only occasionally in journal articles (eg K Mortelmans, 'Towards Convergence in the Application of the Rules on Free Movement and on Competition, (2001) 38 *CML Rev* 613 at 617). The French equivalent speaks of *'les quatre libertés fondamentales à fonction économique'*: J Boulot, *Droit institutionel des communautés européennes* (1993), 211. In one Spanish academic textbook the collective term *'las libertades básicas'* can be found: JNS Solis, *Fundamentis y políticas de la Unión Europea* (1998), 91.

It is uncertain who holds the copyright for the term *Grundfreiheiten.*[4] It is however possible to trace its gradual appearance and acceptance to the first half of the 1990s. Since the mid-1980s, case law on the fundamental freedoms had gradually become increasingly inconsistent. The demarcation between Member State measures which have negative effects on the common market and such which have only internal effects could be hardly comprehended: from rulings on extended retail opening hours,[5] to the restriction of employment on Sundays[6] and the maintenance of the private law concept of *culpa in contrahendo*,[7] each measure intended to regulate economic life seemed to require strict justification on the basis of the fundamental freedoms. Legal uncertainty reigned. Although German legal literature on European law had for decades concentrated upon the decisions of the ECJ, the judgment in *Keck and Mithouard* in 1993, which served to restrict the area protected by the fundamental freedoms, signalled the end of the period of ECJ positivism. This re-orientation was favoured by the Court's theoretically ineffectual reasoning for the change in judicial approach, which had to be understood as a virtual request to develop new theoretical concepts on the subject. For the "increasing tendency of traders to invoke Art 30 of the Treaty as a way of challenging any rules limiting their commercial freedom,"[8] was a methodically unsatisfactory reasoning for the change in approach.

After the *Keck* judgment, an evident change in methodology and approach can be observed in German-speaking literature, which is responsible for the emergence of the linguistic term *Grundfreiheiten*. Alongside the treatment of individual themes, publications appeared for the first time tackling issues relating to the methodology of the common theoretical principles of the fundamental freedoms. Generic terms were born, as it was felt that they would stress common elements. In this way, the new terms stand for the recognition that a general theory on fundamental freedoms was required. This German legal analysis was strengthened by the case law of the ECJ, which took pains to emphasise that the fundamental freedoms were indeed based upon common dogmatic principles.[9]

The elaboration of a general theory is by far the most important contribution from the German-speaking area to the topic. Such a theory is however only understandable from the perspective of German legal scholars.

[4] The earliest source known to the current author is H Runge, 'Das Recht der Europäischen Gemeinschaften' [1964] *Juristische Schulung* 305 at 307.

[5] See Case 145/88 *Torfaen Borough Council* [1989] ECR 3851.

[6] Cf Case C–312/89 *Conforama* [1991] ECR I–997.

[7] See Case C–93/92 *CMC Motorradcenter* [1993] ECR I–5009.

[8] See Cases C–267 and C–268/91 *Keck and Mithouard* [1993] ECR I–6097, para 14; see also Part 1. c).

[9] See Case C–106/91 *Ramrath* [1992] ECR I–3351, para 17; Case C–55/94 *Gebhard* [1995] ECR I–4165, para 37.

German scholars become familiar with legal science as they attempt to impose a systematic order onto the sheer plenitude of positivistic individual regulations, decisions and legal opinions. The result of this learning process is legal doctrine. Legal doctrine insists not primarily on the suitability of a certain system, moreover on the construction of this system. It intends to create abstract common principles for related rules and concepts, in order to facilitate the application of law.[10] It offers assistance in the concretisation of the norms of valid law[11] and makes law—which should not simply be memorised—infinitely both teachable and learnable.

The altered, further-reaching methodological approach to the fundamental freedoms has been demonstrated in all genres of legal writing.[12] In academic literature, this can be best comprehended at the example of the development of Rudolf Streinz's standard work on European law. Not only has the sheer number of pages relating to the fundamental freedoms in his book almost doubled between the first edition in 1992 and the sixth edition in 2003, the structure of his approach has also fundamentally altered during this decade. Whilst in the first edition, the fundamental freedoms were structured in chapters and the general principles were discussed in the context of the free movement of persons and were restricted to a discussion spanning some three pages,[13] the fifth edition contains a separate chapter on the issue entitled "The Fundamental Freedoms of the Common Market/Internal Market" and almost half of it is dedicated to a description of the general principles.[14] A comparable development is evident in legal commentaries: whilst in the older texts only passing reference is made to the fundamental freedoms, today the term and concept is to be found in every index[15] and its systematic and dogmatic processing following German legal theory on fundamental rights under the Basic Law is constantly strengthened;[16] and all this despite the immanent limitations of the single-norm concepts contained within standard legal commentaries. Particularly evident in this respect is the development of analytical literature. Following Peter

[10] J Harenburg, *Die Rechtsdogmatik zwischen Wissenschaft und Praxis* (1986), 189.

[11] F Müller, *Juristische Methodik* (1995), 229; cf KF Röhl, *Allgemeine Rechtslehre* (2001), 414.

[12] This contribution sees its task in the analysis of the German 'state of the art' in the area of the fundamental freedoms; it therefore essentially confines itself to German literature.

[13] R Streinz, *Europarecht* (1992), paras 701 to 713.

[14] R Streinz, *Europarecht* (2003), paras 652 to 710. More recent textbooks such as M Herdegen, *Europarecht* (1997)—even in the first edition—commence with a general theory of the fundamental freedoms and then continue with a description of each fundamental freedom: see the 4th ed (2002), paras 281–285; cf H Lecheler, *Einführung in das Europarecht* (2000), 219.

[15] See the more recent commentaries from C Calliess and M Ruffert (eds), *Kommentar zu EU-Vertrag und EG-Vertrag* (2002); J Schwarze (ed), *EU-Kommentar* (2000); R Streinz (ed), *EUV/EGV* (2003).

[16] A good example of this is the commentary on Art 28 EC by U Becker in Schwarze, above n 15, Art 28 EC, para 5.

Behrens' remark in 1992 upon an apparent convergence of the economic freedoms in European Community law,[17] since 1995, essays on the topic of the so-called *Allgemeine Lehren* (general theory)[18] and on an apparent convergence of the fundamental freedoms[19] respectively have appeared regularly. Even individual dogmatic issues, in particular those pertaining to the horizontal effect and the grounds for justification, are handled in the context of all fundamental freedoms.[20] A perusal of the numerous dissertations and miscellaneous monographs rounds off this sketched view of the literary situation.[21]

It can therefore safely be stated that academic interest in German-speaking areas during the past decade has gradually moved away from a concentration upon the individual fundamental freedoms towards the elaboration of their common dogmatic structure. Its importance is stressed by the title of this article.

II. THE FUNDAMENTAL FREEDOMS IN THE PROCESSES OF EUROPEANISATION AND CONSTITUTIONALISATION

The traditional doctrine of the fundamental freedoms suffers somewhat to the extent that it is unclear what the fundamental freedoms actually are. One assumes that they are something similar to the fundamental rights, but at the same time something quite different. This "otherness" is given clearer boundaries through the integration of the fundamental freedoms into their constitutional environment. Just as any other legal norm, the fundamental freedoms are dependent upon their legal and political context.

[17] P Behrens, 'Die Konvergenz der wirtschaftlichen Freiheiten im europäischen Gemeinschaftsrecht' [1992] *Europarecht* 145.

[18] D Ehlers, 'Die Grundfreiheiten des europäischen Gemeinschaftsrechts' [2001] *Juristische Ausbildung* 266 *et seq* and 482 *et seq*; HD Jarass, 'Elemente einer Dogmatik der Grundfreiheiten' [1995] *Europarecht* 202 and, by the same author, 'Elemente einer Dogmatik der Grundfreiheiten II' [2000] *Europarecht* 705.

[19] See C-D Classen, 'Auf dem Weg zu einer einheitlichen Dogmatik der EG-Grundfreiheiten?' [1995] *Europäisches Wirtschafts- und Steuerrecht* 97; M Eberhartinger, 'Konvergenz und Neustrukturierung der Grundfreiheiten' [1997] *Europäisches Wirtschafts- und Steuerrecht* 43; T Eilmansberger, 'Zur Reichweite der Grundfreiheiten des Binnenmarktes' [1999] *Juristische Blätter* 345 *et seq* and 434 *et seq*; M Nettesheim, 'Die europarechtlichen Grundrechte auf wirtschaftliche Mobilität' [1996] *Neue Zeitschrift für Verwaltungsrecht* 342; H Schneider, 'Zum Funktionswandel der Grundfreiheiten des EGV und zu seinen Auswirkungen auf das nationale Recht' [1996] *Neue Justiz* 512; M Zuleeg, 'Die Grundfreiheiten des Gemeinsamen Marktes im Wandel' in O Due (ed), *Festschrift für Ulrich Everling* (1995), 1717.

[20] See eg the comments in Parts III.2.b) and IV.

[21] See M Hoffmann, *Die Grundfreiheiten des EG-Vertrags als koordinationsrechtliche und gleichheitsrechtliche Abwehrrechte* (2000); T Kingreen, *Die Struktur der Grundfreiheiten des europäischen Gemeinschaftsrechts* (1999); K Mojzesowicz, *Möglichkeiten und Grenzen einer einheitlichen Dogmatik der Grundfreiheiten* (2001); A Mühl, *Diskriminierung und Beschränkung: Grundansätze einer einheitlichen Dogmatik der wirtschaftlichen Grundfreiheiten des EG-Vertrages* (2004).

Recently, European constitutional discourse on the fundamental freedoms has become a little quieter. Instead, another group of individual rights has come to the fore: the fundamental rights, which for some time had the dubious reputation of being Europe's late starter. Through the Proclamation of the Charter of Fundamental Rights for the European Union in Nice, they received a vital impetus[22] and are in the meantime experiencing a level of attention equal to that of the fundamental freedoms in every way. Since the ideas of constitution and of human rights are historically connected, they form the centrepiece (Part II) of the Constitutional Treaty.

This constitutional and political shift in emphasis between fundamental rights and fundamental freedoms cannot be explained solely by the increased interest in fundamental rights evoked by the preparation of the Charter of Human Rights. It is rather also due to the specific function of the fundamental freedoms in the historical process of Europeanisation and constitutionalisation. For a more elaborate analysis of this function and in order to clarify the dogmatic structure of the fundamental freedoms by consequence, the latter are to be put into the context of the European and Member State constitutions.[23]

1. The Political-institutional Context I: The Horizontal Relationship Between the ECJ and the European Legislator

a) The Fundamental Freedoms During the EC Crisis

Historically, the prominent contribution of the fundamental freedoms for the successes of the internal market is on the one hand a consequence of the weakness of the European legislator, and on the other, a result of the ECJ considering itself as a catalyst for integration. From this stems the typical complementary relationship between *acteur* and *souffleur*, to the extent that when the legislative organs, initially in particular the Council, lacked the political ability to fulfil the task of integration, the ECJ would fill the gap and sweep away any hindrances for the internal market.

As in the famous *van Gend & Loos* judgment of 1963, the ECJ rendered the individual a direct subject of Community law,[24] and as in the *Costa v ENEL* judgment of 1964 it confirmed the primacy of Community law over any rule of national law,[25] the political process of integration was at the

[22] See J Kühling in this volume.

[23] See Case 283/81 *CILFIT* [1982] ECR 3415, para 20, in which 'every provision of Community law must be placed in its context and interpreted in light of the provisions of Community law as a whole'.

[24] See Case 26/62 *van Gend & Loos* [1963] ECR 1 at 12.

[25] See Case 6/64 *Costa* [1964] ECR 585 at 593 *et seq.*

same time on the verge of slipping into its first deep crisis. After the initial euphoria concerning the development of a new Europe, the fundamental differences between the main players with regard to the process of integration began to emerge, culminating in 1965 in the French "empty chair policy".[26] The French resistance was ostensibly related to the financing of the common agricultural policy, but was in reality targeted at the constitutional structure of the Community and specifically at the rejection of majority decisions within the Council and the strengthening of the Council by means of restrictive handling of the Commission's political discretion.[27] The crisis was in fact solved by the Luxembourg Compromise of 29 January 1966, but at a high political price, since the requirements of unanimity within the Council remained in effect, which in the future hindered necessary legal harmonisation for the development of the internal market within the Community.[28] The problem peaked in 1973 as a result of the successful entry of new Member States (United Kingdom, Republic of Ireland and Denmark), which served to once again increase the problems of harmonisation and render the decision-making process more burdensome.

The clearer the functional weakness of the legislative became evident, the more obvious the functional advantages of the Court became. An obligatory jurisdiction imposed on the Member States was in any case on the international political stage a truly revolutionary innovation. The Court was at least in the position to be able to give a burst of life to the at the time somewhat flagging vehicle of integration: in comparison to the Council, the Court must, when asked, make a decision, and in any case it had never been disputed that judgments of the ECJ were—again in comparison to political decisions—to be accepted, albeit with the occasional grumble.[29] In a situation of a standstill of efforts towards harmonisation, two particular judgments of the Court, which until today strongly influence the doctrine of the fundamental freedoms, must have seemed like the light at the end of the tunnel.

Since the *Dassonville* decision in 1974, the ECJ has interpreted national trade rules which "are capable of hindering, directly or indirectly, actually or potentially, intra-community trade"[30] as a violation of the principle of

[26] For a chronology and analysis of the incidents see JH Kaiser, 'Das Europarecht in der Krise der Gemeinschaften' [1966] *Europarecht* 4.

[27] T Oppermann, *Europarecht* (1999), paras 29 *et seq*.

[28] T von Danwitz and R Lukes, 'Rechtsetzung und Rechtsangleichung' in M Dauses (ed), *Handbuch des EU-Wirtschaftsrechts* (looseleaf, last update 2000), B. II, para 87, in which it is claimed that the 1970s represented a practical standstill for harmonisation.

[29] A Wolf-Niedermaier, *Der Europäische Gerichtshof zwischen Recht und Politik* (1997), 259.

[30] See Case 8/74 *Dassonville* [1974] ECR 837, para 5. The same applies to the freedom to provide services: see Case 33/74 *van Binsbergen* [1974] ECR 1299, paras 10–12. After some initial reluctance the ECJ now applies the principle of the free movement of persons to all trans-national interferences. This is particularly evident in the following cases: Case 107/83 *Klopp* [1984] ECR 2971, para 19, on the freedom of establishment, and Case C–415/93 *Bosman* [1995] ECR I–4921, paras 90 and 96, on the free movement of workers.

free movement of goods. This was a double-headed breakthrough. Firstly, the individual was now in the position to bring violations of the fundamental freedoms before all domestic courts. Secondly, the *Dassonville* formula contained no restriction on particular forms of impairment, and therefore protects not only against discrimination, but also against all other forms of constraint. The *Dassonville* decision requests that all limitations on trade in the common market are to adhere to the basic standard of the fundamental freedoms. Such limitations would of course have been those hindrances which could not have been precluded initially by the means of legislative harmonisation. Although national measures which contained such unjustified hindrances were not invalid but rather rendered inapplicable in cross-border trade, the decisions of the ECJ exercised on the domestic level a pressure on the national legislative towards harmonisation, so as to ensure that domestic circumstances were not placed in a worse position than those of a cross-border nature (reverse discrimination).[31] Therefore, any adjudication on the application of the fundamental freedoms leads to a shift in emphasis of the constitutionally intended balance of power between legislature and judicature.[32] The wider the ECJ interprets the fundamental freedoms, the stronger the shift in balance from the principles of legal harmonisation (in particular Art 95 EC) towards those of the fundamental freedoms, and from the legislator towards the ECJ, becomes. This precarious constitutional shift in balance was in the European context nevertheless perceived to be an opportunity rather than a problem. This is also due to the fact that legislative powers were concentrated within the executive, lacking a directly democratically legitimised legislator, whose political primacy would have had to be taken into account.

In the second influential decision of *Cassis de Dijon* from 1979, the ECJ once again slipped into the role of *souffleur* within the political process of integration. The Court derived from the principle of free movement of goods the requirement that the import of goods which were legitimately manufactured and marketed in another Member State must not be subject to any hindrance.[33] This was a clear rejection to the widespread opinion at the time that such restrictions were to be accepted until the overall harmonisation of the Community had been achieved.[34] At the same time, the ECJ had given itself the role of precursor of the principle of mutual recognition (the so-called "originating state principle"), which was since then discovered

[31] In particular see U Everling, 'Rechtsvereinheitlichung durch Richterrecht in der Europäischen Gemeinschaft' (1986) 50 *Rabels Zeitschrift* 193 at 214.

[32] GF Schuppert, *Funktionell-rechtliche Grenzen der Verfassungsinterpretation* (1980), 3.

[33] See Case 120/78 *Rewe* [1979] ECR 649, para 14.

[34] See I Schwartz, '30 Jahre EG-Rechtsangleichung' in EJ Mestmäcker (ed), *Eine Ordnungspolitik für Europa: Festschrift für H von der Groeben* (1987), 333 at 355.

and practised by the other organs as a "new strategy".[35] The decision of *Cassis de Dijon* also was a dogmatic milestone. The ECJ had implied immanent restrictions into Art 28 EC, which have since then been included in case law alongside codified law (e.g. Art 30 EC) in relation to all fundamental freedoms: any impediment on internal trade within the Community which may arise out of differences in domestic rules on the marketing of products must be accepted insofar as these provisions are necessary to fulfil urgent demands.[36] This formula satisfied the demands of the time: on the one hand, the wide scope of application of the *Dassonville* formula needed recapturing on the level of justification; one the other hand, in this critical phase of the process of integration, the necessary flexibility of judicial legal harmonisation was preserved. As a result, Art 28 EC began to develop shadowy contours: other than stating that all unjustified hindrances on the internal market were forbidden, case law did not provide further elaboration on this stance. Nevertheless, firm theoretical principles did appear—in a time of faltering legislative harmonisation—as un-opportune restrictions on the praetoric process of legal harmonisation.

The dogmatic foundation of the fundamental freedoms was therefore laid in the 1970s. The ECJ became the motor of legal harmonisation and the fundamental freedoms became its fuel. The recognition of subjective rights (not only in primary, but also in secondary law) made the citizen an important functionary of integration;[37] his own interest was mobilised and used as a contribution to the achievement of a Community legal order above the national systems.[38] But this is far less remarkable than the fact that until today the decisions *Dassonville* and *Cassis de Dijon*—with their wideness and pallid dogmatic contour only understandable in the particular political constellation of the 1970s—have a formative influence on ECJ case law, even in a fundamentally changed political environment.

b) The Fundamental Freedoms After the Single European Act

Without a continuously self-renewing *political* will for integration, European unification would not have been possible in the long term, and as such, this political will had to manifest itself in progressive legislation.[39] Thus, the various institutional reforms in the area of legislation in particular contributed to rescuing the Community from pending crisis in the 1960s and 70s.

[35] See '*Completing the Internal Market*': *White Paper from the Commission to the European Council*, COM(1985) 310, paras 61 *et seq*.

[36] See Case 120/78, above n 33, para 8.

[37] See C-D Classen, 'Der einzelne als Instrument zur Durchsetzung des Gemeinschaftsrechts' [1997] *Verwaltungsarchiv* 645 at 671.

[38] J Masing, *Die Mobilisierung des Bürgers für die Durchsetzung des Rechts* (1997), 175 *et seq*.

[39] J Schwarze, 'Funktion des Rechts in der Europäischen Gemeinschaft' in *id* (ed), *Gesetzgebung in der Europäischen Gemeinschaft* (1985), 9 at 26.

A significant development was the rise of the European Parliament to a democratic co-legislator—albeit timid and because of the special supra-national constellation incomparable with a national parliament. The first direct voting in 1979 did not alter its limited powers, but it did change the basis of legitimation and thereby its self-conception. This was expressed above all in a constitutional initiative,[40] which was a significant impetus for the Single European Act in 1987 and in which the Parliament, for the first time in the legislative process, actively participated. Since then, the participation of the Parliament has gradually been expanded—in particular through the co-decision procedure under Art 251 EC and now due to the legislative procedure provided by Art III-302 CT-Conv (Art 396 CT-IGC)—making the Parliament a co-legislator with equal rights.

The second foundational institutional change concerned the decision-making process in the Council pertaining to legal harmonisation. With the Single European Act, the principle of unanimity for measures relating to legal harmonisation was for the first time overcome by introducing Art 100a EEC Treaty, in order to bring into practical effect the Commission's ambitious internal market programme from 1985.[41] As a result of this, one important reason for the lagging progress in harmonisation dating from the 1960s and 1970s was finally conquered: until 31 December 1992, it became possible to achieve the realisation of over 90 per cent of the notified legal acts contained in the White Paper.[42]

It could now be presumed that the realisation of the legal process and the strengthened legislative activity on the part of the European legislative must also have had an effect on the interpretation and theory of individual rights (fundamental rights, fundamental freedoms). In relation to the fundamental rights, this was proven to be the case: whilst by the end of the 1980s the number of decisions relating to fundamental rights could be counted on ten fingers, it increased significantly in the beginning of the 1990s.[43] A praetorical catalogue of fundamental rights took shape, which was no longer solely restricted to the exercise of economic rights, and with it, the first elements of a European theory of fundamental rights.[44] The reasons for this are clear: along with strengthened legislative activity, the Community rose to become an adversary of individual spheres protected by fundamental rights, and thus the need for supra-national legitimation increased, especially after the ECJ had made clear that national law and fundamental rights could not be a legal standard for legal acts given by the Community.[45]

[40] Resolution on the Draft Treaty Establishing the European Union [1984] OJ C 77/53.
[41] See above n 35.
[42] A Hatje in Schwarze, above n 15, Art 14 EC, para 18.
[43] For a more elaborate compilation, see T Kingreen in Calliess and Ruffert, above n 15, Art 6 EU, paras 93 *et seq*.
[44] See J Kühling in this volume.
[45] See Case 11/70 *Internationale Handelsgesellschaft* [1970] ECR 1125, para 3.

It could have been expected that comparable balancing acts would also take place in the application of the fundamental freedoms, because the former doctrine could only be explained by reference to the specific constitutional situation of the 1960s and 70s. Far from it, the principles demonstrated in the cases of *Dassonville* and *Cassis de Dijon* remained relatively unchanged, at least until the beginning of the 1990s. Largely supported by the literature, all fundamental freedoms were gradually developed from principles of non-discrimination into freedom rights.[46] Though the requirement of a cross-border reference point was formally maintained,[47] an increasing number of measures which no longer had anything to do with the problem of national borders within the internal market found themselves stranded at the ECJ. The reason for this was that each national regulation could always potentially have an effect upon cross-border transactions and the boundless *Dassonville*-formula could not be utilised as a filter. The market participants had discovered the fundamental freedoms as a sharp sword, which opened the hitherto unforeseen opportunity to shuffle of the 'old traditions', the elimination of which could not be accomplished in the national political process. Object of the gravamen were often such measures whose burdensome character resulted from the dissimilarity of the natural legal systems alone. It was in this way that the German prohibition on price comparisons was regarded as an interference, as the various systems of advertisement and sales promotion would result in the entrepreneur in each Member State having to constantly adapt to a new system.[48] In this case, however, the Court ran the risk of making a judicial determination as to which norm system would be the most suitable.[49]

c) The Fundamental Freedoms in the Era of Constitutionalisation

Through the Treaty of Maastricht the process of integration entered a new phase, best described as the period of constitutionalisation.[50] At the same time as the deepening of economic integration through economic and monetary union, the necessity to understand Europe as a political entity was articulated, thus requiring the EC and EU Treaties to develop a form of

[46] For an overview of the developments in jurisprudence and legal literature see Kingreen, above n 21, 40.

[47] There is an emphasis on the inapplicability of the fundamental freedoms to 'internal matters' in Case C–41/90 *Höfner* [1991] ECR I–1979, para 37; Case C–332/90 *Steen* [1992] ECR I–341, para 9.

[48] See Case C–126/91 *Yves Rocher* [1993] ECR I–2361, para 10.

[49] R Joliet, 'Das Recht des unlauteren Wettbewerbsrechts und der freie Warenverkehr' [1994] *Gewerblicher Rechtsschutz und Urheberrecht International* 1 at 14.

[50] See also A Wiener in this volume.

constitutional legal system which would overcome the traditional links between state, citizen and constitution.[51]

Nevertheless, the theory of the fundamental freedoms essentially remains at the status of the 1970s. This assessment is not substantially shaken by the 1993 judgment in *Keck and Mithouard*.[52] At most, it is possible to speak of a cautious change,[53] as the main principles as enumerated in *Dassonville* and *Cassis de Dijon* have not been subject to significant correction. Since the decision in *Keck*, the ECJ has made the well-known distinction between rules which contain provisions relating to the goods themselves (for example their description, form, measurements, weight, constitution, presentation, labelling and packaging), and those that serve to limit or prohibit the various means of sale. Whilst the product-related, indiscriminately valid provisions now as before fall under the auspices of Art 28 EC, measures related to the means of sale no longer represent interferences with that very provision. The requirement clearly is that the relevant provision affects both internal and external products in the same manner, legally as well as factually.[54] It is remarkable from this decision that the requirement of discrimination, which, as a condition for the application of the fundamental freedoms, had been given up in the 70s, is now experiencing a renaissance in relation to the means of sale. It remains unclear even today whether the test in *Keck* could be transferred to the other fundamental freedoms, and if so, the extent of the consequences of such transfer on the level of justification, at which the ECJ would partially differentiate between discriminating and non-discriminating measures.[55]

Much has been speculated on the decision in *Keck*. It seemed reasonable to place the decision in a greater context and in doing so to explain the *Keck* modification by means of the altered constitutional legal norms. As such, the principle of subsidiarity as introduced by the Maastricht Treaty (Art 5(2) EC) has variously been made responsible[56] for the "dramatic judgment"[57] in the so-called "November Revolution"[58]. Others observe the return to a rather more traditional practice of free trade within the internal market.[59]

[51] Evidence on the debate is found in C Calliess in *id* and Ruffert, above n 15, Art 1 EU, paras 17 *et seq*.

[52] See Cases C–267/91 and C–268/91, above n 8.

[53] W Möschel, 'Kehrtwende in der Rechtsprechung des EuGH zur Warenverkehrsfreiheit' [1994] *Neue Juristische Wochenschrift* 429 at 430.

[54] See Cases C–267 and C–268/91, above n 8, para 16, and subsequent case law.

[55] See as a result Part III.2.b).

[56] F Mayer, 'Die Warenverkehrsfreiheit im Europarecht' [2003] *Europarecht* 793 at 812; P Oliver, *Free movement of goods in the European Community* (3rd edn 1996), 100.

[57] N Reich, 'The "November Revolution" of the European Court of Justice' (1994) 31 *CML Rev* 459 at 459.

[58] M Petschke, 'Die Warenverkehrsfreiheit in der neuesten Rechtsprechung des EuGH' [1994] *Europäische Zeitschrift für Wirtschaftsrecht* 107 at 111; E Steindorff, 'Unvollkommener Binnenmarkt' [1994] *Zeitschrift für Handelsrecht* 149 at 149.

[59] See N Reich, 'Urteilsanmerkung' [1993] *Zeitschrift für Wirtschaftsrecht* 1815 at 1816.

One possible first glance explanation suggests a connection with the introduction of the majority principle in the Council, which served to reduce the operating deficit of the European system and which could have resulted in the ECJ in effect resigning itself from its role in the harmonisation of laws. The reasoning of the ECJ itself for this change in approach is, however, much more pragmatic: it merely being a matter of capitulation in the face of its current workload.[60] In fact, the *Keck* judgment led in the short-term to a reduction of the workload of the Court, because the fundamental freedoms did not apply to a section of national regulations any more. Incidentally, for product-related provisions, things remain the same. A recent judgment, *Doc Morris*,[61] moreover raises the question whether the ECJ still adheres to the requirement of discrimination for sales-related regulations.[62] In the end, this shows that the theory developed in *Dassonville* and *Cassis de Dijon* on the fundamental freedoms remains unaffected. The freedoms reach far beyond the protection of specific cross-border limitations; the ECJ carries on by regarding them as general tools for deregulation, at least as far as product-related rules are concerned.[63]

It can therefore be concluded that the foundational elements of the structure of the freedoms as laid down in the 1970s have emerged almost unscathed from the subsequent fundamental constitutional reforms. The wide and contour-less formula, born out of legal urgency, served to guarantee a suitable level of necessary flexibility and have, astonishingly enough, survived to the present day. This is surprising as the fundamental freedoms, just as any other legal principle, are dependent upon their context and can only be interpreted within this particular framework. Judicial interpretation of constitutional norms is adjusted and restricted by the constitutional power structure. The separation of powers is not an abstract idea but rather a concrete concept shaped by the relevant constitutional system. Each theory relating to subjective rights therefore thematises their general character, their normative direction and their substantial scope of application in context of a particular constitution and on the basis of the principles of a constitutional theory or notion of the state.[64] It is from this dependency upon context that the central issue emerges around every theory on subjective rights: whether it is based upon a particular constitution and its historical roots, or whether it contains a comprehensive notion which might eventually prevail over the constitutional-legal situation in which it is found. Before attempting to answer this, the vertical political-institutional context of the matter should be explored.

[60] See Cases C–267 and C–268/91, above n 8, para 14.
[61] See Case C–322/01 *Doc Morris* [2003] ECR I–14887, paras 66 *et seq*.
[62] On this, see also Part III.2.a).
[63] For example, Case C–415/93, above n 30.
[64] See E-W Böckenförde, 'Grundrechtstheorie und Grundrechtsinterpretation' [1994] *Neue Juristische Wochenschrift* 1529 at 1529.

2. The Political-institutional Context II: The Fundamental Freedoms as Multi-Level Norms

The context dependency of the fundamental freedoms also becomes clear when one considers the vertical relationship between the ECJ and the legislative organs of the Member States.

In terms of economic constitutionalism, the fundamental freedoms are, in accordance with Art 14(2) EC (Art III-14(2) CT-Conv; Art 130(2) CT-IGC), components of the internal market. The concept of the internal market aims to merge national markets into one unified market.[65] It is within this market that freedom of individual economic activity should be developed without regard to the borders between the Member States. The individual should, when actively making use of this freedom, consider not the borders between the Member States but the economic efficiency. The economic constitutional concept of the internal market therefore aims for a situation in which the legal differences between the Member States—described by W Hallstein in comparison to the turnpikes at internal crossings as "invisible borders"[66]—are as far as possible irrelevant for private actions. This is where the fundamental freedoms come into play: they are to all intents and purposes the public law trampoline which gives to all participants in the economy the opportunity to vault over the normative barriers between the national markets.

This function of the fundamental freedoms hints at a more fundamental issue: the federal structure of a political association is, for the equality of its subjects, an "open flank".[67] Every federal system entails the danger that each member state will seek to influence the competition with other member states by means of favouritism of its own citizens. One could even speak of *federal risk zones*. Most federally organised states therefore have multi-level norms, which are specially tailored to such risk zones. They are always part of the all-state legal order. Through their inherent supremacy, they declare that the notion of belonging to one member state when receiving treatment at the hands of another is irrelevant. Unequal treatment by a member state for the reason that an individual belongs to another member state is therefore prohibited. All members of the system should in all states be treated equally, regardless of their personal connection to a single other state. Hence, deficits emanating from the fact that non-citizens lack the right to vote and thereby lack an important right to influence the democratic make-up and socio-economic system of this state must also be compensated for. Economic and social participation is instead offered to

[65] See Case 15/81 *Gaston Schul* [1982] ECR 1409, para 33; see also A Hatje in this volume.
[66] See W Hallstein, *Der unvollendete Bundesstaat* (1969), 94.
[67] G Dürig in T Maunz and G Dürig, *Kommentar zum Grundgesetz* (1973), Art 3(1) Basic Law, para 233.

compensate for the lack of political participation. The claim on intra-federal or intra-regional equality of treatment does not stipulate the incorporation of the same laws in each legal system in a mandatory manner. Nevertheless, it tends towards legal unification, as equality of treatment of one's own alongside those citizens of other member states can best be achieved through means of unified national minimum standards.[68]

On the basis of their orientation on federal risk zones, multi-level norms have only really taken a constitutional hold in political systems with a distinctive federal character,[69] for example in the USA (Art IV, section 2(1)—the so-called interstate privileges and immunities clause), in Switzerland (Arts 43(2) and 43(4) of the Bern Constitution), in Art 139(1) of the Constitution of Spain, and in Art 33(1) of the German Basic Law (the so-called common indigenat). Multi-level norms are in any case not restricted to the state level; they appear in those situations in which federal risk zones exist, in other words, the instances of supra-national and international co-operation. Even the fundamental freedoms can therefore be characterised as multi-level norms if the image of the multi-level system is applied to all political associations with a polycentric structure of power. The fundamental freedoms are enhanced by means of further trans-national integration, which seek to serve particular prohibition in relation to discrimination (Art 12(1) EC, furthermore, Art 19(1)(1) EC in relation to municipal voting, Art 71(1) EC for transport and Art 90(1) EC for taxation policies). One particularly remarkable international multi-level norm is contained within Art III(4) GATT.

The ban on rendering personal "membership" to a state as a starting point for differential treatment requires the cohesion of different legal systems, which are superimposed by an all-state legal order. From this can develop a dependency between the multi-level norm on the one hand, and on the other, the furnishing of the separation of powers between all-state and constituent state level. The multi-level norms forge a link among the legal systems of the member states: to the extent to which law is unified through a cross-national legal system, they loose their practical relevance. The historical development in Germany exemplifies this: whereas Art 3(1) of the Constitution of the German Reich of 1871 had a wide scope of application due to the distinct federal structure of the German Reich, Art 33(1) of the Basic Law has the mere status of a "wallflower" in the unitarian federal state of the Federal Republic of Germany.[70] Many German jurists dealing

[68] On this knock-on effect of the fundamental freedoms see Part II.

[69] G Lübbe-Wolff in H Dreier (ed), *Grundgesetz: Kommentar* (1998), Art 33 Basic Law, para 23.

[70] See also U Pfütze, *Die Verfassungsmäßigkeit von Landeskinderklauseln* (1998), 14 and 40 *et seq*.

with the Constitution might hardly know the norm anymore. The US interstate privilege and immunities claim, however, remains a significant principle today and in its scope no less disputed than that of the fundamental freedoms.[71] In relation to Art III(4) GATT, it remains a subject of controversial discussion whether and to what extent the theory developed around the fundamental freedoms can be transferred to the WTO.[72]

In any case it can be said for all multi-level norms that their practical relevance increases to the extent in which the constituent states have competences of their own, but that it decreases to the extent in which the creation of legal uniformity progresses.[73] The insight in the interdependence of multi-level norms and the constitutional allocation of competences is the decisive prerequisite for the formulation of a theory of multi-level norms. It does however also demonstrate that the individual multi-level norm cannot be understood without cross-reference to its concrete constitutional and organisational context.

The breakdown of federal risk zones by the fundamental freedoms tends to have the effect of legal harmonisation, which above all in the formative years of the Community contributed significantly to the establishment of the new legal system.[74] This knock-on effect not only represents opportunity, but also problems, because the claim to equal treatment collides with the competences of the Member States. This is of course perceived most clearly where, for example in social or defence policy, the Member State competences are particularly enhanced. The fundamental freedoms therefore find themselves in a unique, for multi-level norms yet typical, area of conflict: they are to remove discriminatory effects from all co-existing national rules, without levelling federal diversity and differences. This seems to be like putting corners onto a circle.

Upon a more precise examination, this issue is not merely a problem related to de-limitation of powers between the various political elements, rather the realisation of the primacy of politics in trans- and supra-national contexts. In political science, this is referred to as the asymmetry between positive and negative integration.[75] Whilst negative integration refers to the necessary conquering of national restrictions on trade for the implementation of the free internal market by the fundamental freedoms, measures of positive integration are the result of positive Community policy. As opposed to positive integration, negative integration has the advantage of being able to advance the process of integration without having to consider a political

[71] See also L Tribe, *American Constitutional Law* (1988), 528.
[72] See A von Bogdandy, 'Verfassungsrechtliche Dimensionen der Welthandelsorganisation' [2001] *Kritische Justiz* 255 at 278 and 425 at 433.
[73] For an early reference, see P Laband, *Das Staatsrecht des Deutschen Reiches* (1911), i, 186.
[74] See Part II.
[75] See F Scharpf, *Politische Optionen im vollendeten Binnenmarkt* (1996), 109.

process by declaring measures in non-harmonised areas to be unlawful. The scope of the fundamental freedoms depends only on the adjustment of the standard of examination; each alteration in this case can lead to a shift in the vertical and horizontal balance of powers.[76] Indeed, this asymmetry between the ever-advancing negative integration and the apparently stagnating positive integration, for example in social policy, may ultimately cause a problematic splintering of the responsibility for public welfare[77] reflecting the decreasing political steerability of the nation states within the process of internationalisation. The Community lacks the power of positive enforcement, the Member States lose however as "local heroes"[78] the ability to assert the fundamental primacy of politics within the supra-national context and to react to the social and ecologically undesired side effects of cross-border transactions, due to the wide scope of understanding of the fundamental freedoms.

The Commission is therefore correct to emphasise that it must remain the aim of the Community to find an equilibrium between the requirements of the internal market and the consideration of the common welfare interests. The Commission also concedes that this equilibrium is at present "a very tricky balancing act, since the goalposts are constantly moving: the single market is continuing to expand and public services, far from being fixed, are having to adapt to new requirements". The market "mechanisms sometimes have their limits; as a result the potential benefits might not extend to the entire population and the objective of promoting social and territorial cohesion may not be attained. The public authority must then ensure that the general interest is taken into account." The Community must therefore respect the economic and social systems of the Member States. "It is for the Member Sates to make the fundamental choices concerning their society whereas the job of the Community is merely to ensure that the means they employ are compatible with their European commitments."[79]

It can be stated that the theory of the fundamental freedoms on the one hand, and the vertical allocation of competences on the other, are narrowly interrelated. This close dovetailing increases the demand for a theory of the fundamental freedoms. The more complex the entire system becomes, the more it depends on the smooth interplay between its constituent elements and the more sensitive the system becomes for functional difficulties experienced by any element and the more difficult it becomes to replace one element with another. The degree of stability and comfort of the European

[76] See Lukes, above n 28, section B. II, paras 86 *et seq*.
[77] See E-W Böckenförde, *Welchen Weg geht Europa?* (1997), 25.
[78] See H Willke, *Ironie des Staates* (1992), 362 *et seq*.
[79] All quotations are taken from the Commission Communication, *Services of General Interest in Europe* [1996] OJ C 281/3.

house depends to some extent on the fact that the decorator is not responsible for the statics of the building as well. As a result of the independence of the national and the European levels from each other, the hierarchy of norms, i.e. the classic means derived from federal thinking on the reduction of this complexity, can only have system-stabilising effects if applied moderately.[80] The potential of the fundamental freedoms to bring about radical disruption to the system by interferences in the various national legal orders, is just as great as the need to conquer national protectionism. The process of "multi-level constitutionalism" renders urgent the task of precise adjustment of the fundamental freedoms, which takes into account the polycentric base structure of the Union, yet without neglecting the still current task to remove "dysfunctional fragmentation and diffusion".[81]

III. TRANS-NATIONAL INTEGRATION OR (SUPRA-)NATIONAL LEGITIMATION?

1. Fundamental Freedoms and Multi-level Constitutionalism

Significantly, the theory of the fundamental freedoms may contribute to the realisation of a "constitutional networking"[82] which is necessary for the compatibility of European and Member State constitutions. Their categorisation within this constitutional network requires, nevertheless, a clearer enunciation of position as has until now been seen in ECJ case law. The theory of the fundamental freedoms has missed the connection with the constitutional development, from a purpose-built political union in the 1960s and 1970s to that of multi-level constitutionalism (*Verfassungsverbund*) at the beginning of the 21st century. Precisely since the fundamental freedoms can only be properly understood and structured as multi-level norms in a constitutional context, the plain formulae of the 1970s are no longer of much use.

When considering how the fundamental freedoms should be included within the concept of multi-level constitutionalism, the recurring issue is why the fundamental freedoms, as opposed to fundamental rights, play such a insignificant role in the current constitutional discussion.[83] Superficially, the

[80] See F Snyder, *General Course on Constitutional Law of the European Union* (1995), 55: 'The task of the makers of EU constitutional law is how to organize relations of authority in a non-hierarchical and polycentric polity'. For a co-operative and dialogical supra-nationality, see also A von Bogdandy, *Supranationaler Föderalismus als Wirklichkeit und Idee einer Herrschaftsform* (1999), 48.

[81] See in general *ibid*, 50.

[82] R Bieber, 'Verfassungsentwicklung und Verfassungsgebung' in H Wildemann (ed), *Staatswerdung Europas?* (1991), 393 at 396.

[83] See Part I.

question can be answered by stating that the fundamental freedoms, contrary to the fundamental rights, are already present in the Treaties. This however is more of a finding rather than an explanation, though the question as to *why* should again be raised. More is to be gained when this finding is embedded in the historical path from economic community to political union, from purpose built to multi-level constitutionalism and from citizens of the Market to citizens of the Union and when the different functions of fundamental freedoms and of fundamental rights within this very process are considered.

These differences may be clarified with the concepts of *trans-national integration* and *supra-national legitimation*. "Integration" signifies the process by which borders between Member States become irrelevant for economic and non-economic transactions.[84] "Legitimation" is applied in the fundamental legal sense, in other words, the rule of law; on the supranational level, too, the exercise of sovereign power is only legitimate when the limits of such exercise have been fixed (Art 23(1)(1) German Basic Law; Art 6(1) and (2) EU; Art I-2 and Part II CT-Conv; Art 2 and Part II CT-IGC).

When in the 1970s the European Court of Justice determined some of the most elemental matters relating to the fundamental freedoms, case law concerning fundamental rights was still in its infancy. More than the statement that Community law recognises fundamental rights and derives such from the international declarations on human rights and the constitutions of the Member States, could not be gathered from the case law of the Court until around the 1980s.[85] The issue of supra-national legitimation of the newly derived jurisdiction still stood in the shadow of the aim of trans-national integration of the various markets by means of the fundamental freedoms. The relationship between constitution and simple law was therefore more one-dimensional than within the domestic framework. Whilst a constitution conventionally contains not only the rules governing the process of creating new laws, but also the rules which legitimate and restrict such, the EC Treaty, which is today often perceived as a part of the European constitution, served not the legitimation of a pre-existing, quasi pre-constitutional legal system. Instead, the EC Treaty solely served the integration of existing partial orders by means of establishing an entirely new comprehensive order. This explains the early and manifold existence of rules concerning trans-national integration and the initial lack of rules concerning supranational legitimation.

[84] An overview of the theories of integration can be found in Calliess in *id* and Ruffert, above n 15, Art 1 EU, para 9.

[85] See on the development of such Kingreen in Calliess and Ruffert, above n 15, Art 6 EU, paras 20 *et seq*.

However, after the sources of friction augmented with the beginning of the legal activity of the Community, a need for supra-national legitimation emerged, which has been expressed in an increasing number of fundamental rights related decisions in the 1990s. Whilst the Community fundamental rights satisfy the need for legitimation caused by the emerging European legal system, the fundamental freedoms quasi conversely were and are an important element at the creation of this system by having accelerated the process of legal harmonisation, especially in the early years of the Community. Fundamental freedoms were the significant condition for the establishment of the internal market, whereas fundamental rights were the result of this development. Alternatively, expressed in a more simplified way: what the fundamental freedoms have created, the fundamental rights now must seek to legitimate.

In the course of time however, the difference between integration norm and legitimation norm has slipped into oblivion. Two essential dogmatic developments in relation to the fundamental freedoms substantiate this: their expansion to general freedom rights (see below 2.) and their application to Community measures (3.).

2. The Theoretical Structure and Scope of the Fundamental Freedoms

a) The Fundamental Freedoms as Market Access Rights

The difference between fundamental freedoms, serving trans-national integration, and fundamental rights, serving supra-national legitimation, needs to be reflected in the structure of the analyses: whereas the fundamental rights protect against all unjustified restrictions of liberty, the fundamental freedoms only provide protection from specific cross-border infringements.

It is in principle therefore correct that German literature generalises the decision *Keck*[86] accordingly and understands the fundamental freedoms as *market access rights*.[87] Product-related demands tend to hinder the successful introduction of a particular product within a national market if no product series has been produced specifically for this national market or if the manufacturing process did not adhere to the strictest applicable standards. Sales-related modalities do not tend, however, to hinder access to the market. Instead, they affect all participants within the market. The crossing of

[86] See Part II. 1. c).

[87] Becker in Schwarze, above n 15, Art 28 EC, para 49; Ehlers, above n 18, 485; Kingreen, above n 21, 121 *et seq*; C Koenig and A Haratsch, *Europarecht* (2000), 509; P-C Müller-Graff, 'Die Verdichtung des Binnenmarktrechts zwischen Handlungsfreiheiten und Sozialgestaltung' in A Hatje (ed), 'Das Binnenmarktrecht als Daueraufgabe' [2002] *Europarecht* suppl 1, 7 at 36; Streinz, above n 13, para 733.

the border lies, so to speak, already behind them. As far as they do not exceptionally have discriminatory effects on cross-boarder issues, they do not represent an interference, because the protective effect of the fundamental freedoms is only operable in relation to border crossings.

The interpretation of the fundamental freedoms as rights to market access orientates itself around different initial positions: the foreign participants in the market seek to "get a foot in the door" of a market in which internal citizens already find themselves. This interpretation as market access rights has, in contrast to the *Keck* differentiation, the advantage that it is applicable to all fundamental freedoms, and not only to that of the free movement of goods. In addition, it is an advantage that the *material effects* of a regulation, rather than its classification as a product or sales related item, determine whether an interference is present.[88] Namely, it is entirely plausible—for example in the field of advertising—that restrictions in promotion of sales could result in an indirect ban on the import of goods, particularly in cases in which there exists no other means of trade promotion. Thus, the ECJ qualified the Swedish ban on advertisement of alcoholic beverages as a (justified) interference in the free movement of goods, and in doing so explicitly referred to the fact that it rendered more difficult any access to the market by foreign products compared to domestic products, the latter of which the consumer would already be familiar with.[89] In special cases, advertising can therefore also serve as a means of entrance to the market.[90]

The increasing unity on the role of the fundamental freedoms as market access rights should however not lead to the assumption that the big problems have now been eradicated. The debate still rages around the question of transnational integration or also (supra-) national legitimation. In other words, the question is whether one can restrict the fundamental freedoms specifically to the liberalisation of cross-border exchanges (and in doing so filter out measures which affect domestic and cross-border issues in the same way) or whether they should be regarded as general rights to liberalisation prohibiting all disproportionate burdens on the cross-border economic freedom in question.[91] The differentiation of trans-national integration and supra-national legitimation is a question parallel to the

[88] A Epiney in Calliess and Ruffert, above n 15, Art 28 EC, paras 36 and 42; M Simm, *Der Gerichtshof der Europäischen Gemeinschaften im föderalen Kompetenzkonflikt* (1998), 126 *et seq*; J Steiner, 'Drawing the Lines' (1992) 29 *CML Rev* 749 at 773; R Streinz, 'Konvergenz der Grundfreiheiten' in H-W Arndt (ed), *Völkerrecht und deutsches Recht: Festschrift für W Rudolf* (2001), 199 at 219.

[89] See Case C–405/98 *Gourmet International Products* [2001] ECR I–1795, para 21.

[90] See S Leible, 'Urteilsanmerkung' [2001] *Europäische Zeitschrift für Wirtschaftsrecht* 253 at 254.

[91] See also Eilmansberger, above n 19, 355 *et seq*.

question of whether the fundamental freedoms are only equality rights, or also freedom rights which protect from burdens of cross-border transactions even if the cross-border situation is subject to the same burdens as the internal one.

The ECJ seems to prefer, even after the *Keck* decision, an understanding in terms of freedom rights. In the *Bosman* decision, the national transfer rules for professional soccer players were qualified as an interference with the free movement of workers, although these hindered the transfer from Manchester United to both Arsenal London and to Real Madrid.[92] In the case of *Graf*, the question was whether the loss of the right to claim compensation upon termination of an individual's contract of employment in Austria was reconcilable with the notion of the free movement of persons (Art 39 EC). That the loss of this right was independent from citizenship and that it *also* came into play when the employee changed employment to an employer based within Austria, was held to be irrelevant. According to the ECJ, there will always be an interference with the freedom guaranteed in Art 39 EC, when citizens of a Member State are prevented from leaving their native land in order to benefit from the right to free movement.[93]

The decision *DocMorris* momentarily marks the end-point, even possibly a new turning point in the case law of the ECJ.[94] Object of the proceeding was the German ban on mail order business of drugs, which included in particular the distribution via the Internet. In the categories of the *Keck* doctrine, this ban undoubtedly was a sales-related regulation,[95] which under the hitherto valid case law only constituted an interference if it had discriminating consequences.[96] This way the ECJ had classified a Greek regulation in 1995, which restricted the sale of baby food to pharmacies[97] and thus excluded the mail order business for this product. Although foreign pharmacists were not allowed to distribute baby food in Greece, the law was qualified as not discriminating and therefore it did not interfere in the free movement of goods. In a striking contrast to this, the ECJ and the Advocate General avoid a definite classification of the mail order business ban as a sales modality. While the ECJ does not address the cited predecessor decision at all, the opinion of the Advocate of the General contains the little illuminative consideration that the examination of the prerequisites of

[92] See Case C–415/93, above n 30.

[93] See Case C–190/98 *Graf* [2000] ECR I–493, para 23; see also Case C–254/98 *TK-Heimdienst* [2000] ECR I–151, para 15.

[94] See C Lenz, 'Warenverkehrsfreiheit nach der DocMorris-Entscheidung zum Versand von Arzneimitteln' [2004] *Neue Juristische Wochenschrift* 332 at 332 *et seq.*

[95] R Streinz, 'Das Verbot des Apothekenversandhandels mit Arzneimitteln' [2003] *Europäische Zeitschrift für Wirtschaftsrecht* 37 at 43 *et seq.*

[96] See Cases C–267 and C–268/91, above n 8, paras 16 *et seq.*

[97] See Case C–391/92 *Commission v Greece* [1995] ECR I–1621, para 15.

Art 28 EC must not be limited to a "mechanical application" of the two traditional requirements of the *Keck* formula.[98] This is a formulation employed if one wants to distance oneself.

Especially the opinion of the Advocate General was centred on the criterion of market access rather than on the question of an equal treatment of domestic and foreign persons. It was held to be decisive that the method of sales affected by the ban is important for the opening up of a market.[99] With this statement, not much is gained, because for which market or for which market participant the Internet, overcoming all spatial distances, is not important? How, for example, was one to qualify bans on medical or legal advice in a chat room? If the criterion of market access wants to implement the *Keck* formula in relation to sales modalities as well, its examination cannot uncouple itself from the question of the effects of the measure on domestic market participants. However, the relevant statements of the ECJ are rather meagre: although it examines whether a discrimination of foreign market participants exists, it confines itself to the apodictic remark that the ban on the mail order business hits these harder than domestic market participants who would be able to sell drugs in their pharmacies.[100] Nevertheless, this flat rate assertion does not do justice to the complexity of a comparison group formation, which is to include the specific cross-border market access hindrances.[101] A closer analysis of the mail order business ban shows, namely, that it is not foreign as opposed to domestic pharmacists that are put to a disadvantage but non-resident as opposed to resident pharmacists:[102] that is, the necessity of a personal contact between pharmacist and consumer hits the pharmacist in Munich, who wants to gain a foothold on the pharmacy market in Trier by means of a mail order business just as hard as his colleagues in Athens, but considerably harder than the operators of pharmacies in Trier and in Luxembourg.[103] Only the adherence to the requirement of a cross-border reference, i.e. a *specific* discrimination of the foreign situation, procures the filter effect desired by the ECJ itself, which prevents the "increasing tendency of traders to invoke Art 30 of the Treaty as a means of challenging any rules whose effect is to limit their commercial freedom".[104] The target of including specific cross-border

[98] AG Stix-Hackl in Case C–322/01, above n 61, para 73.
[99] *Ibid*, para 88.
[100] See Case C–322/01, above n 61, para 74.
[101] See also the fundamental criticism by W Schroeder in Streinz (ed), above n 15, Art 28 EC, paras 46 *et seq*.
[102] This is the essential difference, for instance, in relation to cases of bans on advertisements which bulkhead off the domestic market for foreign products: see eg Case C–405/98, above n 89.
[103] For criticism of the comparison group formation carried out here, albeit without any substantiation, see AG Stix-Hackl in Case C–322/01, above n 61, para 88.
[104] See Cases C–267 and C–268/91, above n 8, para 14.

burdens is missed, however, if measures similarly hitting domestic and foreign traders are also qualified as interferences because, of course, every measure regulating economy always *also* has cross-border consequences. If this should suffice for the assumption of an interference though, then market access rights become general market design rights; the fundamental freedoms mutate to fundamental rights to defence against all restrictions of economic activity.

This development is precarious also because of the autonomy of the national protection of fundamental rights. Surely, it could be said with good reason that the ban on the mail order business of drugs constitutes a violation of the German fundamental right to free choice of profession (Art 12(1) Basic Law). Community fundamental rights could not be activated, because under Art II-51(1)(1) CT-Conv (Art 111(1)(1) CT-IGC) they are only binding as far as the implementation of Union law is concerned. Here, the relevant norms belonged to a part of drug and pharmacy law which is solely national. The ECJ has overcome this obstacle by giving up the requirement of unequal treatment of domestic and cross-border distribution of drugs. This way however, the fundamental freedoms, which provide protection against all unjustified burdens if only these *also* concern cross-border transactions, develop gradually into a second layer of fundamental rights. The abandonment of the criterion of discrimination therefore heralds a basic functional change: it is not any more merely about integration in the above described meaning, but about the necessity of legitimation of national measures in accordance with the rule of law, which meanwhile already results from the fundamental rights. This doubling-up does not only make little sense. It contradicts the notion that, in relation to the Member States, the binding effect of Community fundamental rights is restricted to the implementation of Community law. It is a little astonishing with which meticulousness it is constantly stressed that the fundamental rights of the Community may not replace the fundamental rights of the Member States and that they may not cause a shift in the allocation of competences, if just this effect is obtained by the mutation of fundamental freedoms to fundamental rights. Here it becomes apparent how narrowly the doctrine of the fundamental freedoms and the basic questions of the interpretation of the European fundamental rights are interrelated.

The decision *DocMorris* once again documents the necessity to sharpen the notion of discrimination and the trans-national integration function of the fundamental freedoms.[105] The notion of discrimination forms the basis for focusing on the fundamental freedoms on federal risk zones, for the concentration on whether a rule specifically serves to hinder any form of

[105] S Plötscher, *Der Begriff der Diskriminierung im Europäischen Gemeinschaftsrecht* (2003).

cross-border transactions. As a result of its formal structure, the equality clause promises a concept of rationality in contrast to the unspecific criterion of perceptibility, which the ECJ occasionally uses in order to restrict the scope of the fundamental freedoms:[106] it is—as opposed to the bi-polar freedom right[107]—tri-polar and therefore requires that a sovereign body treats two circumstances differently, the inland situation on the one hand, and on the other, the cross-border situation. The examination of interference with a fundamental freedom then consists of three steps:

- Comparison between domestic and dross-border circumstances
- Unequal treatment
- Causation between unequal treatment and the prohibited criteria of differentiation (nationality and border crossing).[108]

b) Justification of the Interference

For individual rights, a certain interaction between the level of the protected area and the level of the justification of an interference is characteristic.[109] Therefore, the problematic expansion of the fundamental freedoms to supra-national legitimation norms affects the structure of the examination of the justification: as there are no usable criteria with a filter effect upon the level of the interference with the area protected by the fundamental freedoms, the possibilities of justification must consequently be extended.[110]

Well-known is the fact that the examination of the principles of justification by the ECJ has become somewhat Janus-faced. Interferences in the area protected by the fundamental freedoms cannot only be justified by codified grounds of justification (Arts 30, 39(3), 46(1) and 55 EC), but also through unwritten grounds, which the ECJ itself developed in the *Cassis de Dijon* judgment.[111] The necessity of employing general interests as unwritten grounds of justification stems firstly from the wide *Dassonville* formula, which required adjustment through the addition of

[106] See Case C–190/98 *Graf* [2000] ECR I–493, paras 23 *et seq.*

[107] See G Marenco and K Banks, 'Intellectual Property and the Community Rules on Free Movement' (1990) 15 *ELR* 224 at 238.

[108] For further details see T Kingreen, 'Grundfreiheiten' in A von Bogdandy (ed), *Europäisches Verfassungsrecht* 631 at 662 *et seq.*

[109] For the three-step examination of a subjective right (area protected by the subjective right, interference therein, justification) see J Kühling in this volume.

[110] In this context, see also Streinz, above n 88, 201.

[111] See Case 120/78, above n 33, para 8; see in addition Cases 110 and 111/78 *van Wesemael* [1979] ECR 35, para 35 on the freedom to provide services (the 'general interest'); Case C–255/97 *Pfeiffer* [1999] ECR I–2835, para 19 on the freedom of establishment; see also Case C–237/94 *O'Flynn* [1996] ECR I–2617, para 19 on the freedom of movement of workers. For an extensive analysis, see M Ahlfeld, *Zwingende Erfordernisse im Sinne der Cassis-Rechtsprechung des Europäischen Gerichtshofs zu Art. 30 EGV* (1997).

further general interest rules, and secondly, from a very restrictive interpretation of the codified grounds of justification, in particular the general "public policy" clause.[112]

As such, the *Cassis* formula is at the same time corrective for the wide understanding of the area protected by the fundamental freedoms and for the restrictive interpretation of the codified grounds of justification. This way, it is placed in a dogmatic no man's land between the levels of "interference with the protected area" and "justification". Subsequently, some commentaries interpret the "imperative requirements" as restrictions of the protected area itself,[113] whilst others regard such as grounds for justification.[114] Case law has asserted neither of the opinions. In some decisions, the ECJ speaks of the "imperative requirements" in context with the interpretation of Art 30 EC Treaty (Art 28 EC),[115] but then enunciates the other position (in the case of *Wurmser* even within the same judgment) so that a national law may only be excused compliance with the requirements of Art 28 EC if it can be proven that it is necessary to effectuate the "imperative requirements".[116] Neither variant appears satisfactory. The solution on the level of the protected area is questionable as the ECJ in fact carries out an examination of legal justification and therefore contradicts the principle of transparency of examination. The justification solution remains unconvincing, as well. The creation of unwritten exceptional circumstances counteracts the narrow interpretation of the codified grounds of justification.[117] This serves to demonstrate that the unwritten "imperative requirements" cannot be introduced smoothly into the structure of the fundamental freedoms and that, in addition, they contain no legitimising approval from within the EC Treaty itself.

The *Cassis* formula causes not only theoretical classification difficulties, but it is also responsible for a confusion as regards the content. The central issue appears to be the question as to which form of interference is justifiable by means of Arts 30, 39(3), 46(1) and 55 EC, and by means of the

[112] See further Kingreen, above n 21, 155.

[113] M Ahlt, *Europarecht* (1996), 91; T Jestaedt and F Kaestle, 'Kehrtwende oder Rückbesinnung in der Anwendung von Art. 30 EG-Vertrag' [1994] *Europäisches Wirtschafts- und Steuerrecht* 26 at 27; Hoffmann, above n 21, 111.

[114] U Becker, 'Von "Dassonville" über "Cassis" zu "Keck"' [1994] *Europarecht* 162 at 166; A Epiney, *Umgekehrte Diskriminierungen* (1995), 42; G Hirsch, 'Die aktuelle Rechtsprechung des EuGH zur Warenverkehrsfreiheit' [1999] *Zeitschrift für europäische Studien* 503 at 511; Jarass, above n 18, 719.

[115] See Cases C–1 and C–176/90 *Aragonesa de publicidad exteriror y publivía* [1991] ECR I–4151, para 13; see also Case 25/88 *Wurmser* [1989] ECR 1105, para 11.

[116] See also Case 113/80 *Commission v Ireland* [1981] ECR 1625, para 10; Case 25/88, above n 115, para 11.

[117] See Kingreen, above n 21, 52; W-H Roth, 'Diskriminierende Regelungen des Warenverkehrs und Rechtfertigung durch die "zwingenden Erfordernisse" des Allgemeininteresses' [2000] *Wettbewerb in Recht und Praxis* 979 at 984.

"imperative requirements". This issue has great practical significance, as the ECJ interprets the codified grounds for justification, in particular, that of public policy, very narrowly,[118] and in doing so renders significant principles such as environmental protection to the category of "imperative requirements". The problem springs from a congenital defect of the *Cassis* test: it leaves open—albeit something often overlooked—the decisive issue of determining the comprised forms of interferences. It was not until later that the ECJ extended the *Cassis* formula by one—here italicised—phrase without actually making it clear that the *Cassis* judgment did not ever initially include this statement. In accordance with this, the "obstacles to free movement within the Community resulting from disparities between the national laws must be accepted in so far as such rules, *applicable to domestic and imported products without distinction*, may be recognised as being necessary in order to satisfy mandatory requirements relating *inter alia* to consumer protection".[119] In later cases, the ECJ spoke not of "applicable without distinction", rather of a measure "applied without distinction".[120]

Academic literature has for a long time understood this notion to mean that (overt or covert) discriminatory provisions may only be justified by means of the codified grounds, whilst for discrimination-free measures also the unwritten one of the general public interest can be applied.[121] Indeed, there exists diverse case law dealing with provisions applicable without distinction, but which contain discriminatory effects. Such material discriminations were the reason for the fact that examination of the justification was limited to Art 30 EC.[122] In other cases, the ECJ nevertheless raised, despite the determination of a hidden form of discrimination, the issue of "imperative requirements".[123] Finally, there are also decisions in which the ECJ makes the discriminatory character of a measure disappear by means

[118] See eg Case 177/83 *Kohl* [1984] ECR 3651, para 19. The ECJ justifies this by the exceptional character of the restrictions: see eg Case C–205/89 *Commission v Greece* [1991] ECR I–1361, para 9; this is methodologically doubtful: U Becker, *Der Gestaltungsspielraum der Mitgliedstaaten im Spannungsfeld zwischen Umweltschutz und freiem Warenverkehr* (1991), 71; Kingreen, above n 21, 154; S Leible in E Grabitz and M Hilf (ed), *Das Recht der Europäischen Union* (2000), Art 30 EC, para 2; Roth, above n 117, 983.

[119] Initially see Case 261/81 *Rau* [1982] ECR 3961, para 12.

[120] See also Case 25/88, above n 115, para 10; Cases C–1 and C–176/90, above n 115, para 12.

[121] See also L Defalque, 'Le concept de discrimination en matière de libre circulation des marchandises' (1987) 23 *Cahiers de Droit Européen* 471 at 478; Epiney in Calliess and Ruffert, above n 15, Art 28 EC, para 23.

[122] See Case 177/83 *Kohl* [1984] ECR 3651, paras 15 and 19; Case 229/83 *Leclerc* [1985] ECR 1, paras 26 and 29. See also Case 25/88, above n 115, para 11; Cases C–1 and C–176/90, above n 115, para 13; Case C–224/97 *Ciola* [1999] ECR I–2517, para 16.

[123] See Case 16/83 *Prantl* [1984] ECR 1299, paras 22 *et seq*; see also Case 207/83 *Commission v United Kingdom* [1985] ECR 1201, paras 19 *et seq*; see also Cases C–34/, C–35/ and C–36/95 *De Agostini* [1997] ECR I–3843, paras 44 *et seq* for sales-related forms of discrimination in the sense of the *Keck* formula.

of questionable argumentation. This happens if openly discriminatory acts are to be legitimised by the protection of public interest (for example that of environmental protection) which as a result of narrow judicial interpretation by the ECJ can neither be subsumed under the list of codified grounds (Arts 30, 39(3), 46 and 55 EC), nor be justified by "imperative requirements" on the basis of the *Cassis* formula due to its restriction to non-discriminatory measures.[124] Even in relation to openly discriminatory acts, the ECJ is no longer consequential: the Court rejected the doubtless discriminatory foreign player clause in professional football by using the unwritten restriction in the sense of the *Cassis* test without even mentioning the written basis for justification as contained within Art 39(3) EC.[125] Despite this, the Court once again emphasised in the *Ciola* decision of 1999 that domestic discriminatory regulations were "compatible with Community law only if they can be brought within the scope of an express derogation, such as Art 56 of the EC Treaty (now Art 46(1) EC, TK)".[126]

This inconsistency of legal reasoning has been increasingly thematised within German-language legal literature. Even a former judge of the Court admits that the ECJ is on "shaky ground" and must go in "search for a doctrine of justification".[127] In recent publications, it has been proposed that the border between overt and covert forms of discrimination should be closed and that only the latter should be relevant to the *Cassis* test.[128] As such, the various hidden forms of protectionism would however be primed: why should a provision of hidden discriminatory nature be easier to justify than a stipulation overtly based on one of the prohibited criteria

[124] See Case C–2/90 *Commission v Belgium* [1992] ECR I–4431, paras 34 and 36, in which, in reliance upon Art 174(2) EC, it was held that there was no discrimination, even though waste from Belgium was treated differently from that of other Member States and the Advocate General had suggested a violation of Art 28 EC. This was confirmed in Case C–379/98 *PreußenElektra* [2001] ECR I–2099, paras 73 *et seq*, even though AG Jacobs explicitly reproves the earlier case law as 'faulty' (*ibid*, para 225); in an earlier opinion, AG Jacobs already expressed reservations, [1991] ECR I–4431 at 4457. For a critical analysis see C Nowak, 'Die Grundfreiheiten des EG-Vertrages und der Umweltschutz' [2002] *Verwaltungsarchiv* 368 at 389; S Heselhaus, 'Rechtfertigung unmittelbar diskriminierender Eingriffe in die Warenverkehrsfreiheit' [2001] *Europäische Zeitschrift für Wirtschaftsrecht* 645 at 646.

[125] See Case C–415/93, above n 30, paras 121 *et seq*. The ECJ proceeds in the same manner for example in relation to restrictions on cross-border health claims, which can only be categorised as open forms of discrimination. See C Nowak and J Schnitzler, 'Erweiterte Rechtfertigungsmöglichkeiten für mitgliedstaatliche Beschränkungen der EG-Grundfreiheiten' [2000] *Europäische Zeitschrift für Wirtschaftsrecht* 627 at 629.

[126] See Case C–224/97, above n 122, para 16.

[127] See Hirsch, above n 114, 510.

[128] See Ehlers, above n 18, 487; J Gundel, 'Die Rechtfertigung von faktisch diskriminierenden Eingriffen in die Grundfreiheiten des EGV' [2001] *Jura* 79 at 82; Nowak, above n 124, 392 *et seq*; see also Kluth in Calliess and Ruffert, above n 15, Art 50 EC, para 57, and P Steinberg, 'Zur Konvergenz der Grundfreiheiten auf der Tatbestands- und Rechtfertigungsebene' [2002] *Europäische Zeitschrift für Wirtschaftrecht* 13 at 20.

of differentiation? Therefore, increasingly the insight prevails that the *Cassis* test should be valid for all types of interferences.[129] In principle this is convincing: why should for example the protection, contained within Art 30 EC, of specifically named elements of national culture justify even overt forms of discrimination, whilst the matter of environmental protection, hardly less insignificant, does not?

The real root of the problem is in fact scarcely discussed: it is the nature of the *Cassis* test itself.[130] This criticism-free acceptance of the praetorical creation of the unwritten grounds for justification is in any case surprising for a lawyer trained in German constitutional law: if one were to dare place unwritten grounds for justification alongside the written ones in a publication on the fundamental rights of the German Basic Law, one would be sure to gain the disapproval of one's colleagues. Students who attempt this in examinations or essays would find themselves at the lower end of the grade spectrum. Whereas in relation to the *Cassis* test, the number of amici curiae remains high. It is incomprehensible when, on the one hand, the Court tends to emphasise the unique character of the written grounds for justification and with such, justifies their own narrow interpretation, yet on the other, constantly enumerates other unwritten circumstances which may justify an interference with the area protected by the fundamental freedoms. This serves to counteract the Court's own development *singularia non sunt extenda*. Repeatedly new "imperative requirements" are asserted, for which in the text of the Treaties there appears to be no immediate point of reference. A conclusive catalogue of these general interests is not presented in relation to any fundamental freedom.[131] This gives the impression that there is in fact hardly any single aspect of public life that cannot be subsumed under the *Cassis* criteria.[132] Even objects of legal protection expressly cited in Art 30 EC are classified as "imperative requirements".[133] In such circumstances the case law would benefit from a more a positivistic stance: all grounds for justification should be established where they are mentioned

[129] See Becker in Schwarze, above n 15, Art 30 EC, para 43; Leible in Grabitz and Hilf, above n 118, Art 28 EC, para 20; W Weiß, 'Nationales Steuerrecht und Niederlassungsfreiheit' [1999] *Europäische Zeitschrift für Wirtschaftsrecht* 493 at 497; Müller-Graff spots a 'synchronisation of the issue of justification': see above n 87, 53 *et seq*.

[130] See Kingreen, above n 21, 104 and 162.

[131] See also the formulation contained within Case 120/78, above n 33, para 8: 'in particular'. Cf Case C–353/89 *Commission v Netherlands* [1991] ECR I–4069, para 18, in relation to Art 49 EC.

[132] W Schroeder, 'Kein Glücksspiel ohne Grenzen' [1994] *Europäische Grundrechte-Zeitschrift* 373 at 378; also Nowak, above n 124, 390 *et seq*.

[133] See also the issue of health provision in Case 120/78, above n 33, para 8, which the ECJ included in the list of imperative requirements, but then discovered that this consideration was already included within the context of Art 30 EC: Cases C–1 and C–176/90, above n 115, para 13.

by the Treaty, in other words, Arts 30, 39(3), 46(1) and 55 EC. They all contain the thematically unlimited clause of "public policy" and therefore the classic "security outlet for the national interest"[134] of international treaties. By means of the "public policy" provision the "imperative requirements" can be integrated and legitimised and then be included in the required examination of proportionality.[135]

In conclusion, the inconsistent case law of the ECJ demonstrates that the unwritten "imperative requirements" are not only alien bodies in the examination of the legal grounds for justification, but also within the entire structure of the fundamental freedoms. The *Cassis* formula attempts to correct what cannot be corrected, in other words, the renunciation of the requirement of an incident of unequal treatment on the level of "interference with the protected area". As such, the concept as developed by the ECJ and the prevailing legal opinion remains somewhat half-hearted: the fundamental freedoms should not provide protection from all burdens arising from cross-border transactions, but rather from only some of them. They should indeed be freedom rights, but at the same time different from fundamental rights. The precise form of this 'otherness' remains however unresolved, and it is not surprising that case law on the fundamental freedoms is being steered further by weak formulae inhering a particular form of arbitrariness. The inconsequential theory of justification stands paradigmatically for the precarious rigidity of traditional theory of the fundamental freedoms. As such, it appears that the *Dassonville* and *Cassis* tests cannot in the long term provide any reliable basis for a consistent theory of the fundamental freedoms.

3. The Union as Addressee of the Fundamental Freedoms?

Whilst the first decision served to level out the difference between trans-national integration through the fundamental freedoms and *national* legitimation through Member State fundamental rights, the second decision deals with the delimitation between trans-national integration and *supranational* legitimation: the binding nature of fundamental freedoms even for Union bodies, to which the ECJ refers in current case law, even if the Court

[134] See also H Schneider, *Die öffentliche Ordnung als Schranke der Grundfreiheiten im EG-Vertrag* (1998), 57 *et seq.*

[135] P-C Müller-Graff in H von der Groeben and J Schwarze (eds), *Kommentar zum EU-/EG-Vertrag* (2003), Art 30 EC, para 29; in addition see T Jürgensen and I Schlünder, 'EG-Grundrechtsschutz gegenüber Maßnahmen der Mitgliedstaaten' (1996) 121 *Archiv des öffentlichen Rechts* 200 at 217; Kingreen, above n 21, 156; Roth, above n 117, 984. Cf eg Gundel, above n 128, 83 and Heselhaus, above n 124, 647. For a discussion of proportionality in relation to the fundamental freedoms, above Kingreen, see n 21, 168 *et seq.*

has never assumed a breach in the application of such.[136] Exactly what such was intended to achieve, remains however unclear: if one limits the fundamental freedoms—other than the understanding in relation to the Member States—to the function of trans-national norms of integration, it may indeed be possible to approve a binding effect in relation to the European organs. However, this binding effect would never become of practical use, as the Community legislative, rather than building hindrances between national markets, should serve to deconstruct obstacles between the national markets. Furthermore, an explanation is required as to why there have been different standards established for, on the one hand the European organs, and on the other, the Member States.

If, however, one were to apply the same standards as applied to Member State measures, the fundamental freedoms mutate into supra-national norms of legitimation. They then step into a new relationship with Community fundamental rights, albeit one which requires clarification, because the fundamental rights serve just this precise need for supra-national legitimation.[137]

IV. THE HORIZONTAL EFFECT OF THE FUNDAMENTAL FREEDOMS

In addition to the vertical scope of the fundamental freedoms as against Member States, their horizontal impact on private autonomous actions is increasingly becoming the subject of discussion. The question is whether the fundamental freedoms only procure public law rights or whether in certain cases they also have horizontal effect against private parties. Within the case law of the Court, two dissimilar approaches may be observed.

1. Direct Horizontal Effect

It can be seen that the ECJ appears to accept the horizontal application of the fundamental freedoms in particular in relation to those private individuals who, based on special position, have the capacity for autonomous

[136] See Case 15/83 *Denkavit* [1984] ECR 2171, paras 15 to 17; Case C–51/93 *Meyhui* [1994] ECR I–3879, paras 11 *et seq*; Case C–114/96 *Kieffer* [1997] ECR I–3629, paras 29 *et seq*; see also Becker in Schwarze, above n 15, Art 28 EC, paras 101 *et seq*.

[137] See in relation to the Directive on tobacco advertising and with an appropriate reference to the different functions of basic rights and fundamental freedoms: M Möstl, 'Grenzen der Rechtsangleichung im europäischen Binnenmarkt' [2002] *Europarecht* 318 at 322, 328 and 349.

regulation of parts of economic life, for example sports associations.[138] Behind this stands the consideration that the individual can evade application of the rules of an association just as infrequently as public legal norms, and that the border between private and state exercise of functions is often differently configured in the Member States.[139] In order to ensure the comparability with national legislative powers, it has been proposed in legal literature that the relevant association must have a certain "social power" or even a monopoly position.[140]

Whether the ECJ will accept this limitation, or assume an unlimited direct effect amongst private individuals, is unclear. In particular, the case law on the free movement of goods gives rise to a good few volts of action. First, it appeared as if the Court had assumed a position of directly enforceable rights amongst private individuals. In the *Deutsche Grammophon* judgment, it was deemed that the coming together of the national markets to form one unified market would not be attainable "if, under the various legal systems of the Member States, nationals of those States were able to partition the market and bring about arbitrary discrimination or disguised restrictions on trade between Member States."[141] Certainly, this statement was drafted in general terms and could also be understood to mean that only private law provisions, rather than the private exercise of these provisions, would fall under the scope of Art 28 EC.[142] Subsequently however, the ECJ has regularly distinguished between the status as provided by a protective law and the exercise of such, and in doing so has applied Art 28 EC only to the latter.[143] Indeed, the judgment in *Dansk Supermarked* from 1981 speaks clearly in favour of an unlimited horizontal effect of the

[138] See Case 36/74 *Walrave* [1974] ECR 1405, paras 16 to 19; Case 13/76 *Donà* [1976] ECR 1333, paras 17 to 18; Case C–415/93, above n 30, paras 82 *et seq*; Cases C–51/96 and C–191/97 *Deliège* [2000] ECR I–2549, para 47; Case C–176/96, *Lehtonen* [2000] ECR I–2681, paras 47 *et seq*. For an extensive analysis in the commentaries, see M Burgi, 'Mitgliedstaatliche Garantenpflicht statt unmittelbare Drittwirkung der Grundfreiheiten' [1999] *Europäisches Wirtschafts- und Steuerrecht* 327; W Kluth, 'Die Bindung privater Wirtschaftsteilnehmer an die Grundfreiheiten des EG-Vertrages' (1997) 122 *Archiv des öffentlichen Rechts* 557; B Remmert, 'Grundfreiheiten und Privatrechtsordnung' [2003] *Juristische Ausbildung* 13; A Röthel, 'Grundfreiheiten und private Normgebung' [2001] *Europarecht* 908; W-H Roth, 'Drittwirkung der Grundfreiheiten?' in Due (ed), above n 19, 1231 *et seq*; D Schindler, *Die Kollision von Grundfreiheiten und Grundrechten* (2001), 62 *et seq*; R Streinz and S Leible, 'Die unmittelbare Drittwirkung der Grundfreiheiten' [2000] *Europäische Zeitschrift für Wirtschaftsrecht* 459.

[139] See also eg Kingreen, above n 21, 199; Roth, above n 117, 1246; J-C Séché, 'Quand les juges tirent au but' (1996) 32 *Cahiers de Droit Européen* 355 at 377; in this context, see also Case C–281/98 *Angonese* [2000] ECR I–4139, para 33.

[140] See Ehlers, above n 18, 274; F Kainer, 'Grundfreiheiten und staatliche Schutzpflichten' [2000] *Juristische Schulung* 431 at 432; Roth, above n 138, 1246.

[141] See Case 78/70 *Deutsche Grammophon* [1971] ECR 487, para 12.

[142] See Roth, above n 138, 1233.

[143] See Case 16/74 *Centrafarm* [1974] ECR 1183, paras 4 *et seq*; Case 119/75 *Terrapin* [1976] ECR 1039, paras 4 *et seq*.

fundamental freedoms. In this case, it was deemed "impossible in any circumstances for agreements between individuals to derogate from the mandatory provisions of the Treaty on the free movement of goods".[144] In further proceedings, such statements do not appear to emerge: indeed relevant decisions do not even refer to *Dansk Supermarked*.[145] It rather becomes clear that the ECJ does not want to involve private stipulations themselves in the context of Art 28 EC, rather only the legal norms granting rights which do not correspond with Art 28 EC. Accordingly the Court held in 1988, in relation to a non-aggression clause of a patent licensing agreement, that "it must be borne in mind that those articles (Arts 28 EC *et seq* TK) form part of the rules intended to ensure the free movement of goods and to eliminate for that purpose any measures of Member States likely to form, in any way, a barrier thereto". Agreements between undertakings, on the other hand, are governed by the rules on competition in Arts 85 *et seq* of the Treaty (Arts 81 *et seq* EC, TK), whose aim is to maintain effective competition within the common market".[146] As such, it appeared, at least for the free movement of goods, that the concept of direct horizontal applicability outside private regulations by associations has been cleared from the table.

In the *Angonese* decision from 2000, the ECJ appears to wish to undertake a partial U-turn. The subject matter of the proceedings was a job advertisement placed by a private banking institution in the area of the South Tyrol requiring of applicants a certain qualification as awarded after examination in the Province of Bolzano, which would demonstrate German-Italian bilingual ability. The ECJ affirmed the applicability of the fundamental freedoms in relation to the banking institution: Art 39 EC is "formulated generally" and "is not aimed specifically at the Member States".[147] Just as Art 141 EC, the rule should guarantee "a non-discriminatory treatment within the employment market", which requires that "the prohibition of discrimination applied equally to all agreements intended to regulate paid labour collectively, as well as to contracts between individuals".[148] Without any further differentiation, the Court infers that the "prohibition of discrimination on grounds of nationality laid down in Art 48 (Art 39 EC, TK) of the Treaty must be regarded as applying to private persons as well".[149] It remains unresolved, however, whether the renaissance of

[144] Case 58/80 *Dansk Supermarked* [1981] ECR 181, paras 17 *et seq*.

[145] See Case 311/85 *VVR* [1987] ECR 3801, para 30; Case C–9/93 *IHT Internationale Heiztechnik* [1994] ECR I–2789, paras 33 *et seq*.

[146] See Case 65/86 *Bayer* [1988] ECR 5249, para 11.

[147] See Case C–281/98, above n 139, para 30.

[148] *Ibid*, paras 34 *et seq*.

[149] *Ibid*, para 36.

horizontal effect in fact only concerns the free movement of persons. Much would appear to suggest that, in any case in relation to the free movement of goods, no new trend is intended, particularly since in the context of entrepreneurial trade the application of anti-trust law is more obvious.[150]

2. The Alternative—The Right to Protection

Interestingly, another development emerges, parallel to that of the seemingly re-emphasised horizontal direct effect of the freedom of free movement of people.

In 1998 the ECJ approved a duty incumbent on a Member State to protect the free movement of products and persons by means of active measures to avoid incursions by private individuals. In the decision concerning the violent protests of French farmers against fruit and vegetable traders from other Member States, the Court recognised that Art 28 EC "also applies where a Member State abstains from adopting the measures required in order to deal with obstacles to the free movement of goods which are not caused by the State".[151] Art 28 EC obliges the Member States in connection with Art 10 EC "to take all necessary and appropriate measures to ensure that that fundamental freedom is respected on their territory".[152] The Member State is therefore the guarantor of the fundamental freedoms, which implies the obligation to remove hindrances for the fundamental freedoms caused by individuals, by means of positive action. The non-guarantee of protection for foreign participants within the market constitutes a discrimination. The difference from the horizontal-effect-concept is obvious, as the obligation is addressed to the Member State rather than the individual. The Member State has nevertheless a certain prerogative of assessment. According to the ECJ, it is a matter for the Member State itself to determine which measures are necessary for the maintenance of public security and order.[153] The Court can only examine whether the Member State has adopted appropriate measures for the securing of the free movement of goods. In the French farmer case, the Court approved the violation of the duty of protection, and in doing so a claim to a guarantee for protection was established, as over many years there had been increasingly serious incidents of violence against farm traders from other Member States

[150] K Vieweg and A Röthel, 'Verbandsautonomie und Grundfreiheiten' [2002] *Zeitschrift für Handelsrecht* 6 at 20.
[151] See Case C–265/95 *Commission v France* [1997] ECR I–6959, para 30.
[152] *Ibid*, para 32.
[153] *Ibid*, para 33.

without France undertaking suitable counter-measures—despite numerous demands issued by the Commission.[154]

Now, this case law has been confirmed in the decision *Schmidberger*: according to the ECJ, Austria has interfered with the free movement of goods by not taking the necessary measures for the protection of the transit traffic against the blockade of the Brenner-freeway by environmentalists.[155] However, the interference was held to be justified, because by safeguarding the freedom of assembly Austria had tended to a legitimate interest.[156]

The relationship between private effect and the state duty to protect, however, remains unclear. Why was the horizontal construct selected in relation to sports associations, while in relation to rebelling farmers and blockading environmentalists the concept of protection was employed? The notion that the infuriated farmers and environmentalists, unlike the Belgian Football Association, do not have an address to which a writ of summons can be served, may well form a factual explanation, but is yet in terms of legal theory unsatisfactory.

The concept of the right to protection is, however, somewhat more convincing.[157] It takes into account the legislative and administrative competences of the Member States, which do indeed have a duty to protect, but who themselves can decide how this duty is to be implemented. As such, direct incursions into the domestic private law systems can be avoided and their coherence can be maintained.[158] Alongside this, the concept of horizontal effect does tend to suffer from the fact that it changes the function of the fundamental freedoms from individual rights against the public power to obligations in relation to all citizens.[159] Structurally, the fundamental freedoms are not designed for the obligation of private individuals: if any sense can be deduced from the distinction between state and society really, then this sense should be that the private individual who is bound by the fundamental freedoms cannot have the power to justify his own actions with reference to public policy or security.[160] It appears as if the ECJ itself is aware of this problem: in many horizontal effect cases, the basis of justification remains nebulous. The examination of any grounds

[154] *Ibid*, paras 38 *et seq*.

[155] See Case C–112/00 *Schmidberger* [2003] ECR I–5659, para 59; for more information on this decision, see S Kadelbach and N Petersen, 'Europäische Grundrechte als Schranken der Grundfreiheiten' [2003] *Europäische Grundrechte-Zeitschrift* 693.

[156] See Case C–112/00, above n 155, para 74.

[157] See for further discussion Kingreen, above n 21, 195 *et seq*; Burgi, above n 138, 330 *et seq*; Streinz and Leible, above n 138, 464 *et seq*.

[158] See Burgi, above n 138, 330; Streinz and Leible, above n 138, 466.

[159] See on the fundamental right in the German Basic Law, B Pieroth and B Schlink, *Grundrechte: Staatsrecht II* (2002), para 175.

[160] See Roth, above n 138, 1241.

for justification begins simply with the question as to whether the interference is "objectively justified".[161]

The concept of a right to protection also serves to avoid procedural weaknesses. Within actions for failure to fulfil obligations in accordance with Art 226 EC, only breaches of the Treaties by state bodies and organs may be pursued, excluding breaches emanating from private individuals.[162] The concept of horizontal effect therefore significantly limits the legal remedies available to the Commission, because according to the prevailing opinion the legal possibility to institute proceedings under Art 226 EC depends upon the proof, to be presented by the Commission, that the Member State has an influence on the interfering natural or legal person.[163] The differentiation between private and sovereign restrictions is not understandable;[164] if the non-protection appears to be a form of discrimination, it cannot procedurally be handled any differently from an interference emanating directly from a Member State.

V. CONCLUSION

The fundamental freedoms remain a fascinating subject matter of research within the field of European constitutional law.

At first sight, this is the case because we are dealing with a body of case law which still offers several avenues of attack and for which legal commentators have assumed the role of developing their own concepts, which go beyond the details of individual decisions. Indeed, the interest in such an area stretches further than the merely theoretical issues of discussion. It seems that the main issue relates to what the fundamental freedoms are in reality and, in particular, where they stand in relation to fundamental rights or whether they are actually fundamental rights themselves. The second part of this contribution should have demonstrated that this is far more than terminological to-ing and fro-ing, but rather a fundamental constitutional issue. The Constitutional Treaty, in many areas containing ambiguous doublings in the relation of fundamental freedoms and fundamental rights, shows this clearly. One example is the general right to free movement, which is so far only regulated by Art 18 EC. In literature, Art 18 EC is regarded as lex generalis particularly in relation to the free movement of workers,[165] because its field of application encompasses not only employees

[161] See eg Case C–176/96 *Lehtonen* [2000] ECR I–2681, para 51.
[162] See C Koenig and C Sander, *EG-Prozeßrecht* (1997), paras 200 *et seq*.
[163] See Koenig and Sander, above n 162, para 203.
[164] See Vieweg and Röthel, above n 150, 19 *et seq*.
[165] See eg W Kluth in: Calliess and Ruffert, above n 15, Art 18 EC, para 2 *et seq*.

and family members but all Union citizens. In the Constitutional Treaty, it is therefore placed in its old context of Union citizenship, concretely in Art I-8(2) CT-Conv (Art 10(2) CT-IGC) with provisions for the justification in Art I-8(3) CT-Conv (Art 10(2)(2) CT-IGC). But it is apparently not only a fundamental freedom detached from the economic context, but also a fundamental right for it appears a second time in Part II, in Art II-45(1) CT-Conv (Art 105(1) CT-IGC). Concerning the fundamental right to free movement, however, the general provision of justification contained in Art II-52(1) CT-Conv (Art 112(1) CT-IGC) is consequently applied. Moreover—even much more explosive—according to Art II-51(1)(1) CT-Conv (Art 111(1)(1) CT-IGC) the binding effect in relation to the Member States is restricted to the implementation of Union law. Are these restrictions only applicable as to the free movement in its capacity of a fundamental right? The freedom taken with the freedom of movement irritates and once again shows the necessity for a greater emphasis on the functional differences between fundamental freedoms and fundamental rights. Legal theorists can be part of this process, insofar as they can analyse the function and manner of operation of subjective rights within multi-level systems, in particular from the comparative constitutional and historical perspectives. Such a comprehensive theory of subjective rights in multi-level systems remains yet to be developed. It would in more detail have to consider the interdependence between subjective right and the federal allocation of competences, and in doing so, it could also bring to light important conclusions of the constitutional function of the fundamental freedoms. With regard to the commencing constitutionalisation of the World Trade Organisation, such a project is more than urgent, so that the de-coupling of law and politics in the supra-national context will not be repeated or permitted to continue.[166]

[166] See also von Bogdandy, above n 72, 265 *et seq* and 425.

Part IV
Constitutional Aspects of Economic Law

14

The Economic Constitution

BY ARMIN HATJE

I. ECONOMIC CONSTITUTION AND EUROPEAN INTEGRATION

1. Relevance of the Subject

THE RELEVANCE OF the subject of the European economic constitution remains unchanged. In the *horizontal dimension*, the systematic decision of the EC Treaty for an open market economy with free competition is subject to various relativisations. The legal significance of these relativisations for the economic constitution and the political constitution has not yet been sufficiently clarified. Particularly the discussions on the importance of the services of general economic interest[1] and the limits to liberalisation of regulated markets[2] have been exemplary in displaying the necessity of asserting and maintaining the guarantees of a free market order in a network rife with tension and in the midst of economic and socio-political objectives.[3] In this respect, it follows that the relationship of welfare state and other regulatory policies to basic system decisions and related guarantees, such as the freedoms of the Treaty and fundamental rights as well as the guarantee of undistorted competition, must be dogmatically apprehended as precisely as possible. However, the legal sediments of

[1] Eg, P Badura, 'Wirtschaftliche Betätigung der öffentlichen Hand zur Gewährleistung von Daseinsvorsorge' in J Schwarze (ed), *Daseinsvorsorge im Lichte des Wettbewerbsrechts* (2001), 25; W Frenz, 'Dienste von allgemeinem wirtschaftlichen Interesse' [2000] *Europarecht* 901; see also the findings of the Commission in Document COM(2000) 580 final of 20 September 2000 on the services of general interest in Europe, and in the Communication from the Commission on services of general interest in Europe [2001] OJ C 17/4.

[2] See only the judgment of the ECJ regarding exclusive imports rights for Electricity, Case C–157/94 *Commission v Spain* [1997] ECR I–5699; Case C–158/94 *Commission v Italy* [1997] ECR I–5789; Case C–159/94 *Commission v France* [1997] ECR I–5815; Case C–160/94 *Commission v Spain* [1997] ECR I–5851.

[3] This topic is currently enjoying increased attention: see eg P-C Müller-Graff, 'Die Verdichtung des Binnenmarktrechts zwischen Handlungsfreiheiten und Sozialgestaltung' in A Hatje (ed), *Das Binnenmarktrecht als Daueraufgabe* [2002] *Europarecht* suppl 1, 7.

highly diverse economic political conceptions have settled in this Treaty[4] and the European Constitution. Therefore, from the very beginning, limits have been set for the development of solutions, capable of generalisation, to possible conflicts between market and intervention.

In the *vertical dimension,* because of the enlargement of the EU, the European economic constitution encounters national economies which mostly still find themselves in a process of transformation from planned economy to market economy. From the perspective of these countries, it should be of considerable interest to analyse which legal constraints and political clearances exist when adapting to the intensified competition in the internal market. This difficulty points to the controversial relationship between the European economic constitution and its national counterparts, and there to those guarantees which are not compatible with the market concept of the EC Treaty. However, also in the other direction, national conceptions have an effect on the European economic constitution. It would here be of interest to analyse which pressures towards change, recognisable in basic legal constitutional decisions, could have a reactionary effect on the European Union. Hence, at least a rough inspection of the national economic constitutions is needed, in order to acquire a somewhat complete picture of the legal situation of the economic constitution in the European Union.

Although superficially related to functional correlations with the economy, the economic constitution remains an integral part of the common legal fundamental order of the multi-level European system, i.e., part of its currently, at least in a substantive sense, existing constitution. The discourse on the economic constitution therefore plays an important role in the development of a European Constitution, and has now achieved a new quality with the appointment of the European Convention. In conclusion, it will be of value to discuss in detail which contribution the economic constitution can provide for the further constitutional development of Europe.

2. Terminology and Functions of the Economic Constitution

It is true that the term economic constitution, as formulated primarily by Walter Eucken and Franz Boehm,[5] has pertained for decades to the permanent

[4] See T Oppermann, *Europarecht* (1999), para 927.

[5] See, eg, DJ Gerber, 'Constitutionalizing the Economy: German Neoliberalism, Competition Law and the "New" Europe' (1994) 42 *AJCL* 25; W Noerr, '"Economic Constitution": On the Roots of a legal Concept' [1994/95] *Journal of Law and Religion* 343; W Eucken, *Grundlagen der Nationalökonomie* (1965); F Böhm, *Wettbewerb und Monopolkampf* (1933); *ibid*, *Wirtschaftsordnung und Staatsverfassung* (1950). W Fikentscher, *Wirtschaftsrecht* (1983), ii, 21, traces the term back to 1919. The economic system discussion owes further theoretical findings to E-J Mestmäcker. From his comprehensive works, see in particular the collection of fundamental essays, *Recht und ökonomisches Gesetz* (1984).

inventory of German jurisprudence and also to European jurisprudence in particular.[6] However, meaning and utilisation of the term remain disputed.

a) The Approach

The term economic constitution is found in the intersection between economy and jurisprudence. For this reason, the interpretative meaning differs depending on the particular context. The common starting point of all efforts of a definition is regulatory or proper political thought, which views economic systems as protected by institutions and rules, and which therefore must almost inevitably allocate the state and its legal systems a specified guarantee function. In the broadest sense, the term economic constitution can be understood as the "global political decisions determining the order of national economic life"[7], i.e., those factual and functional contexts that involve the distribution of scarce commodities by means of price systems.[8] In this respect, the term can conduce to differentiate between various national economic models of ideal typical economies. This is, however, less productive for legal purposes. Additionally, an understanding of the economic constitution as the totality of all legal rules that control the economic process of political economy cannot go beyond a bare description of the legal framework of economic activity.[9] This may very well be sensible for an economic analysis of the existing law, whereas the juristic debate of the last decades on a not-yet accomplished theory of the economic constitution is striving towards special goals. This applies to a normative extraction of commercial law as the rights of an economic system in which the conditions are set as to who may have access to scarce commodities and services, and under which conditions.[10] At the same time, the economic constitution

[6] Cp eg the contributions of C-F Ophüls, 'Grundzüge europäischer Wirtschaftsverfassung' [1962] *Zeitschrift für das gesamte Handelsrecht und Wirtschaftsrecht* 136; E Günther, 'Die ordnungspolitischen Grundlagen des EWG-Vertrages' [1963] *Wirtschaft und Wettbewerb* 191; H Zacher, 'Aufgaben eine Theorie der Wirtschaftsverfassung' in H Coing (ed), *Wirtschaftsordnung und Rechtsordnung: Festschrift für F Böhm* (1965), 63; J Scherer, *Die Wirtschaftsverfassung der EWG* (1970) gives a good overview of the discussions of the 1960s. See also M Poiares Maduro, *We the Court* (1998); J Baquero Cruz, *Between Competition and Free Movement* (2002).

[7] Cp F Böhm, W Eucken and H Grossmann-Dörth, 'Unsere Aufgabe' in: F Böhm (ed), *Die Ordnung der Wirtschaft als geschichtliche Aufgabe und rechtsschöpferische Leistung* (1937), xix; reprinted in Walter Eucken Institute (ed), *Wirtschaftswissenschaftliche und wirtschaftsrechtliche Untersuchungen* (1971), 87; see also W Eucken, *Grundsätze der Wirtschaftspolitik* (1990), 250: 'Common Regulatory Political Decisions'.

[8] See P Behrens, 'Die Wirtschaftsverfassung der Europäischen Gemeinschaft' in G Brüggemeier (ed), *Verfassungen für Europa* (1994), 73 at 74 on the problem of scarcity as a core topic of the economy.

[9] For an overview of the meanings and uses of the term 'economic constitution', see F Rittner, *Wirtschaftsrecht* (1987), 25.

[10] E-J Mestmäcker, 'Wirtschaftrecht' (1990) 54 *Rabels Zeitschrift für ausländisches und internationales Privatrecht* 409 at 410 and 415.

marks the area of economic policy that should remain predominantly free of change, and therefore removed from current political processes.

b) Definitions

On the one hand, the legal concept of the economic constitution concerns the clarification of the systematic relationship between economic system and legal system, whereby the economic functional conditions of the economic system and its legal safeguards remain the focal point. On the other hand, economy and economic policy should relate to one another according to legal criteria, in order to gain generalised statements on the relationship between economic freedom and sovereign interventions.[11] Thus, not only the present situation must be recorded and legally defined, but also which goals are to be aimed at for the future, and how conflicts between divergent options are to be solved, must also be established. The heart of the matter is, independent of concrete economic systems, the use of law to establish controls and limitations of power, a power which can be exerted by the state as well as private protagonists.[12] The solution to the question of power, which belongs to the fundamental tasks of every constitution, is therefore the key to understanding the legal function of the economic constitution. The solution assigns the economic constitution not only an important standard function for private and governmental protagonists, but also connects the fundamental legal order of the factual and functional areas of economy with the political section of the constitution.[13]

Accordingly, we have the formula of the juristic economic constitution as "the sum of legal constitutional structural elements of the system of economy"[14] widely recognised today. However, this formula has proven to be in need of expansion, since the process of European integration, based on a common market with straightforward competition, has clearly shifted the balance between the constitutional levels. The question of the economic constitution is now more than ever directed at the legal foundations of the European Union. Above all, substantial statements as to the regulatory principles and guarantees of economic activities can be inferred from the EC Treaty, so that the Treaty's written and unwritten norms contain the valid formative elements of the economy for the Member States.[15]

[11] Succinctly addressed by P Behrens, above n 8, 74 *et seq.*

[12] See especially J Basedow, *Von der deutschen zur europäischen Wirtschaftsverfassung* (1992), 10.

[13] See Behrens, above n 8, 75.

[14] See R Schmidt, *Öffentliches Wirtschaftsrecht* (1990), 70; see also Gerber, above n 5, 44.

[15] See also Oppermann, above n 4, para 926.

c) Delimitations

The function of the European economic constitution is most certainly not to equip a particular economic political model with legal administrative finality.[16] What gives an economic constitution legal strength and which limits it sets to sovereigns and private parties, is not primarily derived from a specific economic model but rather from the concrete applied standard of norms.[17] The relevant regulations are, particularly in Community law, less an expression of an ordered and coherent economic political concept, but rather the result of different economic and political goals, which have altered and shifted through the decades. Indeed, elements of "ordo-liberal" and social-market economic conceptions can be recognised. They also guide the following analysis. However, upon closer perusal, even the express decision in favour of a market economy is relativised by opposite principles and powers of intervention, so that immediately reverting to certain economic models to assist interpretation is forbidden.[18] Inasmuch as a particular economic model is legally guaranteed, the normative relevance of establishing such regulations is recurrently limited to making reference to the fundamental functional conditions of the current model, but not to limiting the state or European Community institutions to a simple execution of certain fundamental economic policy principles.

3. The European Economic Constitution

Through the integration of the Basic Law into the constitutional network of the European Union, the question of an economic constitution situated in a new and superior system is raised, the structural and functional peculiarities of which are also characteristics of the European economic constitution.

a) Expansion of the Debate

The issue of the economic constitution of the Basic Law, discussed in Germany for some time now, has found itself faced with a new and superior system of references since Germany joined the European Community. The question of whether a central administrative economy or derived forms are to be permitted, or of whether the social market economy or other forms of market economy have been enacted should now be directed to the

[16] The same approach is made by G Nicolaysen, *Europarecht II* (1996), 318; a different approach is taken by Poiares Maduro, above n 6, 103 *et seq.*
[17] See Nicolaysen, above n 16.
[18] For more details, see II. 1.

Treaties of the three Communities. Interestingly enough, their constitutional nature in this connection has not been seriously addressed.[19] Especially the EEC Treaty has proven to be a prototypical economic constitution: in fact, rump regulations without real political chapter, but in association with the national constitution laying a decisive legal basis for the creation of business life.[20] Seen from the German perspective, the EC Treaty with its undisguised preference in favour of the market presents a clear and definite contrast to the "economic political neutrality" of the German Basic Law. Thus, Community law was positioned against centrally managed economic system concepts, as at the end of the sixties the economic miracle abated and plan-oriented economic forms enjoyed a renaissance as a political option.[21]

Today the emphasis has been shifted. The contemporary discussion is concerned with those guarantees and securities, assured by a welfare state, which have been declared indispensable by the national constitution, in order to avoid being forced to submit them to "unbridled capitalism"[22] in the European internal market[23]. The discussion is also concerned with what value is to be placed on consumer protection and health and safety, should these limit the freedom of movement in any way. One constant of this discussion has proven to be the knowledge of the fragmentary nature of Community law in the area of constitutional law.[24]

b) The Co-operative Character of the European Economic Constitution

One the one hand, the EC Treaty contains a number of substantial structural elements of the economy, which have been specially secured against divergent national concepts through direct effect and the primacy of Community law. On the other hand, the EC Treaty remains a fragmentary regulatory instrument, even after the latest reforms, with primary areas of general economic policies to a great extent left in the hands of national authorities. When considering the aspect of exercise of power, not only the Community and major private interests must have legal limitations. Also the Member States, as an important third factor, must be made subject to

[19] Cp Ophüls, above n 6, 140 *et seq*, who takes the constitutional nature of the EEC Treaty for granted.

[20] See Scherer, above n 6, 82 referred to the EEC Treaty as an 'Economic Constitution per se'.

[21] Cp W von Simson, 'Die Marktwirtschaft als Verfassungsprinzip in den Europäischen Gemeinschaften' in Rechts- und Staatswissenschaftliche Fakultät der Albert-Ludwig-Universität Freiburg/Breisgau, *Zur Einheit der Rechts- und Staatswissenschaften* (1967), 55.

[22] E-W Böckenförde, 'Welchen Weg geht Europa?' in *id*, *Staat, Nation, Europa* (1999), 68 at 100 *et seq*, perceives this danger if one sticks uncritically to the logic of economical-functional integration.

[23] Concerning the welfare state principle in the European Union, see the recent work by T Kingreen, *Das Sozialstaatsprinzip im europäischen Verfassungsverbund* (2003).

[24] For further information, cp Ophüls, above n 6, 141 and 175.

legal and political control.[25] This obligation must be fulfilled by co-operation between European constitutions, which in this respect also means a co-operation of the economic constitutions.[26]

c) Peculiarities of the European Economic Constitution

Moreover, there is a special additional function of the Community economic constitution: it is, as before, the core of European Community law, the "engine" of the integration process, which can utilise business as the initial basis for creating interstate unification without, however, stopping at the borders of the economy. It combines the concept of *negative integration* by means of the prohibition of obstacles addressed to the states and of *positive integration* by means of active political formulation.[27] The European Court of Justice has emphasised repeatedly that neither the internal market nor competition are goals in themselves but rather means of achieving higher goals of integration, which are placed above the economy.[28] In this respect, the European economic constitution has not only a conserving, canalising function but also a pronounced dynamic character. Yet, this goal imprints the regulatory authority of Community rights as well, which can lead to conflicts with fundamental economic policy decisions.

4. Scope for Economic Policy Formation

The European economic constitution forms no static order, but creates a thoroughly flexible legal framework, which opens considerable room for manoeuvre for the Member States and the institutions, in the evaluation and formation as well as in the interpretation and the application of the relevant Treaty provisions.

The ECJ has always respected the economic political autonomy of evaluation and formation of the Council, the Parliament and of the Commission, as laid out in the firmly anchored control maxims of Art 33(1) of the European Coal and Steel Community Treaty. It states that judicial review absolutely precludes "the evaluation of the situation, resulting from economic facts or circumstances"[29]. It has also left a considerable margin of free decision to the Member States. The renouncement of control leads to a

[25] See W Mussler, *Die Wirtschaftsverfassung der Europäischen Gemeinschaft im Wandel* (1998), 86.

[26] On the idea of co-operation in multilevel constitutionalism, see, *ibid*, 58.

[27] See in particular Mussler, above n 25, 62 for more information on this differentiation which can be traced back to J Tinbergen, *International Economic Integration* (1954).

[28] Opinion 1/91 *EEA I* [1991] ECR I–6079, para 50.

[29] See Case C–233/94 *Germany v Parliament and Council* [1997] ECR I–240, para 55.

so-called elastic relationship between competition and intervention. Therefore, the autonomy of evaluation is the central dogmatic category of the European economic constitution, the hinge between the principles of the market and the political competences of the Treaties. This would mean, however, that much too little has been gained for a juridical theory of the constitution. Because legally it is of crucial importance whether the Treaty sets the priority of market and competition ahead of those goals that can only be reached by interference with the market; or whether other basic principles of reciprocal assignments count. European economic constitutional law requires therefore a "leeway dogmatic" (*Spielraum-Dogmatik*),[30] in order to apprehend the reciprocal assignments of market economy and sovereign regulation juristically and predictably.

II. SYSTEMATIC DECISION AND LEGAL GUARANTEES

A characteristic feature of Community law is the fundamental decision in favour of an open market economy with free competition. This decision is further equipped with a series of legal guarantees,[31] which provide a sufficiently precise scale control by the ECJ and by national courts. At the same time, the Community institutions and the Member States possess important competence potentials, granting them considerable influence in the economic process.[32] The normative content of the economic constitution of the European Union follows at first from the synopsis of market economic guarantees, on the one hand, and the economic policy powers of the Community and the Member States on the other. It is rightly apostrophised as a "mixed constitution".[33] Admittedly, little is gained from a legal viewpoint with this reference. The mixture ratios and rules which determine how much competition and how much economic policy formations are to be allowed, are decisive.

1. The Decision in Favour of an Open Market Economy and Free Competition

According to Arts 4(1) and 98 EC, the economic policy of the Community and its Member States are expressly bound to the "principle of an open

[30] Following R Alexy, 'Verfassungsrecht und einfaches Recht—Verfassungsgerichtsbarkeit und Fachgerichtsbarkeit' (2002) 61 *Veröffentlichungen der Vereinigung der Deutschen Staatsrechtslehrer* 8 at 13.

[31] On the idea of co-operation in multilevel constitutionalism see Mussler, above n 25, 58.

[32] See also the critical analyses of Behrens, above n 8, 86; H-U Petersmann, 'Thesen zur Wirtschaftsverfassung der EG' [1993] *Europäische Zeitschrift für Wirtschaftsrecht* 593; for an economics perspective, see Mussler, above n 25, esp 166 *et seq*.

[33] See Poiares Maduro, above n 6, 160; Nicolaysen, above n 16, 320.

market economy with free competition". In the same way, the European monetary policy should be orientated according to this principle, as stated in Art 4(2) and in Art 5 of the EC Treaty. The European Constitution will also bind the national and European level to this decision (Arts 178 and 185 CT-IGC), but underlines the social responsibility in Art 3 CT-IGC (social market economy). After all, this will not change the general direction of the above-mentioned decision.

a) Legal Quality

The legal significance of a decision in favour of a system of open market economy is certainly under dispute. Its juridical value is prevailingly estimated to be rather low.[34] Often in this context, the questions of the capacity of being adjudicated and the speciality are kept insufficiently apart from one another. The "principle of an open market economy with free competition" is a legal term and therefore justiciable in principle.[35] It offers no great difficulty in the application of law, somewhat comparable to the principle of subsidiarity, because the sum of its terms definitely allows specific legal features to be assigned, lending it substance. They may be very indefinite and abstract; this is however not a problem of the capacity of being adjudicated but rather a question of speciality in relationship to legal conceptions which serve to more precisely define these features. Nevertheless, the individual cannot appeal directly to the systematic decision in favour of an open market, due to a lack of sufficient certainty. As a result, this alone forms no basis for the subjective right of a citizen of the Union to claim maintenance of a market economic system. As an objective principle, however, this systematic decision has a *material* and a *structural* component.

b) Contents

Materially it refers to the functional conditions of a competition controlled market economy. Regardless of possible system variations, this includes economic freedom, the co-ordination of supply and demand in competition and free entry to and exit from the market.[36] The expressly stated openness of the European economic area refers principally to the internal and the

[34] See Nicolayen, above n 16, 320.

[35] In contrast, the German Federal Constitutional Court has refused to deduce an economic constitution in the sense of a self-contained normative system from the Constitution: *Entscheidungen des Bundesverfassungsgerichts* 50, 290 at 336 *et seq* (*Mitbestimmung*).

[36] F von Estorff and B Molitor in H von der Groeben, J Thiesing and C-D Ehlermann (eds), *Kommentar zum EU-/EG-Vertrag* (1997), Art 3a EC Treaty, paras 19, 20; Wittelsberger in H von der Groeben and J Schwarze (eds), *Kommentar zum Vertrag über die Europäische Union und zur Gründung der Europäischen Gemeinschaft* (2003), Art 98 EC, para 6.

world market.[37] The lack of reference to social orientation is not to be equated to an indifference of the Treaty to these protected goods. This aspect of European economic policy is already firmly anchored in Art 2 EC, whereby a high level of social protection is to be strived for. *Structurally* the establishment of a competition driven market economy justifies, for one, the prohibition of a change of the system.[38] Thus, binding centrally-administered or over-planned economic systems may not be introduced, neither by the Member States nor by the Community, unless the elimination or limitation of market principle is expressly allowed, as it is the case in agricultural policy and in the European Atomic Energy Community area. Furthermore, the principle of an open market economy allows for a general 'exception to the rules' relationship, in which each intervention into economic freedom of action is subject to compulsory justification according to the standards of proportionality.[39] Finally, the principle of an open market economy with free competition is the all-important guideline for interpretation of economically relevant guarantees and authorisations of the Community's primary law as well as for the measures of secondary law.[40]

2. Guarantees of a Market Economic Order

The basic principles of a market economy are configured in a series of guarantees capable of adjudication under the protection of constitutional Community law, as succinctly described by Jürgen Basedow.[41] On the one hand, they concern core elements of the market economic system; on the other hand, through them the specific integrating function of the European economic constitution is legally mapped out.

a) Private Autonomy as Fundamental Requirement for a Market Economic System

A market economic system is characterised by the fact that the economic subjects engage in economic activity, and thereby realise private autonomous self-made goals.[42] Private autonomy, for one, especially refers to access to one's own source of labour and income. Furthermore it is

[37] See Von Estorff and Molitor, above n 36, Art 3a EC Treaty, para 20.
[38] See A Hatje in J Schwarze (ed), *EU-Kommentar* (2000), Art 4 EC, para 9.
[39] See Wittelsberger, above n 36, Art 98 EC, para 6.
[40] See Case C–9/99 *Echirolles Distribution* [2000] ECR I–8207, para 25, on the function and legal quality of this principle; Baquero Cruz, above n 6, 79.
[41] For the following, see the groundbreaking work by Basedow, above n 12, 15 and 26.
[42] See Mussler, above n 25, 35.

concerned with the freedom to decide where and how much capital is to be invested and what sorts of goods and services are to be produced or provided. Legally, it is distinguished in particular by legal personality, individual and entrepreneurial freedom of trade, and the reciprocal classification of spheres of liberty according to the principle of equality under the European law.

aa) Economic Participant as Legal Person Legal personality of individuals is presumed and recognised by Community law. It has existed for natural persons in many Member States of the EU for over a hundred years, and enables self-determining participation in commerce.[43] In this connection, the legal capacity to act, beyond its importance for human rights, is appreciated as an essential element of market economic system. The Treaties contain, however, no general regulations on the legal status of natural persons corresponding to paragraph 1 of the German Civil Code. Yet, the Union citizenship of Art 17 EC (see Art 10 CT-IGC) indicates a legal personality of the individual. The practice of the ECJ is instructive on (unwritten) basic rights. According to this, the Court counts, as for example in the Stauder judgment, on the "Rights of the Person" expressly amongst the inventory of Community guarantees.[44] Further evidence for assigning subjective rights through the direct effect of the freedoms of the Treaty can be inferred from various judgments of the ECJ.[45]

For the economy, the possibility for natural persons to organise themselves under the rooftop of legal persons is hardly of less importance. This organisation expands the areas of individual freedom and can simplify participation in legal relations in principal. This status is recognised by Community law, as Art 48 EC (see Art 137 CT-IGC) on the equality of companies illustrates. For realisation of the freedom of settlement, companies, which can also be organised as legal persons, are equated with natural persons who are citizens of Member States. Further reference is found in Art 230(4) EC (see Art 365 CT-IGC), which states that legal persons can also apply for legal protection before the European Court of Justice.

bb) Individual and Entrepreneurial Capacity to Act The individual and the entrepreneurial capacity to act are connected with legal personality, and enjoy basic legal protection under Community law. In particular the previously legally non-binding Fundamental Rights Charter of the EU has codified a range of rights relevant for business activities, such as freedom to choose a profession (see Art 75 CT-IGC), entrepreneurial freedom (see

[43] See Basedow, above n 12, 33.
[44] See Case 29/69 *Stauder* [1969] ECR 419, para 7.
[45] See the pathbreaking Case 26/62 *van Gend & Loos* [1963] ECR 1.

Art 76 CT-IGC), and private property rights (see Art 77 CT-IGC). These and other related rights are already today recognised as general unwritten fundamental principles of law. A "general economic freedom" is especially inferred from the provisions of the common market, which possesses subjective legal character at the same time as it safeguards the fundamental decision in favour of a market economy.[46] Through Art 6(1) EU (see Art 2 CT-IGC), these rights and freedoms become legally binding contents of the national economic constitution. They form the necessary foundation for the unfolding of individual business initiatives and responsibilities at all levels of the European Community constitutional association. The legal framework in which the economic processes take place is accordingly private law.[47] Its existence is presumed and recognised by Community law as well but is, however, subject to increasing European legal influences.[48]

cc) Equal Rights for Market Participants A further characteristic of market economies constituted on a competitive basis is the principle of equality under the law for market participants in trade and industry. It is ensured by the generally accepted unwritten principle of equality combined with special anti-discrimination regulations.[49] These prohibitions preclude discrimination based on nationality (Art 12 EC; see Art 123 CT-IGC) and the immediacy of the economically relevant commandment, "equal pay for equal work" for women and men (Art 141 EC; see Art 214 CT-IGC). In addition, we have the fundamental freedoms (*Grundfreiheiten*) which, in their undisputed core, at least prohibit discrimination.[50] They are, however, partly valid solely for native citizens of the Member States, such as the free movement of workers, with the exception of special regulations in secondary law or international obligations. This does not change anything in the fundamental findings concerning an economic system resting on the equality of the protagonists.[51]

b) Co-ordination Through Trade on the Open Markets

The core principle of a market economic system is the balance between supply and demand of scarce goods and services. This balance is created by

[46] See T Schubert, *Der Gemeinsame Markt als Rechtsbegriff: Die allgemeine Wirtschaftsfreiheit des EG-Vertrages* (1999), 333, on system guarantees in particular, 403.

[47] On the 'structural counterparts of a market economy and of private law' see E-J Mestmäcker, 'Macht-Recht-Wirtschaftsverfassung' in *id*, *Die sichtbare Hand des Rechts* (1978), 9 at 13; F Böhm, 'Privatrechtsgesellschaft und Marktwirtschaft' [1966] *ORDO* 7.

[48] See, eg, E Steindorff, *EG-Vertrag und Privatrecht* (1996); P-C Müller-Graff (ed), *Gemeinsames Privatrecht in der Europäischen Union* (1999).

[49] See J Schwarze's detailed work *European Administrative Law* (1992), 545.

[50] Cf Scherer, above n 6, 110, for an overview of this conception of fundamental freedoms.

[51] H-P Ipsen, *Europäisches Gemeinschaftsrecht* (1972), 567, characterises the economic constitution of the Communities similarly.

numerous individual decisions by the market partners. The process involves an anonymous co-ordination process by which it can be determined who can provide access to scarce goods and services at what price.

aa) Assured Availability of Products and Services A prerequisite for private autonomous decision-making in this respect is an assured availability of products, services, and a stable currency.[52]

(1) Private Property

A primary constitutional element of a market economic system is the private ownership of the means of production.[53] The European Community legal system has two levels of guarantees, which are in an apparent state of tension and conflict with one another. On the one hand, according to Art 295 EC (see Art 425 CT-IGC) "this Treaty shall in no way prejudice the rules in the Member States governing the system of property ownership". This would specifically allow the Member States rights of disposition in private property to the means of production, in accordance with current economic and other policy preferences.[54] Interesting from the perspective of the Community, the reservation of competence is valid not only for legal property of the citizen but also for all other legally protected positions of private ownership, such as trademark rights, copyright protection and company shares.[55]

On the other hand, there is the need to respect the right to private ownership guaranteed by Community law, which is legally binding not only for Community institutions but also for the Member States, insofar as they act within the scope of application of the Treaty. The fundamental right to private ownership was thoroughly developed by the European Court of Justice in the Hauer decision.[56] The Court stated that European law protects private property rights in accordance with Art 1 of the first aditional protocol of the ECHR. Accordingly, although interference with property rights is allowed, it requires legal justification and must be proportional. The Charter of Fundamental Rights of the European Union takes up this concept in its Art 17 (see Art 77 CT-IGC), and even expands it to the express protection of intellectual property and explicitly only permitting expropriation against compensation.[57] Private property is therefore by no means at the unlimited disposal of the Member States and the European Community.

[52] See Eucken, above n 7, 256, for a description of the requirements of a stable currency. He however only claims a 'certain level of stability'.

[53] See Eucken, above n 7, 271.

[54] See I Brinker in Schwarze (ed), above n 38, Art 295 EC, para 1.

[55] Cp, eg, Case C–10/89 *CNL-SUCAL* [1990] ECR I–3711, para 12.

[56] See Case 44/79 *Hauer* [1979] ECR 3727, para 15.

[57] See C Grabenwarter, 'Die Charta der Grundrechte für die Europäische Union' [2001] *Deutsches Verwaltungsblatt* 1, who points out the limited scope of application of the Charter.

(2) Stable Currency

A stable currency is another integral aspect in assuring availability of products and services. The institutional and legal precautions involved in establishing a stable common currency are quite considerable. They range from the independence of the European Central Bank from instructions of national governments (Art 108 EC; see Art 188 CT-IGC) and their banknote monopoly (Art 106 EC; see Art 186 CT-IGC); from the alignment of the common monetary policies with the primary target of price stability (Art 105(1) EC; see Art 185 CT-IGC) to the duty of the Member States to avoid excessive fiscal deficits. From the perspective of market economic systems, more legal reinforcement for securing a stable currency is hardly conceivable.[58] According to Art 2 EC, the national central banks which are integrated within the European System of Central Banks have, however, the additional duty—whilst safeguarding the goals of stability—to support common economic policy goals: namely, growth and employment policies (Art 105(1) EC; see Art 185 CT-IGC). Possible friction resulting from the structure of the European economic constitution will be addressed later.

bb) Reduction of Market Barriers Through Fundamental Freedoms An important objective for the European economic constitution is the opening of the national markets for supply and demand of goods, persons, and services from all Member States. It constitutes an area without internal frontiers in which "the free movement of goods, persons, services and capital is ensured in accordance with the provisions of this Treaty", as formulated in Art 14 EC (see Art 130 CT-IGC). The openness of the markets consequently secures the exercise of private autonomy within the European Union.[59]

The related fundamental freedoms of free movement of goods, persons and services follow the economic insight that politically-defined territories do not necessarily have the optimal calibre for economy. They are supposed to promote Community-wide competition as well as freedom of movement, and therefore trigger the expected affluence of the internal market according to the principle of comparative costing advantages.[60] In addition, they spearhead the actual integration goals, which assume the erosion of those walls protecting the economy in order to render political unification possible. In this fashion, they are just as much an integral part of the economic constitution as the political constitution of the Union. The fundamental

[58] However, for a critical view, see M Seidel, 'Konstitutionelle Schwächen der Währungsunion' [2000] *Europarecht* 861.

[59] See P-C Müller-Graff in von der Groeben and Schwarze (eds), above n 36, pre Art 28 EC, para 3.

[60] *Ibid*, paras 3 *et seq*.

freedoms grant the direct applicable individual right of discrimination-free economic occupation[61] beyond national borders.[62]

Moreover, they prohibit practically every state, community and private hindrance to cross-border activities, unless there are legal justifications for such obstacles.[63] Especially, the expansion of the fundamental freedoms—largely achieved by the European Court of Justice to include prohibitions against obstruction of freedom of movement—has increased the scope of application of the Community economic constitution considerably. Accordingly, in modification of the famous Court of Justice Dassonville formula, an interference with the fundamental freedoms has already taken place when a measure limits or prevents an activity guaranteed under the freedoms of the Treaty "in actuality or potentially, directly or indirectly".[64]

Also the "mandatory requirements" of the Cassis decision and the "selling arrangements" of the Keck case law have not been able to prevent potentially all regulatory areas of the national economic and social order from being obliged to legitimise themselves by measuring up to the testing standards of the fundamental freedoms.[65] The contemporary discussion on the position of the social security system in the internal market, such as, for example, the use of medical services in other Member States, is typical for this tendency.[66] In addition, the Court has consistently interpreted exceptions to the fundamental freedoms very strictly. From the perspective of the systematic decision in favour of a market economy, this extension of those guarantees, which are part of an open market system, is positive. However with a view to the political scope for activity, namely of the Member States, a close critical eye should be kept on these extensions.

cc) Freedom of Communication Freedom of communication is of primary importance for the accessibility of the market and the functional capacity of competition.[67] In a highly differentiated economic system, the freedom of communication has proven to be a prerequisite for competition. Without the freedom of communication, initial contact and exchange of information

[61] See Case 83/78 *Pigs Marketing Board* [1978] ECR 2347, paras 66 *et seq* (Freight Traffic); Case 41/74 *Van Duyn* [1974] ECR 1337, paras 5 and 7 (Freedom of Movement); Case 2/74 *Reyners* [1974] ECR 631, paras 29 *et seq* (Freedom of Residency); Case 33/74 *Van Binsbergen* [1974] ECR 1299, paras 24 *et seq* (Freedom of Service Provision); Cases C–163, C–165 and C–250/94 *Sanz de Lera et al* [1995] ECR I–4821, para 691.

[62] See, eg, R Streinz, *Europarecht* (2001), para 667.

[63] See *ibid*, para 671, pointing out the differences between the fundamental freedoms.

[64] *Ibid*.

[65] T Kingreen, *Die Struktur der Grundfreiheiten* (1999), 104; see also Poiares Maduro, above n 6, 78.

[66] See, eg, Case C–157/99 *Smits* [2001] ECR I–5473, with comment from C Nowak, [2001] *Europarecht* 741.

[67] Basedow, above n 12, 17, has called attention to this aspect.

between suppliers and potential purchasers would hardly be possible. Competition can only function when the economic subjects'[68] "constitutive lack of knowledge" can be removed by provision of information. To achieve this end, free communication is essential. Still, its most important manifestation in the form of advertising is understood simply as an annex of economic freedom, which is unsuitable[69] for both the special characteristics of communication processes and their importance for a competitively systemised economy. For this reason, especially the case law of the European Court of Human Rights on the protection of commercial communication by the freedom of speech of Art 10 ECHR should be gradually taken over by the ECJ. [70] Until now, the European Court of Justice views advertising as above all a protected commodity of the free movement of goods and services.[71]

dd) Limited External Access The openness of the European market to external areas is less distinct in comparison to the interior.[72] This is because the customs union amongst the Member States necessarily presumes a delineation of the "internal market" towards third party states. Each import and export requires at the very least an administrative procedure designed to ensure legally regulated processing of the goods. In addition, the rights of the employee to freedom of movement, right of establishment and free movement of persons and services are reserved for Union citizens.[73] The free movement of capital in relationship to third party states is guaranteed as well; however, it is subject to more extensive limitations than the movement of internal domestic capital.[74]

In this respect, Hans Peter Ipsen's well-known formula which distinguishes the common market as "internal freedom and external unity" is absolutely justified.[75] This unity in relation to third countries has also been assured by the Court of Justice, which has only allowed direct applicability of international treaties in the EU under very limited conditions. As a rule,

[68] See M Streit, *Theorie der Wirtschaftspolitik* (1991), 82.
[69] Cp also A Hatje, 'Werbung und Grundrechtsschutz in rechtsvergleichender Perspektive' in J Schwarze (ed), *Werbung und Werbeverbote im Lichte des europäischen Gemeinschaftsrechts* (1999), 37 at 48 *et seq*; in detail see J Kühling, *Die Kommunikationsfreiheit als europäisches Gemeinschaftsgrundrecht* (1999).
[70] See *Casado Coca v Spain* Series A No 285, (1994) 15, paras 32 *et seq*; *Jacubowski v Germany,* Series A No 291, (1994) 12, paras 23 *et seq*; see also Art 71 CT-IGC.
[71] See especially C Timmermans, 'Werbung und Grundfreiheiten' in Schwarze (ed), above n 69, 26.
[72] For an economic viewpoint, see Mussel, above n 25, 123.
[73] See Streinz, above n 62, paras 660–663, who is also giving an overview.
[74] See Nicolaysen, above n 16, 398.
[75] See Ipsen, above n 51, 551.

trade and industry participants are unable to derive any rights from these treaties that would allow the validity of secondary law of the Community to be questioned. This is true for the rules and regulations of the World Trade Organisation agreements. The political prerogatives of Council and Commission predominate here.[76] They come to fruition in cases of a Community economic embargo of third countries. According to Art 301 EC (see Art 322 CT-IGC), foreign trade can be restricted when this has been decided within the framework of the Common Foreign and Security Policy or, although disputed, under the common trade policies agreed upon according to Art 133 EC (see Arts 314 and 315 CT-IGC).[77] The openness of the market, in consequence limited at any rate, is here used as an instrument of foreign policy.

c) Competition as an Instrument of Co-ordination

Competition law, as stated in Art 81 EC (see Art 161 CT-IGC) and following passages, secures the openness of the markets in the Community against market limitations and distortions, whether originating from companies or the state. It is the expression of an open market economy with free competition, in particular of the task outlined in Art 3(1)(g) EC that a "system of undistorted competition" should be established. The principal contribution of European competition law for securing the systematic decision for a market economy through justiciable guarantees is dealt with here.[78]

aa) Legal framework In this respect, the prohibition of restrictive practises (Art 81 EC) and the prohibition of abuse of a dominant position within the common market (Art 82 EC) secure the openness of the market primarily against interventions by private enterprises. Violations lead, in accordance with Art 81 EC, directly to invalidity of the underlying legal transactions. The provisions are directly applicable and can thus be evoked by individuals to defend themselves against restrictive practices and abuse of dominant positions of competitors.[79] In contrast to freedom of movement, competition rules are not solely connected with cross-border related issues, but also include domestic national processes when they hinder free international trade.[80] The scope of application of European competition law further

[76] Cp also M Hilf and F Schorkopf, 'WTO und EG: Rechtskonflikte vor dem EuGH?' [2000] *Europarecht* 74.

[77] For a description of the allocation of competences, see, eg, H-J Cremer in C Calliess and M Ruffert (eds), *Kommentar zu EU-Vertrag und EG-Vertrag* (2002), Art 301 EC, para 12.

[78] See J Drexl in this volume for more information on competitive systems and on competition law.

[79] W Weiß in Calliess and Ruffert (eds), above n 77, Art 82 EC, para 72.

[80] See Basedow, above n 12, 51.

includes activities of companies in third countries, covering activities that could have a negative influence on undistorted competition within the internal market.[81] The merger control is legally anchored in secondary law only, but is therefore not less important.[82] Public enterprises, enterprises with special or exclusive rights and undertakings that offer services of general economic interests as well as financial monopolies must observe the entire Treaty in principle, and align themselves with the system of undistorted competition (Art 86 EC). Art 86 EC is a compromise between states with primarily privately organised economies and those with a pronounced public sector. The system treats the two economic systems equally, and herein lays the importance for the European economic constitution.[83] Furthermore, state aids are subject to Community monitoring, when an effect on cross-border trade between the Member States (Arts 87 *et seq* EC) is established. It limits the economic political power of the Member States considerably, with the intention to hinder discriminatory treatment of trade participants. Finally, Member States, according to the jurisprudence of the European Court of Justice on Art 10 EC, are obliged to desist from all measures that could endanger the realisation of a system of undistorted competition.[84] The rules of competition therefore are therefore a yardstick for measuring legal acts of the state.[85]

bb) Areas Excluded from Competition Furthermore, certain economic areas, products, and services are excluded from competition principles and subject to special regimes. An important example is the Common Agricultural Policy (Arts 32 *et seq* EC; see Arts 225 *et seq* CT-IGC), to which competition law is only applicable to the extent that the Council determines (Art 36 EC). The Treaty does not consequently obstruct a strong market-directed farming economy, but refers this change to a previous legislative decision. Furthermore, in transport policy (Arts 70 EC *et seq*; see Arts 236 *et seq* CT-IGC)[86] and for the distribution regime of nuclear materials according to the Treaty on the European Atomic Community (Arts 52 *et seq* EA), the principle of competition is only valid with limitations. The reasons

[81] See I Brinker in Schwarze (ed), above n 38, Art 81 EC, paras 21 *et seq*.

[82] Council Reg 4064/89 [1989] OJ L 139/1.

[83] For the principle of equal treatment of public and private enterprises, see Case 303/88 *Italy v Commission* [1991] ECR I–1433, para 19.

[84] See J Schwarze, 'Der Staat als Adressat des europäischen Wettbewerbsrechts' [2000] *Europäische Zeitschrift für Wirtschaftsrecht* 613.

[85] For an in-depth analysis, see A Bach, *Wettbewerbsrechtliche Schranken für staatliche Maßnahmen nach europäischem Gemeinschaftsrecht* (1992).

[86] In the decision on community transport policies, the Court of Justice has emphasised that this area should principally be integrated in the regime of the common market: Case 13/83 *Parliament v Council* [1985] ECR 1513, para 62.

for this are assurance of supply, administration of limited or scarce resources, but also consideration of structures and political resistance in Member States. The special position of the coal and steel industry has been largely transferred into the legal framework of the internal market with the expiration of the European Coal and Steel Community Treaty.

cc) Competition and Market Malfunction The system of free and undistorted competition can be disturbed for a variety of reasons. For example, information deficits, negative external effects, ruinous competition, or natural or technical monopolies can lead to a more or less pronounced "market malfunction", which cannot be altered by supervision of competition alone.[87] These deficits in the allocation efficiency of the market are largely correctible only by regulative interventions. They can thoroughly strengthen market mechanisms and are therefore, when appropriately conceived, not a foreign body in the market economic constitution of the EU. In any case, such corrections are legally part of the economic political competences of the Community and Member States, which can have conceptual consequences for the market within the Union.

3. Guarantees of the Market and Economic Policies

The Community and Member States can intercede in the market processes for different reasons, and therefore either limit or promote the free economic development of market participants. The legal framework contains, on the one hand, a legally binding principle of an open market economy and its corresponding safeguards and, on the other hand, a variety of political goals and matching powers, which open a wide area of appreciation and discretion.

a) Goals of Community Activities

The fundamental goals of Community activities are stipulated in Art 2 EC. The comparatively modest canon of goals of the Treaty of the European Economic Community of 1957, according to Art 2, strives for a harmonious development of business life, continual and balanced economic expansion, greater stability, an accelerated improvement in the quality of life, and closer relationships amongst the Member States. In the meantime, the catalogue of goals has expanded and now contains a grand eleven primary goals for determining Community dealings. In addition to

[87] See Basedow, above n 12, 14 for more information on the importance of a market breakdown for the economic constitution.

the immediate economic-related duties of the EC, the following goals are included: harmonious, balanced and sustainable development of economic activities, a high level of employment and of social protection, equality between men and women, sustainable and non-inflationary growth, a high degree of competitiveness and convergence of economic performance, a high level of protection and improvement of the quality of the environment, raising the standard of living and quality of life, and economic and social cohesion and solidarity among Member States. The Constitution does not change the general direction (Arts 2 and 3 CT-IGC).

b) Instruments

Corresponding to the economic emphasis of Art 2 EC, the establishment of a common market and an economic and monetary union (Art 4 EC) are essential instruments in the realisation of these goals.[88] An economic policy should be introduced to serve as a fundament for a common currency, realised by the Member States and the Community within their respective competences. The term "economic policy" can, in the broadest sense, be taken to mean the entirety of measures that should serve specific goals and be used to influence and steer the economic process.[89] This understanding of the term also forms the basis of the requirements of Arts 4 and 98 EC.[90] In addition, the activities of Art 3 are mentioned, which in part stand for independent policy fields of the Community, where they can have a regulating, co-ordinating, or supportive effect. The catalogue of Art 3 EC has also been steadily expanded on in recent decades.[91] In its development, the rather different intervention concerns of the Member States are reflected, which at the very least can no longer be exclusive national pursuits in a "de-bordered market" with crossovers in national competition and, above all, a framework of a monetary union. Regardless of factual classification into specific political areas, most of these activities allow interventions into the economic process. Whether these interventions conform to the market or distort competition depends particularly on their concrete form and the circumstances. In any case, they reveal an integration potential of central importance for a dogmatic of the European economic constitution.

[88] See M Zuleeg in von der Groeben and Schwarze (eds), above n 36, Art 2 EC, para 13, for more information on the instrumental character of these policies, which, however, can be interpreted as objectives.

[89] See A Heertje and H-D Wenzel, *Grundlagen der Volkswirtschaftslehre* (2001), 369.

[90] See CC Steinle, *Europäische Beschäftigungspolitik* (2001), 79, who gives more examples of differing views trying to limit economic policy in the sense of the Treaty to general supervision only and which are thus too narrow. Regarding the limited competences of the Community, their approach is not persuasive if the Member States and the Community are to maintain their own economic policies at the same time.

[91] See, eg, L Vollmer, 'Wirtschaftsverfassung und Wirtschaftspolitik der EG nach "Maastricht"' [1993] *Der Betrieb* 25 for a critical view about the 'political enrichment' of the Treaty; see also Art 3 CT-IGC.

c) Legal Consequences for an Economic Constitution

The central legal task to systematise the relationship between the guarantees of a market economic order, economic policy structuring authorisations and exception clauses can only be carried out when economic policies of the Community and national economic policies are appropriately differentiated between, according to the distribution of competences. Both levels in the league of European economic constitutions take measures which have an effect on the factual and functional connections of the economy. However, Community law—Union law plays no essential role in this context—due to its wide scope of applicability and its supremacy, functions as a yardstick for the actions of the Member States. Admittedly, the boundaries should not be drawn too strictly where both protagonists co-ordinate their respective policies or where national measures are subject to Community supervision. These intersections must be accounted for. However, they change nothing in the principal dominance of Community law, which leads and limits in different ways the institutions, on the one hand, and the Member States, on the other, in market relevant measures.

III. FORMATIVE SCOPE OF THE COMMUNITY IN ECONOMIC POLICY

The judicial profile of Community economic policy results from study of the following themes: (1) the instruments of economic policy, (2) political areas and (3) legal limits of the decision-making process. A separate examination is required by institutional independent monetary policy, in part 4.

1. Instruments of Economic Policies

A primary parameter allowing an estimation of the integration potential of the Treaties in the area of economic policy are the legal instruments of economic political decisions. In this respect, regulating interventions made by Community legislation and co-ordination on the basis of non-compulsory recommendations are to be distinguished from one another. In addition comes assistance in the form of financial aid or grants, given either to the Member States or to private economic participants.[92]

The legislation of the Community stands in the foreground of legal consideration. This is natural, because it enrobes the legal framework of economic activities within the internal market and can also influence the course

[92] In this respect, there is an immense variety of subdivisions and nuances of definition, above all concerned with separating sovereign intervention in the broadest sense from factual results of private activity.

of economic processes. The legislation is directly connected with an operating mode specific to Community law, particularly the direct effect, its primacy, and liability of the Member States. Added to these are the Union citizens rights, which can be used not only to defend market freedoms but also to secure general public interests. This has become a matter of practical importance in the area of environmental protection.[93]

2. Areas of Community Economic Policies

At the centre of the enforcement potentials are areas of Community economic policy and their corresponding powers, which can be arranged, according to the target areas of the instruments, in the categories of regulatory policy, progressive policy, and distribution and social policy.

a) Regulatory Policy (Ordnungspolitik)

An essential feature of the European economic constitution is the comparatively precise layout of the framework of economic activity in the form of the basic decision of Art 4(1) EC and the related guarantees of an open market economy with free competition. However, this does not deal with a closed system, inaccessible to later modification, limiting economic policy to a strict execution of norms. Rather, the institutions are empowered to equip the market economic layout with regulatory policies.

aa) Opening the Market by Approximation An important series of rules and regulations should result in an effective opening of the market through approximation of national laws. This is directly connected to the goal of realising the European internal market. A particular element of achieving this goal is the enabling clauses of Arts 94 and 95 EC (see Arts 173 and 172 CT-IGC), as well as special competences within the framework of the freedoms of the Treaty or the area of tax harmonisation.[94] These rules, however, have proven to be ambivalent in relation to regulatory policy. They begin where basic freedoms allow different legal frameworks of conditions for trade and industry in the Member States, which serve to hinder the openness of the market and therefore work against "an area without internal frontiers". Ideally, approximation of the law should enhance the cross-border openness of the market by disassembling legal hurdles and so augment the equality of market participants. It is true that Community regulations

[93] The expansion of subjective legal positions in Community law is no longer limited to the implementation of the internal market; see A Hatje, *Die gemeinschaftsrechtliche Steuerung der Wirtschaftsverwaltung* (1998), 307.

[94] A thorough overview is provided by W Kahl in Calliess and Ruffert (eds), above n 77, Art 95 EC, paras 2 *et seq*.

from the perspective of the economic participants could just as well hinder the economic freedoms of trade and industry.[95] However, the equality of competitive conditions has generally acquired a corresponding liberal benefit, which has a positive effect on the market. There is a tendency to overload approximation under the influence of "crossover clauses" (*Querschnittsklauseln*) containing goals outside the bounds of economics, such as the protection of public health or environmental protection. This is in itself a problem and will be given more attention in the following paragraphs. In the hands of a legislator preoccupied with intervention measures, this may well become the vehicle of functional interests opposed to competition.[96] The example of the directive, later declared void, absolutely forbidding advertisement for the promotion of tobacco products, marked a low point of this tendency.[97] However, the European Court of Justice limits in its decision on the Tobacco directive the competences of the Community to the approximation of such differences which have not only a hypothetical effect but also a tangible effect on commerce within the internal market.[98] This limits "social formulation" by the European legislators on the one hand, and extends the scope of national policy of the Member States, on the other.[99]

bb) Liberalising Regulated Markets A further area of regulatory policy measures is the liberalisation of regulated markets. Liberalisation policies are partially based on Art 86(3) EC (see Art 166 CT-IGC), which, in addition to Art 95 EC, provided the legal basis for a series of directives for liberalisation of telecommunications service.[100] The rules further allow the edict of individual decisions, which can deal with special problems for regulated services or the activities of public undertakings in individual Member States.[101] Furthermore, these categories of measures are based on the internal market competence of Art 95 EC, which has been used to liberalise the postal services.[102]

[95] See Mussler, above n 25, 134 for more information on the problem of Communitarian approximation of laws as opposed to the competition of various national regulation systems.
[96] See C-D Ehlermann, 'The Internal Market Following the Single European Act' (1987) 24 *CML Rev* 361 at 389, for more information on the existing broad margin of appreciation; P-C Müller-Graff, 'Die Rechtsangleichung zur Verwirklichung des Binnenmarktes' [1989] *Europarecht* 136.
[97] See Case C–376/98 *Germany v Parliament and Council* [2000] ECR I–8419.
[98] *Ibid*, para 106.
[99] See also Müller-Graff, above n 3, 58; C Calliess, 'Nach dem "Tabakwerbung"-Urteil des EuGH' [2001] *Jura* 311.
[100] See the overview by C Jung in Calliess and Ruffert (eds), above n 77, Art 86 EC, paras 60 *et seq*.
[101] *Ibid*, Art 86 EC, paras 62 *et seq*.
[102] For details, see Jung, above n 100, Art 86 EC, para 61a.

b) Procedural Policy

The sphere of possible influence which the Community has on the individual steps of the economic process requires more differentiated considerations. In conjunction with these considerations, the policies governing monetary and currency policies will be analysed in a separate section.

aa) Financial Policy Financial policy does not play a decisive role in Community economic policy. Firstly, the budget volume of the Community is too small to effectively be used as an instrument of financial global control. Secondly, the Community lacks the authority to specifically determine the type and the amount of its revenues by itself. The Community's own revenues, are, according to Art 269 EC (see Art 54 CT-IGC), allocated to it by way of primary law; neither the keys to imposition nor the upper limits are at the disposal of the institutions.[103] Even import and export duties are subject to legally binding rules within the framework of the WTO. At all events, the authorisation to introduce economic policy-motivated steering contributions, which was granted by the European Court of Justice based on aggregate competence, gave the institutions to a certain degree a radius of action in the area of financial policy.[104] These instruments have not yet attained any real practical significance.

bb) Structural Assistance Measures A further group of rules empowers the Community, partly in co-operation with the Member States, to undertake measures for providing structural assistance. Structural policy is the correlative of competition control, which should serve to actively strengthen competition through market-revitalising initiatives. It can therefore be seen as a sort of "completion to regulatory economic policy", with an influence on the frame of the economic process.[105] On the other hand, assistance measures are an integral part of policy instruments which should primarily serve to promote economic growth. This double function can also be seen in the pertinent authorisations of the Treaty. Some examples are the industrial policy (Arts 157 *et seq* EC; see Art 279 CT-IGC), the research and development policy (Arts 163 *et seq* EC; see Arts 248 *et seq* CT-IGC), and the active support of trans-European networks (Arts 154–156 EC; see Arts 246 *et seq* CT-IGC), which should serve to strengthen the international competitive capabilities of the European economy and its infrastructure.

First, structural funds (regional, social, agrarian, cohesion) are at the service of regional competition capabilities. Simultaneously, they are intended

[103] See Oppermann, above n 4, para 837.
[104] See Case 138/78 *Stölting* [1979] ECR 713; Case 108/81 *Amylum v Council* [1982] 3109.
[105] See U Teichmann, *Wirtschaftspolitik* (2000), 189, for more information on this dual function.

to be an instrument of Community solidarity, although it would be a mistake to consider them to be a surrogate for a federal fiscal adjustment.[106] The redistribution effect of the funds is too small for such an objective.[107] The volume of financing is, nonetheless, worth mentioning. For the assistance period of 2000–2006, a total of 195 billion euros have been designated for the structural funds. Meanwhile, the funds have developed into an independent sub-branch of the law, distinguished by a high degree of technicality as well as complex regulatory and decision-making structures. The principle of co-financing increases the financial volume of the measures considerably; the incentive effect of Community promises of financial aid gives the funds a considerable influence on national structural policy.[108] The unclear supervision of achievement is an essential deficiency of the structural funds.

cc) Employment Policy The title "employment" was introduced by the Treaty of Amsterdam (Arts 125–130 EC; see Arts 203 *et seq* CT-IGC). Although such policy initiatives had previously existed at the European level, it was with the entry into force of the Amsterdam amendments in 1999 that this subject was recognised in a Treaty for the first time. These rules were created, above all, under the pressure of growing unemployment figures in the EU. They provide a tool for the fulfilment of the employment goals of Art 2 EC, but are, however, limited to co-ordination of strategies and of supporting measures. The responsibility of employment policy remains in the hands of the Member States, although promotion of employment is viewed as a "matter of common concern" (Art 126(2) EC). National strategies are co-ordinated by "Employment Policy Guidelines", issued by the Council based on a report on the situation in the EU. These guidelines are not legally enforceable, but rather recommendations for measures, which merely must be considered by the Member States.[109]

dd) Environmental Policy Environmental policy has attained importance through the embedding of environmental protection in Art 2 EC as well as in the crossover clauses of Art 6 EC (see Arts 3, 119 and Art 233 CT-IGC). In general, environmental policy can be defined as the sum of all economic policy measures intended to contribute to the improvement or preservation of environmental quality. Community environmental competences include not only protective measures concerning environmental media, i.e., earth,

[106] Outlined by A Glaesner, *Der Grundsatz des wirtschaftlichen und sozialen Zusammenhalts im Recht der Europäischen Wirtschaftsgemeinschaft* (1990).

[107] See T Hieronymi, *Solidarität als Rechtsprinzip in der EU* (2003).

[108] See R Priebe in Schwarze (ed), above n 38, Art 158 EC, paras 1 *et seq*, for detailed information on the impact of this instrument.

[109] For details, see Steinle, above n 90, 351.

air and water, or human health, for a prudent and rational utilisation of natural resources (Art 175(1) EC; see Art 233 CT-IGC), but also consist of important decisions relating to infrastructure, touching on the choice of a Member State between various forms of energy production or their regional planning (Art 175(2) EC).[110] As central guiding maxim, we find the "polluter pays" principle and the principle of sustainable development.[111]

The competences permit measures of approximation in every form of secondary legislation of Art 249 EC, whereby in practice the directives dominate.[112] Furthermore, the crossover clauses of Art 6 EC give additional enforcement powers to environmental protection. Hence, recent practice of the European Commission has rendered the goal of environmental protection, based on the crossover clause of Art 6 EC, as a base for decisions in competition law on exemptions from Art 81 EC. In the *CECED*-decision of 1999, an agreement amongst French washing machine manufacturers was released from cartel prohibitions, because the agreement created energy saving production norms; these norms, however, resulted in a limitation of competition on this market and exerted a negative influence on interstate trade.[113] The questionable gain for consumers, who were now forced to pay higher prices for the technically superior appliances, was, according to the Commission compensated for by gains in the area of environmental protection (Art 6 EC). This decision shows the potential for imposition of crossover clauses in the core areas of Community economic constitutions, even when carefully evaluated.

The market relevance of direct environmental policy measures should also not be overlooked, when legal permissible limits of certain substances, introduction of new processing procedures such as the EIA Directive, and authorised admission of industrial plants are made dependent upon an integrated examination of their influences on the essential environmental media. The effects on economic freedom and national legal dogmatic can be far-reaching, especially when in Germany precautionary limits, in opposition to the previous legal status, confer subjective rights and can therefore be enforced before the courts by the individual.[114] At the same time, it

[110] See J Jahns-Böhm in Schwarze (ed), above n 38, Art 174 EC, para 2.

[111] See M Schröder, 'Umweltschutz als Gemeinschaftsziel und Grundsätze des Umweltschutzes' in H-W Rengeling (ed), *Handbuch zum deutschen und europäischen Umweltrecht* (1998), i, § 9, especially paras 40 and 82.

[112] See, eg, G Lübbe-Wolff, 'Der Vollzug des europäischen Umweltrechts und seine Bedeutung für die Umweltpolitik der EU' in *id* (ed), *Der Vollzug des europäischen Umweltrechts* (1996), 1; see also Art 33 CT-IGC.

[113] Commission Dec 2000/475/EC [2000] OJ L 187/47; for a detailed discussion of this problem, see J-P Terhechte, 'Der Umweltschutz und die Wettbewerbspolitik in der Europäischen Gemeinschaft' [2002] *Zeitschrift für Umweltrecht* 274.

[114] For a detailed view, see M Ruffert, *Subjektive Rechte im Umweltrecht der EG* (1996).

would be a mistake to assume a quasi-natural antagonism between ecology and economy. Above all, such an antagonism does not exist per se from the point of view of the European economic constitution. Rather, an "*environmentally compatible* rate of growth" is one of the major goals of the Community, according to Art 2 EC (see Art 3 CT-IGC). Therefore, it is a legitimate concern of European economic policy to internalise particularly the negative external effects of the utilisation of the commodity "environment", such as the pollution of the freely available supply of air caused when producing a product, and to factor these costs into the cost accounting of the perpetrators.

c) Distribution and Social Policies

The responsibilities of the Community in the area of distribution policy, understood as property, income and social policy, require a more differentiated examination.[115] The "social" aspect of the European market model is anchored in this area. Characteristic of this sector is the division of responsibilities between the Community and the Member States, legally embodied in common goal perspectives and areas of competence, which secure the socially binding nature of European economic policy but leave the measures largely in the hands of the Member States.

aa) Distribution Policy Goals of the Community Among other goals, the Community strives to reach a "high level of social protections" and an "increase in the standard of living and the quality of life", as set out in Art 2 EC (see Art CT-IGC). The commitment of the Treaty to a high level of social protection, guarantees the essential elements of a social state, without forcing for example the German principle of social justice and the welfare state upon the Member States.[116] In addition, the Community principle of solidarity, referred to especially in Art 1 EU Treaty as well as in Art 2 EC, relates primarily to the relationships of the Member States amongst themselves, and not to the mutual introductory duties of a community of Union citizens.[117] Nonetheless, the Union citizenship in Arts 17 *et seq* EC offers in itself a potential, which has so far not been made use of. In spite of its derivative character, it forms the basis of a European category of citizens' rights and equality under the law, the consequences of which—as social participatory rights—are becoming increasingly distinct. The Court of Justice has recently decided that Union citizenship in connection with the discrimination prohibition of Art 12 EC (see Art 123 CT-IGC) stands in opposition to

[115] See Böckenförde, above n 22, 79, who remains too general on this topic.
[116] For more details, see Kingreen, above n 23.
[117] Cp eg Kingreen, above n 23; also E-A Marias, *Solidarity as an objective of the European Union and the European Community* (1994), 85.

a regulation that makes the granting of financial support for one's livelihood dependent upon nationality.[118] This also has to do with access to national benefit systems, the continuance of which the Member States, in principal, have at their free disposal.

Aside from the question of desirability, the main obstacle to an independent and completely comprehensive European social policy is the fact that the Community does not possess the instruments necessary to achieve such goals as providing social benefits, or guaranteeing equal opportunities or a just social order. This is true as well for the goal of raising the standard of living, which should be understood in the sense of an increase in the average income level. Above all, the financial autonomy of the Community is also limited to achieve redistribution effects worth mentioning through its budget policies. The ponderousness of the approximation competences in the area of taxes, which requires a unanimous vote, is another factor limiting community access to those instruments of just social distribution.[119] Regardless of this, the authorisations of the Community in these areas in the last round of reforms have been continually expanded and supplemented with instruments which open a new dimension of social interventions at the European level as well.[120]

bb) Supplementary Social Policy According to Art 3(1)(j) EC, the activities of the Community shall include "a policy in the social sphere comprising a European Social Fund". Title XI establishes parity between socio-political rules and other policies of the community (see Arts 209 *et seq* CT-IGC). The emphasis of socio-political competences lies, meanwhile, at the national level. This is especially valid for systems providing social services, such as health insurance, annuity insurance, and social insurance, but also for the various forms of contribution to the standard of living, for instance, social security benefits.

(1) Co-ordination of the Systems Providing Social Services

The Community has merely a co-ordinating role in this area. Nevertheless, measures have been taken for the realisation of the free movement of persons: mutual recognition of insurance time periods, rights to benefit support payments and so forth. Although they are functionally related to the freedom of movement, they are not an expression of any particular socio-political formative interests of the EC.[121] Quite the opposite, the Court of Justice,

[118] See Case C–184/99 *Grzelczyk* [2001] ECR I–6193.

[119] See Art 93 EC (indirect taxation) and Art 94 EC (direct taxation).

[120] See also Badura, above n 1, 28, who speaks of the intrinsic necessity of further development towards a 'Welfare and Distribution Community'.

[121] See Case C–158/96 *Kohll* [1998] ECR I–1931; Case C–120/95 *Decker* [1998] ECR I–1831.

beginning with the cases of Kohll und Decker,[122] has emphasised the fundamental importance of internal market regulations for national social insurance, namely health insurance, and allowed only such limitations which should serve to assure the efficiency of the service provider involved.[123]

(2) Supplementation of National Activities

The European Social Fund (Arts 146–148 EC) is meant to improve the employment possibilities of the workforce in the internal market, and thus contribute to an increase of the standard of living. Its primary duty is to support national measures (supplementary principle). Their socio-political goal is also related to the internal market, thus leaving the guarantees of an open market economy unaffected. At the same time, the fund belongs in the context of economic and social cohesion (Art 159 (1) EC) and has the general goal of reducing the differences between the levels of development of the various regions (Arts 3(1)(k), 158 EC).

cc) Starting Points for European Employment and Social Order The Communities competences based on the "social regulations" of Arts 136–145 EC, introduced on the basis of the Treaty of Amsterdam, are much more important for the market-economic orientation of the European economic constitution. The provisions of Arts 137 *et seq* EC are concerned with employment law, above all the legal relationship between employer and employee, as well as matters of collective employment law. Additionally, questions of social welfare law are regulated whereas special rules are to be observed for social protection (Art 137(3) EC) and social security (Arts 42, 137(3) EC). Socially oriented rules and regulations create an independent competence title for social policy. It has been freed from its functional linkage to internal market policy, in which framework socio-political questions have been treated under the aspect of unfair competitive practices.[124] Herein lies the first step to an independent European social policy, the conceptual orientation of which, however, is still relatively unclear. Subjective rights are merely conferred by the precept of equal pay for equal work for men and women (Art 141 EC). In addition, the provisions and regulations of Arts 137 to 140 EC place a wealth of instruments within reach.

[122] Cp U Becker, 'Brillen aus Luxemburg und Zahnbehandlung in Brüssel' [1998] *Neue Zeitschrift für Sozialrecht* 359.

[123] For this, see Case C–157/99 *Smits* [2001] ECR I–5473, with remarks by Nowak, above n 66.

[124] R Rebhahn in Schwarze (ed), above n 38, Art 136 EC, para 5; see also the dissenting work of S Krebber in Calliess and Ruffert (eds), above n 77, Art 136 EC, para 6, who still sees, basically, a competitive policy concept as an important guideline behind European social policy, more precisely the illusion that successful economic policy has a positive effect on social integration.

d) Freedom of Choice in the Framework of Comprehensive Clauses

Finally, the Community legislator has general authorisations available in Art 308 EC, which can also be used for economically relevant measures. As shown in application practices of the last decade, the Council has often used Art 308 EC (see Art 18 CT-IGC) for the introduction of policies which some time later were incorporated into the canon of primary law competences. Environmental and regional policies are examples of this.[125] The restrictive conditions, which can be mobilised under the comprehensive clause of Art 308 EC, therefore change nothing of their principle meaning for the effective scope of market economy guarantees.

3. Formative Boundaries

In the face of a widely spread tableau of economic policy goals and their corresponding authorisations, the limits of formation build the core of a "leeway dogmatic" (*Spielraum-Dogmatik*) of European economic law. The search for crossover principles and rules which determine the relationship between guarantees and the powers of intervention of the Community is in the centre. The prohibitions against system change, anchored in Art 4(1) and (2) and in Art 98 EC, could be simultaneously connected with the principle of rule-exception, which make interventions into economic freedom and other guarantees of a competitively constituted market economy an exception requiring legal justification. Beyond these general boundaries, further written and unwritten legal guidelines for relating competition and intervention can be inferred from the Treaty.

a) Increased Effectiveness of Market Integrative Instruments

Market integrative guarantees tend to have access to a higher capacity for carrying through than competence titles which display interventionist tendencies. This is made visible in the graded autonomy of the regulation areas, in procedural safeguards and, even if in diminishing measure, in the legal instruments available.[126]

aa) Levels of Autonomy One indication of the precedence of competitive market-integrative means is the increased independence of market-integrative

[125] See, eg, the overview by M Rossi in Calliess and Ruffert (eds), above n 77, Art 308 EC, para 6.

[126] See especially J Basedow, 'Zielkonflikte und Zielhierarchien im Vertrag über die Europäische Gemeinschaft' in O Due, M Lutter and J Schwarze (eds), *Festschrift für U Everling* (1995), 49 at 49 and 60.

Community policies.[127] They create their own assignments, which, especially with the assistance of the fundamental freedoms, of competition law and approximation competences, are able to assert themselves. On the other hand, health and consumer policies are limited to a supportive or auxiliary contribution. Even the industrial policy has a complementary character, which manifests itself above all when the Community wishes to resort to specific measures. According to Art 157(3) EC, these must serve to "support" national efforts. The weakest form of these is co-ordination, such as in the area of employment policy, which should merely serve to match up mainly independent decision-making parties with one another.

bb) Procedural Safeguards Procedural safeguards are also a way of protecting the decision in favour of an open market economy with free competition from competition-distorting influences. Important progress was made with the introduction of Art 95 EC (see Art 172 CT-IGC), which allows a qualified majority vote for measures conducive to the establishment and functioning of the internal market. The opposite is true for particularly disputed areas of policy such as industrial politics, in which the conflict potential of the various national economic philosophies is obvious to everyone: these areas are kept under the control with the requirement of a unanimous vote. The same is also true for the general comprehensive clause of Art 308 EC (see Art 18 CT-IGC), which has often served in the past as the legal basis of economic policy measures such as the introduction of a common regional policy. Additionally, such bodies as the Economic and Social Committee and the Committee of the regions must be involved, which can place a burden of justification on the institutions for their measures. However, this indication of a greater capability to enforce the market concept is fading rapidly, as in all areas of the Treaty the tendency is being seen towards expanding the use of the majority decision, as shown by the Reform of Nice.[128]

b) Substantive Safeguards

Much more concrete are a range of substantive safeguards for a competitively constituted market economy. In this respect, one can distinguish amongst subsidiarity, functionality, and effectiveness as limiting principles.

aa) Principle of Subsidiarity The subsidiarity principle of Art 5(2) EC (see Art 11 CT-IGC) can be observed in connection with numerous economic political measures. Although its effectiveness has proven to be relatively

[127] See *ibid*.
[128] For an in-depth study, see A Hatje, 'Die institutionelle Reform der Europäischen Union' [2001] *Europarecht* 143 at 154.

limited in previous applications, it still directs, if only as a policy maxim, the activities of the Community above all on the basis of such competences which are not exclusive.[129] To these belong economic and social cohesion and the protection of collective goods and interests.

bb) Reservation Clauses The functional capacities of the internal market and the system of undistorted competition are additionally secured through reservations, which can be found in a manifold of provisions.

(1) Provisions Supporting the Establishment and Functioning of the Internal Market

The measures of judicial approximation must target the goals of realisation of the fundamental freedoms and the establishment and functioning of the internal market.[130] At the same time, these substantive requirements contain a command to conformity with reference to the guarantees of an open market. These are also valid inasmuch as crossover clauses load up judicial harmonisation with objectives for meeting the needs of non-economic interests such as health or environmental protection. This is often achieved at the expense of economic freedoms.[131] Although they grant the institutions broad latitude of evaluation and formation, they do not give them the right to utilise harmonisation competences for the creation of new market barriers or even for the exclusion of the market.[132] For this reason, prohibitions such as the Communities' prohibition of certain types of advertising, supported by Art 95 EC (See Art 172 CT-IGC), create fundamental problems of limitations to communication, because they interfere with a functional guarantee of the market economic order.

(2) Provisions Ensuring Undistorted Competition

Beyond this, there are several powers limiting Community intervention in market processes to those measures which do not result in a distortion of competition. Especially the controversial industrial policies of Arts 157 *et seq* EC are expressly bound to a "system of open and competitive markets" (Art 157(1) and (2) EC; see Art 279 CT-IGC), and block the use of

[129] In this regard, neither the fears of the first years (see P Pescatore, 'Mit der Subsidiarität leben' in above n 127, *Festschrift für U Everling*, above n 127, 1071) nor the hopes have been fulfilled, with the result that contemporary commentary ranges from sober and empty to negative.

[130] See AG Jacobs Opinion in Case C–350/92 *Spain v Council* [1995] ECR I–1985, para 4; the necessity of an appropriate, not merely opportunistic, harmonisation effect is emphasised by the ECJ in Case C–15/91 *Commission v Council* [1993] ECR I–939, para 19.

[131] See B Langeheine in E Grabitz and M Hilf (eds), *Das Recht der Europäischen Union* (looseleaf, last update 2001), Art 100a EC Treaty, para 73, for the necessity of co-ordination with the requirements of the common market.

[132] See I Schwartz, 'EG-Kompetenz für das Verbot der Tabakwerbung?' [1998] *Archiv für Presserecht* 558.

these competences for measures which could lead to a "distortion of competition" (Art 157(2) and (3) EC). Even so, the Community contribution to the expansion of a trans-European network in the areas of traffic, telecommunications, and energy infrastructures (Art 154 EC; see Art 246 CT-IGC) is bound up with the "structure of a system of open and competitive markets". In this sense, at least from a legal viewpoint, they are conceptualised as compatible with the guarantees of a market economy. Even Community social policies must stop at the point where "the competitive capacity of Community economy" could be negatively influenced. Moreover, the Court has inferred a guarantee from Art 3(g) EC which prescribes a system ensuring undistorted competition that legitimates the further development judge-made law in this area.[133]

(3) Effectiveness

The uncertainty of these provisions does not impede their legal effectiveness. As shown in the case law of the Court of Justice, they may very well give the internal market clauses, as well as the various formulations of competition principles, thoroughly effective supervisory contours.[134] In these cases, "competitive capacity" as a barrier to European social policies opens latitude of evaluation to the political institutions for making economic decisions far removed from judicial scrutiny. In any case, these barriers substantiate a burden of justification for measures which are objectively suited to hinder certain parts of, or the European economy as a whole, in its ability to participate in a competition in performance in the internal market.[135]

c) Burden of Justification

The burden of justification is integrally connected with the guarantees of an open market with free competition. These create overwhelmingly subjective rights, which only allow proportional interventions.

aa) Subjective Rights and the Necessity of Justification Above all, the institutions must protect the fundamental rights of the affected parties. They do not only form the basis of a market economic constitution, but also

[133] See Case 6/72 *Continental Can v Commission* [1973] ECR 215, para 24.

[134] The judgment on the ban on tobacco advertising shows that the Court of Justice controls the Community approximation of laws if it intervenes in economic freedoms from the perspective of functional guarantees of a market economy. See also the critical review by J van Scherpenberg, 'Ordnungspolitische Konflikte im Binnenmarkt' in M Jachtenfuchs and B Kohler-Koch (eds), *Europäische Integration* (1996), 345, especially 350, for more information on the approximation of laws.

[135] See, eg, J Schwarze, *European Administrative Law* (1992), 1412 *et seq*, for more information on the burden of justification institutions with such powers have to meet.

the negative limits of competences for sovereign interferences with economic freedoms. The connection between constitutional liberties and market economy, emphasised by Walter Eucken,[136] is present in Community law. The fundamental freedoms may allow the institutions a broad scope for formulation; however, they substantiate, together with the objective decision in favour of an open market economy with free competition, a burden of justification. Free trade activities represent the presumed rule, and sovereign intervention, for whatever purpose, is the exception which needs justification.[137] Added to this is the prohibition against discrimination, which must be observed when intervening in subjective rights.[138] Its effect, however, is held in check, since the Court of Justice usually limits the examination to whether a factual reason for the differentiating measure is present. In this respect, one of the few examples of setting aside a Community regulation in economic law due to a violation of the constitution was based upon a violation of the discrimination prohibition.[139] In the end, the fundamental freedoms seen as subjective constitutional rights create a barrier for Community interventions in the market.

bb) Proportionality or a Minimum of Intervention Rule The fine-tuning amongst the impaired guarantees of Community measures, such as fundamental rights and freedoms follows, as a rule, the path of an inspection as to proportionality.[140] This is undertaken with various degrees of strictness by the European Court of Justice, depending on whether legislative or administrative interventions are intended. The Community legislator has the already mentioned broad latitude of evaluation and formation, which is dogmatically established on both choice of goals and the levels of suitability and necessity present.[141] Should an examination of proportionality, in a narrow sense, occur, which is not usually the case, the protected goods are weighed in a concrete evaluation. Thus, freedom of economy and competition can, in individual cases, retreat behind the interests to their limitations.[142] Nonetheless, the burden of justification for interventions into economic freedoms leads to a relative minimum of intervention.

[136] *Ibid.*

[137] In general, Cases 46/87 and 227/88 *Hoechst v Commission* [1989] ECR 2859, para 19, express such a burden of justification for interventions.

[138] See R Priebe in M Dauses (ed), *Handbuch des EU-Wirtschaftsrechts* (looseleaf, last update 2001), paras 285 *et seq*, for more information on the prohibition of discrimination in the particularly dense Communitarion agricultural law.

[139] See Case 114/76 *Bela-Mills* [1977] ECR 1211, para 7.

[140] See Case C–284/95 *Safety Hi-Tech* [1998] ECR I–4301, paras 65 *et seq*.

[141] See Case 37/83 *Rewe* [1984] ECR 1229, paras 19 *et seq*; see also the in-depth analysis of U Kischel, 'Die Kontrolle der Verhältnismäßigkeit durch den Europäischen Gerichtshof' [2000] *Europarecht* 380, especially 386.

[142] the 'BSE Cases', Case C–180/96 *United Kingdom v Commission* [1998] ECR I–2265, paras 96 *et seq*; Case C–157/96 *National Farmers Union* [1998] ECR I–2211, paras 60 *et seq* are prominent examples for this.

4. The Monetary Union in the Economic Constitution

A special role is given the monetary system. Although it is an integral element of primary law, it is separated from the rest of the institutional system on the European as well as the national level, by the independent status of the European Central Bank and the European System of Central Banks.[143] The Treaty further formulates a clear objective preference, with price stability as the leading maxim of the monetary union, which conceals a considerable potential for conflict between both the goals of Community and of national economic policies.[144] For this reason, the monetary system cannot be integrated into the remaining economic constitution without friction.

a) Stability Before Unity

The relative unity of the European currency area will probably give way to a new and not unusual variety of currencies with the entry of Central and Eastern European countries. Most new members and candidates do not fulfil the convergence criteria, at least not at present. In this respect, stability goes before unity. However, even the non-participating states remain bound to the criteria of economic convergence, which means that some rather large efforts must be undertaken in order to consolidate public budgets and to lower inflation rates.[145] Until these goals are reached, different degrees of stability within the Union as well remain a possibility, influencing exchanges of trade and services in the internal market.

b) Stability Before Prosperity?

Another aspect is the delineation of objective conflicts within the monetary union, particularly in times of weaker economic activity. A quasi-horizontal conflict is an element of the regulation of the monetary union itself, although Art 105 EC states that the European System of Central Banks (ESCB) should follow the "primary objective" of price stability (also Art 185 CT-IGC). The possibility of a Community business cycle policy is therefore limited from the beginning. As far as possible, the ESCB, under the leadership of the ECB, must support the economic policies of the Community, when this has no negative influence on this objective, in order to contribute to the realisation of the aims of Art 2 EC. The relevant political

[143] See only Arts 107, 108 EC, and Arts 7 and 14 of the Protocol on the Statute of the European System of Central Banks and of the European Central Bank.
[144] Art 105(1) EC.
[145] See U Häde in Calliess and Ruffert (eds), above n 77, Art 122 EC, paras 11 *et seq*, for more information on this commitment.

goals include, among others, a high level of employment, a balanced and sustainable development of economic activities, and a sustainable and non-inflationary growth, that is, a typical economic policy agenda.

Key terms are price stability and non-inflation. How the monetary policy of the ECB is to be created is substantially dependent on their interpretation. On the one hand, this has consequences for the stability of a common currency and therefore for conditions of the market; on the other hand, the economic political creative potential of the ECB can be inferred from this.[146] This in turn has repercussions on the market model of the European economic constitution. The term "price stability" is indefinite, and therefore open to multiple interpretations. A restrictive interpretation in the sense of a rate of zero inflation stands opposed to the fact that this objective is not very realistic and not necessarily economically sensible; above all, it would hardly be possible in practice for the ECB with a view to the clear precedence of price stability to take into account the additional goals referred to in Art 105(1) EC. The same is true for the term "non-inflationary" growth. With good reason, a plea is made in favour of an interpretation as a term of relative stability, permitting a low percentage of devaluation and otherwise allowing the ECB a certain scope of decision-making and evaluation.[147] This also fits in the convergence criteria, which also prescribe a relatively low rate but not zero inflation.[148] In that regard, this section of the European economic constitution is open to monetary policy measures, which for the interests of employment are only satisfied with relative price stability. To this end, the basic principle of an open market economy with free competition is expressly to be followed, according to Arts 4 and 105(1) EC.

c) Vertical Conflicts

From this can be concluded that Community monetary policies and national economic policies can come into conflict with one another. This could be the result of the ECB's somewhat restrictive monetary supply growth colliding with the Member States "deficit spending": for the open flank of the European economic constitution is the far-reaching competence provision in favour of the Member States in the area of general economic policy. The corresponding Arts 98 to 104 EC (see Arts 178 to 184 CT-IGC) merely formulate a relatively broad margin within which the Member States can in principle freely choose their political options, bound solely by the basics of

[146] For details, see R Stadler, *Der rechtliche Handlungsspielraum des Europäischen Systems der Zentralbanken* (1996).

[147] See M Potacs in Schwarze (ed), above n 38, Art 105 EC, para 3.

[148] See Art 1 of the Protocol on the convergence criteria referred to in Art 121 EC.

open market economy and general guidelines for economic policy. The monitoring of the development of the budgetary situation, in order to hinder excessive government deficits, changes in the end nothing in the possibility of following a separate subsidy policy, for example, by restructuring the national budget.[149]

IV. THE DISCRETIONARY POWER OF THE MEMBER STATES IN THE FIELD OF ECONOMIC POLICY

The basic decision in the association of the European economic constitution in favour of an open market with free competition can be additionally limited, above all through the economic policies of the Member States. A broad scope of discretion is the starting point from which the dogmatic of vertical relationships within the constitutional system can be developed.

1. National Constitutional Law

The European economic constitution forms a link between the fundamental judicial regulations of the Member States, especially such regulations which, as creative elements in the national economic constitution, limit the possibilities and boundaries of national economic politics from "below". A precise analysis would stretch the limits of this study; first, the terms of justiciability of the national economic constitutions must be included. Here, tendencies and prominent features of material economic law could simply be given prominence, connected with the stimulus to take up this set of questions separately.[150]

a) System Decisions

None of the constitutions of the former fifteen Member States takes an express system decision comparable to the legal requirements of Arts 4 and 98 EC (see Arts 3 and 178 CT-IGC).[151] Only Art 38 of the Spanish

149 However, it should not be ignored that the increasing Communitarian subsidy control of the past twenty years has put this sector of national economic autonomy under Community control as well.

150 See the important contribution of P-C Müller-Graff, 'Die wettbewerbsverfaßte Marktwirtschaft als gemeineuropäisches Verfassungsprinzip' [1997] *Europarecht* 433.

151 However, for the Federal Republic of Germany, Art 1(3) of the Treaty on the Creation of a Monetary, Economic and Social Union of 25 June 1990 between the FRG and the GDR establishes the 'social market economy' as binding in the sense of a normative declaration about a the practised economic order. For details, see M Schmidt-Preuß, 'Soziale Marktwirtschaft und Grundgesetz vor dem Hintergrund des Staatsvertrages zur Währungs, Wirtschafts- und Sozialunion' [1993] *Deutsches Verwaltungsblatt* 236.

Constitution recognises "the freedom of enterprise in the framework of market economy", which in itself is a remarkable basic statement of regulatory policy. In contrast to this position, several of the constitutions of the new Member States contain express decisions for a particular economic constitution. For example, the Constitution of the Republic of Poland declares in Art 20 that a "social market economy, resting on the freedoms of economic development, private property, solidarity, dialogue, and co-operation between social partners as well" is intended to be the basis of the Polish economic constitution.[152] A similar formulation is contained in Art 55(1) of the Slovakian Constitution, which states that the "economy of the Slovakian Republic is based on a socially and ecologically oriented market economy". Moreover, the Slovakian Republic "protects and supports economic competition" according to Art 55(2) of the Constitution. Hungary also acknowledges market economy in Art 9(1) of its Constitution, but adds that "public and private property enjoy equal protection and equal rights under the law".

b) Guarantees of a Market Economy

The constitutions of all Member States contain additional legal guarantees, which represent a fundamentally justiciable basis for the protection of market economic order. In this respect, they are compatible with the European market constitution, at least in principle. This is valid for freedom of trade for individuals or enterprises, but equally so for the guarantee of private property. The Hungarian Constitution emphasises "the right to enterprise" and the "freedom of economic competition" in Art 9(2); the latter, however, only as a fundamental aim of the state, as far as can be observed. The Irish Constitution names competition as a protected good, too. Art 45(1)(c) states that the politics of the state should be especially constructed so that "an accumulation of property and the control of essential goods do not remain in the hands of the few, leading to general injury to free competition". These normative guidelines allow the state institutions a broad economic political scope for activity, which however can be limited by contrary state intervention in favour of goals requiring such measures.

c) Interventionist Tendencies

In this respect, the guarantees of a market economic order and the interventionist goals of state policies and their corresponding authorisations face one another in concurrence, and in the meantime, in conflict as well. Thus,

[152] For more information on the constitutional law of all European nations, see the CD-ROM, *Die europäischen Verfassungen*, a compilation created within the framework of an EU project. It contains the most important sources of law and an explanatory introduction.

the previously quoted provision of Art 45 of the Spanish Constitution guarantees not only the freedom of enterprise within the framework of a market economy, but also places support, dependent on unison, equal with the "requirements of planning". Furthermore, the constitutions of some Member States vouch for social rights, and contain catalogues of imposing goals, which could justify measures limiting markets and competition.[153] An initial perusal of the national constitutions speaks for a broad scope of economic policy formulation of the national legislator, which should obviously include certain planning elements, such as in the case of Spain or France.

2. Market Relevant Discretionary Powers

The effective extent that these can have on the association of the European economic constitution is first defined by the Treaty and its provisions. In this respect, it can be distinguished whether the area in question falls under the jurisdiction of the Member States or is opened through exceptions in Community policies. In this matter, they consequently form a counterpart to those areas which the Community has not been allowed to regulate, or that until now have not yet been regulated.

a) Regulatory Policy Regulations

Regulatory policy provisions of the Community economic constitution in favour of the Member States concern above all regulations governing the areas of private property and provisions of elementary requirements.

aa) National Systems of Property Ownership The guarantee of Art 295 EC (see Art 425 CT-IGC), which leaves the national regulations governing private property untouched, secures national prerogatives in the area of property regulations. The wide meaning of the term "property" which includes, in addition to physical property, above all intellectual property as stated in the case law of the Court of Justice, opens a principally broad area of configuration discretion to the Member States, which are not prevented from nationalising enterprises.[154] A practical application of this was the wave of nationalisation in France, which occurred after the election victory of the Socialist Party in the beginning of the 1980s.[155] The reverse is also

[153] For more examples, see Müller-Graff, above n 150, 454.
[154] See W Berg in: Schwarze (ed), above n 38, Art 295 EC, para 3; among earlier literature, see G Burghardt, *Die Eigentumsordnung in den Mitgliedstaaten und der EWG-Vertrag* (1969), 107, who qualifies the regulations as 'an enemy to integration', is still worth reading.
[155] See H Weis, 'Verstaatlichungen aus gemeinschaftsrechtlicher Sicht' [1982] *Neue Juristische Wochenschrift* 1910.

true, as the Member States have not been hindered in privatising public enterprises. In this respect, Art 295 EC guarantees the neutrality of Community as regards those regulatory policy decisions of Member States, whose effects can penetrate into the centre of guarantees of an open market economy with free competition.[156] It is not the purpose of Art 295 EC to make an "opting-out" of the Community market constitution possible for the Member States, although it is formulated without reservations. For this reason, at least the practical applications and the effects of public and private ownership laws underlie the general limits of the Treaty. Above all, a comprehensive nationalisation of trade and industry would no longer be covered by Art 295 EC, as it would inevitably involve planning that might not be reconcilable with the fundamental freedoms of the internal market nor with competition rules.[157]

bb) Guarantees in Favour of Services of General Economic Interest The lines of conflict between various concepts of national economic policies are drawn together as in a burning glass in the current discussions on the position of services of general economic interest in a competition-controlled economy.[158] This concerns those businesses that have been assigned particular duties by the Member States; the Treaty mentions in this respect provisions of services of general economic interest. In order to strengthen their position, Art 16 EC (see Art 122 CT-IGC) was introduced by the Treaty reform of Amsterdam, not least with a view to a more restrictive interpretation of Art 86 (see Art 166 CT-IGC) by the Commission and the European Court of Justice. At the same time, like a mirror image, from the point of view of such services, Art 36 of the yet non-compulsory European Charter of Fundamental Rights underlines the rights of Union citizens to access. Items of regulation are the previously mentioned "services of general economic interest". With a view to these services and undertakings, and according to Art 16 EC, "the Community and its Member States, each within their respective powers and within the scope of application of this Treaty, shall take care that such services operate on the basis of principles and conditions which enable them to fulfil their missions". This is also valid without prejudice to Arts 73, 86 and 87 EC, which state that these forms of services are subject to Community controls regarding conformation to the standards of competition law.

[156] T Kingreen in Calliess and Ruffert (eds), above n 77, Art 295 EC, para 2.

[157] See also A Bleckmann, *Europarecht* (1990), para 450; E Klein in *id et al* (eds), *Handkommentar zum Vertrag über die Europäische Union (EUV/ EGV)* (1998), Art 222 EC Treaty, para 10.

[158] J Schwarze, *Daseinsvorsorge im Lichte des Wettbewerbsrechts* (2001) gives a good overview of the current discussion on the basic problems of this area; see F Löwenberg, *Service public und öffentliche Daseinsvorsorge* (2001), 207, for more information on the creation of Art 16 EC.

The content as well as the legal effects of these norms are anything but clear. They are supposed to strengthen, as shown in previous incidents, economic forms of operating for the good of society in the framework of a Community economic constitution in opposition to the model of a market economy governed purely by competition.[159] In this regard, Art 16 EC establishes a duty for the Community and Member States without in itself placing concrete powers at their disposal.[160] The regulations give no grounds for neither citizen's rights to provision of neither services nor the rights of affected businesses to self-defence. They make clear, as plainly shown in the remark as to "the place occupied by services of general economic interest in the shared values of the Union" and incidentally, recently supported, by Art 36 of the Charter, that these economic forms are an independent protected good of the EC Treaty. The regulation supports no reasons for equal alternatives to the market concept, as has been claimed in individual accusations, but rather allows recognition of the provisions of competitive conformity in Arts 73, 86 and 87 EC insist upon the principle compatibility of the provisions of elementary requirements with competition and market. Nothing other than this is valid for Art 36 of the Charter, which places access to services of general economic interest under the provisions of conformity with the EC Treaty.

b) Scope for Procedural Policy Formulation

A variety of possibilities for influencing the economic process is available to the Member States. The instruments of the Community are limited to supplementary or supportive interventions, with the exception of the all-important field of monetary policy. Budgetary policy measures in particular, such as forced public investment and national taxation policies, can have an influence on the business activities or can serve external fiscal interests. The framework conditions of the Community economic constitution must be observed, as in the cases of the newly named Eco-Tax or national debt policies. Particularly the budgetary supervision of the Commission under the auspices of Art 104 EC and the "Stability and Growth Pact",[161] developed as a supplement to aid in the avoidance of an "excessive government

[159] For more details, see S Rodriguez, 'Les services publics et le Traité d'Amsterdam' [1998], *Revue du Marché Commun* 37 at 40 *et seq*.

[160] CO Lenz in *id* (ed), *EG-Vertrag: Kommentar* (1999), Art 16 EC, para 6; A Hatje in Schwarze (ed), above n 38, Art 16 EC, para 7.

[161] This Pact consists of three acts: Resolution of the European Council on the Stability and Growth Pact [1997] OJ C 236/1; Council Reg 1466/97 on the strengthening of the surveillance of budgetary positions and the surveillance and coordination of economic policies [1997] OJ L 209/1; Council Reg 1467/97 on speeding up and clarifying the implementation of the excessive deficit procedure [1997] OJ L 209/6.

deficit" limit national scope for policy formulation immensely, as illustrated in the discussion about an "official warning" to the Federal Republic of Germany and to Portugal for accumulating new debt at or beyond the set limits. However, a wide spectrum of instruments remains available, which should be able to effect economic processes in the form of focussed employment policy.[162]

c) Scope for Distribution Policy

The scope for distribution policy formulation is in this respect more far-reaching than the creation of rate scales in the area of direct taxation, i.e. income tax, once left in the hands of national legislators.[163] Additionally in the area of creation of social security systems, the Member States retain a free hand, while at the same time the co-ordination and expansion of claims for services from other Member States have in this sense affected an opening. The basic decisions as to whether and how certain claims for social services (health insurance, annuity insurance, etc), are to be filled, are still reserved for the Member States. In this respect, the Member States have a broad scope for distribution, with the exception of those—moderate—influences subject to Community social regulations outlined above, which can be filled out by autonomous national political drafts.[164]

d) The Problem of System Competition

In these sectors of autonomous formulation, a "system competition" is taking place, whose legal classification in the framework of the EC Treaty is widely disputed. The thesis primarily represented in economic science, that trade rivalry is supplemented by the competition of national economic policy,[165] stands opposed to the Communities' goals (see Art 2 EC) of a harmonious, balanced and sustainable development of economic activities, a high degree of social protection and solidarity amongst the Member States. As such, competition between the systems is neither legally commanded nor forbidden; however, this competition is subject to Community controls

[162] See Steinle, above n 90, 45, provides a careful analysis of employment policy instruments.

[163] An approximation of direct taxation laws, if this makes sense at all from an economic point of view, can be based only on Art 94 EC, which requires a unanimous Council vote. The approximation of indirect taxation laws according to Art 93 EC is also subject to this procedural restriction.

[164] See, eg, U Becker, *Staat und autonome Träger im Sozialleistungsgesetz* (1996), 494 who discusses, in order to give examples, the various ways of providing social security in Europe in their respective constitutional surroundings.

[165] For more details, see Mussler, above n 25, 77; targeted on taxation competition and its limitations is J Wieland, 'Steuerwettbewerb in Europa' [2001] *Europarecht* 119, who, rather restrictively, perceives tax equity as a criterion for permissible competition, also considering Art 23(1) GG.

according to the Treaty goals and specific provisions concerning the co-ordination of national and European economic policies.

3. Limits of Discretionary Powers

The limits of economic policies of the States are formed, on the one hand, by the market economic orientation of the European economic constitution, which extends the prohibition against system change to the national level. On the other hand, the boundaries are defined by qualitative and quantitative standards of European law.

a) Market Economic Orientation

State economic policy as well as that of the Community must orient itself on the basic principles of an open market economy with free competition according to Arts 4 and 98 EC (see Arts 3 and 178 CT-IGC). The decision-making system thus also becomes an essential part of the national economic constitution, and must be in agreement with it. A change in system to a planned or centrally administered economy can therefore not be tolerated, even in the face of a broader scope for formulation. A positive aspect of this is that the orientation according to this basic principle should render "an efficient allocation of resources" possible, although judicial control is difficult to exercise.[166] Furthermore, national economic policy under Art 98 EC is bound to the goals of Art 2 EC, and should strive to reach a particularly stable, non-inflationary rate of growth.[167] With this comparatively general orientation, state activities below the barrier of system change cannot be hindered from causing delicate disturbances in the market mechanism. The Treaty, therefore, prescribes series of additional safeguards, which can be viewed as a system because of their connection with the goals of protection of market and competition. They limit financial as well as regulatory potential for intervention.

b) Quantitative Limitation of Financial Intervention Potential

The potential for financial intervention is limited above all by budget discipline based on Art 104 EC (see Art 184 CT-IGC), whereby the Member

[166] D Hattenberger in Schwarze (ed), above n 38, Art 98 EC, para 7, supports a normative commitment, as opposed to an explanation of the characteristics of an open competitive economy.

[167] As the reference in Art 98(2) EC to Art 4 EC shows, the economic union shall be above all a stability union. This norm provides for stable prices, healthy public finances and basic monetary conditions, as well as a regulated balance of payments. See R Bandilla in Grabitz and Hilf (eds), above n 131, Art 102a EC Treaty, para 5.

States must avoid "excessive government deficits". It serves the goals of stability of the monetary union, which would be endangered by expansive budget policies of the Member States as compensation for common European monetary policy instruments. The Commission's supervision of public debt levels installed for this purpose tangibly limits the scope for economic policy of most of the Member States. Particularly the 3 per cent mark for new debts incurred to the budget mentioned in the deficit protocol, relating the gross domestic product to market prices, proves to be a thoroughly effective boundary to short-term politically motivated intervention in trade of the Member States.

c) Proportionality as a Limit to Intervention

In the definition of market and competition protection, the basic principle of proportionality limits much more precisely financial and regulatory interventions by the state. Its application rests on the rule-exception principle, whereby the openness of the market and undistorted competition are the rule, and interferences with these guarantees of the European economic constitution require justification. As described many times, the Court of Justice has developed a finely-woven inspection programme out of the principle of proportionality, which can be used to test the compatibility of state economic policies with the guidelines of Community regulation and the guarantees contained within the system.

aa) Legitimisation Based upon European standards State interference with market freedoms and competition must be justified by legitimate purposes. This is just as valid for the fundamental freedoms of the Treaty as it is for the competition rules of Arts 81 *et seq* EC (see Arts 161 *et seq* CT-IGC). Regardless of whether an expressly protected good included in the list of permitted exceptions from freedoms is written or unwritten, there must be justification for interference. The fundamental freedoms are further limited by the fact that the reasons must be of a non-economic nature.

The granting of national subsidies under Art 87(3) EC follows according to the standards of European-defined support goals.[168] Solely in the area of services of general economic interest under Art 86 EC do the Member States have a final bit of state power of definition as to the goals and methods of the execution of public duties, for which a relative exemption of the service provider from the Treaties regulations can be claimed. The extent of the exemption is subject anew to a control regarding Community interests in an internal market with free competition.[169]

[168] For more information on the impact on the economic constitution, see, eg, Müller-Graff, above n 150, 443.

[169] F von Burchard, in Schwarze (ed), above n 38, Art 86 EC, para 77.

bb) Aptitude and Necessity as Precept of Minimum Intervention Interference must be both appropriate and necessary. The appropriateness of a measure for legitimate Community purposes opens a certain margin of appreciation for decision making to the Member States. However, the reasons must possibly be made clear for why the measure will have the desired effect.[170] The necessity of a measure is the obvious limit to state intervention. In the case of interventions in the fundamental freedoms in particular, the Court of Justice has emphasised that the intervening measures instigated by the State are only necessary when there are no other, equally efficient but less onerous, means available to serve the Communities aim. According to this, a measure is only allowed, as emphasised by the Court of Justice for free movement of goods, when "the same objective cannot be achieved by any measure which restricts the free movement of goods less".[171]

The granting of state aids follows a similar test, which contains a special comparison with the presumed results of an "undistorted self-powered competition".[172] First, when a prognostic benefit in favour of state interventions is established, the necessity can be confirmed. Furthermore, the relevant means or interventions in freedoms of the Treaty must be the least restrictive measures. Even exceptions to the competition rules of the Treaty especially for services of general economic interest in the sense of Art 86 EC (see Art 166 CT-IGC) can follow only within the boundaries of suitability, necessity, and appropriateness. On the other hand, the more recent judgments of the Court of Justice allow the conclusion that in accordance with general Community policies and the basic principle of Art 16 EC (see Art 122 CT-IGC), the Member States will be granted a relatively wide discretion within which they can make their decisions as to the type and means of such service provisions.[173] However, these conditions change nothing of the basic requirement for justification for exceptions to the "pure" market principle.

In this, the Community as well as the national potential for intervention has proven that a relatively clear preference in favour of cross-border freedom of competition is present. This relevant pre-adjustment of economically-oriented normative stipulations of Community law becomes clear at two points of the Treaty: Art 86 EC stipulates that undistorted competition may not be obstructed, even in the area of services of general economic interest, unless there are legitimate objectives for such limitations. The Treaty defines all forms of enterprise, whether public or private, as equal to one

[170] See U Kischel, 'Die Kontrolle der Verhältnismäßigkeit durch den Europäischen Gerichtshof' [2000] *Europarecht* 380 at 386 *et seq*.

[171] See Case 216/84 *Commission v France* [1988] ECR 793, para 7.

[172] See Müller-Graff, above n 153, 443.

[173] See Case C–320/91 *Corbeau* [1993] ECR I–2533; Case C–393/92 *Almelo* [1994] ECR I–1477; Case C–159/94 *Commission v France* [1997] ECR I–5815.

another and in this sense, is neutral. However, this neutrality finds its limits there where commercial activity "radiates" negatively on the competition in the internal market. It does not deal with a relationship of equality between activities conforming to or opposing competition, but only with the possibility of justifying forbidden interventions into competition within the framework of proportionality in the interest of the public. This is equally valid for the freedoms of the Treaty, which can only be limited under the requirements of strict proportionality.

V. PERSPECTIVES

The project of a European Constitution will fundamentally alter the architecture of primary law. Whether events cause an actual leap in the quality of the constitutional condition of the European Union is hardly predictable. Should this occur, the legal economic constitutional segments would surely be made relative, and fitted into a primary political framework of regulations within which the economy forms only a partial social system, and which must be subject to the primacy of politics, in case of doubt. For this very reason, effective protection of individual liberties is an absolute necessity, including the freedom of cross-border commerce and industry. This is not only an essential foundation for personal development, but also the central guarantee of a competitively constituted economic order.[174] Its express anchoring in the pattern of Art 4(1) EC and Arts 178 and 185 CT-IGC, has the invaluable advantage of giving economic policies a comparatively clear line. Above all, individual liberties cannot be minimised for economic policy reasons. Through this, equally effective forms of protection for social and other interests, which, as we have experienced, can only assert themselves in competition with great difficulty, would by no means be excluded if the EU were equipped with appropriate competences. In any case, the rule-exception ratio between competition and intervention as outlined above would remain.

[174] On the fundamental connection between economic freedom and personal freedom, see F Böhm, *Wirtschaftsordnung und Staatsverfassung* (1950), 50.

15

Competition Law as Part of the European Constitution

JOSEF DREXL

I. INTRODUCTION

1. Competition Law as Substantive Constitutional Law

THE LAW AGAINST restraints of competition—competition law—constitutes one of the central fields of regulation of European primary law. EC competition law relates neither to the organisation of European institutions nor to the rights of the citizens to be invoked against the Member States or the Union, and, in the context of a national legal system, competition law is not considered part of the political constitution. Nonetheless, inclusion of competition rules in the EC Treaty and a future Constitutional Treaty[1] provides sufficient reason for asking whether competition law should be considered part of the European economic constitution.[2]

The answer depends on the understanding of the term "constitution" in general and the term "economic constitution" in particular. The economic constitution has been a central theme of German legal and economic debate after World War II. The following analysis looks at this debate in order to gain a better understanding of the European situation.

There is no common understanding of the term "constitution". The term can be understood in the legal sense of the state constitution or as the

[1] On the 'economic constitution' of the Constitutional Treaty, see generally J Schwarze, 'Das wirtschaftsverfassungsrechtliche Konzept des Verfassungsentwurfs des Europäischen Konvents' [2004] *Zeitschrift für Europäisches Wirtschaftsrecht* 135.

[2] Even at an early stage, the ECJ viewed the EEC Treaty as the written constitution of the Community: Case 294/93 *Les Verts v Parliament* [1986] ECR 1339, para 23; Opinion 1/91, *EEA* [1991] ECR I–6079, para 21. In principle, supporting attribution of competition law to the constitution of the EU is D Briand-Méledo, 'Droit de la concurrence, droit constitutionnel substantiel de la Communauté européenne' [2004] *Revue trimestrielle de droit commercial* 205 at 208 *et seq* (reacting to the earlier version of this article).

description of the actual state of a given society. Accordingly, a distinction should be made between the normative reading on the one hand and a purely economic reading of the term "economic constitution" on the other hand. From a legal perspective, the EC Treaty's rules on competition law, contained in Arts 81 *et seq* EC, would be part of this European economic constitution.[3]

However, this normative understanding has to face counterarguments. On the one hand, the EC Treaty, as part of the current European constitutional document, and the Constitutional Treaty include detailed provisions on the economy which would not necessarily be taken up in a nation's constitution. On the other hand, defining the European constitution only by primary Community law proves to be much too narrow in the case of competition law. Today, merger law, regulated by secondary law, constitutes an essential part of European competition law.[4] Implementation Regulation No 1/2003[5] defines the relationship between Community competition law and the law of its Member States, which strongly influences the enforcement mechanism and the whole institutional and constitutional power structure of enforcement bodies in the field.

For further analysis, only a mixed economic-normative understanding of the economic constitution can provide theoretical insights.[6] In post-war Germany, Nipperdey defined the economic constitution as the complete body of rules and provisions designed to guarantee the necessary elements and safeguards of the economic model that is deemed to be best.[7] This mixed economic-normative understanding separates the essential normative guarantees of the ideal economic system from less important regulatory provisions. Economic thought defines which rules and provisions are essential for the establishment of the ideal economic system and which already existing rules and provisions merit inclusion in the economic constitution, whether they are included in the written state constitution or not. In addition, in a democratic society in which the constitution leaves it to the parliament to decide on economic regulation, the term "economic constitution" has to be interpreted openly. In this sense, Fikentscher formulates as follows:[8]

> The economic constitution, in a contemporary sense, is constituted by the sum of constitutional and other fundamental legal provisions, even by the lack of

[3] See C-D Ehlermann, 'Wettbewerbspolitik im Binnenmarkt' [1993] *Recht der Internationalen Wirtschaft* 793, naming competition as a European constitutional principle.

[4] Reg 139/2004 on the control of concentrations between undertakings (the EC Merger Regulation) [2004] OJ L 24/1.

[5] Reg 1/2003 on the implementation of the rules on competition laid down in Arts 81 and 82 of the Treaty [2003] OJ L 1/1.

[6] On different definitions of the economic constitution, see J Drexl, *Die wirtschaftliche Selbstbestimmung des Verbrauchers* (1998), 221 *et seq*.

[7] HC Nipperdey, 'Die Grundprinzipien des Wirtschaftsverfassungsrechts' in H Wandersleb and E Traumann (eds), *Recht—Staat—Wirtschaft* (1951), iii, 223 at 225.

[8] W Fikentscher, *Wirtschaftsrecht* (1983), ii, 23.

> such provisions, which regulate the fundamental relationship of the economy, the state and its citizens. This constitution may be based on a conscious decision either for or against planning and order or on a more or less conscious decision against interference in the economy.[9]

This is where one has to locate the political decision in favour of competition. Franz Böhm, the most renowned ordoliberal legal scholar,[10] characterised competition as a constitutional institution (*Verfassungseinrichtung*).[11] Accordingly, the European orientation of the Maastricht Treaty, as expressed in Art 4(1) EC and Art III-69(1) CT-Conv (Art 177(1) CT-IGC), aims towards an "open market economy with free competition"; this marks the European economic constitution's favour for a particular economic system. From a normative perspective, the safeguards of particular economic functions, in the framework of the European economic constitution, consist first and foremost in the fundamental freedoms and in European competition law. Only these functional guarantees may be applied by the courts effectively;[12] at the same time, they give more precision to the decision in favour of the market economy with free competition. With those functional guarantees, European competition law protects the market economy and the competition model against restraints of competition. Additional reference to the social market economy in Art I-3(3) CT-Conv (Art 3(3) CT-IGC) confirms that, in applying the fundamental freedoms, Member States may set rules to safeguard certain mandatory requirements, and that competition promotes broader social distribution of wealth than does a monopoly. Consequently, European competition law, irrespective of its legal basis in primary or secondary law, constitutes an integral part of the substantive constitutional law of the European Community.

2. Competition Law and Constitutional Principles

Having attributed competition law to substantive European law, the resulting question relates to the integration of competition law within European constitutional law. Analysing the possible interaction between European competition law and general principles of the European constitution would underline the coherence of European constitutional law. From this research, important consequences might be drawn for Community law at large and even for the solution of individual legal problems.

Recently, Armin von Bogdandy discussed the influence of general constitutional principles on European competition law.[13] Such homogeneity of the

[9] Translation by the author.

[10] See DJ Gerber, *Law and Competition in Twentieth Century Europe* (1998), 234.

[11] F Böhm, 'Wettbewerbsfreiheit und Kartellrecht' [1958] *ORDO* 167 at 196.

[12] For a similar result see J Basedow, *Von der deutschen zur europäischen Wirtschaftsverfassung* (1992), 32.

[13] A von Bogdandy, 'Rechtsgleichheit, Rechtssicherheit und Subsidiarität im transnationalen Wirtschaftsrecht' [2001] *Zeitschrift für Europäisches Wirtschaftsrecht* 357.

political and the economic constitutions can easily be argued in the light of the ordoliberal ideas of the Freiburg School,[14] which assigns the state an active role in guaranteeing the principal elements of the order on which the ideal form of the economy relies. This school, with its idea of interrelating orders, especially of the constitutional and the economic orders (*Interdependenz der Ordnungen*), had a direct influence on the inclusion of competition law as part of the new Community law.[15] According to ordoliberal thought, the economic order has to conform to the constitutional principles of the social order and has to transpose these principles into the economic sphere. The economic constitution, consequently, shares the objectives and the principles of the constitution of the society and the state. Competition law, along with its economic objectives, gains a political, i.e., a democratic and freedom-oriented dimension.

So far, the impact of the economic constitution on the understanding of general constitutional principles of Community law has not been analysed. But one must take care not to analyse exclusively the impact of general constitutional principles on competition law without considering the reverse impact. This would raise an imminent concern that well-known constitutional principles, like democracy, equal rights and subsidiarity,[16] would be misapplied to competition law by not taking into account the particular economic background and reasoning of the economic constitution. Furthermore, consideration of the impact of competition law on general constitutional principles may influence the theoretical understanding of Community law wherever Community law is applied in an economic context.

In the following, we will first look a little closer at the subject matter of the economic constitution (II) in order to analyse the impact of general constitutional principles on competition law (III) and the impact of competition law on the understanding of constitutional principles (IV). As a conclusion, a number of European constitutional principles emerging from competition law will be formulated (IV. 3).

II. COMPETITION LAW AS PART OF THE ECONOMIC CONSTITUTION

1. The German Concept of the Economic Constitution

The understanding of the term economic constitution, as it was developed in Germany since 1949, can be traced back to two sources. The first source

[14] See generally DJ Gerber, 'Constitutionalizing the Economy: German Neoliberalism, Competition Law and the "New" Europe' (1995) 42 *AJCL* 25; Gerber, above n 10, 232 *et seq.*

[15] *Ibid*, 261 *et seq.*

[16] These are the principles considered by von Bogdandy, above n 13, 362 *et seq.*

relates to the debate concerning the new Constitution, the *Grundgesetz*, and the question of whether the Constitution makes a particular economic model legally binding. The second source has already been mentioned: the Freiburg School, which argued in favour of a particular economic model not just on the basis of economics, but also with political and constitutional arguments flowing from the idea of interrelating orders of economy and society.

a) German Constitutional Debate After 1949

In Germany, existence of an "economic constitution" was known from the Weimar Constitution which, in its provisions beginning with Art 151, included principles and rules relating to the economy.[17] Nipperdey, after 1949, tried to explain that the new *Grundgesetz* would constitutionally guarantee the "social market economy".[18]

However, the Federal Constitutional Court rejected this theory in 1954 and today opts for an understanding of the "relative economic openness" of the *Grundgesetz*.[19] Despite the lack of any clear statement in the *Grundgesetz* on a particular economic model, its provisions prohibit extreme economic models. The principle of social justice (*Sozialstaat*) contradicts a totally unregulated *laissez-faire* liberalism. A centralised socialist command-economy would conflict with the constitutional guarantees of individual freedom and private property. Consequently, the economic constitution as such is no independent argument for testing the constitutionality of the law.[20] Nevertheless, the legislator is especially bound by the economic fundamental rights.[21] In order to identify the German economic constitution in the mixed economic-normative sense, the law inferior to the constitution has to be considered as well.

b) The Ordoliberal Model (Freiburg School)

Ordoliberal ideas of the Freiburg School had a crucial impact on the development of the economic system in post-war West Germany. Most influential were the theories of the economist Walter Eucken.

[17] Most interestingly, Art 165 even provided for a particular institutional arrangement, namely a hierarchy of Economic Councils.

[18] HC Nipperdey, *Die soziale Marktwirtschaft in der Verfassung der Bundesrepublik Deutschland* (1954); HC Nipperdey, *Soziale Marktwirtschaft und Grundgesetz* (1965).

[19] *Entscheidungen des Bundesverfassungsgerichts* 4, 7 at 17 *et seq* (*Investitionshilfe*); affirmed by 12, 354 (*VW-Privatisierung*); 30, 292 (*Erdölbevorratung*); explicitly 50, 290 at 338 (*Mitbestimmung*).

[20] In 1990 the social market economy was legally declared to be the economic model of reunified Germany in Art 1(3) of the Treaty on the Creation of a Monetary, Economic and Social Union. This Treaty, however, has no constitutional character. See P Häberle, 'Soziale Marktwirtschaft als "Dritter Weg"' [1993] *Zeitschrift für Rechtspolitik* 383 at 388 *et seq*.

[21] In more depth see Drexl, above n 6, 220 *et seq*.

Shaped by the experience with Nazi dictatorship and the war, he quested for the most appropriate, i.e., most human economic model. Thereby, he crossed the border from descriptive to normative economics. Eucken called for protection of individual freedom in all respects, i.e., in the context of different "orders", the political order of the society and the economic order. According to his view, society should prefer the "order" that protects most effectively the individual freedom of the citizens from economic dominance.[22]

According to Eucken, neither the economy of central planning nor the unregulated *laissez-faire* market economy offers an appropriate answer to his question of the most appropriate economic order. Economic dominance and dependence can also develop in the context of the market economy in the form of monopolistic structures.[23] Consequently, only a particular form of the market economy should be established, namely the economy of competition.[24] Political freedom as such would not guarantee economic freedom to all members of society. On the contrary, competitors would abuse their freedoms in order to exclude competition through cartels and monopolisation and, hence, to restrain the economic freedom of other market participants.[25]

Thereby, Eucken managed to transfer the freedom paradox from politics to economics. Individual freedom needs to be protected against self-abolition. According to Eucken, the state has a duty to establish the economy according to specific principles. It has to guarantee the conditions under which a well-functioning and humane economic order—in the form of an order of competition—may flourish.[26] At the same time, the state must restrict itself to the establishment of the framework in which the competition order can develop on the basis of self-determined planning by the economic agents. By no means should the state itself direct economic processes.[27]

In view of the institutional guarantees of the competition order, Eucken distinguished constitutive and regulatory principles.[28] The constitutive principles are designed to establish the competition order; the regulatory principles

[22] W Eucken, 'Das ordnungspolitische Problem' [1948] *ORDO* 56. See also P Oberender, 'Der Einfluß theoretischer Prinzipien Walter Euckens auf die deutsche Wirtschaftspolitik nach dem Zweiten Weltkrieg' [1989] *ORDO* 321.

[23] *Ibid*, 199.

[24] Eucken advocated what he called 'complete competition' (*vollständiger Wettbewerb*): Eucken, above n 22, 201. Under the conditions of complete competition, market data cannot be influenced by the acts of individual market participants. This concept was rightly rejected in Germany in early years: see K Borchardt and W Fikentscher, *Wettbewerb, Wettbewerbsbeschränkung, Marktbeherrschung* (1957). See also the more recent publication by W Fikentscher, 'Competition Rules for Private Agents in the GATT/WTO System' [1994] *Außenwirtschaft* 281 at 305 *et seq*.

[25] See, eg, W Eucken, 'Die Wettbewerbsordnung und ihre Verwirklichung' [1949] *ORDO* 1 at 4 *et seq*.

[26] *Ibid*, 7.

[27] *Ibid*, 93.

[28] For more details on these principles, see 2 below.

keep this order in a well-functioning state.[29] In this context, Eucken himself used the term "economic constitution". All these principles would serve to establish a functioning price-system of complete competition as a fundamental principle of the economic constitution and as a criterion for controlling economic measures taken by the state.[30]

Eucken did not envision legal protection of these principles as part of the state constitution. He rather advocated a purely political commitment of decision makers to the establishment of the most appropriate competition order.

c) Concept of Interrelating Orders

With the idea of interrelating orders, ordoliberalism associates the economic order with the constitutional, legal and state orders. Establishment of the "most humane" order—in Eucken's sense—corresponds with the *Grundgesetz*, which in its Art 1(1) protects human dignity as the most important value of the new constitution.

In Germany, the idea of interrelating orders still has force, though largely unnoticed. More recent developments in German constitutional law, especially the concept of a constitutional obligation of the legislature and the courts to "materialise" the understanding of the freedom of contract principle,[31] are characterised by ordoliberal thought. Accordingly, intervention by state authorities in the field of contract law is not, at least not decisively, justified by social reasoning; rather, it results from a "material" understanding of freedom of contract, protected as a particular expression of individual freedom by Art 2(1) of the *Grundgesetz*. Such a constitutional obligation changes the private law understanding of freedom of contract from 1900, the year when the German Civil Code came into effect. Nevertheless, it corresponds with the principles of the market economy.[32]

2. The Private Law Society as the Basis of a Social Competition Order

According to ordoliberal thinking, guaranteeing competition by legal means deserves highest priority. Eucken defines control of monopolies as one of his regulatory principles. As constitutive principles, he lists the importance of

[29] See Eucken, above n 25, 32 *et seq*.
[30] *Ibid*, 33.
[31] See, eg, the decision of the Federal Constitutional Court of 19 October 1993: *Entscheidungen des Bundesverfassungsgerichts* 89, 214 (controlling personal securities given by family members); see also 81, 242 (protecting commercial representatives against post-contractual prohibitions of competition).
[32] Eucken claimed control of standard contract terms deviating from non-mandatory contract rules of the Code: *id*, above n 25, 64 *et seq*. Even before Eucken, the ordoliberal lawyer H Großmann-Doerth, *Das selbstgeschaffene Recht der Wirtschaft* (1933), submitted a similar proposal.

monetary policy, the principle of open markets, consistent economic policy, private property, freedom of contract as well as contractual and tort liability. These principles unveil that competition law has to rely on the existence of central elements of the private law system.

It was left to the Freiburg law professor Franz Böhm to bring more legal precision to the interrelation between the competition order and the private law society. Relying on concepts of justice, Böhm characterises competition as a social institution:[33]

> Competition defines not only the level of economic performance, in which politicians concerned with growth are understandably most interested, but also the level of freedom and social justice attained in a free market society.[34]

According to Böhm, existence of the private law society is a constitutional condition for the market economy.[35] With the principle of party autonomy, the private law society expresses itself as a society of peers. This society provides the conditions under which competition can work to steer the economy.

Thereby, Böhm successfully explains the mutually functional relationship between economic behaviour based on party autonomy and competition. Namely, commercial freedom as a particular form of party autonomy can only be justified where competition is capable of producing social results.[36] Freedom of contract—and abuse of it—is controlled by competition. Conversely, competition can only exist and develop on the basis of freedom of contract and the private law society.

Ordoliberalism does not advocate pushing the state away from involvement in the economy. Rather, the state has a positive role and the responsibility for an order-principled design of market rules. Therefore, Böhm claims that the state should formulate the "rules of the game" and intervene whenever individuals abuse their freedom of contract. Böhm opposes any "cheating as a source of income", such as unfair competition, usury, monopolising and political pressure on the legislator with the intention to establish "cheating" as part of the legislative programme.[37]

From a constitutional law perspective, the arguments put forward by Böhm are still of major interest for several reasons: (i) Böhm adopts a material concept of freedom of contract by acknowledging the danger of its abuse. In this sense, he anticipates the case-law of the German Federal Constitutional Court mentioned above.[38] (ii) Based on the ideas of Böhm, it

[33] F Böhm, 'Freiheit und Ordnung in der Marktwirtschaft' [1971] *ORDO* 11 at 20.
[34] Translated by the author.
[35] For more details, see F Böhm, 'Privatrechtsgesellschaft und Marktwirtschaft' [1966] *ORDO* 75.
[36] See Böhm, above n 33, 21.
[37] See Böhm, above n 35, 140.
[38] See above n 31.

is possible to explain why the material, not formal interpretation of freedom of contract makes perfect economic sense. The market can only fulfil its steering function for the economy if the individual market participants can make their economic decisions without suffering restraints from monopoly power. (iii) The ordoliberal and the constitutional understandings of individual freedom coincide. Individual freedom is the purpose and the precondition of a functioning market economy and the competition order. (iv) Both the private law society and individual freedom require legal protection of competition. Competition law thus has a constitutive function for the private law society and individual freedom.

In ordoliberal thought, constitutional and private law reasoning converge in the field of competition law. Therefore, competition law can be considered substantive constitutional law. This is why it is possible to analyse competition law in the light of general constitutional principles and why we may even try to discuss and solve problems of constitutional law with arguments drawn from competition law and private law.

3. The European Economic Constitution from a German Perspective

In the following, the analysis will determine whether the constitutional understanding of competition law also holds true in the context of Community law. As first step, it will be necessary to ascertain the existence of a European economic constitution in the ordoliberal sense. As second step, different views of the European economic constitution need to be evaluated on the background of existing Community law (see 4).

a) The Economic Constitution of the EC Treaty

The EC Treaty includes essential elements of an economic constitution, as ordoliberal theories prescribe for the establishment of the preferred competition order. In light of Art 4(1) EC, obliging the Member States and the Community to adapt their economic policies to the model of an "open market economy with free competition", the constitutional commitment of the EC to the competition model cannot be denied. Nevertheless, the existence of a number of special policies with an interventionist approach conflicts with an ordoliberal understanding of the European economic constitution. This is especially true for the poorly market-oriented Common Agricultural Policy and the industrial policy provision of Art 157 EC.[39] However, these exceptions to the system do not in principle disprove the order-minded decision in favour of the market economy and the competition order.[40]

[39] Neither of these areas will be revised by the Constitutional Treaty: see Arts III–121–128 and III–180 CT–Conv (Arts 225–232 and 279 CT–IGC).

[40] Because of these frictions, Basedow characterises Art 4(1) EC as a Bohemian decision: *id*, above n 12, 32.

Whereas it is possible to identify an economic constitution within the establishing Treaties or the future European Constitution without particular problems, it is rather difficult to describe the precise nature of this constitution. In the following, we will discuss four different interpretations supported in German scholarship.

b) Functional Integration Model According to Ipsen

Hans Peter Ipsen characterises the Community as a "purposeful unit of functional integration" (*Zweckverband funktionaler Integration*).[41] Indeed, Community law pursues economic integration of the Member States. The major projects of European unification—the common market, the internal market, the economic and monetary union—mark the progress of this integration.

From a constitutional perspective, Ipsen relies on a powerful and regulatory state.[42] This view is very convincing with regard to Community agricultural policy. Nevertheless, European competition law would also fit into the picture. Competition law pursues the overall objectives of establishing the common market (Art 81 *et seq* EC) and the internal market (Art 3(1)(g) EC). This particular integrationist functionality distinguishes European from national competition law. European competition law has to prevent private parties from dividing the common market among themselves by restraints of competition. With the view that the common market and the internal market need to be established and guaranteed by law, especially against restraints of competition, the functional approach of the drafters of the establishing Treaties reflect ordoliberal thought.

c) The Liberal Model According to Mestmäcker

Beyond the mere integration objective, Ernst-Joachim Mestmäcker proposes a particular substantive law character of the European economic constitution. According to Mestmäcker, Europe accepted the establishment of an open society of citizens as the ultimate purpose of the European economic constitution.[43] European constitutional law should guarantee this society of the citizens (*Bürgergesellschaft*).[44]

Mestmäcker introduces another level of legitimacy which relies on a particular understanding of the relationship between the state and the economy.

[41] HP Ipsen, *Europäisches Gemeinschaftsrecht* (1972), 196 and 1055.

[42] For this reason, A von Bogdandy, 'Beobachtungen zur Wissenschaft vom Europarecht' [2001] *Der Staat* 3 at 28, identifies Ipsen as a representative of traditional German public economic law.

[43] On this purpose, even beyond Community law, see E-J Mestmäcker, 'Der Kampf ums Recht in der offenen Gesellschaft' [1989] *Rechtstheorie* 273.

[44] See E-J Mestmäcker, 'On the Legitimacy of European Law' [1994] *Rabels Zeitschrift für ausländisches und internationales Privatrecht* 615 at 633 *et seq*; E-J Mestmäcker, 'Zur Wirtschaftsverfassung in der Europäischen Union in R Hasse (ed), *Ordnung in Freiheit* (1994), 263.

Accordingly, Community law restrains the regulatory power of the Member States with the objective of deregulating the economy, thereby providing room for the evolution of the European society of the citizens. The advantages of Community law are not to be found in the establishment of a centralised regulatory unit for the whole of the European Union, but in controlling the power of Member States in regulating the economy.[45]

Mestmäcker and ordoliberal theory share the particular orientation toward individual freedom. However, Mestmäcker distrusts the state, whereas ordoliberal thinking only rejects the interventionist state in favour of a powerful state, which sets rules and guarantees the conditions for a functioning economy. Mestmäcker is closer to Friedrich August von Hayek, who deemed it more important to protect individual freedom against the state than against economic dominance of other private market participants.[46]

Mestmäcker's concepts risk to collide with existing Community law. Certainly, essential elements of a deregulating law may be identified in the body of primary Community law, in particular to the extent that it limits the regulatory power of the Member States. This is especially true for the fundamental freedoms. However, the free flow of goods, persons, services and capital is not guaranteed without exception. National limitations to the fundamental freedoms may still be justified by mandatory requirements. In addition, the fundamental freedoms only provide for the application of the principle of the country of origin. Consequently, cross-border transactions are not totally freed from national limitations. Traders and consumers are only protected in that they may trade and buy products according to the law of the country of origin. Finally, the European legislature itself may pass specific regulation provided that the conditions for the internal market are thereby improved.[47] In doing so, the European legislature is obliged to protect certain requirements, in particular those of consumer protection (Arts 95(3) and 153(3)(a) EC) and protection of the environment (Arts 95(3) and 174(2) EC). Whereas Mestmäcker considers only a constitution of freedom as the legitimate European constitution, the existing European constitution integrates a whole range of different substantive policies.

The approach by Mestmäcker and Hayek does not take due account of the existing constitution. No wonder Hayek at one point proposed a constitutional reform[48] in order to abolish the welfare state.[49] In contrast,

[45] See E-J Mestmäcker, 'Soziale Marktwirtschaft und Europäisierung des Rechts' in E-J Mestmäcker, *Wirtschaft und Verfassung in der Europäischen Union* (2003), 288 at 294 (on the functionality of harmonisation in the internal market).

[46] For a comparison of Hayek's and Eucken's theories, see Drexl, above n 6, 103 *et seq*.

[47] This is explicitly stated in Case C–376/98 *Germany v Parliament and Council* [2000] ECR I–8599 (Tobacco Advertising Directive).

[48] See FA von Hayek, *The Constitution of Liberty* (1960).

[49] See FA von Hayek, 'The Weasel Word "Social"' (1983) 1 *The Salisbury Review* 4 (criticising the lack of precision of the word 'social').

ordoliberalism and its concept of interrelating orders are in conformity with the existing constitution. The social argument is part of ordoliberalism which supports a material understanding of individual freedom. Ordoliberalism was further developed in the model of the so-called social market economy.[50] Conversely, the approach of Mestmäcker cannot provide a conclusive explanation for the relationship between competition law and general European constitutional law.

d) Constitution of the Citizens According to Reich

Similar to Mestmäcker, Norbert Reich also supports an understanding of Community law as a constitution of the citizens. Unlike Mestmäcker, however, Reich does not pursue acceptance of a concept of economic freedom. He rather looks at Community law as the legal basis of extensive rights of the citizens.[51]

In the field of European economic law, Reich argues in favour of a transfer of constitutional principles. In doing so, Reich draws conclusions that, he himself fully admits, are not in conformity with the ECJ's interpretation of Community law. Nevertheless, Reich promotes his conclusions as an expression of the civil society.

The most striking example of this relates to the interpretation and application of fundamental freedoms in light of the equal protection principle. Reich prefers an understanding of these freedoms as generally applicable civil rights, granted not only to foreigners but also to the Member States' own nationals. Under Art 12(1) EC, reverse discrimination would have to be considered illegal,[52] whereas the ECJ traditionally adheres to the concept that the fundamental freedoms only apply to cross-border situations.

Reich defines fundamental freedoms as "subjective public rights".[53] This seems to be justified by the fact that the freedoms are addressed to the Member States. At the least, the application of the equal protection principle and the concept of fundamental freedoms as civil rights are not convincing with respect to domestic law provisions relating to private law. Actually, such cases arise frequently, as in the area of national intellectual property, domestic provisions on unfair competition and mandatory contract law.[54]

[50] See eg A Müller-Armack, 'Die Wirtschaftsordnungen sozial gesehen' [1948] *ORDO* 125.

[51] See N Reich, *Bürgerrechte in der Europäischen Union* (1999).

[52] *Ibid*, 65. In an earlier article, N Reich, 'Binnenmarkt als Rechtsbegriff' [1991] *Europäische Zeitschrift für Wirtschaftsrecht* 203, tried to justify the illegality of reverse discrimination by the internal market concept. See also the criticism of Reich's approach by J Drexl, 'Review' (2001) 38 *CML Rev* 471 at 476 *et seq*.

[53] See Reich, above n 51, 450 *et seq*.

[54] As to the last situation, see Case C–93/92 *CMC Motorradcenter* [1993] ECR I–5009, on the German precontractual liability rule of *culpa in contrahendo*, with some not very convincing reasoning by the Court.

In the field of private law, equal protection is not a generally accepted principle. On the contrary, the rules of private international law—conflict of laws—frequently lead to the application of different national rules in national and transnational cases. The potential relevance of foreign law may even mandate different treatment in a given case.[55] As a matter of justice, the principle of the application of the most adequate law has to override formally equal protection.

These very few ideas do not contradict an understanding of fundamental freedoms as subjective public rights. However, as the following will show, Reich's approach does not sufficiently take into account the private law perspective. For the development of a counter-approach, one might consider a transfer of competition and private law reasoning to the interpretation of fundamental freedoms.

e) Subjective Private Rights According to Fikentscher and Schubert and the European Private Law Development

In view of placing competition law within the framework of the European constitution, it may be most successful to construe economic freedom as a subjective right protected under Community law.

In Germany, Wolfgang Fikentscher argues in favour of an "economic personality right".[56] This right has been developed on the basis of a private law understanding of the market freedoms in the EC Treaty as the source of the general acceptance of a corresponding subjective private right of economic freedom.[57]

More extensively than Fikentscher, Thure Schubert, in a more recent publication, presented an explanation of why the economic freedoms of the EC Treaty should be understood not only as subjective public rights directed against state authorities but also in a private law sense as an economic personality right.[58] Schubert relies on the notion of the common market of the EC Treaty and distinguishes between the functions of the fundamental freedoms and of competition law. The fundamental freedoms are conceived of as specific rights of freedom.[59] From competition law he draws a subjective law guarantee of the freedom to compete.[60] According to Schubert, this

[55] See eg K Siehr, *Internationales Privatrecht* (2001), 358.
[56] See Finkentscher, above n 8, 112 *et seq* and 132 *et seq*. This right constitutes an analogy with the acceptance of a 'general personality right' (*Allgemeines Persönlichkeitsrecht*) protecting the interests of a person against interference especially with his or her privacy by others under German tort law. This development took place after World War II under the influence of the human dignity clause of Art 1(1) of the Grundgesetz.
[57] *Ibid*, 132.
[58] See T Schubert, *Der Gemeinsame Markt als Rechtsbegriff* (1999), 418.
[59] *Ibid*, 186 *et seq*.
[60] *Ibid*, 220 *et seq*.

freedom to compete constitutes a value protected by European competition law.[61]

Both Fikentscher and Schubert develop their ideas in light of tort protection of economic freedom against other private parties, which may be justified under German law with the recognition of an economic personality right. According to the general clause of § 823(1) of the German Civil Code, tort liability in principle depends on a violation of a specific right protected against everybody else (absolute rights). The wording of the provision is flexible enough to enable the courts to recognise new absolutely protected rights. By acknowledging an economic personality right that meets the requirements of § 823(1) it would no longer be necessary to prove that a certain act violates a law specifically protecting the claimant as required by § 823(2) of the Code.[62]

It is interesting to see that, in the *Courage* case,[63] the ECJ accepted the Community law principle according to which national law has to provide for a right of private parties to recover damages suffered from a restraint of competition. However, this case-law still requires a violation of European competition law. Therefore, under German law, the claim would still have to be based on § 823(2) of the Civil Code along with Art 81(1) EC.

It is not necessary to decide on the merits of broader tort protection based on § 823(1) of the Code. It suffices to note that the ideas of Fikentscher and Schubert are important for a private law understanding of European competition law. Rooted firmly in the tradition of Franz Böhm, they transfer ordoliberal theory on the interaction of competition law and the private legal order to Community law and apply this theory to European economic law at large.

The growing literature on European private law is also developing similar ideas. The fundamental freedoms are increasingly considered for their relevance to private law at large and, more specifically, as the Community law basis for contractual freedom.[64] According to a modern understanding, the fundamental freedoms and European competition law do not themselves constitute the legal basis for the principle of freedom of contract. They recognise and thereby guarantee the existence and legal effect of this principle as part of the legal systems of the Member States.[65] The private law of

[61] *Ibid*, 259.

[62] In this sense, see Schubert, above n 58, 429 *et seq*, arguing in favour of special protection of small and medium-sized businesses as a matter of European competition law, although only German competition law contains specific rules on such protection.

[63] See Case C–453/99, above n 63; see also AP Komninos, 'New Prospects for Private Enforcement of EC Competition' (2002) 39 *CML Rev* 447; T Eilmansberger, 'Schadenersatz wegen Kartellverstoßes' [2002] *ecolex* 28.

[64] According to S Grundmann, 'EG-Richtlinie und nationales Privatrecht' [1996] *Juristenzeitung* 274 at 278; *id*, *Europäisches Schuldvertragsrecht* (1999), para 52, the fundamental freedoms have the objective of extending freedom of contract beyond borders.

[65] In a similar sense see P von Wilmowsky, 'Der internationale Verbrauchervertrag im EG-Binnenmarkt' [1995] *Zeitschrift für Europäisches Privatrecht* 735 at 736 *et seq*.

the Member States enables private economic actors to take advantage of the fundamental freedoms and thereby have an impact on European law.[66]

It follows that the fundamental freedoms protect the freedom to conclude cross-border contracts. This protection is two-pronged: on the one hand, the freedom of the individual to conclude contracts across borders is protected against undue interference by the Member States. On the other hand, freedom of contract is also a principle applied between private parties. This principle vests power in the individual economic agent to regulate her or his own legal affairs in co-ordination with the other parties of the contract. Following German legal terminology, one might be tempted to characterise the fundamental freedoms as both subjective public and subjective private rights.

The interpretation of the fundamental freedoms as subjective private rights is supported by the ECJ's interpretation of the fundamental freedoms not only as rights of undertakings but also of consumers.[67]

Nevertheless, it would not be appropriate to conceive of the fundamental freedoms as a guarantee of economic freedom in the most liberal and formal Hayekian sense. Member States may justify limitations of the freedom-of-contract principle by mandatory requirements. In particular, such requirements may arise from the need to protect consumers,[68] especially in the context of contract law.[69] For application of the fundamental freedoms in consumer contract cases, the rights of all private parties involved need to be considered with regard to the principle of proportionality. Community law shares this particular legal methodology with the recognition of fundamental rights in the framework of German private law. Under European law, however, it is more difficult to discover the conflicting rights of different private parties behind the veil of the conflict between the fundamental freedoms and the domestic law of the Member States. Nevertheless, this conflict between private rights exists and should be taken into account for the application of the fundamental freedoms.

[66] In this sense see P-C Müller-Graff, 'Privatrecht und europäisches Gemeinschaftsrecht' in *id* (ed), *Gemeinsames Privatrecht in der Europäischen Gemeinschaft* (1993) 195 at 203 *et seq*; *id*, 'Europäisches Gemeinschaftsrecht und Privatrecht' [1993] *Neue Juristische Wochenschrift* 13 at 14; see also O Remien, 'Illusion und Realität eines europäischen Privatrechts' [1992] *Juristenzeitung* 277 at 283 *et seq*; C Schmidt-Leithoff, 'Gedanken über die Privatrechtsordnungen als Grundlage zum EWG-Vertrag' in M Löwisch (ed), *Beiträge zum Handels- und Wirtschaftsrecht* (1991), 597.

[67] See Case C–362/88 *GB-Inno-BM* [1990] ECR I–667, para 8, expressly acknowledging a consumer's right to buy in another Member State according to the legal rules of that State. The meaning of the fundamental freedoms as consumer rights is also pointed out by Schubert, above n 58, 189 *et seq*. The consumer orientation of the fundamental freedoms is most apparent in respect of the freedom to provide services. A consumer who crosses borders in order to buy services may not be discriminated against under the law of the receiving state: see Case 186/87 *Cowan* [1989] ECR 195.

[68] See, in particular, for the principle of free movement of goods, the *Cassis de Dijon* case: Case 120/78 *Rewe* [1979] ECR 649.

[69] See Case 382/87 *Buet* [1989] ECR 1235 (on the French prohibition on doorstep selling of educational products).

4. The Economic Constitution from a Community Law Perspective

a) Legitimacy of an Ordoliberal Approach to the European Economic Constitution

Doubts may be expressed as to whether an ordoliberal understanding of the European economic constitution is legitimate in the first place. Indeed, the particularly German concept of the relationship between the state and the economy does not necessarily correlate with the experiences and the economic and political beliefs and traditions in other Member States.[70]

However, there is historical evidence of the influence of German ordoliberalism on the Rome "constitution" of the EEC Treaty. Important European figures of German origin contributed to the drafting of the Treaty and the development of Community law during the first few years; Walter Hallstein and Hans von der Groeben, in particular, had direct contacts with the Freiburg School and were strongly influenced by their ideas.[71] In addition, the purpose of the discussion of ordoliberal theory in this analysis is not to draw mandatory conclusions for the interpretation of Community law. The analysis is rather an attempt to integrate the economic part of Community law into the European constitution, from which conclusions can be drawn for the understanding and interpretation of Community law. Consequently, the analysis has to focus on existing Community law.

b) Objectives of European Competition Law

A detailed analysis of European competition law in light of the practice of the relevant institutions (i.e., the Commission, the European Court of First Instance and the European Court of Justice) produces a whole bundle of different objectives. Such an analysis has already been undertaken several times[72] and, therefore, will not be repeated here in detail.

The particular integrationist objective of European competition law is expressed in many decisions. This is why especially the territorial division of the common market is considered a restraint of competition.[73]

In addition, EC competition law has to combat all restraints of competition affecting the common market in order to guarantee the steering function of competition law in the market economy. In the terminology of neoclassical economics, competition has to guarantee efficient market results. Competition and competition law are thought to achieve economic benefits for the European economy.

In a number of decisions, the ECJ has associated a restraint of competition with a restraint of the freedom of economic agents to make independent

[70] See Mélédo, above n 2 (expressing a French reaction to the ideas presented here on the German ordoliberal concept of an economic constitution).

[71] For further information, see Gerber, above n 10, 263–5.

[72] See Schubert above n 58, 235 *et seq*.

[73] As a first important case, see Case 56/64 *Consten et al v Commission* [1966] ECR 321, paras 16 and 28 *et seq*.

decisions.[74] Thus the ECJ holds that European competition law protects in principle the freedom to select one's own contractual partner, on the levels of both the customer and the provider, and the freedom to design one's own business strategy in the common market.[75] The legal basis of the economic freedom approach of European competition law is to be found in Art 81(1) EC, taking a restriction of such freedom as an indicative test for the existence of a restriction of competition.

Finally, European competition law has the objective of pursuing social (distributive) justice.[76] Here, European law coincides with the German understanding of competition as a social institution. Under existing law, this objective is expressed with the reference to consumer interests, e.g., in Art 81(3) EC. It also matters how the welfare gains of competition are distributed within the society.

It is true that European competition law nowadays adopts a stronger market-oriented economic approach. This becomes very clear in the introduction of the new market-share approach of recent Block Exemption Regulations[77] and under the Guidelines for the Application of Art 81(3) EC[78] following Implementation Regulation 1/2003.[79] The concept of Art 81(3) EC as a legal exemption with direct effect begins to merge Art 81(1) and (3) EC into a uniform provision. Art 2 of Regulation 1/2003 puts the burden of proof on the undertaking seeking the legal exemption under Art 81(3) EC; nonetheless, the importance of the freedom-of-action test for a restriction of competition under Art 81(1) EC has lost weight to the extent that pro-competitive considerations, in the sense of a rule-of-reason approach,[80] now have to be considered on equal footing with anticompetitive effects.[81] It is no wonder that

[74] Eg, see Case C–393/92 *Almelo* [1994] ECR I–1477, paras 35 *et seq*.

[75] See, eg, Cases 40–48/73 *et al, Suiker Unie* [1975] ECR 1663, paras 173 *et seq*.

[76] Also in this sense, see I Schmidt and S Binder, *Wettbewerbspolitik im internationalen Vergleich* (1996), 93.

[77] Reg 2790/1999 on the application of Art 81(3) of the Treaty to categories of vertical agreements and concerted practices [1999] OJ L 336/1; see also V Verouden, 'Vertical Agreements and Article 81(1) EC' (2003) 71 *Antitrust LJ* 525; recently Reg 772/2004 on the application of Art 81(3) of the Treaty to categories of technology transfer agreements [2004] OJ L 123/11; see J Drexl, 'Die neue Gruppenfreistellungsverordnung über Technologietransfer-Vereinbarungen im Spannungsfeld von Ökonomisierung und Rechtssicherheit' [2004] *Gewerblicher Rechtsschutz und Urheberrecht Internationaler Teil* 716.

[78] Communication from the Commission, Notice: Guidelines on the application of Art 81(3) of the Treaty, [2004] OJ C 101/97.

[79] See above n 5.

[80] In the past, the CFI rejected the idea that a rule-of-reason approach can be applied under Art 81(1) EC and, simultaneously, characterised Art 81(3) EC as the European rule of reason: see Case T–112/99 *Métropole télévision (MG) v Commission* [2001] ECR II–2459, paras 72–77.

[81] According to economic theory, the legal distinction between a restriction of competition under Art 81(1) EC and the exemption formula of Art 81(3) EC does not make any sense. In economic theory, conduct which, on balance, is efficiency-enhancing does not restrict competition. It is interesting to see that the Guidelines on the application of the new Transfer of Technology Block Exemption Regulation, for the application of Art 81(3) EC outside the scope of the block exemption, no longer distinguish between the two paragraphs of Art 81 EC: see Commission Notice, above n 78, 2.

German competition lawyers in the tradition of the Freiburg School criticise this development.[82]

Whether the economic approach will finally replace the more normative approach remains to be seen. Today, EC competition law is still in line with ordoliberal ideas, as evidenced by the protection of the competition order as the most efficient form of the economy, the protection of individual freedom and the recognition of positive (social) effects as to the distribution of wealth. A stronger economic approach to competition law would not necessarily conflict with a constitutional approach as long as economic analysis better explains the functioning of the market. But it makes a fundamental difference whether we protect economic freedom as a mere means of promoting economic efficiency or whether we use economic analysis as a means to identify market failures which limit the scope of freedom to act.

c) Economic Freedom as a Subjective Right of European Competition Law?

We must distinguish between the issue of whether protection of individual freedom is an objective of competition law and the question of whether competition law grants a corresponding subjective right to market participants and economic agents. In fact, the wording of Arts 81 and 82 EC and European merger control law[83] do not reflect such a subjective rights approach.

The decision of the ECJ of 20 September 2001 in *Courage*[84] has considerably reinforced legal protection of individual economic agents. The ECJ argued in favour of a right to recover damages based on Community law.[85] The operator of an English pub had been sued by his landlord, a brewery, for unpaid deliveries of beer. The effectiveness of the underlying lease contract, including a beer-tie with an obligation to buy a minimum quantity of beer at pre-fixed prices exclusively from the brewery, was questioned under ex-Art 85(1) EC Treaty (Art 81(1) EC). The English Court of Appeal seemed to be ready to accept the nullity of the beer-tie according to ex-Art 85(2) EC Treaty but saw itself unable to grant damages on the counterclaim of the pub operator. English law would not allow a party to an illegal agreement to claim damages from the other party.[86] However, the ECJ decided

[82] See W Möschel, 'Juristisches versus ökonomisches Verständnis eines Rechts der Wettbewerbsbeschränkungen' in E Keller (ed), *Festschrift für Winfried Tilmann* (2003), 705.

[83] See above n 4.

[84] See Case C–453/99, above n 63.

[85] For a similar interpretation, see Komninos, above n 63, 466. AG Van Gerven had previously argued for such a Community right in his Opinion on Case C–128/92 *Banks* [1994] ECR I–1209, paras 36–45. Later CA Jones, *Private Enforcement of Antitrust Law in the EU, UK and USA* (1999) vigorously claimed introduction of a private enforcement system for European competition law.

[86] See also the decision of the Court of Appeal in *Gibs Mex v Gemmel* [1998] ELR 588. On the background of English law, see R Whish, *Competition Law* (46th ed, 2001), 270 *et seq*; Komninos, above n 63, 461 *et seq*, the latter indicating that the Court of Appeal's decision was not totally clear on the point whether the pub operator brought in a claim for restitution or a tort claim for breach of statutory duty.

that ex-Art 85 EC Treaty would preclude a rule of national law under which a party to a contract, leading to a restraint or distortion of competition within that provision, is barred from claiming damages for loss caused by performance of that contract on the sole ground that the claimant is a party to that contract.

Since the ECJ still requires a violation of European competition law, the decision may not be understood as a recognition of a general "economic personality right" (Fikentscher, Schubert) as the basis of a right to recover damages according to § 823(1) German Civil Code. In the German situation, the right to recover damages may still be derived from § 823(2) German Civil Code along with Art 81(1) EC.[87]

However, one must also reject an interpretation of the decision as the adoption of a subjective rights approach, as far as the right to compensation is concerned. Qualification of the pub operator's right to recover damages as a subjective right is based on a German reading of the decision. In its decision, the ECJ explicitly argues that Arts 81 and 82 EC give rise to "rights for the individuals".[88] As the term "subjective right" is not a familiar one in English legal language, the Court's own term "individual rights" seems more appropriate.[89] This term was also used in the early *Van Gend & Loos* case.[90] In both decisions, existence of individual rights is argued identically.

d) "Individual Rights" as Part of European Competition Law

According to the ECJ, individual rights arise not only where they are expressly granted by the Treaty but also by virtue of obligations the Treaty imposes in a clearly defined manner. In the *Van Gend & Loos* case, the ECJ already held that this is also true for obligations imposed on individuals.[91]

Art 81(2) EC left no doubt as to the direct effect of Art 81(1) EC.[92] In *Courage*, the English Court of Appeal also allowed the pub operator to

[87] On the discussion in Germany before the *Courage* decision, see A Birk, 'Belieferungsansprüche bei Verstoß gegen Art 81 EG' [2000] *Europäische Zeitschrift für Wirtschafts- und Steuerrecht* 485; A von Winterfeld, 'Zum Schutzzweck des Art 81 EG-Vertrag und zu den Rechtsfolgen eines Verstoßes nach nationalem Recht' in HE Brandner, H Hagen and R Stürner (eds), *Festschrift für Karlmann Geiss* (2000), 667. See also G Mäsch, 'Diskriminierung leicht gemacht?' [1999] *Zeitschrift für Wirtschaftsrecht* 1507 at 1512–4.

[88] See Case C–453/99, above n 63, para 23, following Case 127/73 *BRT and SABAM* [1974] ECR 51, para 16; Case C–282/95 P *Guérin Automobiles v Commission* [1997] ECR I–1503, para 39. On the basis of *Guérin*, even before *Courage*, it was argued that a Community right to recover damages would have to be granted; see CA Jones, 'Trilateralism in Private Antitrust Enforcement: Japan, the USA and the European Union' in CA Jones and M Matsushita (eds), *Competition Policy in the Global Trading System* (2002), 211 at 218.

[89] However, one has to admit that in English legal writing this term is used in a very unspecific way: see AC Geddes, *Protection of Individual Rights under EC Law* (1995).

[90] See Case 26/62 *Van Gend & Loos* [1963] ECR 1, para 10.

[91] *Ibid*. However, in *Van Gend & Loos*, reference to obligations imposed on individuals constituted only *obiter dicta*.

[92] Several times affirmed by the ECJ. See only Case 22/71 *Béguelin* [1971] ECR 949, para 24. The ECJ is also very explicit in Case C–453/99, above n 63, para 24.

invoke that provision.[93] For purposes of enforcement, *Courage* adds an individual right to recover damages to the already accepted right to invoke the nullity of a contract under Art 81(2) EC.

The question which remained unanswered for competition law after *Van Gend & Loos* was which rights arise from a violation of competition rules and which persons may invoke such rights. In *Courage*, the answer is drawn from the principle of full effectiveness of Community law (*effet utile*):[94]

> [25] As regards the possibility of seeking compensation for loss caused by a contract or by conduct liable to restrict or distort competition, it should be remembered from the outset that, in accordance with settled case-law, the national courts whose task it is to apply the provisions of Community law in areas within their jurisdiction must ensure that those rules take full effect and must protect the rights which they confer on individuals.[95]
>
> [26] The full effectiveness of Article 85 of the Treaty and, in particular, the practical effect of the prohibition laid down in Article 85(1) would be put at risk if it were not open to any individual to claim damages for loss caused to him by a contract or by conduct liable to restrict or distort competition.
>
> [27] Indeed, the existence of such a right strengthens the working of the Community competition rules and discourages agreements or practices, which are frequently covert, which are liable to restrict or distort competition. From that point of view, actions for damages before the national courts can make a significant contribution to the maintenance of effective competition in the Community.

According to the ECJ, individual rights are granted, beyond positive effects for the legal protection of the individual, in order to strengthen competition as an institution. The private plaintiff acquires an individual right in her or his role as the advocate of Community law.[96] *Courage* is positioned on the same level with *Francovich*. Taken together, the two decisions form a general Community law principle according to which whoever—Member State, the Community itself or another private party—does not respect the obligations imposed by Community law has to compensate the victim.[97]

Hence, the pub operator's right to compensation does not result from the objective of European competition law to protect the pub operator

[93] See Whish, above n 86, 269 *et seq*, indicating that the English court had to decide whether Art 81(2) EC made the agreement only 'void' or even 'illegal'. Only in the latter case would a claim for compensation under the tort of breach of statutory duty be justified.

[94] See Case C–453/99, above n 63, paras 25–7.

[95] Here, the decision refers to Case 106/77 *Simmenthal* [1978] ECR 629, para 16; Case C–213/89, *Factortame* [1990] ECR I–2433, para 19.

[96] Also in this sense, see Komninos, above n 63, 468.

[97] In a similar sense see *ibid*, 476. Para 23 of the cited decision in *Courage*, hinting at the full effectiveness of Community law, can also be found in almost identical wording in Cases C–6 & 9/90, *Francovich* [1991] ECR I–5357, para 22 (also citing *Simmenthal* and *Factortame*).

specifically. Rather, the individual right is justified by the objective Community interest in efficient enforcement of competition law. Strengthening private enforcement of Community competition law seems crucial after the entry into force of Implementation Regulation 1/2003[98] on 1 May 2004, which made Art 81(3) EC directly applicable by the domestic courts of the Member States. Competition law will only be enforced effectively if there is a strong incentive for private action. In this sense, *Courage* is most helpful in terms of the development of the enforcement mechanisms of competition law.

In addition, it is not simple to justify an individual right to recover damages. In the *Courage* situation, Art 81(1) EC reacts to a market access problem. The European cartel prohibition would only intervene if the market were considerably foreclosed by the cumulative effect of the beer-tie and similar contracts to the disadvantage of competitors of the brewery and if the individual conduct of the brewery contributed considerably to the foreclosure (so-called "bundle" theory).[99] In light of the objectives of competition law, the excluded competitor would deserve protection. Additional protection of the customers of the foreclosing breweries as a goal of Community law, however, is not self-evident.[100]

e) European Competition Law and Contract Law

According to the preceding analysis, it seems that acceptance of the right to recover damages in *Courage* cannot be interpreted as a strengthening of competition law as part of an ordoliberal economic constitution. The Court grants individual rights for the sake of effective enforcement and not for the sake of the individual and the protection of the individual's economic freedom.

Nevertheless, this is not the complete picture. After answering the crucial question of whether European competition law should include claims of private parties to recover damages, the ECJ had to give direction as to the requirements under which the pub operator could argue such a claim. In this context, the ECJ made important statements on the intersection of competition law and contract law.[101]

The ECJ allows national law to regulate the modalities of the Community right. Participation of the claimant in the restraint of competition may be taken into account.[102] However, national law has to guarantee

[98] See above n 5.

[99] See in particular Case C–234/89 *Delimitis* [1991] ECR I–935, para 24.

[100] Indeed, Eilmansberger, above n 63, 29 *et seq*, criticises that such detaching of the right to compensation from the goals of competition law would make it impossible to individualise the group of protected persons.

[101] The contract law aspect of the decision has been neglected in the comments on the decision so far. This is also the case for the otherwise very instructive contribution by Komninos, above n 63.

[102] See Case C–453/99, above n 63, para 31.

that such rules are not less favourable than those governing similar domestic actions (principle of equivalence) and that they do not render practically impossible or excessively difficult the exercise of rights conferred by Community law (principle of effectiveness).[103] In addition, the ECJ instructs the domestic court to take into account the economic and legal context in which the parties find themselves and the respective bargaining power and conduct of the two parties to the contract.[104] In particular, the national court will have to ascertain whether the injured party "found himself in a markedly weaker position than the other party, such as seriously to compromise or even eliminate his freedom to negotiate the terms of the contract and his capacity to avoid the loss or reduce its extent"[105].

Thereby, the ECJ accepts European competition law as a legal instrument for the control of unfair contracts. Similar to Franz Böhm, the ECJ combines competition law and private law arguments in a way which is typical for the ordoliberal school.[106]

Courage can be seen as being in line with the German Federal Constitutional Court and its decision in 1993 on private securities given by family members.[107] As explained above,[108] the Constitutional Court imposes an obligation on the legislature and the courts to develop a "material" private law understanding of the freedom-of-contract principle protected under Art 2(1) of the *Grundgesetz*; one important consequence is an obligation to monitor contracts that are only formally covered by party autonomy. The ECJ reaches a similar result in application of European competition law, which thereby acquires a "constitutional" function comparable to the fundamental rights of the German Constitution.

The preceding reasoning sheds more light on the objectives of European competition law. In the case of exclusive dealing arrangements, competition law not only pursues protection of the excluded foreign competitor, who may not enter the market because of a network of similar contracts. It also protects the competition market for the sake of the customers and their interest in contracting with competing providers at fair prices and conditions.[109]

f) The Nature of "Individual Rights" of European Economic Law

At this stage of the analysis a characterisation of the "individual rights" that can be found in European economic law becomes possible. Individual

103 *Ibid*, para 29; citing Case C–261/95, *Palmisani* [1997] ECR I–4025, para 27.
104 See Case C–453/99, above n 63, para 32.
105 *Ibid*, para 33.
106 See above II. 2.
107 *Entscheidungen des Bundesverfassungsgerichts*, above n 41.
108 See above II. 1. c).
109 In contrast, Eilmansberger, above n 63, 29, rejects the idea that the interests of the customers are covered by the objectives of Art 81(1) EC.

rights of European law are oriented toward enforcement and procedure. They more closely resemble common law remedies than, e.g., German-style subjective rights.[110] This is why the term "subjective rights", used in German constitutional and private law, should be avoided in the context of Community law. The remedy approach, however, does not exclude a constitutional understanding of competition law. We have to remember that the ordoliberal school did not claim subjective rights as a necessary element of its economic constitution. Ordoliberal thought pursues individual freedom by the establishment of a constitution of freedom. In this context, competition law has to guarantee the legal preconditions enabling the individual to take advantage of her or his economic freedom and to enter into contracts freely.[111] *Courage* does not change this perspective. The decision adds individual legal protection to the picture in order to guarantee effective enforcement of competition law. Thereby, the European economic constitution is strengthened in respect of its procedural guarantees.

Whereas legal literature has already accepted the fundamental freedoms as the Community law basis for guaranteeing the freedom of cross-border transactions,[112] *Courage* adds competition law as another instrument for the protection of contractual freedom. In this regard competition law and the fundamental freedoms share their character as constitutive law.

g) Concluding Characterisation of the European Economic Constitution

The European economic constitution may be characterised as follows: under the influence of the principle of full effectiveness, Community law grants procedural "individual rights" to economic agents in pursuit of effective enforcement of the European economic order. Thereby, competition law and the fundamental freedoms both guarantee contractual and economic freedom in a constitutive way. These two legal devices are designed to enable the individual economic agent to take advantage of the economic freedoms of the European market on the basis of self-determined decisions. Thereby, Community law adopts a material understanding of freedom which mandates intervention by the law in cases of restraints and distortions of competition and other failures of the contractual system.

The functional identity with European competition law justifies an interpretation of the fundamental freedoms that is based in competition law.[113]

[110] Cf Komninos, above n 63, 479, describing the decision in *Courage* as common law friendly. Komninos also hints at familiarities with the remedy approach.

[111] Because of this functionality, the author of this article described competition law as belonging to the 'constitutive' part of consumer law: Drexl, above n 6, 296–300.

[112] See above II. 3. e).

[113] See below IV. 2. a).

III. IMPACT OF CONSTITUTIONAL PRINCIPLES ON COMPETITION LAW

The constitutional character of European competition law—in the sense of an ordoliberal economic constitution—allows analysis of the impact of constitutional principles on competition law. The objective of the following part of the analysis consists in promoting greater systematic homogeneity between the different parts of the European constitution and developing and evaluating competition law in light of general constitutional principles.

1. Methodology for the Identification of the Relevant Principles

As a first step, it is necessary to identify the relevant constitutional principles. This is not a simple task, since there is no agreement on whether such principles exist at all, which functions particular principles exercise and which principles deserve to be accepted.

According to Armin von Bogdandy, the evolution of constitutional principles in general is not only important for the purpose of giving more structure to the law. It also gives self-assurance to a society about its legal foundations.[114] Since the European consensus on common values is much smaller than the national one and since the establishing Treaties contribute little or nothing to enlighten us as to the principles of the European constitution, European constitutional principles cannot be taken for granted.

Armin von Bogdandy mentions four "complexes" that have gained consideration in the discussion so far:[115] (1.) adaptation of constitutional principles already presented in national constitutions, (2.) development of proper constitutional principles of European law, (3.) orientation towards Union citizenship and (4.) the economic constitution of the Community. Finally, to these Community sources, he would add the role of the European Union as a global player, namely via the Community's WTO membership.[116]

This list indicates a considerable methodological danger. According to the individual preferences of scholars, politicians and judges, for particular complexes, individual principles will be preferred to others without convincing justification. A solution to the methodological dilemma can only be based on a normative analysis that accepts the legal effectiveness of the different complexes and simultaneously takes these complexes into account. Thereby, two issues may be distinguished: the first one relates to the effect of particular principles in their original meaning in the field of competition law. As a second issue, we have to consider whether competition law as such reflects constitutional principles like democracy, the rule of law, equal protection, social

[114] Von Bogdandy, above n 42, 34 *et seq*.
[115] *Ibid*, 35.
[116] *Ibid*, 40.

justice, or individual freedom. The question to be asked—in the sense of interrelating orders—is that of homogeneity of competition law with the constitutional principles of European law. Only in the framework of existing homogeneity is it possible to evaluate the impact of constitutional principles on competition law and to evaluate and develop competition law in light of these principles (3.).

2. Effectiveness of Constitutional Principles in Competition Law

From the perspective of the political constitution, it is necessary to consider the meaning of the rule of law, democracy, equal protection and individual freedom as effective principles in the field of competition law, as well. Additionally, the principle of solidarity (social justice) deserves consideration as a value and objective laid down in Community law.

Of course, the rule of law is accepted as a principle of competition law. It is expressed by the Community's very nature as a Community of law; it has broad direct application in relation to the citizens of the Union and provides a well-designed system of judicial protection. However, as will be seen below, the new Implementation Regulation 1/2003 does not take sufficient account of the rule of law.

Because of the often invoked democratic deficit,[117] effectiveness of the democratic principle under the European constitution is not unproblematic. To a considerable extent, European competition law is laid down in primary Community law. Therefore, these parts are even protected against amendment by the European legislature. Primary law can only be changed through amendment of the establishing Treaties (Art 48 EU). Hence, the Treaty provisions on competition policy are protected in a truly constitutional sense. An amendment requires at least approval by the national parliaments equipped with full democratic legitimacy. However, the democratic legitimacy of primary law contrasts with secondary law based on Art 83 EC, which has extremely little participation of the European Parliament. This is an obvious problem concerning the new Implementation Regulation 1/2003.[118] Secondary law adopted on the basis of Art 83 EC must not alter the substantive rules of Arts 81 and 82 EC.[119] In the framework of Art 86(3) EC, the Commission is even able to adopt directives without the participation of the European Parliament and the Council.[120]

[117] See, eg, R Streinz, *Europarecht* (2003), paras 281–283a.

[118] See above n 5.

[119] The German Monopoly Commission hinted at such an unacceptable change under the new Implementation Regulation 1/2003: Monopolkommission, *Kartellpolitische Wende in der Europäischen Union?* (1999), para 21. Also critical is Mélédo, above n 2, 214. Denying a conflict with primary law is CD Ehlermann, 'The Modernization of EC Antitrust Policy' (2000) 37 *CML Rev* 537 at 539 *et seq* and 553 *et seq*.

[120] Affirmed in Cases 188–190/80 *French Republic et al v Commission* [1982] ECR 2545, paras 4 *et seq*.

The principle of equal protection requires equal application of competition law to all economic agents. This principle also creates problems for the recent reform of European competition law. To the extent that the reform transfers enforcement powers to the authorities and the courts of the Member States, European law has to guarantee equal (uniform) application and equally efficient enforcement of Community law.[121] Therefore, the Commission initially proposed imposing an obligation on national courts of the Member States to avoid decisions in conflict with the general practice of the Commission.[122] Thereby, the Regulation would have postulated legal primacy of the equal protection principle and the Community principle of full effectiveness over the rule of law, subjecting courts to the authority of administrative decisions of the Commission. According to Art 16 in its final and much more moderate version, national courts have to respect decisions and pending cases only in the individual case.[123] In addition, the rule of law is explicitly safeguarded by reference to the possibility of referring cases to the ECJ (last sentence of Art 16(1) of Regulation 1/2003).[124] However, these rules remain problematic in light of the rule of law by giving the Commission power to stop judicial proceedings before a Member State court by simply taking up its own investigation of the case.[125]

In European competition law, the principle of solidarity (social justice) is laid down in those provisions where an exemption from European competition rules is justified by the contribution of a fair share of the resulting benefit to consumers. The relevant provisions—Art 81(3) EC, Art 2(1)(b) of Merger Control Regulation 139/2004[126]—have the objective of guaranteeing that such exemptions in favour of restraints that promote technical and economic progress are not granted against the interests of consumers. These provisions are evidence of the fact that pursuit of economic efficiency is not the only objective of European competition law. European law also looks at

[121] The new Regulation, above n 5, reacts to this requirement with guarantees of substantive law and certain procedural rules. From a substantive law perspective, Art 3(1) of the Regulation imposes a duty on national authorities and courts to apply European competition law, within its scope of application, along with national competition law. Under certain conditions provided for in Art 3(2), conflicting national law may not be applied. A number of procedural rules (Arts 11–16) try to guarantee co-operation between national authorities and the Commission.

[122] Art 16 of the Proposal of 27 September 2000 for a Council Reg on the implementation of the rules on competition laid down in Arts 81 and 82 of the Treaty, COM(2000) 582 final.

[123] See Reg 1/2003, above n 5. This rule is in line with the early decision by the ECJ in Case C–344/98 *Masterfoods* [2000] ECR I–11369, paras 48 and 51 *et seq*.

[124] A similar indication was included in the commentary on Art 16 of the earlier Commission Proposal, above n 122, which would only insufficiently have guaranteed the rule of law given the broad obligation of national courts to respect the Commission's general practice.

[125] According to Art 16(1), 2nd and 3rd sentence of Reg 1/2003, above n 5, the domestic court has to avoid a conflicting decision and, therefore, has to consider whether it is necessary to stay its proceedings.

[126] See the EC Merger Regulation, above n 4.

how efficiency gains are distributed in society. Beyond these clauses, however, the term "social" and the concept of solidarity remain ambiguous. However, the EC Treaty implements the principle of solidarity in the framework of the other, already mentioned policies whose legal relevance needs to be respected.

Of course, the constitutional principle of individual freedom is also effective with regard to the application of competition law. Based on its original function, undertakings can rely on their economic freedoms as a defence against measures taken by competition authorities. According to this "first" interpretation, i.e., as a right of the economic agent directed against state authorities, the principle of individual freedom applies when competition authorities do not respect the limits of their legal powers.

3. "Homogeneity" of Competition Law with General Constitutional Principles

It is necessary to distinguish the effectiveness of general constitutional principles from the question of whether these principles are also reflected in competition law in a homogeneous sense.

a) Competition Law as an Expression of a European Constitution of Individual Freedom and the Rule of Law

The already stated concept of a European economic constitution reflects homogeneity of the general constitutional principle of individual freedom with the constitutional guarantee of economic freedoms safeguarded by European competition law.

Some irritation, however, arises from the diverging legal basis of the guarantee of individual freedom. Whereas, in the political constitution, individual freedom is justified by theories of fundamental rights, within the European constitution, protection of economic freedoms lies above all in the pursuit of effective enforcement. As can be seen from the comparison with the above-mentioned decision of the German Federal Constitutional Court,[127] European competition law was able to guarantee individual freedom without a clear legal justification on the basis of fundamental rights.

Nevertheless, the concept of individual freedom as a fundamental rights concept can be referred to as a criterion for a positive evaluation of recent case-law, especially the ECJ's decision in *Courage*.[128] The fundamental rights concept provides special constitutional legitimacy for the current state of interpretation and application of European competition law.

[127] See *Entscheidungen des Bundesverfassungsgerichts*, above n 31. See also above II. 4. e).
[128] See Case C–453/99, above n 63. See also above II. 4. c)-f).

b) A Democratic Concept of the Market?

Attempts to establish an analogy between economic competition and democracy are well known. From an ordoliberal perspective, Franz Böhm characterised democracy and the market as political and economic expressions of the same phenomenon. Accordingly, he equated market processes with a "democratic process".[129] In line with the approach of this analysis, Böhm argued a homogeneity of the political and the economic orders.

Nevertheless, a democratic concept of the market has to face particular concerns. Democratic elections require the equality of votes. In the market, however, some market participants have better economic means at their disposal and, therefore, are better equipped to influence the market. Additionally, the democratic state and the market constitute fundamentally different systems of co-ordination. Even in the democratic state, citizens are subjected to the authority of the state. In a market, provided that competition is guaranteed, nobody is subjected to the authority of anybody. Hence, competition guarantees more individual freedom than the democratic state. The market receives its legitimacy from the consent of the economic citizen to individual transactions. Its legal foundation consists in the freedom-of-contract principle.

In the political arena, the democratic principle needs to be complemented by individual freedom in order to protect the citizen against the dangers of the centralised system of political decision-making. With the market as a decentralised order of co-ordination, central decision-making is not required in the economy. Decentralised decision-making between the parties of the contract is to be preferred because the individual economic preferences of numerous economic agents would be outvoted in a democratic system of centralised decision-making. Of course, the result of democratic voting would not reflect the economic data, especially the scarcity of resources, which need to be taken into account by an efficient economy. In a model of a democratic economic constitution, collective decisions would collide with the principles of individual freedom and self-determination.[130]

Hence, a constitutional understanding of the competition order can only be found in the principle of individual freedom and not in the principle of democracy.[131]

c) Social Justice and Equal Protection?

There seems to be a fundamental conflict between the principles of economic freedom and those of equality and social justice. The market does not and

[129] F Böhm, *Wirtschaftsverfassung und Staatsverfassung* (1950), 50 *et seq*; *id*, 'Privatrechtsgesellschaft und Marktwirtschaft' [1966] *ORDO* 75 at 92. See also W Fikentscher, *Wirtschaftsrecht* (1983), i, 10, characterising the market as a 'dialogue on values'.

[130] See also S Scholten, 'Die ordnungspolitische Dimension der Verbraucherpolitik in der Sozialen Marktwirtschaft' in H Piepenbrock (ed), *Verbraucherpolitik in der Sozialen Marktwirtschaft* (1984), 95 at 116.

[131] See also the earlier publication: Drexl, above n 6, 243.

cannot guarantee equal income and total satisfaction of the needs and preferences of all citizens. Despite these arguments, it is possible to explain why the competition order deserves to be considered a truly social order.[132]

Competition does not just privilege the most efficient actor. It also guarantees participation of all economic agents in the welfare gains.[133] Since the market economy is the "presumably most social institution for the distribution of scarce products",[134] competition law is situated at the core of the social market economy.[135]

Nevertheless, only a particular model of competition law can operate as a means of social policy. The contrary will be the case if competition laws are not just indifferent towards a transfer of wealth from the bottom to the top, but even promote it. According to Chicago School theory, such transfer would be advocated if, for example, in the case of a merger, economies of scale produced gains in productive efficiency that outweighed losses in allocative efficiency as a consequence of less intensive competition.[136] The situation is significantly different in the case of a competition law that protects competition as such and has a consumer orientation. Only the latter merits being called a social institution.

From a legal perspective, however, the social character of the competition order cannot be made operational, primarily because the word "social" is much too imprecise to be applied in the field of competition law. Social effects are produced as a consequence of the protection of competition as an institution and a material concept of the individual freedom of all economic agents. Therefore, European competition law does not cite the consumer in the prohibition of restraints of competition (Art 81(1) EC), but only then, when it comes to limitations of the exemption clause (e.g. Art 81(3) EC). In the field of competition law, even this analysis of the principle of solidarity finally refers to the central role of the principle of individual freedom.

The situation is similar in respect of the principle of equality and equal protection. In *Courage*,[137] the ECJ did not mention this principle. Nevertheless, one sees its influence in how the Court deals with the control of the contract in order to protect the weaker party.[138] In instructing the national court to evaluate in the relevant case whether the party to the contract, bound by the beer-tie, "found himself in a markedly weaker position than the other party",[139] the Court postulates not only a principle of material freedom,

[132] See also above II. 2.
[133] See Müller-Armack, above n 50, 144.
[134] See Fikentscher, above n 8, 32.
[135] *Ibid*, 13 *et seq*. For a similar view, see H Willgerodt, 'Soziale Marktwirtschaft—ein unbestimmter Begriff?' in U Immenga (ed), *Festschrift für Ernst-Joachim Mestmäcker* (1996), 329 at 338.
[136] See H Hovenkamp, 'Antitrust Policy After Chicago' (1985) 84 *Michigan L Rev* 213 at 231, criticising the Chicago School.
[137] See Case C–453/99, above n 63. See also above II. 4. c)-f).
[138] See in particular above II. 4. e).
[139] See Case C–453/99, above n 63, para 33.

but also one of "equal guarantee of freedom".[140] According to this principle, nobody is allowed to abuse market mechanisms with the intent to violate others' legally protected freedom of contract. In this context, the principle of equality remains a mere qualification of the constitutional guarantee of individual freedom. It is not the objective of competition law to guarantee equal market results. Competition law aims at equal freedoms for all economic agents.

4. European Rights of the Citizens

In his study on European rights of the citizens, Norbert Reich was only able to indicate an "indirect" protection of the consumer on the basis of competition law.[141] Writing before *Courage*, he had to express himself cautiously. Especially against the background of the decision as it relates to contract law,[142] it would be appropriate today to accept, in the sense of Reich, individual rights of the citizens in the economic field.

With his concept of rights of the citizens, Reich refers to an issue that remains unclear in *Courage*. For Reich, it is crucial to explain that European law protects not only undertakings as market citizens but all private parties and especially consumers. This is why he expressly complains that the ECJ has not yet accepted a right of consumers to recover damages in cases of violation of competition law.[143]

The ECJ does not expressly state in *Courage* whether such a right should also be accorded to consumers. The Court decided that *even* the party to the contract liable to restrict and distort competition may have a right to compensation. Obviously, the ECJ would not exclude, in principle, similar claims by other economic agents. The ECJ even argues that full effectiveness of Community law would be put at risk if it were not open to *any* individual to claim damages for loss caused to him by a contract or by conduct liable to restrict or distort competition.[144]

Especially claims of consumers, as U.S. experience shows, can contribute considerably to effective enforcement of competition law. For the ECJ, it was not necessary to refer to the broader understanding of rights of the citizens. The principle of full effectiveness (*effet utile*) argues against a limitation of the persons who may claim compensation. Indeed, protection of the consumer could also be explained in light of the principle of individual freedom. Restraints of competition also reduce room for alternative decisions of consumers. Therefore, they cannot and should not be excluded from protection.

[140] On this principle, see also A von Bogdandy, 'Europäische Prinzipienlehre' in *id* (ed), *Europäisches Verfassungsrecht* (2003), 149 at 164 *et seq*; see also A von Bogdandy in this volume.

[141] See above II. 3. d).

[142] See Case C–453/99, above n 63, paras 32–34.

[143] See Reich, above n 51, 344.

[144] See Case C–453/99, above n 63, para 26; see also the citation above, at II. 4. d).

However, it is not absolutely necessary to refer to the concept of rights of the citizens in order to justify adequate results in application of competition law.

5. Subsidiarity and the Problem of Multilevel Governance

Finally, consideration has to be given to the character of the European constitution as a constitution of multilevel governance. Under this aspect, competition law plays a particular role. Regulating the substantive standards of competition law through Community law is in line with the general approach of Community law to regulation. But almost exclusive enforcement through Community institutions in the past seems to conflict with the Community's overall federal structure, which, in most cases, entrusts administrative enforcement to the Member States on the basis of Art 10(1) EC (Art I-10(2) CT-Conv; Art 5(2) CT-IGC). Though the principle of subsidiarity, laid down in Art 5(2) EC (Art I-9(3) CT-Conv; Art 11(3) CT-IGC), has no relevance within the scope of the exclusive Community competence for competition policy, there seems to be a systematic friction in the federal structure of the Community.[145] In fact, the new approach of Regulation 1/2003 for the implementation of Arts 81 and 82 EC, consisting in a transfer of enforcement powers to national courts and authorities, seems to correspond to the principle of subsidiarity.[146] This analysis, however, only follows the original, i.e., the political perspective of the issue of multilevel governance. The picture changes with an analysis of whether substantive competition law contributes to the spirit of subsidiarity.

This question transcends the narrow-mindedness of the conflict of competences between the Community and its Member States. From a perspective of substantive law, the decision-making competence of authorities on different levels of a federal system cannot be the problem. Substantive competition law rather pursues an attribution and protection of decision-making competence in the market to individual economic players. This substantive law analysis, therefore, adds another level of decision-making to the multilevel dimension of the subsidiarity principle, namely the private law level. For the design of multilevel competition law, the issue is one of effectiveness: which level, the Community level or the national level, is the more adequate to guarantee self-determined decisions of economic agents?[147] It follows that attribution of competences in the field of competition law should not be directed by a political understanding of the subsidiarity principle, but in light of effective enforcement of the objectives of competition law.

[145] See Ehlermann, above n 119, 540, states that there is an 'unusual degree of centralisation'.
[146] Even the Commission referred to the principle of subsidiarity in its proposal for the new Implementation Regulation: see above n 122, part III. Cf also von Bogdandy, above n 13, 362.
[147] Cf W Kerber, 'An International Multi-Level System of Competition Laws: Federalism in Antitrust' in J Drexl (ed), *The Future of Transnational Antitrust Law* (2003), 269 (with an economic analysis on the appropriate level of antitrust regulation and enforcement).

6. Conclusions

The preceding analysis demonstrates that general constitutional principles may be discussed in the framework of competition law. However, competition law should not be applied and interpreted in light of indiscriminate principles. The question is rather whether and to what extent European competition law reflects such principles of the political constitution.

The principle of individual freedom turns out to be most important, since European competition law is designed to guarantee in a constitutive way the economic freedoms of individual economic agents. Enforcement of this principle is strengthened with acceptance of an individual right to compensation. An interpretation of competition law in light of the general constitutional principle of individual freedom leads to a positive evaluation of the ECJ's decision in *Courage*.

European competition law also reflects the principles of equality and solidarity (social justice). However, homogeneity of competition law with these principles only exists in the sense of an equal guarantee of economic freedoms to all market participants and of innate social effects of the competition order. Both principles give more precision to the characterisation of the European competition order as a Constitution of Individual Freedoms.

The democratic principle is no useful tool for an adequate characterisation of European competition law. The concept of a constitution of the citizens underlines the guarantee of equal freedoms for all market participants based on European competition law.

Finally, the analysis of substantive competition law sheds more light on the subsidiarity debate in the field of competition law. Subsidiarity as an instrument for attribution of competences between the Community and the Member States is no satisfying criterion for the design of European competition law. In light of the objective of guaranteeing a competition order as a Constitution of Individual Freedoms, attribution of competences has to follow the criterion of efficient enforcement alone.

Based on this characterisation of European competition law in light of general constitutional principle, the following analysis will try to achieve the reverse by answering the question of whether substantive competition law can contribute to the development of general principles of the European constitution.

IV. IMPACT OF COMPETITION LAW ON THE EUROPEAN CONSTITUTION

The analysis of substantive competition law underlines the role of the active market citizen in the constitutional system of European law. Arguments of the economic constitution identify European competition law as "enabling" law. In a constitutive sense, it is designed to enable the market citizen to participate actively in the economic process of the internal market and to take part in European integration. In this last part of the analysis, the question is whether this enabling character of competition law has any impact on other fields of Community law.

1. The Market Citizen as the Constitutive Force of Parts of the European Constitution

From the outset, and in the sense of a limitation, it has to be admitted that an impact of competition law on general European constitutional law can only be discussed in terms of European law applied in an economic context. An impact on the purely political part of the European constitution seems doubtful at least, since co-ordination of individual preferences in politics follows rules and principles that are fundamentally different from those of the market.

2. Impact on the Interpretation of Substantive Community Law: Taking into Account the Competition Law Dimension

The following analysis will turn to a few examples which will demonstrate the systematic context of different fields of regulation of Community law at large.

a) Application of the Fundamental Freedoms

The preceding analysis argues for a harmonised interpretation of competition law and the fundamental freedoms. Considering the structure of the Constitutional Treaty this argument seems even more convincing, given the fact that the fundamental freedoms (Arts III-18 to III-49 CT-Conv; Arts 133 to 160 CT-IGC) and competition policy (Arts III-50 to III-58 CT-Conv; Arts 161 to 169 CT-IGC) would be dealt with as the two core elements, apart from harmonisation, guaranteeing the functioning of the internal market.[148] In fact, the fundamental freedoms and competition policy pursue identical objectives.[149] They accord individual rights in order to guarantee economic freedom to act in a constitutive sense.

The dominant view of the fundamental freedoms is so far one of individual rights of the market citizen in relation to the Member States—an

[148] The Draft Constitutional Treaty finally replaces the words 'common market' with 'internal market' in formulating the competition rules of the European Union.

[149] See also P Oliver and W-H Roth, 'The Internal Market and the Four Freedoms' (2004) 41 *CML Rev* 407 at 413, arguing that the fundamental freedoms are characterised by the two goals of allowing access to the markets of the Member States and of guaranteeing undistorted competition in the market.

understanding that resembles the German concept of subjective public rights. In contrast, the analogy to competition law as "enabling (constitutive)" law would also promote an understanding of the fundamental freedoms in their private law dimension. This private law dimension has to be taken into account for the interpretation of the fundamental freedoms. This can be illustrated in respect of the *Keck* decision of the ECJ and the debate on reverse discrimination.

aa) Keck Revisited In *Keck*,[150] the ECJ explicitly tried to limit attempts by economic agents to invoke the very broad *Dassonville* formula[151] for the free movement of goods principle.[152] The core idea of the decision consists in the function of Art 28 EC as prohibiting measures of the Member States that restrict market access. The ECJ held that provisions concerning selling arrangements are prohibited by Art 28 EC if they discriminate against goods originating from another Member State. In doing so, the Court apparently introduced a fundamental distinction between two groups of provisions: those relating to the product as such and those on selling arrangements. According to a somewhat different reading, one would even have to distinguish between three groups of provisions,[153] since the Court seemed to single out prohibitions on "certain" selling arrangements as different from others which are not mentioned explicitly.[154] Such "other" arrangements—i.e., those that discriminate, in law or in fact, between the marketing of domestic products and of those of other Member States to the disadvantage of the latter—do restrict market access and, therefore, fall within the scope of Art 28 EC.[155] In this latter situation, the ECJ maintains its earlier case-law according to which such provisions are prohibited unless justified by mandatory requirements in the sense of the *Cassis de Dijon*[156] formula.[157]

The obvious problem with the *Keck* decision is two-fold: on the one hand, with its distinction concerning the term "selling arrangements", the Court introduced a purely formal criterion for the application of Art 28 EC without sufficient explanation why this criterion should be relevant.[158]

[150] See Cases C–267 and C-268/91 *Keck & Mithouard* [1993] ECR I–6097.

[151] See Case 8/74 *Dassonville* [1974] ECR 837, para 5.

[152] See Cases C–267 and C–268/91, above n 150, para 14.

[153] See, eg, W-H Roth, 'Annotation to Keck and Hünermund' (1994) 31 *CML Rev* 846 at 852; Schubert, above n 58, 162. See also AG Léger's Opinion in Case C–470/93 *Mars* [1995] ECR I–1923, para 29.

[154] See Cases C–267 and C–268/91, above n 150, para 16.

[155] Later decisions deal with such provisions: see Case C–189/95 *Franzén* [1997] ECR I–5909 (on the Swedish alcohol monopoly); Case C–405/98 *Gourmet International Products* [2001] ECR I–1795 (on the Swedish advertising prohibition on alcoholic products); Case C–322/01 *Deutscher Apothekerverband* [2003] ECR I–14887. See also Case C–387/93 *Banchero* [1995] ECR I–4663 (on the Italian tobacco monopoly).

[156] See Case 120/78, above n 68.

[157] See Cases C–34–36/1995 *de Agostini* [1997] ECR I–3843, paras 52 *et seq*.

[158] The criterion was initially proposed by EL White, 'In Search of the Limits to Art 30 of the EEC Treaty' (1989) 26 *CML Rev* 235 at 246 *et seq*.

Therefore, the *Keck* formula should only be applied against the background of a functional understanding of Art 28 EC so as to avoid judicial formalism.[159] On the other hand, the *Keck* formula cannot avoid recourse to market analysis, which can prove extremely difficult in the problematic cases of "other" selling arrangements.[160] Seen in this light, it appears that the ECJ, in *Keck*, was not successful in defining a workable formula for the application of Art 28 EC. The decision deserves to be approved only for the unproblematic cases of rules exclusively applied to internal marketing and their exclusion from the scope of Art 28 EC.[161]

A better theoretical handling of Art 28 EC derives from a private law understanding of the fundamental freedoms. As stated above,[162] the fundamental freedoms protect *cross-border* economic activity of both sides of the contract. Application of the fundamental freedoms, therefore, requires a cross-border transaction. This is explicitly formulated by Art 49 EC for the free movement of services; it also holds true in the field of free movement of goods. Accordingly, the free movement of goods principle protects the power of the individual supplier and the individual customer to engage in cross-border delivery and supply of goods. Whether such a cross-border transaction exists can be tested legally without any additional formula. Application of the formal criterion of selling arrangements is not required. Consequently, purely internal marketing activities have to be dealt with differently than cross-border activities. In the *Keck* situation, in which the operator of a supermarket trades both national and foreign products, a prohibition of sale at an economic loss only restricts internal transactions. It does not restrict the preceding cross-border transaction, namely the sale of products from foreign suppliers to the operator of the domestic supermarket. The situation would be fundamentally different if national marketing rules were applied to cross-border marketing activities. Cross-border advertising, e.g., constitutes a preparatory act in respect of the later cross-border

[159] For a similar critique see E Steindorff, 'Unvollkommener Binnenmarkt' [1994] *Zeitschrift für das gesamte Handelsrecht* 149 at 161 *et seq*; N Reich, 'The "November Revolution" of the European Court of Justice' (1994) 31 *CML Rev* 459 at 465 and 470 *et seq*; J Snell, *Goods and Services in EC Law* (2002), 81 and 96. For a completely different perspective, see S Enchelmaier, 'The Awkward Selling of a Good Idea' (2003) 22 *YEL* 249 at 281–7 and 306–11; *id*, 'Four Freedoms, How Many Principles?' (2004) 24 *OJLS* 155 at 158 *et seq* and 162–5. For other interpretations of Art 28 EC and the judgment in *Keck*, see also M Poiares Maduro, *We the Court* (1998), 73–7; J Baquero Cruz, *Between Competition and Free Movement* (2002), 119.

[160] See the decisions of the ECJ on the Swedish trading monopoly for alcoholic products and the Italian trading monopoly for tobacco products, above n 155.

[161] This holds true, in particular, for the regulation of shopping hours. In the pre-*Keck* era, the ECJ had difficulties with the British Sunday trading cases; see Case C–145/88 *Torfaen Borough Council* [1989] ECR I–3851; Case C–169/91 *Stoke-on-Trent* [1992] ECR I–6635; see also Case C–312/89 *Union départementale des syndicats d'Aisne* [1991] ECR I–997; Case C–332/89 *André Marchandise* [1991] ECR I–1027. In the post-*Keck* era, see Cases C–401 and C–402/92 *Tankstation 't Heukske* [1994] ECR I–2199; Cases C–69 and C–258/93 *Puno Casa* [1994] ECR I–2355.

[162] See above II. 3. e).

transaction and, therefore, deserves to be protected equally under Art 28 EC.

However, non-application of all national rules to cross-border transactions would not be appropriate. The fundamental freedoms do not protect against every restraining measure of the Member States but only against those that put a burden on specific cross-border transactions. Therefore, it is necessary to define a criterion for permissible restrictions. In the *Cassis de Dijon* decision,[163] the ECJ correctly developed the principle of the country of origin. Instead of a right of total freedom from regulation, the Court only accepted a right of the supplier to market goods in other Member States according to the legal standards provided for in the country of origin (mutual recognition). Conversely, there is only a right of the customer to buy goods according to these standards of the country of origin. Consequently, the Member State of the customer's domicile may not apply its law to cross-border advertising which is in conformity with the law of the country of origin, unless application of the law of the customer's domicile is justified by mandatory requirements or the requirements of Art 30 EC.

To sum up, it is possible to apply Art 28 EC without the formal distinction between provisions relating to the marketed good as such and those on selling arrangements. The proposed application avoids any concept of the free movement of goods principle as a mere prohibition of discrimination. The prohibition provided for by Art 28 EC covers all restrictions on cross-border transactions in respect of goods.

However, this kind of prohibition does not exhaust the scope of application of Art 28 EC. This provision contains, as seen in more recent case-law on "other" selling arrangements, an individual right to market access which is independent of the legal situation in the country of origin. For instance, it is irrelevant for the assessment of legality of the Swedish trading monopoly in alcoholic products under Art 28 EC whether a similar system exists in the country of origin.[164] In this situation, the prohibition is justified by the discriminatory effect of the law of the country of importation to the disadvantage of foreign goods. The same holds true in respect of an absolute prohibition on advertising; here, whether a similar prohibition exists in the country of origin cannot be decisive. A violation of Art 28 EC would not be based on the principle of the country of origin (mutual recognition) but purely on the discriminatory effect of the national rule that restricts market access. In these cases, an analysis of the market conditions cannot be avoided. This does not come as a surprise. Economically, these cases involve restraints of competition caused by legal provisions of the importing Member State, and such restraints must be addressed by an individual right

[163] See Case 120/78, above n 68.

[164] See Case C–189/95 *Franzén* [1997] ECR I–5909.

to market access.[165] Market analysis is a typical approach to investigating the existence of distortions of competition. Absolute advertising prohibitions, as on the marketing of tobacco and alcoholic products, protect better-known domestic brands against competing foreign products whose market availability may not sufficiently be communicated to the domestic consumer without advertising. These prohibitions distort competition.

As an alternative to the *Keck* approach, it is possible to formulate the following two-level test: on a *first level*, the question is whether the economic agent concerned (either supplier of goods or customer) may invoke an individual right to engage in a particular cross-border transaction under the legal requirements of the country of origin in order to avoid the legal requirements of the country of importation. In the framework of this first test, Art 28 EC works as a prohibition of any restriction; a discriminatory effect is not required. If the claimant cannot invoke application of more favourable legal requirements in the country of origin, then, on the *second level*, Art 28 EC will have to be applied as a prohibition of discrimination. In this function, Art 28 EC works as a prohibition of distortions of competition, caused by state action, to the disadvantage of foreign goods. Even in this respect, Art 28 EC creates individual rights of suppliers and customers in the sense of power to pursue their own economic preferences relying on the freedom-of-contract principle. This interpretation rests on a competition concept of the fundamental freedoms. The second-level test directly protects the competition order; indirectly, i.e., in a constitutive sense, it also protects individual freedom of contract by increasing the possibilities of choice of the economic agents in the internal market. Whereas, under the first-level test, Art 28 EC protects conclusion of the contract according to the legal requirements of the country of origin, under the second-level test, Art 28 EC, protecting the right to market access, increases the likelihood that the supplier will find a customer in the internal market.

bb) The Problem of Reverse Discrimination Reverse discrimination is the classic field where, based on a constitution of the citizens, it would be possible to argue for an approach different from that of the ECJ. Whereas the ECJ continues to allow reverse discrimination as a consequence of the cross-border functionality of the fundamental freedoms, these freedoms are interpreted by Reich as fundamental principles of the internal market that do not depend on a transnational character of their scope of application.[166]

165 See, presumably in this sense Case C–405/98, above n 155.

166 See Reich, above n 51, 204 *et seq*; in a similar sense see, K-H Fezer, 'Europäisierung des Wettbewerbsrechts' [1994] *Juristenzeitung* 317 at 325 *et seq*. See also G Nicolaysen, 'Inländerdiskriminierung im Warenverkehr' [1991] *Europarecht* 95; H Weyer, 'Freier Warenverkehr, rein innerstaatliche Sachverhalte und umgekehrte Diskriminierung' [1998] *Europarecht* 435; D Koenig, 'Das Problem der Inländerdiskriminierung' [1993] *Archiv für öffentliches Recht* 591.

The constitution of the citizens according to Reich rests on the principle of non-discrimination of European citizens under Art 12(1) EC. The Constitutional Treaty will not change that situation. Art I-4(2) CT-Conv (Art 4(2) CT-IGC) is in line with the wording of Art 12(1) EC. In the framework of a constitution of the citizens, it would be unacceptable to grant more rights to foreign European citizens than to domestic ones. Actually there is discussion in some Member States on whether at least the equal-protection clause of the national constitutions should prohibit reverse discrimination.[167]

A competition-law approach, however, still argues for allowing reverse discrimination under European law and domestic constitutional law.

As demonstrated above, in the model of the economic constitution, the problem would have to be analysed in light of the principle of individual freedom whereas the principle of equal protection only requires an equal attribution of individual freedom to all citizens.

Indeed, under existing Community law, with admissible reverse discrimination, all Union citizens have to be granted the same amount of legally guaranteed freedom. Each Union citizen, as a supplier of goods or services, can choose to settle in the territory of the Member State which provides the most favourable economic and legal conditions. Equally, each Union citizen as a customer has the right, in principle, to buy goods and services from other Member States according to the legal rules of the country of origin of those goods. On the basis of the very principle of the country of origin, the supplier selling to domestic customers may only rely on domestic law and may not claim a better right of the foreign competitor. Hence, the ostensible discrimination is only the consequence of the decision of the business operator to settle in a particular Member State. Since Community law also protects the freedom of settlement, the business operator has to bear the negative consequences resulting from the use of that freedom.

A prohibition of reverse discrimination, after all, would change the understanding of individual freedom in the internal market. Such prohibition would allow the domestic business operator to invoke treatment on the same footing with the most favoured foreign competitor. Such interpretation would generally bring down protection to the lowest national level of

[167] In Austria, the Constitutional Court has held, in application of the non-discrimination clause of Art 14 ECHR, that Austrian citizens may not be discriminated against in comparison to the citizens of other Member States of the EU and the European Economic Area. However, this decision does not relate to the equal protection principle as such, but to the protection of private life which, under the Convention, must be guaranteed to the same extent for foreigners and Austrians; see the decision of 17 June 1997: [1997] *Europäische Grundrechte-Zeitschrift* 362. In Germany, courts generally rejected a violation of the constitutional equal protection clause in Art 3(1) Grundgesetz in advertising cases of conflicting European and national law: see Federal Court of Justice (*Bundesgerichtshof*) [1985] *Gewerblicher Rechtsschutz und Urheberrecht* 886 (*Cocktail-Getränk*); Court of Appeal (*Oberlandesgericht*) Hamm [1992] *Gewerblicher Rechtsschutz und Urheberrecht Internationaler Teil* 834 at 836 (*Typ Mozzarella*).

a country of origin which still survives the justification test of the fundamental freedoms.

Claiming a prohibition of reverse discrimination, therefore, contradicts the competition order as understood in the sense of an economic constitution. Implicitly, the prohibition of reverse discrimination would implement a concept of the fundamental freedoms as general principles of economic liberalisation, similar to libertarian concepts of the European economic constitution.[168] According to the present analysis, in contrast, reverse discrimination conflicts with neither the principle of individual freedom nor the idea of competition. Competition even argues for allowing reverse discrimination. The European legislature, relying on Art 95 EC in particular, has a choice between harmonisation and leaving issues to competition between the legal systems of the Member States. The fundamental freedoms intensify this latter legal competition by suspending the application of domestic law in cases of cross-border transactions. A prohibition of reverse discrimination would conversely restrain legal competition. In many cases, the national legislature does not tolerate the application of the principle of the country of origin and instead abolishes the national rule in order to improve opportunities for domestic businesses.[169] Such reaction does not contradict the intention of the fundamental freedoms. On the contrary, the costs for maintaining the national rule had turned out to be—politically and economically—too high and, therefore, in the system of competing legal orders, the national rule was quite rightly abolished.

b) The Internal Market Concept (Art 95 EC)

Because of the possibility of justification, the fundamental freedoms do not always exclude the application of the domestic law of the Member States to cross-border situations. In order to establish the internal market, the European legislature is therefore required to harmonise national law for many issues. The concepts of the approximation of national law constitute another field for which we can analyse the impact of European competition law in its constitutional understanding. The first sub-issue relates to the limits of Community competence for the harmonisation of national law.

Art 95 EC constitutes the most important provision conferring harmonisation power to the Community for the establishment of the internal market. In its decision on the Tobacco Advertising Directive of 2000, the ECJ was able to clarify the limits of this competence.[170]

168 See above II. 3. c).

169 Eg, in summer 2001, the German legislature abolished the prohibition on consumer rebates, thereby reacting to the general introduction of the principle of the country of origin through the Electronic Commerce Directive: see H Köhler, 'Rabattgesetz und Zugabeverordnung' [2001] *Betriebsberater* 265.

170 See Case C–376/98, above n 47. This was confirmed in the later judgment relating to the Tobacco Labelling Directive: Case C–491/01 *British American Tobacco* [2002] ECR I–11453.

Even before the decision, two alternative reasons for harmonisation in view of the internal market were accepted: remaining obstacles to the free movement of goods and services on the one hand and distortions of competition on the other hand. As can be seen from a comparison with the preceding analysis, measures for the approximation of national law also have the objectives of enforcing individual economic freedoms to act and of implementing a competition order.

In light of Art 95(3) EC, power to harmonise national law does not constitute a mere competence for liberalisation. The decision on the Tobacco Advertising Directive had to deal with the conflict between the internal market objective and protection of public health and thus provided the opportunity for clarification of the concepts of the internal market as part of the European economic constitution.

The decision added two elements to the earlier understanding of Art 95 EC. Firstly, the Court rejected a view of Art 95 EC as a general Community legal basis for the regulation of the economy. The Court underlined that the provision would only confer legislative power if the conditions for the establishment and the functioning of the internal market were effectively improved.[171] Distortions of competition need to be "considerable" in order to justify harmonisation.[172] In light of these principles, the total ban on advertising, which would have made it more difficult for foreign brands to enter the national market rather than facilitating access, had to attract critique.[173] Similarly, another critique related to the mere minimum-harmonisation approach of the Directive, which would have allowed diverging national rules and obstacles to the exercise of the fundamental freedoms in the future.[174]

Secondly, the Court emphasised that the Community is allowed to pursue particular protective policies in the framework of Art 95 EC, provided that the above-mentioned requirements in respect of the establishment and functioning of the internal market are met. Even a Directive, motivated primarily by health protection, would be acceptable.[175]

It is possible to solve the conflict. The decision of the ECJ may be integrated into the system of the European economic constitution. The fundamental freedoms and the European competition order are not opposed to regulation as such. Community law does not grant a right of individual freedom directed against every form of regulation of the economy, but has the constitutive objective of creating room for autonomous private law transactions in the transnational context. The Community's various protective policies (health, environment, consumers, etc) enhance the quality of

[171] See Case C–376/98, above n 47, paras 83 *et seq*.
[172] *Ibid*, paras 106–8.
[173] *Ibid*, para 113.
[174] *Ibid*, para 104.
[175] *Ibid*, para 88.

both the private law society, based on freedom of action, and the competition order. To the extent that harmonising measures contribute to the free movement of goods and services and strengthen competition in the internal market, there will be a higher probability that these measures will also implement a material understanding of individual freedom. If the limits drawn by the ECJ were not respected, harmonisation would risk patronising the individual, restraining individual freedom, distorting competition in the internal market and, finally, affecting growth and social welfare in the European Union.

3. Competition Law Principles of the European Constitution

From a perspective of competition law and a European economic constitution, the preceding analysis of European economic law, lying outside the scope of competition law, leads to the following three constitutional principles of competition law: (i) Existence of an individual right to conclude contracts across borders and existence of an individual right to market access, (ii) denial of a general guarantee of freedom from regulation, and (iii) guarantee of a material concept of individual freedom in economic law and private law.

The individual right to conclude contracts across borders and the right to market access are protected, though not without exception, by the fundamental freedoms. In a constitutive sense, these rights are also protected by European competition law and are even further promoted in the framework of the internal market policy of harmonisation.

The existence of these concepts of European competition law as well as the now accepted individual rights approach demonstrate a material understanding of individual freedom in European economic law and private law. Community law is designed, with its competition law and other policies protecting specific interests, to establish the conditions for the market that will allow citizens of the European Union to take advantage of their market freedoms. This material understanding explains why, for example, the Member States are still authorised to restrict the fundamental freedoms for particular reasons, like consumer protection and public health.

V. CONCLUDING REMARKS

Of course, the preceding analysis has not exhausted its subject matter. The particular challenge consisted in testing the validity of theories on the economic constitution for Community law, in combining them with a theory of principles of the European constitution, in unveiling the interaction between principles of the political and the economic constitution and, finally, in enriching principles of the European constitution with principles of competition law which can prove valuable for the interpretation, understanding and development of Community law.

This would be a good time to turn back to competition law and the analysis of its problems in light of the principles developed above. Recent reforms of European competition law, following an economic-market approach, would require much deeper analysis than was possible here.

In the end, the analysis was limited to the internal dimension of Community law. However, large and important parts of Community law relate to the external dimension, to third states and international organisations. Competition law has to deal increasingly often with restraints of an international, even global scope. The European Community has to define its policy with regard to these developments, but can only do so by taking into account its own economic constitution. Simultaneously, the Community has to accept that its trading partners have developed somewhat different economic constitutions and, therefore, will not necessarily be ready to establish principles similar to those of the European economic constitution on the international level.

Part V
On Finality: Contending Legal Visions

16

The European Union Between Community and National Policies and Legal Orders

BY ULRICH EVERLING

I. INTRODUCTION

THE INSTITUTIONALISED EUROPEAN integration in the European Union and Community is one of the most significant and remarkable evolutions in the history of the last century. After a gradual start, at the present almost all of the states in Central and Western Europe as well as recently in Central Eastern Europe are united in a comprehensive organisation with far-reaching sovereign rights which it exercises independently by its own institutions.

The Union was agreed to freely, by treaty and, unlike historical precedents, did not come about by use of force, dictatorship or hegemony. It first united the victorious powers of the Second World War with a defeated and proscribed Germany. Germany was not, as after the First World War, to be suppressed in perpetuity by requirements and supervision, which could not have succeeded, but was instead accepted into the circle of states concerned as an equally entitled member.[1] On this basis, over five decades, a European order has gradually emerged that more or less intensely comprehends, or at least touches upon, most areas of public and private life of the Member States and their citizens. The Member States support this order on the one hand as founders and central actors and are, on the other hand, subject to this order as members and addressees of the law. The citizens of the Member States are immediately connected to the Union and its law by direct rights and obligations.

[1]Cf on the historical contexts K-D Bracher, 'Gedanken zur Entstehung und Entwicklung der Europäischen Gemeinschaft' in R Hrbek and V Schwarz, *40 Jahre Römische Verträge: Der deutsche Beitrag* (1998), 17; M Burgess, *Federalism and European Union—The Building of Europe* (2000), 55 *et seq*; J-B Duroselle, '1948: Les débuts de la construction européenne' in R Poidevin (ed), *Histoire des debuts de la construction européenne* (1986), 11.

Yet, the historical dimension of this development is scarcely appreciated in the public discussion and it is barely still visible behind the daily disagreements over different interests. The political avowals of high-ranking politicians upon European integration do often not correspond to the readiness to act concretely, and they frequently serve to hide national interests. Scepticism and uneasiness are also evident amongst scholars, who often lose sight of the overall goal.[2]

The broader public has become increasingly aware of the scope of the development that has already taken place above all since the Single European Act and the Treaties of Maastricht, Amsterdam and Nice. Their divided reactions have been played out in delicate ratification debates with plebiscites and constitutional disagreements. These disagreements have at the same time, however, also led to an increased occupation with the theoretical foundations of European integration.[3] New impulses were set in the follow-up of the Nice Treaty by the European Convention presenting in July 2003 the Draft of a Treaty establishing a Constitution for Europe. The Treaty was signed, after some amendments, by the Member States in October 2004,[4] but the required ratifications are suspended, at present, after failure of the referendums in France and the Netherlands.[5]

[2] As a recent example of an economist see R Vaubel, *Europa-Chauvinismus: Der Hochmut der Institutionen* (2001); from legal scholarship see, eg, P Neill, 'The European Court of Justice: a Case Study in Judicial Activism' [1995] *European Policy Forum*; KA Schachtschneider, 'Der Vertrag über die Europäische Union und das Grundgesetz' [1993] *Juristenzeitung* 751; A Milward, *The European Rescue of the Nation State* (1992).

[3] From the latest German language literature, in addition to the well-known earlier publications, several comprehensive works may be mentioned, especially T Giegerich, *Europäische Verfassung und deutsche Verfassung im transnationalen Konstitutionalisierungsprozess* (2003); P Häberle, *Europäische Verfassungslehre* (2002); FC Mayer, *Kompetenzüberschreitung und Letztentscheidung* (2000); A Peters, *Elemente einer Theorie der Verfassung Europas* (2002): T Schmitz, *Integration in der supranationalen Union* (2001); W Schroeder, *Das Gemeinschaftsrechtssystem* (2002).

[4] Treaty establishing a Constitution for Europe, signed in Rome at 29 October 2004 (hereinafter CT–IGC).

[5] On the Convention's Draft Constitutional Treaty see T Oppermann, 'Eine Verfassung für die Europäische Union' [2003] *Deutsches Verwaltungsblatt* 1165 and 1234; A Mattera (ed), *Pénélope: projet de Constitution de l'Union europénne* (2003); J Schwarze, 'Ein pragmatischer Verfassungsentwurf' [2003] *Europarecht* 535; J Kokott and A Rüth, 'The European Convention and its Draft Treaty Establishing a Constitution for Europe' (2003) 40 *CML Rev* 1325; J Meyer and S Hölscheidt, 'Die Europäische Verfassung des Europäischen Konvents' [2003] *Europäische Zeitschrift für Wirtschaftsrecht* 613; V Epping, 'Die Verfassung Europas?' [2003] *Juristenzeitung* 821; W Wessels *et al*, 'Der Verfassungsentwurf des Europäischen Konvents' [2003] *Integration*, Special issue 4, 283; F Chaltiel, 'Une constitution pour l'Europe: An 1 de la République européenne' [2003] *RMC* 493; J-V Louis, 'Le projet de constitution: continuité ou rupture?' (2003) 39 *CDE* 215; M Dougan, 'The Convention's Draft Constitutional Treaty?' (2003) 28 *EL Rev* 763; P Birkinshaw, 'A Constitution for the European Union?' (2004) 10 *European Public Law* 57; A Peters, 'European Democracy after the 2003 Convention' (2004) 41 *CML Rev* 37; J Schwarze (ed), *Der Verfassungsentwurf des Europäischen Konvents* (2004); M Ruffert, 'Schlüsselfragen der Europäischen Verfassung der Zukunft' [2004] *Europarecht* 165.

For this author, as a member of the war generation, European integration and the diminishing of the disastrous role of the classical nation-state associated with it was and is a historical response to dictatorship, war and genocide. Since the beginnings of the EEC, the author was mainly active at the intersection of the Union[6] and its Member States and constantly had to make efforts to balance the two.[7] On the base of this experience, he is of the opinion that the Union is characterised by the tensions between the Union and her Member States, and between the Member States themselves. He intends to contribute this personal view of the present state of the Union to the discussion on the European Constitution. He will begin with the foundation of the Union and its political and economic vocation.[8]

II. FOUNDATIONS OF THE EUROPEAN UNION

1. Goals of the Union

The European integration in the European Union and Community can, as already observed, only be seen against the background of the catastrophes of the preceding century.[9] As a reaction to war, despotism and genocide and in the intention to permanently prevent its recurrence, the free part of Germany made two fundamental decisions, above all, in order to build its state order following its total collapse. First, with the *Grundgesetz* and the founding of the *Bundesverfassungsgericht*, it established the conditions for a free, western oriented, democratic constitutional state. Second, it decided to participate in a supranational union of European states. This second aspect is the one to be discussed here.

This short summery simplifies in retrospect yearlong hard and difficult struggles and discussions, whose results must permanently anew be strengthened. They were complicated by the fact that both processes mutually affected each other, but also soon collided, because democracy and rule of law in the young Federal Republic were exposed to supranational

[6] As a rule, and in the interest of simplification, provided the context does not require otherwise, this article will refer to the Union as including the Community, although the latter remains as before its own legal entity.

[7] The author has always reflected on this. See the volumes of selected articles: *Das Europäische Gemeinschaftsrecht im Spannungsfeld von Politik und Wirtschaft* (1985) and: *Unterwegs zur Europäischen Union* (2001). The following text is largely based on the views set out there in more detail, and referred to generally here.

[8] The author presumes that the course of events in the development of the Union and Community is known and therefore believes that he does not need to supply references.

[9] This aspect is little considered by many authors, including especially Anglo-Saxon authors, as for example in the much heeded book by L Siedentop, *Democracy in Europe* (2000).

influences. The conflicts based on this situation became evident at the latest in the well-known *Solange* and *Maastricht* decisions of the *Bundesverfassungsgericht*.

The opening of the Federal Republic vis-à-vis the unification of Europe corresponded to comparable efforts in the other states of Western Europe that had suffered under war and occupation. The roots of these efforts reach far back into the past and were propagated especially in the 1920s by associations such as the Pan-European movement. They failed already at the outset due to the exaggerated nationalism of the pre-war era and in the end, in the Second World War, were perverted by the imperialistic *Großraumpolitik* of the Nazi regime.[10] Only under the influence of the devastating results of the war did the call for a union of European states and their peoples have a chance of being realised. Survivors of the war generation on all sides rose up, disregarding much resistance, to make the recurrence of such a catastrophe impossible.[11]

The concrete impetus for the integration institutionalised in the Union was the well-known declaration by the French foreign minister *Schuman*, which proposed the union of the mining industry of the core states of Europe, calling this a "first concrete foundation for a European federation." The epoch-making, future-oriented significance of this initiative was that all participating states were to subject themselves in the same manner to the Community regime. This basic principle, which excluded every discrimination and hegemony of individual Member States, remained the foundation for all further steps of integration up until today.

This offer gave the newly created Federal Republic of Germany the opportunity to emerge from the general ostracism and isolation after the war and the opportunity to return as an equally entitled member of the community of states. This led to the lifting of the Ruhr statute and later also the occupation statute. Connected with it was the fundamental orientation of the new Federal Republic toward the West, which destined its future. Alignment with the Western democracies was to strengthen internal stability and at the same time, at the start of the Cold War, guarantee external security within the framework of the Western alliance.

The motives of the partner states were nearly the opposite, but corresponded in result with the German motives in the effort to avoid a recurrence of inner-European military hostilities. The Allies wanted to tie a West

[10] See, eg, HW Heulen, *Europa und das 3. Reich* (1987), further J Laughland, *The Tainted Source: The Undemocratic Origins of the European Idea* (1988), whose attempt to project these efforts onto today's Union ignores the complete upheaval at the end of the war and has nothing to do with reality.

[11] On the origin and genesis of the Community see W Loth, *Der Weg nach Europa* (1996); DW Urwin, *The Community of Europe* (1991); D Weigall and P Stirk, *The Origins and Development of the European Community* (1992).

Germany, that once again was economically strengthened and whose rearmament was being discussed, firmly to a supranational context. By grasping at coal and steel, which according to the current state of technology at the time was seen as the basis for armaments, they, at the same time wanted to preclude Germany from acting unilaterally in the future.[12] Whether individual Member States were also, as has been argued, pursuing hegemonial goals,[13] may remain an open question. In any case, such ambitions, if they did exist, were resisted and could not prevail in the long run.

In addition to the political motives, economic motives appeared and became equally, in the eyes of some historians[14] even more important. With the common market for coal and steel, the partners wanted to obtain access to the resources especially of the Ruhr region, which were needed for the reconstruction of the regions destroyed by war.[15] For Germany, this opened up the opportunity to commute limits and requirements of the occupying power. Nevertheless, it was precisely the economic effects that were much debated, since the rules were seen as comprising dirigisme and discriminations, and industry and unions mainly rejected them. In the end, the German Parliament, because of the political perspectives it opened up, accepted the ECSC Treaty.[16]

As is known, efforts to continue integration in the political arena at first remained unsuccessful. Acceptance of the Treaty on the European Defence Community and of the Statute of the European Political Community, which had been drafted by an ad-hoc Assembly of the Council of Europe, would have been a downright revolutionary leap into a constituted Europe. It is idle to inquire whether in the current international situation at the time and in view of the domestic debates in all Member States, this would have been

[12] On the varied motives, simplified here, see R Poidevin (ed), *Histoire des debuts de la construction européenne* (1986); H Mosler, 'Die europäische Integration aus der Sicht der Gründerphase' in O Due, M Lutter and J Schwarze (eds), *Festschrift für Ulrich Everling* (1995), 911; U Böttger, *Ziele und Mittel europäischer Integration* (2002); for further authors see above n 11.

[13] Siedentop, above n 9, 169 *et seq*, imputes such ambitions to France and believes that they were by and large accomplished by means of the transfer of the French administrative structure first to the ECSC and then to the EC. If such intentions really existed, they did not succeed in the long run. But do we not, on the other hand, today see an increasing influence of the principles of English law in the Union by means of the overall use of the English language?

[14] Cf, eg, Milward, above n 2.

[15] There a is detailed discussion in the introduction to P Reuter, *La Communauté européenne du charbon et de l'acier* (1953). See also J Gillingham, *Coal, Steel, and the Rebirth of Europe* (1991).

[16] W Loth, 'Vertragsverhandlungen bei abklingender Europabegeisterung' [1989] *Integration* 107; cf further the memoirs of a leading social-democrat: C Schmid, *Erinnerungen* (1979), 519 *et seq.*

at all viable. In any event, after the failure of the genuine political impetus, economic goal setting moved into the forefront. The EEC, with the common market as its core, soon gained its own weight and increasingly pushed the original understanding of the political sense of the European integration, which had been directed at overcoming the mental and material effects of war, into the background.[17]

In the consciousness of today's actors, the successors to the war generation, the original impetus may scarcely still be present, since the relations between the Member States have by in large been normalised and national borders barely play a role for their citizens in day-to-day life. This change of the motivation is evident by the alterations of the preambles of the Treaties. Whilst the Preamble of the ECSC Treaty referred to "age-old rivalries" and divisions by "bloody conflicts" and the Preamble of the EEC Treaty referred to "barriers which divide Europe" that are to be eliminated, the Preamble of the Constitutional Treaty underlines the "cultural, religious and humanist inheritance of Europe" and the determination to "transcend their former divisions and ... to forge a common destiny".[18] The recognition has now come to the fore that the individual Member States are no longer in the position to effectively look after their chances for survival in the open world. This is not only true for the economic and social functions, which under the influence of globalisation and the economic and environmental crises have rather increased in importance. At present, the political goals of a common foreign, security and defence policy are of central importance because the European states can only exercise sufficient influence together, to secure the freedom for their citizens and to contribute to peace in the world as an equal partner on the same footing to the USA.[19]

Whether, though, the Union should completely change its goals and choose the enforcement of human rights in the world as their pressing task,[20] must be questioned. Surely, the regard for human rights in all measures the Union takes belongs to the foundations of its existence, but that alone cannot justify a union of states and peoples with far-reaching encroachments into their traditional status. The task of contributing to freedom, security and welfare must continue to be at the forefront.[21]

[17] On the change in the goals of integration in the practice of the German federal governments see M Tarama, *Struktur und Wandel der Legitimationsideen deutscher Europapolitik* (2001).

[18] On the importance of the Preamble of the Constitutional Treaty see A von Bogdandy, 'Europäische Verfassung und Europäische Identität' [2004] *Juristenzeitung* 53; *id*, 'The Preamble' in B de Witte (ed), *Ten Reflections on the Constitutional Treaty for Europe* (2003), 3.

[19] On the current German views, see H Schneider, M Jopp and U Schmalz (eds), *Eine neue deutsche Europapolitik?* (2002).

[20] See P Alston and JHH Weiler, 'An "Ever Closer Union" in Need of a Human Rights Policy' in P Alston (ed), *The EU and Human Rights* (1999), 3.

[21] See A von Bogdandy, 'The European Union as a Human Rights Organization?' (2000) 37 *CML Rev* 1307; see also with reference to the Constitutional Treaty A Williams, 'EU Human Rights Policy and the Convention on the Future of Europe' (2003) 28 *EL Rev* 794.

That the original goals continue subliminally in spite of all transformations was evidenced in German reunification, which was regarded by some of the neighbour states with distrust. But the German government made clear from the start that the united Germany would remain a member of the Union and the Western Alliance and thereby still be bound in their context, which excluded every special development. It seems that only for this reason the negotiations with the four powers having had yet certain prerogatives over Germany as a whole could relatively smoothly be terminated.[22] Also part of this context are the proceedings in connection with the participation of the Liberal Party of Austria, considered a right radical party, in the government of Austria, a country which shares historical baggage with Germany.[23] From a German perspective this may simply be observed; it appears to be as impossible to rule off the past in Europe as it is to rule off domestic disputes.

Which form the desired political unity should assume remained unclear from the beginning. The political declarations of the governments and parties fluctuated insofar but, in the practice of the Union, the organisational end goal remained open. The Union develops in an ongoing process, in a direction that is difficult to predetermine.[24] There is no consensus as to a final legal form; the Union will for the present remain undecided in the balance.[25]

2. Building up the Union into a Political Union

After the failure of the Defence Community, the political substance of the integration process remained largely in the background in comparison to the economic goals, which were pursued as a priority. Nevertheless, economic policy is also policy and often determines the fate of the states and the individual citizens more strongly than genuine political actions. In all

[22] See G Langguth, 'Deutschland, die EG und die Architektur Europas' (1991) 42 *Außenpolitik* 136; M Fromont, 'L'union de l'Allemagne dans la liberté 1989–1990' (1991) 27 *Revue de Droit Public* 121; W Heisenberg (ed), *Die Vereinigung Deutschlands in europäischer Perspektive* (1992), and therein particularly the contributions of P Ludlow, 17, and R Fritsch-Bournazel, 55.

[23] Cf F Schorkopf, *Die Maßnahmen der XIV EU-Mitgliedstaaten gegen Österreich* (2001); M Hippold, 'Fourteen against One' (2000) 49 *ICLQ* 953; S Schmahl, 'Die Reaktionen auf den Einzug der freiheitlichen Partei Österreichs in das österreichische Regierungskabinett' [2000] *Europarecht* 819.

[24] The procedural character of integration in the Union is shown in the anthology by R Hrbek *et al* (eds), *Die Europäische Union als Prozess* (1998). See also P Craig and G de Búrca (eds), *The Evolution of EU Law* (1999).

[25] See T Oppermann, 'Der europäische Traum zur Jahrhundertwende' [1999] *Juristenzeitung* 317.

Member States, the measures to establish the common market continually led to considerable encroachments into existing structures, traditions, and gained assets. As a rule, they could be enforced in face of opposition of those affected not in referring to technical rationality of market integration, but rather only by political decision overruling domestic resistance.[26]

For that reason, in Brussels even regulations concerning measures of seeming technical character had to—and still must—be disputed and fought over again and again, to find political compromises and decisions, often after difficult consultations with the groups concerned in the Member States.[27] The connection between economic measures and political effects is obvious in the commercial policy of the Union. Commercial Policy is always simultaneously part of foreign policy, which was long-time exclusively and is now mainly in the domain of the Member States. This was seen especially clearly in the frequently discussed economic sanctions against third countries.[28]

In these circumstances the Member States, or at least some of them, attempted since the sixties to lay down political framework conditions for the European institutions, which were increasingly gaining their own weight, in order to control and direct them. Most such efforts concerned with preference the Council as the organ of states in which the influence of the individual Member States was diminishing due to the majority vote principle and the increasing activities of the Communities. On this point, it suffices to name the catchwords Fouchet Plan, the proceedings surrounding the so-called Luxembourg Protocol, the summit conferences in The Hague and Paris, and the European Council. However, since the enlargements of the Communities in the seventies and eighties the limits of these approaches have become evident. The principle of unanimity and the decision-making structure of that period could not be retained in face of increasing activities of the enlarged Community. The direct election and gradual strengthening of the European Parliament promoted the Union's autonomy from Member

[26] For this reason the attempt, by HP Ipsen in *Europäisches Gemeinschaftsrecht* (1972) and other authors following him, to conceptualise the EEC based on its subject matter orientation and economic rationality (*Zweckverband*) could not be proved true to reality, because decisions in the Community always depend on political consensus building. See U Everling, 'Vom Zweckverband zur Europäischen Union' in R Stödter and W Thieme (eds), *Hamburg—Deutschland—Europa: Festschrift für HP Ipsen* (1977), 595.

[27] See U Everling, 'Zur konsensualen Willensbildung in der föderal verfassten Europäischen Union' in M Brenner, PM Huber and M Möstl, *Der Staat des Grundgesetzes—Kontinuität und Wandel: Festschrift für P Badura* (2004), 1053.

[28] See W Meng, 'Die Kompetenz der EWG zur Verhängung von Wirtschaftssanktionen gegen Drittländer' (1982) 42 *Zeitschrift für ausländisches öffentliches Recht und Völkerrecht* 780; M Vaucher, 'L'évolution recente de la pratique des sanctions communautaires à l'encontre des Etats tiers' (1993) 29 *Revue trimestrielle de droit européen* 39; H-K Ress, *Das Handelsembargo* (2000).

States, and that was moreover furthered by the Single European Act and the Treaties of Maastricht, Amsterdam and Nice. Nevertheless, it is still considered incomplete and shall be developed by the Constitutional Treaty.[29]

The interdependence of the Union's activities and the politics of the Member States leads necessarily in the direction that the Member States must co-ordinate the core of their politics and step by step introduce in the Treaty. The summit conference in The Hague in 1969 already set the course for a common foreign policy by creating the co-called European Political Co-operation. At the beginning, it rested only on informal deliberations and was first anchored by Treaty in the Single European Act. Then in the Treaty of *Maastricht* the Common Foreign and Security Policy became part of the Union Treaty, and in the Treaty of *Amsterdam*, its defence-political components were extended.[30] These rules are still not formally subject to the Community law, but this affects them in many ways.[31] In the last few years, a supplementary organisational structure external to the Treaties, with the pretentious name of European Defence and Security policy, has been built up by means of informal decisions.[32]

At the same time, the Co-operation in the fields of Justice and Home Affairs was drawn into the Treaties. By the *Maastricht* Treaty it was incorporated into the EU Treaty largely in form of co-ordination, but already in the Treaty of Amsterdam essential provisions on the movement of persons including the *Schengen* attainments and the law of asylum, were transferred into the EC Treaty, albeit with certain special rules.[33] This is also true for judicial co-operation in civil matters, so that only co-operation in criminal matters is still carried out in the largely co-operative form of the EU Treaty.[34]

The foreign and domestic policy regulations mentioned encroach considerably into the substance of national policy. Even if they are not yet subject to Community law to the same full extent and in the same manner as the

[29] This is well known and need not be described here. See eg Urwin, above n 11, and Weigall and Stirk, above n 11; see further Burgess, above n 1.

[30] See F Fink-Hooijer, 'The Common Foreign and Security Policy of the European Union' [1994] *EJIL* 173; H-G Ehrhart (ed), *Die Europäische Sicherheits- und Verteidigungspolitik* (2002).

[31] See CWA Timmermans, 'The Uneasy Relationship between the Communities and the Second Union Pillar'(1996) 26 *Legal Issues of European Integration* 61; J Burkhard, *Die Gemeinsame Außen- und Sicherheitspolitik und ihre Berührungspunkte mit der Europäischen Gemeinschaft* (2001).

[32] See A Deighton, 'The European Security and Defence Policy' (2002) 40 *JCMS* 173.

[33] B Meyring, 'Die Reform der Bereiche Justiz und Inneres durch den Amsterdamer Vertrag' [1999] *Europarecht* 309; PJ Kuijper, 'Some Legal Problems Associated with the Communitarisation of Policy on Visas, Asylum and Immigration under the Amsterdam Treaty and the Incorporation of the Schengen acquis' (2000) 37 *CML Rev* 345.

[34] See JM Soria, 'Die polizeiliche Zusammenarbeit in Europa und der Rechtsschutz des Bürgers' (1998) 89 *Verwaltungsarchiv* 400; C Chevallier-Goverts, *De la coopération policière dans l'Union européenne* (1999).

Community matters, they do constrain the Member States' possibility for action in existential matters. The Member States are thus dependent upon resolutions of European bodies or upon co-ordination and at least consultation with them in decisions such as about their political relations with third countries, ranging from the United States to developing countries, or about their positions on crisis situations in the world, as to their peacekeeping missions and their defence measures. Also, the policy on immigration from third country foreigners as well as combating international criminality must be mentioned. Consequently, the Member States lose an essential part of their independence to act.

True, the Member States are already largely subject to international obligations, for example in the United Nations and NATO, and also co-operation mechanisms already existed since the seventies within the Union. However, the development of the last decade contains a new dimension, and it is generally acknowledged that additional measures must be taken after the experiences in the Balkans.[35] The Constitutional Treaty provides further steps and especially competences for the Council to decide under certain conditions.[36] The cautious manner in which progress is gradually made in this area and in which legal obligations are initially being avoided shows the dilemma of the Member States. On the one hand, they wish to retain their responsibility for the fate of their citizens, and on the other hand, for bearing this responsibility, they must act commonly.

To summarise, it can be concluded that the Union is about to return to the beginnings of integration. In the 1950s, the European Defence Community should indicate the way into the common political future, but the time was not ripe. After more than fifty years, the Union, under the pressures of international conflicts, is approaching a state of integration that at that time had been sought in vain. The core difficulty, which was already evident then, that the transfer of existential decisions from the Member States to the Union leads to constant tensions between the Union and the Member States, exists just as much today and must constantly be overcome in practical politics. The result of all this is that for some time now, but at least since the most recent developments, the Union can be characterised as a political union—albeit a partial and incomplete one.

3. Building up the Union into an Economic Union

Economic integration has always stood and still stands at the centre of the policy of the Union. From the beginning, it was not an end in itself but

[35] See J Wouters and F Naert, 'How Effective is the European Security Architecture?' (2001) 50 *ICLQ* 540.

[36] See Arts 41 and 309 *et seq* CT–IGC. See M Jopp and E Regelsberger, 'GASP und ESVP im Verfassungsvertrag' in Wessels *et al* (eds), above n 5, 550.

served the stated political goals. By means of the merger of the markets and national economies, a process was initiated that should turn to a political entity.[37] This functional proceeding was successful in its result, even if it did not lead automatically, as some advocates believed it would, to a "spill-over"-effect and thus to further integration. In fact a new decision was necessary for each further step of integration, but it was provoked nearly unavoidable by the inherent consequence of the steps already completed.

In the beginning the transition from sectoral integration of coal and steel to a union encompassing the entire economy was, in contrast to the retrospective effulgence common today, vehemently controversial. German politicians supporting liberal economics feared a continuation of the assumed elements of dirigisme and control of authorities inherent to the ECSC Treaty and in addition a locking in and closing effect of the customs union.[38] In the early years of the EEC, the challenge of Germany and other Member States of a fundamentally liberal economic and competition policy with rejection of a *planification* according to the French model, and of an open trade policy with low levels of external protection within the framework of a large free economic area was heavily debated.[39]

Contrary to such comprehensions, in this area, looking at it long-term, a liberal approach was able to prevail. The principle formulated in the Maastricht Treaty, of an "open market economy with free competition" (now Art 4 EC) largely influences the economic policy of the Union and Member States. The markets are fundamentally open, internally and with respect to third states and the Union now encompasses almost all West European states and is recently enlarged to the east.[40] With this, important opportunities for overcoming economic and social problems are largely taken away from the Member States and transferred instead to the Union.

The common market, having developed into the internal market, has ever since been the inviolable core of the union. The European Court of Justice has gradually developed the fundamental freedoms of the internal

[37] On different theories of integration see JHH Weiler, I Begg and J Peterson (eds), *Integration in an Expanding European Union* (2003); C Giering, *Europa zwischen Zweckverband und Superstaat* (1997). For a foundational work, see EB Haas, *The Uniting of Europe* (1958).

[38] Cf HJ Küsters, *Die Gründung der Europäischen Wirtschaftsgemeinschaft* (1982). See among the early critics eg W Röpke, 'Gemeinsamer Markt und Freihandelszone' [1958] *ORDO* 31.

[39] See H von der Groeben, *Aufbaujahre Europas* (1982); U Everling, *Die Koordinierung der Wirtschaftspolitik in der Europäischen Wirtschaftsgemeinschaft als Rechtsproblem* (1964).

[40] See M Schulze-Steinen, *Rechtsfragen zur Wirtschaftsunion* (1997); D McGoldrick, 'A New International Economic Order for Europe?' (1993) 12 *YEL* 433; E-J Mestmäcker, 'Zur Wirtschaftsverfassung in der Europäischen Union' in RH Hasse, J Molsberger and C Watrin, (eds), *Ordnung in Freiheit: Festgabe für H Willgerodt* (1994), 263; W-H Roth, 'Der rechtliche Rahmen der Wirtschafts- und Währungsunion' [1994] *Europarecht* Beiheft 1, 45.

market from prohibitions on discrimination to prohibitions on restrictions. National regulations which limit economic transactions between Member States may only be applied to the extent they are justified by a public order reservation or by other reasons of general public interest that are applied in a non-discriminatory fashion and in respect of the principle of proportionality.[41] The obstacles thus remaining can only be eliminated by mutual recognition of the regulations or, since this seems difficult in such matters, by approximation of laws in the interest of the establishment and functioning of the internal market.[42] Such harmonisation has already been taking place to a considerable extent for a long time and is constantly being expanded. The internal market program of the Single European Act had its effect above all as a program of legal harmonisation.[43]

The steadily increasing legal harmonisation already includes most of the areas of economic law more or less intensively. Thus, it limits the latitude for action of the Member States and their constituent parts like regions or *Länder* and constantly leads to conflicts between Community law and national law.[44] These conflicts are viewed as all the more serious, since legal harmonisation is not a technical process that can be left to experts to search for the best of the existing regulations, but is rather truly material legislation and leads as a rule to encroachments into the various traditions, structures, interests and assets of those affected in the Member States. Consequently, there are often considerable difficulties in reaching consensus in the institutions.

The common market can only work if there is undistorted competition, thus the competition policy has always been an indispensable part of the Community economic order.[45] The Commission has over years intensified

[41] This point has often been made. See eg D O'Keeffe and A Bavasso, 'Four Freedoms, One Market and National Competence' in D O'Keeffe (ed), *Judicial Review in European Union Law: Liber amicorum in Honour of Lord Slynn of Hadley* (2000), i, 541; M Eberhartinger, 'Konvergenz und Neustrukturierung der Grundfreiheiten' [1997] *Europäisches Wirtschafts- und Steuerrecht* 43; T Eilmannsberger, 'Zur Reichweite der Grundfreiheiten des Binnenmarktes' [1999] *Juristische Blätter*, 345 *et seq* and 453 *et seq*; N Bernard, 'La libre circulation des marchandies, des personnes et des services dans le Traité CE sous l'angle de la competence' (1998) 38 *CDE* 11.

[42] See J Currall, 'Some Aspects of the Relation between Articles 30–36 and Article 100 of the EEC Treaty, with a Closer Look at Optional Harmonisation' (1985) 5 *YEL* 169; HC Taschner, 'Rechtsangleichung in der Bewährung' in G Lüke, G Ress and MR Will (eds), *Rechtsvergleichung, Europarecht und Staatenintegration: Gedächtnisschrift für L-J Constantinesco* (1983), 765.

[43] U Everling, 'Probleme der Rechtsangleichung zur Verwirklichung des europäischen Binnenmarktes' in JF Baur, K Hopt and KP Mailänder (eds), *Festschrift für E Steindorff* (1990), 1155.

[44] S Weatherill, 'Regulating the Internal Market' (1992) 17 *EL Rev* 299; F Rittner, 'Wieviel Europa braucht Europa?' [1998] *Europarecht* 3.

[45] See the authors named in above n 40.

the application of the competition rules, including the merger and subventions rules. Thus it put often old traditions of the Member States to the test such as the public saving banks (*Sparkassen)* or the book price fixing that have existed for a long time without being challenged. The Member States view this as a serious limitation on their margin for economic-political actions, and this is also true for the dispute as to application of the competition rules to services in the general economic interest, which are labelled too simply as measures for public services.[46] They show clearly the tensions that constantly exist between national and common economic policy measures.

Neither this topic nor specialised areas of economic policy such as agricultural, traffic, environment, consumer, labour and social, regional, tax nor industrial policies can be pursued in more depth here. In these policy areas, the Union is more or less intensely active and is constantly in conflicts of interests with the Member States, which continue to feel responsible for the common welfare.

Since the introduction of the euro, the currency policy is the function of the Union's institutions organ created for that purpose. With this, yet a further essential area of economic policy—after foreign trade policy and competition policy—is taken away from the Member States which participate on the euro. General economic policy as such, however, has not yet been really conferred to the Union, and this will not principally change by the Constitutional Treaty. Particularly financial, employment, social, education, and cultural policies remain essentially within the jurisdiction of the Member States, even if the Union is competent for supporting actions. Yet, all these areas are also connected in many respects to the policy and the law of the Union. In particular the goal of stability and the stability pact in the framework of the currency union exert considerable pressure on the financial policy and thus on the overall policy of the Member States. Therefore, an intensive co-ordination in all fields will be unavoidable.[47]

In conclusion, it can be stated that policy and law of the Union and Community dovetail closely with each other in all areas. The Member States are dependent to a considerable degree on the assistance of the Community, and in reverse, the Community often cannot act without the assistance of the Member States. The danger of a mutual blockage is evident. There is a relationship of constant tension between the Union and

[46] From the extensive literature see A Lyon-Caen and V Champeil-Desplats (eds), *Services publics et droits fondamentaux dans la construction européenne* (2000); M Andenas and W-H Roth Roth (eds), *Services and Free Movement in EU Law* (2002); F Löwenberg, *Service public und öffentliche Dienstleistungen in Europa* (2001); J Schwarze, 'Daseinsvorsorge im Lichte des europäischen Wettbewerbsrechts' [2001] *Europäische Zeitschrift für Wirtschaftsrecht* 324.

[47] See Schulze-Steinen, above n 40; A Buzelay, 'De la coordination des politiques économiques nationales au sein de l'Union européenne' [2003] *RMC* 235.

the Member States as well as amongst the States, which must be steadily resolved by co-operation and compromise.[48]

III. CONSOLIDATION OF THE INSTITUTIONAL SYSTEM OF THE EUROPEAN UNION

1. Peculiarities of the Institutional System of the Union

The Treaty combined elements of functional and institutional methods of integration which were long-times disputed. On the one hand, it ordered open markets and undistorted competition in order to give the enterprises the chances to use the great economic area, and on the other hand it transferred to the institutions the authority to enforce and complete the frame of the market order. This conception demands an institutional system that meets the requirements of effectiveness and is able to resolve the tense relations between national and Community concerns sketched out above. For this, the Treaty sees the Commission as the organ for proposing and enforcing and the Council, composed of state representatives, as decision-making organ, both limited to the competences attributed to them by the Treaty. The European Parliament, at first only to be heard and now largely co-deciding, embodies the democratic element, which Council can only indirect and incomplete mediate by the responsibility of its members before the national parliaments. Finally, the ECJ guarantees legality and legal protection.

The attempt to analyse this sufficiently familiar and proven system must begin with the explanation that consensus building in the Union fundamentally differs from that in the Member States. At the level of the Union, unlike in the Member States, majorities and coalitions are not formed by parties on the basis of elections, who attempt to put through their programs and who face an opposition. Rather the representatives of different political systems and ideas existing in the Member States co-operate at the Community level in concrete material questions united less in political convictions than rather in the interest of common goals.[49] However, in doing so they are burdened by the respective domestic political disputes with regard to their electors.

[48] See FW Scharpf, *Regieren in Europa—effektiv und demokratisch?* (1999), 64; A Dashwood, 'States in the European Union' (1998) 23 *EL Rev* 201; Everling, above n 27.

[49] This situation is often described as a network: see RO Keohane and S Hoffmann, 'Conclusions: Community Politics and International Change' in W Wallace (ed), *The Dynamics of European Integration* (1992), 276; C Joerges, 'Markt ohne Staat?' in R Wildenmann (ed), *Staatswerdung Europas?* (1991), 225.

This is especially evident in the Council. There, majorities are not formed on the basis of common political party programs or at least on basic political consensus, but rather according to the interests in concrete substantive areas, which in each Member State are influenced by the domestic political constellation. On the contrary, in the European Parliament there are parliamentary groups formed between the representatives of various national parties having certain similar orientations. But in spite of such similarities, the differences between them are mostly great so that they are, perhaps with the exception of the greens, no political parties but party alliances coming together in common pursuit of European integration.[50] Also the Commission is not homogenous with respect to party politics and political orientation of their members. Usually domestic political considerations are determinative in the naming of its members, but not a homogenous political orientation on the Union level.

Under these conditions, the proposals of the Commission are based more on a subject matter rationality that is oriented toward the goal of integration, than on programmatic policy. Following those proposals, also in the European Parliament and in the Council compromises are made that often do not correspond to the political inclination of the individual representatives or of the governments. The system may be labelled as polycentric[51] or compared with a government of all parties.[52] It is not caused by an imperfect organisation, which could be changed simply by procedural amendments, but rather on the fact that the essential political orientations still are decided in the national party-based democracies. These decisions express often with very different points of view orientations of the Member States, which must be brought to a compromise in the Council.

The particularities sketched here affect the process of decision taking. The Commission takes a central position in lawmaking on the basis of its right and monopoly to propose decisions, all the more so because its proposals may only be changed by unanimous vote of the Council. The detailed

[50] On the role of political parties in the Union see S Tsatsos, 'Europäische politische Parteien?' (1994) 21 *Europäische Grundrechte-Zeitschrift* 45; R Bieber, 'Les perspectives d'un statut pour les parties politiques européennes' (1999) 35 *Revue trimestrielle de droit européen* 349; PM Huber, 'Die politischen Parteien als Partizipations-instrument auf Unionsebene' [1999] *Europarecht* 579.

[51] See Peters, above n 3, 217 *et seq*.

[52] In this context, Switzerland is to be mentioned, in whose system orientated on consent (*Konkordanzdemokratie*) the Bundesrat, which serves as the government, is traditionally composed by representatives of the four main parties; see W Linder, § 64, para 27, and L Mader, § 67, paras 11 *et seq* in D Thürer, J-F Aubert and JP Müller (eds), *Verfassungsrecht der Schweiz* (2001). The system is based on Switzerland's historical and structural particularities, so it may not simply be compared with the Union; on this point see S Oeter, 'Souveränität und Demokratie als Probleme in der "Verfassungsentwicklung" der Europäischen Union' (1995) 55 *Zeitschrift für ausländisches öffentliches Recht und Völkerrecht* 659 at 699.

and technical character of most of the rules strengthens the Commission even more. Ministers in the Council are regularly neither ready nor in the position to discuss those matters. The negotiations are therefore necessarily shifted to the level of the civil servants, especially to the working groups of the Council composed of representatives of national administrations and the services of the Commission and, finally, to the Committee of Permanent Representatives of the Member States. These groups and committees attempt to reach a broad consensus and present to the Council drafts in which only a few politically significant points rest open to decision and to co-ordination with the European Parliament.[53]

Through this process, the national administrations also hold a central position, in addition to the Commission, in the decision-making process. This has strengthened the criticism of the system as "bureaucratic" and "far from the citizen" and has contributed to the notion that consensus building in the Union is essentially a task of the civil servants. But notwithstanding the fact that the influence of the administration on the law-making is also considerable in the Member States,[54] so that some criticism sounds somewhat self-righteous, it must be acknowledged that effective decision making in the Council is only possible if it is well prepared and the remaining questions are limited to politically important points.

This is especially true in times in which decision-making in the Council is largely blocked due to differences of opinion over fundamental questions. It is due mainly to the co-operation of administrations on all levels, that even in the times of crisis of the seventies and early eighties the then-EEC was continually expanded through a profusion of integrating rules. Preparation of legislation by committees will be even more necessary after the Union's enlargement to 25 Member States, because now the opposing interests and the controversial opinions within the Council will increase.

Finally, reference must be made to the fact that the ministers in the capital cities mostly determine the conduct of the national representatives in the committees, after parliaments and the regions and *Länder* as well as the associations of the affected economic groups have been consulted. The politically responsible minister, who is also guided in this process by the negotiating situation and the general interest in integration, then gives the vote in the Council, often after discussion in the government. Therefore, the criticism frequently put forward that the proceeding in the Council must be regarded as "legislation by civil servants" is not justified. In addition, the

[53] See A Dashwood, 'The Role of the Council of the European Union' in D Curtin and T Heukels (eds), *Institutional Dynamics of European Integration: Essays in Honour of HG Schermers* (1994), ii, 117 at 126.

[54] Cf A von Bogdandy, *Gubernative Rechtsetzung* (2000).

increased role of the European Parliament must be taken in account, which mostly participates actively on the decision-making by the far-reaching procedure of co-decision.

Accordingly, it can be said that the particularities of the institutional system of the Union are caused by the influence of the different interests and political orientations traditions of the Member States. Procedures must be applied to settle the tensions between Community policy and the Member States that are based on those differences.[55]

2. The Legislative Process of the Union

In the political discussion the decision making process is criticised above all as too ponderous and ineffective. Improvement of the decision making process is expected mostly through an increased admissibility and energetic use of the majority principle in the Council.[56] However, such demands mostly neglect the mentioned essential function of the Council, of bringing together the different traditions and interests of the Member States in order to guarantee the acceptance of the rules by those affected. The majority principle is valid already, with few exceptions, in nearly all important economic areas, and it will be strengthened by the Constitutional Treaty, which provides it as the regular standard. It is in practice often applied if no consensus between the ministers in the Council can be reached.[57] However, such a consensus is first sought in the interest of cohesion of the Community before the majority overrules the opponents. In pursuit of compromise, the pressure for agreement that is exercised by the threat of a majority decision is often beneficial.

The remaining exceptions in which unanimity is required concern primarily those cases in which the core of the policy of the Member States is affected, such as tax, immigration and foreign policy, or the foundations of the Community, such as enlargement of the Union or amendments to the Treaties. With regard to the first group, it is understandable that the Member States will not accept that they may be overruled in the Council. On the other hand, the capability to acting was very restraint already in the

[55] See Everling, above n 27.

[56] See G Tsebellis and X Giataganas, 'Veto Players and Decision-making in the EU after Nice' (2002) 40 *JCMS* 283; A Maurer, 'Entscheidungseffizienz und Handlungsfähigkeit nach Nizza' in M Jopp, B Lippert and H Schneider (eds), *Das Vertragswerk von Nizza und die Zukunft der Europäischen Union* (2001), 79.

[57] A Dashwood, 'Majority Voting in the Council' in J Schwarze (ed), *Legislation for Europe 1992* (1989), 79; V Götz, 'Mehrheitsbeschlüsse des Rates der Europäischen Union' in Due *et al* (eds), above n 12, 339. The debate over the majority principle must for this reason be characterised as disproportionately overblown.

Union with 15 Member States. In the enlarged Union of 25 Member States, the chances to reach unanimity in the Council are even more diminished. Propositions to fix a "super-majority" which excludes that one or two opponents are able to block the decision-making were not accepted. At least the Constitutional Treaty provides as future solution that the European Council may decide by unanimity,[58] without applying the ordinary Treaty amendment procedure, that in domains with special procedures the ordinary legislative procedure including majority voting shall be applicable.[59]

With regard to the second group concerning the foundations of the Union, particularly amendments of the Treaties, the media demanded majority rules under the impression of the disastrous Treaty negotiations at Nice. However, this demand is unrealistic at the current stage of development of the Union since it is based on a Treaty concluded with the consent of the national parliaments and not on a constitutional act, which may be autonomously changed. The often-used formula that the Member States are "masters of the Treaties",[60] is expression of the constitutional reality, that according to Art 48 EU formal amendments of the EU or EC Treaties can only be undertaken by means of a Treaty of all Member States. However, in acting so, they are not totally free but bound by the procedures determined in the cited provision, especially with regard to the participation of the Community institutions.[61] Notwithstanding changes of the procedure, equally Arts 443 and 445 CT-IGC provides that amendments of the Treaty, as at present, shall enter into force after being ratified by all the Member States according to their constitutional requirements.

If Member States could be forced to accept amendments of the Treaty and by this, transfers of sovereign rights to the Union without the agreement of their constitutional organs, in particular of their parliaments, the complex status of pending balance between Member States and Union, which is an essential characteristic of the current system, would be pushed in the direction of a federal state. But the required conditions for such a step, particularly the foundation in the consciousness of the European

[58] According to Art 444(3) CT–IGC, the European Council decides after obtaining the consent of the EP and in the absence of opposition from a national parliament.

[59] See P-C Müller-Graff, 'Systemrationalität in Kontinuität und Änderung des Europäischen Verfassungsvertrages' in Wessels *et al* (eds), above n 5, 301 at 313. Such procedures of autonomous Treaty amendments were foreseen in the EEC Treaty. In the limited manner now available they can be regarded as covered by the consent of the national parliaments to the Constitution. For scruples, see Schwarze, above n 5, 552.

[60] See *Entscheidungen des Bundesverfassungsgerichts* 89, 155 at 190 (*Maastricht*).

[61] See U Everling, 'Zur Stellung der Mitgliedstaaten der Europäischen Union als "Herren der Verträge"' in U Beyerlin *et al* (eds), *Recht zwischen Umbruch und Bewährung: Festschrift für R Bernhardt* (1995), 1161. On the problem see PG Xuereb, 'The Future of Europe' (2002) 27 *EL Rev* 643.

peoples to legitimate such an unit might neither at present nor in the foreseeable future be realised. It may be that rules of some international organisations are less strong.[62] For example, amendments of the Statute of the Council of Europe enter into force after ratification by two-third of the Member States. This Statute, however, is not at all comparable to the Union and EC Treaties with their broad attribution of sovereign rights, and as far as organs of the Council dispose of decision power as foreseen in the European Human Rights Convention the majority rule is not applicable to amendments.[63]

On the other hand, the notion that a single Member State of the expanded union could block the further development of the Treaties must be a startling one.[64] In such a case, the only choice would be the attempt to proceed according to the procedure on strengthened co-operation. Consequently the Constitutional Treaty provides deliberations in the European Council if, two years after its signature, an amendment treaty has not yet been ratified by at least one fifth of the Member States. In summary, it should be stressed that on the one hand the majority principle is certainly indispensable for the ongoing activity of the Union; but that on the other hand the margin for expanding it further than the present state seems to be relatively small.[65]

An instrument which has been promoted for long time to make the decision-making more effective is the delegation of legislative powers to the Commission. The demands to increased delegations concern in the first line enforcement measures of Community regulations, which are because of their technical character not suitable to be discussed by ministers in the Council. However, these measures often contain the most important provisions for the practice of the enterprises and are connected to national traditions and interests. Therefore, the Member States are not ready to transfer them totally to the Commission. They intend to influence these measures in order to bring the interests of the Member States and the Community largely into balance.

Thus, since the first negotiations as to the agricultural market regulation at the start of the sixties, delegation of regulation power to the Commission has been tied to the obligation to involve committees of experts from the

[62] This argument is used by C Tomuschat, 'Schwäche durch Starrheit', *Frankfurter Allgemeine Zeitung*, 27 April 2004.

[63] Amendments of the Convention are possible only by protocols which are binding for Member States which have ratified them.

[64] Such a result had been threatened owing to the failure of the first Irish referendum on the Treaty of Nice; see G Hogan, 'The Nice Treaty and the Irish Constitution' (2001) 7 *European Public Law* 565. The danger was, however, overcome by the positive vote in the second referendum: see JA Kämmerer, 'Das *dejà vu* von Dublin' [2002] *Neue Juristische Wochenschrift* 3596.

[65] See Everling, above n 27, 1072; M Seidel, 'Die Einstimmigkeit im EU' [2000] *Europäische Zeitschrift für Wirtschaftsrecht* 65.

national administrations, whose decisions the Commission must take into account, in accordance to certain particular determined models, whereby in certain cases the decision may fall back on the Council.[66] This process of so-called comitology is criticised by the public in particular for lack of transparency.[67] Yet must be considered, that the committees contribute only to consensus building in the Commission and belong thus to its internal procedures to which the public cannot have access without limit. Besides, in the meantime the transparency of the procedure has been bettered by the new regulations concerning the access to documents.[68]

Through this process the expert knowledge of the national administrations, which have to apply the regulations in the practice, is brought into forming the opinions of the Commission. At the same time, mutual interests are asserted and solutions sought which find the widest possible consensus.[69] To this extent, the committees replace the Council without reducing the efficiency of the decision taking by the Commission, which is normally able to find adequate solutions in the committees. The procedure corresponds to a high degree to the requirements of the institutional system of the Union because it moderates the centralised, hierarchical law-making imposed upon the Member States and contributes to balancing the tensions between the Union and the Member States, as well as those between the Member States themselves.[70]

The European Parliament plays a decisive role in decision making in the Union.[71] The comprehensive activities of the Union and in particular its

[66] See K Lenaerts and A Verhoeven, 'Towards a Legal Framework for Executive Rule-making in the EU?' (2000) 37 *CML Rev* 645; C Mensching, 'Der neue Komitologie-Beschluss des Rates' [2000] *Europäische Zeitschrift für Wirtschaftsrecht* 268. On case law see C Demmke and G Haibach, 'Die Rolle der Komitologieausschüsse bei der Durchführung des Gemeinschaftsrechts' [2000] *Die Öffentliche Verwaltung* 710.

[67] See the diverging assessments in the articles in M Adenas and A Türk (eds), *Delegated Legislation and the Role of Committees in the EC* (2000); further see K Bradley, 'Comitology and the Law' (1992) 29 *CML Rev* 693.

[68] See D Curtin, 'Citizens Fundamental Rights of Access to EU Information' (2000) 29 *CML Rev* 7; B Wägenbaur, 'Der Zugang zu EU-Dokumenten' [2001] *Europäische Zeitschrift für Wirtschaftsrecht* 680.

[69] See RH Pedler and GF Schaefer, *Shaping European Law and Policy* (1996). C Joerges and J Falke (eds), *Das Ausschusswesen der Europäischen Union* (2000).

[70] C Joerges and J Neyer, 'From International Bargaining to Deliberative Political Processes' (1997) 3 *ELJ* 273; GJ Buitendijk and M van Schendelen, 'Brussels Advisory Committees' (1995) 20 *EL Rev* 37; Everling, above n 27, 1066.

[71] The literature is unmanageable. Here I mention only P Allott, 'European Governance and the Re-branding of Democracy' (2002) 37 *EL Rev* 60; W Kluth, *Die demokratische Legitimation der Europäischen Union* (1995); C Harlow, *Accountability in the European Union* (2001); M Kaufmann, *Europäische Integration und Demokratieprinzip* (1997); A Verhoeven, *The European Union in Search of a Democratic and Constitutional Theory* (2002); Peters, above n 3, 627 and *id*, above n 5; H-P Folz, *Demokratie und Integration* (1999); M Telo (ed), *Democratie et construction européenne* (1995).

policy and law-making require the legitimacy by the citizens. It is mediated in part indirectly by the Council through its members, who are responsible to their parliaments, and in part directly through the representatives in the European Parliament, who are elected immediately by the peoples of the Member States.[72] The chain of legitimacy from the national parliaments and their electors to the Union, which the *Bundesverfassungsgericht* has placed in the foreground,[73] is indeed relatively long and does not appear overly robust. The Constitutional Treaty introduces a consultative participation of the national parliaments in the legislative process.[74] Whether this will enforce the connections between Union and the peoples in the Member States remains to be seen.

Thus, hopes are directed toward the European Parliament as second bearer of legitimacy. Its competences have been gradually expanded since introduction of the direct vote, especially through participation in the staffing of the Commission and through co-decision in legislation.[75] The public discussion calls for additional strengthening,[76] but as desirable as this might be, the possibility is limited in the current situation.[77]

For one, the weight of the votes of the citizens of the individual Member States in the election is not equal, because the distribution of the representatives' seats among the individual Member States does not correspond to the population, even if taking into account a base for the smaller Member States.[78] Additionally, for taking a full role in the decision making the Parliament needs the basis in a trans-boundary European Public that includes all parts of the society as social groups, media and citizens. At present, such a public is lacking to a large degree, even if there may be exist remarkable developments in the consciousness of the citizen.[79] For these

[72] See F Brosius-Gersdorf, 'Die doppelte Legitimationsbasis der Europäischen Union' [1999] *Europarecht* 133; K Lenaerts and M Desomer, 'New Models of Constitution-Making in Europe' (2002) 39 *CML Rev* 1217.

[73] See *Entscheidungen des Bundesverfassungsgerichts* 89, 155 at 207 (*Maastricht*).

[74] See Protocol on the Role of the National Parliaments in the European Union and Protocol on the Application of the Principles of Subsidiarity and Proportionality, annexed to the Constitutional Treaty as an integral part in accordance with its Art 442 CT–IGC.

[75] See S Byron, 'Maastricht and the Codecision Procedure' (1996) 46 *ICLQ* 293; D Reich, *Rechte des Europäischen Parlaments in Gegenwart und Zukunft* (1999).

[76] See A Maurer, *Le pouvoir renforcé du Parlement européen après Amsterdam* (2000).

[77] See K Neureither and A Wiener (eds), *European Integration after Amsterdam* (2000); P Badura, 'Bewahrung und Veränderung demokratischer und föderativer Verfassungsprinzipien der in Europa verbundenen Staaten' (1990) 109 *Zeitschrift für Schweizerisches Recht* 115 at 120.

[78] See Schmitz, above n 3, 496.

[79] See D Curtin, *Postnational Democracy* (1997); Scharpf, above n 48. CD Classen, 'Europäische Integration und demokratische Legitimation' (1994) 119 *Archiv des öffentlichen Rechts* 238 at 257, refers to remarkable beginnings.

reasons the Parliament may for now only be strengthened so far as participating equally with the Council in Union law-making.

This is unsatisfactory from the perspective of democratic legitimacy.[80] But it is rightly pointed out that, in the international and supranational area, parliamentary democracy can only be incompletely realised,[81] and that in the Member States it comprises more than the central position of the parliaments.[82] Democracy is also realised by elements such as the rule of law, separation of powers, human rights, legal protections and the participation of societal groups, which are far developed in the Union and compensate the incompleteness of the parliamentary system.

In summary, it can be said that the distribution of the various functions among the European Parliament, Council and Commission, joined also by the Court of Justice, which will be handled later[83], creates an appropriate balance inside the Union. This system is very well suited to settle the various tensions that exist due to the diverse interests, traditions and ideas between the Union and the Member States, and amongst the Member States themselves, and corresponds to the special conditions of the Union. Improvements of the procedures on special points as foreseen in the Constitutional Treaty may be necessary, but as a whole the system seems essentially to comply with the requirements of the democratic foundation, the balancing of interests and the ability to reach decisions.

3. Distribution of Competences in the Union

A key problem in the Union, as in any system with several levels of decision-making, is the vertical distribution of competences. The competence norms are scattered throughout the Treaties according to the principle of specific attribution of power (*"Einzelermächtigung")* pursuant to Art 5(1) EC, and they are not always drafted clearly and unequivocally[84]. From the

[80] This is often asserted: see G Ress, 'Democratic Decision-Making in the European Union and the Role of the European Parliament' in Curtin and Heukels (eds), above n 53, ii, 153.

[81] See A Randelshofer, 'Zum behaupteten Demokratiedefizit der Europäischen Gemeinschaft', in: P Hommelhoff and P Kirchhof (eds), *Der Staatenverbund der Europäischen Union* (1994), 39.

[82] Cf eg the comprehensive discussion by E-W Böckenförde, 'Demokratie als Verfassungsprinzip' in P Kirchhof and J Isensee (eds), *Handbuch des Staatsrechts*, i, § 22 (1987); at length on this problem see also Peters, above n 3, 626 *et seq*; Allott, above n 71.

[83] In this article, the Court (ECJ) is understood also to include the Court of First Instance (CFI), unless otherwise indicated by the context.

[84] See A Dashwood, 'The Limits of European Communities Powers' (1996) 21 *EL Rev* 113; H-P Kraußer, *Das Prinzip begrenzter Ermächtigung im Gemeinschaftsrecht als Strukturprinzip des EWG-Vertrages* (1991); A von Bogdandy and J Bast, 'The European Union's Vertical Order of Competences' (2002) 39 *CML Rev* 227.

beginning, Member States and institutions of the Union disagreed as to their interpretation what was primarily carried out in the Council. It is true that the Commission first stepped in with its proposals for a comprehensive and often extensive interpretation and application of the Treaty provisions. Because of its strong position in the process of decision-making and the mostly assured support of the Parliament and some in the concrete case interested Member States, it could often succeed in the Council. In the end, it was then the Member States in the Council, or at least their majority, who were ready to accept a broad understanding of the competences of the Union. Limiting by this their own competences, they often expected from this a more effective acknowledgement of the protection of common interests, and hesitant Member States often abandoned their resistance in the general interests of integration.

In the same understanding, the Council often made use, after initial hesitation and on request of the Paris Summit Conference of 1972, of the general authorisation in Art 235 EEC Treaty (Art 308 EC), to round out and supplement incomplete or controversial competences[85]. The Treaty was then amended accordingly, above all in the Single European Act and the Treaty of *Maastricht*. Today, due to the expansive interpretation of the regularly competence norms, the need to appeal to Art 308 EC is limited. Therefore, this disposition may hardly be considered as a back door for extending competences, all the more since the Court interprets them restrictively.[86] Eliminating them would thus not increase the protection against the widening of competences, but would restrict the flexibility in marginal questions. Accordingly, the Constitutional Treaty upholds the provision in its Art 18 CT-IGC but limits its field of application to the domains included in Part III and demands the consent of the EP.

Yet the Member States have contributed to the expansion of Community competences not only by their decisions in the Council, but above all by the Treaty amendments of the last decade, about which they now complain. Nevertheless, their criticisms, including those of their constitutional courts,[87] are addressed primarily to the ECJ.[88] It is true that the ECJ has seldom

[85] See A Tizzano, 'L'article 235 CEE et le développement des compétences communautaires' in Lüke *et al* (eds), above n 42, 781.

[86] See M Bungenberg, *Art 235 EGV nach Maastricht* (1999); P Kapteyn, P VerLoren van Themaat and L Gormley, *Introduction to the Law of the European Communities* (1998), 235 *et seq*; IE Schwartz in H von der Groeben and J Schwarze (eds), *Kommentar zum Vertrag über die Europäische Union und zur Gründung der Europäischen Gemeinschaft* (2004), on Art 308 EC.

[87] See the *Maastricht* Judgment of the Federal Constitutional Court: above n 73, 209.

[88] U Goll and M Kenntner, 'Brauchen wir ein Europäisches Kompetenzgericht?' [2002] *Europäische Zeitschrift für Wirtschaftsrecht* 101. This article reflects the widespread criticism of German politicians; against: N Colneric, 'Der Gerichtshof der Europäischen Gemeinschaften als Kompetenzgericht' [2002] *Europäische Zeitschrift für Wirtschaftsrecht* 709.

declared legal provisions of the Community legislator void for exceeding competences.[89] Evidently, the Court gives an increased weight to the fact that in the procedure of co-decision the Member States in the Council and the elected representatives in the EP agree to a rule giving it a high legitimacy. However, in the Union, in which the participation of the EP is limited, review by the Court to protect the rights of outvoted Member States and of citizens affected by measures has a special significance.[90]

As important as the protective function of the ECJ may be in this context, it cannot be fundamentally objected that it interprets the competence norms and the Treaty as a whole not restrictively to preserve the rights of the Member States but objectively and *teleological* according to the goals of the Treaty.[91] The Court orients itself at the meaning and systematic location of the dispositions in the Treaty and at the *effet utile*, the "practical effectiveness", of the provisions affected, this means an interpretation in which the provision can fulfil the function for which it is insert in the Treaty.[92] Even if several wide interpretations may be disputed, as a whole this practice corresponds to the character of the Union as an independent entity, equipped with sovereign rights, which has to be understood from the perspective of its own legal order. Analysis of the judgments of the ECJ shows that their tendency runs largely parallel to that of the general political orientation of the Union.[93]

In light of interlacing of the policy of the Union with that of the Member States, and their diverse, often opposing interests, there is no easy solution for a clearer order of competences, something which has long been called for.[94] It is doubtful whether a competence catalogue as has been often

[89] But see recently the ECJ judgment on the tobacco advertising directive, Case C–376/98 *Germany v Parliament and Council* [2000] ECR I–8419. Cf the note by V Götz [2001] *Juristenzeitung* 334; T Hervey, 'Up in Smoke?' (2001) 26 *EL Rev* 101.

[90] See J Mischo, 'The Contribution of the Court of Justice to the Protection of the "Federal Balance" in the European Community' in O'Keefe (ed), above n 41, 59; U Everling, 'Die Kontrolle des Gemeinschaftsgesetzgebers durch die Europäischen Gerichte' in CO Lenz, W Thieme and F Graf von Westphalen (eds), *Beiträge zum deutschen und europäischen Recht: Freundesgabe für J Gündisch* (1999), 89.

[91] See A Arnull, *The European Union and its Court of Justice* (1999), 515 *et seq*; J Annweiler, *Die Auslegungsmethoden des Gerichtshofs der Europäischen Gemeinschaften* (1997); C Buck, *Über die Auslegungsmethoden des Gerichtshofs der Europäischen Gemeinschaften* (1998).

[92] See R Streinz, 'Der "effet utile" in der Rechtsprechung des Gerichtshofs der Europäischen Gemeinschaften' in Due *et al* (eds), above n 12, 1491; N Emiliou, 'Opening Pandoras Box' (1994) 19 *EL Rev* 488.

[93] See U Everling, 'On the Judge-Made Law of the European Community's Courts' in O'Keeffe (ed), above n 41, 29 at 38.

[94] On this problem see eg I Pernice, 'Kompetenzabgrenzung im Europäischen Verfassungsverbund' [2000] *Juristenzeitung* 866; A Dashwood, 'The Limits of European Community Powers' (1996) 21 *EL Rev* 113; G de Búrca, *The Constitutional Limits of EU Action* (2001); J Schwarze, 'Kompetenzverteilung in der Europäischen Union und föderales Gleichgewicht' [1995] *Deutsches Verwaltungsblatt* 1265.

demanded would bring any more clarity than the present rules, because the notions and domains of such a list must be specified later on in special parts of the Treaty in more details[95]. The same is true of the proposal to establish bipolar competences on the upper and lower levels, which needs clarifications. Every catalogue would have to use general terms for the authorisations, which would each be understood differently in the now more than 20 languages of the Community, so that in the end, as has been the case up to present, a uniform interpretation would have to occur through a central instance, namely through the ECJ, so that little would change.[96]

In spite of these objections, the Constitutional Treaty presents in its Arts Arts 12 *et seq* CT-IGC a list of competences grouped in exclusive and shared competences as well as competences to promote, co-ordinate and support certain areas of politics of the Member States, completed by a common foreign and security policy including defence policy.[97] But the domains are only to understand in the light of the special chapters of Part III, which explained more precisely the domains and needs the interpretation by the Union legislator and in last instance by the ECJ. Insofar the Constitutional Treaty presents no essential change to the present state.

Regarding central position of the ECJ, some critical Member States and particularly German *Länder* have called for a special competence court in which active national judges participate.[98] They believe that the ECJ exercises its interpretation function in favouring the Union to the debit of the competences of the Member States, what may be certainly rejected.[99] But for organisational reasons alone such a special court would barely be capable of functioning and would inevitably conflict with the two existing Courts, because questions of competence and questions of substance are inextricable interweaving. Consequently, the effectiveness and coherence of the whole system of legal protection would be endangered.[100]

The Constitutional Treaty does, therefore, rightly not foresee such a special Court. The Treaty is however, taking care of the respect to the subsidiarity principle, which certainly can contribute little to the competence debate, since it does not affect the distribution of competences but rather

[95] See FC Mayer, 'Die drei Dimensionen der europäischen Kompetenzdebatte' (2001) 61 *Zeitschrift für ausländisches öffentliches Recht und Völkerrecht* 577 at 583.

[96] See Von Bogdandy and Bast, above n 84, 227; Schwarze, above n 94, 1268.

[97] See D Hanf and T Baumé, 'Vers une classification de la répartition des compétences entre l'Union et ses Etats Membres' (2003) 38 *CDE* 135; M Schroeder, 'Vertikale Kompetenzverteilung und Subsidiarität im Konvententwurf für eine europäische Verfassung' [2004] *Juristenzeitung* 8.

[98] See eg Goll and Kenntner, above n 88.

[99] See Colneric, above n 88, and Everling, above n 93.

[100] See U Everling, 'Quis custodiet custodes ipsos?' [2002] *Europäische Zeitschrift für Wirtschaftsrecht* 357; Mayer, above n 3, 330 *et seq*, with reference to US experiences.

their practical application.[101] According to the Protocols attached to the Constitutional Treaty the national parliaments shall be entitled to send to the institutions reasoned opinions on the legislative proposals of the Commission stating why it considers that the proposal in question does not comply with the principle of subsidiarity.[102] The institutions are obliged to take into account these opinions, but it remains to see whether they are ready to correct their proposals and whether they also regard critical opinions of the national parliament concerning the competences, though these are not foreseen in the Protocol.[103]

After all the only promising approach seems the attempt to specify the individual competence norms more precisely.[104] This has already occurred in part in the Treaties of Maastricht and Amsterdam, and now the Constitutional Treaty presents further specifications. However, due to the differing interests of the Member States such negotiations are difficult and must not be misused to strive for retrogression in integration. The authorisations may also not be so narrowly formulated that the organs do not have the necessary flexibility. Just one example of this difficulty is set out here.

In practice, the harmonisation of laws toward realisation of the internal market is the most important back door in the jurisdiction of the Member States, as it encroaches extensively into public and private economic law. But harmonisation of laws, as already discussed, is necessary in order to eliminate restrictions on the basic freedoms which the Member States may still undertake through rules in the interest of the common wealth.[105] Whoever wants to limit harmonisation of laws also has to understand the basic freedoms more narrowly than they have been developed until now in the years-long practice and jurisprudence. They still belong, though, to the core of the Union and may therefore not be placed in question. The latitude for restrictive formulations is for this reason small.

In sum, what results is that in the Union a clear and unequivocal separation of the levels of decision-making is hardly attainable. The policies of the Union and the Member States are so variously interwoven and their interests so different, that a clear demarcation of competences runs into difficulties. Member States and the Union must co-operate in common with the

[101] See A Epiney, 'Das Subsidiaritätsprinzip—Eine Kompetenzausübungsregel zur Begrenzung gemeinschaftlicher Tätigkeit' [1993] *Aktuelle juristische Praxis* 951; R von Borries and M Hauschild, 'Implementing the Subsidiarity Principle' (2000) 5 *Columbia Journal of European Law* 369.

[102] See above n 74.

[103] On the defectiveness of the procedure see U Everling, 'Rechtschutz im Europäischen Wirtschaftsrecht auf der Grundlage der Konventsregelungen' in Schwarze (ed), above n 5, 363 at 378; Schröder, above n 97.

[104] See on this point J Schwarze, 'Europäische Verfassungsprobleme nach Nizza' [2002] *Neue Juristische Wochenschrift* 993 at 995.

[105] See above n 42.

loyalty required by the Treaty in order to reach agreement as to the limits of the competences and their performance according to the subsidiarity principle. In any case this requires of the political actors a high degree of moderation and restraint and readiness to co-ordination and compromise. It must be admitted that this is not always found in the struggle for political power, which is always at issue where competences are concerned.

IV. FORMING THE CONSTITUTIONAL AND LEGAL ORDER OF THE EUROPEAN UNION

1. The Constitutional Structure of the Union

For years it has been discussed whether the Union should be invested by a constitution, and particularly the EP has presented such propositions, the sense and advantages of which are discussed controversially.[106] This debate is unsatisfactory to the extent that politicians and scholars use the concept of a constitution differently. It is traditionally related to the state[107] and characterised comprehensively as its legal fundamental order.[108] However, according to a further use of speech, the notion "constitution" can also be applied to an independent inter-state or supra-state entity, which is organisationally and legally fully equipped. Then it must be made clear that thereby no state-like quality will be attributed to it.[109] In a technical sense the Union has long possessed, in the Treaties and in the general legal principles developed by the ECJ, a widely drawn-out constitution as a legal order for its organisation and institutions, for its instruments and procedures for decision making, for its relationship to the Member States and citizens as well as to third countries and for its system of legal protection through jurisdiction. It is applied and confirmed daily in practice.[110]

[106] Cf the summary of important proposals in W Loth, *Entwürfe einer europäischen Verfassung: Eine historische Bilanz* (2002).

[107] See eg J Isensee, 'Staat und Verfassung' in *id* and Kirchhof (eds), above n 82, i, § 13, 591.

[108] See the well-known formula of W Kägi, *Die rechtliche Grundordnung des Staates* (1945).

[109] See N Walker, 'European Constitutionalism and European Integration' [1996] *Public Law* 266; I Pernice, 'Die Verfassungsfrage aus rechtswissenschaftlicher Sicht' in T Bruha, J Hesse and C Nowak (eds), *Welche Verfassung für Europa?* (2001), 19; D Edwards, 'The Community Constitution—Rigid or Flexible?' in O'Keefe (ed), above n 41, 57.

[110] See GC Rodríguez Iglesias, 'Zur "Verfassung" der Europäischen Gemeinschaft' [1996] *Europäische Grundrechte-Zeitschrift* 125, with references to the judicial practice of the ECJ; I Harden, 'The Constitution of the European Union' [1994] *Public Law* 609; JL Seurin, 'Towards a European Constitution?' [1994] *Public Law* 625; JA Frowein, 'Die Verfassung der Europäischen Union aus der Sicht der Mitgliedstaaten' [1995] *Europarecht* 315; Pernice, above n 109, 26.

Nevertheless, the public at the same time calls for a European Constitution, and the Convention proposed and the Member States signed a Treaty establishing a "Constitution" though a Constitution already exists in practice. The motivations to denominate the Union's order as "Constitution" are manifold and differential. Mainly they are based on a formal understanding of the "Constitution" and intend to bring the Union Treaty in a clearer form and to better its functioning. In addition, some political actors may in first line aim the strengthening of the Union in view of the present enlargement, some others may, however, also envisage the original function of a constitution, of limiting the exercise of sovereign power. But thereby it is in their view evidently not, as with the historical precedents the citizens that are to be protected in the first place, but rather the Member States and their constituent parts, especially the *Länder*. The positively expressed calls for a constitution appear sometimes to pursue less the improvement of the Union and more its regression and the restriction of its activities.[111]

Further reaching notions are often behind the call for a constitution for the Union. In the tradition of the enlightenment and the American Convention or the French Revolution, a material sense is tied to the constitution, namely the expression of the will of a group of people to integrate itself as a nation or similarly established human entity for action and to give itself an identity that is determined by common values.[112] The Union is still very far from a constitution in this meaning, as is particularly clear by the fact that the European Constitution will be not established by a common act of the peoples but by a Treaty, which remains its fundament. Above all, the citizens of the Member States, in spite of Europe's common cultural foundations[113] and in spite of the progress achieved over the past years, can only be bound to a limited extent by a common consciousness that could serve as the foundation for a constitution in this sense.[114]

The actual structure of the Union and the Communities is scarcely appropriate to promote such a consciousness because it presents a confusing picture. The relations of these organisations to each other are hardly

[111] This appears eg to be the tendency of W Clement, 'Europa gestalten—nicht verwalten' in Walter Hallstein-Institut (ed), *Die Reform der europäischen Institutionen* (2002), 177, and also of most of the German *Länder*.

[112] On the significance of the development of the Union into a community of values, see M Böhner, *Integration und Legitimität in der Europäischen Union* (1998); JHH Weiler, 'Ideaux et construction européenne' in Telo (ed), above n 71, 99. See on this the text below at n 197.

[113] This is stressed above all by P Häberle in many publications. See above n 3, 64 *et seq*.

[114] Cf M Kaufmann, 'Verfassungspatriotismus, substantielle Gleichheit und Demokratieprinzip im europäischen Staatenverbund' in A Brockmöller (ed), *Ethische und strukturelle Herausforderungen des Rechts* (1997) 66 *Archiv für Rechts- und Sozialphilosophie*, Beiheft, 40; P Eleftheriadic, 'Aspects of European Constitutionalism' (1996) 21 *EL Rev* 32.

comprehensible, even for experts, and create a barrier to the citizens' acceptance of the Union.[115] The three Communities are since their founding separate legal personalities; only the institutions were merged and since then act according to different rules in the Treaties.[116] In practice, the application of these rules has over time to a certain extent been approximated.[117] This still manageable legal situation was made more unclear by the already mentioned investiture of the European Council and Political Co-operation and made completely opaque by the Maastricht Treaty. It placed above the Communities the additionally established Union with the European Council as its core and the special areas of external and security policy as well as co-operation in the areas of justice and internal affairs.[118] Protocols, declarations, informal decisions and inter-institutional agreements as well as a vast mass of secondary legal acts complete the impression of disorder.

The idiosyncratic construction of the Treaties is often explained by use of the popular image of a temple with three pillars, whereby the Union is understood in a double sense, namely on the one hand as the structure that encompasses all parts and, on the other hand, as the roof over those of the Communities, the Common Foreign and Security Policy and the co-operation in justice matters. As accessible as this metaphor is, it obscures the legal uncertainty more than it illuminates the understanding.[119] It leads to the odd result that the "pillar" with the legally secured, supra-national Communities stands under the "roof" with the mostly co-operatively acting European Council, which cannot give the Communities any orders,[120] and the latter are placed on the same level as the equally largely co-operatively organised other "pillars". The image also veils the many links and relationships that exist between the different areas and the Communities.[121]

[115] See eg D Curtin, 'The Constitutional Structure of the Union' (1993) 30 *CML Rev* 17. On the terminological imbroglio see S Hölscheidt and C Baldus, 'EU und EG als terminologisches Problem' [1996] *Deutsches Verwaltungsblatt* 1409.

[116] Here it should be pointed out that the European Coal and Steel Community Treaty expired, with no replacement, on 23 July 2002. See W Oberwexer, 'Das Ende der Europäischen Gemeinschaft für Kohle und Stahl' [2000] *Europäische Zeitschrift für Wirtschaftsrecht* 517.

[117] See U Everling, 'From European Communities to European Union' in A von Bogdandy, PC Mavroidis and Y Mény, *European Integration and International Co-ordination, Studies in Honour of CD Ehlermann* (2002), 139.

[118] Through the Amsterdam Treaty, essential parts of the cited areas of co-operation were taken over from the EU Treaty into the EC Treaty, so that this pillar is limited to provisions on the police and justice co-operation in criminal matters.

[119] See Schmitz, above n 3, 149.

[120] See CA Timmermans, 'The Uneasy Relationship between the Community and the Second Union Pillar' (1996) 26 *Legal Issues of European Integration* 61. See also below n 130.

[121] For theses see the contributions in A von Bogdandy and C-D Ehlermann (eds), *Konsolidierung und Kohärenz des Primärrechts nach Amsterdam*, *Europarecht* (1998), Beiheft 2.

How the construction is to be understood legally is the topic of intense discussion.[122] Some authors want to conceive of the Union, including the Communities and the other two areas, as a legal unit and place them collectively under Community law.[123] It is, however, questionable whether this can be reconciled with the text of the Treaties, since these provide formally for a separation of Union and Communities. The opposite view derive from the text a complete separation; according to this the Union and the substantive areas attached to it, are to be seen as an international law framework for the Communities, which are still acting according to the law of integration.[124] This view comes to the unrealistic result that Council and Commission, when they act in the context of the Union, act for the Member States according to rules of international law.[125]

The practice has long surpassed these theoretical debates and treats the Union and the Communities as a uniform association for integration. This is justified in light of the common goals and institutions as well as their mutual inter-weaving. Nonetheless, the fact cannot be ignored that the Treaty parties consciously did not merge the Union and Community into one legal unit. Under these circumstances, the organisation as a whole, similar to the three Communities up to this point, is to be seen not as a legal, but as a political and economic unit to which the principles of the law of integration are to be applied.[126]

In face of such a disorderly confusion, the establishing of a constitution opens up the opportunity to create clearer structures enabling the institutions to fulfil their functions more effective and present an understandable organisation to the citizens. Indeed, the Constitutional Treaty will eliminate the diffuse division in parts and defines the Union as political and legal unit with a more comprehensive and transparent structure. The text of the Treaty has been assorted with individual rights and symbolic elements for this purpose.[127] It is an open question whether the politicians, economics and citizens on all levels of the society will be already prepared to accept

[122] See *ibid*; T Heukels and J de Zwaan, 'The Configuration of the European Union' in Curtin and Heukels (eds), above n 53, ii (1994), 195; JC Wichard, 'Wer ist Herr im europäischen Haus?' [1999] *Europarecht* 170.

[123] See A von Bogdandy and M Nettesheim, 'Die Europäische Union, ein einheitlicher Verband mit einheitlicher Rechtsordnung' [1995] *Europarecht* 3.

[124] See C Koenig and M Pechstein, *Die Europäische Union* (2000), 282.

[125] This discussion was influenced by the different opinions on the question whether the Union possesses legal personality. Whereas this at first, in the light of the Maastricht Treaty, was mostly denied, now, because of the growing activities of the Union which are broadly accepted as legally obligating, the opposite seems to be the case. At any rate, it should no longer be doubted after the amendment of Art 24 EU by the Treaty of Nice. See Everling, above n 117, 151.

[126] For more detail, see Everling, above n 117, further Wichard, above n 122.

[127] See von Bogdandy, above n 21.

the Constitution as object of identification in the sense designed above. Much speaks for the position that in spite of these developments the Union remains in its state between independent entity and organisation based on the Member States for the time within sight.

2. The Position of the Member States in the Union

These reflections give rise to go into more detail as to the position of the Member States in the Union. The hope expressed in part after the war, that the states would have exhausted their central status, quickly proved to be an illusion. Granted, nation-states of the classic mould of the 19th century, with their claims to power and exclusivity have largely been overtaken by global opening and co-operation. In any event, states remain present for now as a framework for order and an object of identification for citizens.[128] In the states, the citizens reach voting decisions on political orientation, and states continue to feel responsible for the existence of the politically formed society in freedom, peace and welfare, and they are confirmed by the citizens' expectations.

However, the Member States can only do limited justice to their responsibility because important parts of their essential functions have been transferred to the Union. It performs them according to their own rules, and thereby retreat them increasingly from the influence of the Member States. The French government early on recognised the effects of Community measures on Member States' position and ability to act and, with the *Fouchet* Plan, proposed procedures to durable secure the dominance and control of the Member States over the then EEC long-term even in the case of including political substantive areas.[129]

As is known, this project, already named Union, failed but the basic idea was pursued persistently by all of the subsequent French governments, beginning with the Luxembourg Protocols for preserving unanimity. It took shape for the first time in the European Council created 1974 and was then established legally in the Union Treaty of *Maastricht*.[130] However, the original concepts of the Fouchet Plan, to subject the Community to the

[128] On the transformation of state's functions and their continuing importance, see P Saladin *Wozu noch Staaten*? (1995); P Allott, 'The Crisis of European Constitutionalism' (1997) 34 *CML Rev* 439; U di Fabio, *Das Recht offener Staaten* (1998); I Ward, 'The European Constitution and the Nation State' (1996) 16 *Oxford Journal of Legal Studies* 161.

[129] See W Lipgens (ed), *45 Jahre Ringen um die Europäische Verfassung* (1986), 436; R Bloes, *Le Plan Fouchet et le problème de l'Europe politique* (1970); Burgess, above n 1, 78 *et seq*.

[130] See U Everling, 'Überlegungen zur Struktur der Europäischen Union und zum neuen Europa-Artikel des Grundgesetzes' [1993] *Deutsches Verwaltungsblatt* 936 at 940; Timmermans, above n 120.

direction of the united governments of the Member States, could no longer be realised. The Union had already freed itself so far from the Member States, that the Member States are still only placed above them to the extent they can amend the Treaty through the process provided for this. Insofar they may still be called "masters of the Treaties".[131] Decisions of the European Council are not, however, binding for the Community organs, except it is explicitly foreseen in the Treaty, since the Union Treaty expressly leaves the Community Treaties untouched.[132] They have influence not on legal grounds but rather because of the authority of the high members of the European Council and are for this reason respected in practice.

The position of the Member States in the Union is thus ambivalent. On the one hand, they are founders and bearers of the Union and participate authoritatively through their representatives in the European Council and in the Council and through diverse contacts of all kinds toward consensus building. They determine in dialogue with the EP and the Commission the fundamental direction of the policy of the Union; they also largely execute the Community law and, together, can amend the Treaties. Furthermore, there exist domains in which they may act outside the rules of the Union autonomously. In particular, they remain subjects of the international law, even if their discretion is limited by international activities of the Union. Finally, Art 6(3) EU assures that the Union shall respect the identity of the Member States.[133]

On the other hand, the Member States are also members of the Union in the sense that they are subject to its politic and legal order and must give it priority over national politics and national law. In many, if not most areas of public life, they are now only limited capable to act alone, as has been demonstrated. Community law also determines the framework conditions for their constitutional and legal orders. Art 6 EU declares not only that the Union rests on the principles of freedom, democracy, regard for human rights and fundamental freedoms as well as the rule of law, but it also states that these principles are common to all Member States. Thus it establishes as for the Union also for the Member States the obligation to organise themselves according to the rules of a free democracy and to make these the foundation of their policy.[134] This obligation is emphasised by Art 7 EU,

[131] See the text above at n 60, also Everling, above n 61.

[132] See Timmermans, above n 120; H-J Glaesner, 'Der Europäische Rat' [1994] *Europarecht* 22.

[133] See E Pache, 'Europäische und nationale Identität, Integration durch Verfassungsrecht?' [2002] *Deutsches Verwaltungsblatt* 1154.

[134] See F Schorkopf, *Homogenität in der Europäischen Union* (2000); B Beutler in Groeben and Schwarze (eds), above n 86, on Arts 6 and 7 EU; J Schwarze (ed), *Die Entstehung einer europäischen Verfassungsordnung* (2000); P Manin, 'The Treaty of Amsterdam' (1998) 4 *Columbia Journal of European Law* 1 at 23.

which provides for the possibility of sanctions for Member States violating these fundamental principles.

Furthermore, Art 13 EC provides for decisions against discrimination on the basis of sex, race, ethnic origin, religion or worldview, disability, age or sexual orientation.[135] Art 4 EC determines for the economic order that the activity of the Member States and of the Community in the economic field encompasses co-ordination of economic policy, which is bound to the principle of a free market economy and free competition. This sets narrow boundaries for the economic policy of the Member States in the areas remaining to them, particularly in the financial policy.[136] Also, the direct connection of the Union to the citizens beyond the Member States and without their mediation shows the transformation of the position of the Member States. With this the Union removes from the Member States portions of their personal sovereignty, which states traditionally claim. Community law provides subjective rights, on which everybody may rely, but also confirms duties for them that are overseen by the local authorities.[137] The inclusion of the citizen is expressed by the Union citizenship according to Art 17 EC. It has increasingly become of substantial importance by the interpretation of the ECJ.[138]

The development of Community law has led to a constant increase in European influences on the national constitutions.[139] This evolutionary process is described as the Europeanisation of the national constitutions and is to be understood as a longer term European harmonisation, but still leaves plenty of latitude for national peculiarities.[140]

It appears highly questionable whether under these circumstances the Member States can still be characterised as sovereign.[141] To the extent that

[135] See L Flynn, 'The Implications of Article 13 EC' (1999) 36 *CML Rev* 1127; D Rosenberg, 'La lutte contre le racisme et la xenophobie dans L'union européenne' (1999) 35 *Revue trimestrielle de droit européen* 201; E Picker, 'Antidiskriminierung als Zivilrechtsprogramm' [2003] *Juristenzeitung* 540.

[136] See above n 47.

[137] See N Reich, *Bürgerrechte in der Europäischen Union* (1999).

[138] On the newer developments see C Jacqueson, 'Union Citizenship and the Court of Justice' (2002) 27 *EL Rev* 260; S Fries and J Shaw, 'Citizenship of the Union' (1998) 4 *European Public Law* 533. Cf also S Hobe, 'Die Unionsbürgerschaft nach dem Vertrag von Maastricht' (1993) 32 *Der Staat* 245.

[139] See the explanations by Peters, above n 3, *passim* and 375 *et seq*; Häberle, above n 3, 220, even speaks of a *Relativierung der nationalen Verfassungen zu Teilverfassungen* (reduction of the national constitutions into partial constitutions); P de Rossa, *Revolt or Revolution* (1997) is critical of this evolution.

[140] See Schwarze (ed), above n 134; N MacCormick, 'Risking Constitutional Collision in Europe?' (1998) 3 *Oxford Journal of Legal Studies* 157; JA Frowein, 'Die Europäisierung des Verfassungsrechts' in P Badura and H Dreier (eds), *Festschrift 50 Jahre Bundesverfassungsgericht* (2001), 209; T de Berranger, *Constitutions nationales et construction communautaire* (1995).

[141] See on the problem Oeter, above note 52; R Bellamy and D Castiglione, 'Building the Union' in N MacCormick (ed), *Constructing Legal Systems* (1997), 91; *id*, 'Beyond the Sovereign State' (1993) 56 *MLR* 1.

sovereignty in the sense of an unlimited legal capacity to act in the modern, internationally interwoven world can still be spoken of at all, the Member States can at best be regarded as possessing a "divided" or "amputated" sovereignty.[142] In face of substantial concerns having been raised about this construction the picture of a commonly exercised or "mixed" sovereignty should be more fitting.[143] The discussion shows that the traditional understanding of sovereignty cannot contribute to the clarification of the relationship between Union and Member States.[144] but that its real core consists in the relationship between national and European constitutions and their legitimacy. In France, where national sovereignty is anchored in the constitution, the question of sovereignty has not yet had the effect of hindering the progress of integration, thanks to a flexible jurisprudence of the *Conseil constitutionnel* and various constitutional amendments.[145]

In the foregoing context, only the extent to which the Member States have retained the ability to decide over fundamental questions of the polity is determinative.[146] Significant above all in this regard, apart from co-decision on Treaty amendments, is the state of emergency clause in Art 297 EC. According to the view of the author, this clause can be understood as the residual of the sovereignty of the Member States,[147] but according to Art 298 EC they are thereby subject to Community law commitments, especially to review by the ECJ. Of course, the Union possesses no police or military means of coercion against a violation of corresponding judgments by Member States, only financial sanctions under Art 228(2) EC are thinkable even if scarcely imaginable in such fundamental controversies.

In summary, it can be said that the Member States are already relatively firmly inserted in the constitutional system of the Union, but that they have retained some latitude for action. The Constitutional Treaty will bring no principal changes in this regard. It may on the one hand the political and legal coherence of the Union and their Member States strengthen and on the other bring clearer delimitations and precisions of the rights and obligations

[142] See K Doehring, 'Staat und Verfassung in einem zusammenwachsenden Europa' (1993) 26 *Zeitschrift für Rechtspolitik* 98; I Pernice, 'Die dritte Gewalt im europäischen Verfassungsverbund' [1996] *Europarecht* 27 at 31. On this concept see D Obranovic, 'Community Law and the Doctrine of Divisible Sovereignty' [1993] *Legal Issues of European Integration* 1; Schmitz, above n 3, 190 *et seq*.

[143] See Bellamy and Castiglione, above n 141, 111.

[144] See Frowein, above n 110, 319; Peters, above n 3, 148.

[145] See F Luchaire, 'Le Conseil constitutionnel et la souveraineté nationale' [1991] *Revue de Droit Public* 1499; J-M Favret, 'L'intégration européenne et la France' [1999] *Revue de Droit Public* 1741; J Hecker, *Europäische Integration als Verfassungsproblem in Frankreich* (1998).

[146] See S Oeter, 'Vertrag oder Verfassung?' in Bruha *et al* (eds), above n 109, 243.

[147] Thus see U Everling, 'Brauchen wir Solange III?' [1990] *Europarecht* 195 at 223. Mostly the disposition is interpreted as an escapeclause; see P Koutrakos, 'Is Article 297 EC a "Reserve of Sovereignty"?' (2000) 37 *CML Rev* 1339.

of both sides. But in principle the position of the Member States within the Union will not change and persist in continuity. Tensions and conflicts in the Union are therefore unavoidable and must be resolved time and again.

3. Constitutional Perspectives of the Union's Legal Order

In view of the dilemma set forth, the cohesion that the law of the Union can give takes on special importance. The Community is—in the dictum of *Walter Hallstein*—a community of law,[148] and the same now is true of the Union as a whole. Community and Union are created by Treaties, which are instruments of law and these are their foundations up to present. The rule of law is expressively named in Art 6 EU as one of the basic elements of the Union. Together with the other principles listed there of freedom, democracy and the respect for human rights, it is an essential element of a materially understood European constitutional order. It possesses special significance because law works to a great extent as an integrating factor. It harmonises national law, requires conforming conduct and creates a framework for a common policy.[149]

Law regulates the institutions' composition, powers and forms of action, their relation to each other and to the Member States and citizens, the rights of these vis-à-vis the Community and finally legal protection. This has already largely been discussed in another context of this paper. It should be complemented by pointing at the rules about the transparency of the documents of the Community institutions, which fulfil a fundamental requirement of the rule of law.[150] However, it is dubious if also the decision-making process and in particular the deliberations of the Council should be transparent for the public, as often demanded and now foreseen in the Constitutional Treaty. The procedures in the Council are often more comparable to international negotiations than to lawmaking activities, and compromises are seldom closed in the light of the media. The deliberations would be more than before relocated to the working groups of the Council, as is also the case in the German *Bundesrat,* and the requirements of the rule of law would not be bettered.

[148] See W Hallstein, *Die Europäische Gemeinschaft* (5th ed, 1979), 53 *et seq*. See M Zuleeg, 'Die Europäische Gemeinschaft als Rechtsgemeinschaft' [1994] *Neue Juristische Wochenschrift* 545.

[149] See M Cappelletti, M Secombe and JHH Weiler (eds), *Integration through Law* (1986); R Dehousse and JHH Weiler, 'The Legal Dimension' [1994] in Wallace (ed), above n 49, 242; T Möllers, *Die Rolle des Rechts im Rahmen der europäischen Integration* (1999).

[150] See B Wägenbaur, 'Der Zugang zu EU-Dokumenten' [2001] *Europäische Zeitschrift für Wirtschaftsrecht* 681; K Bradley, 'La transparance de l'Union européenne, une évidence ou un trompe d'oeil?' (1999) 35 *CDE* 283; D Curtin, 'Citizens Fundamental Right of Access to EU Information' (2000) 37 *CML Rev* 7.

An essential element of the rule of law in the continental understanding (“*Rechtsstaat*”, “*Etat de droit*”) is the principle of separation of powers. In the modern constitutional state, it is not understood as the separation of the state powers, that can never be purely enforced, but rather as a balance between the functions of the state institutions in order to restrain the exercise of power. It should also at the same time serve the proper allocation of functions to the institutions.[151] Above all, it cannot simply be assigned in its original understanding of *Montesquieu* to the Union, with its special form of organisation. In the Union the functions are distributed so that a one sided accumulation of the power of decision is not possible. This is true horizontally between the institutions of the Union as well as vertically between these and the Member States.[152]

The legislative function rests with the Council and the European Parliament, upon proposal of the Commission, for whose co-operation rules have been laid down. No institution can prevail of it’s own, and the Member States participate in the Council. Governance functions, to the extent they even accrue to the Union, are carried out by the Council or the Commission, but also in part by the European Council or the Member States acting together. The administration is assigned to the Commission as far as it is executed at the Community level, but the administrations of the Member States participate in part in the context of comitology discussed above[153]. As a rule, the administrative execution lies with the authorities of the Member States who act in this capacity on the basis of the law made by the Community organs. The judicial function is entrusted to the ECJ and the CFI, but at the same time, the national courts are called upon in the context of proceedings pending before them to apply Community law, whereby they may or, in the last instance must, obtain a preliminary decision of the ECJ.

As a whole, this system can secure a balance between the various bearers of functions. It is characterised by the Court primarily as a system of institutional balance.[154] With this, the Court expresses that it cannot apply the system of separation of powers in the classical sense, but rather that it must be based on the separation of functions undertaken by the parties to the Treaty, which can be shifted only by amendment to the Treaties. Thus, the balancing of the function-bearers in the Union is circumscribed in the sense of the separation of powers required by the rule of law in the continental understanding of the *Rechtsstaat*.[155]

[151] See E Schmidt-Aßmann, ‘Der Rechtsstaat’ in Isensee and Kirchhof (eds), above n 82, i, § 24, para 49; P Lerche, ‘Gewaltenteilung’ in J Isensee (ed), *Gewaltenteilung heute* (2000), 75.

[152] See T Oppermann, *Europarecht* (1999), 104.

[153] See the above text at n 66 *et seq*.

[154] See eg Case 138/79 *Roquette* [1980] ECR 333, para 33.

[155] See K Lennaerts and A Verhoeven, ‘Institutional Balance as a Guarantee for Democracy in EU Governance’ in C Joerges and R Dehousse (eds), *Good Governance in Europe’s Integrated Market* (2002), 35; M Herdegen, *Europarecht* (2001), 124.

The ECJ has a significant function in the Union's system of the rule of law. Under Art 220 EC it ensures together with the CFI "that in the interpretation and application of the Treaty the Law is observed".[156] It is to underline that this basic text distinguishes between the Law and the Treaty. Union Law consists not only of the dispositions of the Treaty, but also of general principles of law, which the legal and constitutional orders of the Member States have in common.[157] The Court has accordingly claimed for itself the competence to formulate general legal principles of Community law[158] and to develop the Treaty provisions through judicial law.[159]

The elements of the legal order of the Union have often been set forth and documented. Here a few key-words suffice.[160] The principle of the primacy of Community law over national law, which has in essence been accepted in all Member States, ensures its uniform application and forecloses unilateral actions by the Member States that are not admitted by Community law or outsides of its scope. It will now be expressively confirmed in Art I-10(1) CT-Conv (Art 6 CT-IGC). The principle of direct effect of Community law has already been mentioned, through which a direct connection is created from the Union to the individuals, whose position is consolidated by the adjudication of the citizenship. They can call on Community law before the national courts, and this not only for regulations that are characterised as generally valid but rather also for direct applicable provisions of primary Community law. This is especially true of the fundamental freedoms of the internal market and also for those provisions in the directives directed to the Member States which are clear and

[156] On the ECJ see eg H Kutscher, 'Über den Gerichtshof der Europäischen Gemeinschaft' [1981] *Europarecht* 392; R Lecourt, *L'Europe des Juges* (1976); A Arnull, *The European Union and its Court of Justice* (1999); HG Schermers and D Waelbroeck, *Judicial Protection in the European Communities* (1992).

[157] On this see M Schmidt, 'Die vorpositive Bedeutung des Rechts in Art. 164 EGV, 136 EAV und 31 EGKSV' (1996) 60 *Rabels Zeitschrift für ausländisches und internationales Privatrecht* 616. This is comparable to the formula of Art 20(3) Grundgesetz according to which executive power and jurisdiction are bound to *Gesetz und Recht* (statute and law); cf R Dreier, 'Der Rechtsstaat im Spannungsverhältnis zwischen Gesetz und Recht' [1985] *Juristenzeitung* 353.

[158] See T Tridimas, *The General Principles of EC Law* (1999); S Jacoby, *Allgemeine Rechtsgrundsätze: Begriffsentwicklung und Funktion in der Europäischen Rechtsgeschichte* (1997); A Arnull, *The General Principles of EEC Law and the Individual* (1990).

[159] Cf eg J Ukrow, *Richterliche Rechtsfortbildung durch den EuGH* (1995); D Edwards, 'Judicial Activism' in A Cambell *et al* (eds), *Legal Reasoning and Judicial Interpretation: Essays in Honour of Lord MacKenzie Stuart* (1996) 29; T Tridimas, 'The Court of Justice and Judicial Activism' (1996) 21 *EL Rev* 199; D Berlin, 'Interactions between the Lawmakers and the Judiciary within the EC' [1992]/2 *LegIssDrEur* 17; P Mittmann, *Die Rechtsfortbildung durch den Gerichtshof der Europäischen Gemeinschaften und die Rechtsstellung der Mitgliedstaaten* (2000); Everling, above n 93. See also *Entscheidungen des Bundesverfassungsgerichts* 75, 223 at 242 (*Kloppenburg*).

[160] See on the following the overviews in Kapteyn and VerLoren van Themaat, above n 86, 77 *et seq*; Oppermann, above n 152, 143 *et seq*.

unconditional and require no measures for their implementation. In addition, the Constitutional Treaty in its Art 45 CT-IGC as well as many other provisions confirms this principle. Both of these principles are the supporting pillars of the Community legal order and significantly curtail the Member States' latitude for action.

In this context is also to mention the understanding of the basic freedoms of the market not only as prohibition on discrimination but on restraints, furthermore also principles such as those of proportionality, protection of confidences, legality and efficiency of administration, and subsidiarity. The same is to underline with regard to the principle of non-discrimination on grounds of nationality as well as of race and comparable motives.[161] Also, in all these points the Constitutional Treaty confirms, specifies and strengthens the existing rules.

The protection of the fundamental rights of the citizen in Community law is at the heart of the general legal principles set up by the ECJ. Through development of law the ECJ has expanded them into a comprehensive system that made it possible for the *Bundesverfassungsgericht* and the Supreme Courts of other Member States to refrain from applying their national fundamental rights to European law as long as the ECJ assures equivalent protection.[162] The Charter of Fundamental Rights, albeit initially as non-binding guidelines, spells it out, and the Charter's transfer in the Constitutional Treaty will confirm the protection of human rights with regard to Union's measures.[163]

The central reference point of the legal order is the system of legal protection.[164] It assures, as already mentioned, that the law is observed in the relations between the Institutions under each other and between the Union and the Member States and their citizens. The system serves on the one hand the enforcement of Community law vis-à-vis the Member States through the action for infringement of the Treaty, and on the other hand the protection of the Member States, companies and citizens through actions of

[161] See the references above in n 135.

[162] Entscheidungen des Bundesverfassungsgerichts 73, 339 at 387 (*Solange* II). There is an overview eg in HW Rengeling, *Grundrechtschutz in der Europäischen Gemeinschaft* (1993); P Oliver, 'Fundamental Rights in European Union Law after the Treaty of Amsterdam' in O'Keeffe (ed), above n 41, 319; N Neuwahl and A Rosas, *Protection of individual Rights in EC Law* (1995); J Kokott, 'Der Grundrechtsschutz im Europäischen Gemeinschaftsrecht' (1996) 121 *Archiv für öffentliches Recht* 599; A Cassese, A Clapham and JHH Weiler (eds), *Human Rights and the European Community* (1991).

[163] See G Hirsch, 'Die Aufnahme der Grundrechtecharta in den Verfassungsvertrag' in Schwarze (ed), above n 5, 111.

[164] See the overview in Schermers and Waelbroeck, above n 156; W Rengeling, A Middeke and M Gellermann, *Rechtsschutz in der Europäischen Union* (2002); K Lasok, *The European Court of Justice* (1994); J Gündisch und S Wienhues, *Rechtsschutz in der Europäischen Gemeinschaft* (2003).

annulment of decision and for failure to act as well as claims for damages against the institutions of the Union. The procedure for preliminary rulings on the basis of presentations from national courts is to secure the uniform interpretation and application of Community law by the courts of the Member States. At the same time, it serves the legal protection of the citizens, who call on Community law before the national courts, and it is a significant instrument for the further development of the law.

Details as to the right of private parties to bring suit, or damages for illegal regulations are being discussed. The reform of jurisdiction introduced by the Treaty of Nice, which especially makes possible a transfer of proceedings from the ECJ to the CFI, is to ensure legal protection in spite of the constantly increasing load of the Courts and in view of the recent enlargement.[165] The Constitutional Treaty adapts this reform with little changes.[166] Altogether, it can be acknowledged that effective legal protection is guaranteed.

In summary, it can be said that principles of the rule of law are realised in the Union. With this, an essential precondition is achieved that the envisaged constitutional system of the Union may function in spite of manifold internal tensions exhibited. The Constitutional Treaty is built up on this basis and completes and reinforces it in many aspects.

V. LEGAL NATURE AND FUTURE OF THE EUROPEAN UNION

1. Characteristics of the Union's Structure

This presentation of the main problems of the Union was focused throughout on making clear the tension between the policy and the law of the Union and of the Member States and the latter amongst each other. Those tensions are for the author, following decades of experience, characteristic for the Union system. They are well known from federal states[167] and typical for every entity with several decision levels, but in the Union, which has not been formed into a federal state, they are considerably significant. The

[165] See U Everling, P-C Müller-Graff and J Schwarze (eds), *Die Zukunft der Europäischen Gerichtsbarkeit nach Nizza* [2003] *Europarecht* Beiheft, 1; B Vesterdorf, 'The Community Court System Ten Years from Now and Beyond' (2003) 28 *EL Rev* 303; A Johnston, 'Judicial Reform and the Treaty of Nice' (2001) 38 *CML Rev* 499; O Tambou, 'Le système juridictionnel communautaire revu et corrigé par le Traité de Nice' [2001] *RevMC* 164;

[166] See Everling, above n 103.

[167] For this, the fitting term *Politikverflechtung* (interwoven policy) was minted: see F Scharpf, 'Politikverflechtung' in *id*, B Reissert and F Schnabel (eds), *Politikverflechtung* (1976), 13; see also F Scharpf, 'The Joint Decision Trap' (1988) 66 *Public Administration* 230.

Member States exist as much as ever and according their historical tradition, they feel responsibility for the existence of their people. Nevertheless, they are bound in the Union's system and obliged to apply its rules. Therefore, they try to influence these rules and collide with the concurrent intentions of other Member States.

Tensions in the Union arise already from the different initial positions after the war, subliminal persisting even today, from the undefined notions as to goals, which in turn relate to the Member States' various conceptions of nationhood, from the interplay between opening the Community market with genuine competition and national needs for regulation in the interest of the common welfare, from the Union's tendencies to harmonise and the national need for maintenance of the broadest possible diversity, from the inclusion of political and military policy areas, which are judged differently, and finally from the transfer of different concepts about the state, democracy, rule of law and legal protection into decision making process on the level of the Union.

The disagreements based on such tensions are not crises, that is, they are not exceptional situations limited in time and subject matter,[168] but rather they are characteristic as a long term situation for the constantly necessary balancing of interests. The Union is to understand as finding a framework holding these tensions together, and the Union can only be further developed in resolving or at least attempting to reduce them. In the authors' view, policy and theory must take this into consideration when they attempt to conceive the essence and legal nature of the Union.

The nature of the Communities and their law has been discussed since their founding in all of the then Member States.[169] In the extensive literature, there was soon agreement that the received teachings of state relations, especially paired concepts such as *Staatenbund* and *Bundesstaat* (confederation and federal state), did not do justice to the special character of the Community.[170] Granted, until recently politicians use to draw the popular image of a European federal state or a United States of Europe modelled on the USA, but in the practice they were scarcely ready to renounce on national domains and try to preserve the dominance of the States.[171]

Scholars have always sought a solution somewhere between the extremes, which were formulated in the times of nation state building in the

[168] In the main they are treated as such; but see JC Koecke, 'Krisen und Krisengerede' in R Kirt (ed), *Die Europäische Union und ihre Krisen* (2001), 41.

[169] Some seem to overlook this fact. See eg J Shaw, 'European Union Legal Studies in Crisis? Towards a New Dynamic' (1996) 16 *Oxford Journal of Legal Studies* 231.

[170] See eg E Wohlfarth in *id*, U Everling, H-J Glaesner and R Sprung, *Die Europäische Wirtschaftsgemeinschaft: Kommentar zum Vertrag* (1960), Art 1, para 3.

[171] The only recent serious pleading for state building, as the author sees, is the last publication of the late judge GF Mancini, 'Europe: The Case for Statehood' (1998) 4 *ELJ* 29; JHH Weiler, 'Europe: The Case against The Case for Statehood', 4 *ELJ* 43 argues against this.

19th century. That has been intensified in the nineties when the project of the internal market demonstrated even to the specialists of constitutional law that the state is changing. It is nearly impossible to take all the theories and opinions in consideration, which are submitted in the overwhelming discussion.[172] To find a route in the jungle it shall be tried in the following to present the most characteristic of the opinions developed in the literature by groups according to their central thesis.

It is clear that such a short presentation of important characteristic views about the nature of the Union can only convey an incomplete overview of the variety of opinions, and important authors may be disregarded. In addition, the brief comments on each of the opinions can hardly do justice to the differentiated argumentation of the authors, and insofar must be referred to the foregoing explanations in this paper. However, even if only a somewhat accidental selection will be discussed it may perhaps help to more transparency. Some authors are certainly not as one-sided as their classification may suggest, and some are not mentioned because their views may difficult to classify.

Particularly the Anglo-Saxon or French authors are not easy to set in the proposed order. Their respective understanding of state, constitution and sovereignty is different by history, public consciousness and legal philosophy. Therefore, their opinions cannot easy be compared with the groups build up on the base of German authors, who seem to be inclined to present sharpened or even extreme theses explained by stiffing terms. They may be, therefore, the starting points of the overview.

2. Grouping the Views on the Union's Legal Nature

As explained and under the reserves exposed, it shall be attempted to present the most characteristic theories on the Union in four main groups.

a.) Primarily, those theories may be treated which put the technical rationality or the inherent economic dynamic of Community law in the centre, thereby contesting the political character of union building. The famous interpretation of the former EEC by *Hans Peter Ipsen* as a "*Zweckverband funktionaler Integration*" (special-purpose association for functional integration) which was long-times mostly followed in the German doctrine corresponds to the neo-functionalistic approach of the opening of the markets

[172] Comprehensive and instructive overviews are thus all the more noteworthy. See e.g. A von Bogdandy, 'A Bird's Eye View on the Science of European Law' (2000) 6 *ELJ* 208, and Peters, above n 3, 205 *et seq.* See also P Craig, 'The Nature of the Community' in *id* and de Búrca (eds), above n 24, 1. On the integration theories from a political science perspective see C Giering, *Europa zwischen Zweckverband und Superstaat* (1997). See also W Loth and W Wessels (eds), *Theorien europäischer Integration* (2001).

and to the mostly technical rules of economic law.[173] The basic intention of the author was apparently to give the EC an a-political understanding in order to let the identity of the Member States and their political organisation as far as possible untouched. This interpretation is based on strong separation of state and society, well-known in German doctrine, and means that the Community institutions act according to objective knowledge and not to political will, and that they only deal with non-controversial agendas of procedural calculability.

This theory has—insofar as the author sees—scarcely been directly echoed in the Anglo-Saxon and Roman doctrine, but in substance, similar opinions were widespread. British politicians have up to the eighties only spoken of the "Common market" and not from the "Community",[174] and scholars often limited their understanding of the Union in the first line to the economic effect.[175]

But the picture designed by this theory does not reflect the reality as quickly was evident in practice. Economic policy is genuine policy and the harmonisation of policy and legal dispositions encroaches in rights and interests of the Member States and their citizens as has been shown in this paper.[176] In the end, the mainly economic understanding of the Community and Union was overtaken by the progressive development, especially through the European Political Co-operation and, following this, the common foreign policy. The attempt, based on this understanding, to leave the Member States largely untouched in their substance failed because of the political character of integration. But it is perhaps precipitate if it is said that the formulation of "special purpose association" today, in face of recent developments, "can only command a weary smile".[177] Recently this view of the Union has been at least partly rediscovered in the discussion about comitology and agencies.[178]

[173] See Ipsen, above n 26.

[174] The declarations of the former British Prime Minister are well known. The author remembers that during the 1970s when he was active in a German ministry, his British counterparts were always speaking of the EC as the Common Market, whereas the author answered using the term Community—really an absurd *dialogue de sourdes*.

[175] See the neo-functionalists L Lindberg and S Scheingold, *Europe's Would-be Polity* (1970); further A Morawcsik, 'Preferences and Power in the European Community' (1993) 31 *JCMS* 473; G Majone, 'Europe's "Democracy Deficit"' (1998) 4 *ELJ* 5.

[176] See Everling, above n 27.

[177] See S Oeter, 'Europäische Integration als Konstitutionalisierungsprozess' (1999) 59 *Zeitschrift für ausländisches öffentliches Recht und Völkerrecht* 901 at 904.

[178] See K-H Ladeur, *The European Environment Agency and Prospects for a European Network of Environmental Administration*, EUI Working Paper RSC, No 96/50 (1996). On this see M Shapiro, 'The Problems of Independent Agencies in the United States and the European Union' (1997) 4 *Journal of European Public Policy* 276.

A similar, but special approach is based on the economic functionalism and impressing promoted by *Ernst-Joachim Mestmäcker.* It tries to justify and legitimise the Union and Community by the economic dynamic and rationality of the opened markets with undistorted competition, which expands the freedoms of the citizens.[179] As important and proper as these beginnings in market and competition were and still are, they cannot alone explain the construction and core of a political entity that is capable of acting and that is qualified to consider the interests of common welfare in matters extending even to foreign and defence policy.

b.) A second group of views seeks to preserve the integrity of the States less by emphasising the allegedly a-political character of the Union but on the contrary by deriving it from the Member States.[180] The designation of the Union as "*Staatenverbund*" ("compound of states", or "union of states"), promoted in the first line of *Paul Kirchhof* and adopted by the *Bundesverfassungsgericht,* underlines rightly that the core of the Union consists of states, which are not only supporters and founders but also members of the Union, as has been shown. The formula also stresses, albeit in a fashion that is almost impossible to convey in other languages, that the Member States are bound more tightly in the Union than in the traditional confederation of states. However, this theory suggests the dominance of the States over the Union, and this is underlined by the perception that it should obtain its legitimacy and authority to act solely or at least primarily from the limited authorisation by the national statutes of ratification. Following these statutes are regarded as base of the validity of Union Law and the steadily checked measure for its application in the Member States.[181]

This theory corresponds, if not literarily, but in substance to opinions expressed in other Member States by politicians or scholars. Remembered may be to the famous French slogan of "*Europe des patries*" and the attempts to insist on the sovereignty of the States.[182] In the British doctrine the opinion that the Member States are dominant in the Union also is widespread.[183]

[179] See Mestmäcker, above n 40, further: 'On the Legitimacy of European Law' (1994) 58 *Rabels Zeitschrift für ausländisches und internationales Privatrecht* 616. See also C Joerges, '"Good Governance" im Europäischen Binnenmarkt' [2002] *Europarecht* 17. See also Vaubel and Neill, both above n 2.

[180] See P Kirchhof, 'Der deutsche Staat im Prozess der europäischen Integration' in Isensee and *id* (eds), above n 82, vii (1992) § 183, para 50; see also *id* in this volume; further particularly the well-known *Maastricht* Judgment of the Federal Constitutional Court, *Entscheidungen des Bundesverfassungsgerichts* 89, 155 at 188.

[181] On the Bridge theory derived from this, according to which Community law should flow over the bridge of the respective national statute for ratification into the Member States under control of the national constitutional courts, see Everling, above n 93, 226.

[182] See Luchaire and Favret, both above n 145.

[183] See only T Hartley, *Constitutional Problems of the European Union* (1999); I Harden, 'The Constitution of the European Union' [1994] *Public Law* 609; Ward, above n 128; Milward, above n 2.

The reality of the Union, however, is otherwise than it is suggested by this theory. It cannot be ignored that the Union, as explained in this paper, is equipped with its own competences, which it autonomously exercises by its own institutions and by its own legal order with primacy over the law of the Member States without being bound to their consent. These authors try to deprive the Union of its inherent dynamic for self-legitimacy, which rendered the development possible up to present. Above all, this understanding does not make clear the comprehensive and direct inclusion of the citizens in the rules of the Union, which distinguishes this from all other traditional international models.[184] The Union is not only a union of states, but also a union of citizens. Nevertheless, this doctrine equipped with the authority of the Federal Constitutional Court is even today very popular among German scholars.[185]

Some authors answer the objections against this theory by explaining the Union from the perspective of the open constitutional state.[186] As correct as this open understanding of the modern state is, and as much as it is suited to loosen the understanding of the *Staatenverbund*, it can still not explain the particularities of the Union, because this is not understood for its own value but rather as a reflection of the States which constitute it.

c.) A third group of views, inspired by *Ingolf Pernice*, does not start with the states but with their constitutions. The Union is seen as a "*Verfassungsverbund*" ("constitutional compound", or "compound of constitutions").[187] This expresses the idea that in the Union the Member States between each other and with the institutions of the Union are interlacing on all levels of policy, economy, law and society and mutually permeate or at least influence each other. This formulation is useful as a counter concept to that of the *Staatenverbund*, and can aptly characterise the interweaving

[184] Cf JA Frowein, 'Das Maastricht-Urteil und die Grenzen der Verfassungsgerichtsbarkeit' (1994) 54 *Zeitschrift für ausländisches öffentliches Recht und Völkerrecht* 1; C Tomuschat, 'Die europäische Union unter der Aufsicht des Bundesverfassungsgerichts' [1993] *Europäische Grundrechte-Zeitschrift* 489; JHH Weiler, 'The State "über alles"' in Due *et al* (eds), above n 12, 1651; M Herdegen, 'Maastricht and the German Constitutional Court' (1994) 31 *CML Rev* 235.

[185] Cf eg PM Huber, 'Der Staatenverbund der Europäischen Union' in J Ipsen (ed), *Verfassungsrecht im Wandel: Festschrift 180 Jahre Carl Heymanns Verlag* (1995), 349; M Kaufmann, *Europäische Integration und Demokratieprinzip* (1997), 214 *et seq*; Oppermann, above n 152, 337.

[186] See U Di Fabio, *Das Recht offener Staaten* (1998); S Hobe, *Der offene Verfassungsstaat zwischen Souveränität und Interdependenz* (1998), 330 *et seq*.

[187] See I Pernice, 'Der europäische Verfassungsverbund auf dem Wege der Konsolidierung' (2000) 48 *Jahrbuch des öffentlichen Rechts* 205 at 214; I Pernice, 'Multilevel Constitutionalism and the Treaty of Amsterdam: European Constitution-Making Revisited?' (1999) 36 *CML Rev* 703; I Pernice and F Mayer, 'De la constitution composée de l'Europe' (2000) 36 *Revue trimestrielle de droit européen* 623.

of the state functions on the level of the Union. Insofar this theory is near to the reality, which daily shows the dilemma of the institutions of the Member States posed between the obligations founded on their national constitution and those imposed by the Union.

But is must be asked if this opinion does not go too far by collectively seizing the Member States and evidently tending to assume their complete inclusion into the Union, so that their considerable room for manoeuvring within and outside of the Union is unidentifiable. This concept rests on the underlying understanding of the state, according to which it is the constitution that constitutes the states so that the connection between the constitutions on the Union level binds also the States in a common order.[188] Under these circumstances, it can be said that this concept is near to the understanding of the Union as a "*Bundesstaat*" (Federation), which is certainly not intended by the protagonists of this theory.[189]

For this reason other authors like *Jürgen Schwarze* more cautiously speak not of the compound but of the "Europeanisation" of the national constitutions in order to clarify the connection between the organisational structures of the Union and the Member States, without completely receiving them.[190] On the same line, other authors demonstrate the process of constitutionalisation.[191] Opinions of this sort are also common among Anglo-Saxon authors, even if they are difficult to classify in this formal scale.[192] The polycentric network character of the institutional and legal system of the Union and of its compound constitution is emphasised,[193] and the national constitutions, limited in its application by the Union, are even called as partial constitutions.[194] The characterising of the Union as process also underlines the evolutionary character of the integration and the interaction that takes places between the actors at the different levels.[195] This, however, does not suffice for understanding the organised form of the Union.

d.) For a fourth group of authors, as *Armin von Bogdandy* among others, mostly based on German historical experiences, the principle of federalism

[188] See the interesting study by I Pernice, 'Carl Schmitt, Rudolf Smend und die europäische Integration' (1995) 120 *Archiv des öffentlichen Rechts* 100.

[189] See von Bogdandy, above n 172, 27.

[190] See Schwarze (ed), above n 134; see also Frowein and Berranger, both above n 140.

[191] See eg Oeter, above n 177; Peters, above n 3, 360 *et seq*; Giegerich, above n 3.

[192] For profound studies by prominent authors, see N MacCormick, 'Democracy, Subsidiarity, and Citizenship in the "European Commonwealth"' in *id*, above n 141, 1; Craig, above n 172; JHH Weiler, *The Constitution of Europe* (1999).

[193] See Keohane and Hoffmann, above n 49; Peters, above n 3, 218 *et seq*.

[194] See Häberle, above n 3, 220; see further 'Das Grundgesetz als Teilverfassung im Konzert der EU/EG' in D Dörr *et al* (eds), *Die Macht des Geistes: Festschrift für H Schiedermair* (2001), 81.

[195] See H Schneider and R Hrbek, 'Die Europäische Union im Werden' in von der Groeben and H Möller (eds), *Die Europäische Union als Prozess* (1980), 209 at 436.

is the key to understanding the Union.[196] This principle seems especially significant to circumscribe the different levels of decision-making, which are typical for the Union as for similar entities. First, there is the level of the Union and, second, the level of the Member States, both with its own sovereign rights and structures, and third, beneath and inside the Member States, additional levels as regions or *Länder* and Communes. In the political science, therefore the designation of the Union as a multilevel system is widespread.[197] This metaphor is exceedingly vivid and shows the vertical construction of the decision system. However, it evokes the impression of a hierarchic order of the levels and does not illustrate their mutual influences and interlacing.

In this regard, the federal principle is more explicit. It comprises the idea of a political entity, which is pursuing common goals by different decision-making bodies, which are at the same time interwoven and autonomous. The interplay between the Union on the one hand, with the sovereign competences transferred to it and, on the other, the Member States as its constituents which retain a certain measure of independence, may be understood as typical federal. The institutions and the organisational structure of the Union follows largely the forms of federation, particularly the Council is similar to the model of the German *Bundesrat*, the chamber of the *Länder*.[198] The balance between the several levels is significant for this system, and it is underlined by the principle of subsidiarity which is anchored in Art 5(2) EC and in Art 11(3) CT-IGC.

This federal system is the contrary of centralisation as politicians and scholars of Member States who, unlike Germany, do not have a federal tradition often misunderstand it.[199] They frequently believe inherent to this system the tendency to the federal state. But the characteristics of federalism are realised also outside of state organisations, and that the Union takes a development in that direction seems not to be possible in the foreseeable future.[200] In spite of the widespread scepticism, also the notion of federal

[196] See eg A von Bogdandy, *Supranationaler Föderalismus als Wirklichkeit und Idee einer neuen Herrschaftsform* (1999); H Laufer and T Fischer, *Föderalismus als Strukturprinzip für die Europäische Union* (1996); K Heckel, *Der Föderalismus als Prinzip überstaatlicher Gemeinschaftsbildung* (1998); P Badura, 'Die föderative Verfassung der Europäischen Union' in KH Kästner, KW Nörr and K Schlaich (eds), *Festschrift für M Heckel* (1999), 695; among English authors, see in particular Burgess, above n 1.

[197] See eg M Jachtenfuchs and B Kohler-Koch, 'Einleitung: Regieren im dynamischen Mehrebenensystem' in *id* (eds), *Europäische Integration* (1996), 15; Scharpf, above n 48.

[198] See U Everling, 'Zur föderalen Struktur der Europäischen Gemeinschaft' in K Hailbronner, G Ress and T Stein (eds), *Staat und Völkerrechtsordnung: Festschrift für K Doehring* (1989) 179; M Zuleeg, 'Die föderativen Grundsätze der Europäischen Union' [2000] *Neue Juristische Wochenschrift* 2846.

[199] See T Koopmans, 'Federalism: The Wrong Debate' (1992) 29 *CML Rev* 1047.

[200] See Epiney, above n 101.

structure of the Union seems to be increasingly accepted outside the German scholarship.[201]

But also the federal principle alone is not sufficient to explain the complex reality of the Union. Thus, the relationship of the different levels to the citizens and the position of the Member States partly outside the Union are not expressed, so that broader declaration must be found.

3. Conclusions and Outlook

The opinions presented all have a true core, but due to their one-sidedness, none comprehends completely the reality of the Union. Certainly, it is correct that the functions of the Union are focussed to economic aims and technical measures and that they especially use the dynamic of open markets and competition as is expressed by the metaphor of "*Zweckverband*". Equally true is that the Member States, as is made clear with the formulation of "*Staatenverbund*", persist to be essential elements of the Union, whereby they are open to the outside and no longer present themselves as nation-states of the classic mould. The mutual penetration and interlinkage of the Union and its Member States on all levels including the citizen is expressed by the characterisation of the Union as a constitutional compound and by the emphasis on the Europeanisation of the national constitutional and legal orders. Finally, the basic principle of federalism as the organisational form of the Union characterises the interweaving of all levels of policy, economy and society, without cutting off entirely the Member States' ability to act inside and outside of the Union.

In all attempts dealt with here to comprehend the substance of the Union, however, the tension between the Union and the Member States as well as the Member States amongst each other, which has in this study proved to be a central element of the Union, is expressed only incompletely. At all events, it is hinted at in the metaphor of polycentric network or in the federal principal. According to these, to understand the Union the pertinent elements of the various opinions presented here must be brought together and complemented by the tensions between the levels of decision-making that so influence the practice. Taking all together, the Union can be understood as a federally constituted compound system of states and citizens, in which the constitutions of the states are increasingly Europeanised

[201] In particular see Burgess, above n 1; see further D Sidjanski, *The Federal Future of Europe* (2000); J Pinder, 'European Community and Nation State (1986) 62 *International Affairs* 41; K Lenaerts, 'Federalism: Essential Concepts in Evolution (1998) 21 *Fordham International Law Journal* 746.

and the decision makers on all levels interweave in a polycentric network, in which reciprocal tensions exist and must constantly be resolved.

It is difficult to predict whether the Union can exist in the long term as a new form of constituted political entity with the capacity to act, yet beneath the quality of a state. Two developments are to be taken into consideration. First, the enlargement of the Union incorporating ten new Member States which have a low level of development and industrialisation, different burdens of history and structure and certainly many problems which differ of those of the former Member States. Thus, the interests, tensions and traditions inside the Union, which must be brought together in the decision-making processes will be drastically augmented. Compromises and consensus-forming will be more difficult and demand of all the actors a high measure of mutual solidarity.

For this reason the second development is of special importance. The Constitutional Treaty, which only will be in force after ratification by all—old and new—Member States what actually seems to be uncertain, may bring numerous amendments of the EU and EC Treaties, particularly the fusion of the EU and EC Treaties and its so-called "pillars" as well as improvements in general and in detail. As important as this may be, the substance of the difficult relationship between Union and the Member States and their citizen will not change in substance and remains to be in the balance. Also the problems treated here will persist.

Much about the further development of the enlarged Union formed under the Constitutional Treaty will depend upon whether, beyond policy and economy, the societies of the Member States will be integrated beyond their borders. Early on, it was emphasised that European integration would require an intellectual development process.[202] Just as the state is confirmed by the daily plebiscite of its citizens (Renan) and realised by the integration of the citizens (Smend), the Union must also find its basis long-term in the consciousness of the citizens. Up until now, the citizens are directed mainly toward the state and bound to it in loyalty, but this does not preclude a simultaneous orientation toward the larger entity.

This process of consciousness has begun at all levels of society, but requires patience extending over generations.[203] It rests on a common European culture and history, which can be the foundation of the required intellectual development process.[204] Values are found there that are common to all Europeans,[205] as has been shown in this study. But whether such

[202] See U Meyer-Cording, 'Die Europäische Integration als geistiger Entwicklungsprozess' (1962) 10 *Archiv des Völkerrechts* 42.

[203] Cf H Kaelble, *Auf dem Weg zu einer europäischen Gesellschaft* (1987).

[204] See Häberle, above n 3, 487 *et seq.*

[205] See Böhner, above n 112, 55.

general ideas of values suffice for that the Union in the foreseeable future is anchored in the peoples so that they legitimate it without mediation of the Member States may be called in question with weighty arguments.[206]

It may be even questioned whether a far-reaching degree of assimilation of the societies is desirable and whether the force of the Union does not consists in the variety of their peoples. The Constitutional Treaty comprises many elements, which may promote the search for the identity of the new Europe. However, it also underlines the respect of the identity of the Member States. It cannot be predicted what conclusions will result from this dichotomy and what direction it will take in the future. It rest to be seen whether the Union as understood in this study will be able to fulfil its mission under the changed conditions, that is to contribute to freedom and peace in Europe and in the world. The chance exists, and it is a challenge for future generations.

[206] Sceptial under the current conditions: Weiler, above n 112; and *id*, 'Fin-de-siecle Europe' in Curtin and Heukels (eds), above n 53, 23; H Schneider, 'Österreich in Acht und Bann?' [2000] *Integration* 120 is also sceptical.

17

On Finality

BY ULRICH HALTERN*

I. FINALITY AND THE DRAFT CONSTITUTION

THE SCHUMAN DECLARATION left the question of Europe's ends unanswered; a space where "war ... becomes not merely unthinkable, but materially impossible" was utopia, a focus imaginarius worth pursuing but impossible to reach. The famous "ever closer union among the peoples of Europe" from the Preamble of the Treaty establishing the European Community was lofty in its aspirations even though later it became the foundation of a whole strand of supranational thought.[1] To be sure, it was widely felt that "ever closer union" was needed to avert war and create prosperity, but could that be all? There seemed to be a cold modernist void, a spiritual absence at the heart of the European integration project.[2] The Treaty on European Union tried to fill this void with values, hopes, rights, and cultural artefacts. With the difficult ratification process, however, and a growing lack of popularity it provided little guidance as to the Union's finality. If we do not know who we, as Europeans, are, and if we cannot even be sure of the gestalt of the Union, how will it be possible to say anything of import about its finality? If we do not know what it is, we cannot know what it is for.

The Draft Treaty establishing a Constitution for Europe tries for an *aufbruch* as well as a *schlusstrich*. It abandons the cautious state-neutral wording (e.g. it speaks of "European laws"), and although it does not mention

* Prof. Dr. iur., LL.M. (Yale), Chair of German and European Constitutional and Administrative Law; Director of the Hannover Institute of National and Transnational Integration Studies, Hannover University. Lecturer at St. Gallen University and at the Postgraduate Programme in European Studies, Berlin. Parts of this article have been published before: U Haltern, 'Pathos and Patina—The Failure and Promise of Constitutionalism in the European Imagination' (2003) 9 *ELJ* 14; U Haltern, 'Integration Through Law' in A Wiener and T Diez (eds), *European Integration Theory* (2004), 177. Email: LS.Haltern@jura.uni-hannover.de

[1] See JHH Weiler, *The Constitution of Europe* (1999).

[2] See P Allott, 'The European Community is not the True European Community' (1991) 100 *Yale LJ* 2485 at 2499.

the F-word, the white noise surrounding the Draft and its discussion hums with it. Its Preamble aspires to put an end to the self-deprecating doubts about the idea of Europe. Many people have ceased to believe in such ideas as the civilising power of European modernity because they remember that the idea of Europe embodies prejudices that lie deep in the history of Europe. Delanty writes that "the idea of Europe cannot be disengaged from the atrocities committed in its name", reminding us of Benjamin's famous dictum that "there is no document of civilisation which is not at the same time a document of barbarism".[3] European history does not lead from culture to civilisation. The Preamble, however, does away with this insight. In the Convention's Draft, it even claims that "Europe is a continent that has brought forth civilisation" and that "its inhabitants, arriving in successive waves from earliest times, have gradually developed the values underlying humanism: equality of persons, freedom, respect for reason". The Preamble promises the dawning of Europe's future: Europe is now "united in its diversity" and thus a "special area of human hope", a space where the peoples "transcend their ancient divisions" and "forge a common destiny". Europe intends to "continue along the path of civilisation, progress and prosperity", and to "strive for peace, justice and solidarity throughout the world". The future delineated by the Preamble is a horizon of good possibilities and intentions. At the same time, the Preamble asserts continuity. The historical trajectory leading to the Draft Constitution is a great arc that reaches from antiquity to the 21st century. Portraying European integration as a project that spans time and generations is, perhaps, the Preamble's most ostentatious claim. In the Convention's Draft, we have the Thucydides quote, successive waves of arrivals of inhabitants, earliest times and gradual development of values, all in less than five lines. Europe draws inspiration from its various "inheritance" and believes in values still present in its "heritage". Thus, the arc that is to circumscribe European identity, gestalt, and finality, is an arc with invisible ends, something that like a parabolic curve tends towards infinity. The past reaches back to foggy "earliest times", the future is utopia: a "great venture" and a special area of human hope even for the "weakest and most deprived" committed to virtually everything good, like peace, prosperity, culture, knowledge, social progress, equality, justice, solidarity, learning, transparent democracy, and respect for law and reason.

Europe wants to "continue" as well as "remain", to "forge" a future as well as to accept a "destiny"; it is already "reunited" and at the same time strives for being "united ever more closely". What are we to make of this? What of the stringing together of good aspirations, hopes and values, without any hint at priorities? And what, finally, of the breathtakingly shameless

[3] See G Delanty, *Inventing Europe: Idea, Identity, Reality* (1995), 157.

Thucydides quote? My suspicion is that neither the Preamble nor the Constitutional Treaty as a whole will have satisfactory answers to the question that vex Europe today: Who are we, and where are we going. The Draft promises, in its garrulity, a revelation, but reveals too much (all those values) and leaves out too much (all those messy ambiguities) to be more than idle chatter. With the parabolic arc of Europe's projected trajectory tending toward infinity, it is impossible to see the ends; how can we talk of finality if there is no *fin*?

In order to find answers we must look beyond the Constitutional Treaty—but where? As jurists, we are tempted, if not doomed, to look to the law as it stands. That makes little sense, at first glance, when investigating "finality". Finality seems to have to do with political action, is future-oriented, and is part of a promise of novelty. Law, in contrast, is inevitably turned to the past. Law's rule is an exercise in the maintenance of political meanings already achieved. It links the future to the past in that the future of the political order should be the same as its past.[4] Can the past, and law as its maintenance project, tell us anything serious about the promises of future European horizons?

I submit they can. Not only has law been the major leitmotiv of European integration. Above all, law deserves attention from a cultural perspective which is able to yield insights into the possibilities and promises of a Union to come. Law is not just a body of rules. It is a social practice, a way of being in the world. A social practice is not merely a set of prescribed actions, but rather a way of understanding self and others, and thus, a way to make actions meaningful. To live under the rule of law is to maintain a set of beliefs about the self and community, time and space, authority and representation. Law's rule is a system of beliefs—a structure of meaning within which we experience public order as the rule of law.[5] If there is any merit to this suggestion, law is a marker that points not only to a community's past and memory, but to its future and hopes as well. A polity imagines itself in part through law. More often than not, such a legal imagination also yields a political imagination.

The Union's political imagination today is very different from nation state imaginations. If citizens are mostly indifferent towards the Union, that is because EU law is not "theirs". EU law fails in its attempt to create and maintain a collective identity. It does not carry forward rooted meaning, but a precarious form of post-politics (II).

[4] See PW Kahn, *The Reign of Law* (1997), 19.

[5] This cultural approach to symbolic meaning goes back to Ernst Cassirer, Clifford Geertz and Michel Foucault and has been developed most forcefully by PW Kahn, *The Reign of Law* (1997); *id*, *The Cultural Study of Law* (1999); *id*, *Law and Love* (2000); *id*, *Putting Liberalism in Its Place* (2005).

However, things may be changing. Europe has begun an urgent search for its own political imagination.[6] The Constitution-To-Be is but the very visible sign of this search. Europe is about to decide whether the political, for the Union, signifies the market, or humanity, or a self-narrative that reaches back to the symbolic arsenal of cultural mythology so well known from nation-state political rhetoric. We see this everywhere, not simply in the overused cultural artefacts of flag, anthem, Europe day and Jean Monnet prizes, but also in documents such as the Charter of Fundamental Rights, the Constitutional Treaty, and, above all, the European Court's jurisprudence in the fields of human rights and Union citizenship. Partly, these artefacts and documents have proved unsuccessful in forging a political imagination. I will use consumer aesthetics to explain this failure (III). Partly, however, there is much potential, especially in the Court's jurisprudence. It is, above all, the Court's changing human rights and citizenship discourse that is indicative of a major shift in law's role in the quest for European identity. I will explain the recent change of heart and its consequences (IV).

The political has entered the European stage and will not easily go away. Today, we find ourselves in a legal, psychological, and discursive universe different from the one ten or fifteen years ago. European discourse is no longer attracted to the question of what we should do (for instance, with a view to the democratic deficit). It is now fascinated by the question of who we are. Europe's discursive nodal points are defined by contested notions of identity. Therefore, we will have to inquire what meaning we read into Union law, and how this act of reading and understanding interacts with our beliefs about ourselves, and our ends (V.). No functional analysis can grasp this dimension of the law.

II. POST-POLITICS AND LAW: THE STATE OF THE UNION

1. A Cultural Study of Law

The starting point for a cultural-legal investigation of European constitutionalism is a conception of law other than that offered by our dominant legal discourses. As Paul Kahn points out, the rule of law is a shorthand expression for the imaginative construction of a complete social-political order.[7] It is a way of perceiving events and actors, and a framework of understanding that makes it possible to perceive legal meaning in every event. It provides a temporal and geographical shape to events, a normative

[6] See I Ward, 'Beyond Constitutionalism' (2001) 7 *ELJ* 24.

[7] See Kahn (2000), above n 5, 171.

grounds for claims of authority, and an understanding of the self and others as subjects with rights and responsibilities. It has its own imaginative universe, and it is the imagination that constructs the past and the future of the polity, just as it constructs, at the same time, the political identity of the citizen. In the political imagination of citizens of Germany, for instance, the rule of law echoes with the memory of World War II and Auschwitz; American citizens' political imagination of the rule of law echoes with the memory of revolution and civil war, with a continuity between the citizens and the Founders, etc. In other words, the rule of law is a structure of beliefs about the meaning of the polity. Its value lies not in objective facts but in the deployment of power to sustain these beliefs. What we must investigate, then, is the structure of meaning within our experience of public order as the rule of law occurs.

National law usually has a richly textured cushion of cultural resources that it can rely on. It is a symbolic form which establishes a world of preexisting rules to which individuals appeal in order to make sense of their lives. It serves as a community's memory in that it preserves existing meanings. Many of those meanings derive from a different symbolic form—political action—competing with law. Political action's world creates new, rather than preserves, meaning, and locates meaning in individuals performing unique acts. Political action takes revolution, not constitutional preservation, as its paradigmatic political act. The conflict between law and political action is a conflict between past and future, tradition and possibility, loyalty and responsibility. Most obviously, the tension arises at law's origin. Political action and law co-opt each other at the point of law's myth of origin, revolution. Revolutions create meaning, law preserves that meaning. The need for permanence requires the establishment of a historical memory, a text—not just any text, but a text that bears the meaning of law's source. The first text of the revolution is the bodies of the revolutionaries: revolutionary ideas become the foundation of a new political order only when individuals are willing to engage in acts of sacrifice and invest their bodies in that new set of ideas. Sacrifice is the inscription on the body of ideal meaning. The body lends the authenticity of its sacrifice to the legal text that is the product of revolution—the product of the spent body, in other words, is the legal text. The sacrificed body establishes the legal text as "ours".[8] This is the deep structure underneath law's smooth, liberal surface design. It is myth and memory (not rationality), sacrifice (not contract), will (not reason and interest). A legitimate nation-state's legal system exerts

[8] See Kahn (1997), above n 5; *id* (1999), above n 5. Sacrifice becomes the crucial paradigm in this context. Sacrifice is the process by which ideas are embodied in historical artefacts. Law, then, begins with the act of reading the body. Interpretation is the reverse process: it realises the ideal content of the artefact. This is an old religious theme, of course, that has found its way prominently into literature, popular fiction, and movies.

a tremendous normative pull not because of the threat of punishment or some basic consensus. Rather, the legal regime expresses, in traditional terms, the "sovereign will" of the community. To disconnect law from the idea of sovereignty fails to see the crucial connection of the rule of law to self-rule. In a democratic regime, sovereignty and law are tightly linked. The sovereign people govern through the rule of law; and by following the law, citizens participate in popular sovereignty and achieve self-government.[9]

The maintenance project of the law is a project of instantiation: the individual becomes a citizen and, ultimately, the sovereign. Law, then, is not simply about the promise of order; it is about identity. As such, it is incredibly erotic, political, and dangerous.

The meaning of law in the European Union is very different from the meaning I have just laid out. Union law lacks the erotic component so distinctive of nation-state politics. It epitomises the project of a rational rule of law. I will give a few examples, and will attempt to show that the differences in the conception of the rule of law have decisive consequences for the Union's finality and future gestalt.

2. The Union's Birth From Reason

The Union was not born from belief, visionary revolution, shared sacrifices, emotions, or love, but rather from the spirit of reason and enlightenment. How could it be otherwise?[10] Europe was a macabre unity, coming together in infinite destruction, with camps of POWs and millions dead, as an expanse of rubble. Auschwitz was the absolute zero, and the hatred was great enough to spawn serious suggestions to "strew Germany with salt". To build Europe upon emotional appeals to feelings of sharedness and community would necessarily have had to fail. Still, there were two imminent problems to solve: first, what to do with Germany, second, how to rebuild Europe?[11] The Schuman plan was the well-planned and deliberate response to these questions. One cannot be deceived by its pathos: note that it speaks of "de facto

[9] See Kahn (2005), above n 5.

[10] To be sure, there is the Schuman Declaration's pathos; there is also Churchill's Zurich speech on 19 September 1946, calling for a 'United States of Europe': W Churchill, *His Complete Speeches*, 1897–1963, 1943–1949 (ed RR James, 1974), reprinted in: BF Nelsen and AC-G Stubb (eds), *The European Union* (1998) 7. However, Churchill was out of office at the time. What is more, it seems the Zurich speech was just another example of that typically British motto, 'Don't do what I do, do what I tell you to do': JHH Weiler and SC Fries, 'A Human Rights Policy for the European Community and Union' in P Alston (ed), *The EU and Human Rights* (1999), 147. It was Churchill himself who, a few years earlier, had maintained that 'We are with Europe, but not of it', quoted in: D Heater, *The Idea of European Unity* (1992), 148.

[11] See Monnet's text, published in the first issue of the Journal of Common Market Studies: J Monnet, 'A Ferment of Change' (1962) 1 *JCMS* 203, reprinted in: Nelsen and Stubb (eds), above n 10, 19.

solidarity" only. The lack of grand vision and the tangible pragmatism of the Declaration have been noted too often to be repeated here. What is important, though, is the fact that European integration was conceived as a contract and as a project guided by enlightened rationality. We see this in many details. Take the original gestalt the Union. There is no doubt that the Union, irrespective of its subsequent constitutionalisation, was constructed through classic international law treaties. International law, with few exceptions, is basically law through consent between states. Governments represent states, and international law is the product of governmental actors striving for coordination of their mutual interests. International law, in other words, is the apotheosis of the social contract: it is predicated on the analogy between the sovereign state and the unified self. Purvis points out that liberalism in international law, as elsewhere, can be understood as a philosophy that combines an atomistic psychological assumption with a radical epistemology about morality. The liberal psychological understanding is sovereign-centered, with world order representing nothing more than a social contract among sovereigns. The epistemological assumption is the principle of subjective value, leading to the claim that decisions about morality can only be made by the international order's atomic components, its sovereigns.[12] There is no need to explain at length the lack of sacrifice and of the erotic in international law. We can, again and again, study the unerotic consequences of liberalism and universality by looking to nation-states' unwillingness to invest bodies, money, or meaning into NATO or UN projects.

3. Europe as Style, Expertise, and Project

Europe's cultural artefacts and symbols, too, received their share of this ethos. The world of Brussels' office towers was designed to embody the technical coolness and the modernisation of the old continent. It was a world of xeroxed working documents and greyish-greenish office furniture, of simultaneous translators in soundproof cabins featuring multi-channel cables, of license plates in blue-white-red and of new European schools teaching transnational history and more than three foreign languages. This sat well with the then zeitgeist of sky-scrapers, autobahns and nuclear power plants: where such controlled technique was to rule, national idiosyncrasies and peculiarities became mere folklore and, thus, superfluous. Europe was in the hands of technocrats.[13]

The international element of the Union (e.g. the European Council and the Council of Ministers) is closely associated with contractarianism and

[12] See N Purvis, 'Critical Legal Studies in Public International Law' (1991), 32 *Harvard ILJ* 81 at 93–4.

[13] See D Schümer, *Das Gesicht Europas* (2000), 45.

liberalism. Both are political theories which are speechless in the face of sacrifice. A similar charge may be levelled at the Commission whose mode of governance is hostile to the idea of sacrifice, too. The Commission pools expert knowledge and seems like governance through management and technocracy epitomised. There is a diffusion of accountability through the rise of comitology. Expert management, however, may produce an efficient and perhaps even satisfactory distribution of society's resources, but it cannot produce the historical-communal understanding of self-identity that characterises the rule of law as an experience of political order. To the expert, it doesn't matter how the present state of affairs came about. Loyalty may appear irrational. Management, as a form of science, knows no borders. Law is silenced by claims of expert knowledge that purport to provide their own grounds of authority. Scientific expertise always speaks for itself. Like every scientific voice, management exists in the present. It tests the past and future against present interests, whereas law tests the present against the past. Management is in history but is not itself historical.[14] Without history, however, there can be no identity.

Another facet of Europe as a project of modernity becomes visible in the oft-used metaphor of Europe *as a project*. This is one of the central motifs of modernity.[15] "In modernity, Man's finitude becomes reconciled with the infinite and eternal, in terms of progression ... [as] an interim apotheosis, one which rejects the preceding being but which also contains that being and prefigures all the object is yet to become."[16] European academic literature will not tire in emphasising the project nature of integration, and the procedural nature of Union law. The Treaty of Rome, is what we read, did not lay down a static legal order which was complete from the beginning. Rather, European integration is said to be a legislative process characterising the Union as a legal system evolving over time. The Court, too, cashes in on the myth of progression by privileging the teleological method of interpretation.[17] Progression, it seems, becomes an essential element in the mythical structure of the Community legal order. The Union cannot compete with the law of nation-states as a source of order or transcendent being in terms of what it is. It can only attempt to do so in terms of what it is not, and in terms of what it will be.[18]

The Union legal order, as a purely rational legal order, is unable to use the same imaginative and cultural resources as the nation-state. Unlike

[14] See Kahn (1997), above n 5, 182.

[15] Incidentally, the notions of 'project' and of 'project-maker' are in themselves highly modern notions and deserve more attention. For a cultural genealogy see M Krajewski (ed), *Projektemacher* (2004).

[16] See P Fitzpatrick, *The Mythology of Modern Law* (1992), 40.

[17] See T Oppermann, *Europarecht* (1999), para 685.

[18] See JH Bergeron, 'An Ever Whiter Myth' in P Fitzpatrick and JH Bergeron (eds), *Europe's Other* (1998), 3 at 14.

national legal orders, the Union legal order is only what it professes to be: a legal order originating from contract and exhausting itself in reason and interest. The Union has no subtext of will, and hence battles with the fatal difficulty to explain to us, its citizens, why its legal order is uniquely "ours".

4. Europe as Imagined Community

The Union, of course, has not turned a blind eye on this dilemma. The Commission, above all, has commissioned countless studies, initiated working groups, and written up White Papers in order to test social acceptance of the Union, to define problem areas, and to work out solutions. In addition, the Commission, long before 1993, embarked upon various initiatives in the fields of media and information policy to promote integration in the sphere of culture by enhancing what it saw as "the European identity". These initiatives are not very successful—I will return to this in a moment—which is why scholars tend to underestimate the Commission's prowess. The Union's demiurges know their political theory. They have read Hobsbawm and have learned that history is central to the imagining of community, for how people experience the past is intrinsic to their perception of the present. History, they know, is also fundamental to their conception of themselves as subjects and members of a collectivity. Following Hobsbawm and Ranger,[19] they have focused on the "invention of European traditions" and on practices which seek to inculcate certain values and norms of behaviour by implying continuity with the past. The past, like social memory, is a construction, actively invented and reinvented. The Commission might also have learned from Benedict Anderson's highly influential "Imagined Communities". Anderson defines nations as "imagined political communities" because its members will never know, meet or even hear of most of their fellow-members, yet in the minds of each lives the image of their communion. His theoretical point of departure is, indeed, mass-sacrifice for the nation and, ultimately, death. Death brings the threat of oblivion. In a secular age we increasingly look to posterity to keep our memory alive, and the collective memory and solidarity of the nation helps us to overcome the threat of oblivion. Nations are characterised by symbols of commemoration, notably the Tombs of Unknown Soldiers, which suggests that nationalism, like religion, takes death and suffering seriously (in a way that Marxism and liberalism do not). It does so by "transforming

[19] See E Hobsbawm and T Ranger, 'Introduction' in E Hobsbawm and T Ranger (eds), *The Invention of Tradition* (1983).

fatality into continuity", by linking the dead to the yet unborn. The nation, according to Anderson, is particularly suited to this "secular transformation of fatality into continuity, contingency into meaning", since nations "always loom out of an immemorial past, and, still more important, glide into a limitless future. It is the magic of nationalism to turn chance into destiny."[20] This is just what the Commission had in mind: transforming contingency into meaning. However—unfortunately, if you want—the Commission had no fatalities at its disposal to turn into continuity. Perhaps here is the reason why its initiatives to enhance European consciousness and Europeanise the cultural sector all too often appear unconvincing.[21]

[20] See B Anderson, *Imagined Communities* (1991), 11–12.

[21] One early example of the Commission's attempt to define a cultural foundation for European unification is the signing of the 'Declaration on the European Identity' in 1973: Commission of the European Communities, 'Declaration on the European Identity', Bull EC 12 (1973), cl 2501, 118–27; see the wonderfully evocative account by C Shore, *Building Europe* (2000). This approach to Europe is still very much in fashion, as the Decision of 14 February 2000, establishing the Culture 2000 programme demonstrates: Dec 508/2000/EC of the European Parliament and of the Council [2000] OJ L 63/1. Consider, for instance, the following passages: 'If citizens give their full support to, and participate fully in, European integration, greater emphasis should be placed on their common cultural values and roots as a key element of their identity and their membership of a society founded on freedom, democracy, tolerance and solidarity' (5th recital); 'To bring to life the cultural area common to the European people, it is essential to encourage creative activities, promote cultural heritage with a European dimension, encourage mutual awareness of the culture and history of the peoples of Europe and support cultural exchanges with a view to improving the dissemination of knowledge and stimulating cooperation and creative activities' (8th recital). Activities and implementing measures include, among many others, 'the European Capital of Culture and the European Cultural Month', 'organising innovative cultural events which have a strong appeal and are accessible to citizens in general, particularly in the field of cultural heritage', and 'European prizes in the various cultural spheres: literature, translation, architecture, etc' (Annex 1, Activities and Implementing Measures for the Culture 2000 Programme). Another prominent example is the White Paper on 'European Governance' and the attendant Working Group reports (European Commission, *European Governance: A White Paper*, COM(2001) 428 final). Working Group 1a dealt with 'Broadening and Enriching the Public Debate on European Matters'. It found its purpose 'in the sobering and well-documented reality that, despite all of the efforts made by Europe's institutions over the last decade, very few convincing answers have yet been found to the cry: "how can we take Europe closer to its citizens"?': *Report of Working Group on Broadening and Enriching the Public Debate (Group 1a)*, White Paper on European Governance, Work Area No 1, Broadening and Enriching the Public Debate on European Matters (2001), <http://europa.eu.int/comm/governance/areas/group1/report_en.pdf> (4 October 2004), 8. While the Union's competences and responsibilities closely resemble those of most nation-States, its institutions do not have a relationship with the general public 'that remotely compares with that of national institutions' (*ibid*, 9). Public support, therefore, is far from overwhelming. Knowledge of European affairs is low; prevailing attitudes to the Union are characterised by either indifference or lack of knowledge or a combination of both (*ibid*, 11). The Working Group maps the way forward by pointing out that decision-makers need the support of an informed European public and the creation of a 'collective intelligence' on European issues. Then you'll find the heading 'Enlightenment could lead to more popular support' (*ibid*, 14). In practical terms, the Group suggests partnership networks of journalists, teachers, professors, associations, etc, to foster dialogue 'close to the ground' and 'establish links between EU institutions and civil society'. One of the most important proposals is that 'The EU must be taught' (*ibid*, 16).

5. Europe's Iconography

The Union has recognised the overwhelming importance of symbols. Being not a "natural" but an "imagined" community, it needs to be constructed through complicated ideological, political and cultural mechanisms and procedures. Such construction and re-construction takes place discursively. The re-construction of community as European Union touches upon the self-understanding and the practices of its members, their bodies, and their construction of the "Other". Discursive constructions build on communication in order to develop, and generalise, an image of the self. They make use, not only of narratives, but of images, media, and cultural artefacts of all kinds. "Imagined communities" have to do with "imago", too. Objects become images of meaning.[22]

It is here that EU iconography comes to the fore. The Adonnino Committee recommended various "symbolic measures" for enhancing the Community's profile. Foremost among these was the creation of a new EC emblem and flag. That flag was taken from the logo of the Council of Europe. It boasts twelve golden stars which form a circle against a blue background, and professes to be a symbol of everything that is said to make Europeans European: from the Occidental via the Religious to the Esoteric. The number of stars is fixed, twelve being (as the Council of Europe has it) a symbol of perfection and plenitude, associated equally with the apostles, the sons of Jacob, the tables of the Roman legislator, the labours of Hercules, the hours of the day, the months of the year, or the signs of the Zodiac. Twelve is also a representation of the Virgin Mary's halo of stars in the Revelation (from which, according to some interpretations, the new Messiah will be born). Thus, it seemed the symbol par excellence of European identity and European unification, a rallying point for all citizens of the EU.

There are countless other symbolic vehicles for communicating the "European idea". Take, above all, the European anthem, which is the overplayed "Ode to Joy" from Beethoven's Ninth Symphony.[23] Take the Jean Monnet Awards, the European Woman of the Year Awards, the variety of European Year of the Cinema, Culture, or the Environment, or the officially designated Europe Day. Take the European Literature Prizes, the standardised European passport, the European license plates, the stamps bearing

[22] See the excellent collection of essays in U Bielefeld and G Engel (eds), *Bilder der Nation* (1998).

[23] Available as either a high-quality recording or, perhaps for the busy, a compressed recording on the Union's website: <http://europa.eu.int/abc/symbols/anthem/index_en.htm> (4 October 2004).

portraits of EC pioneers, or the European city of culture initiatives. The political aim behind these initiatives was ambitious, trying nothing less than to reconfigure the symbolic ordering of time, space, information, education, and the media, to reflect the "European dimension". In the end, all this pathos has failed.[24] What, after all, is pathos? Formulas of pathos are designed to formally inject new tension into a frozen, rigid world and make it move again.[25] The distinctly European problem of pathos is not life's eventful turbulence, but rather the paralysis of all expression in a hieratic world of gestures. Pathos is thus a final escape from problems of meaning—and *that* is the context to discuss the European pathos not just of anthems and flags, but of the Constitution-To-Be and the Charter of Fundamental Rights as well.

To speak of pathos is to speak of the aesthetic. It is impossible, through purely functional description and analysis, to capture the gestalt of the Union. Description and analysis today will have to move on to, or at least include, the level of the aesthetic. The much despised and oft-scolded world of consumerism has taken this to heart long ago. Legal analysis has not. Recent studies of consumerism show what I mean. They attempt to recover the suppressed aesthetic data of our lives and to make the vast archive of subliminal images accessible to conscious analysis. They describe consumerism on the level on which the consumer actually experiences it: on the visceral level of the senses, the bodies, "from the point of view of the hand reaching for the soup can on the store shelf, the ears listening to the boom box broadcasting the sounds of a cool, refreshing soft drink splashing into a frosted glass, and the eyes fixed on the screen of the multiplex as the *Titanic* sinks".[26]

The Union, too, should be the subject of aesthetic discourse. It is a bit surprising that it practically is not because for decades now, the Commission has been talking about "A Citizens' Europe". The citizen perspective should be important then, and it would be helpful to examine the Union on the visceral level on which the Union citizen actually experiences it. Much less surprising than the lack of aesthetic discourse would be the analytical result, which is, mostly, nothing less than disastrous. The Commission continually bemoans the fact that Europeans feel alienated from the Union, that they have disappointed expectations, that there is a widening gulf between the Union and the people it serves—and wonders

[24] A recent study confirms this finding: OPTEM Sàrl., *Perceptions of the European Union A Qualitative Study of the Public's Attitudes to and Expectations of the European Union in the 15 Member States and in 9 Candidate Countries* (2000) <http://europa.eu.int/comm/governance/areas/studies/optem-report_en.pdf> (4 October 2004).

[25] See N Bolz, *Die Konformisten des Andersseins* (1999), 119–20.

[26] See D Harris, *Cute, Quaint, Hungry and Romantic: The Aesthetics of Consumerism* (2000), p. xiv.

why.[27] The answer is right there, on its own web site. Whoever looks up the flag, the anthem, and the prizes, will have an intuitive understanding of the citizens' indifference towards "their" Union.

6. A Cultural-Legal Study of the Union's Problem

The European Union's problem of meaning is precisely this: that its citizens are more or less indifferent towards it. The Union produces texts which nobody reads and nobody knows. Nobody is interested. That has fatal consequences. Texts, legal texts above all, are a polity's memory, if you want the hard disk storing authentic witness. In nation-states, some legal texts—constitutions—embody ideal historical meaning which links the present to the past, to some point of origin, like a revolution and the consecutive writing of the constitution. They construct an imaginative fabric that allows a state to inscribe its own identity into the identity of its citizens. They form a metaphysical and political deep structure that is largely ignored by theory but still has an important place in political practice.[28] Such texts constitute states as "imagined communities" and continue them over time. They can claim loyalty as their source of moral support because they are "ours".

Union texts are not "ours". They are just texts, empty shells with no roots. Rather than an embodied set of meanings they are seen as a set of ideas without the power to make a claim upon the citizen. They do not bear the deep social meaning. There is no myth of origin; there are no bodies willing to be invested into ideas, no traces, no sacrifices. There is nothing that could convey authenticity on EU texts. Ultimate meaning disappears behind the semantics of rationality. Because of the lack of sacrificial meaning, Europe, in contrast to all its rhetoric, is not a new beginning really, since what is missing is the founding, creative power. The political future will look like the political past: belief in novelty, which is behind sacrifice, is non-existent. In the Union, then, there is nothing to remember, and hence nothing to maintain. Union texts do not constitute a collective self; rather, they constitute a Common Market. Markets cannot tell us who we are. They operate through desires, which are mere placeholders. As market placeholders, "we have no character, only desires. The desiring body is not read, it is satisfied. It leaves no trace; its very existence is a matter of

[27] For a recent example of the Commission's stunned disbelief and disappointment see European Commission, above n 21, 5.

[28] See C Geertz, *Local Knowledge* (1983), 146: 'The "political theology" (to revert to Kantorowicz's term) of the twentieth century has not been written . . . But it exists . . . and until it is understood at least as well as that of the Tudors, the Majapahits, or the Alawites, a great deal of the public life of our times is going to remain obscure. The extraordinary has not gone out of modern politics, however much the banal may have entered'.

indifference to others."[29] Money, the universal means of exchange on the market, is the perfect example. There is nothing with less memory than money. An old saying says you should not conduct money business with friends or foes. The perfect business partner is thus someone completely indifferent, gauged neither for nor against us.[30] The category of price, it seems, makes history and individuality disappear. Remarkably, it is precisely at the point of this total indifference where the European rationality of the market and the European social contract—concluded by unencumbered selves behind the veil of ignorance—converge.

With no history, no identity, and no individuality you cannot produce and maintain social and political meaning. We do not reach ourselves through markets and reason alone. We cannot reason about, or trade in, the symbolic dimension of meaning. Whereas money and reason create borderless fluidity, political and social meaning needs to be rooted. The Union's legal texts are lacking in the way they look to the past, and they are unable to stabilise anything deeper than the ever-changing fluid surface of trade, travel, and consumption. That is the reason why the EU, in the eye of the beholder, appears so breathless. As there is no memory to store meaning, meaning needs to be generated through political action, again and again. Meaning, in the Union, exists only within transitory and forgetful moments. It is a-historical and respects neither borders nor authenticity. Without reservoirs of meaning, there can be no room or time to have a breather, read the legal texts and realise their ideal content. There can be no stable meaning; there can be only frantic, restless and ceaseless production of ever-new meaning. Europe, in this sense, is truly revolutionary, because political action may never come to an end. In the conflict between loyalty and responsibility, the latter prevails. Responsibility, however, is the mode not of law, but of political action.[31] Citizens, therefore, see Europe as politicians negotiating and re-negotiating. Politicians speak the discourse of responsibility; the future is a horizon of possibilities. Europe is the never-ending project. History is being rewritten and re-rewritten. It is in the nature of revolutions to break with the past—and here is the reason why all references to occidental culture, Christendom and Latin (or French) as the once lingua franca seem so unpersuasive. Revelation, which shares a temporal structure with revolution, constructs meaning not from history, but from truth which manifests itself in and through action. That is why we are hardly able to read through the Treaty of Nice before, with its ink not dried yet, we hear talk of the post-Nice process and plans for the next Intergovernmental Conference.

[29] See Kahn (1997), above n 5, 86.
[30] See G Simmel, *Philosophie des Geldes* (1989), 290–1.
[31] See Kahn (1997), above n 5, 76–84.

III. THE MIDDLE GROUND: POLITICS GONE AWRY

The Union, in its attempt to be close to its citizens, has initiated countermeasures. Most of them can best be understood, I believe, from the perspective of consumer aesthetics. There is no substance in them, they are an effort in aesthetics. What lies behind them is a principle of consumerism. They denote the middle ground between post-politics and politics; they are politics gone awry.

1. Europe and Consumer Aesthetics

One of the most important functions of the aesthetics of consumerism, writes Harris, is to provide us with an emotional cushion, a form of camouflage, a credible disguise for a culture that refuses to admit the truth about itself. We do not like to see ourselves as consumers, or our culture as that of consumerism. We continue to pretend that our values are those of an intimate world full of Mom-and-Pop businesses, rather than an overpopulated megalopolis dominated by multinational cartels. The aesthetics of consumerism helps us keep that faith by hiding consumerism from consumers. They combat our estrangement from a world packaged in plastic by restoring the "aura" of the handmade to our commodities. They also shore up our sense of selfhood and individuality, which have been deeply compromised by the conditions of urban society. The aesthetics of consumerism have incorporated our distrust into their marketing techniques. They have built into consumerism symbolic forms of resistance to it: ineffectual strategies of rebellion that make consumers believe they are loners or oddballs, immune to advertising strategies rather than at the mercy of Madison Avenue.[32] The perfect disguise for conformity has become rebelliousness. You buy shoes, for example, which remind you of running shoes, and feel like a rebel battling the conformist obligation to wear conservative shoes with dark laces to work. You're being in control, capable of action and rebellion, rather than being controlled: you "dare to 'be different'". In fact, all you actually do is wear fashionable shoes, just like everybody else.

It is possible to identify a number of broad principles that govern the appearance of popular culture, among them cuteness, zaniness, coolness, and idyllic quaintness. Quaintness responds to the discontent of a culture trapped in an eternal present. It disfigures things to eradicate the stigma of their newness, their disturbingly characterless perfection which smacks of the alienating anonymity of assembly lines. Quaintness also compensates for the absence of real personal history. We hide our sense of uprootedness by creating a sepia-tinted simulacrum of history and "instant" traditions.

[32] See Harris, above n 26, pp. xxi–xxiii.

Even, and especially, those who are cut off from history, like we often are, feel the need to establish something like continuity with the past. The result is quaintness riding roughshod over authenticity. It often mourns the loss of cohesion in family life and of the intimate circle brought together around the fireplace by darkness and cold weather. Quaintness is the industry's tool to help reduce our deep-seated distrust of advertising and our fear of shoddy goods. It rectifies problems that consumerism itself creates, and allows us to express our discontent with consumer culture and society.

Quaintness is also what the Union is after. As vehicles, the Union has chosen a number of romantic idyllic items; one of them is the Constitution-To-Be; another is the Charter of Fundamental Rights.

2. The Charter of Fundamental Rights as Consumer Aesthetics

The Charter serves the same purposes as quaintness in consumer aesthetics. Both, the appearance of popular culture in the form of quaintness and the Charter, are meant to offer us symbolic ways of expressing discontent, and to neutralise our feelings of inferiority, caused by our status as objects, not subjects, of globalisation and international trade.

The Charter has little other use than that associated with consumer aesthetics. The European Court of Justice has developed, for more than three decades now, a rich and differentiated human rights case law. Since 1969, at least, the Court has been ready to invalidate Community legislation that violates EC fundamental rights. Does the newly proclaimed Charter offer better protection of fundamental rights? The Charter itself says no. In its Chapter VII, it admits that neither the scope of the rights it guarantees is broader, nor the level of protection is higher, than the case law status quo.

Clarity is another common justification for the Charter. However, like all human rights documents, the Charter is drafted in magisterial, sometimes cloudy language. While there is much to say in favour of such constitutional traditions, clarity is not one of its features.[33]

Finally, it is not a symbol of shared European identity. While it was solemnly proclaimed, it has no binding legal force. Some regard this as a symbol, not of shared identity, but of European impotence and of refusal to take rights seriously.[34] Even if it is bound to become law as part of the Constitutional Treaty, doubts remain about its integrative force. Europe already has a pronounced culture of rights, with a tightly knit web of fundamental rights protecting its citizens: bills of rights in *Länder* and federal constitutions, the EJC rights jurisprudence, the ECHR and its human rights

[33] JHH Weiler, 'Editorial: Does the European Union Truly Need a Charter of Rights?' (2000) 6 *ELJ* 95 at 96.
[34] *Ibid.*

court in Strasbourg, and the two 1969 UN Covenants on Civil and Political Rights, and on Economic, Social, and Cultural Rights. Waving yet another catalogue of rights in a culture of rights saturation will not take the citizen any closer to the Union.[35]

Why, then, is it that so much money, and so many resources, are lavished on the Charter if there is so little to say for it, either legally or symbolically? The answer is, it is aesthetic. The Union wants the Charter to de-stigmatise itself and to neutralise our distrust. The vehicle is quaintness. The Charter compensates for the lack of real European history. Notwithstanding all rhetoric the Union is a young entity with no model or predecessor. Europe has, not one story, but a multitude of stories which are contradictory, competing, and violent, and which need to be reconciled with each other. Europeans think of "their" Union as faceless Brussels bureaucrats, smooth, modern, insipid, and characterless. The Union suffers from its unrooted newness. Its insatiable surge forward cuts it off from the past. That provokes its citizens' distrust, and they refuse it their loyalty. The Union is seen as the epitome of bureaucratisation and centralisation. It rationalises life (through international division of labour) and depersonalises the market (through internationalisation). It emphasises competition and trans-border trade of goods through the Common Market, thus appearing as commodification of values personified. In addition, there is the peculiarly modern angst because truths and certainties crumble, identities become fragmented and transitory, feelings of displacement and uprootedness grow, and all that is solid melts into air. The Union ideally attends to such anxieties.[36]

The Charter of Fundamental Rights is the Union's designers' program to steer in the opposite direction. The Charter's solemn declaration evokes the spirit of the Virginia Bill of Rights of 1776 and of the Déclaration des droits de l'homme et du citoyen of 1789. In part, this is deliberately done in order to create the impression that the Union's roots reach back to the origins of modern democracies. Perhaps, what is hoped for is not merely a solution to the problem of lacking history and character, but to that of democratic legitimacy as well. By proclaiming a catalogue of rights, the Union adorns itself with the embellishments of the fountains of democracy—among them, the principle of popular sovereignty.[37]

At the same time, in reaching back to 1776 and 1789, the Union creates patina for itself. Patina is a physical property of material culture which consists in the small signs of age that accumulate on the surface of objects. The surface of objects, originally in pristine condition, takes on a surface of

[35] I am by no means alone in this judgment. See eg Weiler, above n 1, 334–5.

[36] See *ibid*, 260–1.

[37] This connection has also been detected by P Craig, 'Constitutions, Constitutionalism, and the European Union' (2001) 7 *ELJ* 125.

its own, being dented, chipped, oxidised, and worn away. This physical property is treated as symbolic property: it encodes a status message and is exploited to social purpose. That purpose is the legitimation, authentication, and verification of status claims.[38] Just as newly acquired wealth, in a world of traditional hierarchy, was under pressure to provide visual evidence of the authenticity of its status claim, the Union is trying to secure and verify its status in a world of nation-states. The Union is the nouveau riche in Europe and needs to prove its wealth is not fraudulent. The gatekeeper that controls status mobility is patina. The Charter, of course, is meant to be the chipping and oxidisation on the EU's pristine surface.

The Charter also conjures up an atmosphere of solidarity, brotherly love, and transgenerational community (the political theory equivalent of the intimate circle gathering around a fireplace).[39] Here is a world resurrected before our eyes that has never known the critique of rights developed by legal realism, CLS, communitarianism, feminism, and postmodernism. The Charter appears as a means to develop a moral and ethical foundation for the Union. It draws on the twin sources of the Ideal and the Other. On the one hand, it refers us to the informing ideal of an ethos of collective societal responsibility for the welfare of the individual and of the community as a whole. On the other hand, the Charter refers to the Other, that which is excluded but nevertheless there, such as stories of injustice and fear, or the barbaric orient. However, both references are (aesthetically, at least) unconvincing. They remain wooden and simplistic in a saturated liberal society. One accepts them the same way one accepts a shoe manufacturer's claim that its shoes aren't shoes but the result of a dream.[40]

The creation of the Charter also speaks for my thesis that it is designed to create an atmosphere of quaintness. The European Council, meeting in Tampere in October 1999, decided to establish an ad hoc body. On its first meeting, that body called itself "Convention"—a name that smacks of Philadelphia and Paris.[41] Atmospherically, this is not insignificant. It fits

[38] On the function of patina in material culture see G McCracken, *Culture and Consumption* (1988), 31–43; Architektenkammer Hessen and R Toyka (eds), *Patina* (1996).

[39] The Preamble, for instance, provides that '[e]njoyment of these rights entails responsibilities and duties with regard to other persons, to the human community and to future generations'. The Charter's individual chapters have the following headings: I—Dignity; II—Freedoms; III—Equality; IV—Solidarity; V—Citizens' Rights; VI—Justice.

[40] That is what the print on a shoebox by Camper, a Spanish-based company that is all the rage in Germany, says: see U Haltern, 'Europe Goes Camper', *Constitutionalism Web-Paper* No 3/2001, <http://www.qub.ac.uk/schools/SchoolofPoliticsInternationalStudies/FileStore/ConWEBFiles/Filetoupload,5325,en.pdf> (4 October 2004), and its German version in [2002] *Kritische Vierteljahresschrift für Gesetzgebung und Rechtswissenschaft* 261.

[41] The German version is even more telling than the English one. The body is called 'Konvent'—according to *Duden Fremdwörterbuch* (6th edn 1997), a Konvent being 1. a) a community, esp. of nuns, bound by vows to a religious life under a superior; b) a gathering of protestant priests for further education; 2. a) a weekly gathering of the [active] members of a fraternity; b) collectivity of lecturers at a university; 3. (no pl., hist.) the convention during the French Revolution.

well with the name of the web site that documented the drafting process of the Charter: http://db.consilium.eu.int. "Consilium" is Latin, the former European lingua franca, and conjures up the image of a Roman council of wise old men, white-bearded and clad in togas. That image is linked to progress and modernity surging forward. "Consilium" is amended by "eu.int"—a cipher of globalisation ("int") à la Europe ("eu") –, and it appears in the internet, the most progressive medium of communication with virtually unlimited possibilities. Such connection of Old and New, of tradition and modernity, of local roots and global aspirations, also shows in the Convention's email address: fundamental.rights@consilium.eu.int. The old lingua franca appears in the same breath, the same address even, as the new lingua franca, the world language English.

Finally, the choice of the Convention's President fits well into the picture, too. Roman Herzog is a former professor of constitutional law and Justice and President of Germany's Federal Constitutional Court—thus standing for cool rationality, academic smartness, and legal expertise beyond doubt. He is also the former President of the Federal Republic of Germany—standing for political vision and statesman-like stature. Most importantly though, he was born in a small town in Bavaria (Landshut), was married, and has two sons. Despite his steep career, Herzog conveys the impression of somehow being native and rooted in the soil, sometimes even of that specifically Bavarian snugness.

All these phenomena serve an aesthetic purpose. That purpose is to soothe our deep-seated distrust of the smooth European machinery and its faceless bureaucracy. A "Convention" is neither a machinery nor a bureaucracy. Its members have a distinctive personal image. The listen to "us" (represented by pressure groups) and take into account our reservations and suggestions. Herr Herzog even talks like someone from Landshut: How can he not be one of us? The stroke of genius that shows in the idea of a Convention is that in spite of all the idyllic cosiness, the Union's twin attributes—rationality and expertise—are not weakened. On the contrary, they grow stronger because the drafting of the Charter rests with a body of experts which bears the name of a gathering of university lecturers, of a community of monks or nuns, or of a political body during the French Revolution—in Latin still. It must seem to the Union's architects that such a body will be able to scatter peoples' doubts without giving up the tried and true Union standard of administrative expertise. Under such conditions, anything becomes possible—even to talk Latin and Bavarian at the same time. Things that seemed incompatible become compatible. There is nothing that cannot be achieved. Is it any wonder that the Convention method was used to draft the Constitutional Treaty, and that it will be brought up every single time a new text must be drafted and another Intergovernmental Conference needs to be prepared? It must seem like the golden bullet that is able to blast a hole in the Gordian knot which blocks communication between the Union and the citizens that it wants to be close to.

3. The Problem with Consumer Aesthetics

There is much logical consistency in the Union's deliberate use of the aesthetics of consumerism. Today's citizens have turned, to a large degree, into consumers. Our personal salvation experiences are often founded upon consumption. "It is the consumer attitude which makes my life into my individual affair; and it is the consumer activity which makes me into the individual," writes Bauman[42], and Urry maintains that "citizenship is more a matter of consumption than of political rights and duties."[43] Saatchi & Saatchi Europe is a reality, and not a bad one at that. There is no reason, then, why Europe should not print the Charter's text on the wrapping of its product "European Union" in order to sell it.

The problem is that the Union actually believes that the Charter really is a step towards shared European identity.[44] That is as if a shoe manufacturer, convinced by its own ads, actually believed its shoes were no shoes but the result of a dream. It simply is wrong to suppose that under the Charter's influence, the people living in Europe will turn into European subjects, coming together in solidarity as a European Community. We have already seen where such belief leads: to the comical attempt to make use of nation-state artefacts. Indeed, those artefacts, in the nation-state, *are* able to transport political and social meaning. The Union's texts, like the Charter, however, are not. It is true that subjectivity, in the times of globalisation, has come under increasing pressure. When locality gets devalued, and geographical space is cancelled out, people begin to feel like objects of transnational interests. Fundamental rights, however, the nth catalogue at that, are no cure. The cure, as Bauman says, is playing the mobility game. Scope and speed of movement make all the difference between being in control and being controlled; between shaping the conditions of interaction and being shaped by them.[45] It seems that to participate in the competition that races along before our eyes is to reconstitute subjectivity. Perhaps, the perils of the market are met effectively only by the weapons of the market. Next to that, fundamental rights pale into near-insignificance and seem like anachronistic window-dressing, at least if injected into the rationality of money and the market.

42 See Z Bauman, 'Soil, Blood and Identity' (1992) 40 *Sociological Review* 205.

43 See J Urry, *Consuming Places* (1995), 165.

44 See Vertretung der Europäischen Kommission in der Bundesrepublik Deutschland (ed), *Europäische Gespräche Heft 2/1999: Eine europäische Charta der Grundrechte, Beitrag zur gemeinsamen Identität* (1999).

45 See Z Bauman, *In Search of Politics* (1999), 26.

But let us be honest. In times in which society itself seems like a fancy-dress party, with identities designed, tried on, worn for the evening and then traded in for the next, we actually like anachronistic window-dressing. That is why we are delighted about the Charter and the Constitution-To-Be. "If there is kitsch in our daily lives," writes Daniel Harris, the theorist of consumerism, "it is because there is kitsch in our minds."[46]

IV. POST POST-POLITICS: THE COURT STEPS IN

What looks unconvincing coming from political actors such as the Commission, the Council, or member state governments, may look different when uttered by the ECJ. The Court has recently taken a leaf out of the Commission's book by entering into what we might term "political rhetoric". Its vehicle was, to little surprise, its citizenship and rights jurisprudence. After all, human rights mark the boundary between "us" and "them". Rights are distributed as a token of membership; little wonder, then, that it is here where law and identity connect. The language of rights introduces a range of values into the Community's legal and policy-making processes. These values differ sharply and ostentatiously from the Community's legacy of economic focus. Rights-talk, in this reading, denotes a certain moral content to Community law and policies, and thus offers a means of developing a moral and ethical foundation for the Community.[47] Rights are commonly conceived of as an integrating force and relied on as a logic for creating group identity that transcends national barriers. It is here that the rhetoric of rights and the rhetoric of citizenship interlock.[48]

Initially, the Court promoted identity forging through human rights and citizenship with extreme caution only. The *Konstantinidis* case of 1993[49] is a good example (1.). Recently, however, the Court has switched gears and has used Union citizenship to table its revamped notion of what Union law and European identity are about (2.). I believe this road to be problematic (V).

1. Cautious Beginnings: Konstantinidis

The case begins simply, but ultimately implicates no less than the warring visions of the identity of Europe. It starts with a Greek national living in

[46] See Harris, above n 26, p. xx.

[47] See G de Búrca, 'The Language of Rights and European Integration' in J Shaw and G More (eds), *New Legal Dynamics of European Union* (1995), 29 at 52. But see A von Bogdandy, 'The European Union as a Human Rights Organization?' (2000) 37 *CML Rev* 1307.

[48] See Y Soysal, *Limits of Citizenship* (1994); J Shaw, 'Citizenship of the Union', *Harvard Jean Monnet Working Paper* 6/97 (1997).

[49] See Case C–168/91 *Konstantinidis* [1993] ECR I–1191.

Germany, Χρήστοζ Κωνσταντινίδηζ, transliterated in his passport as Christos Konstantinidis, who became engaged in a Kafkaesque dispute with the German authorities over nothing less than his right to his name. In 1990 Mr Konstantinidis applied to the German Registry Office to correct a misspelling of his name in the marriage register. Upon examining his application, however, the German authorities determined that his name had, from the first, been improperly transliterated under German law. The spelling, they found, did not comply with the system of transliteration established by the International Organization for Standardization (ISO), the use of which is mandated by a 1973 treaty to which both Germany and Greece are parties. They ordered that pursuant to the ISO he must henceforth be known as Hréstos Kónstantinidés.

The poor man was horrified. The new spelling disguised his ethnic origin (Hréstos, as the Advocate General observed to the ECJ, does not look or sound like a Greek name and has a vaguely Slavonic flavor) and offended his religious sentiments by destroying the Christian character of the name.[50] Mr Konstantinidis was also a self-employed masseur and hydrotherapist, and envisioned the inconvenience and loss of business from having to either change the name by which he was known to his clientele.

The newly christened Hréstos sought protection from the German courts, which referred the matter to the European Court of Justice for a preliminary ruling under the Art 234 EC procedure.

In his Opinion of 9 December 1992, Advocate General Jacobs gave voice to the common-sense intuition that Mr Konstantinidis must be protected by human rights. He suggested that Mr Konstantinidis should be able to invoke European Community human rights against Germany. Wherever a Community national goes to earn his living in the European Community, he argued, "he will be treated in accordance with a common code of fundamental values". Then AG Jacobs said: "In other words, he is entitled to say 'civis europeus sum'," I am a European citizen, "and to invoke that status in order to oppose any violation of his fundamental rights." The ECJ was not so sure. It chose to stay out of the human rights/citizenship business. While the Luxembourg Judges saw fit to afford some protection to Mr Konstantinidis, they did not buy into, or even refer to, AG Jacobs's sweeping concept. Rather, they decided the case exclusively on the basis of Art 52 EEC Treaty (embodying the economic freedom of establishment, now Art 43 EC) and the principle of non-discrimination on the basis of nationality. The German authorities, concluded the Court, were not entitled to insist on

[50] At the hearing, according to AG Jacobs, Mr Konstantinidis pointed out that 'he owes his name to his date of birth (25 December), Christos being the Greek name for the founder of the Christian—not "Hréstian"—religion'. Opinion of AG Jacobs, Case C–168/91, above n 49, para 40.

spelling the applicant's name in such a way as to misrepresent its pronunciation since such "distortion exposes him to the risk that potential clients confuse him with other persons".

a) Advocate General Jacobs

While the doctrinal implications of the case are simple,[51] on a deeper level, as the Advocate General acknowledges himself (para 46), the case is about the depth and foundations of European integration. It is the concept of citizenship that, in its understanding as a membership right, connects the polity and the rights-bearer. "Civis europeus sum", Jacobs has the European consumer say, and attempts to trade in the traditional, and much-despised, market-citizen (or *homo economicus*, or *Marktbürger*[52]) for citizenship cast in terms of human rights, and in modernist, almost cosmopolitan terms at that. His mind-set is best illustrated by an example he gives. Right before he suggests that any individual should be able to claim "civis europeus sum" and rely on the "common code of fundamental values", he hypothesises about the ECJ's right to intervene if a Member State instituted a draconian penal code under which theft was punishable by amputation of the right hand. The reader's immediate reaction will be, "We're *Europeans*, this can't be legal, there must be human rights protecting us." Identifying a form of oppression which horrifies us and which we have reason to expect would horrify anyone from our cultural or social background is a great strategy to argue for a universal claim.[53] AG Jacobs makes a strong appeal to what he,

[51] It was generally accepted that, with the exception of two small, narrowly circumscribed exceptions, the Court lacked competence to review Members States' actions for fundamental rights violations. That was the task of Member States' courts; the Luxembourg Court would review only Community actions. This orthodox view was expressed in Case 43/75 *Defrenne* [1978] ECR 1365, by AG Capotorti. The two exceptions are as follows. First, Member States' actions implementing Community measures will be reviewed according to human rights ('agency' situation). The hallmark case is Case 5/88 *Wachauf* [1989] ECR 2609. Secondly, Member States' measures adopted in derogation from the prohibition on restricting the free movement of the four factors of production will also be scrutinised according to human rights. The hallmark case here is Case C–260/89, *ERT* [1991] ECR I–2925. In view of this, the novelty and breadth of AG Jacobs's position becomes fully apparent. He suggests that whenever an EC national goes to another Member State in reliance on the rights of free movement in the Treaty, any failure to respect a fundamental human right of that national, whether or not it is connected with his or her work, should constitute an infringement of EC law. Clearly, AG Jacobs's view would significantly expand human rights review through the ECJ.

[52] See M Everson, 'The Legacy of the Market Citizen' in Shaw and More (eds), above n 47, 73; HP Ipsen, *Europäisches Gemeinschaftsrecht* (1972), 102.

[53] Even though we are aware that it may be a common practice as part of a cultural tradition in other societies, it is nevertheless abhorred—*rightly* abhorred. One may accept the relativist's anthropological point that sensibilities, moral ideas and ideas of respect for persons and minimally decent treatment vary from society to society. This particular practice, however, so excites our sympathies for those who suffer from it, and so offends our sensibilities, that the example invites us to condemn the practice notwithstanding its establishment in a culture: J Waldron, 'How to Argue for a Universal Claim' (1999) 30 *Columbia HRL Rev* 305.

and surely we, his western readers, associate with the *humanity* of the individual. Viewed in this way, AG Jacobs is a cosmopolitan. He identifies a core of what makes us human—in his penal code hypothetical, bodily integrity; in his argument in the case itself, identity conferred through a name—and entrusts a national court with upholding it across all boundaries.[54]

Ironically, in a cultural reading, these arguments are put to work for a very situated, bounded, geographically and historically sharply defined communal self. Consider, *first*, that the draconian penal code hypothetical conjures up the stereotyped epitome of Europe's Other. Iran, Afghanistan—backward countries under Sharia, in far-away corners of the world, rejecting not only the enlightened wall between the church and the state but also the essentialist notion that common human rights standards can be arrived at and ought to be upheld everywhere in the world. Invoking the Other, and provoking the foreseeable response, reifies a distinctly Western liberal democratic identity. Inventing Europe in the mirror of the Orient, by inventing the orient, has a long tradition in Europe.[55] Hence, surprisingly, at the heart of the human rights argument lies the almost racist image of the bedeviled Orient.[56]

Remember, *second*, that AG Jacobs uses Latin ("civis europeus sum") to voice his citizenship concept. Latin was the European lingua franca, the language of diplomacy and polite society, far into the sixteenth century, until French replaced it. Latin, as a bygone common language, still conjures up a common Europeanness, much more so than French does. It is considered the root of European civilisation.

Consider, *third*, that it was the Apostle Paul who repeatedly said to the Romans, "Civis Romanus sum", to keep the Roman soldiers from physically abusing him and his followers.[57] AG Jacobs, in using the parallel phrase, appeals to the deep strata of Latin Christendom, which, as a cultural framework, has become interchangeable with the idea of Europe. Christianity, moreover, is not only the undercurrent of contemporary European culture.

[54] If law is to embody this universalist claim, its apparent origin must be in (one universal, not a context-specific) reason, not will. With law being the expression of (universal) reason, the inevitable momentum will be towards empire, away from multiple states: see Kahn (1999), above n 5, 58. And the empire, logically, must be ruled by one emperor, who holds all the strings, who will perhaps delegate but never divide his authority, and who can, jealously yet legitimately, claim exclusive loyalty. It is here that the unified European constitutionalism has its deeper roots.

[55] For details see Delanty, above n 3, 84–99.

[56] The irony is highlighted by the fact that, if at all, the argument is made precisely the other way round. Hervey for instance suggests that the *market* construction of rights within the EU raises what she terms the 'racist implications of Community law': TK Hervey, 'Migrant Workers and Their Families in the European Union' in Shaw and More (eds), above n 47, 91 at 95–6.

[57] Cf the narrative, inter alia, in Acts 16, 37; 22, 25–29.

It also carries with it a siege-mentality. Islamic invasions along with the barbarian and Persian gave a European identity to Christendom as the bulwark against the non-Christian world.[58] Note that it also provided Western monarchies with a powerful myth of legitimation. The Advocate General, in surprisingly few words, summons up the rich texture that is part of the idea of Europe.

Thus, there are two layers in the Advocate General's argument. On the one hand, he claims that names are cultural universals, and that to tamper with them is to deprive individuals of their identity. In a way, he protests Germany's distorting Christos's *first name*, which signifies his uniqueness and individuality as a human being. This is a violation sufficiently egregious to evoke our universalist, abhorred response, which is why Christos Konstantinidis needs the Court's protection under the blanket of human rights. On the other hand, he argues that Germany has violated the rights of "one of us", a *European* citizen who can claim membership in the same polity as the rest of us. Here, AG Jacobs protests Germany's distorting of Mr Konstantinidis's *last name*, which provides the bearer with family and extended kinship ties. It identifies Konstantinidis as a Greek national, and hence as part of the Community family. The violation should be made good not because it is so egregious, but because this is no way to treat a member of your extended family.

These two layers do not necessarily contradict each other. In fact, they work well together in that they provide the notion of citizenship, as used by the Advocate General, with a core of organic essentialism. This core—in the first version of the argument, Aristotelian; in the second, European-centered—undermines competing claims to identity and loyalty. If the organic-cultural core of what defines membership in a community is as AG Jacobs claims it is, how can there be a different one when it comes to a different polity? Is it possible that there even *is* a different polity that can lay a claim to loyalty?

The problem with this vision is its displacement of nationality, and thus the finality of just another super-state. The distribution of human rights in the European Union becomes the thick wall separating Us from Them, those who belong from those who don't, and Europe from the Other.[59] This flies in the face of Art 17(1) EC, which reads: "Citizenship of the Union shall complement and not replace national citizenship." Moreover, it is out of touch with reality. Citizens do not identify with the Union whatsoever; rather, they feel alienated, and do not trust Brussels.[60] The reason may be

[58] See Delanty, above n 3, 26.
[59] See JHH Weiler, 'Thou Shalt Not Oppress a Stranger' (1992) 3 *EJIL* 65, with respect to non-Community nationals.
[60] See OPTEM, above n 24.

that the nation, through its myths, provides a social home, a shared history and a common destination. It is the emotional, romantic side of belonging. Weiler calls it the Eros, while the national is Civilisation.[61] If this is true, the Advocate General's effort to wave yet another catalogue of rights before the public will be meaningless in the attempt to create an effective attachment of the European citizens to their new polity, and bring them to accept the redrawn political boundaries. It would also fail to reflect the complicated multilayered structure of European integration, citizenship, or individual identity.[62] It is impossible to funnel polycentricity, legal and cultural pluralism, and plurality into the old vessels of unity and exclusivity.

b) The Court

Far from taking up AG Jacobs's proposals, the Court in its brief decision does not even mention human rights. Still, the Court has a theory on citizenship and identity. That theory emerges from the Court's elaborate silence[63] and its use of *economic* law to protect Mr Konstantinidis.

The context of the Court's theory is that of economic existence. Markets require a fluidity of capital, human and fixed. Market actors, both on the production and the consumption end, must be open to the reshaping of their own conception of the self over time. Identities, in other words, can be adopted and discarded like a change of costume. Bauman has likened modern life to a pilgrimage into the desert where one is in constant danger of losing one's identity. That exactly is what happens to Konstantinidis: He loses his name, unquestionably the main bearer of identity. He learns, through painful experience, that mobility means to subject oneself to forces

[61] See Weiler, above n 1, 324–57. See Anderson, above n 20: While the nation is the place of culture, and culture is the domain of feeling, there is no culture in nationalism, only an elegant, decorous absence of feeling.

[62] See N MacCormick, *Questioning Sovereignty* (1999); H Schepel, 'Legal Pluralism in the European Union' in P Fitzpatrick and HJ Bergeron (eds), above n 18, 47; U Haltern, 'Europäischer Kulturkampf' (1998) 37 *Der Staat* 591.

[63] While it may seem strange, at first glance, to distil a theory from silence, it is not so far-fetched for those who are familiar with the Court's jurisprudential culture. The Court and the Advocate General often seem to engage in a peculiar instance of division of labour. The Advocate General eloquently summarises arguments and precedents, and does not shy away from openly pointing to considerations that go well beyond narrow legal reasoning. The Court, by contrast, more often than not hides the ball. While it is far from being positivist—in fact, the ECJ is acutely aware of the political environment it adjudicates in, and is very often driven by considerations relating to it—it is not exactly outspoken with regard to the 'true' rationales that drive it. The reason might be the necessity to 'speak strict legalese' in its dialogue with its national counterparts. Whatever the merit of that speculation, the result is that in order to obtain a complete picture one has to look not only to the decision, but to the Advocate General's opinion as well. Only in superimposing one on the other, like two transparencies layered together against the light, can one see the meaning shining through the silence.

that will change identity in unknown ways, and that he is not the sole master of his identity.

The Court, then, essentially negates what the Advocate General believes. AG Jacobs is a modernist: identity is in the hands of the individual, and the goal is not to impinge upon it. He believes in a manageable world and rationality. History, to the Advocate General, is progress. The task is an impossible one: humanity as such, order, harmony, and certainty. While the horizon can never be reached, it is precisely the *foci imaginarii* that make the path feasible and even inescapable. If humanity is essentialist, human rights protect at least an essentialist core. The more human rights the better, and the more encompassing their scope the better, too. It is a matter of logic, therefore, to apply human rights judicial review against the Member States. It protects Konstantinidis in his being human (or at least, in his being one of us). His humanity is, inter alia, his autonomy, and as an autonomous sovereign agent, he has the capacity to choose to travel beyond the boundaries of his known world. Protecting that autonomy means absorbing the risk involved in this endeavour. Choice and morality are private; risk is public. Konstantinidis's freedom must be unharmed—it is the job of the government to protect it. The tools of protection are, of course, human rights, as the ultimate weapon at the disposal of the enlightened agent.

The Court is sceptical. It appears comfortable with the notion of citizenship as consumer identity. Commentators are uniformly and customarily critical of such suggestions. Weiler, for example, speaks of "bread-and-circus democracy" and a "Saatchi & Saatchi Europe".[64] However, there is strong evidence that today "we can learn more about the operations and values of social communication from Saatchi & Saatchi than from [Justices on the US Supreme Court] Holmes and Brandeis".[65] Rather than mourning a world we have lost, and condemning consumer culture as a social pathology that is both hedonistic and parasitic, we should accept that individuals use consumption—understood as rituals and codes which form a flow of information—to say something about themselves, their families, and their loyalties. The kinds of statements they make reflect only the kind of universe surrounding them. The meanings and rituals of consumption mark out the categories and classifications which constitute social order. We might want to imagine the postmodern consumer as ironic and knowing, reflexive and aware of the games being played. The consumer has considerable cultural capital.[66]

[64] See JHH Weiler, 'Bread and Circus' (1998) 4 *Columbia Journal of European Law* 223.
[65] See RKL Collins and DM Skover, *The Death of Discourse* (1996), 70.
[66] Some strands of sociological literature even emphasise the communal nature of consumption. According to this view, consumption takes on more and more social functions as a form of sociality, even solidarity: R Shields, *Lifestyle Shopping* (1992), 110.

The Court, it seems, understands this. It has refused to pretend that Europe is composed of individuals carrying their immutable identities around with them, and has recognised instead the risk that identities will be changed, perhaps erased, by forces beyond individual control. Identities are not pre-social, monolithic, or unchanging. They are multilayered, complex, and impacted in unpredictable ways by disordered cultural spaces. The Court recognises that Konstantinidis, like all of us, is not just a self-defined independent agent. Power is exercised not primarily by him, but by the changing social environment around him. The Court displays a postmodern sensibility by limiting that power as is appropriate to Konstantinidis's endeavour as an economic pilgrim.

c) Conclusion and Critique

In a way, the Court takes up AG Jacobs's suggestion of linking the Konstantinidis case to the notion of citizenship. European citizenship, however, will not be defined through essentialist human rights, or exclusive demands on loyalty. According to the Court, a theory of European citizenship has to take into account the practice of citizenship in Europe. That practice does not support liberal, communitarian, or republican theories of citizenship. Beyond its glossy surface of liberal human rights, or communitarian Europeanness, the European experience of citizenship is exactly as Art 17 EC has it: it is framed by the "limitations and conditions laid down in this Treaty and by the measures adopted to give it effect", that is, by economic ratio. There is a gap, then, between the projected nature of the European polity on the one hand, which has appropriated cherished symbols of statehood and which lays claim to its citizens' political loyalty, and the nature of the European citizens' experience of citizenship on the other hand, which is dominated by rituals of trade, travel and consumption. The Advocate General models his vision of citizenship according to the nature of the polity, and embraces the notion that citizenship in Europe is still a project. Applying human rights against Member State actions would accomplish the project of rights-based citizenship, and at the same time the project of an ever-more federal Europe. The Court, in contrast, models its vision of citizenship after the practice, and experience, of citizenship. It refuses to bridge the gap between Europe's reach and citizenship's practice by projecting onto the individual attributes that have long dissolved, and hopes that have proved illusory.

European identity, as understood by the Court in 1993, proves to be fleeting, unstable, and insecure, and hinges on participation in the market. It is just as complex and multilayered as the law that supports it. The upside is that the Union, in sustaining nothing more than weak and thin post-political identity, is able to perform its role as Civilisation. The downside is that postmodern superficiality squashes hopes for a vibrant political life and European Eros.

2. The Way Forward?—Evolving Union Citizenship

Obviously, this state of affairs sits squarely with the increasingly shrill discourse of shared values and a European identity rooted in commonness, feelings of belonging and a shared fate. The mounting pressure is nowhere more evident than in the Court's own documents, namely its Advocate Generals' opinions. In *Konstantinidis*, AG Jacobs seems to have started something of a tradition. A little later, AG Léger in *Boukhalfa*[67], AG La Pergola in *Martínez Sala*[68], and, again, AG Jacobs in *Bickel & Franz*[69], made sweeping statements. The most extensive and fervent treatment of Union citizenship comes from AG Cosmas in *Wijsenbeek*. He first turned against the notion that Art 18 EC might not in itself have regulatory scope:

> First, it underestimates the constitutive task of the Community's constitutional legislature, presenting it as being devoid of substance. Secondly, it disregards the Community's evolutive dynamics at a time when those dynamics are obvious at all stages in the evolution of the written rules and case-law on the

[67] See Case C–214/94 *Boukhalfa* [1996] ECR I–2253, Opinion of AG Léger, para 63: 'Admittedly the concept embraces aspects which have already largely been established in the development of Community law and in this respect it represents a consolidation of existing Community law. However, it is for the Court to ensure that its full scope is attained. If all the conclusions inherent in that concept are drawn, every citizen of the Union must, whatever his nationality, enjoy exactly the same rights and be subject to the same obligations. Taken to its ultimate conclusion, the concept should lead to citizens of the Union being treated absolutely equally, irrespective of their nationality. Such equal treatment should be manifested in the same way as among nationals of one and the same State.'

[68] See Case C–85/96 *Martínez Sala* [1998] ECR I–2691, Opinion of AG La Pergola, para 18: 'Article 8a *extracted* the kernel from the other freedoms of movement—the freedom which we now find characterised as the right, not only to move, but also to *reside* in every Member State: a primary right, in the sense that it appears as the first of the rights ascribed to citizenship of the Union. That is how freedom of residence is conceived and systematised in the Treaty. It is not simply a derived right, but a right *inseparable* from citizenship of the Union in the same way as the other rights expressly crafted as necessary corollaries of such *status* (see Article 8b, c and d)—a new right, common to all citizens of the Member States without distinction. Citizenship of the Union comes through the fiat of the primary norm, being conferred directly on the individual, who is henceforth formally recognised as a subject of law who acquires and loses it together with citizenship of the national state to which he belongs and in no other way. Let us say that it is the *fundamental* legal status guaranteed to the citizen of every Member State by the legal order of the Community and now of the Union.'

[69] See Case C–274/96 *Bickel & Franz* [1998] ECR I–7637, Opinion of AG Jacobs, paras 23 and 24: 'The notion of citizenship of the Union implies a commonality of rights and obligations uniting Union citizens by a common bond transcending Member State nationality. The introduction of that notion was largely inspired by the concern to bring the Union closer to its citizens and to give expression to its character as more than a purely economic union. That concern is reflected in the removal of the word 'economic' from the Community's name (also effected by the Treaty on European Union) and by the progressive introduction into the EC Treaty of a wide range of activities and policies transcending the field of the economy. . . . Freedom from discrimination on grounds of nationality is the most fundamental right conferred by the Treaty and must be seen as a basic ingredient of Union citizenship.'

> free movement of persons. Lastly, my objection is based primarily on the very wording and spirit of the article in question ...[70]

Up to the Maastricht Treaty,

> ... the text of the Treaties establishing the Communities gave the impression that persons were not considered to possess rights, in other words as autonomous holders of rights and obligations, except indirectly; it is only by repercussion that they benefit from the favourable consequences of the direct application of a rule of Community law and, more generally, of the implementation of the economic objectives of the Community legal order. The central objective of the Community rule lay in principle in the development of the Community itself and in the promotion of its fundamental aspirations ... [para 82].

This, however, has changed, according to AG Cosmas, with the insertion of Art 18 EC:

> The article in question is inspired by the same *anthropocentric philosophy* as the other provisions of the body of rules of which it forms part. One class of persons, the citizens of the Union, become holders of a specific right—in the present case the right to move and reside freely within the territory of the Member States—irrespective of whether the enjoyment of this right is accompanied by the promotion of other Community aspirations or objectives.
>
> This is where one of the most essential differences between Article 8a [now 18] and Article 48 [now 39] et seq is to be found. The latter articles have established a *functional* possibility for nationals of the Member States, which they are granted so that they exercise it with a view to the creation of a common market, the objective of which can only be to permit persons to pursue their economic activities in optimum conditions. Article 8a [now 18], by contrast, establishes for nationals of the Member States (now designated citizens of the Union) a possibility of a *substantive nature*, namely a right, in the true meaning of the word, which exists with a view to the autonomous pursuit of a goal, to the benefit of the holder of that right and not to the benefit of the Community and the attainment of its objectives. [paras 83 and 84]

What follows must be a fundamental change:

> In other words, Article 8a does not simply enshrine in constitutional terms the acquis communautaire as it existed when it was inserted into the Treaty and complement it by broadening the category of persons entitled to freedom of movement to include other classes of person not pursuing economic activities. Article 8a [now 18] also enshrines a *right of a different kind, a true right of movement, stemming from the status as a citizen of the Union*, which is not

[70] See Case 378/97 *Wijsenbeek* [1999] ECR I–6238, Opinion of AG Cosmas, para 80.

> subsidiary in relation to European unification, whether economic or not. [para 85]

Citizenship, therefore, is not structured through the parameters of the common market (para 86). As can be seen from "the body of European constitutional literature", citizenship is not so much linked to Arts 39 *et seq* EC, but to "the fundamental right to personal freedom, which is at the apex of individual rights" (para 89).

The Court did not follow its emphatic Advocate Generals. Rather, it developed Union citizenship in small, incremental, but ultimately very powerful steps. While it remained hesitant in *Bickel & Franz* and *Wijsenbeek*, it regrouped in a series of cases which led to a consistent and potent citizenship jurisprudence.[71] The first of this series was *Martínez Sala*.[72] Art 17(2) EC "attaches" to the citizen the rights and duties existing under the EC Treaty, especially the non-discrimination principle in Art 12. Ms Martínez Sala could claim equality of treatment, in this case access to a German child-raising benefit for her new-born child, even if she was solely dependent on welfare and could bring herself within the personal scope of Community law by no other means than that she was a Union citizen lawfully residing in another Member State. The only material condition was that the benefit she claimed must fall within the scope of EU law.[73] Some have concluded that this is something close to a universal right of access to all kinds of welfare benefits to all those who are Union citizens and are lawfully resident in a Member State.[74]

The next step was *Grzelczyk*.[75] The Court's reasoning resembled that of *Martínez Sala* but was more far-reaching. The ECJ used citizenship to determine the sphere of *ratione personae* for the application of Art 12 EC; it is because Mr Grzelczyk is a Union citizen lawfully residing in Belgium that he can avail himself of Art 12 EC, in all situations that come within the scope *ratione materiae* of Community law. The very scope *ratione materiae* is defined in part by the right to move and reside freely in another Member State.[76] Also, the Court held that

> Union citizenship is destined to be the fundamental status of nationals of the Member States, enabling those who find themselves in the same situation to enjoy the same treatment in law irrespective of their nationality, subject to such exceptions as are expressly provided for. [para 31]

[71] For a detailed analysis see U Haltern, 'Das Janusgesicht der Unionsbürgerschaft' [2005] 11 *Swiss Political Science Review* 87.
[72] See Case 85/96, above n 68.
[73] *Ibid*, para 63.
[74] See SC Fries and J Shaw, 'Citizenship of the Union' (1998) 4 *EPL* 533.
[75] See Case C–184/99 *Grzelczyk* [2001] ECR I–6193.
[76] *Ibid*, paras 32 and 34.

This line of reasoning was finally confirmed in *d'Hoop*.[77] If *Konstantinidis* came to the Court today rather than in 1993, the ECJ's decision would look very different from what it did eleven years ago. In fact, a similar case involving the changing of names did come to the Court, and the ECJ did decide on the basis of the citizenship provisions. The case *Garcia Avello*[78] concerns the surname borne by children born in Belgium to a married couple resident there. The father is a Spanish national, the mother Belgian, and the children have dual nationality. On registration of their births in Belgium, the children were given the double surname borne by their father—Garcia Avello—composed in accordance with Spanish law and custom of the first element of his own father's surname and the first element of his mother's surname. The parents subsequently applied to the Belgian authorities to have the children's surname changed to Garcia Weber so that it reflected the Spanish pattern and comprised the first element of their father's surname, followed by their mother's (maiden) surname. That application was refused as contrary to Belgian practice. To little surprise, the Court decided in favour of the parents. Importantly, it continued its citizenship jurisprudence and heavily relied on *Martínez Sala*, *Grzelczyk*, and *d'Hoop*.

This jurisprudence, in conclusion, is interesting in more than one respect. First, the Court decides to use, for the first time in the field of Union citizenship, rather emphatic language. Union citizenship rises to be the "fundamental status" of Member State nationals. If it is "fundamental", nationality consequently loses its hitherto fundamental character. Secondly, the Court does not follow its Advovate Generals' doctrinal submissions. It does not sketch Union citizenship as a "fundamental right to personal freedom" which, according to AG Cosmas in *Wijsenbeek*, is at the "apex of individual rights". Citizenship, according to the Court, is not foremost about freedom, but about equality. The ECJ links the citizenship clause with Art 12 EC and its principle of non-discrimination on the grounds of nationality. Belongingness mediated through nationality thus becomes less relevant; citizenship of the Union becomes fundamental. Behind this doctrinal construction stands the notion of transnational equality of European citizens. Citizenship is defined through the idea that Europeans across borders are equal, or that they are, at least, not unequal because of their respective nationalities. What is implied is that European citizens are part of a whole. While AG Cosmas's right to personal freedom is about solitary individuals, their individual will and their individual ends, the principle of non-discrimination hinges on some form of commonality that makes them part of a larger organism. The gestalt of citizenship is not simply one of liberal individualism and rights so prominent in the Advocate

[77] See Case C–224/98 *d'Hoop* [2002] ECR I–6191.

[78] See Case C–148/02, *Garcia Avello* [2003] ECR I–11613.

Generals' opinions, but is enriched through a collective dimension. Of course, this dimension is "imagined", to borrow Anderson's wonderful phrase. The Court, in other words, starts to construct an imagined community. This is the truly revolutionary moment in the Court's citizenship jurisprudence. The difference between the Advocate Generals' conception of citizenship and that of the Court is not merely academic. Rather, it marks the difference between rights-based individualism and collective imagination of *gemeinschaft*. From the first speaks a logic of enlightenment and its aspiration to place the individual, freedom, and autonomy at the center of communities—this is what AG Cosmas means when he speaks of "anthropocentric philosophy". The Court, on the other hand, displays a good deal of sensitivity towards collective identity as part of individuals' lives.

It may be that the Court has embarked on a journey towards political rhetoric. Political rhetoric invokes physical participation in a transtemporal community that is the physical corpus of the polity. Our century-long experience identifies that community as the state. Political rhetoric is about the realisation of the idea of the state in the individual citizen's body.[79] While political rhetoric is usually wary of law, just as law more often than not excludes political rhetoric, there are instances when these two come together. Prominent examples are the topos of sovereignty, and the mythical point of origin of a community. In such instances, constitutional discourse becomes an important source of political rhetoric. Constitutional courts show us the high political rhetoric of the nation. Courts speak in the name of the sovereign people and tell us who we are, and who we are not. The ECJ's recent jurisprudence on citizenship may mean it is ready to take on its role to elaborate the character of the political subject who is the citizen, and to identify the relevant community as the Union.[80]

[79] See Kahn (2005), above n 5, 244.

[80] It is no coincidence that the Court assumes a new role and turns to political rhetoric and identity. The discursive environment accompanying the citizenship jurisprudence since 1998 has exerted much pressure on Community law to reflect identity in its structures, programmes and meanings. There has been increasing politicisation and a distinct turn away from the primacy of legal and economic integration. The question of the political, the search for Europe's political, imagination and the debate about its identity, foundations, and ends have entered the stream of European discourse with such vigour that debates about democratic structures, transparency, effective administration etc have been, if not replaced, at least contextualised. What does Europe mean to its citizens if the turnout at elections for the European Parliament is extremely low? What is the Community about if the logic of economic growth seems exhausted after Seattle? Is there a democratic identity in sight if in the centre of Europe, a party is represented in the Austrian government that in the eyes of many is intolerant and xenophobic and that sends ministers to the Council? What does our common money mean to us after the dispiriting Duisenberg/Trichet compromise and the drop of the euro below the par of exchange with the dollar in January 2000? Who are we as Europeans if the CFSP is disgraced by the violent conflict in Kosovo? All these questions pressed for an immediate answer; all involved European identity. We have seen part of that answer in the debates on the future of Europe and the quest for a Constitution for Europe. Mostly, however, this has been symbolic politics. The more important, if less showy, part of the answer is the Court's new role and, above all, law's changing meaning.

V. POLITICS AND POST-POLITICS

1. The Murmuring Nation

The turn towards identity in European law is fraught with ambiguity. This comes as no surprise taking into account the historical conditions of the discursive interlocking of citizenship and human rights: the disintegration of European natural law, the rise of social contract theories, and the development of states in the modern sense. The success of the nation-state within the last two centuries is conditioned by ambivalent semantics. On the one hand, state and nation mark the rise of modern, post-traditionally organised polities that have rid themselves of all organic bonds. All premodern commitments, such as family, religion, etc, have weakened and discharged the citizen into a mobile environment. The modern nation-state is constituted through citizens as abstract individuals, not through members of preformed groups. On the other hand, modernity has produced its own anti-thesis. In an environment of an abstract public domain and a gestalt-less levelling of social bonds, individuals look for traces of true commonality in secluded spaces.[81] The pre-modern character of Volk and nation is not premodern at all, but the effect precisely of modernity. The language of common roots, shared history, or cultural unity is the by-product of the modern aseptic language of the nation-state. Today, more than ever, it is intertwined with the rhetoric of the initiated, the unspeakable, and the secret, which makes the political appear ambivalent and ambiguous. At the same time, it is the very condition of modernity, comparable to vampires, which are portrayed as remains from the past, while their existence is in reality constituted by modernity.[82] The state speaks the language of citizenship, rights and universality, but it means some unspeakable remnants, from which it is possible to sniff out the Unique, the Authentic and the unmistakable Commonality. It is this interlocking of efficient bureaucracy and cloudy identity that makes the nation demonic.

The arcane underside of the political drifts to the surface as soon as a polity turns to identity discourse. This is true whether or not it is a transnational polity. Little wonder, then, that Europe today struggles with old demons.[83] Jurists should be aware, too, that law is not immune from such ghosts from the past. Just as the nation murmurs beneath the surface of transnational integration, the mythical and the mystical whisper beneath

[81] See J Vogl, 'Einleitung' in *id* (ed), *Gemeinschaften: Positionen zu einer Philosophie des Politischen* (1994), 7 at 17.

[82] See S Žižek, *Genieße Deine Nation wie Dich selbst!* in Vogl (ed), above n 81, 133 at 154.

[83] See, eg, C Joerges and NS Ghaleigh (eds), *Darker Legacies of Law in Europe* (2003); J Laughland, *The Tainted Source* (1997).

the aseptic surface of the law. As Europe turns to identity, research must turn to Europe's law's deep structure.

2. Europe's Legal Imagination of the Political

The debate on EU constitutional legitimacy has moved from formal validity (the legitimacy of the Court's constitutionalising legal discourse) via deontological concerns (the democratic deficit) to foundational myths (issues of European identity and demos).[84] Europe is redefining its political imagination. Most legal research, as instructive as it is, has little, or the wrong things, to contribute to this search. Trawling the bowels of the regulatory state will not yield a European imagination of the political.[85] Perhaps, we are witnessing the move away from Civilisation, towards Eros.

The political, of course, is a contested domain. Its imagination is contingent upon the reality that surrounds it. Living in a world of economic transactions, consumption, and markets—a world, that is, in which (in the words of the Schuman Declaration) "war becomes unthinkable"—the political is largely replaced by the market. Identity is as fluid as money-flows, citizenship becomes more a matter of consumption than of political rights and duties[86], and Shore writes, "The citizen-hero of the new Europe thus appears to be the Euro-consumer".[87]

That, however, may quickly change. Political meanings are as contingent as any others: they can slip away with a slight change of perspective, and they can just as easily slip back into place. As soon as the political enters the domain of ultimate values and meanings, it becomes incommensurable with the values of the market. We need no reminder of this after September 11. At the center of such imagination stands the nation-state. It is the sole source, and the only end, of its own existence; it loves only itself. It exists as a meaning borne by citizens willing to invest their bodies in its continued existence as an order of law. Its power rests on the willingness of individuals to take up, as their own self-identity, the identity of the state. Maintenance of the state, then, becomes a meaning worth fighting and dying for. That is the nature of sacrifice: to take on, in one's own body, the

[84] See JHH Weiler, 'Epilogue: The European Courts of Justice' in A-M Slaughter, A Stone Sweet and JHH Weiler (eds), *The European Courts and National Courts* (1998), 365 at 372–8.

[85] This may be the reason much of the debate on European good governance (see, eg, the helpful writing in EO Eriksen, C Joerges and J Neyer (eds), *European Governance, Deliberation and the Quest for Democratisation* (2003), and vol 8, issue 1 of the *ELJ* (2002)) seems strangely out of touch with the questions that vex Europe today.

[86] See J Urry, *Consuming Places* (1995), 165.

[87] See Shore, above n 21, 84.

meaning that informs and sustains a larger community. The modern nation-state has been extremely successful in mobilising its population to make sacrifices in order to help sustain the state's continued historical existence.[88]

We stand dismayed and helpless before the tenacity of the nation-state's political imagination.[89] Living in Europe, we like to think we have outgrown the autonomy of the political and have entered the age of post-politics.[90] We describe politics as a site of competition between interest groups. Ultimate political meanings have given way to a multiplicity of particular interests. Many of those interests are just the same as those advanced through the market. Politics, therefore, appears as an alternative means of accomplishing market-ends. We have long lost sight of the notion of sacrificial politics at home. "Who," asked Benedict Anderson in 1983, "will willingly die for Comecon or the EEC?"[91] In part, this is a matter of perspective. It was none other than Carl Schmitt, in 1932, who realised that nowhere in liberal accounts of the state, does anyone die; there is only protection from the state, no dying or killing for the state.[92] Liberalism—a theory of contractual origins of law, whether or not behind a veil of ignorance—fails to see law's move from contract to sacrifice, and the collective nature of sovereignty.[93] Yet, this is not just another version of the story of the blind men and the elephant. There are signs that the political and the market are in fact increasingly being conflated, with "citizens" and "consumers" becoming essentially one and the same thing.[94] Can we really deny a blurring and flattening of modernist (not to mention pre-modernist) distinctions? Is it not true that to a large extent, values have first materialised, then dematerialised and now exist purely as signs circulating within a political economy of signs? The plane of signs and culture can no longer be anchored in "finalities" in the external world (e.g. consumption is no longer anchored in the finality of need, nor knowledge in truth, technocracy in progress, history in a meta-narrative of causation and teleology etc). It often seems there is little credible beneath or beyond the flat landscape of endless signification.[95]

[88] See Kahn (2005), above n 5.

[89] For an impressive example see M Ignatieff, *Blood and Belonging* (1994), 248: 'I began the journey as a liberal and I end as one, but I cannot help thinking that liberal civilisation—the rule of laws, not men, of argument in place of force, of compromise in place of violence—runs deeply against the human grain and is achieved and sustained only by the most unremitting struggle against human nature.'

[90] See S Žižek, 'Carl Schmitt in the Age of Post-Politics' in C Mouffe (ed), *The Challenge of Carl Schmitt* (1999), 18.

[91] See Anderson, above n 20, 53.

[92] See C Schmitt, *The Concept of the Political* (G Schwab transl, orig 1932) (1996), 71.

[93] See U Haltern, 'Recht als kulturelle Existenz' in E Jayme (ed), *Kulturelle Identität und Internationales Privatrecht* (2003), 15.

[94] See U Haltern, 'Gestalt und Finalität' in A von Bogdandy, *Europäisches Verfassungsrecht* (2003), 803; but see Weiler, above n 1, 332–5.

[95] See D Slater, *Consumer Culture and Modernity* (1997).

Perhaps, in Europe, the outlines of a liberal order—a post-political order stripped of its attachment to a popular sovereign—are emerging, something that Kahn calls the "European model".[96]

I fear that while Europe is increasingly postmodern in relation to its Member States, it becomes just as increasingly modern with respect to its own identity. A slight change of perspective may yank us back onto a terrain where we distinguish between friends and enemies, believe in ultimate values, crave for meaning that we derive from standing for some larger community which will outlive ourselves, and are ready to invest our bodies into the continued existence of the polity we live in. Do we want such a political imagination for Europe? If so, how do we get there? If not, can we prevent it? These are questions that concern the meaning of the political just as they concern the meaning of law. Law is memory, and we are witnessing the Court feeding it with its new notion of collective identity. Jurists cannot leave this field to political science or politics.

3. Finality: Eros? Civilisation?

It will get more and more difficult to say what we actually mean when we speak of "European law". What was thought of as a single body of rules has developed into a rich and inter-related patchwork of legal regimes, orders, and spaces. The emergence of cross-referenced legal fields[97] makes it pretty much impossible to maintain a single, coherent way of thinking about Community law. Research will doubtless break up into diverse disciplines: material and institutional, grand theory and micro theory,[98] and subject areas. Much of EU legal studies have already moved into this direction.[99] Integrating political and legal analysis[100] will not hold all those diverse strands together under one roof. That, however, is not a sign of law's demise, but of its maturity. It is law that in the future may help forge a European identity, and re-model a post-political finality into genuinely political ends. With Union law's changing meaning, Europe may change its direction.

To be sure, rethinking the meaning of law in European integration means in no way a diminishing role of the European Court. We should not expect

[96] See Kahn (2005), above n 5.

[97] See C Harding, 'The Identity of European Law' (2000) 6 *ELJ* 128; Z Bańkowski and E Christodoulidis, 'The European Union as an Essentially Contested Project' (1998) 4 *ELJ* 341; Jo Shaw, 'Postnational Constitutionalism in the European Union' (1999) 6 *JEPP* 579.

[98] See J Shaw, 'Introduction' in *eadem* and More (eds), above n 47, 1 at 8.

[99] See, eg, P Craig and G de Búrca (eds), *The Evolution of EU Law* (1999).

[100] See D Wincott, 'Political Theory, Law, and European Union' in Shaw and More (eds), above n 47, 293.

lessening influence, or even a decreasing docket, in Luxembourg, quite on the contrary. Once the Union and its Court enter the stage of the political, we may expect the constitutional discourse of the ECJ to become our most important source of political rhetoric. In a political community with symbolic narratives of self-creation, the Court's legitimacy will be located not merely in the "science of law" but in politics. Political identity will focus on a legal text, which may or may not be the future Constitution. The political, which will define our self-understanding, will merge into our understanding of ourselves as a community under the rule of law. The myth will be that through the law, uttered by the Court, we participate in a sovereign act of self-government.

There is a profound temptation in awakening Europe's political imagination. Yet, a polity imagines itself as a trans-temporal community only from the perspective of the will. There is no will in the abstract, and no universal will, only the narrative of self-creation of a particular community. Thus, Europe is at a decisive crossroads. Aspiring to a world of deep politics, it may easily overcome the social legitimacy deficit; at the same time, it enters the field of belonging, imagined authenticity, possibly of friends and enemies and blood and soil. The law would indeed be not about what we should do, but about who we are. On the other hand, Europe aspires just as much to a world of post-politics, where we imagine ourselves as fluid, multiple, and fragmented. Here, the political looks like the economical, the state does not love only itself but looks like the market. This is the world of networks, a world stripped of flesh and bodies.

The European model, if it is to be the second model, is not the model of the rest of the world, not even the American model. It is my suspicion, however, that the political will not simply go away, not even in Europe. Yugoslavia has taught us about the fragility of post-politics; political rhetoric from Luxembourg will do little to rekindle our belief in the dawning of the age of post-politics. Law in the Union may soon take on a meaning different from what it is today, and while this would lead to a vibrant political life, it is not difficult to spot the problems. In this light, maybe there is something to say for striving for Civilisation rather than Eros.

18

The Legal Structure of the European Union as a Union of States

BY PAUL KIRCHHOF

I. CONSTITUTIONAL STATES IN A EUROPEAN BASIC ORDER

1. The Legal Community as a Community of Measurement

a) The "ever closer" Union

ACCORDING TO THE Preamble of the EC Treaty, the European Community was established to create the foundations "for an ever closer union among the peoples of Europe". The European Union presents a new stage in the realisation of an "ever closer union among the peoples of Europe" (Art 1(2) EU). This fundamental notion is extenuated in the Preamble of the Draft Constitutional Treaty: "Convinced that, while remaining proud of their own national identities and history, the peoples of Europe are determined to transcend their ancient divisions and, united ever more closely, to forge a common destiny." The Union thereby bases itself on the "peoples" (*Staatsvölker*) and on the democratic states and attempts—through uniting "ever more closely"—to initiate a development of a never ending dynamic. The ambiguity of the European community of law (*Rechtsgemeinschaft*) lies in this finality of unlimitedness: whereas the law passes on to the next generation fundamentally proven institutions, tested values and reliable political experience in a binding way and in this legal continuity defines the instruments of renewal—especially the guarantee of individual liberty as well as the decision-making competences of parliament and government—thus making them a reality bounded by legal limits, the European treaties seek to initiate a development in which neither goal nor endpoint are legally identified. But law is measure and effects measurement. The European Community would lose its character as a community of law if it did not provide a sound legal threshold, thus asserting no standard of measurement and falling into measurelessness.

Granted, superlatives—linguistically indicating the infinite—are not unknown to the law. Economic and competition law recognise the individual search for profit maximisation, a theory of fundamental rights seeks to "optimise" protection of these individual rights, legal safety standards demand the "greatest possible care". But these maximum legal requirements are embedded in the restraining and balancing framework of a law against unfair competition, in a doctrine on the scope of protection and the limits of fundamental rights, in a standard of care for a theory of unlawfulness and negligence.

Law functions especially as circumscribed authorisation and binding limitation when it confirms and restrains sovereign power. The principles of the constitutional state, especially democracy and the rule of law, recognise only legally formed sovereignty, thus making the legal measure the condition for every sovereign act. For this reason the European community of law can only preserve its legal character when the "ever closer" Union does not mean a lovers' embrace that in the end suffocates the participants, and it most certainly is not reminiscent of the culprit who chokes the life out of the parties, rather it characterises a developmental impulse which guides the purpose, manner and tempo of the merger into the binding tracks of the law.

b) The Treaties' Anticipation of That Which is Hoped for

Of course it is the dynamic of European integration that is both the historical principle of success and the current condition of the European Union. The Union is perceived by political decision makers as a work in progress,[1] appears to thrive on the "charm of the incomplete" in legal science,[2] has expanded from 15 to 25 Member States and is planning to expand ever further, distinguishes within the Union between a currency union, the Schengen countries and the area of European defence, each with different Member States, and thus promotes a Europe of gradated commitments.

The treaties also stress developmental openness and the task of renewal with premature legal terminology when they seek to talk their way around that which is currently unattainable. When the European assembly, possessing no legislative or budgetary rights, is called "Parliament", when those entitled to liberties are identified as "citizens of the Union" without having to belong to a European people (*Staatsvolk*), when the part-European community qualifies as the "European" Union, when the title "Economic and Monetary Policy" is given to the experiment of a monetary union that had

[1] As per Federal Chancellor Gerhard Schröder, cf T Oppermann, *Der europäische Traum zur Jahrhundertwende* (2001), 62 *et seq.*

[2] See J Isensee, 'Europa—die politische Erfindung eines Erdteil' in *id et al* (eds), *Europa als politische Idee und als rechtliche Form* (1994), 103 *et seq.*

no predecessor economic union, and when a re-conceptualised EU Treaty presents itself as a treaty on a "Constitution" of Europe, then these treaty terms lay claim to something that does not presently exist but might exist in the future. This terminological generosity recognises that the Union has not yet reached the finally intended state, but this terminological alienation can become a revolutionary tactic that seeks to accomplish more in the application of a dynamic law than is currently desired through formal treaty amendments by the governments, parliaments and peoples of the Member States.

Legal experience teaches that stated goals which are over anticipated unduly burden the law: When the obligation of "stability and growth" (§ 1 Stabilitätsgesetz) promises constant and reasonable economic growth in the "magic square", it brings magic into the law and must fail for that reason.[3] When the announcement of an "Alliance for Employment" ("Bündnis für Arbeit") is supposed to unite opponents in a common goal, or a "round table" is supposed to resolve what had previously rather been a squarish problem, these are political declarations of intent and action, but not statements with legally binding content. The judge applying the law cannot here take over the role of "engine" for such a development.

2. The Term "Constitution"

The ability of the law to conceive of reality and legal ideas in concepts must prove itself above all when the legal foundation of the European community of law is to be designated—that is, a legal statement is to be made—as to the grounds for its coming into being, as to the binding character and claim of its regulations, as to the tasks, content and function of its sovereign organs and their standards. In the current debate, the draft of a new EU Treaty is labelled a "Treaty establishing a Constitution for Europe", with some authors going further, calling it—as a matter of course—a "constitutional treaty"[4] or even a

[3] Translator's note: the 'magische Viereck' refers to the 'magic square' of the four goals of the German Federal Law on the Promotion of Economic Stability and Growth (1967) which requires the federation and the States, in their financial and economic policies, to observe four factors: price level stability, increased employment, foreign balance of trade, and appropriate economic growth.

[4] The term 'constitutional treaty' was applied to the German Treaty on the Creation of a Monetary, Economic and Social Union of 25 June 1990 and to the Unification Treaty of 31 August 1990 to identify the way towards the constitution that henceforth would be used for all of Germany, namely the already existing Grundgesetz (Basic Law): K Stern and B Schmidt-Bleibtreu, *Staatsvertrag* (1990), i, 43. Cf on this point F Cromme, 'Verfassungsvertrag der Europäischen Union' [2002] *Die öffentliche Verwaltung* 593.

"constitution".[5] By now this terminology has acquired widespread usage: It, however, designates a legal term to the Treaty which does not correspond with the Treaty. Rather it has a destructive effect on the Member States and their constitutions, as it carries with it an uncertainty, thereby undermining the foundation of the European union of states (*Staatenverbund*, literally "compound of states").

a) The Goal of this Planned Use of Language

In public law, the existence of a constitution is fundamentally attributed only to the basic order of a state. It does not do conceptual justice to the reality of the European Union, because the Union's legal foundation can only be changed by way of treaty supplement and treaty amendment through the Member States,[6] but not through a constitution-making authority. Rather, the Member States—according to the express wording of Art I-1(1) of the draft of a "constitutional treaty"—confer competences to the European Union in order to attain objectives they have in common. This creation of competences is thus based on an act of transferral by the Member States and not on an act of constitution-making. Consequently, the Union competences are governed by the principle of conferral, it is obliged to respect the national identity of the Member States and their essential state functions and it is dependent on their financial and enforcement powers. Due to its limited power to organise and shape policy and, more importantly, due to its indirect legitimation through the peoples of its members (*Staatsvölker*) and not through a European people (*europäisches Staatsvolk*), the European Union cannot lay claim to the legitimation, the universal nature and the power of re-innovation of a constitutional state.

The strong support among politicians and scholars for the term European "constitution" or at least "constitutional treaty" pursues the goal of bringing an end to the legal uncertainty regarding the compound of public authority of the European Union by means of a terminological promise of unity and democracy. The "constitution" advocates a comprehensive—public, i.e. state based—political power to act and a legal responsibility that admittedly does not attribute the quality of a state to the European Union but nonetheless attempts to loosen the clear opposite character of

[5] See the contributions to the Leipziger Staatsrechtslehrertagung by I Pernice, (2001) 60 *Veröffentlichungen der Vereinigung der Deutschen Staatsrechtslehrer* 148 *et seq*; PM Huber, *ibid*, 194 *et seq*; G Lübbe-Wolff, *ibid*, 246 *et seq*; but cf also JH Kaiser, (1966) 23 *Veröffentlichungen der Vereinigung der Deutschen Staatsrechtslehrer* 1 at 17 *et seq*; HP Ipsen, *Europäisches Gemeinschaftsrecht* (1972), 64; *Entscheidungen des Bundesverfassungsgerichts* 22, 293 at 296 (*EWG-Verordnungen*) ('gewissermaßen' or 'in some measure').

[6] Cf *Entscheidungen des Bundesverfassungsgerichts* 89, 155 at 181 and 191 *et seq* (*Maastricht*).

ultimately responsible states and a Union that is empowered by exactly these states.[7] Occasionally and operating under a "postnational" constitutional understanding,[8] the term "constitution" rings the death knell for the state and the nation, thereby unintentionally destroying the very foundation of the European house.

A "constitutional treaty" renders the constituted corporate body independent with respect to the authorising Member States, weakens the democratic-parliamentarian link of the Union vis-à-vis the peoples (*Staatsvölker*) and appears to call into question their function as "masters of the treaties"[9]. In this case the term "constitution" intimates a basic order constituted and legitimated by a democratic *Staatsvolk*, and thus seeks to mask the yet unresolved problem of a weak[10] and, for the increasingly expanded competences, insufficiently democratically legitimated European Union without a European people (*Unionsvolk*). A constitution rests on itself, has duration and continuity as its object, constitutes a corporation that is secure and immutable in its core content.[11] The European "constitutional treaty" on the other hand could only guarantee an in-between status for a community of law which is grounded in an ongoing development and dynamic, and could only codify an *aquis communautaire*, serving as a legal basis for the further development of the Union.

But above all the term "constitution" includes the claim to stipulate a comprehensive basic order of public life, which renews itself from within, takes on new tasks independently and empowers the corporation that it constitutes for autonomous further development. With this terminology the principle of conferral and the prohibition of treaty expansion by the treaty institutions is loosened or even lifted. The more the Union gains a constitutional foundation, the stronger its independence gets, the weaker the Member States' power to determinate the Union, its organisational statute and its material commitment becomes.

The strict legal significance of a European constitution lies in its claim to validity, which is supposed to supplant the validity of the Member State constitutions and thus supplant the provisions that first authorise the respective state to a constitutionally binding co-operation within the European Union. Moreover, the "constitution" is the internal constitution of a state, and thus claims in the transfer to the European Union that its influence on the Member States has come to mean more domestic than foreign

[7] See D Grimm, 'Braucht Europa eine neue Verfassung?' [1995] *Juristenzeitung* 581 at 587.

[8] See I Pernice, 'Europäische Grundrechts-Charta und Konventsverfahren' [2001] *Integration* 194.

[9] *Entscheidungen des Bundesverfassungsgerichts* 89, 155 at 190 (*Maastricht*).

[10] *Ibid*, 181; see further M Kaufmann, *Europäische Integration und Demokratieprinzip* (1997).

[11] Cf R Smend, 'Verfassung und Verfassungsrecht' (1928) in *id*, *Staatsrechtliche Abhandlungen* (1955), 189.

policy.[12] Finally, the term "constitution" possesses its own legitimating and sympathy-inducing value that is supposed to invest the organisational statute of the EU and the EC Treaties with more of the lustre of democratic legitimation and law-like completeness.

b) The Function of Legal Terminology

To be sure, the term "constitution" is often applied carelessly. One considers a healthy person to be of "good constitution", labels the organisational statute of businesses as an "economic constitution", binds municipalities in a "communal constitutional law" or seeks to understand developments ranging from the *magna charta libertatum* (1215) to the UN Charter as constitutional development. This terminology, which is imprecise and almost devoid of meaning, might have prompted the usage of the term "European constitution", as the Treaty on European Union places limitations on public power and protects the citizens by way of fundamental rights, thereby borrowing substantial content from the state constitutions. However, when using such terminology, it is necessary to clearly distinguish the European common usage of the term from the public law (*staatsrechtlich*) concept of constitution.

As a legal term, a constitution accommodates the reality of a state by doing justice to its actual circumstances[13] and, in keeping with the mandate of certainty, formulates in a sufficiently comprehensible and reliably predictable fashion the regulatory intent of democratic legitimation and legal unity.[14] When language must convey legal obligation, the legal intent must be conceived and expressed in the rationality of language.

c) The Limited Primacy of European Law

The current discussion as to the tasks and competences of the European Union and its Member States concerns the legal relationship between constitutional states and the European union of states, and thus the distinction between constitution-making and the conclusion of a treaty, statehood and supranationality, universal mandate with the competence to decide freely

[12] Using the term *Verfassungsverbund* (literally 'compound of constitutions') it remains open who binds whom; see I Pernice, 'Die dritte Gewalt im europäischen Verfassungsverbund' [1996], *Europarecht* 27 at 29 *et seq*.

[13] On the requirement of satisfying reality, see *Entscheidungen des Bundesverfassungsgerichts* 87, 153 at 172 (*Grundfreibetrag*) for an existential need; 93, 121 at 136 (*Vermögensteuer*) for the assessment of economic goods; 84, 239 at 281 *et seq* (*Zinsurteil*) for the efficiency of a process; [2002] *Neue Juristische Wochenschrift* 1103 at 1109 for the analysis of a partial legal order.

[14] On the requirement of certainty see *Entscheidungen des Bundesverfassungsgerichts* 49, 168 at 181 (*Aufenthaltserlaubnis*); 59, 104 at 114; 64, 261 at 280 (*Hafturlaub*); 69, 1 at 43 (*Kriegsdienstverweigerung*); 71, 354 at 362; E Schmidt-Aßmann, 'Der Rechtsstaat' in J Isensee and P Kirchhof (eds), *Handbuch des Staatsrechts* (1987), i, § 24, para 60; H Schneider, *Gesetzgebungslehre* (2002), paras 66 *et seq*.

on its own competences (*Kompetenz-Kompetenz*) and a public authority based on conferred powers, executive law-making and parliamentary law-making, European and national jurisdiction. At the centre of these legal questions is the foundational public law term "constitution". By contrast, whoever attributes constitutional quality to a treaty or conflates the difference between constitution and treaty in the term "constitutional treaty" moves from a secured elementary finding of modern constitutional statehood to a legally non-committed terminology.

Member States participate in the European Union on the basis of an authorisation in their constitutional law,[15] thus acting in a framework sketched out by constitutional law that in part prescribes a certain legal structure of the European Union[16] and a residual constitutional and state structure of the Member States[17] as well as a special procedure[18] and makes

[15] In addition to Art 23(1) Grundgesetz, the Constitutions of France (Arts 88–1 to 88–4), Ireland (Art 29(4)) and Sweden (ch 10 § 5(1) RF) specifically authorise the transfer of sovereign power to the European Communities. The Constitutions of Spain (Art 93 1st sentence), the Netherlands (Art 92), Denmark (Art 20(1)) and Belgium (Art 34) authorise the transfer of sovereign power to supra-state organisations more generally. Cf also the corresponding provision in the Polish Constitution (Art 90(1)).

[16] Constitutional norms containing a structural guarantee clause directly related to the European Union are Art 23(1), 1st sentence Grundgesetz (a Union that is obligated to the democratic, rule of law, social and federative principles and the principle of subsidiarity and guarantees protection of fundamental rights essentially comparable to the Grundgesetz); Chapter 10 § 5(1) RF of the Swedish Constitution (freedoms and legal protections corresponding to the constitution and the ECHR); in more abstract form see also Arts 88–1 *et seq* of the French Constitution (voluntary common exercise of competences, condition of mutuality). Art 7(6) of the Portuguese Constitution authorises the transfer of sovereignty under the condition of mutuality, while observing the principle of subsidiarity and with the goal of realising the economic and social cohesion; Art 7(5) continues that Portugal supports the process of European unification for democracy, peace, economic progress and justice between peoples. Art 20(1) of the Danish Constitution generally foresees the transfer of sovereign rights only to organisations for the promotion of interstate legal order and co-operation.

[17] Art 23(1), 3rd sentence Grundgesetz, referring to the standards of Art 79(3). In many Member States, the reservation of the remaining constitutional and state structure is taken from unwritten parts of the constitutional order, especially the principle of sovereignty. See on this in particular the decisions of the Spanish Constitutional Court of 1 July 1992 [1993] Europäische Grundrechte-Zeitschrift 285, of the French Constitutional Council of 31 December 1997 [1998] Europäische Grundrechte-Zeitschrift 27 and of the Danish High Court of 6 April 1998 (on this point G Ring and L Olsen-Ring, 'Souveränitätsübertragung nach dänischem Verfassungsrecht' [1998] *Europäische Zeitschrift für Wirtschaftsrecht 589 et seq*). On the corresponding concept of sovereignty in Italy see A Carrino, Verfassung und Souveränität in Europa am Beispiel Italiens' [1998] *Zeitschrift für Europarechtliche Studien* 427 *et seq*.

[18] Procedural requirements for the transfer of competences to the European Communities are found, in addition to those in Art 23(1), 2nd and 3rd sentence Grundgesetz (approval by the Bundesrat majority required for constitutional amendment), in Art 168 of the Belgian Constitution (participation of the chambers) and ch 10 § 5(1) RF of the Swedish Constitution (three quarters majority of cast votes or the majority required for constitutional amendment). For any kind of transfers of sovereign power Art 93, 1st sentence of the Spanish Constitution requires a constitutional implementing law and Art 20(2) of the Danish Constitution requires a five-sixths majority of the members of the Folketing. Cf also the corresponding provision in Art 90(2)–(4) of the Polish Constitution (majority requirements, plebiscite).

them a condition for the participation of the respective Member State. These constitutional law articles especially demand precedence also over European law because they constitute the conditions for European law to be valid in the respective Member State and the condition for the command to apply European law, which is granted in the parliamentary act of assent. Hence, European law finds its impassable boundaries in these constitutional law premises of the respective Member State. The theory that European law also has primacy over national constitutional law is valid to the extent that the respective constitution opens itself to European law and the constitutional state has made use of this opening clause—consequentially, under Art 23(1) *Grundgesetz* (German Basic Law) in a procedure of constitutional amendment without actually amending the constitutional document. But European law remains subordinate to the opening clause itself because this clause is the condition for European law to be valid in the respective constitutional state.

Many Member State constitutions promote and thus shape European integration by also guaranteeing elementary principles of constitutional law in the process of integration. This legal claim of direct validity in relation to the Member State, and indirect with respect to the European Union—mediated by means of participation of the Member State –, is placed in question when one sets the Member State constitution opposite a European constitution. Hypothetically speaking, if the amended Treaty of the European Union were a constitution, the scope of application of the Member States' constitutions would be curtailed by the scope of application of the European constitution. Precisely in a time of change, during which new Member States with short-lived democratic traditions and without extensive experience with the principle of the rule of law (*Rechtsstaatsprinzip*) have been admitted to the Union and during which the institutions of the European Union are acting with a lack of orientation regarding the most fundamental constitutional questions—questions such as democracy in Europe, an industrial policy instead of social market economy, an institutional and material stabilisation of the Euro –, the European integration requires the legal foundation of constitutional guarantees of democracy, rule of law (*Rechtsstaat*), fundamental rights and social principles, guarantees which can only be granted by the Member States.

d) The Becoming of the European Union

In addition, the European Union would be incorrectly characterised by the legal concept of a "constitution". The Union is a union of states (*Staatenverbund*),[19] in which constitutional states have so obligated

[19] *Entscheidungen des Bundesverfassungsgerichts* 89, 155 at 156, 181 and passim (*Maastricht*); cf P Kirchhof, 'Der deutsche Staat im Prozess der europäischen Integration' in J Isensee and *id* (eds), *Handbuch des Staatsrechts* (1993), vii, § 183, para 38 et passim.

themselves, that the intensity of this commitment clearly exceeds a confederation (*Staatenbund*), but nonetheless does not reach the statehood of a federal state (*Bundesstaat*). The European Union is rooted in the Member States, but neither seeks or is able to fill their universal functions, nor does it lay claim to the competence to decide freely on its own competences (*Kompetenz-Kompetenz*) by assuming new and other functions out of its own jurisdiction without assignment from the Member States.[20] Precisely now, when the still young democratic constitutional states in Central and Eastern Europe have become members of the European Union, this Union should not claim with the term of a European constitution to seek to place a supplanting legal order over these states in their new constitutions. Europe is more demanding: the community of law lives from the overlapping and complementary circles of European law and the constitutional law of the Member States, and in this cohesion of multi-levelled legislation and determination of the law it develops a legal culture, that would not be possible in a legal system that was centred solely on the Europe level.

According to the democratic understanding of the constitution, the constitution-making authority is the people (*Staatsvolk*) acting as *pouvoir constituant*. Granted, in a Europe that is open to human rights and international law, such a constitution-making is not conceived of as an original development of new legal structures, but is only meant as a further development and specification of general legal principles, so that the constitution-making authority is more an authority that passes along the constitution. Nonetheless, such a constitution-making may not be declared binding in a process of treaty amendment, but rather the *Staatsvolk* must be directly answerable for it. Such a European *Staatsvolk* does not exist, however. The postulate of a European constitution-making thus reaches too far—perhaps even into the utopian. Should a European *Staatsvolk* ever exist which is conscious of its cultural cohesions and therefore ready for the common making and enforcement of law, which economically and politically desires to form a community for actions and endangerments, which at a minimum has as its objective exchange in a common general second language, then the European institutions would have to begin today to work towards this future. They would have to organise political parties that are active Europe-wide, promote a media reporting in which this belonging to Europe and this capacity to be Europe are made self evident in a common language, an internal market, a cultural and scientific exchange, and also to make the decisions and the decision-making processes of the European institutions more visible and understandable for all citizens of the Union. Who indeed currently speaks of European constitution-making obfuscates that these efforts have not yet been attained and thereby endangers any further integration.

[20] Cf also H Schambeck, 'Über die Idee einer EU-Verfassung' in C Baudenbacher (ed), *Ein Leben in Praxis und Wissenschaft: Festschrift für W Barfuss* (2002), 227 at 236 *et seq*.

At the same time, the catchword of a European constitution claims a democratic starting condition that does not currently exist. The model of European integration is not a democratic state to be created but rather the existing union of states, which essentially acts through the governments of the Member States and legitimates itself democratically in their parliaments. The European Communities have by virtue of their original functions rather an administrative-technocratic structure and follow the dominion of the experts.[21] The Council legitimates itself in the national sources of Member States' parliaments and governments, which for their part are legitimated in the required social and institutional cohesion;[22] the European Parliament currently has only a supporting role in the context of democratic legitimation.[23]

A "European" constitution appears also to lay claim to commitment with respect to organs of the Member States. With this, the independence of the constitutional states, the unique features of their constitutions and the accomplishments of their constitutional courts would be sucked into the vortex of a European constitution and would be swallowed up there. Here, too, the question is posed of whether the European Union can currently do without the diversity of the European constitutional culture that advances a Europe-wide constitutional statehood, in the juxtaposition of written and unwritten constitutions, of centuries-long constitutional traditions and recent constitutional renaissances, of organisational constitutions and those of material values, of court oriented and appellative constitutions.

e) The Written Catalogue of Fundamental Rights

Those who hope that the European constitution will provide above all else the reliability of a written catalogue of fundamental rights must first be clear that, while the conference of governments in Nice solemnly proclaimed a Charter of Fundamental Rights through the European Council, the proclamation nonetheless was—so far—a mere declaration of a political will. The Charter of Fundamental Rights is to be included as part II of the "constitutional treaty"; however, this treaty amendment has so far not been implemented through either Member States' parliaments act of assent or through a corresponding plebiscite, and thus remains—at this point in time—not binding. Nevertheless the expectation is expressed, that this non-law will be treated by the ECJ as binding law. This raises a red flag: the

[21] See E-W Böckenförde, *Welchen Weg geht Europa?* (1997), 37 *et seq*.

[22] See J Isensee, 'Europäische Union—Mitgliedstaaten im Spannungsfeld von Integration und nationaler Selbstbehauptung, Effizienz und Idee' in Konferenz der Deutschen Akademien der Wissenschaften und der Akademie der Wissenschaften und Literatur in Mainz (ed), *Europa—Idee, Geschichte, Realität* (1996), 91 *et seq*.

[23] *Entscheidungen des Bundesverfassungsgerichts* 89, 155 at 186 (*Maastricht*).

steps toward integration are becoming ever more laboured and cautious, the promises for the future ever more far-reaching and fundamental, the exorbitant demands on the community of law and its organs is reaching its limits. This Europe of small steps and big plans preserves not only its ability to develop in the realm of the politically possible but also the distance between European desires and European realities, endangering thereby the rootedness of the European Union in the democracies of the Member States and thereby possibly alienating governments from citizens.

Until now, fundamental rights arise in the common constitutional traditions of the Member States and are recognised in a "valuative comparative law" that first determines the different legal solutions of the Member State legal orders and then ascertains the "best" answer discoverable in national law.[24] If, from this point on, fundamental rights were to be included in the Community Treaty, this interplay between Member State and European fundamental rights cultures would fall away in the pursuit of improved protection of fundamental rights. The codification of fundamental rights in the treaty might lay down in a document the fundamental rights standard already reached and bring it to a preliminary conclusion. Nevertheless it must be determined whether the variety of human rights cultures in the current and future Member States has proven itself as the impulse for the continuous improvement in the protection of fundamental rights and whether the informal co-operation of the European constitutional courts works more purposefully towards a high European standard of fundamental rights[25] than does a fundamental rights case law of the ECJ that is limited in its possibility of application.

f) The Perpetualising Constitution and the Dynamic Basic Order

Constitutions are the memory of democracy.[26] The constitution documents in a single charter the assured and recognised stock of traditional public law, shapes it in the rationality of a text, generalises it in the publication of a general, comprehensible rule, at the same time makes available enunciators of constitutional law—the *Recht-Sprechung* or statement of the law—and also a process for amending the constitution, in order to further develop and expand the organising statute and fundamental rights in a manner that does justice to the present day. But the European Union is, in its decidedly future orientation, almost a composite without its own established

[24] See T Oppermann, *Europarecht* (1999), paras 483 and 491.

[25] Cf P Kirchhof, 'Die Gewaltenbalance zwischen staatlichen und europäischen Organen' [1998] *Juristenzeitung* 965 at 972 *et seq*; Ring and Olsen-Ring, above n 17, 589; Carrino, above n 17, 427, each with references to judicial decisions.

[26] P Kirchhof, 'Das Grundgesetz als Gedächtnis der Demokratie' in M Heckel, *Die innere Einheit Deutschlands inmitten der europäischen Einigung* (1996), 35.

legal tradition. The dynamic for integration, already laid down in the founding treaties and renewed in the current phase of expansion, subjects the communitising to a process of development which under the currently envisioned expansion in no way works towards a European federal state,[27] but currently rather loosens and downgrades the composite entity. In this expansion phase of integration with graded and in part reduced intensity of integration there exist neither the task nor occasion for European constitution-making.

As a result, the condition of the legal foundation of the European Union remains too exacting and novel to be placed within a traditional legal category. The integration treaties are legal documents which seek to perpetualise a legal foundation for the European Union and protect it from treaty infringement.[28] The treaties substantiate a basic order of the Community, which preserves an *acquis communautaire* and promotes its further development (Art 2(1) EU), is partially superior to the constitutions of the Member States in the rank of validity and application, and also brings about from within a certain growth of opportunities for action by the Union and thus elucidates the sovereignty of the Member States in their openness to Europe[29] without the competence to decide freely on its own competences (*Kompetenz-Kompetenz*) (Arts 5(1), 7(1) EC), and also has as its objective an interwoven and successively referential co-operation with the constitutional orders of the Member States. The European Union is a union of states with an autonomous basic order that supports, confirms and further develops this union.

g) There is no Verfassungsverbund

In any event, the union of states (*Staatenverbund*) is not a polity of multi-level constitutionalism (*Verfassungsverbund*, literally "compound of constitutions").[30]

[27] Cf G Ress, 'Die EU und die neue juristische Qualität der Beziehungen zu den EC' [1992] *Juristische Schulung* 985 at 986; C Tomuschat, 'Das Endziel der europäischen Integration, Maastricht ad infinitum?' [1992] *Deutsches Verwaltungsblatt* 1073 *et seq*; for a critical view see J Isensee, 'Integrationsziel Europastaat?' in O Due (ed), *Festschrift für U Everling* (1995), 567 at 572 *et seq*.

[28] In this respect the ECJ speaks of a 'basic constitutional charter' of 'a Community based on the rule of law': Case 294/83 *Les Verts* [1986] ECR 1339, para 23; Opinion 1/91, *EEA I* [1991] ECR I–1679, para 1.

[29] See K Doehring, 'Staat und Verfassung in einem zusammenwachsenden Europa' [1993] *Zeitschrift für Rechtspolitik* 98 *et seq*; G Ress, 'Menschenrechte, Europäisches Gemeinschaftsrecht und nationales Verfassungsrecht' in H Haller *et al* (eds), *Staat und Recht: Festschrift für Winkler* (1997), 897 at 901.

[30] Cf on this point I Pernice, above n 12, 27 at 29 *et seq*; M Heintzen, 'Gemeineuropäisches Verfassungsrecht in der EU' [1997] *Europarecht* 1 *et seq*; P Häberle, 'Verfassungsrechtliche Fragen im Prozess der europäischen Einigung' [1992] *Europäische Grundrechte-Zeitschrift* 429 *et seq*; C Calliess in *id* and M Ruffert (eds), *Kommentar des Vertrages über die Europäische Union und des Vertrages zur Gründung der Europäischen* Gemeinschaft (1999), Art 1 EU, para 26.

Granted, the European basic order together with the constitutions of the Member States and also the ECHR seeks to substantiate an all-European legal order, in which the various sources for the coming into existence and cognition of this law support, strengthen and further shape each other. Nonetheless, this legal composite, precisely in distinguishing between the constitutions, the Union Treaty, the EC Treaty and the ECHR, has as its object the allocation of tasks, competences and powers and thus distributing legal responsibilities, legitimating of authority and substantiating of supervisory responsibilities. The states are bound in their autonomous—and to this extent non-committed—condition of being constituted. The union of states—borne by the respective will of the Member States—is a unique, sophisticated concept of commonly exercising public authority, without placing the individual state in an inescapable straitjacket of a European legal order. Rather, the fascination of the European idea is so convincing for the states that the Member States continue their membership in the European Union. The basis for the European union of states is the willingness for integration of the states concerned and not a coercive power of the European Union which would subdue states which did not wish to be members any longer. This self-confidence—built on current consensus—and the trustworthiness of the European institutions, which has been confirmed by the development of integration until today, should not be put into question now.

h) The Current Ratification Procedure

The renewed Treaty of the European Union requires the approval of the Member States. Such approval can be granted either through parliaments or through plebiscites in the respective Member States. This method clarifies that what is meant is not bringing about a constitution, which would require the perception of the power of the founding authority through the 25 people of the Member States and also through a—non-existing—European people (*Staatsvolk*). Rather, the Member States consequentially retain the form of concluding an international treaty instead of giving birth to a constitution.

In the case that some states should not give their approval, the project of such a "founding authority" would obviously have failed. Sparing solutions, which would retain the *status quo* for a state refusing to approve the new "constitution", would be excluded when creating a constitution; this is so because a fundamental legal basis for the Union either exists or does not exist, while a treaty in its further development does not necessarily have to include all Member States. This is best exemplified through the European Monetary Union.

Thus, the procedure on treaty amendment also confirms that an extensive qualification of the Treaty as a "constitutional treaty" raises legal expectations, which cannot be fulfilled by the Treaty—which can rather overstrain the Treaty in its genesis. Legal dignity must therefore qualify the reform of the Treaty of the European Union according to what it is: an amended treaty. We should abandon the terminology of European "constitution" as expeditiously as possible if Europe is to remain in good health and if Europe is to retain its good constitution.

II. THE MEMBER STATES IN THE EUROPEAN UNION

1. The European Union of States

The European Community is a "union of states for the realisation of an ever closer union of the peoples of Europe—organised in states".[31] In this three-level union of states[32] the democratic universal jurisdiction and legal responsibility lies with the Member States; these Member States co-operate in many political areas—especially domestic and judicial policy as well as foreign and defence policy—and have formed above this co-operation—supranationally—a corporate body that exercises its own authority in the territory of the Union, that is, directly in the Member States. This union of states corresponds to a three level legal composite: the basis of the European Union are the self-supporting[33] state constitutions, which are legitimised by the respective people (*Staatsvolk*) and which establish a constitutional state with comprehensive jurisdiction.[34] These constitutional states then bind themselves in the Union Treaty—in the non- or only partially communitised political areas—to a co-operation that is borne and determined respectively by the actual will of the Member States in a simplified negotiation procedure, on the basis of a legal duty to be faithful to the Union and with flanking support through institutions of the Union, including the European Court of Justice. The Union's means of action and decision is a supranational body legitimated by the Member States, but also made independent in its actions with respect to them, which was established by the Member States in order to perform collectively some of their functions and, to that extent, collectively to exercise their sovereignty.[35]

This legal concept of the European Union is without precedent, requires a new sense of a statehood that is open to the world and possesses a sovereignty with an openness to Europe, insists upon especially clear political

[31] *Entscheidungen des Bundesverfassungsgerichts* 89, 155 at 156 (*Maastricht*).
[32] See above n 19.
[33] See E-W Böckenförde, *Staat, Verfassung, Demokratie* (1991), 29 *et seq*.
[34] See J Isensee, 'Staat und Verfassung' in *id* and Kirchhof (eds), above n 14, § 13, para 45.
[35] *Entscheidungen des Bundesverfassungsgerichts* 89, 155 at 189 (*Maastricht*); cf also Art 23(1), 2nd sentence Grundgesetz (transfer of sovereign rights).

responsibilities, bases of legitimation and accountabilities. For this reason it is natural to create a new legal framework for this three-level political power and sovereignty that clearly assigns tasks, competences and powers in an organisational statute and thus legally shapes and tempers responsibilities but at the same time also makes clear the status of the Union citizen in a European community of values determined by fundamental rights, lifts him out of legal anonymity and adjusts anew the balance between well organised mass federations and individual citizens in Europe.

a) Supranationality

The special characteristic of this Community intimated in the codeword of supranationality lies in its considerable but limited body of autonomous responsibilities, in the progressively stronger Community authority and direct obligations of Community authority in the Member States.[36]

The political and legal weight of the Community shows itself in the breadth of its tasks, its obligation to common political basic values (political Union), the autonomous and intensive law-making power with a competence to make law that is directly binding in the Member States, in the autonomy of the Community institutions, which can form a European common will, in the financial—albeit dependent on the Member States—autonomy of the Community, in extensive and effective legal protection and in a lasting but uncompleted Union.[37]

State-like characteristics are recognisable in this structure of the Community, but without the Community being a state or having reached only the preliminary stages of statehood. The Union lacks the essential characteristics[38] of a modern state.[39] The European Union possesses no comprehensive territorial sovereignty, but rather exercises selectively the individual competences granted to it in the territorial "scope" of the Treaties (cf Art 299 EC). It has no comprehensive personal sovereignty over citizens of the Union (Art 17 EC), but rather includes the members of its Member States through the Community to an extent foreseen by treaty. It is an association of the peoples of Europe (Art 1 EU), not a state borne by a European *Unionsvolk*. The Community authority is restricted in principle by conferral (Art 5 EU, Art 5(1) EC); it thus lacks the comprehensive tasks and competences typical of a state, the competence to decide freely on its

[36] See Oppermann, above n 24, paras 889 *et seq*.

[37] Cf *ibid*, paras 893 *et seq*.

[38] Cf G Jellinek, *Allgemeine Staatslehre* (3rd ed 1914), 394 *et seq*; CFW von Gerber, *Grundzüge des deutschen Staatsrechts* (3rd ed 1880); P Laband, *Das Staatsrecht des Deutschen Reiches*, 2 vols (5th ed 1911–14); for a recent contribution, see R Zippelius, *Allgemeine Staatslehre* (1994), 52 *et seq*.

[39] See Oppermann, above n 24, paras 902 *et seq*.

own competences (*Kompetenz-Kompetenz*), in order to open up for itself new tasks, competences and powers. The Community does not have at its disposal, as a community of law, "the sovereignty reserve of its own political power".[40]

But the Community has currently solidified into a corporate body that permanently brings together the Member States in an association legally rendered independent, performs there a portion of their functions in a legally binding manner, makes law and also Europeanises the law of the Member States, and accomplishes better than the Member States a portion of the tasks that have become trans-national.

b) The Ever More Powerful but also Increasingly Vulnerable European Union

In this development of an "ever closer" union of the peoples of Europe the European union of states establishes a community of law between especially tightly bound States, which exercise collectively some of their competences in steady concentration and want to come across as a community based on the rule of law vis-à-vis the citizens of the Union and third states. Certainly this community is not—other than as with constitution-making and state formation in Germany and the United States[41]—borne by a common will of people who belong to each other, who seek to form a new state, but is rather accompanied by the respective Member States and their citizens in differing expectations and political goal settings.[42] Germany sees in the European Union initially the chance of equal membership in the community of states, today primarily a sphere of facilitated economic management. France expects in particular from the Union a European independence from the United States. Great Britain affirms its nation state—proven since the 11th century—and from this perspective is influenced more by the pull of events, i.e. the practical advantages and successes of the European Union. For Poland, with its turbulent history in Europe, the idea of integration of all of Europe under the condition of continuing statehood is a dream. For the states in Eastern and Southeastern Europe who seek to join, the European Union appears at least economically desirable, but culturally more of a foreign entity.

In these differing goal settings and impulses, the European Union is a movement that presents itself as a "work in progress"[43] which, granted, already holds at the ready rooms that can well be inhabited, but is still not

[40] *Ibid*, para 905: '*Souveränitätsreserve eigener politischer Macht*'.

[41] Cf on this point HW Rengeling, 'Eine Europäische Charta der Grundrechte' in J Ipsen (ed), *Recht, Staat, Gemeinwohl: Festschrift für D Rauschning* (2001), 225 at 244 *et seq*.

[42] Cf T Oppermann, *Der europäische Traum zur Jahrhundertwende* (2001), 18 *et seq*.

[43] Cf above n 1.

finished with its overall structure and moving its residents in. Integration is still more a self-occurring union than an accomplished unity, more an organisation in development than a bearer of sovereignty in a firmly constructed legal framework. The institutions of the European Union also are currently more predetermined than still to be fully developed ("mehr vorgegeben als aufgegeben"). The Council, as the central political decision-making organ, with its composition and its procedure, takes vigorous decisions only with difficulty, which strengthen and guide the association of participating constitutional states. The European Parliament lacks the people (*Staatsvolk*); for this reason it cannot originally perform the essential parliamentary functions of law-making and the right to budget. The Commission, in fulfilling its task to form the aggregate will of the union of states, seems to be in a crises that, in the unformed influence of the Member States, appears to be structural.

In this phase of an ever more powerful but also vulnerable European Union, law and jurisprudence are given the classical task of guaranteeing continuity and equalisation, of developing cohesion and Community competences, of giving effect to fundamental values in individual and unique cases. Thereby the judiciary is challenged to exceptional performance because, in this development of the European union of states, it must hold together diverging powers and at the same time strengthen the community of law.

c) The Intersecting Sources for Coming into Existence and Cognition of Law

The multi-level European Union supports itself at the core on two complementary and intersecting sources for the coming into existence and cognition of law.

European law becomes binding by both the conclusion of the treaty by Member States as well as by the issuance of the act of assent through the parliamentary ratification statute or through a plebiscite in the respective Member States.[44] European law is first of all a legal concept produced by the institutions of the EC, then agreed to by the Member States by international treaty, but only becomes binding through the respective parliamentary command to apply the law, which embeds European law in the Member State legal order. European law reaches Germany as a territory of application via the bridge of the German act of assent, but receives its content from the law-making will of the EC institutions and the readiness of

[44] Cf Arts 1, 313 EC, Arts 1, 52 EU, Art 23(1), 3rd sentence, Grundgesetz; *Entscheidungen des Bundesverfassungsgerichts* 31, 145 at 173 *et seq* (*Milchpulver*); 73, 339 at 375 (*Solange* II); 75, 223 at 244 (*Kloppenburg*); 89, 155 at 184 (*Maastricht*).

the Member States to integrate. The binding framework for the validity of European law in Germany[45] is set by the *Grundgesetz*. On this basis, the domestic command to apply the law can decree the validity and application primacy of European law over domestic law. This occurred through the command to apply the law in the ratification statute for the EC Treaty,[46] there—on the basis of Art 24(1) *Grundgesetz*, old version—with an express reservation of identity for the valid constitutional order of the Federal Republic of Germany.

The combined efforts of German constitutional law and European Community law take on practical significance especially for the protection of fundamental rights. The condition of Germany's participation in the development of the European Union is the guarantee of protections for fundamental rights essentially comparable to those contained in the *Grundgesetz* (Art 23(1), 1st sentence).[47] Yet the *Grundgesetz* does not require that in individual cases the protection of fundamental rights is also to be guaranteed respectively directly by the *Bundesverfassungsgericht* (Federal Constitutional Court). Much more it is the openness of the constitution to international co-operation, in the sense of the goals of the Preamble, which determines that the *Bundesverfassungsgericht* does not need to exercise its jurisdiction when a supranational protection of fundamental rights which is essentially comparable to that in the *Grundgesetz* is guaranteed. The *Bundesverfassungsgericht* reviews only whether the requirements resulting from its case law are generally guaranteed to this extent; if the lack of these conditions is not evident, the appellant bears the burden of demonstrating it.[48]

Judicial interpretation of the EC Treaty expounds law from European and German legal sources. The EC Treaty is a constituent part of the German act of assent, which came about under the constraints of Art 23 *Grundgesetz*, and thus requires of the German judges an interpretation according to the meaning and purpose of a European law that is uniformly binding for all Member States[49] in the context of the German legal system. Hence, a continual bringing together of law from different sources is required from the judges.

The view of the judge who applies European law thus constantly shifts back and forth between German statutory law, European law and constitutional law. It stands for a legal order in which these interwoven and successively referential legal circles lead in the individual case to a clear binding

[45] See above nn 15–18, also dealing with the laws of other Member States.
[46] *Entscheidungen des Bundesverfassungsgerichts* 73, 339 at 375 (*Solange* II).
[47] For the cases of Art 24(1) Grundgesetz see Bundesverfassungsgericht, 2 BVR 2368/99, (2001) *Deutsches Verwaltungsblatt*, 1130.
[48] *Ibid*, 1131 *et seq*.
[49] *Entscheidungen des Bundesverfassungsgerichts* 75, 223 at 234 (*Kloppenburg*).

legal obligation. First when these legal statements, which have co-operation as their object, do not reliably let themselves be co-ordinated with each other, the judge must, by means of submission under Art 100(1) *Grundgesetz* or under Art 234 EC, obtain a decision of the respectively responsible court of last instance and decide the case according to the legal standard clarified by that court.

2. The Counterpart: The State

a) Statehood and Openness to Europe

The constitutional state is the organisational form in which the citizens and their representatives act politically and substantiate a legal order. With the instrument of the law the state creates conditions for communal life that offer the individual peace and security and stable foundations for economic, cultural and legal existence, mediates individual membership as persons entitled to benefits and allows democratic participation, organises division of labour and substantiates an ongoing legal and life culture in the succession of generations. Today the human being develops his personality, his language, his ability to interact and be in community, his leisure culture and his democratic involvement, his working life and his provisions for the future by means of membership in a state.

The state constitution, which attributes to the state the power of sovereign functions, organisation and means to act, but also legally limits this power, builds on the democratic cohesion of the *Staatsvolk*: a people which has become conscious of its solidarity and is capable of making and enforcing law, organises itself in a certain territory into a ruling alliance and creates for itself organs capable of decision and with effective means of acting. In this concrete condition of being constituted, the constitutional state shapes universal human rights and the general principles of state organisation into an order which suffices for the needs of the respective community of law, and is grown historically. The securing of existence by the social state guarantees in one state a handful of rice, in another modern mobility and a share in the media. The guarantee of peace in one state is essentially built on the strength of military defence, in another on its system of agreement in international law. The right to property and the freedom of occupation occurs in one state through participation in agriculture, in another on the basis of a highly developed industrialisation, education and a world wide economic management.

Each state lays claim to state sovereignty, the highest and last authority, in order to guarantee domestic law and peace, preserve independence from other states and to represent the state community vis-à-vis third parties. State sovereignty secures the cohesion of the state when groups within the state endanger its unity or the authority of law and thereby weaken domestic peace. Externally the state lays claim to sovereignty vis-à-vis other states to speak with the only authoritative voice for the people (*Staatsvolk*), to dispose of its own territory, to decide on legal relationships with other states.

To be sure, these state functions exceed from time immemorial the capabilities of an individual state. Universal human rights are rooted in a trans-state community of values and urge international systems of guarantee and control. World peace can only be guaranteed in a world-wide system of collective security. Businesses that are active globally have long surpassed the borders of a "political" or "national economy". Environmental protection requires common, trans-generational measures by all states. Information and news systems do not acknowledge state borders. Mass migration of immigrants and refugees can encompass several continents. Science and technology have for centuries cultivated co-operation throughout the world. The media, sports and tourism now find sufficient standards only in trans-state law. For this reason, states make it their object to co-operate in overarching organisations.

b) The Staatsvolk Already Existing in a State of Freedom

The democratic constitutional state builds on a people (*Staatsvolk*) that came together in freedom in order to, in its cohesiveness, build a state to which it felt it belonged. The *Staatsvolk* is the initial fact of democracy, which is the result of free cultural and communal formation, not organisation or legal mandate by the authorities. This principle of liberty is a foundation for the creation of democratic states and the definition of citizenship.

Since the end of the 15th century an understanding of the state developed that finds its central focus in the concept of the nation, and—since the end of the 18th century—in the concept of the people. Nation and people denote human beings who live in cultural, linguistic and political community.[50] Since the early romantic period the terms nation and people signify a community of human beings who generate or have already generated in their working together a common culture (*Kulturgemeinschaft*);[51] who through common political activity form a unit and live together in an autonomous common entity (political community); who speak a common language as the reflection of a common way of thinking and world view (linguistic community);[52] who live in the same area and due to geographic and especially climatic circumstances exhibit similar physiological, dispositional, intellectual characteristics and abilities (geographic community), and who are

[50] See JA Bär, *Universalpoesie und grammatischer Kosmopolitismus*, Diss Phil Heidelberg (1997/1998), 444.
[51] Cf AW Schlegel, 'Vorlesungen über schöne Literatur und Kunst, 2. Teil (1802/3)' in *id*, *Kritische Ausgabe der Vorlesungen* (1989), i, 533.
[52] *Ibid*, 336.

related to each other by descent (community of descent). People and nation continually form an historically grown community, which finds its cohesion in common concerns, in mutual affairs, in corresponding values and experiences.[53]

Notwithstanding certain romantic influences on these ideas,[54] a topical core of this development still remains determinative today:[55] the cultural nation and likewise the *Willensnation*, i.e. a nation which is held together alone by the will to a common state, build on the community already existing in freedom that develops a will for statehood.

To this extent, a European integration can only originate in these conditions. With a *Willensnation*, which is essentially borne by the common will toward a common policy, the requirement of voluntary membership and cohesion also remains a condition of democracy. The state today is also determined by the *Staatsvolk*, the citizens. The German *Bundesverfassungsgericht* has expressly recognised that, in the democracy of the *Grundgesetz*, the state authority is legitimised by the Germans, that is by the already existing community of citizens shaped by cultural and political commonalities. The German people ("*Volk*"), from which all state authority emanates (Art 20(2), 1st sentence *Grundgesetz*), is the community of legitimation and of responsibility for the German state.[56] For this process of legitimation and participation in the formation of a political will, citizens are to be distinguished from others entitled to human rights who also live in the state who, although they have the status of guaranteed welcome and the possibility to develop themselves, do not belong to the legitimising and democratically participating citizens.

c) Sovereignty

aa) The Tradition of a Bound Sovereignty The membership of a state in the union of states of the European Union affects its sovereignty, which is conceived as absolute and lasting power and final responsibility of the state.[57] This sovereignty has nevertheless continually been constrained in three ways: the highest and lasting state authority does not establish an arbitrary dominion, but is rather a power for the preservation of law and peace. Although sovereignty defends its own state against the influence of other states, this does not release it from obligations in the international

[53] See Bär, above n 50, 444 *et seq.*
[54] Cf Schlegel, above n 51, 533.
[55] See E-W Böckenförde, 'Die Nation—Identität in Differenz' in *id*, *Staat, Nation, Europa* (1999), 34 *et seq.*
[56] *Entscheidungen des Bundesverfassungsgerichts* 83, 37 *et seq*; 83, 60 *et seq* (*Ausländerwahlrecht* I).
[57] Cf J Bodin, *Les six livres de la Republique* (1583), reprint edn by C Mayer-Tasch (1981) Book 1, ch 8, 205.

legal order that binds all states[58] and, for the modern constitutional state, in national constitutional law. Traditionally the sovereign was to observe divine law and natural law, later the customary principles of the monarchy, the *leges imperii*,[59] then found legitimation and limits in the fundamental state goal of security[60] and, according to the concept of social contract, became a partner to this contract and its obligations,[61] and in the end transferred sovereignty to the people (*Staatsvolk*), which created concrete legal grounds for justification and responsibilities in the state it legitimated.[62] It pursues a just reign that proves itself in the observation of the law—of that which is god-given, naturally existing, legitimated through state goals, agreed to through binding social contract (by the state as well), and delivered within the limits of the constitution of democratic majority decision-making.[63] This sovereignty is the expression of unity and cohesion: when the society threatens to break up through religious wars, or the opposition between nobility, classes and farmers appears to be growing irreconcilable, or the power of industrial capital, labour organisation or military seeks to gain the upper hand, the state maintains internal cohesion in that it keeps open certain controversial questions—of religion, of class legitimation or of the economic constitution—and thus secures the peaceableness within the state in spite of the disagreement.

The openness of the sovereign to supranational influences is seen especially in the centuries-long competence of the Catholic church to be involved in the development of governing associations and citizens, in a European economic community established by the Roman law, in co-operation with individual political territories such as the Hanseatic cities, in family associations of European nobility with governing effect for various political communities, in the development of modern public international law and universal human rights.

Second, sovereign state authority is limited territorially, thus it has as its object and is dependent upon co-operation with other, equally sovereign states. Therewith, sovereignty is the capability of entering into a treaty and the readiness to reach agreement in the international community. It recognises legal commitments within this community and currently seeks to obli-

[58] See R von Mohl, *Staatsrecht, Völkerrecht und Politik* (1860), i, 529 *et seq*; K Doehring, *Völkerrecht* (1999), § 124.

[59] See H Schulze, *Staat und Nation in der europäischen Geschichte* (1995), 66 *et seq*.

[60] See U Di Fabio, *Das Recht offener Staaten* (1998), 18 *et seq*.

[61] See S Hobe, *Der offene Verfassungsstaat zwischen Souveränität und Interdependenz* (1998), 46.

[62] See Di Fabio, above n 60, 18.

[63] Cf Schulze, above n 59, 66 *et seq*.

gate the states in particular to universal human rights[64] and a constitution-making authority reserved to the people (*Staatsvolk*).

Third, finally, the sovereign state builds upon a division of labour, leaving essential areas of life in the hands of the society of those entitled to liberty. The modern conception of the state distinguishes between the state obligated to respect freedoms and the society entitled to those; today that conception must organise a triangle of state, economy and cultural society corresponding to actual power relationships, in any case placing in non-state hands such essential functions of significance to the community as provision of goods and the areas of employment, cultural society and religion, family and parental responsibility, and diversity of opinion, and thus means a sovereignty with a limited range of functions.

bb) Final Responsibility of the State in the Union This sovereignty developed within the tradition of a legal commitment now meets with a European union of states that can exercise authority directly in the territory of the Member States even against the will of the state and, although it has—in the sense of public international law—not reached the status of a sovereign state, has gained the rights of interstate commerce, especially immunities, privileges, dispensations and claims to non-interference.[65]

This division of functions between the Member State and the European union of states modifies the sovereignty of the Member States in a special legal commitment, so that some already speak of a "relinquishment of sovereignty of the Member States".[66] However this analysis is over-subscribed. The Union has no competence to decide freely on its own competences (*Kompetenz-Kompetenz*), is only set up as a community of law, exercises practically no sort of compulsory authority in the nature of police, enforcement or military power, and thus especially as a community of law has no access to a sovereignty reserve of its own political power. The Member States remain "masters of the treaties".[67] They established the European Union in order to carry out a portion of their functions in common and to this extent collectively to exercise their sovereignty.[68] Accordingly, the Union Treaty says expressly that the Union is to "respect the national

[64] See O Höffe, 'Universalistische Ethik und Urteilskraft' in L Honnefelder (ed), *Sittliche Lebensform und praktische Vernunft* (1992), 59 at 61; O Marquard, *Apologie des Zufälligen, Philosophische Studien* (1986), 131; K Stern, 'Idee der Menschenrechte und Positivität der Grundrechte' in J Isensee and P Kirchhof (eds), *Handbuch des Staatsrechts* (1992), v, § 108, para 48; H Quaritsch, 'Der grundrechtliche Status der Ausländer' in *ibid* (2000), v, § 120, paras 27 *et seq*; P Kirchhof, 'Der demokratische Rechtsstaat' in *ibid* (1997), ix, § 221, para 61.

[65] See Oppermann, above n 24, para 1725.

[66] See Doehring, above n 58, para 236.

[67] See *Entscheidungen des Bundesverfassungsgerichts* 89, 155 at 190 (*Maastricht*); Oppermann, above n 24, para 905.

[68] See *Entscheidungen des Bundesverfassungsgerichts* 89, 155 at 189 (*Maastricht*); this is clear also in Art 88 of the French Constitution.

identities of its Member States" (Art 6(3) EU). The Community is equipped with only limited competences and powers (Art 5 EC), follows the principle of subsidiarity (Art 5(2) EC), builds on a long-term membership of the Member States (Art 51 EU), without in the end taking from them the right to revoke their membership.[69]

In this manner, membership in the European union of states leaves the Member State its sovereignty in the sense of final responsibility for the authority of the European Community exercised in the state's territory and its responsibility vis-à-vis its people (*Staatsvolk*). The question of sovereignty does not remain open:[70] The democratic responsibility vis-à-vis an addressee of that responsibility strengthens the sovereignty, European integration binds it in the service of the principles of peace, state co-operation and concrete human rights policy in the form of Union civil rights. The democratic state holds together the domestic and external sovereignty and also justifies its performance within the European Union vis-à-vis its *Staatsvolk*. The union of states is a striking expression of the fact that sovereign states make co-operation their objective due to their limited spheres of sovereignty, that this co-operation takes place in concentrated association, but that the democratic forms of action of the *Staatsvolk* remain the starting point and goal of this union of states.

The Union rests on the principles of liberty, democracy, respect for human rights and fundamental freedoms, and the rule of law, principles which are common to all Member States (Art 6(1) EU), and thus must preserve this foundation, so familiar to public law, of direct and daily palpable responsibility for democracy and the rule of law, must for this reason stand up to all risks of unclear responsibilities, shifting limits of competences and powers, and avoidable de-parliamentising of law-making and budgetary sovereignty in the Community, which by necessity acts governmentally. This elucidation of responsibilities—of tasks, competences, powers and duties of justification—is especially urgent now when young democratic constitutional states have joined the union of states and expect there a confirmation and deepening of their constitutional statehood gained only a few years ago.

III. LEGAL IMPLICATIONS OF THE SPECIAL STATUS OF THE EU

The European Union is accordingly a union of states supported by the Member States, which, in its three-stage organisation based on overlapping legal circles, is established and borne by constitutional states, acts through

[69] See *Entscheidungen des Bundesverfassungsgerichts* 89, 155 at 190 (*Maastricht*); cf also Doehring, above n 58, para 242.

[70] According to C Schmitt, *Verfassungslehre* (4th ed 1954), 371 *et seq*, the fact that this question remains open belongs to the essence of a federation.

Community institutions in communitised tasks and competences, and through close co-operation of the Member States, promoted by loyalty to the Community,[71] influences further policy areas. This demanding form of organisation and action requires a special co-operation (1), establishes a modern manifestation of the balance of powers (2) and creates the need for structural renewal (3).

1. The Mandate of Co-operation

The Community Treaties establish for the working together of Community institutions and Member State organs a "relation of co-operation",[72] but likewise for the co-operation of the institutions of the European Union amongst themselves,[73] for the working together of the Member States in the policy areas that have not or only partially been "communitised" and in the framework of the dynamic legal development of European integration, which is in the midst of a constant process of renewal.

Consequently, the Union Treaty and the Member State constitutions are so geared toward each other that each source of law directs, complements and completes the other. According to Art 48 EU and Art 313 EC the competence for amending the treaties lies with the Member States, who ratify amendments "in accordance with their respective constitutional requirements". On the other hand, the Community institutions are fundamentally responsible for interpretation and application of the treaty, for which the ECJ has the final responsibility (Art 220 EC, Art 46 EU). Development of law in the internal area of the treaty is a matter for the ECJ,[74] creation of law through expanding the treaty on the other hand is for the Member States. Correspondingly, the constitutions of the Member States set the appropriate constitutional conditions for amendments to the founding treaties and similar regulations. The German *Grundgesetz* requires, in Art 23(1), 2nd sentence, a law from the *Bundestag* and the approval of the *Bundesrat* for every further transfer of competences to the European Union. To the extent to which amendments to the treaty bases of the European Union or similar regulations change or supplement the content of the *Grundgesetz*, or enable such a change or supplementation, this requires a

[71] Cf M Zuleeg, 'Die föderativen Grundsätze der Europäischen Union' [2000] *Neue Juristische Wochenschrift* 284 *et seq*.

[72] *See Entscheidungen des Bundesverfassungsgerichts* 89, 155 at 175 (*Maastricht*): '*Kooperationsverhältnis*', describes the relation between the ECJ and the Federal Constitutional Court.

[73] On this function of the separation of powers in respect of the EC cf P Kirchhof, 'Gewaltenbalance zwischen europäischen und mitgliedstaatlichen Organen' in J Isensee (ed), *Gewaltenteilung heute* (2000), 99 at 119 *et seq*.

[74] Cf *Entscheidungen des Bundesverfassungsgerichts* 75, 223 at 240 *et seq* (*Kloppenburg*).

constitutional amending two-thirds majority in the *Bundestag* and *Bundesrat*. This shows that the participation of the states in the European Union does not mean submission to every additional development in integration urged by the Union institutions, but much more is bound and conditioned by constitutional law.[75] The German *Bundesverfassungsgericht* took this division of functions between development and amendment of the treaty as the opportunity to make clear the limits of legal development by interpretation.[76] In the future, the Community institutions must observe in their interpretation of competences and empowering provisions the fact that the Union Treaty distinguishes fundamentally between the exercise of powers granted by treaty and the treaty amendment, and may not allow an interpretation that results in an expansion of the treaty or—as Art 23(1), 3rd sentence *Grundgesetz* says: in a regulation comparable to a treaty amendment. Such an interpretation of competences and empowering clauses—the Court adds—[77] would not give rise to any binding effect for Germany.

This distinction between treaty interpretation and amendment requires a clear and sufficient allocation of tasks and competences. This is the essential goal of the European basic order that is to be created, a task that is however not achieved. An elucidation of the responsibilities also clarifies the functions of the European Court of Justice and the *Bundesverfassungsgericht*. The *Grundgesetz* "vested" the *Bundesverfassungsgericht* with the task (Art 92 reads "anvertraut"), of watching over the constitutional law limits of the act of assent that gives effect to European law in Germany. The *Bundesverfassungsgericht* must guarantee that German competences are transferred to the Union only through treaty amendments by virtue of the ratification statute. The Court thereby assumes a competence and responsibility for the constitutionality of primary Community law in Germany. A constitutional court cannot dispose of this duty and this constitutional obligation; it can especially not renounce this mandate that has been entrusted to it.

The ECJ is bound in the same way by the Union Treaty, which alone legitimates its jurisprudence and in addition is the only legal basis for its competence to decide cases. For this reason the ECJ, a treaty institution, cannot amend the treaty. The adjudication of the ECJ has authority if and to the extent the Member States assign it such.

Whereas co-operation lies in the mutual interaction of treaty application and supervision of the treaty limits, and thus the securing of these basic limits is not exclusively entrusted to a Community institution or a Member

[75] See above n 15–18.

[76] See *Entscheidungen des Bundesverfassungsgerichts* 89, 155 at 210 (*Maastricht*); today, in addition, a reference to the harmonising competence of Art 95 EC would be something to consider.

[77] *Ibid*.

State, the area of co-operation is broader for secondary Community law produced on the sure treaty basis. The constitutional law limits of a treaty amendment can only be guaranteed by the Member State constitutional court; the ECJ may not even base its decisions on this constitutional standard. In the interpretation of secondary Community law the ECJ may only confirm obligations for all Member States. The decisive competence to guarantee and further develop the law belongs to the ECJ. Therefore the German *Bundesverfassungsgericht* exercises this competence in a relationship of co-operation[78], in principle recognising the respective initial interpretation of norms given by the ECJ. The latter guarantees the protection of fundamental rights in each individual case for the entire territory of the European Union; the *Bundesverfassungsgericht* can to this extent limit itself to the general guarantee of unconditional fundamental rights standards.

A constitution for the Union would by contrast also make the ECJ into a constitutional court, thereby grant it terminologically the competence to supervise on the measuring stick of this comprehensive constitution all organs and all exercises of sovereignty constituted under it, and also to this extent judge the encroachment of European law into national constitutional law, and possibly also to determine the final standards for the actions of state organs in the Member States and to supplant the national constitutional courts. A topical part of European legal culture would be lost through such centralisation.

Regarding the non-communitised tasks, Member States act in the context of their general openness to European and public international law, indeed support this co-operation on the basis of a tried and true *acquis communautaire* (Art 3(1) EU) and the stated goals of a fundamental duty of loyalty with respect to the Community (Art 10 EC). The general openness to co-operation and willingness to be bound under public international law is strengthened and made clear here in the institutional and material framework of the European Community.

Lastly, every organ has as its objective a continuity-preserving co-operation with other organs. Here, too, the Union Treaty requires a collaboration that goes beyond a traditional co-operation between government, parliament and judiciary: the policy instruments held by the European Community as a bearer of public power rest on means of coercion by the Member States. The power to enforce and the responsibility to implement the law, including European law, lies fundamentally with the Member States and not with the European Union. The tax sovereignty lies exclusively with the States. The competence for financial and economic distribution in the Member States comes close to 50 percent of gross domestic product, whereas the European Union distributes significantly less than two percent of the

[78] See above n 72.

national product generated in the Union. But above all the Community institutions are supported by the foundation of a statehood guaranteed in the Member States, in which the State and Union citizen finds his peaceful order, his securing of subsistence, his education and vocational training, protection of his health, his local and professional infrastructure. If the Community would seek to take over these functions it would be entirely overburdened in its institutions, bodies and legal standards. For this reason European public power is one that is ancillary to state sovereignty, which grows out of and rests upon the state foundation.

2. Modern Forms of Balance of Powers

Modern constitutional law confirms an essential element of the balance of powers when it expressly opens the respective state to the international community and to the European Union.[79] State authority is joined by a European authority which finds its legitimation, its partition and its standards for action not only in the constitutional law of the Member States, but in European treaty law and, especially in the independence of Community institutions vis-à-vis state organs, opens up a new scope of application for the concept of the separation of powers.

a) The Legal Sources

Whereas the constitutional state rests on a homogenous state constitution and the constitution-making authority of the people (*Staatsvolk*), the European Union builds on a genesis and renewal of Europe which separates powers. Both legal circles of European law and state constitutional law are so tied to each other that the Member State constitutions support the genesis and the development of the Union Treaties, the European institutions initiate and promote it, and the interaction of constitutional and European law stakes out the standard for the area of development of European law.

This gradated and reciprocally balanced guarantee of fundamental legal culture would be threatened if the development of the treaty would be centralised under European law, the openness of the states for Europe and the state foundation of the European Union would be displaced by a legal partitioning off of the Union in spite of the actual dependence on the states. The element of separation of powers that is the object of the co-operation of Member State and European Union gains an even greater significance in that the traditional separation of powers appears weakened in a parliamen-

[79] See K Vogel, *Die Verfassungsentscheidung des Grundgesetzes für die internationale Zusammenarbeit* (1964), 33 *et seq*, 42 *et seq*; P Badura, 'Arten der Verfassungsrechtssätze' in Isensee and Kirchhof (eds), above n 19, § 159, para 16; Di Fabio, above n 60, 17 *et seq*.

tary system of political parties and threatened in a parliament-poor European Union.

b) The Liberty-ensuring Balance of Powers

In its human rights origins[80] the separation of powers serves to protect the human being who is entitled to fundamental rights vis-à-vis state authority. If public authority is divided between legislation and enforcement, between government and administration, between regulatory and fiscal sovereignty, and if the person entitled to fundamental rights has available to him for the enforcement of his rights a separate, the third power, then the protection of fundamental rights rests especially on the principle of the separation of powers.

In the relation between European Union and Member State, it is above all the state that guarantees this liberty-securing balance of powers, that offers the citizen the conditions for liberty of its tried and trusted legal order, proffers him the foundations of liberty of his own language, of customary legal principles, of social participation in appropriate and expected gross national product of his own national economy, of cultural community thanks to similar education in school and university, of influence through religion, art, science and life habits. The state, always guarantor and opponent of liberty,[81] also assumes the task of continually guaranteeing the conditions of free development, as mediator of understanding in a concrete order. The state must reliably form the world of sovereignty and law, the diversity of jurisdictions and legal standards that have become unintelligible by virtue of the European Union and to convey them in clear responsibilities. The state must also win back for its citizens in *a res publica* the certitude of life that has been weakened in part by a global economy, by the dominion of the media, by the progress in medicine, information technology and data processing. The democratic cohesion in a people (*Staatsvolk*) and its cultural commonality expects a comprehensive responsibility for the guaranteeing of existence and peace, for cultural community and economy, for a fostering of the capability and readiness to be bound long term.

On the other hand, the European Union has the task of opening the state borders, guaranteeing trans-boundary freedom of the market, conveying by

[80] Cf Art 16 of the Declaration of the Rights of Man and of the Citizen (1789); Title III Arts 1–5 of the French Constitution of 1791; cf R Thoma, 'Grundrechte und Polizeigewalt' in H Triepel (ed), *Festgabe zur Feier des 50-jährigen Bestehens des Preußischen Oberverwaltungsgerichts* (1925), 183 at 187, n 4.

[81] P Kirchhof, 'Der Staat als Organisationsform politischer Herrschaft und rechtlicher Bindung' [1999] *Deutsches Verwaltungsblatt* 637 at 639; J Isensee, 'Die alte Frage nach der Rechtfertigung des Staates' [1999] *Juristenzeitung* 265 *et seq.*

means of a common currency the European minted freedom,[82] maintaining and further developing the Union "as an area of freedom, security and justice" (Art 2 EU).

Such a division of tasks and powers expects legal conflicts that should be resolved institutionally in this balance of powers but not suppressed by a central competence for dispute resolution. For this reason, the Commission, the Council, the Member States, the European Court of Justice and the national constitutional courts must balance and assign powers so that the Member States' and Community legal orders do not exist "unmediated and isolated next to each other" but rather are "connected to each other in diverse ways, interwoven with each other and open to mutual influences".[83] Neither the fact that constitutional law is the final standard for the application of European law in the respective Member State nor the cohesion of the European community of law in European treaty law and its final responsibility for interpretation by the European Court of Justice must be reinterpreted in one hierarchy or another. It is precisely the judiciary that fosters the culture of standards, equalisation and co-operation, not of predominance, submission and rejection. To this extent Europe offers the chance to discover anew the classic legal ideal of the balance of powers.

c) Correctness of and Responsibility for Decisions

In its function of appropriate division of labour and responsibility, the principle of the separation of powers seeks to reserve for each power a core area of tasks that this organ can best fulfil with its personnel, equipment and procedure.[84] This separation of powers requires a clear allocation of tasks, competences and powers between Union and Member States, but is then also supplemented by the principle of subsidiarity (Art 5(2) EC, Art 23(1), 1st sentence*Grundgesetz*), which the organs must observe in carrying out[85] their competences.[86]

This subsidiarity principle cautions, in the original concerns of its intellectual history,[87] against an overburdening of the state that, in an impoverishment of the forms of social society, sees itself directly and exclusively

[82] Cf *Entscheidungen des Bundesverfassungsgerichts* 97, 350 at 371 (*Euro*): '*Geld ist geprägte Freiheit*' ('money is minted freedom').

[83] See *Entscheidungen des Bundesverfassungsgerichts* 73, 339 at 368 (*Solange* II).

[84] See *Entscheidungen des Bundesverfassungsgerichts* 68, 1 at 86 (*Atomwaffenstationierung*); Badura, above n 79, para 6; more clearly subjecting the principle to the principle of democracy see E-W Böckenförde, 'Die Demokratie als Verfassungsprinzip' in Isensee and Kirchhof (eds), above n 14, § 22, paras 87 *et seq*.

[85] See *Entscheidungen des Bundesverfassungsgerichts* 89, 155 at 193 (*Maastricht*).

[86] On the Community law principle of subsidiarity see C Calliess, *Subsidiaritäts- und Solidaritätsprinzip in der Europäischen Union* (1999).

[87] See *Enzyclica quadragesimo anno* (1931); on this point see J Isensee, *Subsidiaritätsprinzip und Verfassungsrecht* (1968), 18 *et seq*.

juxtaposed to the individual person and cannot alone do him justice. The individual person is not sufficient for himself and therefore requires the *subsidium*, the assistance, which is expected in the first instance from his more immediate social surroundings and then from the larger societal institutions, and thereafter from the state.

If one transfers these concepts to the relation between the European Union and the Member States, then the subsidiarity principle finds a concrete starting point in the idea of a union of states, the principle of individual empowerment, the form of action of the directive (in the future called "framework law") and the dependence of the Union on Member State competence to execute, and its financial power: the Union sees itself less as juxtaposed to the individual, but much more meets him through the respective Member State and its conveyance of European law and European action.

This concept of the separation of powers does not contradict the concept of state sovereignty. The highest and most lasting public authority does not establish an arbitrary rule, but rather a power for the preservation of law and peace.[88] Sovereignty was imparted to the state in order to put an end to civil war and to establish perpetual peace.[89] Today this legal openness is in particular openness to Europe.

d) Organisations for the Future and the Present

In an ongoing, continuity-preserving constitution, the principle of the separation of powers also contains a chronological plan.[90] The legislator anticipates the future, the administration is occupied with the present, the judiciary judges the past. These responsibilities for time do not find the conventional framework conditions in the European Union. The European Union is in its entire organisational structure a future oriented authority and thus needs in the Member States an authority for the present.

aa) The Future-oriented European Power The European Union has as its objective, according to Arts 1(2), 2 and 3(1) EU, a constant dynamic development. The *Grundgesetz* assigns the German state organs the task of participating "in the development of the European Union" (Art 23(1), 1st sentence *Grundgesetz*). For that reason the Union preserves less what already exists, the Union Treaty ensures not only—similar to a constitution as the memory of a democracy—proven organisational structures and tested values, but rather lives in the constantly incomplete, in the development towards a better condition, in the approaching of the not yet accomplished

88 Cf above II. 2. c. aa.

89 Cf J Bodin, *Les six livres de la Republique* (1583) reprint edn by C Mayer-Tasch (1981), book 1, ch 8, 2. 205.

90 See G Husserl, *Recht und Zeit* (1955), 42 *et seq.*

completion. This is especially the case in the current phase of a clear expansion of the European Union.

After all, in its basic structure the European Union occasionally appears almost to be an organisation forging into the future without a present. The executive produces laws. The enforcing power lies essentially with the Member States, so that the Community has hardly any organ at its disposal that is affiliated with the present. The ECJ traditionally views itself as the "engine of integration", is likewise less occupied with the past than with the future. The Union appears trapped in a continual striving toward the constant growth of competences, but must in its current profusion of competences—other than as in the early years—effectively secure the stability of a community of law. For this reason, the chronological balancing of powers, the condition for openness to development in continuity and consciousness of history, appears to be not yet reached, the balance between an inviolable law and its ability to develop not yet assured.

Of course the forward moving European Union develops its own organs for perpetualising and guaranteeing continuity—especially the European Central Bank, the European Court of Auditors and increasingly a European judiciary that emphasises its judicial character. Here, too, the European Community—as a community of law—faces the task of gaining structures of constancy, and therewith predictability and trustworthiness.

bb) The Present-oriented Member States' Power A European Union that is currently conceived of more as a future-oriented power is linked back in its actions to the jurisdiction and responsibility of the Member States and, in particular, significantly legitimated democratically through the Member States and their parliaments.[91] The separation of powers between European law-making and Member State execution of laws, European financial requirements and Member State financial foundations, but above all a European "communitising" on the basis of a statehood that guarantees a citizen-friendly basis of existence, substantiates a new balance between stability and shaping the future. The continuity of the constitutional state forming the basis of the European Union also offers for the Union an institutionalised responsibility for the present, and thus "planability" and predictability.

The planned European basic order must for this reason also newly structure the balance between guarantee of continuity and renewal, between responsibility for future, present and past in the collaboration between the Union and the Member State. The European community of law needs a stable law that secures continuity, predictability and responsibility; it rests on the known law, which alone can breed confidence in the law; it requires a

[91] *Entscheidungen des Bundesverfassungsgerichts* 89, 155 at 185 (*Maastricht*).

careful transition that secures balance in the time scheme and also avoids excess there.

e) Co-operation Between Powers

Finally, the separation of powers is the foundation for a continuous co-operation, in which the separate powers combine in the constancy of law into a mutually complementary and completing unit of action.[92]

This European co-operation is more than a co-operation between state organs. It is rooted in two autonomous legal orders which, granted, are related to each other but have different content, is partially influenced by different legislative, administrative and judicial cultures, has to overcome the movement in the opposite direction of a broad central organisation that is mindful of the expansion of its competences and a grown Member Statehood that preserves democratic-cultural autonomy, and must especially mediate between governmental structures of organisation and parliamentary democracy. Thus it involves more than the fact that separate state functions have co-operation as their object. European co-operation means above all co-operation in preserving time-tested cultural differences and in overcoming those that can be changed.

3. Prospects for Reform of the European Basic Order

The European Union has again slipped into gear as the number of Member States has expanded from 15 to 25. The distribution of political responsibility is barely transparent and understandable for the citizen, the harmonisation of the economic community and the community of political values has not yet found a clear legal framework, the overlapping legal and jurisdictional circles complicate affiliation and internal orientation for the citizens, the democratic legitimation appears too weak.

a) New Order of Responsibilities

Democracy and the rule of law demand clear responsibilities for the distribution of tasks, competences and powers between the Union and the Member States; they demand distinct parliamentary responsibility, dependable liability for wrongful action as well as comprehensive procedures for administrative self-supervision and jurisdiction.

In the context of a treaty amendment to clarify, and also to revise aberrations, the Community must be responsible for the supranational tasks, the Member States for the national tasks. To the Member States' sole power

[92] Cf above at III.1.

of decision belong especially the democratic self-organisation of the state and its organs, domestic security and justice, education and vocational training (universities, colleges, educational system), research and science, pension and public welfare, transportation and housing, tax and budgetary sovereignty, the most important areas of industrial policy, regional policy and structural policy, media and television, whose products must not deteriorate into commodities under European law.

By contrast, the supranational activity of the Community encompasses primarily the internal market, a common trade policy, currency policy, all procedures for trans-boundary movement of persons and economic goods including their co-ordinated encumbrance by tax law, agriculture and fisheries (with limited financial authority), co-determination authority in the area of transport, competition, employment policy, environmental policy, trans-European networks, consumer protection, energy, protection against disasters and tourism. However, this structural adjustment will remain illusive. The allocation of competences will largely remain the same as will their complexity, their indeterminate limits and the lack of clear responsibilities.

The foreign and defence policies push more and more towards supranationality. But the actual state of the European Union and its expansion appears to speak against a communitising of these sovereign functions at this point in time. After all, the Union shall have two highly visible representatives for foreign policy, a President and a Union Minister for Foreign Affairs. The new full-time position of President represents the Union externally at his or her level, prepares the summit meetings and co-ordinates the 25 governments of the Member States. The Union Minister for Foreign Affairs serves as Vice-President of the Commission, chairs the meetings of the Council of Ministers for Foreign Affairs, and under its mandate the Union Minister prepares proposals for the common foreign policy of the Member States; in addition, the Union Minister commands a separate foreign affairs service.

In the context of their functions the Union takes decisions directly for the Member States, but harmonises these with their legal systems and state structures so that they can be carried out there. In law-making the Union should—once again, in the framework of its tasks—give precedent to standardising the law of the Member States, that is, choose the instrument of the directive (European framework law) and less often that of the regulation (European law), and so Europeanise the national law rather than supplant it by European law.

The European union of states takes the significant decisions of Community policy, law-making and implementation of the law in the Council. It acts there through the governments of its Member States. The European Parliament is limited to the powers of an assisting organ. Considerations whether to strengthen the legitimising power of the

European Parliament by having it elected not by the respective peoples (*Staatsvölker*) but rather formed by Members of the elected parliaments in the Member States deserve critical consideration. In any case, the right of initiating legislation should no longer be monopolised in the Commission as the administrative organ responsible for the Community. Here it should be considered whether the national parliaments—as individual parliaments or in a parliamentary majority—could be granted a right of initiative and the programmatic structuring for the future could be supported legally by the Council.

Even according to the planned "constitutional treaty", the Commission remains a strong, maybe an even stronger institution. Its ability to act is strengthened as the number of Commissioners will be decreased to two thirds of the Member States by 2014; if the Union will have 27 members by then—including Romania and Bulgaria—nine Commissioners must vacate their seats in steady rotation. In the future, the President of the Commission will lay down the guidelines for the Commission's work and the resources; the President may also request a Commissioner's resignation.

The President of the Commission will be elected "taking into account the elections to the European Parliament" by a majority of the members of the European Parliament; Member State governments have the right to submit proposals. In this regard, a creative function of the European Parliament emerges, similar to that assigned to national parliaments in Member State constitutions.

The most important competences remain in the hands of the European executive. The European Council unites the 25 Heads of State and Government in one institution, which defines the general political directions and priorities and which meets periodically every three months. The Council of Ministers, with the respective ministers of the 25 Member States, adopts the legislative acts. Starting in 2009, the Council of Ministers decides with qualified majority, i.e. at least 55 per cent of the states and 65 per cent of the Union citizens. This gives the countries of the Mediterranean a blocking minority so that decisions on agricultural subsidies cannot be taken against their will. The new Member States together with Spain, Greece, Portugal and Ireland can—as cohesion countries—block a change in the structural policy. Majority decisions with a powerfully invigorating character are therefore impossible. In a number of important fields, such as the common foreign and security policy, tax policy and financial planning, social policy, police and judicial co-operation in combating cross-border criminality and in parts of refugee and immigration policy, unanimity remains the mode of taking decisions. The respective Member State remains responsible for the tasks which are of concern for itself, but which must be determined taking into account a community perspective. The European Parliament gains influence in an extended co-decision procedure, but more importantly, in the field of budget planning. However, a democratic parlamentarianism remains—in line with the structure of a union of states—barred from becoming reality.

The Growth and Stability Pact, which has been crudely violated in the recent past, could ultimately not be strengthened. As in the past, the competence on taking final decisions on sanctions lies with the Council of Finance Ministers, i.e. with the budget sinners, who at any rate can reject with qualified majority concrete proposals with regard to reducing the deficit issued by the Commission. The European Union lacks the determination in this area to enforce internal stability against the Member States. Grand visions for a heretofore successful Euro only lead to small steps and sometimes even to regression.

b) Democracy in Europe

The problem—perceived on all sides, if not often intentionally kept quiet—of democracy in Europe consists in the fact that the performance of functions by the European Union is legitimised first and foremost by the peoples (*Staatsvölker*) of the Member States through the national parliaments, and hence that democratic legitimation is produced by the tying back of the actions of the European institutions to the parliaments of the Member States.[93] Within the organisational structure of the European Union, the growing mediation of democratic legitimation through the European Parliament elected by the citizens of the Member States is a further contributing factor.[94] But the more the Union gains in competences and powers, the more problematic this relativised democratic legitimation will become. With this, the task presents itself of not, in the midst of fascination with Europe, abandoning enthralment with democracy.

Currently three considerations are offered that seek to escape this dilemma but not to solve it. The first declares the protection of fundamental rights to be a focus of the principle of democracy and thereby seeks to get around the parliamentary prerogatives. The second seeks to give the European community of law a democratic legal basis in a constitution, which is, however, not produced by a democratic, constitution-making authority. The third attempts to understand democracy primarily as a principle of the state constitution, that is to give effect to the parliamentary representation of the people (*Staatsvolk*) in the Member State parliaments, but not in the European Union.

By contrast, the European Union must be aware of the initial condition of increasing powers of the union of states and weakening democratic-parliamentary legitimation. A parliament is the organ which, as the directly elected representative of the *Staatsvolk,* takes the essential fundamental decisions of a democracy—above all by legislation, including the budgetary right. This democracy can only be realised in modified fashion in a union

[93] See *Entscheidungen des Bundesverfassungsgerichts* 89, 155 at 182 *et seq* (*Maastricht*). See in detail: M Kaufmann, *Europäische Integration und Demokratieprinzip* (1997).

[94] See *Entscheidungen des Bundesverfassungsgerichts* 89, 155 at 182 *et seq* (*Maastricht*).

of states in which the states meet primarily through their executives and cannot support itself on any *Staatsvolk*. Therefore the influence of the Member State parliaments on the European Union must above all be strengthened, if possible by organising a European co-operation of these parliaments and giving more effect to the supporting function of the uropean Parliament—in an increased responsibility especially of the Commission vis-à-vis the Parliament, in an improved participation of the Parliament in executive law-making in the Council and in a right of initiative.

Then the power of the Council to decide by majority voting should be designed to be closer to democracy: the votes of the Member States in the Council are to be weighted appropriately according to the number of citizens they represent. The principle of democracy is one of the classic European ideas, which must become cognisant and effective in times of development, in a time during which the European Union develops from an economic community to a political community.

c) The Community of Values in Fundamental Rights

The European Union has problems to afford its citizens in the Treaty text what is self-evident for every democracy: fundamental rights. The European Charter of Fundamental Rights so far remains non-binding, but it shall form part of the "constitutional treaty". However, today the Charter of Fundamental Rights may not be celebrated as the core of a European constitution. Such anticipation of the uncertain future claims to be current law, although for now the Charter has precisely not achieved legal binding effect. This postulate of simultaneous expansion and deepening of the European community of law proves to be unrealistic.

In addition, the European union of states as well as the candidate states are currently unprepared in many questions of fundamental rights, and occasionally even overburdened. The right to property is traditionally seen as the economic foundation for individual liberty and as the expression of personal entrepreneurial responsibility, but today is often legal title for a financial policy and for equity funds, in which the entitled owner scarcely assumes any responsibility for the effects of his capital contribution and solely claims the profits. The freedom of the press as an essential foundation of modern democracy is only insufficiently harmonised with the law of defamation, which traditionally belongs to the four liberal basic liberties as the right of psychological inviolability.[95] The criminal law presumption of innocence for each person until found guilty loses its actual constitutive power in any event for politicians and entertainers. The capacity for the future of society and state in the guarantee of marriage and family, in the

[95] Cf H Kube, 'Ehrenschutz im Verfassungsrecht des Frühkonstitutionalismus und im Grundgesetz' (2000) 125 *Archiv des öffentlichen Rechts* 341 *et seq.*

existence of sufficient children raised to be capable of independence, to guarantee the future of the people (*Staatsvolk*) appears to be threatened in the discussions regarding marriage and family, which deal only with the self-realisation of the adults and not with the future of the child. In many states the elementary liberal right of privacy, including sexual privacy, runs into new legal institutions of life partnerships, which gives persons an incentive to "out" themselves as same-sex partners without any such declaration being significant for the future of the commonwealth. The principle of competition and rivalry, essential for basic liberty is also often applied to the public sector—especially in "competition" of legal and tax systems—thereby obliterating the fundamental border between the society that is entitled to liberty and the state that is obligated to respect it.

We thus do not have at our disposal secure and well rounded constitutional law conceptions as to individual rights of liberty and equality that need only be generalised in European law. The most reliable starting point is still that of Art 6(2) EU, according to which the Union respects fundamental rights, as they are guaranteed in the European Convention on Human Rights and as they result from the common constitutional traditions of the Member States, as general principles of Community law. It appears to be a call of our times to comprehend in this constitutional comparison the constitutional traditions secured in the Member States and to seek the best solutions in this context. If the European Union on the other hand seeks to conceive of its foundation of values, the specifically European fundamental rights, in an act of fundamental reforms and renewals, it endangers itself. A Europe of small steps and big visions should not now become a field of experimentation for the projection of new values.

4. A Europe of States as an Opportunity for Peace and Freedom

The development of the states in Europe currently strengthens the traditional foundations of European law: statehood and fundamental rights. With each new constitutional state the opportunity for peace and human rights in Europe grows. Where peoples and nations had not yet come together in a constitutional state, the danger of non-peacefulness and violation of human rights grew—as in Yugoslavia. For the community between states, the European Union has developed the new legal form of a union of states (*Staatenverbund*) instituted by constitutional states which are autonomous, democratic and open to Europe. In the working together of the organisational principles of constitutional state and union of states, the European Union gains a basic order which co-ordinates the actions of its Member States, in part also regulates but above all organises the common performance of tasks. In this relatedness, Europe offers the contractual organisational form of a union of states which, in its legally defined tasks, competences and powers, rests upon constitutional states open to co-operation.

19

The Advantages of the European Constitution—A German Perspective

BY MANFRED ZULEEG

I. THE EUROPEAN CONSTITUTION—A PHANTOM?

THE EUROPEAN UNION (EU) is an international organisation with its own legal personality.[1] Its heart, the European Community (EC), exercises sovereign power. This means that the Member States and individuals are required to comply with orders that were made without their express consent. In short, the EU makes law. It is empowered to undertake and implement administrative measures. A European jurisdiction makes legal judgments and other decisions that are binding on the parties. The European Court of Justice (ECJ) creates judge-made law which the Member States and individuals must obey. The Member States must transpose European law into their legal order. They must apply European law through their administrative bodies and courts. The European legal order gives individuals rights and imposes duties on them. The EC interacts internationally with other subjects of international law. The EU is thus not very far from being a state.[2] States have constitutions. This notion comprises legal rules and principles organising the human resources to govern an association and establishing guidelines for the exercise of sovereign powers. Should the EU be deprived of such a fundament in spite of its similarity to states?

Considering the literature on European integration, one still encounters the notion of governance without a constitution. In Germany, the view is

[1] For the reasoning, see A von Bogdandy and M Nettesheim, 'Die Europäische Union' [1986] *Europarecht* 3; A von Bogdandy, 'Die Europäische Union als einheitlicher Verband' in A von Bogdandy and CD Ehlermann (eds), *Konsolidierung und Kohärenz des Primärrechts nach Amsterdam* [1998] *Europarecht* suppl 2 165; M Zuleeg, 'Die Organisationsstruktur der Europäischen Union' in *ibid*, 151.

[2] See M Zuleeg in E Denninger *et al* (eds), *Kommentar zum Grundgesetz für die Bundesrepublik Deutschland* (2001), Art 23, para 15. See further, A von Bogdandy, *Supranationaler Föderalismus als Wirklichkeit und Idee einer neuen Herrschaftsform* (1999), 35 *et seq*.

quite common that constitutions are reserved to states only. It is alleged that they alone are equipped with the legal rules and principles that give them a position of prominence. This view is often based on the idea that only sovereign entities can have constitutions. Then the sub-national states such as the German and Austrian Länder, the various states of the United States and the Swiss cantons could not be said to have constitutions, which is incorrect. Nevertheless, many observers perceive no inconsistency. However, both the dependent entities and the EU are not sovereign. Even the sovereignty of the Member States is eroding. They are no longer omnipotent. The differentiating criterion of sovereignty is thus becoming increasingly blurred.[3] Therefore a constitution is no longer consistently considered to be exclusively an attribute of states, but rather a network of relations between various subjects and a form of social self-organisation.[4] Hence the EU may have a constitution.

Other authors tie constitutions to democracy. Yet even states that are under a dictatorship have basic rules and principles. The concept of constitution is meaningful in order to recognise, sort and compare these basic rules and principles. However, proponents of the nation-state distance themselves from a neutral conception of a constitution. They conceive of the state as being composed of a homogeneous people, the nation. Democracy, then, is derived from this kind of nation, which is a necessary element of a constitution. Under such a premise, the state and the constitution are conditions for each other.[5] Homogeneity brings with it the danger of deforming a free society and hindering the association of states, especially when the other states have members of an ethnic or religious group that are considered to be potential enemies.[6] On the basis of such a conception of democracy one can reserve the constitution to the state. Yet democracy is not dependent on homogeneity. Democratic rights and freedoms preclude such conformity. The United States is an outstanding example of a multi-ethnic, multi-cultural and multi-religious

[3] See C Tomuschat, 'Die internationale Gemeinschaft' (1995) 33 *Archiv des Völkerrechts* 1 at 20.

[4] I Pernice, 'Europäisches und nationales Verfassungsrecht' (2001) 60 *Veröffentlichungen der Vereinigung der Deutschen Staatsrechtslehrer* 148 at 149 *et seq* is pathbreaking.

[5] See J Isensee, 'Staat und Verfassung' in J Isensee and P Kirchhof (eds), *Handbuch des Staatsrechts der Bundesrepublik Deutschland* (1995), i, 591 at § 13 *et seq*.

[6] See P Kirchhof, 'Der deutsche Staat im Prozeß der europäischen Integration' in Isensee and Kirchhof (eds), above n 5, vii, 855; *Entscheidungen des Bundesverfassungsgerichts* 89, 155 at 185 *et seq* (*Maastricht*). BO Bryde, 'Die bundesrepublikanische Volksdemokratie als Irrweg der Demokratietheorie' (1994) 5 *Staatswissenschaften und Staatspraxis* 305 *et seq*; I Pernice, 'Carl Schmitt, Rudolf Smend und die europäische Integration' (1995) 120 *Archiv des öffentlichen Rechts* 100; JHH Weiler, 'Der Staat "über alles": Demos, Telos und die Maastricht-Entscheidung des Bundesverfassungsgerichts' (1996) 44 *Jahrbuch des öffentlichen Rechts* 91, all convincingly put forward the opposite view.

democracy.[7] This example shows that democracy is not bound to a homogeneous people. Democracy is moreover based on the free will of the people. Likewise, the EU recognises the principle of democracy and grants rights and freedoms.[8] Thus, the EU can be counted among the governing entities that have a constitution.[9]

It remains to discover wherein the constitution of the Union of European States lies. In 1967 the German Constitutional Court already determined that the European Economic Community (EEC) constituted a new public power and that this power was autonomous and independent from the powers of the Member States. In a certain way the EEC Treaty represents the Community's constitution.[10] According to the ECJ, "the EEC Treaty, albeit concluded in the form of an international agreement, nonetheless constitutes the constitutional charter of a Community based on the rule of law. The Community treaties established a new legal order for the benefit of which the states have limited their sovereign rights and the subjects of which comprise not only Member States but also their nationals".[11] For the court, the fact that the EU is based on international treaties does not prevent the conclusion that a constitution is present. It is not the legal form, but rather the content that is decisive.[12] The Community Treaties incorporated elements of the Member States' constitutions into the European legal order. Yet basic constitutional principles such as democracy, the rule of law and fundamental freedoms were missing. The ECJ closed these loopholes by developing principles on the base of its own jurisprudence. These constitutional principles are now to be found in Art 6(1) EU. There, human rights are explicitly mentioned. In addition, Art 6(2) EU requires the Union to respect human rights, as guaranteed by the European Convention for the Protection of Human Rights and Fundamental Freedoms and common constitutional traditions of the Member States, as general principles of law. Though a provision of the EU Treaty, its content is also valid for the Communities due to the unity of the Union and the Communities. The treaties do not, however, represent a complete constitution. There are still elements that are only secured by judge-made law. An example is the Community's obligation to co-operate with the Member States, the so-

[7] See M Zuleeg, 'What Holds a Nation together?' (1997) XLV *The American Journal of Comparative Law* 505; M Zuleeg, 'Zusammenhalt durch Demokratie in den Vereinigten Staaten von Amerika und in der Europäischen Union' (2003) 51 *Jahrbuch des öffentlichen Rechts der Gegenwart* 81.

[8] See M Zuleeg, 'Demokratie in der Europäischen Gemeinschaft' [1993] *Juristenzeitung* 1069; M Zuleeg, *Der rechtliche Zusammenhalt der Europäischen Union* (2004).

[9] See PM Huber, 'Europäisches und nationales Verfassungsrecht' (2001) 60 *Veröffentlichungen der Vereinigung der Deutschen Staatsrechtslehrer* 194 at 208 *et seq*.

[10] See *Entscheidungen des Bundesverfassungsgerichts* 22, 293 at 296 (*EWG-Verordnungen*).

[11] See Opinion 1/91, *EEA* [1991] ECR I–6079, para 21.

[12] See Pernice, above n 4, 168 *et seq*.

called loyalty clause.[13] In other areas interplay between treaty formulation and judge-made law takes place, above all in the field of fundamental freedoms.[14] In sum, the European constitution is composed of treaty law and judge-made law. The numerous elements of this constitution exert influence on the EU itself, its Member States and its individuals.[15] Thus, the European constitution is not a phantom.

II. THE ADVANTAGES IN DETAIL

1. The Organisational Structure

A sovereign entity's constitution must set forth who exercises sovereign power, according to which procedures and the manner in which this power is to be exercised. A statute of organisation is therefore a *sine qua non.* The founding treaties of the EU and the two Communities, together with the amendments, annexes and protocols, create institutions and secondary organs. They lay out these bodies' composition and procedures as well as their relationships to each other.[16] The EU's statute of organisation is notable for its creation of a plethora of institutions. It is not the object of this contribution to delineate all of them,[17] but rather to make clear what characterises the EU as an autonomous organisation. In this connection, the Commission—an institution that finds no parallel in the states—must be mentioned first.

The Commission is a supranational institution, which means that it exercises powers and fulfils tasks throughout the whole Union and even beyond in international relations. Not only the individuals within the Member States, but also these states themselves are subject to the Commission's powers. Its members are independent during their period of office. The European Parliament (EP) controls the policy of the Commission. The EP is able to remove the Commission from office, a procedure that has thus far never been used, although the threat of this procedure did once move the Commission to resign. The Commission monitors compliance with Community law, in particular with respect to the Member States. In legislation it usually has the sole right of initiative. It is only exceptionally

[13] See Case 2/88 Imm *Zwartveld* [1990] ECR I–3365, paras 16 *et seq*.

[14] See M Zuleeg, 'Zum Verhältnis nationaler und europäischer Grundrechte' [2000] *Europäische Grundrechte-Zeitschrift* 511 *et seq*.

[15] See JA Frowein, 'Die Verfassung der Europäischen Union' [1995] *Europarecht* 315 at 333.

[16] See T Oppermann, *Europarecht* (1999), paras 236 *et seq*.

[17] See in detail, M Hilf, *Die Organisationsstruktur der Europäischen Gemeinschaften* (1982).

empowered to create law by itself. As an example, the supervision of public undertakings to which the Member States have granted special or exclusive rights should be mentioned (Art 86(3) EC). The Commission may make delegated law upon authorisation by the Council. The Commission is empowered to apply the law on the basis of a specific delegation. It has broad competence to engage in administrative activities. This position is suitable for an authority of a governance that has not yet reached the level of statehood but nonetheless is equipped with numerous sovereign powers. The Commission deserves the title of a "motor of integration". Its role is not comparable to that of governments in a parliamentary democracy because its success largely depends on the Council, since this institution decides at first instance if the Commission's proposals are to be accepted. However, as a monitoring institution it is able to influence the behaviour of the Member States toward integration.[18]

The Council is composed of representatives of the Member States. Its main task is legislating, a task which it must, in certain fields, share with the EP. In other fields it decides alone. Transparency of the procedures within the Council is deficient.[19] As compensation, though, the Member States carry the responsibility for important decisions made at the European level, above all for legislation. If this were not guaranteed, integration would come to a standstill because the Member States are not ready to give up their key position in Europe.

Step by step, the EP has won greater influence. Yet it still does not possess a comprehensive right of co-decision for legislation. Insofar as it is involved, its influence does not measure up to that enjoyed by the Member States' parliaments. This is largely due to the fact that the Council is not, as a partner, dependent on the EP. The public perceives the role of the EP rather as a brake or at least as an unimportant actor in legislation. A fundamental change could only be brought about by reducing the powers of the Member States. This, however, would jeopardise further integration.[20]

Art 220 EC assigns a clear task to the ECJ: the Court of Justice shall ensure that in the interpretation and application of this Treaty the law is observed. It is assisted in this regard by the Court of First Instance. By their jurisprudence, these courts are considerable factors for integration. The ECJ is also marked as a "motor of integration". The European courts are bound by legal norms and principles. In developing unwritten law, the courts

[18] See KO Nass, 'Eine Institution im Wandel' in U Immenga (ed), *Festschrift E-J Mestmäcker* (1996), 411.

[19] See recently on this subject C Sobotta, *Transparenz in den Rechtsetzungsverfahren der Europäischen Union* (2001).

[20] See A Maurer, 'Regieren nach Maastricht: Die Bilanz des Europäischen Parlaments nach fünf Jahren "Mitentscheidung"' [1998] *Integration* 212.

loosen to a certain degree the connection to the existing legal order but do not sever it. The ECJ takes recourse to the Member States' common constitutional principles as well as to international treaties to which the Members belong.[21]

Finally, the European Council must be mentioned. It brings together the heads of state or government of the Member States and the President of the Commission (Art 4(2) EU). According to Art 4(1) EU the task of the European Council is to provide the Union with the necessary impetus for its development and to define the general political outlines thereof. The European Council is organised in the EU Treaty, whereas other institutions are defined in the EC Treaty. As a complex, but united organisation, the EU may, however, distribute institutions all over its parts.

This brief overview is sufficient to demonstrate that the EU's statute of organisation is tailored to a sovereign supranational entity. In this form it is able to further European integration.

With regard to the prescribed procedures, a unique aspect of the European legal order deserves special attention. Art 253 EC and Art 162 European Atomic Energy Community Treaty (EA) oblige the Community organs to provide reasons for all legal acts. In this way, the object and purpose of a legal norm may be ascertained from its reasons. The courts are not required to take recourse to the statements made during the legislative process. Such statements do not reliably reflect legislative intent, since one cannot know whether the final version is based on those statements. Moreover, law-making in the Council is not exposed to the public. The legal text often permits several interpretations. Due to the obligation to provide reasons for all legal acts of the Community, the courts are enabled to find out the authentic motives.[22]

While the EU's and Communities' statutes of organisation are extensively prescribed in the Treaties, there is still room for the development of law by courts in this area. Above all the ECJ has stressed that a balanced relationship between the institutions is important. This institutional balance requires every institution to respect the competences of the other institutions when exercising its power. It also demands that violations of this principle can be sanctioned.[23] In this way, the institutions are in the best position to realise the interests they represent.

[21] See GG Sander, *Der Europäische Gerichtshof als Förderer und Hüter der Integration* (1998). See, eg, Case 44/79 *Hauer* [1979] ECR 3727, paras 13 *et seq*.

[22] See in detail, T Müller-Ibold, *Die Begründungspflicht im europäischen Gemeinschaftsrecht* (1999).

[23] See Case C–70/88 *Parliament v Council* [1990] ECR I–2041, paras 21 *et seq*.

2. Tasks and Objectives

In national constitutions one rarely encounters tasks and objectives.[24] The Community Treaties are replete with such obligations. They oblige the Union's institutions to realise the founders' aims. Tasks and objectives determine the object and purpose of legislation and administrative activity. The Community's objectives restrict its regulatory competence with respect to the Member States. The principle of enumerated powers in Art 5(1) EC provides that the Community's activity not only remain within the scope of the competence provided by the Treaty but also within the scope of the enumerated objectives. Art 2 EC establishes very broad tasks. The list of activities in Art 3 EC obliges the Community's institutions to be active in the listed sectors. Within the individual fields there are more concretised objectives, e.g. Art 14 EC for the internal market and Art 33 EC for agriculture.[25]

3. The Distribution of Powers

In a federative association the larger entity must decide how powers are to be distributed, otherwise there will be chaos.[26] The danger lies either in an area's being left unregulated despite the need for regulation or in the emergence or persistence of contradictory regulations. The fundamental decision is to be found in Art 5 EC according to which the EC has only those powers conferred upon it by the Treaty. These may be conferred exclusively on the EC, but this is a rare occurrence. Usually, the EC's powers are concurrent or parallel. Generally the EC is granted the competence to regulate a certain sector. There are, however, also competences based on the Community's aims. These types of competences are limited to the harmonisation necessary for the completion of the internal market (Arts 94, 95 EC) and to the complementary clause of Art 308 EC. These provisions are criticised as arbitrary because of their imprecise wording.[27] Admittedly, they are broad,

[24] For good arguments, see K Redeker and U Karpenstein, 'Über Nutzen und Notwendigkeiten, Gesetze zu begründen' [2001] *Neue Juristische Wochenschrift* 2825, argue that laws in Germany should provide the law's motives.

[25] For further details, see PC Müller-Graff in MA Dauses (ed), *Handbuch des EU-Wirtschaftsrechts* (looseleaf, last update 2000), A I; M Zuleeg in H von der Groeben and J Schwarze (eds), *Kommentar zum EU-/EG-Vertrag* (2003), on Arts 2 and 3 EC.

[26] The terms 'powers' and 'competences' are used interchangeably in this contribution since the Treaties do so and no difference is to be seen. The importance of the distribution of competences is shown by A von Bogdandy and J Bast, 'Die vertikale Kompetenzordnung der Europäischen Union' [2001] *Europäische Grundrechte-Zeitschrift* 441, English version: 'The European Union's Vertical Order of Competences: The Current Law and Proposals for its Reform' (2002) 39 *CML Rev* 227.

[27] See P Kirchhof, 'Deutsches Verfassungsrecht und Europäisches Gemeinschaftsrecht' [1991] *Europarecht* suppl 1, 11 at 16 *et seq.*

but it must be borne in mind that these competences are not only goal oriented. The exigencies of the internal market must be fulfilled. The European legal order also comprises competences based on a close connection to an explicit competence, the so-called implied powers. Otherwise, the Member States retain their powers. The exercise of supranational competences is furthermore limited by the exercise of the principle of subsidiarity. An appropriate distribution of powers is thus achieved.

It must be noted that distribution may differ according to the function of a specific power. A large proportion of legislation has been transferred to the European level. The Communities are tied to the Member States if directives are issued. The Member States must transform the directives into their respective national law. The EC is entrusted with the administration of certain sectors. On the whole, however, the administrative execution of Community law lies in the Member States' hands. The European courts decide upon litigation within the European legal order. The ECJ controls whether the Member States observe European law. Although institutionally the Member States' courts are not Community courts, functionally they are.[28] The procedure of preliminary decision pursuant to Art 234 EC creates a co-operative relationship between the ECJ and the Member States' courts.[29]

Despite the division of powers described above, a collision between European and Member State law can still occur. The ECJ has therefore developed a rule on the collision of laws, namely the principle of supremacy of Community law. This supremacy does not lead to the invalidity of conflicting national law but only to the inapplicability of this law. Intervention in the Member State's legal order is thus reduced to a minimum.[30] Furthermore, certain strategies have been developed to avoid collisions. In the first place, the interpretation of domestic law in conformity with EC law and legal development through the judiciary must be mentioned.[31] Friction does not occur when the EU adopts elements from the Member States' legal orders. This has happened on a broad scale. It also works the other way around: the Member States must observe their obligations arising from Community law and integrate European provisions into their legal orders. This has also occurred on a broad scale. Both the EU and

[28] See M Zuleeg, 'Die Rolle der rechtsprechenden Gewalt in der europäischen Integration' [1994] *Juristenzeitung* 1 at 2.

[29] See Zuleeg, above n 8, 58 *et seq*. See also M Zuleeg, 'Die Aufteilung der Hoheitsgewalt zwischen der Europäischen Union und ihren Mitgliedstaaten aus der Sicht der deutschen Verfassung' in Walter Hallstein-Institut für Europäisches Verfassungsrecht (ed), *Grundfragen der europäischen Verfassungsentwicklung* (2000), 91 *et seq*.

[30] In this sense, see M Zuleeg, *Das Recht der Europäischen Gemeinschaften im innerstaatlichen Bereich* (1969), 136 *et seq*. See also Zuleeg, above n 8, 104 *et seq*.

[31] See M Zuleeg, 'Die gemeinschaftskonforme Auslegung und Fortbildung mitgliedstaatlichen Rechts' in R Schulze (ed), *Auslegung europäischen Privatrechts und angeglichenen Rechts* (1999), 163.

the Member States can avoid collisions by adjusting their legal orders to the other's. Co-operation between the institutions helps to avert clashes of law. Finally, supervision and sanctions help to prevent or remedy collisions. Nevertheless, specific structural elements of the European constitution intensify the danger of conflicts, namely the principle of effectiveness, the rights granted to individuals and the unity of Community law.[32] Notwithstanding possible conflicts, the European legal order needs such instruments to uphold its binding force.

4. Constitutional Principles

a) Democracy

The EU's constitution is based on democracy. For the ECJ, the EP's participation in the Community's legislative process reflects a fundamental democratic principle: the peoples' participation in the exercise of sovereign power through an assembly of their representatives.[33] The preambles of the Single European Act and of the Treaty of Maastricht proclaim democracy as the basis of the Community. The Treaty of Amsterdam introduced this principle into the Treaty on European Union (Art 6(1) EU). The specific democratic characteristics of the European governance have become more pronounced in the course of time.[34] They are based on the will of the Union's peoples (Art 189(1) EC) and on the Union's citizens' right to self-determination.[35] The EU's legitimacy also flows from the Member States' participation in the exercise of the EU's powers.[36]

There are still complaints about a democratic deficit in the EU. The Treaty of Amsterdam once again increased the EP's powers. Nonetheless in important areas it does not have a right to co-decision, e.g. in agriculture and pursuant to Art 308 EC. In such areas the legitimacy is derived from Member States' decision-making power. The principle of democracy is thus respected. Yet some observers deny that the European governance can be democratic. The lack of a common language, so it is claimed, hinders political forces in their struggle over the best concepts. It is alleged that European parties and interest groups do not exist, nor is a European public perceptible. The EP is not in a position to take speedy or effective action.

[32] See in detail, M Zuleeg, 'Deutsches und europäisches Verwaltungsrecht' (1994) 53 *Veröffentlichungen der Vereinigung der Deutschen Staatsrechtslehrer* 153.

[33] See Case 138/79 *Roquette Frères v Council* [1980] ECR 3333, para 33; Case C–300/89 *Commission v Council* [1991] ECR I–2867, paras 17 *et seq*. On this, see Zuleeg, above n 8, 1069.

[34] J Schwarze, 'Das Staatsrecht in Europa' *Juristenzeitung* (1993) 585 at 588 *et seq*.

[35] See W Kluth, *Die demokratische Legitimation der Europäischen Union* (1995), 30 *et seq*; Zuleeg, above n 8, 1069.

[36] *Entscheidungen des Bundesverfassungsgerichts* 89, 155 at 186 (*Maastricht*).

In short, Europe lacks a living democracy.[37] However, thus far the EP has made use of and asserted its competences. It has matured into a real power in the European Union. Public awareness of European politics has grown with the enlargement of decision-making powers. There is certainly a need to expand democratic rule at the European level. The inadequacies that still remain, however, are insufficient to call the European democracy into question.[38]

The German Federal Constitutional Court (*BVerfG*) assumes two different conceptions of democracy in its judgment on the Treaty of Maastricht. The Court held that, on the European level, a living democracy must exist—a proposition which the Court found doubtful. On the national level a homogeneous people is required that expresses its will in uniformity intellectually, socially and politically.[39] Intellectual and political homogeneity means that the people think and decide in the same way. This is a caricature of democracy and the reverse of a living democracy. The transfer of sovereign powers to the EU allegedly threatens the Member States' statehood without the possibility of establishing an adequate democracy at the European level owing to the lack of a single people.[40] The *BVerfG* had previously enunciated a different conception of democracy. In this earlier judgment it placed the free self-determination of every person at the centre of its reasoning.[41] Democracy is centred on the individual. Such a conception of democracy can be applied to the European level.

Another objection is brought forward against the thesis that the EU is capable of supporting a democracy. Democracy is also based on the principle of equality. From this, one concludes that, without equal weighting of votes in the election to the EP, a fundamental democratic right is injured, thus violating a determinative element of true representation of the people.[42] Equality in weighting of votes would transform the EP into a bloated assembly unable to make decisions if even the smallest Member States had to be proportionally represented. On the other hand, a parliament with no

[37] Namely, D Grimm, 'Braucht Europa eine Verfassung?' [1995] *Juristenzeitung* 581. Against this view is J Habermas, 'Remarks on Dieter Grimm's "Does Europe Need a Constitution?"' (1995) 1 *ELJ* 303. See also P Häberle, 'Gibt es eine europäische Öffentlichkeit?' [1998] *Thüringer Verwaltungsblätter* 121; I Pernice, 'Maastricht, Staat und Demokratie' (1993) 26 *Die Verwaltung* 449 at 479 *et seq*; Zuleeg, above n 7, 505.

[38] See M Zuleeg, 'Demokratie ohne Volk oder Demokratie der Völker?' in J Drexl *et al* (eds), *Europäische Demokratie* (1999), 11 at 20 *et seq*.

[39] See *Entscheidungen des Bundesverfassungsgerichts* 89, 155 at 185 *et seq* (*Maastricht*).

[40] See Kirchhof, above n 6, § 183, in particular para 57 *et seq*. For criticism, see R Bieber, 'Steigerungsform der europäischen Union' in J Ipsen (ed), *Verfassungsrecht im Wandel* (1995), 291 at 299 *et seq*; BO Bryde, above n 6, 305 *et seq*; Pernice, above n 6, 100; Weiler, above n 6, 91; Zuleeg, above n 38, 12 *et seq*.

[41] See *Entscheidungen des Bundesverfassungsgerichts* 44, 125 at 142 (*Öffentlichkeitsarbeit*).

[42] See M Seidel, 'Zur Verfassung der Europäischen Gemeinschaft nach Maastricht' [1992] *Europarecht* 125 at 127.

or only marginal representation of the individual peoples would be a political absurdity. The solution to this dilemma is to recognise that a federation permits—and may even require—derogation from the strict principle of equality to satisfy the need to grant a certain independence and protection to smaller entities. It is a permissible derogation to integrate states or other public entities into a federation without threatening their existence. The EU is a federative democracy *sui generis*, one that is not based on a single people, but rather on peoples.[43]

b) The Rule of Law

Both the English and the German texts of Art 6(1) EU employ well-known terminology for another basic principle: the rule of law, or *Rechtsstaatlichkeit* in German. The rule of law characterises a state-like entity, meaning that the European Communities were obliged to observe the requirements of the rule of law even before the Treaty of Maastricht. The ECJ characterised the European Community as a community of law, or *Rechtsgemeinschaft* in German.[44] The protection of human rights and fundamental freedoms is to be emphasised under these principles. General principles of law derived from the rule of law are a most prominent part of the European legal order.[45] Of particular importance is the principle of proportionality that is now explicitly expressed in Art 5(3) EC.[46] The principles of legal certainty and legitimate expectations are also valid in European law.[47] The administration is bound by law. Administrative measures that impose a burden on individuals require a legal basis.[48] Administrative procedures that comply with the requirements of the rule of law must be guaranteed.[49] Insofar as European law is applicable, legal protection before an

[43] See PM Huber and 27; C Grewe both in Drexl *et al* (eds), above n 38, 27 and 59; Pernice, above n 37, 481 *et seq*.

[44] See Case 294/83 *Les Verts v Parliament* [1986] ECR 1339, paras 23 *et seq*; Opinion 1/91, above n 11, para 21. See in more detail, M Zuleeg, 'Die Europäische Gemeinschaft als Rechtsgemeinschaft' [1994] *Neue Juristische Wochenschrift* 545.

[45] See Case C–13/92 *Driessen* [1993] ECR I–4751, paras 30 *et seq*.

[46] See Case 265/87 *Schräder* [1989] ECR 2237, paras 21 *et seq*;. See in summary, E Pache, 'Der Grundsatz der Verhältnismäßigkeit in der Rechtsprechung der Gerichte der Europäischen Gemeinschaften' [1999] *Neue Zeitschrift für Verwaltungsrecht* 1033.

[47] See Case 66/79 *Salumi* [1980] ECR 1237, paras 10 *et seq*; Case C–31/91 *Lageder* [1993] ECR I–1761, paras 33 *et seq*. On legal certainty, see J Schwarze, *Europäisches Verwaltungsrecht* (1988), ii, 843 *et seq*; on protection of legitimate expectations, see KD Borchardt, *Der Grundsatz des Vertrauensschutzes im europäischen Gemeinschaftsrechts* (1988); B Berninghausen, *Die Europäisierung des Vertrauensschutzes* (1998).

[48] See Case C–8/88 *Germany v Commission* [1990] ECR I–2321, paras 13 *et seq*; Case 46/87 *Hoechst v Commission* [1989] ECR 2859, para 19. On this, see Schwarze, above n 47, i, 193 *et seq*; D Triantafyllou, *Vom Vertrags- zum Gesetzesvorbehalt* (1996).

[49] See Case C–269/90 *Technische Universität München* [1991] ECR I–5469, paras 13 *et seq*. On this see, HW Rengeling, *Rechtsgrundsätze beim Verwaltungsvollzug des europäischen Gemeinschaftsrechts* (1977), 254 *et seq*.

independent court must be granted not only against the powers of the Community but also against those of the Member States.[50] The Member States are required to effectively enforce Community law in their respective jurisdictions.[51] While the principle of the separation of powers as it is known in the German Constitution is not comprehensively applicable to the Union, at least the requirement of an independent judiciary must be respected.[52]

c) Federative Principles

The German Constitution assumes that the EU will follow federative principles (Art 23(1) Basic Law). Although this concept is not explicitly mentioned in the European legal order, it characterises important elements of the Union's constitution.[53] The loyalty clause deserves to be mentioned first. Art 10 EC obliges the Member States to fulfil their obligations arising out of the Treaty, to facilitate the achievement of the Union's tasks and to abstain from any measure which could jeopardise the Treaty objectives. The ECJ emphasises the duty to co-operate[54] and has found that it is an independent obligation.[55] If the Member States' obligation is formulated in a specific provision of European law, then the obligation to co-operate is of auxiliary character.[56] The effectiveness of European law is closely related to the obligation to co-operate.[57] The ECJ increases the effectiveness of European law by extending the obligations of the Member States to subordinate corporations and agencies. The loyalty clause imposes a duty on the Member States to co-operate with the EU's institutions, to eliminate obstacles to the effective application and enforcement of European law and to provide the Union with assistance.[58] The Member States cannot rely on provisions or practices of their internal legal or financial orders to justify breaches of Community law.[59] Practical difficulties do not create a justification for not applying Community law.[60]

[50] See Case 294/83, above n 44, paras 23 *et seq*; Case 222/84 *Johnston* [1986] ECR 1651, paras 16 *et seq*. For a comprehensive review, see HW Rengeling, A Middeke and M Gellermann (eds), *Rechtsschutz in der Europäischen Union* (1994).

[51] See S Magiera, 'Die Durchsetzung des Gemeinschaftsrechts im europäischen Integrationsprozeß' [1998] *Die Öffentliche Verwaltung* 173.

[52] See Opinion 1/91, above n 11, paras 26 *et seq*.

[53] See in detail, M Zuleeg, 'Die föderativen Grundsätze der Europäischen Union' [2000] *Neue Juristische Wochenschrift* 2846.

[54] See Case 230/81 *Luxembourg v Parliament* [1983] ECR 255, paras 35 *et seq*.

[55] For further references, see R Söllner, *Artikel 5 EWG-Vertrag in der Rechtsprechung des Europäischen Gerichtshofes* (1985), 49 *et seq*.

[56] See Cases C–332, 333 and 335/92 *Eurico Italia et al* [1994] ECR I–711, para 22.

[57] On the duties of the Member States, see above Zuleeg, see n 32, 184 *et seq*.

[58] See Case C–217/88 *Commission v Germany* [1990] ECR I–2879, paras 32 *et seq*.

[59] See Case C–290/89 *Commission v Belgium* [1991] ECR I–2851, para 9.

[60] See Case C–244/89 *Commission v France* [1991] ECR I–163, paras 20 *et seq*.

Through judicial development of the law, the ECJ has extended the application of the loyalty clause to the EU.[61] Hence, the Union's institutions are obliged to co-operate with the Member States.[62] According to the ECJ's jurisprudence,[63] however, these obligations do not generally protect elements of the national legal order from the influence of European law simply because they belong to the Member States' constitutional law.[64] The Union's institutions must nevertheless take legitimate interests of the Member States into account.[65] In practice, the principle of proportionality is a means of finding an appropriate balance of interests. Furthermore, the loyalty clause extends to the relations of the Member States to each other and requires them to work together.[66] The division of powers between the EU and its Member States belongs to the federative principles. The European legal order is intertwined with the Member States' legal orders. The Member States take legislative and administrative measures on behalf of the Union. These actions may be categorised as execution of European law.[67] The EU impacts the Member States' legislation. They may exceptionally be empowered to derogate from European law. The EU can obligate the Member States to enact legislation. The transformation of directives into domestic law is the best example of this duty (Art 249(4) EC), although other legal acts of the EU and Treaty law may also impact the Member States' legislation. Law created in this way belongs to the Member States' legal orders and is subject to their laws, regulations and rules, yet it must nonetheless be consistent with European law.[68]

If an institution of a Member State attributes legal effect to European law in any particular case, then the application of Community law becomes an issue. The question then arises whether the Community norm at hand has direct effect.[69] Provisions of European law may be insufficient to be applied in an efficient and direct way because they do not provide for procedural rules. Therefore the Member States' administrative bodies must apply their national law to fill the gaps. However, the Member States' administration must observe the primacy of Community law and fulfil the obligations arising from membership in the EU.[70] The

[61] See Case 44/84 *Hurd* [1986] ECR 29, paras 37 *et seq.*

[62] See Case C–2/88 Imm, above n 13, paras 22 *et seq.*

[63] See Case C–213/89, *Factortame et al* [1990] ECR I–2433, paras 18 *et seq.*

[64] See the opposite view in A Epiney, 'Gemeinschaftsrecht und Föderalismus' [1994] *Europarecht* 301.

[65] See Cases C–213/88 and C–39/89 *Luxembourg v Parliament* [1991] ECR 5643, para 29.

[66] See Case 251/89 *Athanasopoulos et al* [1991] ECR I–2797, para 57.

[67] See Cases 15 and 16/76 *France v Commission* [1979] ECR 321, para 31.

[68] Already formulated in Zuleeg, above n 30, 48, 225 *et seq.*

[69] See S Kadelbach, *Allgemeines Verwaltungsrecht unter europäischem Einfluß* (1999), 57 *et seq*; Oppermann, above n 16, 234 *et seq*, para 629 *et seq.*

[70] See in detail, Kadelbach, above n 69, 108. See also Magiera, above n 51, 173; J Suerbaum, *Die Kompetenzverteilung beim Verwaltungsvollzug des Europäischen Gemeinschaftsrechts in Deutschland* (1998), 119 *et seq.*

"Europeanisation" of the Member States' administrative law has thus been set into motion.[71]

The equivalence and effectiveness of administrative execution based on European law must be guaranteed.[72] Furthermore, because European law is superimposed on Member State law, equality before the law must be uniform throughout the Union. It cannot be expected that a single administrative system will develop in the foreseeable future.[73] Consequently, the Member States must accept the fact that there will continue to be two systems of administrative law: the one is adjusted to European law and the other is a purely national one.[74]

When the Member States' courts apply European law, they must apply the Member States' procedural law. The framework provided by European law must, however, be respected.[75] The Member States' procedures must not be more burdensome for the individuals in cases involving the application of EC law than they are in cases being solely governed by domestic law (principle of equivalence). The exercise of rights arising from European law may not be impossible or unduly burdensome in practice (principle of effectiveness).[76]

The Member States are subject to Community monitoring. This supervisory capacity permits the EU to ensure that the Member States comply with Community law. This began with the Treaty on the European Coal and Steel Community. Art 88 of this Treaty provided for sanctions in case of

[71] See M Brenner, *Der Gestaltungsauftrag der Verwaltung in der Europäischen Union* (1996); CD Classen in KF Kreuzer *et al* (eds), *Die Europäisierung der mitgliedstaatlichen Rechtsordnungen in der Europäischen Union* (1997), 107; Kadelbach, above n 69, 296 *et seq*; DH Scheuing, 'Rechtsprobleme bei der Durchsetzung des Gemeinschaftsrechts in der Bundesrepublik Deutschland' [1985] *Europarecht* 229; DH Scheuing, 'Europarechtliche Impulse für innovative Ansätze im deutschen Verwaltungsrecht' in W Hoffmann-Riem and E Schmidt-Aßmann (eds), *Innovation und Flexibilität des Verwaltungshandelns* (1994), 289; E Schmidt-Aßmann, 'Deutsches und Europäisches Verwaltungsrecht' [1993] *Deutsches Verwaltungsblatt* 924; E Schmidt-Aßmann, 'Zur Europäisierung des allgemeinen Verwaltungsrechts' in P Badura and R Scholz (eds), *Festschrift P Lerche* (1993), 513; J Schwarze, 'Konvergenz im Verwaltungsrecht der EU-Mitgliedstaaten' [1996] *Deutsches Verwaltungsblatt* 881; J Schwarze (ed), *Das Verwaltungsrecht unter europäischem Einfluss* (1996); M Schweitzer (ed), *Europäisches Verwaltungsrecht* (1991); KP Sommermann, 'Europäisches Verwaltungsrecht oder Europäisierung des Verwaltungsrechts' [1996] *Deutsches Verwaltungsblatt* 889. See also CD Classen, *Die Europäisierung der Verwaltungsgerichtsbarkeit* (1996).

[72] See GC Rodriguez Iglesias, 'Zu den Grenzen der verfahrensrechtlichen Autonomie der Mitgliedstaaten bei der Anwendung des Gemeinschaftsrechts' [1997] *Europäische Grundrechte-Zeitschrift* 289.

[73] For a single system, see C Engel, 'Die Einwirkungen des europäischen Gemeinschaftsrechts auf das deutsche Verwaltungsrecht' [1992] *Die Verwaltung* 437 at 475 *et seq*.

[74] See S Kadelbach, 'Der Einfluß des EG-Rechts auf das nationale Allgemeine Verwaltungsrecht' in T von Danwitz *et al* (eds), *Auf dem Wege zu einer europäischen Staatlichkeit* (1993), 132.

[75] See J Schwarze, 'Europäische Rahmenbedingungen für die Verwaltungsgerichtsbarkeit' [2000] *Neue Zeitschrift für Verwaltungsrecht* 241.

[76] See Case C–326/96 *Levez* [1998] ECR I–7835, paras 18 *et seq*.

violations against Community law, but they hardly appeared promising. The Rome Treaties originally contented themselves with a finding of a breach by the Member States (currently Art 226 EC, Art 141 EA). The Commission prosecutes the case, the ECJ makes the finding of a breach of the Treaty. Exceptionally, the Commission may make the finding itself, e.g. in the law of state aids under the EC Treaty. Since the Treaty of Maastricht, the ECJ can impose a lump sum or penalty payment pursuant to the Commission's proposal (Art 228(3), (4) EC, Art 143(2) EA).[77]

The Treaty of Amsterdam introduced a type of constitutional monitoring concerning the respect of constitutional principles (Art 7 EU).[78] On a proposal by one third of the Member States or by the Commission and after obtaining the consent of the EP, the Council may determine the existence of a serious and persistent breach by a Member State of the principles mentioned in Art 6(1) EU. The EP and the Council, meeting in the composition of the heads of state or government, thus have the power to make determinations on freedom, democracy, respect for human rights and fundamental freedoms as well as the rule of law. The Council may suspend certain rights of the respective Member State, above all it may suspend its voting rights in the Council.

d) Protection of Fundamental Rights

The ECJ has developed European fundamental rights through its jurisprudence.[79] At first, the ECJ found the basis for this jurisprudence in the constitutional traditions common to the Member States. Later, it also referred to international human rights treaties. Furthermore, a basis for fundamental freedoms may be found in the Treaties themselves, even if the relevant provisions do not explicitly determine such rights.[80] Art 6(2) EU now provides that the Union shall respect fundamental rights, as guaranteed by the European Convention for the Protection of Human Rights and Fundamental Freedoms (ECHR) and as they result from the constitutional traditions common to the Member States, as general principles of Community law. The material provisions of the ECHR are thus an integral part of European law. The supplementary protocols, though not explicitly mentioned, are also incorporated. Art 3(1) EU stipulates the consistency and continuity of activities exerted by the EU's institutional framework. This challenge includes the fundamental rights as guaranteed by Art 6(2) EU.

[77] On the monitoring procedures, see KD Borchardt, 'Vertragsverletzungsverfahren' in Dauses (ed), above n 25, P I sec 1.

[78] See in greater detail, von Bogdandy, above n 2, 14 *et seq*.

[79] See B Beutler in von der Groeben and Schwarze (eds), above n 25, Art 6, paras 39 and 51 *et seq*; HW Rengeling, *Grundrechtsschutz in der Europäischen Gemeinschaft* (1993).

[80] For further evidence, see M Zuleeg, 'Der Schutz der Menschenrechte im Gemeinschaftsrecht' [1992] *Die Öffentliche Verwaltung* 937 at 940 *et seq*.

While the fundamental rights are conceived as a protection against acts taken by the EU, they are also applicable to the Member States to the extent that European law is applicable.[81] The Charter of Fundamental Rights of the European Union[82] is capable of bringing the standards of protection of fundamental rights within the EU and the Member States closer together even if it remains non-binding. It can strengthen the effective protection of individuals and create greater public awareness of fundamental freedoms.[83] In addition, European courts are able to take the Charter as a confirmation of the existence of constitutional rights.[84]

5. The European Legal Order's Structural Characteristics

Structural characteristics are requirements that must be respected throughout the European legal order. The unity of the legal order is important to the ECJ.[85] It follows that contradictions within the legal order must be eliminated. Rules of collision serve this purpose. Furthermore, the unity of the legal order demands that the Member States' laws do not interfere with the equal application and effect of European law, as otherwise the rights of individuals could be undermined and equality before the law could not be guaranteed. Additionally, competitive conditions within the single market would be distorted. Finally, legal protection would be inadequate if the Member States' courts were able to judge the validity of a legal act by the Community differently.[86] Therefore only the European courts are capable of declaring a European act inapplicable or even null and void.

The unity of the legal order is closely connected to the effectiveness of European law.[87] Early in its jurisprudence, the ECJ emphasised the practical effectiveness (*effet utile*) of Community law to ensure that the Community's institutions are able to fulfil their tasks.[88] The result is that the Member States cannot plead internal provisions, practices or circumstances of their legal or financial orders to justify non-compliance with their

[81] See Case 5/88 *Wachauf* [1989] ECR 2609, paras 17 *et seq*.

[82] Proclamation of the Presidents of the Council, the Parliament and the Commission on the occasion of the European Council at Nice on 7 Dec. 2000 [2000] OJ C 364/1.

[83] See Zuleeg, above n 14, 511. A von Bogdandy, 'Grundrechtsgemeinschaft als Integrationsziel?' [2001] *Juristenzeitung* 157, warns against including the protection of fundamental rights and freedoms as an aim of integration.

[84] See Case T–54/99 *max.mobil Telekommunikation Service v Commission* [2002] ECR II–313, para 48; Case T–177/01 *Jégo-Quéré v Commission* [2002] ECR II–2365, para 41.

[85] See Case 106/77 *Simmenthal* [1978] ECR 629, paras 14 *et seq*; Case C–213/89, above n 63, paras 18 *et seq*.

[86] See Case 314/85 *Foto-Frost* [1987] ECR 4199, paras 12 *et seq*.

[87] See M Nettesheim, 'Der Grundsatz der einheitlichen Wirksamkeit des Gemeinschaftsrechts' in A Randelzhofer (ed), *Gedächtnisschrift E Grabitz* (1995), 447; see also M Zuleeg, 'Die Einheit des Gemeinschaftsrechts steht auf dem Spiel' in V Götz (ed), *Festschrift G Jaenicke* (1998), 899.

[88] Case 8/55, *Fédéchar* [1956] ECR 297 at 312.

obligations resulting from Community law.[89] Practical difficulties are not to prevent the application of Community law.[90] If a Member State frustrates the implementation of a Community measure granting an individual rights and the Member State is at fault, it is liable to the individual for damages.[91] If it is expected that an individual will actively oppose Community law, securing compliance with the law requires the imposition of sanctions.[92]

The ECJ emphasises that the founding Treaties, which serve as the constitutional basis of a community of law, have created a new legal order, the legal subjects of which are not only the Member States but also its citizens.[93] The ECJ was already concerned with providing protection of individuals' rights arising from Community law in 1963.[94] Such rights not only arise when Community law explicitly grants rights to the individuals. Rather, it is sufficient that a legal provision allocates a benefit to individuals if the provision is clear and exact, is neither subject to any exception or condition nor subject to deferment and does not require the intervention of any act of either the Community's institutions or the Member States.[95] In other words, the Community measure must impose a clear, precise and complete obligation on the Member States in favour of the individuals.[96] The Member States, in their realm, must protect the rights arising from European law.[97] In Germany this has met with resistance because this jurisprudence allegedly endangers the administrative legal system.[98] These objections may not weaken the effect of individuals' rights arising from European law.[99]

6. The Constitution's Scope

The EU's constitution is composed of Treaty law and judge-made law. The European constitution is thus extensive. By comparison, the Member States' constitutions are relatively short, though, in interpreting constitutional law, high courts or constitutional courts usually produce an impressive jurispru-

[89] See Case 254/83 *Commission v Italy* [1984] ECR 3395, para 3.
[90] See Case C–244/89 above n 60, para 20; Case C–52/95 *Commission v France* [1995] ECR I–4443, para 28.
[91] See Cases C–6 and 9/90 *Francovich and Bonifaci v Italy* [1991] ECR I–5357, paras 11 *et seq.*
[92] See Case 14/83 *von Colson and Kamann* [1984] ECR 1891, paras 22 *et seq.*
[93] See Opinion 1/91, above n 11, para 21.
[94] See Case 26/62 *van Gend & Loos* [1963] ECR 1, paras 24 *et seq.*
[95] See Cases 2 and 3/69 *Brachfeld* [1969] ECR 211, paras 22 *et seq*; Case 41/74 *van Duyn* [1974] ECR 1337, paras 12 *et seq*; Case 8/81 *Becker* [1982] ECR 53, paras 23 *et seq.*
[96] See P Craig and G de Búrca, *EU Law: Texts, Cases and Materials* (1998), 188.
[97] See Case C–208/90 *Emmott* [1991] ECR I–4269, paras 16 *et seq.*
[98] See T von Danwitz, *Verwaltungsrechtliches System und Europäische Integration* (1996).
[99] For references, see M Zuleeg, 'Beschränkung gerichtlicher Kontrolldichte durch das Gemeinschaftsrecht' in S Magiera and KP Sommermann (eds), *Verwaltung in der Europäischen Union* (2001), 223.

dence concretising the provisions of the constitution. Such a development is necessary to maintain a living constitution, do justice to new developments and challenges, increase the protection it offers and define more precisely broadly formulated wording. Nevertheless, the EU's constitution is much more complicated. The broad scope of the Treaties is therefore the first problem: two Communities each have a founding Treaty that covers a vast array of material. Furthermore, one must take into account the supplements, protocols and declarations. Overarching all this is the EU Treaty, which also contains addenda, many parts of which are incorporated into the Community Treaties, while others remain only in the EU Treaty. One speaks of "pillars" in order to achieve at least a minimal overview. To this must be added the "independent treaties" that cover a subject matter under the jurisdiction of the ECJ and thus part of the European legal order. It is not surprising that the complicated European constitution is not popular.

There are, however, good reasons to maintain such a constitution for the EU. With every leap of European integration there is the danger that a treaty will fail, as the planned European Defence Community Treaty has demonstrated. If an earlier treaty were to be incorporated into a later one in order to have a distinct draft, then the earlier treaty may be endangered if the latter one is rejected. The Treaty establishing the European Coal and Steel Community would have remained in existence if the Treaties of Rome had failed. The Treaty establishing the European Economic Community and the Treaty establishing the European Atomic Energy Community were separately ratified. The double ratification of the Treaties of Rome had the advantage that at least one Treaty could come into effect even if the other one were rejected. The explanation for the Single European Act's complicated structure and later that of the EU Treaty is that the Member States wanted to tackle some subject matters at the European level without, however, granting the supranational authorities competences over them.[100] The future may hold further occasions for such a proceeding. As creators of the EU's constitution, the Member States have thus far been anxious to retain control over certain subject matters. To protect these matters from legislation by the Union's institutions, the Member States regulate the subject matter in question themselves through the Treaties if European law is needed. The Treaties are thus replete with provisions of this kind. Member States may have reservations as to one or another part of the European Treaties. Exceptions, derogations or supplements are introduced into the Treaties to satisfy the concerns of the Members. This attitude further swells the European constitution.

[100] See the contributions by von Bogdandy and Bast, above n 26.

III. FUTURE DEVELOPMENT

1. The Call for a European Constitution

The call to draft a European constitution came from Germany. In other Member States, the public reacted to the proposal hesitantly at first. Gradually, however, politicians followed suit, and citizens did likewise. It was, and still is, widely believed that the EU does not have a constitution. Others did assume the existence of a constitution but hoped to achieve an even better one.[101] Anticipating a constitutional draft, the Charter of Fundamental Rights of the European Union developed, though it is still not binding.[102] A European draft Constitution began to take form. The Member States left the drafting to a Convention, the members of which were representatives of the EU as well as the respective Member States. But the citizens were not included in the convention; instead, the public was called upon to take part in the constitutional debate—a call which it answered on a broad scale. The Convention submitted the draft to the President of the European Council. The political leaders of the Member States still must approve the draft, if it is to enter into force. If it does, the next step would be for each Member State to enter into the treaty under its constitutional procedure, which would in some states require a referendum. Thus, the new Constitution must yet overcome difficult obstacles.

2. The Content of the New Constitution

a) The Clarity of the New Constitution

Proponents of a Constitution hoped to formulate a clear and concise document.[103] This they did not achieve. The proposed constitutional treaty comprises four parts. The first part is the core of the Constitution, and it also includes subject areas of lesser integration. This part is based on the current EU Treaty. The second part contains the Charter of Fundamental Rights. A third part follows and catalogues a great number of foundational provisions. This part extends the present EC Treaty. Here, the level of integration is high. The fourth part brings the resolution: the symbols of the Union and

[101] See for an insight S Oeter, 'Ansichten zur Gemeinschaftsverfassung' [2002] *Europarecht* suppl 3, 43.

[102] See J Schwarze, 'Auf dem Wege zu einer europäischen Verfassung' [2000] *Europarecht* suppl, 7.

[103] Namely, R Bieber, 'Die Vereinfachung der Verträge zur Errichtung der Europäischen Union' [1996] *Deutsches Verwaltungsblatt* 1337.

the final provisions regarding the Treaty as a whole. Orienting oneself amidst this (dis)array is difficult. The Charter separates regulations and principles that belong together. Protocols and addenda contribute further to the overload. Retaining the cumbersome Euratom Treaty in its entirety is a mistake. Certain treaties with a connection to the Union are also retained, others disappear. Hopes for clarity in the new Constitution have largely been dashed. This, though, does not imply that the current construction should be discarded. The Constitution must account for a great many factors, which cannot be compressed into a concise draft.[104]

b) Form and Content of the EU

The debate over the legal personality of the EU will be resolved, if the proposed Constitution enters into force. It succinctly states: the Union shall have legal personality. In contrast to current terms, voluntary withdrawal from the EU is to be permitted. This permission is not regrettable, since at any rate a member cannot be forcibly held within an organisation, when it is resolved not to be. Germany, however, has legally committed itself to membership. To wit, Art 23(1) Basic Law states that, with a view to establishing a united Europe, the Federal Republic of Germany shall participate in the development of the European Union. Germany could, of course, overcome this obligation with a constitutional amendment.[105]

c) The Institutional Structure

The new Constitution largely leaves the institutional structure of the European Union intact. A transition to a single state is not foreseen, although some changes are noteworthy. The EP works with the Council as legislator and exercises the budgetary function. It elects the President of the European Commission and has influence over its formation.[106] Thereby, democracy in Europe is strengthened. The European Council remains a body that gives the necessary impetus for development in the EU, though it is explicitly excluded from legislative functions. The President of the Council does, however, ensure the external representation of the Union regarding its common foreign and security policy. These innovations do not

[104] For a detailed catalogue of some of the advantages, see FC Mayer, 'Verfassungsstruktur und Verfassungskohärenz' [2003] *Integration* 398.

[105] For further evidence, see M Zuleeg in Denninger *et al* (eds), above n 2, Art 23, para 9; D König, *Die Übertragung von Hoheitsrechten im Rahmen des europäischen Integrationsprozesses* (2000), 265 *et seq*, comes to the same conclusion, based on Germany's close connection with continued intergration among the Member States.

[106] For further detail, see D Nickel, 'Das Europäische Parlament als Legislativorgan' [2003] *Integration* 501.

overly empower the European Council, but its President can officially represent the Union in foreign relations.[107] The Council of Ministers, together with the EP, enacts legislation and carries out budgetary competences. Nonetheless, the role of the Council stays largely the same. The term of the Council Chair is extended to at least one year, from which one would expect greater efficiency of operations.[108]

The European Commission maintains its role. Except where otherwise specified in the Constitution, a legislative act can only be adopted based on a Commission proposal. The Commission is thus in a position to propose important drafts. The EP and the Council, then, are placed on a high level, but without having significantly to sacrifice autonomy. The Commission consists of its President, the Minister of Foreign Affairs who is also the Vice-President and 13 voting Commissioners. The President appoints non-voting commissioners. The European Council proposes the President of the European Commission, and the EP elects the candidate by a majority of its members. A Commissioner must resign, if the President so requests. The Commission remains, as previously, answerable to the EP. These regulations increase the Commission's political clout. It is kept small, allowing it to work efficiently. Every Member State is connected to the Commission through its voting and non-voting Commissioners.[109] The Treaty of Nice rearranged the Union's judiciary; hence, only slight changes are foreseen.[110] This is to be welcomed, since frequent alterations interfere with the working of the Courts.[111]

d) Division of Competences Between the EU and the Member States

During the drafting of the new Constitution, extensive curtailment of Union competences was recommended.[112] Above all else, critics hoped to eliminate the so-called "final" competences. This concerns the approximation of laws and the complementary clause for unforeseen cases in matters of the common market. Allegedly, the components of these provisions will lead to an unbounded extension of competences.[113] This accusation is not well-founded.

[107] Set out in P de Schoutheete, 'Die Debatte des Konvents über den Europäischen Rat' [2003] *Integration* 468.

[108] See A Maurer and S Matl, 'Steuerbarkeit und Handlungsfähigkeit' [2003] *Integration* 483.

[109] See J Schild, 'Die Reform der Kommission' [2003] *Integration* 493.

[110] See U Everling, '50 Jahre Gerichtshof der Europäischen Gemeinschaften' [2002] *Deutsches Verwaltungsblatt* 1293; KJ Hopt, 'Reform der europäischen Gerichtsbarkeit' (2002) 66 *Rabels Zeitschrift für ausländisches und internationales Privatrecht*, 589.

[111] For more detail, see T Läufer, 'Der Europäische Gerichtshof' [2003] *Integration* 510.

[112] For a summary, see M ter Steeg, 'Eine neue Kompetenzordnung für die EU' [2003] *Europäische Zeitschrift für Wirtschaftsrecht* 325; against see R Bieber, 'Abwegige und zielführende Vorschläge' [2001] *Integration* 309.

[113] See Kirchhof, above n 27, 11.

The provisions are indeed broad, but they are certainly limited, as shown by the ECJ's judgment on the advertising and sponsorship of tobacco products.[114] Limitations of competences are still governed by the fundamental principles of conferred powers, subsidiarity and proportionality. A rearrangement could vulnerably weaken European integration. The danger was averted only shortly before the end of the debates. The previous legal bases return with only minor modifications in the third part of the Constitution. Henceforth, the two main types of competences will be exclusive competences and areas with shared competence.[115]

The prospective legally binding acts, by which Union competences are exercised, are to some extent composed differently than in the past. The European law replaces the regulation and inherits the legal consequences of regulations. Renaming the act stresses the primacy of the European law, as opposed to national regulation within Member States. More importantly, the EP's participation is incorporated consistently. European framework laws replace directives, while still keeping their content. The European regulation is a non-legislative act of general application. A European regulation can be binding as a whole and directly effective in each Member State, as is a current regulation. However, a European regulation can also correspond to a current directive. The European decision is non-legislative but binding in its entirety. Its legal predecessor is the current legal order's decision. As at present, recommendations and opinions adopted by the institutions are not legally binding. This structure brings the Union closer to a state. The European Constitution and the law derived therefrom have primacy over the law of Member States—which are to take all general or particular measures to fulfil duties arising out of the Constitution or acts of Union institutions. Thus, the constitutional legislator explicitly adopts the principle of primacy from the ECJ's case law.[116]

e) Rights of the Individual

The extensive Charter of Fundamental Rights of the European Union was wedged—without losing any of its substance—between the constitutive provisions of the first part and the implementing provisions of the third part. If the new Constitution enters into force, the Charter will be realised through the obligatory force of the other parts. Many have already

[114] See Case C–376/98 *Germany v Parliament and Council* [2000] ECR I–8419. See also C Calliess, 'Nach dem "Tabakwerbung-Urteil" des EuGH' [2001] *Juristische Ausbildung* 311; R Streinz, 'Fehlende EG-Kompetenz für Tabakwerberichtlinie' [2001] *Juristische Schulung* 288.

[115] For more details, see A von Bogdandy, J Bast and D Westphal, 'Die vertikale Kompetenzordnung im Entwurf des Verfassungsvertrags' [2003] *Integration* 414.

[116] On the current legal situation, see Zuleeg, above n 8, 104.

discussed its significance and legal consequences.[117] But one should not forget that the EU has a myriad of further individual rights. Foremost among these are the fundamental freedoms within the internal market.[118] The rights derived from Union citizenship are mostly directed against the Member States, whereas the right to vote for members of the EP implicates the EU as such.[119] Additional rights of the individual are scattered about the European legal order. They can be characterised as simple rights. As with other rights, they are to be protected.[120]

[117] See especially J Meyer (ed), *Kommentar zur Charta der Grundrechte der Europäischen Union* (2002). See also S Alber, 'Die EU-Charta der Grundrechte und ihre Auswirkungen auf die Rechtsprechung' [2000] *Europäische Grundrechte-Zeitschrift* 497; M Hilf, 'Die Charta der Grundrechte der EU in der Perspektive 2004' [2002] *Europarecht* suppl 3, 13; Zuleeg, above n 14, 511.

[118] For an insightful overview, see D Ehlers (ed), *Europäische Grundrechte und Grundfreiheiten* (2003), 147, with contributions by D Ehlers, A Epiney, U Becker, C Tietje, E Pache and P von Wilmowsky.

[119] See M Nettesheim, 'Die Unionsbürgerschaft im Verfassungsentwurf' [2003] *Integration* 428.

[120] For an extensive analysis, see Zuleeg, above n 8, 136.

Index